1 MONTH OF
FREE
READING

at
www.ForgottenBooks.com

By purchasing this book you are eligible for one month membership to ForgottenBooks.com, giving you unlimited access to our entire collection of over 1,000,000 titles via our web site and mobile apps.

To claim your free month visit: www.forgottenbooks.com/free965307

ISBN 978-0-260-70464-1
PIBN 10965307

Produce TODAY*

VICTORY

OFFICIAL WEEKLY BULLETIN OF THE AGENCIES IN THE OFFICE FOR EMERGENCY MANAGEMENT

WASHINGTON, D. C.   APRIL 7, 1942   VOLUME 3, NUMBER 14

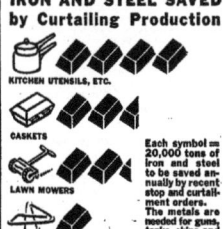

IRON AND STEEL SAVED by Curtailing Production

KITCHEN UTENSILS, ETC.

CASKETS

LAWN MOWERS

OFFICE SUPPLIES*

Each symbol = 20,000 tons of iron and steel to be saved annually by recent stop and curtailment orders. The metals are needed for guns, tanks, ships and war planes.

* SAVING, APR. 1 TO DEC. 1, 1942

WPB stops or cuts many lines of products to save thousands of tons of materials and convert vital machines to war

Evidences of the ever-increasing manufacture of weapons multiplied last week when the War Production Board moved in on a long list of civilian products with curtailment or stop orders. The industries involved represented 'a host of machines for war production, some already turning out military items and others to be converted shortly. WPB counted some three-quarters of a million tons of iron and steel to be conserved annually by these actions, along with other, uncounted amounts of these metals and untold quantities of other vital materials.

At or near the top in the list of lines to be curtailed was metal office equipment. With the tools and facilities of the $100,000,000 metal office equipment industry soon to be converted to war production, an end to the manufacture of virtually all types of such furniture and equipment, effective May 31, has been ordered.

Except for insulated metal filing cabinets, safes, visible record equipment and metal shelving, the manufacture, assembly, processing or fabrication of a long list of equipment is to be discontinued after that date, and strict restrictions on production are to be in effect for all items in the meantime.

500,000 tons of steel from furniture

In addition, beginning April 1, manufacturers may not sell, lease, or otherwise transfer any metal office furniture or equipment produced after April 1, except for Army, Navy, Maritime Commission or orders with a preference rating higher than A-2.

The industry last year used about 275,-000 tons of steel and employed about 18,000 workers. It is estimated that approximately 215,000 tons of steel will be saved by the order, which, together with recent restrictions on the production of metal household furniture and equipment, will bring total savings to about 500,000 tons of steel.

Already producing airplane wings

Conferences are now being held with the industry on a program for full conversion to the output of essential war materials. The industry is already partly converted and has produced subassembly airplane wings, demolition bombs, incendiary bombs, and practice bombs for the Government.

The order (Limitation Order L–13–a) was effective April 1. Metal office furniture is segregated by the order into three groups of products, while manufacturers are divided into a similar number of classes according to the use of steel in the year ended June 30, 1941.

Other restrictions made effective by the order are:

1. Manufacture or assembly of insulated metal filing cabinets, safes, and metal visible record equipment (Group I) is to end imme-

*MEETING PLANE AND TANK SCHEDULES—PAGE 17

452385°—42

Review of the Week

Cautioning again that however much we do will not be enough, War Production Board Chairman Nelson last week gave the Nation the news that we are ahead of our schedule for tanks, up to schedule on planes. Also, he said, we should meet this year's schedule for guns and merchant ships.

Savings in metals and machines

The proportions of our gathering industrial effort became clearer as WPB moved in on many lines of civilian products with orders to stop or curtail output or cut metal consumption, and counted huge savings in materials and machines by these actions. Lines affected included metal office furniture, office supplies, kitchen and household utensils, vacuum cleaners, lawn mowers, caskets, fluorescent lighting fixtures, tin tops, tin tubes, toys, and household electrical appliances from toasters to shavers. Many facilities of these industries already are in war production, WPB announced.

Encouraging news came from yet another level when the WPB Production Division revealed 20,307 machine tools were delivered in February as compared with 19,266 in January. Nevertheless, the division repeated the warning that most of the increase in war manufacture must come from existing machines.

And to spur accomplishment of this increase at the workbenches and in the offices of existing plants, Production Drive Headquarters issued a supplement to its Official Plan Book—with a foreword by Mr. Nelson warning that management, labor, and Government are on trial before the American public.

Guarding limited supplies

While new sacrifices to win the war were being announced, the Office of Price Administration acted to prevent hardships that are unnecessary to the war effort. OPA prescribed maximum prices that may be charged at retail for 44 household electrical items that will be made scarce by the WPB order. At the same time, however, the assistant administrator of OPA in charge of the Consumer Division warned that "today we are losing the battle against inflation,"

and urged the public to do its part against scarcity by refraining from hoarding.

To accomplish better distribution of available supplies, WPB confined sugar deliveries by eastern refineries to their home areas, and also moved to regulate sales of that increasingly important vehicle, the bicycle.

Pig iron under allocation

A few metal-consuming products of peacetime escaped the WPB ax because of their continued importance in war. Among them were kerosene refrigerators and nails. Since most types of mechanical refrigerators will not be made any more, WPB moved to get more "iceboxes" out of the existing metal supply by cutting the steel used in each one to 20 pounds. More metal was allotted to manufacture of farm implements to meet increased demands for food.

The shortage of pig iron resulted in an order placing it under complete allocation. A similar fate overtook antimony, and all orders of glycerine over 50 pounds a month. WPB warned that additional drastic curtailments will be necessary in civilian use of copper. Rubber consumption of many articles was reduced further, and a coordinator was appointed to integrate all current programs dealing with that commodity.

Rents curbed in another area

OPA allowed a slight increase in North Atlantic refiners' prices for sugar, to take care of added costs. Hard coal prices at the mine were stopped at existing levels, with customary discounts. Baltimore was added to the list of areas which must curb rents or submit to Federal control.

Other OPA activities concerned iron and steel scrap; iron and steel products; boring machines; zinc oxides; pig tin; primary lead; antimonial lead; reagent oxalic acid; cast iron soil pipe; lumber; paper; paper shipping bags; old manila rope; tea; and canned fruits and vegetables.

The Office of Civilian Defense allotted protective helmets and arm bands to cities in strategic coastal areas.

Civilian goods curtailed

(Continued from page 1)

diately except for orders placed by the Army, Navy, Maritime Commission or for an order bearing higher than an A-2 rating.

2. Beginning April 1, no manufacturer can use in the production of metal shelving (Group II) more than 50 percent of steel used in the base period.

3. For the 2 months beginning April 1 large manufacturers (those who used more than 12,000 tons of steel in the base period) may not use each month more than 40 percent of average monthly steel consumption in the following products (Group III):

Metal filing cabinets other than insulated cabinets; metal lockers; metal office storage cabinets; metal desks; office chairs containing more than two pounds of metal other than swivel irons; metal office tables, including typewriter and office machine stands; metal bank vault equipment; metal office counters; movable metal partitions; doors, etc., for such partitions; other equipment including wastepaper baskets, metal trays and wire baskets; any other office furniture not specifically mentioned in Group I or Group II, containing more than 5 percent of metal in the net weight of the finished product other than swivel irons and joining hardware.

The percentages allowable for other manufacturers are 50 percent and 60 percent, depending on the size of the manufacturer.

May shift quotas among products

4. Any manufacturers making Group III products may adjust the amounts of steel to be used in any one product up to 120 percent of the amount permitted, provided that the total amounts used conform to the limitations of the order.

5. Beginning April 1, no manufacturer can sell, deliver, or otherwise transfer inventories of steel intended for use in metal office furniture, except as parts of furniture or equipment permitted by the order to other manufacturers to fill A-2 or better, orders to the Defense Supplies Corporation or other agencies of the RFC or as ordered by the Director of Industry Operations.

6. Manufacturers may not process, fabricate, work on, or assemble any steel in their inventories, except as such steel is intended for use in equipment permitted by the order, or on specific authorization of the Director of Industry Operations.

7. The restrictions contained in the order do not apply to "special orders" involving certain essential Army and Navy needs for metal desks, lockers, and chairs for use on combatant vessels or troop ships, or to be used outside the limits of continental United States where the tropical climate requires the use of such metal furniture.

★ ★ ★

WAR EFFORT'S PROGRESS TOLD VISUALLY

The charts appearing every week on the front cover of VICTORY tell the story of America's battle as it is fought here at home. One-column mats are available for publication by newspapers and others who may desire them.

VICTORY

OFFICIAL BULLETIN of the Office for Emergency Management. Published weekly by the Division of Information, Office for Emergency Management, and printed at the United States Government Printing Office, Washington, D. C.

Subscription rates by mail: 75¢ for 52 issues; 25¢ for 13 issues; single copies 5¢, payable in advance. Remit money order payable directly to the Superintendent of Documents, Government Printing Office, Washington, D. C.

On the Home Front

This Thursday is the anniversary of the Nazi invasion of Norway. The Axis powers have stained the months with such bitter anniversaries. They have been able to do this because they work with a single purpose, although a loathsome purpose. The Nazi purpose is conquest and enslavement. The Nazis knew that only through machines could they achieve this goal and so they let nothing interfere with the drive for machines.

"We learned slowly"

We know now that the only answer to a tank is two tanks, that the only answer to an airplane is two airplanes, and that the answer to a gun is a lot of guns—and better guns.

But we did not learn this all at once. Like the British, we learned slowly. For a long while we thought we could exist in two worlds, the ruthless world of total war and the comfortable world of peace. Other countries thought that way, too, and now—except for those gallant men who escaped to keep on fighting—they are slave countries. The British won a second chance at Dunkerque; they have made good use of that second chance and today their home front is a real front, with every man and woman a soldier.

Reminders of what it means to lose

We, of course, remember Pearl Harbor and realize that all of us must produce and save and sacrifice so that we may make the machines which will fight for us. But it is a good thing not to forget anniversaries like next Thursday, either. They remind us of what we must have to win, and of what it means to lose.

America, engaged in the gigantic task of building at top speed a colossal mechanized army, a vast air force, and a navy the like of which the world has never seen before, has still other commitments. America must supply her friends and allies, too, with tremendous quantities of finished weapons and raw materials and machine tools and food and clothing. And she must build the merchant ships in which these supplies are transported, build them at a rate to offset the work of Hitler's submarines.

That is why every ounce of almost every material counts, why last week brought War Production Board conservation orders which reach almost from the cradle to the grave, why we are to have less and less and less of virtually everything.

Did it seem a trifling thing to you when WPB took the cuffs from men's trousers to save wool? In total war there are no trifles. Cuffs average about 2 percent of the total cloth in a man's suit. The cuffs from 19,500,000 pairs of men's and youths' trousers—about 4 months stock—would make more than 300,000 suits.

Or put the saving in terms of uniforms. There's about 5.18 pounds of wool in a soldier's uniform, about 24 one-hundredths of a pound in a pair of trouser cuffs. Nine pairs of cuffs would equal enough cloth for a pair of Army trousers, 12 pairs would give the material used for an average Army coat. Twenty-one pairs of cuffs, then, and you have a soldier's uniform.

Our problems are bigger than we are

Cooperation between management and labor is the basis of our great War Production Drive. "Every one of the problems we face," said Donald M. Nelson in a supplement to the Official Plan Book for that drive, "is bigger than any of us . . . It isn't easy, and it's going to be harder. But we've got to stick together."

Cooperation is the root of such plans as that of the Office of Defense Transportation to have farmers pool the trucks they drive to market—so that trucks and tires may last longer. And even such a simple and sensible program as that requiring that everyone buying toilet goods in collapsible tubes turn over a used tube to his druggist in exchange cannot succeed without cooperation. Another little thing, that— but we need tin quite as much as we need wool.

Short shrift if you don't play the game

The basic necessity for working together is implicit in every WPB priority order, in every Office of Price Administration rationing regulation. For both the priority system of putting first things first and the rationing system of distributing fairly that which is scarce are essentially great adventures in national cooperation.

Because almost all of us realize this, we're going to give very short shrift to anybody who doesn't play the game. We are going to get tough with such people and just how tough was explained the other day by Acting Price Administrator John E. Hamm.

Mr. Hamm warned that under the new Second War Powers Act willful violators of WPB priority orders or OPA rationing regulations face maximum penalties up to $10,000 fines and a year's imprisonment.

Metals, plastics to be banned for toys

Childhood and death and the life of the years between were touched last week by WPB orders designed to save metals and materials for the uses of war.

One order, which will save an estimated 50,000 tons of iron and steel alone, limited use of those metals in caskets and for other burial purposes and prohibited use of other metals—except gold and silver—altogether.

A second order prohibits manufacture of toys containing metals or plastics after June 30 while a third limits the use of iron, steel, and zinc in a long list of kitchen utensils and miscellaneous household articles. WPB's consumers durable goods branch urged, in this connection, that such utensils and articles, wherever possible, be made of glass and wood and earthenware.

War work for 4,000,000 women

There'll be fewer lawn mowers, too—and that should save some 45,000 tons of iron and steel . . . WPB ordered that production of vacuum cleaners must be discontinued after April 30 and prohibited use of copper and brass base alloy in manufacture of slide fasteners (zippers), hooks and eyes, grippers, etc. . . . There's some rubber for repairing tires of "List B" users this month but OPA warns that it's almost entirely reclaimed rubber and tires recapped with it had better be driven below 35 miles an hour . . . Life at low speeds, around 5,000 miles . . . WPB's Labor Division estimates that at least 4,000,000 women workers will be required for war industry by the end of next year . . . Control of all glycerine deliveries above 50 pounds a month has been taken over by WPB . . . Glycerine is a by-product of soap making and our British allies use it in manufacturing their most important military explosive, cordite . . . Soap in turn is made from fats and maybe we'll all be saving fats, someday . . . Another proof that everything counts: WPB's order cutting in half the iron and steel which can be used for paper clips, thumb tacks, office supplies . . . Enamel won't decorate the ends of tin cans any more because it is needed to coat military supplies . . . Keep the distilled water level up in your automobile battery, don't keep your stove on high after the pot comes to a boil . . . Everything saved, everything made to last, contributes toward Victory.

INDUSTRIAL OPERATIONS . . .

Electric appliances—toasters to shavers— to get no more pig tin, alloy steel, nickel plate, copper, or aluminum

The War Production Board on March 30 ordered manufacturers of electrical appliances to discontinue at once the use of certain critical materials in the manufacture of a long list of electrical appliances commonly found in American homes.

Between March 30 and May 31 these manufacturers, some 200 concerns that normally produced approximately $60,-000,000 worth of appliances annually, may produce appliances at a rate of approximately one and a half times their rate of production in 1941, though without the use of critical materials prohibited by the March 30 order.

Only for A-2 after May 31

After May 31 they must halt production of all orders except to fill orders or contracts bearing preference ratings higher than A-2.

The production of replacement parts is not affected.

The order (L-65) affects such common household appliances as electric toasters, waffle irons, flat irons, roasters, grills, table stoves, portable heaters, food mixers, juice extractors, percolators, dishwashing equipment, dry shavers, hair dryers, permanent wave equipment, hair clippers, cigar and cigarette lighters, and heating units for new electric ranges, water heaters, and radiating heaters.

50 listed but that isn't all

Attached to the order is a list of 50 varieties of appliances covered by the order, but it is explained that this list is not intended to be exhaustive, since all appliances coming within the definitions contained in the order are affected.

Electrical appliances are defined in the order as meaning "any domestic or commercial appliances which have as functional parts electric heating elements of a total rated wattage of not more than 2,500 watts, or powered by an electrical vibrator or electrical fractional horsepower motor." The order also applies to heating units of any wattage to be incorporated in electrical appliances or in any new domestic electric range. It does not apply to heating units already in use.

Exceptions mostly covered elsewhere

The order specifically states that it does not apply to the following: laundry equipment, vacuum cleaners, refrigerating and air conditioning equipment, commercial dishwashing equipment, fans and electric heating pads, record-players, oil furnaces, vending and gaming machines, and other electrical items not customarily classified as domestic or commercial electrical appliances. For the most part these items are covered by orders previously issued or by orders about to be issued.

The prohibition on materials is as follows:

Effective immediately, no manufacturer may put into process any pig tin; or any alloy steel, copper, or copper base alloy, or aluminum that was not processed beyond the first stage when the order was issued.

Beginning April 1, no nickel may be used for nickel plating.

The provision as to production between March 30 and May 31 is as follows: During that period, each manufacturer may produce electrical appliances having a total factory sales value of up to 25 percent of the total value of the appliances produced by him in 1941, provided that such appliances do not contain more than 15 percent, by weight, of the amount of electrical resistance material such manufacturer used in 1941.

Must set aside materials

The order contains additional restrictions on the use of electrical resistance material. It requires each manufacturer to: (a) set aside sufficient electrical resistance material to fill all orders bearing an A-10 or higher rating; (b) set aside and hold as reserve for future disposition by WPB 15 percent by weight of the balance of such material; (c) set aside, at his option, enough such material to complete appliances permitted under the order; (d) set aside, at his option, a reserve for replacement parts not to exceed one and a half times the amount of such materials he used for replacements in 1940; (e) set aside all remaining electrical resistance material for future disposition by WPB, except that he may sell to other manufacturers such quantities as are needed by them to complete production of their quotas.

An inventory restriction prohibits a manufacturer from accepting delivery of more materials than are necessary to produce the appliances permitted him under the order.

Industry already producing weapons

The order does not restrict the manufacture of replacement parts.

The 200 plants affected by the order normally employ between 20,000 and 25,000 workers.

Some of the plants are already engaged in direct war work and the entire industry is expected to be converted within a few months. They already have war contracts totalling $15,000,000. War production already under way includes the manufacture of fuzes, 20 millimeter feed mechanism, shot and shell, bomb carriers, gas tanks, and gun mounts.

Robert Beatty, chief of the electrical appliances section of WPB, said that when the industry is fully converted it will employ more persons than it did at its peak of peacetime operation.

★ ★ ★

APRIL ZINC POOL

The zinc pool for April was set March 28 by the Director of Industry Operations at these percentages:

High grade and special high grade— 60 percent of January 1942 production; all other grades—40 percent of January; zinc oxide—none; zinc dust—none.

At the same time, General Preference Order M-11, under which the zinc pool is operated, was extended to May 31, 1942. It was due to expire on March 31 and the extension was made pending completion of a revised zinc order.

★ ★ ★

Canners using leased machines get owners' ratings for repairs

Canners who use leased machinery are entitled to the same preference ratings under Order P-115 for repair and maintenance as if they owned the machinery, the WPB has ruled in an interpretation of the order.

Manufacture of lawn mowers banned after June 30 to save steel, free machines for war

The song of the lawn mower will be heard in the land this summer, but it will be a muted tune.

To conserve iron and steel for military uses and more important civilian requirements, WPB on March 30 issued an order drastically curtailing production during the next 3 months of all types of mowers, except those used to harvest crops, and prohibiting manufacture after June 30.

Effective at once, the order directs manufacturers to cut their use of iron and steel in lawn mowers, from now to the end of June, to one-half of the amount which went into this production during the same period last year, or to three times one-half of the average monthly use during the 12 months from July 1, 1940, to June 30, 1941.

It is estimated that about 45,000 tons of iron and steel will be made available for essential uses each year as a result of the ordered shut-down, which will also free metal-working machinery for war.

⌃ ⌃ ⌃

Pig iron put under complete allocation

Because the pig iron shortage is increasing, the Director of Industry Operations on March 28 issued Amendment No. 2 and Extension No. 2 to General Preference Order M–17, completely allocating pig iron supplies.

The amendment eliminates the reserve tonnage pool and, instead, places all tonnage produced under mandatory control. Steel companies that produce and use their own pig iron are required to report priority ratings on their production schedules.

Pig iron buyers are required to fill out Form PD–69 by the fifth day of the month before they purchase pig iron. By the same date buyers must file reports on Form PD–70 with the War Production Board, showing inventories and pig iron consumption.

Producers of pig iron must file reports on orders, schedules, and shipments by the 12th day of each month hereafter. Producers may ship pig iron only in accordance with delivery schedules filed on Form PD–71, as approved or modified by the Director of Industry Operations.

The pig iron order has also been extended to remain in effect until revoked.

Kitchen and household articles cut 30 to 50 percent in use of iron, steel, zinc; no metal for nonessentials after July 1

The effects of the war were felt in the American home March 31 when the War Production Board curtailed the use of iron, steel, and zinc in the manufacture of a long list of kitchen, household, and miscellaneous articles.

The order (L–30), which took effect March 31, divides such equipment into three groups. During April, May, and June the use of iron, steel, and zinc in each group is reduced by various amounts in accordance with the utility of the product, and also with a view to the possibility of substituting a less critical material, such as glass, wood, or earthenware.

Three groups defined

The three groups and the reductions in the use of metals in each during April, May, and June are as follows:

1. Cooking utensils. Reduction: iron and steel, 10 percent.

2. Kitchen ware and essential household articles. Reduction: iron and steel, 30 percent; zinc, 50 percent.

3. Nonessential household and other miscellaneous articles. Reduction: iron, steel, and zinc, 50 percent.

A manufacturer may use any part of his iron and steel quota for less essential products in the production of articles in the more essential groups.

Beginning July 1, no metal of any kind may be used in the manufacture of articles in group 3.

Base is year ended June 30, 1941

All of the iron and steel reductions in April, May, and June are based on the total amount of iron, steel, tin, aluminum, nickel, copper and copper alloys, chromium and lead used in such articles in the 12 months ended June 30, 1941, expressed in a daily average. In the case of zinc, the reduction is based on the amount of zinc used in such articles during the same base period.

The order does not apply to electrical appliances, cutlery, or silver-plated hollow ware.

The consumers' durable goods branch said that despite the March 31 order and previous WPB metal restrictions, the available supplies of household articles, plus production which will be allowed under L–30, will be sufficient for essential requirements of the Nation. Housewives are urged to take care of their present equipment so that it will last as long as possible. The branch urged that wherever possible articles made of noncritical materials, particularly of glass, wood, and earthenware, be substituted for items made of critical materials.

Ash cans to towel racks

Products in group 1 include kitchen utensils used primarily in the preparation, cooking, and storage of foods for household, institutional, and commercial uses.

Products in group 2 include the following, whether manufactured for household or for any other purpose: wash basins, dish pans, rinsing pans, wash boilers, ash cans, garbage cans and pails (including step-on cans), wringer buckets, clothes wringers, pails (except dairy pails), commodes, chambers and chamber covers, combinets, bread boxes, funnels, liquid measures, galvanized and other portable tubs, wash boards, ironing boards, carpet sweepers, dust pans, refrigerator pans and all kitchen tools, including (but not limited to) can openers, jar openers, bottle openers, beaters, ice cream dippers or scoops, corers, and mashers.

Products in group 3 include the following, whether manufactured for household or for any other purpose: all closet accessories, including (but not limited to) coat and garment hangers and hooks, tie racks and boot and shoetrees; all articles of fireplace equipment except fire screens; towel bars and racks, toothbrush holders, soap dishes, soap savers, toilet and other paper holders, pot chains, fly swatters, sink drainers, dish drainers, cuspidors, vegetable bins, curtain rods and fixtures, clothespins, candlesticks, carpet beaters, pot cover holders, picnic stoves, camp grids, cup frames, and cake coolers.

To save 80,000 tons a year

A manufacturer of a product in any group may not accumulate greater inventories of raw materials, semiprocessed materials or of finished parts than are necessary to maintain operations at the rates specified in L–30.

It is estimated that the order will save more than 80,000 tons of iron and steel annually and bring about substantial savings in zinc.

APRIL LEAD POOL

The April lead pool March 30 was set at 15 percent of February 1942 production by the Director of Industry Operations. The percentage is unchanged from last month and the amount to be set aside varies only slightly from recent months.

WPB takes all copper out of zippers, hooks and eyes, buttons, snap fasteners; steel, zinc for them limited drastically

The War Production Board on March 30 prohibited the use of copper and copper base alloy in the manufacture of slide fasteners (zippers), hooks and eyes, brassiere hooks, snap fasteners and grippers, and other garment closures. More than 8,000 tons of copper were used in such products in 1941.

The same order (L-68) restricts the use of steel, zinc, and zinc base alloy in the manufacture of the same items.

In addition, the order prohibits the use not only of copper and copper base alloy but also steel, zinc, and zinc base alloy in zippers now found in a long list of everyday items enumerated in an appendix to the order.

Effective April 1

All of the prohibitions and restrictions became effective April 1.

The order does not apply to orders or contracts for the Army, Navy and other war agencies, and Lend-Lease.

The order affects five different groups of items, as follows: slide fasteners; hooks and eyes and brassiere hooks; snap-fasteners or grippers; metal buttons, rivets and burrs; and a general group including buckles, corset clasps, garter trimmings, etc.

Since the restrictions on each group are different, they are dealt with separately in this description of the order.

Length of zippers restricted too

Restrictions on the manufacture and use of slide fasteners are as follows:

1. The use of copper or copper base alloy in the manufacture of slide fasteners is prohibited.

2. The use of steel, zinc, or zinc base alloy in any calendar quarter, beginning April 1, is restricted to 50 percent of the quarterly poundage of metals used by a manufacturer for similar purposes during the year ending June 30, 1941. (It should be noticed that the restriction is based on the poundage of metals, not necessarily steel or zinc, used during the base period, inasmuch as copper or copper alloy rather than steel or zinc may have been the metal largely used during the base period. Consequently, a restriction based on the quantity of steel or zinc used in the base period might have permitted little or no production after April 1, when the copper prohibition goes into effect).

3. Regardless of the materials used in the manufacture of zippers—whether metals or plastic—the order prohibits the manufacture of zippers of more than 10 inches in length, except that up to 12 inches is permitted for fly fasteners on trousers and up to 20 inches for work jackets.

4. No manufacturer may produce or deliver any zippers or zipper parts made from copper, steel, or zinc for use on any of the articles or garments listed in an appendix to the order. The list includes bags of all sorts, bathrobes, billfolds and pocketbooks, all sorts of coats, corsets and foundation garments, cosmetic sets and kits, coveralls and one-piece work suits, all sorts of covers such as seat covers and slip covers, footwear of all types, gloves, hoods, toilet and novelty kits, linings, luggage, muffs, negligees and lingerie, notebooks and checkbooks, overalls, pads such as heating pads, all types of pouches, purses, raincoats, robes, shirts, slips and petticoats, sporting goods, sport jackets, sweaters, swim suits and beachwear, toys and upholstery. This does not apply to zippers or zipper parts already manufactured and not adaptable for any other use. Nor does it apply to zippers for garment pockets.

5. The manufacture of bead pulls, chain pulls, or similar items from steel, zinc, or copper is also prohibited, except for such items that were in process of manufacture on March 28, 1942.

6. In the production of zippers for sale on notion cards, for home use, a manufacturer may use in any quarter more steel, zinc, or zinc base alloy than 50 percent of the weight of metals he used quarterly for such purposes during the base period. Such steel and zinc must be taken out of the total amount of steel and zinc permitted for zippers under the order.

7. The prohibition against the use of zippers for the articles and garments listed in the appendix applies not only to the zipper manufacturer but equally to the person who uses zippers in the manufacture of the articles or garments.

Hooks and eyes

Restrictions on the manufacture of hooks and eyes and brassiere hooks are as follows:

1. No copper or copper base alloy may be used.

2. During any calendar quarter beginning April 1, no manufacturer may use more steel, zinc, or zinc base alloy in the production of hooks and eyes and brassiere hooks than 100 percent of the weight of all metals he used for such items during a similar period in the base year.

3. In the production of such items for home use he may use not more steel and zinc than 50 percent of the weight of metals he used for the same items in the base year. This steel and zinc must come out of the 100 percent quota permitted him under the order.

Snap fasteners

Restrictions on the manufacture of sew-on, machine-attached, or riveted snap fasteners or grippers are as follows:

1. No copper or copper base alloy may be used.

2. In the production of such items for work clothes and women's and children's wear, a manufacturer may use quarterly in steel and zinc up to 100 percent of his quarterly poundage of metals in the base year.

3. For these same items for other purposes, a manufacturer may use quarterly in steel and zinc only 50 percent of his quarterly poundage of metals during the base year.

4. The use of steel and zinc for these same items for sale on notion cards, for home use, is restricted to 50 percent of his quarterly poundage of metals during the base year. This 50 percent comes out of his total allocation of steel and zinc.

Metal buttons

Restrictions on the manufacture of metal buttons, rivets, and burrs and insignia are as follows: -

1. No copper may be used in the manufacture of such items except for Army, Navy, Marine, Coast Guard, and Coast and Geodetic officers, United States Government Military and Naval Academy and Training School students, and Maritime Commission employes.

2. As a further exception, metal buttons for uniforms of, and identification badges for, public-carrier employes, police and fire departments and military school students, may be plated with copper or copper base alloys.

The use of copper and copper base alloy is also prohibited in the manufacture of the following items: buckles (other than dress buckles covered by a previous order), corset clasps, eyelets, furniture glides, garter trimmings, hose supporters, identification badges, and similar items (with the exceptions already mentioned), loops, mattress buttons, personal hardware, pin fasteners, staples, slides, tacks, and trouser trimmings.

Simplifying radiators to save 11,500 tons of cast iron a year

Issuance of an additional simplification schedule establishing types and sizes for tubular radiators was announced March 30 by the Director of Industry Operations. The schedule, effective April 16, is expected to save about 11,500 tons of cast iron annually.

This saving is due to the fact that the schedule (No. VI to Limitation Order L-42) eliminates production of large-tube radiators.

Simplification of other plumbing and heating equipment items ordered by previous schedules covered valves, pipe fittings, metal jackets, fusible plugs and tricocks, soil pipes and soil pipe fittings.

Copper for 1,000,000 fuses saved

According to data compiled by the WPB plumbing and heating branch, the simplified schedule on pipe fittings will save over 1,000,000 pounds of copper base alloy, sufficient to produce about 1 million 50 mm. fuses.

Other material savings already accomplished by various simplification schedules of L-42 include 19,000 tons of cast iron and 500 tons of brass through the simplification of soil pipes and fittings, and 18,000 tons of steel through the elimination of metal jackets from boilers.

Casket metals going into war; all to be banned except gold, silver, hardware of iron, steel

WPB on March 30 ordered a curtailment in the use of iron and steel and prohibited the use of all other metals, except gold and silver, in the manufacture of caskets, casket shipping cases, and burial vaults.

The order (L–64) cuts the amount of iron and steel that may be used in such burial equipment by 25 percent during April, by 50 percent during May, and 75 percent during June, as compared with average monthly use in 1940. These reductions, however, do not include the use of an amount not exceeding 10 pounds of casket hardware, shell hardware, or fastenings, or the amount of iron and steel necessary for the production of metal liners for wooden caskets or of metal shipping cases which are required by State laws for the transportation of human corpses.

Iron and steel out July 1

Beginning July 1, the order prohibits entirely the use of iron and steel in the production of burial equipment, except in hardware and metal liners under the prescribed restrictions.

A purchaser of metal liners or of metal shipping cases is required to file an affidavit with the manufacturer outlining the use of the article and the requirements of the State law.

With the exception of gold and silver, the use of other metals, such as bronze, copper, zinc, and lead, is prohibited upon the issuance of the order.

The reductions in the 3-month period ending June 30 are based on the average monthly amount of iron and steel used for caskets, shipping cases, and burial vaults during 1940. A manufacturer who used any other metal during 1940 may add the weight of such metal to iron and steel in computing his full quota for the base period.

To save 50,000 tons of 2 metals

The order immediately freezes a manufacturer's inventory of any metal, except iron, steel, gold and silver, and on July 1, the inventory of iron and steel will be frozen.

M. D. Moore, of the consumers durable goods branch, WPB, estimated that 50,-000 tons of iron and steel will be saved annually by the order, and that substantial metal-working capacity will be released for the production of war goods.

Iron and steel limited for office supplies to release 19,300 tons; copper, nickel, tin, chromium, crude rubber forbidden

Curtailment in the use of iron and steel in the manufacture of metal office supplies, such as paper clips, thumb tacks, pencil sharpeners, and various desk accessories, was ordered by the War Production Board March 29.

The program is designed to release approximately 19,300 tons of iron and steel this year for ships, guns, tanks, and other war products, in addition to large amounts of other critical materials.

Office supplies covered by the order are essential to Army, Navy, Government, and Lend-Lease operations. The program is designed to take care of these needs and at the same time meet essential civilian demands. The ordinary consumer will not be able to obtain supplies in usual quantities. However, no shortages should occur if consumers make careful use of supplies on hand.

Zinc restricted

The limitation order, L–73, prohibits manufacturers of office supplies from using any copper, tin, nickel, chromium, cadmium, or crude rubber unless already processed beyond the first stage of cutting or stamping. Use of zinc is restricted to galvanizing necessary for practicable use and wear.

Effective immediately, the order imposes restrictions on iron and steel consumption in three classes of office supplies beginning April 1, using 1940 as the base period. That year is regarded as the most recent normal production year. Production last year was from 30 to 50 percent above the 1940 rate, depending upon the product.

With one exception, the restrictions on iron and steel consumption for the three months beginning April 1 will remain in force during each three-month period thereafter.

Wire staples at 1940 rate

Expressed in percentages of the average rate of consumption of all metals for 1940, the reductions are as follows:

Wire staples, which contain only a small amount of iron and steel, are classed alone in group 1, and iron and steel may be used in producing them at the same rate as during 1940.

Use of iron and steel in products in group 2 must be cut during the next 8 months by 20 percent below the 1940 rate of consumption. Products included in this group are: clips, clamps, pins, and thumb tacks; copy holders; eyelet and round and flat-head fasteners; eyeleters; file fasteners; pencil sharpeners; punches and perforators, and stapling and fastening machines. For each quarter beginning July 1, the rate of curtailment for this group will be increased to 40 percent.

A 50 percent cut below the 1940 consumption rate was ordered for iron and steel consumption in products in group 3. This group covers adhesive and gummed tape dispensers; arch and clip board files; calender stands; desk accessories; inked ribbon spools and containers; list finders; rulers and yardsticks; staple removers, and any stationery sundries not classified in groups 1 or 2.

Producers may exceed their quotas in order to take care of Government contracts, but the excess must be deducted from subsequent quotas.

An important feature of the order is that all manufacturers, regardless of whether they are working on a Government or civilian order, must adhere to Federal specifications for metal office supplies issued from time to time by the Director of Procurement. These specifications are designed to reduce the amount of critical materials required to produce these supplies.

How civilians can help

Commenting on the part the average consumer can play, M. D. Moore, chief of the WPB section charged with administering the order, said:

"The order was drafted to provide sufficiently for the requirements of the Army, Navy and civilian industries. While there will be permitted under its terms sufficient production to meet the demand, it is, nevertheless, advisable to caution the public to conserve to the utmost the use of these small office supply items.

"For example, clips should not be used for permanent filing. A staple will do the job. Nor should two clips or two staples be used where one will do. Clips and other fasteners should be removed when material is finally filed. Typewriter ribbon spools can be used over and over again and should be saved by the typist and returned in the old container upon receipt of a new typewriter ribbon."

Heater simplifying formalized

The ban contained in Order M–9–c on use of copper or copper base alloy in hot water heaters and piping systems has been formalized in a simplification schedule to plumbing Order L–42, it was announced March 30 by Industry Operations Director Knowlson.

"Iceboxes" cut to 20 pounds of steel each to increase output for new civilian need without boosting total supply of metal

A program to keep steel consumption at a low level in the manufacture of non-mechanical ice refrigerators ("iceboxes") and at the same time permit output of enough units to meet increasing civilian demands was announced March 31 by the War Production Board.

Ban on other types increases demand

Since production of domestic mechanical refrigerators must be halted April 30, civilian demands for household refrigeration for the duration of the war must be filled largely by the manufacturers of nonmechanical refrigerators. Ice-making facilities are far in excess of normal demands.

Under Supplementary General Limitation Order L-7-b, WPB ordered continuation during April, May, and June of the existing 40-percent cut on use of steel in the manufacture of domestic nonmechanical refrigerators. The same rate of curtailment below average monthly use during the 3-year or 12-month period ending June 30, 1941, will prevail during subsequent quarters unless otherwise ordered.

Manufacturers must turn to wood

After June 30, however, manufacturers will be prohibited from using more than 20 pounds of steel in each box produced. The average weight of metal per unit is 85 pounds. The effect of this restriction on unit consumption will be to compel manufacturers to turn to wood or wood base cabinets as a substitute for steel.

With substitution of less critical materials, manufacturers may make in the year beginning July 1 approximately 495,000 units, as compared with an output of about 200,000 units during the year ended June 30, 1941, but at the same time the cut in use of steel will result in reducing consumption of this vital material from 8,250 tons in the base year to 4,950 tons this year.

May use rest of old quotas

During the next 3 months, manufacturers may add to their quotas unused balances of quotas granted earlier, provided a report is filed with the consumers' durable goods branch showing the amount of steel intended to be used. This privilege expires June 30. Beginning April 1, Government orders no longer can be exempted from quotas.

In order to check use of steel under the 20-pound restriction, the order provides that no manufacturer may sell any nonmechanical refrigerator produced after June 30 unless he files with the branch a bill of material for each model produced.

★ ★ ★

Kerosene refrigerators get reprieve; needed by U. S.

WPB, acting to provide for essential Government requirements, on March 31 excluded kerosene refrigerators from the order halting production of domestic mechanical refrigerators after April 30.

It is estimated that approximately 15,500 of this type of refrigerator, which is used widely by Government agencies in areas where power facilities are not available for other mechanical types, will be needed this year and next for essential Government purposes. Should production be stopped April 30, only about 3,500 would be available to meet these demands.

Under an amendment to Order L-5-c, specific permission of the Director of Industry Operations must be obtained in order to continue production beginning May 1, and manufacturers must comply with minimum specifications for the kerosene-type established by the Army and other Government agencies.

★ ★

Asbestos textiles reserved for essential uses

With the Army preparing to let bids for more than 300,000 pairs of asbestos gloves, WPB issued on March 31 an order designed to conserve the supply of asbestos textiles for essential military and civilian uses.

By the terms of Conservation Order M-123, manufacturers are prohibited from making deliveries of asbestos textiles except for use in the manufacture of industrial packings, or to fill orders bearing a preference rating of A-10, or higher.

Industrial packings include gaskets, pump packing and other uses in machinery.

Metal signs out July 1; materials cut in half till then

WPB has ordered a curtailment of the use of steel and iron in metal signs.

The order (L-29) applies to signs which are 36 square inches or larger in size and of which at least 5 percent of the weight of the sign consists of metal.

The order cuts in half the amount of iron and steel that may go into such signs during the 3-month period beginning April 1, and prohibits the use of any metals in such signs beginning July 1, 1942. The 50-percent reduction for the 3-month period is based on the amount of all metal used for signs during the year ended June 30, 1941. From March 27 to April 1, the use of steel and iron was cut to not more than the average amount of metal used in a similar period of the base year.

The order involves the construction and installation of signs and accessories such as billboards, electric, indoor, neon, porcelain enamel, and store-front signs. Accessories include such items as electrical equipment (other than light bulbs) frames, hanging brackets, and poles. The order does not include any type of plate, tag, or emblem used by a governmental unit for licensing or registration purposes. Such items are already under a curtailment order.

Wood and other signs which do not contain 5 percent of their weight in metal, are not affected by the order.

Effective March 27, sign manufacturers' inventories, raw and semiprocessed iron and steel were frozen. Any manufacturer of metal signs or accessories may not sell or deliver any materials except by consent of the Director of Industry Operations, WPB; or to persons having a preference rating of A-3 or higher, to the Defense Supplies Corporation, to the Metals Reserve Co., or to any other agency formed under the Reconstruction Finance Corporation Act.

A sign manufacturer may not accumulate more materials in his inventory than are necessary to maintain operations at rates permitted by L-29.

★ ★

Dickinson executive director of WPB Planning Committee

Appointment of Edward T. Dickinson, Jr., as executive director of the Planning Committee, WPB, was announced April 1 by Robert R. Nathan, chairman of the committee.

Vacuum-cleaner production to end April 30 for 100 percent conversion to war

Production of vacuum cleaners must be discontinued after April 30, the War Production Board ruled March 31 in a move to concentrate the industry's facilities 100 percent on war work.

During April, the industry will operate at the same rate of curtailment as during January, February, and March. Class A manufacturers, whose average monthly factory sales in the 12 months ended June 30, 1941, were 5,200 or more units, are required to curtail output by 40 percent below the base period. Class B manufacturers whose average was less than 5,200 units, must cut 25 percent.

The industry now joins others in the consumers' durable goods field whose facilities are being converted to war work. Eighteen companies, with factory employment of approximately 12,000 workers, will be affected by the shutdown order, Supplementary General Limitation Order L–18–b.

Approximately one-fourth of the industry already has been converted 100 percent and all companies are now in production of various types of war supplies.

The initial curtailment for the industry, a 10 percent cut for Class A manufacturers, covered the period October 1–December 31, 1941.

NAILS ESCAPE AX—WPB ASKS MORE OF THEM

Because lumber is largely replacing steel in wartime building construction, nail manufacturers are being asked to increase production during coming months.

Twenty-six common nail manufacturers have been authorized by the Director of Industry Operations to produce a total of 72,000 tons of nails a month during April, May, June, and July. The announcement was made by C. E. Adams, chief, iron and steel branch.

Nail production averaged 55,000 tons a month in 1940 and had climbed to 65,000 tons a month by 1941.

Nail manufacturers have been directed to sell their products only on orders carrying preference ratings. Large consumers buy a portion of the output directly from manufacturers, but jobbers still distribute a large percentage of total production.

War invades Santa's workshop, takes metals, plastics, colors

The War Production Board has invaded Santa's workshop.

It issued an order (L–81) that will stop production, after June 30, of toys and games made of metal, plastic, and other materials needed for the war.

The order permits use of enough metal to hold together pieces of wood or other noncritical materials which are expected to be used as substitutes.

The order divides the needed war materials into two groups. One, consisting of iron, steel, zinc, and rayon, is listed as Critical Material. Toys containing more than 7 percent, by weight, of these materials are affected by the order; those containing 7 percent or less may continue to be manufactured.

Supply cut off after June 30

As to those affected, the order provides that between now and June 30 toy and game manufacturers may use up to 25 percent of the amount of Critical Material in the manufacture of such toys which they used in a corresponding period in 1941. After June 30 they may use none—except in toys containing 7 percent or less of their weight of Critical Material.

The second group consists of Prohibited Material and is treated still more drastically. Prohibited Material consists of a long list of metals, cloth, plastics, colors, oils, and chemicals. The order provides, among other things, that, effective at once, none of these materials in their raw state may be put into process. The prohibition does not apply to such materials already in a semiprocessed or processed state. After June 30 none of the Prohibited Material may be used in toys or games, not even by the assembly of parts containing any of the Prohibited Material.

Prohibited Material includes alloy steels, chromium plating, copper, antimony, tin, cork, silk, plastics, certain bright colors, certain oils, and certain chemicals. The only colors permitted are domestic earth colors, ultramarine blue, carbon black, lampblack, boneblack, titanium dioxide, and lithopone. A few bright colors are permitted only for stripes or bands.

Substitution cited

M. D. Moore of the WPB consumers' durable goods branch cited, as an example of the use of substitutes, the case of a large children's play vehicle manufacturing firm that has already perfected a wood tricycle requiring no more steel than is permitted by the order. Similar substitutions are being made in boys' coaster wagons.

Some of the toy manufacturers are already engaged in direct war work. The largest electric-train manufacturer is now making binnacles, compasses, and other precision instruments for the Navy. Another concern is making flares and other products.

Of the more than 600 toy and game companies, about 30 now have war contracts and more are expected to be able to convert.

Production of all outboard motors halted except for war

The War Production Board March 27 halted the production of all outboard motors except for war orders.

At the same time it froze stocks of all outboard motors of 6 horsepower and over in the hands of manufacturers, permitting delivery only of those in transit at the close of business March 27.

The freeze order does not apply to motors under 6 horsepower in the hands of manufacturers, nor does it apply to motors of any size in the hands of distributors or dealers.

The Order, L–80, permits continued manufacture of repair and replacement parts up to 75 percent of a manufacturer's average monthly production of such parts in 1941.

The motors being frozen—6 horsepower and over—will be made available to the Army, Navy, Maritime Commission and other Government war agencies not restricted by the order. Motors under 6 horsepower, referred to generally as fishing motors, will be made available to the public until the present stock is exhausted, but no more will be manufactured. Repair and replacement parts may be made in April and succeeding months up to 75 percent of each manufacturer's average monthly production in 1941.

All of the motors have been manufactured by seven companies, located in the Middle West area. All are already engaged in some direct war production and within a short time almost their entire capacity will be devoted to such work.

Crude rubber, latex cut for 50 items, banned in 20, to save 1,000 tons a month

In a move to save more than 1,000 tons of crude rubber and latex a month, WPB on March 30 amended Supplementary Order M-15-b, reducing the permitted consumption of crude rubber or latex in more than 50 products, and eliminating entirely the use of crude rubber or latex in about 20 products.

15 more under strict control

The Amendment (No. 7) also transfers more than 15 products from the lists which allow use of rubber up to certain percentages of a base period to lists of products for which manufacturers must have specific permission for the use of rubber or latex from the rubber branch of WPB.

The new list "A" of the order—that listing products for which crude may be used only up to certain percentages of the average monthly consumption for the year ended March 31, 1941—now contains 23 groups compared with the previous list of 31.

List B—products for which manufacturers must have specific permission—has been increased from 10 to 27.

Reductions listed

Reductions in the permitted rates of consumption include the following:

Concentrator belts, industrial brake lining and clutch facings, polishing belts, and screen diaphragms, from 125 percent to 100 percent.

Cleats and bucket pads, last puller belts, pulley lagging, round belts, and streetsweeper belts, from 100 percent to 80 percent.

Acid, chemical, high-pressure, jetting and hydraulic, railroad, rotary drillers', and sandblast hose, from 125 percent to 100 percent.

Fire and mill hose, from 40 percent to 30 percent.

Hard rubber pipe and fittings, rubber buckets, pails, etc., rubber insulators, fume ducts, etc., for handling corrosive materials, rubber pumps, and rubber covered rolls (except wringers, printers, fingerprint, and business machines), from 100 percent to 85 percent.

Storage battery parts, hard rubber sheets, insulated tools, and magneto parts, from 125 percent to 80 percent.

Respirators, gas masks, mine safety battery and lamp parts, from 125 percent to 100 percent.

Chute linings, oil well specialties, sheet, strip and mechanical packings, and nonautomotive vibration dampers, from 100 percent to 80 percent.

Automotive parts, 75 percent to 50 percent.

Electricians' gloves, 150 percent to 100 percent.

Mortuary gloves, 100 percent to 20 percent.

Surgical tape, 100 percent to 85 percent.

Automotive fan belts, 30 percent to 20 percent.

Water bottles and syringes, 75 percent to 50 percent.

Among the products transferred from List A to List B (requiring application to the rubber branch for an allotment of crude rubber) are:

Commercial diving equipment; belt splicing and repair materials; elevator and conveyor belts; automotive V-belts; flat transmission and hog beater belts; rubber-lined tanks, drums, and pipes; cable splicing compounds; loom pickers; feeding nipples; surgeons' gloves; press die pads; and cements for repair and manufacturing of shoes.

Completely eliminated from the use of crude rubber by the March 30 amendment are:

Wire braid hose, brewers' hose, hatters' belts and hat-forming bags, vacuum cleaner belts, switchboard mats and matting, wringer rolls, acoustic aids, hard-rubber syringes, dental dam, and fountain syringes.

The revised order permits an increase from 80 percent to 100 percent in the consumption rate for gasoline, oil tank wagon, and sanitary hose.

Newly permitted products

Added to the permitted products are cement gun hose, grease gun hose, hydraulic control hose, and molded seals for dam and lock gates, 100 percent; molded cable connectors, and terminal blocks, 80 percent; and self-adhering gauze bandages and pneumatic truss pads, 50 percent. A new classification is set up for autopsy, mortuary gloves, and net-lined and all-rubber gloves for handling corrosive or severely abrasive materals at a 20 percent rate.

Changes in List C—products in which latex can be consumed only in specific percentages—are as follows:

Use in flat and round belts is reduced from 85 percent to 75 percent; in latex insulation for fume ducts, fans, racks, pumps, valves, etc., from 25 percent to 15 percent; in industrial rubberized fabric gloves for handling corrosives, from 50 percent to 20 percent.

Transferred to List D—products which require permission for use of latex—are: Feeding nipples, surgeons' gloves; nonautomotive V-belts; and cements for manufacture of shoes. Completely eliminated from use of latex are: Blood pressure bags; inhalation bags and face pieces (medical, surgical, etc.); operating cushions, sinus, and cautery bulbs; and compounds for treating tire cords.

★ ★ ★

THOMAS, WESTBERG ADVANCED

Appointment of Fred W. Thomas, formerly head of the feed and grain unit of OPA, as associate price executive in the food section and advancement of John K. Westberg to Mr. Thomas' former post was announced April 1 by Assistant Administrator H. R. Tolley.

Newhall named rubber - coordinator to direct and integrate all current programs

Appointment of Arthur B. Newhall as coordinator for rubber, with broad powers to direct and integrate all current programs dealing with the use, control, or production of natural and synthetic rubber, was announced March 31 by Donald M. Nelson, chairman of the WPB.

Subject to the direction of the chairman, Mr. Newhall as rubber coordinator will:

1. Exercise general supervision over the work of the rubber and rubber products branch of the Division of Industry Operations, WPB;

2. Exercise general supervision over the work of the synthetic rubber section of the Division of Materials, WPB;

3. Determine, whenever and to the extent he deems it necessary, policies and standards to govern priorities and allocations with respect to rubber, including both allocations as between essential civilian needs and other broad classes of demand and allocations among particular civilian needs;

4. Exercise general supervision over the activities of the Bureau of Industrial Conservation of the War Production Board relating to rubber, with particular reference to salvage, conservation, and substitution;

5. Coordinate and exercise general supervision over all work within the War Production Board relating to military or civilian specifications involving the use of rubber;

To represent WPB chairman

6. Coordinate the rationing of rubber tires and tubes by the Office of Price Administration with activities within the War Production Board relating to rubber;

7. Represent the chairman of the War Production Board in relation to the activities of the Reconstruction Finance Corporation or any subsidiary thereof, and the Office of the Petroleum Coordinator for National Defense, with respect to: (a) The provision of additional facilities for the production of synthetic rubber or any of the raw materials therefor; (b) the stockpiling of rubber; (c) the purchase or sale of rubber or rubber products; and (d) the financing of additional production facilities or of transactions in rubber or rubber products;

8. Coordinate measures for enlisting public support for the conservation and salvaging of rubber.

★ ★ ★

Power curtailing plan changed to help seasonal users

WPB Order L-46 providing for curtailment of electric power in the Niagara Falls frontier area in time of shortage, has been amended to change the base period for limiting increases in deliveries from the maximum demand during the month of January 1942, to the maximum demand occurring during any month within the 12-month period ending January 31, 1942. The original provision worked a hardship on seasonal consumers who may not operate in January.

Antimony under allocation May 1; restricted till then

Allocation control over antimony, important lead and tin alloy, was ordered March 30 by the Director of Industry Operations with issuance of General Preference Order M-112. Complete allocation will become effective May 1.

Special directions have been issued for the control of deliveries during the period from the issuance date to May 1. These provide that:

During April, deliveries to any one customer must not exceed deliveries to him. for either January or February of this year.

No deliveries may be made in April on preference ratings lower than A-10.

Effective July 1, use of antimony in any form is prohibited in the manufacture of pigments or opacifiers for paints, lacquers, and enamels, or for toys and decorative and ornamental objects.

Effective on July 1 also is a limitation on the amount of new antimony which may be used in the production of alloys for automotive batteries. New antimony for such purposes is limited to 7 percent of the total used, with the remainder coming from scrap and secondary metal.

The antimony content of alloys for use in battery grids must not exceed 7.5 percent by weight.

Effective immediately, the weight of antimony in any alloy is limited to 0.5 percent unless specifications call for more, and then the limit is 0.5 percent additional.

Consumers of antimony are required to file, by April 20, and by the 20th of every month thereafter, their orders on Form PD-381 with suppliers and a report on Form PD-380 with the War Production Board.

Possessors of antimony in excess of 100 pounds must file an inventory report by April 20 on Form PD-380.

Persons requiring small amounts of antimony monthly are not required to file monthly reports, provided they have filed the inventory report by April 20.

★ ★ ★

Allocating semifinished steel discontinued for seamless tube

To assure maximum steel usage in the direct war effort, semifinished steel will no longer be allocated to manufacturers of seamless tubing who do not make their own steel, C. E. Adams, chief, iron and steel branch, announced March 30.

Instead, manufacturers of this type must rely in the future on the use of priority ratings, except in cases where the tubing itself is allocated.

Nonintegrated producers of steel sheets and pipe (those that do not make their own steel) who have been buying their semifinished steel from integrated manufacturers, must also rely on priority ratings in the future.

This decision was announced in a telegram to all manufacturers.

GUN INVENTORY UNDER WAY

Dealers and wholesalers who have shotguns, pistols, and rifles in stock have been ordered to report to the Government on their inventories of such firearms, many of which will be bought by the Government through the Defense Supplies Corporation. Forms PD-382 and PD-383 have been sent to them for this purpose.

Sales of firearms have been restricted by the WPB in Limitation Order L-60, issued on February 27, except for sales for State, local, and Federal Government use, to Allied Governments, or for Lend-Lease purposes. Information on other permitted exceptions should be secured from the Governmental Requirements Bureau, which is administering the order.

Officials of the Bureau said that as soon as the report forms are tabulated, steps will be taken to unfreeze the stocks which the Government does not need. Meanwhile, users such as war plants may ask the Governmental Requirements Bureau for permission to buy arms.

★ ★ ★

Tin tops for glass containers limited or forbidden

Use of tinplate and terneplate as closures for glass containers was brought under control by WPB April 3 with the issuance of Conservation Order M-104.

The order restricts the production of tinplate or terneplate crown caps for bottled beer and soft-drinks after a four-week period, and lists other specific products for which tinplate or terneplate closures may not be produced after a similar interim period.

Cover caps made of tinplate or terneplate, designed as closures for tomato catsup, chili sauce, and for home-use jars of jelly, jam, marmalade or preserves may no longer be produced. This restriction was effective immediately.

The WPB containers branch, which is administering the order, said that approximately 1,600 tons of tin annually would be saved by the order.

★ ★ ★

WPB asks fewer tacks in shoes

The shoe and leather products section, WPB, suggested April 1 that shoe manufacturers immediately cut the use of tacks by 20 percent to reduce the amount of tack plate and other metal for tacks consumed by the industry.

10 yellow to brown dyes, needed for uniforms, banned for civilians; others cut

Because dyestuffs are necessary for the manufacture of military uniforms the Director of Industry Operations issued on March 29 Conservation Order M-103, curtailing civilian use of organic coloring matter

The order, effective immediately, provides that 10 dyes with colors ranging from orange and yellow to brown, khaki and olive drab, be set aside entirely for war use.

Civilian use of all other anthraquinone vat dyes and other derivative dyes is limited for the second quarter of 1942 to 12½ percent of the amount used during 1941.

The order provides that no producer may export more than 8 percent of his total dyes requiring anthraquinone or derivatives in their manufacture. This requirement is expected to place civilians of Allied countries on an approximately equal footing with civilians in the United States.

According to the order a producer may export 3 percent of his total production of those basic dyes set aside for war use. WPB officials expect this will make available to the Allied countries the dyes with which they can dye uniforms for their armed forces. These include the Latin American nations, India, the Netherlands Indies, and the Free French forces.

Anyone who is not a manufacturer of dyestuffs but who has any of the 10 dyes on list "A" of the order in excess of the amount scheduled to be used by him prior to April 30, 1942, must resell or return the excess dyes to their manufacturer.

★ ★ ★

Persons buying trousers unfinished warned of rule

The apparel section of WPB said April 2 that it has been advised from several sources that some persons are buying suits or trousers at retail and having them delivered to their homes with the trousers unfinished or finished with more than a reasonable turn-up.

The Apparel Section called attention to paragraph (c) (2) of the men's and boys' clothing simplification order (M-73-a), which reads:

"No person shall finish a pair of trousers made of wool cloth with cuffs or cause such to be finished with cuffs by others for his account."

Use of scarce materials limited for ink making; high rating aids manufacturers

The WPB indicated March 30 that it intends to assist the printing and publishing industry isofar as possible, by the issuance of two orders governing the manufacture of printing inks.

The first, M-53, limits in varying percentages the amount of scarce materials which can be used in the manufacture of inks, and the second, P-94, assigns the high preference rating of A-5 to enable manufacturers to obtain these materials.

M-53 limits to 70 percent by quarters, compared to 1941, the use of these materials in the manufacture of printing inks: Chrome yellows and oranges, molybdate orange, chrome green, orange mineral and organic pigments. Iron blue is similarly restricted to 100 percent.

Other provisions

Use of oil soluble toners in any black ink or news ink is prohibited. Use of alkali blue or other organic toner in black ink is restricted to 8 percent by weight in paste form or 4 percent in the form of dry color.

Use of glycerol phthalate or phenolic resins in the production of gloss inks is prohibited. A number of substitutes are available in this field.

P-94 assigns a preference rating of A-5 to 50 percent of the average monthly use in 1941 of the inorganic colors and organio pigments restricted by M-53 to 70 percent use. Iron blues, zincated resins and ester gum may be purchased under the rating up to 80 percent of 1941 use.

Form PD-345 is provided for reports from producers monthly. This form will be available in about 10 days.

Both orders are effective immediately. P-94 expires on June 30, 1942, and M-53 has no terminal date.

Neither order places any restriction as to how a manufacturer of printing ink shall use the materials he can obtain nor any restriction on end uses of inks so produced.

★ ★ ★

LAIDLAW APPOINTED

Defense Transportation Director Eastman announced April 1 the appointment of Neil S. Laidlaw as associate director of the division of coastwise and intercoastal transport.

PRIORITY ACTIONS			• From March 28 • Through April 1		
Subject	Order number	Related form	Issued	Exp. date	Rating
Alcohol:					
a. Methyl:					
1. Assigns preference ratings to shipments in classifications I and II of M-25.	M-31 amend No. 4.		3-31-42		B-2; B-3.
Antimony:					
a. Allocation order	M-112	PD-380, 381	3-30-42	12-31-42	
Asbestos textiles:					
a. Conservation order	M-123		3-30-42		A-10 or higher.
Canning:					
a. Maintenance and expansion of plants canning fruits and vegetables:					
1. Canners who use leased machinery entitled to same preference ratings as if they owned the machinery.	P-115 Int. No. 1.	PD-81a, 285	3-27-42		
Caskets, Shipping Cases and Burial Vaults:					
a. Curtails use of certain metals in manufacture.	L-64		3-28-42		
Chemicals:					
a. Materials for maintenance, repair and operating supplies:					
1. Further clarification of "operating supplies".	P-89 as amended, Int. No. 1.		3-27-42		
b. Solvents (chlorinated hydrocarbon):					
1. Extension	M-41 ext. No. 1		3-30-42	5-15-42	
c. Chlorine:					
1. Postpones effective date to May 1, 1942.	M-19 as amended, amend. No. 2.		3-30-42	Until revoked.	
Chromium—Supply and direct distribution:					
a. Supplementary order:					
1. Limits use of chromium in chemicals.	M-18-b	PD-54	3-26-42	do	A-10 or higher.
Closures and Associated Items:					
a. Prohibits use of copper and copper base alloy, steel, zinc, and zinc base alloy in manufacture of certain items.	L-68		3-18-42		
Copper:					
a. Clarifies use of bronze powder, ink, paste, and lead by printing and publishing industry.	M-9-c as amended.		3-28-42		
b. Supplementary order:					
1. Permits public utilities to use in own operations wire or cable that has become scrap through obsolescence, provided lengths are in excess of 5 feet and monthly total less than 5 tons.	M-9-b as amended and extended.	PD-121, 130, 226, 249.	3-31-42	Until revoked.	
Cork:					
a. To insure equal distribution.	M-8-a amend. No. 1.	PD-384	3-26-42	do	
Cotton (Egyptian, imported):					
a. Conservation order:					
1. Restricts sale, use and delivery of certain grades of imported Egyptian cotton to defense orders and sewing thread.	M-117		4-1-42		
Dyestuffs:					
a. Conservation order	M-103		3-26-42	Until revoked.	
Electrical Appliances:					
a. Discontinues use of critical materials in manufacture after May 31 production halted except orders rated higher than A-2.	L-65	PD-370	3-30-42	do	Varies.
Farm Machinery and Equipment:					
a. Material for production:					
1. Includes irrigation equipment and increases manufacturing percentage quotas of various types of machinery.	P-95 amend No. 1.		3-30-42		A-3.
b. To restrict production:					
1. Additional equipment not included in original program.	L-26 amend No. 1.		3-30-42		
Flashlights:					
a. Cases and batteries:					
1. Prohibits use of critical materials in production of.	L-71		3-27-42	Until revoked.	
Glycerine:					
a. Deliveries in excess of 80 pounds a month placed under allocation control.	M-58	PD-361, 362, 363.	3-30-42	do	
Goatskins, Kidskins, and Cabrettas:					
a. Conservation order	M-114	PD-373	3-30-42		
Honey:					
a. To conserve present stocks	M-118		3-26-42		

Subject	Order number	Related form	Issued	Exp. date	Rating
Kitchen, Household, and other Miscellaneous Articles:					
a. Curtails use of iron, steel, and zinc in manufacture of certain kitchen, household and miscellaneous articles.	L–30		3–31–42	Until revoked.	
Laboratory Equipment and Reagent Chemicals:					
a. Materials for production	P–62	PD–63	11–15–41	3–31–42	A–3.
1. Extension; amended to abolish PD–93	P–62 ext. No. 1 Amend. No. 1.		3–30–42	6–30–42	
Lauric Acid Oils:					
a. Correction	M–60		3–31–42		
Lawn Mowers:					
a. To curtail production:					
1. Iron and steel used in manufacture cut in half; prohibits entirely manufacture after June 30.	L–67		3–30–42		
Lead:					
a. Supplementary Order:					
1. April lead pool set at 15 percent of February 1942.	M–38–g		3–30–42		
Manila Cordage:					
a. Cordage manufacturer need not include in sales quota defense orders placed and ready for delivery prior to Mar. 2, 1942, but which could not be delivered by them for reasons beyond his control.	M–36 amend No. 8.		4–1–42		
Metal Signs:					
a. Curtails use of steel and iron in manufacture.	M–29		3–25–42	Until revoked.	
Molasses:					
a. Operational changes made	M–54 as amended.		3–27–42	do.	
Nickel:					
a. Definitions changed; amended and extended.	M–6–a amended and extended.	PD–27	3–30–42	do.	
Office machinery:					
a. Restrictions made applicable to wide-carriage typewriters.	L–54–a amend. No. 1.		3–27–42		
Office supplies:					
a. Curtails use of certain materials in manufacture of metal office supplies.	L–73		3–26–42	Until revoked.	
Outboard motors and parts:					
a. To restrict production:					
1. Halts production except for defense orders.	L–60		3–27–42		
Plumbing and heating:					
a. Cast iron tubular radiators.	Schedule No. 6 to L–42.		3–30–42		
b. Prohibits use of copper or copper base alloy in certain items.	Schedule No. 7 to L–42.		3–30–42 (eff. 4–1–42)		
Power (electric):					
a. Changes base period for limiting increases in deliveries from maximum demand during January 1942 to maximum demand during any month within 12-month period ending Jan. 31, 1942.	L–46 amend. No. 1		3–30–42		
Printing ink:					
a. Conservation order:					
1. Limits in varying percentages amount of scarce materials which can be used in manufacture of inks.	M–53	PD–344	3–30–42		
b. Assigns preference rating to 50 percent of average monthly use in 1941 of inorganic colors and organic pigments restricted by M–53 to 70 percent use.	P–04	PD–345	3–30–42	6–30–42	A–5.
Refrigerators (domestic mechanical):					
a. Kerosene:					
1. Kerosene refrigerators excluded from order halting production after Apr. 30.	L–5–c amend. No. 3.		3–26–42		
b. Domestic mechanical:					
1. Dealers permitted to sell entire stocks.	L–5–b amend. No. 2.		3–26–42		
c. Permits acquisition of strategic materials from refrigerator manufacturers by any company organized under RFC Act.	L–5–c amend. No. 2.		3–27–42		
d. Domestic nonmechanical:					
1. Supplementary order—reduces steel consumption in manufacture.	L–7–b		3–30–42		
Research work:					
a. Preference rating covering material entering into experimental and research for aircraft raised and order extended.	P–24 amend. No. 1 and ext. No. 2.		3–25–42	6–30–42	A–1–a.
Rough Diamonds:					
a. Provides for inventory	M–109	PD–376, 377, 378.	3–27–42		

(Continued on page 14)

Publishers given stay of ban on bronze powder, paste, ink

An interpretation and supplement to Copper Order M–9–c covering the use of bronze powder, ink, paste, and lead by the printing and publishing industry were issued March 28 by Industry Operations Director Knowlson.

The effect of the order and interpretation is to permit a limited use of these materials for 2 months, after which their use must be discontinued entirely.

The interpretation points out that the use of these copper derivatives in printing and publishing is deemed decorative and would be prohibited after March 31, 1942, under the terms of the order.

However, because some confusion has existed in regard to the application of M–9–c to the use of these materials, Supplementary Order M–9–c–3 was issued March 28, postponing for 2 months the prohibition against use of these materials in the printing and publishing industry and permitting consumption of inventory stocks.

After May 31, 1942, the complete prohibition becomes effective. Each printer and publisher who intends to take advantage of this 60-day stay must file with the War Production Board before April 20, 1942, his inventory as of March 31 of all bronze powder, ink, paste, and lead and a statement of his uses in the year 1941. In the ensuing 60 days he may use 16⅔ percent, all from present inventory, of the amount he used in 1941.

Other uses of copper and copper products by the printing and publishing industry are not deemed decorative and are governed by the general provisions of Order M–9–c which limits the use of copper in any quarter to approximately 70 percent of the amount used in the last quarter of 1940.

Drums, containers, packing supplies under chemical rating

Drums, containers, and other packages, and materials to be physically incorporated in them, are included in "operating supplies" under the terms of the preference rating order for the chemical industry, P–89, it was explained March 28 in an official interpretation of the order issued by the Director of Industry Operations.

Also included in "operating supplies," for which a preference rating of A–3 may be assigned by producers as defined in the order, are materials to be used for sealing or fastening packages.

WPB orders national inventory of rough diamonds

A Nation-wide inventory of rough diamonds, used in making machine tools and for numerous other phases of the war effort, was announced March 28 by Industry Operations Director Knowlson.

Conservation Order M–109, issued and effective March 27, provides that all persons, who, on March 31, 1942, had in their possession or had title to 10 carats or more of rough diamonds must report them to the War Production Board by April 15, 1942. Subsequent reports must be made quarterly. Form PD–376 is provided for this purpose.

Also must report sales, transfers

Sales, transfers, and imports of rough diamonds also must be reported. Sales of rough diamonds in quantities of more than 5 carats must be reported within 10 days on Form PD–377. Imports also must be reported within 10 days on Form PD–377. Sales or transfers of less than 5 carats must be reported monthly on Form PD–378. Forms PD–376, 377 and 378 will be available in about ten days from March 28.

The order does not apply to cut or polished diamonds used as gems nor to rough diamonds incorporated in a tool in use. Diamonds in unused tools must be reported.

In addition to the inventory aspect, the purpose of WPB is to channel industrial diamonds directly into war uses and to eliminate insofar as possible sales of rough diamonds for purposes of speculation and hoarding.

Machine tool rebuilding order is extended

Preference Rating Order P–77, covering material for the rebuilding of machine tools, has been extended to May 1, 1942. This order, which applies only in the case of companies to which an individual copy of the order has been addressed with a serial number, was scheduled to expire April 1.

Companies operating under the order have been advised that they will be expected as soon as possible to shift over to use of the Production Requirements Plan. However, some special problems have arisen in connection with application of PRP to this industry, and the extension is designed to permit further study and any necessary adjustments.

PRIORITY ACTIONS

*From March 28
*Through April 1

(Continued from page 13)

Subject	Order number	Related form	Issued	Exp. date	Rating
Rubber:					
a. Reduces consumption of crude rubber or latex in more than 50 products, and eliminates their use entirely in more than 20 products.	M-15-b amend. No. 7.		3-30-42		
b. Corrections	M-15-b-1		3-28-42		
c. Rubber yarn or elastic thread:					
1. Conservation order	M-124		3-28-42		
Steel and Iron:					
a. Corrosion and heat resistant chrome steel.	M-21-d amend. No. 1.		3-27-42		A-1-k or higher.
b. Pig iron:					
1. Complete allocation of pig iron supplies.	M-17 amend. No. 2 and ext. No. 2.	PD-09, 70, 71, 71d..	3-28-42	Until revoked.	
Sugar—to conserve supply and direct distribution:					
a. Refiners may fulfill sugar requirements of beekeepers and the USO without charge to their quotas.	Amend. No. 2 to to M-55 as amended and extended.		3-26-42		
b. Supplementary order:					
1. Restrictions on primary distributors.	M-55-c		3-27-42	12-31-42	
c. Supplementary order:					
1. Definitions of zones.	M-55-d		3-27-42	12-31-42	
d. Supplementary order:					
1. Sets quotas.	M-55-e		3-27-42		
e. Supplementary order:					
1. Quotas for raw or invert direct-consumption sugar.	M-55-f		3-27-42	12-31-42	
f. Supplementary order:					
1. Raises raw sugar for period Jan. 1 to Sept. 30, 1942.	M-98-a amended.		3-27-42		
Tea—to restrict distribution:					
a. Places restrictions on deliveries and receipts.	M-111	PD-374	3-27-42		
b. Supplementary order:					
1. Quotas provided for.	M-111-a.	PD-374	3-27-42		
Tin:					
a. Collapsible tin, tin-coated and alloy tubes:					
(a) Completely eliminates use for foods, cosmetics and most toilet preparations.	M-118		4-1-42	Until revoked	
Tools:					
a. Machine tools:					
1. Production and delivery of machine tools, gages, and chucks.	E-1-a amend. No. 1.		3-26-42		
b. Extension	P-77 ext. No. 2.		3-31-42	5-1-42.	
Toys and games:					
a. Production of toys and games made of metal, plastic and other critical materials stopped after June 30.	L-81		3-30-42 (eff. 4-1-42)		
Utilities:					
a. Maintenance, repair and supplies—materials necessary for Vacuum cleaners (domestic):	P-46 amended		3-26-42	6-30-42	As assigned.
a. Supplementary order:					
1. Production discontinued after Apr. 30.	L-18-b		3-30-42 (eff. 4-1-42)		
Zinc:					
a. Extension	Ext. of M-11 as extended.		3-26-42	5-31-42.	
b. Supplementary order:					
1. Zinc pool for April.	M-11-j		3-28-42		

SUSPENSION ORDERS

Company	Order No.	Violations	Penalty	Issued	Exp. date
Lubbock Hardware & Supply Co., Lubbock, Tex.	8-18	Acceptance of deliveries in excess of its quota pursuant to Supplementary Order M-21-b.	Reduction of deliveries.	3-27-42	6-30-42
Hunter and Havens, Inc., Bridgeport, Conn.	8-20	....do....	....do....	3-27-42	6-30-42
Huron Steel Co., Detroit, Mich.	8-21	....do....	....do....	3-27-42	6-30-42
Gadsen Hardware Co., Gadsen, Ala.	8-22	....do....	....do....	3-27-42	6-30-42
Genesee Bridge Co., Inc., Rochester, N. Y.	8-23	....do....	....do....	3-27-42	6-30-42
The Faeth Co., Kansas City, Mo.	8-24	....do....	....do....	3-27-42	6-30-42
Baker Steel and Tube Co., Los Angeles, Calif.	8-25	....do....	Suspension of deliveries.	3-27-42	6-30-42
Swedish Steel Mills' A. A., Inc., New York City, N. Y.	8-26	....do....	Reduction of deliveries.	3-27-42	6-30-42
J. B. Beaird Corporation, Shreveport, La.		....do....	....do....	3-27-42	6-30-42

Company	Order No.	Violations	Penalty	Issued	Exp. date
Austin-Hastings Co., Cambridge, Mass.	8-28	Acceptance of deliveries—Con.	Reduction of deliveries—Con.	3-27-42	6-30-42
N. H. Bragg & Sons, Bangor, Maine.	8-28	......do..................	.....do..............	3-27-42	6-30-42
Coulter, Sibbett & Burke, Los Angeles, Calif.	8-28	......do..................	Suspension of deliveries.	3-27-42	6-30-42
Dayton Hardware & Supply Co., Dayton, Ohio.	8-28	......do..................	Reduction of deliveries.	3-27-42	6-30-42
Delaware Hardware Co., Wilmington, Del.	8-28	......do..................	.....do..............	3-27-42	6-30-42
Fable & Co., Philadelphia, Pa...	8-28	......do..................	.....do..............	3-27-42	6-30-42
Fairmont Supply Co., Fairmont W. Va.	8-28	......do..................	.....do..............	3-27-42	6-30-42
Polisk Steel Co., Cincinnati, Ohio.	8-28	......do..................	.....do..............	3-27-42	6-30-42
Ross-Frazer Iron Co., St. Joseph, Mo.	8-28	......do..................	.....do..............	3-27-42	6-30-42
Chas. G. Stevens Co., Chicago, Ill.	8-28	......do..................	Suspension of deliveries.	3-27-42	6-30-42
Stratton & Terstegge Co., Louisville, Ky.	8-28	......do..................	.....do..............	3-27-42	6-30-42
Super Steels, Inc., Cleveland, Ohio.	8-28	......do..................	Reduction of deliveries.	3-27-42	6-30-42
Penn. Metal Co., Inc., Los Angeles, Calif.	8-20	......do..................	.....do..............	3-27-42	6-30-42

Most of U. S. industry to be brought under Production Requirements Plan in move for closer control of scarce materials

A fundamental change in the priorities system was announced March 21 by Director of Industry Operations Knowlson.

Blanket ratings to go

A specific requirements approach to the control and distribution of scarce materials will replace the use of general or blanket priority rating orders as rapidly as the necessary new orders and procedures can be put into effect. Between April 1 and June 30, most of the blanket rating orders will be revoked or allowed to expire, and companies which have been operating under blanket ratings will be required to apply for priority assistance under the Production Requirements Plan.

Under the Production Requirements Plan, a company makes a single application for priority assistance covering all of its estimated materials needs over a 3-month period. Interim applications may be filed when a company needs additional quantities of material during the quarter because of increased war or other essential business.

A Modified Production Requirements Plan has been developed to meet the needs of small firms whose business is less than $100,000 a year. Such companies may use a simplified application form, PD-25X.

The effect of placing virtually all of American industry, including producers who supply the Army and Navy, under the Production Requirements Plan will be to give the War Production Board closer control of the distribution and use of all scarce materials.

Because it would be physically impossible to handle the load of PRP applications if they were to be submitted immediately from all companies in all industries, the change-over from the use of blanket ratings will be continuous over a period of 3 months, and each industry will be notified as to the date by which the change must be completed.

To gear economy to war

New limitation or conservation orders will continue to be issued to curtail production by nonessential and less essential industries which still use scarce materials and to force substitutions for scarce materials wherever possible in essential industries. All ratings assigned under PRP will be subject to such controls.

The extension of PRP to cover a much broader field, and its substitution for "P" orders, will constitute another long step toward gearing the whole American economy into the war program. When the change-over is completed, priority assistance will be granted only for specified quantities of materials or products, and the War Production Board will then be in a position to go as far toward complete allocation as war needs may require.

Financial advice to contractors controlled by new bureau

Organization of a bureau of finance in the Division of Industry Operations to assist contractors and subcontractors in solving financial problems which may arise in connection with the handling of war orders was announced March 28 by Director of Industry Operations Knowlson.

Closer contacts with industry branches

The bureau will take over the functions and personnel of the financial section of the Contract Distribution Branch of the WPB Production Division. Bradley Nash, who has been head of this financial section since June 1941, will be chief of the new unit.

Transfer of the bureau to the Division of Industry Operations will make possible closer contact between the bureau's financial experts and the staffs of the industry branches in the division, with special reference to financial problems involved in converting civilian industries to war work.

Acts in advisory capacity

The bureau of finance does not make any loans or dispense any funds to contractors, but furnishes advice and assistance about financial matters to companies engaged in war production or desirous of obtaining war contracts or subcontracts. It also endeavors to be helpful in working out the financial requirements when a group of manufacturers undertakes to pool facilities for war work.

The bureau of finance now has about 35 representatives located in WPB field offices. The staff has recently been handling about 500 new cases a month involving amounts running from as little as one thousand dollars up into millions.

To help arrange financing

The bureau endeavors wherever possible to arrange financing of war work through commercial banks. When the required financial assistance cannot be so arranged the bureau assists the contractor to make the proper application to the Reconstruction Finance Corporation, a Federal Reserve bank, or other Government financing agency.

Financial advice and assistance are provided by the bureau for companies which have difficulty in obtaining sufficient working capital to handle war contracts as well as for those which need to expand or alter their production facilities.

LABOR . . .

Board declines jurisdiction of wage case while binding contract is still in force

The National War Labor Board last week issued a decision in one case, declined to take jurisdiction in another on the ground that a binding contract is still in existence, closed the primary hearings in the Little Steel case, reached agreement in one case, made an arbitration award in another case and received certification of 10 new disputes.

Postal Telegraph

For a second time since its creation, the National War Labor Board unanimously declined to take jurisdiction in a dispute and returned the case to the Secretary of Labor. The case involved the Postal Telegraph Cable Co., New York, N. Y., and the American Communications Association, CIO. The union is asking for wage increases. The Board's decision was based upon the grounds that a contract is in existence between the parties which may not be altered under its terms without the mutual consent of the parties.

In announcing the action of the Board, Mr. Davis, chairman, said:

"The present wage structure is set by the terms of a contract agreed upon by the company and the union, which binds the parties until October 1, 1942. No changes can be made under this contract except by mutual consent. This Board will not be used by either management or labor to escape from the terms of any voluntary collective bargaining agreement while that agreement is still in effect. To adopt any other course would do irreparable harm to the whole structure of industrial relations in this country and endanger successful prosecution of the war."

The dispute was certified to the Board March 25 and involves 10,710 employees.

Little Steel

The fact-finding Panel of the Board hearing the dispute between four steel companies and the Steel Workers Organizing Committee, CIO, began last week the task of digesting over 8,000 pages of testimony taken during more than a month of hearings. The union and the companies involved—Bethlehem Steel Co., Republic Steel Corp., Youngstown Sheet and Tube Co., and Inland Steel Co.—have been given until April 15 to file rebuttals, and on April 22 the panel and the parties will reconvene for questioning by the panel on the basis of their study of the record and the rebuttals. The panel will then make its report to the full Board.

The Panel in the case is composed of Arthur S. Meyer, chairman of the New York State Board of Mediation; Cyrus Ching, Vice president of United States Rubber Co. and Richard Frankensteen, director of aircraft organization of the United Automobile Workers, CIO. Hearings began February 26 over the union's demands for $1 per day wage increase and the union shop. The dispute involves a total of 182,000 employees of the four companies.

Food Machinery Corporation

After only two days of hearings, a voluntary agreement was reached settling all issues in dispute between the Food Machinery Corp., Lakeland, Fla. and the International Brotherhood of Boiler Makers, Iron Shipbuilders and Helpers, AFL.

An increase in the base rate from 96 cents to $1.05 per hour retroactive to December 30, 1941, was agreed upon and on July 1, 1942, the wage question is to be again subject to discussion. The union security issue was settled by a clause to be inserted into the contract advocating maintenance of membership for the duration of the workers' employment and the company is to furnish all new employees with a copy of the contract and will advise them to become members of the union. The agreement will affect 185 employees of the company.

The panel which heard the case was composed of Professor I. L. Sharfman, Fred Krafft, and Richard Gray.

Toledo, Peoria & Western Railroad

Judge Benjamin C. Hilliard of the Supreme Court of Colorado was appointed by the Board last week as arbitrator of all issues in dispute between the Toledo, Peoria & Western Railroad and the Brotherhood of Locomotive Firemen and Enginemen and the Brotherhood of Railroad Trainmen. The appointment was made in accordance with the Board's decision of February 27 ordering the dispute to be arbitrated. Refusal by Mr. George P. McNear, president of the road, to accept the Board's order resulted on March 21 in Federal seizure and operation of the road.

In the Executive order, the President directed the Director of the Office of Defense Transportation to manage the railroad "pending such termination of the existing labor dispute as may be approved by the National War Labor Board."

The telegram to Mr. McNear announcing Judge Hilliard's appointment stated that "final settlement of the controversy will depend upon your compliance with the President's order that the dispute be arbitrated" and asked him to notify the Board if and when he is ready to proceed with arbitration.

Federated Fishing Boats

In a 4-to-2 decision, with the labor members dissenting, the Board ordered that the war risk insurance dispute between the Federated Fishing Boats of New England and New York, Inc., Boston, Mass., and the Atlantic Fishermen's Union, AFL, should be settled by dividing that cost evenly between the fishermen and the employers. Radio officers serving on fishing vessels of the employers were also granted war risk bonuses with the expense of such additional compensation to be shared equally by employers and fishermen.

At the time the case was certified to the Board in January, some 800 men were on strike and 57 boats were tied up in Boston Harbor. The employers at first refused to comply with the Board's request that they advance the premium for the insurance until a final determination of the issue could be made by the Board, but on February 14 the employers finally agreed to the Board's order.

A public hearing was held in the case on March 12, and it was on the basis of that hearing that the decision was made. Both decisions were written by Dr. George W. Taylor, Vice chairman of the Board, and were concurred in by Frank P. Graham, public member, and Roger Lapham and George H. Mead, employer members. The dissenting

labor members were Robert J. Watt and R. J. Thomas.

American Smelting and Refining

A three-man arbitration board last week made its award settling the dispute between two plants of the American Smelting & Refining Co., at San Francisco and Selby, Calif., and two locals of the International Union of Mine, Mill and Smelter Workers, CIO. The arbitration board was composed of Judge Walter P. Stacy, John E. Connelly, and Sherman Dalrymple, with Mr. Dalrymple dissenting from the award which was that the wage scales and conditions prevailing at the two plants should not "be further disturbed during the remaining term" of the two contracts.

The case was certified to the Board on February 5 and at the hearings before the panel in March it was agreed that the dispute be settled by arbitration with the members of the panel acting as arbitrators. The award will affect 250 employees at the San Francisco plant and 550 at the Selby plant.

New cases

The new cases certified to the Board last week involved the following: Western Electric Co., Kearny, N. J. and the Western Electric Employees Assn., affiliated with the National Federation of Telephone Workers and the Assn. of Communications Equipment Workers, both independent; Committee of Employers, Seattle, Wash. and the Int. Woodworkers of America, CIO; the Shell Oil Co., Houston, Texas and the Oil Workers International Union, CIO; Roller Bearing Co. of America, Trenton, N. J. and the United Automobile Workers, CIO; Johns Manville Co., Billerica, Mass. and Nashua, N. H. and District 50, United Mine Workers, CIO; Frank Foundries Corp., Moline, Ill. and the United Automobile Workers, CIO; Cornell Dubilier Condenser Corp., South Plainfield, N. J. and the Int. Brotherhood of Electrical Workers, AFL, and the United Electrical, Radio and Machine Workers, CIO; Westinghouse Air Brake Co., Wilmerding, Pa. and the United Electrical, Radio and Machine Workers, CIO; Armour Leather Co., Williamsport, Pa. and the Int. Fur and Leather Workers, CIO; and Nevada Consolidated Copper Co., Santa Rita and Hurley, New Mexico and the Metal Department, AFL.

★ ★ ★

Fluorescent lighting fixture production halted by WPB

WPB on April 2 ordered an immediate end to the production of fluorescent lighting fixtures except for use of existing inventories for a period of 20 days and certain other excepted purposes.

The order (Limitation Order L–78) is expected to result in the saving of 35,000 tons of steel, 2,200 tons of copper, and 5,200 pounds of mercury.

The terms of the order prohibit the manufacture or assembly of any fluorescent lighting fixture or part, notwithstanding existing contracts or agreements, except on orders bearing a preference rating of A–2 or better.

Meeting plane schedules, ahead on tanks, says Nelson, but warns we must do more

Excerpts from an address by Donald M. Nelson, Chairman, War Production Board, before a banquet of the Military Order of the World War, April 4:

When you look back, I am sure you will agree that we set out to do the impossible. We have not yet done the impossible—but we are doing it. The achievements this Nation has recorded during the last 20-odd months are as remarkable as anything in our history. We cannot be satisfied, because the sky is the limit; but do not let the fact that we are not satisfied delude you into the feeling that nothing much has been accomplished.

An "impossible" program

The airplane production program adopted after Pearl Harbor was presumed by practically everyone to be bigger than could possibly be attained. It was an "impossible" program if there ever was one. We met our schedules in January and we made 23 percent more planes than we had made in December. We exceeded our schedules in February which, of course, called for an increase over January. In March again we met the schedule which increases in line with the President's objective.

We are ahead of schedule on tank production. Our production of merchant shipping is rising rapidly; we should meet this year's schedule. The same is true of our production of anti-aircraft and anti-tank guns.

Yet this is no time for easy optimism. Measured by any ordinary standard, this Nation has done extremely well; but we aren't measuring by ordinary standards any more. Instead, we are measuring our performance against the greatest emergency the country has ever faced. What would be superlative performance at any other time could easily turn out to be short of the goal we must reach. It has been said often, but we must continue to say it—no matter how well we are doing, we must do even better.

Speaking for the millions of men and women engaged on the home front in the great job of providing those weapons and that support, I want to say this to our fighting men everywhere:

You have given us hope and courage. We will live up to the ideal you have set for us. We know what your need is; we are going to move ahead and meet that need in spite of any and all obstacles. We will not let you down.

Tool plant's production committee cited for heroic effort to keep going in flood

Donald M. Nelson, Chairman of the War Production Board, on March 28 personally cited the management-labor production committee in the Batavia, N. Y., plant of the Doehler Die Casting Co. for heroic efforts to keep production going during the recent Tonawanda Creek flood.

Worked in water up to knees

The plant's management-labor committee sent a graphic report to Production Drive headquarters detailing efforts made to keep the plant going. At times officials and workers labored in water up to their knees to continue operations. Mr. Nelson wrote the plant management-labor committee, known as the Victory Production Board:

"I have just received your full report of the way labor and management worked tirelessly together to keep production going during the Tonawanda Creek flood.

"That is precisely the kind of enthusiastic cooperative effort we are asking for in our production drive, and it represents the spirit which will carry this Nation to victory. When we are ready to award recognition formally for outstanding achievements your committee will certainly be eligible for consideration for an award.

As good as firing a gun

"Meanwhile, please extend my congratulations to all the men who proved themselves heroes of production during the flood. They are destroying our enemies as surely as if they were firing a gun."

The committee reported that the first warning of the flood came at 11 a. m. March 17:

"Both management and labor worked as a body to save all equipment and materials in the plant. No one was concerned whether he was a plant official or a worker in the plant. They worked in water which at times was up to their knees and continued to operate equipment in the plant until the water forced them to stop production. The quantities of metal and packing material which were saved through coordination of management and labor amounted to many thousands of dollars. Because of such action, only 16 hours elapsed before the plant was in operation again."

The committee singled out for special praise the maintenance crew under Harry Heller, Sr.; Ted Pickering, plant

manager, and the traffic department under William McCue.

The National Association of Die Cast Workers (CIO) which has a closed-shop contract with the company waived provisions of its agreement to permit men to work regardless of their shift without overtime for the first eight hours.

The Victory Production Board was organized at the plant on November 11, 1941. Its membership is made up as follows:

Raymond Wood, chief steward of the union, and chairman of the board; John McGarigal, plant superintendent; Francis Kennedy, union president; A. E. Swanson, assistant plant superintendent; George Hodgson, plant metallurgist; William Schaefer, maintenance department; William Kane, personnel director; Ernest Pawnell, casting machine operator; John Rhoads, superintendent of the brass division; Arthur Griswold, permanent mould pourer; Mr. Wood was named chairman of the Board.

When Chairman Nelson announced the Production Drive, the Victory Boards in the Doehler plants volunteered to participate in the drive.

We are all on trial, Nelson warns in Supplement to Production Drive book

WPB Chairman Nelson on March 31 told labor and management they are on trial before the American public and that "this is our last chance to show that a free economy can survive and be strong." His statement appeared in a foreword to a supplement to the Official Plan Book, the master plan for the War Production Drive. The supplement was mailed last week to primary war contractors.

New posters that will be available during April are reproduced. Accompanying the supplement is a master military map which, it is suggested, may be enlarged by plant War Production Drive committees. From time to time, the supplement reports, the War and Navy Departments will issue official communiques describing the performance of equipment in action. This will enable committees to indicate on the map spots where equipment made in their own factory is proving its worth in the war.

RATIONING . . .

Sugar refiners' deliveries restricted to nearby areas, to conserve East's supply

The War Production Board has ordered sugar refiners to restrict deliveries of refined domestic cane sugar to certain areas adjacent to their refineries.

The action (Supplementary Order M-55-d) was taken to prevent further depletion of the sugar supply in the East, particularly in the New England States.

Simultaneously, the WPB issued three other supplementary orders, M-55-c, M-55-e, M-55-f, and an amendment to order M-98-a.

April quota set

These orders and amendment do the following things:

Fix the April refined sugar delivery quota at 80 percent of April 1941 deliveries, and extend restrictions to all industrial users.

Set aside 15 percent of the stocks of beet sugar and 15 percent of future beet sugar production for shipment as directed by the WPB.

Establish a special annual quota for invert refined sugar. Invert refined sugar is a type of glucose.

Raise certain raw sugar quotas.

Zones defined

Supplementary order M-55-d restricts the sale and shipment of domestic refined sugar to specific zones, which are as follows:

1. Refiners in New England may ship to points only in the six New England States.
2. Refiners in New York, Philadelphia, and Baltimore may ship to points only in Massachusetts, Rhode Island, Connecticut, New York, New Jersey, Pennsylvania, Delaware, Maryland, Virginia, West Virginia, and the District of Columbia.
3. Refiners in North Carolina may ship to points only in that State.
4. Refiners in South Carolina, Georgia, and Florida east of the Apalachicola River may ship to points within that area, plus North Carolina, Tennessee, and Kentucky.
5. Refiners in Tennessee and Kentucky may ship to points only in that area.
6. Refiners in Alabama, Mississippi, Louisiana, Arkansas, Oklahoma, Texas, Missouri, Illinois, Indiana, Ohio and Florida west of the Apalachicola River, may ship to points in this area plus Tennessee and Kentucky.
7. Refiners in any State outside of the specified zones may ship to any point in the continental United States (excluding Alaska and the Canal Zone) and in Texas, Oklahoma, Missouri, and Illinois, but not to any point within the specified zones.

Some special sugars excepted

A refiner may, however, sell or ship the following sugars outside of his specified zone: refined sugar processed outside continental United States, soft sugars in bulk, confectioners', brown, loaf, tablet, and other specialty refined sugars in 1- and 2-pound packages, and raw sugar.

Supplementary order M-55-c directs any beet sugar processor to set aside for a period of 60 days 15 percent of his existing stock and 15 percent of his future monthly production of refined sugar for shipment as ordered by the Director of Industry Operations, WPB.

Within 15 days from the issuance of this order (March 27) and within 5 days after the end of each subsequent month, he is required to notify the WPB in writing of the location and amount of such sugar. If the WPB does not specify shipment of the sugar within 60 days it is automatically released to the processor.

The purpose of orders M-55-c and M-55-d is to prevent the overlapping of sugar distribution by a beet processor and a cane refiner, and thereby prevent further depletion of the supply of sugar in the Eastern States. WPB and the Defense Supplies Corporation have agreed that the DSC will compensate a beet processor for losses incident to shipping east of his normal trading area, which, in the case of a western processor, usually is west of Chicago. By operating in a smaller territory, a cane refiner will be better able to serve the trade in that area.

All industrial uses controlled

In addition to fixing the April refined quota, supplementary order M-55-e extends control to include all industrial uses of sugar. Furthermore, any jobber or wholesaler may not deliver more sugar to such a user than his quota.

In addition, any receiver may not have in his possession, at any time, more than a minimum practicable working inventory.

Supplementary M-55-f establishes for any user of raw or invert refined sugar, except in the processing of refined sugar, a special annual quota of as much as 70 percent of his 1941 deliveries, but not more than 10,000 pounds in any one month.

To take advantage of the order, a user is required to certify in writing to the War Production Board by April 15, his use of raw or invert refined sugar during each month of 1941 and 1942. A user not taking advantage of the order is governed by the general provisions of the other sugar orders.

The amendment of M-98-a raises the raw sugar quota for the period January 1 to September 30, 1942, to a total of 2,659,372 short tons, raw value, an increase of 72,004 short tons over the quota in the original order. The increase was made after complete data on the sugar industry made it necessary to revise the 9-month allotment of some refiners. The original allotment had been fixed on preliminary data.

★ ★ ⊥

RED CROSS TO COLLECT WOOL CLIPPED FROM TROUSERS

The clothing section of WPB announced April 3 that arrangements have been made for the American Red Cross to act as a central agency in collecting from clothing stores throughout the country wool clips that will become available by reason of the prohibition against cuffs on men's and boys' trousers.

April tire recaps for "B" cars mostly from reclaimed rubber

The extremely serious rubber situation has made it necessary to allocate tire recapping material made almost wholly of reclaimed rubber for use on List B passenger cars during April, OPA Acting Administrator Hamm said March 28.

The camelback which will go to retreading shops for use in meeting requirements under certificates issued to List B passenger car operators in April is made of reclaimed rubber with only about 2 percent of new crude used in the mixture for cohesion.

"Tires recapped with this lower grade camelback should be driven at speeds no greater than 35 miles an hour," Mr. Hamm said.

✕   ✕

Late pleas for camelbacks must give reason for delay

Retreaders and recappers entitled to an initial allotment of truck camelback but who did not apply for it before the March 1 deadline, still may get their allotments on a showing of valid reason for failure to apply before expiration of the time limit, Acting Price Administrator Hamm announced April 1. A late applicant must file with his local board, in addition to the regular OPA form, an affidavit stating the reason for the delay.

•   •

6 indicted on charge of violating tire order

One of the most important cases prosecuted by the Federal Government in connection with consumer rationing was brought to a head successfully April 1 when a Los Angeles Federal grand jury returned an indictment charging Guy O. Bryan, tire dealer, and five others with conspiracy to violate the tire rationing regulations, OPA announced April 2.

The indictment charged the defendants with conspiring to commit offenses and fraud against the United States in the retail sale of new tires and tubes to consumers without certificates from local rationing boards. They were also charged with conspiring to violate a temporary restraining order issued on March 14 against any more such sales.

OPA to release certain classes of new passenger autos now in Government pool

Certain classes of new passenger automobiles now held in the Government pool may be released by the OPA under Amendment No. 4 to Rationing Order No. 2A, announced March 28 by Acting Administrator Hamm. The effective date of the amendment was March 24, 1942.

Less than 1 percent of total

The pool is made up of new passenger cars which were not shipped by the manufacturer prior to January 16, 1942, to an agency other than one controlled by the manufacturer.

The cars affected by the amendment are those which the OPA may determine will not serve the purposes for which the pool was created. The amendment also provides for the removal of pool stickers erroneously attached to nonpool automobiles. The number of automobiles which will be released under Amendment No. 4 will probably not amount to as much as 1 percent of the pool total.

As a condition to release of a car from the pool, the OPA may require the dealer or manufacturer to put another new car into the pool as a substitute. Even after an automobile is released, it still may not be sold except to the holder of a certificate issued by a local rationing board.

Cars affected

Among the cars which the OPA will consider releasing from the pool under the new amendment are:

1. Those ordered on or before January 1, 1942, by agencies of Federal, State, local or foreign governments or by the American Red Cross.
2. Automobiles specially built, painted, or equipped on order of specific buyer.
3. Automobiles with list price above $2,000.
4. Automobiles manufactured prior to March 2, 1942, for experimental purposes.
5. Automobiles that on or before January 16 were in the hands of or in transit to a manufacturer's branch engaged primarily in selling cars at retail, or were consigned, invoiced, or billed to an agency not controlled by the manufacturer.
6. Automobiles as to which registration had been effected or applied for prior to January 1 and for which rationing certificates were given under Rationing Order No. 2.

The amendment outlines the procedure for withdrawing cars from the pool and for the substitution of others for those removed. Applications for all releases are to be made to OPA headquarters in Washington and not to the local rationing boards.

Collapsible tin tubes banned for foods, cosmetics; regulated for other uses

Drastic regulations on the use and production of collapsible tin tubes, completely eliminating their use for foods, cosmetics, and most toilet preparations, were put into effect April 1 by the War Production Board in a further move to conserve this country's supply of the metal.

Used tubes must be turned in

In the first provision of its kind, the order (M–115) also requires that every individual purchaser of a tube of tooth paste or shaving cream, when buying from a retailer, from April 1 on must turn in a used tin, tin-coated, or tin-alloy collapsible tube of any kind for each new tube bought.

Retailers, and dealers in possession of used tubes, are required to hold them, subject to further order of the Director of Industry Operations.

The regulations permit the use of 100 percent tin tubes only for certain medical ointments and pharmaceutical preparations, and allow the use of a tin-coated tube for certain other pharmaceutical preparations, for tooth pastes, and shaving creams.

Three classes set up

The order sets up three classes of tubes.

Class I allows the use of 100 percent tin tubes for medicinal and pharmaceutical ointments compounded by pharmacists according to a prescription by a doctor, dentist, or veterinarian.

Class II permits the use of a tube containing 7½ percent of tin for medicinal and pharmaceutical ointments not included in Class I, and for ointments intended for use in the body orifices.

Class III permits the use of a tube containing 7½ percent tin for tooth pastes and shaving creams.

Other provisions

Collapsible tube makers are required by the order, effective April 1, to halt the manufacture of tubes containing more than 7½ percent of tin, except for Class I products. In addition, manufacturers of dental and shaving creams may not pack during the period of April 1 to June 30, 1942, more than 100 percent (by volume) of the tooth pastes and shaving creams packed in the corresponding period of 1940.

Tube blanks already manufactured by the effective date of the order may be made into "nonessential tubes," and may be sold and used for products not listed by Tables I, II, and III. Manufacture or use of tubes for nonessential purposes,

however, is to end with the issuance of the order, except to the extent of existing inventory.

All manufacturers of tubes are required by the order to cooperate in reducing the thickness of tin coatings for tubes allowed by the order to the "minimum thickness which will be sufficient for satisfactory packing of the particular product packed." Manufacturers are also ordered to concentrate to the greatest possible extent on larger-sized tubes, and to subsitute other types of containers where practicable.

A further restriction of the order prohibits the use of tin-coated tubes by those who did not use such tubes for their products prior to January 1, 1941.

Officials of the containers branch, which is administering the order, said that the regulations would reduce the use of tin by the collapsible tube industry to about 150 tons in the second quarter of the year.

In permitting the use of pure tin tubes for Class I products, the order announced April 1 supersedes the applicable provisions of Tin Conservation Order M–43–a.

∧ ∧ ∧

ADULT BICYCLES FROZEN

The War Production Board on April 2 froze the sale, shipment, delivery, or transfer of all new adult bicycles. The order became effective at 11:59 p. m, April 2.

The freeze order applies to all bicycles except those actually in transit at the time the order went into effect. Those may be delivered to their imediate destination and be frozen there, unless the destination is an ultimate consumer.

"New adult bicycle" means any bicycle, with a frame measurement from the center of the crank to the top of the saddle staff post of more than 19 inches, which has never been used by an ultimate consumer.

M. D. Moore, section chief of the WPB durable goods branch, said that "stocks frozen and future production will be made available on the basis of essential needs, with defense workers getting first call, essential civilian needs second, and then anyone else, if more are available."

PRICE ADMINISTRATION . . .

Retail ceiling on 44 electric appliances follows WPB stop-production order

Retail prices of 44 common electrical household appliances, ranging from curling irons to toasters, last week were ordered frozen by the Office of Price Administration at levels no higher than those in effect on March 30.

The temporary maximum price order applies also to wholesalers and manufacturers and was to become effective April 7, Acting Administrator Hamm announced.

"This action has been taken to prevent runaway prices in view of the War Production Board's order of March 30 halting production of these and other electrical appliances on May 31," Mr. Hamm explained.

Rationing not now planned

"Rationing of these articles is not now contemplated," he said. Sufficient stocks are in distributors' hands or in the process of manufacture to last through most of this year, it is believed.

The temporary ceiling will apply until June 5 unless superseded earlier by a permanent schedule of maximum prices.

Evasions barred

Implementing the order on electrical appliances, OPA issued a prohibition against evasion through a decrease in allowances for transportation, and for cash quantity or other discounts, or through an increase in charges for time payments and repair service. Manipulating price increases through pyramiding of the Federal excise tax is also prohibited.

Affected items listed

The order applies to the following electrical appliances with a rated electrical capacity up to 2,500 watts, or powered by an electrical vibrator or electrical fractional horsepower motor:

Biscuit and muffin bakers, bottle warmers, bread toasters, broilers, casseroles, chafing dishes, cigar and cigarette lighters, clothes dryers, coffee makers, corn poppers, curling irons, deep fat fryers, double boilers, dry shavers, egg cookers, fan type heaters, fans, flatirons, food and plate warmers, food mixers, griddles, hair clippers, hair dryers, hotplates and disc stoves, immersion heaters, juice extractors, massage vibrators, neckwear and trouser pressers, portable air heaters, roasters, percolators, sandwich toasters, smoothing irons, table stoves, tea kettles, tea tables, unit radiator heaters, urns, vaporizers, waffle irons, water heaters, and whippers.

The order applies also to parts and accessories for items on this list.

★ ★ ★

BALTIMORE AREA GIVEN 60 DAYS TO CURB RENTS

The strategic war production and military center of Baltimore, Md., and its six surrounding counties was placed April 3 on the list of defense-rental areas by the Office of Price Administration and will be subject to Federal regulation if the recommendations made are not complied with.

Acting Price Administrator Hamm recommended that rents be reduced to the levels prevailing in the area on April 1, 1941. Under the Emergency Price Control Act, the affected area is given 60 days to meet these recommendations. The Baltimore defense-rental area, having a 1940 population of 1,083,300, includes the city of Baltimore and the counties of Anne Arundel, Baltimore, Carroll, Cecil, Harford, and Howard.

In the area are located aviation factories, shipbuilding yards, and other war establishments.

★ ★

China teas put under specific price maximums

Specific maximum prices for China teas at the wholesale level have been set in Amendment No. 3 to Revised Price Schedule No. 91, Acting Price Administrator Hamm stated April 2. These ceiling prices were effective April 2, 1942.

Following tabulation indicates the maximum prices set for China tea in cents per pound ex dock New York:

China grade	Common	Medium	Fine
	Cents	Cents	Cents
Young Hyson	27½	35½	48½
Congou	41	45	57
Gun powder No. 1		48	
Gun powder No. 2		41	
Gun powder No. 3		38	
Gun powder No. 4		35	
Gun powder No. 5		32½	
Gun powder No. 6		31½	
Gun powder No. 7		29	
Gun powder No. 8		27½	
First imperial		33½	
Second imperial		30½	
Third imperial		27½	

Hard coal price at mine halted at existing level; customary discounts ordered

Possibility of higher producers' prices for Pennsylvania anthracite was removed March 31 by the OPA with the issuance of Maximum Price Regulation No. 112, which keeps hard coal prices at the mine at existing levels and orders customary seasonal discounts on domestic sizes, beginning with 50 cents per net ton during April 1942.

The regulation, announced by Acting Price Administrator Hamm went into effect on April 1, 1942.

The ceilings established in the regulation are the prices that prevailed in the period October 1-15, 1941, and which have been maintained since that time at the request of OPA.

Acting Administrator Hamm pointed out that an anthracite price increase, apparently imminent, would militate against the national price stabilization program.

Under the price regulation the following maximum prices are established for anthracite f. o. b. transportation facilities at the mine or preparation plant from which delivery is made:

Size:	Price per net ton
Domestic:	
Broken, egg, stove, and chestnut	$6.75
Pea	5.25
Steam:	
No. 1 Buckwheat	3.75
Rice (No. 2 Buckwheat)	2.90
Barley (No. 3 Buckwheat)	2.15

The maximum prices for domestic sizes shall be reduced by not less than the following amounts during the months of April to July, inclusive:

April, $0.50; May, $0.40; June, $0.25; and July, $0.10.

Special service charges

The price regulation provides that there shall be deducted from the maximum prices established in the section covering maximums and seasonal discounts the cash, quantity or other discounts or allowances in effect during the period October 1-15, 1941, inclusive. It provides also that certain interest and service charges shall not exceed rates during the period October 1-15, 1941, inclusive, and requires producers and distributors to file with OPA not later than May 1 1942, a statement of these discounts and charges as of the October 1-15 period.

Rationing violators face fines, imprisonment, under new law

Willful violators of rationing orders and rationing regulations issued by the Office of Price Administration now face direct prosecution and severe penalties under provisions of the Second War Powers Act, 1942, Acting Price Administrator John E. Hamm warned March 31.

The act, which became effective March 28 when signed by President Roosevelt, provides a maximum penalty of $10,000 fine and imprisonment for one year for willful violation of priority orders of the War Production Board or of rationing orders or regulations of OPA.

Mr. Hamm disclosed that OPA, working in close cooperation with the Department of Justice, has adopted a comprehensive plan for investigation and criminal prosecution of those persons who flout the rationing rules.

MOLASSES ORDER CHANGED

Operational changes in the molasses Order, M-54, were made in an amended version of the order issued March 28 by Industry Operations Director Knowlson.

The amendments to the order cover these points:

1. Hydrol, corn sugar molasses, is included in the definition of molasses and is subject to all terms of the order.
2. Distributors are divided into two classes, primary and secondary. Deliveries of molasses may not be made by a primary distributor without specific authorization. Secondary distributors are not thus restricted.
3. Definitions of various classes of purchasers have been rewritten to include all users of molasses.
4. Manufacturers of yeast, citric acid and vinegar and users of molasses for foundry purposes are granted a quota of 110 percent of their consumption for the year ending June 30, 1941.
5. Manufacturers of yeast, citric acid, edible molasses, and edible sirup may purchase molasses on a yearly rather than a quarterly basis.
6. Deliveries of edible molasses and edible sirup may be made without reference to the terms of the order.
7. Molasses may not be exported without express permission of the Director of Industry Operations.

CUBAN SUGAR SURVEY

Officials from the War Production Board, Department of Agriculture, and Defense Supplies Corporation are leaving for Cuba this week to gather statistics and information on the Cuban sugar industry, the sugar section of the WPB announced.

Cane sugar ceiling raised 15 cents per 100 pounds in North Atlantic area

Because cane sugar refiners in the North Atlantic area cannot operate on the current basis price of $5.45 per hundred pounds without incurring substantial losses, Acting Price Administrator Hamm March 31 raised the ceiling 15 cents per hundred pounds.

Small rise in cost to consumer

The increase, effective March 31, 1942, under Amendment No. 1, Revised Price Schedule No. 60 (Direct-Consumption Sugars), applies only to sugars processed by refineries in Pennsylvania, New York, New Jersey, and Massachusetts.

This action, however, is not expected to increase the ultimate cost of refined sugar to the consumer in these States by more than 1 cent on each 5-pound package, the Acting Price Administrator cautioned.

Other provisions

Other features of the new OPA amendment include:

1. A provision that sugar is at its point of delivery, within the meaning of the schedule, when it has arrived at the siding or dock in the vicinity of the buyer's warehouse or place of business at or from which it is to be used or resold.
2. Clarification of the maximum price calculation in cases where sugar is delivered by the seller within a refinery city metropolitan area.
3. Applicable maximum prices are set where transportation is performed by means of a motor vehicle owned, controlled, or hired by the buyer.

Conditions for using buyer's vehicle

4. Before a buyer may use transportation by a vehicle owned, controlled, or hired by him, the seller first must offer to deliver the sugar at a price calculated delivered in carload quantities, freight prepaid to the point of delivery. In those cases where it is more economical for a buyer to transport sugar by his own, a controlled, or hired vehicle, he may refuse the seller's offer and be free to take delivery and transport sugar by such vehicle.
5. Another clause provides clarification of maximum prices for sales of direct-consumption sugars at wholesale.
6. Where persons made no sales of direct-consumption sugars at wholesale during either base period, they now are permitted to sell at the market price prevailing on date of sale. However, this is with the proviso that (a) the seller submit to OPA a statement specifying grade, package and amount sold; and (b) name, address, type of purchase, price to be charged, and whether purchase includes delivery to buyer's place of business. Furthermore, such statement must be submitted to and the price approved by OPA prior to delivery of the sugar sold.

Purchases and sales of DSC

7. Clause is provided covering purchases by Defense Supplies Corporation—or any designee of that R. F. C. subsidiary that it names—from persons not in the business principally of selling sugars.

8. Prospective sales by Defense Supplies Corporation—or its designee, if any—also are covered by the new amendment.
9. Final DSC provision covers the possibility that the DSC—or its designee—may have to purchase or sell sugar in large lots. In order to implement this program, such sales contract may allow payment of an adjusted price not to exceed the maximum price in effect at time of shipment.

OPA granted permission for the advance in the refined cane sugar price ceiling in the North Atlantic seaboard area to $5.60 per hundred pounds, following extensive analysis of the recent Tariff Commission report on refining cost studies.

Beet crop competes on West Coast

Refined sugar price increases are considered unnecessary in the South Atlantic and Gulf Coast areas.

The cost survey indicates that West Coast refiners currently are operating at a loss under a $5.45 refined ceiling. However, an advance in that area would be useless, as cane refiners could not take advantage of it in view of the heavy competition from beet sugar.

On shipments to adjacent areas

The Acting Administrator clarified what possible maximum prices refiners might charge on shipments made to adjacent areas. For example, under the amendment, the ceiling price on refined sugar will remain $5.45 per hundred pounds for sugar refined in Baltimore, although it will be lifted to $5.60 in the case of sugar refined in Philadelphia.

However, if a Baltimore refiner sells in the Philadelphia area, such Baltimore sales cannot be made at higher than the $5.45 basis price, it was emphasized. OPA quarters pointed out that the basis price is dependent upon the refinery point at which the sugar was processed.

★ ★ ★

Some tea sales above ceilings allowed New York firm

Exception has been granted to Volkart Bros. Inc., New York, permitting it to sell certain listed quantities of tea at higher prices than the maximum prices established by Revised Price Schedule No. 91, but not higher than its cost for such tea, OPA Acting Administrator Hamm announced March 28. The exception is granted in Order No. 2 under that schedule.

OPA moves to stimulate flow of iron, steel products into domestic, foreign commerce

In a move designed to stimulate the flow of iron and steel products into domestic and foreign commerce, Acting Price Administrator Hamm issued Amendment No. 1 to Revised Price Schedule No. 49 (Resale of Iron and Steel Products).

The amendment, directed specifically toward streamlining activity in three hitherto somewhat clogged distributive channels, was evolved by the OPA's export price control committee, working in close collaboration with a like committee from the Board of Economic Warfare.

Inventory sales

Highlights of the amendment, which became effective March 28, 1942, follow:

1. Inventories acquired prior to December 15, 1941—effective date of the original sched-

ule—may be sold voluntarily in the export market only at the regular ceiling prices, plus the addition of storage charges, demurrage and similar charges accumulated because of failure to secure shipping space, and the same commissions allowed to exporters under the initial order.

2. Special cognizance is taken of distress and stranded iron and steel products, which were destined for export and shipped to a port of exportation prior to March 1, 1942, so incurring charges for ocean freight, marine or war-risk insurance, or storage as a result of failure to secure necessary shipping space. In this category also are included certain shipments on the high seas December 7, 1941, which were ordered back to West Coast ports, unloaded, and have piled up charges there since then. It also covers shipments originally destined for France, the Netherlands or similar European destinations.

3. A third phase of the amendment provides for export shipments in exceptional cases where the Board of Economic Warfare certifies that a price above the ceiling is necessary for considerations of political or military necessity, or because of the requirements of economic warfare.

Retailers need allies to win war against inflation, says Keezer

"In spite of the fact that many retailers have been fighting a good fight to keep prices down, they must have allies if the war against the terror of inflation is to be won," Dexter M. Keezer, assistant administrator of OPA in charge of the Consumer Division, told members of the National Conference of Business Paper Editors at a meeting March 27.

Further excerpts:

The simple fact is that today we are losing the battle against inflation. Prices are going up all along the line and at a dangerously accelerated pace.

While there have been cases of profiteering, it is not fair to blame the retailer indiscriminately for this. The records indicate, that, as a whole, retailers have exercised considerable restraint in raising their prices. They, along with the rest of us, are caught by forces which are exercising a tremendous upward pressure on prices. Often they have resisted this pressure and thus foregone profits they might have had.

The nature of this pressure can be indicated by the fact that national supplies available for civilians are being cut about 1 percent a month to meet military needs while money available to buy these supplies (in the form of wages, salaries, profits, etc.) is increasing about 3½ percent a month. This sets up a situation which, left alone, can result in a monthly increase of 3½ percent in the cost of living, a ruinous rate of inflation.

It was both to combat inflation and protect consumers from paying unreasonably high prices that the OPA recently set maximum prices, effective March 30, that retailers can charge for seven important household appliances. The surest aid to the retailers in fighting inflation would be larger supplies of the things they sell. While we cannot hope for great aid along this line while the war continues, the situation would be materially eased by the elimination of hoarding, both by consumers and in trade.

Price ceiling raised on antimonial lead

The maximum price of antimonial lead is increased by an amendment to Revised Price Schedule No. 70 (the scrap and secondary lead schedule) issued April 1 by Acting Price Administrator Hamm.

The increase amounts to 1½ cents a pound for the antimony content of antimonial lead and reflects a similar increase in the price of primary antimony metal recently authorized by the OPA.

Need not test for total metal content

The amendment also changes the language of the section by which the maximum prices for battery lead plates are computed so as to require an assay only for lead and antimony content, instead of for the total metal content.

Antimonial lead is defined in the schedule as "any lead antimony alloy in the form of pigs or special shapes containing not less than 98 percent lead and antimony combined; not less than 2 percent antimony; and not more than ½ percent tin." The maximum price per pound, f. o. b. point of shipment, for any grade or type of antimonial lead sold in pigs in carload lots, according to the amendment, shall be equal to 15½ cents (instead of 14 cents as formerly) a pound for the antimony content, plus the base price of lead for the remainder. The base price of lead varies from 6.35 to 6.55 cents a pound, depending upon the basing point given in the schedule.

Change in the language of the schedule regarding assays is to conform to industry practice and make it clear that consumers need not test for and pay for unimportant amounts of metals other than lead and antimony.

Above ceiling contracts for No. 1 old manila rope can be fulfilled in some instances

Contracts made before February 8, 1942, to supply manufacturers with No. 1 old manila rope at prices above the ceiling of $115 per ton may now be completed by dealers under certain conditions outlined in Amendment No. 1 to Revised Price Schedule No. 47 (Old Rags), announced March 31 by Acting Price Administrator Hamm.

Must meet certain conditions

Old manila rope is used by rope-paper manufacturers in production of such essential products as gas masks, cables, parachute flares, and electric insulating paper.

Many dealers acquired rope from collectors prior to issuance of the schedule at prices above the established maximum level in order to fulfill contracts already made. Accordingly, under the amendment, these contracts can be fulfilled at contract price if both the purchase of the rope by the dealer and its contract for resale were made before February 8, 1942, the date the schedule was made public.

However, dealers must make all deliveries on such contracts on or before April 15, 1942, and must keep records showing the dates and names of persons from whom the dealer bought the rope and the price paid. In addition, the dealers must show the amount of rope acquired before February 8 in order to meet contracted orders, the dates these contracts were made, the dates of delivery, and the contract prices.

The maximum price for No. 1 old manila rope is not changed by the amendment, nor has there been any change made in the number or names of grades defined in the schedule.

★ ★ ★

Scrap hoarders won't profit, says Henderson

Price ceilings on scrap metals set by the Office of Price Administration will not be raised, it was emphasized in a letter from Leon Henderson, OPA Administrator, to Lessing J. Rosenwald, chief of the Bureau of Industrial Conservation.

"There will be no profit in hoarding—only a loss of self-respect by anyone gambling for personal gain at the expense of the common effort to whip our enemies," Mr. Henderson's letter also declared.

Butcher shops, meat markets asked not to raise pork cut prices over mid-March levels

Butcher shops and retail meat markets were called upon March 27 not to raise prices of ham, bacon, pork chops, and other pork above mid-March prices in an appeal by Dan A. West, Director of the Consumer Division of the OPA.

Protest marked increase, consumers told

He advised consumers to question any increase over middle-of-March prices on fresh pork cuts. Any marked increase in retail pork prices should be protested to the storekeeper and reported immediately to the Office of Price Administration in Washington, he said.

Present retail prices for pork cuts are close to the highest previous prices for this season of the year and supplies are limited. The pork supply situation will be relieved when the present pig crop gets to market next fall.

The wholesale pork prices prevailing between March 3 and March 7 were taken as the basis for the OPA wholesale price ceilings. Since retail prices frequently lag behind changes in wholesale prices, Mr. West said, the advance in retail pork prices between the beginning and middle of March may partly represent previous wholesale increases. He advised consumers to check back on the retail pork prices they paid during the middle of March as the basis for judging whether they were being gouged by present prices.

★ ★ ★

Ceilings adjusted on variety of special kinds of scrap

An amendment affecting the maximum prices of a variety of special kinds of scrap covered by Revised Price Schedule No. 4 (Iron and Steel Scrap) was announced March 31 by Acting Price Administrator Hamm.

By the amendment, which is effective at once, a change is made in the premium for cast iron borings for chemical use; a new premium is set for high manganese steel scrap for electric furnace use only; price differentials are fixed for briquetting, and premiums are allowed for several railroad specialty items shipped from a dealer's yard.

Other changes made by Amendment No. 2 reduce the price at which railroads may sell certain unprepared scrap to consumers and further restrict mixed shipments.

"CARLOAD LOT" OF PRIMARY LEAD REDEFINED

Redefinition of a "carload lot" of primary lead, in order to conform with industry practice, is contained in Amendment No. 1 to Revised Price Schedule No. 69 (Primary Lead), Acting Price Administrator Hamm announced March 27.

A carload lot is defined as a shipment equal to or greater than the minimum weight as set forth in established tariffs of railroads. In addition, the definition of a carload lot includes any quantity which would move from point of shipment to point of destination at the carload rate, rather than at a less-than-carload rate, because a lower total charge is produced thereby.

A seller who ships a quantity less than the minimum carload weight specified in the tariff, but nevertheless a carload lot within the meaning of the amendment, may add to the carload lot prices specified in the price schedule an amount per pound not to exceed the difference between

(a) the rail transportation charge on a per pound basis actually paid for the quantity shipped and
(b) the usual railroad carload rate on a per pound basis applicable to a shipment between the same points.

★ ★ ★

Sellers of canned goods put on equal basis by amendment

Disparities existing between sellers of canned fruits and vegetables under the ceiling price provisions of Temporary Maximum Price Regulation No. 6 have been eliminated by issuance of Amendment No. 1, Acting Administrator Hamm announced April 1.

Under the original regulation, it was provided that the maximum prices for certain designated kinds of canned fruits and vegetables shall be or shall be determined by reference to "the highest price at which the seller sold, contracted to be sold for delivery within sixty days, delivered or transferred" such kinds during the period February 23–27, 1942.

The new amendment, however, changes the pricing clause to read "the highest price at which the seller sold or contracted to sell for delivery within 60 days."

In many instances, deliveries or transfers were made on contracts entered into at an earlier time, when prices were much lower.

2,500 paper merchants asked to sign agreements on maximum wholesale mark-ups

Individual agreements, which list maximum wholesale mark-ups for many fine and coarse paper items, have been sent to more than 2,500 paper merchants for signature, Acting Price Administrator Hamm announced March 30.

Accompanying the copies of the agreements was a letter in which Mr. Hamm requested the coarse paper merchants to sign by April 10 and fine paper merchants by April 15.

Premiums over ceilings allowed on export sales of pig tin

Premiums over the maximum prices permitted under Revised Price Schedule No. 17 will be allowed on export sales of pig tin under Amendment No. 1, OPA Acting Administrator Hamm stated March 27. The new amendment became effective March 30, 1942.

Under the amendment, in the case of export pig tin sales, in addition to the maximum price set in the schedule, the following premiums may be added:

Quantity:	Premium
11,200 pounds or more	1 cent per pound
2,240 to 11,199 pounds	1½ cents per pound
Less than 2,240 pounds	2 cents per pound

Where the export shipment requires packaging of pig tin, the actual cost to the exporter of such packaging may be added to the maximum price.

Other provisions

The amendment provides assistance to permit the seller to make sales on a delivered basis. One provision is that where expenses of delivery actually and legitimately are incurred, the seller may add to the maximum prices transportation charges, specified additional standard charges under the terms of sale, and foreign agent's commission. No part of the foreign agent's commission can be added if it is received by the exporter directly or indirectly for his own use.

Another provision is for the completion at contract prices of all pig tin export sales contracts from a steamer with transshipment privileges, where such contracts were entered into prior to March 30, 1942.

Jobbers of No. 1 and 2 fuel oils denied increase in margin

Maximum prices for Number 1 and Number 2 fuel oils will not be increased on the Eastern Seaboard at this time to afford higher jobber margins, Acting Price Administrator Hamm announced April 1. OPA has had under consideration a request from numerous fuel oil jobbers that their margins be raised.

An increase of four-tenths of a cent per gallon in the maximum prices on these fuel oils was allowed in Amendment No. 4 to Revised Price Schedule No. 88 for petroleum and petroleum products, effective March 26. This was to compensate for higher transportation costs.

SHIP RATING LIMITED

Only material which becomes a part of a merchant ship, and perishable tools, expendible materials and temporary equipment used up by the shipbuilder in constructing ships can be assigned preference ratings under General Preference Order P–7, the WPB ruled April 3 in an official interpretation.

Used paper shipping sacks in demand; OPA suggests prices

Suggested maximum prices for used multiwall paper bags, or paper shipping sacks, aimed to encourage conservation of kraft paper and to relieve the pressure of demand on burlap bags, were made public April 1 by Acting Price Administrator Hamm.

The suggested prices for dumpers or users and dealers, for No. 100 bags, are presented in the following table:

	Four-ply bags		Five-ply bags	
	Plain (each)	Printed (each)	Plain (each)	Printed (each)
Price paid to dumper by dealer	$0.030	$0.0225	$0.0375	$0.030
Price paid to dealer by user	.050	.0425	.0575	.050

Above prices are for carload lot transactions. Recommended l. c. l. prices may be determined as follows: (1) Deduct 10 percent from price paid by dealer to dumper. (2) Add 10 percent to price paid to dealer by user. Bags will be bought by dealer f.-o. b. source and sold by dealer f. o. b. destination or "full freight allowed basis."

RUBBER YARN EXCEPTION

Knitters, weavers, and other users of rubber yarn and elastic thread are permitted by an amendment issued April 2 to Conservation Order M–124 to knit, weave, or otherwise use rubber yarn and elastic thread which, prior to 12:01 a. m., March 29, 1942, had been placed on a knitting machine, braider or loom, or which had been removed from the vendor's containers, wrapping, packing, or "put up" and placed on quills, cones, cops, spools, bobbins, tubes, beams, or warps prior to 12:01 a. m., March 29, 1942.

★ ★ ★

Reagent grade of oxalic acid permitted higher prices

The reagent grade of oxalic acid (used in comparatively small quantities in laboratory work) is exempted from the provisions of the maximum price schedule by Amendment No. 1 to Revised Price Schedule No. 78 for Oxalic Acid, announced April 1 by Acting Price Administration Hamm.

The amendment redefines the product put under a price ceiling by OPA in these terms:

"'Oxalic acid' means crystalline and powdered oxalic acid of technical grade."

OPA permits increase for leaded zinc oxides

Producers of zinc oxides will be asked shortly to enter into new voluntary agreements with the OPA, increasing the maximum permissible price on leaded zinc oxides containing 35 percent or more lead to 7 cents per pound, Acting Administrator Hamm announced March 28.

Producers usually make contracts each quarter with their customers. The new producers' list was due to go out April 1. By permission of OPA, the increase may be made effective April 1, 1942, allowing producers to take account of it in new contracts.

★ ★ ★

Elastic threads frozen

Stocks of rubber yarns and elastic threads have been frozen in the hands of manufacturers and mills by a temporary order effective for 30 days beginning 12:01 o'clock a. m. on March 29, it was announced March 28 by Industry Operations Director Knowlson.

OPA field operations to reach all war industry areas

Plans to expand its field operations far beyond the 11 regional offices already established were announced March 31 by the OPA with the opening of the first group of field offices in 16 cities.

Cities in which the field offices are located, and the regional offices out of which they will operate follow: *Hartford, Conn.,* Boston area; *Newark, N. J.,* and *Buffalo, N. Y.,* New York area; *Pittsburgh, Pa.,* Philadelphia area; *Birmingham, Ala.,* and *Memphis, Tenn.,* Atlanta area; *Detroit, Mich.,* Cleveland area; *Milwaukee, Wis.,* and *Indianapolis, Ind.,* Chicago area; *St. Louis, Mo.,* Kansas City area; *New Orleans, La.,* and *Houston, Tex.,* Dallas area; *Salt Lake City, Utah,* Denver area; *Los Angeles, Calif.,* and *Seattle, Wash.,* San Francisco area; and *Richmond, Va.,* Baltimore area.

★ ★ ★

Changes for Southern lumber

Three changes—a modified basis for pricing tough white ash lumber, permission for the seller to add inspection charges under certain circumstances, and a redefinition of the terms "mill" and "distribution yards" for the purposes of price e s t a b l i s h m e n t—are made in Amendment No. 2 to Revised Price Schedule No. 97 for Southern Hardwood Lumber, announced April 1 by Acting Price Administrator Hamm. The amendment was effective as of April 6, 1942.

★ ★

Fischel named cocoa consultant

Appointment of Alwyn N. Fischel, vice president of W. Bartholomew & Co., Inc., New York, as a cocoa consultant to the food section of OPA, was announced March 30 by Assistant Administrator H. R. Tolley.

★ ★ ★

Schemers to defeat grey goods ceiling warned by OPA

Willful violations of OPA cotton and rayon grey goods ceilings through manipulative schemes recently advised by some members of the textile trade must be halted immediately, Acting Price Administrator Hamm declared April 3.

Preliminary investigation by the OPA has confirmed reports from the textile market that some mills, which formerly sold "grey," or unfinished, goods exclusively, have been refusing to furnish such goods to their regular trade. Instead, these concerns have been requiring buyers to accept bleached or partially finished goods at exorbitant mark-ups.

Sheet steel for drums limited to ratings June 1

Beginning June 1, requirements for sheet metal for the manufacture of steel drums, heretofore met by allocation, will be obtainable only by preference ratings, except for urgent military needs, and allocations in April and May will be curtailed sharply, C. E. Adams, chief of the WPB iron and steel branch, announced April 3.

WPB arranges allocation to mills of excess rayon cut staple

The War Production Board, April 2, wired worsted mills that rayon cut staple set aside for them for March and April has not been exhausted because certain users failed to take up their allotments. The excess quantity may be allocated to those mills which can put it into process before May 1.

★ ★ ★

Certain war orders excluded from cordage sales quotas

A cordage manufacturer need not include in his cordage sales quota, permitted under Manila Fiber Cordage Order M-36, war orders placed and ready for delivery prior to March 2, 1942, but which could not be delivered by March 2 for reasons beyond the control of the manufacturer. This is provided for in Amendment No. 5 to M-36, effective April 1.

★ ★ ★

Some Egyptian cotton restricted to war orders, sewing thread

The use, sale, and delivery of certain grades of Egyptian cotton henceforth imported into this country were restricted April 2, by the WPB to war orders and orders for cotton to be used in the manufacture of sewing thread.

The order (M-117) applies to cotton of the following specifications in accordance with recognized Egyptian standards of grading:

Giza—7: Grade—"Good to Fully Good" and better; Staple—Nothing below "Good" staple.
Sakha—4; Sudan; Giza—26 (Malaki); Giza—29 (Karnak): Grade—"Fully Good" and better; Staple—Nothing below "Good" staple.

GLYCERINE DELIVERIES TO BE ALLOCATED

All deliveries of glycerine in excess of 50 pounds a month were placed under allocation control March 30 by the Director of Industry Operations, effective May 1.

Emergency soil pipe pricing method changed

Permission for manufacturers of cast iron soil pipe and fittings to compute maximum delivered prices on emergency shipments of less than 250 pounds in the same manner as maximum delivered prices for warehouse shipments are determined was granted in Amendment No. 2 to Revised Price Schedule No. 100 (Cast Iron Soil Pipe and Fittings), Acting Price Administrator Hamm announced April 1.

To avoid unjustified price increases in some sections of the country, the amendment also specifically requires the use of the lowest railroad carload rate from Birmingham, Ala., in computing maximum delivered prices for all shipments.

Chlorinated hydrocarbon solvents order extended

General Preference Order M-41, which limits the use of chlorinated hydrocarbon solvents, has been extended to May 15, 1942. It was scheduled to expire on March 31.

The solvents included in the terms of the order are carbon tetrachloride, trichlorethylene, perchlorethylene, and ethylenedichloride. They are used in charging fire extinguishers, in grain fumigation, the manufacture of refrigerants, the processing and manufacturing of food, chemicals, and petroleum.

NICKEL ALLOCATION EXTENDED

General Preference Order M-6-a, which provides general allocations control over nickel, was extended indefinitely by amendment March 30 by the Director of Industry Operations. It was due to expire on March 31.

Several changes are made in the order.

Civilian copper to be cut more, says Requirements Committee

Rapid acceleration of the Nation's arms production has resulted in a shortage of copper that will result in additional drastic curtailments of the amount assigned to civilian uses, William L. Batt, chairman of the WPB Requirements Committee, announced April 3.

The Committee has adopted an over-all program allocating the available supply of copper for the current quarter of 1942, Mr. Batt said. It calls for a drastic reduction in copper consumption by civilian users.

Direct military and shipbuilding requirements and the vital needs of the United Nations for the quarter will require practically all the copper available, in spite of the fact supplies of the metal have reached an all-time record.

Orders now being issued

At the same time, some copper is necessary for the maintenance of vital civilian operations, even at the expense of military production. The program contemplates a cut of approximately 60 percent in civilian use of copper from that of 1940, with a large proportion of the remaining 40 percent devoted to "behind the lines" uses that support the military establishment.

It was pointed out by the War Production Board that orders implementing the program now are being issued and that further orders would be issued in the immediate future.

The program is the first in a series which will be issued by the Requirements Committee in an effort for a unified and planned disposition of the basic scarce materials.

★ ★

Copper scrap rule extended

Supplementary Order M-9-b, relating to copper scrap and copper alloy scrap, which was due to expire on March 31, has been extended until it is revoked, the Director of Industry Operations announced April 1.

Two minor changes are made in the order as reissued:

The first permits public utilities to use in their own operations wire or cable that has become scrap through obsolescence, provided the wire or cable is in lengths in excess of 5 feet and that the total so used in any month does not exceed 5 tons.
The second forbids any person to accept delivery of copper alloys or castings made from scrap obtained in violation of this order.

AGRICULTURE

(Information furnished through Office of Agricultural Defense Relations, U. S. Department of Agriculture)

Hemp seed increase of 3,300 percent asked, to offset loss of imports

Farmers are being asked by the Secretary of Agriculture this year to increase hemp seed production by at least 33 times the 1941 production in an effort to obtain a substantial domestic production of hemp fiber in 1943 to overcome shortages created by a stoppage of imports from the Philippines and Netherlands East Indies.

Farmers offered CCC sales agreements

The Commodity Credit Corporation is contracting to purchase at the price of $8 per bushel of 44 pounds—cleaned basis—hemp seed from the 1942 crop. It is expected that about 350,000 bushels of seed will be produced for planting for fiber production in 1943.

The offer of the Commodity Credit Corporation to purchase the seed produced in 1942 at the guaranteed price is available only to those growers who agree to sell their seed to the corporation. AAA farmer committeemen will contact prospective producers in order to explain the program to them and give them an opportunity to sign the CCC sales agreements.

Most satisfactory substitute

Fiber from the American hemp plant is the most satisfactory substitute for abaca, sisal, and henequen, the three principal hard fibers used for rope and twine whose supply has been sharply curtailed by the loss of imports.

Normally the United States obtains practically all (98%) of its abaca from the Philippines and about one-half of its sisal from the Netherlands East Indies. The remainder of its sisal requirements comes largely from British East Africa. Imports from the Orient are virtually stopped and there is no assurance that imports from Africa will continue.

240,000,000 pounds of fiber needed

For this reason, the Department of Agriculture finds imperative a seed production program in the United States in 1942 which will provide enough seed for planting an acreage of hemp in 1943 that will produce a minimum of 240,-000,000 pounds of fiber.

To produce 240,000,000 pounds of hemp fiber would require about 300,000 acres of hemp in 1943. This calls for 350,000 bushels of seed. To produce this seed in 1942, assuming a yield of 10 bushels per acre, would require 35,000 acres and, roughly, 3,000 to 3,500 bushels of seed.

Apparently, according to Department estimates, there are more than 15,000 bushels of hemp seed in the United States. This seed was grown in Kentucky, where most of the 1942 expansion of seed production is expected to take place.

Commodity Credit Corporation has been given priority of purchase of the seed by the WPB which now has control over seed stocks. CCC has already purchased more than 3,200 bushels, and has made a blanket offer under its priority rating to purchase all seed in excess of the amount holders expect to plant.

3,747,000,000 pounds of farm products delivered for Lend-Lease shipment to Feb. 1

A total of 3,747,000,000 pounds of agricultural commodities was delivered to representatives of the United Nations for Lend-Lease shipment up to February 1, 1942, the Department of Agriculture announced March 17. Total cost of these commodities, bought by the AMA and delivered at shipping points since operations started last April, was about $417,000,000.

Principal commodities

During January, more than 435,000,000 pounds of food and other agricultural commodities were delivered for shipment, at a cost of about $50,000,000.

Outstanding among commodity groups delivered, with cumulative values up to February 1, were: dairy products and eggs, about $131,000,000; meat, fish and fowl, $106,000,000; lard, fats and oils, $30,000,000; fruits and vegetables, $43,-000,000. Other deliveries included grain and cereal products, concentrated fruit juices, vitamin concentrates, miscellaneous foodstuffs, and nonfood agricultural commodities including cotton, tobacco and naval stores. A large proportion of the nonfood supplies was made available for Lend-Lease operations by the Commodity Credit Corporation.

Old manila rope needed to keep insulating-paper plants working

Acting to avert a threatened shutdown of certain plants manufacturing electrical insulating papers vitally needed for many war purposes, the industrial salvage section of the Bureau of Industrial Conservation issued on March 30 an urgent appeal for the salvage of old manila rope.

Supply nearly gone

Six plants, according to George T. Weymouth, chief of the industrial salvage section, produce more than 75 percent of the Nation's supply of insulating papers. Representatives of these plants have declared that they had on hand only a few weeks' supply of No. 1 old manila rope, from which the papers are made. The insulating material is used, it was explained, in electrical apparatus such as motors, generators, and transformers, where the strength of manila fiber papers permits a reduction in the size of the apparatus and promotes maximum speed in the application of the insulation.

Dealers ready to handle it

Dealers are available throughout the country to handle the old rope and move it promptly to the mills which need it.

Mr. Weymouth telegraphed the managers of 13 regional offices of the industrial salvage section that "scarcity of manila rope threatens to cause shutdown of practically all plants engaged in manufacturing electrical insulating papers, parachute flare papers, gasket papers used in manufacture of tanks and airplanes, and other special papers used by the Navy. Only solution is immediate and thorough collection of manila rope scrap normally used by steamship companies; barge, tug, and ferry lines; marine stores handling boat supplies which get back old rope in exchange for new; railroad freight yards; fisheries, coal mines; quarries; electrical repair companies, yacht clubs, and stevedore companies."

To touch 30,000 organizations

The regional managers were instructed to transmit the appeal to industrial salvage committees in 58 key cities. The committees, in turn, will be instructed to emphasize the old rope shortage to persons in charge of salvage operations in some 30,000 plants, mines, mills, and public utilities.

10,000-ton cache of scrap metal seized for war use

Using its requisitioning powers for the second time within 3 weeks to eliminate bottlenecks in the movement of scrap metal needed for war production, the Bureau of Industrial Conservation, WPB, March 31 seized an accumulation of refrigerators and miscellaneous metal scrap which had been dumped into a ravine near Dayton, Ohio, over a period of 10 years.

It was estimated that the cache weighed approximately 10,000 tons.

As in the case of the requisitioning of an automobile graveyard at Valparaiso, Ind., on March 13th, Metals Reserve, subsidiary of R. F. C., will pay for the seized metal and will sell it to a dealer.

"Under peacetime conditions, the defective cases would not be in demand as scrap metal, because of their heavy porcelain surfacing, which must be removed before the metal is usable," George T. Weymouth, chief of the industrial salvage section, said. "However, with the vastly increased demand for scrap metals of all kinds essential to the war effort, the refrigerator cases can be promptly and efficiently utilized for the production of new metal."

WPB controls all goatskins suitable for military purposes

WPB on April 1, by Conservation Order M–114, took control of all supplies of goatskins suitable for military purposes. It also limited the amount of raw goatskins, raw kidskins, raw cabretta skins, and India-tanned goatskins that may be put into process by any tanner during the month of April to 80 percent of the monthly average of skins put into process during 1941. This percentage will be revised from month to month in accordance with the number of skins imported.

Under the April 1 order, approximately 15 percent of the total supply of skins will be earmarked for a military stock pile. The skins will be primarily for the manufacture of military leather gloves and jackets.

The order directed that any raw or in-process goatskin that could be processed into more than 5¾ square feet must be set aside for military purposes. The only exceptions are extreme reject skins, extremely heavy (bull) skins and India-tanned goatskins.

Farm equipment allotted more metal to take care of increased food demands

The War Production Board revised its 1942 farm equipment program April 1 to meet increased food demands being made upon the country's farmers as the result of the war.

Changes in the program, designed to provide machinery for greater production of edible oil, sugar, potatoes, and general food products, are expected to add approximately 25,000 tons of materials, mostly steel and iron, to estimated requirements of farm equipment manufacturers for the period from November 1, 1941, to October 31, 1942.

An A–3 preference rating is made available to manufacturers to obtain materials going into the equipment. The original program, announced December 28, 1941, carried the same rating and was based on estimated requirements of 1,793,647 tons of materials for new machines, repairs and export operations during the 12-month period.

Irrigation equipment included

In amendments to Preference Rating Order P–95 and Limitation Order L–26, WPB revised the program to include irrigation equipment, vitally needed in certain Western States, and increased the manufacturing percentage quotas of various types of machinery needed to carry out the Department of Agriculture's expanded food program.

The increase in estimated material requirements as the result of revision of the program is brought about as follows:

Irrigation equipment not included in the original program, approximately 17,000 tons.

3,600 peanut pickers required to produce more edible oil because of the loss of normal sources in the Far East, 1,733 tons.

Cultivators added

One-row tractor-drawn or mounted cultivators, for which no percentage quota was fixed in the original program because insufficient data were available, approximately 4,800 tons.

The remaining tonnage is distributed among various types of machinery needed to meet increased demands for sugar, potatoes and general food products, such as beet cultivators, drills and lifters, potato planters, and steel plow shares. For example, manufacturers were permitted to make during the 12-month period under the original program up to 64 percent of the number of beet cultivators they

produced or sold during 1940. The revised program permits them to make up to 100 percent.

Some of the other changes in percentages are: horse or tractor drawn potato planters, 58 percent to 72 percent; horse or tractor drawn beet drills, 57 percent to 100 percent; steel plow shapes or shares, 71 percent to 140 percent; horse or tractor drawn beet lifters, 84 percent to 130 percent; cylinder-type power corn shellers, 33 percent to 80 percent, and harness hardware, 75 percent to 100 percent.

Company quotas for peanut pickers

The percentage quota system is not used to bring about production of the peanut pickers urgently requested by the Agriculture Department. Instead, individual company quotas are established.

In addition to increasing material requirements for essential machinery, the amendments make several technical changes in the original program.

Chief change is the setting up of an alternate production percentage schedule, known as Schedule A–1, fixing percentages for entire groups of products rather than for individual items so that manufacturers can concentrate on those products for which they have greater demand, provided the overall tonnage is not exceeded.

Manufacturers may use the new schedule or continue operations under the existing Schedule A, which sets up percentages for individual products, but they must notify WPB immediately if they intend to change. Once a choice is made, they cannot shift back and forth between the two schedules.

★ ★ ★

Domestic shorn wool regulations modified

Two changes in regulations applying to domestic shorn wool were announced March 30 by Acting Price Administrator Hamm.

The first requires a deduction of 10 cents per pound for inferior wools if the wool is tied with sisal or binder twine, under Amendment No. 2 to Maximum Price Regulation No. 106 (Domestic Shorn Wool).

The second change deletes section 1410.8 of Regulation 106. This concerned scoured domestic shorn wool, but since Revised Price Schedule No. 58 as amended now sets maximum prices for scoured domestic shorn wool, this section is no longer necessary.

7 new industry advisory committees

BEDDING COMMITTEE

Government presiding officer — William A. Adams.

Members:

A. J. Schob, vice president, Nachman Springfilled Corporation, Chicago, Ill.; J. L. Moore, president, Hager Manufacturing Co., Muncie, Ind.; George Holmes, sales manager, Kay Manufacturing Corporation, Brooklyn, N. Y.; John V. Hubbell, assistant to the president, Simmons Co., main office, New York, N. Y.; H. G. Brandwein, vice president, A. Brandwein Co., Chicago, Ill.; L. P. Best, sales manager, Mebane-Royall Co., Mebane, N. C.; A. Brewer, president, Premier Bed & Spring Co., San Franciso, Calif.; William Lamey, president, Haggard & Marcusson Co., Chicago, Ill.; Irving Weisglass, president, Eclipse Sleep Products, Brooklyn, N. Y.; Harry R. Olson, president, Land-O-Nod Co., Minneapolis, Minn.; Walter J. Schob, president, Honor-Bilt Products Co., Philadelphia, Pa.

BREWING INDUSTRY COMMITTEE

Government presiding officer—John B. Smiley, chief, beverage and tobacco branch.

Members:

S. E. Abrams, Jos. Schlitz Brewing Co., Milwaukee, Wis.; Carl W. Badenhausen, P. Ballantine & Sons, Newark, N. J.; August A. Busch, Jr., Anheuser-Busch, Inc., St. Louis, Mo.; H. J. Charles, Theo. Hamm Brewing Co., St. Paul, Minn.; Adolph Coors, Jr., Adolph Coors Co., Golden, Colo.; Joseph F. Hein, Monarch Brewing Co., Chicago, Ill.; Wm. G. Koerber, Koerber Brewing Co., Toledo, Ohio; Edward V. Lahey, Smith Bros., Inc., New Bedford, Mass.; Karl H. Lang, Oertel Brewing, Louisville, Ky.; B. B. McGimsey, San Antonio Brewing Association, San Antonio, Tex.; Harris Perlstein, Pabst Brewing Corporation, Milwaukee, Wis.; Charles J. Reuss, Centlivre Brewing Corporation, Fort Wayne, Ind.; Rudolph J. Schaefer, F. & M. Schaefer Brewing Co., Milwaukee, Wis.; Edward A. Schmidt, C. Schmidt & Sons, Inc., Philadelphia, Pa.; Karl F. Schuster, Acme Breweries, San Francisco, Calif.; Emil G. Sick, Seattle Brewing & Malting Co., Seattle, Wash.; Frank B. Sullivan, American Brewing Co., New Orleans, La.; F. Brooke Whiting, Queen City Brewing Co., Cumberland, Md.

JUTE COMMITTEE

Government presiding officer—Arthur R. Howe.

Members:

Walter Guthrie, Lehigh Spinning Co., Allentown, Pa.; E. D. Martin, Hooven & Allison Co., Xenia, Ohio; J. F. Malcolm, Revonah Spinning Mills, Hanover, Pa.; R. C. Utess, American Mfg. Co., Brooklyn, N. Y.; Alfred Bessel, Southern Bagging Co., Houston, Tex.; Willard Lewis, Riverside Mills, Atlanta, Ga.; Frank E. Willsher, Schricter Jute Cordage Co., Philadelphia, Pa.; Malcolm B. Stone, Ludlow Mfg. & Sales Co., Boston, Mass.; J. C. Gordon, Allen Industries, Detroit, Mich.; J. S. Jenkins, Dixie Jute Bagging Co., Norfolk, Va.; E. F. Parham, Carolina Bagging Co., Henderson, N. C.; W C. Brown, Jr., Belton Bagging Co., Belton, S. C.; R. J. Paisley, Pritchard & Co., 90 Wall Street, New York, N. Y.; J. P. Anastasiadi, Ralli Bros., 25 Broadway, New York, N. Y.; Chas. E. Bingham, Bingham & Co., 90 Wall Street, New York, N. Y.; Ed Kuhnle, No. American Trading Co., 26 Broadway, New York, N. Y.

PHOTOGRAPHIC EQUIPMENT COMMITTEE

PHOTOGRAPHIC ACCESSORIES SUBCOMMITTEE

Government presiding officer—M. D. Moore.

Members:

A. C. Brandt, G. M. Laboratories, Inc., 4326 Knox Avenue, Chicago, Ill.; Dalton Craig, president, Craig Movie Supply Co., 1053 South Olive Street, Los Angeles, Calif.; L. Fisch, president, Motion Picture Screen and Accessory Co., Inc., 534 West Thirtieth Street, New York, N. Y.; James Forrestal, general manager, Agfa Ansco, Binghamton, N. Y.; Jean Foute, general manager, Raven Screen Corporation, 314 East Thirty-fifth Street, New York, N. Y.; J. S. Heck, president, Da-Lite Screen Co., Inc., 2723 North Pulaski Street, Chicago, Ill.; Miss Marie Witham, president, Society for Visual Education, 100 East Ohio Street, Chicago, Ill.; Homer Hilton, vice president, Argus, Inc., Fourth and William Streets, Ann Arbor, Mich.; J. J. Kuscher, sales manager, DeJur Amsco Corporation, 6 Bridge Street, Shelton, Conn.; W. L. Lawson, vice president, Chardelle, Inc., 10 East Fortieth Street, New York, N. Y.; S. Mendelsohn, president, Mendelsohn Speed Gun Co., 46 Ferrand Street, Bloomfield, N. J.; F. Neubauer, president, Effen Products, 79 Woodruff Avenue, Brooklyn, N. Y.; Benjamin W. Price, president, Price Industries, 130 West Seventeenth Street, New York, N. Y.; E. C. Rogers, president Elwood Pattern Works, 125 North East Street, Indianapolis, Ind.; Morris Schwartz, president, Kalart Co., Inc., 114 Manhattan Street, Stamford, Conn.; Fred Simmon, president, Simmon Brothers, Inc., 37-06 Thirty-sixth Street, Long Island City, N. Y.; H. M. Smith, president, J. H. Smith & Sons Corporation, Lake and Colfax Streets, Griffith, Ind.; W. S. Vaughn, production manager, Eastman Kodak Co., 343 State Street, Rochester, N. Y.; L. Weston, Weston Electrical Instrument Corporation, 614 Frelinghuysen Avenue, Newark, N. J.

PLUMBING AND HEATING COMMITTEE

SANITARY CAST IRON; AND FORMED ENAMELWARE SUBCOMMITTEE

Government presiding officer—Walter W. Timmis, chief of the plumbing and heating branch.

Members:

M. L. Ondo, (director Washington Office), Youngstown Pressed Steel Division, Mullins Co., Normandy Building, Wash., D. C.; C. A. Ferguson, president, Maryland Sanitary Mfg. Co., Baltimore, Md.; W. G. Moore, president, Humphreys Mfg. Co., Mansfield, Ohio; E. O. Brady, asst. sales manager, Briggs Mfg. Co., Detroit, Mich.; J. M. Carbeau, Ellwood Co., Ellwood City, Pa.; C. C. Adams, vice president, Richmond Radiator, Uniontown, Pa.; T. M. Hodges, vice president, U. S. Sanitary Mfg. Co., Pittsburgh, Pa.; P. P. Uphues, assistant manager, Crane Co., Chicago, Ill.; Thos. J. Hannah, Jr., American Radiator & Standard Sanitary Corporation, Bessemer Bldg., Pittsburgh, Pa.; C. A. Morrow, Mullins Mfg. Co., Warren, Ohio; R. R. Crane, vice president, Eljer Co., Ford City, Pa.; C L. Stoup, Auburn, Central Mfg. Corporation, Connersville, Ind.; A. G. Zibbell, Kohler Co., Kohler, Wis.; H. C. Beresford, department manager, Murray Corporation of America, Detroit, Mich.; H. J. Held, vice president, Rundle Mfg. Co., Milwaukee, Wis.; Louis Probst, vice president, National Sanitary Co., Salem, Ohio; James M. Bonner, secretary, Washington-Eljer Co., Los Angeles, Calif.; R. J. Trubey, president, Davidson Enamel Co., Clyde, Ohio.

TRACKLAYING TRACTOR COMMITTEE

Government presiding officer—William Parrish.

Members:

E. B. English, Caterpillar Tractor Co., Washington, D. C.; M. L. Noel, Allis Chalmers Tractor Co., Milwaukee, Wis.; W. E. Miles, Cleveland Tractor Co., Cleveland, Ohio; Neal Higgins, International Harvester Co., Chicago, Ill.

WOODPULP ALLOCATION COMMITTEE

Government presiding officer—David Graham.

Members:

G. B. Gibson, Union Bag & Paper Corporation, New York, N. Y.; George E. Dyke, Robert Gair Co., Inc., New York, N. Y.; H. O. Nichols, Crown-Zellerbach, New York, N. Y.; L. K. Larson, Weyerhaeuser Timber Co., New York, N. Y.; Charles Conrad, Rayonier, Inc., New York, N. Y.; F. W. Brainerd, Scott Paper Co., Chester, Pa.; S. E. Kay, International Paper Co., New York, N. Y.; Rex W. Hovey, Oxford Paper Co., New York, N. Y.; H. H. Hanson, W. C. Hamilton & Sons, Inc., Miquon, Montgomery County, Pa.; Dwight L. Stocker, Michigan Paper Co. of Plainwell, Plainwell, Mich.; Douglas Crocker, Crocker, Burbank & Co. Association, Fitchburg, Mass.; Amor Hollingsworth, Penobscot Chemical Fibre Co., Boston, Mass.

★

Program for war traffic control described in OCD booklet

A plan for emergency control of highway traffic during air raids, blackouts, and evacuations is described in a booklet entitled "War Traffic Control" issued April 3 by the OCD.

The program was developed for the Office of Civilian Defense by the International Association of Chiefs of Police, working with the Federal Bureau of Investigation, Office of Provost Marshal General of the War Department, U. S. Conference of Mayors, Public Roads Administration, Institute of Traffic Engineers, Automotive Safety Foundation, and Society of Automotive Engineers.

Calling on enforcement officials to assume positive leadership in case of disaster, the booklet emphasizes immediate need for machinery to control traffic during air raids, blackouts, and evacuations.

If an area within the United States becomes a theatre of active military operation, civil police traffic control activities will be coordinated and directed by military authorities administering martial law, according to the publication.

The 19-page pamphlet is on sale by the Superintendent of Documents, Washington, D. C., for 10 cents a copy.

Dairy committee presents tire-saving program

Clyde E. Beardslee, chief of the dairy section, WPB, announced April 3 that the dairy industry advisory committee has recommended to WPB a four-point program to conserve transportation facilities in the ice cream industry by approximately 30 percent. The Office of Defense Transportation expressed approval of the procedure followed by the committee in formulating the program. The recommendations follow:

1. Eliminate all special deliveries.
2. Eliminate all home deliveries.
3. Reduce the number of days when deliveries will be made and make no more than one delivery on any one day to a customer.
4. Use common carriers to serve scattered trade.

Local groups should inform ODT of what they are doing along these lines, and can request the ODT to clear local programs with the Justice Department if they have any doubts as to their legality.

★ ★ ★

Rail sale allowed above ceiling price

L. B. Foster Co., Inc., of New York City, was authorized by OPA April 1 to sell 300 tons of relaying rail at a price above the ceiling established last December 1.

The authority was granted by Amendment No. 1 to the price schedule for relaying rail (No. 46). The amendment permits completion of a contract signed three months before adoption of the schedule. The rail was acquired by the Foster firm in August 1941 at a price in excess of the ceiling subsequently established.

★ ★ ★

Food distributors to discuss delivery cuts to save rubber

A meeting of the food distributors' advisory committee has been called by Burt Flickinger, chief of the distributors' section of the food supply branch, WPB. The meeting will be held April 21, in Washington, to submit recommendations for the conservation of strategic war materials.

RAILWAY TRANSPORT EXECUTIVES

Appointment of three executives to positions in the division of railway transport was announced March 28 by Defense Transportation Director Eastman. Harry G. Brandt, of Wichita, Kans., has been named associate director of the division, in charge of rail-truck coordination in the western region. O. C. Castle, of Houston, Tex., has been appointed assistant director in charge of freight service. W. C. Kirby, of Norfolk, Va., has been named terminal assistant to J. M. Hood, associate director in charge of the southern region.

V. V. Boatner is director of the division of railway transport.

Mr. Brandt will work in cooperation with staff members of the division of motor transport to bring about a higher degree of coordination in rail and truck operations. He will maintain headquarters in Chicago.

Mr. Castle will maintain a close check on railroad freight operations with a view to improving efficiency through heavier loading of cars, pooling of equipment, and other expedients. He will be stationed in Washington, D. C.

Mr. Kirby will maintain a close check on port and terminal operations in the Norfolk, Va., area.

★ ★ ★

FARMERS' HAULING POOL BEING WORKED OUT

A plan under which farmers of a community will be asked to plan their marketing together and eliminate unnecessary truck mileage is being worked out by the Division of Motor Transport, ODT, in cooperation with the United States Department of Agriculture and other governmental agencies.

Pooling equipment and cooperative hauling of products and supplies is the keystone of the plan by which, ODT officials believe, farm truck mileage can be reduced from 35 to 50 percent without undue hardship to anyone.

Pending announcement of further detailed suggestions, the ODT will be glad to consider and advise with any group operating or formulating a cooperative conservation program. Until establishment of field offices by the ODT, suggestions or questions should be submitted in written form to John L. Rogers, Director, Division of Motor Transport, Office of Defense Transportation, Washington, D. C.

Truck owners asked to check and recheck to prevent rubber waste

Truck owners who permit waste of rubber through carelessness and reckless use of equipment are aiding the enemy as certainly as if they deliberately set fire to rubber supplies, Joseph B. Eastman, ODT Director, said April 2.

Applications for new trucks are cleared through the Office of Defense Transportation. Mr. Eastman said that the ODT could not recommend new trucks to operators who had permitted careless or reckless use of their old ones, and particularly of tires.

Truck owners were asked by John L. Rogers, director of motor transport of the ODT, to check and recheck constantly to prevent rubber waste caused by any of the following: 1. Speed—greatest thief of tire mileage; 2. Improper air pressure; 3. Overloads; 4. Cuts, snags, and wear; 5. Improper adjustments; 6. Recklessness; and 7. Excess mileage.

Baking industry asked to cut mileage $\frac{1}{4}$ to save facilities

The baking advisory committee, WPB, April 2, recommended that the baking industry reduce mileage by 25 percent to conserve transportation facilities, John T. McCarthy, chief of the bread and baking production section, announced.

The committee also outlined methods for improvement and maintenance of tires and vehicles.

The recommendations, made with the approval of the ODT, are designed to conserve available equipment and materials.

Ripley named consultant on Diesel engine equipment

Charles T. Ripley, chief engineer of the technical board of the Wrought Steel Wheel Industry, Chicago, has been named consultant on Diesel engine propulsion equipment in the materials and equipment section, ODT, it was announced March 27.

H. L. Hamilton of La Grange, Ill., whose appointment as consultant in this field was previously announced, was unable to accept the post.

CIVILIAN DEFENSE . . .

Practical measures for concealing vital civilian installations from the air graphically portrayed in OCD booklet

Camouflage methods for industrial plants, factory buildings, railroad yards, airfields, routes of communication, conspicuous landmarks and transportation systems are described in a profusely illustrated 68-page booklet entitled "Protective Concealment," issued March 30 by the OCD.

Prepared by War Department

The booklet was prepared by the War Department under the direction of the Chief of Engineers, United States Army, by the Engineer Board, with suggestions of the National Technological Civil Protection Committee.

The booklet emphasizes the fact that any use of camouflage should be carefully considered and planned with the technical assistance of trained personnel.

In the opening chapter the booklet declares: "This bulletin is concerned with practical measures for the concealment of important civilian installations and equipment from aerial observation. Concealment from the observation of attacking ground troops is not treated."

Bombing technique described

Accompanied by graphic sketches, the booklet describes the technique of precision bombing and declares:

At least five circumstances combine to oppose the bomber and simplify the defender's concealment problem . . . high altitude, the oblique view required to pick up the target, the brief period available for aiming the bombsight, the possibility of haze or thick weather, and the obscurity of nightfall.

Although an enemy may have accurate maps and photographs he must rely on visual identification of the target (or a close landmark) in order to properly aim and release the bombs. Any concealment measure that serves to reduce the visibility or confuse the identity of an installation may therefore be considered of value to be weighed in conjunction with the importance of the installation and the probability of attack.

There is discussion of the comparison of photographic reconnaissance and the effect of shadows at different times of day or of different dates. This is followed by description of "Aids to Concealment" such as dummy, or decoy installations, the use of smoke and artificial fog such as provided by smudge-pots, etc.

On concealment of roads

On the subject of "Routes of Communication," the booklet declares "the concealment of main highways and railroads is for the most part impracticable. However, all types of road surfaces can be made relatively inconspicuous by application of a surface coloration appropriate to the surroundings." The booklet then appraises the possibility of affording protective concealment to new roads, narrow roads in wooded areas, city blocks, and intersections.

Conspicuous landmarks a problem

Difficulties in effectively concealing conspicuous landmarks are described. In its consideration of the protective concealment of transport, the booklet declares "the visibility of highway vehicles can be greatly reduced by the use of dull, lusterless colors. The flash of windshields from sunlight or from artificial illumination at night may be eliminated by the use of horizontal louvres or, if that is considered impracticable, by the removal of the windshields." This chapter also describes the technique of protective concealment for watercraft and grounded aircraft against aerial attack.

Should observe site from air

"For the study of existing installations, plans and elevations are usually needed. Rough outside dimensions rather than details are desirable. For proposed installations as well as existing ones, maps and air photographs of the area concerned are essential. In addition, the individuals most intimately concerned with the creative concept of the concealment plan and the persons having final authority in accepting it should personally observe the site from the air.

Camouflage treatment

The four appendices give detailed description of bombing methods and technique employed; the methods for creating artificial smoke and fog; and the treatment to reduce visibility of existing concrete wearing surfaces.

The final appendix entitled "Materials for Protective Concealment" is a catalogue of specifications and uses for paints, fabrics, and other items suitable for camouflage.

Advance shipments of protective equipment sent to shore cities

A limited number of protective helmets and arm bands are being provided to cities in the "strategic areas" of the East and West Coasts, according to OCD Director Landis.

To reach more than 40 cities

During the first week in April more than 40 cities along the shores of the Atlantic and Pacific will receive advance shipments of equipment of this type for air raid wardens, auxiliary firemen, and auxiliary police.

Mr. Landis announced that the first shipment of this material is now being sent to municipalities in California, Washington, and Oregon.

Loaned to communities

The allocation of this material is based on fixed ratios of the population of the cities to the number of helmets and arm bands available.

All protective equipment supplied by the Government is loaned to communities, Director Landis explained. Its distribution is governed by the military situation at the time, and if an emergency should arise in any locality, shipments may be rerouted or supplies drawn from communities that have some on hand.

Through the cooperation of the District of Columbia Civilian Defense organization, the Office of Civilian Defense was able to "borrow" equipment of this character which has been contracted for by the District.

Veterans of Foreign Wars offer services to civilian defense

Voluntary mobilization of the services and facilities of the Veterans of Foreign Wars of the United States to aid in the civilian defense program was announced March 5 by OCD Director Landis and Max Singer, commander in chief of the veterans' organization.

Under the joint arrangement, the 3,600 Posts of the Veterans of Foreign Wars will be encouraged to enroll with the local defense councils as auxiliary police and firemen.

FACTS AND FIGURES . . .

Axis radiocasters try to put their hooks into U. S. primary elections

Enemy propagandists jumped into American politics March 31, OFF revealed.

In the role of volunteer campaign orators, they took to the air in anticipation of the coming primary elections.

The Nazis beamed a new program at the United States from their so-called "American Freedom" station, with one "Joe Scanlon," claiming to be an American, as the speaker. He exhorted:

"Join us in our endeavor to save our boys from foreign battle fields. You can compel the Government to act. The elections are coming again and our people will have a last opportunity to reassert themselves. Organize as free Americans to fight the dictatorship being set up in Washington. The only real enemies sit right within the ranks of our Government today."

Tokyo's "America First"

Tokyo named a new short-wave broadcast the "America First" program and the Japanese "America Firster" declared:

"The isolationists were right."

From Tokyo, too, came the assurance that, "Japan would be a charming partner to any nation which would understand Japan's ideals correctly," and the promise that Japan would share with the United States its newly won rubber and tin if only Americans "will get rid of Roosevelt."

At almost the same time, in an official broadcast to Japanese youth, the Tokyo radio was declaring that Japan's goal must be the "ultimate destruction of Britain and the United States."

Abandoning promises of plenty, Germany admits she can't feed self or victims

Hitler's Europe is hungry. Hitler propagandists admit it.

Recent broadcasts from the Reich and from countries where the "New Order" is in force, show that the Nazis have repudiated Hitler's earlier promise of abun-

---

Illustration on this page is by Fitzgerald, from OFF pamphlet "Divide and Conquer." (See VICTORY, *March 31.)*

---

dance. Monitored by the Federal Communications Commission and described April 1 by the Office of Facts and Figures, the propaganda line tells the story of a Europe in which all available food supplies have had to go to feed Hitler's army.

The propaganda line shifts.

Drastic cuts in rations, seizures of crops from farmers, and "black market" operations are revealed by radio broadcasts within Europe. No longer denying shortages, Axis propaganda takes the cue from Goebbels and floods the people of Europe with appeals for greater sacrifices, particularly within Germany.

In Germany, the people were promised adequate food supplies as late as February 23. State Secretary Becker, of the Reich Ministry of Food and Agriculture, announced, "Germany's supplies of foodstuffs will enable her to maintain the same rations this year as in 1941. The Reich is now able to meet the greater foodstuffs requirements."

Early in March, the line suddenly changed and Becker said, "There are two reasons for readjusting food rationing at the end of the third winter of the war. First, harvests throughout Europe for the past 2 years have been only average because of unfavorable weather, and second, foodstuffs demands have risen considerably because of the war."

The Vichy radio reports that, beginning in April, Germany will have to reduce food rations, such as those for bread, fats, and meats.

Nurses get death sentence

Goebbels, commenting on new and drastic penalties for food hoarding, recently said, "Soon it will not pay to risk one's head for particularly good feeding."

A Berlin broadcast to Europe reports that nurses in the Koenigsburg children's hospital had been sentenced to death for stealing food from the kitchen.

Reich gets Italy's food

In Italy, the amount of wheat that a farmer may keep for his own use has been reduced, and bread rations were cut nearly a quarter. The Italian freedom station, Radio Italia, charges that Italian food shortages are a result of food shipments to Germany. An official broadcast to the Italian people in March stated that Germany was "assured" all food production not absolutely essential to Italy.

In France, Marshall Petain has appealed to French peasants immediately to hand over all wheat supplies. He said, "All concealment, all waste of wheat would constitute an unpardonable crime. If all producers let themselves hold back or waste even one bag of wheat, this wrongful act would result in depriving all the French of bread for 1 month."

Norway and Holland

The Berlin radio admits that Norwegian farmers are feeding synthetic fodder to their cattle.

In Holland, Director General Ruyter of Dutch Agriculture, has urged farmers to increase production this year to meet a "severe food situation." Farmers have been asked to sacrifice a considerable number of their young cattle, so that milk cows will have sufficient feed.

Assassination tale backfires when Quezon reaches Australia

The Japanese propaganda machine backfired March 27, OFF revealed.

Ever since Gen. Douglas MacArthur's arrival in Australia, the Tokyo radio had been telling the world that Manuel Quezon, president of the Philippine Commonwealth, had been assassinated on orders of the American general.

Then General MacArthur's headquarters announced that President Quezon had arrived safely in Australia.

BELSLEY SUCCEEDS EMMERICH AS EXECUTIVE SECRETARY, WPB

Appointment of G. Lyle Belsley as executive secretary of the War Production Board was announced March 28 by Donald M. Nelson, chairman.

Belsley, who has been assistant executive secretary for the past 6 months, succeeds Herbert Emmerich, who was appointed Commissioner of the Federal Public Housing Authority.

★ ★ ★

Campaign to finance USO second year to be discussed by McNutt, civic leaders

Six thousand civic leaders in all parts of the United States have been invited by Federal Security Administrator Paul V. McNutt to attend a 1-day conference in Washington, April 12, to discuss a campaign to finance the second year of United Service Organizations' operations. The USO provides recreation facilities for members of the armed forces on leave and for industrial war workers. The public appeal for funds amounting to $32,000,000 will be made from May 11 to July 4.

Within a year, according to Mr. McNutt, the total number of Americans in uniform will increase twofold. On that basis the money sought by the USO in its forthcoming campaign will come to about 2 cents per day for each soldier and sailor.

WPB to use punitive powers whenever needed, Knowlson says

James S. Knowlson, Director of Industry Operations, said April 1 that, while the War Production Board is relying on the voluntary support of the war production program by industry, the board is prepared to use the punitive provisions of the Second War Powers Act swiftly and without hesitation whenever necessary to insure compliance with WPB regulations, including all priorities rules and orders.

The Second War Powers Act provides penalties of up to $10,000 fine and one year's imprisonment for each violation of WPB regulations or orders.

★ ★ ★

Machine tool deliveries continue to go up

Value of new machine tools, presses, and other metal working machinery shipped during February was $93,100,000, it was announced April 3 by George C. Brainard, chief of the tools branch of the War Production Board.

Shipments of machine tools alone amounted to 20,307 units with a total value of $84,355,000. During January 19,266 units, valued at $83,546,794, were shipped.

"Production of new machine tools continues to go up month by month," Mr. Brainard said.

WAR EFFORT INDICES

MANPOWER

National labor force, Feb.	52,600,000
Unemployed, Feb.	4,000,000
Nonagricultural workers, Feb.	39,842,000
Percent increase since June 1940.	11
Farm employment, Mar. 1, 1942.	8,940,000
Percent decrease since June 1940.	25

FINANCE

	In millions of dollars
Authorized program June 1940–Mar. 31, 1942	‡186,954
Ordnance	32,417
Airplanes	26,802
Misc. munitions	17,789
Naval ships	15,223
Industrial facilities	13,968
Merchant ships	7,550
Posts, depots, etc.	7,078
Stock pile, food exports	5,791
Pay, subsistence, travel for the armed forces	4,131
Housing	1,392
Miscellaneous	4,623
Total expenditures, June 1940–Mar. 31, 1942	*22,860
Sales of Defense Bonds, Cumulative, May 1941–Mar. 1942	4,860
March 1942	558

PRODUCTION

	In millions of dollars
June 1940 to latest reporting date	
Paid on contracts, Feb. 28	*16,200
Gov. commitments for plant expansion; 1,060 projects, Feb. 28	9,281
Private commitments for plant expansion; 6,237 projects, Feb. 28	1,978

EARNINGS, HOURS AND COST OF LIVING

		Percent increase from June 1940
Manufacturing industries—January		
Average weekly earnings	$35.10	36.1
Average hours worked per week	41.5	10.7
Average hourly earnings	80.1¢	19.2
Cost of Living, Feb. (1935–39 = 100)	Index 112.6	12.0

*Preliminary.
‡Preliminary and excludes authorizations in Naval Supply Act for fiscal year 1943.

OFFICE FOR EMERGENCY MANAGEMENT

WAYNE COY, *Liaison Officer*

CENTRAL ADMINISTRATIVE SERVICES: Dallas Dort, *Director.*

DEFENSE COMMUNICATIONS BOARD: James Lawrence Fly, *Chairman.*

DEFENSE HOUSING DIVISION: C. F. Palmer, *Coordinator.*

INFORMATION DIVISION: Robert W. Horton, *Director.*

NATIONAL WAR LABOR BOARD: Wm. H. Davis, *Chairman.*

OFFICE OF SCIENTIFIC RESEARCH AND DEVELOPMENT: Dr. Vannevar Bush, *Director.*

OFFICE OF CIVILIAN DEFENSE: James M. Landis, *Director.*

OFFICE OF THE COORDINATOR OF INTER-AMERICAN AFFAIRS: Nelson Rockefeller, *Coordinator.*

OFFICE OF DEFENSE HEALTH AND WELFARE SERVICES: Paul V. McNutt, *Director.*

OFFICE OF DEFENSE TRANSPORTATION: Joseph B. Eastman, *Director.*

OFFICE OF FACTS AND FIGURES: Archibald MacLeish, *Director.*

OFFICE OF LEND-LEASE ADMINISTRATION: E. R. Stettinius, Jr., *Administrator.*

OFFICE OF PRICE ADMINISTRATION: Leon Henderson, *Administrator.*

CONSUMER DIVISION: Dexter M. Keezer, *Assistant Administrator,* in charge. Dan A. West, *Director.*

WAR PRODUCTION BOARD:

Donald M. Nelson, *Chairman.*
Henry L. Stimson.
Frank Knox.
Jesse H. Jones.
William S. Knudsen.
Sidney Hillman.
Leon Henderson.
Henry A. Wallace.
Harry Hopkins.

WAR PRODUCTION BOARD DIVISIONS:

Donald M. Nelson, *Chairman.*
Executive Secretary, G. Lyle Belsley.

PLANNING BOARD: Robert R. Nathan, *Chairman.*

PURCHASES DIVISION: Douglas MacKeachie, *Director.*

PRODUCTION DIVISION: W. H. Harrison, *Director.*

MATERIALS DIVISION: Wm. L. Batt, *Director.*

DIVISION OF INDUSTRY OPERATIONS: J. S. Knowlson, *Director.*

LABOR DIVISION: Sidney Hillman, *Director.*

CIVILIAN SUPPLY DIVISION: Leon Henderson, *Director.*

PROGRESS REPORTING: Stacy May, *Chief.*

REQUIREMENTS COMMITTEE: Wm. L. Batt, *Chief.*

STATISTICS DIVISION: Stacy May, *Chief.*

INFORMATION DIVISION: Robert W. Horton, *Director.*

LEGAL DIVISION: John Lord O'Brian, *General Counsel.*

*Produce TODAY**

VICTORY

OFFICIAL WEEKLY BULLETIN OF THE AGENCIES IN THE OFFICE FOR EMERGENCY MANAGEMENT

WASHINGTON, D. C.   APRIL 14, 1942   VOLUME 3, NUMBER 15

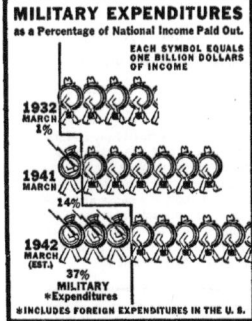

MILITARY EXPENDITURES
as a Percentage of National Income Paid Out.

EACH SYMBOL EQUALS ONE BILLION DOLLARS OF INCOME

1932 MARCH 1%

1941 MARCH 14%

1942 MARCH (EST.) 37%

MILITARY
*Expenditures
*INCLUDES FOREIGN EXPENDITURES IN THE U. S.

Consumers' durable goods metal industry and civilian construction suspended to make way for conversion to war work

Donald M. Nelson, chairman of the War Production Board, said April 7 that WPB orders already issued or about to be signed provide for the virtual cessation of consumers' durable goods industries using critical metals in the United States and the conversion of their men, plants, and facilities to an all-out war effort.

Some production is still being carried on, but within 3 months almost all of it will be stopped except for that production necessary for war and essential civilian purposes. The elimination of less-essential production and the conversion program have already changed the face of American industry and are now harnessing the entire economy to war.

Automobiles, washing machines, refrigerators, radios, lawn mowers, oil burners, and metal furniture are only a few of the many items which can no longer be produced with critical metals after cut-off dates provided in the various orders.

Two sweeping new orders

Illustrating his point, Mr. Nelson announced that two new orders with sweeping effect were in their final stages. One is a construction order which will confine all new construction to relatively small projects and defense work. (*Issued* last week—*See page 4.*) The other is a new steel limitation order which prohibits the use of iron and steel in hundreds of items.

With his statement, Mr. Nelson issued a 'list showing many consumers' goods which are being cut off under existing orders.

Mr. Nelson's statement follows:

The War Production Board has issued a series of orders cutting off in the next 3 months the production of hundreds of civilian metal products.

Actions change face of industry

These orders change the face of American industry. They show that the Nation has learned the first lesson of total war—that it means not business as usual, but production for victory.

The most important field of curtailment for war is, of course, the great metal-working industry. The climax of this program is the preparation this week of two major orders which, in another phase, are as important to victory as the winning of a major battle. These orders are a stop-construction order and a steel-conservation order. Their impact here and abroad will be widespread and sweeping.

They mark the suspension of the consumers' durable goods metal industry
(Continued on page 5)

*472 PLANTS REPORT PRODUCTION COMMITTEES—Page 17

Review of the Week

Within 3 months, American industry will devote all its effort to essentials of war. Two orders prepared last week will mark, in the words of War Production Board Chairman Nelson, "the suspension of the consumers' durable goods metal industry and the civilian construction industry."

The construction order has already been issued, on April 9. It permits construction in certain instances essential to the war; it allows farm construction up to $1,000, and residential construction up to $500 o: to restore property damaged by catastrophes. Other construction must have specific approval.

An encouraging glimpse

To a Nation that knows these measures are only a part of the supreme effort which still lies ahead, WPB issued some encouragement last week in a glimpse of what is already being done. Monetary expenditures for war, the only yardstick permitted by wartime secrecy, amounted in March to more than 3 billion dollars. This is over three times as great as the figure of March 1941, and indicates that physical commodities and construction for our military effort are now going ahead at an annual rate greater than our total physical output in 1932.

Moreover it was announced that deliveries of steel plate, styled by Mr. Nelson as the "limiting factor" in the crucial shipbuilding industry, broke all records in March. But Mr. Nelson revealed that, despite the fact that we are now meeting the Maritime Commission's schedule for plate, ship production is now being slowed by past shortages and we will have to do better than the schedule to catch up.

Idle stocks are seized

Showing that it means business, the Division of Industry Operations announced the results of a priorities survey which took in 3,500 firms. About 1,600 of these were found to have committed minor violations and received letters explaining the rules. A small number appeared to have transgressed more seriously, and punishment is being studied. One large vacuum cleaner company was penalized for diverting aluminum from war needs.

The inventory and requisitioning branch of WPB listed idle inventories in 17 categories seized for war. Large quantities of copper sheet and aluminum were taken over in two actions last week when the owners refused to sell.

Further tightening controls to get materials and machines for wartime needs, WPB issued new restrictions on tin, electrical appliances and heating pads, many types of industrial machinery, liquefied petroleum gas equipment, copper screening, tracklaying tractors, plumbing fixtures, lead foil, enamel can coatings, loofa sponges, jute, and quinine. Inventories of 19 kinds of supplies were frozen in the hands of wholesalers, retailers and others.

Gasoline cut again

The Division of Materials warned that war production at the instance of the United States may cause some curtailment in Canadian power for civilian use late in 1942. This would affect supplies of newsprint.

At the same time, deliveries of gasoline to the East and the far Northwest were cut again, this time to two-thirds of the December - January - February average. WPB granted additional sugar to more than 40 areas where war activity has caused concentrations of population. To provide a limited quantity of tire retreads for war workers, WPB amended its rubber orders so that passenger car capping stock can be made from reclaimed rubber with a little crude for cushioning.

New rolling stock to be controlled

The railroad industry was notified that materials will be made available during the rest of 1942 for 18,000 additional freight cars and 300 more locomotives, and that WPB will schedule production, and will control distribution of all new equipment on recommendation of the Office of Defense Transportation.

WPB also issued last week its limitation on women's clothes, eliminating such cloth-consuming extras as wide flares, all-around pleats and patch pockets but preserving essentials of present styles so that clothes will not be "dated."

The Office of Price Administration froze prices of plumbing fixtures to make sure that speculation does not follow WPB limitations.

Other OPA actions dealt with iron ore, anthracite, crude petroleum and motor fuel, lithopone, leather, pine products, paperboard, paper, sugar, dressed hogs, cocoa beans and cocoa butter.

Canadian power may be limited late in 1942 because of war needs

Some curtailment of nonwar uses of electric power may be necessary in Canada late in 1942 as a result of war industries being established there, William L. Batt, chairman, U. S.-Canada Materials Coordinating Committee, announced April 10 after a conference with Canadian officials.

Such a curtailment would affect United States supplies of newsprint, as this industry is one of Canada's largest users of electric power. The time or extent of this possible curtailment, however, is uncertain.

The ruling factor will be waterfall in Canada. Low water may bring drastic curtailment, and plenty of water would reduce it to a minimum.

Aluminum and chemical plants now projected for Canada, at the request of the United States, will take the bulk of the Dominion's available power.

WPB and other agencies authorized to make audit

President Roosevelt has designated the War Production Board, the War Department, the Navy Department, the Treasury Department, the United States Maritime Commission, and the Reconstruction Finance Corporation as the governmental agencies authorized to inspect the plants and audit the books and records of defense contractors, under Title XIII of the Second War Powers Act, of 1942. Designation was made in Executive order 9127, dated April 10.

VICTORY

OFFICIAL BULLETIN of the Office for Emergency Management. Published weekly by the Division of Information, Office for Emergency Management, and printed at the United States Government Printing Office, Washington, D. C.

Subscription rates by mail: 75¢ for 52 issues; 25¢ for 13 issues; single copies 5¢, payable in advance. Remit money order payable directly to the Superintendent of Documents, Government Printing Office, Washington, D. C.

On the Home Front

The past few days have been dangerous days, really, because we made so much progress in so many different ways that there's a temptation to sum it all up and lean back.

The score is still against us

"Well, well," we might say—if we didn't know better, if we didn't know how things are going in the Far East—"Look what we've accomplished! Here we are halting every bit of nonessential civilian production. Stopping almost all building, too—except the sort of building that's our only business now, the building of ships and tanks and planes and guns. We're getting results from our War Production Drive, what with steel plants smashing record after record and our daily rate of war expenditure well above the 114-million dollar mark. Furthermore, we're showing again and again that we're still an ingenious people, a people who can make a little go a long, long way. Not so bad, America—not so bad!"

Not so bad, indeed. In ordinary times we could be excused for taking a complacent breather, but not today. Today we must catch up with a ruthless, determined enemy who has had a head start and is making the most of it.

Here's something you can do now

The best antidote to leaning back is to do something that carries you forward, and do that something right away. There is a job at hand, a job that is with the Home Front always but at which we should get unusually good results in this time of Spring housecleaning.

That job, of course, is the job of salvage—the job of getting old metals and rags and paper and rubber back to the mills and furnaces and processing plants and into the war effort.

If, when you're searching the house from basement to attic, you'll remember that you're not collecting junk but guns and bombs and shells and hand grenades, the job will be more fun. And that's just what you'll be doing.

Add up items for a gun

Suppose, for instance, that in the course of your adventure in household mining you came up with the following collection: Item, 1 pair of roller skates (broken). Item, 2 door hinges. Item, 1 door lock. Item, 1 battered spade. Item, 1 trash burner, ditto. Item, 1 trash basket.

What have you got there? Just a lot of junk? No, Sir or Madam, you have the metal that will make one .30 cal. machine gun. And, by the way—that 5-pound flatiron over there would make four hand grenades.

Here's something that will be done

There's the biggest sort of news for the Home Front, obviously, in those two inclusive orders issued last week by the War Production Board; the order which will end the use of iron and steel and other metals and even plastics in nonessential civilian industry and the order which puts a virtual stop to all nonmilitary construction.

WPB has long been slicing away at civilian manufacture, at the output of nonessential goods and gadgets, and these far-reaching orders complete the process, funnel vast quantities of metal and materials (and men and machines, too) away from the channels of peace and into the stream—the swelling stream—of ships and weapons.

And we know why

All this means we shall have to accept a lower standard of living but this won't bother us because we know why. We have seen what has happened to peoples who weren't ready to put everything they had into war machines to combat the war machines of the Axis. Right now we're producing these machines of war for our soldiers and sailors and the soldiers and sailors of our allies at the rate of about 30 billion dollars' worth a year. That's three times what we were doing last year and infinitely more than we did during the last war—in the last war we didn't even get around to restricting the output of automobiles until the middle of 1918. Never in the last war, however, was our situation as serious as it is today—today we must sacrifice for our allies as well as for ourselves and today we must save as we did not save in 1917–18 because we are cut off from sources of materials which then were open to us.

Last week the necessity for saving operated to change women's styles. The results were scarcely comparable to what took place in the field of men's clothing. About the only parallel is that there will be no cuffs on women's slacks as there are no cuffs on men's trousers. Basically, the purpose of WPB's order on women's clothing is to save materials and at the same time avoid drastic and arbitrary interference with style.

Next to the problem of production the most important problems confronting the Home Front today are the problems of shortages, transportation, and inflation. All three endanger the war effort.

Transportation is going to grow more difficult every day. The Office of Defense Transportation urges care in ordering rail transportation; make reservations only when you're sure you're going to use them.

The problems of motor transport increase every day, too, and if you drive to your war work you'd better make arrangements to pool use of cars with a neighbor or fellow worker.

More price ceilings

The OPA is combating inflation and the rising cost of living and that is a fight that must be won if we are to win the war. In the past few days OPA has added more articles, including 44 electric appliances, ranging from curling irons to toasters, to a long list of products over which it has set maximum prices. Meanwhile national income continues to rise and we have more money with which to buy fewer things. That means higher prices, that means inflation. That means we shall get less than our money's worth of guns and planes and ships—and it means that we face the danger of grave economic crisis. We must beat inflation to win the war.

WPB in addition to its blanket order on iron and steel and other metals, recently has taken other measures to save vital materials. One such measure forbids cigarette manufacturers from using lead foil to wrap their packages after May 1. Another forbids the use of rubber as a seal for glass containers containing certain nonessential products. One sufferer from this is Fido.

From bottles to battles

Twenty-four distilleries are sending beverage alcohol, known in the trade as "high wines" and running 120 to 140 proof, to industrial alcohol plants where they'll be redistilled into 190 proof industrial alcohol—the kind used in making smokeless powder. That's an example of American ingenuity, that's getting things done . . . OPA warns you'd better buy your coal now . . . next winter there may not be transportation available to get it from the mines . . . The supply of adult bicycles has been "frozen" and bikes will be made available to war workers first, other civilians afterward . . . After June 30 tin may be used to can only a limited variety of condensed soups.

INDUSTRIAL OPERATIONS . . .

WPB stops nonessential construction; specific permission necessary to build in all but a few limited categories

The War Production Board on April 9 called a halt to nonessential construction.

Effective immediately, Conservation Order L-41 prohibits the start of unauthorized construction projects which use material and construction equipment needed in the war effort. It also places all new publicly and privately financed construction under rigid control, except for certain strictly limited categories.

The action was taken by the WPB because the war requirements of the United States have created a shortage of materials for war production and construction. It is in the national interest, the Board stated, that all construction which is not essential, directly or indirectly, to the successful prosecution of the war, and which involves the use of labor, material or equipment urgently needed in the war effort, be deferred for the duration of the emergency.

Materials going into weapons

Many of the same materials, such as iron, steel, and copper, are used by both essential and nonessential construction, and the same materials are largely used for war production. Since there is not enough of these materials for both war production and less essential use, the order, in effect, allocates these materials away from unnecessary construction, and into ships, planes, tanks, guns, war housing, and other essential production.

This step goes much further than the SPAB policy announcement of October 9, 1941. In that announcement, it was made clear that no priority assistance would be given to nonessential construction. In the April 9 order, however, it is provided that no construction may be started (except in a few specified cases) without permission.

$500 limit on home construction

Equally binding upon property owners, builders, and suppliers, the order prohibits not only the start of construction in most categories, but also the withdrawal from inventory and the purchase, sale, or delivery of any material for use in such construction unless expressly authorized by WPB.

The order specifically provides that no residential construction except for maintenance and repair work may be started without permission if its estimated cost is $500 or more. Similarly, no new agricultural construction may be started if the estimated cost is $1,000 or more for the particular building or project involved. No other construction, including commercial, industrial, recreational, institutional, highway, roadway, subsurface, and utilities construction, whether publicly or privately financed, may be initiated without permission if the cost of the project amounts to $5,000 or more.

In computing such costs, the amount spent on the project within 12 months of the date of beginning construction, and subsequent to April 7, 1942, is included.

Exempt classes listed

Specific types of construction, however, are necessarily exempt from the provisions of the order. These include:

1. Projects which will be the property of the Army, Navy, Coast Guard, Maritime Commission and certain other listed agencies of the Federal Government.

2. Projects to reconstruct or restore residential property damaged or destroyed on or after January 1, 1942, by fire, flood, tornado, earthquake, or the public enemy.

3. Projects of the type restricted or controlled by provisions of the orders of the M-68 series, which cover the production and distribution of petroleum.

It was emphasized however, that the order does not affect ordinary maintenance and repair work to return a structure to sound working condition without a change of design.

Although the order applies only to construction not yet commenced, projects already under construction are being carefully examined by WPB on an individual basis. Such projects may be stopped if the scarce materials to be used in them can be put to more effective use in the war program.

Where priority assistance is granted by WPB, authority to commence construction will be issued by the Director of Industry

Operations on appropriate forms of orders in the P series.

These include preference rating orders of the P-14 series, P-19 series, P-41, P-46, P-55, P-98, P-110, and P-115. Preference ratings extended on PD-1 or PD-1A forms or by any other P order than those listed in the L-41 order do not constitute authorization to begin construction.

FHA to help administration

Facilities of the Federal Housing Administration have been made available to WPB in the administration of this order and applications for authority to start construction will be filed with the local offices of the Federal Housing Administration on Forms PD-200 and PD-200A, copies of which may be obtained at any of the district War Production Board offices or at any local office of the Federal Housing Administration. The public is urged to file only emergency applications during the next month, as it is anticipated that authorization will be given only for emergency projects. Authority to begin construction will be granted only when the design and specifications conform with the standards established for the minimum use of critical materials, and no materials will be used on the project that do not conform with the conditions of the authorization granted to begin construction.

On the basis of criteria established by the Director of Industry Operations of WPB, the local Officer of the Federal Housing Administration will decide whether or not the project is eligible for recommendation to WPB. If the project is deemed eligible, the application will be forwarded by FHA to the administrator of the order for final consideration.

If the application is denied by the local FHA office, on the basis of the WPB criteria, provision is made for an appeal to an appeals board to consist of the administrator of the order, a representative of labor and a third member who will represent the end product branch of WPB within whose jurisdiction the class of project or construction would fall.

★ ★ ★

Enamel limited for tops of glass containers

To save scarce materials such as tung oil, resins, and solvents, the Director of Industry Operations on April 6 announced the issuance of Conservation Order M-116, limiting the use of enamel coatings for glass container tops.

The order prohibits further use of enamel coating on the exterior surfaces of tinplate or terneplate closures for glass containers, subject to certain exceptions.

Reduction of the weight of the interior and exterior enamel coating on all closures for glass containers to not more than nine-tenths of the standard weight in 1940, wherever practicable, is also directed by the order.

WPB officials expect that through the order approximately 1,500,000 pounds of scarce protective coating raw materials will be conserved.

Small remodeling jobs to furnish war housing granted A–5 preference

WPB moved April 10 to make it easier for owners to remodel housing that can provide additional living accommodations essential to the war program.

In order P–110, effective immediately, an A–5 preference rating is assigned to deliveries to builders and their subcontractors of materials entering into low cost remodeling projects in areas important to the war effort.

It is limited to projects for which the cost of materials which are on the Defense Housing Critical List does not exceed an average of $100 per room for each dwelling unit. The scarce materials for each structure cannot cost more than $800.

Projects must be located in Defense Housing Critical Areas and the material for which a rating is granted is limited to that specified on the Defense Housing Critical List. Owners are not permitted to sell or rent any dwelling unit included in the project at prices higher than those approved on the application. In any case the monthly rental—less certain service charges—cannot exceed $50 for each dwelling unit and the sales price cannot exceed $6,000 for each single family accommodation.

Builders may apply for rating on Form PD–406 which should be filed in the local office of the Federal Housing Administration. Copies of PD–406 soon will be available at any local office of the FHA, at any priority office of the Bureau of Field Operations of WPB, or at banks, building and loan associations, or other housing institutions. Information regarding the Defense Housing Critical Areas List and the Defense Housing Critical List may be obtained at any local office of the FHA.

Remodeling projects rated under P–110 are exempt from the provision of Conservation Order L–41, issued April 9, 1942, which restricts construction.

★ ★ ★

Steel plate sets all-time mark in March; deliveries for ships up 30 percent in one month

Steel plate shipments in March set an all-time record of 878,726 tons, C. E. Adams, chief, iron and steel branch, announced April 10. February shipments were 758,723 tons.

Deliveries from strip mills totaled 306,195 tons in March, a substantial increase over February's total of 268,988 tons.

Deliveries to shipyards for the Maritime Commission's merchant ship program increased 30 percent in March over February.

April deliveries are expected to equal the March total, despite the fact this month has one less working day.

Orders to stop civilian production

(Continued from page 1)

and the civilian construction industry. They make possible the complete conversion of the men, materials, and machine tools formerly devoted to these pursuits to war production.

Metals, plastics barred

The steel order, to be issued shortly, will prohibit at an early date the use of iron and steel in hundreds of specifically listed metal products. But it is more than a steel order. It also prohibits the use of specifically listed materials as a substitute. This list of materials includes all of the metals and the scarce plastics.

The construction order will place severe limitations upon new construction of all types, confining it to relatively small projects and defense works.

These two orders mark the high point in the execution of a policy that was initiated with the closure of the gigantic automobile industry in the first days of February.

Since the issuance of the automobile orders, the War Production Board has moved quietly but swiftly for the curtailment of one consumers durable goods industry after another.

A new weapon of total war

Soon there will be no more processing of such articles as electric refrigerators, vacuum cleaners, laundry equipment, radio receivers, vending machines, amusement machines, and a host of electrical appliances.

Other industries producing metal signs, metal windows, metal furniture, metal kitchen and household utensils, metal toys, lawn mowers, domestic oil burners and coal stokers will be equally affected. Even such items as mortician's goods cannot be produced in the metal-working field.

This drastic type of order that results in a complete stoppage of production is a new and important weapon of total war. Those who are old enough to recollect, or who have had occasion to study the subject, know the role which American industry played in winning the last war.

It is worth bearing in mind that during the entire course of the first world war, not a single limitation order was issued which completely prohibited the output of any civilian product.

In August of 1918, or a year and four months after the United States entered the war, an agreement was made between the automobile industry and the War

Industries Board to limit the output of the auto industry for the second half of 1918 to a quarter of its normal output.

Difficult adjustments ahead

The next 2 or 3 months will be a period of difficult adjustment for the Nation in general and the industrial producers and employees engaged in the operations which are restricted. The American consumer will shortly find that many of the items which he would purchase in the normal course cannot be secured at all, or, at least cannot be secured without recourse to rationing procedures.

All this is dictated, however, by a carefully worked out plan and program, planned to accord with the necessities of war and the desirability of maintaining the production of relatively essential civilian items and services. The metal working industries which consume vast amounts of important raw materials, labor and machine tools, can now be diverted in large part to war production. This is a part of the process of total war in which our enemies have excelled. With our more abundant supplies of the consumers' goods in the homes and in stock, the Nation will bring its metal industries completely into war production in an orderly fashion. This is the way of total all-out war and the price of early victory.

NO RUBBER YARN PLANNED FOR CIVILIAN USE

Ben Alexander, acting chief of the WPB textile, clothing, and leather goods branch, said April 10 that it is not contemplated to amend the Rubber Conservation Order M–124 to release any rubber yarns for civilian use.

"These yarns are needed for military purposes and simply cannot be made available for civilian purposes," Mr. Alexander said.

The enemy says—

Professor Kunihiko Okura said April 9 in a Japanese-language broadcast: "We are engaged in a great war and we must not slacken our determination to crush once and for all Britain, America and the Netherlands." (Recorded by FCC and reported by OFF.)

19 kinds of supplies limited in hands of wholesalers, retailers, and others

Inventories of 19 kinds of supplies, whether in the hands of wholesalers, distributors, jobbers, dealers, retailers, or branch warehouses are strictly limited by Suppliers' Inventory Limitation Order L–63, issued April 6 by the Director of Industry Operations.

Wholesalers and dealers affected by the order who are located in the eastern and central time zones are required to limit their inventories to twice the dollar value of sales of the specified types of supplies which they shipped from stock in the second preceding calendar month. Suppliers located in other time zones may have inventories equal to three times the corresponding amount. Shipments made directly from producers to customers in which the distributor acts only as an agent may not be included as a basis for calculating permissible inventory.

Small suppliers exempt

Suppliers whose total inventory at cost is less than $20,000, and less than $10,000 for any one of the listed types of supplies, are exempt. Special provision is made for inventories of seasonal supplies.

The new order supersedes Suppliers' Order M–67, covering plumbing, heating, and electrical supplies, which is revoked. The types of supplies covered by Order L–63 are:

Automotive, aviation, builders, construction, dairy, electrical, farm, foundry, grain elevator, hardware, health, industrial, plumbing and heating, railroad, refrigeration, restaurant, textile mill, transmission, and welding and cutting.

Suppliers affected by the order are required to keep records of their inventory and sales on Form PD–336, and to keep this form in their files for at least two years. Separate records must be kept for each type of supplies handled by the distributor or dealer.

Must record frozen inventories

Inventories of material frozen by the "L" or other orders should be included in the inventory records. The provisions of L–63 do not relieve suppliers from responsibility of compliance with any other applicable order or orders.

Suppliers affected by the new order whose inventories on hand at the time the order was issued exceed the permissible maximum must not receive any deliveries of such supplies until the inventories are reduced below the maximum. However, when inventories are below maximum, suppliers may receive deliveries of minimum commercially procurable quantities, even though such deliveries would raise their inventories above the maximum.

Distribution of quinine limited to build stock pile

In order to build a stock pile for military needs, WPB on April 5 established control over the supply and distribution of quinine.

The order (Conservation Order M–131) affects all pharmaceutical and medicinal chemical companies, botanical supply houses, wholesale drug and supply houses, retail drug stores, and all other persons who deal in quinine—except the ultimate consumer.

Permitted as anti-malarial agent

The terms of the order permit sale and delivery of quinine only for use as an anti-malarial agent or an ingredient of quinine and urea hydrochloride.

This restriction does not apply to any stock of quinine in combination with any other medicinal ingredient.

Persons owning or having control of 50 pounds of cinchona bark or 50 ounces of quinine must report such stocks to the War Production Board on Form PD–401. This form will be available in about a week.

95 percent from Far East

Ninety-five percent of cinchona bark from which quinine is derived comes from Java in the Dutch East Indies. The Federal Government has built a substantial stock pile, and in addition, there is available a large supply in the hands of manufacturers and distributors.

The estimated military requirements for the balance of this year will exceed the production expected to be obtained from South American sources of cinchona bark.

A–3 for medium, heavy trucks is extended to May 31

An extension of Limited Preference Rating Order P–54 until May 31 was ordered by WPB April 7 to enable producers of medium and heavy trucks to obtain materials necessary to complete authorized production quotas.

The extended order makes available an A–3 rating for materials going into the production of medium and heavy trucks.

This action is supplementary to orders issued recently permitting manufacturers to clean up February civilian production quotas by April 30, and to dispose of March quotas for trucks having a gross weight of 16,000 pounds or more by May 31.

WPB asks wool users to submit blending programs

The War Production Board April 4 sent letters to all woolen manufacturers advising them to submit to WPB before April 30 estimates of their blending programs for the third and fourth quarters of 1942 showing the maximum yardage of satisfactory fabrics they will be able to produce with the minimum amount of new wool, after taking care of Government contracts.

✦ ✦ ✦

Mechanical rubber goods specifications discussed

Methods of developing specifications for mechanical rubber goods products have been discussed with the industry committee at a recent meeting, it was announced April 6 by the rubber and rubber products branch. The products affected are used primarily by industry.

Water softener company voluntarily cancels increase

Permutit Co. of New York City, one of the largest manufacturers of industrial water softeners in the United States, has voluntarily withdrawn a general advance in prices effective October 15, 1941, and returned to its October 1 prices, Acting Price Administrator Hamm announced April 4.

The increase, which affected Permutit's entire line of carbonaceous zeolite water softening equipment, was made effective before the company and others in the field were asked by Mr. Hamm in January of this year to return to October 1, 1941, prices

MOTOR FUEL ORDER IS L–70

The order restricting delivery of motor fuel was styled as L–7 in the list of priorities actions appearing in VICTORY March 31. The correct number of this order is L–70.

WPB sets up section to use prison industries for war

Creation of a separate section within the Bureau of Governmental Requirements to cooperate with State governments and Federal procurement agencies in utilizing the fully equipped shops and skilled labor of prison industries in the war effort was announced April 4 by Maury Maverick, chief of the bureau.

Guidance of the program will be in the hands of Dan Turner, former Governor of Iowa.

The bureau has been promised the cooperation of virtually all States in making the facilities of prison shops available for the production of war goods, most of which would be purchased by other governments warring against Hitler. The prison industries section of the bureau is now studying procedures which would enable the prison industries to sell to the Defense Supplies Corporation for Lend-Lease purposes.

It was pointed out that before the Federal Government can contract with the several States for prison-made goods, it would be necessary temporarily to suspend certain portions of the Walsh-Healey and other Acts.

A survey of the textile prison industries made by the bureau shows that cotton mills operated by State prisons have 51,-000 cotton spindles with a 7,000,000-pound annual capacity.

A total of 1,671 cotton looms, operated by 3,100 inmates, have an annual capacity of 19,000,000 square yards of 5½-ounce fabric, based on one shift of 40 hours a week.

Surveys of the metal and wood-working industries are being completed.

Ban on toy paint materials postponed to June 30

The toys and games limitation order (L-81) has been amended to take certain colors, oils, and chemicals out of the category of Prohibited Material whose use was forbidden as of the date the order was issued, and prohibit their use, after June 30, "in any form whatsoever in paints, lacquers, varnishes, or any other surface or protective coatings in the manufacture of toys or games."

The effect of the amendment is to permit unrestricted use of these materials between now and June 30 and to restrict their use after that time.

ALLOCATIONS TO AMERICAS

The United States Government, in accordance with the policy of close inter-American cooperation, has announced a list of commodities allocated to the other American republics for the second quarter of 1942. This announcement was made jointly by the Department of State, War Production Board, and Board of Economic Warfare. The announced list comprises the following materials:

Acetic acid; acetone; aconite; ammonium sulphate; anhydrous ammonia; aniline; camphor; carbon tetrachloride; castor oil; caustic soda; chlorine; copper; cotton linters; dibutyl phthalate; electrodes; farm equipment; formaldehyde; glycerin; leather; ferro-manganese; methanol; molybdenum; neat's-foot oil; phenol; phosphorous; phthalic anhydride; plastics; potash salts; potassium permanganate; rayon; red squill; household electric refrigerators; soda ash; strontium chemicals; sulphuric acid; superphosphate; tanning materials; toluol; tricresyl phosphate; light trucks; tungsten and ferro-tungsten; ferro-vanadium; wood pulp.

It is anticipated that there may be further announcements of additional materials to be made available during this quarter, the State Department said.

. . .

Control of soles extended to manufacturers' stocks

WPB on April 4 took control of 80 percent of all available stocks of manufacturers' type cut outer and inner shoe soles of military weight and quality. The restriction applies to all soles in the hands of manufacturers whether cut by them or not, as well as in the hands of sole cutters. The order (amendment to M-80) does not refer to finders type soles, such as those in the hands of shoe repair shops.

Jute for rugs cut again because of events in Asia

WPB on April 4 ordered a 50-percent cut in the amount of jute previously allocated for April to rug and carpet mills. The action was necessary because of recent developments in the vicinity of Calcutta, from which all jute is shipped. Pending issuance of a formal order, the WPB wired the restriction to all carpet mills and producers of carpet yarns.

New liquefied petroleum gas equipment may not be installed

Installations of new liquefied petroleum gas equipment were prohibited April 8 by the Director of Industry Operations.

Liquefied petroleum gas includes butane, propane, propylene, and similar products which are commonly used for cooking and heating in localities where gas from central plants is not available.

The order forbids new installations of equipment to contain, distribute, or dispense liquefied petroleum gas, except facilities used in transportation and refining.

The limitation order, L-86, does not apply to material for maintenance and repair of existing equipment or to exchange of containers on the premises of any person in the normal course of distribution of liquefied petroleum gas.

Installations which were begun before January 14, 1942, may be completed, provided the work of installation is finished on or before May 15. Exceptions to the order may also be made in special cases by the Director of Industry Operations upon application in accordance with Form PD-397.

Use of preference ratings under the Petroleum order, P-98, and the Utilities order, P-46, for operations affected by Limitation Order 86, is specifically forbidden.

Typewriter parts manufacture allowed in economical lots

Typewriter manufacturers can produce some parts and subassemblies in economical manufacturing lots, even though the result is production in excess of established quotas for completed typewriters, according to an official interpretation of Conservation Order L-54-a, announced April 4 by the Director of Industry Operations.

This relaxation does not apply generally to part production but is restricted to those parts which, because of their nature, cannot be produced economically in small quantities.

★ ★ ★

Jewelry makers get 41 days to use up plated, alloyed copper

The jewelry industry on April 4 was granted until May 15 to use up such of its copper in inventory as has been plated or alloyed with gold or silver.

1,600 minor priority violations, and some more serious, revealed by WPB inquiry

The operations of 3,500 firms have been surveyed for priorities violations by the compliance branch of the War Production Board since it was set up last June, L. J. Martin, assistant chief of the Bureau of Priorities, announced April 5. The operations of 10,500 additional companies are now being investigated, and reviews of the work of 7,100 companies are now being prepared, the branch reported.

Of the 3,500 completed reports received by the branch, more than 1,600 revealed no violations of priority orders. Approximately the same number of firms were found to have committed minor violations, largely through misunderstanding. These received letters explaining priority regulations.

Some serious violations

A small number of the reports indicate violations of varying degrees of seriousness. These reports are now being studied, and punitive action will probably be recommended in the case of the more serious examples.

Of the 35 suspension orders, affecting 46 firms and 1 individual, issued so far as a result of the compliance branch's findings, 5 were in cases disclosed in the course of industry-wide surveys, and 30 were the result of information supplied by other branches of WPB, Government agencies, and the public.

The industry-wide surveys are conducted with the assistance of investigation staffs loaned for the purpose by other Federal agencies. Cooperating with the WPB to date have been the Wage and Hour Division of the Department of Labor, Federal Trade Commission, Home Owners Loan Corporation, and the Geological Survey, General Land Office, and National Park Service of the Interior Department. Relations have been established with a total of 13 Federal agencies, which will make available to the WPB the services of approximately 3,550 investigators.

New law increases severity

Under the provisions of the Second War Powers Bill the activities of the compliance branch will take on a greater severity, since the bill provides for criminal prosecution of violators of priority regulations. Penalties of up to 1 year in jail and a $10,000 fine may be imposed in cases of proven violation.

Heretofore, it has been possible to impose penalties only by the issuance of suspension orders, which deny to the violating company the right to deal in or fabricate the scarce material involved in its illegal activities. While these orders have been effective as punitive measures in many cases, there are instances in which their use would impair the war effort by cutting off needed production.

Field operations planned

A "flying squadron" of special investigators is being set up by the branch so that prompt action may be taken in special cases, and plans for the development of field operations include the establishment of investigation units in each of WPB's regional and district offices.

Compliance commissioners will be assigned to the 13 regional offices. They will sit in conference with the respondent companies, and hear explanations offered by those charged with violations. After a study of evidence, a compliance commissioner will report his findings and recommendations to Washington. If his recommendations are for punitive action, and are accepted, the Director of Industry Operations will issue a suspension order, or refer the case to the Department of Justice for criminal proceedings, depending upon the circumstances and the degree of culpability involved.

Lead foil for cigarettes forbidden May 1

Manufacturers of cigarettes were ordered on April 6 to cease the use of lead foil for cigarette packaging on May 1, regardless of inventories on hand. The manufacture of metal foil for this purpose has already been prohibited.

Director of Industry Operations Knowlson issued Amendment No. 1 to Conservation Order M-38-c setting the termination date.

Other changes in Lists "A" and "B" of the order:

The use of lead is prohibited immediately in buttons, costume jewelry, novelties and trophies. They are added to List "A."

Cames, the grooved lead rods that hold fitted pieces of stained glass windows together, are removed from the list, thus permitting their manufacture.

Foil for condensers, electrotyping and moulding lead, and dental X-ray equipment and supplies are placed on List "B" which permits their manufacture when other materials are impractical.

Large vacuum cleaner producer penalized for diverting aluminum from war needs

The Hoover Co., of North Canton, Ohio, third largest producer of vacuum cleaners in the country, with a normal annual output of more than 200,000 units, is prohibited from fabricating or dealing in aluminum for a period of 3 months by terms of a suspension order announced April 8 by the Director of Industry Operations.

The violations for which the Hoover Co. is penalized resulted in the diversion of approximately half a million pounds of secondary aluminum from the requirements of the war program, the announcement stated.

Not used as intended by OPM

During the period July-October, 1941, the company made shipments of 23,615 pounds of aluminum, which had been approved by the OPM on the company's statement that this aluminum was to be used for circuit breakers. Actually it went into motor bases and small motor parts, uses which would not have been authorized had full disclosure been made.

During approximately the same period, it was announced, the Hoover Co. shipped 140,382 pounds of aluminum under unauthorized toll agreements. In addition, the company accepted deliveries of 179,274 pounds of scrap aluminum, although no preference rating had been assigned to these deliveries, nor had other authorization to accept them been obtained.

Suspension Order S-14 provides that the Hoover Co. may not deliver or accept any form of aluminum for a period of 3 months, and also enjoins it from entering into any contracts for purchase or delivery of the metal.

The Hoover Co. is permitted to continue processing of aluminum for 10 days following issuance of the order. At the end of this grace period, the company must cease all manufacturing operations calling for the use of aluminum.

Textile firm punished

Announced at the same time as the Hoover Co. case were orders which prohibit a New York City textile processor from accepting delivery of any yarn subject to priority control, and prohibited a yarn jobber from accepting or making delivery of such yarn. These Suspension Orders are S-30 and S-31.

The penalized companies are David Ritter, Inc., 1239 Broadway, New York, N. Y., and the Jesam Yarn Co., of the same address.

Connett beads goatskin unit

The appointment of Harold Connett of Philadelphia as chief of the newly created goatskin unit of the leather and shoe section was announced April 6.

WPB seizes aluminum after owner refuses to sell; other cases studied

The inventory and requisitioning branch moved April 6 to take over a quantity of aluminum, which its owners had refused to sell at prices established by the WPB. This was the first action of the kind to become necessary since the inauguration in February of a Nation-wide campaign to salvage all idle stocks of aluminum in fabricators' hands.

J. Clem Kline & Son, of Easton, Pa., in filing their report of stocks on hand, had claimed that 1,000 pounds of high grade commercial aluminum ingot in their possession were required to fill rated orders. Subsequent investigation disclosed that the material was not needed for this purpose and the requisitioning orders were drawn up. They were served April 6 by a United States Marshal.

Other cases of refusal to sell are being studied by the branch, and it is expected that the WPB's requisitioning authority will be invoked in a number of them.

11,000,000 pounds made available

Since the beginning of the program to purchase idle aluminum, the inventory section of the branch has received replies from approximately half of the 1,000 fabricators circularized. Those accepting the proposed terms have made immediatley available for war production more than 11,000,000 pounds of this critical material.

An additional 500 manufacturing users will shortly have questionnaires sent to them, and it is expected the campaign when completed will have salvaged in the neighborhood of 35 million pounds of aluminum.

... ...

78,000 pounds of copper seized

Two lots of copper sheet, totaling 78,000 pounds, the property of J. M. Katz, 261 Broadway, New York, N. Y., were seized April 6 for war purposes at Allentown, Pa., and Peru, Ill., by order of the inventory and requisitioning branch. Mr. Katz, who had previously refused an offer by Metals Reserve Corporation to purchase this copper, is a supplier of bathroom accessories. The material taken over represents inventories, in excess of requirements to fill rated orders, which he could not otherwise dispose of because of the terms of the copper conservation order.

Large amounts of metals, fibers, toluol rescued for war by requisition branch

In his first over-all report to the War Production Board on the activities of the inventory and requisitioning branch since its organization last December, L. J. Martin, assistant chief of the Bureau of Priorities, revealed that by some 60 separate requisitioning actions large quantities of commodities in 17 categories and the entire cargo of an Axis ship, have been seized for war uses by Government agencies.

Much also negotiated

In addition to the material obtained as the result of these requisitioning orders, the branch has succeeded in negotiating voluntary sales which have made available to war industries large quantities of critical materials frozen by conservation orders because they had been purchased before the outbreak of war for export to enemy and occupied countries, or for other reasons.

Another method employed by the branch to direct idle inventories of badly needed supplies into war production is represented by the broad salvage campaigns carried on with the assistance of the RFC. In these campaigns the branch establishes a schedule of prices to be paid from RFC funds for raw, semiprocessed and scrap materials found to be in the possession of manufacturers prohibited by priority regulations from making use of them.

At present such programs are being conducted to salvage inventories of aluminum, white metal and nickel anodes held by owners not engaged in war production.

Similar programs will be initiated shortly to acquire known stocks of copper, brass and bronze, iron and steel, manila hemp and other critical items.

List of materials seized

Critical material seized under requisitioning orders up to March 25, 1942, includes the following:

Copper, 7,230,301 pounds; lead, 550 tons; manila hemp, 570 bales; silk, 26,772 bales; steel, 11,000 tons; tin plate, 1,354 tons; iron and steel scrap, 4,000 tons; tin, 278,864 pounds; toluol, 262,544 gallons; wax, 119 bags; wood pulp, 10,972,569 pounds; zinc concentrates, 5,000 tons; boats, 6; cargo, 5,000 tons, miscellaneous; steel containers, 2,700 drums; machinery, miscellaneous, three plants; rail track, 49.7 miles.

Voluntary sales

Voluntary sales by owners to fabricators, negotiated by materials disposition

section of the inventory and requisitioning branch, involved transfers of:

Copper and brass, 4,066,705 pounds; steel, 8,760 tons; tin plate, 2,311 boxes; iron and steel scrap, 3,294 tons; tin, 883,942 pounds; lead, 494,402 pounds; antimony, 15,400 pounds; type metal, 189,523 pounds; zinc, 34,000 pounds; tungsten ore, 129,655 pounds; molybdenum wire, 3,341,000 meters; molybdenum concentrates, 45 tons; chrome silicate, 500,000 pounds; wolframite, 82 tons; rubber, 2,348 tons; rubber tires and tubes, 1,640 approximately; toluol, 41 tons; sugar, 40,000 tons; kapok, 700 bales approximately; marine engines, $89,000; tractors, 31; trucks, 296; steel mill equipment; tools and miscellaneous machinery, 81 lots.

★ ★ ★

Loofa sponges, needed by Navy, limited to A–1–a ratings

WPB on April 8 restricted deliveries of loofa sponges to orders bearing an A–1–a preference rating.

The loofa sponge is made from the fiber of the luffa or loofah plant. The sponge is unique for its property of oil absorption, and, therefore, is useful in oil-filtration. It is used by the Navy extensively.

Under the order (M–125) a dealer may not sell, transfer, or deliver loofa sponges to persons other than those having a rating of A–1–a or better. Moreover, no person may use, cut, or process loofa sponges for any purpose except upon orders having a similar rating.

The plant is grown on a commercial basis almost exclusively in Japan. Plans are under way to put production on a commercial basis in the United States, as well as in Central and South America.

★ ★ ★

Tin regulations revised

Regulations governing tin usage, which was brought under WPB conservation control by Order M–43–a on March 18, are revised under the terms of Amendment No. 1A to the order, announced April 16.

Subparagraph (c) (2) (ii) of the order is amended to allow the use of enough solder to manufacture the cans permitted by Conservation Order M–81.

Terne metal used for terneplating cans under Conservation Order M–81 must be limited in tin content to 15 percent by weight. Terne metal used to coat long ternes may not contain more than 10 percent tin by weight.

The term "automobile body solder" is defined to include any tin-bearing material used as a filler or smoother for automobile or truck bodies or fenders.

WPB curbs extremes in women's clothes; coat or dress bought today will be good for duration—and order saves cloth

The War Production Board acted April 8 to assure the women and girls of America that there will be no extremes in dress styles during this war as there were during the last war, and that their present wardrobes will not be made obsolete by radical fashion changes.

No hems to let down

It issued an order L–85 in effect stabilizing for the duration of the war the present length and fullness of skirts. This will guard against extreme variations such as long, full skirts and sleeves that would waste millions of yards of material.

The order will not affect clothes for this spring and summer, most of which are already made. The restrictions on woolen garments became effective April 9 in time to apply to the production of most of next fall and winter's clothes. Restrictions on cotton, rayon, and other materials do not go into effect until June 19, by which time production of clothes for this summer will have been completed. Restrictions on existing retailers' stocks of ensembles will go into effect August 17.

Through conservation and prevention measures, the order is expected to make possible the production of at least 15 percent more garments out of the same yardage of cloth. The conservation measures consist mainly of eliminating such things as French cuffs on sleeves, balloon sleeves, patch pockets of wool, and the prohibition of suit and coat ensembles of more than two pieces at one unit price. The prevention measures consist of fixing maximum coat and skirt lengths and sweeps, thus heading off possible extreme style changes to lengthen skirts and coats and thus increase cloth requirements.

Designers still have lots of leeway

The measurements fixed in the order represent present averages in women's clothing.

The measurements were purposely made liberal in order not to outmode present wardrobes and stocks, which would have defeated the purpose of the order—to conserve cloth. The order does not mean the standardization of women's clothes. Within the limitations fixed in the order, fashion designers, dress manufacturers, and housewives are free to use their ingenuity in creating whatever fashions may strike their fancy.

The lengths represent the present average. Likewise, the sweeps are neither the narrowest nor the widest found today, but strike a middle ground. Specifically, the survey showed that the American woman wears a jacket today that varies from 23 to 27 inches in length; the order strikes a medium of 25 inches. The skirt of her dress now varies

Sketches on this page were released by WPB to show examples of the changes in dress. One-column mats are available to publications. Address Distribution Section, Information Division, OEM, Washington, D. C.

from 68 to 108 inches in width; the order sets maximum widths at 78 inches for a size 16.

In each case, the measurements fixed in the order permit variations, to accommodate the requirements of "regular women," "little women," "stout women," "misses," "junior misses," "teen age," "girls," and "children."

The order does not apply to infants' and toddler apparel (sizes from 1 to 4), bridal gowns, maternity dresses, clothing for persons of abnormal size, burial gowns, and robes and vestments as required by the rules of religious orders or sects.

Restrictions as to ensembles apply only to the unit price and not to the garments themselves. The order permits not more than two pieces of an ensemble to be sold at one unit price. This is done in

DRESSES for peace and for war. Dress at right is pleated in clusters with sweep of 78 instead of 136 inches; sleeves are bracelet-length.

COATS before and after WPB changes. Model at right is in same style but eliminates full sleeves, patch pockets, turn-back cuffs

SUITS approved and disapproved. Jacket changes from 27-inch length to 25, pockets from patch to set-in, skirt from 96-inch flare to 64 inches.

the hope of saving material by discouraging women from buying matching jackets and blouses. A matching jacket can be worn with only one dress, whereas a jacket of neutral color or pattern might be worn with several dresses.

Other than that, the order provides no sweeping curtailment.

Essential details of the order, as they affect the different apparel in a woman's wardrobe, are:

GENERAL RESTRICTIONS ON ALL GARMENTS

1. Not more than two articles of apparel at one unit price.
2. No dress may be sold with a jacket, bolero, cape, coat, or redingote at a unit price.
3. No French cuffs on sleeves.
4. No double material yokes.
5. No balloon, dolman, or leg-of-mutton sleeves.
6. No fabrics which have been reduced from normal width or length by all-over tucking, shirring, pleating, except for minor trimmings.
7. No inside pockets of wool cloth.
8. No patch pockets of wool cloth on a lined wool garment.
9. No interlinings containing any virgin or reprocessed wool.

COATS

1. No cuffs.
2. No wool evening wraps.
3. No wool linings.
4. No sleeves cut on the bias.
5. No belt wider than 2 inches.
6. No wool cloth lining under fur trimming.
7. No hem more than 2 inches.
8. Maximum lengths for size 16, with other lengths in proportion to size: 42 inches for a box coat, 43 inches for a fitted coat. This compares with a present average length of 41 to 42 inches for a box coat, and 42 to 43 inches for a fitted coat.
9. Maximum sweeps for size 16, with other measurements in proportion to size: 60 inches for a box coat, and 70 inches for a fitted coat. This compares with present range of 58 to 65 inches for a box coat, and 68 to 80 inches for a fitted coat.

DRESSES

1. No sleeves wider than 14 inches in circumference for a size 16.
2. No hoods, shawls, capes, scarfs, petticoats, overskirts, or aprons made with dress.
3. No belt more than 2 inches wide.
4. No hems of more than 2 inches.
5. Maximum length of size 16 dresses, with proportionate lengths for other sizes: 43 inches, compared with present range of 41½ to 44 inches.
6. Maximum sweeps for size 16 :
(a) Rayon and cotton—73 inches. Present lengths vary from 66 to 96 inches.
(b) Wool (9 ounces and less)—75 inches. Present lengths, 66 to 96 inches.
(c) Wool over 9 ounces—64 inches. Present lengths, 66 to 96 inches.

EVENING DRESSES

1. No overskirts or aprons.
2. No wool evening dresses.
3. No belt or sash more than 2 inches.
4. No hoods.
5. No slips with dresses of nontransparent materials.
6. Maximum length for size 16—59 inches. Present average is 59 to 61 inches.
7. Maximum sweep for all sizes, 144 inches. Present average, 130 to 216 inches.

SUITS, JACKETS, AND SKIRTS

1. Length of suit skirts, 28 inches (present range, 26 to 28 inches).

2. Length of jackets, 25 inches (present range, 25 to 27 inches).
3. Sweep of suit skirts, made of wool material of 9 ounces and under, 72 inches; made of wool material of over 9 ounces, 64 inches. This compares with present range of 54 to 86 inches.
4. No hems of more than 2 inches.
5. Other restrictions on skirts:
(a) No matching or contrasting belts.
(b) No wool-lined skirts.
(c) No evening skirts of wool.
(d) No hems exceeding 2 inches.
6. Other restrictions on jackets:
(a) No jackets longer than 25 inches for size 16; present lengths 23 inches to 27 inches.
(b) No vents, no bi-sweep, no Norfolk styles.
(c) No bias cut sleeves.
(d) No cuffs.
(e) No hoods, capes, scarfs, muffs, bags, or vests with jackets.

SLACKS

1. No cuffs.
2. No patch pockets or flaps.
3. No belts.
4. No slacks measuring more than 44½ inches outseam measurements nor more than 19 inches at the bottom—present average bottoms measure from 19 inches to 22 inches.

BLOUSES

1. No hoods or scarfs.
2. No more than one patch pocket.
3. No blouse larger than 22 inches for a size 32; present average 21 inches to 23 inches.

CHILDREN'S

Same general specifications as on all other garments with proper gradations for lengths and sweeps for the various size ranges.

OTHER GENERAL RESTRICTIONS

1. No pants or leggings with coats in the teen age range, 10–16.
2. No hoods on wool coats.
3. No separate hoods on snow suits.
4. No hats or caps with coats.

HEATING PADS CURTAILED

WPB has restricted the production of electric heating pads. It also has prohibited the use of chromium and curtailed the use of rubber, nickel, and electrical resistance material in the manufacture of such pads.

Under order L–84, effective April 4, the 1942 production of hospital-type electric heating pads is limited to the amount manufactured in 1940, and the production of pads for home use is limited to 50 percent of the amount manufactured in 1940.

The health supplies branch of WPB said that the order will permit, at most, production during 1942 of approximately 150,000 hospital-type pads and 675,000 pads for home use.

A manufacturer, after date of the order, may not purchase or accept delivery of critical materials from any market, except such critical materials as he can obtain from other manufacturers in the electric heating pad industry.

Loophole in import order is stopped by amendment

Because General Imports Order M–63 failed, in a few instances, to keep private purchasers out of foreign markets for critical materials, Industry Operations Director Knowlson on April 8 issued Amendment No. 4 to accomplish that result.

The original order provided that private persons could not arrange or contract to import materials listed in the order without specific authorization. To clarify the question of whether or not the order referred to purchases, the amendment specifically lists "purchase for import" as prohibited along with arranging or contracting.

The amendment does not change the provision of the order permitting imports under contracts existing at the time of passage of the order.

A number of additional commodities are placed under the order. They are:

Babassu nuts, kernels and oil; castor beans and castor oil, and oiticica oil.

Cashew nuts, shells, kernels, and oil.

Cohune nuts and kernels, imported from Honduras.

Columbite and columbium ore, a steel alloy.

Chemical and munitions grades of cotton linters.

Certain grades of flax, graphite, seed lac, and tantalum ore.

ALL COPPER SCREEN FROZEN

All stocks of copper screening in the United States, including uncut rolls in the hands of retailers, were frozen April 9 by an amendment to Copper Order M–9–c issued by the Director of Industry Operations.

Manufacture of copper screening was stopped on March 31. Large stocks exist in the country in the hands of manufacturers, wholesalers, and retailers that can be used by the Military Services, thus avoiding the use of additional copper to make new screening for them.

Adequate amounts of steel wire screening are available for civilian use.

The amended order provides no person shall deliver, install or cut any copper screening except for certain Government agencies or upon specific permission of the Director of Industry Operations. It does not apply to used or second-hand screening or to rolls which were partly used on April 9.

Interim manufacture of electrical appliances is further restricted

WPB on April 9 further restricted the production of electrical appliances.

It issued an amendment to order L–65 providing a further reduction in the number of electrical appliances that may be made before production must cease altogether on May 31, and providing tighter restrictions on the metals that may be used in the appliances that may be manufactured under the order.

The original order permitted manufacturers to produce, between the issuance date of May 31, appliances having a factory sales value up to 25 percent of the factory sales value of their products in all of 1941, exclusive of orders having ratings of A–10 or higher.

The April 9 amendment reduces the production permitted under the order to 20 percent of factory sales value in 1941, exclusive of A–10 and higher orders.

Metal limit restored

The amendment also tightens restrictions on the use of critical metals in the electrical appliances that may be produced under the order. The original order provided that Conservation Orders M–1–a, M–6–b, M–9–c, M–21–d, and M–43–a restricting the use by manufacturers of aluminum, nickel, copper and copper base alloys, alloy steel and tin in the production of electrical appliances would no longer apply to production permitted under the order but would be superseded by the provisions of L–65.

The new amendment provides that the conservation orders will apply in all cases in which their restrictions are more severe than the restrictions under L–65. The only exception to this rule is in the use of electrical resistance material (nickel or chromium), which may be used, out of inventory, up to 15 percent of the amount of such material used in 1941.

Electric appliance sellers may pass along tax

Under the temporary maximum price regulation recently issued for domestic electrical appliances, sellers may continue to pass on the Federal manufacturers' excise tax, OPA announced April 10.

PRIORITY ACTIONS
*From April 1
*Through April 9

Subject	Order number	Related form	Issued	Expired date	Rating
Bicycles:					
a. Supplementary order—to restrict sale and delivery of new adult bicycles:	L–52–a		4–2–42		
1. Includes all bicycles having frames of more than 17 inches.	L–52–a amend. #1		4–7–42		
Burlap and burlap products:					
a. Eases restrictions on receipts of burlap by bag users; Removes restrictions on importation of burlap into this country.	M–47 amend. #4		4–4–42		
Closure enamel:					
a. Conservation order: Limits use of enamel coatings for glass container tops.	M–118		4–4–42		
Construction:					
a. Conservation order: 1. Prohibits the start of unauthorized construction projects which use material and construction equipment needed in the war effort; places all new publicly and privately financed construction under rigid control.	L–41	P D–200, 200 A	4–9–42		
Copper:					
a. Supplementary conservation order: 1. Jewelry industry granted until May 15 to use up such of its copper in inventory as has been plated or alloyed with gold or silver.	M–9–c–2		4–4–42		
b. All stocks of copper screening in the U. S. including uncut rolls in hands of retailers frozen.	Amend. to M–9–c (as amend. 12–10–41).		4–9–42		
Cotton duck:					
a. Releases from all restrictions cotton duck of any width, weight, or construction manufactured in rug and carpet mills and on looms heretofore producing drapery or upholstery.	M–91 amend. #1		4–3–42		
Electric heating pads—to restrict production:					
a. Prohibits use of chromium and curtails use of rubber, nickel, and electrical resistance material in manufacture.	L–84		4–4–42	Until revoked.	
Feminine apparel:					
a. Stabilizes for the duration the present length and fullness of skirts, sleeves, etc.	L–85		4–8–42		
Fluorescent lighting fixtures:					
a. Production ended immediately except for essential uses or on contracts accepted prior to today on which work has begun.	L–78		4–2–42	6–30–42	A–2 or higher.
Furniture (metal office):					
a. Supplementary order: 1. An end to the manufacture of virtually all types of metal office furniture and equipment ordered.	L–13–a		4–1–42		
General imports order:					
a. Keeps private purchasers out of foreign markets for critical materials.	M–63 amend. #4	P D–222–c	4–8–42 (eff. 4–9–42).		
Lead:					
a. Prohibits use of lead foil for cigarette packaging on May 1; changes in lists "A" and "B."	M–38–c amend. #1		4–6–42		
Leather (sole):					
a. Control established of 80 percent of all available stocks of manufacturers type cut outer and inner shoe soles of military weight and quality.	M–80 amend. #1		4–4–42		
Liquefied petroleum gas equipment:					
a. Prohibits installations of new liquefied petroleum gas equipment except those used in transportation and refining	L–86	P D–307	4–8–42	Until revoked.	

Subject	Order number	Related form	Issued	Expired date	Rating
Loofa sponges: a. Conservation order: 1. Restricts deliveries to orders bearing A-1-a rating.	M-125		4-8-42		A-1-a or higher.
Motor carriers: a. Trucks, truck trailers, and passenger cars: i. Establishes separate definition for off-the-highway trucks.	L-1-a amend. #5		4-2-42		
b. Permits manufacturers to assemble fabricated or semi-fabricated materials on hand 2-28-42 in either knock-down or built-up form to provide estimated 28,000 additional vehicles.	L-1-a amend. #6		4-2-42		
c. Establishes separate definition for off-the-highway trucks.	P-54 amend. #3		4-2-42		
d. Motor trucks, truck trailers, and passenger carriers: 1. Extended to enable producers of medium and heavy trucks to obtain materials necessary to complete authorized production quotas.	P-54 ext. #5 (eff. 3-1-42)		4-7-42	5-31-42	A-3
e. Supplementary order: 1. Producers granted additional 30 days until Apr. 30 to complete February quotas; until May 31 for March quotas.	L-1-f		4-2-42		
Motor fuel: a. Cuts percentage of deliveries of gasoline to service stations and bulk consumers in areas where curtailment is in effect.	L-70 amend. #1	PD-368	4-8-42 (eff. 4-16-42).		
Office machinery: a. Typewriter manufacturers can produce some parts and subassemblies in economic manufacturing lots, even though it results in production in excess of established quotas for completed typewriters.	L-54-n int. #1		4-3-42		
Plumbing and heating: a. Certain types of pipe fittings required for shipbuilding have been exempted.	L-42 amend. #1 to Schedule #2.		4-4-42		
b. Plumbing fixture fittings and trimmings: 1. Additional articles for which use of copper or copper base alloy prohibited.	L-42 Schedule #5-a		4-9-42		
Quinine: a. Conservation order—to conserve supply and direct distribution.	M-131	PD-401	4-4-42		
Railroad equipment: a. Locomotives: 1. Prohibits production or delivery except in accordance with announced schedules.	L-97		4-4-42	Until revoked.	
b. Railroad cars: 1. Prohibits production or delivery except in accordance with announced schedules.	L-97-a		4-4-42	Until revoked.	
Rubber: a. Rubber yarn and elastic thread: 1. Knitters, weavers and other users permitted to use rubber yarn and elastic thread by meeting certain requirements.	M-124 amend. #1		4-1-42		
b. Permits manufacture of pass. car capping stock entirely from reclaimed rubber together with a small quantity of crude for cushion stock.	M-15-b-1 amend. #3.		4-8-42		

c. Rubber sealed closures for glass containers:
  1. Conservation order:
    a. Prohibits use of rubber on containers for packaging more than 40 groups of products effective in 30 days.
	M-119		4-9-42	Until revoked.	

(Continued on page 14)

Small tracklaying tractors discontinued to get more of larger military type

Seeking to hasten production of large tracklaying tractors urgently needed for military, export, and essential civilian uses, WPB on April 9 ordered immediate and drastic curtailment in the output of smaller types used principally in agricultural operations.

Supplementary Limitation Order L-53–a prohibits production of the smaller types—those in the 17–35 horsepower class—after September 1. Tracklaying tractors are those which obtain traction from a crawler or track-type device, and not from wheels.

3,035 more permitted

Between April 9 and the closing production date, manufacturers will be permitted to make 3,035 tractors in the 17–35 horsepower class, as compared with their estimated possible production of 6,973 tractors for the balance of this year. This is a reduction of 3,398 units.

The industry consists of only four companies, and the permitted production will be distributed as follows:

Allis-Chalmers Manufacturing Co., Milwaukee, Wis._____ 1,000
Caterpillar Tractor Co., Peoria, Ill _____ 1,000
International Harvester Co., Chicago, Ill_____ 600
Cleveland Tractor Co., Cleveland, Ohio_____ 435

Tractors to be produced under the program will be distributed by WPB in accordance with the provisions of Limitation Order L-53, which prohibits distributors from making deliveries except upon specific authorization of the Director of Industry Operations.

Some pipe fittings for ships exempted from limits

Certain types of pipe fittings required for shipbuilding have been exempted from the operation of Schedule II to Limitation Order L-42, it was announced April 4 by the Division of Industry Operations.

An amendment to the schedule, effective April 4, alters the definition of pipe fittings to exclude hydraulic or high pressure types; cast or forged steel fittings; and brazed or soldered brass or bronze fittings, whether screwed or flanged at any outlet.

Copper banned for 13 more plumbing fixture articles

The addition of 13 plumbing fixture products to a list of articles for which use of copper or copper base alloy is prohibited was announced April 9 by the Director of Industry Operations.

A new schedule (V–a) to Limitation Order L–42 becomes effective on June 15. It is expected that the regulations will result in a saving of approximately 1,000 tons of copper and brass a year.

The articles affected are: Bath tub fillers and nozzles; shower fittings; lavatory compression faucets; lavatory combination faucets; sink compression faucets; combination sink faucets and spout; combination faucets for laundry tubs and spouts; combination faucets for wash sinks; laundry tray faucets; outlet plugs and strainers; tail pieces; flush ells; flush valves for closet tanks.

Allowed for certain parts

Copper or copper base alloy, however, may be used in certain component parts of all the above items, except for the last four, if such use is limited to the minimum amount practicable.

The prohibitions and restrictions in the schedule do not apply to the use of copper or copper base alloy in products being made for use in chemical plants, research laboratories; hospitals, or for nonplumbing vessels or aircraft where use of other materials is impracticable. Although the requirements of the schedule do not go into effect until June 15, Army procurement officers are already specifying plumbing equipment items as permitted by the schedule.

★ ★ ★

Requirements plan simplified

Two modifications in the use of preference ratings under the production requirements plan were announced April 6 by A. L. Williams, chief of the production requirements branch.

In cases where a rating assigned under PRP is subsequently raised to a higher rating after appeal to the production requirements branch, the applicant may notify his suppliers of the higher rating by letter instead of making out completely new purchase orders.

The other change in the application of PRP preference ratings permits a producer to make out a single order covering his requirements for the same material or product, even though he uses two or more different preference ratings which have been assigned to him.

PRIORITY ACTIONS
*From April 1
*Through April 9

(Continued from page 13)

Subject	Order number	Related form	Issued	Expired date	Rating
Sanitary napkins: a. Reduces amount of cotton gauze and wood cellulose in sanitary napkins.	L–95		4–9–42	Until revoked.	
Ships (merchant): a. Restricts preference ratings to certain materials and tools.	P–7 int. #1		4–3–42		
Sugar (direct consumption): a. Canners and packers may obtain quota exempt sugar under M–55 in amounts needed for first processing of fruits and vegetables; sugar needed for secondary processing not quota exempt.	M–55 int. #2 (as amend.).		4–4–42		
b. Additional sugar quotas for April granted to more than 40 defense areas whose population has increased 10 percent or more during the past year.	Issued by letter pursuant to M–55 and M–55–e.		4–8–42		
Suppliers' order: a. Revocation of order (revoked by L–63).	M–67		4–6–42		
b. Strictly limits inventories of 19 kinds of supplies.	L–63 (Revokes M–67)	PD–336 (PD–IX).	4–6–42	Until revoked.	
Tin: a. Regulations governing tin usage revised.	M–43–a amend. #1 (as amended).		4–4–42		
b. Tin plate and terneplate: 1. Limits packing of condensed soups in tin plate after June 30 to certain specified kinds.	M–81 amend. #1		4–6–42		
c. Tin closures: 1. Conservation order: a. Use of tin plate and terneplate as closures for glass containers brought under control.	M–104		4–3–42		
Toys and games: a. Takes certain colors, oils, and chemicals out of the category of prohibited material.	L–81 amend. #1	—	4–6–42		
Track-laying tractors: a. Immediate and drastic curtailment in output of smaller types used principally in agricultural operations.	I–53–a		4–9–42		
Waste paper: a. General inventory order: 1. Permits manufacturers of paper, paperboard and paper products who consume waste paper to accumulate inventories without restriction.	M–129	PD–240	4–6–42	Until revoked.	
Wool: a. O.D. wool clips, rags, and wastes: 1. Certain types of olive drab wool wastes excluded from restrictions of M–87.	M–87 amend. #1		4–2–42		
b. Clarifies "putting into process" of tops on any system other than the worsted system.	Amend. #3 to M–73 (as amend. and ext. 7–4–42).		4–8–42		

SUSPENSION ORDERS

Company	Order number	Violation	Penalty	Issued	Exp. date
Hoover Co., North Canton, Ohio.	S–14	Made shipments of aluminum for unauthorized purposes and under unauthorized toll agreements, accepted deliveries of scrap aluminum to which no preference rating had been assigned.	Suspension of all manufacturing operations calling for use of aluminum 10 days after issuance of order.	4–6–42	7–6–42

Company	Order number	Violation	Penalty	Issue	Exp. date
David Ritter, Inc., 1239 Broadway, New York, N. Y.	8-80	Sold or exchanged 8 cases of reserved rayon yarn which had been allocated to it in violation of M-37-a.	Enjoined from accepting any deliveries of yarn; no deliveries to them of other material or equipment will be granted preference ratings.	4-6-42	6-21-42
Jesam Yarn Co., 1239 Broadway New York, N. Y.	8-81	Accepted transfer of the yarn from David Ritter, Inc., although not entitled to such acceptance.	Enjoined from accepting any deliveries of yarn; no deliveries to them of other material or equipment will be granted preference ratings; further enjoined from making any deliveries of reserved rayon yarn.	4-6-42	6-21-42

WPB controls manufacture, distribution of many types of industrial machinery

The War Production Board assumed control over the manufacture and distribution of many types of industrial machinery April 10 in an effort to stimulate conversion of machine tools and skilled labor to the output of war materials.

Under General Limitation Order L-83, effective immediately, manufacturers are prohibited from filling any orders for the production or delivery of certain types of new, second-hand or reconditioned machinery unless they bear WPB approval.

A-9 orders approved

Approved orders include those for the Army and Navy, certain other Government agencies, the governments of the United Nations, Lend-Lease operations, and any orders bearing an A-9 or higher preference rating issued at any time on an original PD-1, PD-1A, or P-19h certificate or on a PD-3 or PD-3A certificate countersigned before April 10.

Certain orders involving less than $200, and, in the case of pulp and paper making machinery, less than $1,000, are not restricted. Likewise, no prohibition is placed on deliveries of less than $1,000 worth of parts to repair or maintain a single piece of existing machinery or a single piece delivered hereafter, or on deliveries of parts worth more than $1,000 in cases where there has been an actual breakdown or suspension of operations because of damage or destruction of machinery.

List of machinery covered

Machinery covered by the order follows:

Leather working—all orders.
Tanning—all orders.
All types of textile machinery and equipment—all orders.
Packaging and labeling (except machinery to be used to package or label fruits and vegetables packed in hermetically sealed and heat sterilized containers)—orders in excess of $200.
Pulp and paper making—orders in excess of $1,000.
Paper converting—orders in excess of $200.
Printing and Publishing—orders in excess of $200.
Bakery—orders in excess of $200.
Confectionery—orders in excess of $200.
Beverage bottling—orders in excess of $200.
Industrial sewing—orders in excess of $200.
Cotton ginning and delinting—all orders.
Shoe manufacturing—all orders.
Shoe repairing—all orders.

Explaining the need for the order, L. S. Greenleaf, Jr., chief of the special industrial machinery branch, said:

"The order has two primary purposes—one, the obvious one of conserving critical raw materials which might otherwise be used in the manufacture of machinery which in turn would be used for the manufacture of articles considered nonessential under the war economy;

"Second, to control and limit the manufacture of industrial machinery so that such machinery will henceforth be produced primarily for the armed forces, the Lend-Lease countries, and for necessary civilian requirements. In this manner, we can promote the rapid conversion to war work of these machinery manufacturers.

"Industrial machinery manufacturers are in an ideal position to manufacture ordnance and other material for the armed forces."

Keep stovepipe, WPB advises

Home owners are urged by the War Production Board's plumbing and heating branch not to throw away stovepipes this spring when the pipes are taken down in preparation for warm weather. Scarcity of steel will limit the amount of available stove pipe.

Soup to be canned in tin plate to be limited to 21 kinds

Amendment of Conservation Order M-81 on tin plate and terneplate to limit the packing of condensed soup in tin plate after June 30 to certain specified kinds was announced April 7 by the Director of Industry Operations.

These soups are chicken, chicken gumbo, chicken noodle, gumbo creole, consomme, bouillon, tomato, asparagus, spinach, fresh green pea, clam or fish chowder, Scotch broth, vegetable, vegetable-vegetarian, pepper pot, oxtail, mock turtle, country style chicken, corn chowder, beef, and vegetable beef.

The amendment specifies the percentages of solids which the above soups are to contain after June 30, 1942, in order to improve their nutritive content.

The amendment also provides that only No. 1 picnic or larger cans may be used, and that canners may use 100 percent of the tin plate used in the corresponding period of 1941 for packing forms of the soups requiring the addition of water or other liquids. Canners who packaged these soups in "ready-to-serve" form in 1941 may use only 70 percent of the tin plate consumed for such purposes in the corresponding period of 1941.

Until June 30, canners may not use more tin plate than they did for these soups in the corresponding period of 1941.

Packaging of soups, broths, and chowders other than those provided for by the amendment may not exceed 25 percent of the 1940 pack before June 30, after which date packing of such products in tin plate is to be discontinued.

Burlap quota base changed

The War Production Board has amended the burlap conservation order (M-47) to ease restrictions on receipts of burlap by bag users. Because the use of burlap is seasonal, quotas based on a past year create unnecessary hardships. This is corrected in the new amendment (No. 4), effective April 4.

The amendment also removes restrictions on the importation of burlap into this country. Previously no provision was made for the nonimporting bag manufacturer to import burlap should he be in a position to do so.

How war production campaigns get under way described in reports of two committees

War Production Drive Headquarters April 12 offered a picture of how war production campaigns get under way by making public in considerable detail the reports of two labor-management committees.

Typical of hundreds of others

These were two of hundreds of labor-management committees that have been formed in war plants at the invitation of Donald M. Nelson, Chairman of the War Production Board, to bring the production of planes, tanks, guns, and machine tools up to war-winning totals.

The reports came from the labor-management committee of the Continental Roll & Steel Foundry Co., of East Chicago, Ind.; and from the labor-management committee of the Niles-Bement-Pond Co. Division of Pratt & Whitney, of West Hartford, Conn. Michael W. Straus, Chief of War Production Drive Headquarters, said the reports were representative.

No work stoppages or slow-ups

"We are giving you an outline of what we, labor and management, of this organization have accomplished and hope to accomplish in aiding the war effort," the Continental's committee report said.

"From the date of the American Federation of Labor, Local No. 22636, negotiating and signing a contract with the Continental Roll & Steel Foundry, there have been no work stoppages or work slow-ups; in fact there has not been 1 man-hour lost in this plant. We are, and we have been working 24 hours per day, 7 days per week, and employees are paid at the rate of time and one-half for all hours worked in excess of 40 hours in any 1 week.

"The shop stewards have been appointed by the AFL as safety committeemen. It is the duty of these committeemen to conduct, each Monday, at the beginning of each shift, meetings in all departments relative to safety and war production."

The report said suggestion boxes have been painted red, white, and blue and established in each department. Bulletin boards have been erected and a publicity committee appointed to direct the publicity of the drive through these bulletin boards, the plant magazine, and plant meetings and, with the labor-management committee's approval, release statements to the press.

The report continues:

"Through the cooperation of labor and management, locker rooms and rest rooms have been installed and others are in progress. The management has installed and is installing new machinery and equipment for better production and the comfort of its employees.

"A move is now in progress to stage a War Production and Defense Show, in which the United States Army, the United States Navy and all local government agencies will participate, the proceeds from which are to be turned over to the proper Government agency for aiding in the purchase of a tank.

"The employees of this plant, through voluntary donations, have purchased an American flag for each department."

The committee reported that employees have purchased $500,000 in war bonds and exceeded its Red Cross quota in 2 days.

"Small groups of three, four, and five employees are being formed in which they alternate the use of automobiles in coming to and going from the plant, thereby conserving rubber and gasoline. . . .

"The AFL and the management have agreed that due to the demands for war production, vacations must be waived voluntarily by the employees, but he will receive his vacation compensation . . . in addition to his regular wages for the hours worked."

Provide for men in service

The committee also reported that employees entering the armed service get $25 a year to continue their insurance, etc., that they still get their regular vacation check, and that men returning from

Kinda give it your personal attention, will you?

MORE PRODUCTION

PERSONAL APPEAL . . . The poster reproduced here from the Supplement to the Production Drive Plan Book will be sent shortly to war plants. Two-column mats for newspapers and other publications are available on request to Distribution Section, Division of Information, Office for Emergency Management, Washington, D. C.

the service who will be unable to perform their old duties will be given consideration. The labor-management committee also takes up deferment cases with local draft boards. It reported, "It is our policy to request deferments for only those employees who in our opinion are of more value in the production of war materials than they would be in the armed forces."

The committee is circulating this pledge, to be signed by all employees:

I ...., as a true American, do hereby pledge my wholehearted support to President Franklin D. Roosevelt and Hon. Donald M. Nelson, Chairman of the War Production Board, to do all in my power to cooperate in this War Production Drive.

"Fighting to retain our American way . . ."

The Pratt & Whitney Niles-Bement-Pond Division committee reported it consisted of 12 members, 6 appointed by the management and 6 elected by United Electrical Radio and Machine Workers of America, CIO, Unity Lodge, Local 251.

The committee addressed a notice to all employees announcing it recognized the importance of increasing production. The committee wrote:

By far the greater increase in production can be obtained by more personal efforts on the part of every one of us. That is a means that is in the hands of each of us now—today. It requires no banners, no speeches, no parades, no prizes.

We are told that the time we have to accomplish this result is measured in days. Each hour now is worth 10 a little later. We are fighting to retain our American way of living, which we have no intention of giving up in any measure. Rather should we improve it when the first job is done.

Work through subcommittees

The committee appointed subcommittees to gain publicity, to improve morale, to operate suggestion boxes and to conduct a slogan contest. Another committee has been made to encourage auto pooling to save gas and rubber. The committee further reported:

"We are instituting a definite program to cut down the absence of men from work, or their lateness in reporting, without excuses satisfactory to our committee. This matter is being studied now and probably will be carried out to include merit marks, both good and bad, on clock cards which are on display in racks for all employees to see. . . .

"We have established a Good Housekeeping Subcommittee to see that everything is properly in place and that the personal habits of our men are influenced to avoid unsightly floors, dirty corners, etc. Our shop has always been rigid in this connection, but it is more important now than ever."

472 labor-management committees report launching of War Production Drives

A total of 472 labor-management committees reported to the War Production Board in the first 11 days of April that they have organized to get War Production Drives under way in their plants.

All varieties of plants represented

These committees were organized to increase production to meet the President's goal of 45,000 tanks, 60,000 planes, 20,000 antiaircraft guns, and 8,000,000 tons of shipping this year. They are purely voluntary, organized and operating at the request of Donald M. Nelson, Chairman of the WPB.

All varieties of war production plants are represented by the reporting committees—from units of vast organizations like Westinghouse Electric & Manufacturing Co. and the E. I. du Pont de Nemours Co. with plants scattered throughout the Nation, to small single-plant war producers.

In each instance they had established management-labor Production Drive committees in response to Chairman Nelson's declaration that nothing can "split this great American production team; we will pull together—not apart."

Adapted to local conditions

The organization reports recited how management and labor came together after Mr. Nelson's broadcasts at the President's direction that he "take every possible step to bring home to labor and management alike the supreme importance of war production this spring."

Notable for the absence of labor or management recrimination, the reports told in detail how various plants adapted the pattern of the War Production Drive which Mr. Nelson offered, to local conditions, and how posters, war news, slogans, suggestion boxes, and informational literature were fitted into their efforts. Several labor-management committees stated that their plants were handicapped by lack of materials.

Several labor-management committees have adopted slogans. The committee of the American Car Foundry Co.'s Buffalo plant reported that it had adopted the slogan: "Volume for Victory."

The Erie Concrete & Steel Implement Co. committee, reporting that the company was building ships on the same spot that Admiral Perry built ships in 1812, announced the adoption of this slogan: "Perry did it and so will we."

The Houston (Tex.) Packing Co. committee reported the following slogan: "For glycerine, save fats to make bombs for the Japs."

The Houston committee reported that labor and management were working together on plans to conserve every bit of fat because of its importance in making ingredients for explosives.

Steel workers break records

S. S. Marshall, Jr., vice president of the Jones & Laughlin Steel Corporation, Pittsburgh, where a labor-management committee has been formed, telegraphed Mr. Nelson:

Workmen of the Jones & Laughlin Steel Corporation during the month of March helping to fight the war shattered all previous records and established all-time new highs for the production of coke, pig iron, steel ingots, and finished steel products. All of the previous high records had been established no longer ago than 1941 and in January or February of this year operating 24 hours a day 7 days a week. "Let's go for new records to help win the war!" is the word with men and management.

This committee reports that it is carrying on and extending the work of teaching new men the proper care of tools to make them last longer and to facilitate cooperation between shifts requiring the same company tools.

Three production scoreboards have been erected and more are planned. The committee noted that, since the boards have been operated, "they have evoked much discussion among the men and a general voluntary movement based on pride of workmanship to increase production."

In addition to a safety committee, the management-labor committee reported that an Ex-Service Men's Battalion of firefighters had been recruited and that it now has 300 members, all considered committeemen on the general subject of fire prevention. They are also in charge of air-raid protection.

The committee concluded, "It is the consensus of opinion that if the program can be made to work successfully, it will produce a marked effect on speeding up production."

The reports disclosed that a labor committeeman was chairman of the Continental committee and that a management representative was chairman of the Niles-Bement-Pond committee.

TRANSPORTATION . . .

Materials for 18,000 more freight cars, 300 locomotives, to be allocated in 1942

The railroad industry was advised by the WPB April 8 that materials will be allocated during the remainder of 1942 for construction of an additional 18,000 freight cars and 300 locomotives for domestic use, in an effort to assure adequate transportation of war supplies.

Additional materials will be made available to complete Army and Lend-Lease orders. No assistance will be given for passenger car production beyond that already authorized by WPB.

Approved by Requirements Committee

The program, aproved by the WPB Requirements Committee, was announced by Andrew Stevenson, chief of the transportation branch, at a meeting of the railroad industry advisory committee.

Under the original 1942 railroad construction plan, announced January 2 by the former Supply Priorities and Allocations Board, materials were pledged for production of 36,000 freight cars in February, March, and April, and continued production of 248 steam locomotives, 58 electric locomotives and 620 Diesel locomotives. Mr. Stevenson said that, if necessary, materials will continue to be made available for this initial program. Inventories now held by the entire industry will have to be used for this purpose, and pooling of materials may be necessary. Although locomotive output is ahead of schedule, all car builders probably will not be able to finish production by April 30.

No more for refrigerator cars

The Requirements Committee, Mr. Stevenson said, agreed that for the nine months ending December 31, materials should be allocated for an additional 250 steam locomotives, 50 Diesel locomotives, and 18,000 freight cars. No materials will be made available for further production of refrigerator cars, and provision will be made for materials for "only a minimum number of tank-cars" as determined by the transportation branch in consultation with the Office of Defense Transportation.

Construction of the additional Diesel locomotives must not interfere with output of Diesel engine crankshafts for military use, the industry representatives were told. The additional freight cars, Mr. Stevenson said, "shall be constructed

with the fullest possible substitution of wood for steel in their superstructure."

Materials for rails provided

The Requirements Committee, which on March 17 announced approval of the railroad industry's 1942 requirements for 1,260,000 tons of heavy rail, also has agreed to the allocation of approximately 450,000 tons of materials for the rail program for the 3 months beginning April 1. Approximately 350,000 tons were made available in the first quarter of this year.

Mr. Stevenson said that the transportation branch will schedule the construction of all new equipment, so that added facilities can be made available for war work as the construction program proceeds. The branch also will direct the types of locomotives and cars to be built and determine to whom they should be delivered, acting upon recommendations of the Office of Defense Transportation.

Limitation Orders L-97 and L-97-a, designed to effectuate the scheduling program, were issued April 4. The orders prohibit production or delivery of locomotives and freight and passenger cars except in accordance with schedules issued by WPB from time to time.

Miller named assistant chief of WPB transportation branch

Appointment of Sidney L. Miller, of Iowa City, Iowa, as assistant chief of the transportation branch was announced April 7 by Andrew Stevenson, branch chief.

Mr. Stevenson also announced the following additional appointments:

Edward S. Pardoe, of Washington, D. C., chief of the bus, electric railway and other transportation equipment section.

David W. Odiorne, of Yonkers, N. Y., chief of the rolling stock section.

E. Carroll Hanly, of Harrisburg, Pa., chief of the motive power section.

Berkeley Robins, of Richmond, Va., chief of the maintenance and supply section.

George M. Cornell, of Huntington, W. Va., technical consultant.

Buy next winter's coal now while there's transportation, Henderson urges home owners

Added emphasis to the Government's "Buy Coal Now" drive came from Price Administrator Henderson April 7 in a statement urging every home owner who burns coal to purchase next winter's supply immediately.

"The advice to buy coal now may develop into a 'now or never' appeal for many coal users," declared Mr. Henderson. "Transportation now is available to haul coal from the mine to consumers' coal bins but by fall our railroad and truck lines will be loaded to capacity hauling war shipments."

With Mr. Henderson's statement, the OPA has joined two other Government agencies—the Office of the Solid Fuel Coordinator, and the Bituminous Coal Consumers' Counsel—in getting the public to avert the possibility of heatless days next winter by buying coal this spring.

Aid of Federal employees sought in preventing traffic congestion

The Office of Defense Transportation on April 7 requested all Federal Government agencies to aid in preventing passenger traffic congestion on railroads and bus lines by instructing employees to exercise greater care in buying tickets and reserving space accommodations when traveling on official business.

Government employees should buy tickets and Pullman space well in advance of train departure, should reserve space accommodations only for trips which are reasonably definite, and should notify carriers immediately if cancelation of reservations becomes necessary, the ODT said.

In making public the request, Joseph B. Eastman, Director of Defense Transportation, urged private firms to issue similar instructions to their employees. "By exercising reasonable care in buying tickets and reserving space accommodations," Mr. Eastman said, "business concerns can do much to aid transportation companies in accommodating passengers and in handling the growing volume of passenger traffic."

No intention of closing outside offices, Eastman declares

The Office of Defense Transportation April 10 assured railroads, bus and truck lines, and other carriers that no plans for ordering the abandonment of off-line offices engaged in sales and service activities are now under consideration.

In a statement addressed to all carriers, Joseph B. Eastman, Director of Defense Transportation, said:

Decision regarding continuance of outside agencies and the scope of their activities is primarily a responsibility of carrier management, which we do not wish to influence beyond pointing out that in making these decisions preponderant weight must be given to the fact that during the war the interest of individual lines must be subordinated to the maximum utilization of all our transportation facilities for the successful prosecution of the war. Cooperation must be the watchword rather than competition.

Rebuild worn parts, truck operators urged

"Thousands of dollars' worth of automotive parts that are now finding their way into scrap piles can be saved by regular check-ups and by building up worn parts by approved methods," William J. Cumming, chief of the vehicle maintenance section of the ODT, told a safety school for truck and bus operators at the University of South Carolina, April 7.

In an appeal to truck owners and repairmen to give vehicles special maintenance attention to prolong truck life and conserve gasoline, parts, and tires, Mr. Cumming emphasized the necessity of rebuilding and repairing worn parts instead of sending them to the junk yard.

★ ★ ★

New appointments announced to transport personnel staff

Joseph B. Eastman, Director of Defense Transportation April 7 announced the appointment of Edwin M. Fitch and Dorothy Sells to the staff of the division of transport personnel.

Mr. Fitch, former chief statistician of the Railroad Retirement Board, will serve as assistant to Otto S. Beyer, director of the Division.

Miss Sells has been named chief of the personnel supply section of the division of transport personnel.

Pooling of available storage space by group warehousing plan to simplify Government dealings, assure best use

A group warehousing plan designed to permit more efficient use of storage facilities and to simplify dealings between warehousing companies and Government procurement agencies has been worked out by the Office of Defense Transportation, the War Department, and other Government agencies, it was announced April 9.

To be located in distribution centers

The plan calls for the pooling of available storage space through emergency warehouse associations formed by public merchandise warehousemen in distribution centers throughout the country.

The plan is already in operation in Kansas City, Mo., where a contract has been signed on behalf of the War Department and a newly formed Federal Emergency Warehouse Association of Kansas City, made up of 11 local warehousing companies. The ODT's division of storage, of which Col. Leo M. Nicolson is director, is aiding in the establishment of similar associations in New York City, Philadelphia, Boston, Chicago, and other cities where shortages of storage space are expected.

Government signs a single contract

Under the group warehousing plan, a Government procurement agency, instead of negotiating separate contracts with a number of individual companies, signs a single contract with a local warehouse association for a large block of space. A single Government order may be issued for storage or shipment of materials by different companies. Each company is bonded to the association, to which it bills all charges. The manager of the association in turn bills all charges to the Government.

On a voluntary basis

All group contracts drawn up under the plan will be carefully studied by the ODT to assure that the rates to be charged and the terms and conditions of storage are reasonable. The plan will be conducted on a voluntary basis, all owners of storage facilities in a given locality being given an opportunity to take part in the pool. Under an arrangement agreed to by the Department of Justice, warehouse operators entering into group contracts which have been approved by the ODT during the war

emergency will not be subject to prosecution under the anti-trust laws.

By making it possible for Government agencies to obtain small units of storage space operated by many different companies, the pooling plan is expected to result in fuller use of existing warehouse facilities, while reducing the need for construction of new facilities to meet expanding war production needs.

The simplified procedure saves time and paper work both for Government agencies and for warehouse operators.

★ ★ ★

Civil Air Patrol proves value of courier service to Army

The Civil Air Patrol of the OCD has released regular Army pilots for more important duties by establishing a courier service along the East Coast, it was reported April 8 to James M. Landis, OCD Director, by Earle L. Johnson, National Commander of the CAP.

During the first 20 days of operations, five Civil Air Patrol planes of the Pennsylvanian Wing of CAP flew 2,277,000 pound-miles of cargo from Maine to Florida in 270 hours of flying time in an experiment to test the value of this service. The cargo included Army equipment and supplies urgently needed at Army air bases.

William M. Anderson, CAP Wing Commander of Pennsylvania, reported to National Commander Johnson that the service already has proved so successful that recommendations have been made to continue it on a permanent basis.

Relieves Army of routine tasks

Before the experimental courier service was initiated, Army planes were used for the transport of the material.

Already 38,000 members have been enrolled in the Civil Air Patrol, including more than half of the eligible civilian pilots in the Nation. With applications pouring in to the Wing Commanders in each of the 48 States, the test of the courier service indicates but one of the many functions the Civil Air Patrol is capable of performing, and thus relieving the Army air forces of many of the purely routine tasks with which it is now confronted, Commander Johnson reported to Director Landis.

RATIONING . . .

WPB grants additional sugar to 40 areas where war has concentrated population

The War Production Board has granted additional sugar quotas for April to more than 40 areas of war-essential activity, whose population has increased 10 percent or more during the past year. Similar relief had been granted in some of the areas in March.

A. E. Bowman, chief of the sugar section, has sent a letter to manufacturers and importers authorizing them to deliver a "relief quota" of sugar during April to receivers in specified areas, in addition to the regular quota already assigned under the sugar limitation order, M-55, as amended.

Regular quota was 80 percent

Under the regular quota of Supplementary Order M-55-e, issued on March 30, a receiver, during April, may accept 80 percent of the amount of sugar used or sold by him in the corresponding month of 1941.

The new action will allow all receivers in the specified areas to receive more than this basic quota during the month. For example, receivers in Detroit will receive 95 percent of the amount used or sold in April 1941; in Baltimore, 90 percent; in Seattle, 100 percent; in Louisville, 90 percent; in Wichita, Kans., 100 percent; and in Bridgeport, Conn., 100 percent. The quota for Washington, D. C., has also been raised to 100 percent to provide sufficient sugar for the increased number of war workers in the capital.

How to calculate increase

The increase for receivers who distribute sugar is calculated by applying the additional percentage to each receiver's resale of sugar within the area during the corresponding period of 1941; and the additional sugar obtained on this basis must be sold for consumption within the same area.

The increase in the quota of a receiver who is an industrial user is calculated by applying the additional percentage to the amount of sugar physically incorporated into the products manufactured during the base period for sale within the area. The sugar used in products sold outside the area during the base period is excluded in calculating the "relief quotas."

WPB announced that the remaining areas showing a population increase of as much as 10 percent within the last year were being relieved during the first part of April.

Areas and quotas

The following are the specified defense areas receiving "relief quotas" in March and April, and the revised total quota for April [1] in each case:

Alabama—Decatur 95, Talladega County 95; *Arizona*—Phoenix, met. district 90; *California*—Los Angeles 90, San Diego, met. district 100, Santa Barbara 90; *Colorado*—Colorado Springs 90; *Connecticut*—Bridgeport 90; *District of Columbia*—Washington 100; *Georgia*—Augusta 100; *Illinois*—Marion 90; *Iowa*—Burlington 100; *Kansas*—Wichita, met. district 100; *Kentucky*—Elizabeth Town, Hardin County 95, Louisville 90.
Louisiana—[2] Alexandra, Rapides Parish.105; *Maine*—Bath, B r u n s w i c k 90, Portland, South Portland 90; *Maryland*—[2] Baltimore met. district 90; *Michigan*—Detroit 95; *Missouri*—Joplin 90; *New York*—Messena 95; *North Carolina*—Fayetteville 145, [2] Jacksonville 115, [2] Kinston 115, [2] Morehead City 115, [2] New Bern 115, Wilmington 130; *Oregon*—[2] Portland 100; *South Carolina*—Charleston 95.
Texas—Austin 90, Abilene 100, Corpus Christi, met. district 100, Wichita Falls area 95, Dallas, Tarrant Counties 90, Jefferson, Orange Counties 100, [2] Texarkana 95; *Virginia*—Hampton 110, Newport News 110, Norfolk 110, Phoebus 110, Portsmouth 110. South Norfolk 110; *Washington*—S e a t t l e 100, Tacoma, met. district 95; *West Virginia*—Charleston, met. district 90.

[1] Supersedes 80 percent regular quota under Limitation Order M-55-e.
[2] Adjustment applies to April only. Other areas had received a "relief quota" during the latter part of March.

No conflict on sugar rationing, Henderson and Nelson announce

The following statement was issued April 4 by Donald M. Nelson, chairman, War Production Board, and Leon Henderson, administrator, Office of Price Administration:

Newspaper and radio stories indicating existence of a dispute as to the need for sugar rationing between the War Production Board and the Office of Price Administration are without foundation in fact. The sugar rationing program will proceed as scheduled and the public should not permit unauthorized sources to confuse the necessity for this policy.

All bicycles with frames over 17 inches taken into freeze

The bicycle freeze order (L-52-a) was amended April 7 by WPB to include all bicycles having frames of more than 17 inches.

The original freeze order, issued the previous week, applied to bicycles having frames of more than 19 inches. Subsequently it was pointed out that an 18-inch "camel-back" frame (a frame with a double bar) is the same as the conventional 20-inch "diamond frame," and both are adult size. Adult bicycles for women run about the same sizes as "camel-back" frames.

★ ★ ★

First-processing sugar for canners is exempt from quota

WPB has notified canners and packers that they may obtain quota-exempt sugar under Order M-55 in amounts needed for the first processing of fruits and vegetables.

Sugar needed for any secondary processing is not quota exempt. The ruling (Interpretation No. 2 of Order M-55, amended) was made following many inquiries.

War workers to get recaps only if necessary to jobs

Tires will be made available to war workers only when they cannot get to their jobs without them, OPA Administrator Henderson said April 7.

"The restrictions applying to issuance of recapping certificates to List B applicants are in no way relaxed," the administrator said. "Moreover, it is not certain that the War Production Board will continue to make even reclaimed rubber available to permit the OPA to allot quotas for List B passenger cars in future months. The amount of reclaimed rubber we can produce in this country is governed in large part by the amount of scrap or junk rubber. How much of that there is, no one knows definitely, but we do know that the rate of its flow to reclaimers has decreased."

Mr. Henderson called upon war workers to be just as thrifty as anyone else in the matter of tires.

Special board to consider appeals based on rationing of commercial vehicles

Joseph B. Eastman, Director of the Office of Defense Transportation, announced April 8, establishment of a special Appeal Board in Washington, D. C., to consider appeals from decisions of the ODT's local allocation offices under the commercial-vehicle rationing program.

The special Board has been set up pending creation of local appeal boards in the field.

Members of the Board are M. V. Fredehagen, liaison officer, Board for Civilian Protection, Office of Civilian Defense, Washington, D. C.; W. Foster Banks, president, Motor Haulage Co., Brooklyn, N. Y., and J. B. Pymer, secretary-treasurer, The City Baking Co., Baltimore, Md.

★ ★ ★

WPB formalizes permission for combination capping stock

In order to provide retreading materials for a limited number of tires to be used by workers in war industries, WPB on April 3 amended rubber order M–15–b–1 to permit the manufacture of passenger car capping stock entirely from reclaimed rubber together with a small quantity of crude for cushion stock.

No rubber for farm tractors if steel wheels can be put back

Farm tractors which were originally fitted with steel wheels but have changed to rubber tires will not be granted certificates to purchase tires whenever steel wheels are locally available and can be put back into service, State rationing administrators were informed April 6 in a letter issued by OPA.

Mud, snow tires not replaceable by others until worn out

Purchase certificates for tires to replace mud and snow tires now on vehicles may not be issued by local rationing boards except under conditions that ordinarily govern issuance of certificates. OPA announced April 7.

CHANGE TO OBSOLETE TIRES ALL RIGHT WHILE THEY LAST

OPA has no objection to issuance of purchase certificates for new tires of obsolete sizes to List B vehicle owners who have changed wheels and rims to permit use of those sizes instead of the recapped casings that otherwise would be the only kind available to them.

This stand is taken by OPA in a letter to State rationing administrators.

"However", the OPA letter says, "administrators or boards may well point out to such applicants that there is considerable risk incurred in these changeover expenditures, since the available tire supply is limited to those obsolete sizes now on hand."

Rules for camelback and new tubes

Authority under which retreaders and recappers will be able to get initial allotments of camelback for passenger car tires and local rationing boards may issue certificates for purchase of new tubes for List B passenger cars and trucks is contained in Amendment No. 4 to the Revised Tire Rationing Regulations, announced April 7 by Price Administrator Henderson.

The amendment, which was to go into effect April 10, prohibits the application of truck type camelback to tires to be used on passenger cars and the application of passenger type material to truck tires.

By the terms of the amendment, a retreader or recapper who as of midnight March 22 had passenger type camelback inventory equal to less than 500 pounds for each mold or curing table in his establishment capable of treading only tires smaller than 7.50–20 can get a certificate for purchase of enough to bring his stock as of March 23 up to that level.

To get such a certificate, he must apply not later than April 30, 1942, to the local rationing board which serves the area in which his principal office is located. Application forms will be furnished the board any time after the effective date of the amendment.

Taking into consideration the amount of the retreader's inventory as of March 22, the board may issue a certificate which will permit him to buy the difference between that amount and the permitted initial allotment of 500 pounds per mold or curing table which can handle only tires smaller than 7.50–20.

The recipient of such a certificate may use it for purchase of the material from a supplier of camelback any time before June 1, 1942. If one supplier is unable to fill the entire order, the certificate holder may return to the local board which then may issue as many certificates as are necessary to permit spreading the purchase among several suppliers.

Gasoline cut again; curtailed areas to get two-thirds of December–February average

Effective April 16, deliveries of gasoline to service stations and bulk consumers in the areas where curtailment is in effect will be cut from 80 percent to 66⅔ percent of average deliveries last December, January, and February, adjusted for seasonal variations, the Division of Industry Operations announced April 9.

To the 17 Eastern States, the District of Columbia, Oregon, and Washington, where gasoline deliveries have been reduced since March 19, the City of Bristol, Tenn., has been added. This action was taken because Bristol is partly in Virginia and partly in Tennessee.

To clarify the intent of the original order, the section limiting service stations to operations 12 hours a day and 72 hours a week has been amended to exempt deliveries to commercial vehicles, ambulances, or for the use of physicians, Federal, State, and local governments, agricultural machinery, and other categories listed in section (f) of Limitation Order L–70 as issued on March 14.

Reports of expectations eliminated

Another amendment to the order removes the requirement that suppliers of gasoline must file monthly reports on Form PD–368 showing anticipated deliveries of motor fuel in the curtailment area. Reports of actual deliveries in preceding months, on Form PD–369, must continue to be filed on or before the 20th of each month as previously required.

Deliveries during the second half of April must be reduced proportionately in accordance with the amendment announced April 9. Service stations and bulk consumers may thus receive 80 percent of half their monthly quota before April 16th, and 66⅔ percent of half of the quota during the remainder of the month.

★ ★ ★

Names of intelligence officers getting tires not to be revealed

The names of Federal Government intelligence officers whose work depends upon secrecy will be withheld hereafter by local rationing boards when they release lists of recipients of tire purchase certificates to newspapers or post the lists in the rationing offices. Instructions were sent to all State rationing administrators by the Office of Price Administration April 9.

PRICE ADMINISTRATION . . .

Lake Superior iron ore ceiling set approximately at last year's prices

Lake Superior iron ore, now beginning to move through the Great Lakes to steel making centers, is brought under a price ceiling which closely approximates last season's prices by a new regulation issued April 7 by Price Administrator Henderson.

The regulation, No. 113, is effective April 10, and applies to all market iron ore produced in Minnesota, Wisconsin, and Michigan (the so-called Lake Superior District), whether sold by "spot" or long-term contracts.

"Lake Erie" price is base

The published, or "Lake Erie," 1941 season price of $4.45 per gross ton for Mesabi non-Bessemer ore, 51.50 percent iron content, delivered at Lower Lake ports, is recognized in the regulation as a base for relating prices of ores of different grades, as well as a base from which discounts are calculated. However, the regulation forbids sales of ore under continuing long-term contracts at prices exceeding those at which deliveries were made last season. Since the bulk of all market ore normally moves under long-term contracts, this means that the 1942 price of this important tonnage will be unchanged from 1941.

In the case of long-term contracts that expired at the end of last season and are up for renewal, the regulation requires the seller to base his maximum price on the weighted average price at which his "spot" (i.e. one season) sales were made in 1941. Maximum price to be charged under new "spot" contracts for the 1942 season must be computed similarly.

Escalator clauses eliminated

One feature of the new regulation makes all "escalator" clauses in existing contracts inoperative for price purposes. These clauses, in general, provide for automatic price advances to the extent that certain increases in costs, such as transportation, occur. Where ore was sold in 1941 under contracts with escalator clauses, the new regulation allows it to be sold this year at the price to which the escalation may have carried it in 1941, but no higher.

When ore is sold f. o. b. an Upper Lake port, the maximum price cannot exceed the Lower Lake price, less lake freight, according to the regulation, and in cases where ore is sold f. o. b. mine, the maximum price cannot be above the Lower Lake price, less lake freight and rail freight.

New producer encouraged

Because Lake Superior ore producers are being called upon to furnish the Nation's steel furnaces with a record total of 90,000,000 tons in the current season, the OPA regulation contains a special provision to make the opening of new operations attractive from a price standpoint. Ore shipped from a mine which was idle in 1940 and 1941 and from which no ore was shipped except from stock pile may carry a maximum price equivalent to $4.45 per gross ton delivered at Lower Lake ports for Mesabi non-Bessemer 51.50

per cent iron, natural content. However, before any sales on this basis can be made, the producer must file with OPA an affidavit describing the operation and must await written OPA permission before proceeding with any sale at the $4.45 price. New sellers, that is, persons who did not sell ore during the 1941 season, must price their ore at a figure not above the weighted average spot price of a seller situated in substantially similar circumstances. OPA will furnish this information to any new seller upon application.

Prices adequate to maximum production

An extensive OPA study of the iron ore industry indicated that the prices provided in the regulation are adequate to insure the maximum production of ore for the war programs.

The regulation also provides for records and reports.

The provisions of the present regulation apply only to market, merchant, and non-captive ore. The Office of Price Administration plans immediately to institute an investigation covering sales of captive ore.

* * *

Cocoa butter, cocoa bean export pricing changed

Some changes and additions to the export provisions on maximum prices for cocoa beans and cocoa butter are covered in Amendment No. 1 to Revised Price Schedule No. 51, announced April 5 by Acting Price Administrator Hamm. There is also a provision specifying charges which may be made for credit extensions.

Highlights of amendment

Highlights of the new amendment which becomes effective April 6, 1942, include the following:

1. The export clause, permitting sales at prices 10 percent in excess of the maximum domestic prices, is revised to except Canada from such export category.

2. "Consular fees actually incurred by the seller" may be added to the maximum prices for cocoa beans and cocoa butter when sold for export.

3. Where cocoa is bought on credit terms, OPA ruled that interest charges by the seller may not exceed a 6-percent-per-annum rate for the first two months; interest charges may be made at a 3-percent-per-annum rate for not more than 10 months thereafter. Such credit charges, which are considered desirable for small manufacturers who operate on a deferred-payment basis, may be added to the maximum prices established by the schedule.

4. The section permitting a 7½-percent premium on small-lot sales of 25 bags or less is clarified by a specific provision, emphasizing that the premium may be added only for those sales."

Export price policies and methods outlined by OPA, Board of Economic Warfare

Export problems and policies as they relate to the prices of domestic commodities and products destined to be sold to friendly foreign countries are outlined in a joint memorandum issued April 6 by the Office of Price Administration and the Board of Economic Warfare. (*Press release PM 2857.*)

The memorandum summarizes the functions of the OPA and BEW as regards exports; gives a seven-point "OPA export price policy" and outlines the machinery established for close collaboration between the two agencies in connection with export ceiling prices.

OPA's export policy

The OPA export price policy is stated as follows:

The OPA is gradually establishing export ceilings in commodities and end products where export trade is significant. Before a ceiling is fixed the OPA consults with the BEW and the industries affected by the proposed ceilings.

In the formulation of export price ceilings, the policy of the OPA is:

1. To set a fair price which covers the additional costs involved in exporting.

2. To set a price, which is neutral in its effects on the distribution of sales between export and domestic markets. While excessive export prices endanger the maintenance of domestic ceilings and thus endanger morale at home, on the other hand insufficient export margins will result in a loss of foreign markets at a time when export markets are already jeopardized by shipping difficulties and contracted supply at home. The OPA carefully weighs both considerations.

3. To fix export margins at different levels according to the functions performed by the sellers; the highest margin is allowed to the middlemen who incur the largest costs, inclusive of risks.

4. To establish export differentials in a manner (which follows from "3") which will not disturb established methods of doing business. Where additional middlemen insert themselves as a result of disturbed market conditions, export margins are not raised in order to support the unnecessary middlemen. If, on the other hand, producers refuse to sell to exporters and take over the export market, the OPA is not disposed to allow the producer the margin which otherwise would have gone to the exporter.

5. To give special consideration to hardship cases: distress sales resulting from war conditions, sales required by strong political or military considerations, purchases in the pre-ceiling period of exports at prices much above ceiling prices.

6. To err on the side of liberality where generous treatment will enable exporters who have lost much of their trade to maintain export contacts for the post-war period.

7. To cooperate and collaborate with BEW in such a manner that exporters who appeal selling price provisions will be instructed in the most expeditious manner of treatment.

Price rise allowed on two types of drilling machines to permit subcontracting

In order to facilitate an increase in production of necessary drilling machines by subcontracting, the OPA amended on April 7 the maximum price schedule on machine tools to permit the Defiance Machine Works, of Defiance, Ohio, to sell certain machines built by its subcontractor, the Power Gates Company, of Louisville, Ky., at increased prices.

WPB had requested that Defiance arrange for additional production through subcontracting, and the amendment is intended to permit prices which defray the increased cost of subcontracting.

Under Price Schedule No. 67, maximum prices were established at list prices in effect on October 1, 1941. The April 7 amendment, No. 5, permits the Defiance concern to sell the following specified quantities and types of production drilling machines manufactured for it by Power Gates Company as subcontractor:

100 Model No. 112–21″ at maximum price of $1,600 each;

50 Model No. 200–26″ at maximum price of $2,062 each.

The October list prices for these machines by the Defiance concern were $1,524 and $1,964, respectively.

Price of tool needed for planes increased to aid subcontracts

By approving a small increase in the maximum price for a machine tool used to make airplane engine piston rings, Price Administrator Henderson on April 7 cleared the way for production by subcontractors of 150 additional urgently needed units.

Amendment No. 6 to Revised Price Schedule No. 67—New Machine Tools—authorizes an increase from $7,025 to $7,290 each, or slightly less than 3.8 percent in the price of 150 Model No. 26 Hyprolap Machines in order that the Norton Co., of Worcester, Mass., can arrange to subcontract for the immediate production of these machines. The Army Air Corps at Wright Field and the War Production Board had requested the Norton Co., to arrange for increased production by subcontracting.

CEILING LIFTED TO ASSURE VIRGIN ISLANDS KEROSENE

To assure a continued and sufficient supply of kerosene for the Virgin Islands, pending adjustment of questions regarding an excise tax on kerosene collected by the government of Puerto Rico, Price Schedule No. 88 (Petroleum and Petroleum Products) was amended April 7 to permit, for a period of 30 days, a charge of 3 cents per gallon above the maximum set for kerosene in the Virgin Islands.

The amendment, No. 6 to the schedule, announced by Acting Price Administrator Hamm, was effective April 7, 1942, and expires May 6, 1942, by which time the tax question is expected to be settled.

★ ★ ★

Gas stations allowed 3-cent margin in curtailment area

Retailers of motor fuel in the curtailment area (17 Eastern States and the District of Columbia and Oregon and Washington) are permitted to charge 3 cents per gallon above the cost to them, under Amendment No. 2 to Temporary Maximum Price Regulation No. 11, announced April 7 by Price Administrator Henderson. The amendment was effective April 11, 1942.

The amendment was issued after a preliminary field study by the Office of Price Administration revealed that most service stations selling motor fuel in the curtailment area operate on a margin of at least 3 cents per gallon. In the past, a minority of service stations, generally known as independent stations, have sold motor fuel at prices below prevailing prices and at margins below 3 cents.

Permission to charge prices at the 3-cent margin is contingent upon the seller providing for OPA a certified statement of the price charged to him for each grade of motor fuel and the maximum price otherwise applicable under Temporary Regulation No. 11.

Brumbaum joins OPA

Appointment of Harold R. Brumbaum, sales manager of the department store division of Landers, Frary, and Clark, New Britain, Conn., as senior business specialist in charge of cutlery and allied products for the hardware and housewares unit in the consumers' durable goods section, was announced April 7.

Plumbing fixtures under ceiling to forestall speculative rises as result of any curtailments

In an effort to avert speculative price increases likely to follow a forthcoming War Production Board order curtailing manufacture of some types of plumbing fixtures, the Office of Price Administration on April 4 froze prices for such products at levels in effect on March 30, 1942.

Temporary Maximum Price Regulation No. 17, establishing the plumbing fixture prices, was announced by Acting Price Administrator Hamm. It became effective April 7, 1942, and continues in force through June 5, 1942.

Affected by the regulation are "plumbing fixtures of all types, kinds, sizes, shapes and colors, whether made of vitreous china, porcelain, enameled cast iron or formed metal, and their accessories."

The regulation stipulates that maximum prices, during the period set, shall be such that the cost to the purchaser is not in excess of what it was or would have been to such purchaser on March 30, 1942, on the basis of the prices, trade, quantity and cash discounts, charges, deposits and allowances, whether published or unpublished, then listed or quoted by the seller, and on the basis of the freight and delivery practices recognized by the seller on that date for like transactions.

OPA moves for uniform prices in oil pools with new wells

Means for establishing uniform maximum prices for crude petroleum in pools where new wells have been opened or old wells reopened subsequent to October 1, 1941, are provided in Amendment No. 5 to Revised Price Schedule No. 88.

The amendment became effective April 9, 1942.

The price schedule previously provided that where there was no purchase price posted as of October 1, 1941, for the pool in which a well completed or reopened after October 1, 1941, is located, a temporary price for crude petroleum produced from the new or reopened well, provided the price and a description of the crude petroleum were reported to OPA within 10 days.

The new amendment provides that such temporary price now shall be subject to disapproval by OPA. If the temporary price is a posted price, it shall, unless disapproved by OPA, be the maximum price at the well for crude petroleum produced from any wells located in the pool in which such new or reopened well is situated. The provision also covers wells representing discovery and development of new pools subsequent to October 1, 1941.

Paperboard exports, except "f. a. s.," excluded from ceiling

All export sales of paperboard, except those sold by producers on f. a. s. (free along side) vessel basis, are excluded from Revised Price Schedule No. 32 as the result of Amendment No. 1 to the schedule (Paperboard sold East of the Rocky Mountains) issued April 9 by Price Administrator Henderson.

The amendment, which became effective April 9, 1942, also clarifies the definitions of "paperboard," "person," and "producer."

Producers who export paperboard f. a. s. vessel now may add to the maximum prices established for domestic sales the actual costs for the extra packing required for export shipment plus the actual cost of the extra freight occasioned by such packing. All other export sales, which previously were covered by the schedule, will be treated in individual agreements with the producers and exporters, Mr. Henderson said.

As amended, the term "paperboard" now refers to all kinds, grades, types, calipers, colors, and patterns of paperboard described in the schedule and leaves specialty paperboard for separate treatment as was intended by Amendment No. 6 to the original schedule on Feb. 8, 1942.

The definition of "person" has been expanded to include in its meaning the United States, the States, or any of their political subdivisions or agencies.

To correct an unintended variance in the scope of the meaning of "producer," the term has now been broadened to include agents or representatives of producers.

★ ★ ★

OPA HARDWOOD LUMBER ADVISORY COMMITTEE

Twelve men identified with the southern hardwood lumber industry have been invited by the Office of Price Administration, Leon Henderson, Administrator, to serve on an industry advisory committee to cooperate with OPA in studies of the price situation concerning the industry.

Letters of invitation have gone to the following:

Lee Robinson, Mobile River Saw Mill Co., Mt. Vernon, Ala.; L. A. Mizener, Chicago Mill & Lumber Co., Chicago, Ill.; J. B. Edwards, Hillyer-Deutsch-Edwards, Inc., Oakdale, La.; J. W. Foreman, Foreman-Blades Lumber Co., Elizabeth City, N. C.; W. M. Camp, Camp Manufacturing Co., Marion, S. C.; H. C. Parrish, Richmond Cedar Works, Norfolk, Va.; Maurice W. Grundy, Commission, Wholesale, New Orleans, La.; George Henderson, Angelina Hardwood Co., Keltys, Tex.; C. W. Parham, Parham Hardwood Co., Memphis, Tenn.; J. W. Wells, J. W. Wells Lumber Co., Montgomery, Ala.; W. W. Kellogg, Kellogg Lumber Co., Monroe, La.; and H. L. Hayes, Jr., Wilson Lumber Co. of Florida, Perry, Fla.

LEATHER PRICING REVISED

Additional methods of determining maximum prices that may be charged for leather by tanners, jobbers, exporters, and importers, and provisions permitting sellers to have their price lists approved by OPA are provided in a further revision of Revised Price Schedule No. 61 (Leather) announced April 7 by Acting Administrator Hamm.

Original ceilings to halt speculation

The original schedule was an emergency measure to halt inflationary and speculative advances in leather prices issued shortly after the entrance of the United States into the war.

Under the present revisions, which became effective April 9, 1942, all maximum prices of leather, even though no sales were made during the base period, must be in line with the general level of prices prevailing during the November 6–December 6 period, with consideration given to the relative market value of each type, quality and grade of leather and to the class of purchaser to whom sold. This will eliminate high prices out of line with the general market established by some sellers during the base period.

Other changes and additions are contained in the revision.

★ ★ ★

Long-term contracts calling for OPA maximum are approved

Sales of anthracite under long-term contracts which stipulate that the price shall be the OPA maximum price in effect as of the date of delivery are allowed by Amendment No. 1 to Maximum Price Regulation No. 112 (Pennsylvania Anthracite) issued April 9 by Price Administrator Henderson.

The amendment was effective immediately.

Small gear makers exempted from reporting

Manufacturers of gears, pinions, sprockets, or speed reducers whose gross sales of such items during 1941 were less than $5,000 are exempted from submitting monthly reports to OPA as originally required under provisions of Revised Price Schedule No. 105, Price Administrator Leon Henderson announced April 9. The change is covered in Amendment No. 1 to that schedule, which was effective April 9, 1942.

Fine paper merchants advised of changes in bristol mark-up

Two changes in dealers' mark-up tables, which were included in individual agreements sent March 25 to 1,800 fine paper merchants, were announced April 7 by Price Administrator Henderson.

The changes permit merchants to use their customary practice in computing maximum prices in the sale of bristol paper, and are as follows:

Change "*1 package to less than 1 carton base price per pound plus 60 percent*" to read as follows:

1 package to less than 1 carton

Base price per pound less than 12 cents per pound. Add 3 cents per pound to the per pound carton maximum selling price.
Base price per pound 12 cents per pound to less than 24 cents per pound. Add 4 cents per pound to the per pound carton maximum selling price.
Base price per pound 24 cents per pound and over. Add 5 cents per pound to the per pound carton maximum selling price.

Change "*When selling in lots of less than 1 package, the paper merchants may add 50 percent to his per pound package maximum selling price*," to read as follows:

Less than 1 package

Base price per pound less than 12 cents per pound. Add 6 cents per pound to the per pound package maximum selling price.
Base price per pound 12 cents per pound to less than 24 cents per pound. Add 7 cents per pound to the per pound package maximum selling price.
Base price per pound 24 cents per pound and over. Add 8 cents per pound to the per pound package maximum selling price.

Agreements signed and returned to OPA will be treated as amended, Mr. Henderson said.

One regional, six new field offices announced by OPA

Opening of one new regional office and six field offices was announced April 7 by OPA.

The new office in Minneapolis (326 Midland Bank Building) becomes the twelfth OPA regional office. It will take over supervision of price control, rationing, investigation, and enforcement operations in North Dakota, South Dakota, and Minnesota. These three States were formerly in the Chicago region.

The new field offices are located at Des Moines, Iowa, Crocker Building (Chicago Region); Oklahoma City, Okla., 440 Key Building (Dallas Region); Portland, Oreg., Bedell Building (San Francisco Region); Omaha, Nebr., Grain Exchange Building, (Kansas City Region); Cincinnati, Ohio, Union Trust Building, and Louisville, Ky., Todd Building (both Cleveland Region).

New industry advisory committees

The Bureau of Industry Advisory Committees, WPB, has announced the formation of the following new industry advisory committees:

AUTOMOTIVE BATTERY COMMITTEE

Government presiding officer—R. L. Vaniman.

Members:

A. J. Baracree, Am-Plus Storage Battery Co., Chicago, Ill.; Edward Becker, Merry-Bean Co., San Francisco, Calif.; G. W. Douglas, Douglas Battery Mfg. Co., Winston-Salem, N. C.; E. T. Foote, Globe-Union, Inc., Milwaukee, Wis.; A. Foster, Battery Division, Norwalk Tire & Rubber Co., Norwalk, Conn.; J. H. McDuffee, The Electric Auto-Lite Co., Toledo, Ohio; B. F. Morris, Battery Division, Thomas A. Edison, Inc., Kearney, N. J.; Lester Perrine, Perrine Quality Products Corporation, Waltham, Mass.; Arthur G. Phelps, Delco-Remy Division, General Motors, Anderson, Ind.; W. F. Price, Price Battery Corporation, Hamburg, Pa.; L. B. Raycroft, The Electric Storage Battery Co., Philadelphia, Pa.; G. W. Taylor, American Battery Co., Nashville, Tenn.

BEET SUGAR PROCESSING COMMITTEE

Government presiding officer—A. E. Bowman, chief of the sugar section.

Members:

H. A. Bonning, Amalgamated Sugar Co., Ogden, Utah; W. N. Wilds, American Crystal Sugar Co., Denver, Colo.; H. C. McMillen, Central Sugar Co., Decatur, Ind.; J. Stewart, The Garden City Co., Garden City, Kans.; Frank A. Kemp, Great Western Sugar Co., Denver, Colo.; Wiley Blair, Jr., Holly Sugar Corporation, Colorado Springs, Colo.; A. W. Beebe, Lake Shore Sugar Co., Detroit, Mich.; R. E. Lies, Menominee Sugar Co., Green Bay, Wis.; W. W. Patterson, Michigan Sugar Co., Saginaw, Mich.; A. A. Schupp, Paulding Sugar Co., Paulding, Ohio; F. J. Belcher, Jr., Spreckels Sugar Co., San Francisco, Calif.; J. W. Timpson, Utah-Idaho Sugar Co., Salt Lake City, Utah.

CIGAR MANUFACTURERS INDUSTRY ADVISORY COMMITTEE

Government presiding officer—John B. Smiley, chief, beverage and tobacco branch.

Members:

H. P. Wurman, vice president, Bayuk Cigars, Inc., Ninth and Columbia Avenue, Philadelphia, Pa.; T. E. Brooks, partner, J. S. Brooks & Co., Red Lion, Pa.; Alvaro Garcia, partner, Garcia & Vega, 570 Seventh Avenue, New York, N. Y.; R. C. Bondy, vice president, General Cigar Co., 119 West Fortieth Street, New York, N. Y.; E. Wile, vice president, D. Emil Klein, 438 East Ninety-first Street, New York, N. Y.; George Whitfield, Lorillard Co., 119 West Fortieth Street, New York, N. Y.; J. C. Newman, president, M. & N. Cigar Co., 922 Woodland Avenue, Cleveland, Ohio; Tom Horton, president, Van Slyke & Horton, Kingston, N. Y.; Daniel McCarthy, secretary, H. Fendrich & Co., Evansville, Ind.; H. B. Michener, president, H. Marsh & Sons, Inc., Wheeling, W. Va.

ELEVATOR, ESCALATOR AND DUMB-WAITER COMMITTEE

Government presiding officer—C. S. Williams, chief, general industrial equipment branch.

Members:

C. F. Carlson, president, Monarch Elevator & Machine Co., Greensboro, N. C.; J. E. Martin, Montgomery Elevator Co., Moline, Ill.; L. A. Peterson, vice president, Otis Elevator Co., New York, N. Y.; Stanley Rowe, Shepard Elevator Co., Cincinnati, Ohio; J. G. Gosney, vice president, Westbrook Elevator Manufacturing Co., Inc., Danville, Va.; G. L. McKesson, president, Haughton Elevator Co., Toledo, Ohio; F. E. Brust, vice president, Atlantic Elevator Co., Philadelphia, Pa.

FLUORESCENT LIGHTING FIXTURES COMMITTEE

Government presiding officer—J. L. Haynes, chief, building materials branch.

Members:

Arthur Miller, vice president, The Miller Co., Meriden, Conn.; W. P. Lowell, Jr., Hygrade Sylvania Co., Salem, Mass.; Joseph Markel, president, Markel Electric Products, Inc., Buffalo, N. Y.; Nathan H. Eglowstein, president, Fluoro-O-Lite Manufacturing Co., Newark, N. J.; E. C. Huerkamp, Westinghouse Electric & Manufacturing Co., Cleveland, Ohio; Ward Harrison, General Electric Co., Cleveland, Ohio; A. K. Wakefield, president, F. W. Wakefield Brass Co., Vermilion, Ohio; Thomas G. Beckett, president, Beckett Electric Co., Inc., Dallas, Tex.; R. W. Staud, Benjamin Electric Manufacturing Co., Des Plaines, Ill.; Leon F. Moore, general sales manager, Electrical Products Consolidated, Denver, Colo.

IRON AND STEEL COMMITTEE

GENERAL STEEL WAREHOUSE SUBCOMMITTEE

Government presiding officer—C. E. Adams, chief of the iron and steel branch.

Members:

Guy P. Bible, Horace T. Potts Co., Philadelphia, Pa.; C. H. Bradley, W. J. Holliday & Co., Indianapolis, Ind.; Lester A. Brion, Peter A. Frasse & Co., New York, N. Y.; A. C. Castle, A. M. Castle & Co., Chicago, Ill.; W. S. Doxsey Warehouse, American Steel Association, Cleveland, Ohio; Sol Friedman, Reliance Steel Corporation, Cleveland, Ohio; Everett D. Graff, Jessie T. Ryerson & Sons, Chicago, Ill.; Earle M. Jorgensen, Earle M. Jorgensen Co., Los Angeles, Calif.; W. Kurtz, Peninsular Steel Co., Cleveland, Ohio; Richmond Lewis, Charles C. Lewis Co., Springfield, Mass.; N. R. Patterson, Patterson Steel Co., Tulsa, Okla.; J. H. Peebles, Peden Iron & Steel Co., Houston, Tex.

MEN'S, WOMEN'S AND CHILDREN'S ROBE, NEGLIGEE AND HOUSECOAT COMMITTEE

Government presiding officer—H. Stanley Marcus.

Members:

Louis M. Brown, B. Brown & Sons, 105 Madison Avenue, New York, N. Y.; Irving Caro, Caro & Co., Inc., 10 East Thirty-second Street, New York, N. Y.; Edward Glazier, President, Rothley Inc., 307 West Van Buren Street, Chicago, Ill.; Harry H. Greenberg, President, Royal Robes, Inc., 16 East Thirty-fourth Street, New York, N. Y.; Raymond Halpern, President, Raymodes Negligees Inc., 105 Madison Avenue, New York, N. Y.; Alfred Van Baalen, Van Baalen Heilbrun & Co., 1239 Broadway, New York, N. Y.; George Jebaily, Jebaily Lonschein Co., 105 Madison Avenue, New York, N. Y.; Benjamin Levin, C. N. Mack Soud Corporation, 1 East Thirty-third Street, New York, N. Y.; A. A. Normandin, President, Robes. Negligees, Housecoats, Lounging Robe Manufacturing Co., 2715 South Main Street, Los Angeles, Calif.; Leo Safir, president, Rabhor Co., Empire State Building, New York, N. Y.; Elias Sayour, President, Elias Sayour Co., 31 East Thirty-first Street, New York, N. Y.

OFFICE MACHINERY COMMITTEE

Government presiding officer—N. G. Burleigh, chief, industrial and office machinery branch.

Members:

Carl W. Brenn, Autographic Register Co., Hoboken, N. J.; Harland W. Rippey, Bircher Co., Inc., Rochester, N. Y.; Lawrence V. Britt, Burroughs Adding Machine Co., Detroit, Mich.; T. B. Hiranberg, Jr., Check-O-Meter Sales Co., Chicago, Ill.; Ralph C. Coxhead, Ralph C. Coxhead Corporation, New York, N. Y.; Merrill B. Sands, Dictaphone Corporation, New York, N. Y.; Theodore W. Robinson, Sr., Ditto, Incorporated, Chicago, Ill.; Harmon P. Elliott, Elliott Addressing Machine Company, Cambridge, Mass.; Carl M. Friden, Friden Calculating Co., Inc., San Leandro, Calif.; Thomas J. Watson, International Business Machines Corporation, New York, N. Y.; Norman Sheras, A. D. Joslin Mfg. Co.. Manistee, Mich.; Stanley C. Allyn, National Cash Register Co., Dayton, Ohio; C. G. Watkins, Simplex Time Recorder Co., Gardner, Mass.; W. J. Bernart, Jr., Pitney-Bowes Postage Meter Co., Stamford, Conn.

PLUMBING AND HEATING COMMITTEE

WARM AIR FURNACE SUBCOMMITTEE

Government presiding officer—W. W. Timmis.

Members:

H. S. Sharp, vice president, Henry Furnace & Foundry Co., Cleveland, Ohio; Cliff Ackerson, vice president, Agricola Furnace Co., Gadsden, Ala.; W. L. McGrath, vice president, Williamson Heater Co., Cincinnati, Ohio; L. B. Taylor, vice president, International Heater Co., Utica, N. Y.; Frank C. Packer, Payne Furnace & Supply Co., Beverly Hills, Calif.; A. W. Wrieden, Lennox Furnace Co., Syracuse, N. Y.; R. S. McNanney, president, Dowagiac Steel Furnace, Dowagiac, Mich.; F. H. Faust, General Electric Co., Bloomfield, N. J.; Robin Bell, Surface Combustion Co., Toledo, Ohio.

WINE COMMITTEE

Government presiding officer—John B. Smiley, chief, beverage and tobacco branch.

Members:

Fred Bechtold, manager, Italian Swiss Colony, Chicago, Ill.; J. B. Cella, president, Roma Wine Co., Fresno, Calif.; B. V. Granfeld, treasurer and general manager, Engels & Kurdwig Wine Co., Sandusky, Ohio; John E. Laird, president and general manager, Laird & Co., Scobeyville, N. J.; Edward A. Lavin, president and general manager, Granada Wine Co., Inc., Cambridge, Mass.; John A. Margolis, president and treasurer, Bisceglia Brothers Corporation, Philadelphia, Pa.; E. S. Underhill, Jr., president, Urbana Wine Co., Inc., Hammondsport, N. Y.; Erich Steinborg, general manager, Upland Winery, Sunnyside, Wash.; J. Campbell Moore, vice president, Garrett & Co., Inc., Brooklyn, N. Y.; Albert M. Paul, president and general manager, California Products Co., Fresno, Calif.; Edward F. Pooley, Hood River Distillers, Inc., Hood River, Oreg.; Calvin L. Russell, chairman board, Central California Wineries, Inc., Fresno, Calif.; Irvin M. Schlenker, manager, Gulflex Drug Co., Houston, Tex.; Greyton H. Taylor, co-owner, The Taylor Wine Co., Hammondsport, N. Y.; Walter E. Taylor, secretary-treasurer and general manager, Fruit Industries Limited, San Francisco, Calif.

LABOR . . .

Board grants "union security" by 8-4 vote in Walker-Turner dispute, other issues settled unanimously; 10 new cases

The National War Labor Board last week issued its first important union security decision, directive orders in two other cases, reached an agreement in a fourth case and received certification of 10 new disputes.

Walker-Turner Co., Inc.

At his first press conference since the creation of the Board, William H. Davis, chairman, announced on April 10, the decision of the full Board in the dispute between the Walker-Turner Co., Inc., Plainfield, N. J. and the United Electrical, Radio and Machine Workers, CIO, affecting 293 workers. Two of the three issues in the case were settled by unanimous decision while the third was decided by a vote of 8 to 4 with the employer members of the Board dissenting.

Wage increases were granted and grievance machinery was set up in accordance with the unanimous panel recommendations which the Board unanimously adopted as its own. On the question of union security, both the panel and the Board were divided with the employer members dissenting from the public and labor members in each case.

The majority decision on union security provides for inclusion in the contract the following clauses:

1. All members of the union who were members in good standing on November 27, 1941, or who have since become members shall remain members in good standing for the period of the contract.
2. The union shall waive claims to the dues and initiation fees which accrued prior to April 1, 1942, the date of the Board's decision.
3. The present dues and initiation fees of the union shall not be increased except by the international organization.
4. Each employee who may hereafter join the union shall sign a card which voluntarily binds him to the provisions of the article. The union shall not coerce any employee to join the union and any employee who claims he has been coerced shall have a right to impartial trial by an umpire.
5. In the event a union member is certified by the local not to be in good standing in accordance with the constitution and by-laws of the union, and the company wants a review of this certification it may treat the matter as a grievance under the grievance machinery set up by the contract. If the arbitrator supports the union he shall, (a) Direct the company to discharge the man, or (b) Direct the company to deduct from his wages the amount of his financial obligations to the union for the period of the contract, and the employee shall lose his seniority rights under the contract.

The majority decision, written by Mr. Davis, listed the following reasons for this recommendation:

1. The company's attitude toward organized labor was "certainly not one of cooperation or helpfulness."
2. Substandard wages, due to a large extent to the company's reinvestment of its funds in plant and equipment during the past year in preference to increasing wages to standard levels.
3. The great decline in the number of dues-paying members because of the above facts and because the union was living up to its no-strike agreement.

"This Board was created," Mr. Davis said, "on the assumption that the peaceful cooperation of responsible organized labor and responsible management is essential in carrying on the war. It follows as a close corollary that the Board in peacefully settling the labor disputes which come before it, must continually bear in mind the broad principle that neither management nor labor shall take advantage of one another as a result of the changed conditions brought about by the war, either by direct aggression or by indirectly bringing about a situation which leads to a natural process of disintegration."

Thomas Kennedy, R. J. Thomas, George Meany, and Martin Durkin wrote a concurring opinion in which they said that although they were dissatisfied with certain aspects of the decision including the limitation of union dues, they concurred because they believed it "makes a considerable approach to an adequate solution of the issue presented."

The dissenting opinion written by Roger D. Lapham and concurred in by E. J. McMillan, R. R. Deupree, and George H. Mead, representing employers, pointed out that the union members should not be required to maintain their membership in good standing unless they voluntarily agreed in writing to be so bound. "We are convinced," the dissenting opinion said, "that persuasion, rather than compulsion, produces the best results and that within the framework of law we should leave it to management and the representatives of the workers to solve the difficult problem of union status."

Toledo, Peoria & Western Railroad

On April 9, Chairman Davis sent a telegram in answer to one received from George P. McNear, president of the Toledo, Peoria & Western Railroad, raising questions about the appointment of Justice Benjamin C. Hilliard of the Colorado Supreme Court as arbitrator in McNear's dispute with the Brotherhood of Locomotive Firemen and Enginemen and the Brotherhood of Railroad Trainmen. Mr. Davis' wire stated that failure to notify the WLB "immediately" of his willingness to arbitrate the dispute as the Board had ordered would result in the Board's proceeding without delay "to take such steps as are necessary to determine the merits of the dispute ex parte."

The Executive order of March 21, which ordered the director of the Office of Defense Transportation to take over and manage the railroad, also imposed on the WLB the obligation of finally settling the dispute. Judge Hilliard was appointed by the Board in accordance with its order of arbitration of February 27.

San Francisco Hotel Employers

An interim directive order was issued last week providing for the return to work without discrimination of all members of the San Francisco Local Joint Executive Board of Hotel and Restaurant Employees, AFL, who have been on strike against the Hotel Employers' Association of San Francisco. The order was a unanimous one of the Board. A public hearing in the dispute, which involves wages and the union shop, was held April 2 and the final decision of the Board will be made later.

Chase Brass & Copper Co.

Another interim directive order was issued, by unanimous decision of the Board, in the dispute between the Chase Brass & Copper Co., Cleveland, Ohio and the International Association of Machinists, AFL. The order made retroactive to January 1 any wage adjustments that may later be ordered when the final decision is made.

The panel which had heard the parties early in March had made a unanimous recommendation to the Board that the issuance of such an order "would tend to reduce unrest and uncertainty among the company's employees."

The dispute over the union's demand for a 10 cent per hour general wage increase involves 1,600 employees. The panel composed of Robert J. Myers,

Frederick Fales, and Joseph McDonagh is now preparing its complete recommendations to the Board.

Pullman Standard Car Manufacturing Co.

A voluntary agreement between the Pullman Standard Car Manufacturing Co., Bessemer, Ala. and three unions followed 6 days of hearings before a panel of Herman B. Wells, for the public, Thomas R. Jones, and Frederick Fales for employers, Frank Tobin and Milton Murray for labor. The three unions in the case are the Steel Workers' Organizing Committee, CIO, the International Association of Machinists and the International Brotherhood of Electrical Workers, both AFL.

Wages and union security were the issues in dispute with about 1,100 employees involved. The union security question was, with all three unions, settled by an agreement that the company will not discriminate against union members, will not discourage membership in any of the unions or encourage membership in any other union.

The SWOC and the IAM wage demands were settled by the granting of a 5½ cent increase over the present hourly day rate and a 5 cent increase over the hourly piece rate, with an increase in the minimum rates for various classifications of machinists. These increases are retroactive to March 9 and after 6 months either party may reopen the question of wages.

The wage question in the case of the International Brotherhood of Electrical Workers was settled by an agreement for voluntary arbitration which will be final and binding on both parties. Mr. Jones, one of the panel, will act as arbitrator and the rates determined by him will be made retroactive to March 9, also.

RADIO PROGRAM SETS RECORD

"You Can't Do Business With Hitler," a 15-minute recorded radio program, has broken best-selling broadcasting records.

The program is distributed weekly, at their own request, to 720 of the 850 radio stations in the United States.

"You Can't Do Business With Hitler" is based on the best-selling book by Douglas Miller, who was Commercial Attaché of the American Embassy in Berlin for 14 years. It is prepared by the Radio Section of the OEM with Miller's collaboration.

It was first distributed, with no advance fanfare, in January. Its growth since then has been largely by neighbor-to-neighbor build-up.

OEM Information Division field offices

OEM has issued the following list of Information Division field offices and officers:

ATLANTA—Marvin Cox, 1507 Candler Building; Tel. Jackson 5880; *territory,* Georgia, Florida, Alabama, Tennessee, Mississippi.
BALTIMORE (Branch of Philadelphia).— Thomas Stevens, 1528 Baltimore Trust Building; Tel. Plaza 8170.
BIRMINGHAM (Branch of Atlanta).— Irving H. Belman, 301 Phoenix Building; Tel. 4–7761.
BOSTON.—E. Bigelow Thompson, 17 Court Street; Tel. Lafayette 7500, Ext. 204–205; Evenings: Lafayette 7502, 7503, 30 Cornhill.
BUFFALO (Branch of New York).—Harry S. Mullany, 432 M & T Building; Tel. Washington 2077–2078.
CHICAGO (Branch of Detroit).—William F. Sullivan, 2600 Civic Opera Building; Tel. Andover 3600, Ext. 21 22, Evenings: Andover 3604.
CLEVELAND.—Samuel Slotky (consultant), 472 Union Bank of Commerce Building; Tel. Cherry 5984; *territory,* Ohio, Kentucky, West Virginia.
DALLAS.—L. L. Sisk, 419 Fidelity Building; Tel. Riverside 4651, Evenings: Riverside 4651, 4652; *territory,* Texas, Oklahoma, Louisiana.
DENVER.—Eugene Cervi, 505 United States National Bank Building; Tel. Main 4231; *territory,* Colorado, Wyoming, New Mexico, Utah, Montana, Idaho.
DETROIT.—Paul Jordan, Boulevard Building, 7310 Woodward Avenue; Tel. Trinity 1–5500, Ext. 53; *territory,* Illinois, Wisconsin, Michigan, Indiana.
HOUSTON (Branch of Dallas).—Maurice Gardner, 1011 Electric Building.
INDIANAPOLIS (Branch of Detroit).— Joseph Collier, Tenth Floor, Circle Tower Building; Ma. 9411, Ext. 18.
JACKSONVILLE (Branch of Atlanta).— William Bennett, 520 Lynch Building; Tel. 5–1846 or 5–1847.
KANSAS CITY—Marvin McAlister, 300 Mutual Building; Tel. Victor 7780; *territory,* Missouri, Nebraska, Kansas, Arkansas.
LOS ANGELES (Branch of San Francisco).—Richard Washburne, 724 Western Pacific Building, 1031 South Broadway; Tel. Richmond 0311.
MEMPHIS (Branch of Atlanta).—Ewing Johnson, 2111 Sterick Building; Tel. 5–7421, Ext. 17.
MILWAUKEE (Branch of Detroit).— George A. Mann, 7002 Plankinton Arcade; Tel. Broadway 4440.
MINNEAPOLIS.—Dowsley Clark, 326 Midland Bank Building; Tel. Main 3244, Night, 5032; *territory,* Minnesota, North Dakota, Iowa, South Dakota.
NEWARK (Branch of New York).—James J. Kennedy, Globe Indemnity Building, 20 Washington Place.
NEW ORLEANS (Branch of Dallas).— David McGuire, 409 Canal Building.
NEW YORK.—Clifton Read, 703 Chanin Building, 122 East Forty-second Street; Tel. Murray Hill 3–6805, after 7:00 p. m. Murray Hill 3–6828; *territory,* New York State, New Jersey.
OKLAHOMA CITY (Branch of Dallas).— Harrington Wimberly, 422 Key Building, Oklahoma City; Tel. 7–0919.
OMAHA (Branch of Kansas City).—Lawrence May, 504 Grain Exchange Building; Tel. Jackson 6466.
PHILADELPHIA.—Howard Browning, 666 Pennsylvania R. R., Suburban Building; *territory,* Pennsylvania, Delaware, Maryland.
PITTSBURGH (Branch of Philadelphia).— William Schoyer, Fulton Building; Tel. Grant 3790.
RALEIGH (Branch of Richmond).—William Sharpe, Sir Walter Hotel; Tel. 3–1901.
RICHMOND—William Bourne, 2d Floor, Johnson Publishing Co. Building; Tel. 7–2331;

territory, Virginia, North Carolina, South Carolina.
SAN FRANCISCO.—Dean Jennings, Western Merchandise Mart, 1355 Market Street; Tel. Klondike 2–2300; *territory,* California, Washington, Oregon, Nevada, Arizona.
SEATTLE (Branch of San Francisco).— Howard Macgowan, 234 Henry Building; Tel. Elliott 0200.
SALT LAKE CITY (Branch of Denver).— Ottis Peterson, 308 David Keith Building; Tel. 3–7676, Night 3–7679.

★ ★ ★

10 concerns told to stop discrimination

Ten concerns having millions of dollars in war contracts were told to cease discriminating against available workers because of their race or religion, in "Findings and Directions" which they received April 13 from the President's Committee on Fair Employment Practice.

Firms in Chicago, Milwaukee areas

The concerns are in the Chicago and Milwaukee areas, and the findings and directions are based on 2 days of public hearings held January 19–20 in Chicago. Since January the Committee, of which Dr. Malcolm S. MacLean, president of Hampton Institute, is chairman, had studied the record before taking the action announced April 13.

The companies involved in the Chicago area are: the Stewart-Warner Corporation, the Buick Aviation plant at Melrose, Ill., a unit of General Motors Corporation; the Bearse Manufacturing Co., Simpson Manufacturing Co., and the Studebaker branch factory. Those in the Milwaukee area are: the Nordberg Manufacturing Co., A. O. Smith Corporation, Heil Co., Allis-Chalmers Corporation and the Harnischfeger Corporation.

Jurisdiction to continue

The complaints filed against the several companies included allegations that they had refused to employ either Negroes or Jews, or both; that they had given restrictive orders to either public or private employment agencies, asking for only white or only Gentile workers; that they had advertised in newspapers for help and specified "Gentile" or "Protestant" or "white," or that they had refused to give workers of certain races and creeds opportunity for promotion in keeping with their qualifications.

The companies for the most part denied that they were discriminating, but in each case the Committee found that the evidence supported the charges of discrimination.

AGRICULTURE

(Information furnished through Office of Agricultural Defense Relations, U. S. Department of Agriculture)

Rapid progress reported in guayule rubber production project; planting now under way

Rapid progress in the guayule rubber production project is reported by the Department of Agriculture's Forest Service. Seed sowing for 500 acres of nursery beds near Salinas, Calif., started the last week of March, plowing and discing of the nursery beds, and soil surveys and maps having been completed. Sowing will follow progressively behind installation of irrigation systems in the nursery.

Since March 5, when the guayule rubber production act was signed, a seed treating building, 80 feet by 109 feet has been completed and is now in operation. Some 13,000 pounds of screened sawdust, in which seed is mixed before sowing, have been delivered.

Over 3 million feet of lumber is being delivered for 911 miles of 1-inch by 8-inch cleated tracks or duckboards on which equipment is operated over the 48-inch wide seed beds.

To plant 10,500,000 seedlings

About 25 miles of windbreak fencing has been transferred from the Prairie States Forestry Project. A total of 100 miles will be needed for protection of the entire nursery. The Forest Service's Central States Region has also supplied some windbreaks.

Digging and field planting the 10,500,000 seedlings acquired from the Intercontinental Rubber Co. started the day the act was signed. Planting will proceed at an increased pace as weather permits, utilizing six planting machines that have been obtained and repaired. About 875 acres of field planting will be completed this week.

Equipment from various sources

Camp facilities are being constructed to house labor used on the project. One 200-man unit is ready for occupancy. A considerable amount of CCC camp equipment will be transferred to the guayule project.

Some equipment needed on the project has been transferred from the Civilian Conservation Corps and Departmental bureaus, some has been rented and some purchased, either new or second-hand. Altogether more than 125 trucks, 85 tractors, and 420 pieces of farm machinery

have been started toward Salinas or are actually in service on the job. Equipment repair and machine shop buildings, as well as a warehouse for small equipment and tools, have been established and are in operation.

500 workers on the job

Some 500 workers are on the job in California, including Forest Service personnel detailed from several regions, and local laborers. A contract has been let to furnish food, bedding, and other housekeeping facilities for laborers who will occupy the Forest Service camp. Investigations by the Bureau of Plant Industry looking to the establishment of test plots for guayule production are under way in other areas, including Mexico, and the Bureau of Agriculture Chemistry and Engineering is checking on guayule rubber manufacturing facilities.

Transportation, storage of 1942 crops to be discussed at series of meetings

Anticipating a shortage of storage space, representatives of agriculture, transportation agencies, and the grain trade will attend a series of meetings during April in 11 western cities to discuss methods of facilitating grain storage and movements.

Problems more critical

The USDA grain experts point out that problems in connection with housing the 1942 crops promise to be more critical than they were a year ago because of the larger carry-over, above average crop prospects, increased nonagricultural demand for railroad facilities, no great increase in commercial fireproof storage during the year, and the growing scarcity of labor and structural materials.

May set up grain marketing committees

Consideration will be given to setting up representative grain marketing committees similar to those established in 1941 to alleviate the storage and transportation situation.

10,000 acres of sorgo planned in experiment to produce molasses for alcohol

The United States Department of Agriculture has announced an experimental project in cooperation with the American Sugar Cane League for the production of up to 10,000 acres of sorgo in the cane belt of Louisiana to produce molasses for conversion into alcohol.

Would conserve sugar

The use on a substantial scale of sorgo, or "sorghum" molasses, in producing ethyl alcohol for war requirements would conserve sugar, which, in the form of high test molasses, has constituted the principal raw material for that purpose. Since sorgo matures in approximately 120 days from the time of planting, it will be possible for the sugar mills in the area to complete the processing of the sorgo before their normal sugarcane grinding operations get under way.

1,000,000 gallons of alcohol anticipated

It is hoped that the planting of 10,000 acres will yield approximately 2,400,000 gallons of standard density molasses,

from which approximately 1,000,000 gallons of alcohol should be obtained. To encourage this production, the Commodity Credit Corporation has agreed to purchase the molasses at the mills at a price comprised of the following: $4 per ton to growers of sorgo delivered at the nearest hoist; $1 per ton for processing; and the actual cost of transportation, but not more than an average of $0.50 per ton. The molasses or sirup will be delivered to distillers for conversion into alcohol.

Technical aid from Bureaus

The Bureau of Plant Industry will assist the mills and growers in the acquisition and distribution of the seed and will give technical advice in the production of the crop. Representatives of the Bureau of Agricultural Chemistry and Engineering will assist mills in meeting technical problems in connection with the processing of the sorgo into molasses.

The extent to which this project proves successful will determine future developments.

Judge rules city must not sell goods over ceiling

Judge Lee N. Murlin in Common Pleas Court, Toledo, Ohio, on April 6 ruled that municipalities making sales of any commodity covered by Office of Price Administration ceilings must comply with such maximum price provisions, rather than sell to the highest bidder as required by State statute.

The decision, the first of its kind, enjoins the City of Toledo at the plea of taxpayer Harold B. Rosenblatt from selling 320 tons of salvage scrap rail at higher than the ceiling figure for scrap iron under OPA Price Schedule No. 4.

Judge Murlin ruled that in the case of identical bids the material must be sold to the bidder having the greatest need for serving war production.

Three types of waste-paper users freed of inventory limit

Manufacturers of paper, paperboard, and paper products who consume waste paper will be permitted to accumulate inventories of this essential material without restriction under an order issued April 6 by WPB. General Inventory Order M-129 removes the inventory restrictions imposed on waste paper consuming mills by Priorities Regulation No. 1.

The purpose of the order is to encourage mills to stock up with waste paper now, while Government-sponsored collection agencies are gathering supplies in ever increasing quantities.

Paper mills consuming waste paper must continue to make weekly inventory reports to the War Production Board on Form PD-240.

"Putting into process" clarified for wool tops

WPB has issued an amendment to Wool Conservation Order M-73 clarifying "putting into process" of tops on any system other than the worsted system. Under the amendment (No. 3), tops are regarded as being put into process when the first physical change in form occurs, and the dyeing of tops is not regarded as putting into process.

CONSERVATION . . .

WPB calls for Nation-wide spring housecleaning to salvage waste for war

A Nation-wide spring housecleaning for materials that can be salvaged for war production was called for April 8 by the Bureau of Industrial Conservation, WPB.

Need should be plain to all of us

"Vast quantities of the things we need would be brought to light by a concerted spring housecleaning," Lessing J. Rosenwald, chief of the bureau, said.

"This year the need for the return of waste materials into new production should be plain to all of us . Old metal ornaments, obsolete plumbing and heating equipment, broken tools—these can become parts of guns, planes and tanks; old tires and tubes, hot water bottles and bath mats can go into the production of reclaimed rubber so critically needed to replace our lost supply of crude rubber from the East; old rags will be made into wiping rags for use in war plants, and wastepaper is in demand for conversions into cartons . . ."

Through State and local salvage committees organized by the bureau, the public has been instructed to sell waste material to local dealers or give the collections to any one of a number of charitable organizations active in the salvage field. In rural areas, the Department of Agriculture is cooperating through its County War Boards, and in country sections where collection facilities were not available, Work Projects Administration trucks and labor are being utilized.

What to look for

Noting that many persons are uncertain about the variety of household articles that may be returned to production when they are obsolete or useless, Mr. Rosenwald made public the following list of suggested items for the housecleaner:

IN THE ATTIC

Beds made of brass or iron.
Electric cords (they contain copper wire).
Electric toasters, irons, heaters, fans, or any electrical equipment.
Hardware—door knobs, hinges, keys, locks, trim, springs, etc.
Kitchen Utensils—old knives, pans, pots, scissors.
Lamps and lighting fixtures made of brass, copper, or iron.
Ornaments—metal ash trays, bowls, statues, vases.
Porch and garden furniture made of metal.
Radios—broken parts containing metal.
Screens made of brass or copper.
Toys—sleds, ice skates, roller skates.

Vacuum Cleaners—broken parts made of metal.
Old rubber overshoes, raincoats, bathing caps.

IN THE CELLAR

Coal stoves that are worn out.
Fireplace Equipment—andirons, grates, pokers.
Fire extinguishers.
Furnace Parts—old grates, doors.
Iron and nickel parts of old gas stoves.
Pipes,—pieces of iron, brass, or copper piping.
Plumbing Fixtures—bathtubs, faucets, sinks.
Radiators.
Refrigerator Parts—ice trays, inside linings.
Tools—all old tools.

IN THE GARAGE

Tires, tubes.
Automobile Parts—batteries, chains, license plates, parts of motors.
Bicycles and tricycles.
Garden tools—lawn mowers, hoes, pickaxes, rakes, shovels.

IN THE YARD OR ON THE FARM

Old tires, inner tubes.
Farm tools.
Logging chains.
Wire fencing and fence posts.
Motors and motor parts.
Playground equipment.
Pieces of old metal—well handles.
Ploughs.
Wheelbarrows.

★ ★ ★

OPA clarifies difference between reusable and scrap material

Maximum delivered prices for reusable iron and steel products of certain types are covered under Revised Maximum Price Schedule No. 49, Price Administrator Henderson emphasized April 7. The interpretation is designed specifically to clarify the distinction between reusable and scrap material.

"Professed ignorance or misunderstanding of the schedule's provisions," the administrator warned, "cannot be used as an excuse for evasion. The Emergency Price Control Act of 1942 empowers OPA to deal sharply with violators. If necessary, we shall not hesitate to use such powers to punish offenders."

The administrator explained that prices of all reusable iron and steel products not covered by other specific schedules "after such shearing, cutting, straightening, bending or pickling as may be necessary, shall be computed in the same manner used by the seller on April 16, 1941, provided that such prices do not exceed the maximum delivered prices for comparable iron or steel products of prime quality." This ruling follows the language of Section 1306.159 (1) of the schedule as amended March 31.

"Unless this material is offered by the seller in such condition that no further operations are necessary to class it as similar to iron or steel products of prime quality," the administrator cautioned, "it cannot be classed as used and reusable, but instead must be classed as scrap."

CIVILIAN DEFENSE . . .

U. S. industrial areas can be bombed, managements must prepare, says Woodward

In an address before the War Conference for the Protection of Workers and Plants, under the auspices of the Office of Civilian Defense of the Chicago Metropolitan Area, in Chicago, April 9, Rear Admiral Clark H. Woodward, U. S. Navy (Retired), declared:

"Some will scoff at the idea that an air raid can be made on this particular industrial area. Don't be misled by erroneous information, for the answer definitely is *yes it can!*"

Further excerpts:

The United States has been engaged in total war for more than 4 months.

Many believe that because of our vast resources of manpower, machines, ingenuity, and courage we are bound to win the final victory, no matter how serious may be our early military and naval defeats.

Though we have magnificent resources and manpower, unequalled mass-production machinery, and skilled men to operate it, these all count for little in total war unless we use them efficiently and to the maximum limit. The enemy will not wait for us to get in full gear.

Can't fight this war in the future

Though the richest nation on earth and the strongest potential military Power, unless we get on a real wartime basis soon, we cannot win. We can't fight this war in the future.

We only have to look at Japan's record to see the urgency of this matter. In less than 4 months the Japanese juggernaut, in its southern sweep, has successfully crushed all Allied opposition from Shanghai down to and including the Dutch East Indies and seized all strategical points in the Southwest Pacific—a military feat which, prior to December 7, seemed absolutely fantastic and beyond the realms of possibility.

Plants must be well guarded

Being engaged in total war, we must not only consider production as the key to our military effort, but also we must give serious thought to the protection of the plants which produce the vital sinews of war. They must be well guarded against sabotage, fires, and other unusual hazards, including air raids.

However, plant protection should by no means be limited to those concerns manufacturing military equipment and arms. It applies also, though to a lesser degree, to plants supplying the home defense legions with food, clothing, housing, and other necessities of life.

It is a matter of common sense, then, that in every industrial area we prepare as quickly and as thoroughly as possible complete air raid protection for all plants, for we know not when, where, or how hard the enemy will strike.

Hit-and-run raid possible

Some will scoff at the idea that an air raid can be made on this particular industrial area. Don't be misled by erroneous information, for the answer definitely is *yes it can!*

We know that the Nazis have bombers with 4,500-mile range. That, in itself, permits an easy flight from Brest to Cleveland (3,400 miles), Detroit (3,500 miles), or Chicago (3,700 miles) with time to spare for pop calls on all three cities. Naturally, it would be only a token hit-and-run raid, and probably would be of the suicide type. However, it is not at all necessary to sacrifice a skilled bomber's crew in any such suicide attack. Because of the vast expanse of the ocean and the relatively small space occupied by a ship—even a large vessel representing only a pin point—it is possible for an aircraft carrier to arrive, undetected, at some point 800–1,000 miles off our Atlantic coast and send off a flock of bombers with a fair chance of the majority returning after their raid.

Why wait for the first bomb?

We have been forewarned of what may come. Why wait for the first bomb? Why not prepare against it now?

Civilian defense against enemy action unquestionably is one of our major problems, as it still is in England after 2½ years of war. It concerns the protection not only of citizens of each community, but also the protection of vital plants in the immediate area. With specific regard to the latter I cannot overemphasize the fact that the responsibility for such preparation falls directly on management. If this is an all-out war, it must be all-out effort at production.

Every coastal State has held or plans to hold schools for plant protection

In a report to James M. Landis, Director of the Office of Civilian Defense, Rear Admiral Clark H. Woodward, U. S. N. (Retired), head of the plant protection division, April 12 declared that every State along our coast lines has already held or intends to hold plant protection schools. At these schools plant executives are given a general over-all picture of the necessity for protection against air raids and of the means of carrying it out.

"Some bombers will get through"

"Some bombers will get through," Admiral Woodward declared, "and it is up to the plants to prepare themselves so that each plant has a proper organization with its personnel trained and ready to minimize and control damage resulting from enemy action. Plant protection is a subject that requires technical instruction and training to achieve a measure of success in combating the effects of possible enemy air attacks."

The Plant Protection Schools program, initiated early in August 1941, has been accelerated since December 7. By the end of January 1942, approximately 4,500 executives had attended, representing approximately 5 million employees. Since then the number of graduates has been greatly increased as Protection Schools have been held in 20 States, the greater number in the States lying within the target areas of the East, West, and Gulf Coasts.

Pamphlets outline protective measures

An important part of the Plant Protection program has been the distribution of literature on the subject. The pamphlet, "Protection of Industrial Plants and Public Buildings," issued by the Office of Civilian Defense, is on the "best-seller" list of OCD publications, over half a million copies having gone to readers. A new booklet, "Protection of Industrial Plants," prepared by the industrial advisory committee of the Plant Protection Division, to be issued shortly, discusses protective measures which should be taken by large and small industrial establishments.

FACTS AND FIGURES . . .

Millions moved about conquered Europe to labor under the yoke of Germany

Hitler is moving with "blitz" speed to extend his system of slave labor throughout subjugated Europe, the Office of Facts and Figures reported April 6. Nazi propagandists are boasting of the pace attained in putting millions of once-free men and women under the yoke for labor in the Reich.

Foreign broadcasts monitored by the Federal Communications Commission show that Nazi labor bosses are reaching from Rome to Riga for manpower to ship into Germany. Branches of the German Employment Office are strategically located throughout all of occupied Europe. In Poland alone, there are 22 German labor offices, with 70 branches and 500 subbranches. In occupied Russia, 140 labor offices have been set up to recruit workers.

Plan to use 4 million

A Berlin broadcast boasted recently that Germany will increase the number of foreign workers in the Reich to more than 4 million.

Field Marshal Goering in a broadcast to German farmers said, "The crushing need, the pressing need, for necessary labor forces for agriculture will be met by the application of usable auxiliary laborers from occupied eastern territories, and by the use of foreigners and prisoners of war."

Mussolini—once the bellicose, but now the pliant partner of Hitler—is sending manpower, as well as food, to the Reich. A Berlin broadcast said Italy had provided 300,000 workers to Germany in 1941, eight percent of them women. Berlin predicted that the number of Italian workers in Germany would soon reach 400,000. Another German broadcast revealed that Italian workers are also being sent to occupied Russia.

1,100,000 Poles claimed

The German-controlled Polish radio reported the total number of Poles working in Germany as 1,100,000. Excluding war prisoners, the number is 655,000, with 517,000 of them in agriculture, according to the Weischel radio. Two hundred and fifty thousand Polish women are in Germany, and one-fourth of them are on farms, Berlin said.

Evidence that the Poles do not accept their unhappy role as slave workers comes from the Berlin radio which reported that Stefan Wlodara, a Polish civilian laborer, had been executed. His crime was that, "he had shown a rebellious attitude, threatened his German employer and attacked him several times."

Latvia sends girls

Latvia, which the Nazis claim they liberated from Russia, is sending girls to the Reich. The Berlin radio announced that, "A number of Latvian girls, from 16 to 25 years old, have recently arrived from Riga to work as farm and industrial hands in Northern Germany. All of them concluded contracts with the German Employment Office in Riga and will stay in the Reich for 1 year. The German Labor Front will care for the girls by controlling their working conditions and organizing their leisure time." The Berlin radio also told of using Latvian labor on the Russian front to repair and rebuild roads.

The Berlin radio, reporting that 150,000 French workers were in Germany, boasted, "Four special trains leave France weekly with French volunteers to Germany." And later, "Since the beginning of March, a weekly average of 30 trains with about 1,000 workers each have been leaving France for the Reich. This is another proof of the fact that France is taking an active part in the construction of the new Europe."

250,000 from Belgium

Belgium supplied the Nazis with 200,000 workers in January, and this was increased by 50,000 in February, Berlin said. Additional Belgian workers will go to France for farm labor. Labor camps have been established in Luxembourg to train farm workers.

Holland has supplied 200,000 workers for Germany, the Axis radio declared. Berlin mentioned Lithuanians and Esthonians working in Germany, but did not give numbers.

Immigrants from Poland and the Balkans who came to France before the war are being conscripted by the Nazis for labor in Germany. The clandestine "European Revolution" station said that Russian peasants from occupied territories are being shipped by the thousands to Germany in freight cars.

Work where you like—if you don't want to eat

German citizens enjoy freedom of employment—if they do not mind going without food. The Berlin radio said Germans would be told where to work and the penalty for refusal was withdrawal of food rations. Berlin asserted, "A labor dictator, so to speak, has been appointed," as it explained the new labor decrees.

Japan admits year's preparation for attack on Pearl Harbor

Admission by Japan that she had been secretly preparing for the attack on Pearl Harbor as much as a year in advance was contained April 6 in an official Japanese broadcast recorded by the FCC and reported by the Office of Facts and Figures.

Trained and studied secretly

Praising the members of a suicide squad who lost their lives in the attack, the Tokyo commentator declared:

"When I heard of the special unit that took part in the demolition of Pearl Harbor, my head bowed unconsciously. They were youths of Japan, at the height of blooming manhood. They had voluntarily trained and studied secretly for a long year, during which time no one was ever aware of their secret plans."

MIXED SIGNALS DEPARTMENT

In a propaganda broadcast to the United States, a Japanese commentator said, "Japan would be glad to share the riches of Asia with the Western nations."

In a broadcast in Japanese for domestic consumption, Radio Tokyo said, "The most important task is the expulsion from East Asia of Britain and America. The outbreak of the Greater East Asia War may be said to be the beginning of the fight to put an end to Britain and America."

The broadcasts were recorded by the FCC and reported by the Office of Facts and Figures.

U. S. war output exceeds 1932 rate of all physical production, spending shows

Preliminary figures for the month of March indicate that the total war effort of the United States in March exceeded 3 billion dollars, WPB announced last week. Of this total, more than 2½ billion represents munitions and war construction as distinct from pay and subsistence. Thus the United States today is producing war goods at a rate of not less than 30 billion dollars a year.

Threefold over March 1941

In March of 1941 less than 1 billion dollars' worth of war expenditures and value of production was put in place, indicating a more than threefold increase over the past year.

At the low point of the depression of 1932 the total national income of the country was forty billion dollars. Of this amount, about two-thirds represented tangible or physical production and one-third represented services. In March of this year the comparable output of physical production for war purposes alone exceeded an annual rate of 30 billion as compared with approximately 25 billions of net physical output in 1932. Prices are higher now than in 1932, but even taking into account the price increase it is probable that at present the United States' contribution to the war effort in physical commodities and construction is greater than the total physical output of the Nation in 1932. Reflecting the increasing production

effort, the daily rate of Government spending for war purposes in March jumped more than 15 percent to $114,-900,000, compared with $99,600,000 in February.

This was 73 percent greater than the daily expenditure rate in November, the month before the attack on Pearl Harbor, and almost four times the rate of a year earlier.

Contracts and other commitments in February amounted to $20,892,000,000, compared with $8,414,000,000 in January, $5,132,000 in December, and $1,782,-000,000 in November.

Commitments embrace contracts, letters of intent, and other obligations incurred by the United States Government for war purposes, including expenditures for the pay, subsistence, and travel of the armed forces during the month. Between June 1940, and the end of February 1942, such commitments reached a total of $81,835,000,000.

BOX MEETING POSTPONED

The joint industry meeting of folding carton and set-up box manufacturers with OPA officials, originally scheduled for Friday, April 10, has been postponed to April 24, Administrator Henderson announced April 8.

WAR EFFORT INDICES

MANPOWER

National labor force, Mar.	54,000,000
Unemployed, Mar.	3,600,000
Nonagricultural workers, Feb.	39,842,000
Percent increase since June 1940	11
Farm employment, Mar. 1, 1942	8,940,000
Percent decrease since June 1940	25

FINANCE *(In millions of dollars)*

Authorized program June 1940-Mar. 31, 1942	‡136,894
Ordnance	32,417
Airplanes	26,802
Misc. munitions	17,789
Naval ships	15,223
Industrial facilities	13,898
Merchant ships	7,550
Posts, depots, etc.	7,078
Stock pile, food exports	5,791
Pay, subsistence, travel for the armed forces	4,181
Housing	1,392
Miscellaneous	4,823
Total expenditures, June 1940-Mar. 31, 1942	*22,860
Federal Debt outstanding under statutory limitation as of March 31, 1942	63,748

PRODUCTION *(In millions of dollars)*

June 1940 to latest reporting date	
Paid on contracts, Feb. 28	*16,200
Gov. commitments for plant expansion; 1,060 projects, Feb. 28	9,281
Private commitments for plant expansion; 6,237 projects, Feb. 28	1,978

EARNINGS, HOURS, AND COST OF LIVING

		Percent increase from June 1940
Manufacturing industries— January		
Average weekly earnings	$35.10	36.1
Average hours worked per week	41.5	10.7
Average hourly earnings	80.1¢	19.2
Cost of Living, Feb. (1935-39=100)	*Index* 112.6	12.0

* Preliminary.
‡ Preliminary and excludes authorizations in Naval Supply Act for fiscal year 1943.

OFFICE FOR EMERGENCY MANAGEMENT

WAYNE COY, *Liaison Officer*

CENTRAL ADMINISTRATIVE SERVICES: Dallas Dort, *Director.*

DEFENSE COMMUNICATIONS BOARD: James Lawrence Fly, *Chairman.*

INFORMATION DIVISION: Robert W. Horton, *Director.*

NATIONAL WAR LABOR BOARD: Wm. H. Davis, *Chairman.*

OFFICE OF SCIENTIFIC RESEARCH AND DEVELOPMENT: Dr. Vannevar Bush, *Director.*

OFFICE OF CIVILIAN DEFENSE: James M. Landis, *Director.*

OFFICE OF THE COORDINATOR OF INTER-AMERICAN AFFAIRS: Nelson Rockefeller, *Coordinator.*

OFFICE OF DEFENSE HEALTH AND WELFARE SERVICES: Paul V. McNutt, *Director.*

OFFICE OF DEFENSE TRANSPORTATION: Joseph B. Eastman, *Director.*

OFFICE OF FACTS AND FIGURES: Archibald MacLeish, *Director.*

OFFICE OF LEND-LEASE ADMINISTRATION: E. R. Stettinius, Jr., *Administrator.*

OFFICE OF PRICE ADMINISTRATION: Leon Henderson, *Administrator.*

    CONSUMER DIVISION: Dexter M. Keezer, *Assistant Administrator*, in charge. Dan A. West, *Director.*

OFFICE OF ALIEN PROPERTY CUSTODIAN: Leo T. Crowley, *Custodian.*

WAR RELOCATION AUTHORITY: Milton Eisenhower, *Director.*

WAR SHIPPING ADMINISTRATION: Rear Admiral Emory S. Land, U. S. N. (Retired), *Administrator.*

WAR PRODUCTION BOARD:
    Donald M. Nelson, *Chairman.*
    Henry L. Stimson.
    Frank W. Knox.
    Jesse H. Jones.
    William S. Knudsen.
    Sidney Hillman.
    Leon Henderson.
    Henry A. Wallace.
    Harry L. Hopkins.

WAR PRODUCTION BOARD DIVISIONS:
    Donald M. Nelson, *Chairman.*
        Executive Secretary, G. Lyle Belsley.
    PLANNING COMMITTEE: Robert R. Nathan, *Chairman.*
    PURCHASES DIVISION: Houlder Hudgins, *Acting Director.*
    PRODUCTION DIVISION: W. H. Harrison, *Director.*
    MATERIALS DIVISION: Wm. L. Batt, *Director.*
    DIVISION OF INDUSTRY OPERATIONS: J. S. Knowlson, *Director.*
    LABOR DIVISION: Sidney Hillman, *Director.*
    CIVILIAN SUPPLY DIVISION: Leon Henderson, *Director.*
    OFFICE OF PROGRESS REPORTS: Stacy May, *Director.*
    REQUIREMENTS COMMITTEE: Wm. L. Batt, *Chairman.*
    STATISTICS DIVISION: Stacy May, *Director.*
    INFORMATION DIVISION: Robert W. Horton, *Director.*
    LEGAL DIVISION: John Lord O'Brian, *General Counsel.*

VICTORY

OFFICIAL WEEKLY BULLETIN OF THE AGENCIES IN THE OFFICE FOR EMERGENCY MANAGEMENT

WASHINGTON, D. C. APRIL 21, 1942 VOLUME 3, NUMBER 16

The "INFLATIONARY GAP" In our 1942 Individual Incomes

31 BILLION DOLLARS — personal taxes and savings

EACH DISC EQUALS 10 BILLIONS OF $ $

21 BILLION DOLLARS — THIS SURPLUS

65 BILLION DOLLARS IN TERMS OF 1941 PRICES — available supply of consumers' goods and services

If not controlled and absorbed in further savings and taxes, will be converted into price increases resulting in further INFLATION

117 BILLION DOLLARS TOTAL INDIVIDUAL INCOMES

ESTIMATED DATA FROM OPA

President creates Manpower Commission within OEM, with McNutt at head

A War Manpower Commission within the Office for Emergency Management, with Federal Security Administrator Paul V. McNutt as chairman, was created by Executive order of President Roosevelt April 18.

WPB division reorganized

The new agency takes over the labor supply and training functions of the War Production Board's Labor Division, which—according to a White House announcement—will be reorganized into a Labor Production Division reporting to WPB Chairman Nelson. This division, as well as various other agencies including the Selective Service System, the Civil Service Commission, the Office of Defense Transportation, and the Department of Agriculture, are made subject within certain limits to the policies and directives of the War Manpower Commission.

An excerpt from the Executive order, outlining the composition and duties of the War Manpower Commission, follows:

The commission shall consist of the Federal Security Administrator as chairman, and a representative of each of the following departments and agencies: The Department of War, the Department of the Navy, the Department of Agriculture, the Department of Labor, the War Production Board, the Labor Production Division of the War Production Board, the Selective Service System, and the United States Civil Service Commission.

The chairman, after consultation with the members of the commission, shall:

A. Formulate plans and programs and establish basic national policies to assure the most effective mobilization and maximum utilization of the Nation's manpower in the prosecution of the war; and issue such policy and operating directives as may be necessary thereto.

B. Estimate the requirements of manpower for industry; review all other estimates of needs for military, agricultural, and civilian manpower; and direct the several departments and agencies of the Government as to the proper allocation of available manpower.

C. Determine basic policies for, and take such other steps as are necessary to coordinate, the collection and compilation of labor market data by Federal departments and agencies.

To formulate legislative programs

D. Establish policies and prescribe regulations governing all Federal programs relating to the recruitment, vocational training, and placement of workers to meet the needs of industry and agriculture.

E. Prescribe basic policies governing the filling of the Federal Government's requirements for manpower, excluding those of the military and naval forces, and issue such operating directives as may be necessary thereto.

F. Formulate legislative programs designed to facilitate the most effective mobilization and utilization of the manpower of the country, and, with the approval of the President, recommend such legislation as may be necessary for this purpose.

Review of the Week

Manpower—without which the guns won't shoot, the machines won't run, the food won't grow—has become the responsibility of a new 9-member commission, headed by Federal Security Administrator Paul V. McNutt. The War Manpower Commission, created within the Office for Emergency Management last week by Executive order, numbers among its broad functions the formulation of plans and proposing of legislation for the most effective use of men. Various agencies must conform to the policies and directives the commission lays down in the performance of its duties. These agencies include the Selective Service System and the Civil Service Commission, within certain limits, and a Labor Production Division which—according to White House announcement—will be formed by a reorganization of the War Production Board's Labor Division. The labor supply and training functions of the WPB Labor Division are transferred, by the Executive order, to the War Manpower Commission.

Rising prices continue to threaten

Officials of the Office of Price Administration were warning, meanwhile, that the gap between expected income and expected goods and services purchasable with that income threatens us with rapidly rising prices and a loss of the battle against the high cost of living. To save small mine operators from possible ruin, OPA removed its requirement of seasonal discounts for sales of hard coal at the mines. At the same time, however, OPA moved to foil wholesalers of pork who tried to get around the ceiling. Some had posted artificially high prices in the period on which the ceiling was based, so that they might continue to charge those prices if they chose. OPA changed the base period, taking an earlier one.

OPA revealed that the initial ration of sugar for individuals will be 1 pound for 2 weeks. Distribution of forms was begun for registration April 28 and 29 of some 2,000,000 retailers, wholesalers, and industrial and institutional users of sugar. A booklet of instructions for officials of the household sugar rationing, which will take place May 4, 5, 6, and 7, also was released.

The War Production Board, in the meantime, went ahead with its drastic restrictions to save machines and materials for the war effort. WPB ordered an end to the manufacture of oil burners and coal stokers for residential use, May 31; to the production of medium and heavy trucks for civilian use after existing quotas have been completed; to the production for civilians of 349 of the 710 types of radio tubes. A reduction was ordered in the amounts of iron and steel for warm-air furnaces. On June 1, manufacture of cast iron soil pipe will be limited to a single weight.

Other restrictions

A limitation on shellac cuts its use for phonograph records to 30 percent of the 1941 figure. Natural resins are under a conservation order. Rhodium is banned from jewelry because it is needed for searchlight reflectors. Heavy compressors, urgently necessary for war production, were put under complete allocation, and plumbing and heating equipment was frozen except for orders with high ratings. The insecticide rotenone was forbidden for some purposes.

Manufacturers were ordered to stop immediately putting any wool into process for floor coverings and drapery and upholstery fabrics, except for Army, Navy and Maritime Commission orders.

Benefiting by new or higher priority ratings were mines; makers of mining equipment; steel producers; and manufacturers of farm machinery.

500 plants report on war drive

To head off a threatened shortage of refrigerator cars, Transportation Director Eastman ordered that they be used for perishable products only.

The Office of Price Administration was active in other fields besides pork and coal. Other subjects of its attention were copper and copper scrap; refrigerators; linoleum; paraffin wax; southern pine lumber; wood pulp; newsprint, and hide glue.

War Production Drive headquarters revealed that with the report of the Douglas Aircraft Company, 500 war contractors now have announced their organization for the campaign.

We have passed Axis output but must overcome reserve to win the war, says Nelson

Speaking to the American Society of Newspaper Editors in New York April 17, Donald M. Nelson, WPA Chairman, declared:

. . . We are over the hump on war production. Today the combined production of America, Russia, and England undoubtedly is greater than the combined Axis production.

That does not mean that we are going to win the war next month, or that we can start out tomorrow to take the offensive, of course. Japan began piling up armaments as far back as 1930; Germany started in 1933. Each nation built up an enormous reserve of arms and munitions, to which has been added the booty seized in conquered countries.

So it is not enough merely to top their current production; we also have to overcome that accumulated reserve, which means that we must go on increasing our effort as rapidly as we can. But I believe it is safe to predict that by the end of the year we will have overcome that reserve and will from then on have our enemies at an increasing disadvantage. . . .

Wood pulp ceilings

Maximum prices at which the various grades of domestic and foreign wood-pulp, basic raw material used in the production of paper, can be sold in the United States or for export are established in Maximum Price Regulation No. 114 (Woodpulp), issued April 16 by Price Administrator Henderson. The regulation, effective April 20, replaces prices which producers at the OPA's request, have maintained since July 1, 1940.

Supplanting current pricing systems, such as the "on dock Atlantic Seaboard" method, which caused certain price inequities, the regulation establishes a single price system with freight allowances based on geographic location of the producing mill.

With respect to the price level, an increase is effected only in the price of groundwood pulp

VICTORY

OFFICIAL BULLETIN of the Office for Emergency Management. Published weekly by the Division of Information, Office for Emergency Management, and printed at the United States Government Printing Office, Washington, D. C.

Subscription rates by mail: 75¢ for 52 issues; 25¢ for 13 issues; single copies 5¢, payable in advance. Remit money order payable directly to the Superintendent of Documents, Government Printing Office, Washington, D. C.

On the Home Front

All of us here on the Home Front are engaged in building a future and the future we are building is a future in which the Axis oppressors will get what is coming to them.

Last week we had a foretaste of that future. Last week our bombers roared up to the Philippines out of Australia and the Japs got a preview of things to come, of things to come when we have translated the fat of peace into the lean sinews of war.

"Fighting men gave double value"

The fighting men who flew those bombers gave us double value for every ounce of material, every moment of labor, every small bit of sacrifice, which entered into their making.

Which proves again what has been demonstrated before—that the key to victory is here at home, that victory depends upon our ability to get tough with ourselves.

Stream of civilian goods now a trickle

We are making rapid progress at that and it is fortunate, because this is no time to move slowly. The great stream of civilian goods has dried to a damp trickle. We have dammed that stream, and altered its course. Now in increasing flood it races along the deep channel of war production, carrying with it materials and machines and men.

Last week saw such diverse products as household furnace stokers and phonograph records swept into the current, to emerge as vital parts of the more and more and yet more weapons we must provide.

Less shellac for rug-cutting

The purpose behind the WPB order which halts manufacture of oil burners and coal stokers for residential use is an obvious one, to save iron and steel for guns and ships. But there's something pretty fascinating in the reasons which moved WPB to issue an edict which will cut by 70 percent our output of phonograph records.

WPB's order which will cut America's quota of dance band platters and radio transcriptions is one of those little things—like the fact that we can't spare resin any more to put that slick finish on playing cards—which remind us that we are engaged in a war which must enlist almost every material as well as almost every man and woman if we are to win. We need such reminders.

And fewer rugs to cut

The reason why we'll only have 30 percent as many new phonograph records as we used to have is that you need shellac to make records and almost all our shellac comes from India. That's where we get most of our jute, too, and because we're not going to be able to

REPRINTING PERMISSIBLE

Requests have been received for permission to reprint "On the Home Front" in whole or in part. This column, like all other material in VICTORY, may be reprinted without special permission. If excerpts are used, the editors ask only that they be taken in such a way that their original meaning is preserved.

spare jute any more there'll be fewer rugs and carpets.

We must save our jute for camouflage and for sandbags, among other things.

Two ounces of shellac = one signal flare

We are saving shellac because every time an officer fires a signal flare into the Pacific night from his Very pistol he is using up shellac; because shellac protects our ammunition nesting against the day when it whistles into the lines of our enemies; because shellac cements the jeweled bearings of the navigational instruments which keep our swift cruisers on course.

We are saving shellac because it binds the abrasives used on the grinding wheels of our war industry, goes into the making of our military explosives and pyrotechnics, coats the wooden patterns for the metal castings which become weapons, may be used to preserve the hulls of dauntless torpedo craft and other vessels of war.

A 10-inch phonograph record contains about 2 ounces of shellac.

And 2 ounces of shellac is just about the amount that goes into the manufacture of one signal flare, or Very light.

The transportation situation grows increasingly complicated and OPA which recently warned that people who don't order coal this spring may not be able to get it next autumn, now urges everyone on the Eastern Seaboard or in the Pacific Northwest who is using oil heat to convert to coal, if possible.

The railroads are suffering from a serious shortage of manpower and railway leaders met in Washington last week with Office of Defense Transportation officials to discuss this problem . . . Motor transport of war workers is another problem which grows more serious as tires wear thin. . . . Pooling the use of private autos is one way of lessening this problem, there may be prospect of a solution in the big bus which ambled into Washington last week from Indiana . . . It will carry 141 passengers.

Consumer sugar registration May 4–7

WPB, for obvious reasons, has forbidden manufacture of blowout shoes . . . To prevent existing plumbing and heating supplies from being dissipated on projects not related to the war, WPB has frozen stocks . . . Retail sales amounting to $5 or less, however, will be permitted . . . With sugar rationing no further away than the beginning of next month—May 4, 5, 6 and 7 are the days set for consumer registration—instruction books are being sent out to guide the 1,250,000 elementary school teachers who will act as volunteer registrars . . .

"The Home Front delivers"

The drive to save iron and steel has caught up with the game of golf . . . After May 31 iron or steel may not be used to make golf clubs . . . Golfers, however, won't feel the effect of this until next year—this year's production is almost completed . . . Lots of things are going to be different next year . . . They must be . . . More machines and more work in our industrial Midwest—the skilled labor soon will be released for war men and machines which have been busy turning out our final complement of trucks . . . WPB's Bureau of Industrial Conservation has announced that the drive to salvage old paper has been so successful that paper mills now are able to meet most current orders . . . Which proves that when the Home Front knows what is expected of it, the Home Front delivers.

The rubber shortage has hit the fire houses . . . WPB has prohibited use of rubber tires on new auxiliary trailers for fire apparatus . . . The Office of Price Administration has refused to allow linoleum manufacturers to raise prices . . . And OPA continues to fight to keep down the high cost of living, to keep prices stable . . .

PRICE ADMINISTRATION . . .

Gap between incomes and goods available creates serious situation, says Ginsburg

The dangers of a situation in which the Nation's individuals have billions of dollars more to buy goods than there are goods to buy was described by David Ginsburg, OPA General Counsel, April 13. In his address before the War Conference of Controllers in New York City, he also called attention to the fact that the Price Control Act gives the Administrator discretion as to whether he shall put ceilings over individual commodities or a ceiling over all commodities.

Excerpts:

The reason we're all troubled about inflation is that as a Nation we have more money to spend than we have consumer goods to buy. We've either got to reduce or immobilize a substantial portion of the Nation's spendable income, or increase the supply of consumer goods. And we can't do the latter because we're arming the forces of the United Nations.

Wholesale prices up .31 percent

Last year we had 74 billion dollars left to spend after personal taxes and savings were deducted from our individual incomes. At the same time we had just about an equal amount of consumer goods and services available to be bought. We came through the year with some price increases, but on the whole we did pretty well. This year, if income payments continue at their present accelerated rate, and even if the present proposed tax program is enacted, we figure that after deducting personal taxes and savings, spendable incomes will be increased from 74 billion to 86 billion dollars. At the same time the supply of consumer goods and services, we estimate, will fall from 74 billion to 69 billion dollars at current prices. This leaves a menacing inflationary gap of about 17 billion dollars. (Note: Mr. Ginsburg is speaking in terms of current prices, whereas the chart on page 1 is drawn in terms of 1941 prices.) That's probably more than any Government price controller can handle. Seventeen billion dollars bidding for a short supply of goods in a tight market will get around any price control and any rationing schemes that any government can devise.

Since the outbreak of the war in September 1939, a period of about thirty months, prices of basic raw materials have increased 66 percent, wholesale prices 31 percent, and retail prices at least 25 percent. Today I imagine retail prices have just about caught up with wholesale increases. But the significant fact is that half of the raw material price increase, two-thirds of the wholesale, and three-fourths of the retail price increase have taken place during the past twelve months. It's the accelerating rate of increase that's most frightening.

Each 1 percent equals a billion

The last war cost this country 31 billion dollars. Of this, 13½ billion dollars represented not ships and guns but inflated prices. The rise of prices since September 1939 has already increased the prospective cost of this war by more than the total cost of the last war. If the present rise in prices were permitted to continue, it would add at least 50 billion dollars to the cost of the war by the end of 1943.

Assuming a national income of about 100 billion dollars, each 1 percent we keep the price level from rising yields a profit to the Nation of a billion dollars.

As most of you are aware, the price control contemplated by the legislation (Emergency Price Control Act of 1942) is control over the maximum prices of all articles, products and materials, whether raw materials, foodstuffs or finished products, and whether at the manufacturers', wholesalers' or retailers' level. This authority extends over imports and exports and over sales and purchases by the United States and the States.

The Administrator may take action whenever in his judgment the price or prices of a commodity or commodities have risen or threaten to rise to an extent or in a manner inconsistent with the purposes of the Act. The Administrator, therefore, has discretion either to establish maximum prices for particular commodities or groups of commodities in furtherance of a policy of selective price control, or if it should prove necessary, to establish a ceiling over prices for all or a number of commodities at one time.

OPA abandons seasonal discounts for anthracite at mine, to save small producers

To save the small producers of anthracite from operating at a loss through a period when the Government is calling for an unusually high level of production, Price Administrator Henderson on April 16 amended Maximum Price Regulation No. 112 (Pennsylvania Anthracite) to eliminate the requirement for seasonal discounts in sales at the mines. The amendment is effective as of April 16, 1942.

At the same time OPA refused industry requests for a 25-cent-per-ton price increase for domestic and pea sizes over the maximum prices established in the price regulation.

It was contended by members of the industry that in 1941 the industry earned little more than 1 percent on its claimed invested capital. It was maintained that the spring loss under discount requirements would be too great to be offset by profits later in the year, because of the Government call for heavy production in the earlier months of the year.

OPA disapproves coal price increase for Akron

Fourteen retail coal dealers in Akron, Ohio, have been informed by OPA that they have not furnished justification for any increase in retail coal prices above those prevailing during the period December 15–31, 1941.

★ ★

Company allowed premium

A premium charge of 25 cents per ton for certain high quality anthracite produced and marketed by Jeddo Highland Coal Co. of Jeddo, Pa., is permitted in Amendment No. 2 to Maximum Price Regulation No. 112 (Pennsylvania Anthracite), announced April 14 by OPA Administrator Henderson. The amendment was effective April 15, 1942.

The premium applies to the price at the mine and affects domestic and pea sizes and two of three steam sizes, with no premium permitted on Barley (No. 3 Buckwheat) steam size.

Cartoon by Elderman for OEM. Two-column mats available for publication, on request to Distribution Section, Division of Information, Washington, D. C.

Financing plan for abnormal sugar movements under way

A self-sustaining plan to finance abnormal movements of both beet and cane sugar, necessitated by the war, is being worked out by the OPA in cooperation with processors and refiners, Harold B. Rowe, chief of the food rationing section of the OPA rationing division, announced April 17. Details of the program will be presented at a later date.

Officials of Defense Supplies Corporation, the Department of Agriculture and WPB were present at conferences held in Washington, D. C., with the country's beet refiners April 16 and cane refiners and offshore distributors April 17.

A definitive program, designed to facilitate payment of freight charges for the movement of sugar to places in need of supplies but out of the normal selling areas, was presented to the trade for their ideas and suggestions, at the request of WPB.

Pending working out of the program, OPA has sent a telegram to all refiners and primary distributors of sugar in this country, requesting them to limit their sales to "immediate shipment" terms. An "immediate shipment" is defined by OPA as sugar shipped within 3 days of the order's date.

OPA hangs pork prices on Feb. 16–20 to foil sellers who overquoted in old base period

To offset the advantage gained by certain sellers, who made unwarranted price advantages in anticipation of OPA's regulation setting maximum prices for dressed hogs and wholesale pork cuts, Price Administrator Henderson on April 15 made a sweeping revision.

Amendment No. 6 to Temporary Maximum Price Regulation No. 8 requires all sellers to compute their maximum prices by reference to their price list quotations and highest sales of the period February 16–20, 1942, plus certain additions which are expressly stated in the amendment. These additions are based upon the actual rise in prices of raw materials from this period to March 3–7, 1942. The new amendment became effective April 20.

Principal purpose of the new amendment is to remove great inequalities among sellers caused by the fact that some merchandisers took advantage of advance and—in several instances—confidential information by establishing artificially high ceilings for themselves. They accomplished this by arbitrarily raising prices quoted in their lists during the periods February 23–28, 1942, and March 3–7, 1942, and by making a small number of sales at the quoted prices during this time.

"The new price basis," Mr. Henderson declared, "will not increase the cost of pork products to the ultimate consumer, and, possibly, may effect a slight decrease."

Following are the specified additions which may be made to the seller's highest listed prices or actual sales made during the period February 16–20, 1942:

Regular hams fresh or frozen, ½¢; regular hams boned and rolled, ¾¢; regular hams cured ½¢; regular hams smoked, ¾¢; regular hams boiled, 1¢; regular hams baked, 1¼¢; picnics fresh or frozen, 1¢; picnics cured, 1¢; picnics smoked, 1¼¢; picnics boned and rolled, 1½¢; shoulders fresh or frozen, 1¢; shoulders cured, 1¢; shoulders smoked, 1¼¢ shoulders boned and rolled, 1½¢; regular pork loins fresh or frozen, 2¢; boneless pork loins, 3¢.

Skinned hams fresh or frozen, 1¢; skinned hams boned and rolled, 1½¢; skinned hams cured, 1¢; skinned hams smoked, 1¼¢; skinned hams boiled, 1¾¢; skinned hams baked, 2¢; Boston butts fresh or frozen, 1¼¢; bellies fresh or frozen, ¾¢; bellies dry cured, ¾¢; bellies dry salt cured, 1½¢; bellies sweet pickle cured, ¾¢; bellies dry salt cured and smoked, 1¾¢; smoked slab bacon, 1¢; Canadian bacon, 4¢; Canadian sliced bacon, 4¢; sliced bacon, 1¼¢.

Canned or packaged spiced luncheon meat made entirely from pork, 1½¢; fat backs fresh or frozen, ⅝¢; fat backs cured, ⅝¢; spare ribs fresh or frozen, ½¢; canned or packaged spiced ham, 1½¢.

DSC or designees allowed to raise price on several grades of sugar in 10 States

Price Administrator Henderson April 12 gave Defense Supplies Corporation—or its designees—permission to advance the selling price to $5.60 per hundred pounds on several grades of offshore refined sugar and domestic refined beet sugar in 10 specified Northeastern States.

To relieve tight supply situation

The broad permission, contained in Order No. 1 under Revised Price Schedule No. 60 (Direct-Consumption Sugars), is designed for the twin purpose of relieving the current tight North Atlantic States' supply situation and partially reimbursing DSC for the additional freight expenses in moving sugar there from outlying areas. It became effective April 13, 1942.

The permission granted by the order is conditioned on payment of a difference between the maximum basis prices permitted for each type under the schedule and the $5.60 figure to DSC reimbursing that agency for part of the additional freight expenses incurred.

The section providing that DSC may apply for approval to sell direct-consumption sugars at higher than the maximum ceilings was contained in Amendment No. 1 to Revised Price Schedule No. 60, issued March 30.

The section was inserted to help DSC recoup extra freight charges, where sugars must be shipped to abnormal territories for the particular sugars involved or in an unusual combination of transportation facilities.

States in which such $5.60 sales may be made are: Maine, New Hampshire, Vermont, Massachusetts, Rhode Island, Connecticut, New York, New Jersey, Pennsylvania, and Delaware.

Types of sugar and basis for sales

Following are the types of sugar, and the basis which DSC or its designees now may sell at, in the 10 named States:

1. Fine granulated beet sugar manufactured in the continental United States—$5.60 per 100 pounds, f. o. b. United States seaboard cane sugar refinery nearest freightwise to point of delivery.
2. Fine granulated sugar from offshore areas, domestic (such as Puerto Rico) or foreign—$5.60 per 100 pounds duty paid basis f. o. b. United States seaboard cane sugar refinery nearest freightwise to point of delivery.
3. Turbinado, washed-white or similar sugar for direct consumption, from offshore areas, domestic or foreign—$5.60 per 100 pounds duty paid basis f. o. b. United States seaboard cane sugar refinery nearest freightwise to point of delivery.
4. The balance of approximately 861,991 bags of 100 pounds each of fine granulated sugar purchased by DSC from The Coca-Cola Co., by agreement made February 19, 1942—$5.60 per 100 pounds f. o. b. United States seaboard cane sugar refinery nearest freightwise to point of delivery.

"The $5.60 price permitted to be paid for these offshore sugars and domestic refined beet sugar," the administrator explained, "merely matches the new ceiling price permitted for sales of refined cane sugar processed in four of the ten Northeastern States named in the current order. Therefore, it should not result in any increase in retail prices to the consumer."

★ ★ ★

OPA grants three of six pleas

Six orders replying to trade petitions for exception or amendment of Revised Price Schedule No. 49—Resale of Iron or Steel Products—were issued April 11 by Price Administrator Henderson.

Order No. 1: Jacobs & Gile, Inc., Portland, Ore., was denied a petition requesting that its price on a particular gage of galvanized sheet be raised $5 per ton.

Order No. 2: A petition for amendment filed by H. Schultz & Sons, Newark, N. J., was dismissed. The request for permission to raise prices on merchant wire products had already been granted through provisions of Amendment No. 2 which does away with the inadequate spread between the cost and the sale price for these products.

Order No. 3: The American Near East Corporation, New York City, was granted partial exception to the schedule on sales and deliveries of specified kinds, grades, and quantities of steel to designated buyers in the Near East.

Order No. 4: Trans-Atlantic Export Corporation, New York City, is denied a request for an addition to the margin permitted it as an exporter in order to compensate an agent in South Africa who participated in the transaction.

Order No. 5: The Simons Iron and Metal Co., Newark, N. J., is granted a petition permitting it to sell specified kinds, grades, and quantities of steel products at prices approximating the cost of these items.

Order No. 6: A partial exception is granted to American Steel Export Co., New York City, permitting it to sell a specified inventory of iron and steel products for export at cost.

Southern pine lumber schedule tightened

A tightening up of Revised Price Schedule No. 19 for Southern Pine Lumber, to halt some evasion practices and to codify interpretations issued in the past, is accomplished in Amendment No. 1 to the schedule, announced April 16 by OPA Administrator Henderson. The amendment became effective April 21, 1942.

The amendment does these things:

1. Clarifies the point that wholesalers' discounts were taken into account in computing maximum prices;
2. Prohibits the sale at a single flat price of any lot consisting of lumber subject to the schedule and lumber not subject to price control;
3. Prohibits elimination or reduction of cash discounts in effect before issuance of the price schedule;
4. Prohibits the buying of lumber at random lengths and its reselling on a specified length basis;
5. Refuses permission for charges made for workings, specifications, services or other extras not specifically provided for in the schedule.

Manufacturers' request to raise linoleum prices refused by OPA

Declaring that "increased costs of production are not alone sufficient grounds for authorizing a price increase," the OPA announced April 14 that it had refused to allow linoleum manufacturers to raise prices as an offset to higher freight rates.

Piece goods ceiling not to be pushed up by "escalator"

Sellers of finished piece goods made of cotton, rayon or their mixtures subject to Temporary Maximum Price Regulation No. 10 may not rely on "escalator" clauses to increase their prices above the maximum levels established by that regulation, Price Administrator Henderson made clear April 16.

Ceilings set for makers' sales of new domestic refrigerators on A–10 or higher rating

Maximum prices at which manufacturers may sell new domestic refrigerators directly to persons assigned a preference rating of A–10 or higher by the WPB are established in Amendment No. 1 to Revised Price Schedule No. 102, issued April 11 by Price Administrator Henderson. The amendment became effective April 16. .

Revised Price Schedule No. 102 (Household Mechanical Refrigerators) established maximum prices for sales of domestic mechanical refrigerators by manufacturers to distributors and dealers.

Supplies of domestic mechanical refrigerators in the hands of manufacturers, distributors and dealers, on February 14, 1942, were "frozen" by WPB's supplementary general limitation order L–5–b. Since then the order has been amended so that sales could be made to meet the needs of the Army, Navy, Maritime Commission, Panama Canal Zone, defense projects or defense housing projects with an A–10 preference rating or higher. The amendment was drawn to cover these sales, since the sales covered by the original schedule from manufacturer to dealer and distributor are no longer permitted by WPB.

The base price established in the amendment is the same as the base price to distributors fixed in the schedule, but to this the manufacturer may add the actual amount of the excise tax, and the actual charges for servicing when special services are requested by the purchaser.

However, allowances for cooperative advertising must be deducted as cooperative advertising will not enter into sales permitted by WPB.

The amendment allows the manufacturer to add a 2 percent charge of the base price in shipment of less-than-carload lots.

If the refrigerators were ready for delivery on February 14, 1942, an amount equal to 1 percent of the base price for each month, or fraction of each month, which elapses between February 1942 and the date of sale may be added, to cover the "freeze" costs such as storing, financing, insuring and handling. If the unit was not ready for delivery February 14, the allowable amount shall be 1 percent of the base price for each month which elapses between the date the refrigerator was ready for delivery and the date of sale.

"SLIDING-SCALE" COTTON COVERAGE BROADENED

"Sliding-scale" tables of OPA maximum price schedules for cotton yarns and textiles are extended to brackets that take in a 22-cent 10-market "spot" cotton price, and specific margins for print-cloth bed linens are provided in amendments to five cotton yarn and textile schedules issued April 9 by Price Administrator Henderson.

Rise in average price of spot cotton

As these schedules stood, the tables which set forth the sliding scales of yarn and textile maximum prices as they relate to the 10-market average price of "spot" cotton covered a range of cotton prices from approximately 16 cents up to 20 cents per pound. Recently the average price of spot cotton has risen above 20 cents, thus, in effect, "running off the page" for pricing purposes. The cotton-price range covered by the sliding scales is now extended to take in 22-cent cotton and to list appropriate price ceilings for yarns and textiles.

The price schedules affected are: No. 7—Combed Cotton Yarns; No. 11—Fine Cotton Grey Goods; No. 33—Carded Cotton yarns; No. 35—Carded Grey and Colored-Yarn Cotton Goods; and No. 89—Bed Linens.

For Bed Linens, an amendment also provides specific margins which may be added to the price of print-cloth in determining applicable maximum prices for print-cloth bed linens. Such margins are based on price lists of manufacturers of print-cloth bed linens in effect from October 1 to October 15, 1941.

Hide glue prices changed to aid rail shipment to East

The hide glue revised price schedule was amended by OPA April 15 to encourage rail shipments of the product from the West Coast to the Eastern Seaboard.

Amendment No. 2 to Revised Price Schedule No. 76 makes this provision on transportation charges:

"Regardless of any other provision of this Revised Price Schedule No. 76, there may be added to the maximum prices set forth in this section the amount of transportation charges in excess of 75 cents per hundredweight."

The amendment b e c a m e effective April 18.

Paraffin wax ceilings may be revised to cover higher packaging

The additional cost of shipping paraffin wax in cotton bags (above the cost of burlap bags customarily used when Revised Price Schedule No. 42 for paraffin wax was issued on November 21, 1941) may be added to maximum prices, according to an interpretation of the price schedule issued April 13 by OPA.

The interpretation was outlined in a letter to a member of the paraffin wax industry who had pointed out the additional packaging costs which followed the virtual stoppage of burlap shipments from India due to the war.

Under Revised Price Schedule No. 42, maximum prices for various grades of paraffin wax were established for shipments in tank cars, barrels, and bags. Another section of the schedule provided for maximum prices when shipments were in "other containers."

In its response to the industry query, OPA explained that the term "bags" as used in the schedule referred to burlap bags. The maximum prices for such wax sold in cotton bags, the letter said, are determined under paragraph (e) in section 1335.460 appendix A of the price schedule.

Paragraph (e) permits the addition to maximum prices of "a reasonable charge for additional costs, if any, of the containers" if containers other than those specified in the schedule are used. It is required, however, that such additional charges shall be shown as separate items on all records and invoices.

Gasoline cost, tax, plus 3 cents gives total price

Certain retail gasoline dealers in the East were told by the Office of Price Administration April 15 how to compute the 3-cents-per-gallon margin permitted them under Amendment No. 2 to Temporary Price Regulation No. 11.

The regulation and its amendments apply only to the curtailment area—17 Eastern States and the District of Columbia, and Oregon, and Washington.

Amendment No. 2 applies only to retailers who have been operating on a margin of less than 3 cents per gallon.

The explanation declares that only the price paid by the retailer to his supplier, and the tax, may be considered in fixing a base upon which to impose a 3-cents-per-gallon margin. All other charges which are not for gasoline must be excluded.

Charges for rent, for payments on account, and other such charges are not permitted in computing the cost to which the 3-cent margin may be added.

RATIONING . . .

OPA sends forms for sugar registration, April 28-29, of wholesalers, retailers, institutional and industrial users

Two forms which will be filled out and filed by nearly 1,000,000 institutional and industrial users of sugar, and one form by more than 1,000,000 retailers and wholesalers, when registering on April 28-29 under the Nation-wide sugar rationing program, have been released by the Office of Price Administration.

Asked to fill out blanks in advance

Distribution of the forms began at once, and it is expected that copies will be available through the local rationing boards several days before the registration, which will take place in high schools in each locality.

The registration form to be used by wholesalers and retailers is officially designated as OPA Form No. R-305.

Industrial and institutional users of sugar will fill out two forms. One form, officially designated as OPA Form R-310, is designed for the registration of such users of sugar and for recording all information about past usage of sugar, stocks on hand and other information. The other form, OPA R-314, is for making application for sugar purchase certificates authorizing the acceptance of delivery of sugar. Registrants will be able to obtain sugar as soon as certificates are issued, OPA pointed out, and there will be no interruption in shipments.

Registrars and trade rationing advisers will be available at the high schools on the registration dates to assist those who need help in filling out their blanks. However, instructions about their use are attached to the blanks which should be filled out in advance whenever possible, OPA officials emphasize. Registrants will then only need to appear at the local registration sites on one of the registration days for the purpose of signing and filing their registration blanks. Each registration must be signed in the presence of the registrar.

Why registration is necessary

The registration of retailers and wholesalers is necessary in order to make possible the adjustment of sugar stocks so that each establishment will have an equal opportunity to serve its customers under the rationing plan. This adjustment is accomplished by computing from information called for by the form an "allowable inventory" which is intended to approximate a reasonable working stock for the business.

Registration of institutional and industrial users of sugar is necessary in order to obtain the information necessary for

---

FIRST SUGAR RATIONS: 1 POUND FOR 2 WEEKS

According to the OPA official instructions in War Ration Book One, each of the first four stamps will be good for one pound of sugar. Each of these four stamps covers two weeks' ration for one person.

---

determining the amount of sugar which each registrant is entitled to receive under the rationing regulation.

PROCEDURE FOR RETAILERS AND WHOLESALERS

If the "allowable inventory" exceeds the inventory on hand at the time of registration, sugar purchase certificates will be issued authorizing the registrant to accept delivery of sugar to make up the difference. On the other hand, if the "allowable inventory" is smaller than the inventory already on hand, the registrant will be required to surrender stamps or certificates obtained through the sale of sugar to the amount of the difference before additional deliveries may be accepted.

Basis for replenishing stocks

After the rationing program is in operation, both retailers and wholesalers will replenish their stocks on the basis of rationing stamps and certificates received from their customers. From the time rationing begins, no further sales of sugar will be permitted except on the basis of these stamps and certificates.

All applicants for sugar, whether wholesalers or retailers, may obtain their permitted quota in more than one certificate, but not in more than four, for any one month. This is to enable the registrants to purchase sugar in such quantities as they are normally accustomed to obtain deliveries.

On the registration form the applicant enters his "registering unit," its location, name of the owner and his address. He then fills out either the information required for retailers or that required for wholesalers.

Determination of quantity allowed

In both cases the amount of sugar to which the "registering unit" will be entitled through a certificate will depend on the volume of his business during a specific period in the past, and his present sugar inventory.

In the case of retail registering units, this volume will be determined on the basis of either his gross sales of "all meats, groceries, fruits, and vegetables, etc.", for the week ending April 25, 1942, or of the weekly average of sugar delivered to and accepted by him during last November. In the gross sales method of computation the unit will be allowed 1 pound of sugar for each dollar of his gross sales, but this amount will be used only if it is less than his weekly average of sugar deliveries in November. Whichever figure is smaller will be noted as the unit's "allowable inventory." From this amount is to be deducted the number of pounds of sugar the owner has on hand for sale, and a certificate for sugar purchase will be issued for the difference.

Registrants are expected to state the quantity of sugar delivered to and accepted by them during the month of November 1941, OPA officials point out, and only when such information is unobtainable will permission be given to use the alternative computation.

"Allowable inventories" for wholesalers

Wholesalers use the same form as retail dealers of sugar, but they fill out a different set of items in computing their "allowable inventories."

In the case of wholesalers, after stating the number of months in 1941 during which the registering unit made deliveries of sugar, they are required to state the customary unit by which they normally took deliveries on or about December 1, 1941. If a wholesaler, for example, customarily bought three carloads of sugar at a time, the amount to be entered is the weight of one carload, not the total quantity.

The purpose of this provision is to enable wholesalers to continue to operate in the manner in which they have been accustomed, since some prefer to take shipment in large quantities while others, operating on a quick turn-over basis, normally take shipment in smaller quantities.

The registrant must next state the quantity of sugar delivered to and accepted by the registering unit during 1941, and this quantity is to be divided by twice the number of months during which the registering unit made deliveries in 1941. For example, if a total of 400,000 pounds of sugar was delivered to the registering unit in 1940–41 and it operated for 10 months, the amount to be entered will be 20,000 pounds. The allowable inventory will then be obtained by adding the customary shipping unit of the registrant to the quantity obtained in the previous computation.

Should apply only for actual needs

The amount of sugar for which a certificate may be issued to wholesalers will be determined by subtracting the number of pounds of sugar now owned by the registering unit for sale from his allowable inventory.

Registrants do not need to apply for certificates to purchase the whole amount of sugar to which they are entitled, it is pointed out.

PROCEDURE FOR INDUSTRIAL AND INSTITUTIONAL USERS

Certificates authorizing users of sugar to accept delivery of the product will be issued to industrial and institutional users on the basis of the information furnished in the registration and application forms. It is pointed out that all applicants may obtain their permitted quota in more than one certificate up to a reasonable number.

This flexibility, OPA officials explained, has been made to enable registrants to purchase sugar in such quantities as they were normally accustomed to obtain deliveries.

The amount of sugar to which institutional and industrial users are entitled will be determined in two different ways. First, some users will obtain sugar in proportion to their estimated production. Others will receive allotments based on the amount used last year.

Some may obtain "provisional allowance"

Registrants requiring sugar for canning fruits, vegetables, or juices, for freezing fruits, for curing or canning meats, fish, or poultry, and for feeding bees, are required to limit the amount of sugar used per case or other unit of their production, but are not restricted as to the volume they can produce. Industrial users in this category may obtain a "provisional allowance" of sugar equal to the amount they will require in carrying on their business in conformity with the schedule of the regulations which specifies the amount of sugar that may be used for each unit of product. Registrants who receive such allowances are required to report later the

2½ million pamphlets on registration for sugar rationing en route to county clerks

Half a million copies of a pamphlet giving detailed official information and instructions for all those who will be engaged in conducting the trade registration in connection with sugar rationing and two million copies of a pamphlet on registration for individual rationing have been printed and are now being distributed throughout the country, the Office of Price Administration announced April 16.

Trade registration, which includes wholesalers and retailers of sugar, as well as all industrial and institutional users, will take place in high schools on April 28 and 29. Consumer registration will take place in elementary schools on May 4, 5, 6 and 7, and will be carried out by the 1,250,000 elementary school teachers

in the country and by other volunteers under the supervision of "school site administrators."

The first-mentioned 30-page book of instructions, officially called "The Plan for Trade Registration," is being sent to county clerks. The custodian, who will usually be the local county clerk, will make available copies of the booklet and all other documents in connection with trade registration to the local rationing boards for distribution to the registration sites.

The second book of instructions, officially called "The Plan for Distributing War Ration Book One," 56 pages, is being sent to the county courts, from where it will be distributed to the public elementary schools and placed in the hands of registrars.

---

actual volume of each product produced to show that their use was in accordance with the authorization.

Those registrants who use sugar either for meals or for food services, or as an ingredient in a manufactured product may obtain an allotment computed on the basis of the quantity used during the corresponding period of last year, and a percentage quota to be announced later by the Office of Price Administration.

Allotments for several purposes

Allotments will be made for the following purposes:

Meals or food services; (b) bread; (c) other bakery products; (d) cereal products, batters, and mixes; (e) confectionery, candy, chocolate, chewing gum and cocoa; (f) ice cream, ices, sherbets, and frozen custards; (g) other dairy products, condensed milk, cheese, etc.; (h) preserves, jam, jellies, and fruit butter; (j) production of bottled beverages, flavoring extracts, and syrups; (k) specialties, such as desserts, puddings, drink mixes, pickles, table syrups, mincemeat, catsup, chili sauce, salad dressing, soups, and tomato sauces; (l) nonfood products, such as drugs and medicines, soaps, tobacco, insecticides, and leather; and (m) all other industrial uses of sugar not previously specified.

Sugar for these purposes will be allotted under the rationing scheme on the basis of information with regard to the amount of sugar used in 1941 that will be furnished in the registration form. The quantity used during the corresponding period last year will be multiplied by the percentage allotment established by the OPA, which will determine the amount of sugar to which the applicant will be entitled.

The exact percentage that will be allowed to various types of industrial users

will be announced before the registration dates.

In the case of sugar for meals or food services, registrants will have the option of entering under each month of 1941 either the quantity used in March 1942 or figures of the amount of sugar actually used during each month of last year.

"Registering unit" flexible

When registering on April 28 and 29, the owner or authorized agent must state on the registration form his "registering unit," its location, and the name and address of the owner, the type of business in which the unit is engaged, and the date of commencement of operations (if subsequent to January 1, 1941), the number of pounds of sugar now in the possession of the "registering unit," and the amount of sugar used during each month in 1941, as well as the purposes for which the sugar was used.

If a person owns but one industrial or institutional establishment which uses sugar in its operations, that establishment is the "registering unit." If a person owns two or more such establishments the "registering unit" is the establishment or group of establishments selected by the owner to be treated as a single unit for the purposes of the Sugar Rationing Regulations.

Flexibility in the definition of "registering unit" was provided, OPA officials explained, in order that an owner might continue to operate his business under rationing with the same organizational setup he had been operating under previously.

Clothes won't change much, but for your information, this is how you'll look

The average civilian in wartime will bear no resemblance whatever to the pitiably clothed figure pictured in some recent cartoons, according to the Consumer Division of the Office of Price Administration. He will encounter changes in style and fabric, and reductions in the range of selection to which he has been accustomed, but on the whole there will be no noticeable difference in the appearance of his clothes. He will continue to dress warmly and well.

This is how the average man will look when manufacturers begin to turn out wartime styles in quantity, probably by next fall. Some stores already are carrying men's wear embodying certain of these changes:

SUITS AND OVERCOATS

He will wear conservatively cut suits and coats made of softer but serviceable fabrics, woven from larger quantities of reused or reprocessed wool, cotton, and rayon mixtures. His worsteds will be made of a crossweave of rayon or cotton, and mixed fibers also will be used in his gabardines and covert cloths. His overcoat will be as warm as it ever was and probably fashioned out of reused or reprocessed wool, mohair or other fleecy fabrics, in contrast to the hard, smooth fabrics.

His suits, minus trouser cuffs, pleats, tucks, gussets, and all the other fancy details, won't seem very different to him from those he wore before the war. Nor will shorter and slimmer overcoats affect his appearance to any marked extent.

He will have cotton gabardines, seersuckers and other warm weather materials in satisfactory quantities and will find their use a saving on his heavier garments.

SHIRTS

His dyed shirts will tend to be lighter in color, but shirts will be among the last to feel the chlorine shortage. Sheets, pillowcases and underwear of unbleached cotton will appear long before white shirts take on a yellowish tinge. He will have fewer patterns from which to choose, but enough to satisfy anyone but a professional Beau Brummel. He will find pleated, fancy shirts a rarity, but the popular styles will remain on the market. Only the most expensive varieties of shirt fabrics are likely to go out of stock. Those that remain will be serviceable, but qualities equivalent to those of peacetime are already higher priced

The same trends apply to pajamas, shorts, handkerchiefs and other items of men's wear, commonly made of cotton, rayon, and their mixtures. Existing price ceilings on finished piece goods employing these fabrics will aid in regulating retail prices on men's clothing. Consumers are advised to shop around for the best buys in the makes they have found satisfactory in the past.

SOCKS

The average man's socks may be of cotton or rayon, instead of wool or silk, and he will select them from a narrower range of colors and patterns.

HATS

His hat may be the fur felt he has worn before, but fur and wool felt mixtures probably will be more common. During the summer he may sport one of the up-and-coming straw substitutes, visca, cellophane, or celtafal. Chances are he'll want a panama from Ecuador, still available in the higher price brackets. He'll certainly want to have his old straw renovated for continued use.

SHOES

His shoes will be conservative in style and will not show off the thick soles, expensive leathers and color varieties of peacetime. Because the upper part of his footgear will outlast the soles by a longer period, he will walk to his office or factory more frequently in shoes renovated to look just like new.

Wing tips, one-piece uppers, woven leather uppers and heavy brogues requiring double soles will probably not be made. Curtailments will be felt in general among those shoe patterns that cause a waste of leather in cutting from the hide.

With the Government needing a large percentage of top-grade sole leathers, the long-range result will be lighter, plainer shoes. Colors may be limited to black, Yankee brown, natural brown, tan and light tan. Everyday shoes will look very much like current conservative styles, but heavy sports shoes will be rare and those using rubber or crepe soles nonexistent. As the law stands now, only reclaimed rubber may be used for rubber heels, and the supply for this purpose has been cut in half.

GLOVES

The average man's gloves also will show the effects of Army demand for good leathers. Gloves employing less leather, more fabric weaves, knitted rayon and cotton mixtures, will keep his hands warm in winter.

In general, these changes are coming because of the need for materials and looms to weave fabrics for the armed forces. Wool and leather stocks are curtailed further by the sharp drop in shipments from Australia and South America. Fur for felts formerly came from countries in the war area; straw from the Far East. Two examples demonstrate how rapidly the war is using up supplies: A civilian uses about 9 pounds of raw wool a year; a soldier needs 162 pounds. A civilian's shoes last a year and longer with proper repair; a soldier on combat duty can go through a pair in 10 days.

41,000 new autos released by rationing boards; liberalizing change prepared

Approximately 41,000 new passenger automobiles had been released by local rationing boards throughout the country by the end of March, figures compiled by OPA indicate.

Of the total, 23,952 consisted of cars purchased, but not delivered, before 6 p. m., January 1, 1942.

In the 33 States for which figures are available, the rationing boards acted favorably on 72 percent of the applications received.

Commenting on the first month of automobile rationing Rolf Nugent, chief of the OPA automobile rationing section, said:

"The slow movement of passenger automobiles under the Rationing Order has frequently been blamed upon local rationing boards. This is highly unfair. These boards, the members of which serve without pay as a contribution to the war effort, have done a remarkable job in the face of great handicaps and they are entitled to the thanks of everyone. It was their duty to adhere strictly to the provisions of the rationing order and if these provisions are too strict, it is the responsibility of Washington and not of the local rationing boards to liberalize them. Now that it is clear that the movement of passenger automobiles is slower than had been intended, an amendment designed to liberalize the order is being prepared."

Two convicted on criminal charge arising from rationing program

The first criminal indictments arising out of the tire rationing program have resulted in a plea of guilty on the part of the LaSalle Motor Sales Corporation of Boonville, Ind., the Office of Price Administration announced April 13.

Convicted on all eight counts of the indictment were Charles L. Hart, president, and Russell W. Baker, secretary and treasurer.

The defendants, appearing in the United States District Court of Judge Robert C. Baltzell, of Evansville, Ind., admitted falsifying a report submitted to the Government concerning the number of tires and tubes on hand on December 12, 1941, the date following the tire "freeze" order which was issued 4 days after the bombing of Pearl Harbor.

Hart and Baker also admitted storing a substantial stock of new tires and tubes belonging to the LaSalle Motor Sales Corporation in Hart's residence in Boonville, as well as falsifying an invoice and a promissory note for $1,400 covering a large number of tires removed to the Boonville Mills on January 15. Both note and invoice, it was admitted, were falsely dated, as was a floor stocks tax return filed with the Bureau of Internal Revenue on October 1 of last year.

· · ·

Rubber tires banned on auxiliary trailers for fire apparatus

Because of the critical shortage of rubber, the WPB April 14 prohibited the use of rubber tires on auxiliary trailers for fire apparatus manufactured or delivered after that day.

The order (Amendment 1 to General Limitation Order L–43) also corrects typographical errors in Appendix A of the order.

The fire equipment section said that steel-rimmed wheels will be satisfactory for use on the auxiliary trailer units during the emergency.

It was also announced that Preference Rating Orders P–45 and P–108 covering material entering into production of motorized fire apparatus and fire protective equipment have been extended until June 30.

The orders would have expired on April 18.

Typewriter rationing delayed to April 20; more persons eligible

Postponement of the date for rationing typewriters from April 13 to April 20 was announced April 12 by the OPA in an amendment to the rationing order that also broadens the eligibility base for purchase of new and used machines.

Pending distribution of forms

The amendment (No. 1 to Revised Rationing Order No. 4) also provides a procedure for release of specially built typewriters from manufacturers, and shifted the deadline for filing manufacturers', wholesalers', and dealers' inventory reports from April 6 to April 13.

The date announced in the Revised Rationing Order for releasing typewriters for sale or purchase under rationing was postponed in order to relieve confusion in congested areas, which had not received supplies of application forms and certificates for rationing.

The amendment announced April 12 enlarges the groups of persons eligible to receive new, or used, nonportable typewriters upon presentation of a rationing certificate to include manufacturers of parts and materials essential to the making of specified war products, providing such parts and materials are actually used for the manufacture of the specified war products and constitute 70 percent or more of the manufacturer's production. It is also required that these parts and materials be made or processed under a priority rating of A–1–d, or higher, from the War Production Board.

Other provisions

Under the amendment, portables may be sold to, or purchased by, any plant, project or facility operating under a War Production Board priority rating of A–3 or higher; or under a priority rating of A–3 or higher for 60 percent of its combined billings and accepted, but unbilled, orders during the 3-month period preceding the month in which the application is filed; or under a priority rating of A–3 or higher granted for 60 percent or more of its production requirements upon the last previous rating by the WPB under its Production Requirements Plan.

Any special typewriter ordered from a manufacturer prior to March 6, 1942, when all typewriter stocks were "frozen," may be delivered subject to certain provisions as soon as such typewriters are allocated by the War Production Board to the Office of Price Administration.

The section of the Revised Rationing Order on the restriction of sales and deliveries of typewriters was clarified by the stipulation that no manufacturer, wholesaler, or dealer shall transfer to his use any typewriter from his stock carried for resale, or rental, except in accordance with provisions of the order. Manufacturers, wholesalers, and dealers in typewriters are eligible to receive new typewriters without application "for the purpose of permissible resale or other permissible transfers," as was provided in the original order.

★ ★ ★

Private plants controlled by Government can get new typewriters only by rationing

WPB on April 13 issued an interpretation of its typewriter industry conversion order to clear up the status of privately operated plants or shipyards controlled by the Army, Navy or other Government agencies engaged in financing output of war supplies.

Under this interpretation (No. 2) of Conversion Order L–54–a, WPB will not make new standard or portable typewriters available to private plants or shipyards financed by or controlled by Government agencies involved in procuring war material.

Privately operated plants or shipyards covered by the interpretation can obtain new typewriters only through the rationing system set up by the OPA.

The interpretation applies to plants or shipyards privately operated on a cost-plus-fixed-fee basis, as well as to those privately operated and financed or controlled by the Army or Navy, the Defense Plant Corporation, the Maritime Commission, or any other Government agency engaged in financing or sponsoring production of war supplies.

★ ★ ★

Box meeting postponed again

The joint industry meeting of folding carton and set-up box manufacturers with OPA officials, which was recently rescheduled for April 24 in New York, has been indefinitely postponed, Administrator Henderson announced April 15. It is expected that the meeting will be held early in May.

INDUSTRIAL OPERATIONS . . .

WPB stops manufacture of oil burners and coal stokers for residential use

WPB on April 15 ordered an end to the manufacture of oil burners and coal stokers for residential use after May 31, and limited the production of commercial and industrial types to orders bearing a preference rating of A–10 or better.

These actions, supplementing a recent cut in furnace production, were embodied in Limitation Orders L–74 (oil burners) and L–75 (coal stokers), both effective on April 15, 1942.

92,000 tons of iron and steel saved

The orders are expected to save large amounts of ferrous material and considerable quantities of other critical materials which would have been required for the manufacture of the necessary automatic controls and fractional horsepower motors. According to officials of the plumbing and heating branch, the stoker order will result in the saving of about 80,000 tons of iron and steel, and 142,000 sets of the controls and small horsepower motors.

Similarly, the oil burner order will enable producers of war goods to use 12,000 tons of iron and steel, and material for 211,000 sets of controls and motors which would otherwise have been wasted in nonessential articles.

The orders segregate burners and stokers according to capacity. The larger ones in each case are those commonly used for industrial purposes, while the smaller ones normally are residential types.

Order L–74 defines a "Class A oil burner" as any which has a capacity for burning oil at a rate in excess of 15 gallons per hour. A "Class B oil burner" is any with a lesser maximum capacity.

Order L–75 defines a "Class A coal stoker" as any which has a capacity for feeding coal at a rate in excess of 60 pounds per hour. A "Class B coal stoker" is any with a lesser maximum capacity.

Limitations outlined

The terms of both orders establish these limitations:

1. Beginning April 15, no person shall produce, fabricate, or assemble any Class A oil burner or coal stoker except to fill an order with an A–10 or higher rating.

2. For the period April 1 to May 31, fabrication or assembly of Class B oil burners or stokers must not exceed $\frac{1}{12}$ of the production of these types during 1941.

3. After May 31, 1942, no person shall produce, fabricate, or assemble any Class B oil burner or coal stoker.

The manufacture of replacement parts for all types of burners and stokers is specifically permitted by the two orders.

Rapid conversion expected

Officials revealed that manufacturers have inventories of approximately 35,000 coal stokers and about 60,000 oil burners. It is expected that an additional 30,000 stokers will be fabricated before May 31, while about 60,000 additional oil burners are now in the process of fabrication.

Production of coal stokers in 1941 amounted to approximately 200,000 units, compared with 150,000 units in 1940. Oil burner production totaled 320,000 units in 1941, against 265,000 units during the previous year.

Conversion of the oil burner industry to production of essential war goods has already made considerable progress and the order announced April 15 is expected to expedite conversion programs for the entire industry. A rapid conversion of the coal stoker industry is also expected to result from the curtailment order.

WPB denies great demand for small wood boat facilities

Requirements for small wooden boats are insufficient to use all the shipyards capable of producing them, the contract distribution branch of the WPB said April 13.

The Maritime Commission buys steel life boats for new merchant vessels, it was pointed out, and wooden boat requirements of the Navy and the United Nations are not large enough to engage existing facilities at anything like capacity.

The statement was occasioned by erroneous reports that facilities to make small wooden boats were in great demand.

WPB cuts iron and steel for warm-air furnaces

WPB has ordered a reduction in the amounts of iron and steel which may be consumed in the manufacture of warm-air furnaces.

The order (L–22) was effective on April 11, and covers all warm-air furnaces designed to heat the interior of a building, except those commonly known as space heaters or floor furnaces.

The terms of the order limit larger manufacturers to the use during 1942 of 50 percent of the iron and steel consumed in 1940. Smaller manufacturers, or those who made or assembled fewer than 8,000 furnaces in 1940, are required to reduce iron and steel consumption 10 percent.

It is estimated by the WPB plumbing and heating branch that the regulations will result in the saving of approximately 100,000 tons of iron and steel, and reduce the consumption of the industry to about 200,000 tons. This is the amount of iron and steel calculated to be needed for the manufacture of furnaces for military, wartime housing, and essential civilian replacement purposes.

Expected to produce war goods

Officials said that the restrictions would mean a 50-percent cut in the production of furnaces available for civilian replacements. If furnace users take proper care of existing equipment, it was added, there will be an ample supply of new furnaces for the minimum civilian requirements.

The curtailment is expected to speed the conversion of the larger manufacturers to the production of urgently needed war goods. Difficult problems, however, are expected to arise in the conversion of smaller manufacturers whose facilities are not readily adaptable to uses other than those for which they were originally designed.

★ ★ ★

Rough diamond report date postponed to April 30

Because of delay in printing necessary forms, the filing date for reports on rough diamonds required by Order M–109 has been postponed from April 15 to April 30, the Director of Industry Operations announced April 14.

Change back to coal heat, householders in East and Northwest are warned

Home owners in Atlantic Coast States, and in Washington and Oregon were warned April 15 to change back from oil to coal heating by Dan A. West, director of the Consumer Division, OPA.

"Because of oil transportation difficulties, householders in these areas who have coal furnaces and boilers which have been converted to oil should change to coal at once by reinstalling the grates," Mr. West said.

Transfer of some tankers to war service and loss of some others through enemy action caused the War Production Board to issue a curtailment order through the Office of Petroleum Coordinator on March 14 limiting consumption of fuel oil used for industrial and commercial purposes and for house heating and water heating.

Mr. West issued these suggestions:

1. Home owners in these States who have coal boilers and furnaces which have been converted to oil, and for which grates are on hand or available from manufacturers, should install grates now. In addition, they should order their coal for next heating season now.
2. Householders in these States who up to now have planned to use any type of oil heating equipment next winter, including oil-fired "space heaters" and parlor stoves, should consider switching to stoves which will be fired by wood, coal, or coke.
3. Where possible, water heating equipment fired by wood, coal, or coke should be used in place of water heating equipment fired by kerosene or fuel oil.
4. Home owners who continue to use fuel oil or kerosene for house heating and water heating, in the affected States, should make especially intensive efforts to avoid wasting fuel.

Indications are that as the war continues there may be need for additional steps to curtail the consumption of petroleum products in the Pacific Northwestern and the Atlantic Coast States.

★ ★

WPB prohibits blowout shoes, restricts making of reliners

WPB on April 11 amended Rubber Order M-15-b to prohibit the manufacture of blowout shoes, regarded as an uneconomical form of tire repair, and to restrict the manufacture of reliners, many of which are being used to repair tires on nonessential vehicles.

It was also announced that the amounts of reclaimed rubber which may be consumed in the manufacture of reliners will be authorized directly by the Director of Industry Operations after April 30.

Construction industry, converted to war, faces largest program in Nation's history

Converted almost entirely to military and other essential construction, the construction industry faces this year the largest building program in the Nation's history, the War Production Board announced April 16.

Latest estimate of the volume of military and civilian construction such as airfields, war plants, camps, shipyards, and war housing scheduled for this year is $13,750,000,000—more than a 20 percent increase over the figure for total construction in 1941 when an all-time record was set.

Nonessential building halted

Nonessential civilian construction, which had been declining sharply since the fall of last year, was virtually brought to a halt April 9 when Conservation Order L-41 became effective. This order places all civilian construction, whether publicly or privately financed, under rigid control. Except in certain limited categories, no construction will be permitted unless authorized by WPB.

It is estimated that construction of the type controlled by L-41 amounted to approximately $4,000,000,000 during 1941. When the order became effective, the volume of this type of construction already had been cut in half and was estimated to be going at a rate of only $2,000,000,000 a year.

Further reductions, under the order, are expected to keep the total of nonessential construction for the entire year to less than one-fourth of the 1941 amount.

250,000 laborers freed for war work

By shutting down nonessential building, approximately 250,000 laborers now engaged on projects of this type will be freed to work on essential programs. Total employment on all types of construction, including maintenance and repair, was estimated to be approximately 2,500,000 in February—the last monthly figure available.

In order to complete the huge program of military and essential construction, the volume must reach about $1,250,000,000 a month. This will need a labor force of approximately 3,000,000. With the 2,500,000 already at work on essential construction programs and the 250,000 to be freed from nonessential projects, there is need for approximately 250,000 addi-

tional employees to handle the anticipated volume.

Total construction last year amounted to nearly $11,500,000,000, of which nearly $7,500,000,000 was classed as essential—military and civilian—and nearly $4,000,000,000 as nonessential. It is estimated that the total construction for this year will be approximately $14,750,000,000 divided roughly into $13,800,000,000 essential and $900,000,000 nonessential.

Cast iron soil pipe limited to single weight June 1

Amendment of Schedule IV to Limitation Order L-42 to limit manufacture of cast iron soil pipe to a single weight was announced April 13 by the Director of Industry Operations.

The specifications ordered by the WPB are for a pipe slightly heavier than soil pipe known commercially as "standard," but lighter than pipe now classed as "medium." Effective June 1, only the new weight pipe may be produced.

This will also replace the current soil pipe simplification program, in effect since April 1.

The schedule, in limiting nonessential production of cast iron soil pipe, is expected to save about 80,000 tons of pig and cast scrap iron this year.

The new restrictions permit the production of fittings at weights heretofore known commercially as "standard" or "medium," but the use of brass for plugs and other parts of the fittings is prohibited.

WPB requires export boxes for Services' canned foods

WPB on April 14 amended Supplementary Order M-86-a, which requires canners to set aside certain percentages of their 1942 pack of canned foods for the armed forces. The amendment (No. 1) requires canners to provide themselves with the materials necessary to pack such canned goods adequately in export boxes. Such boxes may be nailed wooden boxes, weatherproof solid fiber boxes, or wirebound wood boxes.

Attached to the amendment are detailed specifications for the boxes.

Plumbing and heating stocks frozen except for $5 sales or ratings of A-10

In order to prevent the dissipation of existing plumbing and heating equipment stocks for nonwar building, modernization, or unnecessary replacements, WPB on April 16 froze all such stocks, except for retail sales of $5 or less, or for any sale on an A-10 or better preference rating.

The order (L–79) covers all new plumbing and heating equipment, including any equipment, fixture, fitting, pipe, or accessory of a type used in or connected to a water, sewer, or gas system; or any primary heating unit or accessory designed to provide building warmth.

Doesn't cover used items

The order does not cover used plumbing and heating equipment, or tools used for installation and repair, or hoses, sprinklers, and similar devices commonly attached to outdoor faucets.

In effect, the order prevents the sale or delivery by a dealer or any other person of furnaces, oil burners, coal stokers, and a wide range of other plumbing and heating equipment if the item is to be used for nonessential purposes.

The general restrictions of the freeze order prohibit the sale or delivery of new plumbing and heating equipment to any person, except that:

1. Retailers may sell or deliver items being sold for no more than $5.
2. Sale and delivery on orders bearing an A-10 or better preference rating is permitted.
3. Retailers may sell or deliver to other retailers, and to distributors, jobbers, wholesalers, or manufacturers of plumbing and heating equipment.
4. Distributors, jobbers and wholesalers may sell and deliver to any jobber, or to other wholesalers, distributors, or manufacturers.
5. Any new plumbing and heating equipment actually in transit on the date of issuance of the order may be delivered to its immediate destination.
6. Any person may sell to a purchaser who certifies that the item is necessary for the installation of specifically listed farm machinery and equipment.

Plumbing and heating branch officials said that certain classes of items will be released from the terms of the order if studies now being made show that some types of equipment cannot be directly used in the war effort.

All persons affected by the order are required to keep accurate records on inventories and sales for at least two years. Sellers are also required to keep the signed statements received in connection with sales to purchasers in the farm machinery and equipment field.

Electric pad inventories to be used if otherwise worthless, but all output stops June 30

The WPB April 16 amended the electric heating pad order (L–84) to permit manufacturers to use up inventories which cannot be used for other purposes, but to stop production entirely on June 30, 1942.

The original order restricted 1942 production of home-type electric heating pads to 50 percent of the number manufactured in 1940 and restricted production of hospital-type pads to 100 percent of the number produced in 1940.

If can't be used otherwise

The amendment No. 1 allows a manufacturer to use up inventory even though resultant production exceeds his original quota. It permits a manufacturer to use up in the production of electric heating pads any materials, including critical materials, which on April 4, 1942, were in his inventory and which had been cut, processed or fabricated to such an extent that they could not practically be used for any purpose other than heating pads.

However, all production of heating pads must stop on June 30, 1942, regardless of whether a manufacturer has used up his inventory by that time.

Uniforms, fire hose excluded from A–10 rating

Neither uniforms nor fire hose may be ordered with a preference rating assigned under the terms of the Repair, Maintenance, and Operating Supplies Order, P-100, it was explained April 16 in an official interpretation issued by the Director of Industry Operations

Production of medium, heavy trucks for civilians to stop when quotas are complete

The WPB April 12 ordered all production of medium and heavy trucks for civilian use discontinued after existing quotas have been completed.

Thus, another large segment of the automotive industry must convert its facilities to the output of war weapons. Production of passenger cars and light trucks was halted February 1.

The stop-production order, Supplementary General Limitation Order L–1–e, applies also to off-the-highway vehicles for civilian use.

Chief reason for the production ban is the shortage of rubber. No tires are available.

Trucks automatically frozen

Trucks produced between now and the time permitted for cleaning up present quotas will automatically be frozen under General Conservation Order M-100, which put into effect the truck rationing plan now being administered through the joint facilities of WPB and the Office of Defense Transportation.

Under Supplementary Limitation Order L-1-f, producers of medium trucks (weighing from 9,000 to 16,000 pounds) will have until April 30 to complete production quotas fixed for February.

Producers of heavy trucks (weighing 16,000 pounds or more) will have until May 31 to clean up amended March quotas. These trucks cannot be equipped by the manufacturer with tires, casings or tubes.

When production ceases, it is estimated that 97,070 medium and heavy trucks will have been produced for civilian use since January 1, as compared with an output of 88,085 medium and heavy trucks during the first 3 months of 1941.

Off-the-highway vehicles weighing 24,000 pounds or more produced under March quotas may be equipped with tires and tubes only if they are specially designed to transport materials or equipment on mining, construction, logging, or petroleum development projects.

An A–3 preference rating for materials going into the production of medium, heavy and off-the-highway trucks will continue to be made available under Limited Preference Rating Order P-54.

The stop-production order does not apply to output of truck trailers, bodies or passenger carrier buses of certain types.

Novelty firm penalized
for diversion of metals
from war effort

The Mills Novelty Co., Chicago, Ill., producers of "Panorams" and other coin-operated amusement. machines, is the first manufacturer to be penalized for wartime violation of priority orders, WPB announced April 14.

Suspension Order S-37 holds that in the period beginning December 22, 15 days after the attack upon Pearl Harbor, and ending February 7, the Mills Co. illegally diverted substantial amounts of aluminum, copper, steel, and other scarce materials from the war program.

The specific violations for which the company is penalized include the use of aluminum in the manufacture of "Panorams," coin-operated machines which show motion pictures accompanied by music. This was prohibited by the terms of Conservation Order L-21, issued on December 10, 1941.

In further disregard of the conservation order, the Mills Co. was said to have turned out 2,332 amusement and gaming machines in excess of its allotted quotas.

The suspension order announced April 14 enjoins the Mills Co. from selling or delivering any of the machines manufactured in excess of its quota, and further curtails the number of amusement machines which it may produce during the months of March and April.

Additional penalties imposed include refusal of all priority assistance and allocations of any restricted material until the expiration of the order on July 10.

Mines given A-1-c
rating for explosives

Use of a higher preference rating to obtain explosives and explosive equipment is granted to mining enterprises operating under Preference Rating Order P-56 by Amendment No. 5, issued April 14 by the Director of Industry Operations.

Under the order as originally issued, a preference rating of A-8 was assigned to deliveries of operating supplies, including explosives. The new amendment, which adds explosives and explosive equipment to the types of machinery and supplies listed in Schedule A of the order, will allow mining enterprises to use a rating of A-1-c to obtain them, subject to quota restrictions.

STEEL PRODUCERS GET A-1-C
ON 30 PERCENT OF SUPPLIES

Steel producers were granted on April 13 a higher preference rating for materials for maintenance and repair and may extend the higher rating to their suppliers, it was announced by Industry Operations Director Knowlson.

Amendment No. 3 to Preference Rating Order P-68 grants a rating of A-1-c to 30 percent of the dollar value of repair and maintenance materials and operating supplies ordered in any one quarter. An A-3 rating continues applicable to the remaining 70 percent.

Producers are required to file monthly reports on Form PD-228 with WPB showing applications of the A-1-c rating.

A-1-a ratings in case of actual breakdowns and A-1-c ratings to make reasonable advance provisions against break-downs are not changed.

Two more companies suspended
for diverting aluminum from war

Two more wartime violators of priority regulations governing use of critical materials are penalized in suspension orders announced April 15 by the WPB.

Suspension Order S-34 prohibits the Walleck Brass Co., Cleveland, Ohio, from fabricating or dealing in aluminum for a period of 4 months, and S-36 imposes the same restrictions for a period of 3 months on the Aluminum Bronze Powder Co., Bedford, Ohio.

Records in the case indicate that the Walleck Co., aluminum founders, during the periods from September 13 through October 13 and from December, 1941, through February, 1942, shipped aluminum for prohibited nonwar purposes, and accepted and processed unauthorized deliveries of aluminum scrap.

The Aluminum Bronze Powder Co., manufacturer of aluminum powder, was said to have made deliveries through December 1941, totalling 20,834 pounds of its product, on orders bearing no preference ratings. During the same period, the announcement added, it accepted unauthorized deliveries of 19,740 pounds of aluminum scrap.

These transactions by the two companies resulted in diversion from the war program of substantial quantities of the critically needed light metal.

The suspension orders provide that, until their expiration, the Walleck Brass Co. and the Aluminum Bronze Powder Co. shall not accept or make any deliveries of aluminum and that no preference ratings shall be assigned to any orders for materials placed by them.

In addition, the Aluminum Bronze Powder Co. is prohibited immediately from processing or fabricating any aluminum in its possession, while the Walleck Brass Co., after a 10-day grace period, must likewise cease all fabrication involving the use of aluminum.

Suspension order punishes
zipper company for failing
to report supply in plea

Talon, Inc., Meadville, Pa., world's largest manufacturers of "zippers," is the latest company to be subjected to a WPB suspension order.

Talon, Inc., was one of the first industries to base its appeal for scarce material on the fact that lack of it would throw its workers out of employment. The company appeared before OPM last summer with reports of the serious hardships which, it said, would develop in Meadville if supplies of copper were not immediately made available.

In filing its application for priority assistance, the company contended that serious unemployment faced its workers, but failed to reveal that there was available to it a sufficient supply of copper to maintain its output.

Rated for 350,000 pounds of alloy

Upon these representations, and to keep operations going, the OPM assigned preference ratings to deliveries to Talon of 350,000 pounds of alloy, 87½ percent copper and 12½ percent zinc, which it said it required to keep going.

Meadville had previously been certified as a distressed area on the strength of Talon's statements, and as a result had been awarded substantial contracts by the Army.

Talon, Inc., later made a second application for preference ratings on an equal amount of alloy. This application was denied by OPM, as by that time it had been established that the company had had on order (but not delivered) at the time of making its first application 3,000,000 pounds of imported copper, which was not at that time under priority control. This amount of control-free copper, if delivered to its suppliers of the alloy, would have filled Talon's total requirements and kept its employees at work, without depletion of the domestic supply of the critically needed metal.

Suspension Order S-33 prohibits Talon, Inc., until July 1, from using steel, zinc, or zinc-base alloys in the manufacture of slide fasteners in excess of 40 percent of the average quarterly poundage of all metals used for this purpose during the year ending June 30, 1941.

No deliveries of any materials to Talon, Inc., shall be assigned any preference ratings, and no allocations of any material under priority control shall be made to it during the life of the order, which is to expire on June 30, 1942.

First 500 war plants to launch production drives report progress on many fronts

The first 500 war plants in the United States to set up voluntary labor-management committees and launch War Production Drives, at the invitation of Donald M. Nelson, Chairman of the WPB, were listed April 17.

Workmen number millions

The 500th report accepted was from the labor-management committee of the Douglas Aircraft Company of California, where organization was completed several days ago.

No estimates were made of the number of American workmen officially enlisted in the Production Drive to meet the President's goal of 60,000 planes, 45,000 tanks, 20,000 antiaircraft guns, and 8,000,000 tons of shipping this year. Since there are more than 500,000 men in the plants of only three of the large corporations which have joined the drive, the total number runs into the millions.

The Douglas Aircraft report came from a joint meeting of labor-management committees in three plants of the company. Committee members included management representatives, draftsmen, welders, assemblers, planners, mechanics, sheet metal workers and toolmakers.

Drive had already begun

The Douglas committee reported that in addition to announcing a slogan contest, a contest was inaugurated for the naming of various Douglas products. The committee also reported that several elements of the War Production Drive were already in operation in its plants. In one plant, a total of 5,841 suggestions have been received and a total of 1,090 awards made. Effective April 1, the awards were increased 500 percent, the committee reported.

The report from the Crosley Corporation of Cincinnati related that the War Production Drive committee consisted of 12 management representatives and 12 labor representatives, drawn from every department and including women, a large number of whom is employed in the plant.

Program linked to sons at war

The most unusual feature of the Crosley report was a section devoted to a special 30-minute recorded program explaining to union employees and group meetings of everyone in the company, including stenographers, engineers, supervisors and labor and management representatives, the need of increased production.

The program linked the drama of the war with the need for more production, and the need for more production with the men in the Crosley plant. For instance, a father with a son on Bataan was called upon to tell what the plant would do for his comrades. Workers in the plant were freely mentioned by name.

In addition to bulletin boards, information stands and posters, the Crosley labor-management committee reported on production charts.

The labor-management committee of the A. O. Smith Corporation of Milwaukee reported organizing with eight men from labor and five men from management. The eight represented seven different unions. This committee also drafted a letter to former employees in the armed forces asking them for letters, within the limits of censorship, telling how things made in the plants are performing.

The 500 plants reporting produce almost every manner of war equipment in use today. The names of the companies more often serve to shield the type of their product than to identify it.

Every mail brings more reports. The 500 include only those plants whose reports have been received and processed in the Drive Headquarters, and which then have been formally posted as officially participating plants with joint labor-management committees.

He's a fighting fool give him the best you've got

MORE PRODUCTION

KEEP HIM FIRING * * * The poster reproduced here from the Supplement to the Production Drive Plan Book will go out shortly to war plants. Two-column mats are available to newspapers and other publications on request to Distribution Section, Division of Information, Office for Emergency Management, Washington, D. C.

LABOR . . .

Membership maintenance approved by 8-4 vote in Harvester dispute; 25,000 employees in 8 plants get wage increase

A maintenance of membership clause which must bear the approval of a majority of union members at a Government-conducted election was ordered by the National War Labor Board last week in a far-reaching decision settling the International Harvester Company dispute.

Also ordered was a 4½-cent an hour wage increase for 25,000 employees working in eight plants of the giant farm equipment concern, which is now doing war work, and a provision to prevent union representatives from losing pay during the time spent handling grievances within the plant. The unions had asked an increase of 12½ cents an hour. Both were unanimously approved.

To vote on membership clause

Under the maintenance of membership clause, which was approved by an 8 to 4 vote with the employer members dissenting, union members in good standing must remain in good standing as a condition of continued employment. This clause does not go into effect unless a majority of the union members vote in favor of it in a secret ballot election conducted by the Board.

Unions whose members will vote as soon as contracts are signed include the Farm Equipment Workers Organizing Committee, CIO, the United Automobile Workers, CIO, and two federal labor unions of the AFL. The decision marks the first time that a Government agency has agreed to hold an intra-union election.

Another high point in the decision was an anti-coercion clause binding the union not to coerce or intimidate employees into joining, and to discipline members who are guilty of coercion or intimidation.

Appeal for "industrial statesmanship".

Issuing an appeal for "industrial statesmanship devoid of selfish partisan or class-conscious motivation," Wayne L. Morse, public member of the Board who wrote the majority opinion in the case, pointed out that "This is a crisis hour about which historians will render judgments as to the quality of leadership which those responsible for the program of American labor and industry give to our country today.

"Great issues such as those involved in this case place upon the leaders of labor and industry and upon the representatives of the public solemn obligations and duties which they must not hesitate to perform," Morse wrote. . . . It is in such a spirit that the National War Labor Board calls upon the parties in this and in other cases as well as upon the American people, to accept its decrees.

"It is submitted," the majority opinion states, "that the foregoing union membership provision is eminently fair and reasonable in light of the facts and circumstances of this case as shown by the lengthy record. It would seem to be a foregone conclusion that industrial harmony with resulting maximum war production will be difficult to obtain in the International Harvester Company's plants unless the question of union maintenance is determined by the union membership itself.

Scope of union security plan

"The plan will dissipate much of the cause for ill-feeling and distrust which now exists between management and the union. It will place very definite responsibilities and obligations upon the union to keep its house in order. It will protect management from many of the abuses of which it now complains. If the majority of the members vote for this plan of union security, it will tend to eliminate rival union organization activities because it will 'freeze' membership of that union now possessing the collective bargaining rights for the life of the contract, thus making ineffective any attempted raids upon its membership. It will give the union effective disciplinary powers over any member who violates the terms of the contract or who is guilty of those abuses of which employers so frequently complain.

"When the majority has spoken . . ."

"One of the great cries of American employers and union critics generally in recent months has been for the adoption of safeguards, guaranteeing to the individual union member the right to a secret vote or referendum on union maintenance policies. This plan approves and adopts that principle. It provides that when the majority has spoken the minority must be bound by the majority. Such a procedure is democracy in action."

Asked to consider "minimum guarantees"

The majority opinion asked that the following "minimum guarantees" be considered by the Board in any wage issue "for the duration of the war."

"*First*, all workmen shall receive wages sufficiently high to enable them to maintain a standard of living compatible with health and decency.

"*Second*, the real wage levels which have been previously arrived at through the channels of collective bargaining and which do not impede maximum production of war materials shall be reasonably protected. This does not mean that labor can expect to receive throughout the war upward changes in its wage structure which will enable it to keep pace with upward changes in the cost of living.

"On the other hand, every attempt should be made to protect the real wages of labor to the point that they do not drop below a standard of living sufficient to maintain health and decency. Without doubt wages in substandard brackets should not only be increased to meet changes in cost of living, but whenever possible, they should be raised to the standard level.

"*Third*, to the extent that it can be done without inflationary effects, labor should be encouraged to negotiate through the processes of collective bargaining for fair and reasonable upward wage adjustments as an offset against increases in the cost of living. Labor should not be put in an economic strait jacket during the war without redress to some such agency as the War Labor Board which has authority to grant fair and deserved wage adjustments."

Four employer members dissent

In dissenting from the majority decision on union security, the four employer members of the Board stated that they were in favor of a maintenance of membership clause if the union members either individually signified their willingness to be bound or if individual members could resign from the union in 10 days if they did not want to be bound.

Phonograph records, radio transcriptions cut to 30 percent by limiting shellac as war moves across path of supply

The War Production Board on April 14 reduced the output of phonograph records and radio transcriptions to approximately 30 percent of 1941 production by limiting the amount of shellac available to that amount.

50 percent of large stocks frozen

Order M–106, issued April 14 by J. S. Knowlson, Director of Industry Operations, also freezes 50 percent of all inventories of shellac of 10,000 pounds or more and 50 percent of all future imports.

Uses other than the manufacture of recordings are restricted to 75 percent of the corresponding period of 1941 until June 30 and 35 percent by quarters thereafter.

India practically sole source

Reason for the drastic action is that India is practically our sole source of shellac and supplies are subject to shipping hazards. Direct military requirements are heavy and use of shellac is necessary in certain essential civilian processes.

These uses are excepted from the restrictions of the order:

Electrical equipment, coatings for munitions, military explosives and pyrotechnics, navigational and scientific instruments, communication instruments, marine paints for vessels other than pleasure craft, grinding wheels, wood patterns for metal castings, health supplies as defined in P–29, and in scientific research.

Records used one-third

Reason for the action on phonograph and transcription records is that these uses normally consume approximately one-third of the Nation's annual shellac consumption. Experiments now are being made to find a suitable substitute for these uses and reclaiming of old records probably will be tried out.

Persons who had on April 1 possession or control of five thousand pounds of shellac are required to file with the War Production Board by May 9 a report on Form PD–334.

Salable to Defense Supplies Corporation

Shellac is defined in the order as lac of all grades, but does not include lac which has been bleached, cut, or incorporated into protective or technical coatings.

Stocks frozen by the order may be sold to the Defense Supplies Corporation.

The order is effective immediately.

Use of natural resins restricted as supplies grow scarce

Natural resins which have been substituted in civilian use for the synthetic resins needed for war purposes, have also become scarce, so the WPB April 16, limited the use of natural resins.

Unfortunately, natural resins come only from such widely separated parts of the world as New Zealand, the Philippines, Batavia, Singapore, the East Indies, India, and Africa. None are found in this hemisphere.

This is accomplished by Conservation Order M–56, issued April 16 by J. S. Knowlson, Director of Industry Operations. In the main, it restricts the use of natural resins in any calendar quarter to 50 percent of the amount used in the corresponding quarter of 1941.

In the manufacture of rotogravure inks the restriction is to 75 percent of the amount used in the corresponding period.

Some uses banned entirely

Use of natural resins in barn paint, farm equipment finishes, floor finishes, freight car paints, interior house paints, pencil finishes, playing card finishes, porch and deck paints, road marking paints, spirit label varnishes and toy and novelty finishes is prohibited entirely. Asphaltic and pitch bases can be used for some of these products and pine rosin is adaptable to others. For the slick varnish finish on pencils and playing cards, however, no substitute is known.

The restrictions do not apply to Army, Navy, or Lend-Lease contracts; nor to use as a noncorrosive finish in chemical plants; in research laboratories; in vessels other than pleasure craft, or in health supplies.

Form PD–339 is provided for quarterly inventory reports.

The order applies to the manufacture of products containing natural resins and does not restrict the sale of paints or varnishes already manufactured. It became effective immediately.

Used electric generating equipment, steam boilers "frozen" for war use

Used electric generating equipment and used steam boilers were frozen April 11 by order of the WPB. This action was taken to promote efficient use of such equipment in the war effort, when it becomes available.

Dealers in such equipment have been notified by telegram that they may not sell, lease, or option used electric generating equipment or used steam boilers without specific authorization from the Director of Industry Operations. Order L–102 extends the prohibition to cover all persons with such equipment in their possession.

The order became effective at 11:59 p. m. April 11.

"Used electrical generating equipment" is defined in the order to mean any used or reconditioned stationary steam-turbine generator unit. "Used steam boiler" is defined as any used or reconditioned stationary steam generating boiler. Equipment which has an actual or market value of less than $1,000 per unit is exempt from the terms of the order.

Modified mine order extends deliveries of materials for machinery, equipment

Broader application of priority assistance for the production of mining machinery and equipment is provided by amendments to Preference Rating Order P–56–a issued April 13.

As originally announced on March 3, paragraph (b) (1) of the order permitted the assignment of ratings only for material to be delivered to operators as defined in Preference Rating Order P–56, the general mine order.

The April 13 amendments will permit companies using ratings assigned by P–56–a to make deliveries to South American copper companies operating under Preference Rating Order P–58, to iron and steel producers under P–68, to smelters under P–73.

Upon application, special permission may also be given by the Director of Industry Operations for deliveries of material obtained by use of ratings assigned under P–65–a to fill other rated orders.

Wool forbidden for carpets, drapery, upholstery

Manufacturers were ordered by the WPB April 17 to stop putting wool into process after 11:59 p. m. April 17 in the manufacture of floor coverings and drapery and upholstery fabrics except to fill Army, Navy, and Maritime Commission orders.

The April 17 action is in the form of an amendment (Amendment No. 4) to the Wool Conservation Order, M-73. It replaces the second quarter allocation of carpet wool provided for in the order.

Civilian production of laundry, dry cleaning equipment to stop

Commercial laundry and dry cleaning machinery were added April 18 to the list of durable goods for which civilian production is to end for the duration of the war.

Existing stocks frozen

Limitation Order L-91, effective April 18, bans production of the laundry equipment after June 1, and of the dry cleaning equipment after July 1, except for Army, Navy, or Maritime Commission orders.

In addition, the regulations freeze existing equipment and stocks to be manufactured until the cut-off date, except for Army, Navy or Maritime Commission orders, or for deliveries specifically authorized by the Director of Industry Operations.

Java sisal banned for wrapping, binder twine; other changes

The agave fiber order (M-84) was amended by the WPB April 13 as follows:

1. The use of Java agave sisalana, commonly known in the trade as Java sisal, for manufacturing wrapping twine or binder twine is prohibited. Previously a limited use was permitted.

2. Inventory restrictions of the order as to import shipments of wrapping twine are lifted as to importers of agave cordage and agave twine.

Rug makers warned of serious jute shortage; asked to consider diversion of carpet wool stocks to blankets, apparel

Due to the present jute shortage and the improbability of obtaining additional supplies from Calcutta, it is extremely unlikely that there will be any further allocation of jute yarns for floor coverings after this month, the soft fiber section of the WPB said April 13.

Advised not to start production

The seriousness of the jute situation was explained to the wool floor covering industry at a recent industry advisory committee meeting in Washington in order to prevent manufacturers from beginning production on rugs and carpets that they might not be able to finish for lack of jute. Some members of the committee said it would be wise if manufacturers of wool floor coverings stopped putting into production any more virgin wool for rugs and carpets, inasmuch as they would not be able to complete the products if sufficient jute were not available.

War Production Board officials asked that the industry make an immediate study to determine what stocks of carpet wool now in this country could be diverted into more essential civilian uses, such as the manufacture of blankets and apparel of various kinds. Wool conservation order M-73 does not make wool available to floor covering manufacturers for suit purposes, but WPB officials indicated that this could be worked out.

Storage space for wool needed

WPB officials said that creating a large stock pile of wool for military purposes has resulted in an immediate need for storage space. They suggested that the mills and warehouses of the floor covering industry could assist in solving this problem. Distributors' warehouses could also be used for this purpose as they became empty. The industry was referred to the Defense Supplies Corporation, Washington, D. C., for particulars.

Alexis Sommaripa, of the WPB Office of Civilian Supply, urged the immediate study of the manufacture of burlap substitutes and similar cloths which are in great demand. He recommended that the industry experiment with a material made of low cotton and waste which might serve the purpose of 8- or 10-ounce burlap. The War Production Board will be interested in seeing samples.

The project of spinning coarse cotton yarns on the wool spinning equipment of the carpet industry was discussed. The WPB officials urged that experiments be continued, as the only requirement of bagging yarn is strength, and the shortage of burlap will result in an increased market for these yarns.

The committee expressed great interest in the possibility of making blankets for the armed forces. A committee member displayed a blanket made to Army specifications.

A-1-a on farm equipment speeds production of foodstuffs

To speed production of foodstuffs vitally needed by the armed forces of this Nation and its allies, the WPB April 18 granted an A-1-a rating to manufacturers of certain types of farm equipment and machinery.

Designed to hasten the output of foodstuffs under the Department of Agriculture's 1942 program, the new arrangement is necessary to give farm machinery makers materials which could not be obtained with sufficient speed under lower ratings.

Production stopped on 349 types of radio tubes for civilians

The WPB April 17 ordered radio tube manufacturers to discontinue within 7 days production for civilian use of 349 of the 710 types of radio tubes now on the market.

Heavy compressors placed under complete allocation

The WPB April 17 placed heavy compressors, urgently needed in the war production program, under a system of complete allocations. War requirements for heavy compressors have put a strain on existing supplies.

Questions and Answers on Priorities

1. Q. How does the priorities system work?

A. The Priorities System directs strategic and critical materials away from nonessential production to production essential for war. It organizes, mobilizes, and directs materials and productive facilities where they will be most useful to the military effort. This is accomplished by preference ratings which put more important orders ahead of those which are less important, and in some cases by direct allocation.

2. Q. How are ratings assigned?

A. They are assigned in various ways. The most widely used are (1) Individual Preference Rating Certificates, (2) Blanket Ratings, (3) Project Ratings, (4) and ratings obtained through the Production Requirements Plan.

3. Q. What are the advantages of the Production Requirements Plan?

A. It sums up in a single application all the materials needed by a producer over a three-month period, granting one or more preference ratings for continued deliveries, including repair, maintenance, and operating supplies. Under it each manufacturer has a rating good for three months for the materials named, and by requiring full information on each application as to the kind of materials needed, the amount on hand and the importance of their use to the war effort, it enables WPB to give every industry concerned fair and uniform treatment.

4. Q. Is there a printed list available of priority orders and forms?

A. Yes. A printed compilation of priority orders and forms is now available for distribution at the Public Service Unit, WPB, and is entitled PRIORITIES IN FORCE. Supplements are printed weekly in VICTORY, and are available also in mimeographed form to a Public Service Unit mailing list open to manufacturers and others who may need the extra service.

PRIORITY ACTIONS

*From April 9
*Through April 16

Subject	Order number	Related form	Issued	Expiration date	Rating
Agave fiber:					
a. Prohibits use of Java sisal for certain manufacturing purposes; changes inventory restrictions.	M-84 amend. No. 3.		4-13-42.		
Amusement machines:					
a. Clarifies provisions for cutting and stamping copper; sale, transfer or delivery of parts and filing of inventory form.	L-21-a int. No. 1.		4-13-42.		
Canned foods:					
a. Requires canners to provide themselves with materials necessary to pack canned goods for the armed forces adequately in export boxes.	M-86-a amend. No. 1.		4-13-42.		
Coal stokers:					
a. Prohibits manufacture for residential use after May 31; limits production of commercial and industrial types to orders rated A-10 or higher.	L-75.		4-15-42.	Until revoked.	A-10 or higher.
Electrical appliances:					
a. Further restricts production and tightens restrictions on metals that may be used.	L-65 amend. No. 1.		4-9-42.		
Electric generating equipment and steam boilers (Used):					
a. Sale, lease, or option prohibited without specific authorization.	L-102.		4-11-42.		
Electric heating pads:					
a. Permits manufacturers to use up inventories which cannot be used for other purposes, but stops production on June 30, 1942.	L-84 amend. No. 1.		4-15-42.		
Farm machinery:					
a. Makes plain that the intent of the order is to prohibit all sales and exports of farm machinery and equipment in excess of quantities permitted to be manufactured.	L-26 amend. No. 2.		4-13-42.		
Fire-fighting apparatus:					
a. Motorised:					
1. Prohibits use o. rubber tires on auxiliary trailers for fire apparatus manufactured or delivered after date of issuance.	L-43 amend. No. 1.		4-14-42.		
2. Fire apparatus extended.	P-45 (as revised) Ext. No. 1.		4-13-42.	6-30-42.	
3. Fire protective equipment extended.	P-108 ext. No. 1.		4-13-42.	6-30-42.	
Furnaces:					
a. Reduces amounts of iron and steel which may be consumed in manufacture of warm-air furnaces.	L-22.		4-11-42.	Until revoked.	
Golf clubs:					
a. Cuts off use of iron and steel, other critical metals, plastics and cork in manufacture after May 31; limited production permitted meanwhile:	L-93.		4-9-42.		
1. Permits manufacturers to acquire from inventories of other manufacturers finished parts containing iron and steel for assembly in golf clubs.	L-93 amend. No. 1.		4-16-42.		
Industrial machinery:					
a. Assumes control over manufacture and distribution of many types.	L-83.	P-D-1, 1a, 3, 3a, 200, 200a.	4-9-42.	Until revoked.	A-9 or higher.
Kitchen, household and other miscellaneous articles:					
a. Curtain rods, fixtures and drapery attachments all brought under control of L-30.	L-30 amend. No. 1.		4-11-42		
Maintenance and repair:					
a. Iron and steel production:					
1. Steel producers granted a higher preference rating for materials for maintenance and repair and may extend the higher rating to their supplies.	P-68 amend. No. 3	PD-228	4-11-42		A-3; A-1-a; A-1-c.

Subject	Order number	Related form	Issued	Expiration date	Rating
b. Neither uniforms nor fire hose may be ordered with a preference rating assigned under terms of P-100.	P-100 (as amend.) Int. No. 3.		4-16-42		
Metal household furniture:					
a. Transfers control over "drapery attachments" from L-62 to L-30.	L-62 amend. No. 1.		4-11-42		
Mining machinery and equipment:					
a. Permits companies using ratings assigned by P-56-a to make deliveries to South American Copper Companies operating under P-58, to iron and steel producers under P-66.	P-56-a amend. No. 2.	PD-25A	4-13-42		
b. Grants use of higher preference rating to obtain explosives and explosive equipment.	P-56 amend. No. 5.		4-13-42		
Motor carriers:					
a. Motor trucks, truck-trailers and passenger carriers:					
1. Supplementary order:					
(a) Discontinues all production of medium and heavy trucks for civilian use after existing quotas completed.	L-1-e		4-11-42		
Natural resins:					
a. Conservation order:					
1. Restricts use in any calendar quarter to 50 percent of amount used in corresponding quarter of 1941; restrictions do not apply to Army, Navy or Lend-Lease and other specified uses.	M-56	PD-339	4-15-42	Until revoked.	
Office machinery:					
a. Clarifies status of privately operated plants or shipyards controlled by the Army, Navy or other Government agencies.	L-54-a int. No. 2.		4-11-42		
Oil burners:					
a. Prohibits manufacture for residential use after May 31; limits production of commercial and industrial types to orders rated A-10 or higher.	L-74		4-15-42	Until revoked.	A-10 or higher.
Plumbing and heating:					
a. Cast iron soil pipe and fittings:					
1. Amended to limit manufacturers of cast iron soil pipe to a single weight.	Schedule 4 to L-42 (as amend.).		4-13-42	6-1-42	
b. Plumbing and heating equipment:					
1. To prevent dissipation of existing plumbing and heating equipment stocks for nondefense building, modernization or unnecessary replacements freezes all such stocks, except retail sales of $5 or less or A-10 or better.	L-79		4-16-42	Until revoked.	Do.
Remodeling projects (low-cost):					
a. Makes it easier for owners to remodel housing that can provide additional living accomodations essential to the war program.	P-110	PD-406	4-10-42	Until revoked.	
Rotenone:					
a. Conservation order—to conserve supply and direct distribution.	M-133		4-13-42	Until revoked.	
Rough diamonds:					
a. Filing date for reports postponed from Apr. 15 to Apr. 30, 1942.	M-109 amend. No. 1.	PD-375	4-13-42		
Rubber:					
a. Prohibits manufacture of blowout shoes and restricts manufacture of reliners.	M-15-b amend. No. 8.		4-11-42		
b. Specifications governing use of rubber as insulation on neutral electrical wires effective on May 1.	M-15-b-1 amend. No. 4.		4-11-42		

(Continued on page 22)

Restrict steel shoe shanks to 3 sizes, WPB requests

The leather and shoe section of WPB has requested manufacturers of steel for shoe shanks to restrict their production to three specific thicknesses.

A shoe shank is a sheet steel stamping which is inserted between the insole and the outsole of a shoe to reinforce the part that supports the arch of the foot. Steel shanks are used in more than 60 percent of the total production of shoes, exclusive of slippers.

The leather and shoe section said that while steel shanks will continue to be used in some types of shoes, the use of wood shanks is advocated. The section added that the request is designed to save steel for war purposes by encouraging the standardization of steel shanks of light gages.

The leather and shoe section sent telegrams to ten steel manufacturers requesting them to discontinue the manufacture of all shoe shank steel except for 18-gage shanks of 0.045-inch thickness, 21-gauge shanks of 0.032-inch thickness, and 19 gage shanks of 0.040-inch thickness.

The telegram further specified that the steel of 0.045-inch and 0.032-inch thickness be made of 50 carbon steel, and the 0.040-inch thickness of low carbon steel.

Present stocks of shank steel in the hands of shoe manufacturers, shoe shank manufacturers, or suppliers of shoe shank steel are not affected by the request. Any application of shank manufacturers for priorities for the second quarter of 1942 must comply with the requested specifications.

★ ★ ★

HONEY QUOTA EXPLAINED

The honey conservation order (M-118) was amended April 17 to clarify the quota provision for small industrial users of sugar.

The original order permitted any person to use, in the manufacture of any product, not over 60 pounds of honey in any month of 1942. This provision was misconstrued by some to mean that a person might use up to 60 pounds of honey per month in the production of each of several products.

The order was not intended to permit such use, and the April 17 amendment changes the language to read: "any person may use, in the manufacture of other products, a total of not more than 60 pounds of honey in any month of 1942."

Mine machinery makers assured materials for equipment, repairs by high rating on allotted quota

WPB has granted an A-1-a rating to manufacturers of mining machinery operating under Order P–56–a. This rating is to be assigned to specified percentages of the manufacturers' requirements as listed by them and submitted on Form PD–25–A in connection with the order, and will be in effect during the second calendar quarter ending June 30, 1942.

To insure deliveries of specified quantities

Effect of the action will be to insure deliveries of specified quantities of materials to the hundred-odd makers of mining and smelting machinery operating under the order, and will provide a steady flow of equipment and repairs to the essential mine and smelting operations providing minerals vital to the war effort.

Manufacturers' requirements for raw, semifabricated and fabricated materials totaling about 50 million dollars for the quarter were approved by the Requirements Committee. This represents approximately 30 percent of the total for the year.

J. S. Knowlson, Director of Industry Operations, has implemented the Requirements Committee action by providing for the use of the high ratings for materials.

Control of the ratings will be in the hands of the mining branch. Mining machinery manufacturers affected by the action must report to the branch each Monday all orders they have placed through the previous Saturday.

Amounts of each of the 81 items purchased will be entered against the quota for that particular company and further purchases must cease when the quota is reached. Likewise, the total quota for the industry for any particular item may not be exceeded.

⁂

Waterman to head lighting and fixtures section

Appointment of Marshall N. Waterman as chief of the lighting and fixtures section of the WPB building materials branch was announced April 17, by John L. Haynes, chief of the branch.

Charles L. Harold, who preceded Mr. Waterman as chief of the section, has transferred to the Bureau of Industrial Conservation as a special consultant.

PRIORITY ACTIONS

*From April 9
*Through April 16

(Continued from page 21)

Subject	Order number	Related form	Issued	Expiration date	Rating
Shellac: a. Conservation order—reduces output of phonograph records and radio transcriptions to approximately 30 percent of 1941 production by limiting amount of shellac; freezes 50 percent of all inventories of shellac of 10,000 pounds or more and 50 percent of all future imports.	M-106	PD-334	4-14-42		
Special conservation order: a. Order issued to halt auction at Foos Gas Engine Co., Springfield, Ohio, revoked.	Revocation		4-14-42		
Sugar: a. Lifts shipping zone restrictions on sugar for the Army, Navy, or Lend-Lease.	M-55-d amend. No. 1.		4-13-42		—
Tea: a. Extends to Apr. 25 the date on which a receiver or packer must file a complete report of tea inventories of 500 pounds or more.	M-111 amend. No. 1.		4-11-42		
Tin: a. Restricts all persons except retailers from selling any solder with tin content of more than 16 percent, any tin-bearing babbit metal or tin oxide with certain exceptions.	M-43 amend. No. 2.		4-10-42		As assigned.
b. Removes limitations on uses of tin for manufacture of implements of war.	Amend. No. 2 to M-43-a (as amend.)		4-10-42		
Vitamin A: a. Permits unrestricted use in feeds of vitamin A oils blended prior to Feb. 10.	L-40 as amended April 10, 1942.		4-10-42		
Wood pulp: a. Permits producers and consumers to receive, after May 1, without approval of the Director of Industry Operations, pulp of domestic origin ordered and actually in transit prior to midnight, Apr. 30.	M-93 Int. No. 1.		4-13-42		

SUSPENSION ORDERS

Company	Order number	Violation	Penalty	Issued	Expiration date
Talon, Inc., Meadville, Pa.	S-33	Failed to disclose existence of available supply of import copper in any applications for preference ratings.	Prohibited, until July 1, from using steel, zinc or zinc-base alloys in manufacture of slide fasteners in excess of 40 percent of average quarterly poundage of all metals used for this purpose during year ending June 30, 1941; no deliveries of any materials shall be assigned any preference ratings and no allocations of any material under priority control shall be made.	4-11-42	7-1-42
Walleck Brass Co., Cleveland, Ohio	S-34	Shipped aluminum for prohibited nonwar purposes and accepted and processed unauthorized deliveries of aluminum scrap.	Shall not accept or make any deliveries of aluminum and no preference ratings shall be assigned to any orders for materials placed by the company.	4-13-42	

Company	Order number	Violation	Penalty	Issued	Expiration date
Aluminum Bronze Powder Co., Bedford, Ohio.	S-36	Made deliveries on orders bearing no preference ratings and accepted unauthorized deliveries of aluminum scrap.	Shall not accept or make any deliveries of aluminum and no preference ratings shall be assigned to any orders placed by the company; after a ten-day grace period must cease all fabrication involving use of aluminum.	4-13-42	
Mills Novelty Co., Chicago, Ill.	S-37	Used aluminum in the manufacture of coin-operated machines; turned out 2,332 amusement and gaming machines in excess of its alloted quota.	Enjoined from selling or delivering any of the machines manufactured in excess of its quota, and further curtails the number of amusement machines it may produce during months of March and April; refusal of all priority assistance and allocations of any restricted material until expiration of order.	4-11-42	7-10-42

P-83 revoked; assigned ratings to some petroleum supply houses

Preference rating order P-83, under which priority ratings have been assigned to a considerable number of petroleum supply houses, was revoked April 16 by the Director of Industry Operations.

This action was taken because the supply houses affected may now obtain priority assistance either by extending the ratings on orders received by them from petroleum enterprises, or by applying for preference ratings on the distributors' Form PD-1X.

All serially numbered copies of P-83, as issued to individual supply houses, are immediately revoked. However, deliveries already rated under the terms of P-83 may be completed in accordance with the rating.

Shipping zone restrictions lifted for Military, Lend-Lease

The WPB April 13 amended Supplementary Order M-55-d to lift shipping zone restrictions on sugar for the Army, Navy, or Lend-Lease.

The action was taken in Amendment 1 to Supplementary Order M-55-d. The supplementary order, issued March 27, originally restricted the sale and shipment of domestic refined sugar to specific zones near sugar refineries. These restrictions were lifted to the extent nec-

essary to facilitate deliveries by or for the armed forces or for Lend-Lease.

★ ★ ★

War risk insurance revised by Shipping Administration

The War Shipping Administration announced April 13 a revised schedule of war risk insurance rates covering shipments of cargoes made on American merchant vessels.

These rates will apply to all quotations made on and after April 13, 1942, but are subject to change thereafter without notice. In accordance with the provisions of General Order No. 6, the new rates are contained in Bulletin No. C-1 of the War Shipping Administration.

★ ★ ★

All uses of rhodium now banned for jewelry making

All use of rhodium, one of the metals of the platinum group, in the manufacture of jewelry was prohibited April 17 by the Director of Industry Operations in Amendment No. 1 to Order M-95.

The order, issued March 11, stopped electroplating of rhodium on jewelry but did not affect its use in alloy or other forms. The April 17 amendment stops all uses of the metal in jewelry making.

In a letter accompanying the order, the Director of Industry Operations authorized jewelry manufacturers to use up stocks on hand.

The important war use of rhodium is to coat reflectors in antiaircraft searchlights. Its civilian use is to give a non-tarnishable finish to vanity and cigarette cases and the like.

Steel companies not bound by ratings in shipping specimens for test purposes

Steel companies melting National Emergency Alloy Steels have been given authority to ship specimens to laboratories or manufacturers without regard to preference ratings, the WPB announced April 14.

To obtain widest possible testing

The purpose is to obtain the widest possible testing of these new steel alloys, which reduce quantities of alloys used and are based upon the principle that small quantities of various elements are more effective than larger quantities of a single element.

Those receiving these steels must certify in their purchase orders that the material will be used for experimental purpose; that the amount ordered, together with any on hand or on order from other mills, will not exceed 500 pounds for any one specification, and that the total on hand or ordered for all types does not exceed 10 tons.

The authority extends until July 31.

Warehouse steel listed in M-21-b exempt from L-63 provisions

Warehouses carrying steel bars, ingots, wire, and other products listed in Schedules A and B of the Steel Warehouse Order, M-21-b, may omit these products from the inventory reports required by Suppliers' Limitation Order L-63, it was explained April 17 by the Director of Industry Operations.

How it works

Exemption No. 1 of Limitation Order L-63 specifically exempts warehouses coming under the provisions of Order M-21-b from the provisions of L-63 insofar as material listed in the schedules attached to M-21-b are concerned.

The distributors' branch of the Division of Industry Operations explained at the same time that no priority assistance will be granted on the distributors' application form, PD-IX, for any materials listed in Schedules A or B of Supplementary Order M-21-b, and such materials should not be included in any PD-IX application.

CONSERVATION . . .

Paper salvage overcomes shortage; mills now able to meet current orders

The salvage-for-victory program has been so successful in stimulating the movement of wastepaper back into production that paper mills throughout the country are now able to meet current orders, Lessing J. Rosenwald, chief of the Bureau of Industrial Conservation, declared April 14.

"Public response to the War Production Board's appeal for a continuous return of wastepaper to meet the vastly increased demands of war production is an outstanding demonstration of patriotic and unified action," Mr. Rosenwald said. "Only a few months ago, many of the country's paper mills were on the verge of shutting down completely because of a lack of wastepaper.

Bottleneck explained

"Today, as a result of the activities of State, local, and industrial salvage committees, and the many volunteer organizations making collections, in every part of the country, wastepaper is being collected and returned for re-use at an unprecedented rate. In fact, the flow of paper has been accelerated to such a degree that in certain areas dealers are having difficulty in moving their material to the mills.

"The bureau has received reports from several sections of the country that certain mills have refused to buy wastepaper from dealers. Not only the dealers but the general public can be assured that this is a temporary and localized situation which is being promptly corrected."

Part of the recent bottleneck in the movement of wastepaper from dealers to consuming mills, Mr. Rosenwald explained, was due to the fact that Priorities Regulation No. 1 prohibited mills from building up more than very limited inventories. However, at the request of the bureau, the Division of Industry Operations on April 6 lifted these restrictions to permit paper consumers to build up unlimited reserve supplies, during this period when civilian industries are being curtailed, with a consequent lessening of the demand for paper board for civilian goods.

Careful sorting urged

In addition, Mr. Rosenwald pointed out, the wastepaper-consuming indus-

tries have been urged to take advantage of the current increase in the return of paper in order to be prepared for any future emergency demands.

The consuming mills have explained that part of their inability to handle the tremendously increased flow of wastepaper has been due to the fact that much of the material being returned by dealers has been inadequately or badly packed, or is of inferior quality. In many instances, mills have lowered the prices paid to dealers for wastepaper of inferior quality.

Dealers have been urged to pack their paper shipments more carefully and to direct their efforts toward moving paper of higher grades. In addition, it was pointed out, the public can aid in this respect by segregating household wastepaper, bundling it carefully. All dirty, oily, or wet paper should be eliminated, and magazines, newspapers, and cartons should be bundled separately.

Public should concentrate on rubber now

After explaining the temporary delay in the movement of paper from dealers to mills, Mr. Rosenwald also said:

"We are now confronted with a scrap rubber shortage much like the crisis that developed in the wastepaper field some months ago. It is essential that the public concentrate its most intensive efforts at this time on salvaging every possible pound of old rubber. Old tires and inner tubes, hot water bottles, rubber bath mats, old raincoats, rubber jar rings—these and any similar items made of rubber can be found in nearly every home.

"Naturally, we do not want any one to give up rubber articles which are still usable. But if our rubber-reclaiming plants are to be able to produce on the vast scale needed, we must rely upon American housewives for the unstinted cooperation they are giving the paper salvage campaign."

★ ★ ★

Sentner to head tin plate unit

Richard F. Sentner of Wheeling, W. Va., has been appointed head of the tin plate unit of the iron and steel branch, C. E. Adams, branch chief, announced April 15.

OPA to survey scrap flow under ceiling in New England

A comprehensive survey of the scrap materials situation in New England will be undertaken in the near future by OPA, Administrator Henderson announced April 15.

Beginning April 27 a staff of 35 or 40 OPA representatives will make spot checks over a period of 3 or 4 weeks at the establishments of New England scrap peddlers, collectors, small and large dealers, and brokers. Information will be sought on all scrap materials, including rubber, waste paper, old rags, and ferrous and nonferrous scrap. Analysis of the data gathered is expected to afford OPA a comprehensive picture of the structure of the scrap industry in New England.

In connection with this survey, a special attempt will be made to secure information on the flow of iron and steel scrap under Price Schedule No. 4, which has been in operation for slightly more than a year. This latter information will be compared with the scrap flow in New England before imposition of maximum prices.

It is expected that the New England area will exhibit many characteristics common to other scrap producing regions; if so, it may be possible to apply the results of the survey quite broadly. However, Mr. Henderson said future plans contemplate additional surveys in two or three other scrap producing areas somewhat smaller than the New England region.

WPB releases machinery plant after study of war value

The WPB revoked on April 14 its special conservation order, issued February 21, which halted the sale at auction of the machinery, tools, and equipment situated at the plant formerly owned by the Foos Gas Engine Co., at Springfield, Ohio.

Purpose of the order was to permit a survey of the plant and its facilities to determine whether they could be used intact for war production. Subsequent investigation by the Navy Department and the WPB failed to disclose any valuable use which could be made of the plant as it stands.

OPA alters brass scrap ceilings to aid electrolytic copper

Supplementing the Metals Reserve Company program for increasing the copper supply in this country by encouraging the copper refiners to buy yellow brass scrap for conversion into electrolytic copper, OPA has fixed maximum prices for all yellow brass castings on a copper content basis. The prices are set forth in Amendment No. 3 to Revised Price Schedule No. 20 (Copper and Copper Alloy Scrap), announced April 17 by Administrator Henderson.

The Administrator said a decision could be expected shortly on other amendments discussed with representative members of the industry in Washington on March 30 and 31.

Highlights of the new amendment, which became effective April 17, are provisions which:

1. Remove from the schedule heavy yellow brass, cast yellow brass borings, light brass and yellow brass breakage grades and add a grade called refinery brass.
2. Establish a method for determining maximum prices for any kind or grade of copper scrap and copper alloy scrap not previously specified in the February 27, 1942, ceiling. Some 30 kinds or grades were covered at that time.

The maximum price for the new grade is fixed at dry copper content times 9.25 cents where the assay is 60.01 percent or more and at dry copper content times 9.00 cents where the assay is 50.01 percent to 60.00 percent.

Since April 1, 1942, certain copper refiners, as Metals Reserve Company's agents have bought yellow brass scrap for conversion into electrolytic copper. The new amendment is issued, in part, to insure that these refiners who have never bought and are not equipped to buy sorted yellow brass do not violate the schedule by purchasing this material on a copper content basis and in part to prevent an unnecessary and wasteful use of dealer's time and manpower in sorting material for a buyer who can more readily handle unsorted material.

Inasmuch as yellow brass castings remain in the schedule, any ingot maker or foundry still will be able to purchase sorted yellow brass material. Yellow brass castings can be separated relatively easily and quickly from the general run of yellow brass material.

★ ★ ★

Dodge named assistant deputy director

Appointment of H. W. Dodge, of Bronxville, N. Y., as assistant deputy director of the Materials Division was announced April 16 by Materials Director Batt.

With his new appointment Mr. Dodge becomes third in command of the Materials Division and will take over a part of the duties of A. I Henderson, deputy director.

MATERIALS . . .

Vitally needed nickel to be got from vast Cuban deposits for first time

Cuba is on its way to become a new source of badly needed nickel, Materials Director Batt announced April 16.

Large deposits of low-grade ores blanketing the wooded plateau of northeastern Cuba are to be treated by a complicated chemical and metallurgical process to yield nickel for armor plate and for other tough steels required for warships, planes, tanks, and guns.

The job is being tackled by Nicaro Nickel Co., a new subsidiary of the Freeport Sulphur Co., which through another subsidiary also produces manganese in Cuba. Since early 1940 the company has conducted research on nickel recovery. The work has had the close attention of officials and technicians of the WPB and other Government agencies.

Financed by RFC

After a technical committee representing the Government had approved Nicaro's research results, the WPB authorized a project for a $20,000,000 plant and facilities. The construction is being financed by Reconstruction Finance Corporation and the plant will be operated by Nicaro for the Government.

At the Government's request, Nicaro began purchasing the materials and making construction plans even before the final design was completed and final contracts were signed. The first crew of several hundred engineers and workers, the bulk of them Cubans, is already on the scene, dredging waterways, laying electric lines and building temporary structures.

Practically all of the United States' supply of nickel has to be imported. With the exception of a very small trickle from New Caledonia, the United States' supply—and Great Britain's as well—comes from one area in Canada. In fact, Canada accounts for about 85 percent of world nickel production.

Demand surpasses Canadian supply

The flow of nickel from Canada, although at peak levels, has been overtaken by the mounting needs of the national war effort. Nickel was one of the first materials to be put under priority control and now is under allocation. Less essential uses were curtailed months ago and finally prohibited entirely.

In this crisis, Nicaro put its chemists and metallurgists on a 24-hour day and accelerated its laboratory work. A small pilot plant, which Government officials subsequently visited and examined, was built and put into operation late in the summer at Freeport's sulphur plant in Texas.

In 1901 two American geologists started from Santiago with a pack train bound for the opposite coast of the island.

The geologists drew a geological cross-section of the district and wrote the following description of the hilly region reaching back from the sea:

"Upon the top of this sierra there are many large areas which are practically level, and these are always covered by a thick mantle of red clay, which contains a large proportion of iron in the form of spherical pellets. Locally particles are cemented together by ferruginous materials, making a spongy mass of brown iron ore."

Deposits stretch for miles

Later more exhaustive surveys of the deposits were made by engineers interested in their iron content. It was found that they stretch for miles, constituting an almost horizontal mantle from a few inches to 80 feet in thickness. In these later geological reports, iron averaging about 46 percent, and in places nickel in quantities ranging up to 1½ percent were recorded. Bethlehem Steel Co. uses this ore extensively to produce a nickel iron widely used in this country.

In 1909 shipments of iron ore to the United States were begun. The following year the International Geological Congress in Sweden in a publication on the world's iron ore reserves estimated the Cuban deposits to contain about 2,000,000,000 tons. Analyses of the raw ore during these early operations revealed an average of 1 percent of nickel.

Although no nickel was actually produced, its existence in these extensive deposits became a fascinating metallurgical nut for scientists to try to crack. Some of the best brains in the United States, England, France, Germany, and Japan were put to work on the baffling problem of recovering nickel from low-grade ores.

TRANSPORTATION . . .

Eastman rejects Texas-Savannah pipe line, but thinks others might be "necessary;" relayings, reversals under consideration

Joseph B. Eastman, Director of Defense Transportation, April 16 refused a request by the Trans-American Pipe Line Corporation that he certify that a crude oil pipe line which the corporation proposed to build is necessary for the war effort.

Basis for decision

The corporation sought to obtain permission to build a pipe line reaching from Texas to the Atlantic Coast. Mr. Eastman was asked to recommend to the President that he issue a proclamation under the Cole Pipe Line Act declaring that the proposed pipe line "is or may be necessary for national defense purposes."

Mr. Eastman's decision was based on the report of a three-member board which held a public hearing February 19 on the corporation's application, and on a statement of views by the War Department.

In rejecting the application of the corporation, Mr. Eastman declared, "However, I am of the opinion that additional pipe line facilities which can substantially increase the flow of oil to the Atlantic Seaboard area are 'necessary for national defense purposes'."

The proposed pipe line was described by the corporation as being 1,050 miles in length, stretching from Wichita County, Tex., to Savannah, Ga. It would have cost an estimated $25,000,000 and would have had an estimated daily capacity of 70,000 barrels of oil.

No support from Armed Services

In describing the drawbacks of the proposed project, Mr. Eastman said, "the steel requirements were estimated at about 85,000 net tons. There was no showing that the necessary pipe, pumps, and other materials are available under present conditions."

Though representatives of both the Army and Navy attended the hearing on the corporation's application, neither Armed Service offered support of the project, Mr. Eastman said. Instead, the War Department wrote him after the hearing, actively opposing its construc-

tion, contending that because of its location, it would be of relatively little value to the war program.

Best use of existing facilities stressed

Stressing the need for realism, Mr. Eastman said, "If these were normal times the steel necessary for new pipe lines would be readily available and whatever lines are needed could be built within a relatively short time. But the imperative steel requirements of the war effort are such that it is necessary to make maximum use of existing facilities before allocation of existing materials can reasonably be asked.

"In the case of pipe lines, this may well mean an extensive relaying of existing pipe in new locations as well as the reversal of some lines in their present locations. Some measures of this character have been taken and others are contemplated.

"I shall be glad to join any other governmental agencies in an investigation of the necessity for additional pipe line facilities and have designated R. W. Shields, engineer for pipe lines, of the Interstate Commerce Commission, to represent me in any such investigation. It is my opinion that a study of this character must consider the relative merits of all proposed projects, including that of the Trans-American Pipe Line Corporation."

★ ★ ★

Hauer named assistant director of railway transport division

To increase further the efficiency of the Nation's railway equipment, ODT Director Eastman announced April 16 the appointment of E. R. Hauer of Cleveland, Ohio, as assistant director of the division of railway transport, in charge of mechanical operations.

Mr. Hauer's duties will include reviewing and reporting on the efficient use of motive power, its availability and sufficiency; the state of repair of railway equipment, and the adequacy of tools and repair facilities required to keep railway plants in the condition necessary to operate at maximum capacity.

Mammoth bus trailer, designed to carry 141 workers, provides "stop-gap" in transportation

As one answer to the problem of transporting hundreds of thousands of war workers from central points in cities to outlying industrial plants, representatives of the Office of Defense Transportation, with the aid of officials of the War Production Board and a number of private companies, have designed and built in less than 30 days a simplified type of oversize bus trailer made almost entirely of noncritical materials.

Can haul 141 persons

The trailer chassis embodies an ingenious application of a conventional design steel frame with a plywood and masonite superstructure. It rolls on eight standard truck-size tires, with the usual six tires on the power units. Because of the light weight of the unit in relation to the load carried, and the use of a modern-type floating axle, efficiency in the use of tires will be far greater than in any other type of rubber-tired passenger carrier so far developed.

Maximum load of the trailer is 141 persons.

The trailer is intended primarily as a stop-gap vehicle for mass transportation of workers to plants located in areas where no other public transportation facilities are available.

★ ★ ★

ODT shifting coal transport for East from water to rail

Steps are being taken by the Office of Defense Transportation to insure the movement into the Eastern Seaboard region of large amounts of coal which formerly moved by water along the coast, ODT Director Eastman said April 15.

Curtailment of coastwise shipping as a result of enemy submarine activity and other factors has made railroad routing necessary. Much of the coal that formerly moved by rail to tidewater for transshipment by collier must now move the entire distance to Baltimore, Norfolk, Philadelphia, and New England points by rail.

Samuel S. Bruce, of Pittsburgh, has been appointed assistant director of the Division of Railway Transport in charge of coal movement and equipment.

Don't apply for new trucks, truck-tractors, trailers unless qualified, ODT requests

With some 50,000 applications received during the first month's operation of the commercial-vehicle rationing program, the ODT April 16 asked operators who cannot meet minimum qualifications to refrain from applying for new trucks, truck-tractors, or trailers.

Only small supply available

ODT officials said it was apparent that many of the applications were from operators seeking to buy commercial vehicles as they normally would under a business-as-usual economy.

The rationing plan, which is administered jointly by the ODT and the WPB, went into effect March 9.

Because of the small supply of trucks available to meet present and future civilian demands, and the necessity for maintaining a reserve to meet unpredictable military needs, ODT officials said, each operator before applying for a new truck should ask himself this question:

"Would a new truck in my possession actually help, directly or indirectly, in winning the war?"

General Conservation Order M–100, which set up the rationing plan (described in the March 10 issue of VICTORY), shows the order in which the demand for new vehicles will be met. Five classes were established.

Should exhaust other avenues first

Those who can qualify in the higher classes should resort to application for new vehicles only after they have exhausted the following possibilities: The used-truck market, leasing vehicles not being fully utilized by other operators, pooling equipment with other operators, maintaining present equipment better than ever before, working present equipment longer hours and more days, and salvaging equipment which in normal times would not be used further.

There will be no production of trucks after the March quotas are completed; trailers are being produced in quantities much below normal production. The only certain supply of trucks is the pool now held by manufacturers and dealers, representing stocks frozen January 2 and the diminishing production of the first months this year.

If persons who are not qualified to get vehicles will refrain from making applications, the work of making speedy decisions on the applications of qualified operators can be speeded, ODT officials said.

Draft deferment not the answer to growing labor shortages, railroads told

Problems of manning and maintaining the nation's railroads in the face of increasing labor shortages cannot be solved by draft deferment of employees, representatives of the Association of American Railroads were told April 14 at a meeting called by the ODT.

Training needed to meet growing demands

At best, the representatives were told, granting of deferment to railroad employees must be considered only as an opportunity to train workers to replace those called to duty with the Armed Services.

Training is also necessary, it was pointed out, to meet the increasing number of railroad employees made necessary by the growing demands placed on railroad transportation by the war effort.

Attending the meeting were M. J. Gormley, executive assistant to J. J. Pelley, president of the Association of American Railroads; Otto S. Beyer, director of the division of transport personnel; J. H. Parmelee, director of the Association's Bureau of Railway Economics; Edwin N. Fitch, Edward E. Goshen, and Dorothy Sells, of the division of transport personnel; Lt. Commander Patrick H. Winston and Major Francis V. Keesling of the Selective Service Board; and William F. Patterson, chief, apprentice training section, Department of Labor.

Suggested self-help measures

Suggested self-help measures that might be adopted by the railroads to meet growing shortages of almost every type of skilled and semiskilled railroad employee included:

1. Raising the hiring-age limits and relaxing physical requirements.
2. Making a drive to rehire former employees, including those who have quit and those who have retired.
3. Utilizing all State and Federal aids to improve apprentice and learner training methods, and speeding up apprentice training by agreement with labor.
4. Surveying situation on each railroad to determine possibilities of upgrading employees to more skilled positions and utilizing more skilled workers to instruct and guide semiskilled workers.
5. Employing women wherever possible.
6. Making full use of governmental employment services.
7. Establishing a clearing-house by which the various railroads can exchange information on manpower and self-help measures.
8. Organizing effective personnel management system for each carrier under appropriate supervision and direction.

At the conference, the creation by the railroads of a permanent committee to study and act on the industry's manpower problems was suggested.

Mr. Parmelee and Mr. Gormley were to carry the suggestions to the railroad industry for further action.

★ ★

Form PD–336 corrected to include railroad supplies

Through a typographical error, "Railroad Supplies" was omitted under "Type of Supplies" in the preparation of Form PD–336, the reporting form used in connection with the distributors' order, L–63. A copy of the form was attached to WPB press release 828.

Copies of the form which have been reproduced for use may be corrected by substituting "Railroad" for "Health" at the top of column three under "Type of Supplies," with a rubber stamp or otherwise. Forms corrected in this manner will be acceptable for keeping the required reports.

The forms should also be identified by stamping or writing "PD–336" in the upper left-hand corner.

★ ★ ★

No violation found in building of New Jersey race track

In response to many inquiries, the compliance branch of the WPB announced April 16 that it had completed an investigation of the construction of a race track, stables, and grandstand near Haddonfield, N. J., and had found no violation of priority regulations or WPB orders.

TWO OFFICIALS NAMED IN TRAFFIC MOVEMENT DIVISION

Two appointments to executive positions in the division of traffic movement were announced April 15 by Defense Transportation Director Eastman.

George A. Warren of Burlingame, Calif., has been appointed assistant director of the division in charge of the section of traffic channels. Mr. Warren succeeds Walter Bockstahler, who has been placed in charge of a newly created section of merchandise traffic.

A. R. Mahaney, of Pittsburgh, Pa., has been appointed chief of the traffic flow unit.

New industry advisory committees

The Bureau of Industry Advisory Committees, WPB, has announced the formation of the following new industry advisory committees:

BUILDERS' HARDWARE COMMITTEE

Government presiding officer—J. L. Haynes, chief of the building materials branch.

Members:

J. J. Meyer, Independent Lock Co., Fitchburg, Mass.; William C. Habbersett, Russell & Erwin Mfg. Co., New Britain, Conn.; R. T. Mitchell, Yale & Towne Mfg. Co., Stamford, Conn.; L. W. Oakes, Sargent & Co., New Haven, Conn.; Duncan Shaw, Reading Hardware Corporation, Reading, Pa.; Charles Kendrick, Schlage Lock Co., San Francisco, Calif.; E. F. Lawrence, Jr., Lawrence Brothers, Inc., Sterling, Ill.; A. L. Hager, Hager & Sons Hinge Mfg. Co., St. Louis, Mo.; E. J. Tower, Master Lock Co., Milwaukee, Wis.; Johann Frohlich, Bommer Spring Hinge Co., Brooklyn, N. Y.; A. H. Schleicher, Oscar C. Rixson Co., Chicago, Ill.; W. A. Heizmann, Sr., Penn Hardware Co., Reading, Pa.

COMBAT INSTRUMENTS COMMITTEE

Government presiding officer—Charles L. Saunders.

Members:

F. G. Vaughen, manager, Meter Division, General Electric Co., Schenectady, N. Y.; Ray R. Simpson, president, Simpson Electric Co., Chicago; H. L. Olesen, assistant general sales manager, Weston Electrical Instrument Co., Newark, N. J.; H. F. Sparkes, sales manager, Meter Division, Westinghouse Electric & Mfg. Co., Newark, N. J.; D. J. Angus, president, Esterline-Angus Co., Inc., Indianapolis, Ind.; R. H. Isaacs, sales manager, Bendix Aviation Corporation, Pioneer Instrument Division, Bendix, N. J.; W. P. Loudon, Electric Auto-Lite Co., Toledo; Victor Carbonara, vice president, Kollsman Instrument Division, Square D Co., Elmhurst, N. Y.; A. D. Hickok, president, Hickok Electric Instrument Co., Cleveland.

DOMESTIC SEWING MACHINE COMMITTEE

Government presiding officer—Louis C. Upton, chief of the consumers' durable goods branch.

Members:

Milton C. Lightner, vice president, The Singer Manufacturing Co., New York, N. Y.; A. S. Rodgers, president, White Sewing Machine Corporation, Cleveland, Ohio; Raymond F. List, president, National Sewing Machine Co., BelVidere, Ill.; Jay Kasler, president, Free Sewing Machine Co., Rockford, Ill.

ISTLE COMMITTEE

Government presiding officer—Arthur R. Howe.

Members:

R. J. Paisley, R. L. Pritchard & Co., New York City; William Garrettson, New York City; Roy J. C. Emmert Hanover Cordage Co., Hanover Pa.; E. D. Martin, HooVen & Allison Co., Xenia, Ohio; T. A. Unsworth, E. B. & A. C. Whiting Co., Burlington, Vt.; Norman F. Smith, Osborn Manufacturing Co., CleVeland; Harry Burkart, F. Burkart & Co., St. Louis Mo.; L. M. Argueso, M. Argueso & Co., New York City; Frederick K. Barbour, Linen Thread Co., Paterson, N. J.; R. C. Utess, American Manufacturing Co., Brooklyn, N. Y.;

L. E. Hohl, Maryland Fibre Products Co., Inc., Baltimore; C. A. Porter, National Brush Co., Aurora, Ill.; O. D. Wiley, Burton-Dixie Corporation, Chicago; Frank W Bird, Smith & Bird, New York City; G A. Moreland, Columbian Rope Co., Auburn, N. Y.; Arthur Nelson, Dolphin Jute Mills, Paterson, N. J.; A. Bloom, Otto Gerdau Co., New York City; F. W. Weitzel, Ox Fibre Brush Co., Frederick, Md.; Jack Gantz, Empire Brush Works, Port Chester, N. Y.; Winthrop Page, National Automotive Fibres, Inc., East Los Angeles, Calif.

MECHANICAL RUBBER GOODS COMMITTEE

Government presiding officer—C. S. Reynolds.

Members:

Willard H. Cobb, U. S. Rubber Co., New York City; F. M. Daley, Sponge Rubber Products Co., Derby, Conn.; J. E. MacDonald, Jr., Whitehead Brothers Rubber Co., Trenton, N. J.; K. H. Glantor, Dayton Rubber Manufacturing Co., Dayton, Ohio; W. S. Richardson, B. F. Goodrich Co., Akron, Ohio; Franklin G. Smith, Ohio Rubber Co., Willoughby, Ohio; W. L White, Raybestos-Manhattan, Inc., Passaic, N. J.; C. W. Yelm, Gates Rubber Co., DenVer, Colo.; H. F Schultz, Republic Rubber Co., Youngstown, Ohio; Paul H. Henkel, Continental Rubber Works, Erie, Pa.; D. E. Harpfer, Goodyear Tire & Rubber Co., Akron, Ohio; George L. Abbott. Garlock Packing Co., Palmyra, N. Y.; J. H. Hayden, Hewitt Rubber Corporation, Buffalo, N. Y.; A. F. Matheis, Thermoid Co. Trenton, N. J.

PLUMBING AND HEATING COMMITTEE
DISTRIBUTORS SUBCOMMITTEE

Government presiding officer—W. W. Timmis, chief of the plumbing and heating branch.

Members:

M. W. Dennison, executive director, Braman Dow & Co., Boston, Mass.; W. A. Brecht, president, Hajoca Corporation, Philadelphia, Pa.; F. W. Swanson, president, Globe Machinery & Supply Co., Des Moines, Iowa; Frank E. Elliott, manager, Crane Co., San Francisco; A. T. Chamercy, Sears Roebuck & Co., Chicago, Ill.; R. W. Conway, Hechinger Co., Washington, D. C.; H. G. Starr, executive secretary, Plumbing & Heating Wholesalers of New England, Inc., Boston, Mass.; N. J. Higinbotham, president, W. A. Case & Sons Manufacturing Co., Buffalo, N. Y.; J. A. Galloup, president, Galloup Pipe & Supply Co., Battle Creek, Mich.; W. J. Spillane, general manager, James B. Clow & Sons, Chicago, Ill.; Milton M. Goldsmith, president, Sam B. Glauber, Inc., New York, N. Y.; John Sepple, diVision manager, Montgomery Ward Co., Chicago, Ill.; Theodore Feinstein, executive director, National Supply Association of America, Boston, Mass.

WOMEN'S AND CHILDREN'S LINGERIE COMMITTEE

Government presiding officer—H. Stanley Marcus.

Members:

Philip Springer, president, Phil Springer Co., Inc., 159 Madison Avenue, New York, N. Y.; Herbert L. Miskend, president, Lande & Miskend, Inc., 16 East Thirty-fourth Street, New York, N. Y.; A R. Balton, president, Chic Lingerie Co., Inc., 1126 Santee Street, Los Angeles, Calif.; A. J. Schneierson, Vice president, I. Schneierson & Sons, Inc., 1350 Broadway, New York, N. Y.; Gerald Ritter,

president, Barbizon Corporation, 148 Madison Avenue, New York, N. Y.; J. D. Croom, Jr., Randolph Underwear Co., Randleman, N. C.; H. B. Snader, Vanity Fair Silk Mills, Reading, Pa.; Walter W. Moyer, Ephrata, Pa.; Harry Berger, president, Kaylon, Inc., 180 Madison Avenue, New York, N. Y.

PULP AND PAPER MACHINERY COMMITTEE

Government presiding officer—L. S. Greenleaf.

Members:

Elmer H. Neese, Beloit Iron Works, Beloit, Wis.; Homer W. Martindale, Black-Clawson Co., Hamilton, Ohio; S. Harley Jones, E. D. Jones & Sons Co., Pittsfield, Mass.; Leonard J. List, Samuel M. Langston Co., Camden, N. J.; Walter L. Barker, Improved Paper Machinery, Nashua, N. H.; William Buchanan, Appleton Wire Works, Appleton, Wis.; William W. Bolton, Emerson Manufacturing Co., Lawrence, Mass.; Samuel J. Campbell, Hudson Sharpe Machinery Co., Green Bay, Wis.

PULP AND PAPER COMMITTEE

Government presiding officer—David Winton, chief, pulp and paper branch.

Members:

W. J. Alford, Jr., Continental Paper Co., Ridgefield Park, N. J.; Walter J. Bergman, Lily-Tulip Cup Corporation, New York, N. Y.; H. S. Dennison, Dennison Manufacturing Co., Framingham, Mass.; George E. Dyke, Robert Gair Co., New York, N. Y.; E. E. Grant, Crystal Tissue Co., Middletown, Ohio; Willard J. Henry, Southern Advance Bag & Paper Co., Chicago, Ill.; Walter A. Starr, Soundview Pulp Co., Everett, Wash.; D. L. Luke, Jr., West Virginia Pulp & Paper Co., New York, N. Y.; Ernst Mahler, Kimberly-Clark Corporation, Neenah, Wis.; Arthur L. Hobson, St. Croix Paper Co., Boston, Mass.; Clyde B. Morgan, Eastern Corporation, Bangor, Maine; W. Irving Osborne, Jr., Cornell Wood Products Co., Chicago, Ill.; D. H. Patterson, Fibreboard Products, Inc., San Francisco, Calif.; Robert F. Nelson, Glassine Paper Co., West Conshohocken, Pa.; J. T. Roach, Southern Central Co., Memphis, Tenn.; Maxwell D. Bardeen, Lee Paper Co., Vicksburg, Mich.; Glen Graham, Sutherland Paper Co., Kalamazoo, Mich.; E. V. Johnson, United States Envelope Co., Springfield, Mass.; Robert B. Wolf, Weyerhauser Timber Co., Longview, Wash.; Stewart E. Kay, International Paper Co., New York, N. Y.

WOOD CASE PENCIL MANUFACTURERS COMMITTEE

Government presiding officer—M. D. Moore, of the consumers' durable goods branch.

Members:

Coburn Musser, Eberhard Faber Pencil Co., Brooklyn, N. Y.; Joseph S. Reckford, American Lead Pencil Co., Hoboken, N. J.; Asa B. Wallace, Wallace Pencil Co., St. Louis, Mo.; M. LeVine, Reliance Pencil Co., Mt. Vernon, N. Y.; W. C. Rucker, Musgrave Pencil Co., Shelbyville, Tenn.; J. H. Schermerhorn, Joseph Dixon Crucible Co., Jersey City, N. J.; Irving P. FaVor, L. & C Hardtmuth, Inc., Bloomsbury, N. J.; Herman Price, Eagle Pencil Co., New York City; Arthur Edelhoff, General Pencil Co., Jersey City, N. J.; J. P. Fitzpatrick, Red Cedar Pencil Co., Lewisburg, Tenn.; Frank Beck, Empire Pencil Co., Shelbyville, Tenn.; Henry Hassenfeld, Hassenfeld Brothers, Inc., Pawtucket, R. I.; Jack P. McClasson, National Pencil Co., Shelbyville, Tenn.; Edward M. Parrish, Gulf Red Cedar Co., Richmond, Va.; M. A. Ferst, M. A. Ferst, Inc., Atlanta, Ga.; A. H. Best, Richard Best Pencil Co., Irvington, N. J.; Garett Roberts, Weldon-Roberts Rubber Co., Newark, N. J.

Over-quota sales, exports of farm machinery, equipment banned

WPB on April 14 issued an amendment (No. 2) to Limitation Order L–26 to make it plain that the intent of the order is to prohibit all sales and exports of farm machinery and equipment in excess of the quantities permitted to be manufactured.

Some confusion over the order's terms has developed, and issuance of the interpretative amendment is considered necessary to prevent production and sales over quotas, to preserve the competitive status of various manufacturers and to conserve raw materials and finished products.

The sales restriction does not apply to equipment or attachments and repair parts which were completely manufactured or completely fabricated and ready for shipment in knock-down form on October 31, 1941.

★ ★ ★

Uses of rotenone limited as Far East sources are shut off

Because imports of rotenone from Malaya and the Netherland Indies have been cut off, limitations on its use were ordered April 14 by the Director of Industry Operations with issuance of Conservation Order M–133, effective immediately.

The chemical is used as a spray for food crops, particularly peas and beans; as a delousing agent; for household insecticides, cattle and poultry powders and as an ingredient in sprays and soaps for dogs, cats, and other household pets.

M–133 permits its continued use as a delousing agent and for food crops other than cotton, tobacco, cranberries, eggplant, cucurbits (plants of the gourd family, such as cucumbers, squashes, and pumpkins), onions, peppers, and sweet corn. Household uses are prohibited.

Doesn't affect products already manufactured

The order applies to manufacture of preparations containing rotenone and does not affect the use of such products already manufactured.

Imports of rotenone from Latin America, normally half the United States' supply, are expected to increase sharply next year. Meantime, shipments of pyrethrum, a satisfactory substitute for household uses, continue to arrive from Africa and are not restricted.

Four new sections will handle problems for specific types of farm machines, equipment

The farm machinery and equipment branch of WPB has set up four sections to handle all problems relating to products formerly handled by the branch in general. These four sections are

To handle all appeals under L–26

Tractor and Farm Engine Section.—Frank Bonnes, chief, formerly supervisor of farm tractor sales of the International Harvester Co., Chicago, Ill.

Harvesting and Marketing Equipment Section.—K. W. Anderson, chief, formerly assistant sales manager of John Deere Harvester Works of Deere & Co., Moline, Ill.

Tillage, Planting and Seeding Equipment Section.—L. P. Richies, chief, formerly assistant secretary of the Oliver Farm Equipment Co., of Chicago, Ill.

Barn, Poultry and Miscellaneous Equipment Section.—Stephen Mahon, chief, formerly executive Vice president of the James Manufacturing Co., Fort Atkinson, Wis.

These sections will handle all appeals under Limitation Order L–26, which regulates the production of all types of farm machinery and equipment.

Each section chief will be responsible only for the equipment assigned to him. Therefore, in making appeals, administrative work will be expedited if separate appeals are sent to the section having control over the equipment covered by the appeal.

All correspondence relating to the limitation order should be addressed to the War Production Board, Ref. L–26, and should be marked for the attention of the section chief handling the equipment involved.

Equipment assigned to each section

TRACTOR AND FARM SECTION

Tractors, wheel, except all purpose; tractors, all purpose; tractors, garden; engines, air cooled, farm; engines, water cooled, farm; pump, jacks; irrigation pumps; irrigation equipment; pumps, hand; wind mills; pumps, cylinder, farm; pumps, jet; pumps, pitcher; pumps, power; pumps, reciprocal; pumps, shallow well; wagons, farm; trucks, farm; trailers, farm.

HARVESTING AND MARKETING EQUIPMENT SECTION

Binders, corn; binders, grain; binders, rice; blowers, agricultural; cleaners, grain; combines, harvester; crushers, feed; cutters, ensilage; cutters, feed; elevators, portable, farm; elevators, stationary, farm; evaporators, syrup; graders, grain; graders, fruit; harvesters, bean; harvesters, ensilage; harvesters, grain; harvesters, hay; harvesters, pea; huskers, corn; loaders, hay; mills, cane, farm; mills, cider, farm; mowers, hay; pickers, corn; pickers, cotton; pickers, peanut; presses, fruit, farm; presses, hay; presses, pick-up, hay; rakes, hay; shellers, corn, hand; shellers, corn, power; shredders, corn; stackers, hay; threshers, bean; threshers, grain; threshers, pea.

TILLAGE, PLANTING, AND SEEDING EQUIPMENT SECTION

Cultivators, beet; cultivators, garden; cultivators, horse; cultivators, tractor; cutters, stalk; diggers, potato; drills, seed; dusters, crop; fertilizing machinery; harrows, agricultural; hoes, rotary; lifters, beet; lifters, peanut; lime spreaders; listers, agricultural; manure spreaders; manure loaders; packers, soil; planters, corn; planters, cotton; planters, garden; planters, potato; plows, disc; plow shapes; plow shares; plows, subsoil; pulverizers, agricultural; rollers, agricultural; seeders, farm; sprayers, farm; sprayers, hand; sprayers, power; transplanters, agricultural; weeders, garden; weeders, horse-drawn; weeders, rod.

BARN, POULTRY, AND MISCELLANEOUS EQUIPMENT SECTION

Beekeepers' supplies; brooders, poultry; butter-making equipment, farm; carriers, feed; carriers, hay; carriers, litter; cookers, feed; coolers, milk, farm; corn cribs; cream separators, farm; drinking cups, livestock; feeders, livestock; feeders, poultry; fence controllers, electric, farm; forks, hay, harpoon, grapple, etc.; gates, farm; grain bins, farm; harness hardware; heaters, tank, livestock; horseshoes; horseshoe nails; incubators poultry; milking machines; partitions, stock; tanks, farm; tanks, livestock; track and hangers, barn door; track, hay and litter carrier; troughs, livestock; trucks, feed; watering bowls, livestock; waterers, poultry.

· · ·

Buying of pork, pork products expedited to meet Allied needs

The Department of Agriculture is expanding its purchase program for pork and pork products to meet the urgent requests of Allied Nations.

The Agricultural Marketing Administration has asked packers operating under Federal inspection to offer for sale to the Federal Surplus Commodities Corporation at least two-fifths of their production of pork cuts and canned pork and two-thirds of their production of lard and hog casings. This action has been taken to assure the availability of sufficient quantities of pork products to meet Lend-Lease requirements during the late spring and early summer months.

These requirements will necessitate a considerable step-up in the weekly rate of purchases. Therefore, if plans work out, the AMA will buy the equivalent of approximately 40 percent of the pork and 65 to 70 percent of the lard produced during the next 3 to 6 months in Federally inspected plants. These packers normally handle about two-thirds of the country's total production of pork.

CIVILIAN DEFENSE . . .

Selected civilian hospitals in three coastal areas promised funds, technical aid in accumulating blood plasma banks

OCD Director Landis announced April 16 that funds have been made available through the United States Public Health Service to enable the medical division of the Office of Civilian Defense to provide technical and financial assistance to selected civilian hospitals, located within 300 miles of the Atlantic, Pacific, and Gulf Coast, so that they can accumulate a local store of blood plasma for the treatment of civilian casualties caused by enemy action.

A reserve supply of dried plasma also will be prepared for prompt shipment to communities whose local plasma bank may be exhausted after air raids or other major catastrophe. At Pearl Harbor many lives were saved because of the availability of blood plasma, Director Landis said.

Dr. George Baehr, chief medical officer of OCD, explained that an adequate supply of blood and of plasma must be promptly available in all exposed communities for the treatment of civilian casualties which may be caused by enemy action, sabotage, or a major disaster.

Dr. Baehr's statement follows (in part):

Such casualties are frequently of a very serious nature. . . . Although whole blood transfusions are indicated when there is bleeding, the condition of shock is more common after severe injuries and burns, and many lives can be saved by transfusions of plasma, the liquid part of the blood.

Civilian plasma depots needed

The Army and the Navy, with the assistance of the Red Cross, have been collecting blood and having it processed into dried plasma in commercial laboratories so that it can be shipped readily to distant parts. Because of the widespread distribution of our major cities along long coast lines, civilian depots of plasma must be established in hundreds of communities. These local supplies can be stored in the liquid or frozen form.

Technical direction provided

In order to increase the amount of reserve plasma in all exposed communities, a portion of the money now available to the Office of Civilian Defense will be employed to assist selected hospitals within the coastal defense zone which do not now have blood or plasma banks, to develop such facilities in accordance with the technique recommended by the National Research Council. In addition to some financial assistance, expert technical direction will be available to such hospitals

through the assignment of Dr. John Alsever as national technical director to the Office of Civilian Defense by the United States Public Health Service, and through a number of other experts who will be designated as regional consultants.

Collections from voluntary donors

The plasma to be collected may be used both to meet current local needs and to establish a reserve supply. Hospitals to be selected must have at least a 300-bed capacity, since that size has been found to be desirable for proper operation of a blood and plasma bank. Each hospital selected will be expected to accumulate a reserve stock of liquid or frozen plasma amounting to at least one unit per bed within 3 months. A unit of plasma is the amount which can be obtained from 500 cc. (1 pint) of blood. The hospital will later be expected to maintain this plasma bank for its own needs.

By this means an adequate supply of plasma should be available in hospitals in the "target areas" of the United States within 3 months time. . . . The blood from which this plasma is to be obtained will be collected by each hospital from voluntary donors.

★ ★ ★

OCD streamlined for war by new order, says Landis

President Roosevelt has established by Executive order a Civilian Defense Board within the Office of Civilian Defense to integrate OCD activities more closely with those of other Federal, State, and local war agencies.

Director Landis had the following comment to make:

The new Executive order is significant to me because it accomplishes two very important things: First, it streamlines OCD for war in a manner in which I believe it should be streamlined, and second, through the creation of the Civilian Defense Board, it integrates the operations of OCD with those of the total government program for prosecution of the war. I am, needless to say, very much pleased with the new order.

Members of the Board are the OCD Director (chairman), the War and Navy Secretaries, the Attorney General, the Director of the Office of Defense Health and Welfare Services, Mayor Maurice J. Tobin of Boston, E. D. Mallery, Executive Director of the American Municipal Association, Red Cross Chairman Davis, and Governor Stassen of Minnesota.

Under the order, Director Landis will perform his duties under supervision of the President, with the advice and assistance of the Board.

More adequate health facilities for war plants urged by McNutt

An assertion that 80,000,000 working days, or enough to build 14,000 bombers, 33,000 tanks, or 10 great battleships, in the next year, could be saved if adequate industrial health measures were taken immediately in the country's war plants, was made by Paul V. McNutt, Federal Security Administrator, at the Fifth National Conference of Governmental Industrial Hygienists held in Washington April 9–11.

War centers inadequately served

Medical services in such war centers as Bremerton, Wash., Valparaiso, Fla., and Hinesville, Ga., are so inadequate that doctors, nurses, and dentists may have to be drafted from other communities, Asst. Surg. Gen. Joseph W. Mountin told the conference.

The conferees were informed by Channing R. Dooley of the Labor Division, WPB, that part of their problems could be met if they would draw on the 6,000 to 8,000 licensed women doctors in the country as plant physicians.

Health needs of small plants stressed

The conferees expressed special concern with two phases of industrial health: the health problems created by large, sudden influxes of persons into war industrial areas, and the problem of providing adequate health services in small industrial plants.

The conference recommended (in part):

1. That the Public Health Services take leadership in mobilizing facilities in war industrial areas.

2. That the present program of research, training, and technical assistance in industrial health to war industry be expanded in order to meet present and future needs.

The latter resolution pointed out that almost none of the small industrial plants employing less than 500 have medical, engineering, or nursing services. Since a large majority of the workers are employed in such plants, the conference recommended that governmental industrial hygienists undertake to develop plans and promote the voluntary establishment of medical, engineering, and nursing services in small plants by industry.

HEALTH AND WELFARE . . .

Very few city families eat all 8 "musts" for nutrition, survey indicates

Very few city families probably make a habit of eating all the protective foods necessary for health and strength, according to preliminary reports on a recent nutrition poll made public April 15 by Federal Security Administrator Paul V. McNutt. The survey, made by Crossley, Inc., at the request of the Office of Defense Health and Welfare Services of which Mr. McNutt is director, was conducted in South Bend, Ind., where an intensive community nutrition program is now under way.

The eight basic food groups about which South Bend housewives were questioned are those listed as daily "musts" in the national nutrition food rules, recommended by the Nation's leading nutritionists: milk and milk products; oranges, grapefruit, tomatoes, raw salad greens; green or yellow vegetables; other vegetables and fruits; whole-grain products or enriched white bread and flour; meat, poultry, and fish; eggs; butter and other spreads.

A third use at least seven

Only a small percentage of the families interviewed use all eight essential groups daily; but the survey shows that a third of the housewives use at least seven of them in the average day's meals; and another third use six. Meat, vegetables (other than green or yellow), and butter are the three groups reported most frequently in the average day's meals.

Children seem to fare much better, nutritionally speaking, than adults. This is especially noticeable in the findings on milk and milk products. Approximately 95 percent of housewives with children believe that milk products should be served daily, whereas no more than 80 percent of adults without children believe they need milk or milk products every day.

About 75 percent of the housewives interviewed had heard of enriched bread; about 20 percent had not, and the remainder were uncertain. Slightly more than half definitely remembered having purchased enriched bread; about one-third did not remember.

Value of tomatoes overlooked

Oranges and grapefruit appear much more frequently on their tables than either salad or tomatoes; the relative frequency might be roughly stated as one for tomatoes and tomato juice, two for the cabbage and salad group, and three for citrus fruits. The regular use of the citrus fruits by so many families is encouraging in the opinion of nutritionists. But, it is pointed out, more people need to know that tomatoes and cabbage grown locally over wide areas are acceptable alternatives with similar protective values. This is particularly important information for the housewife who must see that her family is well fed on a modest budget.

In South Bend, and no doubt other parts of the country, the white potato is eaten more frequently than any other vegetable. Eight out of every 10 of the housewives to whom the interviewers talked serve potatoes practically every day. This is a good showing in the opinion of nutritionists. But the picture is different for green and yellow vegetables, which are particularly high in protective vitamins and minerals; these are included in the average day's meals in only about half the families. A substantial number, perhaps as much as a third to a half, of the total women interviewed, say they never serve spinach or similar leafy vegetables.

Use of tops and skins neglected

There also seems to be considerable room for improvement even in getting all the good out of the vegetables which are used fairly frequently: Only about one-third of the women interviewed believe the tops of beets have high nutritive value and for turnip tops the ratio is only about one-fourth; one-half of these housewives believe the skins of baked potatoes have high food value.

GOLF CLUB ORDER AMENDED

The golf club limitation order, L–93, was amended April 16 to permit manufacturers to acquire from inventories of other manufacturers finished parts containing iron and steel for assembly in golf clubs.

All manufacture and assembly of golf clubs will cease after May 31, 1942.

Physical fitness activities to be integrated into existing FSA programs, says McNutt

Federal Security Administrator McNutt announced April 15 after a study of the operations of the division of physical fitness that a large part of its previous operations will be integrated with existing programs of the Federal Security Agency.

Kelly to be assistant director

Mr. McNutt said that John B. Kelly, director of the physical fitness division, recently transferred from the Office of Civilian Defense, will become assistant director in charge of physical fitness, and will continue to maintain headquarters in Philadelphia with a small staff.

The administrator paid tribute to the excellent work that has been accomplished by Mr. Kelly and his coworkers, and called on those leaders throughout the Nation, who have so generously given their time and effort to this work, to continue to promote these vital community programs in this period of emergency.

Mr. McNutt stated:

The stimulus furnished by the physical fitness division to local and individual initiative in organizing constructive use of leisure time has aided communities throughout the Nation in planning and developing local fitness programs.

Existing facilities to be used

In the Office of Civilian Defense the division operated on a small budget as a coordinating agency for the development of local programs. It has rendered a service in bringing about a more extensive use of existing community resources and encouraging local sponsorship of organized sports activities. An over-all program for ultimate success requires the full cooperation of Federal, State, and local governments, private organizations, and of the people.

This program will be forwarded through the existing facilities of the Office of Education and the Office of Defense Health and Welfare Services, both part of the Federal Security Agency. Field recreation representatives of the Office of Defense Health and Welfare Services will assist local communities in developing plans to meet their recreational needs while representatives of the Office of Education will do similar work with schools and colleges.

Subcontracts may swing balance in war, says Nelson; plants with as few as five or six machines should be used, he asserts

Increased subcontracting may swing the balance in this war, Chairman Donald M. Nelson of the War Production Board said April 15 in an open letter asking major prime contractors to spread more work among other firms whenever deliveries can be hastened by this policy.

Mr. Nelson's letter, designed primarily for contractors on critical items, follows:

More subcontracting will help win the war.

Production speed is the dominant factor in the race with the Axis; we have no time to wait for new tools and new plant facilities.

Every available idle tool that can be put to work must be put to work. This may cost more, but the job must be done fast, and experience has taught us that some prime contracts can be subcontracted as much as 90 percent.

Planes, tanks, guns, and ships—their parts and subassemblies are needed in an ever increasing flow, and only by full use of existing facilities, by sharing the work, can we get them soon enough.

Every prime contractor can help. Every prime contractor should consider having an established subcontracting department. Subcontractors should be given engineering assistance. Plants with as few as five or six machines can

and should be used in subcontracting.

The War Production Board has established field offices throughout the United States, now grouped in 13 regions. One purpose of these offices is to effect the fullest and most efficient utilization of facilities within their areas. For this purpose, they maintain records of machine tool equipment and other facilities of manufacturing establishments. I urge you to make your subcontracting needs known to the nearest office.

With the future of our country at stake, with our Armed Forces in immediate need of more weapons, imagination and boldness are called for on the industrial front. Increased subcontracting may swing the balance.

Production lines are battle lines. Let's use all the production we've got.

Sincerely,

DONALD M. NELSON.

★ ★ ★

Release of "frozen" retreads

Retreaded or recapped passenger car tires "frozen" in the hands of retreaders since February 19 may be released to any of their owners who can qualify for retreading certificates, instructions sent by the OPA to State rationing administrators revealed April 17.

WAR EFFORT INDICES

MANPOWER

National labor force, Mar.	54,000,000
Unemployed, Mar.	3,600,000
Nonagricultural workers, Feb.	39,842,000
Percent increase since June 1940.	**14
Farm employment, April 1, 1942.	9,483,000
Percent decrease since June 1940.	**4

FINANCE *(In millions of dollars)*

Authorized program June 1940-Mar. 31, 1942	‡136,894
Ordnance	32,417
Airplanes	26,802
Misc. munitions	17,789
Naval ships	15,223
Industrial facilities	13,898
Merchant ships	7,550
Posts, depots. etc.	7,078
Stock pile, food exports	5,791
Pay, subsistence, travel for the armed forces	4,131
Housing	1,392
Miscellaneous	4,823
Total expenditures, June 1940-Mar. 31, 1942	*22,860
Sales of War Bonds, cumulative, May 1941-April 15, 1942	5,117
April 1-15	257

PRODUCTION *(In millions of dollars)*

June 1940 to latest reporting date	
Gov. commitments for plant expansion; 1,060 projects, Feb. 28	9,281
Private commitments for plant expansion; 6,237 projects, Feb. 28	1,978

EARNINGS, HOURS, AND COST OF LIVING

		Percent increase from June 1940
Manufacturing industries—February		
Average weekly earnings	$35.76	38.7
Average hours worked per week	42.2	12.5
Average hourly earnings	80.3¢	19.5
Cost of Living, Feb. (1935-39=100)	112.6	12.0

* Preliminary
‡ Preliminary and excludes authorizations in Naval Supply Act for fiscal year 1943.
** Adjusted to avoid reflection of seasonal changes.

OFFICE FOR EMERGENCY MANAGEMENT

WAYNE COY, *Liaison Officer*

CENTRAL ADMINISTRATIVE SERVICES: Dallas Dort, *Director.*

DEFENSE COMMUNICATIONS BOARD: James Lawrence Fly, *Chairman.*

INFORMATION DIVISION: Robert W. Horton, *Director.*

NATIONAL WAR LABOR BOARD: Wm. H. Davis, *Chairman.*

OFFICE OF SCIENTIFIC RESEARCH AND DEVELOPMENT: Dr. VanneVar Bush, *Director.*

OFFICE OF CIVILIAN DEFENSE: James M. Landis, *Director.*

OFFICE OF THE COORDINATOR OF INTER-AMERICAN AFFAIRS: Nelson Rockefeller, *Coordinator.*

OFFICE OF DEFENSE HEALTH AND WELFARE SERVICES: Paul V. McNutt, *Director.*

OFFICE OF DEFENSE TRANSPORTATION: Joseph B. Eastman, *Director.*

OFFICE OF FACTS AND FIGURES: Archibald MacLeish, *Director.*

OFFICE OF LEND-LEASE ADMINISTRATION: E. R. Stettinius, Jr., *Administrator.*

OFFICE OF PRICE ADMINISTRATION: Leon Henderson, *Administrator.*

CONSUMER DIVISION: Dexter M. Keezer, *Assistant Administrator*, in charge. Dan A. West, *Director.*

OFFICE OF ALIEN PROPERTY CUSTODIAN: Leo T. Crowley, *Custodian.*

WAR MANPOWER COMMISSION: Paul V. McNutt, *Chairman.*

WAR RELOCATION AUTHORITY: Milton Eisenhower, *Director.*

WAR SHIPPING ADMINISTRATION: Rear Admiral Emory S. Land, U. S. N. (Retired), *Administrator.*

WAR PRODUCTION BOARD:
  Donald M. Nelson, *Chairman.*
  Henry L. Stimson.
  Frank W. Knox.
  Jesse H. Jones.
  William S. Knudsen.
  Sidney Hillman.
  Leon Henderson.
  Henry A. Wallace.
  Harry L. Hopkins.

WAR PRODUCTION BOARD DIVISIONS:
  Donald M. Nelson, *Chairman.*
    Executive Secretary, G. Lyle Beisley.
  PLANNING COMMITTEE: Robert R. Nathan, *Chairman.*
  PURCHASES DIVISION: Houlder Hudgins, *Acting Director.*
  PRODUCTION DIVISION: W. H. Harrison, *Director.*
  MATERIALS DIVISION: Wm. L. Batt, *Director.*
  DIVISION OF INDUSTRY OPERATIONS: J. S. Knowlson, *Director.*
  LABOR DIVISION: Sidney Hillman, *Director.*
  CIVILIAN SUPPLY DIVISION: Leon Henderson, *Director.*
  OFFICE OF PROGRESS REPORTS: Stacy May, *Director.*
  REQUIREMENTS COMMITTEE: Wm. L. Batt, *Chairman.*
  STATISTICS DIVISION: Stacy May, *Director.*
  INFORMATION DIVISION: Robert W. Horton, *Director.*
  LEGAL DIVISION: John Lord O'Brian, *General Counsel.*

VICTORY

OFFICIAL WEEKLY BULLETIN OF THE AGENCIES IN THE OFFICE FOR EMERGENCY MANAGEMENT

WASHINGTON, D. C.   APRIL 28, 1942   VOLUME 3, NUMBER 17

Gasoline rationing begins May 15 in East; cards to be given out May 12-14

Acting on information supplied by Petroleum Coordinator Ickes and at the direction of the War Production Board, Price Administrator Henderson on April 23 announced that a temporary plan for rationing gasoline in 17 eastern States and the District of Columbia would be instituted May 15.

This plan, designed to meet the immediate emergency in the eastern States affected by the recent gasoline limitation order of the Office of Petroleum Coordinator, is an interim plan, which will probably operate only until July 1, when it is planned to institute a more elaborate and comprehensive coupon rationing system. The amount of gasoline that a user may receive under the plan will be announced before May 15.

The States where gasoline will be rationed under the interim plan are: Connecticut, Delaware, Florida, Georgia, Maine, Maryland, Massachusetts, New Hampshire, New Jersey, New York, North Carolina, Pennsylvania, Rhode Island, South Carolina, Vermont, Virginia, West Virginia, and the District of Columbia.

To assure fair distribution

The plan, the administrator pointed out, was adopted to assure the public of fair distribution of the curtailed supplies of gasoline under the new limitation order, which reduces deliveries to gasoline retailers by 33½ percent.

"The petroleum shortage in the East

arises, not from a scarcity of crude or from refinery facilities, but from a lack of transportation means," Mr. Henderson said. "Normally more than 90 percent of the 1,500,000 barrels of petroleum products we consume daily in the East is brought in by tanker. Since the start of the war many tankers have been sunk by enemy submarine action, and sinkings continue. At the same time the Army and Navy, preparing for offensive action at the earliest possible moment, need every tanker that can be pressed into military service.

Industries must have oil

"There is also an ever growing demand for petroleum products on the home front, and every gallon that comes in to any area must be wisely used. Industries, thousands of which are located in the Eastern States, must have oil, or their production of war materials will stop. Gasoline must be used to get workers employed in those factories to work, or war production again will be hampered. Then there are many other types of gasoline users—the doctor, the nurse, the commercial driver—who need gasoline to carry on activities regarded as essential to civilian efficiency under war economy.

Registration days for obtaining gasoline rationing cards will be May 12, 13, and 14. The registration sites and hours

(Continued on page 26)

SOLDIERS of PRODUCTION

END OF 1941	(symbols)
APR. 1 1942	(symbols)
*MIDDLE OF NOV. 1942	(symbols)
*JAN. 1 1943	(symbols)

Each symbol = 3 million workers in war industry

* REVISED ESTIMATES

SOURCE: U. S. BUREAU OF LABOR STATISTICS

100 MORE PLANTS ORGANIZE FOR TOTAL PRODUCTION—Page 9

Review of the Week

So many tank ships have been sunk by the Axis or diverted to the uses of war that it is no longer possible to move enough gasoline to the East Coast for all needs, the Government announced last week. Motor fuel will be rationed to individual consumers, beginning May 15, under the authority of the Office of Price Administration.

Sugar rationing details

OPA also issued an order setting forth the details of sugar rationing for trade, industrial, and institutional users; and for individual consumers, who will register on May 4, 5, 6, and 7. An allotment of not more than 5 pounds a year per person was announced for home canning. OPA warned, moreover, that an acute shortage of sugar would develop in the Northeast unless wholesalers and industrial users took advantage of supplies of beet sugar.

May quotas allowed passenger cars fewer new tires, but an increase in recapped tires boosted the combined total to a higher figure than for April. OPA authorized a 16-percent increase in prices of new tires and tubes, to cover the cost of the plan whereby overstocked dealers turned supplies over to the Defense Supplies Corporation. Emergency reserves of tires were made available to long-distance bus and truck operators.

Blanket ceiling for export prices

Also last week, OPA advanced into the field of blanket price regulation by applying an over-all ceiling to exports. At home, OPA established maximum prices that may be charged for hundreds of china and pottery articles; extended its control over textiles to cover practically every product of the cotton textile industry; put a temporary ceiling over oil paints and varnishes, and a permanent ceiling over silk waste, now used only for military purposes.

Moving into still another phase of civil life, the War Production Board ordered that military and essential needs be given preference in installation of telephones. Operators of the country's biggest network estimated the restrictions would result in denial of about 200,000 applications for main-line residential service this year.

Sewing-machine output to stop

WPB also called a halt to production of sewing machines June 15, with limited output in the meantime; shut off metals, cork, and plastics for noncommercial fishing tackle; restricted deliveries of iron and steel products to orders with high preference ratings; instructed the cotton textile industry to convert a large part of its capacity from such civilian products as clothing fabric to military items like bag osnaburg and bag sheeting; directed a quick end to manufacture of farm machinery (except combines) requiring rubber tires; reduced the amount of elastic fabric that may be used in foundation garments; extended limitations on delivery of natural and mixed gas into parts of six States; and stopped the use of benzene in motor fuel because it is a necessary ingredient of synthetic rubber.

Materials needed for repairs to air conditioning and refrigeration equipment were granted high preference ratings. Preference ratings were also used to make sure that machinery is kept in good running order to meet demands for dairy products.

Meanwhile, WPB delved into another source for nickel, urgently needed for armor plate and other components of fighting machines. Under a new order, all scrap containing nickel is to be segregated, and melted only for authorized uses.

16,000 doctors sought

Now under the new War Manpower Commission, the Procurement and Assignment Service for Physicians, Dentists, and Veterinarians sent out a questionnaire designed to find 16,000 physicians and 3,000 dentists who can be called to duty with the Armed Services this year without disrupting care of the public's health.

Planned use of networks to give information is announced by OFF

America's 30 million radio-listening families are scheduled for a better planned fare of Government information from now on, the Office of Facts and Figures said last week. "Fewer announcements, but better timing and planning of those which are made is the keynote of the new plan," according to Archibald MacLeish, director of OFF, which has been designated by President Roosevelt as coordinator of Government radio broadcasts.

Under the OFF plan, each night-time program on the networks will carry a Government announcement once every 4 weeks; each daytime serial program on the networks will present an announcement once in 2 weeks. Information from the Government will include such topics as purchase of War Bonds, pooling of cars, salvage of rubber, conservation of oil and gasoline, and recruiting. No definite allocation plan is provided for local station programs, but the station program managers will be provided every 2 weeks with a "Radio War Guide" classifying Government messages in order of their importance.

The OFF plan will not affect news broadcast, public forums, or speeches by Government officials.

★ ★ ★

TRADE DELIVERIES OF SUGAR

Price Administrator Henderson announced April 24 that trade deliveries of sugar on and after April 28 must conform to the regulations in Rationing Order No. 3, even if contracted for beforehand.

WAR EFFORT'S PROGRESS TOLD VISUALLY

The charts appearing every week on the front cover of VICTORY tell the story of America's battle as it is fought here at home. One-column mats are available for publication by newspapers and others who may desire them. Requests should be sent to Distribution Section, Division of Information, OEM, Washington, D. C.

VICTORY

OFFICIAL BULLETIN of the Office for Emergency Management. Published weekly by the Division of Information, Office for Emergency Management, and printed at the United States Government Printing Office, Washington, D. C.

Subscription rates by mail: 75¢ for 52 issues; 25¢ for 13 issues; single copies 5¢, payable in advance. Remit money order payable directly to the Superintendent of Documents, Government Printing Office, Washington, D. C.

On the Home Front

The tinkling tunes of peace are lost in the swelling symphony of war. Time was when our war effort touched only a few people here and there, when War Production Board orders affecting our daily lives were few, when rationing was a possibility of the future, when all of us wondered what would be the nature and the extent of our contribution to victory.

That time is past. These days the orders to the home-front come thick and fast as the war machine gathers momentum and speed. Now we are aware that we must mobilize our total manpower in order to defeat the Axis, and we know that upon all of us devolve specific duties—above everything the duty to avoid waste, to save, to channel every possible iota of energy into this fight for freedom.

There've been some changes made

Last week saw gasoline rationing a certainty for 17 States on the Eastern Seaboard and the District of Columbia. It found the Office of Price Administration preparing to meet this emergency and at the same time proceeding with the program for the Nation-wide sugar rationing registration which takes place this week. The week brought a general order by the Office of Defense Transportation cutting local delivery services to save tires, and saw strict WPB controls established which mean some 200,000 persons won't be able to get main line telephone installations this year.

Add these developments to the others which have taken place in recent months—orders which have altered our dress to save cloth and stopped production of radios and refrigerators and vacuum cleaners and more than a hundred other products—and you realize that the home front has been stripped down to a fighting front.

A seaman or your Sunday spin?

The reasons for rationing gasoline along the Eastern Seaboard are obvious. Tankers which used to bring gasoline from the Gulf and from the Southwest have been sunk by the Nazis, others have been diverted to direct war service. American sailors have lost their lives trying to bring in gasoline needed for war, no one would ask that such lives be risked to preserve motoring-as-usual. And motoring as usual will be impossible, in those States, from about May 15 on. To the patriotic citizen, for that matter, motoring as usual already has ended all over the Nation—to save rubber.

The growing rubber shortage led the ODT last week to issue its general order cutting local delivery services to a single delivery to any one person on a single day, and local carriers now are required to keep mileage records. And ODT also ordered the trucking industry to haul capacity loads over direct routes in order to get the most out of their tires. OPA's tire quotas for May make fewer new tires

REPRINTING PERMISSIBLE

Requests have been received for permission to reprint "On the Home Front" in whole or in part. This column, like all other material in VICTORY, may be reprinted without special permission. If excerpts are used, the editors ask only that they be taken in such a way that their original meaning is preserved.

available than in April but allocate more rubber for tire repair.

Day by day our compulsion to save rubber increases and also the compulsion upon every householder to get every bit of scrap rubber out of the home or the garage, the barn or the attic or the alley, and back to the reclaiming plants.

Beer caps or ships?

Last week brought several additional WPB orders indirectly affecting the home front of the same type as those orders of the week before which cut the output of phonograph records and foreshadowed a rougher finish on playing cards—orders which underline the manner in which we are scraping the bottom of the materials barrel to meet the needs of war.

One of these new orders restricts manufacture of what are called "crown" caps for beer and other beverage bottles, to save steel and cork. Enough steel was used in making crown caps during 1941 to have made more than 30 "ugly duckling" merchant freighters. And still another order directs manufacturers of fishing tackle to stop using metals, plastics, and cork after May 31 in making noncommercial fishing tackle. Since almost all fishing tackle involves use of these materials, the order means the virtual end of such manufacture until after the war. There's easily a year's supply of fishing tackle, however, in the stores. The time may come when we shall have to ration travel. ODT director

Joseph B. Eastman last week issued an appeal urging that vacationists travel during the middle of the week whenever possible . . . OPA continues its drive to prevent inflation, and today practically every product of the cotton textile industry is under price ceiling . . . Prices are rising because the war gives us more money to spend—and less and less to spend it on as materials and machines and manpower work increasingly for war . . . . WPB has reduced still further the amount of elastic fabric which may be used in corsets, girdles, combinations, brassieres . . .

Doctors in demand

WPB has stopped use of benzene as a motor fuel . . . It's needed now to make synthetic rubber . . . The War Manpower Commission announces that the armed forces want 16,000 additional physicians, 3,000 more dentists, before the end of 1942 . . . Traffic accidents in 1941 are reported to have caused enough lost man-hours in industry to have built 26 battleships . . . Drive slowly and save your tires . . . A New England firm that turned from making horse blankets to manufacture of auto upholstery now is turning out woolen cloth for uniforms and canvas for army tents . . . WPB has ordered the radio industry to discontinue manufacture of 349 types of tubes for civilian use . . . But they're duplicate, obsolete, or small-demand types . . . WPB has added machinery for laundries and dry-cleaning establishments to the list of things on which production must stop . . . OPA warns women that they'd better save the zippers when they rip that old slip into dust cloths . . . And that if your stove, furnace, or boiler needs repairs you'd better have them made now . . . You may not be able to get the parts later on . . . A scarcity of sugar threatens part of the Northeastern United States unless wholesalers and industrial users take advantage of available beet-sugar supplies, OPA warns . . . WPB's Bureau of Industrial Conservation is asking America's mayors to start local drives for spring salvage of rags, metals, and rubber . . .

How's that, again?

"The recent U. S. edict against cuffs on trousers in war time shows the decay of American liberty, because it took away from the male the symbol of domination and the right of freedom." (*Tokyo broadcast recorded by FCC and reported by OFF.*)

PRICE ADMINISTRATION . . .

OPA sets blanket ceiling for profits on all goods sold for export

Maximum prices over all commodities and products sold for export were established April 26 by Price Administrator Henderson.

The new order—titled "Maximum Export Price Regulation"—becomes effective April 30. It was formulated by OPA in cooperation with the Board of Economic Warfare and the Department of State. Its provisions apply to all export sales, regardless of whether or not the commodity or product is under an OPA ceiling schedule or regulation, and override all provisions of existing OPA orders that are in conflict with its terms.

An export sale, in the language of the regulation, is a sale of any commodity or product for export to any place outside the territorial limits of the United States—the 48 States and the District of Columbia.

While the new regulation cuts across all outstanding contracts of sale or purchase it does not disturb prices involved in any export made under a validly outstanding export license issued by the Board of Economic Warfare prior to April 30, 1942.

Briefly, the new order provides that the export price of any commodity shall be the cost of acquisition by the exporter plus the average premium charged in the export trade in a similar transaction during July 1 December 31, 1940, or March 1-April 15, 1942, whichever period yields the lower average premium. In addition, the exporter may add an amount sufficient to compensate him for expenses, such as war risk insurance, consular fees, demurrage charges, and shipping charges. Manufacturers or producers who export directly can similarly add the lower of the two average premiums and the export expenses to their domestic price for the product or commodity exported.

Makers of steel screen cloth may raise prices 5 percent

An amendment to Revised Price Schedule No. 6 (Iron and Steel Products) permitting an increase of about 5 percent in manufacturers' prices for steel screen cloth was announced April 22 by Price Administrator Henderson.

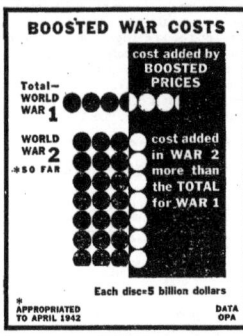

BOOSTED WAR COSTS

Total— WORLD WAR **1** cost added by BOOSTED PRICES

WORLD WAR **2** = 50 FAR

cost added in WAR 2 more than the TOTAL for WAR 1

Each disc=5 billion dollars

*APPROPRIATED TO APRIL 1942

DATA OPA

OPA acts to ease movement of sugar

In order to facilitate the movement of offshore fine granulated sugar and domestic beet sugar into abnormal sales areas, Price Administrator Leon Henderson has granted two requests made by the Defense Supplies Corporation:

(1) To allow such sugars to be sold below the $5.60 per hundred pound maximum selling price in 10 Northeastern States without the necessity of the seller still being forced to pay DSC the full difference between $5.60 and, for example, the $5.35 beet ceiling price allowed in Revised Price Schedule No. 60.

(2) To establish another area in which domestic beet sugar now may sell at a higher price. New States included—in order to conform to zone requirements set up recently by the War Production Board—are Maryland, Virginia, and West Virginia, as well as the District of Columbia. Sellers may merchandise this sugar at as high as $5.45, but must turn over to the DSC the difference between $5.35—the beet ceiling under the schedule—and $5.45 in partial payment of the DSC's excess freight costs for shipping to outlying districts, if they sell at such higher prices.

Passenger car tire price increase of 16 percent allowed to cover cost of return plan

Permission for price increases to cover the cost of the Government's tire return plan, (see VICTORY, Mar. 3) which was set up to check "bootlegging" and to relieve retailers and jobbers of the financial burden of carrying large stocks in a shrunken market, was given April 23 by Price Administrator Henderson.

Maximum retail prices for new tires and tubes of passenger car sizes are increased 16 percent by Amendment No. 1 to Revised Price Schedule No. 63, effective April 25. Manufacturers and mass distributors will be permitted to advance their wholesale prices by the actual dollar amounts of the 16 percent increases in the retail ceilings. They have been notified that the voluntary maximum price agreement with the OPA has been relaxed to allow for the advances to take place April 25.

Truck tires not affected

The price adjustments were made on the basis of preliminary calculations of the cost of the return plan, and it is expected that other minor adjustments will be necessary later when complete information as to costs becomes available.

As truck tires were not included in the return plan, no price adjustment is necessary for them.

The price increases permitted apply not alone on tires that were sold upstream in the return plan, but also to all tires sold to the Defense Supplies Corporation by manufacturers and mass distributors, since the Office of Price Administration spread the cost of the plan over all passenger car tires in the hands of manufacturers and mass distributors.

Applies to tires still held

Moreover, dealers who did not return all their tires and tubes and still have some in inventory are permitted to charge the full 16 percent increase on them as well as on any they purchase for resale from now on.

All retailers of tires must post by May 4, 1942, in a conspicuous place in each retail establishment, the amounts added to the maximum prices on new passenger car tires and tubes on April 25.

Use beet sugar or face shortage, Northeast warned

An acute shortage in the supply of sugar in the scarcity areas of Northeastern United States is threatened unless wholesalers and industrial users move quickly to take advantage of supplies of beet sugar now being offered to them, Price Administrator Henderson said on April 23.

Formal sugar rationing, which goes into effect April 28, will create a heavy demand in these areas. Mr. Henderson urged wholesalers and industrial users to begin buying immediately in anticipation of May quotas, as permitted by WPB Order No. M-55-h. The amount

Cartoon by Dr. Seuss for OEM. Three-column mats available for publication, on request to Distribution Section, Division of Information, OEM, 2743 Temporary R, Washington, D. C.

that buyers are allowed under the order is 50 percent of their May 1941 usage. Beet sugar processors have already been authorized by the Government to begin sales in the scarcity areas.

The offer of beet sugar will continue for an indefinite period. Large quantities of beet sugar must be moved into the Northeast to meet the anticipated demand.

Until sufficient beet sugar is moved into the scarcity areas, no other sugars will be made available.

Rise allowed in coastwise rate on coal from 2 cities

In order to cover higher wartime operating expenses, the War Shipping Administration on April 17 authorized increased surcharges for the coastwise transportation of coal in bulk from Hampton Roads and Philadelphia to ports in the north Atlantic area.

To the basic freight rates, the War Shipping Administration has allowed the addition of a maximum surcharge of $1.70 per gross ton for vessels using the "outside route," and $1.35 per gross ton for vessels using the "inside route."

The new rate is effective on sailings on and after April 1, 1942.

Nearly every product of cotton textile industry now under ceilings as OPA covers carded grey and finished goods

Practically very product of the cotton textile industry will now be under OPA price ceilings as a result of a move April 24 by Price Administrator Henderson extending maximum price regulations to all types of carded grey and finished cotton goods not previously covered by schedules.

The April 24 action, which becomes effective May 4, 1942, under the provisions of Maximum Price Regulation No. 118, covers chiefly manufacturers' sales of "cotton products" and provides a method for determining ceiling prices for many special constructions of textile merchandise prepared by large cotton mills for consumers. Wholesalers, jobbers and retailers who perform their normal service are exempt from the provisions.

Action brings prices down

The regulation, in effect, establishes maximum prices for "cotton products" at considerably lower levels than the present market and brings them substantially into line with cotton yarn and textile prices already under ceilings. Some combed cotton goods are not yet subject to OPA regulation.

It is now apparent that ceilings must be extended to cover virtually the entire cotton textile field," declared Mr. Henderson, in explaining the reasons for the new order. " With some cotton textiles subject to ceilings and others free to rise without any formal restriction, the price structure of the industry has become greatly distorted. On the one hand, prices of ceiling fabrics have remained stable, increasing only to the extent that the cotton market has advanced. Non-ceiling goods have, on the other hand, continued to follow an inflationary trend. This has resulted in a tendency to shift looms to unregulated goods."

Products brought under regulation by the order include such important finished textiles used by consumers as blankets, towels, bedspreads, ginghams, table cloths and napkins, corduroys, diapers, cottonades, whipcords, flannels, and chambrays.

In addition, among the numerous "unfinished" goods covered are wide goods of 42 inches and over, industrial fabrics, ducks, shirting, twills and drills, sateens, gabardine and repps.

A "weighted average" base pricing period from July 21, 1941, through August 15, 1941, inclusive is established. As in other cotton textile and yarn schedules, the maximum prices are allowed to fluctuate in conformity with price changes in raw cotton.

"Cotton products" are defined to mean "products made on a loom and consisting basically of cotton, regardless of the extent to which, during the time when . . . title remains in the producer, they are finished, processed or fabricated."

Certain exceptions to the definition of "cotton products" are set forth. These include products subject to any other maximum price regulation or schedule; products consisting of 50 percent or more by weight, after weaving and before any finishing or fabrication, of combed cotton yarn; garments; yarn-dyed or printed upholstery or drapery fabrics; gauze bandage, adhesive tape and related medical supplies; fabrics less than 6 inches in width; and woven tickings heavier than 4.95 yards per pound and not in weaves requiring a Jacquard loom.

Some products remain under 10

The April 24 cotton products regulation takes into consideration many products of "integrated" mills which combine in part or in whole the spinning, weaving, finishing and fabrication of goods such as towels, bedspreads and flannels.

However, finished piece goods of a character customarily finished and marketed in larger volume by independent converters and finishers than by integrated producers remain subject to Temporary Price Regulation No. 10 (Finished Piece Goods). The schedule directs persons desiring an opinion as to which of these schedules (Maximum Price Regulation No. 118 or Temporary Maximum Price Regulation No. 10) is applicable to their products to communicate in writing with the Office of Price Administration.

Inasmuch as a strict application of the regulation might result in a different ceiling price for each seller for the same product, the Administrator revealed that a list of weighted average market prices is being prepared by a representative group of cotton textile merchants.

Because of the time required to adjust the numerous textile prices to the new basis, the effective date of the regulation is not until May 4, 1942.

Firm to sell dynamite glycerine to U. S. at cost

Harshaw Chemical Co., Cleveland, was authorized April 23 by Price Administrator Henderson to sell to the Treasury Procurement Division approximately 45 tons of dynamite glycerine at a price reflecting only cost, but nevertheless exceeding the maximum prices set by OPA Revised Price Schedule 38.

Contract price exceeded maximums

The glycerine in question was refined from crude glycerine purchased in South America before OPA imposed ceiling prices. The contract price exceeded the maximums thereafter set by OPA. Because of transportation difficulties the crude product was not delivered to Harshaw until recently.

Harshaw converted the crude glycerine into refined glycerine of dynamite grade essential to the war effort and offered to transfer the full amount to the Treasury Procurement Division without profit. By Amendment No. 1 to Revised Price Schedule No. 38, OPA approved this transaction.

★ ★ ★

Price rise on two tool orders allowed to aid subcontractors

Two manufacturers of machine tools, who although already operating at capacity were requested by the War Production Board to increase output, have been authorized to charge more than established maximum prices on two war orders which are to be turned out by subcontractors, Price Administrator Henderson announced April 23.

Higher manufacturing costs

The exceptions to Revised Price Schedule No. 67—New Machine Tools—were granted in view of the subcontractors' higher manufacturing costs.

Amendment 7 to this schedule authorizes Gould & Everhardt of Newark, N. J., to increase its maximum price for 209 industrial shapers manufactured on subcontract by the Henry and Wright Manufacturing Company of Hartford, Conn.

Amendment 8 authorizes an increase in the maximum price from $15,250 each to $16,548.08 for 104 single-spindle automatic machines manufactured on subcontract by the Sullivan Machinery Co. of Claremont, N. H., for the Cleveland Automatic Machine Co.

Permanent silk waste ceilings identical with temporary

Permanent maximum prices for silk waste, now used solely for military purposes such as the manufacture of powder bags, are continued at the identical levels established in a previous temporary OPA regulation, Price Administrator Henderson announced April 21.

Applies to domestic and imported

Maximum Price Regulation No. 115 replaces Temporary Maximum Price Regulation No. 7 (Silk Waste) which sets ceilings for this product for a period of 60 days commencing February 28, 1942.

The ceilings apply both to domestic and imported silk waste, except that imports after February 28, 1942, are excluded because of conditions resulting from the war.

China and pottery prices halted at October 1-15 levels; 5 percent extra for semivitreous

Hundreds of china and pottery articles used in the average American household—dinnerware sets, cups, saucers, bowls, plates, dishes, cream pitchers, cooking and baking dishes, and refrigerator jars, to name a few—are among the items covered by Maximum Price Regulation No. 116 (China and Pottery), announced April 23 by Price Administrator Henderson.

The regulation, effective April 27, 1942, fixes maximum prices for the sale by manufacturers of vitreous and semivitreous ware in the United States or for export. Stoneware and art pottery are not covered, but vitreous and semivitreous ware produced by art potters comes under the terms of the regulation.

Profits going up

Maximum prices and packaging charges for the vitreous ware industry are established at the price levels prevailing between October 1 and 15, 1941, and for the semivitreous ware industry, at 5 percent above the levels prevailing during the same period.

Both classes of manufacturers have maintained their prices at the OPA's request since last February 1, at which time they withdrew a proposed 10 percent advance to give the OPA time to complete its study.

Reflecting increased buying power and drastic curtailment of pottery imports, American pottery manufacturers' profits,

either on a percentage or dollar basis, were larger in 1941 than in previous years.

New articles shall be sold at a price in line with, or lower than, most nearly comparable items in a manufacturer's line during the base period. Such new articles, if a change in body or glaze is involved, must be reported and described to the OPA within 10 days after delivery on the first sale. Reports of sales must be filed with the OPA quarterly by every manufacturer, and records of all transactions must be kept.

Maximum prices for articles not sold during the base period, but sold after October 15, are 100 percent for vitreous and 105 percent for semivitreous of the prices in effect prior to the issuance of the regulation, except that the prices must be kept in line with the prices in effect during the base period for comparable articles. Prices in effect are those quoted in a price list or those at which sales were actually made where there was no price list.

Sales to Government

In sales to Government departments or agencies, according to the regulation, the maximum price shall be the highest price at which any article of china or pottery was contracted to be sold by any manufacturer to that department or agency during the October 1-15 period, or during the period October 15, 1941, to January 1, 1942, if no sales were made during the base period.

In the case of export sales, the maximum prices for domestic sales shall apply, but the exporter may add the actual cost of packing for export if customarily he charged such cost as a separate item, the actual cost of transportation to port of exit, and the normal commission charged by the same general class of exporter to the same foreign market and to a purchaser of the same general class in the period of October 1 to 15. Exporters also may add the actual costs of war risk, ocean freight, marine insurances on sales f. a. s. vessel, f. o. b. vessel, c. i. f. destination or f. o. b. destination.

13 firms, producing 95 percent of brass materials for small arms ammunitions, agree to cut prices 1 cent per pound

Thirteen firms, producing more than 95 percent of the brass materials used for small arms ammunitions, have agreed to reduce prices of these products 1 cent per pound, Price Administrator Henderson announced April 19.

To effect substantial savings

This reduction, the Administrator stated, will effect for the Government substantial savings which will become increasingly larger as production expands.

All deliveries on and after April 20, 1942, of cartridge case cups, bullet jacket cups, and sheet metal required therefor—produced by these companies—were affected.

In a letter to the brass mills, requesting the price cut, Mr. Henderson indicated that OPA has been studying for some months the general price level on all brass mill products. Particular attention has been devoted to those which are being sold in large volume to the Army, Navy, and Maritime Commission for small arms and artillery ammunition and other material.

Cuts warranted by profits

Prices of these materials have been considered in the light of marked increases in brass mills' profits, the Administrator added. Mr. Henderson emphasized the fact that the large volume of business that these mills now do and will continue to do in an even greater degree in these relatively few items have produced these profits. For this reason, the Administrator concluded that a substantial price reduction is warranted.

Mr. Henderson described the current price reduction as only "a preliminary and partial step in dealing with this whole question."

Voluntary cooperation sought

The brass mills were asked to cooperate on a voluntary basis in reducing prices of small arms ammunition material. Favorable replies were received from 13 firms from which such action was asked. These concerns represent a cross-section of a very large majority of the industry.

Only one refusal has been received by OPA to date. This comes from a small mill. OPA will investigate this concern to determine whether or not its refusal is justified.

Mr. Henderson indicated to the brass mills that he fully realized the significance of his request. He expressed his appreciation of their cooperation in the effort "to achieve our objective by voluntary action."

13 firms agree to cut

The cooperating firms were:

American Brass Co.; Bridgeport Brass Co.; Bristol Brass Corporation; Chase Brass & Copper Co., Inc.; Miller Co.; New England Brass Co.; Plume & Atwood Manufacturing Co.; Revere Copper and Brass Co.; The Riverside Metal Co.; Scovill Manufacturing Co.; Seymour Manufacturing Co.; Stamford Rolling Mills Co.; and Waterbury Rolling Mills, Inc.

OPA opens drive to end violations of price ceilings on iron, steel scrap

Signaling a concerted drive to end violations of price ceilings on iron and steel scrap, Price Administrator Henderson announced April 19 the filing of civil action in Chicago against Northwestern Steel and Wire Co. of Sterling, Ill., its broker, and 24 dealers.

Charged with "upgrading"

The Steel and Wire Co. and its broker, M. S. Kaplan Co. of Chicago, were charged with buying and accepting delivery of iron and steel scrap at prices in excess of those established in OPA's Revised Price Schedule No. 4.

The 24 dealers were charged with selling and delivering at prices above the established maximums.

OPA charged all 26 defendants with "upgrading," a device by which inferior grades of scrap are sold at prices allowed for higher grades. The 26 were also charged with failing to keep complete and accurate records as required in the price schedule.

Hearing set for April 28

The OPA request for an injunction was set for hearing April 28 before United States District Judge William H. Holly.

The action is the second OPA has taken against violations of the price schedule for iron and steel scrap but is the first taken simultaneously against dealer, broker, and consumer. Earlier this week OPA obtained a temporary order restraining the Pittsburgh Steel Co. from buying unprepared scrap at the price set for prepared scrap.

"These actions are only the first of a series we are preparing to take throughout the country," Mr. Henderson said.

Violations not to be tolerated

"Iron and steel scrap are vital to war production. The OPA schedule has been adopted to provide fair prices and to insure an orderly market in the face of heavy demands from steel mills working at top speed on war orders.

"We are not going to tolerate violations under any circumstances. Those who fail to comply with the price regulations are subject to criminal penalties."

In the "upgrading" charged to the 26 defendants, OPA officials reported that the top layer in a carload shipment usually corresponded with the grade specified in the invoice but that beneath this layer were inferior grades of scrap and even, in some cases, material worthless to steel mills.

24 dealers charged

The 24 dealers named in the civil action are:

Advance Steel Salvage Corporation, Chicago, Ill.; Alter Co., Davenport, Iowa; Max Falk, doing business as American Auto Parts Co., Sioux City, Iowa; Atlas Iron and Metal Co., Joliet, Ill.; Morris Pollock, doing business as Aurora Auto Wrecking Co., Aurora, Ill.; Morris Max Blum, doing business as Blum Iron and Metal Co., Dubuque, Iowa; Central Paper Stock Co., Chicago, Ill.; Consumers Steel and Supply Co., Racine, Wis.; I. W. Kaufman, Kansas City, Mo.; General Iron and Metal Co., Chicago, Ill.; Henry M. Cohen, doing business as Co-Henry Co., Kansas City, Mo.; Mary Bodow, doing business as Southwest Iron and Metal Co., Kansas City, Mo.; Abe L. Pekarsky, doing business as Kishwaukee Auto Parts and Wrecking Co., Rockford, Ill.; Light Bros. and Co., Sioux Falls, S. Dak.; John A. Robinson, doing business as Norfolk Hide and Metal Co., Norfolk, Nebr.; J. H. Krause, Inc., Rockford, Ill.; Marmis and Solomon, Dubuque, Iowa; Miller Bros. Iron and Metal Co., Milwaukee, Wis.; Miller Iron and Metal Co., Chicago, Ill.; Newtson Iron and Metal Co., Ottawa, Ill.; H. Pitts and Co., Sioux Falls, S. Dak.; Rothstein Iron and Metal Co., Freeport, Ill.; Southern Illinois Scrap Iron and Metal Co., Harrisburg, Ill.; Wolf Bros., Inc., Mason City, Iowa.

★ ★ ★

Only voluntary agreements on zinc oxide, Henderson affirms

Except for individual producer voluntary price agreements, no action has been taken by the OPA with respect to establishing maximum prices for zinc oxides, Administrator Henderson emphasized April 21.

At a meeting of zinc oxide dealers and exporters with OPA representatives held in New York City, April 17, considerable confusion was apparent as to the extent of OPA price action on zinc oxides up to this time.

Producers have been asked individually to enter into agreements with OPA not to sell, offer to sell, deliver, or transfer any zinc oxides at prices higher than the maximums published by OPA on December 16, 1941, and supplemented by a statement issued on March 28, 1942.

Under such circumstances, however, Mr. Henderson indicated April 21 that the margins obtained by others than producers should bear the same relationship to producers' prices as customarily prevailed prior to the present emergency.

Temporary ceilings set on makers' prices for oil paints, varnishes

The OPA moved April 20 to hold steady the price consumers must pay for oil paints and varnishes.

Heeding the danger of threatened serious price advances by producers, Price Administrator Henderson fixed temporary maximum prices at which manufacturers can sell oil paints and varnishes at levels which prevailed on April 12, 1942.

Effective April 22, the action is embodied in Temporary Price Regulation No. 19 (Oil Paints and Varnishes).

Most manufacturers in the paint industry have until now maintained prices at the October 1, 1941, level at the request of OPA.

The new regulation will remain in force for 60 days, during which time OPA will continue its investigation of the pressures on paint prices, such as advancing costs for linseed oil and labor and the curtailment of certain raw materials.

... .

Exporters warned against dealers violating paraffin wax ceilings

Exporters were warned April 18 by Price Administrator Henderson against certain dealers who are attempting to evade maximum price provisions in Revised Price Schedule No. 42 for paraffin wax by splitting shipments into units small enough to obtain price differentials. Such practices are direct violations of the price schedule.

★ ★ ★

Makers of rolled, wire glass to discuss ceilings with OPA

Manufacturers in the rolled and wire glass industry were called, in telegrams sent April 21, to a meeting with OPA officials on April 29, to discuss maximum prices proposed for rolled and wire glass and heat-absorbing rolled glass.

The five manufacturers earlier agreed individually to suspend price advances and to maintain prices at the level existing October 1, 1941, pending completion of OPA's study of the price situation in the industry.

100 more war plants launch Production Drives in week

One hundred war plants have reported in the past week the establishment of voluntary labor-management committees, bringing to 600 the number to launch War Production Drives.

War Production Drive Headquarters April 23 released the names of the 100 plants in which new committees have been recognized.

Seventeen of the new plants reporting are in Pennsylvania, whose total is now 109, the highest in the country. Twenty-one more committees reported from Ohio, bringing that State's total to 75.

Workers sum up war in slogans

How the American workman sums up the war is shown by slogans written in contests in connection with the War Production Drive.

Independent slogan contests are being conducted in plants where voluntary labor-management committees have been formed to speed the production of planes, tanks, guns, ships, and other war goods.

A number of winning slogans have been reported to War Production Drive Headquarters by plant committees. Drive Headquarters, which had suggested the possibility of such contests, released some of the slogans last week.

Earl Myers, a milling department inspector, won the slogan contest in the Propeller Division of Curtis Wright, Beaver, Pa., with this slogan:

Speed 'em for Freedom!

Robert H. Culver, a milling machine hand, won the contest at the Vinco Corporation, Detroit, with this acrostic:

Unity
Service
Action

J. L. McKenna won first prize in a contest at the Guilbert Steel Co., Pittsburgh, with:

Don't ration your cooperation
Increased production will save your Nation

C. E. Steiner, a timekeeper at the Cincinnati, Ohio, Planer Co., won the contest there with:

High production means Axis destruction

Reynolds Johnson, personnel director, won the contest at Hardinge Brothers, Elmira, N. Y., with:

Hardinge Hands Harass
Hitler and Hirohito

Jack R. Campbell of the open hearth department of the Ashland (Ohio) Division of the American Rolling Mills Co., won the contest there with:

Tomorrow's battles will be
decided here today

Incidentally, the day that Mr. Campbell was declared winner (April 14) the mill's whistles were tied down at 7:30 a. m. to celebrate the establishment of the five hundred and twenty-first new record since Pearl Harbor. As high as 70 new peaks were reached in a single day. A safety record was established, too, with only three accidents in 73 days. W. F. Songer, director of the mill's War Production Drive, and Noah Wellman, assistant director, telegraphed Donald M. Nelson Chairman of the War Production Board:

"The only thing these records now mean to us is a bench-mark to exceed in the future."

War Production Drive Headquarters will announce other slogan contest winners later. War Production Drive plans also include the erection of production scoreboards, improvement of plant efficiency and encouragement of suggestions for greater production.

JUST GIVE HIM THE WEAPONS . . . The poster reproduced above from the Supplement to the Production Drive Plan Book will be sent out shortly to war plants. Two-column mats are available for publication, on request to Distribution Section, Division of Information, OEM, 2743 Temporary R, Washington, D. C.

LABOR . . .

Membership maintenance clause ordered in 10-month-old Federal Ship dispute

Settlement of the 10-month-old controversy at the Federal Shipbuilding & Drydock Co., Kearny, N. J., by the National War Labor Board was announced last week by Board Chairman William H. Davis.

The Board by an 8 to 4 vote, with employer members dissenting, ordered the inclusion of a modified maintenance of membership clause in the contract between the company, a subsidiary of the United States Steel Corporation, and Local 16, Industrial Union of Marine and Shipbuilding Workers of America, CIO.

The clause requires all present and future union members to maintain their membership in good standing for the remaining thirteen months of the contract between the company and the union. Union members who fail to remain in good standing may withdraw from the union yet keep their jobs by paying monthly union dues and fines until the present contract expires.

The Board majority rested its case for the maintenance of membership clause on the belief that a union was entitled to be protected from the disintegration which might follow its loyal and patriotic surrender of the right to strike for the duration of the emergency.

Approximately 22,000 workers are employed in the plant. About 12,000 are union members affected by the maintenance of membership clause.

Dr. Frank P. Graham, President of the University of North Carolina and a public member of the Board, wrote the majority opinion for the public and labor members of the Board. In a separate opinion concurring with the majority, Chairman Davis said in part:

"I want to say at the outset that I would vote for the Order for one overwhelming reason—because I think it will increase production of ships and help win the war. This issue has been disturbing the relations between management and the workers at Kearny for just about a year. It is time to put an end to it."

"For all-out uninterrupted production"

Dr. Graham summarized the majority opinion as follows:

"1. This maintenance of membership clause, as implemented in the directive order, has no absolute requirement for the discharge of a member of the union except by his own choice.

"2. It does not require any employee to join the union at any time.

"3. In its original form as proposed by Chief Justice Stacy, it was supported by all the seven public members of the National Defense Mediation Board.

"4. It has merits and values of its own for the maintenance of membership, the maintenance of the contract, and the maintenance of maximum production for winning the war.

"5. It is the decision of the umpire, upon the acceptance of whose decisions depends the survival of the national agreement for all-out uninterrupted production of arms, tanks, planes, and ships.

"6. In the midst of this total and desperate war is no time for defiance of the Government by any labor union or corporation. It is the time for the acceptance of a decision carefully arrived at in accordance with the national agreement between labor, management, and the Government of the People of the United States. The war is wide and desperate, but the time is short. The time is too short for any further delays in the settlement of a dispute in a plant where are built the ships which carry the men and armaments and supplies to support American boys as they fight for the future of America and the future of freedom in the world."

Freedom of choice protected

Other highlights of the majority opinion follow:

"This case came to the National War Labor Board because of the long defiance of the Government of the United States by the Federal Shipbuilding & Drydock Co., a wholly owned subsidiary of the United States Steel Corporation. It is high time that in the midst of a world war involving the future of America and the future of freedom, that a dispute in a plant building most essential ships for America and for freedom be settled without further delay. . . .

"The freedom of choice of the individual worker is protected by a provision already in the contract against any coercion of a worker into membership in the Union. In addition, the individual's right to work is safeguarded by a clause in the Board's order. Under this clause, a member of the Union may withdraw from the Union by not maintaining his membership in good standing. In such case, he must, as a condition of employment, continue to pay his financial obligations to the Union for the duration of the contract, which has little more than a year to run. A member of a club has no more freedom and no lighter obligation. No member of the Union need ever be discharged under this provision, except by his own choice. . . .

"The maintenance of membership clause does not require any worker, at any time, to join the Union. It does not require the Company to employ only members of the Union and is, therefore, not a closed shop. It does not require the employees who have been hired by the Company, to join the Union, and is, therefore, not a union shop. It does not require the Company to give preference in hiring to members of the Union, and, is, therefore, not a preferential union shop. It does not require any old employee, any new employee or any employee whatever to join the Union at any time.

"The maintenance of membership clause requires only that any employee who is a member of good standing, at the time the contract is signed, or who thereafter voluntarily joins the Union, shall remain a member in good standing. This he is required to do as part of his obligation to keep the provisions of the contract made by the Union with the Company on his behalf. Every employee who, since the original recommendation of July 26, 1941, has chosen to remain a member in good standing, or who has since joined the Union, has had full knowledge of this provision and has thus made the choice voluntarily to maintain his membership. Any others have already resigned. . . .

"The umpire may once in a while miscall balls and strikes. But in the midst of a total war for our existence as a free people, let no labor union or no corporation defy the peaceful procedures of the Nation for the settlement of disputes and for unbroken maximum production. It is inconceivable that this subsidiary of even the most powerful corporation in the world shall longer defy the government of the People of the United States.

"In the momentous struggle between the United Nations and the Axis Powers, let us have no defiance of the Nation, no mustering of disunity, no measuring and testing of the comparative sovereignty of the United States Steel Corporation and the United States of America. . . . Failure to settle this dispute would reveal both a lack of the acceptance of the democratic process and a lack of understanding of the decisive role of ships in the world strategy of the United Nations against the long gathered might of the Fascist-Axis Powers."

History of the case

The giant shipbuilding plant had been seized August 26, 1941, by the United States Navy at the order of President Roosevelt after the company had refused to accept a straight maintenance of membership recommendation by the peace-time National Defense Mediation Board.

On January 6, the Navy restored the plant to the company with the understanding that all unsettled disputes "should be settled without interrupting production by recourse to the machinery established by the President."

After the company and the union exhausted all possibilities of settling the union security issue, the Board held a public hearing March 30. Last week, the Board acted and made public its decision.

Employers' dissenting opinion

The majority opinion, written by Dr. Graham, was concurred in by Mr. Davis, Mr. Morse, and Dr. Taylor, public members, and Thomas Kennedy, George Meany, Emil Rieve, and Martin F. Durkin, labor members of the Board. In addition to the separate concurring majority opinion by Mr. Davis, there is also a separate concurring dissenting opinion by E. J. McMillan, representing employers. The dissenting opinion, written by Roger D. Lapham, employer member, and concurred in by E. J. McMillan, Horace P. Horton, and H. L. Derby, reads in part as follows:

"The issues in this case are quite clear. This is not an ordinary case. In July 1941 the same issues were presented to the National Defense Mediation Board; a decision was rendered; the Company refused to accept the recommendation of the Board and offered to turn the yards over to the Government for operation rather than agree to the contract proposed by the National Defense Mediation Board.

"Much has been said about each case being determined on its own merits. Any practical person, and especially the members of this

Board and those who served on the National Defense Mediation Board, know the fallacy of such statements. The National Defense Mediation Board was wrecked on this issue and the resignation of some of the labor members of that Board was predicated on the theory that a previous decision of the Board established a governing precedent.

"However, acting in our capacity as members of a Government agency, we cannot subscribe to any national labor policy which compels an unwilling employer to force an unwilling employee either to join or to remain a member of a labor union in order to play his part in winning this war.

The employer members presented two proposals, both of which the majority rejected, which can be summarized as follows:

"(1) That the Company shall insert a provision in the contract with the Union making continuance of membership a condition of employment for all Union members who voluntarily certify in writing thereafter their willingness to remain members of the Union during the life of the contract.

"(2) That if the Company is directed to insert a provision in the contract requiring Union members who are employees to maintain their membership in the Union in good standing as a condition of employment, then after such contract is entered into each employee who is a Union member shall be given a definite opportunity within a stated time so to resign from the Union. If he fails to resign, he would then be required, as a condition of employment, to remain a member of the Union in good standing for the contract period."

Commenting on the employers' dissent, Chairman Davis told a press conference:

"You see, gentlemen, the fact is that the line which divides the majority and the minority is so fine—a hair, perhaps—that we can't really define it."

No-strike pact hailed as success

Pronouncing the industry-labor no-strike pact an "astonishing success," William H. Davis, Chairman of the National War Labor Board revealed that time lost through strikes on war production during January, February, and March of this year was only 6/100 of 1 percent of total war employment.

During the same period last year, time lost was 9/100 of 1 percent, or 15 times the amount lost this year, Mr. Davis said.

"Nevertheless, we are not satisfied with anything less than perfect," he stated at a press conference. "We want to stop them all if we can."

The statistics on strikes were gathered with the aid of an interdepartmental committee representing six Federal agencies interested in war labor matters—the War, Navy, and Labor Departments, the Maritime Commission, the War Production Board, and the War Labor Board.

"From now on there will be one official list of strikes affecting the war," Mr. Davis said. The new plan for coordinating all strike data into a single list has been adopted to end the confusion of the past and to give the public a clear picture."

Mr. Davis invited all private agencies that collect figures on strikes affecting the war effort to submit their information to the War Labor Board.

War employment triples

There were approximately 332,000 man-days of idleness due to strikes affecting the war effort during the first quarter of 1942 or about one-fourth of the approximately 1,384,000 man-days idle for the first quarter of 1941. At the same time, employment on war materials increased three and two-thirds times since the first quarter of 1941—from about 156 million man-days in the first quarter of 1941 to about 552 million for the first quarter of 1942.

"The statistics on strike activity are useful as a measure of the over-all effectiveness of conciliation methods," Mr. Davis said. "But

WPB extends metals survey to obtain complete picture of U. S. use and needs

A complete survey of the use of metal in the United States during the first quarter of 1942, and of anticipated requirements for the quarter beginning July 1, is being undertaken by the WPB with the mailing of questionnaires to all American users of metal in raw or semi-fabricated form.

Scope broadened

The questionnaire, which is being sent out on Form PD–275, is a refinement of the metals questionnaire which was mailed to 11,000 users on January 30.

The original questionnaire, covering metals used in the last quarter of 1941 and requirements for the second quarter of 1942, was mailed only to manufacturers using metal in their products. The survey initiated April 20 will also cover mines, railroads, shipyards, utilities, construction jobs, and the petroleum industry, as well as military and naval contractors. The list of manufacturers has also been expanded. For all practical purposes, it should provide a complete picture of United States metal use and requirements.

Permanent ceilings set on used egg cases to stabilize price, prolong use

Issuance of a permanent price regulation for used egg cases—a measure designed to stabilize prices and at the same time to encourage reconditioning and longer reuse of cases, with ultimate savings for the consumer—was announced April 23 by Price Administrator Henderson.

The permanent regulation has been prepared to keep prices of emptied cases from spiraling upward as competition for available cases grows, and, at the same time, to assist in the acceleration of movement of cases from egg case emptiers back to the packers.

The new permanent regulation (Maximum Price Regulation No. 117) which replaces Temporary Regulation No. 2, simplifies the classification of used cases to two types: (1) those completely reconditioned, and (2) those sold without reconditioning.

The new permanent regulation recognizes customary price differentials for defined Eastern, Central, and Western areas, contrasted with the more general Eastern and Mid-Continent areas called for in the temporary measure. No maximum prices have been created for Rocky Mountain and Pacific Coast area States.

The ceiling prices established in the new permanent regulation are substantially those prevailing for used cases and parts from October 1 to 15, 1941.

Shipping Administration sets up Gulf, Atlantic districts

The United States Maritime Commission and the War Shipping Administration announced April 20 establishment of an Atlantic Coast district and a Gulf Coast district and appointment of respective directors for those areas.

Capt. Granville Conway has been named director of the Atlantic Coast district, which consists of all United States Atlantic ports north of Florida, and includes Maritime Commission and War Shipping Administration activities in Canadian and Newfoundland ports. Capt. Conway will continue as district manager for the Commission and the Administration at New York and will make his headquarters at 45 Broadway, New York City.

Chester H. Marshall has been designated as director of the Gulf Coast district, which includes all United States ports on the Gulf of Mexico and all ports in Florida. Mr. Marshall will make his headquarters at the Federal Office Building, New Orleans.

the over-all figures do not tell the whole story. The present list includes some strikes that had a very slight effect on war production, regardless of the number of men involved.

"For instance, one of the two largest strikes listed for March—the New Orleans Laundries, accounting for 32,500 man-days of idleness—was included because it was certified to the War Labor Board, though its effect on the war was slight."

Mr. Davis declared that the amount of time lost due to strikes has been "infinitesimally small," and pointed out that the 6/100 of 1 percent represented one workday in 7 years for each man employed on war production.

★ ★ ★

Ceilings raised on crude petroleum in Ritchie field

To correct a subnormal price for crude petroleum in the Ritchie oil field in Acadia Parish, La., maximum prices for that field are increased by Amendment No. 7 to Revised Price Schedule No. 88 (Petroleum and Petroleum Products).

INDUSTRIAL OPERATIONS . . .

War, essentials put first for new phones; others can't be sure of installations

New installations of telephones throughout the country were brought under strict War Production Board control on April 24.

Only persons or organizations engaged in direct war work or in occupations essential to the public welfare can be sure of obtaining new telephone service in the future.

New service may be denied to groups outside the preferred category unless existing exchange line capacity can take care of their needs without disrupting essential service.

200,000 applications may be denied

New installations of exchange line and central office exchange equipment are restricted to essential requirements. An exchange line is the overhead or underground cable which runs from a central office exchange and to which subscribers' telephones are connected. It does not include what are commonly known as the lead-in wires running from a home or office to the cable.

The Bell System, which operates by far the greatest portion of the country's vast telephone network, has estimated for WPB's communications branch that the restrictions will result in denial of approximately 200,000 applications for main line residential service this year.

Exemption clause covers minor extensions

Some relief may be afforded to groups outside the preferred category under an exemption clause permitting minor cable extensions, utilizing less than 100 pounds of copper, when such extensions are required to make use of idle exchange line capacity. Or, if line capacity and the type of central office equipment permits, these groups may be able to obtain service on a party line.

WPB's action, necessary to conserve large quantities of critical materials, is embodied in a general revision of Limitation Order L-50, which limited the engineering practices of telephone companies and their plans for betterment and relocation of plant facilities. The revised order retains all of the original limitations.

As revised, the order is expected to result in total annual savings of approximately 53,000 tons of lead, 35,000 tons of iron and steel, 14,000 tons of copper,

6,500 tons of zinc, 1,890 tons of crude rubber, and large amounts of other critical materials vitally needed for the war program.

New installations, replacement limited

Broadening the definition of an "operator" to include not only the Federal government but also the District of Columbia, State and Territorial governments, and their agencies, the order provides that unless expressly authorized by the Director of Industry Operations, all operators must:

1. Limit replacement of all equipment and facilities to essential maintenance, repair, or protection of service.

2. Limit new installations of exchange central office and exchange line equipment to those required for essential maintenance, to meet the known or "fairly anticipated" demands for service "reasonably required by persons engaged in direct defense or charged with responsibility for public health, welfare, or security," and to set up public pay stations in areas where a demand for such service exists.

3. Limit further installations of residence extensions (additional telephones on the same line in a residence where there already is one phone) to those required for the essential use of persons in the preferred category. Additional lines or additional stations on party lines cannot be provided as a substitute for extension stations.

4. Discontinue the use of open copper line wire to provide local exchange service.

5. Conserve or reuse existing equipment and facilities whenever the result will be to save critical materials.

May require party lines

The order stipulates that when necessary in order to avoid new installations of exchange line equipment and to conserve materials, and to the extent necessary to fulfill the requirements of persons on the preferred list, operators must employ party-line service in place of individual line service, reserve idle facilities in existing exchange lines, and regrade service to the type best fitting into the conservation program, if the requirements of the users will permit.

As a guide to what constitutes a person "engaged in direct defense" or charged with responsibility for public health, welfare, or security, the order sets forth seven groups considered to come within the category, including Army, Navy, Marine Corps, Coast Guard, and civilian defense services; Federal, State, county, and municipal government services; agencies of foreign governments; recognized organizations serving the health,

safety, or welfare of the public; business concerns furnishing materials or facilities to the Federal Government and those furnishing materials or services under "A" priority ratings; building management offices located in new housing developments; and temporary extensions when essential in cases of serious illness.

This is not an irrevocable definition, and additional groups may be added at any time.

The order does not apply in cases where physical installations of equipment had commenced prior to its issuance.

Preference ratings issued

Two preference rating orders—P-129 and P-130—were issued in conjunction with revised L-50. Both expire September 30. L-50 remains in force until revoked.

P-129, applying to radio communication as well as to wire communication, makes available an A-3 rating for deliveries to an operator or his supplier of materials essential for maintenance and repair and protection of service.

P-130, covering only telephone communication, makes an A-3 rating available to an operator or his supplier for deliveries of materials costing under $50 and used in normal construction caused by the connection, disconnection, changes in location, etc., of a subscriber's equipment, and in other small but essential services where operators would be forced to file thousands of individual PD-1A applications with WPB in order to obtain materials.

Some crane makers get extension of old ratings

Makers of certain types of cranes and hoisting equipment were notified April 21 by WPB that they can continue until July 1 using preference ratings assigned to them under Preference Rating Order P-5-b.

✳ ✳ ✳

HEATER TANKS SIMPLIFIED

Storage tanks for hot water heaters of the kind used in most homes will be manufactured in only three sizes after May 15 as a result of a simplification schedule issued April 25 by the War Production Board.

Another Schedule (No. VIII) to the Limitation Order, requires the simplification of vacuum and vapor heating specialties after June 15.

Sewing machine production to stop June 15 to reserve materials, machines for war

A limited number of sewing machines and sewing machine attachments may be produced between now and June 15, 1942, after which production must cease, WPB ordered April 25.

The order, General Limitation Order No. L-98, effective April 25, will result in a substantial saving of critical materials and will make available for war production at least a part of the industry's plant facilities.

Under the order, manufacturers may produce new machines and attachments until June 15 at a rate of 75 percent of the 1940 rate. Machines completely assembled prior to June 15 may be installed in cabinets or on portable bases after the cut-off date, provided they come within the 75 percent quota.

* * *

Bottle cap production further restricted

Manufacture of crown caps for beer and other beverage bottles during the balance of this month was further restricted by WPB on April 24.

* * *

Disposal of used rail, joints under WPB control

WPB has assumed control over all used railroad rail and rail joints so that ample supplies will be available for war requirements.

WPB LIMITS USE OF INDIVIDUAL RATINGS

As a further step toward putting American industry under the Production Requirements Plan, Director of Industry Operations Knowlson announced April 21 that WPB will soon discontinue granting preference ratings on individual applications for material to be used in general manufacturing operations.

Effective immediately, no individual application from a manufacturer for materials to be incorporated in his products over a period of more than 1 month will be approved.

U. S. TAKES OVER ALL CARGO AND TANK SHIPS

Admiral Emory S. Land, Administrator, announced April 18 that the War Shipping Administration has requisitioned possession and use of all essential oceangoing tankers and dry cargo vessels owned by American citizens which are subject to requisition under the Merchant Marine Act, 1936, as amended, and have not been previously acquired by the Government. Such requisitions will become effective as of the time possession is taken by the Government. This action affects several hundred vessels.

* * *

Sugar receivers allowed to anticipate May quotas

The War Production Board issued on April 22 a supplementary order (M-55-h) to the sugar conservation order (M-55) allowing receivers of refined sugar to anticipate their May quotas by accepting, between now and May 1, 50 percent of the amount of sugar they used or resold in May 1941.

The order was issued at the request of the Office of Price Administration to lay a foundation for the sugar rationing system, which began on April 28 for industrial users and will begin on May 5 for household consumers.

The May quotas have not yet been announced.

Under the supplementary order, a receiver (wholesaler, jobber or industrial user) in zones 1, 2, and 3, may receive delivery of beet sugar only in anticipation of the May quota. These zones, set up under Supplementary Order M-55-d on March 27, include the States of Maine, New Hampshire, Vermont, Massachusetts, Rhode Island, Connecticut, New York, New Jersey, Pennsylvania, Delaware, Maryland, Virginia, West Virginia, and the District of Columbia.

Receivers in the other five zones may accept advance delivery of either beet or cane sugar against their May quotas.

A receiver who accepts delivery against his May quota during April may not use the sugar in manufacturing before May 1, nor resell it at any time except upon tender of an OPA ration stamp or certificate.

Make spring housecleaning a city-wide salvage drive, Maverick urges mayors

The mayors of America were asked April 24 to take the initiative in local drives to make traditional spring housecleaning a means of increasing the flow of rags, metals, and rubber to the Nation's war machine.

The appeal, made in letters sent by Maury Maverick, chief of the Bureau of Governmental Requirements of the WPB, to all mayors in the country, is part of the general salvage program sponsored by the Bureau of Industrial Conservation.

Mr. Maverick suggested that the mayors bring the spring housecleaning-salvage program into homes, offices, stores, and plants by the issuance of proclamations. He also suggested that the mayors could set an excellent example by ordering a thorough housecleaning and salvage search on all municipal property.

Mr. Maverick requested that local campaigns be conducted in cooperation with local salvage committees.

MORE BINDER TWINE

Java sisal (Java agave sisalana) put into process on or before April 20, 1942, may be manufactured into wrapping twine or binder twine, under Amendment No. 4 to the agave fiber order, M-84, issued April 21.

The agave fiber order (M-84) has been amended to permit the manufacture of more binder twine than was permitted under a previous order. Under the amendment (Amendment No. 5) a manufacturer may produce during the 11 months ending June 30, 1942, an amount of binder twine which when added to his stocks on hand on November 1, 1941, does not exceed 120 percent of his sales during the 12 months ending October 31, 1941. The amendment also allows production at the 120 percent rate for a four-month period beginning July 1, 1942.

* * *

WOOLEN FIRM PENALIZED

In its first move against a violator of the wool conservation program, the WPB has issued a suspension order against the Susquehanna Woolen Co., New Cumberland, Pa.

Deliveries of iron, steel products will be restricted to A-10 or higher, after May 15

Deliveries of iron and steel products will be restricted to preference ratings of A-10 or higher after May 15, WPB announced April 22, with issuance of Order M–21 as amended.

The order formerly applied to steel products only and the inclusion of iron means that the 2,700 iron foundries in the country must comply with its provisions.

Two exceptions to A-10 requirement

Form PD-73 is abolished, effective May 1. In its place is this system:

Each purchase order for iron or steel must contain a signed statement by a duly authorized official or agent of the purchaser, either stamped or typed on the order, stating that the material is to be used for one of the group classifications set up in the order. These are Army, Navy, Maritime, Defense Projects (war plants), Lend-Lease, Other Export, Railroad, Warehouse, and all other.

Two exceptions are made to the A-10 rating requirement. Warehouses may deliver carbon steel on unrated orders when the purchaser specifies that the material is to be used for repair and maintenance. Each warehouse is limited, by quarters, to 3 percent of its quota for any product for such deliveries. Persons other than producers may deliver on unrated orders, nails, bale ties, and small black or galvanized welded pipe.

New forms have been provided for producers in connection with the amended order. To report shipments, iron and steel producers will use Form PD-138, which must be received by the WPB by the fifteenth of the month following the month of shipment.

First complete steel picture

Form PD-139, which is due in Washington by the tenth of each month, must be used to report tonnages requested for delivery, during that month and the following month, including past-due tonnage on the books of the producer. Both forms will be available shortly at all WPB field offices and at the iron and steel branch, WPB, in Washington.

Information derived from PD-139 will give the WPB, for the first time, total tonnage requested from each producer by product and by recipient. Summarized, it will be the first complete picture of all types of steel being produced and who is getting them.

The new order, designated as Amendment No. 3 and Extension No. 2 of General Preference Order M-21, became effective immediately and will remain in effect until revoked.

Ban on metals, plastics, cork to end nearly all output of pleasure fishing tackle

Fishing tackle manufacturers were ordered April 23 by WPB to stop using metals, plastics and cork in noncommercial fishing tackle manufactured after May 31, 1942.

The only exception is fish hooks, which may be manufactured after June 1 at a rate of 50 percent of each manufacturer's production in 1941.

Since most fishing tackle cannot be made without the use of metals, plastic or cork, the order (L-92) will mean the end of such production for the duration. However, large stocks are now on hand.

Between now and the shutoff date, limited production is permitted out of stocks on hand or on order before April 23. No additional quantities of critical materials may be ordered except iron and steel for the manufacture of fish hooks.

The order restricts the use of iron and steel out of inventory, during the period to May 31, to 75 percent of the rate of use of such metals in 1941. Previously issued metal conservation orders restrict the use of other metals ordinarily used in fishing tackle.

15 percent converted to war

Fishing tackle is defined in the order as products designed primarily for use in noncommercial fishing, including but not limited to: rods, rod fittings, and rod accessories; reels, reel equipment, and reel accessories; lines, leaders, sinkers, swivels, fish hooks, bait boxes, tackle boxes, fly boxes, creels, artificial lures, baits, and flies.

George Moore, chief of the WPB sporting goods unit, pointed out that the order applies only to the manufacture of fishing tackle and not to the sale of tackle already on hand and to be produced until May 31.

A total of 171 firms are in the industry, which is approximately 15 percent converted to war work, with some manufacturers converted 50 percent.

WPB takes control of all nickel scrap and orders segregation

The War Production Board on April 23 went after an additional source of badly needed nickel by establishing complete control over nickel scrap.

Order M-6-c, issued by Director of Industry Operations Knowlson requires segregation of scrap containing more than one-half of 1 percent nickel by weight and prevents its melting only for authorized uses. An increase of 150 percent in available nickel scrap is expected as a result of the order.

To whom deliveries are permitted.

Deliveries of nickel scrap may be made to a scrap dealer, but he may, in turn, deliver only under these circumstances:

To a melter who is currently receiving allocations of nickel, for use in products for which the allocation is made.
To a melter who is not receiving allocations of nickel, but who has orders bearing ratings higher than A-2 which call for nickel.
Persons other than melters are restricted to a 30-day accumulation of nickel scrap, unless the nickel content is less than 100 pounds.

Segregation of nickel scrap by all persons who handle it is required by the order. Nickel scrap must not only be kept separate from other scrap, but various grades and degrees of content of nickel scrap must be segregated.

Purchase orders for nickel scrap or secondary nickel must bear a certification that the purchaser is authorized to receive nickel and that the material will be used only as permitted by the order.

Persons who must report

Reports are required by the 15th of each month from these persons:

Those who generate in their own operations scrap containing more than 500 pounds of nickel content per month.
Those who have on hand at the end of a month scrap containing more than 500 pounds of nickel content.
Those who have on hand at the end of a month more than 30 days accumulation of scrap generated in home operations, if the nickel content is more than 100 pounds.

The order was effective immediately, and will continue in effect until revoked.

★ ★ ★

Priority plea to be returned unless it dates delivery

All applications for priority assistance which do not specify a required delivery date will hereafter be returned to the applicant by the War Production Board, it was announced April 23 by Industry Operations Director Knowlson.

Elastic fabric for foundations cut in half by WPB to make supply on hand last longer

The War Production Board has reduced the amount of elastic fabric that may be used in corsets, girdles, combinations, brassieres, and similar women's apparel, in order to make supplies now on hand last as long as possible.

Number can be doubled

The apparel section, WPB, estimates that as a result of the order the number of garments which can be made available for women will ultimately be doubled, and that production from present stocks of elastic fabric will be extended by at least eight or nine months. Therefore, adequate supplies of corsets, girdles, combinations, and brassieres will be available for many months ahead, particularly since retail stores have large stocks on hand at the present time, Stanley Marcus, chief of the WPB apparel section, said.

Orders L-90 and L-90-a, issued April 23, have the effect of reducing the amount of elastic fabric that may be used in such garments by approximately 50 percent. In addition the number of garments a manufacturer may cut or knit in any month is limited to 75 percent of his average monthly production during the three months ended March 31, 1941. The cut is to be applied pro rata for the balance of April.

Entire industry affected

A manufacturer is prohibited, however, from using any rubber yarn and elastic thread which was frozen under order M-124, on March 28, 1942.

The entire corset, combination, and brassiere industry will be affected, as well as mills knitting and weaving fabrics for use in such apparel.

The order provides different limits for corsets, panty-girdles, and combinations of three types, based upon the character and weights of the various elastic materials:

Class One Garments—This class is the surgical type corset and combination which may depend on front, back, or side lacing for adjustment.

Class Two Garments—This class covers heavy weight foundation type garments.

Class Three Garments—This class covers a lighter weight foundation type garment.

WPB grants air conditioning, refrigeration high ratings on materials for repair

The War Production Board has granted high preference ratings for deliveries of materials needed for repairs to air conditioning and refrigeration equipment.

The top rating—A-1-a—is available in the case of an actual break-down of equipment used primarily to process, transport or store food for the Army, Navy or Maritime Commission, or used in cold storage warehouses, meat-packing houses under U. S. Government inspection and blast furnace air conditioning.

All ratings in "A" class

Other ratings, each in the "A" class, are provided to avert break-downs of essential equipment and to maintain emergency repair service for existing equipment of all types, except domestic mechanical refrigerators. No rating is available for repairs to household refrigerators.

The program is set forth in Preference Rating Order P-126, and will be administered by WPB's air conditioning and commercial refrigeration branch. Ratings assigned under the terms of the order will be available only until June 30.

List of preferences available

In addition to the A-1-a rating in the case of actual break-downs of equipment deemed most essential for the country's health and safety, the order makes available the following ratings:

A-3 to avert an immediately threatened break-down of any of the types of equipment listed above for which the A-1-a rating is available in case of actual break-down.

A-3 in the case of actual break-downs of equipment used generally to process, transport or store food and dairy products, including equipment in retail establishments where food is stored or served, and used in manufacturing plants actually engaged in filling Defense Orders as defined in Priorities Regulation No. 1.

A-8 to avert an immediately threatened break-down of any of the types of equipment covered in the A-3 classification as listed in the preceding paragraph.

A-8 for emergency service to all other types of air conditioning and refrigerating equipment, except domestic mechanical refrigerators, and for deliveries of materials needed to maintain an emergency service inventory.

Usable only by approved agencies

The ratings may be applied only by designated emergency service agencies and their suppliers. In order to obtain designation, an agency must be regularly authorized to represent a manufacturer, owner or lessee of air conditioning or refrigerating equipment, and must obtain a serial number from WPB after first making application on Form PD-399.

★ ★ ★

2 firms get 6-month suspension of priority aid for illegal deals in scarce chemicals

"Black market" operations in scarce chemicals, which had resulted in profits of more than 100 percent to two New York City firms, backfired April 24 as the WPB announced suspension orders directed against the Acme Chemical Company, Inc., Rona Chemicals, and Hans Lowey and Leroy G. Cohen, principals in the illegal transactions.

The orders, S-41 and S-42, effective April 23, state that priority assistance had been extended to the Acme Chemical Company, Inc., to purchase acetic anhydride and salicylic acid for use in the manufacture of aspirin. Some of the material acquired with this assistance was used for the purpose stated in the company's application. However, Rona Chemicals, acting as agent for Acme, sold at least 8,160 pounds of the acetic anhydride and approximately 800 pounds of the salicylic acid. Rona also contracted to sell an additional 5,000 pounds of the acetic anhydride.

Further violations of priority orders by these two companies include the unauthorized extension by Acme of its preference ratings to the purchase of 720 gallons of iso-propyl alcohol, and the sale by Rona, again acting as agent for Acme, of this alcohol.

Chlorine for rag stock process now limited on per ton basis

A change in the method of computing the permissible use of chlorine in the treatment of rag stock under General Limitation Order No. L-11 has been ordered by the War Production Board.

Order L-11 limited the use of chlorine in the treatment of rag stock according to the total amount consumed during a base period. Amendment No. 1, effective April 20, changes the basis of limitation to the amount used per ton of rag stock treated.

30 of 55 makers of civilian radios ceased production on April 22 deadline; remaining 25 given more time to convert

At or before midnight April 22 the major part of the country's radio industry stopped production of radios for civilian use in order to make its entire facilities available for war work. The remainder of the industry will wind up its operations within a few weeks.

Have $780,000,000 in war contracts

Thirty of the 55 companies producing civilian radios ceased putting sets into production when the deadline fixed in WPB order L-44-a was reached. Two other large companies, RCA and Philco, each operating several plants, shut off civilian production at midnight in plants representing more than 80 percent of their total production. These 32 companies already have war contracts totaling $780,000,000, representing 87 percent of all the war contracts let so far to the home radio industry.

Some given additional time

The remaining 25 companies were given additional time, ranging from 1 to 6 weeks, to produce additional sets in order to facilitate their program of conversion to war work, as provided for in L-44-a. Half of the approximately 410,-000 sets to be produced after the shutoff date will be reserved for export to friendly nations, as requested by the Coordinator of Inter-American Affairs and Lend-Lease.

The plants discontinuing civilian production by midnight April 22 produced approximately 57 percent of all the civilian sets, on a dollar basis, sold in 1941. Their sales accounted for approximately $151,000,000 worth of the $263,400,000 worth of home radios manufactured in 1941.

At least six of the concerns stopped civilian production before the first of March. They ranged from General Motor's Delco plant to the small Kingston plant, and included also Noblitt-Sparks, Remler, Gilfillan, and Hammarlund.

RCA's large plant at Camden, representing more than 80 percent of the company's total production, ceased civilian production on March 5 and is now converted to war work. The company was given an additional 2 weeks to operate its plant at Bloomington, Ind., in order to produce sets for export and to better prepare it to start work on a big war contract the first week in May.

Stewart-Warner ceased its civilian radio production on March 31 and is now engaged in war work.

Philco has closed its two plants in Indiana and Ohio and two of its three plants at Philadelphia. It was given a few weeks longer to operate the third of its Philadelphia plants to turn out sets for export. The bulk of Philco's facilities is engaged in war work.

R. C. Berner, chief of the WPB radio section, said that the conversion order of March 7 (L-44-a) greatly expedited the conversion of the radio industry to war work. That was true, he said, not only of the 55 companies producing home radio sets but of the 15 or 20 companies manufacturing phonographs and some 250 companies manufacturing radio parts. In fact, he said, the parts companies began conversion almost immediately after the issuance of the order, because the radio companies, faced with a stop-production order and stop-purchase order, cancelled orders for parts and placed no new orders.

War work to which the industry is being converted includes all sorts of detection equipment, used to detect airplanes and ships, and a variety of receiving and transmitting sets for use in airplanes, tanks, trucks, and other military equipment, and even small sets for individual soldiers.

Gas cooking stoves may be sold only on A–10 or higher orders

Gas cooking stoves are subject to the terms of Limitation Order No. L-79, covering sales and deliveries of plumbing and heating equipment, it was explained April 21 by W. Walter Timmis, chief of the WPB plumbing and heating branch.

Mr. Timmis pointed out that gas ranges are covered by paragraph (1) of the definitions contained in the order.

Gas cooking stoves, and other plumbing and heating items covered by the order, may not be sold except on orders bearing A–10 or better preference ratings, or to other retailers, jobbers, distributors or manufacturers in accordance with the provisions of the order.

Bar to production of critical industrial machines delayed to preserve schedules

Restrictions on production of critical industrial machinery listed in Limitation Order L-83 have been removed until May 15 to avoid disruption of schedules in the output of war supplies.

Provisions of L-83 remaining in force, however, make it unlawful for manufacturers or distributors to accept orders for such equipment or to make deliveries without WPB approval.

Amendment No. 1, delaying restrictions on production until May 15, will permit manufacturers to continue production on orders that were on their books before L-83 became effective. The order as originally issued was effective April 9.

L. S. Greenleaf, Jr., chief of the special industry machinery branch, cautioned manufacturers, however, that there is no guarantee that machinery produced on unapproved orders will be permitted to be delivered to the person or persons from whom the orders were received. Before deliveries will be permitted, he said, WPB must be advised of the type of equipment involved, and the use for which it is intended.

War housing suppliers given 3 months to extend ratings

A supplier of materials entering into the construction of a defense housing project will be permitted to extend a preference rating at any time within 3 months after he becomes entitled to apply it, the WPB ruled in amendments to Preference Rating Orders P–19–c, P–19–d, and P–55, effective April 20.

Formerly such ratings could not be extended after the expiration date of the individual orders.

★ ★ ★

Tin segregation required

Segregation of tin plate and tin alloy scrap from other scrap for delivery to steel mills was ordered April 22 by the Director of Industry Operations.

Order M-24-b, which took effect immediately, prohibits mixture of any tin component in a bundle or car of scrap or delivery of a mixed car or bundle.

Ban lifted on sale of women's, children's ensembles put into process before April 9

The WPB April 21 lifted restrictions on the sale of women's and children's ensembles put into process of manufacture before April 9 1942. This will permit manufacturers, jobbers, and retailers to clean out present stocks of ensembles.

Other changes

This and other changes are provided for in an amendment to Order L–85. Other changes include:

1. Bias sleeves, prohibited in the original order, are now permitted except when the cloth is plaid. Bias sleeves of plaid cloth are still prohibited because of the waste of material involved in matching.
2. Wool interlining, prohibited in the original order, may be used if the cloth was woven prior to April 9.
3. Fur trimmings may be used with a wool cloth lining when the wool under the fur is an integral part of the body of the coat. This provision makes it unnecessary to cut out material under fur when that material is actually a part of the body of the coat.
4. The top of a two-piece dress is required to conform with the length restriction on jackets.
5. The prohibition against cuffs on slacks is extended to riding breeches, jodhpurs, ski pants, play suits, overalls, and coveralls.
6. A blouse made of any material may not have more than one patch pocket. Previously this restriction applied to blouses made of rayon, silk, cotton, linen, or a mixture of these materials.
7. A jacket may have a two-piece back with a belt attached, provided the belt is stitched on in such a way that there is not more than a half inch overlay of wool cloth on wool cloth at the upper and the lower side of the belt. In the original order a belt was not permitted on a wool jacket.
8. Flaps on patch pockets are prohibited. The original order did not refer to flaps.
9. The restrictions on pleats in skirts are lifted, provided the quantity of material used in the skirt comes within the restrictions. That is, if a woman does not care to have a skirt as full as is permitted under the order she may use up the difference in pleats.
10. A schedule of maximum sweeps (circumference of a skirt at the bottom) for suit skirts is added. This was omitted from the original order. It permits a sweep of 78 inches for a size 16, with corresponding sweeps for other sizes.
11. The restrictions of the order are lifted as to historical costumes for theatrical productions, provided that such garments are not sold for other purposes unless altered to conform to the provisions of the order.

★ ★ ★

M–116 postponed to avert hardship on industry

Because manufacturers of enameled closures for bottles, cans, and jars already had started processing tin plate for April when Order M–116 was issued April 4, its effective date was postponed until April 30.

Cotton mills told to divert large part of production to bag osnaburgs and sheetings

The WPB has instructed the cotton textile industry to convert a substantial part of its capacity from civilian to military production.

To alleviate shortage

Limitation Order No. L–99 directs the cotton mills to convert specified percentages of their looms now producing a long list of cotton fabrics commonly used in clothing and in the home to the production of bag osnaburg and bag sheetings.

The loom allocations to osnaburg and bag sheetings were made on a basis that, in the opinion of WPB's Civilian Supply Division, will not reduce the production of the fabrics now being manufactured below a point which will satisfy essential civilian requirements.

The order was issued after months of careful investigation of its feasibility and after it had been dovetailed into a complete conversion plan for the cotton textile industry. It will approximately double the production of osnaburg and bag sheetings needed in the war program for sand bags, camouflage cloth, and food and agricultural bags.

Other orders on civilian fabrics

In explaining the order to the cotton textile industry, at a meeting April 20 of the WPB cotton mill advisory committee, Mr. Walton said that the WPB will issue additional orders soon dealing with essential civilian fabrics, and mills required under these forthcoming orders to manufacture specified essential civilian fabrics will be regarded by the WPB as having converted to war production.

"It is just as important for the winning of the war to provide work clothing for the men and women who work in our bombing plants as it is to provide sand bags to protect our buildings against enemy bombers," Mr. Walton said.

The plan now being worked out by the WPB calls for increasing the production of cotton fabrics from the 9,045,-000,000 square yards in 1939 to 14,000,-000,000 this year and 15,000,000,000 in 1943.

Allocations for bag osnaburg

Under Order L–99 cotton mills are directed to allocate to the production of bag osnaburg the following percentages of their looms:

1. 20 percent of all looms operating on bedtickings. Bedtickings are used mainly in the production of mattresses and pillows.

2. 20 percent of all looms operating on cottonades and suiting coverts. These fabrics are used mainly in men's semidress and work clothing, and industrial uniforms.
3. 20 percent of all looms operating on colored yarn suitings (other than cottonades, suiting coverts and whipcords). These fabrics are used in men's and women's sportswear, such as slacks and shorts, and in other apparel for men.
4. 20 percent of all looms operating on denims. Denim is used mainly in coveralls and other work clothing.
5. 20 percent of all looms operating on pin stripes; pin checks, hickory stripes, etc. This material is similar to denim and has similar uses.
6. 20 percent of all looms operating on drapery, upholstery and tapestry fabrics.
7. 20 percent of all looms operating on turkish and terry woven towels and toweling, used for bath towels, beach towels, beach robes, etc.
8. 20 percent of all looms operating on huck, damask, and jacquard woven towels and toweling, for face towels.
9. 100 percent of all looms operating on osnaburg of any construction. That is, all looms now producing any kind of osnaburg must produce the bag osnaburg specified in the order.

Allocations for bag sheetings

The bag sheetings allocations of loom capacity are as follows:

1. 40 percent of all looms operating on outing flannels, used chiefly in sleeping garments.
2. 40 percent of all looms operating on all other napped fabrics except canton flannels, work shirt flannels, and blankets. Fabrics used in athletic and sports wear, decorative fabrics, trimmings, linings and a long list of other items are included in the conversion program.
3. 40 percent of all looms operating on soft-filled sheetings. This material has many uses in the home.
4. 50 percent of all looms operating on Class C sheetings. This is unbleached sheeting and has a variety of uses.
5. 100 percent of all looms operating on Class A and Class B sheetings. The sheetings in these two classes are coarser than Class C and are used mainly for bagging. Looms manufacturing them must be converted 100 percent to the type of bag sheeting specified in the order.

The percentages are calculated for looms which on February 28, 1942, were operating on the fabrics listed for conversion. The percentages apply to all the looms regardless of the fact that some of them may have been engaged on February 28 in the production of preference-rated civilian or military fabrics.

"Before working out these percentages for conversion," Mr. Walton said, "the cotton section and the conversion section of the WPB, in cooperation with the Civilian Supply Division, had determined the amount of each fabric necessary for essential civilian needs.

"It is planned to allocate for essential civilian needs under separate orders."

Questions and Answers on Priorities

1. Q. Will there be a fundamental change in the priorities system in the near future?

A. Within the next few months blanket ratings of "P" orders to entire industries will gradually be replaced by the Production Requirements Plan, which has a closer check on the amount of material for which priority assistance will be granted. Individual applications for material on PD–1A forms are being discontinued in most cases in favor of single applications on PD–25A forms for each industry under the PRP, covering all their materials requirements for a calendar quarter.

2. Q. Are there any statutory penalties for the violations of the priorities system?

A. The recently enacted Second War Powers Act provides for criminal prosecution with heavy fines or imprisonment for violations of any rule, regulation, or order issued under the priority powers.

3. Q. Are small firms or companies subject to the provisions of Priorities Regulation No. 1?

A. The word "person" as used in this Regulation is all-inclusive and applies to all firms or companies regardless of size. The two main provisions of Priorities Regulation No. 1: (1) forbid hoarding of any kind of material, and (2) provide that orders bearing a priority rating must be accepted and filled, according to the rating and delivery date.

4. Q. What priority assistance is given to distributors who supply retail stores?

A. They may apply to the WPB, Washington, D. C., on the new PD–1X form for ratings for essential supplies to keep their inventories up to a practicable working minimum, which in general means the smallest inventory possible to enable them to meet the demands of their customers. This applies to distributors who deal in supplies in the following 16 categories:

Automotive, aviation, builders' construction, electrical, foundry, hardware, health, industrial, plumbing and heating, railroad, refrigeration, restaurant, transmission, textile mill, welding and cutting.

PRIORITY ACTIONS
*From April 16
*Through April 22

Subject	Order Number	Related form	Issued	Expiration date	Rating
Agave fiber:					
a. Java sisal put into process on or before Apr. 20, 1942, may be manufactured into wrapping twine or binder twine.	M–84 amend. No. 4.		4–20–42		
b. A mfgr. may produce during the 11 months ending June 30, 1942, an amount of binder twine which when added to his stocks on hand on Nov. 1, 1941, does not exceed 120 percent of his sales during the 12 months ending Oct. 31, 1941.	M–84 amend. No. 5.		4–22–42		
Benzene:					
a. Conservation order:					
1. Use in motor fuel stopped immediately, except any producer or distributor may use within next 30 days 1–6 amount used for the three months ending 5–31.	M–137		4–20–42	Until revoked.	
Chemicals:					
a. Chlorine—to restrict use in pulp, paper and paperboard:					
1. Changes basis of limitation to amount used per ton of rag stock treated.	L–11 amend. No. 1.		4–20–42		
Closure enamel:					
a. Postpones effective date until Apr. 30.	M–116 amend. No. 1.		4–20–42		
Communications:					
a. New installations of telephones brought under strict control; only persons or organizations engaged in direct war work or in occupations essential to public welfare can be sure of obtaining new telephone service.	L–50 as amended Apr. 23, 1942.		4–23–42	Until revoked.	
b. Maintenance, repair and operating supplies:					
1. Applies to radio communication as well as wire communication; makes available A–3 rating for deliveries to an operator or his supplier of materials essential for maintenance, repair and protection of service—cannot be used for plant expansion or improvement.	P–129		4–23–42	9–30–42	A–3.
c. Makes available A–3 rating to an operator or his suppliers for deliveries of materials costing under $50 and used in normal construction caused by connection, disconnection, changes in location, etc., of a subscriber's equipment.	P–130		4–23–42	9–30–42	A–3.
Compressors:					
a. Complete system of allocations; prohibits placing or acceptance of orders for compressors covered by the regulations unless specific authorization is made.	L–100	PD–415, 416, 420.	4–17–42	Until revoked.	
Cranes and hoisting equipment:					
a. Extension	P–5–b ext. No. 2.		4–21–42	7–1–42.	
Dairy products:					
a. Repair, maintenance and operation of plants processing or producing dairy products:					
1. Makes available high ratings for deliveries of materials necessary for.	P–118	PD–414, 413.	4–18–42	6–30–42	A–2, A–3.
Farm machinery and equipment:					
a. Equipment, attachments and repair parts:					
1. Grants A–1–a rating to mfgrs. of certain types of farm equipment and machinery.	P–95 amend. No. 2.	PD–81	4–16–42	6–30–42.	
b. Production of farm machinery and equipment requiring rubber tires discontinued after April 30, except for combine harvester · threshers; production of combines requiring rubber tires stopped after July 31.	L–26–a amend. No. 1.		4–20–42		

Subject	Order Number	Related form	Issued	Expiration date	Rating
Feminine apparel: a. Lifts restrictions on sale of women's and children's ensembles put into process of manufacture before Apr. 9, 1942.	L-85 amend. No. 1.		4-20-42		
Fishing tackle: a. Mfrs. ordered to stop using metals, plastics and cork in noncommercial fishing tackle manufactured after May 31, 1942, with the exception of fish hooks, which may be manufactured after June 1 at a rate of 50 percent of each manufacturer's production in 1941.	L-93		4-23-42	Until revoked.	
Furniture (metal office): a. Removes from restrictions of order all metal shelving and metal lockers being produced for Army, Navy, and Maritime Commission, and requires that they be delivered before July 15, 1942.	L-13-a amend. No. 1.		4-20-42		
Honey: a. Clarifies quota provisions for small industrial users.	M-118 amend. No. 1		4-17-42		
Industrial machinery: a. Restrictions removed until May 15 to avoid disruption of schedules in plants preparing to convert to the output of war supplies.	L-83 amend. No. 1.		4-20-42		
Jute: a. Effective date of prohibition against use or use of raw jute imported into the U. S. applies at once; definition of "import."	M-70 amend. No. 1.		4-16-42		
Laundry equipment: a. Commercial laundry and dry cleaning equipment: 1. Bans production of laundry equipment for civilian consumption after June 1; dry cleaning equipment after July 1, except for Army, Navy or Maritime Commission orders.	L-91	PD-25A, 25X, 418, 419.	4-18-42	Until revoked.	
Nickel: a. Supplementary order: 1. Requires segregation of scrap containing more than one-half of one percent nickel by weight and permits its melting only for authorized uses.	M-6-c	PD-149, 150, 151, 394.	4-23-42	Until revoked.	
Osnaburg: a. Bag osnaburg and bag sheetings: 1. Directs cotton mills to convert specified percentage of their looms now producing a long list of cotton fabrics commonly used in clothing and in the home to the production of bag osnaburg and bag sheetings.	L-99		4-20-42		
Petroleum: a. Material stocked by supply houses for distribution to petroleum industry—revocation of order and PD-82a.	P-83 revoked		4-16-42		
Plumbing and heating equipment: a. Gas cooking stoves subject to terms of L-79.	Explanation of L-79.		4-21-42		A-10 or higher.
Projects (defense): a. Material for construction: 1. Supplier of materials entering into the construction of a defense housing project will be permitted to extend a preference rating at any time within three months after he becomes entitled to apply it.	P-19-c amend. No. 1, P-19-d amend. No. 1, P-55 amend. No. 1.		4-20-42	Until revoked.	
Rail and rail joints (used): a. Prohibits any person from selling, transferring or otherwise disposing of used rail of relayer grade, reroll grade or scrap grade without authorization—does not prevent railroads from using rail in own tracks.	L-88		4-22-42	Until revoked.	
Refrigerators (domestic mechanical): a. Any refrigerator built by a mfgr. to meet specifications of the Army, Navy or Maritime Commission for use on vessels built or operated by them is not considered a domestic mechanical refrigerator and therefore does not come under the order.	L-5 int. No. 1		4-20-42		

(Continued on page 20)

Natural, mixed gas deliveries limited for areas in 6 States in Midwest region

Restrictions on the delivery of natural and mixed natural and manufactured gas to consumers, as provided in order L-31 issued February 16, 1942, have been extended to parts of six midwestern States.

After May 15 no utility may deliver natural or mixed gas to new nonresidential consumers in those areas or increase deliveries to existing nonresidential consumers unless such consumer installs stand-by facilities to replace the new or additional delivery during a period of shut-off, or unless such delivery is approved by the WPB.

After May 15 no utility may deliver natural or mixed gas for the operation of a gas-heating system unless such equipment was installed prior to May 15 or unless, in the case of new construction, the gas-heating equipment was specified in the contract and the foundation under the main part of the structure in which the equipment is to be installed was completed prior to May 15. The prohibition also applies to gas-heating equipment which has been converted from another fuel to natural or mixed gas unless conversion takes place prior to May 15.

The new areas brought under the restrictions are:

IOWA—The western part of the State, including Des Moines, Sioux City, and Fort Dodge, served by Northern Natural Gas Co. and utilities obtaining any part of their requirements from that company.

KANSAS—Central Kansas, including Wichita and Hutchinson, served by Cities Service Gas Co, Kansas Power & Light Co,. Kansas-Nebraska Gas Co, Consolidated Gas Utilities Corporation, Drillers' Gas Co., and utilities obtaining any part of their requirements from those companies. The areas in Kansas formerly brought under the order remain under the restrictions.

MINNESOTA—Minneapolis and the area in the southern part of the State served by Northern Natural Gas Co. and distributing utilities.

NEBRASKA—Omaha, Lincoln, and other areas in the eastern and central parts of the State served by the Northern Natural Gas Co., Kansas-Nebraska Gas Co., Cities Service Gas Co., and utilities obtaining any part of their requirements from those companies.

OKLAHOMA—Certain areas throughout the State, served by Cities Service Gas Co., Consolidated Gas Utilities Corporation, and utilities obtaining any part of their requirements from those companies.

SOUTH DAKOTA—Sioux Falls, Yankton, Vermillion, and other areas served by Northern Natural Gas Co., and utilities obtaining any part of their requirements from this company.

These extensions of the areas affected are embodied in Amendment No. 2 to Exhibit A, Limitation Order L-31.

Unbroken dairy output assured by high rating for repairs, upkeep

The WPB has acted to make certain that necessary machinery is kept in good running order to meet increasing demands for milk and other dairy products for the armed forces, the civilian population, and the allied nations.

Preference Rating Order P–118 makes available high ratings for deliveries of materials necessary for repair, maintenance and operation of plants processing or producing dairy products.

An A–2 rating is made available for deliveries of materials required for emergency repairs to avert spoilage due to an actual or threatened break-down of operations.

Materials needed for normal repair, maintenance, operation, or replacement can be obtained with the assistance of an A–3 rating. Neither rating may be used to obtain materials for addition or expansion of operations.

The ratings may be applied by persons engaged in processing or producing dairy products in Canada, provided a copy of the order is specifically issued to them.

* * *

Users with excessive steel plate supplies to get none in May

Following a telegraphic survey of steel plate consumers, C. E. Adams, chief, iron and steel branch, announced April 22 that users with excessive inventories will receive no allocations in May.

A constant check upon inventories of plates is being made, Adams said, because demand continues at least 50 percent in excess of rising plate production. May output is expected to be in excess of 900,000 tons.

* * *

Metal shelving, locker rules removed for military needs

Limitation Order L–13–a, covering metal office furniture and equipment, was amended April 21 to remove from the restrictions of the order all metal shelving and metal lockers being produced under contracts placed by the Army, Navy, and Maritime Commission. The amendment (No. 1) requires that all such metal shelving or lockers be delivered to the Services or to the Maritime Commission before July 15, 1942.

PRIORITY ACTIONS	*From April 16 *Through April 22

(Continued from page 19)

Subject	Order Number	Related form	Issued	Expiration date	Rating
b. Enables dealers who want to get out of business to dispose of entire stock to another dealer; permits mfrs. to transfer refrigerators from one warehouse to another; a person who ordered and paid for a refrigerator prior to issuance of order is entitled to such refrigerator.	L-5-b amend. 3.	No.	4-20-42		
c. Refrigerating and air-conditioning machinery and equipment—material for emergency servicing:	P-126	PD-399	4-20-42	6-30-42	A-1-a, A-3,
1. Grants high preference ratings for deliveries of materials needed for repairs to air conditioning and refrigeration equipment.					
Rhodium:					
a. Prohibits all use of rhodium in the manufacture of jewelry.	M-95 amend. No 1.		4-17-42	12-31-42	
Steel and Iron:					
a. To conserve supply and direct distribution:					
1. Deliveries of iron and steel products will be restricted to preference ratings of A-10 or higher after May 15; abolished PD-73.	Amend. No. 3 and ext. No. 2 to M-21.	PD-138, 139	4-22-42	Until revoked.	A-10 or higher.
b. Iron and steel scrap—supplementary order:					
1. Orders segregation of tin plate and tin alloy scrap from other scrap for delivery to steel mills.	M-24-b		4-22-42	Until revoked.	
Sugar:					
a. Supplementary order:					
1. Allows receivers of refined sugar to anticipate their May quotas by accepting, between now and May 1, 50 percent of the amount of sugar they used or resold in May 1941.	M-55-h		4-21-42	5-1-42	
Sulphur:					
a. General inventory order:					
1. Permits deliveries of sulphur in excess of a practical minimum working inventory; no restrictions placed upon deliveries or acceptances of sulphur from a primary producer.	M-132		4-18-42	Until revoked.	
Suppliers inventory order:					
a. Warehouses carrying steel bars, ingots, wire and other products listed in Schedules "A" and "B" of Steel Warehouse Order M-21-b, may omit these products from inventory reports required by L-63.	L-63 exemption No. 1.		4-17-42	Until revoked.	
Tubes:					
a. Orders radio tube manufacturers to discontinue within seven days production for civilian use of 349 of the 710 types of radio tubes now on the market.	L-76.		4-17-42		
Tung oil and oiticica oil:					
a. Oiticica oil made subject to terms of M-57; restricts use of both oils to certain uses.	M-57 as amended Apr. 15, 1942.		4-15-42	Until revoked.	
Wool:					
a. Mfrs. ordered to stop putting wool into process after 11:59 Apr. 17, 1942, in the manufacture of floor coverings and drapery and upholstery fabrics except to fill Army, Navy, and Maritime Commission orders.	Amend. No. 4 to M-73 (as amend. and ext. to July 4, 1942).		4-17-42		

SUSPENSION ORDERS

Company	Order number	Violation	Penalty	Issued	Expiration date
Anderson & Sons, Westfield, Mass.	S-19	During 1941 shipped 38,926 pounds of products fabricated from aluminum for unauthorized, nonmilitary purposes; willful misrepresentation in the assignment of preference ratings.	Prohibited for a period of 6 months from accepting or delivering any aluminum, copper, or stainless steel.	4-20-42	10-20-42

Fluorescent lamp over 30 watts must rate A-2 after May 16; ban on small fixtures eased

WPB has amended Limitation Order No. L-78, on fluorescent lighting fixtures, to ease the restrictions on production and sale of small fixtures, and to set a definite closing date on the manufacture of other types.

The original order required that production of all fixtures end on April 22, except for certain rated orders and fixtures in process of manufacture. Amendment No. 1, effective April 24, allows the manufacture without restriction of fixtures with a lamp capacity of 30 watts or less if the materials were ordered on or before April 2 and actually on hand by April 20.

The small fluorescent fixtures may also be manufactured if the materials to be incorporated into them are acquired under an A-2 preference rating or under any rating assigned under the Production Requirements Plan.

The amendment bans the manufacture after May 16 of fixtures with a lamp capacity of more than 30 watts, except for orders bearing an A-2 or better preference rating.

Under the terms of the original order, no fluorescent lighting fixture could be sold or delivered after June 1, except on orders bearing a preference rating of A-2 or better, or for purposes of maintenance and repair. The amendment allows the unrestricted sale of the small fixtures and of cold cathode (high voltage) fluorescent lighting fixtures.

★ ★ ★

Production of rubber-tired farm machinery, equipment banned after April 30, except combines

The country's farmers soon will return to using the old-fashioned steel-wheeled wagon.

Because of the critical rubber situation, WPB has ordered production of farm machinery and equipment requiring rubber tires discontinued after April 30, except for combine harvester-threshers.

Production of combines requiring rubber tires must be stopped after July 31.

The action is embodied in Amendment No. 1 to Supplementary Limitation Order L-26-a.

New Industry Advisory Committees

The Bureau of Industry Advisory Committees, WPB, has announced the formation of the following Industry Advisory Committees:

COCOA AND CHOCOLATE COMMITTEE

Government presiding officer—John M. Whittaker, chief of the confectionery section, food supply branch.

Members:

W. F. Crouse, Hershey Chocolate Co., Hershey, Pa.; Russell Burbank, Rockwood & Co., Brooklyn, N. Y.; C. H. Gager, Walter Baker & Co., Dorchester, Mass.; Clive C. Day, Peter Cailler-Kohler, Swiss Chocolate Co., New York, N. Y.; Miss G. B. Schoenleber, Ambrosia Chocolate Co., Milwaukee, Wis.; Alfred Ghirardelli, D. Ghirardelli Co., San Francisco, Calif.; August Merckens, Merckens Chocolate Co., Buffalo, N. Y.; H. R. Horton, United Chocolate Refiners, Inc., Mansfield, Mass.; John Bachman, Bachman Chocolate Co., Mt. Joy, Pa.; O. O. Dickens, E. J. Brach & Sons, Chicago, Ill.

FLUID MILK SHIPPING CONTAINER COMMITTEE

Government presiding officer—Charles Dailey, chief, steel drum and tight cooperage section, containers branch.

Members:

W. H. Lane, Atlantic Stamping Co., Rochester, N. Y.; John M. Breen, Buhl Stamping Co., Detroit, Mich.; George W. Putnam, Creamery Package Mfg. Co., Chicago, Ill.; C. H. Richter, Keiner-Williams Stamping Co., Richmond Hill, N. Y.; C. W. Turner, H. E. Wright Co., Charlestown, Mass.; J. H. Stevenson, Lalance and Grosjean Mfg. Co., WoodhaVen, N. Y.; R. K. Follansbee, Sheet Metal Specialty Co., Pittsburgh, Pa.; R. H. Strickland, Solar Sturges Mfg. Co., Melrose Park, Ill.; J. N. Welscher, Superior Metal Products Co., St. Paul, Minn.; B. Rosenthal, Tennessee Can Co., FayetteVille, Tenn.

LEATHER AND LEATHER GOODS COMMITTEE

WOODSHANK SUBCOMMITTEE

Government presiding officer—Maj. Joseph W. Byron.

Members:

Forrest M. Larchar, United Shoe Machinery Corporation, Boston, Mass.; John Lewis, U. S. Pegwood & Shank Co., BrownVille, Maine; Stacy M. Nickerson, CamPello Shank Co., Campello, Mass.

MOTION PICTURES AND SPEAKING STAGE THEATERS COMMITTEE

Government presiding officer—Jesse Maury, deputy chief of the consumers durable goods branch.

Members:

E. Kuykendall, Motion Picture Theatre Owners of America, Columbus, Miss.; Arthur H. Lockwood, Lockwood & Gordon EnterPrises, Inc., Boston, Mass.; William F. Crockett, Virginia Theatre O ners Association, Virginia Beach, Va.; Carter Barron, Loew's Theatre, Washington, D. C.; Simon Fabian, Fabian Theatres, New York, N. Y.; N. A. Rosenberg, Allied States. Association, Pittsburgh, Pa.;

Joseph Bernhard, Warner Bros. Theatres, New York, N. Y.; Robert H. Poole, Pacific Coast Conference of Theatre Owners, Los Angeles, Calif.; Claude Ezell, Northwest Highway Drive-in Theatre, Dallas, Tex.; Paul Beisman, American Theatre, St. Louis, Mo.; N. B. Carskadon, Music Hall, Keyser, W. Va.; A. Fuller Sams, Jr., State Theatre, Statesville, N. C.

SET-UP BOX COMMITTEE

Government presiding officer—William W. Fitzhugh, chief, folding and set-up box section, containers branch.

Members:

J. H. Patterson, F. N. Burt Co., Inc., Buffalo, N. Y.; Adolph Dorfman, A. Dorfman Co., Inc., New York, N. Y.; Allen K. Schleicher, F. J. Schleicher Paper Box Co., St. Louis, Mo.; Charles A. Allen, Sprowles & Allen, Philadelphia, Pa.; F. R. ZurSchmiede, Finger Paper Box Co., Louisville, Ky.; N. Karasik, Pharmacy Paper Box Co., Chicago, Ill.; Walter P. Miller, Jr., Walter P. Miller Co., Inc., Philadelphia, Pa.; G. R. Kreider, Jr., Lebanon Paper Box Co., Lebanon, Pa.; A. G. Burry, Wayne Paper Box & Printing Corporation, Fort Wayne, Ind.; A. M. Bond, Consolidated Paper Box Co., SomerVille, Mass.; J. W. Scully, Puget Sound Paper Box Co., Seattle, Wash.; W. J. McClintock, Jr., McClintock Corporation, Harrisburg, Pa.

WATERPROOF RUBBER FOOTWEAR COMMITTEE

Government presiding officer—C. S. Reynolds.

Members:

George H. Bingham, Jr., Cambridge Rubber Co., Cambridge, Mass.; Albert H. Wechsler, ConVerse Rubber Co., Malden, Mass.; Charles H. Baker, GoodYear Footwear Corporation, ProVidence, R. I.; C. L. Munch, Hood Rubber Co., Watertown, Mass.; L. J. Larkin, LaCrosse Rubber Mills Co., LaCrosse, Wis.; William Rand, TingleY-Reliance Rubber Corporation, Rahway, N. J.; Hugh Bullock, Tyer Rubber Co., AndoVer, Mass.; H. S. Marior, U. S. Rubber Co., New York, N. Y.; Frank Petrik, Bata Shoe Co., Belcamp, Md.; Maurice C. Smith, Jr., Bristol Manufacturing Corporation, Bristol, R. I.; R. L. Lasser, Endicott-Johnson Corporation, Johnson City, N. Y.; C. M. Parks, GoodYear Rubber Co., Middletown, Conn.; Max Kalter, ServUs Rubber Co., Rock Island, Ill.

WOOD HOUSEHOLD AND UPHOLSTERED FURNITURE COMMITTEE

Government presiding officer—William A. Adams, assistant chief, furniture branch.

Members:

W. G. Mullins, Olive & MYers Mfg. Co., Dallas, Tex.; D. E. Rowe, Kroehler Mfg. Co., NaperVille, Ill.; Earle O. HultQuist, Jamestown-RoYal UphoIstery Corporation, Jamestown, N. Y.; B. L. DaVies, MichÍgan Seating Co., Jackson, Mich.; Hollis Baker, Baker Furniture Factories, Holland, Mich.; F. H. Gillespie, F. H. Gillespie Co., Los Angeles, Calif.; T. Austin Finch, ThomasVille Chair Co., ThomasVille, N. C.; William M. Bassett, W. M. Bassett Furniture Co., MartinsVille, Va.; Charles C. Brooks, Conant Ball Co., Gardner, Mass.; Gleeson MurphY, Jr., MurphY Chair Co., Owensboro, Ky.; H. W. Koehm, The Sikes Co., Inc., Buffalo, N. Y.

(More Industry Committees on page 27)

RATIONING . . .

Sugar rationing details for individuals, trade, industries, and institutions are set forth in new Order No. 3

Rationing Order No. 3, which sets forth in detail the regulations for the sugar rationing program to individual consumers and trade users, as well as the sugar quotas allowed to all forms of industrial and institutional users, has been issued by the OPA, acting under the authority of WPB Directive 1E, which transferred to the OPA the authority to ration sugar.

1 pound with each of first 4 stamps

Consumers, who will register in elementary schools throughout the country on May 4, 5, 6 or 7, will be able to purchase 1 pound of sugar with each one of the first four stamps in their War Ration Books.

Stamp No. 1 will be valid during the period May 5 to May 16, stamp No. 2 will be valid during the period May 17 to May 30, stamp No. 3 will be effective from May 31 until June 13, and consumers will be able to use stamp No. 4 for purchasing 1 pound of sugar during the period of June 14 to June 27.

Restaurants and other food services will be able to obtain 50 percent of the amount of sugar used during the corresponding month last year, while bakers, manufacturers of confectionery, ice cream, dairy products, preserves, bottled beverages, desserts, and other specialties will be entitled to an allotment of 70 percent of past use.

Under the regulations, one adult member of each family unit should register and apply for War Ration Book One for all the members of the family, including those temporarily absent or confined to an institution during the registration period.

Family units which do not contain an adult member should be registered by the oldest member, or by a responsible adult authorized to act on behalf of the minors.

Other provisions

In the case of consumers who are not members of a family unit, the regulations provide that they should register for themselves. Minors, unless they are self-supporting, are to be registered by their parents or guardians. Consumers who are not members of a family are not eligible for registration and cannot obtain a War Ration Book while confined in a public or private hospital, asylum, prison, or similar institution.

Special provisions are made for persons who, while not members of a family unit, and not confined to an institution, are incapacitated and unable to register for themselves during May 4, 5, 6, and 7, the dates set aside for consumer registration. Such individuals may be registered by the person caring for them or by such other persons as they designate.

Children born after the registration dates will be entitled to a normal ration of sugar, and may be registered at any time by parents or guardians at the local rationing board where the parents or guardians are registered. A War Ration Book will be issued upon registration, but the board will remove the ration stamps applicable to all the expired ration periods.

Consumers who did not receive a ration book at the time of registration because of ownership of a quantity of sugar in excess of 6 pounds will receive their ration books by applying to their local boards, but only after "the commencement of the latest ration periods during which stamps become valid having a weight value equal to the excess sugar supply owned on May 4, 1942."

Rules for inductees

Persons inducted into the armed forces of the United States or those leaving the United States for a period of more than 30 days must surrender their war ration books to their local boards. Rationing books must also be returned to the board within ten days after the death of a person for whom the book was issued.

Persons who become confined to an institution for a period likely to exceed 10 days must surrender their ration books to the institution. Their ration books, which will be returned to them upon discharge from the institution.

While army and navy personnel "subsisted in kind" or fed "in organized messes" are not eligible to register for a war ration book, other members of the military establishments who eat at home should register and apply for ration books like all other consumers.

OPA delegated to ration sale and distribution of sugar at all levels

Authority to ration the sale and distribution of sugar at all levels from the refiner to the ultimate consumer was delegated April 21 to the OPA by Supplementary Directive No. 1 E issued by the Director of Industry Operations.

Covers all direct-consumption

Rationing powers delegated by the order cover all direct-consumption sugar, defined to include any sugar which is not to be further refined or otherwise improved in quality, but excluding certain syrups.

Deliveries to Government agencies listed in WPB Directive No. 1 and deliveries for export are exempt from OPA rationing control.

The purpose of the Supplementary Directive is to give OPA control over the distribution of refined sugar to industrial users, wholesalers and retail stores as well as to individual consumers. General rationing authority at the retail level has already been delegated to OPA by WPB Directive No. 1, but control over the distribution of sugar cannot be satisfactorily exercised unless all authority over public distribution is in one agency.

Issuance of the Supplementary Directive formalizes a policy which has already been in effect for some time.

5 pounds annually at most allotted to each holder of War Ration Book for canning

Every person holding a War Ration Book can get a special allotment of not more than 5 pounds of sugar a year for home canning or preserving fresh fruits and vegetables for home consumption, the OPA announced April 19.

Application for more sugar for canning will have to be made to local rationing boards on a special form provided by the OPA (OPA Form No. R-315), and will have to be presented by an adult member of the family or by an authorized agent. The maximum amount of sugar which each holder of a War Ration Book will be entitled to obtain will be 5 pounds.

For this purpose local boards will issue sugar purchase certificates, not stamps. The certificate will state the total amount of sugar the bearer may purchase.

1 pound to "scarcity areas"

Consumers registered with boards located in what are known as "scarcity areas," will be able to obtain only 1 pound of sugar for home canning during the period of May and June. This provision will apply to the District of Columbia and to the States of Virginia, West Virginia, Maryland, Delaware, Connecticut, Pennsylvania, New Jersey, New York, Rhode Island, Massachusetts, New Hampshire, Vermont, and Maine.

On the other hand, army and navy personnel "in furlough status for a period in excess of one week" are entitled to their ration of sugar for the furlough period, and will receive a sugar purchase certificate upon presentation of leave papers to any local rationing board.

"The board issuing the certificate,' the order states, "shall enter on the leave papers the designation of the board and a statement that a certificate has been issued by the board and the date of the issuance."

Special cases

Special provisions are made for consumers who did not register on May 4, 5, 6, and 7. "Upon good cause being shown," they may register after May 21 at the local rationing boards having jurisdiction over the areas in which they reside. In cases of unusual hardship, boards may permit, at their discretion, registration before May 21.

Special provisions are also made for consumers who because of transportation difficulties find it a hardship to buy sugar in the quantities allowed during each ration period. Under the Regulations, such a consumer may apply to his local rationing board for a sugar certificate authorizing him to purchase at one time the total amount of sugar to which he would be eligible during four weeks.

Efforts have been made by the OPA not to disturb the traditional arrangement of those growers of sugarcane or beets who have in the past taken part payment in the form of refined sugar for the crops sold to primary distributors for processing. Such growers may apply to their local rationing boards for sugar purchase certificates authorizing them to take delivery of a maximum of 25 pounds for each member of a family unit. They must, however, surrender their war ration books to the local rationing boards.

Consumers who by reason of illness require more sugar than the normal ration allowance may apply to their local boards for the additional quantity required. The special application form for this purpose, which is officially designated as OPA Form No. R-315, must be accompanied by a doctor's certificate stating the amount of sugar required and explaining why the additional sugar is needed.

Lost ration books

Under the sugar rationing regulations, consumers may apply to local boards for ration books to replace books accidentally lost or destroyed, but replacements will not be made till after 2 months from the date of the application. "To make a false application," it is pointed out, "is a criminal offense."

Industrial and institutional users of sugar, who register at high schools on April 28 and 29, will receive either a provisional allowance or an allotment to cover their sugar needs from the date of registration till June 30, depending on the products for which the sugar is used.

Computing "allotment"

In the case of "institutional users," the base for every month will be determined by the amount used during the corresponding month in 1941, or, at the option of the registering unit, by the amount used in March 1942, which will serve as a base for computing the allotment for every month of 1942.

A primary distributor may deliver sugar on and after April 28 without interruption, but only upon the surrender of stamps or sugar purchase certificates.

A primary distributor is defined as "any person who manufactures sugar or the agent of any such person, or any person who delivers sugar to the continental United States from offshore areas or any person who takes such delivery or the agent of any such person who makes or takes such delivery. The term "agent" shall be deemed to include a broker, factor, commission merchant, or a person who takes title but actually performs functions commonly performed by agents, brokers, factors, or commission merchants.

A primary distributor must keep at his principal business office records of all sugar delivered by him, "the persons to whom such deliveries were made and the amounts thereof, the serial number of all certificates received, the weight value of such certificates, and the amount of sugar delivered against them," the order states.

New establishments, including those which commenced operations subsequent to the effective date of the order, may petition their local boards for registration and for sugar purchase certificates.

Valid only during rationing period

Under the regulations certificates or stamps may be transferred only upon an order to receive sugar, and all other transfers are prohibited. Consumers who use less sugar than they are allowed to purchase, may not give their stamps to friends.

Each stamp is valid only during the ration period assigned to it. A registering unit which has received sugar rationing stamps may use them only within ten days of the close of the period during which the stamps were valid. A certificate authorizes a person to whom it was issued to take delivery within sixty days from the date of the certificate, and it authorizes a primary distributor or wholesaler to whom it has been surrendered to make a delivery of sugar within thirty days from the date of the last endorsement on the reverse side of the certificate.

Retailers receiving stamps from consumers must paste the stamps on a card provided by the Office of Price Administration or upon a similar card containing room for 100 stamps. Only stamps bearing the same number may be affixed to the card.

"A registering unit whose sugar is destroyed, stolen, or spoiled may apply to and obtain from the board a certificate authorizing it to take delivery of an amount of sugar equal to the amount destroyed, stolen, or spoiled," the regulations provide.

May petition for adjustment

Provisions are made in the sugar rationing regulations for petitioning for an adjustment of the base, allotment or of the allowable inventory. Such a petition must be filed with the board with which the unit is registered and must be made on a special form provided by OPA, known as "Special Purpose Application."

Registering units may also appeal to the State Director against an adverse decision by local boards, but the appeal must be filed with the local board within ten days after the decision.

Under the terms of the order, a violation of the regulations is punishable by a maximum fine of $10,000 or imprisonment of not more than 1 year, or both. In addition, a violator of the order in connection with the operation of an establishment using sugar may be required to surrender for cancellation all stamps or sugar purchase certificates held by him "in conjunction with the operation of all such establishments."

Not only can violators of the order be prohibited from receiving stamps or sugar purchase certificates either permanently or for a set period of time, and from receiving and dealing in any other materials which may be subject to rationing or allocation, but the Office of Price Administration has the power under der Rationing Order No. 3 to prohibit any person from delivering or agreeing to deliver to a violator of the order any materials which now or in the future may be subject to rationing or allocation.

Emerson to head OPA region 9

Appointment of Rupert Emerson as regional administrator of the new OPA region No. 9 was announced April 22 by Price Administrator Henderson. Region No. 9 includes Alaska, Puerto Rico, the Virgin Islands, the Canal Zone, Hawaii, and the Philippine Islands.

Mr. Emerson, who has been serving as price executive for the Territories and possessions now grouped in Region No. 9, will be stationed in Washington. He was formerly director of the Division of Territories and Island Possessions in the Department of the Interior.

Long-distance bus and truck operators carrying vital hauls to get emergency reserves of tires and tubes

Emergency reserves of tires and tubes for quick replacements of blow-outs will be made available to some long-distance bus and truck operators to save time and rubber in carrying vital materials, OPA Administrator Henderson announced April 18.

Amendment No. 5 to the Revised Tire Rationing Regulations, effective April 22, allows an emergency reserve of tires and tubes equal to 10 percent of the total number of running wheels on qualified vehicles—in addition to spares already permitted.

OPA will make available either emergency reserve certificates for new tires and tubes, or regular certificates for retreading or recapping when the applicant has extra tire carcasses. Certificate holders may purchase immediately the tires and tubes or turn the certificates over to their drivers for use as need arises.

Vehicles must qualify

If tires are bought immediately, the purchaser may spot them at points along routes over which his vehicles operate.

To qualify for emergency certificates a vehicle must be either operated by a State government or subject to Interstate Commerce Commission regulation. In addition, it must be eligible under List A of the Revised Tire Rationing Regulations and have more than 50 percent of its regular mileage on runs 50 miles or more from the nearest depot where the operator has tires stored.

No applicant qualifies under the plan, unless all his vehicles, except passenger cars, are on List A, which includes vehicles operating only in service deemed most necessary. Where only part of a fleet qualifies, under the long-haul provision of the plan, emergency certificates may be allotted for those vehicles. Tires obtained with emergency certificates may be used on any vehicle in the fleet.

Not to exceed 10 percent computation

Emergency certificates and emergency reserve tires together are not to exceed 10 percent of the total number mounted on running wheels of long-haul eligible trucks in possession of the certificate-holder. In the case of small operators who have so few wheels on qualified vehicles that the 10 percent computation

would show them entitled to less than one tire, at least one emergency reserve certificate will be allotted. The operator of a single eligible truck is not excluded from the plan.

The certificates, to be issued by local rationing boards, will be granted only after the applicant has filled out a form requiring full disclosure of all pertinent information in regard to tires already in his possession. Applications for an original allotment are to be filed not later than May 15, 1942. The person who signs the application must appear before the issuing board for any questioning necessary.

When an operator's emergency reserve falls below the 10 percent level, provision is made for replenishment.

Certificates issued to establish the original emergency reserve are not to be charged against the quota of the board that issues them.

★ ★ ★

Tire ration violator sentenced to 18 months in jail

Violators of rationing regulations will be subject to severe penalties if a precedent set April 17 by Judge Robert C. Baltzell of the Federal Court of Evansville, Ind., is followed.

Charles L. Hart and Russell W. Baker, president and secretary-treasurer, respectively, of the La Salle Motor Sales Corporation of Boonville, Ind., the defendants, were the first to be convicted and sentenced for violating the rationing regulations issued by the Office of Price Administration.

Hart was sentenced to 18 months in jail and fined $500. Baker was fined $250 and sentenced to a year and a day in jail. His sentence was immediately suspended, and he was placed on 3 years' probation. The LaSalle Motor Sales Corporation was fined $1,000.

Hart and Baker admitted concealing and storing large quantities of new tires from the stock of the LaSalle corporation, falsifying the dates on a promissory note covering tires removed to the Boonville Mills, on January 15, and filing a false inventory of floor stocks with the Bureau of Internal Revenue.

Buses may carry entertainers for Services without losing eligibility for tires

Buses may be used on special trips to carry entertainers and other participants in organized morale-building recreational activities, as well as military personnel, to and from Army and Navy establishments without losing eligibility under List A of the Revised Tire Rationing Regulations.

Must have written request

This permission, which is given only where other means of transportation are not available and where the commanding officer makes written request for the service, is contained in Amendment No. 6 to the regulations, announced April 21 by Price Administrator Henderson. The effective date was April 22.

At the same time, provision is made for List A trucks to make deliveries to ultimate consumers when these do not entail special trips or diversions from normal routes, and are only incidental to the performance of eligible services. Until now, such deliveries have been expressly forbidden.

Amendment No. 6 also defines ambulances as vehicles specially designed and equipped to carry sick or injured human beings. Mail carriers, under the terms of the amendment, are made eligible under List A if their vehicles are used principally in transporting mail.

★ ★ ★

Benzene banned in motor fuel

The WPB April 20 stopped the use of benzene in motor fuel because it is a necessary ingredient of synthetic rubber.

Order M-137, issued by J. S. Knowlson, Director of Industry Operations, halted the use of benzene in motor fuel immediately, with the exception that any producer or distributor may use within the next 30 days one-sixth of the amount he used for the 3 months ended March 31.

Benzene is added to motor fuel as an antiknock ingredient, either in addition to or in place of tetraethyl lead. It is a principal source of styrene, one of the main ingredients of Buna rubber. While production is on the increase, both demands cannot be met.

The order specifically exempts benzene used in the production of aviation fuel with an octane rating higher than 87.

Time He Went to School

Cartoon by Elderman for OEM. Publishers may obtain mats of these cartoons weekly in either two- or three-column size. Requests to be put on the mailing list should be addressed to Distribution Section, Division of Information, Office for Emergency Management, 2743 Temporary R, Washington, D. C.

Check-up reveals 60,000 more autos available for rationing

The number of new automobiles available for rationing this year is about 60,000 larger than the 340,000 originally indicated by manufacturers' reports.

Passenger car figures received by OPA in a close count of inventory show 399,565 new cars in the hands of dealers, distributors and manufacturers as of February 11, 1942. This is in addition to the Government "pool" stocks held by them.

The inventory has not been completed.

The 340,000 figure which until now has been used as the inventory of new passenger cars (over and above the estimated 140,000 held in the Government pool for military needs and rationing in 1943) was arrived at on the basis of reports by manufacturers. These reports included inventory figures submitted to the manufacturers by dealers.

May tire quotas allow recaps for first time to List A passenger cars

May quotas that make available fewer certificates for new tires but more for recapping than in April were announced April 24 by OPA Administrator Henderson.

The total of new and recapped tires for May is greater than the combined total for April. This increase follows a seasonal pattern of expansion as warm weather permits a stepping up of industrial and construction activities.

Retreading to be required if possible

The May quota makes available recapping certificates for List A passenger cars and motorcycles for the first time since rationing began. This is in line with provisions of a forthcoming amendment to the rationing regulations which will require that after May 1 passenger car eligibles on List A must accept recapping certificates when the casings in use at the time of application are recappable or retreadable. This requirement has been in effect for some time in regard to all truck applicants. However, it is proposed to release new tires for vehicles that operate in such hazardous services—police and fire department equipment, for instance—that recaps cannot be safely used.

The May quota provides only 55,573 new tires for List A passenger vehicles, but includes 578,092 recapped tires upon which List A eligibles have first call, with the remainder available to List B users. The entire April quota provision for List A passenger vehicles was 101,636 new tires, with a separate quota for List B of 470,317 recapped tires. List A and B cars together are assigned an inner tube quota of 315,058 for May, against 285,977 in April.

List A includes vehicles used in services deemed most essential in the Nation's economy, and List B covers those considered of secondary importance.

For trucks also, the new tire quota for May is less than in April, with the difference more than made up by an increase in the number of recaps made available. The quota provides 238,259 new and 379,060 recapped tires for eligible trucks, buses, farm equipment, and industrial tractors, compared with 275,523 and 246,442, respectively, in April. The truck inner tube quota is 328,836, against 260,983.

The quotas are for the 48 States, the District of Columbia, Alaska, Panama Canal Zone, Puerto Rico, and the Virgin Islands.

Leave gasoline for war needs, don't wait for rationing, war leaders urge

Heads of five war agencies on April 23 put motorists in the East on notice that "motoring-as-usual is out."

The statement, issued jointly by Harold L. Ickes, Petroleum Coördinator; Donald M. Nelson, Chairman of the War Production Board; Leon Henderson, Price Administrator; Joseph B. Eastman, Director of Defense Transportation, and Admiral Emory S. Land, War Shipping Administrator, follows in part:

It is not possible to transport enough petroleum to the 17 eastern States to meet both essential war needs and normal civilian demands. Very substantial reductions in gasoline consumptions must be achieved immediately. Motoring-as-usual is out.

Seamen risking lives

Already hundreds of men have lost their lives at sea trying to bring in the oil needed for war. No patriotic American can or will ask men to risk their lives to preserve motoring-as-usual.

There is a critical deficiency in facilities to transport oil to the Atlantic Seaboard from the producing areas. This deficiency has been increasing ever since the United States entered the war, with the result that it has been impossible to haul enough oil to meet all demand. How long this will continue, it is impossible now for anyone to say.

Consequently, oil companies have had to draw on their reserve stocks and are continuing to draw on them—in order to fill requirements. If this condition were allowed to continue, it would mean that the supply of gasoline would run out entirely, and that we should be entirely dependent on day-to-day shipments, which are not sufficient to meet requirements—and cannot be depended upon because of the uncertainty of ocean movements.

The present system of restricted deliveries to filling stations is to be supplemented by card rationing. If before card rationing goes into effect, some people flout the spirit of the curtailment by going from one station to another and thus keeping their tanks full, others are going to have no gasoline at all.

If a motorist fills up the tank to go to a picnic, some defense worker may not be able to get to his job. If a man drives to work alone every day, instead of working out a car-sharing plan with his neighbors, he may take gasoline from a truck that is hauling for a war plant.

Steps to save gasoline

The Government is, therefore, asking motorists to:

1. Eliminate all unnecessary driving.

2. Form car-sharing pools with neighbors working in the same general area.

When use of the car has been reduced to the minimum, gasoline consumption may be further conserved by observing the following suggestions:

1. Drive under 40 miles an hour. Studies have shown that gasoline consumption increases with the speed of a car. A car getting 16.4 miles on a gallon of gas at a speed of 40 miles an hour will get only 14.6 miles on a gallon at 50 miles an hour; 12.6 at 60 miles; 10.6 at 70 miles, and 8.6 miles at 80 miles an hour.

2. Don't "idle" the motor unnecessarily. The Bureau of Standards report that a 30-second "idle" uses one-sixteenth as much gasoline as would be consumed by a car going 1 mile at 50 miles an hour.

3. Keep your car in good mechanical condition.

4. Align the wheels properly.

5. Lubricate all parts of the car regularly with the proper lubricants.

6. Drive at steady speeds. Avoid spurting.

7. Start slowly. Don't attempt quick get-aways.

8. Keep braking to a safe minimum.

9. Inflate tires properly.

10. Don't drive on curves at speeds that "pull" the car.

Gasoline rationing begins May 15 in East

(Continued from page 1)

for registering will be announced later. However, it was emphasized, the same local rationing boards that administer the rationing of tires, automobiles, and sugar will again be called upon to serve as rationing bodies.

Drivers of all noncommercial passenger cars will need their cards to purchase gasoline beginning May 15, the day after registration closes.

Operators of all trucks and other motor vehicles that are readily recognized as commercial vehicles will not need cards for gasoline purchases. Under the interim plan they are not restricted, and may get gasoline as they formerly did.

Five types of cards

All other operators, including commercial users whose vehicles are not clearly marked as commercial, will need one of five types of cards to be issued upon application.

The basic "A" card will be issued to any passenger automobile owner upon presentation of his car registration card. The owner of two or more automobiles may receive an "A" rationing card for each vehicle in his possession.

Emphasizing the simplicity of the interim plan, Joel Dean, chief of the fuel ration branch of OPA, said automobile owners will not be asked to fill out formal registration blanks to get "A" ration cards.

"When a car owner presents his registration card at an elementary school on one of the registration days," Mr. Dean explained, "the registrar will immediately write the license number on the card, and stamp it as well as the registration certificate so that it cannot be presented at another time for another ration card. The car owner will thereupon be handed his 'A' card."

The "A" card, which will resemble a meal or commutation ticket, will contain seven squares, each representing a unit of gasoline which the holder will be entitled to purchase any time between May 15 and July 1. The number of gallons in each "unit" will be announced shortly before May 15, and may be varied later to meet the supply situation. Service station attendants will tear off, mark, or punch a square for each unit of gasoline delivered to the card holder.

Greater allowance for doctors, others

Doctors, war workers, and others whose vocations require mileage greater than that provided by the basic allowance may apply for supplemental cards. Cards "B1," "B2," and "B3" will be issued to passenger car owners who state in an application that their gasoline needs fall within certain specified mileage limits.

The "B1" cards will contain 11 "unit" squares; the "B2" card will have 15 squares; and the "B3" card 19. As in the case of the "A" card, the amount of gasoline each "unit" will represent has not been determined. An "A" unit may also differ from a "B" unit.

In addition to the "A" and "B" cards there will be an "X" card to be issued to car owners whose gasoline needs cannot be estimated in a definite number of miles. A doctor, for example might qualify for an "X" card.

Forms for making applications for "B" and "X" cards will be supplied at the time of registration, and may be filled out at the registration site. Rationing cards will be issued at that time to those who qualify.

Hardship cases may get more

Any registrant who feels he is suffering especial hardship because of the particular rationing card issued him may appeal later to the local rationing board. He will be issued supplemental rations if he can show need.

Owners of motorcycles will receive a smaller number of gallons for each unit on their ration cards, Mr. Dean said. Small motor cars, however, will get the same gallonage as larger cars.

Inboard motor boats not used commercially will get "A" cards. They will be required to show additional vocational requirements to obtain any supplemental gasoline allowances. A normal supply of gasoline will be allowed for other nonhighway uses, including outboard motor boats, farm tractors, gasoline engines, stoves and furnaces, cleaning establishments, etc. Owners, however, will be required to sign a declaration that the gasoline will be used for nonhighway purposes.

New industry advisory committees

The Bureau of Industry Advisory Committees, WPB, has announced the formation of the following new industry advisory committees:

BICYCLE MANUFACTURERS COMMITTEE

Government presiding officer—M. D. Moore.

Members:

H. Clyde Brokaw, Vice President, Shelby Cycle Co., Shelby, Ohio; Frank Carlton, comptroller, Arnold, Schwinn & Co., Chicago, Ill.; N. R. Clarke, president, Westfield Manufacturing Co., Westfield, Mass.; Jack Dougherty, president, Monark Silver King, Inc., Chicago, Ill.; F. J. Hannon, Vice president, Murray Ohio Manufacturing Co., Cleveland, Ohio; Horace Huffman, president, Huffman Manufacturing Co., Dayton, Ohio; James S. Manton, president, Manton & Smith Co., Chicago, Ill.; Homer L. Mueller, Vice president, Cleveland Welding Co., Cleveland, Ohio; A. H. Myers, Iver Johnson's Arms & Cycle Works, Fitchburg, Mass.; Neely Powers, president, The Colson Corporation, Elyria, Ohio; S. K. Pruett, vice President, Excelsior Manufacturing Co., Inc., Michigan City, Ind.; E. S. Van Valkenburg, President, H. P. Snyder Manufacturing Co., Little Falls, N. Y.

BREWING COMMITTEE

TRAFFIC SUBCOMMITTEE

Government presiding officer—John B. Smiley, chief, beverage and tobacco branch.

Members :

H. Val Haley, president, Eastern Brewers Traffic Assn., Newark, N J.; Van G. Hildebrand, traffic manager, Anheuser-Busch, Inc., St. Louis, Mo.; E. D. Hedstrom, traffic manager, Pabst Brewing Co., Chicago, Ill.; Frank L. Degroat, general traffic manager, Joseph Schlitz Brewing Co., Milwaukee, Wis.; Karl Schuster, president, Acme Breweries, San Francisco, Calif.; W. G. Koerber, president, Koerber Brewing Co., Toledo, Ohio; F. Brooke Whiting, president, Queen City Brewing Co., Cumberland, Md.; Edward V. Lahey, president, Smith Brothers, Inc., New Bedford, Mass.

IRON AND STEEL COMMITTEE

PIPE, WIRE PRODUCTS AND GALVANIZED SHEET JOBBERS SUBCOMMITTEE

Government presiding officer—C. E. Adams, chief, iron and steel branch.

Members:

Henry J. Allison, Glasgow-Allison Co., Charlotte, N. C.; Wakefield Baker, Baker-Hamilton & Pacific, San Francisco, Calif.; A. J. Becker, Ohio Valley Hardware & Refining Co., Evansville, Ind.; Thomas A. Fernley, Jr., National Wholesale Hardware Association, Philadelphia, Pa.; Henry A. Hoeynck, Shapleigh Hardware Co., St Louis, Mo.; Charles Igoe, Igoe Brothers, Brooklyn, N. Y.; A. C. Rankin, Teague Hardware Co., Montgomery, Ala.; M. W. Denison, Braman-Dow & Co., Boston, Mass.; William French, Sr., Moore-Handley Hardware Co., Birmingham, Ala.; S. C. Hinkle, Mine & Smelter Supply Co., Denver, Colo.; N. J. Higginbotham, W. A. Case & Son Mfg. Co., Buffalo, N. Y.; Lucien W. Moore, Crane Co., Chicago, Ill.

LAWN MOWER COMMITTEE

Government presiding officer—M. D. Moore, of the consumers durable goods division.

Members:

P. N. Case, president, Blair Manufacturing Co., Springfield, Mass.; H. M. Cooper, Cooper Manufacturing Co., Inc., Marshalltown, Iowa; W. C. Davis, G. W. Davis Corporation, Richmond, Ind.; K. E. Goit, Toro Manufacturing Corporation, Minneapolis, Minn.; H. L. Heineke, Heineke & Co., Springfield, Ill.; O. T. Jacobsen, president, Jacobsen Manufacturing Co., Racine, Wis.; R. C. Luecke, president, Milbradt Manufacturing Co., St. Louis, Mo.; W. S. McGuire, Dille & McGuire Manufacturing Co., Richmond, Ind.; M. D. Perine, Vice president, Pennsylvania Lawn Mower Works, Primos, Pa.; W. S. Watrous, President, Whirlwind Lawn Mower Co., Milwaukee, Wis.

LEATHER AND LEATHER GOODS COMMITTEE

HORSEHIDE TANNERS SUBCOMMITTEE

Government presiding officer—Joseph W. Byron, chief of the leather section.

Members:

E. H. Foot, president, S. B. Foot Tanning Co., Red Wing, Minn.; Karl Friend, J. Greenebaum Tanning Co., 3057 North Rockwell Street, Chicago, Ill.; O. Plotkin, president, Midwest-Tanning Co., 12 and Davis Avenue, East Milwaukee, Wis.; F. Rulison, Jr., president, F. Rulison & Sons, Johnstown, N. Y.; Solomon Katz, secretary, Superior Tanning Co., 1244 West Division Street, Chicago, Ill.; Gustave Swoboda, Jr., H. Swoboda & Sons, Inc., 1027 North Bodine Street, Philadelphia, Pa.; V. W. Krause, secretary, Wolverine Shoe & Tanning Corporation, Rockford, Mich.

MOTION PICTURE PRODUCERS AND DISTRIBUTORS' COMMITTEE

Government presiding officer—M. D. Moore, of the consumers durable goods branch.

Members:

B. Balaban, president, Paramount Pictures, New York, N. Y.; Carrol Sax, studio manager, Warner Bros. Pictures, Burbank, Calif.; William F. Rodgers, Vice president, Metro Goldwyn Mayer, New York, N. Y.; Jed Buell, president, Commander Pictures, Hollywood, Calif.; A. Montague, sales manager, Columbia Pictures, New York, N. Y.; John J. O'Connor, Universal Pictures, New York, N. Y.; O. Henry Briggs, President, Producers Releasing Corporation, New York. N. Y.; Herman Robbins, president, National Screen Service, New York, N. Y.; M. J. Siegel, president, Republic Pictures Corporation, North Hollywood, Calif.; W. Ray Johnston, president, Monogram Film, New York, N. Y.; Earl I. Sponable, supervisor, Fox Movietone, New York, N. Y.; N. Peter Rathvon, Pathe News, Inc., New York, N. Y.; Louis DeRochemont, president, March of Time, New York, N. Y.; George Weeks, president, Range Busters Pictures Inc., Los Angeles, Calif.; Gradwell L. Sears, Vice president, United Artists, New York N. Y.; Ray Klune, Society of Independent Motion Picture Producers, Los Angeles, Calif.

NONALCOHOLIC BEVERAGE COMMITTEE

Government presiding officer—John B. Smiley, chief, beverage and tobacco branch.

Members:

W. T. Aitken, president, Mission Dry Corporation, Los Angeles, Calif.; Willis Battle, Vice President, Nehi Corporation, Columbus, Ga.; Dr. W. D. Bost, president, Orange Crush Co., Chicago, Ill.; E. W. David, treasurer, The Charles E. Hires Co., Philadelphia, Pa.; J. L. Firmage, president, Nehi Beverage Company of Utah, Salt Lake City, Utah; Talbot O. Freeman, Vice President, Pepsi-Cola Co., Long Island City, N.Y.; H. C. Grigg, Vice president, The Seven-Up Co., St. Louis, Mo.; William Ries, president, Jacob Ries Bottling Works, Inc., Shakopee, Minn.; James Vernor, president, James Vernor Co., Detroit, Mich.; Edward Wagner, president, The W. T. Wagner's Sons Co., Cincinnati, Ohio; Paul F. Glaser, president, Glaser Beverage, Inc., Seattle, Wash.; W. S. Kilborn, Vice president, Dr. Pepper Co., Dallas, Tex.; John F. Leary, owner, C. Leary Co., Newburyport, Mass.; Joseph La Pides, president, Suburban Club Carbonated Beverage Co., Inc., Baltimore, Md.; Benjamin H. Oehlert, Jr., assistant to President, The Coca-Cola Co., Wilmington, Del.; C. V. Rainwater, President, Hygeia Coca-Cola Bottling Works, Inc., Pensacola, Fla.; Wm. J. Williams, secretary, Canada Dry Ginger Ale, Inc., New York, N. Y.; H. A. Canfield, President, A. J. Canfield Co., Inc.; Chicago, Ill.

PLUMBING AND HEATING COMMITTEE

EXTENDED SURFACE HEATING SUBCOMMITTEE

Government presiding officer—W. W. Timmis, chief of the plumbing and heating branch.

Members:

Donald French, Vice president, Carrier Corporation, Syracuse, N. Y.; C. A. Dunham, president, C. A. Dunham Co., Chicago, Ill.; Richard H. Nelson, Herman Nelson Corporation, Moline, Ill.; Henry Mathis, partner, New York Blower Co., Chicago, Ill.; Reuben N. Trane, president, The Trane Co., LaCrosse, Wis.; Harry S. Wheller, Vice president, J. Wing Manufacturing Co., New York, N. Y.; P. T. Miner, Larkin Coils, Inc., Atlanta, Ga.; Israel Kramer, president, Kramer-Trenton Co., Trenton, N. J.; A. G. Dixon, manager heating division, Modine Manufacturing Co., Racine, Wis.; Albert J. Nesbitt, president, John J. Nesbitt, Inc., Holmesburgh, Philadelphia, Pa.; H. W. Rinearson, President, Shaw Perkins Manufacturing Co., Pittsburgh, Pa.; A. A. Ahlff, sales manager, Tuttle & Bailey, Inc., New Britain, Conn.; Max F. May, Vice president, Young Radiator Co., Racine, Wis.

TRUCK TRAILER COMMITTEE

Government presiding officer—R. L. Vaniman.

Members:

Harvey C. Fruehauf, president, Fruehauf Trailer Co., Detroit, Mich.; Bert P. Bates, director, Commercial Division, Highway Trailer Co., Edgerton, Wis.; M. N. Terry, Vice President, Trailmobile Co., Cincinnati, Ohio; W. C. Nabors, president, W. C. Nabors Co., Mansfield, La.; M. J. Neeley, President, Hobbs Manufacturing Co., Fort Worth, Tex.; Harrison Rogers, assistant treasurer, Rogers Brothers, Albion, Pa.; N. A. Carter, president, Carter Manufacturing Co., Memphis, Tenn.; Harry N. Brown, president, Keystone Trailer & Equipment Co., Kansas City, Mo.; Christopher Hammond, Jr., Vice president, Steel Products Co., Savannah, Ga.; H. C. Bennett, president, Utility Trailer Manufacturing Co., Los Angeles, Calif.; A. R. Trombly, president, Trombly Truck Equipment Co., Portland, Oreg.; C. H. Kingham, president, Kingham Trailer Co., Louisville, Ky.; J. L. Glick, president, Truck Engineering Co., Cleveland, Ohio; F. H. McIntyre, president, Carolina Truck & Trailer Co., Charlotte, N. C.; Myles Standish, President, Omaha Standard Body Corporation, Council Bluffs, Iowa; C. G. Farrell, Vice President, Easton Car & Construction Co., Easton, Pa.; G. A. Burns, manager, Oil Equipment Division, Butler Manufacturing Co., Kansas City, Mo.

TRANSPORTATION . . .

ODT issues general orders to truckers to bar short loads and save tires

Moving to counteract a rapidly dwindling supply of motortrucks in the face of increased demands on the country's transportation facilities, the Office of Defense Transportation April 23 ordered the trucking industry to put its over-the-road freight operations on a more efficient basis.

Rules for 3 classes

The ODT issued three orders (General Orders 3, 4, and 5) setting up specific wartime rules for common carriers, contract carriers and private carriers. Compliance with both the letter and the spirit of the orders, the ODT asserted, is "essential to the successful prosecution of the war."

The new regulations go into effect June 1.

The purpose of the orders is twofold:

1. Elimination of less-than-capacity loads through a general overhauling of schedules and, in the case of the common carriers, outright pooling of facilities.

2. Conservation of tires and equipment through establishment of ceilings on overloading and elimination of hauling by circuitous routes.

Except for certain vehicles which are exempt from the regulations because of the nature of the services in which they are engaged, all trucks after June 1 will be expected to be loaded to capacity on the outgoing trips and to at least 75 percent of capacity on the return trips.

Seven possibilities for common carriers

In the cases of contract and private carriers, this would be done, in the main, through revision of shipping schedules. Order No. 3, dealing with common carriers—firms which offer their facilities for public hire—goes a step further.

Not only are the common carriers expected to tighten up their operations through schedule revisions but also to pool their facilities wherever necessary to carry out the provisions of the order.

Order No. 3 sets up seven possible procedures for common carriers. They may:

1. Alternate or stagger schedules.

2. Exchange shipments or property.

3. Pool shipments, revenues or both.

4. Jointly load or operate their trucks.

5. Divert shipments, lease equipment, operate joint terminals or pickup or delivery vehicles.

6. Establish arrangements with other carriers for the interchange of equipment.

7. Appoint a joint agent "to concentrate, receive, load, forward, carry, unload, distribute and deliver property; receive, account for and distribute gross or net revenues therefrom, or otherwise handle or conduct the carrier's business as carriers of property upon just and reasonable terms and conditions."

Carriers contemplating joint action under one or more of these procedures may submit plans to the Office of Defense Transportation for consideration. No such plan may be put into operation, however, without the permission of the Interstate Commerce Commission, the proper State regulatory body or the ODT.

Several categories exempt

Exempt from the provisions of the new regulations are trucks carrying explosives or other "dangerous articles," farm trucks and trucks classified as "special equipment," such as those carrying mounted machinery. Trucks used in the maintenance of public utilities, those operated exclusively in the furtherance of public health and safety, and trucks operated exclusively in the interests of the armed forces are also excluded.

All other motortrucks are expected to eliminate waste in operations and to conserve and properly maintain tires and other equipment.

In the case of the common carriers, trucks not exempt from the provisions of Order No. 3 are directed to eliminate duplication of services and to "curtail schedules and services to the extent necessary" to comply with the order.

In order that shipments not be unduly delayed, the common carriers will be required to divert to other carriers freight held at a terminal 36 hours or at two or more intermediate terminals for an aggregate of 48 hours and to accept such diverted freight from other carriers.

Conversion of 11,500,000 cu. ft. of cooler to freezer sought

To forestall any shortage of freezer (zero) refrigeration space for storage of war-important foods, officials of the Office of Defense Transportation urged the warehousing industry April 22 to convert 11,500,000 cubic feet of cooler (30-degree) space to the freezer type. Conversion of 2 to 3 million cubic feet of that amount is already under way, and the cost is said to be relatively low.

Indications of an all-time high demand for refrigerated storage space by next autumn have inspired a program by ODT's division of storage to prevent future shortages. Besides the effect of increased food production for war, the refrigerated warehouse industry is expected to feel the result of the shortage of tin containers.

★ ★ ★

Moving of empty tank cars is freed from penalties

To relieve owners of tank cars of financial burdens resulting from the shift of these cars from normal routes to emergency service, railroad carriers, at the request of ODT, have agreed to eliminate certain penalty charges previously imposed on tank car companies, it was announced April 24.

The railroads customarily levy a freight charge for every mile a tank car moves empty in excess of the miles it moves loaded.

The new tariff becomes effective May 1.

★ ★ ★

War Shipping Administration ready to write risk insurance

In keeping with the marine war risk insurance law recently signed by the President, the War Shipping Administration on April 20 announced that it is prepared to write war risk insurance on shipments of cargo in foreign commerce to or from the United States, its Territories and possessions, regardless of the flag of the carrying vessel.

The Administration announcement is in accordance with the provisions of General Order No. 6 of the War Shipping Administration.

Government policy for best use of local transport is stated by Eastman

A 12-point statement of Government policy respecting local passenger transportation was issued April 18 by Transportation Director Eastman.

The statement was addressed to local transit operators and public regulatory authorities in communities throughout the country.

To assure maximum utilization of existing passenger transport vehicles, and to conserve rubber, the ODT urged the staggering of working, store, and business hours; discontinuance of bus service on routes where street railways can handle the traffic; elimination of unnecessary service to outlying districts; reduction of the number of stops on streetcar and bus lines; use of school buses where established common carriers are unable to provide service; and revision of traffic regulations and controls to give precedence to the movement of mass transit vehicles rather than automobiles.

Policy on charter buses

With respect to charter buses, the statement said:

Buses not operated in regularly scheduled service whether run on a chartered or individual fare basis, should be operated only to carry workers to and from places of defense employment or to meet similar situations where failure to provide such service will have a definitely unfavorable effect on the war effort.

Acceptable charter or special business includes transportation of selectees, of groups made up principally of members of the armed forces, of participants in organized recreational activities at military posts, and school children, teachers, and other school employees to and from school only, and under appropriate conditions the necessary transportation of underprivileged children.

Unacceptable charter or special business includes civilian parties to beaches, pleasure resorts, picnic places, points of historic interest, race tracks, baseball, and other sporting events.

. . .

Crowe named assistant director of local transport division

Joseph B. Eastman, ODT, Director, April 22, announced the appointment of Robert O. Crowe, of Los Angeles, as assistant director of the division of local transport, in charge of the Pacific Coast region.

He will aid in investigating the acute transport problems arising in war plant areas on the West Coast and will maintain headquarters in San Francisco.

EASTMAN OPPOSES SETTING CLOCK UP IN 3 STATES

Transportation Director Eastman announced April 20 that he had sent telegrams to the Governors of New York, New Jersey, and Pennsylvania, stating the plans under consideration in those States to set clocks ahead an additional hour would be "wasteful of necessary public transportation facilities."

. . .

Farm-truck operators work out plans for best use of vehicles

Representatives of America's million farm-truck operators met with Government officials April 16 under the auspices of the ODT to work out plans for obtaining maximum use of farm vehicles for the duration of the war.

Must conserve existing supply

To lay the basis for an effective program to conserve motor vehicles used to haul farm products and supplies between farm and consumer, the group heard reports on the rubber, spare parts, and maintenance situations.

Speakers included Joseph B. Eastman, director of Defense Transportation; Grover Hill, assistant secretary of Agriculture; M. Clifford Townsend, director of the Office of Agricultural Defense Relations, and Robert Hicks, chief of the farm vehicle section, division of motor transport, Office of Defense Transportation.

Summarizing results of investigations into farm products transportation, Mr. Hicks said, (in part):

The truck and the automobile are so extremely important in the marketing of farm products that it is vital for the farmer to do everything possible to conserve the existing supply of vehicles, tires, and parts.

At the same time, the increased wartime output of farm products must be transported, not only in 1942 but in later years as well, from the farms to the points of consumption here and abroad. . . .

Investigations by the division of motor transport, directed by John L. Rogers, prove that there is a great deal of unnecessary duplication and inefficiency in country assembly and city distribution. Reports received from the Department of Agriculture on dairy products, livestock and other commodities indicate the amount of duplication which exists at the present time.

16 named to head motor transport field offices carrying out war program

Managers have been appointed for 16 of the 51 field offices to be established by the division of motor transport, Joseph B. Eastman, Director of Defense Transportation, announced April 21.

In addition to the administration of the various programs undertaken by the division of motor transport, the field offices will assist the War and Navy Departments and other shippers of war materials in making arrangements for motor transport and will assist in coordinating and mobilizing motor vehicle equipment to meet war requirements.

Location of field offices established to date, and the managers appointed for each, are as follows:

Indianapolis, Ind.—George F. Burnett. Mr. Burnett was formerly president and general manager of his own automobile transport company.

Jacksonville, Fla.—H. E. McDaniel, formerly executive secretary of the Florida Trucking Association, Inc.

New York, N. Y.—William J. Clarke, formerly secretary-treasurer and general manager of the Highway Express Lines, Philadelphia, Pa.

Hartford, Conn.—John Maerz. Mr. Maerz formerly practiced before the Interstate Commerce Commission.

Dallas, Tex.—S. J. Cole, formerly secretary and manager of the Common Carrier Motor Freight Association of Dallas.

Phoenix, Ariz.—William Cox, formerly manager of the motor transport dispatch office established under the Office of Defense Transportation at Phoenix.

Atlanta, Ga.—John G. Caley, formerly general manager of the Carolina Freight Corporation.

Denver, Col.—E. Robert Baker, formerly executive secretary and treasurer of the Colorado Motor Carriers Association.

Portland, Ore.—Herman Sites, formerly President of the Portland-Pendleton Motor Freight.

San Francisco, Calif.—W. B. Grummel, formerly Vice President of the Pacific Intermountain Express.

Boston, Mass.—Eli C. Benway, formerly manager of the Motor Truck Club of Massachusetts, Inc.

Charleston, S. C.—William B. Love, Jr., formerly general manager of the Motor Transportation Association of South Carolina.

Spokane, Wash.—Holly I. Smith, formerly Vice President and general manager of Caters Motor Freight System.

Birmingham, Ala.—W. E. Duncan, formerly vice President of the North Alabama Motor Express, Inc.

Little Rock, Ark.—William R. Atkins, formerly safety inspector for the Interstate Commerce Commission's Bureau of Motor Carriers.

Norfolk, Va.—Maclin Simmons, formerly engaged in the distribution of motor vehicle lubricants in the Norfolk area.

J. H. Hoffman and M. J. Greene, both of Baltimore, Md., and H. S. Blackwell, of Johnson City, Tenn., have been appointed to the Washington office of the division of motor transport.

MANPOWER . . .

New commission charged with providing labor for war production when and where needed

The following statement was issued April 20 by Federal Security Administrator McNutt upon his appointment as chairman of the War Manpower Commission:

The War Manpower Commission which the President, the Commander-in-Chief of our total war effort, has created should provide the machinery for making certain that the manpower we need for war production will be available when and where it is needed.

To establish basic national policies

Through this Commission, all the agencies of the Federal Government, working closely with representatives of labor and industry, will be able to develop and maintain coordinated labor supply policies and programs on a voluntary and democratic basis. At the present time I can see no need for the building up of a large administrative staff to do this work. I believe that we can carry on most of the functions through the existing agencies.

The Commission has been charged by the President with the formulation of plans and programs and the establishment of basic national policies to assure the most effective mobilization and maximum utilization of the Nation's manpower in the prosecution of the war, and the issuance of such policy and operating directives as may be necessary.

Other functions

Its other functions will include "Estimating the requirements of manpower for industry, reviewing all other estimates of needs for military, agricultural, and civilian manpower, and directing the several departments and agencies of the Federal Government as to the proper allocation of available manpower."

It will determine basic policies for the collection and compilation of labor market data by Federal departments and agencies, and it will establish policies and prescribe regulations governing all Federal programs relating to the recruitment, vocational training, and placement of workers to meet the needs of industry and agriculture.

It will also prescribe basic policies governing the filling of the Federal Government's requirements for manpower, excluding those of the military and naval forces, and issue such operating directives as may be necessary.

Does not replace existing machinery

Finally, it is charged with formulating legislative programs designed to facilitate the most effective mobilization and utilization of the manpower of the country.

The Commission does not replace the existing machinery for collective bargaining, mediation, and the settling of labor disputes, which is already being carried on by other Government agencies.

I want to emphasize that in my opinion the primary reason for my designation as chairman of this Commission is that many of the activities with which the Commission will be concerned are already operating within the Federal Security Agency. These include the United States Employment Service, with its basic responsibility for recruiting labor, and the wartime training programs carried out through the United States Office of Education, the Civilian Conservation Corps, and the National Youth Administration.

Takes 18 workers to equip a fighter

It takes 18 industrial workers to equip a single fighting man. Human labor is the one element for which there is no substitute, and unless we devise methods to conserve and allocate our available labor supply, our production machinery and our industrial plants will not be able to provide the armaments we need.

We will need 10,500,000 additional skilled and lesser skilled workers in war production.

At least 2 million additional young men will be drawn from the labor market for service with the armed forces.

Agriculture will need labor to meet its essential production goals.

Serious shortage of skilled workers

Our transportation system will need workers to keep raw materials and finished products flowing to the places where they are required.

There is already a serious deficiency in the number of skilled workers available for industry. These shortages are currently critical in many occupations.

For example, for every skilled tool designer available, 51 are needed. The ratio of demand and supply of tool makers is 25 to 1; for ship carpenters, 7 to 1; for marine machinists, 22 to 1; for aircraft riveters, 4 to 1.

These are among the steps the Commission will have to consider:

1. We shall have to decide where our available labor supply is most urgently needed.

(a) We shall have to make a careful determination of the manpower and woman power required by the armed forces, by war industry, by agriculture, by transportation and by civilian production.

(b) We shall have to obtain the necessary information concerning occupational skills possessed by each man and woman to make sure that all of us are serving where we are most urgently needed. This data is now being obtained from Selective Service registrants through an occupational questionnaire.

(c) Arrangements will have to be made for supplying labor to various war industrial plants in accordance with the urgency of the need for the products each plant turns out.

Need to make most effective use

2. In order to obtain the most effective use of our limited supply of skilled workers we must make sure that:

(a) Employers use their skilled workers only at jobs where such skills are required.

(b) Skilled workers are hired through an orderly process guaranteeing that factories engaged in the most urgent war production receive first call on the available supply.

(c) Manpower is allocated between the armed forces and industry in such a way as to provide for most effective utilization of men whose skills are essential to the war production.

3. In order to make full use of presently unemployed workers we must make sure that:

(a) War contracts are placed in areas in which there are now large numbers of unemployed and that further concentration of war production is avoided in areas of labor shortage.

(b) Effective measures are enforced to insure full utilization of local labor.

Must mobilize full manpower

4. In order to mobilize the full manpower and womanpower of the country to meet the prospective needs of the war program we must:

(a) Utilize women in industries where they are best fitted to serve, and under proper working conditions.

(b) Utilize on a full-time basis in war industry workers who are now partially employed.

(c) Expand our program of industrial training as fully as possible.

(d) Tap all available labor supplies, such as the millions of Negroes and loyal foreign-born workers not now in war production.

Most of the 13,000,000 war production workers who will be placed in jobs during the next year will come from those who are now employed in nonwar industries.

I hope this shift will be accomplished largely by the conversion of plants and their regular labor force from civilian to war production.

Other workers will be drawn from the unemployed. We shall also need at least several million new recruits—women, young people, self-employed persons, and retired workers.

Labor "pirating" decried

At the present time many of our war production plants are obtaining many workers by "pirating" them from other employers in the same or related industries. Labor scouts are now traveling about the country enticing skilled workers to leave their jobs for higher wages without regard for the essential nature of the work at which these workers are now employed. As a matter of fact, one aircraft producer has hired away a number of workers employed by the very firm which was making wings for his own planes.

This "pirating" forces the employer who may be temporarily unable to use all his skilled workers to retain them at all costs, lest some other employer hire them away permanently. The result is labor hoarding—skilled workers being held for future work while nearby plants attempt to secure such workers through advertising and labor scouting.

Other factors intensify shortages

Many employers have continued to assign skilled workers to jobs which workers of lesser skill could perform. They have sought to recruit highly skilled machinists when semiskilled machine operators were fully qualified for the job to be done. Substantial numbers of skilled and semiskilled workers of the kind most needed at present are now engaged in nonwar activities. Many of these workers may be reluctant to transfer to war jobs because they fear that they will lose their seniority rights or because wages and working conditions may be less favorable or because of bad housing and other living conditions in war industry centers.

All of these factors artificially intensify skilled labor shortages which now exist.

Some areas crowded, others short

There are some localities in which we already have not only a shortage of highly skilled labor, but also a general shortage of labor of lesser skill. At the same time, in other parts of the country we have large surpluses of workers whose services are vitally needed in the shortage areas. Part of this current picture

Assignment Service seeks 16,000 doctors for forces in '42, regards public's need

Paul V. McNutt, chairman of the War Manpower Commission, announced April 21 that the Procurement and Assignment Service for Physicians, Dentists, and Veterinarians had started its machinery to secure 16,000 physicians and 3,000 dentists for the armed forces before the end of 1942, without weakening the medical structure for civil and industrial populations.

To round out inventory

An official enrollment form and a new questionnaire is now being mailed to every man licensed in the three professions. There are 186,000 licensed physicians, 71,000 dentists, and 12,000 veterinarians.

"The new questionnaires supplement those circulated as early as 1940 by the professions in order to make inventory of those available for military service," said Mr. McNutt. "They also supplement information previously requested by asking about experiences in foreign countries, the ability to speak and understand foreign languages, by asking about hobbies which may be of value, such as special knowledge of photography, cryptanalysis and similar subjects."

Any physician or dentist who does not receive an enrollment form by May 10 will know his name is not on record and should write for the form to the National Roster of Scientific and Specialized Personnel, Washington, D. C.

Every physician will also have the opportunity to indicate whether he would prefer service with the Army, Navy, field of public health, industry, care of veterans, essential research, teaching, or private practice.

"Dentists and veterinarians will also have the opportunity to indicate their orders of preference," Mr. McNutt continued.

Due regard for public needs

In regard to the needs of the civilian and industrial population in view of the depletion of available physicians in their communities, Mr. McNutt said the President had "charged us with maintaining due regard for the needs of the public."

The first step in this direction is the continuation of medical education.

"The Secretary of the Navy recently approved a change in Navy regulations whereby it is now possible for persons who have been accepted for entrance in the next entering class and all medical students in Class A medical colleges and all dental students in approved dental colleges to be appointed in the United States Naval Reserve with the commission Ensign H-V (P) provided they meet the physical and other requirements for such appointment," said Mr. McNutt.

"The Secretary of War has authorized the commission as Second Lieutenant, Medical Administrative Corps, United States Army, of young men of similar status. These men are not subject to induction under the Selective Service Acts. The Army and Navy authorities will defer calling these officers to active duty until they have completed their medical education, and one year internship."

All interns should apply for commissions as First Lieutenant, Medical or Dental Corps, United States Army, or as Lieutenant (j. g.) United States Navy or Naval Reserve.

arises from the fact that our war industries have not always been expanded in the localities in which there was the greatest amount of available labor. . . .

"Positive action taken in time . . ."

Local labor shortages have been unnecessarily intensified by discriminatory hiring practices. In one overcrowded war industry center, native white workers have been imported from hundreds of miles away although fully qualified Negro and loyal foreign-born workers were available at the plant's doorstep. In other cases employers still turn down fully qualified applicants locally available merely because they are women or too old or physically handicapped.

If this is to be a long war—and I think we must make that assumption—we must now face the fact that we may be confronted with an over-all Nation-wide labor shortage. The task of manpower mobilization will not only involve the problems which I have already described, but also that of planning our labor supply budget to make sure that we will be prepared to meet any general labor shortage which may occur. The experience of England and of other countries clearly proves the necessity for dealing with these problems before they become serious. Positive action taken in time will prevent the necessity for more drastic measures later on.

Landis orders further streamlining of OCD to cut red tape, duplication

A further reorganization of the Washington office of the Office of Civilian Defense has been ordered by Director James M. Landis to eliminate duplication of function, red tape, and unnecessary activities, he announced on April 27.

Abolished is the position of chief of area office supervision through which contacts of the heads of the operating divisions with the field staff were channeled. Abolished also is the office of deputy director. Instead there is created the office of special assistant to the director to perform special duties as they arise. The Federal and State liaison functions are transferred directly to the operating division in accordance with the particular functions of each.

The reports and analysis section and the procedures and distribution section of the area office supervision division are transferred to the administrative division, for coordination with other similar activities of the OCD.

An additional office of special assistant to the director has been created for the purpose of the over-all coordination of policy matters to be brought to the attention of the director and to handle the preliminary clearance of detailed policy matters for the director.

The division of public advice and counsel is created to prepare, review, and pass upon informational, educational, and in-

structional material concerning civilian defense measures to be disseminated to the public and to appropriate officials of the Federal, State, and local governments.

The office of executive assistant to the director will be retained with the duties of providing executive direction in the preparation of regulations, reports, important correspondence, etc. This officer will also act as liaison among the divisions of the office.

A legal division is established to direct the legal activities of the office and provide legal advice and assistance where such problems arise in the activities of the operating divisions.

The duties and responsibilities of the civilian protection division, the medical division, the mobilization division, and the civil air patrol are modified only to relate their activities to the terms of the recent revised Executive order on the Office of Civilian Defense and to eliminate some duplications of function. The office of assistant director in charge of plant protection becomes the office of assistant director in charge of plant defense organization.

The administrative division is reorganized to integrate internal management functions and to assume certain of the administrative activities and responsibilities which were previously conducted in the several divisions.

WAR EFFORT INDICES

MANPOWER

National labor force, Mar.	54,000,000
Unemployed, Mar.	3,600,000
Nonagricultural workers, Feb.	39,842,000
Percent increase since June 1940.	*†14
Farm employment, April 1, 1942.	9,463,000
Percent decrease since June 1940.	**†4

FINANCE *(In millions of dollars)*

Authorized program June 1940-Mar. 31, 1942	‡$137,278
Ordnance	31,394
Airplanes	26,796
Misc. munitions	17,324
Naval ships	15,426
Industrial facilities	14,017
Merchant ships	7,484
Posts, depots, etc.	7,061
Stock pile, food exports.	5,791
Pay, subsistence, travel for the armed forces	4,180
Housing	1,392
Miscellaneous	6,413
Contracts and other commitments June 1940-Mar. 31, 1942	*99,328
Total expenditures, June 1940-Mar. 31, 1942	*22,860

PRODUCTION *(In millions of dollars)*

June 1940 to latest reporting date	
Gov. commitments for plant expansion; 1,060 projects, Feb. 28	9,281
Private commitments for plant expansion; 7,366 projects, Mar. 31	2,333

EARNINGS, HOURS, AND COST OF LIVING *February*

		Percent increase from June 1940
Manufacturing industries—		
Average weekly earnings	$35.76	38.7
Average hours worked per week	42.2	12.5
Average hourly earnings	80.3¢	19.5
Cost of Living, Mar. (1935-39=100)	*Index* 114.3	13.7

* Preliminary.
‡ Preliminary and excludes authorizations in Naval Supply Act for fiscal year 1943.
** Adjusted to avoid reflection of seasonal changes.

OFFICE FOR EMERGENCY MANAGEMENT

WAYNE COY, *Liaison Officer*

CENTRAL ADMINISTRATIVE SERVICES: Dallas Dort, *Director.*

DEFENSE COMMUNICATIONS BOARD: James Lawrence Fly, *Chairman.*

INFORMATION DIVISION: Robert W. Horton, *Director.*

NATIONAL WAR LABOR BOARD: Wm. H. Davis, *Chairman.*

OFFICE OF SCIENTIFIC RESEARCH AND DEVELOPMENT: Dr. Vannevar Bush, *Director.*

OFFICE OF CIVILIAN DEFENSE: James M. Landis, *Director.*

OFFICE OF THE COORDINATOR OF INTER-AMERICAN AFFAIRS: Nelson Rockefeller, *Coordinator.*

OFFICE OF DEFENSE HEALTH AND WELFARE SERVICES: Paul V. McNutt, *Director.*

OFFICE OF DEFENSE TRANSPORTATION: Joseph B. Eastman, *Director.*

OFFICE OF FACTS AND FIGURES: Archibald MacLeish, *Director.*

OFFICE OF LEND-LEASE ADMINISTRATION: E. R. Stettinius, Jr., *Administrator.*

OFFICE OF PRICE ADMINISTRATION: Leon Henderson, *Administrator.*

CONSUMER DIVISION: Dexter M. Keezer, *Assistant Administrator,* in charge. Dan A. West, *Director.*

OFFICE OF ALIEN PROPERTY CUSTODIAN: Leo T. Crowley, *Custodian.*

WAR MANPOWER COMMISSION: Paul V. McNutt, *Chairman.*

WAR RELOCATION AUTHORITY: Milton Eisenhower, *Director.*

WAR SHIPPING ADMINISTRATION: Rear Admiral Emory S. Land, U. S. N. (Retired), *Administrator.*

WAR PRODUCTION BOARD:
Donald M. Nelson, *Chairman.*
Henry L. Stimson
Frank W. Knox.
Jesse H. Jones.
William S. Knudsen.
Sidney Hillman.
Leon Henderson.
Henry A. Wallace.
Harry L. Hopkins.

WAR PRODUCTION BOARD DIVISIONS:

Donald M. Nelson, *Chairman.*
Executive Secretary, G. Lyle Belsley.

PLANNING COMMITTEE: Robert R. Nathan, *Chairman.*

PURCHASES DIVISION: Houlder Hudgins, *Acting Director.*

PRODUCTION DIVISION: W. H. Harrison, *Director.*

MATERIALS DIVISION: Wm. L. Batt, *Director.*

DIVISION OF INDUSTRY OPERATIONS: J. S. Knowlson, *Director.*

LABOR PRODUCTION DIVISION: Wendell Lund, *Director.*

CIVILIAN SUPPLY DIVISION: Leon Henderson, *Director.*

OFFICE OF PROGRESS REPORTS: Stacy May, *Director.*

REQUIREMENTS COMMITTEE: Wm. L. Batt, *Chairman.*

STATISTICS DIVISION: Stacy May, *Director.*

INFORMATION DIVISION: Robert W. Horton, *Director.*

ADMINISTRATIVE DIVISION: James G. Robinson, *Administrative Officer.*

LEGAL DIVISION: John Lord O'Brian, *General Counsel.*

VICTORY

OFFICIAL WEEKLY BULLETIN OF THE AGENCIES IN THE OFFICE FOR EMERGENCY MANAGEMENT

WASHINGTON, D. C'   .MAY 5, 1942   VOLUME 3, NUMBER 18

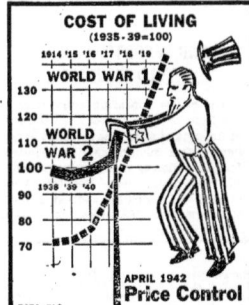

COST OF LIVING
(1935 - 39 = 100)

APRIL 1942
Price Control

DATA - BLS

U. S. puts blanket ceilings on retail and wholesale prices; pegs rents in 302 areas

Rigid Government controls for the war's duration over retail and wholesale prices and rents were announced April 28 by Price Administrator Henderson following President Roosevelt's call for decisive action to halt the swiftly mounting cost-of-living.

In a single sweeping order—the General Maximum Price Regulation—the Administrator set the highest prices charged in March 1942 as an absolute ceiling over virtually everything that Americans eat, wear, and use. The only exemptions are a limited list of food commodities. Companion orders paved the way for Federal control of rents in 302 defense areas in 46 States and Puerto Rico, housing more than 76,000,000 persons, and set separate ceilings for a broad range of commodities and products.

What the order does

By its terms, the General Maximum Price Regulation requires that:

  1. Beginning May 18, retail prices, with a few exceptions, must not exceed the highest levels which each individual seller charged during March 1942.
  2. Beginning May 11, manufacturer and wholesale prices and the prices for wholesale and industrial services must not exceed the highest March levels for each seller.
  3. Beginning July 1, no one may charge more for services sold at retail in connection with a commodity than he charged during March.
  4. Effective *immediately*, all retailers, wholesalers, manufacturers and sellers of services must preserve existing records of sales made during March for maximum pricing purposes when the ceiling goes into effect

Other highlights of the general order include:

The requirement that every retail store must publicly display the ceiling prices for selected "cost-of-living" commodities on and after May 18;

Immediate licensing of all retailers and wholesalers, effective as of the date the ceiling applies to their articles or services; in other words each retailer should consider himself licensed as of May 18 and each wholesaler as of May 11. Later, wholesalers and retailers will be required to register in writing on forms which OPA will provide.

COMMODITIES AND SERVICES COVERED

The general regulation applies to prices at all levels—manufacturer, wholesale, and retail—of every commodity or product, domestic or imported, that is neither covered by a separate OPA regulation nor specifically excluded. All services connected with commodities also come under the ceiling.

Prices on literally millions of articles of all sorts are, by the regulation, automatically controlled. Prices on relatively few products are exempt.

Almost all processed foods

Among those controlled are prices of almost every processed food commodity—such as bread, cake, and bakery products; beef, pork and their products; sugar, fluid milk and cream sold at retail; ice cream; canned meats, soups,

(Continued on page 4)

OVER 1,000,000 WORKING IN PRODUCTION DRIVES—Page 16

Review of the Week

Last week's big news was the general maximum price regulation which set the highest prices charged by the individual seller in March 1942 as the ceiling over virtually everything that Americans eat, wear, and use. Ceilings are effective May 11 for wholesalers, May 18 for retail sales, and June 1 for retail services. Rent control was ordered for 302 areas in addition to the 21 already designated, putting the freeze as of a certain date on regions populated by some 86 million people in the 323 areas.

Farm produce escapes

Excepted from the general ceiling were such things as books, magazines, newspapers, and movies, which do not fall within the Price Control Act's definition of commodities; unprocessed agricultural produce, which cannot be treated under the act until prices rise substantially over parity; some goods like objects of art, for which there is no organized market; and primary raw materials, which are already controlled by individual ceilings. Also excluded were waste materials below the level of the industrial consumer; certain machines and parts made by subcontractors; antimony ore and concentrates; instrument j e w e l bearings.

Solid fuel prices pegged

A number of separate ceilings were issued, mostly pegging prices at levels other than March. Dealers' prices for all solid fuels (except wood) were frozen at December 15–31, 1941, figures. Other separate ceilings were imposed on bituminous coal (producers); miscellaneous solid fuels (producers); rolled zinc products (producers); nonferrous castings (manufacturers); fluorspar (producers); paper, its products and raw materials (manufacturers); standard newsprint (manufacturers, converters, distributors, merchants); camelback (manufacturers); waterproof footwear (manufacturers); farm equipment (retail); construction and road maintenance equipment (rental); mixed fertilizer (retail); machines and parts (manufacturers and wholesalers); standard ferromanganese (producers.)

Premiums on motor fuels in East

Service station prices for motor fuels were frozen in another ceiling, providing premiums over the March level for the East, where use of tank cars boosts costs.

Prices of cotton goods and cotton yarns, governed heretofore by a sliding scale based on cost of "spot" raw cotton, were brought to a rest on the basis of the highest March price for the raw material. Action was taken also on woven cotton tickings; on "finished" cotton piece goods; and on raw and processed wool waste, which is the most important substitute for virgin wool in garments.

New autos easier to get

As the public prepared over the weekend for sugar-rationing registration, which began Monday, and learned the details of the interim gasoline rationing cards which will be given out beginning May 12, the Office of Price Administration announced that it was relaxing the conditions for distribution of new automobiles.

The War Production Board meanwhile restricted deliveries of coffee for large retailers and large restaurants to 75 percent of the amount in the corresponding period of 1941.

War contracts being reviewed

A measure of the growing war effort which underlies these regulations and deprivations was contained in the announcement that funds made available for America's battle now total more than 162 billion dollars—while President Roosevelt during the week asked for additional appropriations which would round the figure out to some 200 billions. WPB Chairman Nelson revealed that war contracts are being reviewed in all cases where it is believed the ever-increasing swing into mass production has lowered costs to the point where refunds or adjustments for the Government are feasible. Substantial savings already have resulted.

Mr. Nelson also announced that voluntary war-production drives in cooperation with the WPB campaign have been organized in plants employing over a million workers.

On the industrial front, WPB set up machinery to handle power shortages wherever and whenever they may occur; regulated the manufacture of storage batteries to save vital materials; got more metal by limiting the size of hairpins; limited production of protective helmets; banned fancy finishes on metalworking machinery, to speed up deliveries; put metallic zinc and "high wine" (new source of industrial alcohol) under complete allocation.

Synthetic rubber program increased

WPB placed all rubber substitutes of the Koroseal and Vinylite type under direct allocation; continued restrictions on scrap and reclaimed rubber; and at the same time authorized the Reconstruction Finance Corporation to provide facilities for an annual production capacity of 700,000 tons of Buna synthetic rubber by the end of 1943—an increase of 100,000 tons over the previous Buna program.

Wool dealers, shippers asked not to overtax Boston storage space

ODT Director Eastman, in a statement issued May 1, called upon wool dealers, shippers, cooperative organizations, and mills to do everything within their power to prevent arrival in the Boston area of more wool than they can handle without delay and with minimum storage and warehouse requirements.

WAR EFFORT'S PROGRESS TOLD VISUALLY

The charts appearing every week on the front cover of VICTORY tell the story of America's battle as it is fought here at home. One-column mats are available for publication by newspapers and others who may desire them. Requests should be sent to Distribution Section, Division of Information, OEM, Washington, D. C.

OFFICIAL BULLETIN of the Office for Emergency Management. Published weekly by the Division of Information, Office for Emergency Management, and printed at the United States Government Printing Office, Washington, D. C.

Subscription rates by mail: 75¢ for 52 issues; 25¢ for 13 issues; single copies 5¢, payable in advance. Remit money order payable directly to the Superintendent of Documents, Government Printing Office, Washington, D. C.

On the Home Front

Today, five months after Pearl Harbor, the U. S. A. has driven the last spike in the framework for total war on the five continents and the seven seas. In one hundred and fifty days we have mobilized our vast reservoir of brains, brawn and spirit—men, materials and machines—for titanic death struggle with the Axis.

Here are the timbers in that stout framework: Our production machine moving toward maximum conversion to war; the flower of our youth training for service in the air, on the land and at sea; our technical skill massing for duty at lathe and punch-press; our scarce supplies of automobiles, rubber, gasoline and sugar rationed in justice to all; our materials guarded by a Nation-wide drive for saving and for salvage and, finally, our economic resources marshalled securely under the price and rent-fixing regulations.

"Strides made by a free people"

Democracy's enemies scoff at its alleged inefficiency but democracy's friends might well exult over this record. For these strides have been made by a free people, acting voluntarily under the direction of their duly-elected leaders. No concentration camps, no dragooning of helpless minorities, no "one-way ballots," no whiplash of invective and harangue accomplished this job. The goal was set, the blueprints mapped, the requirements were explained—and the people responded.

"Privilege"—not "sacrifice"

Americans have dropped the word "sacrifice" from their vocabulary and substituted the word "privileged" because as President Roosevelt said in his last message to Congress, "free men and women, bred in the concepts of democracy, and wedded to the principles of democracy, deem it a privilege rather than a sacrifice to work and to fight for the perpetuation of the democratic ideal."

More ceilings on what we eat and wear

It would have been futile to convert the great automobile industry and other durable goods industries to war work, send our workers to man the machines of war and our boys to foreign fronts, dole out our scarce commodities, conserve our household appliances, collect old scrap iron and share our cars with our neighbors—if at the same time we had permitted our national economy to careen toward certain disaster down the highroad of inflation.

The Office of Price Administration recognized what every housewife and every businessman knew, too—that the cost of living was getting out of hand and that something must be done to halt the inflationary spiral. That's why the OPA

last week imposed a ceiling on almost all prices for the things we eat and wear and use and a roof on rents in areas housing 76,000,000 people.

No "dead" mileage for taxicabs

The importance of transportation as an indispensable link between Democracy's arsenal and her battlefront has been underlined by Joseph B. Eastman, director of the Office of Defense Transportation. Last week he told the taxicab industry that the highly personalized service received by one billion passengers last year must end, that cruising must be abolished and dead mileage pared to the bone.

Other steps to make the Nation's wheels roll farther and carry more: War workers and civilian employees were urged to move as close to their places of work as possible to save millions of miles in tires and gasoline. The use of closed freight cars for transporting shipments within cities was banned wherever motor vehicles can be utilized.

Illustrating his recent statement that "We are over the hump on war production," Donald M. Nelson, Chairman of the War Production Board, remarked on the success of the War Production Drive in a message to the Citizens for Victory Committee of San Francisco. More than a million men and women are on the job in factories where Joint Labor-Management Production Drive Committees have been set up, he said, and such committees will soon be under way in more than a thousand plants.

Women are being shown new ways in which they can contribute to the war effort. Now they are asked to save the metal, glass and plastic containers in which they buy their glamour aids and hold them for refills.

This might seem like a trifle measured against the gigantic panorama of war production, but look at the figures: In 1941, it is estimated, three to five million pounds of plastics, 10,000 tons of steel, 2,250 tons of copper and 550 tons of zinc were consumed by the cosmetics industry. A lipstick holder saved is a bullet gained.

More rubber planned——for war

The Reconstruction Finance Corporation has been authorized to build plants sufficient for the production of 700,000 tons of Buna synthetic rubber a year, starting not later than the end of 1943, an increase of 100,000 tons over the previous program approved by WPB . . . But all this and more too will be needed for military operations, none of it will be available for civilian use . . . Fifty-eight specialists with wide experience in the consumer's field have been appointed to help unravel the knots in the sugar rationing program. They will be on hand in regional and local offices in the 48 States and the District of Columbia when consumers register this week for their War Ration Books . . . Steamship starting voyages may get their sugar just by signing a receipt . . . But OPA is drafting regulations for them. . . . When the President signed the Sixth Supplemental War Appropriation Act, involving 19 billion dollars, it raised the total funds made available by Congress and the RFC for war purposes to $162,416,000,000. . . . The WPB has set up the machinery to prevent power shortages by choking off the flow of electricity to nonessential services and diverting it to war industries and primary civilian needs. . . . War comes to Derbytown: OPA requested the hotel men of Louisville, Ky., not to jack up the rates for war workers caught in the flood of racing fans bound for the Derby. . . . The U. S. coffee supply has been placed under WPB restrictions. Roasters may not deliver to wholesalers more than 75 percent of the brown bean supplied in 1941. It's needed for the Army and Navy . . . Stabilization of the cost of cotton goods for the American wardrobe has been buttressed by the freezing of manufacturers' and wholesalers' selling prices. . . . WPB has released a total of 19,351 trucks and truck trailers under the ration program announced March 9. Most of these have gone to war agencies, Lend-Lease operations, or the export market.

PRICE ADMINISTRATION . . .

U. S. puts blanket ceilings on retail and wholesale prices; pegs rents in 302 areas

(Continued from page 1)

canned fruits and vegetables; canned fish and other canned seafoods; cereals; lard and shortening; coffee, tea, cocoa, salt, and spices. Also covered by the ceiling are all clothing, shoes, dry goods, and yard goods; soap in all forms; every kind of common fuel (even firewood); pipes, cigars, cigarettes, and prepared smoking and chewing tobacco; drugs, toiletries, and sundries; furniture and furnishings; appliances and equipment; and hardware and miscellaneous agricultural supplies.

Specifically mentioned in the regulation are "cost-of-living" items including those which are most significant in the budgets of average low-and-middle-income family groups. Ceiling prices on such items must be publicly displayed by retailers, thus giving consumers every possible assurance that they will not be charged more than the highest prices reached last March.

Existing schedules remain

All of the existing OPA schedules and regulations issued over the past year continue in full force and effect. Those commodities covered by temporary 60-day regulations automatically will come within the provisions of the general ceiling regulation upon their expiration unless otherwise treated by separate orders.

Separate orders, issued simultaneously with the general regulation, impose maximum prices over a broad range of products of a nature requiring special pricing treatment. For the most part, these separate regulations set prices back beyond March 1942—in some cases back to the levels of last October.

In addition to the separate orders, there are several amendments intended for the most part to make outstanding regulations conform with provisions of the general order. One highly important series of amendments eliminates OPA's "sliding-scale" maximum prices for cotton yarns and textiles. By these amendments the maximum prices of all cotton textiles and yarns covered by OPA ceilings are fixed at the levels determined by the highest price quoted for r   :ot-ton on 10 spot markets during /   h— 20.37 cents a pound. Also issu... with

the general regulation was a supplementary order revoking seven temporary maximum price regulations, thus bringing the commodities involved under the new general regulation.

EXCLUSIONS

Commodities not covered by the regulation fall generally into three classifications:

1. Those that are exempt because of provisions of the Emergency Price Control Act of 1942 either (a) because they do not fall within the Act's definition of a "commodity"—this excludes advertising, newspapers, books, magazines, motion pictures, wages, common carrier and public utility rates, insurance, real estate, and professional fees; or (b) by reason of the Act's special treatment of agricultural commodities unless and until they attain a level reflecting a substantial premium over parity.

2. Commodities which do not have organized markets and for which it would be almost impossible to determine maximum prices either on the basis of previous sales or prices for comparable articles. Examples are: highly seasonal fresh vegetables, fresh fish and game, objects of art, and collector's items.

3. Primary raw materials—such as timber and mineral ores—all prices for which are substantially controlled by ceilings already in effect at certain levels.

Administrator Henderson explained that many of the commodities which are left free of price regulation at the present time will be covered in the future by supplementary orders. Among other things, he said, it is planned to set maximum prices for certain agricultural products as soon as such action is consistent with present or future legislation.

Some items specifically excepted

Specifically listed as "excepted" in the regulations are:

1. Any raw and unprocessed agricultural commodity or greenhouse commodity while it remains in substantially its original state, except bananas. In general, prices of such commodities are fixed at the stage of first processing, although fresh fruits and vegetables, plants, flowers and the like are excluded entirely.

2. Eggs and poultry.

3. All milk products, including butter, cheese, condensed and evaporated milk (but not fluid milk sold at retail, cream sold at retail, and ice cream).

4. Flour (but not packaged cake mixes and other packaged flour mixes).

5. Mutton and lamb.

6. Fresh fish and seafood, and game.

7. Dried prunes, dry edible beans, leaf tobacco (whether dried or green), nuts (but not peanuts), linseed oil, linseed cake and linseed meal, mixed feed for animals, and manure.

8. Living animals, whether wild or domestic.

9. Books, magazines, motion pictures, periodicals, newspapers, and materials furnished for publication by any press association or future service.

10. Domestic ores and ore concentrates.

11. Stumpage, logs, and pulpwood.

12. Stamps and coins; precious stones; antiques and knotted oriental rugs; paintings, etchings, sculptures, and other objects of art.

13. Used automobiles.

14. Wood and gum for naval stores (resin, turpentine, etc.) and naval stores prior to sale to industrial consumers, or prior to the first sale to a distributor. (However, all sales of naval stores on any exchange are not exempt.)

15. Securities ("Securities" are defined as any notes, stocks, bonds, or instruments commonly known as securities.)

Supplementary Regulation No. 1 to the general order, issued at the same time, lists several additional exceptions, including sales of all waste materials up to the level of the industrial consumer; zinc, lead and tin industrial residues; certain machines and parts manufactured in the course of subcontracting (and the services performed on these subcontracted materials); antimony ore and concentrates; and instrument jewel bearings.

Individual or special transactions

To make provision for transactions of an individual or special nature the general regulation exempts the following sales and deliveries:

1. By hotels, restaurants, soda fountains, bars, cafes, or other similar establishments, of food or beverages prepared and sold for consumption on the premises.

2. To the United States or any of its agencies of such commodities or in such transactions as may be specified by supplementary regulations. These supplementary regulations will include broad categories of finished military equipment.

3. By a farmer, of commodities grown and processed on his farm, if the total of such sales or deliveries does not exceed $75 in any one calendar month. (This permits the sale of small farm processing items such as smoked ham, bacon, maple syrup, cider, etc.)

4. By an owner, of his used personal or household effects or other personal property used by him.

TEMPORARY CEILINGS REVOKED

The following temporary maximum price regulations are being revoked, bringing the products concerned under the provisions of the general maximum price regulation:

Number of Temporary Regulation	Products
12	Domestic washing machines and ironing machines—distributors and retailers.
13	Resale of new domestic cooking and heating stoves and ranges.
14	Resale of new radio receiving sets and phonographs—distributors and retailers.
15	New typewriters.
17	Plumbing fixtures.
18	Domestic electrical appliances.
19	Oil paints and varnish.

5. By any merchant, farmer, artisan, or person who renders professional services, of his used supplies, or business, farm or professional equipment, not acquired or produced by him for the purpose of sale.

6. At a bona fide auction, of used household or personal effects.

7. By a breeder, trapper, or hunter, of pelts, furs, or other parts of wild animals raised by him, or trapped, shot, or killed by him, if the total of such sales or deliveries does not exceed $75 in any one calendar month.

8. Of commodities sold without private profit in the course of any sale, fair, or bazaar conducted for a period of not more than 15 days by any religious, charitable, or philanthropic organization.

Professional services excluded

Personal services not connected with commodities, and professional services are excluded from the order. All other retail services having to do with the installation, maintenance, preservation, repair, storage, and distribution of commodities must be priced no higher than the highest levels charged in March 1942. (The "retail service" ceiling goes into effect July 1.)

Thus the rates charged by automobile repair shops, garages, tailors, laundries, dry cleaners, shoe repair establishments, etc., are covered by the regulation, while the prices set by barbers and beauty shops (services to the person) and the fees of doctors, dentists, and lawyers, etc. (professional services) are not.

Services that are not rendered at retail, for example, repair of machinery in a manufacturing plant by an outside contractor, come under the ceiling on May 11—the same date on which maximum prices apply to manufacturer and wholesaler.

Text of the general regulation lists "excepted services" as follows:

a. Services of an employee to his employer.
b. Personal services not rendered in connection with a commodity.
c. Professional services.
d. Motion pictures, theaters and other entertainments.
e. Services of a common carrier or public utility.
f. Advertising services, including radio broadcasting.
g. Insurance and underwriting services.
h. Press association and feature services.
i. Services relating solely to real property.
j. Such other services as may be specified by supplementary regulations.

RENTS

The Price Administrator's action on rent applies to defense rental areas in every State of the union except North Dakota and Idaho and extends into Puerto Rico also. Metropolitan New York with close to nine million people is covered as well as King George County, Virginia, with a population of only 5,400.

In effect, Mr. Henderson recommended the maximum rent ceiling for each of 302 groups of communities. If his recommendations are not carried out within the next 60 days, he is empowered by the Emergency Price Control Act to step in and impose Federal controls. This is not OPA'S first action on high rents, since 21 areas with an aggregate population of 10 million persons already are on notice to bring rents down. In four-fifths of the areas so far announced, Mr. Henderson's recommendations would freeze rents as of March 1, 1942, thus wiping out any increases that have occurred during the current spring moving

and leasing period. Because exorbitant increases have taken place in 64 areas, the Price Administrator recommended that rents be cut back to levels in effect on January 1, 1941, April 1, 1941, or July 1, 1941. Ten of the 21 areas previously designated were enlarged.

Appeals to landlords, tenants

"Rent control is a war measure and an essential part of the over-all price ceiling," Mr. Henderson stated. "Rent is second only to food in importance to the average family budget and American families spend 5 to 6 billion dollars a year for rent."

He appealed to every landlord and every tenant to cooperate with each other and with the Government to guarantee success of the program, which he described as "an invaluable contribution to the war effort on the home front." He warned that the March 1, 1942, rent date would not establish fair levels in many cases and that if voluntary adjustments were not sufficient he would reconsider and take appropriate action. "Furthermore," he added, "the designation of 323 areas does not mean that rents would not be checked in the few remaining sections of the country still free of control. We are continuing our study of local conditions and will move immediately into additional areas whenever it appears that the defense activities are likely to result in higher rents."

Three main points are involved in Mr. Henderson's rent recommendations: (1) For housing accommodations rented on the maximum rent date (March 1, 1942 or January 1, April 1, or July 1, 1941, as the case may be) the rent shall not exceed that charged on the maximum rent date. (2) Provision must be made for establishing maximum rents for accommodations not rented on the maximum rent date, or substantially altered subsequently. (3) Provisions must be made to prevent evasion of maximum rents and to protect the tenant against unwarranted eviction.

Of the 323 defense rental areas designated, 132 contain establishments of the armed forces, 63 primarily are centers of ordnance manufacture and storage, 15 are mainly shipbuilding and ship repair centers, 8 are locations of aircraft plants, and the remaining 105 contain establishments engaged in varied war production.

MAXIMUM PRICES

One feature of the General Maximum Price Regulation will result in different prices for the same article in different stores, even though they are under com-
(Continued on page 6)

SEPARATE MAXIMUM PRICE REGULATIONS

Following is a list of the separate maximum price regulations issued April 28 by Price Administrator Henderson in connection with announcement of the general maximum price regulation:

Reg. No.	Commodity or product	To whom ceiling applies	Price level date	Effective date
120	Bituminous coal	Producers	Oct. 1-15, 1941	May 18
121	Miscellaneous solid fuels	Producers	Dec. 15-31, 1941	Do.
122	All solid fuels	Dealers other than producers	Dec. 15-31, 1941	Do.
124	Rolled zinc products	Producers	Nov. 29, 1941	May 11
125	Nonferrous castings	Manufacturers	Oct. 1-15, 1941	Do.
126	Fluorspar	Producers	Jan. 2, 1942	Do.
129	Paper, paper products, raw materials for paper and paper products	Manufacturers	Oct. 1-15, 1941, generally. A later date in a few cases.	Do.
130	Standard newsprint paper	Manufacturers, converters, distributors and merchants.	Oct. 1-15, 1941 same as April 1, 1938.	Do.
131	Camelback for recapping and retreading tires.	Manufacturers	March level	Do.
132	Waterproof footwear	Manufacturers	March level	Do.
133	Farm equipment	Retail	Oct. 1-15, 1941	Do.
134	Construction and road maintenance equipment.	Rental to user	Oct. 1-15, 1941	Do.
135	Mixed fertilizer machines and parts.	Retail	Feb. 16-21, 1942	Apr. 28
		Manufacturers and wholesalers.	Oct. 1, 1941	May 18
.....	Standard ferromanganese	Producers	Oct. 1-15, 1941	
.....	Residential rents	Housing accommodations in specified areas.	Varies from January 1, 1941, to March 1, 1942.	

U. S. imposes blanket price ceilings

(Continued from page 5)

mon ownership or are located in the same neighborhood. This is because the order requires each individual seller (and each store is considered "an individual seller") to charge no more for any article than the highest price charged in that particular store during March 1942. As an example, Mr. Henderson pointed out that a certain brand of tomatoes might have a maximum price of 12 cents per can in one grocery, while in a market around the corner the can of tomatoes of the same brand and size might be priced at 11 cents.

Housewives will recognize that this situation prevails even under ordinary conditions. The only change made by the new regulation is to require each seller not to exceed his maximum price. However, the regulation specifically allows any seller to lower his price; hence, competition may well iron out many of the different prices over a period of time.

How to determine ceilings

The heart of the regulation is contained in Sections 2 and 3—the provisions by which maximum prices are determined.

As a first step, the seller is ordered to take for his maximum the highest price he charged during March 1942 for the same commodity or service sold to a purchaser of the same class.

"Highest price charged" means two things:

First, it means the top price for which an article was delivered during March 1942 in completion of a sale to a purchaser of the same class. Customary allowances, discounts or other price differentials cannot be changed, except to lower the price. Thus a physician who buys bandages or proprietary medicines from a local drugstore will, if he has a professional discount, continue to receive the benefit of a lower maximum price than an ordinary citizen.

Second, if there was no actual delivery of a particular article during March, the seller may establish as his maximum price the highest price at which he offered the article for sale during that month. This permits the use of a list price if no completed sale occurred in March. Conversely however, if there was a completed sale at a price under the list price the actual sale price must be used as the maximum. The "offering price" where used to set the maximum price cannot be a "freak" price quoted to open bargaining or one never intended to apply to a bona fide sale.

These two provisions are expected to permit retailers to arrive readily at ceiling prices for the great majority of their articles.

Articles not sold in March

To cover articles that were not sold during March and had no offering price—such as a new line of canned goods—the seller must establish as his maximum price the highest price charged in March for the most nearly similar article. The seller cannot use his own discretion to adjust the maximum price for the new article up or down because it may vary in grade or quality or size, but must adhere strictly to the "March highest" price of the most similar article.

A "similar commodity" is defined as one that has the same use, gives the buyer fairly equivalent serviceability, and is of a type which ordinarily would be sold in the same price line. Differences merely in style or design which do not affect use, serviceability or the price line cannot be taken into account.

In cases in which a seller did not deal in the same or similar commodities or services during March 1942 (for example, a person who took on a completely new line of goods during April), he must base his maximum price on the highest price charged during March by his most closely competitive seller of the same class. The seller here cannot use the prices of a more pretentious store in a better neighborhood, but must find a store as nearly like his own as possible. If the "competitive seller" does not have, item by item, the same brands and grades of goods, the seller seeking prices must apply the most nearly similar commodity standard as outlined above.

Pricing other items

Inevitably, there will be a small number of commodities which a seller will be unable to price under any of the foregoing methods. These commodities usually will be wholly new and there may be no standard of comparison with any existing article. In this case, a retail or wholesale seller will select the fastest moving comparable commodity of the same general classification; divide its maximum price by his current replacement cost and multiply the percentage result by the cost of the new article. The figure obtained will be the maximum price of the new article and must be reported to the nearest OPA field office within 10 days. In other words, the retailer gets the same percentage margin on his new item as he would get on the comparable fast-selling item if he had to buy that item now.

Manufacturers seeking to price a new article must apply to OPA, giving full information, and then will be told how to calculate the maximum price.

ADMINISTRATION

In order to administer the universal ceiling, OPA has made extensive changes in its organization. A Retail Trade and Service Division has been established in the Washington office. This Division will have responsibility for ironing out irregularities in the ceiling at the retail level and for working with retailers in the administration of the regulation. The present regional offices of the OPA situated in Boston, New York, Cleveland, Atlanta, Dallas, Chicago, Denver and San Francisco are being enlarged and a special staff has been stationed in every regional office to aid in organization for the new program. In addition, State and district offices are being opened to decentralize administration as widely as possible. The process of decentralization

eventually will involve the establishment of local War Prices and Rationing Boards in each community. Further information on the regulation will be made available by OPA through the press and radio. Urgent inquiries should be addressed to the regional office serving the area in which the person resides. To facilitate the work of OPA it is requested that such communications be confined during the next few weeks to those of the most compelling character.

LICENSING AND REGISTRATION

While on May 11 and 18, 1942, respectively, all wholesale and retail sellers of commodities covered by the general regulation or by any other outstanding schedules or regulations of OPA are automatically licensed by the Administrator, there will be no physical evidence of the license issued immediately. Nevertheless, the provisions of the price control law are applicable, which means that a licensee who violates the regulation may, after warning by OPA, have his license suspended by court action.

Sellers of services at retail do not become licensed until July 1, 1942, when the maximum price provisions of the order as applied to them go into effect.

National registration coming

A national registration of every retail and wholesale outlet will be undertaken in the near future. Each store or business establishment must be registered separately. Forms for this purpose will be issued by OPA.

With reference to the posting of "ceiling prices" for the "cost-of-living" items listed, the order requires the article itself or the shelf, box, rack or counter to be marked, or a price list posted for public inspection. Maximum price is to be stated as "Ceiling Price $——" or "Our Ceiling $——." Lines of certain merchandise, such as suits, coats, hosiery, and dresses, may be posted by price-lines in the store and, in addition, the actual selling price (which may be lower than maximum price) must be marked on the article itself.

Penalties that the Emergency Price Control Act provides for violations of the Administrator's regulations, orders, etc., include fines of not more than $5,000 or 1 year's imprisonment, or both; civil suits for treble damages (these suits may not be brought until July 31, 1942); and revocation of the seller's license for not more than 12 months. All sellers are subject to the criminal penalties, but only those buyers who purchase OPA-regulated commodities or services in the course of trade or business.

WHAT HOUSEWIVES SHOULD KNOW ABOUT PRICE CEILING

Q. When does the ceiling become effective?

A. 1. For goods sold at retail, the ceilings apply on May 18, 1942.

2. For services at retail, that is, rendered to the ultimate consumer, the ceiling applies on July 1, 1942.

3. For sales by manufacturers, producers and wholesalers, and services rendered to an industrial consumer, the ceiling applies on May 11, 1942.

Q. Will the ceiling prices be the same at every store for the same article?

A. No. In general, the ceiling is the highest price at which each store sold an article during March. The maximum price will vary from store to store just as prices varied from store to store during March.

Q. How will the housewife know what the maximum prices are?

A. The Regulation lists about 100 of the most important groups of items in the average family's cost of living. The maximum prices of these items must be displayed by any retailer selling them after May 18.

Q. What about prices of goods that are not on the cost-of-living list?

A. Until July 1, the housewife should ask the storekeeper for his maximum prices. After July 1, the retailer must have a prepared statement of the highest prices for all commodities or services which he delivered or supplied during March. This may be examined by any one on request.

Q. What should the housewife do if she believes that she is required to pay more than a storekeeper's maximum?

A. She should ask the storekeeper to explain the price to her. If she still believes that she is required to pay more than his legal maximum, she should communicate the facts to OPA's nearest War Price and Rationing Board or its nearest local office.

Q. How can the shopper obtain a record showing what she paid so that she can make positive comparison with March prices?

A. Every store, when requested by a customer, must give a sales slip or receipt showing the date, the name and address of the store, the item sold, and the price received.

Q. What articles are covered by price ceilings?

A. Practically every article used in the life and work of America.

NOTE.—For an outline of the exceptions to the ceiling, see pages 4 and 5.

Learn ceiling methods, talk to retailer first when in disagreement, OPA urges

Patience and tolerance by the buying public—for which the price control program is being placed in operation—was urged April 30 by the Office of Price Administration.

Americans will recognize that the overall ceiling on prices is their protection against the rising cost of living, Administrator Henderson said.

"Long-run success of the program requires the complete cooperation of the consumer. The housewife and the shopper can help by learning how price ceilings will operate and by showing patience while a program so vast is getting under way. . . .

"Shoppers should realize that by the 18th of May every retailer must reprice his merchandise in keeping with the price regulations and after May 18 he can not make sales above the ceiling. This is a tremendous task, especially for small merchants whose records may be incomplete.

"When disagreements arise, the shopper and the seller should get together and see if they can not reach a common understanding. Only after that has been done and the shopper has facts to warrant a conclusion that price regulations are being violated should the matter be reported to enforcement authorities."

An outline of the part the housewife and shopper can play in making the over-all ceiling of prices effective was contained in this three-point guide from the OPA:

1. Before July 1: Educate yourself and your neighbor on the price regulations and how they operate.

Don't try to be a price-policeman. Leave the policing job to the Office of Price Administration. From the very start, prices will be under the closest surveillance by OPA, which will use trained technicians of the Bureau of Labor Statistics to check price trends.

2. After July 1: By this time War Price and Rationing Boards—committees of your neighbors—will be operating and handling complaints. Know how and where and in what detail to report violations. The boards will sift complaints and make adjustments wherever possible, but will turn special cases over to OPA enforcement officials for final action.

Meanwhile, OPA will train professional shoppers to work with each War Price and Rationing Board and police prices in the area.

3. For the long-run: Realize that you have a personal responsibility to buy only at or below the ceiling price. As goods become scarce, get together with your neighbors to help make the scarce goods go farther, to pool delivery services, and to find substitutes.

★ ★ ★

Territories' ceilings remain unless construed inconsistent

Price ceilings which have been established by Territories and possessions of the United States, through action of their own legislative bodies, are to remain in force unless and until they are construed to be inconsistent with the purposes and provisions of the Emergency Price Control Act or regulations issued under the authority of that act, Price Administrator Henderson stated April 28.

Tin-coated iron and steel scrap prices raised

Revised Price Schedule No. 4 for iron and steel scrap has been amended to provide an upward adjustment in the price of bundles made exclusively of tin-coated materials, Price Administrator Henderson announced April 28.

The amendment, which became effective April 28, 1942, also adds a new requirement to the schedule with regard to rail or vessel shipping notices and stiffens the regulations on mixed shipments of scrap.

The amendment—titled Amendment No. 3—increases by $4 per gross ton the price of bundles made exclusively of tin-coated material. The former provision priced such bundles at $8 per gross ton below No. 2 dealers' bundles.

The reduction of the $8 per ton differential to $4, OPA officials said, was made to assure a more adequate supply.

RUBBER FOOTWEAR CEILINGS

Maximum Price Regulation No. 132, effective May 11, establishes ceilings on manufacturers' wholesale prices for waterproof rubber footwear at the levels that prevailed under voluntary agreement during March.

Rent control ordered for 302 more areas in parts of 46 States, all of Puerto Rico

The 302 "defense-rental" areas designated by OPA April 28 for rent control (see p. 4) have a population of 76,000,000 people. The addition of these areas to the 21 already named places rent control over regions with a total of 86,000,000 inhabitants.

The 323 areas now under control are listed below. Each area is named by its principal center of population or by the geographic name most common to the section. Areas extend beyond the municipal areas of the principal city or cities within them and have been defined chiefly in terms of counties and parishes. The date given in each case is that whose rentals are recommended as the maximum.

ALABAMA: Anniston, Counties of Calhoun and Cleburne—April 1, 1941; Birmingham*—Jefferson County—April 1, 1941; Columbus, Ga.*—In Russell County, Ala., Election Precinct One, including the City of Phenix City; and Muscogee Co., Ga.—January 1, 1941; Dothan-Ozark—Counties of Dale and Houston—March 1, 1942; Gadsden—Etowah County—March 1, 1942; Huntsville—Counties of Limestone, Madison and Morgan—April 1, 1941; Lanett—Chambers County—March 1, 1942; Mobile*—Mobile County—April 1, 1941; Montgomery—Counties of Elmore and Montgomery—March 1, 1942; Muscle Shoals—Counties of Colbert and Lauderdale—April 1, 1941; Selma—Dallas County—March 1, 1942; Talladega—Counties of St. Claire, Shelby, Talladega—April 1, 1941; Tuskegee—Macon County—March 1, 1942.

ARIZONA: Fort Huachuca—Counties of Cochise and Santa Cruz—March 1, 1942; Phoenix-Salt River Valley—Counties of Gila and Maricopa—March 1, 1942; Prescott-Flagstaff—Counties of Coconino and Yavapai—March 1, 1942; Tucson—Pima County—March 1, 1942.

ARKANSAS: Benton-Bauxite—Saline County—March 1, 1942; Blytheville—Mississippi County—March 1, 1942; Camden—Counties of Calhoun and Ouachita—March 1, 1942; El Dorado—Union County—March 1, 1942; Fort Smith—Sebastian County—March 1, 1942; Hope—Hempstead County—March 1, 1942; Little Rock—Counties of Lonoke and Pulaski—March 1, 1942; Memphis, Tenn.—Crittenden County, Ark.; Shelby County, Tenn.—March 1, 1942; Pine Bluff—Jefferson County—March 1, 1942; Texarkana—Miller County, Ark.; Bowie County, Tex.—July 1, 1941.

CALIFORNIA: Bakersfield—Kern County—March 1, 1942; Chico—Butte County—March 1, 1942; Fresno—Fresno County—March 1, 1942; Lassen County—Lassen County—March 1, 1942; Lemoore-Hanford—Kings County—March 1, 1942; Los Angeles—Counties of Los Angeles and Orange—March 1, 1942; Marysville-Yuba City—Counties of Sutter and Yuba—March 1, 1942; Merced—Merced County—March 1, 1942; Monterey Bay—Counties of Monterey and Santa Cruz—March 1, 1942; Riverside-San Bernardino County—March 1, 1942; San Bernardino County—March 1, 1942; San Diego**—Area Extended; now includes all of San Diego County—January 1, 1941; San Francisco Bay—Counties of Alameda, Contra Costa, Marin, Napa, Sacramento, San Francisco, San Joaquin, San Mateo, Santa Clara, Solano, Sonoma, and Yolo—March 1, 1942; San Luis Obispo—San Luis Obispo County—

January 1, 1941; Santa Barbara—Santa Barbara County—March 1, 1942; Visalia-Tulare—Tulare County—March 1, 1942.

COLORADO: Colorado Springs—El Paso County—March 1, 1942; Denver—Counties of Adams, Arapahoo, Denver and Jefferson—March 1, 1942; Pueblo—Pueblo County—March 1, 1942.

CONNECTICUT: Bridgeport**—Area extended; now includes all of Fairfield County—April 1, 1941; Hartford-New Britain**—Area extended; now includes Counties of Hartford, Middlesex and Tolland; and in the County of New Haven, the towns of Meriden and Wallingford—April 1, 1941; New Haven—In the county of New Haven, the towns of Ansonia, Branford, Derby, East Haven, Guilford, Hamden, Madison, Milford, New Haven, North Branford, North Haven, Orange, Seymour, West Haven and Woodbridge—April 1, 1941; New London—Counties of New London and Windham—April 1, 1941; Waterbury**—Area extended; now includes Litchfield County and in the County of New Haven the towns of Beacon Falls, Bethany, Cheshire, Middlebury, Naugatuck, Oxford, Prospect, Southbury, Waterbury, and Wolcott—April 1, 1941.

DELAWARE: Wilmington—New Castle County, Del.; Salem County, N. J.—March 1, 1942.

FLORIDA: Banana River—Brevard County—March 1, 1942; Fort Meyers—Lee County—March 1, 1942; Gainesville-Starke—Counties of Alachua, Bradford and Clay—January 1, 1941; Hobe Sound-Stuart—Martin County—March 1, 1942; Jacksonville—Duval County—April 1, 1941; Key West—Monroe County—March 1, 1942; Orlando—Orange County—March 1, 1942; Panama City—Bay County—March 1, 1942; Pensacola—Escambia County—March 1, 1942; Sebring—Highlands County—

Service station gasoline price set at March level with additions for East Coast

Motor fuel prices at all service stations throughout the country—with the exception of 17 East Coast States and the District of Columbia—have been placed under a ceiling based on the highest prices charged by each individual seller during March 1942, Price Administrator Henderson announced April 28.

These price ceilings were established by OPA in Maximum Price Regulation No. 137. The new maximums become effective May 18, 1942.

In the east coast area, service stations will be allowed to charge the highest prices prevailing during March 1942, plus 0.4-cent per gallon in the case of gasoline and 0.2-cent per gallon in the case of Diesel fuel (used for heavy trucks, buses, and boats). Due to abnormal war conditions, much gasoline customarily arriving in this territory via ocean tanker now is being moved by tank car, which is more expensive.

March 1, 1942; Tallahassee—Leon County—March 1, 1942; Tampa—Counties of Hillsborough, Pinellas and Polk—March 1, 1942; Valparaiso — Okaloosa County — March 1, 1942.

GEORGIA: Albany—Dougherty County—March 1, 1942; Atlanta—Counties of Clayton, Cobb, De Kalb and Fulton—March 1, 1942; Augusta—Richmond County, Ga.; and Aiken County, S. C.—March 1, 1942; Chattanooga, Tenn.—Counties of Catoosa, Dade and Walker, Ga.; Bradley, Hamilton and Marion Counties, Tenn.—March 1, 1942; Columbus*—Muscogee County, Ga.; in Russell County, Ala.; Precinct one, including Phenix City—January 1, 1941; Copperhill-McCaysville—Fannin County, Ga.; Polk County, Tenn.—March 1, 1942; Hinesville—Liberty County—March 1, 1942; Macon—Counties of Bibb, Houston and Peach—April 1, 1941; Moultrie—Colquitt County—March 1, 1942; Savannah—Chatham County—March 1, 1942; Toccoa—Stephens County—March 1, 1942; Valdosta—Lowndes County—March 1, 1942.

ILLINOIS: Burlington, Ia.**—Area extended; now includes Henderson County, Ill.; Des Moines, Henry and Lee Counties, Ia.—January 1, 1941; Chicago—Counties of Cook, Du Page, Kane and Lake—March 1, 1942; Crab Orchard—Counties of Jackson and Williamson—March 1, 1942; Dixon—Lee County—March 1, 1942; Joliet — Will County—April 1, 1941; Peoria—Counties of Peoria and Tazewell—March 1, 1942; Pike-Pike County, Ill.; Pike County, Mo.—March 1, 1942; Quad Cities—Rock Island County, Ill.; Clinton and Scott Counties, Ia.—March 1, 1942; Quincy-Adams County, Ill.; Lewis and Marion Counties, Mo.—March 1, 1942; Rantoul—Champaign County — March 1, 1942; Rockford—Boone and Winnebago Counties—March 1, 1942; Savanna-Carroll County—March 1, 1942; Springfield-Decatur—Counties of Christian, Logan, Macon and Sangamond—March 1, 1942; St. Louis, Mo.—Counties of Madison, Monroe, and St. Clair, Ill.; Counties of Jefferson, St. Charles, St. Louis, Mo., City of St. Louis, Mo.—March 1, 1942.

INDIANA: Bedford—Counties of Lawrence and Martin—March 1, 1942; Clinton-Newport—Counties of Parke and Vermillion—March 1, 1942; Columbus—Counties of Bartholomew and Brown—March 1, 1942; Connersville—Fayette County—March 1, 1942; Evansville-Henderson—Vanderburgh County, Ind.; Henderson County, Ky.—March 1, 1942; Fort Wayne—Allen County—March 1, 1942; Gary-Hammond—Lake County—March 1, 1942; Indianapolis—Marion County—July 1, 1941; La Fayette—Counties of Fountain, Tippecanoe and Warren—March 1, 1942; La Porte-Michigan City—Counties of La Porte and Starke—April 1, 1941; Louisville, Ky.—Counties of Clark and Floyd, Ind.; Jefferson County, Ky.—July 1, 1941; Madison—Jefferson County, Ind.—March 1, 1942; Muncie-Anderson—Counties of Delaware, Grant, Howard and Madison—March 1, 1942; South Bend*—Counties of St. Joseph and Elkhart—January 1, 1941; Terre Haute—Vigo County—March 1, 1942.

IOWA: Burlington*—Area extended; now includes Counties of Des Moines, Henry and Lee, Ia.; Henderson County, Ill.—January 1, 1941; Cedar Rapids—Linn County—March 1, 1942; Des Moines—Polk County—March 1, 1942; Omaha, Nebr.—Pottawattamie County, Ia.; Douglas and Sarpy Counties, Nebr.—March 1, 1942; Quad Cities—Counties of Clinton and Scott, Ia.; Rock Island County, Ill.—March 1, 1942; Waterloo—Black Hawk County—March 1, 1942.

KANSAS: Baxter Springs—Cherokee County, Kans.; Ottawa County, Okla.—March 1, 1942; Junction City-Manhattan—Counties of Geary and Riley—April 1, 1941; Kansas City, Mo.—Counties of Johnson, Leavenworth and Wyandotte, Kans.; Counties of Clay, Jackson and Platte, Mo.—March 1, 1942; Parsons—Labette County—July 1, 1941; Topeka-Lawrence—Counties of Douglas, Franklin and

Shawnee—March 1, 1942; Wichita*—Sedgwick County—July 1, 1941.

KENTUCKY: Cincinnati, Ohio—Counties of Boone, Kenton and Campbell, Ky.; Counties of Butler, Clermont, Hamilton and Warren, Ohio—March 1, 1942; Evansville-Henderson—Henderson County, Ky.; Vanderburgh County, Ind.—March 1, 1942; Fort Knox—Counties of Bullitt, Hardin and Meade—March 1, 1942; Huntington, W. Va.—Counties of Boyd and Greenup. Ky.; Counties of Cabell and Wayne, West Va.; and Lawrence County, Ohio—March 1, 1942; Louisville—Jefferson County, Ky.; Counties of Clark and Floyd, Ind.—July 1, 1941; Morganfield—Union County—March 1, 1942; Paducah—McCracken County—March 1, 1942; Richmond—Madison County—March 1, 1942.

LOUISIANA: Alexandria-Leesville—Beauregard, Rapides, and Vernon Parishes—January 1. 1941; Baton Rouge—East Baton Rouge and West Baton Rouge Parishes—March 1, 1942; Lake Charles—Calcasieu Parish—March 1, 1942; Minden—Webster Parish—July 1, 1941; Monroe-Bastrop—Morehouse, Ouachita, and Union Parishes—March 1, 1942; New Orleans-Jefferson, Orleans, and St. Bernard Parishes—March 1, 1942; Shreveport—Bossier and Caddo Parishes—March 1, 1942.

MAINE: Bangor—Penobscot County—March 1, 1942; Bath—Lincoln and Sagadahoc Counties—April 1, 1941; Portland—Androscoggin and Cumberland Counties—March 1, 1942; Portsmouth, N. H.—York County, Me.; Rockingham and Strafford Counties, N. H.—March 1, 1942; Presque Isle—Aroostook County—March 1, 1942.

MARYLAND: Baltimore***—City of Baltimore and Anne Arundel, Baltimore, Carroll, Cecil, Harford, and Howard Counties—April 1, 1941; District of Columbia Suburbs—Montgomery and Prince Georges Counties, Md.; City of Alexandria and Counties of Arlington and Fairfax, Va.—January 1, 1941; Hagerstown—Washington County—March 1, 1942; Indian Head—Charles County—March 1, 1942.

MASSACHUSETTS: Eastern Massachusetts—Barnstable, Bristol, Essex, Middlesex, Norfolk, Plymouth and Suffolk Counties—March 1, 1942; Greenfield—Franklin County—March 1, 1942; Pittsfield—Berkshire County—March 1, 1942; Springfield—Hampden and Hampshire Counties—March 1, 1942; Worcester—Worcester County—March 1, 1942.

MICHIGAN: Adrian—Lenawee County—March 1, 1942; Detroit**—Area extended; now includes Macomb, Oakland, Washtenaw and Wayne Counties—April 1, 1941; Flint—Genesee County—March 1, 1942; Grand Rapids—Muskegon—Kent, Muskegon and Ottawa Counties—March 1, 1942; Jackson—Jackson County—March 1, 1942; Kalamazoo-Battle Creek—Calhoun and Kalamazoo Counties—March 1, 1942; Lansing—Clinton, Eaton, and Ingham Counties—March 1, 1942; Niles—Berrien County—April 1, 1941; Port Huron—St. Clair County—March 1, 1942; Saginaw-Bay City—Bay, Midland, and Saginaw Counties—March 1, 1942; Toledo, Ohio—Monroe County, Mich.; Lucas and Wood Counties, Ohio—March 1, 1942.

MINNESOTA: Duluth-Superior — Carlton and St. Louis Counties, Minn.; Douglas County, Wis.—March 1, 1942; Minneapolis-St. Paul—Anoka, Dakota, Hennepin, Ramsey, and Washington Counties—March 1, 1942.

MISSISSIPPI: Biloxi-Pascagoula—Harrison and Jackson Counties—April 1, 1941; Columbus — Lowndes County — March 1, 1942; Greenville—Washington County; March 1, 1942; Hattiesburg—Forrest County—April 1, 1941; Jackson—Hinds, Madison and Rankin Counties—March 1, 1942; Meridian—Lauderdale County—March 1, 1942.

MISSOURI: Joplin-Neosho — Jasper and Newton Counties—July 1, 1941; Kansas City—Clay, Jackson and Platte Counties, Mo.; Johnson, Leavenworth and Wyandotte counties, Kans. —March 1, 1942; Pike — Pike County, Mo.; Pike County, Ill.—March 1, 1942; Quincy, Ill.—Lewis and Marion Counties, Mo.; Adams County, Ill.—March 1, 1942;

ADDITIONAL EXCEPTIONS FROM GENERAL CEILING

Additional commodities and services excepted from the provisions of the general maximum price regulation were announced April 28 by Price Administrator Henderson.

Supplementary Regulation No. 1 to the general regulation, issued simultaneously therewith, excludes from the master price order the following:

1. All waste materials up to the level of the industrial consumer.
2. Zinc, lead, and tin industrial residues.
3. Certain machines and parts manufactured in the course of subcontracting—including certain machines and parts specially designed for war production use, also services performed on materials furnished by the customer, which will result in such machines.
4. Antimony ore and concentrates.
5. Instrument jewel bearings.

Supplemental Regulation No. 1 becomes effective May 11, 1942.

Special situations in connection with prices of all these commodities, as well as services performed on materials furnished a subcontractor by the customer led to the exceptions, officials of the OPA stated.

Rolla-Waynesville — Laclede, Phelps and Pulaski Counties—April 1, 1941; Springfield—Greene County—March 1, 1942; St. Louis—City of St. Louis and Counties of Jefferson, St. Charles and St. Louis, Mo.; Madison, Monroe and St. Clair Counties. Ill.—March 1, 1942.

MONTANA: Butte—Silver Bow County—March 1, 1942.

NEBRASKA: Columbus — Butler, Colfax, Platte and Polk Counties—March 1, 1942; Grand Island—Hall County—March 1, 1942; Lincoln—Lancaster County—March 1, 1942; Omaha—Douglas and Sarpy Counties, Nebr.; Pottawattamie County, Ia.—March 1, 1942; Sidney—Cheyenne County—March 1, 1942; Wahoo-Fremont—Dodge and Saunders Counties—March 1, 1942.

NEVADA: Las Vegas—Clark County—March 1, 1942.

NEW HAMPSHIRE: Manchester—Hillsborough County—March 1, 1942; Portsmouth-Rockingham and Strafford Counties, N. H.; York County, Me.—March 1, 1942; Springfield-Windsor, Vt.—Sullivan County, N. H.; Windsor County, Vt.—March 1, 1942.

NEW JERSEY: Allentown-Bethlehem, Pa.—Warren County, N. J.; Northampton and Lehigh Counties, Pa.—March 1, 1942; Bridgeton-Millville—Cumberland County— March 1, 1942; Northeastern New Jersey—Bergen, Essex, Hudson, Middlesex, Monmouth, Morris, Passaic, Somerset, and Union Counties—March 1, 1942; Philadelphia-Camden-Burlington, Camden and Gloucester Counties, N. J.; Bucks, Chester, Delaware, Montgomery and Philadelphia Counties, Pa.—March 1, 1942; Trenton—Hunterdon and Mercer Counties—March 1, 1942; Wilmington, Del.—Salem County, N. J.; New Castle County, Del.—March 1, 1942.

NEW MEXICO: Albuquerque—Bernalillo County—March 1, 1942; Roswell—Chaves County—March 1, 1942; Silver City-Lordsburg—Grant and Hidalgo Counties—March 1, 1942.

NEW YORK: Albany-Troy—Albany and Rensselaer Counties—March 1, 1942; Binghamton—Broome and Tioga Counties—

March 1, 1942; Buffalo—Erie and Niagara Counties—March 1, 1942; Elmira—Chemung and Steuben Counties—March 1, 1942; Essex County—Essex County—March 1, 1942; Jamestown—Chautauqua County—March 1, 1942; Massena—St. Lawrence County—April 1, 1941; New York City—City of New York, including the Boroughs of Bronx, Brooklyn, Manhattan, Queens, and Richmond; and Nassau, Rockland, Suffolk and Westchester Counties—March 1, 1942; Poughkeepsie—Dutchess, Orange and Ulster Counties—March 1, 1942; Rochester—Genesee, Monroe, Orleans and Wayne Counties—March 1, 1942; Schenectady**—Area extended, now includes Montgomery, Saratoga and Schenectady Counties—April 1, 1941; Seneca—Ontario, Seneca and Yates Counties—March 1, 1942; Sidney—Chenango, Delaware and Otsego Counties—March 1, 1942; Syracuse—Cayuga, Onondaga and Oswego Counties—March 1, 1942; Utica-Rome—Herkimer, Madison and Oneida Counties—March 1, 1942; Watertown—Jefferson County—April 1, 1941.

NORTH CAROLINA: Charlotte—Mecklenburg County—March 1, 1942; Durham—Durham County—March 1, 1942; Elizabeth City—Pasquotank—March 1, 1942; Fayetteville—Cumberland and Hoke counties—April 1, 1941; Greensboro—Guilford County—March 1, 1942; Jacksonville—Onslow County—March 1, 1942; Mt. Airy-Elkin—Surry County—March 1, 1942; New Bern—Carteret and Craven Counties—March 1, 1942; Wilmington*—New Hanover County—April 1, 1941.

OHIO: Akron**—Area extended; now includes Medina and Summit Counties—April 1, 1941; Ashtabula—Ashtabula County—March 1, 1942; Canton**—Area extended; now includes Stark and Tuscarawas Counties—April 1, 1941; Celina-St. Mary's—Auglaize and Mercer Counties—March 1, 1942; Cincinnati—Butler, Clermont, Warren and Hamilton Counties, Ohio; Boone, Campbell and Kenton Counties, Ky.—March 1, 1942; Cleveland**—Area extended; now includes Cuyahoga, Geauga and Lake Counties—July 1, 1941; Columbus—Franklin County—March 1, 1942; Dayton—Champaign, Clark, Darke, Greene, Miami, Montgomery and Preble Counties—April 1, 1941; Findlay-Fostoria—Hancock and Seneca Counties—March 1, 1942; Huntington, W. Va.—Lawrence County, Ohio; Cabell and Wayne Counties, W. Va.; Boyd and Greenup Counties, Ky.—March 1, 1942; Lima—Allen County—March 1, 1942; Lorain-Elyria—Lorain County—July 1, 1941; Marion—Marion County—March 1, 1942; Point Pleasant-Gallipolis, W. Va.—Gallia County, Ohio; Mason County, W. Va.—March 1, 1942; Ravenna—Portage County—April 1, 1941; Sandusky-Port Clinton—Erie, Huron, Ottawa and Sandusky Counties—March 1, 1942; Toledo—Lucas and Wood Counties, Ohio; Monroe County, Mich.—March 1, 1942; Wheeling-Steubenville, W. Va.—Belmont, Columbiana and Jefferson Counties, Ohio; Brooke, Hancock, Marshall, Ohio and Wetzel Counties, W. Va.—March 1, 1942; Youngstown-Warren*—Mahoning and Trumbull Counties—April 1, 1941.

OKLAHOMA: Baxter Springs, Kans.—Ottawa County. Okla.; Cherokee County, Kans.—March 1, 1942; Choteau—Craig, Mayes, Rogers, and Wagoner Counties—March 1, 1942; Enid-Garfield County—March 1, 1942; Lawton—Comanche County—April 1, 1941; Muskogee—Muskogee County—March 1, 1942; Oklahoma City—Oklahoma County—March 1, 1942; Paris, Tex.—Choctaw, Okla.; Lamar County, Tex.—March 1, 1942; Tulsa—Creek, Osage and Tulsa Counties—March 1, 1942.

OREGON: Astoria—Clatsop County—March 1, 1942; Corvallis—Benton and Linn Counties—March 1, 1942; Medford—Jackson County—March 1, 1942; Pendleton—Umatilla County—March 1, 1942; Portland-Vancouver—Clackamas, Multnomah, and Washington Counties, Ore.; Clark County, Wash.—March 1, 1942.

PENNSYLVANIA: Allentown-Bethlehem—Lehigh and Northampton Counties, Pa.;

(Continued on page 10)

Rent control ordered for 302 more areas

(Continued from page 9)

Warren County, N. J.—March 1, 1942; Altoona-Johnstown—Blair, Cambria, and Somerset Counties—March 1, 1942; Chambersburg—Franklin County—March 1, 1942; Erie—Erie County—March 1, 1942; Harrisburg—Cumberland, Dauphin, Lebanon, and Perry Counties—March 1, 1942; Lancaster-York—Lancaster and York Counties—March 1, 1942; Meadville-Titusville—Crawford and Venango Counties—March 1, 1942; Milton—Montour, Northumberland, Snyder, and Union Counties—March 1, 1942; Philadelphia-Camden—Bucks, Chester, Delaware, Montgomery, and Philadelphia Counties. Pa.; Burlington, Camden, and Gloucester Counties, N. J.—March 1, 1942; Pittsburgh—Allegheny, Armstrong, Beaver, Butler, Fayette, Greene, Lawrence, Washington, and Westmoreland Counties—March 1, 1942; Reading—Berks County—March 1, 1942; Scranton-Wilkes Barre—Carbon, Columbia, Lackawanna, Luzerne, and Schuylkill Counties—March 1, 1942; Sharon-Farrell—Mercer County—April 1, 1941; Williamsport—Lycoming County—March 1, 1942.

RHODE ISLAND: Newport—New County—March 1, 1942; Providence—Bristol, Kent and Providence Counties—March 1, 1942; Quonset Point—Washington County—March 1, 1942.

SOUTH CAROLINA: Augusta, Ga.—Aiken County, S. C.; Richmond County, Ga.—March 1, 1942; Beaufort—Beaufort County—March 1, 1942; Charleston—Charleston and Dorchester Counties—March 1, 1942; Columbia—Calhoun, Lexington and Richland Counties—March 1, 1942; Greenville — Greenville County—March 1, 1942; Greenwood—Greenwood County—March 1, 1942; Spartanburg—Cherokee, Spartanburg and Union Counties—March 1, 1942; Sumter—Sumter County—March 1, 1942.

SOUTH DAKOTA: Provo-Hot Springs—Fall River County—March 1, 1942; Rapid City-Sturgis—Lawrence, Meade and Pennington Counties—March 1, 1942.

TENNESSEE: Chattanooga—Bradley, Hamilton and Marion Counties, Tenn.; Catoosa, Dade and Walker Counties, Ga.—March 1, 1942; Clarksville — Montgomery County—March 1, 1942; Columbia—Maury County—March 1, 1942; Copperhill-McCaysville—Polk County, Tenn.; Fannin County, Ga.—March 1, 1942; Jackson-Milan-Humboldt—Carroll, Gibson and Madison Counties—January 1, 1941; Knoxville—Blount and Knox Counties—March 1, 1942; Memphis—Shelby County, Tenn.; Crittenden County, Ark.—March 1, 1942; Nashville—Davidson County—March 1, 1942; Paris—Henry County—March 1, 1942; Tullahoma—Bedford, Coffee, Franklin Lincoln and Moore Counties—January 1, 1941.

TEXAS: Abilene—Callahan, Jones and Taylor Counties—April 1, 1941; Amarillo—Potter County—March 1, 1942; Austin—Hays, Travis and Williamson Counties—March 1, 1942; Bastrop—Bastrop County—March 1, 1942; Beaumont-Port Arthur—Jefferson and Orange Counties—April 1, 1941; Bonham—Fannin County—March 1, 1942; Brownwood—Brown, Coleman and Comanche Counties—January 1, 1941; Corpus Christi—Nueces and San Patricio Counties—March 1, 1942; El Paso—El Paso County—April 1, 1941; Fort Worth-Dallas — Dallas and Tarrant Counties—March 1, 1942; Gainesville—Cooke County—March 1, 1942; Houston-Galveston—Brazoria, Chambers, Galveston, Harris, and Liberty Counties—March 1, 1942; Killeen-Temple—Bell and Coryell Counties—March 1, 1942; Lower Rio Grande Valley—Cameron, Hidalgo, and Willacy Counties—March 1, 1942; Lubbock—Lubbock County—March 1, 1942; Marfa—Presidio County—March 1, 1942; Marshall—Harrison, Marion, and Upshur Counties—March 1, 1942; Matagorda Bay—Calhoun, Jackson, and Matagorda Counties—March 1, 1942; Midland-Odessa—Ector and Midland Counties—March 1, 1942; Mineral Wells—Palo Pinto and Parker Counties—January 1, 1941; Paris—Lamar County, Tex.; Choctaw County, Okla.—March 1, 1942; San Angelo—Tom Green County—March 1, 1942; San Antonio-Atascosa, Bandera, Bexar, Comal, Guadalupe, Kendall, Medina, and Wilson Counties—March 1, 1942; Sherman-Denison—Grayson County—March 1, 1942; Texarkana—Bowie County, Tex.; Miller County, Ark.—July 1, 1941; Victoria—Victoria County—March 1, 1942; Waco—McLennan County—March 1, 1942; Wichita Falls—Wichita County—March 1, 1942;

UTAH: Provo — Utah County — March 1, 1942; Salt Lake City-Ogden—Salt Lake, Davis, Morgan, and Weber Counties—March 1, 1942; Tooele-Wendover—Tooele County, Utah—March 1, 1942.

VERMONT: Burlington—Chittenden County—March 1, 1942; Springfield-Windsor—Windsor County, Vt.; Sullivan County, N. H.—March 1, 1942.

VIRGINIA: Blackstone — Nottoway County—March 1, 1942; District of Columbia Suburbs—Alexandria and Counties of Arlington and Fairfax, Va.; Montgomery and Prince Georges Counties, Md.—January 1, 1941; Hampton Roads—Cities of Hampton. Newport News, Norfolk, Portsmouth and South Norfolk; Elizabeth City County; in Norfolk County, Magisterial Districts of Deep Creek, Tanners Creek, Washington and Western Branch; in Princess Anne County, the Magisterial Districts of Kempsville and Lynnhaven; in the County of Warwick the Magisterial District of Newport—April 1, 1941; King George County—King George County—March 1, 1942; Petersburg—City of Petersburg and Dinwiddie and Prince George Counties—April 1, 1941; Quantico—City of Fredericksburg, and Prince William and Stafford Counties—March 1, 1942; Radford-Pulaski—City of Radford; and Montgomery and Pulaski Counties—April 1, 1941; Richmond—City of Richmond; and Chesterfield and Henrico Counties—March 1, 1942; Yorktown—City of Williamsburg; James City and York Counties, and in the County of Warwick, Magisterial Districts of Denbigh and Stanley—March 1, 1942.

WASHINGTON: Bellingham — Whatcom County—March 1, 1942; Everett—Snohomish County—March 1, 1942; Island County—Island County—March 1, 1942; Long View-Kelso—Cowlitz—March 1, 1942; Pasco-Franklin County—March 1, 1942; Port Angeles-Port Townsend—Counties of Clallam and Jefferson—March 1, 1942; Portland-Vancouver, Ore.—Clark County, Wash.; and Counties of Clackamas, Multnomah and Washington, Ore.—March 1, 1942; Puget Sound—Kitsap County and those parts of the counties of King and Pierce lying west of the Snoqualmie National Forest—April 1, 1941; Spokane—Spokane County—March 1, 1942; Walla Walla—Walla Walla County—March 1, 1942.

WEST VIRGINIA: Charleston—Kanawha County—March 1, 1942; Huntington—Counties of Cabell and Wayne, W. Va.; Lawrence County, O.; and Counties of Boyd and Greenup—March 1, 1942; Morgantown—Counties of Marion and Monongalia—April 1, 1941; Point Pleasant-Gallipolis—Mason County, W. Va.; Gallia County, Ohio.—March 1, 1942; Wheeling-Steubenville—Counties of Brooke, Hancock, Marshall, Ohio and Wetzel, W. Va.; Counties of Belmont Columbiana and Jefferson, Ohio.—March 1, 1942.

WISCONSIN: Beloit - Janesville — Rock County—March 1, 1942; Duluth, Superior—Douglas County, Wis.; Carlton and St. Louis Counties, Minn.—March 1, 1942; Madison—Counties of Columbia, Dane and Sauk—March 1, 1942; Manitowoc—Manitowoc County—March 1, 1942; Milwaukee—Counties of Kenosha, Milwaukee, Racine and Waukesha—March 1, 1942; Oshkosh-Fond du Lac—Counties of Fond du Lac and Winnebago—March 1, 1942; Sparta—Monroe County—March 1, 1942; Sturgeon Bay—Door County—March 1, 1942.

WYOMING: Cheyenne—Laramie County—March 1, 1942.

PUERTO RICO: Puerto Rico—The possession in entirety—March 1, 1942.

*Announced March 2, 1942.
**E ended; originally announced March 2, 1942. xt
***Announced April 2, 1942.

20 "defense-rental" areas to be checked for compliance with OPA recommendations

Investigation of housing rents in the 20 "defense-rental" areas designated March 2 (see, VICTORY, March 10) will be undertaken at once to determine whether Federal recommendations for the reduction and stabilization of rents have been met, Price Administrator Henderson announced April 28.

Administrative offices will be opened on or about May 15 in areas where surveys show that recommendations have not been complied with, and in these areas Federal regulation will take effect with June rents.

The 20 areas follow:

Bridgeport, Conn.; Hartford-New Britain, Conn.; Waterbury, Conn.; Schenectady, N. Y.; Birmingham, Ala.; Mobile, Ala.; Columbus, Ga.; Wilmington, N. C.; Hampton Roads, Va., area; Detroit, Mich.; Akron, Ohio; Canton, Ohio; Cleveland, Ohio; Ravenna, Ohio; Youngstown-Warren, Ohio; South Bend, Ind.; Burlington, Iowa; Wichita, Kans.; San Diego, Calif.; Puget Sound, Wash., area.

Five percent rise granted for original auto, truck tires

Following a study of tire companies' operating experience in January and February of this year by OPA, Administrator Henderson has established maximum prices on original equipment tires and tubes for automobiles and trucks allowing 5 percent increases over levels that prevailed throughout 1941.

Maximum Price Regulation No. 119, which establishes the new ceiling, was effective as of April 27.

Prices on original tires and tubes for farm equipment are not to be advanced and will continue at the 1941 levels.

All rented living quarters in Federally controlled towns must be registered, OPA rules

Registration of all rented dwelling accommodations will be required in cities and towns that are brought under Federal rent control, Price Administrator Henderson announced April 29 in making public the text of OPA's Proposed Maximum Rent Regulations covering dwelling units other than hotels and rooming houses.

Scope of registration

The registration will be made by landlords at a local rent administrator's office to cover houses, apartments, trailers, and all other property which is rented for living quarters. A similar registration will be required of persons operating hotels and rooming houses. Regulations covering hotels, rooming and boarding houses will be issued shortly.

Implementing the Emergency Price Control Act, the regulations, not yet in effect in any area, prescribe the methods of rent control by the OPA. They will become effective only on specific order from Mr. Henderson, and only in previously designated war-rental areas where, after a 60-day period, a finding is made that recommendations for stabilizing rents have not been met.

At the end of the 60-day period, the OPA makes an investigation to determine if rents have been brought in line with the Price Administrator's recommendations. If they have not, an area rent director is appointed, a local administrative office is opened, and the regulations for the area are issued. After the effective date of the regulations, tenants in the area are to pay the rent fixed by Mr. Henderson.

In addition to the Registration Statement by landlords, the regulations cover such points as leases, evictions, services, new construction, substantial alterations, adjustments, special relationships between tenant and landlord, off-season rentals, violations and evasions, and penalties.

Hotels asked not to raise war workers' rates in Derby Week

Hotel operators in Louisville, Ky., are asked by Price Administrator Henderson to make no increase in rates during Derby Week for Government employees residing in hotels and engaged in the war effort.

Solid fuel prices put under ceiling for over 45,000 retailers and wholesalers

Maximum prices which may be charged by the more than 45,000 wholesalers and retailers of all solid fuels were established formally April 30 at the highest levels prevailing in the December 15-31, 1941, period through issuance by Price Administrator Henderson of Maximum Price Regulation No. 122. Previously, informal agreements, subject to some exceptions, had held prices at this level.

The regulation will become effective May 18, the effective date of the general maximum price regulation, and will cover all sales of solid fuels in any quantity excepting sales at mines or preparation plants. Sales of the latter types are covered in other regulations issued previously.

Dealers to be licensed

Plans were being formulated by OPA in conjunction with the RFC to make this program effective, particularly as regards the New England area, by taking care of increases in transportation costs in such manner as to prevent retail prices from rising above the December 15-31 level.

All dealers covered by the regulation will be licensed as in the case of persons subject to the general price regulation.

The dealers also are required to post the maximum price per ton of all solid fuels offered for sale.

"Solid fuels" quoted

The term "solid fuels," as used in the regulation, means all solid fuels with the exception of wood and wood products. It includes all anthracite, semianthracite, semibituminous, bituminous, subbituminous, and cannel coal; lignite, all coke, including low-temperature coke and petroleum coke (except byproduct foundry and blast-furnace coke, and beehive oven-furnace coke produced in Pennsylvania), briquettes made from coke and coal, and sea coal used for foundry facings.

The maximum prices provided in appendix A are:

1. The price specified in any advertisement inserted in newspapers or other publications in the same locality between October 1, and December 31, 1941, and in effect during any portion of the period of December 15-31, 1941. This must be the price so specified for the sale of:
   a. The same size, kind and quality of solid fuel;
   b. In quantities taking the same price per ton;
   c. To purchasers of the same general class;
   d. By the same method of delivery; and
   e. Under the same terms of delivery.

2. If the maximum price cannot be established as stated above, the maximum price shall be the same as specified in the last price circular, list or schedule issued by the same person on or before December 31, 1941, and in effect for any portion of the December 15-31, 1941, period;

3. If neither of the above two methods can be used, the maximum price shall be the "average price" obtained by dividing the aggregate of prices charged by the same dealer during the period December 15-31, 1941, by the tonnage sold, on sales of the same price size and quality of fuel, similar quantities and under the same terms and conditions of delivery.

4. If none of the above methods can be used, the maximum price shall be the maximum price specified by any dealer of the same general character and in the same general locality, either in an advertisement placed between October 1 and December 31, 1941 or a circular issued on or before December 31, 1941.

The regulation stipulates that the dealer shall allow deductions from his price of cash and quantity discounts which he permitted during any part of the December 15-31, 1941 period. Charges for special services shall not exceed those for similar services during the December 15-31, 1941 period.

★ ★ ★

Soft coal prices at mine or preparation plant put under OPA maximum

Coincident with the issuance of the general maximum price regulation April 28 Price Administrator Henderson established maximum prices for bituminous coal sold at mines or preparation plants at levels which will permit the industry a realization somewhat higher than during the October 1-15, 1941 period. The regulation—Maximum Price Regulation No. 120—becomes effective May 18, 1942.

Maximum prices at the mines, established by the Price Regulations are set forth in 22 appendices covering specifically mine operations in the 22 production districts set up under the Bituminous Coal Act of 1937 and under which the operators are observing minimum prices established by the Bituminous Coal Division of the Department of the Interior.

In determining these maximum prices at the mines, OPA gave consideration not only to the October 1941 price levels, but also to increased costs of production which the industry stated it has incurred since that time.

Lower prices than the established maximums may be charged, provided that nothing in the regulation shall be deemed to authorize code member producers or distributors to make sales or deliveries at prices lower than the effective minimum prices set from time to time by the Bituminous Coal Division.

Cotton and rayon finished piece goods prices lowered by permanent ceilings

Converters' and wholesalers' prices of "finished" piece goods made of cotton, rayon and their mixtures were placed under a formal OPA price regulation April 28 at substantially lower levels than the temporary ceilings imposed last March.

At the same time Administrator Henderson, in a companion order, established maximum charges which converters may obtain for their costs of transforming "grey" goods into finished textiles, through such processes as bleaching, dyeing, napping, printing or mercerizing.

Broad effect on consumer

These two regulations—one establishing the margin which a converter may charge to cover his overhead and profit and the other setting forth what his costs for processing shall be—are among the broadest yet issued affecting prices of cotton and rayon textiles as they reach the consumer.

Under Maximum Price Regulation No. 127—Finished Piece Goods—the method of determining ceilings for "finished" piece goods is set forth in detail. In general, the regulation provides maximum margins which may be charged by the converter above the sum of his specified cost items. These cost items are stabilized by grey goods ceilings already in effect and by Maximum Price Regulation No. 128—Processing Piece Goods—which is issued simultaneously covering the various finishing operations on the basis of prices charged for each particular service between March 16 and April 15 1942.

"Finished" piece goods under Regulation No. 127 include items ranging from plain bleached fabrics used for such products as sheets and shirts; plain dyed numbers used for linings, dress material, and underwear; and goods printed in their wide variety of colors, patterns and styles for cretonnes and other fabrics such as those used by dress and clothing manufacturers as well as home dressmakers. The regulation does not apply to sales at retail.

Sell to clothing manufacturers

Converters, affected by the April 28 provisions, usually buy "unfinished" grey goods from mills, have them styled and finished, and then sell them to apparel manufacturers or to retailers as piece goods.

The regulation became effective May 4, and is applicable to all deliveries and all contracts made on and after that date regardless of the terms of existing contracts.

The regulation also replaces Temporary Maximum Price Regulation No. 10, and, in practical effect, reduces the maximums which were temporarily "frozen" at the levels prevailing between last March 7 and 11. When the "quick freeze" order was issued on March 13, OPA officials pointed out that it was for the purpose of stopping further advances pending the issuance of a permanent regulation. At that time, Acting Price Administrator Hamm asserted that "there is no justification for the rapid rise in the price of finished goods since basic costs of converters selling such goods have been relatively stable."

Profit based on costs

The method of controlling prices for the finished piece goods covered by Regulation No. 127 is through the control of converters' margins above their direct costs. The five cost elements are carefully defined in detail to prevent obvious abuses of a "cost plus" system. These five costs are:

1. The basic cost of the "grey" goods from which the finished piece goods are produced;
2. The cost of freight for transporting the grey goods to the finishing plant;
3. The actual "working allowances," due to the shrinkage in yardage resulting from the finishing process. In some cases where there is a "working gain" when the finishing process stretches the goods, a deduction from grey goods cost must be made;
4. The cost of finishing, and
5. The cost of "put-up," which represents the packaging by the finisher.

To determine the converter's margin above these direct costs, the sum of these five items is divided by a "division factor" which results in a price higher than the total of the five cost items. The gross margin thus provided covers overhead and profit.

★ ★ ★

TERM "WOOL" REDEFINED

Because a maximum price regulation establishing ceiling prices for wool waste materials became effective April 28, the term "wool" has been redefined by an amendment to Revised Price Schedule No. 58. Under Amendment No. 1, effective April 28, wool waste, clips and rags and reworked wool of all grades and mixtures are eliminated from the definition of wool.

Maximum Price Regulation No. 123 (Raw and Processed Wool Waste Materials) replaces Price Schedule 58 insofar as the latter applies to wool waste materials.

PROCESSING CEILINGS

Ceilings for figures to be calculated as processing costs for rayon, cotton and mixed piece goods, established under Regulation No. 128, are the prices contracted for by each processor for each particular service during the period between March 16 and April 15, 1942, inclusive. In no event, however, may any processor's prices be above the general levels of prices of processing piece goods prevailing during the established base period.

The regulation carries a provision for a processor who made no contract for a particular service during the base period. In such an event, his maximum is his highest outstanding quotation during that period for such service. If he had no such quotation outstanding, then his maximum price is the highest quotation in the thirty days immediately preceding.

If a processor cannot determine his maximums under the foregoing provisions, his ceiling charge is a price in line with the maximum of the most nearly comparable processing service rendered by him during the March 16–April 15 period.

Provision is made in the regulation for reporting maximum prices for each particular process to the Office of Price Administration on or before June 20, 1942. Persons filing may request approval by OPA of such prices as being in line with the general levels prevailing in the base period. If OPA approves such specific prices, they are then considered to be the maximum prices of that person for all purposes.

★ ★ ★

A–2 for agricultural bag fabrics to cover more uses

Order M–107, which assigns a preference rating of A–2 to purchase orders by bag manufacturers for cotton fabrics suitable for "Agricultural Bags," has been amended to include a few additional commodities for which such agricultural bags may be used. They are shellfish, hops, brewers malt, tobacco and nursery stock, ground poultry grit, manufactured and natural abrasive grain, and metal parts.

Cotton picking sacks and sheets are brought within the definition of agricultural bags, so that osnaburg may be used as a substitute for duck.

The list of sheeting constructions specified in the order as being suitable for agricultural bags is enlarged to include one additional construction

Sliding scale for cotton goods pegged on March spot basis

Price Administrator Henderson April 29 gave further assurance to the American people that the cost of cotton goods items in their wardrobes would be stabilized at March 1942 levels by freezing the ceiling price at which manufacturers and wholesalers may sell, virtually all types of cotton goods and cotton yarns.

Six price schedules affected

Supplementing the General Maximum Price Regulation, the Administrator issued amendments to 6 price schedules applying to cotton products. These changes peg the previous sliding-scale "textile" ceilings on the basis of a 'spot" cotton price of 20.37 cents per pound. This represents the highest quotation registered for actual cotton sold at the ten leading southern terminal markets during March 1942.

The Administrator emphasized that, if the objectives of the General Regulation are to be attained, "it is evident that cotton yarns and textiles must not be allowed to advance beyond the highest prices attained in March."

"Sliding scales" eliminated

The April 29 action, which is designed to prevent wholesale prices from creeping up on retail prices, was taken only after exhaustive OPA cost studies showed that the ceilings determined for cotton yarn and textile prices are ample to satisfy the agricultural commodity requirements of the Emergency Price Control Act of 1942.

In eliminating "sliding-scales," Mr. Henderson pointed out that "the essential point to be observed here is that the ceilings now being imposed on cotton textiles are amply high to permit raw cotton prices to rise above any levels specified in Section 3 (a) ('the agricultural section')."

Before taking the April 29 action, OPA studies of costs, mill margins and earnings revealed that mills could pay considerably above the levels specified in Section 3 (a) and still earn a substantial profit on the great majority of cotton goods constructions.

The schedules covered by the April 29 amendments, which became effective May 4, 1942, are: No. 7—Combed Cotton Yarns; No. 11—Fine Cotton Grey Goods; No. 33—Carded Cotton Yarns; No. 35—Carded Grey and Colored-Yarn Cotton Goods; No. 89—Bed Linens; and No. 118—Cotton Products.

Ceiling put on wool waste, most important substitute in making clothes

Ceiling prices for raw and processed wool waste materials, the most important available substitutes for virgin wool in men's and women's clothing and other articles, were established by Maximum Price Regulation No. 123, effective April 28.

Six classes covered

Specific dollars and cents prices set in the April 27 order cover 2,865 items under six general classifications of raw wool waste materials. These are wool waste (wool fibers recovered during manufacturing processes), new wool clips (trimmings from garments), knitted wool clips, graded old wool rags, mixed old wool rags and government new wool clips. The maximum prices are based on levels which prevailed during October 1 to 15, 1941.

For processed wool waste materials, which comprise clips, etc., cleaned and reduced to a fibrous condition, a price formula is designed to allow processors a margin generally equal to the amount they received for their services and materials during the base period of October 1 to December 15, 1941.

Supersedes previous provisions

The new regulation supersedes those provisions of Revised Price Schedule No. 58 as amended (Wool and Wool Tops and Yarns) that applied to wool waste materials. Under the previous provisions, individual maximum prices were determined at the highest prices received by each seller of these products during October 1–December 15.

While the original schedule did not expressly forbid a purchaser to pay more than the individual ceilings, the April 27 order specifically applies both to buyers and sellers of these wool waste materials.

Greatly increased demand

The wool fiber which is reclaimed or processed from wool rags or clips is commonly known as "shoddy." Proper mixing of shoddy with new wool often produces a cloth which is equal in appearance, color and serviceability to cloth made of medium grades of new wool.

Price Administrator Leon Henderson said:

Inasmuch as restrictions have been placed on the volume of virgin wool allocated to the woolen industry for civilian use, the need for these waste materials has been heightened. The ceiling prices will thus be helpful in holding down costs of woolen goods to manufacturers and should stabilize costs of clothing to consumers . . ."

Based on extensive study

In determining the specific maximum prices for the various types and grades of raw wool waste materials, OPA officials studied price reports from some 200 firms and reports of several thousand transactions submitted by producers, dealers, processors and consumers. The ceilings provided are based on tabulations of these reports.

Classifications of types, kinds and grades of wool waste materials and price differentials between classes have been used in the regulation to embody, so far as practicable, existing trade practices.

Price basis

Prices set are on a net weight basis for wool waste and knitted wool clips in accordance with the usual trade practice. For new wool clips, old rags and Government clips, the prices allowed are on a gross weight basis with a provision that tare is not to exceed 5 percent, as is the customary practice.

Discounts may be allowed by sellers at prices less than the maximums.

Maximum prices for rough cloth and overcoats are established on a basis to encourage their use in the manufacture of processed wool and waste materials.

Mr. Henderson expressed the hope that all holders of wool rags, waste and clips would sell these materials to dealers, sorters, shoddy manufactures or consuming mills.

"With the imposition of ceilings, hoarding operations will not result in hoarders obtaining higher prices," he said.

Sales of imported nickel scrap not to exceed domestic ceilings

An amendment requiring imported nickel-bearing scrap and secondary materials to be sold at not more than the maximum prices provided for domestic scrap was announced April 29 by Price Administrator Henderson.

In the past, import charges under the law could be passed on to the ultimate consumer.

The measure—titled Amendment No. 1 to Revised Price Schedule No. 8 on nickel scrap—became effective April 28.

Ceiling prices set on makers' sales affecting hundreds of paper items

Maximum prices at which manufacturers can sell many varieties of converted paper products and industrial papers are established at levels which prevailed late in 1941 in Maximum Price Regulation No. 129 announced April 29 by Price Administrator Henderson with the General Maximum Price Regulation.

Two base periods

The regulation, effective May 11, 1942, fixes manufacturers' maximum prices for hundreds of paper items. Some prices are based on levels prevailing during the period from October 1 to October 15, 1941, others are based on levels of the December 1-15, 1941 period, and for a few other commodities specific prices have been set forth.

Scope of regulation

The Administrator found that the prices established by the regulation are fair and equitable.

Covered by the regulation are:

Waxed paper; envelopes; paper cups, paper containers and liquid-tight containers; sanitary closures and milk bottle caps; drinking straws; certain sulphate and certain sulphite papers; certain tissue papers; rope and jute papers; gummed papers; technical papers; tags, pin tickets, and marking machine tickets; glazed and fancy papers; standard grocer's and variety bags; resale book matches; unprinted single weight crepe paper in folds; certain bag papers; and certain wrapping papers.

The maximum prices established by the regulation for the following commodities are the highest prices a manufacturer charged during the October 1-15 period:

Waxed paper, including such classifications as bread wraps, carton wraps, cutter box papers, waxed glassine, twisting tissue, plain waxed papers, and delicatessen papers; paper cups; envelopes (except those made of specialty papers or of transparent materials); paper containers, and liquid-tight containers; sanitary closures and milk bottle caps; drinking straws, certain sulphate and sulphite papers defined specifically in the order; rope and jute papers; tissue papers under 18 pounds basis weight, excluding cigarette, carbonizing, fruit wrapping and condenser tissues; and technical papers including but not limited to those classified as saturating, impregnating, insulating, shotshell, and photographic papers.

Other provisions

The maximum price a manufacturer now can charge for any gummed papers, tags, pin tickets, marking machine tickets, glazed and fancy papers, are the highest prices he charged in the period from December 1-15, 1941.

Specific maximum prices are established by the regulation for the following: (1) self-opening (automatic) kraft grocer's bag; (2) resale book matches; (3) unprinted single weight crepe paper in folds, and (4) standard kraft bag paper and three grades of wrapping paper. Differentials for other grades of standard grocer's and variety bags and machine glazed kraft bag paper and kraft wrapping paper are established by reference to differentials on sales and deliveries during the period from Oct. 1-15, 1941.

The maximum manufacturer's delivered price for self-opening (automatic) kraft grocer's bag carload lot, Zone A, is 25/5's discount from standard list price. (The zones defined in the order are those generally used by the trade for pricing purposes.)

The manufacturer's maximum delivered price for resale book matches is $3.60 per case of 2,500 books.

The maximum price at which a manufacturer may sell for export is the price determined by the provisions of the Maximum Export Regulation which becomes effective April 30.

★ ★ ★

Public schools asked to stagger paper orders

An appeal to public schools and other public institutions to stagger shipments to them of certain paper products so that deliveries can be spread out over the year was made by the WPB April 30 in an effort to avoid disruption of commercial paper markets.

The pulp and paper branch placed special emphasis on supplies of tissues and paper towels, which most schools and institutions order in vast quantities during a brief period of time.

The branch asked them not to demand delivery within the next few weeks of all such supplies that they will need until the summer of 1943. In so changing their purchasing methods they will contribute to the war effort, branch officials said.

No shortage in tissues and paper towels is anticipated, but a flood of buying orders calling for deliveries a year in advance is threatening to disturb commercial markets seriously because of unusual conditions resulting from the war emergency.

"Standard" newsprint ceilings remain at $50 per ton in permanent regulation

"Standard" newsprint paper prices will remain at 50 dollars per ton as the result of Maximum Price Regulation No. 130 announced April 29 by Price Administrator Henderson with the General Maximum Price Regulation freezing prices of nearly all cost-of-living items at all levels of distribution.

Few changes effected

The new newsprint regulation, effective May 11, 1942, replaces Temporary Maximum Price Regulation No. 16, which on April 1 established maximum prices for standard newsprint at the same levels.

Mr. Henderson explained that the new regulation does not preclude further discussions between OPA and the Canadian Wartime Prices and Trade Board concerning Canadian newsprint mills.

The April 29 regulations effect few changes from the provisions of the temporary order. Maximum prices are fixed to cover the sales of standard newsprint paper by converters—who process newsprint paper from rolls to sheets—and sales by merchants and distributors who purchase standard newsprint paper from converters, as well as from manufacturers.

The regulation also precisely defines standard newsprint paper, with specifications as to weight, rolls, sheets, stock, finish, ash content, degree of sizing, color and thickness, and establishes one level of prices for all sellers.

Sales taxes conform to regulation

Sales taxes, and the possible use of sales taxes, are treated to conform with provisions of the General Maximum Price Regulation, and adjustable pricing—not to exceed the levels established by the regulation—is permitted in conformity with the general order.

Sales by exporters are placed under the Maximum Export Price Regulation controlling prices on all exports, effective April 30. Exporters' contracts entered into prior to April 1, 1942, may be completed even if the prices are above the maximum if the exporter has received delivery of the newsprint he has contracted to resell from a supplier and keeps records of such transactions in accordance with provisions of the regulation.

Zone price differentials frozen

The price of $50 per ton is the "port" price of white standard newsprint for carload lots in rolls. A price of $51 per ton is set for zone 4, and is used in the regulation as a base price to determine the actual prices in the 10 zones into which the United States is divided.

Price differentials for other zones, and for color, sheets, or special packing are frozen in the regulation at the levels prevailing during the period October 1 to October 15, 1941,

Gasoline, oil wholesale price allowed to rise in East

Acting to permit the petroleum industry to recover additional expenses incurred in moving petroleum and petroleum products eastward by high-cost transportation — substituted for tanker shipments curtailed by the war—Price Administrator Henderson on April 29 amended Revised Price Schedule No. 88 to permit increases over established maximum prices on the Eastern Seaboard for fuel oils and gasoline.

The increases permitted in the Amendment to Revised Price Schedule No. 88 on all fuels excluding service stations are:

Gasoline, 4/10¢ per gallon; tractor fuel, gas house oils, distillate Diesel fuel oils, Nos. 2, 3, and 4 fuel oils, 2/10¢ per gallon; No. 2 fuel oil in Washington tank wagon area, 2/10¢ per gallon; residual fuel oils (Nos. 5 and 6 fuel oils, Bunker C, Navy Grade and residual Diesel fuel oils), 25¢ per barrel.

The amendment, No. 10, effective April 28, 1942, affects sales of the products mentioned in Connecticut, Delaware, Maine, Maryland, Massachusetts, New Hampshire, New Jersey, New York, North Carolina, Pennsylvania, Rhode Island, South Carolina, Vermont, Virginia, West Virginia, Georgia, and Florida east of the Apalachicola River, and the District of Columbia. Bristol, Tenn., is included in provisions regulating gasoline prices under Amendment No. 3 to temporary maximum price regulation No. 11, issued April 27, 1942, and made effective as of April 30, 1942.

Maximum prices for Bunker C and No. 6 fuel oils on the East and Gulf coasts in cargo and barge lots f. o. b. refineries and terminals (ex lighterage) are also established by the amendment.

★ ★ ★

Metallic zinc allocation scheduled to begin June 1

Metallic zinc will be placed under complete allocation control beginning June 1, WPB announced May 1. Industry Operations Director Knowlson issued an amended Order M-1 setting up the zinc allocation plan. He issued at the same time Order M-11-a which places zinc oxide and zinc dust under the pool arrangement by which all zinc has been controlled heretofore.

Zinc pool for May

Zinc pool requirements for May also were issued May 1. The metallic zinc pool is set at 75 percent of January production for high grade and special high grade and 50 percent of January production of all other grades of zinc. Zinc oxide is set at 10 percent of January production. No zinc dust need be set aside for the month.

FAINSOD TO HEAD OPA RETAIL DIVISION

Appointment of Merle Fainsod as chief of the retail trade and services division of OPA was announced April 29 by Administrator Henderson.

Named as head of the trade relations branch in the new division was Hector Lazo.

The new division will work in close conjunction with the local boards in administering the details of the price control program. The trade relations branch will be responsible, among other things, for instructing the Nation's retailers in the specific requirements and procedures of the program and will confer and consult with retailers and representatives of retail trade associations.

★ ★ ★

OPA clarifies gasoline price base for East

For the purpose of clarifying the base upon which are calculated the permissible increases in maximum prices for gasoline on the eastern seaboard (above the retail level), Price Administrator Henderson has issued Amendment No. 8 to Revised Price Schedule No. 88 (Petroleum and Petroleum Products), effective April 29.

Amendment No. 4, issued last March 26, stipulated that gasoline sold in 15 States on the eastern seaboard and in the District of Columbia should not be priced in excess of 8/10 of a cent per gallon above the prices on October 1, 1941, and in Georgia and Florida east of the Apalachicola River not in excess of 5/10 of a cent above the prices on the same date.

Amendment No. 8 reestablishes as a base for calculating increases, the stipulations originally ordered in Revised Price Schedule No. 88.

★ ★ ★

Ceilings set on rolled zinc products

Maximum prices for rolled zinc products were announced April 30 by Price Administrator Henderson.

The prices established are those published by the Price Administrator on November 29, 1941, with slight changes in the prices of zinc, boiler, hull, and engravers' plates based upon the receipt of additional information subsequently by the OPA.

The maximum prices are contained in Maximum Price Regulation No. 124, which becomes effective May 11.

Makers' ceilings set on paperboard and specialty items

Maximum manufacturers' prices for specialty paperboard, and many processed paperboard items not covered previously, were established in Amendment No. 2 to Revised Price Schedule No. 32 (Paperboard Sold East of the Rocky Mountains) announced April 30 by Price Administrator Henderson following issuance of the General Maximum Price Regulation.

The amendment has the effect of establishing maximum manufacturers' prices for all paperboard, including specialty paperboards which were not included in the original schedule. The definition of "paperboard" has been expanded by the amendment to include "all kinds, grades, types, calipers, colors and patterns of paperboard."

★ ★ ★

Gasoline ceilings adjusted on some grades in Mid-West areas

Because prices used as standards in establishing maximum tank wagon prices for regular and third-grade gasoline in Midwest and Western territories were protested as not truly reflecting market quotations, Price Administrator Henderson April 29 issued Amendment No. 9 to Revised Price Schedule No. 88 for Petroleum and Petroleum Products. The amendment was effective April 29.

★ ★ ★

Woven cotton tickings put under formal ceiling

Woven cotton tickings, used chiefly in the manufacture of mattresses, pillows, and box springs, were placed under a formal price ceiling April 30 by Price Administrator Henderson through Amendment No. 2 to Revised Price Schedule No. 35—Carded Grey and Colored Yarn Goods.

★ ★ ★

Ceilings set on standard ferromanganese

Maximum prices for standard ferromanganese were fixed April 30 in Maximum Price Regulation No. 138 Price Administrator Henderson has announced.

Review of war contracts, now in progress promises large savings by adjustment, refund; costs drop as mass output begins

A method by which costs and profits on war contracts are being continuously reviewed by Government war agencies in order that savings made possible through mass production of war material will be reflected in savings to the Government was announced April 30 by WPB Chairman Nelson.

The method involves collaboration by the War Department, the Navy Department, the United States Maritime Commission and the War Production Board in studying war contracts and working out adjustments or refunds with the contractors in cases where costs or profits are found to be excessive.

3 discussions save $140,000,000

Direct savings to the Government which will be obtained in this way will be very substantial, Mr. Nelson said, pointing out that recent discussions with three contractors by the War and Navy Departments had resulted in savings of $140,-000,000. He added:

"In our war program we are calling on industrial firms to manufacture hundreds of articles which were never previously made on a mass production basis. It is perfectly obvious that as a company gets into mass production on such articles, its costs go down. But it is also obvious that it is not possible for a new contractor to know in advance just how much those costs are going to drop. It is also true that the primary objective of the procurement officers must be speed in production. Hence it is out of the question to delay signing of all war contracts until everyone is certain that costs and profits have been figured down to the most just and equitable level.

Many firms initiate talks

"The system which has been worked out by the Armed Services and the Maritime Commission, in consultation with the War Production Board, gets us around this difficulty. As production gets into full swing, both the contractor and the Government get a clearer picture of costs and are able to determine what constitutes a fair profit. Contracts are now being so examined in all cases where the agencies involved find it advisable. In cases where an excessive profit is found, the contract can be renegotiated at a lower figure—or, if the contract has

been performed, a refund can be arranged.

"I should like to point out that many business firms are coming in voluntarily to discuss this lowering of profit margins. Our experience so far reveals a very general realization among industrialists that there is no place in our war program for excessive profits."

By a joint memorandum signed by Under Secretary of War Robert P. Patterson, Under Secretary of Navy James Forrestal, Chairman E. S. Land of the Maritime Commission, and Mr. Nelson, a cost analysis section has been set up in each agency to conduct studies and surveys. In addition, price adjustment boards, on each of which the War Production Board is represented, have been established in the War and Navy Departments and in the Maritime Commission, to advise and assist the procurement officers in getting adjustments or refunds in all cases where costs or profits are found to be excessive.

★ ★ ★

$162,416,000,000 in war funds made available since June 1940

War funds made available by Congress or the Reconstruction Finance Corporation since June 1940 totaled $162,416,-000,000 when President Roosevelt signed the Sixth Supplemental War Appropriation Act of 1942 on April 28. This Act carried cash appropriations and net contract authorization of $19,138,000,000.

$8,761,000,000 for airplanes

The $162,416,000,000 total includes approximately $6,000,000,000 for the Navy Department, which does not become available for spending until fiscal 1943, and has not been allocated officially for specific purposes. The total does not include $4,096,000,000 contracted by foreign governments for war production in the United States.

The most important item of expenditure provided for in the latest appropriation is $8,761,000,000 for airplanes. Posts, depots and stations call for $6,-123,000,000, virtually double the amount previously appropriated for such purposes. Miscellaneous munitions and supplies covered in the Act came to $2,268,000,000.

1,000,000 making war material in plants which have Production Drive committees

More than one million men and women are producing war material in factories where joint labor-management Production Drive committees have been set up, Donald M. Nelson, WPB Chairman, said in a message April 30 to the Citizens for Victory Committee meeting in San Francisco.

The Citizens for Victory Committee is a nonpartisan national organization.

Pressure of his duties prevented Mr. Nelson from attending the meeting and a recording of his address was sent.

Excerpts from the text follow:

"I don't need to remind you that as far as we at home are concerned this is a war of production. The war is finally going to be won on the battlefields, of course, but we must never for one moment forget that it could easily be lost in the shops and factories of America. That puts a terrible responsibility on you and me. We're the people who could lose this war. And if by evil chance we should lose it, nobody would care to listen to us while we tried to blame each other for the defeat.

"We would all be guilty—management, labor, and Government alike; and the fires of defeat would quickly consume all of the rights, privileges, and liberties that we are so zealous to guard.

"I believe we have all learned that lesson by now. We know that unless we cheerfully work together for our own liberty we shall some day be forced to work together in slavery. We are up against something that is bigger than any of us. We know now what the price of freedom really is."

BANE LEAVES OPA

Relinquishment by Frank Bane of his temporary post with the OPA to return to the Council of State Governments was announced April 27 by Price Administrator Henderson.

Mr. Bane was lent to the OPA last November to develop a field organization plan. He was later induced to stay on in order to initiate this plan in principal cities, and again in January he agreed, at Mr. Henderson's insistence, to continue further with the OPA in order to set up the organization for rationing tires and other commodities.

Time to Take the Mountain to Mahomet

Cartoon by Elderman for OEM. Publishers may obtain mats of these cartoons weekly in either two- or three-column size. Requests to be put on the mailing list should be addressed to Distribution Section, Division of Information, Office for Emergency Management, 2743 Temporary R, Washington, D. C.

Dairy conservation program

Clyde E. Beardslee, chief of the WPB dairy section recommended on May 1, that the butter and ice cream industries curtail a number of services, discontinue the use of certain packages, and change some distribution methods to conserve materials for the war effort.

Mr. Beardslee said that the recommendations were adopted after conferences with the dairy industry advisory committee and have been approved by Douglas Townson, chief of the food supply branch.

* * *

Save cosmetic containers

American women can help the war effort by saving the increasingly precious metal containers in which they buy their lipsticks, their toiletries, and other beauty aids.

WPB consultants from industry help Services find factories, break bottlenecks

Donald M. Nelson, Chairman of the WPB, announced April 26 that facilities of American civilian industry which can be used to break bottlenecks in war production are being made available to the Armed Services and the Maritime Commission through special industrial consultants in the Bureau of Industry Branches.

Men thoroughly familiar with the existing machinery and facilities in their own industries have been brought into the Government service.

Chief function of these industrial consultants is to furnish information to Army, Navy, and Maritime Commission procurement officers about the types of war work which each industry can handle, both in prime and subcontracts. They do not, however, enter into any direct negotiations for placing orders.

Report on conversion coming

In announcing this industrial approach to the problems of conversion, Mr. Nelson said that first consideration must be given to efficiency in filling war orders. Time does not permit a detailed program of placing war orders with every company affected by a WPB limitation or conservation order.

The activities of the industrial consultants are therefore directed primarily toward finding existing facilities to speed the war effort. A progress report on the whole conversion program will be issued by WPB in the near future.

Consultants named

Consultants actively engaged in this program, with the business connections and the industries concerned, are as follows:

N. L. Etten, American Wringer Corporation, Woonsocket, R. I.—*Household Appliances;* D. G. Smellie, Hoover Vacuum Cleaner, North Canton, Ohio—*Household Appliances;* D. D. Burnside, American Stove Co., St. Louis, Mo.—*Stoves;* E. E. Berry, Beloit Iron Works, Beloit, Wis.—*Pulp and Paper Machinery;* S. H. Arnold, Atlas Steel & Tube, Warsaw, Ind.—*Metal Furniture;* W. E. Chollar, Remington Rand Co., Bridgeport, Conn.—*Office Machinery;* Alvin Haas, Yates American Co., Beloit, Wis.— *Wood Working Machinery;* Fred Erbach, Yates American Co., Beloit, Wis.—*Wood working Machinery;* John Lehman, Harris, Seybold, Potter Co., Cleveland, Ohio—*Printing Machinery;* R. G. Conklin, Vulcan Lead Products, Milwaukee, Wis.—*Lead Products;* A. P. Nichols, Jr., Kansas City Smelting Co., Kansas City, Mo.—*Lead Products;* C. C. Lincoln, Virginia Lincoln Furniture Co., Marion, Va.— *Wood Furniture;* Dr. A. B. Pacini, American Home Products, Jersey City, N. J.—*Toiletries and Cosmetics;* L. C. Wilkoff, Youngstown Steel Car Co., Youngstown, Ohio—*Car Building;* and Col. L. S. Horner, New Haven, Conn.— *Builders' Hardware.*

RATIONING . . .

Moving to ration autos faster, OPA relaxes standards of qualifying

In order to increase the flow of new passenger cars to eligible buyers and to assure more uniform treatment of applicants for automobile rationing certificates throughout the country, the Office of Price Administration has made changes in its automobile rationing regu-

lations, Administrator Henderson announced April 26.

This is in accordance with the Administrator's express policy of releasing all new passenger automobiles, except those in the Government "pool," within a 12-month period after the beginning of rationing on March 2 of this year. Sales so far under rationing have been at a rate considerably less than was expected at the time. quotas were allotted for March, April and May.

Standard of need relaxed

The new amendment revises completely the section of the automobile rationing order which requires an applicant to prove that he needs a new passenger automobile before a local rationing board may issue a certificate. The applicant must still prove that he needs a car to carry on efficiently essential civilian services or war work, but the standard of need has been simplified and relaxed.

An eligible applicant may establish need for an automobile by meeting any of the following conditions:

That he must travel quickly and would be better able to do so by automobile than by other means of transportation;

That he must transport passengers or heavy or bulky tools or materials;

That without a car he would have to walk at least 3 miles in going to and coming from work;

That he would have to spend at least 1½ hours in going to and coming from work without a car, and could save 45 minutes by using one;

That his work is arduous, or his hours unusually long, or that he must travel late at night;

That local transportation services are overcrowded;

That his physical condition would make it a hardship for him to walk or to use public transportation facilities;

That he clearly needs an automobile because of other unusual circumstances.

How to qualify

If the applicant fulfills one or more of the above conditions, he may qualify for a new car purchase certificate by showing that he does not already have an

---

TAKE CARE OF YOUR AUTO—Illustrations ("Drive Slowly," "Form a Car Pool") are from a WPB flier which is being distributed to motorists with cooperation of State motor vehicle departments. Other pictures on the flier get across these ideas: Drive less; grease often, check your oil; start right in cold weather; take care of your battery; protect the finish. Another page tells 10 ways to prolong tire life.

---

automobile adequate for his purposes. A board may decide that a car is inadequate if (a) it is a 1939 or earlier model; or (b) it has been driven more than 40,000 miles; or (c) it has been rendered unserviceable by fire, collision, or otherwise; or (d) it is not reliable enough for the services it is to perform; or (e) demands upon the applicant for the specified services have increased to such an extent that he needs an additional automobile to render such services.

These changes are brought about by Amendment No. 6 to the New Passenger Automobile Rationing Regulations, which was to go into effect April 29, 1942.

Henderson explains reasons

Commenting on the objectives of the new amendment, Mr. Henderson said:

When automobile rationing began there were some 535,000 new passenger automobiles in the hands of dealers, distributors, and manufacturers throughout the United States. It was then and still is our policy to distribute the major part of these cars—roughly 400,000 of them—during the first 12 months of the operation of the rationing system. The remainder—about 135,000—have been earmarked as a reserve pool to meet military and essential civilian needs thereafter.

We are fully aware that the reserve pool is pitifully small to meet our needs after March 1943. Requirements of the Military Services for passenger automobiles will increase next year. Police services must be expanded in certain areas, and thousands of additional cars will be necessary to transport workers to defense plants now under construction. In addition, we will have to replace automobiles that will be worn out or wrecked in important civilian services.

Nevertheless, two primary considerations make it appear desirable to distribute the major part of our passenger car stock over a relatively short period.

Storage taxed, cars depreciating

First, even though a serious scarcity of automobiles is in prospect due to the stoppage of production, the present stock of automobiles is taxing our storage facilities. Reduction of this stock will release warehouse space badly needed for storing other commodities.

Second, automobiles depreciate in storage even under the most favorable storage conditions. Some deterioration is bound to occur with the passage of time. The rate of depreciation is greater where the conditions of storage prevent occasional starting of motors and movements of cars. When automobiles are stored in open lots, exposed to the weather, as is now the case in some areas, depreciation is rapid unless exceptional precautions are taken.

The present amendment to the new Automobile Rationing Regulations results from reports received recently from State rationing administrators which indicate that new passenger automobiles are now moving at about 40 percent of the quota rate. By relaxing the age and mileage requirements for disposal and by establishing relatively liberal tests of need, this amendment undoubtedly will increase the flow of cars into the hands of eligible buyers.

There are, however, other factors which have held up the movement of automobiles. Some eligible persons who need to replace their cars are not doing so because they believe it to be unpatriotic.

To such people, I would like to say that there is nothing unpatriotic about replacing a car which is used to perform essential serv-

ices and which would have to be replaced next year or the year after. To the extent that we can equip those who need automobiles for the performance of essential services with the best available transportation, we will be cutting costs of storage and reducing next year's automobile requirements. Those who obtain new automobiles under the rationing program have, however, a special responsibility for using their cars sparingly, for driving slowly and carefully, and for keeping their automobiles and tires in the best condition possible.

The amendment to the New Passenger Automobile Rationing Regulations does not change the list of eligible services

WPB authorizes 700,000-ton Buna S synthetic rubber program

The WPB has authorized the Reconstruction Finance Corporation to provide facilities for an annual productive capacity of 700,000 tons of Buna S synthetic rubber to be in operation not later than the end of 1943, it was announced April 25 by WPB Chief Donald M. Nelson and Coordinator for Rubber Arthur B. Newhall.

Assured of priority aid

This represents an increase of 100,000 tons in the Buna S program previously authorized by the WPB, and is in addition to the planned capacity for Butyl synthetic rubber and neoprene, totalling 100,000 tons.

The WPB said that the 700,000-ton Buna S program is to be given all the priority and allocation assistance needed to assure the production of not less than 350,000 tons during the calendar year of 1943.

All the synthetic rubber to be produced for many months must be reserved for military uses, and none will be available for civilian uses, such as automobile tires.

Check on tire and tube rationing shows some margin below quotas

Figures released by the OPA April 29 on the amount of tire and tube rationing quotas actually used in January reveal a small but important offset to the serious deterioration that has taken place in the Nation's rubber position since that month's allotments were established.

In the 40 States and the District of Columbia for which January reports are available, certificates issued for new passenger car tires amounted to 45 percent of the combined total of their quotas and the reserves which are set aside in each State for adjustment of emergency situations. A slightly higher percentage of truck tire quotas was used.

These preliminary figures indicating a margin of quota allotment over actual use were welcomed by officials in the OPA tire rationing division, who point out that any saving at this time can be looked upon as an addition to the vitally important inventory for later use.

10,000,000 automobile owners in 17 Eastern States must show ration card to buy gasoline after May 15

The cards by which nearly 10,000,000 passenger-car owners in 17 Eastern States will make their gasoline purchases under rationing after May 15, were described April 28 by the OPA.

Five different ration cards

The cards, as well as the application forms which some gasoline users will be asked to fill out, will be distributed to school registration sites throughout the rationed area before May 12, when registration begins.

Five different ration cards have been prepared, and owners of motor vehicles and inboard motorboats will receive at registration time the type of card for which they qualify. The cards are designated as "A," "B-1," "B-2," "B-3," and "X" cards and are intended to last users to whom they are issued through the 45-day period, from May 15 to July 1, in which the temporary plan announced the previous week will be in effect.

"A" or basic allotment card

No application form whatever will be needed to obtain the "A," or basic allotment card. Owners may receive one of these upon presentation of their car registration cards.

Across the bottom of the "A" card are seven squares, each good for one "unit" of gasoline. The gallonage value of each unit will be announced before May 15. The holder of an "A" card may use up his "units" as fast as he wishes, but he is warned that he will not be eligible for another "A" card after his "units" are gone. The squares on the card will be punched, marked, or torn off by the service station attendant as purchases are made.

Instructions issued with all cards point out that only after the registration dates can the local rationing boards make adjustments, or issue different cards to registered gasoline users.

More units on "B" cards

The "B" cards resemble the "A" cards, except for the number of "unit" squares. The "B-1" card has 11 units; the "B-2" card, 15 units; and the "B-3" card 19 units. The value of these units will also be announced before rationing begins.

In applying for one of the "B" cards an owner must fill out at the time of registration the "B" application form, as well as present the registration card of the motor vehicle for which gasoline is needed.

The information to go on the "B" application will show the applicant's need for more gasoline than he could obtain with an "A" card. Specifically, it will ask for the exact nature of the applicant's work (gainful occupation). Other questions that must be answered are: "If you drive to work, what is the shortest mileage from your home to your regular place of work, or commuting point?" "How many miles do you drive each working day in carrying on your work (other than from home to work and back)?" "What is the total average daily mileage customarily driven in the car described above to get to and from work and to carry on work?" "Are you making every possible effort to reduce this mileage by using public transportation and by 'doubling-up' with your neighbors?"

The applicant will certify that the gasoline obtained with the ration card will be used solely in the motor vehicle described in the application and will not be used for any other purpose.

"X" card "for essential use"

The applicant for an "X" card, which entitles the holder to whatever gasoline he needs "for essential use," must also fill out an "X" application form.

Legitimate uses, which make an owner eligible for an "X" card are listed on the application as follows: (a) As an ambulance, or hearse; (b) as a taxi, bus, jitney or other public conveyance for hire, or as a vehicle available for public rental; (c) for a regularly practicing minister of a religious faith, in the performance of religious duties in meeting the religious needs of the congregation served; (d) for a duly licensed physician, nurse, osteopath, chiropractor, or veterinarian for rendering medical, professional, nursing, or veterinary services; (e) for the official business of Federal, State, local or foreign governments or government agencies; (f) for trucking, hauling, towing, freight-carrying, mail carrying, delivery, or messenger service; (g) for the transportation of materials and equipment for construction or for mechanical, electrical, structural, or highway maintenance or repair work; or for transportation of work crews to enable them to render such services.

Inboard motorboat owners must fill out a form to obtain either the "A" or "X" cards. An "A" card will be issued if the craft is used for nonessential purposes; an "X" card will be issued if the boat is used for specific commercial purposes listed on the application form.

Other gasoline rationing forms prepared by the OPA will (1) serve persons wishing to replace lost, or damaged, ration cards, (2) authorize the transfer of gasoline for use other than in motor vehicles or inboard motorboats, (3) authorize bulk gasoline transfer for ultimate consumption in motor vehicles and inboard motorboats.

Tires to be denied to those who abuse them; recaps will be required where practical

New tires will not be available for list A vehicles after May 1, when use of a recapped tire is practical, and no tires at all will be released after June 1 to anyone who abuses those he now has in use.

These provisions are contained in Amendment No. 7 to the Revised Tire Rationing Regulations, announced April 30 by Price Administrator Henderson. Effective date of the amendment was May 1.

In the case of vehicles operated in hazardous services where the safety factor is a consideration, the local rationing board may issue a new tire certificate. Although this provision is primarily to take care of police and fire vehicles, it is considered broad enough to cover other list A eligibles when the board is convinced of their need for new tires.

After June 1, anyone who presents an inspector's report that a tire cannot be made fit for recapping or retreading will be called upon to show that it did not become unusable through abuse or neglect.

★ ★ ★

TRAILER TOW VEHICLES ELIGIBLE FOR TIRES

Vehicles used to tow house trailers from the factory to sites where they are necessary as living quarters for war workers will be eligible for tires under A of the rationing regulations after May 1, Price Administrator Henderson announced April 30. The tow car must not be used for other than list A purposes, and the length of haul for a house trailer is limited to 200 miles. However, on written consent of the State rationing administrator, a local board may issue a certificate where the distance limit is exceeded. A further provision prohibits issuance of a certificate when it is practicable to move the trailers by rail.

Heavy truck tires provided

WPB has made it possible to equip heavy trucks produced under existing quotas with tires and tubes. Amendment No. 7 to Limitation Order No. L-1-a, effective April 25, rescinds the prohibition against putting tires and tubes on new heavy trucks except for delivery to dealers.

58 SPECIALISTS AID RATIONING IN FIELD

The appointment of 58 specialists to aid in handling the problems which will arise in the sugar-rationing program, which went into effect on April 28, was announced April 30 by OPA Administrator Henderson. They will serve as technical aides in the offices which are maintained in the 48 States and the District of Columbia as well as in the 8 regional offices through which the rationing program is administered.

★ ★ ★

Excess sugar inventories not to be maintained

Retail grocers will not be permitted to maintain stocks of sugar they now have on hand which are in excess of the amount of sugar allowed them as working inventories under the rationing regulations, the OPA said May 1.

While no grocer is required to surrender any present excess sugar inventory, he cannot accept any future delivery of sugar until he has first turned over to his local rationing board for cancelation War Ration Stamps or Sugar Purchase Certificates with a weight value equal to the excess amount.

The same principle applies to wholesalers who have present inventories in excess of their allowable inventories.

★ ★ ★

If you eat in a boarding house . . .

Among the establishments classified by OPA as institutional users of sugar are hotels, restaurants, resorts, fraternities, sororities, dormitories, hospitals, boarding houses, orphanages, convents, monasteries, and State institutions such as prisons and asylums.

Persons who reside or eat their meals in buildings classified as institutions were to register or be registered the same as other consumers in the registration on May 4, 5, 6, and 7.

Consumers who eat 12 or more meals a week in an establishment registered as an institutional user are required to surrender their War Ration Books to the owner or manager of the establishment in order to permit removal of the sugar ration stamps for cancelation by the local rationing board.

"Off-sale" baked goods to get 70 percent of 1941 sugar

OPA on April 27 issued a clarification of sugar rationing regulations as they apply to restaurants manufacturing baked goods or other products for off-sale purposes.

According to OPA, restaurants which in 1941 manufactured products for sale off the premises may receive for that purpose 70 percent of the amount of sugar they used during the corresponding month last year. This regulation applies to the off-sale portion of their business only.

For use in making baked goods or other products for consumption on the premises—as meals or food services—restaurants preparing and serving meals may obtain 50 percent of last year's sugar usage.

★ ★ ★

School teachers commended for handling of sugar registration

Price Administrator Henderson April 30 expressed his gratitude to the thousands of public school teachers throughout the country who conducted the 2-day trade registration for sugar rationing.

★ ★ ★

Ocean shipmasters to get sugar by signing receipts

An ocean-going vessel may for the time being obtain the sugar it needs for the voyage on which it is embarking without a sugar purchase certificate, OPA said April 30.

All that is necessary is that the master of the vessel sign a receipt for the amount of sugar delivered.

The person delivering the sugar can then present this receipt to his local rationing board and receive in exchange a sugar purchase certificate which will permit him to acquire an amount of sugar equal to that delivered to the ship.

★ ★ ★

First industrial sugar quota April 28 or 29 to June 30

The first allotments of sugar to industrial and institutional users—under the new Nation-wide rationing program—were to cover the period from the time of registration, April 28 or 29, to June 30, 1942, OPA announced.

LABOR . . .

President gives Board job of stabilizing wages; labor members to handle jurisdictional disputes for the duration

The National War Labor Board last week received a new job from the President—to stabilize wages—and it set up a system for final settlement of all jurisdictional disputes between labor unions for the duration of the war.

President Roosevelt gave the Board the job of stabilizing wages when he outlined to Congress his 7-point program to keep the cost of living down.

"In respect to the third item," the President said, "seeking to stabilize remuneration for work, legislation is not required under present circumstances. I believe that stabilizing the cost of living will mean that wages in general can and should be kept at existing scales.

"Organized labor has voluntarily given up its right to strike during the war. Therefore all stabilization or adjustment of wages will be settled by the War Labor Board machinery which has been *generally accepted by industry and labor for the settlement of all disputes.*

"All strikes are at a minimum. Existing contracts between employers and employees must, in all fairness, be carried out to the expiration date of those contracts. The existing machinery for labor disputes will, of course, continue to give due consideration to inequalities and the elimination of substandards of living. I repeat that all of these processes, now in existence, will work equitably for the overwhelming proportion of all our workers if we can keep the cost of living down and stabilize their remuneration."

An interdepartmental committee consisting of representatives of the War, Navy, and Labor Departments, the War Production Board, the Maritime Commission, the new Manpower Commission, and the War Labor Board was formed to work in cooperation with the War Labor Board in this difficult task. The committee was created as a result of a conference of high-ranking officials of the agencies involved which was called by Board Chairman William H. Davis to discuss the President's message.

Jurisdictional disputes to be settled

Jurisdictional disputes between labor unions coming to the Board will be re-ferred to the labor members of the Board for settlement from now on, Mr. Davis, Board Chairman, announced. The procedure was evolved as a result of an agreement between William Green, president of the American Federation of Labor, and Philip Murray, president of the Congress of Industrial Organizations.

The jurisdictional disputes agreement will dispose not only of disputes between unions affiliated with the two national organizations, but also disputes between unions within either the AFL or CIO which affect the war effort.

"All jurisdictional questions in cases coming before the War Labor Board," Mr. Davis announced, "will be referred as a matter of course to the labor members of the Board for adjustment.

"If any particular dispute cannot be settled by the labor members, Mr. Murray and Mr. Green will be so notified and they will thereupon promptly appoint a group or individual to make a final and binding determination of the dispute.

"Jurisdictional disputes have always been the most difficult to settle because of their very nature. The American people will welcome this agreement between the two labor organizations for finally determining all jurisdictional disputes until the war is won."

Harvester Company accepts

Mr. Davis last week congratulated the International Harvester Co. on behalf of the Board for its decision to accept a maintenance of membership clause ordered by the Board April 15. The Board is still awaiting word from the United States Steel Corporation that it has accepted a similar clause ordered by the Board in the case of its subsidiary, the Federal Shipbuilding & Drydock Co.

News of the acceptance by this giant farm equipment concern, after deliberation by its board of directors for more than 2 weeks, came in the form of a telegram from Fowler McCormick, company president. In the telegram Mr. McCormick stated that the company "will fully comply" with the Board's decision.

Thomas Fair Neblett, principal mediation officer of the Board, is now in Chicago, setting up machinery to hold secret ballot elections in eight of the company's plants on this clause, Mr. Davis announced. The clause would require all members of the union to maintain their membership in good standing for the duration of the contract. Only members of the majority union in each plant will be eligible to vote.

"I hope and believe," Mr. Davis said in a telegram to the company president, "that under the new contract the relations between your company and its employees will advance toward that cooperative understanding and mutual confidence upon which maximum production depends."

The elections are believed to be the first strictly intraunion elections ever to be held under the auspices of the agency of the Federal Government. The 8 plants employ 25,000 workers.

Complete contract drawn up

The Board unanimously settled the dispute between the Arcade Malleable Iron Co, Inc,. Worcester, Mass., and the Steel Workers Organizing Committee, CIO, by ordering both parties to accept a collective bargaining contract drawn up by the 3-man panel of the Board which heard the case. A total of 400 employees are affected. This marks the first time the Board has had to draw up a complete contract.

The contract drawn up by the panel was sent to both parties. The union signed it, but the company rejected it. The panel then adopted the contract as its unanimous recommendation for a "fair and equitable" settlement of the dispute and referred the matter to the whole Board.

˄ ˄ ˄

WENDELL LUND NAMED LABOR PRODUCTION DIRECTOR

Wendell Lund of Detroit will head the new Labor Production Division of the WPB, Chairman Donald M. Nelson announced May 1.

WPB operations having to do with labor relations and staff activities bearing on production will be continued without interruption, Nelson said.

Lund, 36 years old and a native of Escanaba, Mich., has been executive director of the Michigan Unemployment Compensation Commission during the recent automobile conversion program and is conversant with the Labor Division activities of the WPB.

INDUSTRIAL OPERATIONS...

Production of storage batteries cut for autos, light trucks, to save vital items

The WPB April 26 announced a program to conserve substantial quantities of lead, antimony, rubber, and other critical materials going into the manufacture of storage batteries for passenger automobiles and light trucks.

Sizes and models cut from 75 to 15

In Supplementary Limitation Order L-4-b, the Board:

1. Prohibited production of these batteries after April 30 except in specified minimum ampere hour capacities, thereby reducing the number of sizes and models now being produced from about 75 to 15. This will in no way affect the normal life of a battery.
2. Curtailed production by each manufacturer during the 6 months from April to September 30 to 75 percent of the number of batteries sold by him during the corresponding period of 1941.
3. Ordered retailers to cease selling or delivering after April 30 any new replacement battery to any purchaser unless the purchaser turns in a used battery at the time of the transaction.
4. Placed rigid restrictions on inventories of producers, retailers, jobbers, and warehouses, in order to avoid tying up critical materials.

Quota modified for second quarter

Terms of the order do not apply to batteries produced for the Army and Navy, certain other Government agencies, certain foreign governments, and Lend-Lease requirements.

The limitation on production during the second and third quarters of this year supersedes, as affects the second quarter, the production quota fixed for the first 6 months of this year under Amendment No. 1 to Limitation Order L-4-a, which covered all replacement parts for automobiles and light trucks. Under that order, battery manufacturers were authorized to produce during the 6-month period up to 150 percent of the number of batteries they sold for replacement purposes during 1941.

Inventories restricted

Producers may manufacture, before May 31, batteries from materials on hand at the present time in minimum ampere hour capacities other than those specified, provided no additional material is required and the material on hand cannot be used in batteries of the specified capacities.

No producer is permitted to have in inventory on the first day in any month a stock of batteries in excess of the number sold by him during the 60 day

period in 1941 corresponding to the 60-day period following the date of the inventory.

Retailers, jobbers, and warehouses are prohibited from ordering more than a 45 days' supply of batteries or accepting delivery of batteries which, in combination with existing inventory, will aggregate more than a 45 days' supply. In any month, a 45 days' supply means the number of batteries sold during the corresponding month last year plus one-half the number sold in the next succeeding month in 1941.

The order places a 30-day limit on the time producers, retailers, jobbers, and warehouses may keep used, traded-in, imperfect or condemned batteries, or parts for them, in inventory, in their possession or under their control.

★ ★ ★

Curb on use of scrap and reclaimed rubber continued

Use of scrap and reclaimed rubber during May in a specific list of articles will continue to be limited to 60 percent of a formula based on average monthly use over a base period, Director of Industry Operations Knowlson announced April 27.

It was ordered on March 20 that after May 1, products on list F of rubber order M-15-b could be made only with the prior approval of the Director of Industry Operations. Since information on which specific allotments could be based has not yet been developed, this date has been postponed to June 1 by Amendment No. 9.

List F includes automotive parts, fan belts, business machine rolls, parts for motor-driven electrical apparatus, and certain other items generally used in industry.

The use of scrap or reclaimed rubber which is permitted by the formula for the month of May is 60 percent of an amount comprising the average monthly consumption of reclaimed or scrap in List F products during the last quarter of 1941, plus 166⅔ percent of the average monthly consumption of crude rubber or latex in the List F products in the same period.

Metal windows authorized for certain rated housing projects

Limitation Order L-77 on metal windows has been amended to permit the manufacture of basement windows and residential-type casements for use in certain rated housing projects.

The amendment, effective April 28, authorizes the manufacture of metal windows composed wholly of materials in a manufacturer's inventory prior to March 25 for use in a project to which a preference rating has been assigned by Order P-55 (Defense Housing), Order P-19-d (Publicly Financed Housing) or Order P-110 (Remodeling of Houses in a Defense Area).

This is permitted whether or not the preference rating has been extended to the order or contract for the purchase of the metal windows.

The amendment also permits the manufacture until May 15 of any metal window pursuant to an order received on or before March 25, if the window is for use in a rated project. The provision of the original order which permitted the manufacture of any metal window to fill an order with an A-2 or higher rating is continued by the amendment.

Sale and delivery restricted

After May 1, deliveries of material for the manufacture of metal windows may not be made except under the Production Requirements Plan.

Sale and delivery of metal windows is permitted only for the following purposes:

1. On an order or contract rated A-10 or higher.
2. Until May 31, sale and delivery is permitted on orders received on or before March 25, if the window is for use in a rated project.
3. For use in a project to which a preference rating has been assigned by the three Housing orders mentioned above.
4. Any manufacturer or distributor may sell and deliver any metal window to any other manufacturer or distributor.

~ ~ ~

WINDBLOWN FOR VICTORY

The WPB has restricted the amount of metal to be incorporated in hairpins and bobpins and regulated their length and thickness in order to obtain the maximum number of such articles from the amount of metal that may be used.

The order is L-104, effective April 25.

Fancy painting and finishing of metal-working machinery banned

Fancy painting and finishing of metal-working machinery by machine tool builders were to be banned after April 30, the WPB announced April 27.

Limitation Order No. L-108, effective April 27, provides that only one coat of primer or sealer may be applied to new metal-working equipment. No filler may be applied and not more than two coats of paint, enamel, or lacquer may be used. Any color other than "old machine-tool gray" for the final coat of paint is prohibited.

The order was issued, the Board stated, to reduce the time required for delivery of machine tools and to free the space now used for finishing, for more productive work.

★ ★ ★

"High wine" placed under complete allocation

Beverage alcohol from 100 to 189 proof, known in industry as "high wine," April 28 was placed under complete allocation control so it can be used to augment the Nation's industrial alcohol supply.

Amendment No. 1 to Order M-69 requires distillers to deliver specified quantities to rectifying plants for redistillation into 190 proof alcohol.

Each producer also is required to report to the chemicals branch, WPB, the quantity of high wine his distillery is capable of producing and his entire storage facilities.

★ ★ ★

FORMAL FLUORSPAR CEILINGS

Formal price ceilings for fluorspar at levels generally prevailing on January 2, 1942, were announced April 30 by Price Administrator Henderson.

The maximum prices—contained in Maximum Price Regulation No. 126—become effective May 11.

An informal price ceiling for fluorspar, coinciding for the most part with the new formal maximums, has been observed since January 20, when all persons known to be producing and milling this crystalline mineral were requested not to exceed their prices of January 2.

The Price Administrator said that the formal regulation was necessary to prevent price increases and to limit the prices of individuals or companies that had not complied with the informal request.

Fluorspar is important to the war effort by reason of its uses, among others, in the manufacture of synthetic cryolite for making aluminum, and as a flux in the manufacture of steel and ferro-alloys.

MAGNESIUM CONTROL EXTENDED

The Director of Industry Operations on April 25 extended until October 31 Order M-2-b, which provides for complete allocation of magnesium. The order was due to expire on April 30.

.. .. ..

GAS EQUIPMENT ORDER CLARIFIED

An exemption paragraph in Limitation Order L-86, governing the installation of liquefied petroleum gas equipment, was clarified April 27 in an official interpretation issued by the Director of Industry Operations.

The paragraph in question exempts from the terms of the order equipment "installed and in actual use prior to April 1, 1942 . . . subsequently withdrawn from such use." The interpretation makes it clear that only equipment withdrawn *after* April 1, 1942, is exempt.

.. .

Use of A-1-c for mining machine repairs clarified

An amendment to Preference Rating Order P-56 issued April 13, 1942, added explosives and explosive equipment to the list of mining machinery and equipment in Schedule A of the order. This enables mine operators who have serial numbers under the order to use an A-1-c rating in obtaining repair parts for such equipment.

Not for ordinary operating supplies

To clear up some confusion which has arisen as a result of this amendment, Dr. Wilbur A. Nelson, administrator of the mining branch, explained April 28 that the A-1-c rating is applicable for repairs to blasting machines and similar machinery and equipment, but that the rating may not be used for ordinary operating supplies such as black powder and dynamite, to which the A-8 rating remains applicable.

Mines which do not operate under P-56 may use an A-10 rating under the general repair, maintenance and operating supplies order, P-100, to obtain explosives. The amendment to P-56 does not affect any existing priorities on explosives and explosive equipment, nor does it prevent any mine operator from obtaining explosives in the same way as before the amendment was issued.

General Motors punished on charge of using chrome, aluminum for decoration

General Motors Corporation, Detroit, Mich., was cited May 1 by the WPB for wartime violation of priority regulations in a suspension order charging prohibited uses of substantial quantities of scarce materials.

Suspension Order S-53 states that between January 7 and March 9, 1942, the Ternstedt Manufacturing Division of General Motors used 10,259 pounds of chrome steel in the manufacture of decorative mouldings for automobiles, and that between January 24 and March 13, 1942, it used 9,239 pounds of primary aluminum and 11,492 pounds of secondary aluminum to produce radiator grills and other body hardware, in violation of Supplementary Orders M-1-e and M-21-d.

The suspension order, effective May 2, prohibits General Motors Corporation from manufacturing or producing any replacement parts for passenger automobiles, light, medium, and heavy trucks, truck trailers, passenger carriers, and school bus bodies other than functional replacement parts as defined in General Preference Orders P-57 and P-107. The order is effective for three months.

At the same time, the WPB announced that it had investigated complaints received from various sources that Ternstedt also was using large quantities of copper, nickel and zinc in violation of WPB orders. The investigation showed that Ternstedt's use of these metals did not violate any then existing orders.

★ ★ ★

Dairy processors must use repair ratings before June 30

The WPB April 27 amended Preference Rating Order No. P-118 to restrict application of preference ratings by dairy processors to orders for repair, maintenance and operating materials for use before June 30, 1942, when the order expires.

★ ★ ★

RADIOSONDES ORDER EXTENDED

Preference Rating Order No. P-38 covering materials for the production of radiosondes was extended April 29 to June 30, 1942, by the WPB. The order, issued February 26, 1941, and amended February 18, 1942, was due to expire April 30.

WPB cuts coffee deliveries to 75 percent; war need for ships might affect supply

WPB on April 28 placed restrictions on the distribution of the United States entire coffee supply.

The order reduces the amount of coffee which may be delivered by roasters and the amount which may be accepted by wholesale receivers during any month to 75 percent of deliveries during the corresponding period of 1941.

Ships needed for war

This action was taken to conserve supplies now on hand for the Army, Navy, and civilian population and to make future supplies go as far as possible. The war has created uncertainties about future supplies, since merchant ships that normally transport coffee are needed to carry war materials.

Practically all coffee received in the United States comes from 14 South and Central American countries, with Brazil and Colombia alone supplying about 75 percent of the total. Present stocks of green coffee in this country are about normal.

Conservation Order M–135, issued April 28, specifically requires roasters and wholesalers not to discriminate between customers. The direct order does not attempt control at consumer levels, but receivers affected by the order are expected to pass the cut along to their customers as equitably as possible.

Provisions of orders

Order M–135 and Supplementary Order M–135–a, which fixes the percentage of the reduction in deliveries, restrict the amount of coffee which may be delivered by a roaster or by anyone who has green coffee owned by him roasted by another person. The amount of coffee which may be accepted by a wholesaler, jobber, or any representative of a retail system of four or more stores is similarly restricted. "Wholesale receivers," as defined in the orders, include retailers or other users (such as restaurants), whose purchases during 1941 averaged 2,000 pounds or more of coffee per month.

Each month, until further notice, a coffee roaster may deliver 75 percent of his average monthly deliveries in the corresponding quarter of 1941. The quota also applies, on a pro rata basis, to deliveries during the rest of April. Deliveries against the quota for any month may be begun not more than ten days before the first day of that month.

Inventories under control

A wholesale receiver may not accept delivery of any coffee which, together with his stock on hand, would bring his total inventory above the amount of his monthly quota. If any receiver now has on hand more than his monthly quota of coffee, he may not accept further deliveries until the excess is disposed of at a rate corresponding to the amount he may receive under the quota.

If a wholesale receiver is also a roaster, he does not need to include in the calculation of his inventory any coffee which has already been roasted, or coffee which has been delivered to retail stores.

Quota-exempt deliveries of coffee may be made to certain agencies and persons directly connected with the war program. These include:

The Army, Navy, Defense Supplies Corporation, Veterans' Administration hospital and homes, and any Lend-Lease agency; the American Red Cross and the United Service Organizations; operators of oceangoing vessels; and operators of camp restaurants, post exchanges, and similar camp or ship services for soldiers and sailors.

★ ★ ★

Production and sale of protective helmets curbed

Production and sale of protective helmets, except on order by an agency of the United States or by one of the other United Nations, was forbidden by the WPB April 29 to prevent the waste of critical materials and the manufacture of helmets not conforming to safety standards.

A protective helmet is defined in Limitation Order No. L–105, effective April 29, to include any head covering intended for civilian use during air raids. The term does not include industrial, official, police, fire department, or other helmets not represented as a means of civilian protection from the hazards of war.

★ ★ ★

Worrell succeeds Luke on pulp and paper committee

Rufus I. Worrell, president of Mead Sales Corporation, Chillicothe, Ohio, has been appointed to the pulp and paper industry advisory committee. He succeeds D. L. Luke, Jr.

★ ★ ⌐

Use of totaquine banned except as antimalaria agent

Distribution and use of totaquine, except as an antimalaria agent, was prohibited by WPB April 30 in order to prevent an evasion of the intent of Conservation Order M–131 on quinine.

It was pointed out by the health supplies branch that after issuance of the original quinine order on April 4, some drug manufacturers began to use totaquine, which was not covered by the terms of the order, for the same purpose for which quinine had been prohibited.

Tea quota alternative relieves seasonal hardship

WPB on May 1 issued an amendment to the tea order (M–111) and a new supplementary order (M–111–b), relaxing some of the distribution provisions of the original order.

The amendment will make available more tea than would have been available under the original order. The percentage delivery to dealers remains the same—that is, 50 percent of deliveries in a 1941 base period—but the amended order makes allowance for irregularities in delivery schedules which would have penalized some dealers unduly under the terms of the original order.

The amended order redefines a receiver; provides alternative base periods for computing quotas for May and June, to take care of the seasonal marketing of tea; includes bulk tea as well as packed tea; enables a packer to sell tea to any receiver; extends quota exemptions on deliveries of tea to the following agencies and persons connected with the war program: The Veterans' Administration hospitals and homes; the American Red Cross and the United Service Organizations; operators of oceangoing vessels; and operators of camp restaurants, post exchanges, and similar camp or ship services for soldiers and sailors. Originally, quota-exempt deliveries were permitted only for the Army, Navy, and Lend-Lease agencies.

One of the alternative bases for computing monthly quotas is the same as in the original order. That is, the quotas for May and June are 50 percent, each month, of average monthly deliveries in the corresponding calendar quarter of 1941.

The other alternative basis is 25 percent, for each of the months of May and June, of the difference between deliveries in the first six months of 1941 and the first four months of 1942. This alternative takes care of situations, particularly in the South, where deliveries are seasonal because of the popularity of iced tea.

⌐

Crown cap change rescinded

Amendment No. 1 to Conservation Order M–104 on glass container closures, issued April 23, was rescinded April 25 by the Director of Industry Operations.

This action, effected by Amendment No. 2 to the order, was taken because adequate time was not provided for crown cap manufacturers to secure certificate forms for the shipment of caps with cork discs as required by Amendment No. 1.

Terms of the original order thus again govern the manufacture of crown caps for use on beer and beverage bottles. Production of crown caps made of tinplate and terneplate for these bottles was permitted to the extent that cork was available until May 1, after which date such production was to end.

All heavy sole leather set aside for military use

WPB on April 25 ordered the entire stock and production of heavyweight sole leather set aside to meet military and Lend-Lease requirements for shoes. Previously, 80 percent of such sole leathers was set aside, but that was found insufficient.

The WPB leather and shoe section explained that only heavyweight outersole leather is affected by the order, leaving for civilian shoes the entire supply of ordinary and lightweight outersoles, the kind of soles used for most civilian purposes except in heavy work shoes.

During the coming months, the demand for civilian shoes is not expected to be as great as it was in 1941 because thousands of men who were in civilian life last year are now in the Army. Moreover, indications are that stores and consumers already have large stocks of shoes on hand. In addition, the number of cattle on American farms now is close to an all-time high, and cattle slaughter in 1942 is expected to be at record proportions, increasing the potential leather supply.

Cotton textile orders for industrial tape get A-2 rating

In order to assure an adequate supply of industrial cloth or tape, indispensable as insulation in electrical cables and for other essential purposes, the WPB has issued an order (M-134) assigning a preference rating of A-2 to purchase orders for cotton textile fabrics from which tape is made.

Quick-freeze refrigerators not covered by L-5 orders

The WPB orders in the L-5 series governing the production and sales of domestic mechanical refrigerators do not apply to a low temperature mechanical refrigerator designed for the storage of frozen foods or for the quick-freezing of food, when the low temperature compartment contains more than 75 percent of the total refrigeration space, WPB said April 25 in an amendment (No. 2) to the order. Quick-freeze refrigerators will be covered by another order.

Men's, boys' clothing, imports included, must follow amended rules after May 30

All men's and boys' clothing sold or delivered in this country after May 30, 1942, must comply with the restrictions of the War Production Board except for clothing put into the process of manufacture before May 30. The only exception to this ruling is second-hand clothing.

While the manufacture in this country of men's and boys' clothing has been subject to WPB wool conservation restrictions since March 30 under General Conservation Order M-73-a, the original order did not apply to men's and boys' clothing imported from other countries. The order as amended April 27 will make it necessary for clothing manufacturers outside this country to comply with the simplification order if their products are to be sold or delivered in this country. The recently issued WPB Order L-85 contains the same provision for clothing for women and girls.

Replaces original order

The order as amended April 27, which replaces the original M-73-a, in general follows the lines of the original order. However, it provides some new restrictions and removes some of the restrictions in the original order.

Changes include the following:

1. Lumberjackets and mackinaws, not included in the original order, are brought under the restrictions. The maximum length of a lumberjacket is the same as a sackcoat—29¾ inches for a size 37 regular, 24¾ inches for a boy's size 14, with other sizes in normal proportions. The maximum length for a man's mackinaw is 32 inches. For a boy's size 18 it is 30 inches, with other sizes in normal proportions. Unlined lumberjackets and mackinaws are permitted to have two lower inside patch pockets of wool.

2. The amendment permits coats and overcoats to have a two-piece back with belt stitched on in such a way that there is no overlay of wool cloth on wool cloth greater than a half inch on the upper and the lower side of the belt. This is intended primarily for lumberjackets and mackinaws but may be used on other coats and overcoats.

Religious garb exempt

3. Restrictions of the order are removed as to clothing, robes and vestments of religious orders or sects, and to historical costumes for theatrical performances.

4. Leisure and loafer coats, work pants, slack-suit trousers, work overcoats, fingertip coats, and similar type garments are specifically mentioned in the order as coming under restrictions. A WPB interpretation of Amendment No. 1 of the original order mentioning them by name already made it clear that they were covered.

5. A new category is set up under boys' clothing to include sizes from 2 to 10, inclusive, corresponding with a similar category for girls' clothing in order L-85. This new section of the order provides that:

(a) In sizes 2 to 10, a suit, jacket, mackinaw, topcoat, or overcoat may not be made with separate or attached hood, scarf, helmet, cap, mittens, gloves, or purse of the same or matching material. However, a mackinaw or a jacket may have an attached hood if it is made without a collar.

(b) A snow or ski suit in sizes 2 to 10, inclusive, may not have a wool cloth lining, a separate or detachable hood, a collar if an attached hood is used, an attached hood of wool cloth lined with wool cloth, more than one pair of pants or leggings, self or contrasting wool belt more than two inches wide, or separate or attached cape, muff, scarf, bag, hat, coat, or mittens of the same or matching material.

Tailors' cuffs banned May 9

6. The amendment advances from May 30 to May 9 the effective date of the cuff prohibition on merchant tailors and tailors-to-the-trade. The original order provided that the restrictions under the order, effective on March 30 for manufacturers, would not become effective as to these tailors until May 30. The two-month extension was given to tailors to put them on an equality with clothing merchants who, it was thought, had on hand a two-month supply of ready-made clothing manufactured prior to the issuance of the simplification order. This, however, gave tailors an advantage in the matter of finishing trousers with cuffs and also was a source of many attempted violations of the order. The amendment was intended to put an end to that advantage, but gave these tailors more than a week to make arrangements to put orders on hand into process, which will allow them to be completed without any kind of restrictions.

The amendment also limits the turn-up at the bottom of trousers to three inches. Since the purpose of the no-cuff provision is to save wool cloth, nothing would be gained if the equivalent of a cuff were used in the turn-up.

Curb on iron, steel continued for domestic cooking appliances

Limitation Order L-23 on domestic cooking appliances has been extended for a 15-day period beyond May 1 to permit the conclusion of further studies on a comprehensive order to replace L-23.

Supplementary Order L-23-a permits manufacturers to use iron and steel in the production of domestic cooking appliances in amounts equal to ⅓ of quotas assigned for a 3-month period by the original order. Manufacturers may also use during the additional 15-day period all or any part of quotas granted as a result of appeals under the original order. Quotas for use of iron and steel under L-23 were fixed only for the quarter ending on April 30.

Questions and Answers on Priorities

1. **Q.** Does the Production Requirements Plan in any way compel the elimination of PD–1A certificates?

   A. The PRP does not compel the elimination of PD–1A certificates. It does, however, forbid producers who are operating under it, from using any ratings other than those assigned by the plan.

2. **Q.** What provision is made for producers and distributors to keep their plants and equipment in working order?

   A. A special P order, P–100, replacing the old order P–22, permits specified producers and distributors, such as manufacturers, wholesalers, and warehousemen to use an A–10 rating to obtain repair, maintenance, and operating supplies.

3. **Q.** What materials are excluded from the terms "repair," "maintenance," and "operating supplies" in the sense of P–100?

   A. Since the primary purpose of P–100 is to enable producers, as defined by the order, to maintain their property and equipment, the above does not include replacement of existing equipment, except for purposes of repair, or materials incorporated in a manufactured product, or items such as typewriters or other business machines, or fuel.

4. **Q.** Is the maximum permissible inventory under L–63 uniform for all suppliers?

   A. Wholesalers and distributors in eastern- and central-time zones are required, under L–63, to limit the total value of their inventories at any given moment to twice the value of sales shipped from stock during the second preceding month, while those in other time zones must limit the total value of their inventories to three times the corresponding amount.

LEAD POOL UNCHANGED

The May lead pool was set at 15 percent of March production by the Director of Industry Operations May 1. The percentage is unchanged from previous months.

PRIORITY ACTIONS
*From April 22
*Through April 30

Subject	Order No.	Related form	Issued	Expiration date	Rating
Agricultural bags:					
a. Cotton textile fabrics for use as:					
1. Amended to include a few additional commodities for which such agricultural bags may be used.	M–107 amend. No. 1.		4–27–42		
Alcohol:					
a. Distilled spirits:					
1. Beverage alcohol from 100 to 189 proof placed under complete allocation control: distillers required to deliver specified quantities to rectifying plants for redistillation into 190 proof alcohol.	M–69 amend. No. 1.		4–25–42		
Chemicals:					
a. Polyvinyl chloride:					
1. All rubber substitutes of the general type of Koreseal and Vinylite made subject to direct allocation.	M–10 amend. No. 2.		4–29–42		
Coffee:					
a. Conservation order:					
1. Reduces amount of coffee which may be delivered by roasters and the amount which may be accepted by wholesale receivers during any month to 75 percent of deliveries during the corresponding period of 1941.	M–135		4–26–42		
b. Supplementary order:					
1. Fixes percentage of reduction in deliveries.	M–135–a		4–26–42		
Liquefied petroleum gas equipment:					
a. Exemption paragraph clarified—makes it clear that only equipment withdrawn after Apr. 1, 1942, is exempt.	L–86 int. No. 1		4–27–42	10–31–42	
Magnesium:					
a. Extension	M–2–b extended		4–25–42		
Metal hairpins and metal bob pins:					
a. Restricts amount of metal in production and regulates length and thickness.	L–104		4–25–42		
Metal windows:					
a. Permits manufacture of basement windows and residential-type casements for use in certain rated housing projects; authorizes manufacture of metal windows composed wholly of materials in a manufacturer's inventory prior to Mar. 28 for use in a project to which a preference rating has been assigned by P–55, P–19–d or P–110.	L–77 amend. No. 1.		4–28–42		
Metal working equipment (finishes on):					
a. Only 1 coat of primer or sealer may be applied to new metal-working equipment; no filler may be applied and not more than 2 coats of paint, enamel, or lacquer may be used. Any color other than "old machine-tool gray" for final coat of paint prohibited.	L–108		4–27–42		
Mining machinery and equipment:					
a. A–1–c rating applicable for repairs to blasting machines and similar machinery and equipment, but rating may not be used for ordinary operating supplies such as black powder and dynamite, to which the A–8 rating remains applicable.	Explanation of amend. No. 5 to P–56.		4–28–42		
Cooking appliances (Domestic):					
a. Supplementary order:					
1. Extends L–23 for a 15-day period beyond May 1; permits manufacturers to use iron and steel in production of domestic cooking appliances in amounts equal to one-eighth of quotas assigned for a 3-month period by the original order.	L–23–a		4–25–42		
Corsets, combinations and brassieres:					
a. Reduces amount of elastic fabric that may be used by approximately 50 percent. Manufacturer prohibited from using any rubber yarn and elastic thread frozen under order M–124.	L–90		4–28–42		
b. Supplementary order:					
1. Quota for remainder of month of April 1942.	L–90–a		4–28–42		
Cotton:					
a. Cotton textile fabrics for use as industrial cloth or tape:					
1. To conserve supply and direct distribution—inventories of tape	M–134		4–27–42		A–2.

Subject	Order No.	Related form	Issued	Expiration date	Rating
manufacturers restricted to a 60-day supply of "grey goods" (technically, greige goods)—fabrics suitable for tape but not put into process of manufacture of tape—or a 30-day supply of partially processed cloth.					
Dairy products:					
a. Restricts application of preference ratings by dairy processors to orders for repair, maintenance, and operating materials for use before June 30, 1942.	P-118 amend. No. 1.		4-27-42	6-30-42	A-2; A-3.
Electric lamps and shades (portable):					
a. Extends by 39 days period in which metal, metal parts, lamp cords, and silk may be used in manufacture of portable lamps and lamp shades. Such materials must have been fabricated or semifabricated form in the inventory of the manufacturer or his supplier prior to Mar. 23, 1942.	L-33 amend. No. 1.		4-30-42		
Fire-fighting apparatus:					
a. Fire-protective equipment:					
1. Prohibits transfer, sale, or use of all 2½-inch brass fire-hose couplings except on specific authorization; prohibits use of copper in antifreeze extinguishers.	L-30 amend. No. 1.		4-27-42		
Fluorescent lighting fixtures:					
a. Eases restrictions on production and sale of small fixtures, and sets a definite closing date on manufacture of other types.	L-78 amend. No. 1.		4-23-42		
Leather:					
a. Sole leather:					
1. Sets aside entire stock and production of heavyweight sole leather to meet military and Lend-Lease requirements for shoes.	M-80 amend. No. 2.		4-25-42		
Motor carriers:					
a. Motor Trucks, truck trailers and passenger cars:					
1. Rescinds prohibition against putting tires and tubes on new heavy trucks except for delivery to dealers.	L-1-a amend. No. 7.		4-25-42		
Natural gas:					
a. Restrictions on delivery of natural and mixed natural and manufactured gas to consumers extended to parts of six midwestern States.	L-31 amend. to Exhibit A (No. 2).		4-23-42		
Petroleum:					
a. Material for producing, refining, transportation and marketing of petroleum outside United States limits—revocation of order.	P-98-a revoked		4-25-42		
b. Materials for operation of Standard Oil Co. of New Jersey—revocation of order.	P-103-a revoked		4-26-42		
Plumbing and heating equipment:					
a. Vapor and vacuum heating specialties:					
1. Requires simplification of vapor and vacuum heating specialties after June 15.	L-42 schedule 8		4-25-42		
b. Direct fired gas storage water heaters:					
1. Storage tanks for hot water heaters of the kind used in most homes will be mfg'd. in only three sizes after May 15.	L-42 schedule 9		4-25-42		
Protective helmets:					
a. Prevents production and sale of except on order by an agency of the United States or one of the other United Nations.	L-105		4-29-42		
Radios and phonographs:					
1. Extension	P-38 extended		4-29-42	6-30-42	
Refrigerators (domestic mechanical):					
a. Orders in L-5 series do not apply to a low temperature mechanical refrigerator designed for storage of frozen foods or for quick-freezing of food, when the low temperature compartment contains more than 75 percent of total refrigeration space.	L-5 amend. No. 2.		4-25-42		
Replacement parts:					
a. Materials entering into production of replacement parts for passenger automobiles and light trucks:					
1. To conserve lead, antimony, rubber and other critical materials in manufacture of storage batteries for passenger automobiles and light trucks.	L-4-b		4-25-42		
Rubber:					
a. Use of scrap and reclaimed rubber during May in a specific list of articles will continue to be limited to 60 percent of a formula based on average monthly use over a base period.	M-15-b amend. No. 9.		4-27-42		

(Continued on page 28)

WPB sets up machinery to handle power shortages anywhere in U. S.

The War Production Board on May 1 set up machinery to handle power shortages wherever and whenever they occur in this country.

It issued an order (L-94) of Nation-wide application which may affect every user of electric power in the country. The purpose of the order is to assure a steady flow of power to war industries and essential civilian services by curtailing nonessential uses. Curtailment of electricity for regular consumers, however, will not take place until an area becomes a power shortage area.

Two main lines of action

Two main lines of action against power shortages are set out in the order. The first, which goes into operation at once, requires utilities to operate their systems in a way that will produce the maximum amount of power from their present capacity. In general, this calls for integrating or tying together the systems to permit transfer of power from one locality to another where the power is needed most.

The second part of the program, which will be put into operation when and where a shortage occurs, establishes machinery for mandatory curtailment of power for commercial and industrial consumers. Provision is also made for curtailment of residential consumers.

Makers of portable lamps, shades given more time

The WPB April 30 extended by 39 days the period in which metal, metal parts, lamp cords, and silk may be used in the manufacture of portable lamps and lamp shades. Such materials must have been in fabricated or semifabricated form in the inventory of the manufacturer or his supplier prior to March 23, 1942.

Under the original order (L-33), none of these materials could be used after April 22. The extension to May 31, 1942, was granted in Amendment No. 1 to L-33 to permit manufacturers and suppliers to use up fabricated and semi-fabricated parts.

A manufacturer may not produce during May more lamps or shades than 50 percent of his total quota for May and June, which was fixed in the original order at 60 percent of the 1940 rate.

Rubber substitutes subject to direct allocation

All rubber substitutes of the general type of Koroseal and Vinylite have been made subject to direct allocation by the WPB by Amendment No. 2 to General Preference Order M–10.

The order as originally issued in June 1941 and as amended last December included only polymerized vinyl chloride and its co-polymer with vinyl acetate, containing 92 percent or more of vinyl chloride. The April 29 amendment brings under the restriction all co-polymers of polyvinyl chloride and all co-polymers and polymers of vinyl chloride.

Rubber situation to be explained to public in meetings

A series of meetings in principal cities throughout the United States to explain the seriousness of the rubber situation to shippers, truckers, tire dealers and the general public has been arranged by the Office of Defense Transportation and the Office of Price Administration.

The first meeting in Boston, May 11, will be followed by one in New York the next day. Succeeding meetings are scheduled for Philadelphia, May 13, Atlanta on the 15th, Cincinnati on the 18th, Chicago the 19th, Kansas City the 20th, Dallas the 22d, Denver the 25th, Salt Lake City the 27th, Seattle the 29th, San Francisco June 1, and Los Angeles June 3.

★ ★ ★

Stocks of rubber yarns, elastic threads frozen indefinitely

The WPB has extended indefinitely an order freezing stocks of rubber yarns and elastic threads in the hands of manufacturers. The original order, M–124, expired at midnight April 29.

Form PD–73 required with all iron, steel purchase orders

The filing of Form PD–73 with all purchase orders for steel and iron products to be delivered before June 1 is required by the terms of amendment 4 to General Preference Order M–21, announced April 29 by the WPB.

PRIORITY ACTIONS
*From April 22
*Through April 30

(Continued from page 27)

Subject	Order No.	Related form	Issued	Expiration date	Rating
Sewing machines (domestic): a. Manufacturers may produce new machines and attachments until June 15 at a rate of 75 percent of 1940 rate. Machines completely assembled prior to June 15 may be installed in cabinets or portable cases after cut-off date, provided they come within the 75 percent quota.	L–98		4–25–42	Until revoked.	
Steel and Iron: a. Requires filing of PD–73 with all purchase orders for steel and iron products to be delivered before June 1; will not be necessary for a producer to secure the certification (which will replace PD–73 beginning June 1) in cases of orders previously placed to fill Lend-Lease, other export or warehouse requirements, inasmuch as these classifications remain the same as in PD–73.	M–21 amend. No. 4.	PD–73	4–29–42		
Suppliers inventory order: a. Removes health supplies from list of products subject to control.	L–63 amend. No. 1.		4–27–42		
Tin: a. Tinplate and terneplate closures for glass containers: 1. Further restricts manufacture of crown caps for beer and other beverage bottles during the balance of April.	M–104 amend. No. 1.	PD–384	4–23–42		
b. Tinplate and terneplate closures for glass containers: 1. Repeals amendment No. 1 entirely; production of crown caps permitted to the extent that cork is available until May 1, after which date such production is to end.	Amend. No. 1 (Repealed) amend. No. 2.		4–25–42		
Wool: a. Wool clothing for men and boys: 1. All men's and boys' clothing sold or delivered in this country after May 30 must comply with restrictions of WPB except for clothing put into process of manufacture before May 30; second-hand clothing excepted.	M–73–a as amend. Apr. 27, 1942.		4–27–42		

SUSPENSION ORDERS

Company	No.	Violation	Penalty	Issued	Expiration date
Aluminum and Magnesium, Inc., Sandusky, Ohio.	S–32	Unauthorized deliveries of 45,063 pounds of aluminum, and deliberate misrepresentation in reports.	Prohibited until Sept. 30 from melting any aluminum for use in deoxidizing or alloying steel, or entering into contracts to deliver any aluminum for such purposes.	4–25–42	9–30–42
Tanglefoot Co., Grand Rapids, Mich.	S–35	Applied for and received priority assistance in acquisition of materials of $54,269.44, by representing that the materials was essential to the completion of an Army contract. It was later discovered that the total value of the contract was $45.50, and that the company made use of the rated deliveries to complete not only its Army contract, but also to fill orders to which no preference ratings had been assigned.	No deliveries of any material to the company shall be accorded any preference ratings, and no allocation of restricted materials shall be made for a period of three months.	4–23–42	7–23–42
Lewittes & Sons, 36 East 31st St., New York, N. Y.	S–38	Used large quantities of goose and duck feathers, the entire supply which is reserved for sleeping bags for the armed forces, in the manufacture of upholstered furniture.	Prohibited from accepting deliveries of any goose or duck feathers, or making shipments of any articles containing these materials. No deliveries to them will be accorded preference ratings and no allocations of restricted materials will be made to them for a 4-month period.	4–26–42	8–26–42
Susquehanna Woolen Co., New Cumberland, Pa.	S–39	Put in process approximately 40,000 pounds of wool, of which 19,000 pounds were	Prohibited from putting into process any wool, yarn or cloth for nonmilitary orders for a period	4–26–42	7–26–42

Company	No.	Violation	Penalty	Issued	Expiration date
Acme Chemical Co., Inc., New York, N. Y.	8-41	used for nondefense orders, despite limitations of 18,152 pounds of which only 9,066 pounds were to be used for nondefense orders. Failure to use chemicals for purpose specified in connection with P-29; unauthorized sale of chemicals and extension of preference ratings.	of 3 months; no deliveries to the company will be assigned preference ratings, and no allocation of restricted materials will be made while order is in effect. For a period of 6 months, no preference ratings shall be assigned to delivery of any material, and no allocation of any material restricted by WPB shall be made to it.	4-23-42	10-23-42
Rona Chemicals, N. Y.	8-42	Acting as agent for Acme Chemical Co., made unauthorized sales and contracts for sales.	For a period of 6 months, no preference ratings shall be assigned to delivery of any material, and no allocation of any material restricted by WPB shall be made to it.	4-23-42	10-23-42
Everett Sales & Equipment Corporation, New York, N. Y.	8-44	Willful violation of the cellophane limitation order by manufacturing cellophane packages, for textile products.	Priority assistance withdrawn; prohibited from accepting or delivering any cellophane or similar transparent material derived from cellulose; after 10-day grace period enjoined from cutting or processing any cellophane.	4-30-42	5-31-34

PRIORITIES REGULATIONS

| Priorities Reg. | No. 9..... | Govern issuance and use of ratings for export whenever appropriate forms are approved for specified industries or products. A preference rating assigned under its terms to a product for export may not be applied without an export license or other authorization to export, and the rating will be automatically cancelled if the export license or authorization is revoked. | | 4-25-42 | |

New industry advisory committees

The Bureau of Industry Advisory Committees, WPB, has announced the formation of the following new industry advisory committees:

BABY CARRIAGE INDUSTRY ADVISORY COMMITTEE

Government presiding officer—Louis C. Upton.

Members:

Harvey Hartman, vice president, Hartman Mfg. Co., St. Louis, Mo.; B. Lederman, president, Leader Baby Carriage Co., New York, N. Y.; Wm. Reusch, president, George Cooper Mfg. Co., 362 Jefferson Avenue, Brooklyn, N. Y.; George A. Keyworth, president, Collier Keyworth Co., Gardner, Mass.; W. B. Stearns, general superintendent, Heywood Wakefield Co., Gardner, Mass.; W. N. Muchmore, secretary, Frank F. Taylor Co., Norwood, Cincinnati, Ohio; Paul R. Holman, president, F. A. Whitney Carriage Co., Leominster, Mass.; Wm. Troendle, president, Thayer Co., Gardner, Mass.; Carl Hedstrom, Jr., president, Hedstrom Union Co., Gardner, Mass.; A. D. Welsh, president, Welsh Co., St. Louis, Mo.

FOLDING BOX COMMITTEE

Government presiding officer—William W. Fitzhugh, chief, folding and setup box section, containers branch.

Members:

A. G. Ballenger, Morris Paper Mills, Chicago, Ill.; Joseph P. Thomas, U. S. Printing & Lithographing Co., Cincinnati, Ohio; F. Burroughs, Trenton Folding Box Co., Trenton, N. J.; Sidney L. Wellhouse, National Paper Co., Atlanta, Ga.; Walton D. Lynch, National Folding Box Co., New York, N. Y.; William B. Leavens, Jr., Wilkata Folding Box Co., Kearny, N. J.; Leonard Dalsemer, Lord Baltimore Press, Baltimore, Md.; J. J. Brossard, Container Corporation of America, Chicago, Ill.; W. D. Lane, Eggeras-O'Flyng Co., Omaha, Nebr.; Norman F. Greenway, Robert Gair Co., Inc., New York, N. Y.; Bruce H. Bacon, Spitzer Paper Box Co., Toledo, Ohio; V. C. Hobbs, Fibreboard Products, Inc., San Francisco, Calif.

★ ★ ★

FERTILIZER PUT UNDER PERMANENT CEILING

The Nation's farmers were assured by Price Administrator Henderson April 30 that the prices they pay for mixed fertilizer, superphosphate, and potash will be stabilized at the levels prevailing since February under a previous maximum price regulation.

Maximum Price Regulation No. 135 in effect continues the provisions of Temporary Maximum Price Regulation No. 1, which applied to the same kinds of fertilizers and which expired on April 27, 1942. The permanent regulation became effective April 28.

Under a new provision for adjustable pricing, a person may offer or agree to adjust prices to, or not in excess of, the maximum prices in effect at the time of delivery upon application to, and approval by, the OPA. This changes limitations of the temporary regulation whereby conditional agreements providing for the adjustment of a price to a higher price were prohibited.

127-page indexed digest issued covering OPA releases

Issuance of an indexed digest of all public announcements made by the OPA and its predecessors over the period of slightly more than 1 year and 7 months in which Federal price-control activities were carried out under Executive orders of President Roosevelt was announced May 2, by OPA.

The digest—a 127-page booklet entitled "Federal Price Control"—covers the period from July 1, 1940, when Mr. Henderson was acting as Price Stabilization Commissioner in the National Defense Advisory Commission, up to February 11, 1942, when he took the oath of office as Price Administrator under the Emergency Price Control Act of 1942.

Embodying as it does a comprehensive digest in convenient form, indexed and cross-indexed for ready reference, the booklet is expected to be of considerable value to business establishments, trade and industry associations, purchasing organizations, schools, colleges, students, researchers, and librarians.

The foreword emphasizes that many of the press releases indexed in the booklet are no longer available. However, copies of the formal price schedules and rationing regulations and their amendments, all of which are itemized in special sections can be got from OPA.

The booklet is being placed on general sale by the Superintendent of Documents, Government Printing Office, Washington, D. C., at 20 cents per copy.

★ ★ ★

New export rating plan

A new method of assigning preference ratings to orders for export was adopted April 25 by WPB. Immediate application of the new method is limited to exports for petroleum enterprises outside the United States and Canada.

Priorities Regulation No. 9, issued by the Director of Industry Operations, will govern issuance and use of ratings for export whenever appropriate forms are approved for specified industries or products. The most important provision of the regulation is that a preference rating assigned under its terms to a product for export may not be applied without an export license or other authorization to export, and the rating will be automatically canceled if the export license or authorization is revoked. This will help to prevent burdening transportation and dock facilities with materials which cannot be exported.

CIVILIAN DEFENSE . . .

Volunteers' efforts recognized by creation of new Citizens' Service Corps; Civil Air Patrol gets Federal status

Provision for the organization of a new United States Citizens Service Corps and formal recognition of and basic regulations for the United States Citizens Defense Corps and the Civil Air Patrol are contained in a new series of administrative orders and regulations issued April 30 by Director James M. Landis under the new Presidential Executive order for the Office of Civilian Defense. Certain classes of persons not enrolled in any of these services who may wear arm bands during a blackout are also designated.

In essence, the orders accomplish the following:

1. Give official status to the Citizens Defense Corps for the first time, and prescribe standards of eligibility and training for membership; the regulations provide that no person who is not a member may wear the official insignia or receive or use Federal protective equipment to be issued by the Office of Civilian Defense.

50 hours of work required

2. Create a new U. S. Citizens Service Corps for official recognition of volunteers who have completed 50 hours of work in such activities as conservation, War Bond sales, salvage, education, health, consumers' services, etc., or for those who have completed certain prescribed training courses in volunteer war activities other than the protective services.

3. Make official provisions for special insignia which will permit doctors, nurses, newspaper reporters and photographers, members of the clergy, undertakers and others to carry on essential services or duties during the course of a blackout or air raid.

Must meet basic training standards

In announcing these new regulations, Mr. Landis made it clear that defense workers in protective services will not be entitled to wear the official insignia nor will they be permitted to receive protective equipment under the recent $100,-000,000 grant from Congress unless the basic standards of training are complied with. He pointed out that communities that conform to the new basic regulations which become effective June 1, 1942, may of course adopt provisions to meet special needs if not inconsistent with the regulations.

I

U. S. CITIZENS DEFENSE CORPS

The new regulations prescribe that all citizens shall be eligible for membership with-

out distinction as to race, color, creed, or sex and that appointment shall be made by local authorities, based entirely on ability to perform the prescribed duties.

Eligibility of resident aliens

Resident aliens of Germany, Italy, and Japan are ineligible for membership in the United States Citizens Defense Corps except where State Defense Councils, acting on the favorable recommendation of the particular local defense council, may declare an alien of enemy nationality to be eligible when his loyalty is satisfactorily established. Resident aliens of other countries are eligible for membership except that local defense councils may declare any alien ineligible if the interest of the United States so requires, taking into account his reputation for loyalty.

Approved courses of training must be satisfactorily completed and an oath to defend the Constitution and perform all the required duties, including a statement that a member does not advocate the overthrow of the Constitution by force or violence are among the requirements. Certificates of membership will be issued to enrolled members. Local defense councils or the Director of OCD may terminate or suspend membership of any member improperly appointed or trained or any member who fails to perform his duties. In this connection it is pointed out that the community may continue to permit such persons to act in its protective service but that they will be deprived of membership in the U. S. Citizens Defense Corps and the right to use its insignia.

In order to assure that the Federal supplies and equipment to be procured from the $100,000,000 appropriation are used only by persons qualified and trained under the basic standards of training, the rules provide that no such equipment can be distributed to persons whose appointment and training have not met these standards. The purpose of this regulation is to assure maximum protection for civilians.

II

U. S. CITIZENS SERVICE CORPS

The U. S. Citizens Service Corps for the first time formally organizes the men and women of all ages who volunteer under their local defense councils for work outside of protective services and who meet certain prescribed standards of qualifications, training, and work. This corps will be supervised nationally by the Civilian Mobilization Branch of OCD.

Membership qualifications

Qualifications for membership include completion of prescribed training courses, officially approved by the local defense council, or completion of a prescribed apprenticeship devised by the local civilian Defense Volunteer Office, or completion of 50 hours of work where no specific training is required in a position approved by the local defense council through its volunteer office. Persons already serving in such positions who have completed the re-

quired number of hours are immediately eligible for membership in the U. S. Citizens Service Corps.

Appointment to the U. S. Citizens Service Corps is to be made by the local defense council and each person appointed must take an oath to defense and uphold the Constitution of the United States and to perform all duties to which he is assigned. Members are entitled to a certificate of membership and to wear a newly adopted insigne of the U. S. Citizens Service Corps. Failure to perform duties assigned is ground for dismissal by the local defense council.

The new insigne for the members of the U. S. Citizens Service Corps consist of a red V in the center of a white triangle with a small red C and D placed on the sides of the V, the usual white triangle to be embossed on a circular field of blue.

Members of the U. S. Citizens Service Corps are entitled to wear their insigne either as a lapel button or pin. They are not, however, authorized to use the brassard or sleeve band which entitle members of the protective services of the U. S. Citizens Defense Corps to be in the streets during a blackout.

III

CIVILIAN DEFENSE AUXILIARY GROUP

This is a group of professional or specialized persons who are not otherwise members of the Citizens Defense Corps but whose business or profession might require that they travel on the streets during a blackout or air raid. Upon the authority of the local defense council, these persons will be designated in advance and given the right to wear arm bands which will be in essence "passes" to permit transit on official business. The arm bands will bear, as a special insigne, the basic OCD insigne of the letters CD in a triangle within a circle, except that the letters will be in blue instead of red.

IV

CIVIL AIR PATROL

The Civil Air Patrol is confirmed in the new order as an integral corps of the OCD. Civil Air Patrol is comprised of volunteer pilots and ground personnel usually operating in close cooperation with military authority in the various States.

V

INSIGNIA

Under the act of Congress dated January 27, 1942, and the Executive order issued by the President, the Director of the Office of Civilian Defense is authorized to prescribe official insignia, the unauthorized use of which is a Federal offense. The new rules prohibit the use of the simple CD arm band frequently used by trainees and other persons by Local Civilian Defense Groups, and all prior orders and instructions relative to the use of the CD arm band are rescinded.

The insignia regulations provide that only licensed manufacturers may make and sell articles of identification embodying any prescribed OCD insignia, such as lapel buttons and pins, automobile plates, and arm bands. To guard against unauthorized use of the insignia, the rules further provide that all distribution must be through the local defense councils. Any unauthorized use of insignia will be prosecuted.

TRANSPORTATION . . .

Eastman calls for Nation-wide transport organization, enlists governors, mayors

Joseph B. Eastman, Director of the Office of Defense Transportation, April 28 called for immediate organization of a Nation-wide war transportation program.

Aid sought from each State, town

The call was issued simultaneously to the governors of every State and to the mayors and other chief executives of every town and city with a population of 10,000 or more.

Plans also are under way to mobilize the smaller communities and rural areas in the first systematic drive to get the most efficient service possible from the country's passenger transportation facilities.

In letters to governors and mayors in every State, Mr. Eastman declared:

Any break-down in our local transportation facilities, including the necessary use of automobiles needed to get war workers to their jobs, will seriously interfere with the war production program.

Immediate steps must be taken by each State and by each community to insure the continued and efficient operation of all such facilities essential to war production and to the maintenance of essential civilian activities

The plan proposed by Mr. Eastman has two main objectives:

1. To prolong the life of all transportation facilities now in use.
2. To increase the efficiency of mass transportation.

Emergency transportation programs already have been put into operation in several communities, and the experience thus obtained, according to Mr. Eastman, has shown that the job can be done.

Three conservation methods suggested

Three principal methods are proposed for conservation and more efficient use of present transportation facilities:

1. Systematic staggering of business, school, and working hours.
2. Group riding in private automobiles on a planned, neighborhood-by-neighborhood basis.
3. Improved regulation of local traffic to make possible more efficient movement of passenger vehicles, both private and commercial.

A master plan designed to provide each community with a basis for setting up a war transportation program has been drawn up by the ODT in cooperation with a number of governmental and private agencies.

Responsibility for national direction and coordination of the program has been assumed at Mr. Eastman's request by the National Highway Traffic Advisory Committee to the War Department, under the chairmanship of Commissioner of Public Roads Thomas H. MacDonald.

Each governor is requested to place administration of the program in the hands of the State Highway Traffic Advisory Committee and to designate the chairman as liaison between the State and national committees.

The mayor or other chief executive of every city, borough, or town with a population of 10,000 or more is requested to appoint an administrator to take charge of the program locally.

Manual describes master plan

Methods for dealing with the specialized problems in each phase of the program are provided in a manual containing the ODT's master plan which will be sent to the State and local administrators as soon as they have been designated.

The plan calls for staggering of hours on a community-wide basis, replacing the haphazard, piecemeal attempts made along this line in a number of communities.

Once this phase of the program is under way, it is expected that each community will attack systematically the problem of waste of tires and equipment in the private transportation field.

The average number of passengers per car at present is less than two, including the driver.

Copies of the manual are to be sent to all State and local administrators as soon as Mr. Eastman has been notified of their designation.

★ ★ ★

Eastman suggests war workers try to live near jobs

War workers and other employed persons who do not live near their places of employment can do their country a real service by moving into such locations whenever possible, ODT Director Eastman said April 29.

Such a practice carried out on a large scale would result in valuable conservation of tires, gasoline, and vital transportation equipment.

Local deliveries curtailed to save facilities, equipment

Joseph B. Eastman, Director of Defense Transportation, April 23 issued a general order curtailing local delivery services as a means of conserving transportation facilities and equipment.

Special services affected

The order (General Order ODT No. 6) prohibits most special deliveries and "call-backs," and limits the number of deliveries and the mileage of local delivery carriers.

Effective May 15, local carriers are forbidden to make any special deliveries except to hospitals and the armed forces of the United States, and except emergency deliveries of supplies necessary to protect the public health, life and safety.

As of the same date, the order prohibits call-backs made in a second attempt to deliver shipments on the same day or to make collections and forbids carriers to make more than one delivery to any one person in a single day. However, if deliveries to one person are so large as to require more than one vehicle, they may be considered as a single delivery.

After June 1, local carriers using rubber tires are required to reduce their total mileage by at least 25 percent each month as compared with the corresponding month in 1941. In computing the mileage reduction, mileage saved by cutting down on deliveries and by eliminating special deliveries and call-backs may not be included.

Pooling of deliveries

If local carriers undertake joint action to pool their deliveries or to curtail services, such action must conform to the terms of the joint statement issued by the ODT and the Department of Justice on March 12, 1942.

Excepted vehicles

Vehicles are defined by the order to be any rubber tired vehicles propelled or drawn by mechanical power or by horses. Local carriers include all persons engaged in the transportation of property by vehicle for compensation or as a business service in or near communities or on trips not longer than 15 miles.

Vehicles exempted from the provisions of the order include those operated exclusively for the construction and maintenance of telegraph, telephone, radio, electric light and power, gas, water supply, sewage disposal, garbage disposal, and sanitation services; vehicles owned or operated by the armed forces of the United States or of any State; farm vehicles when transporting produce or farm supplies to market or farm; and vehicles performing pick-up and delivery service for line-haul motor, rail, express, air, or water carriers, or for freight forwarders.

Intracity use forbidden for closed freight cars if motor transport is possible

Use of closed freight cars in any kind of intracity freight movement where utilization of motor vehicles is possible was prohibited April 30 by Defense Transportation Director Eastman, in an amendment to General Order No. 1, which established weight limits for less-than-carload merchandise and directed carriers to conserve freight cars for preferential transportation of war materials.

★ ★ ★

WPB cancels A–2 ratings for freight car materials to use up inventories

In order to make full use of existing inventories in the hands of all freight car makers before permitting them to receive additional raw materials, WPB has issued an order canceling all preference ratings of A-2 or lower on material for car construction which has not already been received by or put in transit to producer.

At the same time, the order, Supplementary General Limitation Order No. L-97-a-1, effective April 29, permits any producer to sell and deliver any material which he has on hand or in transit to any other producer of freight cars.

Railroad labor shortage complicated by needs of war

Already facing an acute labor shortage in many departments of maintenance and operation, American railroads today are confronted with the necessity of finding enough men to fill an estimated 117,-000 new jobs for the remainder of 1942. Current estimates, meanwhile, indicate that employment in war industries will increase from about 7,500,000 to about 15,000,000 men and that about 4,000,000 men will be needed in the armed forces by the end of this year.

This situation was disclosed April 30 by ODT Director Eastman upon receipt of a report by Otto S. Beyer, director of the division of transport personnel, based on information obtained from the Interstate Commerce Commission, Railroad Retirement Board, and the railroad industry.

★ ★ ★

Cabs' fate rests largely on use of equipment, says Eastman

The fate of taxicabs—by which almost one billion passengers were transported last year—depends in large part upon how efficiently existing equipment is used, ODT Director Eastman said April 29.

In any event, he said, highly personalized cab service available in the past cannot be maintained during the war.

WAR EFFORT INDICES

MANPOWER

National labor force, March	54,000,000
Unemployed, March	3,600,000
Nonagricultural workers, March	40,298,000
Percent increase since June 1940	**14
Farm employment, April 1, 1942	9,483,000
Percent decrease since June 1940	**4

FINANCE *(In millions of dollars)*

Authorized program June 1940– April 30, 1942	‡156,416
Airplanes	35,557
Ordnance	32,122
Miscellaneous munitions	19,592
Naval ships	15,457
Industrial facilities	14,365
Posts, depots, etc	13,184
Merchant ships	7,484
Stock pile, food exports	5,791
Pay, subsistence, travel for the armed forces	4,930
Housing	1,392
Miscellaneous	6,542
Total expenditures, June 1940– April 30, 1942	*26,534

PRODUCTION *(In millions of dollars)*

June 1940 to latest reporting date	
Gov. commitments for plant expansion: 1,428 projects, Mar. 31	10,677
Private commitments for plant expansion; 7,366 projects, Mar. 31	2,333

EARNINGS, HOURS, AND COST OF LIVING

		Percent increase from June 1940
Manufacturing industries— February:		
Average weekly earnings	$35.76	38.7
Average hours worked per week	42.2	12.5
Average hourly earnings	80.3¢	19.5
Cost of Living, March (1935–39=100)	114.3	13.7

* Preliminary. Includes revisions in former months.
‡ Preliminary and excludes authorizations in Naval Supply Act for fiscal year 1943.
**Adjusted to avoid reflection of seasonal changes.

OFFICE FOR EMERGENCY MANAGEMENT

WAYNE COY, Liaison Officer

CENTRAL ADMINISTRATIVE SERVICES: Dallas Dort, *Director.*

DEFENSE COMMUNICATIONS BOARD: James Lawrence Fly, *Chairman.*

INFORMATION DIVISION: Robert W. Horton, *Director.*

NATIONAL WAR LABOR BOARD: Wm. H. Davis, *Chairman.*

OFFICE OF SCIENTIFIC RESEARCH AND DEVELOPMENT: Dr. Vannevar Bush, *Director.*

OFFICE OF CIVILIAN DEFENSE: James M. Landis, *Director.*

OFFICE OF THE COORDINATOR OF INTER-AMERICAN AFFAIRS: Nelson Rockefeller, *Coordinator.*

OFFICE OF DEFENSE HEALTH AND WELFARE SERVICES: Paul V. McNutt, *Director.*

OFFICE OF DEFENSE TRANSPORTATION: Joseph B. Eastman, *Director.*

OFFICE OF FACTS AND FIGURES: Archibald MacLeish, *Director.*

OFFICE OF LEND-LEASE ADMINISTRATION: E. R. Stettinius, Jr., *Administrator.*

OFFICE OF PRICE ADMINISTRATION: Leon Henderson, *Administrator.*

CONSUMER DIVISION: Dexter M. Keezer, *Assistant Administrator,* in charge. Dan A. West, *Director.*

OFFICE OF ALIEN PROPERTY CUSTODIAN: Leo T. Crowley, *Custodian.*

WAR MANPOWER COMMISSION: Paul V. McNutt, *Chairman.*

WAR RELOCATION AUTHORITY: Milton Eisenhower, *Director.*

WAR SHIPPING ADMINISTRATION: Rear Admiral Emory S. Land, U. S. N. (Retired), *Administrator.*

WAR PRODUCTION BOARD:
Donald M. Nelson, *Chairman.*
Henry L. Stimson
Frank W. Knox
Jesse H. Jones.
William S. Knudsen.
Sidney Hillman.
Leon Henderson.
Henry A. Wallace.
Harry L. Hopkins.

WAR PRODUCTION BOARD DIVISIONS:
Donald M. Nelson, *Chairman.*
Executive Secretary, G. Lyle Belsley.
PLANNING COMMITTEE: Robert R. Nathan, *Chairman.*

PURCHASES DIVISION: Houlder Hudgins, *Acting Director.*

PRODUCTION DIVISION: W. H. Harrison, *Director.*

MATERIALS DIVISION: Wm. L. Batt, *Director.*

DIVISION OF INDUSTRY OPERATIONS: J. S. Knowlson, *Director.*

LABOR DIVISION: Sidney Hillman, *Director.*

LABOR PRODUCTION DIVISION: Wendell Lund, *Director.*

CIVILIAN SUPPLY DIVISION: Leon Henderson, *Director.*

OFFICE OF PROGRESS REPORTS: Stacy May, *Director.*

REQUIREMENTS COMMITTEE: Wm. L. Batt, *Chairman.*

STATISTICS DIVISION: Stacy May, *Director.*

INFORMATION DIVISION: Robert W. Horton, *Director.*

ADMINISTRATIVE DIVISION: James G. Robinson, *Administrative Officer.*

LEGAL DIVISION: John Lord O'Brian, *General Counsel.*

U. S. GOVERNMENT PRINTING OFFICE: 1942

VICTORY

OFFICIAL WEEKLY BULLETIN OF THE AGENCIES IN THE OFFICE FOR EMERGENCY MANAGEMENT

WASHINGTON, D. C.   **MAY 12, 1942**   **VOLUME 3, NUMBER 19**

TANK CARS IN SERVICE
* Supplying the East Coast

1939 🚃 MAX. EST. BEFORE THE WAR

1942
ESTIMATE
ANYTIME
DURING
WEEK
ENDING
MAY 2

* Each symbol = 1000 tank cars
serving the East Coast with Petroleum and Petroleum Products
(Includes cars on the way back)

DATA
OPC

Iron, steel banned for over 400 products in common use, from tubs to pie plates

Thousands of manufacturing plants were ordered May 5 by WPB to stop using iron and steel in the manufacture of more than 400 common civilian products.

Limited production for 90 days

The list of products to be banned includes such common iron and steel items as bathtubs, pie plates, cash registers, wastebaskets, cigarette lighters, clock cases, mail boxes, and fountain pens.

The sweeping order—General Conservation Order M-126—affects not only the manufacturing plants but also thousands of wholesalers, distributors, jobbers, retailers, employees in all these businesses and the consuming public.

Limited production is permitted for 90 days, but after that manufacture must stop, even for many items customarily used by the armed forces.

Gold, silver only substitutes allowed

Manufacturers have 15 days to deliver or accept delivery of iron and steel to be used in the manufacture of any of the products listed in the order. For 45 days iron and steel may be processed for the manufacture of the items listed, up to an aggregate weight of 75 percent of the average monthly weight of all metals processed by each manufacturer during 1941 in the making of each item. The processing must be completed within the 45 days. For the next 45 days he may assemble items on the list. After that date all use of iron or steel in the manufacture of items on List A of the order must cease.

Manufacturers who have been making items on the list out of iron or steel may not turn to any other metal except gold or silver to make that article. During the 90-day period when fabrication and assemblage is permitted manufacturers

PETROLEUM CHART

Chart on this page shows increased use of high-cost transportation to move petroleum and its products to the Eastern Seaboard, which has caused Office of Price Administration to permit higher prices in that area (see VICTORY, May 5). What chart cannot show is that this huge proportional rise in use of tank cars does not compensate for sinking and diversion of tank ships, hence depleted stocks and supply, and hence rationing registration beginning May 12 (See VICTORY, April 28, and page 25 of this issue). Also, consequent shortage of tank cars, which are needed to carry vital chemicals as well as oil, moved Office of Defense Transportation to inaugurate Nation-wide control of tank cars effective May 15 (see page 27).

may sell iron and steel to others engaged in the same line of business. They may not sell iron and steel from inventory otherwise except on preference ratings of A-10 or higher for other than alloy steel and A-1-k or higher for alloy; to the Metals Reserve Company or its agencies or with the specific authorization of the Director of Industry Operations.

Also included in the order is a List B, which applies only to Army, Navy, or Maritime Commission orders. These may be processed, fabricated or assem-

(Continued on page 8)

Review of the Week

While millions of Americans breathed a sigh of relief over the simplicity of their registration for sugar rationing under the auspices of the Office of Price Administration, and prepared for the gasoline registration which was to begin on May 12, the War Production Board last week did some rationing of its own at the other end of the industrial scale. The WPB action was the other half of its blanket program to cut off all nonessential civilian production—an order forbidding the use of iron and steel for more than 400 articles in common use. Not only that, but the only metals permitted as substitutes are gold and silver.

Further, WPB put an end as of May 15 to the manufacture of replacement parts, except a few specified "functional" ones, for civilian automobiles and light trucks. Copper and its alloys were forbidden for any except essential operating parts for automobiles, and in another sweeping order about a hundred items were added to the general list of those which must not be made of this metal.

Retailers preparing for May 18

As the over-all price ceiling went into effect May 11 for manufacturers and wholesalers, OPA urged retailers to get their records together and survey their prices quickly in preparation for imposition of their ceiling on May 18.

At the same time OPA placed a separate ceiling over used mechanical refrigerators, to bring about savings for householders now that new ones are hard to get. OPA also continued to round out its control of textile prices, prescribing maximum charges for "back-filled" sheetings used by families of low income.

The WPB Production Division revealed that metal-working machinery shipped in March totaled $108,600,000 in value as compared with $84,355,000 in February. The Division of Industry Operations placed all new critical machine tools under limited allocation. The Materials Division announced that increased production is slightly easing the crucial steel plate problem, but held that only the operation of new plate mills will bring a permanent solution. WPB told

suppliers that deliveries for construction of aluminum and magnesium plants must proceed on schedule, even if later orders from other sources bear higher ratings.

Still searching for materials

Still searching out supplies of vital materials for the war effort wherever they may be, WPB forbade the use of scarce metals for "demonstrator" incendiary bombs; asked an end to extension of street lighting systems except where necessary for public safety; eliminated all but the most essential use of rubber tires on hand trucks; ruled out feeding nipples of the type using extra amounts of rubber; banned all metals except iron and steel from pencils; put strict regulation on the consumption of scarce materials in safety equipment; cut deliveries of gasoline and light heating oils 50 percent on the East Coast; and limited the delivery of brass mill, wire mill, and foundry copper products to high-rated orders.

OPA, meanwhile, issued a maximum price regulation to cover all machines and parts not already subject to ceilings.

Warning that restrictions on passenger travel were imminent, Transportation Director Eastman set up a division of transport conservation under authority of a Presidential order, to formulate measures for adjusting services to the war, and if necessary, for restricting them to essential uses. Mr. Eastman also banned grain exports over the Great Lakes, except by special permit, to give preference to movement of iron ore; and set up a Nation-wide system of tank-car control.

★ ★

Imports of cashew nuts curbed

Restriction of the importation of cashew nuts was ordered May 9 by the Director of Industry Operations.

The purpose of the order, M-147, is to insure maximum extraction of oil from cashew nut shells in the exporting country.

Deliveries of principal imported spices placed on monthly quota basis

The WPB May 8 placed restrictions on the distribution of black and white pepper, pimento (allspice), cassia (cinnamon), cloves, ginger, nutmeg, and mace.

Such spices are the principal imported seasoning commodities used by United States industry and consumers.

The order places a quota on the amount of each spice a packer may deliver monthly, and on the amount an industrial or wholesale receiver may accept.

Production of incendiary bombs banned for "demonstrator" use

Because their manufacture calls for the use of scarce materials, including magnesium and metal containers, the production and distribution of incendiary bombs for use as "demonstrators" by civilian groups has been prohibited by Limitation Order L-115, issued May 7 by the WPB. Only permitted exceptions are to fill orders authorized in writing by the Army or Navy.

·   · · ·

Cottonseed oil prices

Price Administrator Henderson May 6 established specific "cents per pound" maximum prices for various grades and qualities of actual spot cottonseed oil and set ceilings on the same commodity for future delivery on the organized exchanges at the identical price level.

★ ★ ★

WAR EFFORT'S PROGRESS TOLD VISUALLY

The charts appearing every week on the front cover of VICTORY tell the story of America's battle as it is fought here at home. One-column mats are available for publication by newspapers and others who may desire them. Requests should be sent to Distribution Section, Division of Information, OEM, Washington, D. C.

VICTORY

OFFICIAL BULLETIN of the Office for Emergency Management. Published weekly by the Division of Information, Office for Emergency Management, and printed at the United States Government Printing Office, Washington, D. C.

Subscription rates by mail: 75¢ for 52 issues; 25¢ for 13 issues; single copies 5¢, payable in advance. Remit money order payable directly to the Superintendent of Documents, Government Printing Office, Washington, D. C.

On the Home Front

We have battened down the hatches of the ship of state, we are set to ride out the gales of war.

Price control and rent control were the first steps to that end, the third step came last week when the Federal Reserve System moved to tighten controls over consumer credit.

Charge accounts discouraged

Federal Reserve's action means heavier down payments on installment purchases, it means that installment balances must be paid off sooner, it means that charge accounts and personal loans up to $1,500 incurred for the purchase of "listed" goods have been placed under strict control. The control over loans even includes bank loans.

The reason for this action, of course, is that unrestrained credit is quite as dangerous as unlimited cash, quite as likely to send the cost of living and the cost of war spiraling upward. Whereas payment of debts and saving of surpluses helps us now and creates a cushion for the postwar period. As President Roosevelt put it: "We must discourage credit and installment buying and encourage the paying off of debts and mortgages."

Bootlegging of goods unpatriotic

With $4 in cash competing for every $3 in goods in the American marketplace, it is obviously to our advantage not to aggravate the situation by applying the pressure of additional purchasing power based on future earnings.

"So vital are the benefits of these restraints to the American people," remarked Price Administrator Leon A. Henderson of the Federal Reserve move, ". . . that support . . . becomes a matter not only of self-interest but of patriotism." The selfish individual who turns to the "bootlegger of goods or money" is a "menace to the welfare of all," he said, while the patriot will buy nothing "not essentially needed" and will try to invest his surplus in "debt retirement and savings for future use."

Gasoline rationing in 17 Eastern States

Gasoline rationing becomes a fact this week in 17 Eastern States and the District of Columbia. The War Production Board has already cut deliveries of gasoline and light heating oils to 50 percent of normal, an indication of what's going to happen to the individual motorist when he drives up to his filling station on May 15.

While the eastern automobile owner is getting the heavy end of the stick, the rest of the country should not congratulate itself on its escape. Gasoline is a national problem, not a sectional one and, as has been emphasized before, it is a problem of distribution, not production. The transportation difficulties of the Atlantic seaboard have a direct effect on the Midwest and the Far West. The

REPRINTING PERMISSIBLE

Requests have been received for permission to reprint "On the Home Front" in whole or in part. This column, like all other material in VICTORY, may be reprinted without special permission. If excerpts are used, the editors ask only that they be taken in such a way that their original meaning is preserved.

death of merchant sailors and the destruction of tanker tonnage are equally the loss of the Southwest and the Northwest. Sooner or later the sorrows and problems of one section become the sorrows and troubles of all sections in total war.

Steel Age suspended for duration

As still another forfeit to victory, the War Production Board has suspended the Steel Age for the duration as far as the civilian is concerned. After a period of 90 days the use of iron and steel in the manufacture of more than 400 household, office, factory, and farm products comprising many hundreds of everyday items will be banned. When the present supply is gone, the housewife must do without her pie plates, the business man without his cash register, the glamour girl without her lipstick, and the man-about-town without his cigarette lighter—if they are made of any metal except gold or silver.

Against these inconveniences and irritations, we can rejoice that unnumbered thousand of tons of iron and steel, the very stuff of war, will be diverted into the stream of victory. No one is apt to grumble at the loss of bathtubs, wastebaskets or fountain pens when he knows that they are going pound for pound into the machine guns, tanks, and submarines which will spell the overthrow of the dictators.

Darkened Main Streets release power

The growing need for power to operate new aluminum and other war material

plants is indicated in another WPB order. Electric utility systems have been asked to discontinue all street lighting extensions except those indispensable to public safety. Suspension of street illumination would not apply to heavily-traveled areas surrounding war factories, airports or military centers nor to essential traffic control signals elsewhere. If one end of Main Street is dark these spring nights it may mean that an extra American pursuit plane is aloft over the Caribbean.

War Ration Books a best seller

Donald M. Nelson, chairman of WPB, has personally appealed to the lumber industry for greater cooperation. He has asked logging and sawmill operators to step up the production of soft-wood construction lumber to the maximum to meet the imperative and immediate needs of the armed forces for housing.

Boy will meet girl in Hollywood from now on against a background costing not more than $5,000 . . . Amplifying a previous conservation order, WPB has specifically authorized that much and no more for the construction of new motion picture sets . . . They used to cost between $10,000 and $150,000 . . . Industrial diamonds have been brought under the price ceiling by the OPA . . . They're vital in the operation of machine tools . . . 57,670,453 persons or 44 percent of the eligible population walked away with War Ration Books in the first 2 days of the 4-day registration . . . Those who did not register must wait until May 21 to get books unless they can prove illness or present an equally good excuse . . . The Bureau of Industrial Conservation has seized 200 junked cars in an automobile graveyard in the Washington, D. C., metropolitan area because the owner refused a fair offer to sell . . .

WPB cracks down on violators

WPB suspended a division of General Motors Corporation for 3 months for violation of priority regulations on the grounds that it used quantities of chrome steel and aluminum in the manufacture of automobile parts . . . And three Puerto Rican rum distillers have been penalized on charges that they continued to distill rum from molasses after January 15. Motorists in 17 Eastern States and the District of Columbia are warned not to hoard gasoline to beat rationing . . . It is not only unpatriotic but it may lead to a serious fire . . .

LABOR . . .

Federal Ship and General Motors yield to decisions of Board

America's two largest corporations, which had questioned the National War Labor Board's authority and threatened its ability to settle wartime disputes, last week agreed to comply with Board orders.

The Federal Shipbuilding & Drydock Co., Kearny, N. J., wholly owned subsidiary of the United States Steel Corporation, agreed to sign a maintenance of membership contract with the Industrial Union of Marine and Shipbuilding Workers of America, CIO, which a majority of the Board had ordered on April 25.

This announcement came on the heels of a dramatic public hearing at which the General Motors Corporation reversed its position and agreed to a Board order it had resisted and apologized for charging that the Board made one-sided decisions.

Compliance by the two great corporations greatly enhanced the Board's prestige and strengthened it in its wartime job of settling labor disputes by peaceful means in the interest of uninterrupted production, it was reported.

Federal Shipbuilding announcement

The announcement by Federal Shipbuilding ended months of controversy during which the yard was taken over by the Navy last August after the steel corporation refused to comply with a maintenance of membership recommendation by the peacetime National Defense Mediation Board. The plant was returned to the corporation on January 6 with the understanding that the issue was to be settled by the War Labor Board. However, the position taken by the corporation at the public hearing before the Board March 30 had led observers to conclude it intended to challenge the government again.

In notifying the Board of its compliance, L. H. Korndorff, president of Federal, stated, "This action has been taken solely because of the war emergency; and this country's great need of ships in order successfully to prosecute the war."

"Happiest effect on production"

Chairman William H. Davis of the Board promptly sent a telegram to Mr. Korndorff expressing the Board's appreciation for the action by the United States Steel Corporation subsidiary.

"Please accept this expression of my appreciation for your letter of today," Mr. Davis wired, "in which you convey to the National War Labor Board the acceptance by the Federal Shipbuilding & Drydock Co. of the Board's directive order of April 25. I believe that this acceptance, which finally determines a long dispute, will have the happiest possible effect upon the war production in which we are all so deeply concerned."

The maintenance of membership clause ordered by the Board requires all present members of the union to maintain their membership in good standing as a condition of continued employment. Any union member, however, who wishes to withdraw from the union may do so by agreeing to have his union dues deducted from his salary for the duration of the contract (about a year).

"To increase production"

The Federal Ship clause will go into effect within ten days, as soon as the company and union formally sign a contract embodying the provision. During the interval before the contract is signed, employees have the privilege of withdrawing from the union without any penalty.

Board's hand strengthened

Federal Ship's compliance gave added weight to the Board's use of the maintenance of membership formula as one means of protecting unions from disintegration under the strain of wartime responsibilities. The shipyard was the third company to announce its acceptance of a maintenance of membership order within a 10-day period. The other two concerns—International Harvester Co., Chicago, Ill., and the Walker Turner Co., Plainfield, N. J.—announced their compliance after more than 2 weeks' delay in each case.

In the Harvester case, the Board ordered an election among the members of the majority union in each of eight plants of the company on the question of incorporating a maintenance of membership clause in the company's collective bargaining contract. This election, which will be held shortly, will be the first intraunion election ever held under government auspices.

In the Walker Turner case, the Board decided that union members in good standing on November 27 of last year must remain in good standing to retain their jobs. As in other union maintenance clauses ordered, employees who join the union in the future will be bound by the clause. All three decisions were reached by eight to four votes, with the employer members of the Board dissenting.

★ ★ ★

GENERAL MOTORS YIELDS

A 3-man panel of the Board began to mediate the dispute between the General Motors Corporation and the United Automobile Workers of America, CIO, last week after the corporation dramatically ended its defiance of the Board by agreeing to comply with a Board order at the conclusion of a tense two-hour public hearing called by unanimous vote of the Board.

Charles E. Wilson, president of the corporation, admitted that he misunderstood the meaning of an order of the Board extending until May 18 all the provisions of a contract between the company and the union including a controversial clause providing for the payment of double-time for Sunday work. At the same time he apologized for having charged that the Board made its order after "ex parte" consideration of the case and stated that he was satisfied that the Board had taken no "unfair advantage of the corporation."

The disputed clause was extended by the Board to provide time to apply the President's formula ending double time for Sunday to the complicated shifts of the more than 85 plants of the General Motors Corporation. A total of 200,000 employees are involved.

The "ex parte" charge

Prior to the hearing, the corporation had announced to the press that it would not comply with the Board's interim order. At the hearing, Mr. Wilson at first reaffirmed his earlier position, but unexpectedly reversed himself at the end of more than two hours of acrimonious debate.

When the order was originally announced by the Board, Chairman Davis said, in part: "I want to say at the outset that I would vote for the order for one overwhelming reason—because I think it will increase production of ships and help win the war. This issue has been disturbing the relations between management and the workers at Kearny for just about a year. It is time to put an end to it."

Dr. Frank P. Graham, public member of the Board, had urged the Steel subsidiary to accept the decision to help win the war.

"In the midst of this total and desperate war," Dr. Graham wrote, "is no time for defiance of the government by any labor union or corporation. It is the time for the acceptance of a decision carefully arrived at in accordance with the national agreement between labor, management and the government of the people of the United States. The war is wide and desperate, but the time is short. The time is too short for any further delays in the settlement of a dispute in a plant where are built the ships which carry the men and armaments and supplies to support American boys as they fight for the future of America and the future of freedom in the world."

With respect to the ex parte charge, Mr. Wilson finally stated: "I don't know what an ex parte hearing is myself."

Then, the following dialogue took place:

"Mr. DAVIS. Now the trouble is that the American people do know what an ex parte hearing is, and you don't, and you went out to the American people and said it was an ex parte hearing which means exactly one thing, and that is that there was a hearing at which one party was present and the other was not.

Now I don't want to press the thing, Mr. Wilson. I think you have come along nicely now, and if you want to say that you didn't understand what ex parte meant, or did not intend to say that there was a hearing in which one party was represented and another was not, and you are not asserting that the union was represented at this hearing before the Board when the company was not, why, say so. It is just for clarification.

Mr. WILSON. Are we going to settle it on a technical basis or on a practical one?

Mr. DAVIS. I say on a practical one, Mr. Wilson, right away.

Mr. WILSON. I would like to say that the ex parte business did not mean that we thought that anyone had taken an unfair advantage of any position that they might have had, that after a view of the whole matter, that I was satisfied that that was so. I think that is better than for me to ask you to make public the minutes and have a technical discussion over whether it was or was not an ex parte hearing. Technically, I don't know whether it was or was not.

Mr. DAVIS. I think the thing, gentlemen, in which the American people are concerned is whether or not the General Motors Corporation thinks that an unfair advantage was taken of them. Now Mr. Wilson says they do not think so, and it seems to me that is satisfactory.

Stand taken by Morse

Earlier in the hearing, Wayne L. Morse, public member of the Board and Dean of the Oregon University Law School, denounced the refusal of General Motors

10 lower craft wage rates raised, 14 of highest unchanged by decision in Detroit building trades dispute

The Board of Review of WPB's Labor Production Division announced May 6 a decision in the Detroit building trades wage disputes, under which 14 of the highest craft wage rates remain unchanged and 10 lower craft wage rates are increased.

Decision final and binding

The decision was made by a Board of Arbitration made up of John P. Coyne, president, Building and Construction Trades Department, AFL; Major James T. O'Connell, chief, Labor Relations Branch, Corps of Engineers, War Department; and Louis K. Comstock, chairman, Board of Review. The Board of Review approved the Arbitration Board's decision and therefore under the Building Trade Stabilization Agreement, the decision is final and binding. This was the agreement entered into between the Government and the AFL Building Trades last August under which all war construction strikes were banned and all

to comply with the Board's order as a "sit-down strike against the best interests of this country at war."

"I want to say that as a lawyer, I think I know when parties stand in contempt before a tribunal," Dean Morse said.

"There is only one issue before this Board, and that is whether or not the tribunal which has been set up by the President of the United States to settle labor disputes, including labor disputes of the General Motors Corporation of America, shall settle them by this Board, or whether they shall be settled in accordance with Mr. Wilson's judgment as to how they should be settled.

"I have no doubt, Mr. Wilson, as to what the American people or what the President of the United States will say to you in answer to the contemptuous position you have taken before a tribunal created by the President of the United States," Dean Morse said. "I want to plead with you as a public member of this Board and as a citizen interested in the successful outcome of this war that you do what every party is supposed to do when he stands before a tribunal and finds that he has misunderstood and mistaken the action of that tribunal . . .

"I ask you in the interests of the suc-

disputes were to be settled by peaceful means.

The 17 building trades unions involved all asked considerably higher wages.

Principal changes in lower levels

The statement announcing the decision said as to this point:

Throughout the discussions in the executive sessions of the Board of Arbitration and the Board of Review, the thought has been ever present that in these days of war emergency, necessitous high production, and extreme care for the preservation of our institutions, and as a helpful hedge against inflation, there should be no attempt to alter the wage scales more than to stabilize them and to bring into line some wage scales that seemed definitely out of line.

Two things stand out in these wage determinations: (1) The highest scales of wages have not been changed and (2) the principal changes have been in the lower levels where the rise in the cost of living (whatever it is) bears a relatively greater ratio to the income received than in the higher levels.

The unions and employer associations involved jointly signed agreements binding themselves in advance to abide by the decision of the arbitrators.

cessful prosecution of this war to express to this tribunal your apology, which is due, and say that you will abide by the decisions of this Board and abide by the decision of May 1."

Near the close of the hearing, Dr. Frank P. Graham, public member of the Board, turned to Mr. Wilson and pleaded with him to change his stand in the interest of the war effort.

"I cannot understand that such a big issue should be made out of this point with the whole world crashing around us, when we ought to be not stirring up things to divide labor organizations from corporations, not raising issues to undermine the influence and value of this Board," Dr. Graham said.

After the hearing concluded with Mr. Wilson's agreement to comply, the three-man mediation panel sat down with the parties to start the business of mediation. Considerable progress was reported at the first meeting. Other issues in the case besides double time are the question of union security, wages, and the negotiation of a new collective bargaining contract to replace the one between the company and union which expired on April 28.

INDUSTRIAL OPERATIONS . . .

Production of spare parts for civilian autos, light trucks sharply curtailed

The WPB May 5 ordered a sharp cut in the present high rate of production of replacement parts for automobiles and light trucks for civilian use.

70 percent production quota

Only specified functional parts may be produced after May 15, and in curtailed quantities designed to satisfy actual demand but eliminate surpluses.

Applying to spare parts for passenger cars, station wagons and taxicabs, and trucks under 9,000 pounds gross weight, WPB's action supersedes, during the period April 1–June 30, the provisions of Amendment No. 1 to Limitation Order L–4–a.

Under the new order, Supplementary Limitation Order L–4–c, producers may make during the period April 1–June 30, and during the period June 30–September 30, 70 percent of the total dollar volume of replacement parts sold by them in the corresponding quarter of 1941. This production quota is accompanied by certain restrictions on inventory of finished parts.

Parts permitted

Effective May 15 (the date was postponed from May 1 by amendment on May 8), producers may manufacture only the following replacement parts:

Engines, clutches, transmissions, propeller shafts, universal joints, axles, brakes, wheels, hubs, drums, starting apparatus, spring suspensions, shock absorbers, exhaust systems, cooling systems, fuel systems, lubricating systems, electrical systems (including generators, lights, and reflectors), gauges, speedometers, rear view mirrors, windshield wipers, windshield wiper motors, control mechanisms, and steering apparatus.

In the manufacture of the specified functional parts, producers are subject to all restrictions on the use of materials covered by M orders issued by WPB. It is estimated that a relatively small amount of additional materials will be needed to produce the permitted quota of parts.

Can maintain low rate to September 30

R. L. Vaniman, deputy chief of the automotive branch, said that as a result of its conversion studies, the branch has found that parts production facilities probably will not be completely taken up by war production, and that, therefore, a low rate of production may be maintained at least until September 30 in order to make available an adequate supply of essential parts to meet estimated needs for the rest of this year and 1943.

"The branch, in its present and continuing program, is laying particular emphasis on the reconditioning or repairing of replacement parts, such as rewinding of starters and generators, rebabbitting of connecting rods, more extensive reconditioning of engines and other items," Mr. Vaniman said.

A distributor requiring a replacement part for the emergency repair of a designated vehicle which cannot be operated without such part must file with a producer a "Certificate for Emergency Order" specifying the make and engine number of the vehicle involved. A producer to whom such a certificate is submitted must give the order precedence in shipment over other orders not of an emergency nature.

★ ★ ★

Deliveries of gasoline and light heating oil are cut 50 percent in East

Acting on the recommendations of the Office of the Petroleum Coordinator, WPB on May 5 ordered deliveries of both gasoline and light heating oils cut 50 percent beginning May 16 in 17 Eastern States and the District of Columbia.

The 50 percent cut will reduce deliveries of both products to half of the normal demand.

The cuts in gasoline deliveries will apply to service stations and to bulk consumers. The cuts in heating oil deliveries will apply to deliveries to suppliers.

Gasoline deliveries, under Limitation Order L–70, are already cut one-third in the 17 States and the District of Columbia.

The fuel oils covered by the May 5 decision are of the type generally used for space heating and central heating, including domestic heating plants. This means, therefore, that the quantity of such fuel available for household purposes will be restricted and controlled under the plans being worked out.

Copper banned from autos except in essential operating parts

WPB on May 6 prohibited the use of copper or copper base alloy products in the manufacture of all but essential operating parts of motor vehicles. The limitation order, L–106, is effective immediately.

The restrictions do not apply to the production of parts for the Army or Navy where use of copper or copper base alloy products is required by the specifications of the prime contract.

Permitted uses listed

Unless specifically authorized by the Director of Industry Operations, producers are prohibited from using the restricted products except in the following:

Radiators; cooling system control devices; electrical equipment; tubing and fittings; bearings, bushings, thrust washers, and similar parts; carburetor parts; plating; gaskets; certain types of transmissions; brazing materials; powdered copper for briquetted bearings; as alloying elements in certain parts, and in some miscellaneous parts, including keys and lock tumblers.

The extent to which the restricted products may be used for the purposes listed is set forth in detail in the order.

.. .. ..

Wheeler heads New England regional office of WPB

Walter H. Wheeler, Jr., has been appointed New England regional director of the War Production Board, it was announced May 7. Mr. Wheeler formerly was chief of the contract distribution branch of the Production Division.

The New England regional office will have its headquarters in Boston and will be responsible for the administration of all WPB field offices in the six New England states. Other regional offices have been established in Cleveland, Atlanta, Philadelphia, Detroit, and Chicago.

Replacing Mr. Wheeler as Chief of the contract distribution branch of WPB is C. E. Hallenborg, formerly assistant chief of the branch.

Supplies to build aluminum, magnesium plants to go ahead of higher-rated but later orders

Suppliers of materials used in the construction of vital aluminum and magnesium plants were advised May 6 by WPB that deliveries should be made on schedule even though subsequent orders assigned under Preference Rating Order P-19-I carry higher preference ratings.

The ruling was made in Interpretation No. 1 of P-19-I which covers materials used in essential civilian construction. It was necessary, the board said, to prevent any delay in delivery which might result from a misunderstanding of the original order.

The Interpretation ruled, however, that this provision does not require or permit a supplier to make deliveries on an order to which a rating has been assigned under P-19-I in preference to deliveries on earlier-accepted orders bearing equal or higher ratings.

* * *

WPB forbids rubber tires for most hand trucks

WPB on May 7 ordered elimination of all but the most essential uses of rubber tires on hand trucks. It is estimated that these required more than 500,000 rubber tires last year.

Limitation Order L-111, effective immediately, prohibits any manufacturer from delivering rubber-tired hand trucks, any person from accepting delivery of such trucks or of rubber tires for replacement purposes, and any person from delivering rubber tires except on authorization to a hand-truck manufacturer for use on such trucks. All other uses of rubber in the manufacture or assembly of these trucks is prohibited.

Exceptions are granted where the use of rubber tires is necessary to prevent explosion hazards, and to avoid accidents in the handling of explosives, damage in transporting unbaked grinding wheels or, green foundry cores, or damage to delicate instruments which are an integral part of the truck. Persons receiving delivery of a truck or a spare rubber tire must certify on the purchase order that the equipment is required for one of the specified essential purposes.

* * *

Indian kyanite, furnace lining, under complete allocation

Indian kyanite (including andalusite and sillimanite); a superduty refractory used in furnaces where extremely high temperatures are necessary, was placed under complete allocation control May 6 by the Director of Industry Operations.

WPB tightens control over all types of rubber-tired construction equipment

The WPB, acting to save substantial amounts of rubber, May 3 assumed rigid control over the production and distribution of all types of rubber-tired construction equipment.

Over 70 items affected

More than 70 items of construction equipment normally equipped with rubber tires are affected by Limitation Order L-82-a.

At the same time, WPB, in Limitation Order L-82, placed restrictions on the sale and production of power cranes and shovels, which are greatly in demand for military and essential civilian activities.

In its order applying to rubber-tired construction equipment, WPB prohibits the future sale, lease, trade, loan, delivery, shipment, or transfer of any new equipment without specific authorization of the Director of Industry Operations, except for orders placed prior to the issuance of L-82-a which carry a preference rating higher than A-2, on which shipments must be made on or before May 1.

Between May 1 and June 1, no rubber-tired construction equipment can be produced except to fill Army, Navy, Maritime Commission, and lend-lease orders, to fill orders for specified items of equipment needed in the war program for which steel wheels or other substitutes for rubber tires are impractical, or on production schedules specifically approved by the Director of Industry Operations. The specified items are: self-propelled earth moving graders, carrying and hauling scrapers, and power cranes and power shovels.

WPB must approve schedules

The order provides that after June 1, each manufacturer's production schedule, regardless of whether or not it is designed to fill war orders or orders for the specified items, must be approved by the Director of Industry Operations. Proposed schedules must be submitted to WPB on form PD-446. This will provide a means of preventing any manufacturer from using critical material to produce equipment that would be useless without rubber tires and of preventing production for nonessential uses.

As defined in the order, construction equipment takes in many items, including snow plows, drilling machines, crushers, excavators, mixers, street sweepers, and others set forth in Schedule A attached to the order.

In order to obtain release of equipment frozen by the terms of the order, a producer, dealer, or an authorized distributor may apply to WPB on form PD-448, unless delivery of the item involved has been assigned a preference rating higher than A-2, in which case no application is necessary. However, such preference rating must have been issued before May 2, must designate the person seeking to purchase equipment, must be issued directly to that person, and shipment must be made on or before June 1.

The order places no restrictions on repossession of equipment in case of a breach of installment contract or other form of conditional sale. Equipment actually in transit to the ultimate consumer on May 27 is exempt from the terms of the orders.

Before May 15, producers, dealers, and distributors must file with WPB on form PD-445 a statement detailing inventories of rubber-tired construction equipment as of May 2.

L-82, covering power cranes and shovels, which can continue to be mounted on rubber tires, contains production and distribution restrictions similar to those set forth in L-82-a. Effective immediately, sales and other transactions are prohibited except upon specific authorization by the Director of Industry Operations and to fill orders placed prior to the issuance of L-82 which carry ratings higher than A-2 and on which shipments must be made on or before June 1. Application for release may be made on Form PD-448.

* * *

Feeding nipples modified to use less rubber

Specifications for the manufacture of feeding nipples, designed to save approximately 45 tons of crude rubber annually, were ordered by the WPB May 6 in Amendment No. 5 to Supplementary Order M-15-b-1.

The specifications, effective on May 15, set forth the maximum amount of rubber which may be contained in each thousand nipples.

The amendment will eliminate the production of the so-called "breast" type nipple, which consumes three times the amount of rubber required to manufacture a nipple, conforming to the specifications.

List of articles for which iron and steel will be forbidden by new WPB order

Following are the over 400 articles for which the use of iron and steel will be forbidden under WPB order of May 5:

LIST A

Access panels, except as required by underwriters code; acoustical ceilings; advertising novelties; air-conditioning systems—except for hospital operating rooms and industrial plants; amusement park devices and roller coasters; area walls; ash sieves; asparagus tongs; atomizers, perfume-boudoir; attic fans; autographic registers; automobile accessories—except as required by law; automotive replacement parts, non-functional; awning frames and supports.

Bag, purse, and pocketbook frames; barber and beauty shop furniture; baskets—except for commercial cooking and manufacturing uses; bathtubs; B-B shot for air rifles; beds—except hospital; bed spring frames—except for hospital link fabric spring type bed; beer kegs—except hoop and fittings for wooden kegs; beer mugs; beer stands; beer steins; bench legs—except industrial; binoculars—except U. S. Government Agencies; bird cages and stands; bird houses and feeders; biscuit boxes; blackboards; blade stroppers, mechanical; bleachers and grandstands; book ends; bottle holders; boxes and trays for jewelry, cutlery, combs, toilet sets; bread racks; bridge splash guards; building ornaments; butter chips; butter knives.

Cabinets—except: (a) Hospital operating and examining rooms; (b) Office furniture as permitted in Limitation Orders L-13-a and L-62; Cake cutters; cake tongs; candy-display dishes; canopies for electric brooders; canopies and supports; cans or containers for anti-freeze, under 5-gallon size; artist supplies; bouillon cubes; candy; caviar; chalk; coffee; gloves; incense; lawn seed; nuts; pencils; pet food; phonograph needles; playing cards; razor blades; sponges; staples; tennis balls; tobacco products; toilet water; yarn. Carpet rods; carving-set holders; cash boxes; cash registers; casket hardware; cattle stanchions—except hangers and fasteners; ceilings; cheese dishes; chicken crates; chick feeders; Christmas-tree holders; Christmas-tree ornaments; cigar and cigarette holders and cases; cigarette lighters; cigar slippers; clock cases—except on recording and controlling industrial instruments; clothes-line pulleys; clothes-line reels; clothes racks and dryers; clothes trees; coal chute and door, household; coal pans; cocktail glasses; cocktail sets; cocktail shakers; coffee-roasting machinery; compacts; cooking stoves, commercial electric; copy holders; corn cribs; corn poppers and machines; counter tops; croquet sets; crumb trays; culverts; cupboard turns; cups of all kinds, drinking; curb guards.

Decorative iron products; dictaphone racks; dinner bells; dishwashing machines—except hospitals; dispensers, hand, for hand lotions, paper products, soap, straws; document stands; door chimes; door knockers; door closers—except fire-prevention as required by Underwriters code; door handles—except shipboard use; door stops; drain boards and tub covers, household; drawer pulls; dress forms; dummy police; dust-collecting systems and equipment—except on A-1-j rating.

Ediphone racks; egg slicers; electric water coolers—except on PD-1a or PD-3a certificates; enamel store fronts; erasing knives; escalators; feed troughs; fence posts—except on A-2 or higher; fences, chain link—except on A-2 or higher; fences, ornamental; finger [illegible] [illegible] equipment except dampers; fireplace screens; fish aquariums; flagpoles; flashlight tubes; floor and ceiling plates for piping; floor and counter covering trim; floor polishing machines; flour, salt and pepper shakers; flower boxes, pot holders, and vases; flower shears; fly traps; foot baths—except hospitals; foot scrapers; fountain pens—except functional parts; fountains, ornamental; furniture—except: (a) wood furniture; (b) as listed in Limitation Orders L-13-a and L-62; (c) hospital operating and examining rooms; (d) hospital beds and cots.

Garage hoists, car lifts, and racks; golf bag supports; grain storage bins—except strapping, hardware, and reinforcing materials; grass shears; grilles; ornamental; sewers—except on A-2 or higher and reinforcing for concrete sewers; gutters, spouting, conductor pipe, and fittings for single family dwellings; hair curlers, non-electric; hair dryers; hand mirrors; hangers and track for garage doors for private use; hanger rings on brushes, brooms etc.; hat frames; hat-making machinery; hedge shears; helmets—except on A-2 or higher; hose reels—except; (a) fire-fighting equipment; (b) industrial uses in direct fire-hazard areas; house numerals; ice-box exteriors—except portable blood banks; ice-cream freezers, household; ice-cube trays; inkwell holders; incinerators—except industrial, commercial, and as allowed in Defense Housing Critical List; insulation, metal reflecting type; jam boxes; jelly molds; jewelry; jewelry cases; kitchenware of stainless steel; knitting needles.

Lard or vegetable oil tubs—except 5 pounds and over and straps for wood containers; laundry chutes; laundry trays—except reinforcing mesh; lavatories—except hangers; lawn sprinklers; letter chutes; letter openers; letter trays; lighting poles and standards; lipstick holders; lobster forks; lobster tongs; lockers—except: (a) oil refinery use; (b) office equipment as limited by Limitation Order L-13-a; looseleaf binding wire, rings, posts, and metal parts; mail boxes—except those required by U. S. postal regulations; mailing tubes; manicure implements; marine hardware for pleasure boats; marquees; match boxes; material for housing not otherwise specified in this order—except as allowed in Defense Housing Critical List; mechanical bookbinding wire; measuring pumps and dispensers for gasoline station, garage and household use, including but not limited to: gasoline dispensing pumps, grease pumps, oil pumps, except barrel pumps and lubesters;

kerosene pumps, air pumps; menu holders; milk bottle cases; millinery wire and gimps; mop wringers; music stands.

Napkin rings; necktie racks; newspaper boxes or holders; novelties and souvenirs of all kinds; office machinery used for: change making, coin handling, check cancelling, check cutting, check dating, check numbering, check signing, check sorting, check writing, envelope handling, envelope opening, envelope sealing, envelope stamping, envelope mailing, folding contents of envelope; ornamental hardware and mouldings; outdoor fireplace parts.

Packing twine holders; pail clasps; paint spray outfits—except industrial; paper rollers, household; park and recreational benches; parking meters; pencils, automatic; pen holders; permanent wave machines; pet beds; pet cages; pet dishes; phonograph motors, hand wound; phonograph record blanks; photographic accessories; physical reducing machines; picture and mirror hardware; pie plates—except commercial or institutional; pipe cases; pipe-cleaner knives; plant and flower supports; pleasure boats; pneumatic tube delivery systems, except industrial; polishing-wax applicators; polishing-wax sprayers; portable bath tubs; posts for fencing—except on A-2 or higher; poultry incubator cabinets; push carts; push plates and kick plates, doors; racquets; radiator enclosures; radio antenna poles—except on ratings of A-2 or higher; refrigerator containers and trays, household; rotary door bells.

Salesmen's display cases and sales kits; salt and pepper holders; sample boxes; scaffolding; screen frames—except industrial processing; scrubbing boards; service food trays; sewer pipe, exterior installations—except for vents and within 5 ft. of buildings; sheet iron or hoop iron packings for cookies and sweet goods; shirt and stocking driers; shoe cleaning kits; shower reception—except frames; shower stalls—except frames; show window lighting and display equipment; sign hanger frames; sign posts; signets; silos—except strapping and reinforcing; sink aprons and legs; sink metal drainboards, both integral and removable; sitz baths; skates, roller and ice; ski racks; slide fasteners; snow shovels and pushers, hand and power propelled—except A-1-j or higher; spittoons; sporting and athletic goods; spray containers, household; stadiums; stamped bakery equipment; stamps and tablets; starter shingle strips; statues; steel wool for household use made from other than waste; store display equipment and show cases; structural steel home construction; subway turnstiles; sugar cube dryer trays; sugar holders; swivel chairs.

Table name-card holders; table tops for household use; tags: identification; key; name; price; tanks (strapping excluded): dipping—for animals; watering—for animals; feeding—for animals; storage, beer; storage, water—except: (a) in tropical climates; (b) heights in excess of 100 feet; (c) boilers, hot water and storage; (d) pneumatic pressure tanks under 31 gallons. Teapots; telephone bell boxes—except bases and where required for safety; telephone booths; telescopes—except U. S. Government Agencies; terrazzo spacers and decorative strips—except hospital operating rooms; thermos jugs and bottles over 1 qt.; thermometer bases, household; tile, steel-back; tongs, food handling and household use; tool boxes—except industrial; tool cases—except industrial; tool handles—except power driven; urinals.

Wagon bodies, frames and wheels, all metal—except for construction; voting machines; wardrobe trunks; wastebaskets; water color paint boxes; weather stripping; wheelbarrows—except wheels; whiskey service sets; window display advertising; window stools; window ventilators—except industrial and hospitals; wine coolers; wine service sets; wire parcel handles and holders; wire racks and baskets—except (a) industrial, (b) scientific laboratory equipment, (c) animal cages for biological work; work benches—except shipboard and industrial where required for safety.

LIST B

Access panels; acoustical ceilings; air-conditioning systems; area walls; ash sieves; attic fans; automobile accessories; automotive replacement parts, nonfunctional; awning frames and supports; barber and beauty shop furniture; baskets; bathtubs; B-B shot for air rifles; beds—except hospital; bed spring frames; beer kegs—except hoop and fittings for wooden kegs; beer mugs; bench legs; binoculars; bird houses and feeders; biscuit boxes; blackboards; bottle holders; bread racks; butter knives.

Cabinets; cake cutters; cake tongs; canopies and supports; cans or containers for: antifreeze, under 8 gal. size; candy, chalk, coffee, nuts, pencils, tobacco products; cash boxes; cash registers; ceilings; cigarette lighters; clock cases; clothes line pulleys; clothes line reels; cocktail shakers; coffee roasting machinery; cooking stoves, commercial electric; counter tops; culverts; cupboard turns; cups of all kinds, drinking; dishwashing machines; dispensers, hand, for: paper products, soap; door closets; door handles; door stops; drawer pulls; dust collecting systems and equipment.

Egg slicers; electric water coolers; erasing knives; escalators; feed troughs; fence posts; fireplace equipment—except dampers; flagpoles; flashlight tubes; floor and ceiling plates for piping; floor polishing machines; flour, salt and pepper shakers; fountain pens; furniture; garage hoists, car lifts and racks; grass shears; grilles—sewer; gutters, spouting, conductor pipe, and fittings for single family dwellings; hand mirrors; hat-making machinery; helmets; hose reels; ice box exteriors; ice cream freezers, household; incinerators; insulation, metal reflecting type; jelly molds.

Kitchenware of stainless steel; lard or vegetable oil tubs; laundry chutes, laundry trays; lavatories; lawn sprinklers; lighting poles and standards; lockers; looseleaf binding wire, rings, posts and metal parts; mail boxes; mailing tubes; measuring pumps and dispensers for gasoline—station, garage, household use, including but not limited to: gasoline dispensing pumps; grease pumps; oil pumps; kerosene pumps; air pumps; millinery wire and glads. Office machinery used for: change making; coin handling; check cancelling; check cutting; check dating; check numbering; check signing; check sorting; check writing; envelope sealing.

Paint spray outfits; pencils, automatic; pen holders; photographic accessories; picture and mirror hardware; pie plates; pneumatic tube

WPB forbids copper and its alloys for a hundred-odd more civilian products

The War Production Board on May 7 prohibited the use of copper and its alloys, including brass and bronze, in an additional hundred-odd civilian products; curtailed other uses after June 15, and ordered a number of other restrictions designed to conserve supplies of the red metal.

The action was taken in a revision of Order M-9-c, issued by Industry Operations Director Knowlson. M-9-c originally was issued on October 21, 1941, and has been amended frequently.

New ban applies May 31

The May 7 order maintains the list A of the previous order in substantially the same form. Use of copper in the manufacture of articles on this list was prohibited after March 31, 1942.

A new list, A-1, is added. Items on this list must not be manufactured, assembled or finished after May 31.

Probably the greatest dislocation the order will cause will be by the ban on manufacture of the common household pin. Approximately one-third of the pins manufactured in 1940 and 1941 were made of brass, with the remainder of steel. There is no ban on steel pins, but the rate of production is limited.

Among other items on list A-1, are bulbs and neon and fluorescent tubes for advertising and display purposes, bulbs and cords for Christmas trees; dog collars, fountain pens and musical instruments.

Unlisted items restricted later

Beginning May 7, manufacturers may not further process copper, brass or bronze plate, sheet, strip, rolls, coils, wire, rod, bar, tube, pipe, extrusions, ingots or powder to make items on list A-1 if

the materials are in substantially the same form in which they were acquired.

Manufacture with copper of every article not on lists A or A-1 must stop on June 15 if any copper is used which was obtained before February 28, 1942, unless the article is being made to fill a purchase order rated A-1-k or higher, or its manufacture has been specifically authorized by an application filed on Form PD-426.

If the raw material has been obtained since February 28 and is being used to make articles not on the lists, it is the attitude of WPB that the copper was properly allocated and no further restriction is necessary.

The previous exemption for parts to conduct electricity is removed. If an article appears on list A or list A-1, use of copper in its manufacture is prohibited for any purpose, unless a specific exception is made in the order.

Plating also restricted

Copper plating of all articles mentioned in the lists also is prohibited after May 31.

The restrictive provisions of the order do not apply to Army, Navy, or Maritime Commission contracts, where the contracts call for copper, brass, or bronze, until August 1.

Form PD-426 is provided to permit manufacturers of items not specifically prohibited to request permission to continue after June 15. It is not an appeal from the order in the usual sense, but an opportunity to review specific cases. It is the intention to grant such request when the circumstances justify this action.

PD-167, as revised, continues to be the regular appeals form.

Rug, carpet makers allowed to use up jute yarn on hand

Restrictions of the jute order (M-70) were relaxed by telegrams sent May 8 to permit rug and carpet manufacturers to use jute yarns on hand in the manufacture of rugs and carpets beyond the previous shutoff date.

The purpose of the relaxation is to make it possible for rug and carpet manufacturers to weave stocks of dyed wool carpet yarn to the extent that jute yarn is available.

delivery systems; portable bath tubs; push carts; push plates and kick plates, doors; radio antennae poles; refrigerator containers and trays, household.

Salt and pepper holders; scaffolding; service food trays; sewer pipe, exterior installations; shoe cleaning kits; shower receptors; shower stalls; show window lighting and display equipment; sink aprons and legs; sink; metal drain boards, both integral and removable; ski racks; slide fasteners; sporting and athletic goods; stamped bakery equipment; stamps and tablets; sugar holders; swivel chairs; tags—identification; name; tanks—storage, water; teapots; telephone bell boxes; telescopes; thermos jugs and bottles over 1 quart; tile, steel-back; tongs, food-handling and household use; tool boxes; tool cases; urinals; wagon bodies, frames and wheels, all metal; wastebaskets; wheelbarrows; wire racks and baskets; work benches.

Furniture makers rapidly shifting production to wide variety of war items

Airplane trainers and gliders instead of wooden office desks; ammunition boxes instead of metal letter-trays and wastebaskets; and airplane fuel lines instead of chrome-plated chair legs—this is the story of the conversion program for the furniture industry, the country's second largest producer of consumers' durable goods.

Over $500,000,000 in contracts

The industry in normal times produces metal and wooden furniture for the home and the office valued at about $1,000,000 annually, second in dollar value to consumers' goods only to the automobile industry.

Today, makers of furniture all over the country are rapidly changing over their tools and facilities not only to the production of wooden airplanes and gliders, but to a wide variety of other war items. Prime contracts and subcontracts held by the industry exceed $500,000,000. Appreciable increases in the rate of production of war goods are expected to be evident by the end of 1942. The rate of war production by the middle of next year is expected to be equal to the recent annual production of civilian items.

War equipment soon to be produced in quantity by metal furniture companies includes ammunition boxes, tail and wing assemblies for airplanes, rear fin struts, and seating equipment for planes, tanks, and ships. The industry, of course, will continue to make types of metal furniture needed by the armed services here and abroad.

At least 3 woodworking furniture plants are now producing airplane parts out of plywood, and eventually, 12 or more companies are expected to be engaged in the production of wooden airplanes and subassemblies.

$108,600,000 in metal-working machinery shipped in March

The value of new machine tools, presses, and other metal working machinery shipped during March was $108,600,000, it was announced May 7 by William H. Harrison, WPB Director of Production.

Shipments of machine tools alone mounted to 24,300 units, with a total value of $98,400,000. During February, 20,307 units, valued at $84,355,000 were shipped.

⋆ ⋆ ⋆

Softwood lumber critically needed, Nelson tells industry

WPB Chairman Donald M. Nelson May 5 appealed to logging and sawmill operators and their employees immediately to bring production of softwood construction lumber to a maximum in order to meet the urgent needs of the Army, Navy, and Maritime Commission for housing and other purposes.

Mr. Nelson, in a telegram to the Lumber and Timber Products War Committee, which represents the lumber manufacturing industry, the American Federation of Labor, and the Congress of Industrial Organizations, said that "the situation is so critical that I ask your immediate cooperation and action."

Higher production eases steel plate problems temporarily

The perplexing steel plate problem is being eased slightly by increasing production, particularly from strip mills, C. E. Adams, chief, iron and steel branch, announced May 9, but any permanent solution will depend upon new plate mills coming into operation.

Shipments for April were 895,971 tons, as compared with 878,726 in March, the previous record. Strip mills accounted for 337,519 tons of the total, an increase from this source of 31,324 tons over March.

For the second successive month, shipments on Maritime Commission orders met the tonnage asked. The total for the month was in excess of 280,000 tons.

⋆ ⋆ ⋆

Toy order clarified

The WPB May 8 issued an interpretation to the toy limitation order (L–81) to clarify the meaning of the term "raw material form" in the order.

The interpretation states that critical material, the use of which is restricted in the order, is considered to be in raw material form when it has not been fabricated or processed for use in toys or games or parts, but is in such form that it can be fabricated or processed for use in any other product.

New critical machine tools under limited allocation, 75 percent for services

All new critical machine tools were placed under a limited allocation system by WPB May 2.

General Preference Order No. E–1–b provides for an apportionment of each producer's monthly deliveries of each size of each type of tool, 75 percent to service purchasers and 25 percent to other purchasers. These allocations may be reduced to the extent in each case that purchase orders are not placed for such percentages months prior to the month of delivery.

The 75 percent for service purchasers is to be divided among the supply arms and bureaus of the Army and Navy and the Maritime Commission in accordance with a percentage table for each type of tool accompanying the order.

The 25 percent for other purchasers is to be divided among foreign purchasers and essential industries in this country and Canada, and will be scheduled for delivery in accordance with preference ratings.

A new numerical master preference list has been formulated to cover the sequence of deliveries to service purchasers, but it will have no effect upon other purchasers.

Halt street light extensions except for safety, WPB asks

WPB's power branch has asked all electric utility systems to discontinue for the duration of the war all street lighting extensions except those needed for public safety.

Agreements between utilities and governmental agencies providing for street and highway lighting extensions should be suspended, the branch said in a letter to all utilities. The utilities were asked in the letter not to apply for priority assistance in obtaining material for such extensions.

The suggestions do not apply to illumination for critical areas "where traffic conditions are enormously aggravated by war industries, camps, airports, etc." Nor do the suggestions apply to traffic-control signals where necessary. Applications for priority assistance where installations are essential to public safety will continue to receive consideration by the WPB power branch.

British release steel, copper scrap to U. S. munitions plants

Through the efforts of WPB officials, more than 27,000,000 pounds of steel and 500,000 pounds of copper have been freed by the British Purchasing Commission for use in American munitions plants working on United Nations war orders.

The steel and copper had been machined into certain field gun projectiles, largely made obsolete by the loss of Allied equipment at Dunkirk. Shipping delays further reduced the potential value of the shells. They were offered to U. S. Army Ordnance, which could make no use of them in their present condition.

The industrial salvage section of WPB announced May 8 that the iron and steel section of the British Purchasing Commission has been authorized by London to dispose of the shells as scrap metal.

This cartoon was drawn especially for OEM by O. Soglow. This notice constitutes full permission to reprint the drawing. Engravings may be made direct from this reproduction, or three-column mats will be furnished on application to Distribution Section, Division of Information, Office for Emergency Management, Washington, D. C.

Fuel oil sales, deliveries not subject to ratings

Because some oil companies have been refusing to deliver fuel oil without preference ratings, the WPB May 5 issued an order cancelling all preference ratings assigned to fuel oil purchases, and providing specifically that sales and deliveries of fuel oil may be made without regard to any preference rating heretofore issued.

Zinc sulphide pigment pool is established

A monthly producers' pool in zinc sulphide pigments, of which lithopone is the principal product, was established May 6 by the Director of Industry Operations.

Lithopone is an opaque white pigment and is, together with titanium dioxide and white lead, a principal ingredient of white and light-colored paints.

The May 6 order, M-128, provides that the Director of Industry Operations will set up by the 15th of each month a percentage of all classes of lithopone manufactured, to be set aside for the following month. Mandatory orders will be filled from this pool, after which other production may be sold without restriction.

Exports of lithopone other than lend-lease cannot be made except upon application to the War Production Board on Form PD–464.

Clearing house set up to handle problems of over 2,900,000 service institutions

Organization of a services branch within the Division of Industry Operations to act as a clearing house for problems confronting the more than 2,900,000 service institutions in the country was announced May 3 by John R. Kimberly, assistant chief of the bureau of industry branches.

Functions of new branch

Service institutions—such as banks, insurance companies, commercial laundries, barber and beauty shops, theaters and other amusement enterprises, hotels, office buildings, retail stores, wholesale houses, and repair shops—employ approximately 8,000,000 persons.

The functions of the branch will include processing priority applications from service industries, and assistance in conversion to war work wherever possible.

The branch is headed by Nathaniel G. Burleigh, who was chief of the former service and distribution, office and service machinery branch and who is a veteran member of the WPB organization. The assistant chief is O. G. Sawyer, of Durham, N. C., formerly supervisor of purchases for Duke University and Duke Hospital.

In addition to serving as the focal point to which all institutions classified as service institutions can bring their problems, the branch has supervision of the office machinery industry and the services machinery industry, including all types of office machinery, domestic laundry machinery, commercial laundry machinery, dry cleaning machinery, industrial vacuum cleaners, floor maintenance machinery, and institutional dish, glass, and silver washing machinery.

Mr. Burleigh announced establishment of eight sections within the branch, the first two dealing with machinery and the remaining six concerned with services to all service institutions.

The sections and the chiefs appointed for each are:

OFFICE MACHINERY SECTION: Arthur Sanders, of Dothan, Ala., who has spent 6 years serving with the Controller of the Currency and who has been engaged in WPB liaison work between the Army and Navy and various war agencies.

SERVICE MACHINERY SECTION: L. L. Frey, of New York City, former industrial engineer for the General Electric Co., American Pencil Co., Cincinnati Planer Co., and other firms.

AMUSEMENTS SECTION: Christopher J. Dunphy, of New York City, former assistant to Adolph Zukor, chairman of the board of Directors of Paramount Pictures, Inc., and former director of advertising and publicity for Paramount.

FINANCIAL AND BUSINESS SERVICES SECTION: James D. Vail, Jr., of Evanston, Ill., who was a partner in Crane, McMahon & Co., a banking and brokerage concern.

RETAIL AND WHOLESALE TRADE SECTION: S. J. Dunaway, of Dover, N. H., former president of Expello Corporation, sales manager of the Lye Department of Hooker Electro Chemical Co., Niagara Falls, N. Y., and advertising manager and assistant sales manager of B. T. Babbitt, Inc., New York City.

OFFICE BUILDINGS, HOTELS, AND RESTAURANTS SECTION: Frank A. Duggan, of Santa Monica, Calif., former president of Greely Square Hotel Co., and executive vice president of Hotel Statler Co., in charge of all hotel operations.

PERSONAL SERVICES SECTION: Orval A. Slater, of Dallas, Tex., former president of National Institute of Dyeing and Cleaning.

REPAIR AND GENERAL SERVICES SECTION: Dewey M. Crim, of Washington, D. C., former executive of Crim's Store & Fixture Co., Memphis, Tenn., and sales engineer for Thomas Grate Bar Co., Birmingham, Ala.

★ ★ ★

WPB PLACARDS TO MARK APPROVED PROJECTS

Placards showing that approval has been granted by WPB were being sent last week to builders of authorized projects to be displayed conspicuously on the premises during construction.

Printed in blue on a white background, the placard carries the initials WPB on which are superimposed the words:

AUTHORIZED CONSTRUCTION
WAR PRODUCTION BOARD

There is space on the placard for a serial number, identifying the individual project, which will be given the project by the War Production Board. The placard may be used only for the particular project for which it is issued and should be destroyed when the project is completed.

Only WPB issues the placards.

Juke box makers may dispose of materials on A-2 orders

Manufacturers of automatic phonographs and other amusement machines, who have on hand inventories of raw materials and semi-processed and finished parts, frozen by the terms of Limitation Order L-21-a, are now permitted, by an amendment to that order, to dispose of such inventories to fill orders bearing preference ratings higher than A-2.

Suppliers may replenish stocks of specific "short" items regardless of total inventory

Wholesalers and distributors covered by the Suppliers' Inventory Limitation Order, L-63, will be permitted to accept deliveries of limited quantities of specific items, regardless of their total inventory, by Amendment No. 2 to the order, issued May 6.

Amendment No. 2 to L-63 is designed to allow suppliers who are subject to the order to replenish stocks of specific items in which they are "short" even when their total inventory exceeds the maximum permitted by the order. The amendment allows a wholesaler or distributor to accept deliveries of specific items of such supplies up to a total dollar volume equal to his sales of these specific items during the preceding month. This will prevent a shortage of such items in communities served by suppliers whose total inventory now exceeds the maximum permitted by the order.

Makers of outboard motors allowed to sell to 10 agencies

An amendment to the outboard motor order (Limitation Order L-80) issued May 2 permits the sale or lease, by manufacturers, of motors of 6 horse-power or more to the Army, Navy, Maritime Commission, Panama Canal, Coast and Geodetic Survey, Coast Guard, Civil Aeronautics Authority, National Advisory Commission for Aeronautics and Office of Scientific Research and Development.

Aluminum supplies removed from restrictions of L-63

Stocks of supplies made of aluminum in the hands of wholesalers and distributors are removed from the restrictions of the suppliers' inventory limitation order, L-63, by Exemption No. 4, announced May 5 by the Director of Industry Operations. The exemption permits suppliers to omit their stocks of aluminum and aluminum products in calculating their total permissible inventory as prescribed by L-63. The action was taken because distribution of aluminum through warehouses is already strictly controlled under Supplementary Order M-1-f.

Use of vital, scarce materials curbed for safety equipment

In order to conserve the supply of materials urgently needed in war production, strict regulations on the use of aluminum, copper, plastics, and several other commodities in the manufacture of safety equipment were put into effect by the WPB May 5.

Safety equipment, as defined by the order, includes guards, shields, containers, harnesses, headgears, belts, shoes, protective clothing or coverings, masks, respirator inhalers, resuscitating apparatus, measuring instruments, indicating instruments, protective creams, treads, warning signs, and all other such safety articles.

The order prohibits the use of scarce materials in these items except:

1. For A-2 or higher-rated orders, if the equipment was manufactured prior to the date of the order, or from parts ready for assembly on the date of the order;
2. As permitted by an appendix to the order; or
3. Within 90 days of the effective date for delivery to the Army, Navy, or Maritime Commission.

The critical materials affected are aluminum, asbestos cloth, chromium, copper, copper base alloys, nickel, corrosion-resisting steel, alloy steel, tin, synthetic plastics, magnesium, rubber, synthetic rubber, and neoprene.

★ ★ ★

Ratings modified on hydrocarbon solvents

Changed preference ratings for all permitted uses of chlorinated hydrocarbon solvents were announced May 2 by the Director of Industry Operations, with amendment of Order M-41.

The order extends A-10 ratings for such solvents to be used in the fumigation of stored products, including grain; for charging and recharging fire extinguishers; for laboratories, hospitals and public institutions; for processing and manufacturing food, chemicals, rubber, petroleum, and plywood; for cleaning metal parts of electrical equipment; for the manufacture of refrigerants; and for degreasing machines used in the manufacture of war materials.

B-2 ratings are assigned for degreasing machines other than those used on Army and Navy contracts, for packaged spotting and cleaning preparations, for dry cleaning establishments, and for manual cleaning of other than metal parts of electrical equipment. B-2 ratings are restricted to 50 percent of average monthly consumption in the base period set up in the order.

No other uses of chlorinated hydrocarbon solvents are permitted with the exception that any person may purchase up to one gallon without a preference certificate or rating. B-2 ratings are restricted to 50 percent of average monthly consumption in the base period set up in the order.

The previous order was due to expire on May 15. The May 2 amendments took effect immediately and will continue in effect until revoked.

ELECTRIC RANGE STOCKS FROZEN

All domestic electric ranges in the hands of manufacturers, distributors and retail dealers were frozen May 2 by WPB.

In order to make existing stocks and future production available for new war housing, Army and Navy and lend-lease orders, Supplementary Limitation Order L-23-b forbids the sale, lease or transfer of any domestic electric range except on a preference rating of A-9 or higher, or by specific authorization by the Director of Industry Operations. Delivery was permitted on ranges actually in transit May 2.

The order provides for increased production of electric ranges during the month of May, above the quotas established for the past 4 months. After June 1, no domestic electric ranges may be produced except to fill orders bearing a preference rating of A-1-k or higher.

2½-inch brass hose couplings frozen for distributors

Issuance of Amendment No. 2 to the Limitation Order on fire protective equipment, freezing all 2½-inch brass fire-hose couplings in the hands of coupling distributors, was announced May 5 by Director of Industry Operations Knowlson.

This provision supplements Amendment No. 1 to the order (L-39), which froze such couplings in the hands of manufacturers.

⊥ ⊥ ⊥

Ban on private imports extended

WPB on May 4 added a number of materials to the restriction on private importation into the United States imposed by General Imports Order M-63.

Added to the order are cube (timbo or barbasco) root, derris root and tuba or tube root, beryl ore and beryllium ore, metallic beryllium and beryllium oxides and salts and two additional classifications of flax.

M-63 prohibits any person, except Government agencies or their authorized representatives, from making arrangements for importing materials listed in the order into the United States, except under contracts existing at the effective date of the order.

Imports made under contract must not be sold, or transferred beyond a place of initial storage, except to a Government agency, under an existing contract, or with special authorization from the Director of Industry Operations.

Czechs, Free French, Turks, Iceland on preference list

Czechoslovakia, Free France, Iceland, and Turkey have been added to the list of countries whose government orders are defined as "defense orders" under the terms of Priorities Regulation No. 1 as amended, by Amendment No. 2 to the regulation.

This means government orders from these countries are automatically assigned a preference rating of A-10 if no higher rating has been assigned by certificate or otherwise, and that such orders must be accepted and placed in production schedules in accordance with the rating.

Warehouses restricted to A-10 in delivering iron and steel

Revision of Order M-21-b, the iron and steel warehouse order, to make it conform to Order M-21 was announced May 4 by the Director of Industry Operations.

M-21 forbids deliveries by producers on ratings lower than A-10 except in certain specified cases. The May 4 order applies the same restriction to warehouses. Warehouses are to receive deliveries on quotas established by the Director of Industry Operations.

. ★ ★ ★

Control tightened on segregation, sale of aluminum scrap

Amendments to Supplementary Order M-1-d designed to place firmer control over the segregation and sale of aluminum scrap were issued May 2 by the Director of Industry Operations.

These changes are made in the order:

The maker of segregated scrap must hereafter furnish the buyer with a signed statement showing the specifications, form, weight, and name and address of the plant where the scrap is generated. The date of sale and names and addresses of the transacting parties must also be shown and any further resale must be similarly endorsed and transferred.

Because dealers have been unable to function effectively under the 1,000-pound limitation formerly in effect, the new order provides that segregated scrap of top quality alloy may be sold to a dealer or an approved smelter as well as to a producer, up to 5,000 pounds per month.

Plant scrap is redefined in the order to hold under strict control for recovery as secondary aluminum all scrap which contains 15 percent or more aluminum by weight. Scrap with less than 15 percent aluminum content may be sold to any buyer.

Questions and Answers on Priorities

1. Q. What is a "subcontract"?

A. It refers to a contract made by a prime contractor with another company for the production of parts necessary for the prime contract. The obvious tendency of subcontracting is to spread war contracts and to enable small companies to undertake essential work on prime contracts, which of necessity are normally held by the larger companies.

2. Q. How does the new "stop" order (conservation order L-41) on construction differ from the old SPAB policy that has been in effect since Oct. 1941?

A. The new order goes further. The SPAB announcement made it clear that no priority assistance would be given to nonessential construction. The new order, however, provides that no construction may be started, except in a few instances, without permission. It also forbids the sale, delivery, or withdrawal from inventory of any construction material in order to begin construction not authorized by WPB.

3. Q. What new appeals system is set up in the sweeping steel order M-126?

A. All appeals under M-126 on the related Form PD-437, must be filed with the field office of the War Production Board in the district in which the plant filing the appeal is located.

4. Q. Can copper still be used after June 15 in the manufacture of an article not specifically prohibited in lists A1 and A of the new freeze order M-9-c as amended?

A. To meet the war demand for copper, the manufacture of such articles must stop on June 15, if any copper used was obtained before Feb. 28, 1942, unless the article bears an A-1-k or higher rating, or unless a specific exception is authorized by an application filed on Form PD-246.

Perkins named to paper branch

Appointment of James A. Perkins as associate price executive of the paper and paper products branch of the OPA was announced May 8 by Herbert F. Taggart, director of the general products division.

PRIORITY ACTIONS
*From April 30
*Through May 7

Subject	Order No.	Related form	Issued	Expiration date	Rating
Aluminum: a. Aluminum scrap: 1. Places firmer control over segregation and sales of aluminum scrap.	M-1-d amendment No. 1.		5-2-42		
Amusement machines: a. Automatic phonographs and weighing, amusement and gaming machines: 1. Mfrs. who have on hand inventories of raw materials and semiprocessed and finished parts, frozen by L-21-a, now permitted to dispose of such inventories to fill orders bearing preference ratings higher than A-2.	L-21-a amendment No. 1.		5-2-42		
Burlap: a. Jute and jute products: 1. Restricts processing of jute for mfr. of carpet yarns during month of April.	M-70 amendment No. 2.		5-1-42		
b. Prohibits use of in mfr. of rugs, carpets and linoleum for civilian use.	M-70 amendment No. 3.	PD-222b.	4-30-42		
Canning: a. Tinplate and Terneplate: 1. Permits utilization of tinplate sheets, usable only for food cans of restricted sizes, if sheets were on hand 2-11-42. Extends indefinitely telegraphic exceptions. Permits use of cans produced from tinplate under terms of this amendment.	M-81 amendment No. 2.		4-30-42		
Chemicals: a. Chlorinated hydrocarbon solvents: 1. Announces changed preference ratings for all permitted uses of chlorinated hydrocarbon solvents.	M-41 as amended 5-2-42.		5-2-42	Until revoked.	A-10, B-2.
b. Napthalene: 1. Conservation order. (a) Distribution placed under field control commencing June 1.	M-105.	PD-434, 435.	5-6-42		
Copper: a. Prohibits use of copper and its alloys, including brass and bronze, in additional hundred-odd civilian products, curtails other uses after June 15, and orders a number of other restrictions designed to conserve supplies of the red metal.	M-9-c as amended 5-7-42.	PD-167, 426.	5-7-42	Until revoked.	
Fire apparatus: a. Fire protective equipment: 1. Freeze all brass fire-hose couplings in hands of coupling distributors.	L-89 amendment No. 2.		5-5-42		
Fuel oil: a. Cancels all preference ratings assigned to fuel oil purchases and provides specifically that sales and deliveries of fuel oil may be made without regard to any preference rating heretofore issued.	M-144.		5-5-42	Until revoked.	
Goatskin, kidskin and cabrettas: a. Limits amount that may be put into process by any tanner during May to 70 percent of monthly average of skins put into process during 1941; removes India-tanned goatskins from restrictions.	M-114 amendment No. 1.		4-30-42		
Hand trucks: a. Eliminates all but the most essential uses of rubber tires on hand trucks.	L-111.	PD-468.	5-7-42	Until revoked.	
Imports order: a. Adds a number of materials to the restricted list on private importation into the U. S. imposed by M-63.	M-63 amendment No. 3.		5-4-42		
Indian kyanite: a. Conservation order. b. To conserve supply and direct distribution.	M-148	PD-466	5-6-42	Until revoked.	
Kapok: a. Prohibits use of as insulation for industrial refrigeration and as stuffing for civilian maritime equipment.	M-86 amendment No. 2.		4-30-42		A-2.

Subject	Order Number	Related form	Issued	Expiration date	Rating
Lead:					
a. Supplementary order: 1. May lead pool set at 15 percent of March production.	M-38-b			5-1-42	
Outboard motors: a. Permits sale or lease, by mfgs., of motors of 6 horsepower or more to the Army, Navy, and other Government agencies.	L-80 amendment No. 1.			5-2-42	*
Pencils (wood-cased): a. Prohibits use of any metal, except limited amounts of iron or steel, in mfr. of; restricts use of pigments and other materials for finishing.	L-113				
Pigments, zinc sulphide: a. Establishes a monthly producers' pool, from which orders will be filled. Production, other than that set aside may be sold without restriction. Exports prohibited except with specific authorization.	M-128	PD 464		5-6-42	Until revoked
Plumbing and heating: a. Permits use of lead and zinc as a preserving finish on plumbing fixtures and trim.	L-42 Schedule V, amendment No. 1.			5-6-42	
b. Permits Dir. of Industry Operations to make exceptions to the Schedule in meritorious cases.	L-42 Schedule VII, amendment No. 1.			5-6-42	
Projects (defense): a. Materials entering into: 1. Suppliers of materials used in construction of vital aluminium and magnesium plants advised that deliveries should be made on schedule even though subsequent orders assigned under P-19-i carry higher preference ratings.	P-19-i, interpretation No. 1.			5-6-42	
Quinine, totaquine and cinchona bark: a. Conservation order: 1. Distribution and use of Totaquine, except as an antimalaria agent, prohibited by WPB in order to prevent an evasion of the intent of M-131 on Quinine; requires that primary use of Cinchona Bark must be for extraction of Quinine or Totaquine.	M-131 (As amended 4-30-42).	PD-401		4-30-42	
Railroad equipment: a. Excludes mining locomotives from provisions of L-97.	L-97 amendment No. 1.			4-29-42	
b. Supplementary order: 1. Cancels all preference ratings of A-2 or lower on material for freight car construction which has not already been received by or placed in transit to the producers; permits any producer to sell and deliver any material which he has on hand or in transit to any other producer of freight cars.	L-97-a-1			4-29-42	
Rubber: a. Specifications for mfr. of feeding nipples.	M-15-b-1 amendment No. 5; M-15-b-1 as amended.			5-6-42 (Effective 5-15-42).	
b. Rubber yarn and elastic thread: 1. Amended and extended	M-124, amendment No. 2.	PD-433		4-29-42	
Steel and iron: a. Conservation order	M-126	PD-437		5-5-42	Until revoked
Suppliers order: a. Wholesalers and distributors covered by L-63 will be permitted to accept deliveries of limited quantities of specific items, regardless of their total inventory.	L-63 amendment No. 2.			5-5-42	
b. Stocks of supplies made of aluminum in the hands of wholesalers and distributors are removed from restrictions of L-63.	L-63 exemption No. 4.			5-4-42	Until revoked
Tea: a. To restrict distribution: 1. Relaxes some distribution provisions of original order and makes available more tea than permitted under original order.	M-111, as amended 5-1-42.			5-1-42	
b. Superseding M-111-a, establishes Tea quotas for any Packer or Wholesale Receiver for months of May and June, 1942.	M-111-b			5-1-42	

(Continued on page 16)

Plant leasing or toll work doesn't excuse manufacturer from preference schedules

Manufacturers cannot escape their responsibility for scheduling deliveries in accordance with preference ratings by leasing their plants or making their products under a toll agreement, it was explained May 7 in an official interpretation of Priorities Regulation No. 1.

It has been a practice of some manufacturers at times to lease all or part of their plants to one of their large customers for a few days a month, while the plant continues to operate with regular personnel and is producing the manufacturers' regular products.

In other cases, manufacturers have processed materials furnished to them by their customers on a fee or toll basis.

The interpretation of Priorities Regulation No. 1, issued May 7 by the Director of Industry Operations points out that in neither of these cases is the manufacturer permitted to interrupt or delay his production schedules or orders bearing preference ratings, but must fill them in accordance with the ratings and delivery dates.

Booklet explains cost methods under United States contracts

A handbook which explains principles for determining costs under Government contracts has just been prepared by the accounting advisory branch of the War Production Board.

For some time costs under Government contracts have been based on a decision of the Treasury ("TD 5000"). The booklet just issued is not a revision or an interpretation of TD 5000 but explains in simple and complete terms the principles of costs as covered by TD 5000. Copies of the booklet can be obtained from the Superintendent of Documents, Government Printing Office, Washington, D. C., at 10 cents each.

Roaster's green coffee inventory limited to 2 months' supply

The WPB May 8 issued Amendment 1 to the Coffee Order, M-135, restricting a roaster's inventory of green coffee to a 2-months' supply. In calculating this inventory, any roaster who has more than 1 month's supply of roasted coffee on hand or in his control must include such coffee with his green coffee. Any amount of roasted coffee less than 1 month's supply may be disregarded.

Restrictions on distribution of new office machines relaxed to aid dealers

The WPB May 8 modified its restrictions on distribution of various types of new office machinery to enable wholesalers, distributors, retailers, and other dealers to return new equipment to manufacturers willing to accept it.

The action, embodied in Amendment No. 2 to Limitation Order L–54–b, is intended to ease financial burdens falling upon dealers as the result of restrictions in the original order, which prohibited sales, rentals, and deliveries of new office machinery except to fill orders rated A–9 or higher on Preference Rating Certificate PD–1A or PD–3A.

Shipments of brass mill, wire mill, foundry copper products limited to A–1–k

Because of the tremendous war demand for brass mill, wire mill, and foundry copper products, the WPB May 7 limited shipments of these products to ratings of A–1–k or higher, unless specific authorization is given for a lower rated shipment. Deliveries previously were permitted down to A–10 ratings.

The action was taken in an amendment to Order M–9–a issued by the Director of Industry Operations.

* * *

$5,000 per movie allowed in new materials for sets

Motion picture producers were given specific authorization by WPB May 6 to spend $5,000 per picture for new material for the construction of movie sets.

Kapok banned for some uses

The use of kapok as insulation for industrial refrigeration and as stuffing for civilian maritime equipment has been prohibited by the WPB in Amendment No. 2 to the kapok conservation order, M–85.

PRIORITY ACTIONS			*From April 30 *Through May 7		

(Continued from page 15)

Subject	Order Number	Related form	Issued	Expiration date	Rating
Tools:					
a. Machine tools—production and delivery of:					
1. All new critical machine tools placed under limited allocation system; provides for an apportionment of each producer's monthly deliveries of each size of each type of tool, 75 percent to service purchasers and 24 percent to other purchasers.	E–1–b...........	PD–3, 3A, 4....	4–30–42 (Effective 5–1–42)	Until revoked.	

SUSPENSION ORDERS

Company	Number	Violation	Penalty	Issued	Expiration date
Southern Scrap Material Co., Inc., New Orleans, La.	S–40	Accepted shipments during Oct., Nov., and Dec. 1941 and Jan. 1942 of copper scrap contrary to terms of Supplementary Order M–9–b.	Prohibited from accepting copper or copper base alloy scrap for three months; withdraws all priority assistance; requires inventory reports and disposition of stocks must be made as directed.	5–2–42	8–2–42.
Jose Del Rio Marovis, Puerto Rico.	S–46	Distilled beverage rum from molasses, which was prohibited by M–54 after Jan. 15. Violation occurred after prohibition date and before appeal was granted for relief from such provisions on Jan. 30.	For period of forty days is prohibited from using or dealing in molasses. From June 23 through Dec. 31, 1942, may not use for distilling rum more than 75 percent of quantity processed during similar period in 1941.	5–4–42 (effective 5–14–42)	12–31–42.
Borinquen Associates, Inc., Carretara Quintana, Hato Rey, Puerto Rico.	S–47	Used molasses in manufacture of distilled beverages after Jan. 15 contrary to M–54 before appeal for relief was granted Jan. 31.	For period of fourteen days shall not use or deal in molasses. From May 28 through Dec. 31, 1942, shall not use for distilling rum more than $5 percent of quantity processed during similar period in 1941.	5–4–42 (effective 5–14–42)	12–31–42.
Compania Ron Carioca Destillera, Inc., San Juan, P. R.	S–48	Used molasses in manufacture of rum although marking it for use in fruit extracts after Jan. 15 contrary to Order M–54 and before appeal for relief was granted Jan. 31.	For period of 40 days shall not use or deal in molasses; shall not use molasses for distilled rum more than 80 percent quantity processed during similar period in 1941 during period from June 23 to Dec. 31, 1942; shall not sell barrels marked "for Fruit Extracts" manufactured after Jan. 15 except for fruit extracts.	5–4–42 (effective 5–14–42)	12–31–42.
Reuben and Ralph Finkelstein, Capital Iron and Metal Co., Capital Compressed Steel Co., Oklahoma City, Okla.; Springfield, Mo., Tulsa, Okla., Topeka, Kans.	S–51	Charged with refusal to execute three iron and steel scrap allocation orders directing shipment of 1,000 tons of steel scrap to Sheffield Steel Corporation and delivering like scrap to other users.	Prohibited from accepting processing, delivering or dealing in iron and steel scrap for 3 months.	5–7–42	8–7–42.
General Motors Corporation, Detroit, Mich. (Ternstedt Mfg. Div.).	S–53	Used chrome steel in manufacture of decorative moldings for automobiles; used primary and secondary aluminum for radiator grills and other body hardware contrary to M–1–e and M–21–d.	Prohibited from manufacturing or producing for 3 months any replacement parts except as defined in P–57 and P–107.	5–2–42	8–2–42.

PRIORITIES REGULATIONS

Number	Subject	Issued
a. Priorities Reg. No. 1 as amended: 1. Interpretation No. 1 of Section 944.2.	Manufacturers cannot escape responsibility for scheduling deliveries in accordance with preference ratings by leasing their plants or making their products under a toll agreement.	5–7–42.
b. Priorities Reg. No. 1, as amended: 1. Amendment No. 2.	Czechoslovakia, Free France, Iceland, and Turkey have been added to the list of countries whose government orders are defined as "defense orders."	5–1–42.
c. Priorities Reg. No. 3: 1. Amendment No. 2.	To discontinue reports required in connection with construction project rating orders of the P–19 series.	5–5–42.

New industry advisory committees

The Bureau of Industry Advisory Committees, WPB, has announced the formation of the following new industry advisory committees:

CAFFEINE AND THEOBROMINE

Government presiding officer—William M. Bristol, Jr.

Members:

A. C. Boylston, president, Mallinckrodt Chemical Works, St. Louis, Mo.; M. J. Hartung, president, Maywood Chemical Co., Maywood, N. J.; J. J. Kerrigan, vice president, Merck & Co., Inc., Rahway, N. J.; Charles Metcalfe, vice president, General Foods Corporation, New York, N. Y.; F. P. Robert, Robert & Co., New York, N. Y.; H. F. Shattuck, washington representative, Monsanto Chemical Co., 1028 Shoreham Bldg., 15th & H Streets NW., washington, D. C.; I. Vandewater, vice president, R. W. Greef & Co., 10 Rockefeller Plaza, New York, N. Y.; W. W. White, president, Citro Chemical Co., Maywood, N. J.

CUTLERY

Government presiding officer—Jesse L. Maury.

Members:

H. Alpern, Pal Blade Co., Holyoke, Mass.; S. L. Berger, president, Rex Cutlery Co., Irvington, N. J.; G. E. Chatillon, president, Foster Bros. Cutlery Div., John Chatillon & Sons, New York, N. Y.; C. H. Corbin, treasurer, Ontario Knife Co., Franklinville, N. Y.; Ralph E. Herman, Sta-Brite Production Corporation, New Haven, Conn.; C. E. Dorrell, vice president, Russell Harrington Cutlery Co., Southbridge, Mass.; Alfred Kastor, president, Camillus Cutlery Co., New York, N. Y.; C. L. F. Wieber, president, Henkel Claus Co., Fremont, Ohio; Norman Wiss, president, J. Wiss & Sons Co., Newark, N. J.

ELECTROPLATING COMMITTEE

Government presiding officer—Robert Beatty, section chief in consumers' durable goods branch.

Members:

Gustave Cropsey, president, Gustave Cropsey, Inc., New York, N. Y.; Fred Pierdon, president, Art Metal Finishing Co., Washington, D. C.; Stan White, president, Cadmium & Nickel Plating Co., Los Angeles, Calif.; V. W. Todd, president, Hanson Van Winkle-Munning Co., Matawan, N. J.; Erwin Sohn, American Radiator & Standard Sanitary Co., Louisville, Ky.; H. Ochs, president, Economy Plating Co., Cleveland, Ohio; B. G. Daw, president, LaSalco Inc., St. Louis, Mo.; T. W. Kirby, president, A. T. Wagner Co., Detroit, Mich.; L. K. Lindahl, president, Udylite Corporation, Detroit, Mich.

FISH COMMITTEE

Government presiding officer—Lawrence T. Hopkinson.

Members:

James Abernethy, secretary, Sunset Packing Co., West Pembroke, Maine; Walter S. Hallet, president, American Fish Co., Fish Pier, Boston, Mass.; Harden F. Taylor, president, Atlantic Coast Fisheries Corporation, New York, N. Y.; Julian McPhillips, president, Southern Shellfish Co., Inc., Harvey, La.; Victor H. Elfendahl, vice-president, Alaska Pacific Salmon Co., Seattle, Wash.;

Harry A. Irving, president, Sea Pride Packaging Corporation, San Francisco, Calif.; Leland B. Irish, vice president, Coast Fishing Co., Wilmington, Calif.; Robert F. Fletcher, Jr., president, Booth Fisheries Corporation, Chicago, Ill.

INDUSTRIAL INSTRUMENTS COMMITTEE

Government presiding officer—Charles L. Saunders.

Members:

E. B. Evleth, vice president, Brown Instrument Co., 4482 Wayne Avenue, Philadelphia, Pa.; R. A. Schoenfeld, vice president, Wheelco Instruments Co., 847 West Harrison Street, Chicago, Ill.; E. M. Jones, general manager, Simplex Valve & Meter Co., 66th & Upland Streets, Philadelphia, Pa.; Barton Jones, president, Morey & Jones, Ltd., 922 South Hemlock Street, Los Angeles, Calif.; L. B. Swift, president, Taylor Instrument Co., 95 Ames Street, Rochester, N. Y.; L. G. Wilson, president, Precision Thermometer & Instrument Co., 1434 Brandywine Street, Philadelphia, Pa.; P. T. Sprague, president, Hays Corporation, P. O. Box 299, Michigan City, Ind.; H. Merrill, general manager, Manning, Maxwell & Moore, Inc., Bridgeport, Conn.; Paul A. Elfers, vice president, Fisher Governor Co., Marshalltown, Iowa; H. C. Mueller, Powers Regulator Co., 2734 Greenview Avenue, Chicago, Ill.; J. V. Geisler, president, Fulton Sylphon Co., Knoxville, Tenn.; C. S. Redding, president, Leeds & Northrup Co., 4970 Stenton Avenue, Philadelphia, Pa.; George Hendricks, vice president, Republic Flow Meters Co., 2249 Diversey Parkway, Chicago, Ill.; Rowland Hazard, vice president, Bristol Co., Waterbury, Conn.

LARGE COMPRESSOR COMMITTEE

Government presiding officer—William K. Frank.

Members:

J. F. Huvane, manager, Compressor Department, Chicago Pneumatic Tool Co., New York, N. Y.; J. B. O'Connor, vice president, Clark Bros. Co., Inc., Olean, N. Y.; T. F. Hudgins, vice president, Cooper-Bessemer Corporation, Mt. Vernon, Ohio; E. F. Schaefer, vice president, Gardner-Denver Co., Quincy, Ill.; M. C. Davison, vice president, Ingersoll-Rand Co., New York, N. Y.; J. M. Dolan, manager, Compressor Department, Sullivan Machinery Co., Michigan City, Ind.; Edwin J. Schwanhausser, vice president, Worthington Pump & Machinery Corporation, Buffalo, N. Y.; Frederick Pope, Chemical Construction Corporation, 30 Rockefeller Plaza, New York, N. Y.

NAVAL STORES SUBCOMMITTEE

Government presiding officer—J. B. Davis.

Members:

W. D. Hodges, Filtered Rosin Products, Inc., Brunswick, Ga.; Thomas J. Taylor, Jr., Taylor, Lowenstein & Co., Mobile, Ala.; E. W. Colledge, Southern Pine Chemical Co., Jacksonville, Fla.; Joseph M. Wafer, Industrial Chemical Sales Division, West Virginia Pulp & Paper Co., New York, N. Y.; W. H. Jennings, Chesapeake Camp Corporation, Franklin, Va.

PATRIOTIC FLAG COMMITTEE

Government presiding officer—Frank L. Walton.

Members:

Digby W. Chandler, Annin & Co., New York, N. Y.; Charles L. Campbell, Dettra Flag Co., Inc., Oaks, Pa.; George H. Schaller, National

Flag Co., Cincinnati, Ohio; W. C. McAllister, Collegeville Flag & Manufacturing Co., Collegeville, Pa.; George L. Glendon, Chicago Flag and Decorating Co., Chicago, Ill.; W. H. Pollock, Paramount Flag Co., San Francisco, Calif.; A. Liberman, Valley Forge Flag Co., New York, N. Y.

SILVERPLATED FLATWARE

Government presiding officer—Jesse L. Maury.

Members:

Miles E. Robertson, Oneida, Ltd., Oneida, N. Y.; J. McKenzie Morrison, Ontario Manufacturing Co., Muncie, Ind.; A. K. Hobson, Hobson & Botta Co., Danbury, Conn.; E. C. Stevens, International Silver Co., Meriden, Conn.

SOFTWOOD PLYWOOD

Government presiding officer—Arthur Upson, chief, lumber and lumber products branch.

Members:

W. E. Difford, managing director, Douglas Fir Plywood Association, Tacoma, Wash.; Frost Snyder, president, Vancouver Plywood & Veneer Co., Vancouver, Wash.; E. W. Daniels, president, Harbor Plywood Corporation, Hoquiam, Wash.; J. R. Robinson, president, Robinson Manufacturing Co., Everett, Wash.; Thomas J. Malarkey, vice president, M & M Woodworking Corporation, Portland, Oreg.; Morris Sekstrom, manager, Olympic Plywoods, Inc., Shelton, Wash.; L. G. Opsahl, sales manager, Red River Lumber Co., Westwood, Calif.; Max D. Tucker, vice president and general manager, Evans Products Co., Plywood Div., Public Service Bldg., Portland, Oreg.

TOBACCO MANUFACTURERS' TRAFFIC

Government presiding officer—John B. Smiley, chief, beverage and tobacco branch.

Members:

J. C. Turner, traffic manager, John H. Swisher & Co., Jacksonville, Fla.; Frank J. McMahon, traffic manager, General Cigar Co., New York City, N. Y.; John J. Ehrardt, H. Fendrich, Inc., Evansville, Ind.; J. A. Bloch, president, Bloch Bros. Tobacco Co., Wheeling, W. Va.; Charles W. Bumstead, president, George W. Helme Co., New York, N. Y.; T. T. Harkrader, Traffic Department, American Tobacco Co., New York, N. Y.; G. E. Goodwin, traffic manager, Liggett & Myers Tobacco Co., St. Louis, Mo.; A. J. Kneesy, traffic manager, Brown & Williamson Tobacco Co., Louisville, Ky.; L. F. Owen, traffic manager, R. J. Reynolds Tobacco Co., Winston-Salem, N. Y.

X-RAY

Government presiding officer—Milton H. Luce, health supplies branch:

Members:

Arthur Albert, president, Standard X-Ray Co., Chicago, Ill.; A. H. Feibel, president, Kelley-Koett Manufacturing Co., Inc., Covington, Ky.; W. S. Kendrick, vice president, General Electric X-Ray Corporation, Chicago, Ill.; R. R. Machlett, president, Machlett Laboratories, Inc., Springdale, Conn.; James Picker, chairman of board, Picker X-Ray Corporation, New York, N. Y.; C. V. Aggers, general manager, Westinghouse Electric & Manufacturing Co., Baltimore, Md.; W. A. Brendecke, general manager, F. Mattern Manufacturing Co., Chicago, Ill.

PRICE ADMINISTRATION . . .

Separate ceilings set on all sales of used mechanical household refrigerators

Substantial savings for the average householder seeking to purchase a used mechanical household refrigerator because of the current difficulty in obtaining a new refrigerator were made possible May 6 as the result of a separate price action by Price Administrator Henderson placing a ceiling of prices, reflecting February 1942 levels, on all sales of used mechanical household refrigerators.

First action of its kind

Maximum prices in specific dollars and cents figures are listed for hundreds of second-hand refrigerators of all brands and models in the order — maximum price regulation No. 139 (Used Mechanical Household Refrigerators).

The action, giving separate price treatment to a second-hand household commodity, was the first of its kind. Previously, used typewriters and used tires were brought under price regulations.

The regulation is effective May 18, the same day on which the General Maximum Price Regulation, freezing prices of virtually all retail commodities at March levels becomes effective. Until the provisions of the order can be applied, OPA has requested that second-hand refrigerators be sold at prices no higher than prices listed in the regulation. Consumers were advised that no price control on the used boxes exists until May 18.

Ceiling includes taxes

The regulation sets specific top prices that may be charged for "as is," "unreconditioned," and "reconditioned" boxes. In general, the ceiling price for a reconditioned refrigerator is less than half the manufacturers' original suggested retail price for the same machine when new. Maximum prices for most unreconditioned boxes run about $30 per unit less, (while for "as is" boxes the ceiling goes down as low as $10.50 each).

All of the maximum prices exclude Federal excise taxes or any State and municipal taxes that are generally passed on separately to the buyer.

Although sellers of used refrigerators realized adequate returns from sales based on February prices, OPA found that, as a result of this pressure, prices in the second-hand market continued to advance in March. The May 6 action was designed to return the prices of the second-hand refrigerators to the reasonable levels prevailing in the latter part of February. Under the provisions of the general maximum price regulation, the March prices would have been established.

Other provisions

While the regulation contains a maximum price for virtually every make and model of refrigerator likely to be sold at second-hand, a formula is given to enable a seller to determine his top price for any box that may have been omitted.

For sales in 11 western states the seller may add $5 to the maximum price allowed by the order. The states included are: Montana, Wyoming, Colorado, New Mexico, Arizona, Utah, Idaho, Nevada, California, Oregon, and Washington.

Evicting tenants won't enable landlords to collect higher rents, says Henderson

Bluntly declaring that "we cannot and will not tolerate wholesale evictions of war workers," Price Administrator Henderson served notice May 3 that landlords who evict tenants in the hope of evading maximum rent regulations "are engaging in a futile and unpatriotic act."

His statement followed reports that in some of the "defense-rental" areas designated earlier that week as the first step toward Federal regulation of rents, landlords were attempting to evict tenants and bring in new tenants at higher rentals.

"We will not permit the war production program to be sabotaged by a few landlords who have the mistaken notion that they can somehow wiggle outside the of the essential war-time program," the Price Administrator said.

"The new tenants will not be required to pay, nor will the landlords be permitted to collect, rents in excess of that collected on the maximum-rent date."

Henderson commends new consumer credit controls by Federal Reserve Board

Prompt action by the Board of Governors of the Federal Reserve System in strengthening controls over consumer credit through amendments to its regulations, announced last week, will be of great importance in supporting other measures being taken by OPA toward keeping down the cost of living, Price Administrator Leon Henderson said May 7.

The Board of Governors has announced adoption of Amendment No. 4 to its Regulation W, effective May 6, enlarging the scope of consumer credit control and increasing restraints against purchase of consumers' goods on credit or with borrowed money.

"The importance of this step will be quickly recognized by the American people. It will be welcomed and wholeheartedly supported as a potent means of self-defense," said Mr. Henderson. "These amendments are designed to effectuate one point of the President's recently announced program, designated by him as the national economic policy to keep the cost of living from spiraling upward. Point 7 of that program states: 'We must discourage credit and installment buying and encourage the paying off of debts,' to the end that excessive buying be retarded and savings be promoted to provide a form of insurance against post-war depression.

"This amendment constitutes virtually a complete revision of the program of control. While utilizing the system of restraints already developed, it increases the deterrents to credit purchases of consumers' goods by requiring substantially heavier cash down payments and by materially shortening the periods during which the indebtedness created must be retired. At the same time, the scope of control is expanded, not only by important additions to the consumers' 'listed' goods on which credit restrictions apply, but also by extending control for the first time to open-account credits, charge accounts, and single-payment 'personal' loans up to $1,500, including bank loans, incurred for purchase of 'listed' goods. These are now added to the field of installment sales and installment loans heretofore covered."

Cartoon by Elderman for OEM. Publishers may obtain mats of these charts weekly in either two- or three-column size. Requests to be put on the mailing list should be addressed to Distribution Section, Division of Information, Office for Emergency Management, 2743 Temporary R, Washington, D. C.

Finished piece goods may be billed at contract prices, pending determination of costs

In order that there may be no further interruption in deliveries of finished piece goods whose price ceiling are established by Maximum Price Regulation No. 127 (Finished Piece Goods), the OPA May 8 outlined conditions under which such deliveries may be made pending the determination of cost elements required by the order.

The OPA will not object to deliveries of finished piece goods under existing contracts being billed on memorandum or billed at contract prices subject to later adjustment if the sellers are unable to ascertain immediately all of the cost elements.

★ ★ ★

Southern hardwood lumber schedule modified

New definitions of "mill" and "distribution yard," designed to adopt a more refined distinction between distribution yards and concentration yards, are set forth in Amendment No. 3 to Revised Price Schedule No. 97, Southern Hardwood Lumber, Price Administrator Henderson announced May 8.

★ ★ ★

Ceilings raised on some lighter weights of relaying rail

Higher maximum prices on certain lighter weights of relaying rail were announced May 8 by Price Administrator Henderson.

★ ★

Copper scrap order modified to include "ingots"

Supplementary Order M–9–b, which controls copper scrap, was amended May 9 by the Director of Industry Operations to include "ingots."

★ ★ ★

Coffee roasters proffered aid in disposing of excess imports

Douglas C. Townson, chief of the food supply, branch, WPB, said May 9 that WPB is willing to aid coffee roasters in disposing of excess coffee imports.

Corn sirup for canning is part of sugar ration

Packers of canned fruits and vegetables were advised May 9 by the OPA that the amount of corn syrup or dextrose used in canning or packing must be computed as part of the maximum amount of sugar per unit allotted any product under rationing regulations.

Aircraft part processing supplies get A–1 rating

In an amendment to Preference Rating Order P–109 the WPB May 8 allowed suppliers of material used in the production of aircraft to apply an A–1–a rating for those operating supplies absolutely necessary in processing the aircraft parts which they furnish on ratings assigned by the order.

Sheeting used by low-income groups gets special recognition in new ceilings

Manufacturers' ceiling prices for a special type of lightweight bed linen widely used by low-income groups were established May 4 by Price Administrator Henderson.

By Amendment No. 5 to Revised Price Schedule No. 89 (Bed Linens), effective May 4, the Price Administrator set maximum prices for the special goods—known in the trade as "back-filled"—which take into consideration their out-of-ordinary specifications.

Won't raise retail price

Prior to the amendment the "back-filled" type was subject to maximum prices applying to substandard materials, a system of pricing which did not recognize their special characteristics.

Mr. Henderson pointed out that the ceilings established for "back-filled" types under the new amendment will readily permit retailers to price these bed linens at no higher than their March 1942 prices and that therefore the action supplements the General Maximum Price Regulation. Maximum prices now determined for these linens are lower than manufacturers charged prior to February 2, Mr. Henderson said.

Two changes applying to all types of bed linens under the schedule are also effected by the amendment. Since sales by jobbers, wholesalers, and retailers are generally exempt from Revised Price Schedule No. 89, one of these changes extends this exemption to retail sales of bed linens by manufacturers who regularly maintain and operate their own bona fide retail outlets. Such sales will be subject to the General Maximum Price Regulation, effective May 11, 1942.

The amendment also eliminates requirements for proper labeling of sheets and pillow cases when a Government agency asks that no label be attached to the goods.

Previous tables appended to the schedule set up a method of determining maximum prices. To these tables is now added a new column for "back-filled" types. These tables include specifications, base prices, and maximum prices for manufacturers.

Finished piece goods prices changed for jobber, wholesaler

An adjustment of the mark-up which wholesalers and jobbers of finished piece goods made of cotton, rayon, or their mixtures may charge was provided May 1 by OPA through Amendment No. 1 to Maximum Price Regulation No. 127—Finished Piece Goods.

In effect, the change allows wholesalers and jobbers a maximum mark-up equivalent to 17 percent of their selling price for goods covered by this regulation. Originally, the order provided a mark-up of no more than 17 percent above the actual cost.

In addition, the May 1 amendment makes clear that freight charges which are incurred by wholesalers and jobbers may be included in determining the cost.

★ ★

Ceilings set on sanitary napkins

Maximum prices for sanitary napkins are established in Maximum Price Regulation No. 140, announced May 6 by the OPA.

Mark-up about the same

The order, effective May 18, is designed to reduce unwarranted price advances which have already taken place.

Although retail prices are lowered, mark-ups for retailers and distributors remain, under the regulation, about the same as prior to July 1, 1941, after which date retail prices were increased about 25 percent. The cost and profit study of the industry by OPA indicates that the 12 producing firms will realize adequate returns despite past and current cost increases.

Under the regulation, the maximum net return to manufacturers on sales made to wholesalers will be $6.90 per case, a reduction of 62 cents from the current price of the two leading brands but 90 cents more than the same brands sold for prior to July 1, 1941. On sales made directly to retailers the maximum net return of the manufacturer will be $7.31 per standard case (48 packages of 12 napkins each), a reduction of 69 cents per case from current prices and about 75 cents more per case than the return to manufacturers before July 1.

The maximum price a wholesaler now can receive per case of any brand is $1.40, which permits him a return about equal to, or slightly more than that he received before July 1. If the wholesalers' differential between the leading brands and the other brands is the same as it was July 1, retailers' margins will be slightly better than they were on that date.

As a result of the decrease in price, the largest selling item, the package containing 12 sanitary napkins, is reduced from 25 cents to 22 cents for the consumer.

WPB studies usefulness of carpet wools for other items

The wool section of the WPB is studying the utility value of carpet wools to ascertain which of the wools are suitable for apparel and blankets and which are useful only in floor coverings.

No action will be taken in the matter until the WPB has obtained opinions from affected industries. One group of wool experts has already submitted its opinions. It is the opinion of this group that the following types of wools, representing about half of the types of wool from which rugs and carpets are made are useful only in floor coverings:

Aleppo—stuffings and pieces (not including fleeces); Persian Gulf—stuffings and pieces (not including fleeces); Egyptian—fleeces and colors (not including white pulled); Awassi-Karadis; Indias—(other than Joria, Kandahar, Vicanere No. 1 and Vicanere super); Cyprus; Oporto; Balkan Pulled Wools; Thibet—(other than No. 1 and No. 2 white); Iceland skin wool; B. A. 5's-6's combing, 12-month growth only; Cordoba 40's-36's combing, 12-month growth only; Devon; Scotch, Irish, and English Blackfaced; Irish Kerry; Haslock; Herdwick; Swalesdale.

All other carpet wools were considered by the group to be usable for apparel and blankets.

Petitions provided in "hardship cases" under wool ceiling

A procedure by which sellers of wool or wool tops or yarns may, in a few "hardship cases," apply to OPA for relief has been provided through issuance of an amendment to the wool schedule.

When a seller finds that his ceiling price as determined by the individual freeze provisions of Revised Price Schedule No. 58 is substantially below the price prevailing for the same type and kind of wool or wool tops or yarns in the same or nearest competitive area, Amendment No. 2 permits him to file a petition for adjustment in accordance with OPA procedural regulations.

The amendment, effective May 2, applies only to those ceilings based upon the highest price at which sellers sold or contracted to sell particular types of wool during the period between October 1, 1941, and December 15, 1941, inclusive.

★ ★ ★

Retail chlorine reports ended

Because the wording of Order M-19 relating to chlorine would have required the filing of monthly reports by thousands of retail stores throughout the country, it has been amended by the Director of Industry Operations to remove that provision.

OPA financial report system to cover 25,000 firms

A general financial reporting program designed to provide basic financial data necessary for studies of price control problems in many industries where adequate information is not now available was instituted May 2 by Price Administrator Henderson.

Reporting forms and an instruction book requiring balance sheet and income account data were to be sent to about 25,000 business corporations, with over $250,000 assets each, engaged in manufacturing, mining, construction, wholesale trade, retail trade and related fields.

The confidential nature of the reports will be strictly observed, the Administrator said, although the reports will be available on a confidential basis to war planning agencies, such as the War Production Board, when needed, thus providing a centralized regularly recurring source of information for such agencies.

The forms ease the burden for some companies of supplying over-all cost data to OPA in connection with individual requests for specific costs of each of a variety of products, since the one report will now be the only request for overall data as to the company's operations. Similarly, time and expense are saved companies which might request special treatment under a price schedule because with general information made available by the report, the preliminary investigational work is eliminated and the actual field work expedited and confined to matters raised by the particular request.

New price regulations explained to retailers in meeting with OPA

Retail trade associations representing somewhat over 700,000 establishments that deal directly with the buying public May 5 were given a detailed explanation of the General Maximum Price Regulation as it applies to retailers at an all-day meeting in Washington with officials of the OPA.

The regulation which becomes effective as to retail sales of commodities on May 18, 1942, places a ceiling with few exceptions over all prices.

The May 5 meeting was one of hundreds to be held in virtually every State in the Union in order to give retailers an opportunity to ask questions regarding the regulation as it affects their various situations.

Retailers urged to gather records, survey prices quickly in preparation for May 18

The Nation's retailers — numbering close to 2,000,000 — were urged May 3 by Price Administrator Henderson to observe three cardinal "do's" and a like number of "don'ts" before seeking special guidance from OPA on immediate problems under the recently issued general maximum price regulation.

THE THREE DO'S

The three "do's" indicate immediate steps to take in getting ready for the May 18 effective date of the regulation in all retail stores.

(1) Assemble and preserve immediately all your records regarding all prices charged for goods in March. In addition, begin preparing your statement of highest base period prices for each item sold, so that it will be completed by July 1, 1942.

(2) Check prices of all goods in your store to be sure that they are no higher than the highest price charged in March 1942. This job must be completed by May 18, after which time you cannot exceed these maximum prices.

(3) Arrange to post or mark and identify as "ceiling price" or "our ceiling," your maximum prices on all "cost-of-living" commodities specified in Appendix A of the Regulation. This must be finished by May 18. In addition, a list of these items and their ceiling prices must be filed with the War Price and Rationing Board in your area by June 1, 1942.

THE THREE DON'TS

The three "don'ts" are:

(1) Don't bring your problems to Washington personally. It would be physically impossible for OPA's staff at this moment to give every retailer the time and individual attention that such a visit ordinarily would warrant.

(2) Don't telephone Washington on your problem, unless it is of the most urgent nature. It probably would be impossible to render a snap decision on your case. You will receive carefully considered guidance from OPA, along with all others, as soon as is humanly possible.

(3) Don't write in before you have carefully read and reread the regulation itself, the official press release issued simultaneously, and the question and answer summary that also accompanied the order. In many cases, clearer reading will reveal that your problem has been anticipated by OPA and answered in this or other material to be released shortly.

"Troubleshooters" from OPA's Retail Trade and Services Division currently are preparing a bulletin of explanations to go out to the retail trade. These explanations are based on questions now coming to OPA's offices from individual merchants and trade leaders. They are expected to provide the answers to a host of questions now in the minds of many retailers. In addition, further question and answer summaries are contemplated

for general press distribution in the near future and will appear in local newspapers.

★ ★ ★

5 temporary ceilings to be superseded by general order

Five temporary maximum price regulations, covering such commodities as canned fruits and vegetables, used typewriters, metal beds and novelty floor coverings, will be superseded automatically by the provisions of the general maximum price regulation, Price Administrator Henderson announced May 2.

The temporary regulations—Nos. 3, 4, 5, 6 and 9—had expired or will expire before the effective dates, May 11 for the manufacturers' and wholesale levels and May 18 for the retail levels, of the general maximum price regulation, which froze prices of nearly all cost-of-living items.

Voluntary compliance in meantime

Until the provisions of the general order apply to the commodities covered by the five temporary regulations, the OPA has requested that these commodities be sold at prices no higher than those which are permitted under the general maximum price regulation. Purchasers of these products are warned by the OPA to take into consideration the fact that there is no price control over these commodities between the dates of expiration of the temporary regulations and the effective dates of the general order.

The following table presents the expiration dates of the temporary regulations and the types of commodities covered:

Temporary maximum price regulation	Covering price level	Commodity	Expiration date of temporary regulation
No. 3	Manufacturers and distributors.	Novelty floor coverings.	April 30.
No. 4	Manufacturers.	Sisal pads.	May 2.
No. 5	Manufacturers.	Bedding, metal beds, mattresses, springs, studio couches.	May 2.
No. 6	Wholesale.	Canned fruits and vegetables.	April 30.
No. 9	Retail.	Used typewriters.	May 11.

Top prices set on machines, parts not already covered by OPA schedules

A comprehensive regulation establishing maximum prices for machines and parts not covered by other price schedules was announced May 2 by Price Administrator Henderson. All outstanding "freeze" letters and "informal agreements" covering machinery are superseded by the new measure—title "Maximum Price Regulation No. 136."

Effective May 18, 1942, the new regulation specifies October 1, 1941, prices, for the machines and parts it covers, at all levels of distribution except retail. October 1 rentals for machines are also established as maximum rentals.

But giving special recognition to the requirements of the contracting-out program, the regulation specifically excludes certain subcontracted parts and subassemblies manufactured for incorporation into another machine by the buyer. This will exclude many specially designed parts for munitions. Informal price action is expected in this field in the near future.

In addition to providing top prices for new machines, the comprehensive regulation states formulas for maximum prices for rebuilt used machines and parts, and other second-hand units.

Maximum prices for rebuilt and guaranteed second-hand machines are established at 85 percent of the October 1, 1941, net price of the nearest equivalent new machine.

For other second-hand machines, maximum prices are set at 55 percent of the October 1, 1941, net price for nearest equivalent new machine.

★ ★ ★

Osnaburg allowed for baling if made on looms outside L-99

The WPB textile branch pointed out May 5 in connection with Limitation Order L-99 that any cotton mill which has made or is making its own baling material, whether of a construction listed in L-99 or some other construction, may continue to use this cloth for the baling of its own product only, but must manufacture it on looms other than those required to comply with the conversion as directed in Limitation Order L-99. L-99 requires that all looms that operated on osnaburg on February 28 be devoted to five constructions of osnaburg and be sold only on war orders.

POSTMEN AND POLICE-TEST RECLAIMED RUBBER

Postmen and policemen in the Nation's Capital are acting as walking laboratories for the Government, so that the millions of pedestrians throughout the country can obtain good rubber heels for the duration.

The Consumer Division of the OPA announced May 4 that many members of the Washington Post Office and Police Department have consented to pound their beats on reclaimed rubber heels which the Division is testing for quality and durability. The raw material for these heels is scrap rubber collected from the Nation's junk yards and attics and then reprocessed.

Paper prices to be discussed in series of industry meetings

The first of a series of more than 40 meetings with representatives of the various branches in the paper industry, including manufacturers and wholesalers, which the OPA has called for the purpose of discussing provisions of the general maximum price regulation and other price actions, was held May 7 in New York City.

OPA price executives and attorneys discussed the background and purpose of the general maximum price regulation, and explained those provisions applicable to the wholesale paper trade.

Another group of wholesalers met in Chicago the following day. About 100 were invited to attend a meeting arranged tentatively for May 11 in Denver and 200 are expected to be present in San Francisco on May 14.

Similar meetings for other branches of the paper trade were to be held in the following two weeks.

Auerbach named price executive

Appointment of Alfred Auerbach as price executive of the consumers' durable goods sections of OPA was announced May 2. Mr. Auerbach succeeds Merle Fainsod, who was recently appointed chief of the retail trade and services division. Named associate price executive was Harvey Mansfield, who has been serving as administrative officer in the section.

Incoming freight rate rise on iron and steel products must be absorbed

A clarification of the effect of the recent 6-percent freight rate increase on the prices of iron and steel products under the provisions of Price Schedules No. 6 and No. 49 was announced May 5 by Price Administrator Henderson.

In general, the Administrator said, the rule is that the increased freight costs must be absorbed by the steel mill or the steel reseller on incoming shipments, but may be added to outgoing shipments in cases where freight is a component and declared part of the maximum price.

For example, the increase in freight rates on incoming scrap must be absorbed by the steel mills, and does not affect the maximum price at which the mills may sell their products.

However, the increase in freight from a mill's governing basing point to destination may be added to the mill delivered price of steel.

There are certain exceptions to this general rule, the Administrator added. For example, under Price Schedule No. 6, some prices are "arbitrary delivered prices," such as the delivered prices applicable to Detroit and eastern Michigan. These may not be increased, except as specific increases have been granted by Amendment No. 4 to Revised Price Schedule No. 6. Also, under Price Schedule No. 49, where the maximum delivered price is limited by the April 16, 1941, prices of named sellers in a "listed city," it is not affected by the freight rate increase.

★ ★ ★

Vacuum cleaner label sets forth possibility of below-ceiling sale

Modification in the price labels on household vacuum cleaners to make clear that sales to the consumer at less than the maximum prices set by the OPA are optional with the retailer as far as the regulations and orders of the office are concerned was announced May 4.

In addition, the labels are to be worded so as to avoid any appearance of being in conflict with State minimum price laws.

Amendment 2 to Maximum Price Regulation No. 111—New Household Vacuum Cleaners and Attachments—effective May 5, provides that the label shall read:

The maximum cash price for this household vacuum cleaner (or attachment) as established by the Office of Price Administration, is $——. Lower prices may be charged without violating any regulation or order of the Office of Price Administration.

The use of the phrase, "lower prices may be charged or demanded," in the last sentence in the label is optional with the seller.

Scrap dealers under ceilings will all be licensed

Practically all dealers selling waste, scrap or salvage material to industrial consumers will be licensed, OPA announced May 7.

The licensing order, Supplementary Order No. 5, becomes effective May 20, 1942, and requires registration by the dealers on or before June 20, 1942.

The order covers dealers selling to industrial consumers waste, scrap or salvage material for which maximum prices are established by 14 price schedules and regulations issued by the Office of Price Administration. Furthermore, the necessary licensing was extended in the case of iron and steel scrap to a dealer selling to a consumer or to a consumer's broker.

First licensing of specific industry

Although retailers and wholesalers generally are licensed by provisions of the General Maximum Price Regulation, this new order marks the first instance of the application of OPA licensing authority to a specific industry. The order affects dealers in a wide range of waste and scrap materials, including aluminum scrap, zinc scrap, iron and steel scrap, nickel scrap, brass mill scrap, copper and copper alloy scrap, waste paper, old rags, second-hand bags, lead scrap materials, scrap rubber, rayon waste, silk waste, and raw and processed wool waste materials.

"Any dealer violating the price schedules or regulations covering such waste or scrap materials," the Price Administrator warned, "may have his license suspended, as provided in the Price Control Act. He thereby will lose his privilege to do business. Activity after suspension of a license would violate the Price Control Act and would subject the offender to civil and criminal prosecution."

Industrial diamonds subject to general price regulations

Industrial diamonds, vital in the war effort because of their widespread use in machine tools for cutting, shaping, drilling, and marking, are subject to the general maximum price regulation, issued April 28, Price Administrator Henderson pointed out May 6.

Premiums raised on sorted quantity shipments of copper, copper alloy scrap

An increase in quantity premiums to three-fourths cents a pound for shipments of 60,000 pounds of a single group of grades of copper scrap or copper alloy scrap is provided in Revised Price Schedule No. 20 as amended, Price Administrator Henderson announced May 7.

An increase to one-half cent in quantity premiums for shipments of 40,000 pounds of two groups of grades is also provided.

Other provisions

Revised Price Schedule No. 20 as amended, effective May 11, also changes the special preparation premiums, includes a provision licensing dealers who sell to consumers and adds prices for six new grades—High-grade Bronze solids and borings, High Lead Bronze solids and borings, Bronze Paper Mill Wire Cloth, and No. 1 Tinned Copper Wire.

It also makes upward or downward adjustments in the base prices of all principal grades except refinery brass and automobile radiators, incorporates new consumer report forms and forbids payment of a quantity premium on material containing 10 percent or more rejections.

The new preparation premiums are:

1. No. 1 Heavy Copper, No. 1 Copper Wire, No. 1 Tinned Copper Wire in crucible shape or briquettes—1¼ cents per pound. No. 2 Copper Wire or Mixed Heavy Copper—1 cent per pound. (These premiums may not be paid by a copper refiner or brass ingot maker.)

2. Copper scrap specially prepared for the direct use of any person except a copper refiner, brass ingot maker, ferrous or nonferrous foundry, or brass mill—1¼ cents a pound.

3. Copper alloy scrap in crucible shape—1¼ cents per pound. (This premium may be paid on either clean, heavy scrap free of all harmful material and suitable for direct use by the consumer or on turnings and borings of uniform content and completely free of impurities. It may not be paid by a copper refiner or a brass ingot maker.)

Bronze Paper Mill Wire Cloth and No. 1 Tinned Copper Wire have been added to the schedule at the request of the industry.

Dutch Government allowed more on extra cost paraffin

Permission has been granted a New York agent of the Netherlands Government in London by OPA to sell a specified lot of fully refined paraffin wax at a price which includes extra expenses involved as a direct result of war influences.

★ ★ ★

Machinery installation costs computed on March basis

Manufacturers who sell machinery on an installed basis may calculate prices of installation on the basis of March 1942 rates for field labor and outbound freight, instead of October 1, 1941, rates, Price Administrator Henderson announced May 8. The equipment must be priced at October levels; it is only the costs of installation which may be computed on the March basis, it was explained.

Permission to compute costs of installation in this manner is granted in Amendment No. 1 to Maximum Price Regulation No. 136, on machines and parts, effective May 18, 1942.

2 types of insurance added to ceiling for 4 imported foods

Coffee, cocoa, tea, and pepper importers may add their entire charges for "deviation" and "frustration" insurance to the maximum prices for such commodities under an interpretation issued May 2 by Price Administrator Henderson. "Deviation" insurance covers such expenses as handling and storing when a vessel is deviated from its original course; "frustration" insurance covers losses due to spoilage and deterioration when a ship is diverted from its course.

★ ★ ★

Restriction on carpet yarn jute is formalized for April

Director of Industry Operations Knowlson has issued Amendment No. 2 to the Jute and Jute Products General Conservation Order, M-70, formalizing the action taken on April 3 by telegram to restrict processing of jute for the manufacture of carpet yarns during the month of April.

Processors were directed at that time not to put more than 20 percent of their average monthly use of jute in 1940 into process during April 1942.

In 1941—the U. S. imported more than 1 MILLION long tons of RUBBER

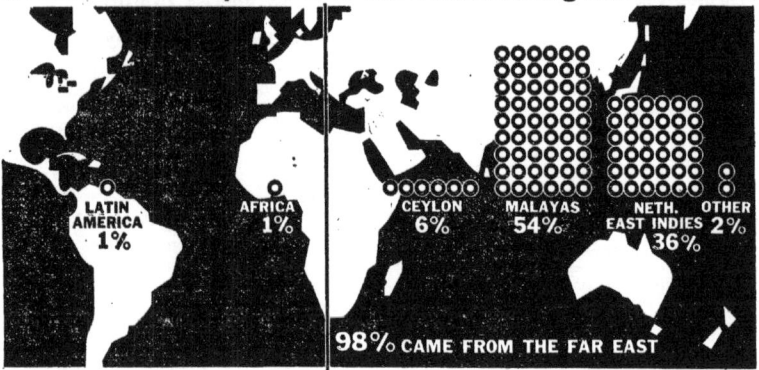

LATIN AMERICA 1% | **AFRICA 1%** | **CEYLON 6%** | **MALAYAS 54%** | **NETH. EAST INDIES 36%** | **OTHER 2%**

98% CAME FROM THE FAR EAST

OPA GIVEN AUTHORITY TO RATION ALL TYPES OF TIRES

Authority to ration all types of tires, including synthetic, for all purposes, including industrial equipment, was delegated to the Office of Price Administration by the War Production Board May 6.

Under previous delegations of authority by the WPB, the OPA had power to ration tires for commercial as well as passenger use, but some confusion existed as to the jurisdiction over tires for certain types of industrial equipment. The new regulation (Amendment No. 1 to Supplementary Directive 1-B) makes clear that power to ration this type of tire resides in the OPA.

The amendment also extends the rationing power delegated to OPA by WPB Directive No. 1 to cover all tires, whether made of crude, scrap, or reclaimed rubber, of any of the substances commonly known as synthetic rubber.

Excepted from OPA control by the amendment are tires to be sold for military use or export, or tires for use on airplanes. The WPB also retains control, under the Rationing Regulations, of tires for vehicles in the hands of manufacturers, distributors, and retailers.

The delegation contained in the amendment supersedes the powers delegated by Rubber Order, M-15-c, but all actions heretofore taken by the OPA pursuant to the latter order, or in accordance with other rationing directives or regulations are ratified, approved, and confirmed.

★ ★ ★

Anyone entitled to rent a typewriter

Any person or business needing a typewriter is entitled to rent a used office machine or new portable directly from any dealer, OPA announced May 7 in a clarification of typewriter-rationing regulations.

3 appointed in auto rationing

Three appointments in the automobile rationing division of OPA were announced May 5. Hubert G. Larson of Hewlett, Long Island, was named an assistant chief of the division. Robert E. Stone, now on leave of absence from the University of California also was appointed an assistant chief of the division. Mr. Stone will be in charge of appeals made from the decisions of local rationing boards and State administrators. Dr. Harry R. De Silva of Hamden, Conn., was named head of the research and quotas unit of the division.

Gasoline hoarding unpatriotic

Hoarding of gasoline in anticipation of rationing constitutes not only an unpatriotic act, but also an invitation to a serious fire, the OPA warned May 2.

At the suggestion of fire insurance and fire protection experts, OPA officials pointed out that gasoline in cans and makeshift containers stored in the basement, garage, or in the car is a dangerous explosive. When gasoline is exposed to the air or when there is any leak or spill, vapor is produced which, when mixed with air, can explode with disastrous results.

WORLD TOTALS for PRODUCTION of RUBBER

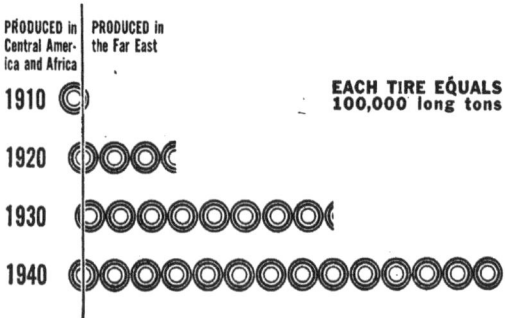

PRODUCED in Central America and Africa	PRODUCED in the Far East
1910	
1920	
1930	
1940	

EACH TIRE EQUALS 100,000 long tons

Mats of 3- and 2-column cuts on this page available on request to Distribution Section, Information Division, OEM.

Commercial and governmental users of gasoline exempt from card rationing plan

All commercial and governmental users of gasoline are exempt from the card rationing plan to be inaugurated May 15 in 17 Eastern States by the OPA.

However, all such gasoline users who are subject to recent orders of the Office of Defense Transportation providing for the elimination of all luxury or nonessential services must comply with the ODT regulations.

Joint statement issued

These points were made clear in a joint statement issued May 4 by the OPA and ODT to clarify previous rulings.

The statement follows:

The card rationing plan to be instituted by the Office of Price Administration on May 15 to 17 Eastern States where a critical petroleum shortage exists is designed to give all commercial and governmental users the gasoline they need to carry on their business.

At the same time, regulations governing rationing of gasoline are not intended to authorize use of a motor vehicle or inboard motorboat in violation of the provisions of any order issued by the Office of Defense Transportation, or any other applicable Government order. Such orders, many of which are already in effect, are operating to effect gasoline economies—one of the purposes of rationing—as well as to move commercial and governmental traffic more expeditiously.

Trucks, buses, and other commercial vehicles will not need ration cards to make gasoline purchases, and do not need to register. They are to be served gasoline in their tanks as usual. However, to avoid delay and confusion in the case of vehicles used commercially and in governmental service, but which may not be clearly marked, it has been provided that X ration cards may be obtained. Such a card will enable them to make whatever gasoline purchases they need for essential use.

Purposes for which an X card may be obtained include: As an ambulance or hearse; as a taxi, ferry, or other public conveyance for hire; or as a vehicle available for public rental; for a regularly practicing minister of a religious faith in the service of his congregation; for a duly licensed physician, surgeon, nurse, osteopath, chiropractor, or veterinarian in professional service; for the official business of Federal, State, local or foreign governments or government agencies; for trucking, hauling, towing, freight-carrying, delivery, or messenger service; for the transportation of materials and equipment for construction or for mechanical, electrical, or structural or highway maintenance or repair service, or for the transportation of work crews to enable them to render such services.

The regulations provide also for the sale of bulk quantities of gasoline for use in motor vehicles and boats and for nonhighway purposes.

Purchase of such bulk quantities may be made by filling out the appropriate certificates, which will be kept by the dealer or supplier. In the category of nonhighway purposes, gasoline may be used, for example, for farm tractors and gasoline engines, and for outboard motors. All such purchases can be made without restriction as to quantity, except in the case of inboard motorboats.

Rationing gives grocer important post along America's home battlefront

The inauguration of the sugar rationing program gives the corner grocer an important role on the civilian front, OPA officials pointed out May 4.

Every day the corner grocer will have to handle dozens of ration stamps. At the beginning, while the whole sugar rationing program is new, he'll probably have to do an awful lot of explaining. One of his best customers may plead for just a "couple of pounds more of sugar" with which to bake a cake for junior's birthday. Somebody may show up without a War Ration Book and ask for sugar and promise to bring in the stamps later. The grocer will have to say, "Very sorry, but that's contrary to regulations."

Must explain and explain

Another customer may bring in some loose stamps and the grocer will have to explain very patiently that he can't accept stamps in such form. He must see them torn out of the War Ration Books in his presence. Another customer may come with a War Ration Book containing stamps whose period of validity has expired.

Another problem is pasting the stamps he gets over the counter on the cards distributed for this purpose by OPA. He has to be careful not to lose them and to turn them in for sugar before their term of validity expires.

Has to keep records

From now on the quantity of sugar which the grocer will be able to get from his wholesaler will depend upon the number of stamps and sugar purchase certificates he surrenders. He will have to keep records. If a standard shipping package or standard shipping unit has a total weight greater than the number of pounds for which a retailer has stamps, the wholesaler must charge the excess against the next stamps surrendered by the grocer. If the grocer hands over stamps which have a greater pound value than what has been delivered to him, he must carefully note that fact, and the excess amount can be accepted by him at the time of the next delivery.

And must be alert for changes

The grocer must be on the lookout for changes in rationing regulations. The amount of sugar which can be bought with each stamp may be changed.

Every time a grocer surrenders a War Ration Stamp Card, he should write across it his name and address.

A lot more than just the equal distribution of sugar depends upon the success of the sugar rationing program. The sugar program is expected to set a pattern for possible rationing of other foods.

Red Cross will be added to eligible buyers of autos

The American Red Cross will be added to the list of those who are eligible to purchase new passenger automobiles under the rationing regulations, Price Administrator Henderson announced May 2.

Other provisions

At the same time, he said that after May 10, on permission of OPA headquarters in Washington, a convertible passenger car may be withdrawn from the Government pool for sale this year if a steel-topped model is substituted for it. He announced also that employers may purchase cars for use of employees who are eligible. Heretofore, employees whose transportation was essential to the war effort were eligible to buy new cars. Now, either the employee or the employer may make the purchase.

Amendment No. 7 to the New Passenger Automobile Rationing Regulations, which becomes effective May 12, contains the authority for these changes.

All Red Cross chapters must apply through their head office in Washington rather than to local rationing boards, and the head office will then apply to OPA for the necessary certificates.

OPA directed to aid ODT policies through rationing

WPB has directed OPA, in exercising rationing authority with respect to tires, passenger cars, gasoline, or other products used in transportation, to implement to the full extent administratively practicable the transportation policies of the Office of Defense Transportation.

TRANSPORTATION . . .

New division charged with planning auto, tire, fuel savings, and adjusting transport service to continuing needs

OTD Director Eastman announced May 5 that he has set up a staff division of transport conservation to administer the new duties given to the ODT by Executive Order 9156 made public May 4 by the White House.

John R. Turney, who has been director of the ODT's division of traffic movement, has been named director of the new division.

Henry F. McCarthy, who has been associate director of the division of traffic movement, will succeed Mr. Turney as director of traffic movement.

Scope of new division

It will be the duty of the new division of transport conservation, Mr. Eastman said, to formulate policies, programs, and measures for (a) the continuous adjustment of national transportation requirements and the transport service available therefor; (b) the conservation of automotive vehicles, tires, fuel, and other materials, and (c) the conservation and distribution of transportation service, and to the extent necessary, its restriction to essential needs.

The program will be carried into effect in part through established divisions of the ODT, and in part through other agencies of the Government, especially the local rationing boards of the OPA, Mr. Eastman said.

"Not a private resource"

The division of transport conservation is expected to work in close cooperation with the Office of the Petroleum Coordinator and the branches of the WPB and the OPA dealing with rubber, gasoline and passenger cars.

"The present supply of automotive vehicles and particularly rubber tires constitutes a national and not a private resource," Mr. Eastman said. "The rubber shortage is a grave reality. Rubber must be conserved. Every owner of a motor vehicle in public or private service should realize that he holds this vehicle in trust for the national war effort and that it should be used only for purposes of necessity."

Mr. Eastman pointed out that he had already asked the Governors of every State and the mayors of all cities above 10,000 population to mobilize local forces for a drive to insure the continued operation of all local transportation facilities through (1) systematic staggering of business, school, and working hours, (2) group riding in private automobiles on a planned neighborhood-by-neighborhood basis, and (3) improved regulation of local traffic to make possible more efficient movement of passenger vehicles.

★ ★ ★

RESTRICTIONS ON TRAVEL IMMINENT, SAYS EASTMAN

Restrictions on passenger travel, elimination of high-speed duplicating service on competing lines, lengthening of limited schedules to include more stops, and reduction or total elimination of all luxury equipment for the duration were declared imminent May 3 by Joseph B. Eastman, Director of Defense Transportation.

In a statement embracing the whole passenger problem Mr. Eastman pointed to the gasoline and rubber shortage as responsible for diverting to public carriers better than fifty percent more passengers than were transported before Pearl Harbor.

Schedules must be readjusted, Mr. Eastman stated, so that essential military and civilian travel will not be impeded, and where it is necessary to discontinue train service, the affected communities must be served by bus.

★ ★ ★

Transportation officers' advisory committee

Formation of a transportation officers' advisory committee to help ODT in mapping plans for closer coordination of rail transportation and freight car handling was announced May 2. Members:

J. D. Clarke, Baltimore, superintendent of freight transportation, Baltimore & Ohio Railroad; J. C. Wroton, general superintendent of transportation of the Seaboard railway, Norfolk, Va.; F. E. Spero, general superintendent of transportation of the Burlington Lines, Chicago, and J. H. Little, superintendent of transportation of the Missouri, Kansas & Texas Railroad Co., Denison, Tex.

Short roads use own methods of observing weight minimum

Short-line railroads, serving far-flung mountain, mining, and agricultural communities, are using their own methods to comply with ODT's General Order No. 1, it was revealed May 2 by Director Eastman in a check-up on more than two-score companies who operate from 2 miles to 26 miles of track.

These small railroads, many of which own no cars at all, were among the first to provide the ODT with a full report on their less-than-carload service, and their ability to meet General Order No. 1's six-ton minimum weight limit after May 1 for this kind or freight. The order provided exceptions which would relieve the small roads of the weight limits when conditions made compliance difficult or impossible without imposing a hardship on patrons and shippers.

Rather than take advantage of the exceptions, however, a number of the lines, Mr. Eastman said, either put into service obsolete cars not permitted in interchange—sometimes borrowing this equipment from connecting roads—or cut down the daily service to two or three days a week.

In many remote sections, such as in the West Virginia mountains, and out on the Western deserts, these short lines provide the only means of freight haul by which farmers and miners may obtain necessities of life, and in all cases where these or similar conditions required, exceptions from the minimum weight load have been granted.

★ ★ ★

Truck tire rationing calls for care by drivers—Rogers

Warning that failure to take proper care of truck tires can produce a "transportation bottleneck," John L. Rogers, director of the ODT division of motor transport, urged truck drivers and owners to safeguard their present tire supply.

While tire rationing regulations provide tires for motor transport engaged in war production or essential civilian activities, Mr. Rogers said that rationing is possible only so long as the utmost caution is used in consumption of available rubber stocks.

Mr. Rogers urged truck operators to observe conservation rules cited by ODT. These rules, drafted by government experts, emphasize the President's request that speed be kept under 40 miles per hour. Maintenance of proper air pressure in the tires is vital. Overloading is second only to high speeds as a cause of rapid tread wear and premature truck tire failure. The rules also call for regular attention to tire valves and valve caps.

Lake grain movement banned except by special permit, to make way for iron ore

Transportation Director Eastman has banned all grain movement over the Great Lakes, except by special permit, from any port or point, in a sweeping order designed to assure cargo space for the preferential movement of iron ore.

ODT's General Order No. 8, which becomes effective May 15, brings under Mr. Eastman's control approximately 340 ships with a gross carrying capacity of nearly 3,000,000 tons, suited to ore cargo, and a number of mixed carriers used in scrap, coal and grain movement.

Diversion of grain tonnage to the railroads, Mr. Eastman said, will be necessary in order to assure maximum carrying capacity for iron ore.

The prospect of an unprecedented movement of ore tonnage, estimated at nearly 90,000,000 tons for the season, prompted the issuance of the order, Mr. Eastman explained.

Master plan for Nation-wide conservation released by ODT

Mobilization of the entire country for war conservation of private and public transportation facilities moved a step forward May 8 with the release of a manual describing in detail methods for setting up systems of staggered hours and group riding in every sizable community.

Eastman urges relaxation of weight, length limits

ODT Director Eastman urged May 7 that peacetime restrictions on weight and length of trucks be changed voluntarily by State action where necessary in order to permit maximum utilization of all highway transport facilities in the war effort.

Lead and zinc finish allowed on plumbing fixtures

Amendment of the plumbing and heating simplification order (L-42) to permit the use of lead and zinc as a preserving finish on plumbing fixtures and trim was announced May 6 by the Director of Industry Operations.

Nation-wide control of tank car movement established, effective on May 15

Defense Transportation Director Eastman issued on May 5 an order establishing a section of tank-car service which will inaugurate a nation-wide system of tank-car control on May 15.

On and after that date, no railroad will be allowed to accept for transport any loaded tank car without special or general permission of the section of tank-car service, except cars specifically exempted.

Movement to East exempted

An exception order issued simultaneously with the general order takes cars used for transporting petroleum into 17 Eastern States and the District of Columbia and into two Northwestern States.

The exception order (ODT No. 7-1) also exempts cars used in hauling any commodity for a distance of more than 100 miles over the shortest available published rail tariff route.

The main order (General Order ODT No. 7) specifically exempts tank-car shipments consigned by or to any Government agency.

Cars subject to transfer on order

In addition, all railroads, tank-car owners, leasing companies or lessees must stand ready to move any or all tank cars in their possession to any point designated by the section of tank-car service, regardless of any contractual arrangements already in force.

Any person or firm may apply for special or general permission to move cars not exempted by the order by filling out forms to be provided by the section of tank-car service.

Such applications must show the extent to which other methods of transportation, including tank trucks, are available for the hauls involved.

In issuing special or general permits, the section of tank-car service may specify commodities to be shipped, routes to be used, and other conditions of shipment.

Owners protected from claims

Where tank cars are operated under the direction of the section of tank-car service, their owners are protected from claims of violation of existing contract with respect to the use of the cars.

It also was emphasized that issuance of a special or general permit will not guarantee that a tank car will be available for the service contemplated. Such a permit merely will authorize movement of such a car over the rails.

The exception order specifically exempts the following shipments:

1. Crude petroleum and petroleum products into the States of Maine, New Hampshire, Vermont, Massachusetts, Rhode Island, Connecticut, New York, Pennsylvania, New Jersey, Delaware, Maryland, Virginia, West Virginia, North Carolina, South Carolina, Georgia, Florida, and the District of Columbia.

2. Crude petroleum and petroleum products into the States of Washington and Oregon.

3. Any commodity billed to a point more than 100 miles from the shipping point by the shortest available published rail tariff route.

Mr. Eastman said that a shortage of tank cars exists by reason of the extraordinary demand on rail transport to meet the needs of the public for petroleum products on the Eastern Seaboard and in the States of Oregon and Washington.

Needed to carry war goods

"Not only are tank cars in great demand for petroleum service, but they are required for chemicals and other liquids of critical importance to the successful prosecution of the war. There is, for example, a growing production of alcohol used in the manufacture of powder. Tank cars must be provided in increasing numbers for transport of this vital commodity."

"Just before Pearl Harbor," Mr. Eastman said, "petroleum products were reaching this area by tank car at the rate of 70,000 barrels a day. This figure has jumped to about 600,000 barrels a day."

Railroads asked to spread maintenance-of-way work to meet peak farm labor needs

ODT Director Eastman appealed May 9 to the eight major railroads serving the Southwest to spread their maintenance-of-way work so that peak railway labor needs will cease to conflict with peak demands for farm labor.

Calling attention to the mild weather prevalent in the Southwest through the winter months, Mr. Eastman asked that the railroads plan as much track and roadbed work as possible from January through the spring and early summer months when agriculture's demands are low. He suggested that maintenance-of-way officers check with the U. S. Employment Service in their districts to determine when local peak demands for farm labor are likely to be reached.

AGRICULTURE . . .

(Information furnished through Office of Agricultural Defense Relations, U. S. Department of Agriculture)

Pooling, exchange of farm labor suggested to meet increased need, reduced supply

United States farmers, with the task in 1942 of producing record amounts of food and fiber in the face of wartime shortages of equipment and labor, can help solve the problem of obtaining adequate farm labor by following three general practices, M. Clifford Townsend, Director of the Office for Agricultural War Relations, United States Department of Agriculture, told representatives of the International Association of Public Services at a meeting at Louisville, Ky. May 7.

New sources also suggested

These three general practices include: *First*, make full use of labor normally employed on farms by operating labor pools, exchanging labor, and using more family workers. *Second*, keep more workers on farms by increasing the attractiveness of farm work through better housing, more continuous employment, and other meth-

ods. *Third*, bring into the farm labor force persons not usually employed in agriculture.

Workers drawn into war, industry

Pointing out that agriculture's No. 1 job today is the production of food and fiber at levels 119 percent of average annual farm production during the 1935-39 period, Director Townsend said that the farm assembly line must be kept running with approximately the same land and equipment as in the 1930's, but with decreasing amounts of labor.

"It is important to note," he said, "that it is the more skilled, the more adaptable, and the better farm workers who are first to leave for industry and who are most acceptable to the armed forces. Yet, the farm assembly line in 1942 will require an estimated 142 million additional man-days of work."

Farm production outlook bright; largest crop acreages since 1933 anticipated

Agriculture Department officials in a monthly review of the farm production situation issued May 4, drew a picture of new records month after month in the production of milk, eggs, meats, and other protective foods.

Possible handling problems

Considerable concern was expressed, however, over possible difficulties in getting farm products transported, processed, distributed, and stored later this year. Federal agricultural agencies are attacking those problems on many fronts.

Farmers' costs of production are considerably higher this spring than last, but the long-standing gap between prices received and prices paid by farmers has been closed. Farm income is rising seasonally now, but less sharply than at this time last year.

Special wartime demands

Crop acreages are expected to be largest since 1933. Livestock numbers are the largest on record, and still increasing. Feed reserves are large, and pastures and range prospects are promising.

Milk production continues to exceed former records—is expected to total more than 12 billion pounds in May, and more than 12.5 billion in June. Production has been running about 4 percent larger this year than last.

Egg production is declining seasonally, but in coming months should be bigger than in the like period last year. Production of all kinds of poultry this year is increasing far above 1941.

Marketing of 1941 fall hogs has been large with prices recently the highest in 16 years. Farmers are producing more pigs and feeding them to relatively heavy weights to produce needed supplies of pork and lard. Total slaughter of cattle, sheep, and lambs in 1942 also will be substantially larger than in 1941.

High-protein feeds a record-breaker

Production of high-protein feeds is likely to break all former records by reason of greatly increased production of the oil crops.

Tobacco will be in large supply this year as measured by prewar averages, but domestic consumption also is far above prewar figures.

Cotton and wool mills are turning out the biggest yardage of fabrics in the Nation's history. Wool and mohair production this year are likely to be in high volume.

Production of truck crops to be marketed as fresh products and to be canned will be considerably larger this year than last, say reports from farmers and processors. Fruits of all kinds—fresh, canned, and dried—will be in good supply.

Lend-lease farm products totaled $524,500,000 on April 1

The Department of Agriculture has announced that up to April 1, 1942, farm products costing $524,500,000 have been delivered to representatives of the United Nations for lend-lease shipment. Total volume of the commodities bought by the Agricultural Marketing Administration and delivered at shipping points since the program began in April 1941, approximates 4,350,000,000 pounds.

Increase in concentrated foods

Commodities costing close to $55,-470,000 and weighing 285,000,000 pounds were delivered during March. During this month there was an increase in the deliveries of such items as dried eggs and meat products and concentrated foods of high value. The per unit cost of all commodities delivered in March for shipment averaged 19.4 cents per pound as compared with 16.5 cents a pound for the February deliveries. During February 309,000,000 pounds were delivered, at a cost of $52,000,000.

High up among the commodity groups delivered, with cumulative values up to April 1, 1942, were:

Dairy products and eggs, $169,706,960; meat, fish and fowl, $142,022,393; fruits, vegetables and nuts, $46,658,112; lards, fats and oils, $39,132,785 and grain and cereal products, $24,620,850.

＊ ＊ ＊

Peddlers allowed premium on unprocessed used bags

Peddlers and dealers in "unprocessed" second-hand cloth bags are entitled to add to their resale price a premium of not more than three-fourths cent per bag when purchased for resale, Price Administrator Henderson announced May 4 in issuing Amendment No. 1 to Maximum Price Regulation No. 55 (Second-Hand Bags).

This premium may be added to the maximum prices established for second-hand bags which have not been subjected to the necessary reconditioning rendering them fit for immediate reuse as containers. Only one such premium is permitted to be added to the maximum even though the same lot of bags is resold more than one time before being processed.

Makers of butter, ice-cream containers asked to use less paperboard

Following request of the WPB food supply branch to the dairy industry, urging the adoption of a program to conserve materials, the containers branch announced May 2 that it had issued suggestions to manufacturers of butter and ice cream containers which would reduce the amounts of paperboard used to pack these products.

Among the suggested specifications are these:

Butter.—Discontinue the use of all individual containers for ¼- and ½-pound sizes.
Ice cream containers and direct-fill pails.—Restrict the number of small packages, reduce thickness and eliminate use of two-fold flaps on certain cartons.
Cups.—Restrict sizes.
Liquid-tight containers.—Restrict sizes and thickness of the paperboard used.

Seek to preserve food without tin, WPB warns

Inasmuch as more drastic tin conservation measures may be necessary before the beginning of the 1943 packing season, canners were requested May 4 by the WPB containers branch to give thought to other forms of food preservation such as freezing, dehydrating, or packaging in materials less critical than tin.

In addition, the branch, after consultation with the Department of Agriculture as well as with the WPB branches, urged careful planning of the production of "secondary" vegetables and the harvesting of "secondary" fruits this year so that the tin allotted for the packing of these products will be adequate for the amounts produced.

The branch warned that the necessity for careful conservation of tin supplies will not permit the allocation of tin for secondary fruits and vegetables beyond the quotas now established by Conservation Order No. M–81, on tinplate and terneplate.

Bean heads flour unit

Appointment of Atherton Bean of Minneapolis as senior business analyst in charge of the flour unit, food section, OPA, was announced May 5 by Assistant Administrator H. R. Tolley.

Agriculture boards pass on farm building applications before authorization by WPB

County war boards of the United States Department of Agriculture will cooperate with the WPB in handling applications for authorization to begin construction work on farms, the WPB announced May 4.

The procedure to be followed by farmers was outlined in a letter to M. Clifford Townsend, director of the Office for Agricultural War Relations, Department of Agriculture, from Esty Foster, administrator of Conservation Order L–41.

Order L–41, issued April 9 by the WPB, prohibits the start of unauthorized construction projects which use materials, labor and construction equipment needed in the war effort, and places all new publicly and privately financed construction under rigid control, except for certain limited categories.

A farmer planning to begin construction which needs authorization should consult his county United States Department of Agriculture war board and follow its instructions. County boards will be sent instructions covering procedure. Application forms PD–200 will be furnished by county boards.

All farm projects, including residential, agricultural and off-the-farm construction, such as warehouses, processing plants, creameries, etc., will be considered first by the United States Department of Agriculture county war boards. Applications for projects recommended by these boards, will be sent to State war boards and then to the Department of Agriculture. The Department will consider the recommendations and send to WPB for final approval those which are deemed essential.

So far as residential construction is concerned, farm dwellings are covered by the same regulations as other residential construction (see VICTORY, April 14). Other farm building and construction costing less than $1,000 per farm may be started without authorization.

3 rum distillers penalized on use of molasses

Three prominent Puerto Rican rum distillers are penalized for violations of WPB regulations in suspension orders announced May 2 and effective May 4. The offending companies are Compania Ron Carioca Destileria, Inc., San Juan; Jose Del Rio, Marovis, and Borinquen Associates, Inc., Carretera Quintana, Hato Rey.

The WPB charges willful disregard by the three companies of General Preference Order No. M–54, which prohibited the distilling of beverage rum from molasses after January 15, 1942.

On January 30, 1942, relief from M–54 was granted to Puerto Rican distillers by permitting them to produce, during the balance of 1942, 90 percent of the rum distilled by them in the corresponding period of 1941.

The violations took place between effective date of M–54 and date of relief. The penalties consist in the main of bans and restrictions for various periods on the use of molasses.

In addition, Compania Ron Carioca Destileria, Inc., is prohibited from selling, except for use in the preparation of fruit extracts, the spirits which it placed in barrels stenciled "For Fruit Extracts."

Distillers must give 75 days' high wine output to war

Beverage alcohol distilleries must devote 75 days' output of high wines in the remainder of 1942 to meet war requirements for industrial alcohol, they were told May 4 by the WPB.

Program extended

This will be in addition to maximum production of 190 proof beverage alcohol by all distilleries having facilities to produce it. The 75-day estimate is based upon current war needs for industrial alcohol and present estimates of maximum high wine capacity of the distilling industry.

Immediate extension of the high wine program, under which 120–140 proof alcohol is shipped to industrial plants for rectifying into 190 proof, is being made by the WPB. Two projects were in operation for the last 10 days of April, one in Kentucky and the other in Maryland. These will be continued and four others operated during May. The new projects will take in distilleries in Pennsylvania, Massachusetts, and New Hampshire, and two additional groups in Kentucky.

The May program is expected to produce in excess of 1,500,000 gallons of 190 proof alcohol.

CIVILIAN DEFENSE . . .

76.6 percent of $97,000,000 for protective equipment allocated, OCD reports

The Office of Civilian Defense May 6 sent a report to Congress on the progress of its protective equipment procurement program:

Excerpts from the report follow:

The amount of $100,000,000 was appropriated on February 21, 1942, to enable the Director of Civilian Defense to provide, under such regulations as the President may prescribe, facilities, supplies, and services for the adequate protection of persons and property from bombing attacks, sabotage or other war hazards in such localities as he may determine to be in need of, but unable to provide such protection.

Scope of OCD responsibilities

On March 6, 1942, Executive Order No. 9088 was issued under which the Director of Civilian Defense will act in carrying out this program.

Under the operating agreement which the Director of Civilian Defense has with the Secretary of War, the Director of Civilian Defense determines the general types and quantities of protective equipment and supplies and establishes priorities of issue of such equipment with respect to localities. He is also responsible for preservation, maintenance, storage, issue and distribution of such equipment after delivery to OCD depots or other localities by the War Department. The War Department undertakes the actual procurement program, engages in research and development as to specifications and standards, and provides, on request, technical advice.

Services of the Chemical Warfare Service, the Corps of Engineers, the Surgeon General and Quartermaster General have been enlisted to procure the facilities, equipment and supplies ordered by the Director of Civilian Defense.

Determining allocations.

Lists of communities, supplied by the War and Navy Departments, having important manufacturing plants producing war materials for these departments have been used to provide specific information for determining primary localities in need of protective equipment and supplies. Regional directors of the OCD have conferred with State Defense Councils and with their assistance have compiled lists of communities which they believe should receive the equipment and supplies.

Pursuant to directives contained in the Executive order of the President, the Director of Civilian Defense has proceeded to take such further action as is necessary to:

1. Determine allocations of equipment and supplies under priorities now being established.

2. Apportion the funds appropriated and make available working funds to the War Department for the procurement of supplies, equipment, and facilities and to defray the incidental administrative expenses of these cooperating branches in connection therewith.

3. Issue procurement directives to the War Department as to supplies, equipment, and facilities to be acquired.

4. Develop and establish machinery prerequisite to control and the distribution of equipment and supplies to the communities, including:

a. The preparation and issuance of Regulation No. 1 governing loans of equipment and supplies to civil authorities.

b. The establishment of storage and assembly depots.

c. The establishment of full and accurate records of all property received by the Office of Civilian Defense and disposition thereof.

5. Distribute available supplies and equipment to the localities.

Status of appropriation

Of the $97,000,000 made available by Congress for the purpose of procuring protective equipment, supplies, etc., $74,320,000 (76.6 percent) has been allocated to the War Department for the procurement of various items of equipment. Of the unallocated amount, approximately $5,000,000 is being held in abeyance until the research and development of protective clothing, now being engaged in by the War Department, is consummated. Approximately $10,000,000 will be made available to the Chemical Warfare Service, supplementing the previous allocation, upon further clarification of the gas mask situation. In view of the priorities restrictions and the changes in specifications, the remainder has been set aside awaiting further developments.

Of the $3,000,000 limitation established for all administrative expenses in connection with the protective equipment procurement program, $1,250,000 has been apportioned for use during the second half of the fiscal year 1942. Of this latter sum, $468,000 has been allocated to the War Department to date, upon their request. The Office of Civilian Defense in establishing the Procurement and Distribution Section, the Allocations Section, and the Salt Lake City assembly depot has allocated $55,000 for their operation and maintenance.

Procurement directives issued to the War Department

To date, the Director of Civilian Defense has issued to the War Department procurement directives totaling $73,014,398.

The procurement directive calls upon the Chemical Warfare Service to design gas masks for civilian use, to develop production facilities for 2,500,000 gas masks per month, and to manufacture an undetermined number of masks within the funds available. The Quartermaster General has been requested to institute research with a view to the development of suitable clothing for the use of decontamination squads, and to procure 1,000,000 civilian defense helmets and 100,000 arm bands. The Surgeon General, pursuant to our request, is to procure 386,000 instruments, 494,720 units of suture material, 68,640 traction splints, and 68,640 miscellaneous items. The Corps of Engineers has been requested to procure 18,000 auxiliary pumping units, including accessories, and 27,360,000 feet of discharge and hard suction hose, as well as 2,258,000 four-gallon pump tank extinguishers.

Procurement progress

The situation with respect to vital war materials has materially intensified as a result of Japanese aggression in the Pacific. The rubber situation is particularly critical. The WPB, in clearing priorities, has been very reluctant to grant more than a very moderate proportion of the amount requested of certain of the protective equipment. . . .

The War Department is endeavoring on our behalf to revise specifications and standards in quite a number of instances where the WPB has turned down our requests for priorities.

Despite the short period of time which has elapsed since the appropriation of the $100,000,000, and despite the manifold problems of procurement, appreciable progress has been made.

Paul assumes new OPA post

D. R. Paul, formerly connected with the truck department of the Chevrolet Motor Division of General Motors Corporation in the Davenport, Iowa, zone, has been appointed by the OPA to head the field management and liaison section of its passenger automobile rationing branch.

Milwaukee firm reports steps to correct discrimination

The Heil Co., of Milwaukee, Wis., 1 of 10 firms recently ordered to cease discriminating against available workers because of their race or religion, is the first one to advise the President's Committee on Fair Employment Practice of its action taken to comply with the directives of the committee, Lawrence W. Cramer, executive secretary of the committee, announced May 3.

Written instructions clarify policies .

The first obligation of the firm, as directed by the committee on April 9, was to give written instruction to each of its employees charged with hiring, and to employment agencies, revoking all orders and policies in violation of Executive Order 8802 which outlaws discrimination against workers in war industries and in government, because of their race, creed, color or national origin.

In the report of the Heil Co. to the committee, C. T. Hibner, works manager, submitted copies of letters sent to the personnel manager and the comptroller of the company, to three branches of the United States Employment Service, and to 17 schools and placement agencies, explaining the policies of the company.

Manpower released for war work

In announcing this first report from the Heil Co., Cramer pointed out that, "although the action taken by the committee will be to the advantage of minority group workers, even more important is the manpower which will be released for essential war industry as all willing, able, and available workers are integrated into producing the instruments of war which are needed by the United Nations. . . ."

+ + +

McIntosh named chief of communications radio section

Frank H. McIntosh, of Toledo, Ohio, has been appointed chief of the radio section of the communications branch, Leighton H. Peebles, branch chief, announced May 6.

In addition to handling problems in the commercial radio field, the communications branch now is charged with the responsibility for problems arising in the domestic radio industry, formerly handled by WPB's consumers' durable goods branch.

MANPOWER . . .

Women will be inducted for war work along voluntary lines as needed, McNutt declares

Following a White House announcement May 2 on the voluntary registration of women, Chairman Paul V. McNutt of the War Manpower Commission declared that the Nation has an adequate supply of womanpower, which will be trained and employed in war and essential civilian industries at an increasing rate during the next 2 years.

Nation-wide registration not needed

The induction of women will be along voluntary lines, utilizing first the women with industrial experience, and training women who are available for such work, Mr. McNutt said.

No early necessity of a Nation-wide registration of all women is foreseen, he added, pointing out that the United States Employment Service has 1,500,000 women registered already who are looking for jobs. Many of these are qualified for war industry employment.

He predicted that a million or more additional women will be employed in war industries this year, and that 1943's expansion of war production will bring women into war jobs rapidly to a probable total of 4,000,000—out of an expected total of 20,000,000 or more war workers.

To meet shortages in war industry

Women will also be placed in essential civilian jobs in increasing numbers, to replace drafted men and war industry workers, and many must be used in the farm regions during this summer's harvest, he said.

In some war industry communities with labor shortages, Mr. McNutt said, there is need for immediate voluntary registration and employment of women, and in these the United States Employment Service will move to increase placements of qualified women workers.

Conditions of employment

Mr. McNutt announced the Employment Service is sending a directive to its 1,500 full-time field offices, outlining conditions under which employment of women is to be handled. The directive says:

Local offices of the United States Employment Service will recruit women for war production industries under the following conditions:
a. The need exists to use women as an additional source of labor.
b. The employers are willing to hire women.
c. The openings cannot be filled by women already registered in the office.

Recruitment should be specific, planned on the basis of the number and kinds of workers needed, as well as the specific time of hiring. It is inadvisable to recruit far in advance of placement opportunities.

Women who are presently unemployed or who will be unemployed because of the conversion of industries should be given first opportunity for employment in the locality. Before undertaking recruitment to bring additional women into the labor market, effort should be made to recruit women who are normally a part of the labor market although not registered with the employment service.

This directive resulted from a recent meeting of the women members of the Social Security Board's Federal Advisory Council for Employment Security, which surveyed the situation.

War plants surveyed

The Employment Service made a special check of 12,500 important war industry establishments and found that immediate prospects of a great increase of women workers were small. Of a total of 675,000 hires which these firms said they would make by July 1, only 79,000 are expected to be women.

The survey showed, however, that these firms could use many more women, and undoubtedly will after the displaced and unemployed workers from civilian jobs are reemployed in the expanding war plants, Mr. McNutt said.

The major war industries which are able and willing to employ women in large numbers are the ammunition, aircraft, and electrical machinery industries, he said.

"Graveyard" cars taken over after offer is refused

The entire stock of wrecked cars in the graveyard of Lenox Motor Co. at Colmar Manor, Md., was requisitioned May 5 by WPB's Bureau of Industrial Conservation.

The automobile graveyard section of the Bureau went into action after Leo F. Donovan, owner of the Lenox Motor Co., refused to move his jalopies and rejected offers which the Bureau considered fair.

Although the yard is not a large one, containing only about 200 junked cars, officials believe it will assay about 150 tons of iron and steel and 7 tons of nonferrous metal.

Industrial, labor leaders pledge support to war production drive

Labor-management committees for war production drives have been formed in 100 additional plants, bringing the total to 700, it was announced May 11 at war production drive headquarters.

These 700 plants are now engaged in stepping up the production of planes, tanks, guns, ships and other war implements under a voluntary plan offered by Donald M. Nelson, Chairman of the War Production Board.

Company finds advantages

William P. Witherow, president of the Blaw-Knox Co., of Pittsburgh, Pa., telegraphed to Mr. Nelson:

The latest survey of our various plants has indicated advantages of the war production drive. This is manifested in greater interest and better understanding by our production employees as to what they are doing, why they are doing it and when it has to be finished. We are convinced that our management-labor committees have helped in increased production and further increases are expected.

Mr. Witherow is also president of the National Association of Manufacturers.

Support from longshoremen

Support of the war production drive has also come from Harry Bridges, of the International Longshoremen's Association and California director of the Congress of Industrial Organizations. An excerpt from his statement follows:

Joint meetings, joint discussion, joint planning, action and understanding of industry's production problems are necessary to gear every cog and wheel, machine and mind in the nation's industry to all-out war effort and victory. One word to win the war: *teamwork!* That is what labor-management production committees are and what they are for.

Endorsement of drive had already come from William Green, president of the AFL, and Philip Murray, president of the CIO.

In addition to the report on the Blaw-Knox Co., many other companies have reported success under the war production drive program. Typical is the report of the Bausch & Lomb Optical Co., Rochester, which announced $5,000 would be awarded, for best suggestions turned in before May 9.

At the Bausch & Lomb plant a $1,000 award was made to Karl Kraemer for a suggestion that eliminated one operation in the manufacture of a war implement.

In addition to the contest, pay envelopes carry production messages; 14 posters, some especially designed, were put up; and the plant paper, local newspapers and radio stations were enlisted to increase the production.

WAR EFFORT INDICES

MANPOWER

National labor force, March	54,000,000
Unemployed, March	3,600,000
Nonagricultural workers, March	40,298,000
Percent increase since June 1940	**14
Farm employment, April 1, 1942	9,483,000
Percent decrease since June 1940	**4

FINANCE

(In millions of dollars)

Authorized program June 1940–	
April 30, 1942	‡158,362
Airplanes	35,557
Ordnance	32,122
Miscellaneous munitions	19,552
Industrial facilities	16,288
Naval ships	15,457
Posts, depots, etc.	13,173
Merchant ships	7,484
Stock pile, food exports	5,791
Pay, subsistence, travel for the armed forces	4,930
Housing	1,392
Miscellaneous	6,613
Total expenditures, June 1940–	
April 30, 1942	*26,534
Sales of War Bonds, cumulative	
May 1941–April 1942	5,389
April 1942	531

PRODUCTION

(In millions of dollars)

June 1940 to latest reporting date	
Gov. commitments for plant expansion; 1,428 projects, Mar. 31	10,677
Private commitments for plant expansion: 7,366 projects, Mar. 31	2,333
Manufacturing industries—February—	

EARNINGS, HOURS, AND COST OF LIVING

	Percent increase from June 1940
Manufacturing industries— February:	
Average weekly earnings	$35.76 / 38.7
Average hours worked per week	42.2 / 12.8
Cost of Living, March (1935– Index 39=100)	114.3 / 13.7

* Prelim. Includes revisions in former months.
‡ Preliminary and excludes authorizations in Naval Supply Act for fiscal year 1943.
** Adjusted for seasonal variations.

OFFICE FOR EMERGENCY MANAGEMENT

WAYNE COY, Liaison Officer

CENTRAL ADMINISTRATIVE SERVICES: Dallas Dort, Director.

DEFENSE COMMUNICATIONS BOARD: James Lawrence Fly, Chairman.

INFORMATION DIVISION: Robert W. Horton, Director.

NATIONAL WAR LABOR BOARD: Wm. H. Davis, Chairman.

OFFICE OF SCIENTIFIC RESEARCH AND DEVELOPMENT: Dr. Vannevar Bush, Director.

OFFICE OF CIVILIAN DEFENSE: James M. Landis, Director.

OFFICE OF THE COORDINATOR OF INTER-AMERICAN AFFAIRS: Nelson Rockefeller, Coordinator.

OFFICE OF DEFENSE HEALTH AND WELFARE SERVICES: Paul V. McNutt, Director.

OFFICE OF DEFENSE TRANSPORTATION: Joseph B. Eastman, Director.

OFFICE OF FACTS AND FIGURES: Archibald MacLeish, Director.

OFFICE OF LEND-LEASE ADMINISTRATION: E. R. Stettinius, Jr., Administrator.

OFFICE OF PRICE ADMINISTRATION: Leon Henderson, Administrator.

CONSUMER DIVISION: Dexter M. Keezer, Assistant Administrator, in charge. Dan A. West, Director.

OFFICE OF ALIEN PROPERTY CUSTODIAN: Leo T. Crowley, Custodian.

WAR MANPOWER COMMISSION: Paul V. McNutt, Chairman.

WAR RELOCATION AUTHORITY: Milton Eisenhower, Director.

WAR SHIPPING ADMINISTRATION: Rear Admiral Emory S. Land, U. S. N. (Retired), Administrator.

WAR PRODUCTION BOARD:
Donald M. Nelson, Chairman.
Henry L. Stimson.
Frank W. Knox.
Jesse H. Jones.
William S. Knudsen.
Sidney Hillman.
Leon Henderson.
Henry A. Wallace.
Harry L. Hopkins.

WAR PRODUCTION BOARD DIVISIONS:
Donald M. Nelson, Chairman.
Executive Secretary, G. Lyle Belsley.

PLANNING COMMITTEE: Robert R. Nathan, Chairman.

PURCHASES DIVISION: Houlder Hudgins, Acting Director.

PRODUCTION DIVISION: W. H. Harrison, Director.

MATERIALS DIVISION: Wm. L. Batt, Director.

DIVISION OF INDUSTRY OPERATIONS: J. S. Knowlson, Director.

LABOR DIVISION: Sidney Hillman, Director.

LABOR PRODUCTION DIVISION: Wendell Lund, Director.

CIVILIAN SUPPLY DIVISION: Leon Henderson, Director.

OFFICE OF PROGRESS REPORTS: Stacy May, Director.

REQUIREMENTS COMMITTEE: Wm. L. Batt, Chairman.

STATISTICS DIVISION: Stacy May, Director.

INFORMATION DIVISION: Robert W. Horton, Director.

ADMINISTRATIVE DIVISION: James G. Robinson, Administrative Officer.

LEGAL DIVISION: John Lord O'Brian, General Counsel.

VICTORY

OFFICIAL WEEKLY BULLETIN OF THE AGENCIES IN THE OFFICE FOR EMERGENCY MANAGEMENT

WASHINGTON, D. C.   MAY 19, 1942   VOLUME 3, NUMBER 20

CONCENTRATING OUTPUT
The Stove Industry

NORMALLY
EMPLOYED
IN STOVE
MANUFACTURE

WORKING IN
SMALL FIRMS
OUTSIDE OF
LABOR
SHORTAGE
AREAS
working in large firms, and small firms within labor shortage areas

THESE WILL
CONTINUE TO
MANUFACTURE
STOVES

THESE ARE
FREED FOR
WAR WORK

DATA
WPB

Each symbol=5,000 workers

First "production concentration" confines stove manufacture to small factories, frees men, metals, plants for war work

The War Production Board on May 14 for the first time adopted the principle of "concentration of production," ordering an end to the manufacture of domestic cooking appliances by large producers after July 31, and permitting the production of a limited number of simplified and light-weight models by smaller companies for civilian use.

The order (L–23–c, effective May 15) thus releases the facilities of the larger firms for war production and permits the essential civilian needs for cooking and heating stoves to be met by the smaller firms. In addition, a b o u t 350,000 tons of iron and steel, on an annual basis, will be conserved for war needs.

To produce only where labor is plentiful

Another unusual feature of the order is the designation of 39 "labor shortage areas" in fifteen States. Any firm—large or small—located in these areas must discontinue production of cooking and heating stoves after July 31.

The order covers the entire domestic cooking appliance industry (except electric), and the entire domestic heating stove industry (except electric), and establishes these three classes of manufacturers:

Class A—Those whose factory sales value for the year ending June 30, 1941 totaled $2,000,000 or more.
Class B—Those whose factory sales in the same period totaled less than $2,-000,000, and who are located in labor shortage areas.

Class C—Those whose sales in the same period totaled less than $2,000,000 and who are *not* located in labor shortage areas.

In each case, the factory sale value applies to both domestic sales and exports.

Types restricted, weight reduced

Eleven general restrictions are set up by the order:

1. After July 31, no person is permitted to manufacture any domestic cooking appliances except "Permitted Types." The order defines permitted type gas ranges, gas hot plates, coal and wood ranges, combination ranges, kerosene ranges, gasoline ranges, kerosene stoves, gasoline stoves, kerosene table stoves, gasoline table stoves, and portable ovens. Simplifications and reduction in weight are ordered for each permitted type of unit.

2. After July 31, Class A and Class B manufacturers may not produce any domestic cooking appliances or any domestic heating stoves.

3. During the period January 1 to July 31, 1942, Class A and Class B manufacturers may use in domestic cooking appliances no more than six times the average monthly consumption of iron and steel in the year ended June 30, 1941.

4. During the period May 15 to July 31, Class A and Class B manufacturers may use in domestic heating stoves no

(Continued on page 21)

Review of the Week

Huge quantities of weapons are rolling out of the new factories we began in the first phase of our production program, War Production Board Chairman Nelson reported last week. And though we are still building new factories, he said, limitations on some raw materials are becoming apparent and the shortness of time in many cases poses the problem of whether we shall use the materials to build factories to make weapons later or use them to make weapons now. The emphasis now has shifted, he observed, to the conversion of every possible existing factory from civilian to war work.

Concentrating civilian production

In line with this latter objective, WPB last week adopted in the first instance the British principle of concentrating civilian production. By confining stove manufacture to small plants outside areas of labor shortage, and by curtailments, WPB expects to free for war work 25,000 of the industry's normal 35,000 workers—as well as invaluable machines and metals.

The Office of Price Administration informed retailers, who were to go under a price ceiling May 18 affecting practically everything that Americans eat, use, and wear, that applications for relief from the maximum prices are expected only "in the most unusual circumstances." OPA extended from June 1 to July 1 the time within which retailers must file price lists of designated "cost-of-living" items with their local boards, but emphasized that they still must post these prices beginning May 18 for the benefit of the public.

Three gallons a week

Veterans of rationing (the first sugar stamp expired Saturday) stood in line for cards that will provide pleasure drivers with gasoline at the rate of 3 gallons a week. Public outcry at the number of persons obtaining X (unlimited) and B-3 (extra gasoline) cards was followed by an OPA decree that names of persons and the types of cards they got be made public. There will be a check, anyway,

to see that persons are entitled to the cards they hold.

At the same time it was announced that Oregon and Washington motorists will have their gasoline rationed by card beginning June 1.

Moving in still further on individual transportation, WPB gave OPA rationing authority over new adult bicycles, which have been frozen since April 2.

OPA commends cooperative landlords

Price Administrator Henderson praised landlords who have written to him promising support of the ceiling on rents he prescribed April 28 for 302 new areas.

OPA also gave retailers a way to price certain warm-weather merchandise not sold in March, the general ceiling base; and established formal ceilings over new tires and tubes at wholesale, shearlings (used to make flying suits), and nonferrous foundry products. Other OPA actions affected machines and parts; woodpulp; unsorted wastepaper; combed cotton yarn; all-cotton goods; 3 kinds of woolen fabrics needed by the Navy; mixed shipments of iron and steel scrap, and specially prepared copper scrap.

New air conditioning limited

The Division of Industry Operations banned new installations of air conditioning and commercial refrigeration except to meet war and essential civilian needs; subjected alloy iron and steel to monthly melting schedules; froze softwood construction lumber; curtailed grinding and pressing of cocoa beans; placed production of antifreeze on a quota basis; decreed thinner and less fancy glass containers; limited use of colors on the outside of pencils; lifted a death sentence on coat hangers. Sperm oil was put under complete allocation, and the use of cashew-nut oil in brake linings except for Army and Navy was prohibited. Acrylonitrile, needed for Buna rubber, also was placed under allocation.

WPB began turning over for conversion to weapons 300,000 tons of copper and brass products manufacturers had been forbidden to use. Suppliers of

maintenance and repair parts to copper and brass mills were given an A-1-c rating.

A. I. Henderson was appointed to head the Materials Division, as W. L. Batt withdrew to give his full time to the chairmanship of the Requirements Committee and other important duties.

Construction bureau formed •

The Production Division organized a bureau to carry out the construction policies of WPB. At the same time the Division of Industry Operations freed certain construction of roads by governmental agencies from individual project rating.

All shipment of grain ceased on the Great Lakes so far as it involved boats suitable to carry vital iron ore for the war effort.

War Production Drive headquarters announced that plant committees, encouraging car pooling by use of maps with thumbtacks and other methods, had reduced the number of automobiles bringing men to work by as much as two-thirds.

··

Phone surcharge canceled
at Henderson's request

The Northwestern Bell Telephone Company has, effective May 15, withdrawn a 15 percent surcharge on telephone service in Iowa which went into effect April 10, OPA announced. The action was taken in response to a request by Price Administrator Henderson who asked that the rate increase be withdrawn to conform with the national program of preventing inflationary increases which add to the cost of living.

··

WAR EFFORT'S PROGRESS
TOLD VISUALLY

The charts appearing every week on the front cover of VICTORY tell the story of America's battle as it is fought here at home. One-column mats are available for publication by newspapers and others who may desire them. Requests should be sent to Distribution Section, Division of Information, OEM, Washington, D. C.

VICTORY OFFICIAL BULLETIN of the Office for Emergency Management. Published weekly by the Division of Information, Office for Emergency Management, and printed at the United States Government Printing Office, Washington, D. C.

Subscription rates by mail: 75¢ for 52 issues; 25¢ for 13 issues; single copies 5¢, payable in advance. Remit money order payable directly to the Superintendent of Documents, Government Printing Office, Washington, D. C.

On the Home Front

For five months we have watched our raw materials being mobilized for victory. One after another—steel, copper, aluminum, rubber—they were marched from the storehouses of civilian life and into the arsenal of war. Until finally only wood remained undrafted.

Wood becomes key material

Last week the War Production Board moved toward marshalling our resources of wood for duty against the Axis, freezing for 60 days sale of softwood construction lumber for nonmilitary purposes. This lumber represents 70 percent of production and thus the order mobilizes the pine trees of Oregon, Michigan, and the Carolinas along with the iron ore of the Mesabi range and the copper of the Anaconda.

While small sawmill operators are not included in the order and there is no provision for extending the freeze beyond the 60-day period, this is probably the first step toward enlisting our vast timber treasure on an all-out basis for the construction of ships, factories, barracks, and supply depots, and other essentials to victory. Wood takes its place alongside metals as a key material, and that place will be a large one, too, if civilian consumption is any gage.

Two average desks = one trainer plane

Last year we used 27½ billion board feet of softwood in general construction, defense housing, railroad operation and maintenance, and boxes and crates for shipping. On that basis we may save as much as 2½ billion feet of lumber by virtue of the order. And as an example of use—two average desks contain enough softwood to supply all the requirements of a medium trainer plane.

All such orders have an end effect on the Home Front, and the lumber order is no exception to the rule. Defense housing, for example, comes within the scope of the new restrictions. Eventually we may find that the stick of pine which might have made chair rungs or bed slats will be part of a box carrying bullets to our fighting forces in Northern Iceland or Red Cross supplies to the wounded in Australia.

Copper last to be conscripted

Copper was the last of the metals to be totally conscripted for war. The recent WPB order which forbids use of copper and its alloys in more than a hundred additional consumer articles means that 300,000 tons of copper and brass which used to go into ash trays, doorknobs and roofing will end up in the crucible of Mars. This copper is enough to produce one-half billion rounds of .30-caliber rifle or machine-gun ammunition, 2 million .75-mm. field howitzer shell casings, 33 destroyers, 28

REPRINTING PERMISSIBLE

Requests have been received for permission to reprint "On the Home Front" in whole or in part. This column, like all other material in VICTORY, may be reprinted without special permission. If excerpts are used, the editors ask only that they be taken in such a way that their original meaning is preserved.

---

cruisers, and 2,000 bombers. In other words, the copper that might have opened your front door may reopen the door to the Far East.

Eastern motorists show ration cards

Gasoline rationing is now a fact in the Eastern Seaboard area and more than 8,500,000 motorists are presenting A, B, or X cards to their filling station operator when their tanks run dry. The Office of Price Administration expects cheerful and honest compliance because motorists understand that we cannot spare tankers for the submarine-infested run from the Gulf—we need those tankers to supply our fronts.

Practical tips for the ladies

Some tips to the ladies: The OPA's Consumer Division advises the woman who would be well dressed in the performance of her war duties to "Buy clothes practically"—"Mix them up"—"Make them last." In buying rayon hose, ask for the high-twist grade, get your exact size in leg and foot, choose the weight best suited to the purpose for which you are going to use them. To prolong the life of foundation garments, combat dirt, heat, strain.

Retailers warned of sacrifices ahead

OPA announced procedure by which retailers—in exceptional circumstances—might apply for adjustment of abnormally low maximum prices. But OPA coupled the announcement with a warning that—in the words of Price Administrator Leon A. Henderson: "The price control order is a war measure and such sacrifices as it requires of retailers must be taken in the light of sacrifices for the country's welfare. There is no more 'business as usual,' nor will there be until we win the war."

WPB sets up 13 regional offices

Large manufacturers of domestic cooking appliances have been ordered by WPB to halt production after July 31, while smaller companies are authorized to make a limited number of simplified "Victory" models. . . Idea is concentration of production. . . Ice cream comes under the general price ceiling at all levels of sellings, says OPA. . . Railroad shop facilities, wherever available for use, will be used for war production by agreement of management and labor. . . WPB has cut the flow of cocoa products, green coffee and spices—black and white pepper—allspice, cinnamon, cloves, ginger, nutmeg and mace—to our dinner tables. Lack of transportation and enemy action make it necessary to conserve supplies. . . WPB has set up 13 regional offices and is appointing regional directors with broad authority to act on the spot. . . Now—as spring cleaning draws to a close—is the time to "get in the scrap against Hitler"—collect your old iron, paper, rags and rubber and call the junk man. . . Drugs, food, liquor and beer will come in thinner and plainer glass containers from now on. WPB has standardized sizes and weights, simplified design, in order to save soda-ash and other materials. At the same time, production will be raised 30 percent to help make up for the shortage of tin cans and other metal containers.

OPA's Consumer Division is aiming at a recapped tire that will travel 10,000 miles and give 2 year's limited service. . . But it's no answer to the ordinary driver's tire problem. . . If you failed to receive a War Ration Book a few weeks ago because you had an excess supply of sugar you are urged to cut your consumption to half-a-pound a person each week so you'll be eligible for a book when you've used it up. Labor-Management Committees charged with conducting the War Production Drive now have been formed in 700 plants and have enlisted more than 1,000,000 men in stepping up the flow o' war materials. . . Tailors and clothing stores are asked to turn their old wool samples and wool clips over to the Red Cross. . . We spent an average of $131,600,000 a day on war purposes in April as compared with $114,900,000 in March, says Donald M. Nelson, Chairman of WPB. . . That means we're making progress toward victory.

PURCHASES . . .

Huge volume of weapons is rolling out of newly-built plants, Nelson reports

A huge volume of weapons is rolling out of the new factories begun in the first phase of our production program, WPB Chairman Nelson said last week. He spoke before the National Institute of Social Sciences. Excerpts:

I think it is worth our while to look back briefly at our entire effort to prepare ourselves for war. It will pay us to understand more clearly what we tried to do.

First emphasis on new plants

There are two ways in which you can do that kind of job. You can divert part of your resources and energy to build brand new factories for war production—or you can adapt the plants you already have so that they will produce war goods. Our chief emphasis from the start, and down until comparatively recently, was on the first of these alternatives. Despite all the criticism that has been voiced because of that procedure, I have no hesitation in saying that we are today reaping very great benefits from that program. The new factories that were planned and ordered during the last two years are now coming into production. They are ideally designed for the job they have to do. We are getting a huge volume of war goods out of them, and that part of our war production program is running more smoothly and efficiently than would be the case if we had relied on our existing plant from the start.

Shift to conversion

But the job is too big to be done entirely in new factories. So the emphasis has shifted during the last 6 months. Now we are undertaking to convert to war production factories which were built to make goods for peace.

We have built and are still building all the new factories and new machinery we can; we are also converting civilian industry to war production to the fullest possible extent. Our goal is and must be the absolute physical maximum of production, attained in both ways and attained in the shortest possible time.

That maximum is going to be very high much higher than we dared to hope as recently as last autumn. But there is a limit. We have been forced to realize that instead of having unlimited supplies of the vital materials, we are

running into some very definite and restrictive limits.

These shortages have very complex results. There is a multiplicity of uses for all of the metals. You need a given metal, let us say, to make certain direct military items. You also need that metal to make some of the machinery with which other military items are made. You need it, furthermore, to build the plants with which still other military items are made; you may need it in order to expand your capacity to produce some other raw material which is equally vital to successful prosecution of the war.

To add to all of these complexities there is the pressure of time.

Of all of the shortages we face, the shortage of time is the most serious. It

is comparatively easy to figure out how this complex production program can move forward to the desired goal *eventually*—but our Army and Navy are in action *today*, and we know that it will do no good whatever to turn out a flood of goods a year from now if we do not have adequate equipment and supplies for the emergencies that are certain to arise this year.

From this point on, the crux of the war production program will be this unending struggle with the double problem of time and materials.

˄ ˄ ˄

Shafter to assist Reed

A. S. Shafter, secretary-treasurer of the United States Manufacturing Co., Decatur, Ill., has been appointed special assistant to Philip D. Reed, chief of the Bureau of Industry Branches.

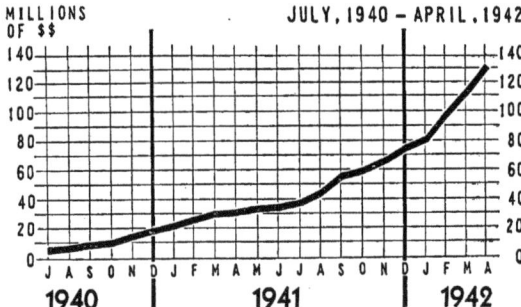

The average daily rate of expenditure for war purposes in April increased to $131,600,000, as compared with $114,900,000 in March, WPB Chairman Nelson reported May 11. Total expenditures for the month, including Treasury checks and Reconstruction Finance Corporation disbursals, were $3,421,000,000 against $2,987,000,000 in March.

"April daily rate expenditures were more than four times those of a year earlier and nearly double those of November 1941' the month before the attack on Pearl Harbor," Mr. Nelson said.

"Expenditures reflect the growth of

the armed forces, as well as increased production. Rising prices affect increased expenditures, but are to some degree offset by increased efficiency in production, which means lower unit costs.

"Hence, the rapidly rising expenditures may be considered as a rough measure of our vast war effort.

"Americans can draw much satisfaction from this picture, which means that a mighty mobilization of materials, machines and manpower is proceeding at a rapid pace. Now we must strive to increase the daily rate of expenditure very greatly."

$55,109,969 loans obtained for war factories in April with aid of Finance Bureau

The Bureau of Finance of the War Production Board reported May 15 that during April it helped manufacturers obtain $55,109,969 of financing for war production from local banks, Federal Reserve Banks, the Reconstruction Finance Corporation, Defense Plant Corporation, Army, Navy, Maritime Commission, and prime contractors.

289 companies aided

The financing went to 289 companies throughout the country, many of which received their loans from local banks.

The Bureau has representatives in 35 WPB field offices (listed below) who give advice and assistance to firms engaged in war production or seeking war orders.

Making no loans itself, the Bureau endeavors wherever possible to arrange financing of war work through local banks. Frequently, it obtains commercial loans for war contractors or potential contractors by helping them to demonstrate that their contracts constitute a sound basis for credit.

War production involves extraordinary credit requirements for many manufacturers, especially smaller firms called upon to do a volume of business far in excess of normal.

FINANCIAL CONSULTANTS

ATLANTA, GA., REGION: *Atlanta, Ga.*—Clarence Knowles, Suite 150, Hurt Building. *Jacksonville, Fla.*—James J. French, Jr., 730 Lynch Building. *Knoxville, Tenn.*—A. P Frierson, 202–304 Goode Building. *Memphis, Tenn.*—St. John Waddell, 2112 Sterick Building.

BOSTON, MASS., REGION: *Boston, Mass.*—Fred R. Hall, 17 Court Street; Asst. Joseph P. Marto. *Hartford, Conn.*—Edward R. Barlow, Phoenix Bank Building, 805 Main Street. *Portland, Maine*—142 High Street. *Providence, R. I.*—580 Industrial Trust Building.

CHICAGO, ILL., REGION: *Chicago, Ill.*—Harry R. Kimbark, 20 North Wacker Drive. *Indianapolis, Ind.*—Henry Ketcham, Circle Tower Building. *Milwaukee, Wis.*—Paul D. Robinson, 161 West Wisconsin Avenue.

CLEVELAND, OHIO, REGION: *Cleveland, Ohio*—Union Commerce Building. *Charleston, W. Va.*—F. O. Lamb, Capital and Quarrier Streets. *Cincinnati, Ohio*—Justin J. Stevenson, Jr., Room 804, Union Trust Bldg. *Louisville, Ky.*—Joseph T. Simmons, 200 Todd Building. *Pittsburgh, Pa.*—406 Fulton Bldg.

DALLAS, TEX., REGION: *Houston, Tex.*—O. W. Jackson, 1016 Walker Avenue. *New Orleans, La.*—G. L. Woolley, Room 423 Canal Building.

DENVER, COLO., REGION: *Denver, Colo.*—Robert W. Frye, 708–714 Kittredge Bldg.

DETROIT, MICH., REGION: *Detroit, Mich.*—Charles W. Renfrew, Boulevard Building.

KANSAS CITY, MO., REGION: *Kansas City, Mo.*—Alexander R. Silverberg, 508 Mutual Building, 13th and Oak Streets. *Little Rock, Ark.*—304 Rector Building. *St. Louis, Mo.*—R. Jewett Jones, Boatmen's Bank Building.

Organizational planning office established, with Gulick at head, to advise Nelson

WPB Chairman Donald M. Nelson May 14 named Dr. Luther Gulick to direct a permanent Office of Organizational Planning which will advise him on methods of simplifying and decentralizing the wide administrative operations of the War Production Board.

The Office of Organizational Planning will operate as a staff agency directly responsible to the chairman of the WPB, and will make recommendations for coordinating and simplifying controls over the mammoth war supply program.

Functions outlined

Functions of the new office will include a continuous study of the responsibilities and operations of the separate units of the WPB. It will search for possible duplication and overlapping of functions and will suggest any changes deemed necessary to the WPB plan of organization.

At the same time, the Office of Organizational Planning will examine organizational relationships between WPB, the Army and Navy and the Maritime Commission—all agencies directly concerned with the war production program.

The office will also study methods of achieving the greatest practicable decentralization of authority and responsibility both in Washington and in the regional offices of the WPB.

Mr. Nelson put careful stress on the permanent advisory status of the new office. He emphasized that there is no question involved of a shakeup or drastic reorganization within the War Production Board.

MINNEAPOLIS, MINN., REGION: *Minneapolis, Minn.*—Guy F. Jensen, 326 Midland Building.

NEW YORK CITY, REGION: *New York City*—Erwin Rankin, Chanin Building, 122 East Forty-second Street; Assts. Harwood Gilder, W. D. L. Starbuck, W. Gordon Brown. *Albany, N. Y.*—State Bank Building, 75 State Street. *Buffalo, N. Y.*—H. L. Underhill, Main and Swan Streets. *Newark, N. J.*—Walter H. Hick, Globe Building, 20 Washington Place. *Syracuse, N. Y.*—Richard A. Robertson, 302 Starret-Syracuse Building, 224 Harrison Street.

PHILADELPHIA, PA., REGION: *Philadelphia, Pa.*—W. W. Moss, Broad Street Station Building 1617 Pennsylvania Boulevard. *Richmond, Va.*—Phillip E. W. Goodwin, Johnson Publishing Building, Fifth and Cary Streets.

SAN FRANCISCO, CALIF., REGION: *San Francisco, Calif.*—Leonard A. Woolams, Furniture Mart, 1355 Market Street. *Los Angeles, Calif.*—Frank C. Mortimer, 1031 South Broadway; Assistant Allen E. Wahlgren.

SEATTLE, WASH., REGION: *Seattle, Wash.*—George W. Klinefelter, Jr., 339 Henry Building. *Portland, Oreg.*—A. C. Ruckdeschel, 815 Bedell Building.

The Office of Organizational Planning will have only a small staff, and will rely heavily on the advice and cooperation of WPB division heads, with whom the office will study possibilities of streamlining and clarification of relations.

Dr. Gulick's office will not supersede the WPB Administrative Division, an agency concerned with internal organizational arrangements. Instead, it will work out broad problems of design which will be put into operation by the Administrative Division.

Dr. Gulick comes to this assignment from the War Department, where, as expert consultant to the Secretary of War, he has served under Lt. Gen. Somervell on supply organization problems. He is Director of the Institute of Public Administration, Columbia University. He was a member of the President's Committee on Administrative Management which developed the plans for Government reorganization effected in 1939. Dr. Gulick has also served as consultant to the Treasury, National Resources Planning Board, Children's Bureau and the Co-ordinator of Inter-American affairs.

Simultaneously with the appointment of Dr. Gulick, Mr. Nelson named Lounsbury S. Fish as assistant director of the new office. Mr. Fish, who has spent 20 years as an organizational planning expert with the Standard Oil Company of California, recently engaged in a broad first-hand study of the over-all plans of management of 30 leading industrial concerns.

War contracts are spread

Primary war contracts are now spread somewhat more broadly among prime contractors than was the case in the months before Pearl Harbor. This is shown in an analysis of supply contracts of $50,000 or more held by 100 corporations to whom the largest volume of contracts has been awarded.

As of the end of September 1941, these 100 companies held approximately 82 percent of the dollar volume of supply contracts of $50,000 or more let by the War and Navy Departments and the Maritime Commission since June 1940. But at the end of February 1942, the 100 companies holding the greatest volume of supply contracts had about 76 percent of the business awarded since June 1940.

RATIONING . . .

Gasoline restrictions lifted outside actual rationing area; boundary revised

The 50-mile border area in which certain gasoline purchases were to be restricted under rationing was eliminated by the OPA May 14, in an amendment to the gasoline rationing regulations that also revised the boundary of the rationed area.

The 50-mile zone was one in which persons from the rationed area would have been required to use cards to buy gasoline, whereas persons living in the zone could have bought without cards.

Supplementary rations for some

Amendment No. 1 to Ration Order No. 5 also provides for the issuance of supplementary rations:

1. To motorists caught away from home with their cars May 15, when the emergency plan for gasoline rationing went into effect, as well as to persons who change their place of residence and need additional gasoline to move their cars to their new residence.

2. To persons who use their cars in taking children to and from school, if the children are too young to walk or to use other methods of transportation.

Persons needing gasoline for vehicles actually engaged in war activity under the official supervision of the Army, Navy, Marine Corps, or Coast Guard may receive gasoline without a card, upon presentation of official identification, another section of the amendment states. Authority is given the military services and law enforcement agencies of the United States to receive "X" cards for their officers, agents, or employees performing duties which depend on secrecy.

Boundary revised

The boundary defining the rationed area has been revised to coincide with changes in the WPB limitation order revising the area in which deliveries to gasoline dealers were curtailed 50 percent beginning May 15. This revision excludes from rationing all of West Virginia except eight eastern counties, as well as 25 counties in Pennsylvania, 10 in New York, one in Maryland and 10 in Virginia. (See page 7.)

The city of Bristol, Tenn., was also removed from the rationed area.

Elimination of the border area, which extended 50 miles beyond the former boundary for rationing, has the effect of removing all rationing restrictions on gasoline purchases, or sales, outside the area actually placed under rationing.

Persons away from home when rationing goes into effect who need gasoline in order to return home may apply to a local rationing board for a supplemental ration.

Persons moving from one place of residence to another will follow the same procedure to obtain gasoline needed to move their cars.

Supplementary rations needed to transport children to school will be issued by a board if more gasoline is needed for this purpose than is provided for by the ration card already in the car owner's possession.

GASOLINE CARD UNIT GOOD FOR 3 GALLONS

Acting to conserve the East's limited gasoline supply for essential use, OPA on May 9 set the value of the units to be rationed beginning May 15 at three gallons.

On this basis pleasure drivers, who hold 7-unit "A" cards, were entitled to purchase a total of 21 gallons for the 47-day period from May 15 to July 1, when the permanent plan will go into effect.

OPA formally authorized to carry out gasoline rationing

The WPB May 11 gave formal authority to the OPA to put into effect the gasoline rationing program which has already been announced.

OPA's authority to ration gasoline is restricted by the directive to the States of Connecticut, Delaware, Florida east of the Apalachicola River, Georgia, Maine, Maryland, Massachusetts, New Hampshire, New Jersey, New York, North Carolina, Pennsylvania, Rhode Island, South Carolina, Vermont, Virginia, West Virginia, the District of Columbia, and the corporate limits of the City of Bristol, Tennessee; except that such authority may further extend to any point within 50 miles of the boundaries of these areas.

The gasoline rationing authorization is contained in Supplementary Directive No. 1H.

Gasoline to be card rationed in Oregon, Washington beginning June 1

Card rationing of gasoline in the States of Washington and Oregon beginning June 1 was announced May 14 by the OPA.

OPA action followed the WPB Limitation Order (L-70, as amended) effective the same date, curtailing deliveries of gasoline to dealers in those States by 50 percent. As in the East, where an emergency plan for rationing went into effect May 15, the rationing area in the two Pacific Coast States will coincide with that covered by the limitation order.

The plan of rationing will be the same as that being put in effect in the East, OPA said. It will operate for a 30-day period, until July 1, when a more comprehensive coupon rationing plan will be instituted.

Fewer units on each card

Registration will take place in the elementary schools on May 28 and 29.

The "A," "B," and "X" cards to be issued the approximately 700,000 car owners, as well as to all owners of inboard motor boats, will be the same as those issued in the East except for one detail—the number of units. In view of the fact that the plan will be in operation for a shorter period—30 days instead of 47—there will be fewer units on each type of card.

An "A" card will contain 5 units (instead of 7) ; a "B-1" card 8 (instead of 11) ; a "B-2" card 10 (instead of 15) ; and a "B-3" card 13 (instead of 19). "X" cards will be issued to a specified group of drivers "for essential use."

The value of each unit will be 3 gallons.

OPA makes gasoline cards a matter of public record

The types of gasoline ration cards issued to motorists were to be made a matter of public record by the OPA in an order issued May 16 revising the confidential status of gasoline rationing records, it was announced by Price Administrator Leon Henderson.

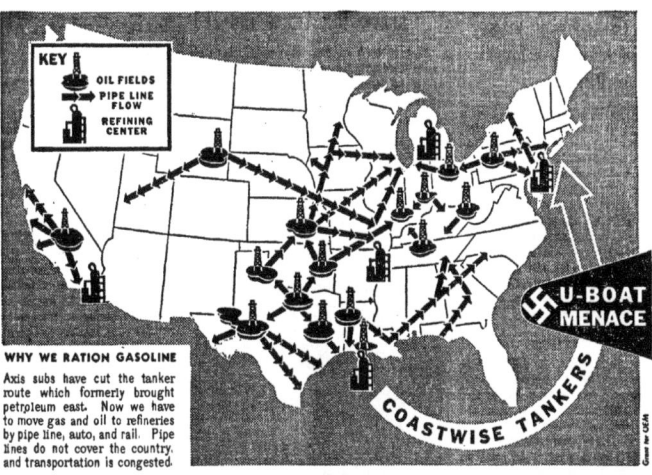

KEY
OIL FIELDS
PIPE LINE FLOW
REFINING CENTER

U-BOAT MENACE

COASTWISE TANKERS

WHY WE RATION GASOLINE

Axis subs have cut the tanker route which formerly brought petroleum east. Now we have to move gas and oil to refineries by pipe line, auto, and rail. Pipe lines do not cover the country, and transportation is congested.

Some counties served by West exempted as 50 percent gasoline cut goes into effect

Implementing the previous week's announcement by the War Production Board that deliveries of gasoline and fuel oil in the Eastern States would be cut to 50 percent of normal, the Director of Industry Operations on May 13 issued amendments to Limitation Orders L-70 and L-56 which made the reductions effective beginning May 15.

The orders require reduction in deliveries of gasoline to filling stations and bulk consumers in seventeen Eastern States and the District of Columbia, except in certain counties.

Effective in Northwest June 1

Effective June 1, there will be a similar 50 percent cut in deliveries of gasoline in Washington and Oregon. Until June 1, the present 33⅓ percent cut from normal deliveries will remain in effect in those States. A 50 percent cut in fuel oil deliveries in those States went into effect May 15.

The amendment to the gasoline order forbids delivery or use of motor fuel for the operation of racing automobiles or racing motor boats in the restricted areas.

Other minor changes in the gasoline order include modification of the provisions with respect to "normal gallonage" on which seasonal adjustments are based, and a provision to make it clear that appeals may be taken from any part of the order.

Exempt counties served from West

The counties which have been exempted from the cuts in gasoline and fuel oil deliveries have been receiving shipments from western points which are not affected by the East Coast shortage.

The restrictions on fuel oil deliveries imposed by the amendment to Order L-56 apply to fuel oil for use in space and central heating, coal spraying, and the operation of domestic and commercial water heating equipment.

In addition, the amendment contains a prohibition against deliveries of fuel oil to be used in equipment installed after June 15 in the following States: Illinois, Indiana, Iowa, Kansas, Kentucky, Michigan, Minnesota, Missouri, Nebraska, North Dakota, Ohio, Oklahoma, South Dakota, Tennessee and Wisconsin. This provision does not, however, apply to new stoves for domestic cooking.

The counties exempt from the new cuts imposed by both the gasoline and fuel oil

MATS FOR PUBLICATION

This map of our oil resources is available in the form of 3-column mats for newspapers, magazines, and other publications. Requests should be addressed to Distribution Section, Division of Information, 2743 Tempo R, Washington, D. C., and should refer to mat V-2. If desired, reproduction may be made directly from this page and no further permission is necessary.

orders are listed below. The 33⅓ percent cut in gasoline deliveries imposed by Order L-70 as previously amended is rescinded in those counties.

NEW YORK.—Monroe, Orleans, Niagara, Genesee, Livingston, Wyoming, Erie, Allegany, Cattaraugus, and Chautauqua.

PENNSYLVANIA.—Potter, McKean, Warren, Erie, Crawford, Mercer, Venango, Forest, Elk, Cameron, Clearfield, Jefferson, Clarion, Lawrence, Butler, Armstrong, Indiana, Cambria, Somerset, West Moreland, Allegheny, Beaver, Washington, Fayette, and Greene.

MARYLAND.—Garrett.

WEST VIRGINIA.—Preston, Monongalia, Marion, Wetzel, Marsh, Ohio, Brooke, Hancock, Tyler, Pleasants, Upshur, Randolph, Pocahontas, Webster, Braxton, Calhoun, Roane, Jackson, Mason, Putnam, Kanawha, Clay, Nicholas, Greenbrier, Harrison, Taylor, Barbour, Tucker, Doddridge, Wood, Ritchie, Wirt, Gilmer, Lewis, Monroe, Summers, Raleigh, Boone, Lincoln, Cabell, Wayne, Mingo, Logan, Wyoming, Mercer, McDowell, and Fayette.

VIRGINIA.—Bland, Tazewell, Buchanan, Dickenson, Smyth, Washington, Russell, Scott, Wise, and Lee.

Rationing control over sales, transfers of new adult bicycles delegated to OPA

The WPB May 13 delegated to the OPA rationing control over the sale, transfer or other disposition of new adult bicycles.

The sale of new adult bicycles has been frozen by the WPB since April 2, 1942. The manufacture of the so-called Victory model bicycle has been under way more than a month. Disposition of such bicycles, as well as adult bicycles of all models on hand when the freeze order was issued, will be under the control of OPA. The WPB retains control over the production of bicycles and the sale of bicycles to defense agencies.

Sales during transition period

To clarify the situation during the period of transition of rationing and allocation powers from the WPB to the OPA, the WPB issued May 13, concurrently with the rationing directive, an amendment to the bicycle freeze order to permit the sale of new adult bicycles to the Army or Navy, United States Maritime Commission, the Panama Canal, the Coast and Geodetic Survey, the Civil Aeronautics Authority, the National Advisory Commission for Aeronautics, the Office of Scientific Research and Development, and Government agencies or other persons acquiring new bicycles for export to or use in any foreign country upon authorization by the Director of Industry Operations.

The amendment also provides for the sale, delivery and transfer of a new adult bicycle to any person who provides a certificate issued by the OPA or complies with conditions prescribed by OPA.

The actions were taken in Supplementary Directive No. 1–G and Amendment No. 2 to Supplementary General Limitation Order L–52–a.

★ ★

Henderson praises sugar registration volunteers

Price Administrator Henderson, whose office of Price Administration made the blueprints for sugar rationing procedure, expressed his thanks May 12 in a telegram to State Governors, to the thousands of American school teachers, school superintendents and principals, and civilian volunteers, who handled the gigantic task of registering virtually the entire population for rationing in a 4-day period.

STAMP NO. 1 EXPIRES

Stamp No. 1 in War Ration Books became unusable by consumers in the purchase of sugar after midnight May 16, OPA reminded individuals.

WHAT RATIONING MEANS: Poster in red, white and black for Office of Price Administration (28 by 40 inches). Two-column mats available for publication, on request to Distribution Section, Division of Information, Office for Emergency Management, 2743 Tempo R, Washington, D. C. Refer to Mat V–3.

Little girl's offer to give up sugar book declined with thanks of Price Administrator

Price Administrator Henderson on May 14 wrote a 10-year-old Los Angeles girl that it was not necessary for her to sacrifice the use of her War Ration Book as she had sought to do in a letter to President Roosevelt.

"We appreciate the fine principles of Americanism which prompted you to do this and we also note with great pleasure your expressed desire to save your money for the purchase of War Savings Stamps," Mr. Henderson wrote. "However, it is not necessary for you or your brother or anyone else to give up the use of sugar to help us give greater support to our soldiers and allies. There is enough sugar for all of us if it is all shared properly and that is the purpose of the sugar rationing program. . . . A proper amount of sugar in our diets is a nutritional necessity and we must keep ourselves physically fit to win the war."

Households denied ration books due to excess sugar advised to regulate use

Households which had excess amounts of sugar and were not issued War Ration Books in the sugar rationing registration were advised May 12 by the OPA to police their own use of sugar in accordance with the designated consumer sugar allotments.

Subject to current consumer allotment

At the present time, the OPA said, no family or individual should consume sugar at a greater rate than a pound a person each 2 weeks, which is the current consumer allotment.

This rule applies to those who did not receive War Ration Books the first week because they possessed sugar in excess of 6 pounds each, as well as to those who were issued War Ration Books.

No War Ration Books will be issued to persons who registered excess amounts of sugar until a sufficient number of ration periods have expired during which the consumer—if he had ration stamps — might have purchased an amount of sugar equal to his excess.

The OPA has received reports that some people who registered excess amounts of sugar think they can obtain War Ration Books as soon as the excess is gone, regardless of the length of time in which it was consumed.

The OPA also issued a warning concerning lost War Ration Books. In the event a book is lost, a person may make application to his local rationing board for a new one but it cannot be issued to him until 2 months after the date of his application. While the boards cannot issue new books until the 2-month period has elapsed, they may in a deserving case permit a person to file a Special Purpose Application for a Sugar Purchase Certificate.

Consumers' excess tires not to be taken in by boards

Local rationing boards will not be asked to take in or resell tires under any plan by which the OPA offers to purchase consumers' excess supplies.

A telegram to this effect was sent May 13 to all regional administrators of the OPA by Paul M. O'Leary, deputy administrator in charge of rationing, who asked that the information be passed on.

PRICE ADMINISTRATION . . .

Retail merchants may seek adjustment of ceiling prices in exceptional cases only, Henderson says in outlining procedure

Procedure by which retailers in exceptional circumstances may apply for adjustment of an abnormally low maximum price under the provisions of the general maximum price regulation was announced May 14 by Price Administrator Henderson.

Not for widespread use

The Administrator emphasized that the machinery—outlined in Temporary Procedural Regulation No. 2—is not intended for widespread use.

The new regulation expires August 1, 1942, at which time it will be replaced by a permanent procedural regulation.

The temporary regulation distinguishes between various classes of application for relief.

In case of an application for adjustment in prices of single items, in one store, or in a group of stores under common ownership, the retailer should use Form OPA-T-1 for each item.

An original and one copy of an application for adjustment must be filed with the appropriate regional office of the OPA. However, where a single application relates to stores of the applicant in more than one region, the original and copy must be filed with the Retail Trade and Services Division of the OPA in Washington, D. C.

Regional office will investigate

An applicant whose application has been denied in whole or in part by the Regional Office, may, within 15 days after the date on which the denial was mailed to him, file with the regional office a request for review by the Administrator. Requests for review must be filed on Form OPA-T-2.

A list of regional offices with which applications may be filed follows:

Region 1. Boston Regional Office; 17 Court Street, Maine, New Hampshire, Vermont, Massachusetts, Rhode Island, and Connecticut.
Region 2. New York Regional Office, 350 Fifth Avenue, New York, New Jersey, Pennsylvania, Delaware, Maryland, and District of Columbia.
Region 3. Cleveland Regional Office, 863 Union Commerce Building, Ohio, Michigan, Indiana, Kentucky, and West Virginia.
Region 4. Atlanta Regional Office, Candler Building, Peachtree Street, Georgia, Alabama, Mississippi, Florida, Tennessee, North Carolina, South Carolina, and Virginia.

Region 5. Dallas Regional Office, Fidelity Union Building, Texas, Oklahoma, Louisiana, Missouri, Arkansas, and Kansas.
Region 6. Chicago Regional Office, 2301 Civic Opera Building, 20 North Wacker Drive, Illinois, Wisconsin, Iowa, Minnesota, North Dakota, South Dakota, and Nebraska.
Region 7. Denver Regional Office, 334 United States National Bank Building, Colorado, New Mexico, Utah, Idaho, Montana, and Wyoming.
Region 8. San Francisco Regional Office, 1355 Market Street, California, Nevada, Arizona, Oregon, and Washington.

Territorial office and territories covered:

Region 9. Territorial Office, Office of Price Administration, Washington, D. C., Alaska, Puerto Rico, Virgin Islands, Canal Zone, Hawaii, and Philippine Islands.

Men's wool gabardine, tropical worsted garments subject to general regulation

Definition of men's summer suits, coats, trousers, and slacks to which the maximum pricing provisions of OPA's summer seasonal goods regulation (No. 142) apply is so worded as to exclude garments made of wool gabardine and tropical worsted fabrics, it was pointed out May 14 by the retail trades and service division of the OPA.

Bulletin explaining ceiling to be distributed over Nation

"What Every Retailer Should Know About the General Maximum Price Regulation"—a bulletin setting forth the A, B, C of price regulations that went into effect May 18, for virtually all goods sold at retail—will be distributed throughout the Nation beginning this week, Price Administrator Henderson announced May 15.

The publication, known as Bulletin 2 on the general maximum price regulations, contains illustrations of methods for displaying a retail store's ceiling prices on cost-of-living items and sets forth specific examples, taken from the operations of typical stores, showing how the pricing regulations apply.

OPA tells how to establish ceilings for seasonal goods not sold in March

Methods by which retailers can readily establish their ceiling prices for a restricted list of summer apparel, furniture, and certain other warm-weather merchandise that was not sold generally in March—the base period used in OPA's general maximum price regulation—are contained in a new and separate order issued May 13 by Price Administrator Henderson.

Briefly, the new regulation—No. 142, Retail Prices for Summer Seasonal Commodities—requires retailers of the seasonal goods listed to obtain maximum prices by applying last "season's" percentage mark-up to a cost figure that cannot be more than the highest manufacturer's price in March and may be less. The seasonal ceiling went into effect May 18 on the following articles:

Men's and boys' clothing.—Summer suits and separate sack and sport coats; summer sport trousers, or slacks; summer slack suits; outerwear shorts; washable summer neckties; straw hats, washable summer hats, and beach helmets; bathing suits, trunks and shorts; toweling or terry-cloth robes, pull-overs, and cardigans and rubber bathing shoes and beach shoes.
Women's and girls' clothing.—Playsuits and sunsuits; bathing suits; terry-cloth or toweling beach robes; rubber bathing shoes and beach shoes; halters; washable hats of woven fabric; and beach bags.
Girls' clothing.—Outerwear shorts, slacks, overalls, and slack suits of cotton or rayon.
Infants' clothing.—Sunsuits; bathing suits; straw or cloth sunbonnets; and carriage or crib netting.
Furniture.—Rattan, metal, and wood chairs; tables, settees, gliders, and umbrellas for outdoor or porch use; beach pads; rubberised or coated slip covers to protect outdoor furniture; and summer rugs made of grass or fiber.
Toys.—Sandboxes and sand for children's play; children's wading pools; toy sail boats; rubber beach toys.
Miscellaneous.—Awnings; sailboats, motorboats, rowboats, and canoes; electric fans and ventilators and room coolers; flower boxes for growing plants; summer holiday novelties; screen doors and windows and screening; wood-slat porch shades; lawn sprinklers; picnic baskets; sunglasses, and wooden trellises and arbors.

★ ★ ★

Woodpulp export ceilings

Manufacturers of woodpulp are permitted to base ceilings on a price f. o. b. producer's mill on sales to persons other than consumers, or their vendors, under the terms of an amendment to the woodpulp regulation issued May 15 by Price Administrator Henderson.

Prices of nonferrous foundry products stabilized at October 1–15, 1941, levels

Maximum prices for nonferrous foundry products based on levels prevailing between October 1 and 15, 1941, were announced May 11 by Price Administrator Henderson.

To insure compliance

Foundries accounting for more than 70 percent of the Nation's output, in compliance with a request of the OPA last January, already had said they would maintain prices based on those of the first half of last October. While there has been no indication that the remaining 30 percent of the foundry industry has not been complying with the OPA request, maximum prices have been formally established "to insure that the whole industry complies."

The new price measure—Maximum Price Regulation No. 125—became effective May 11. Thereafter, regardless of any contract, no company shall sell or deliver nonferrous castings substantially the same as those sold between October 1 and 15, 1941, at prices above the highest prices charged between October 1 and 15, 1941, or castings substantially different at prices higher than would have been charged October 15.

Wholesale ceiling on tires, tubes set at level of agreements

Price Administrator Henderson announced May 15 a formal price order which establishes maximum prices for all wholesale sales of new replacement tires and tubes at the levels which heretofore have applied to manufacturers and mass distributors under voluntary agreement with OPA.

The order, Maximum Price Regulation No. 143, which covers tires and tubes for passenger cars, trucks, and other vehicles, does not depart from the existing informal ceiling levels, but it brings within its scope wholesalers who until now have not been specifically covered. The effective date of the order is May 18.

No advances over the maximums in effect under the voluntary agreements are permitted, as those levels already were high enough to permit sale of passenger car tires and tubes at prices that would compensate for the costs entailed in the Government's tire return plan, based upon preliminary estimates of such costs.

CEILING INTERPRETATIONS

Interpretations of the General Maximum Price Regulation of importance to retailers, for whom the over-all price ceiling went into effect May 18, were issued May 14 by Price Administrator Henderson, in question and answer form (Press Release PM 3286).

Mr. Henderson called particular attention to determinations (1) that prices of cost-of-living commodities must be marked or posted in a manner clearly visible to the public and may not be listed in book form; (2) that the regulation controls prices of retailers established under fair trade contracts; (3) that different brands of the same item are different commodities; (4) that deliveries of sample or memorandum goods by manufacturers or wholesalers during March do not establish their maximum prices.

Date postponed for filing "cost-of-living" item prices; but they must be posted

Extension from June 1 to July 1 of the time within which retail storekeepers must file price lists on cost-of-living items with local War Price and Rationing Boards was announced May 15 by Price Administrator Henderson.

As issued on April 28, the regulation required each retail store to display publicly its ceiling prices for every "cost-of-living" item beginning May 18 and to file a list of these items with an OPA War Price and Rationing Board by June 1.

The May 15 amendment *does not change the May 18 posting requirement.*

Extracted honey regulated

Extracted honey is covered under the general maximum price regulation at all levels, including retailer, wholesaler, bottler, importer, and beekeeper OPA Administrator Henderson ruled May 14 in an opinion directed to the attention of the trade. However, comb honey is excluded from the regulation as a raw agricultural commodity.

Machine ceiling postponed

The Office of Price Administration May 15 postponed until June 1 the effective date of Maximum Price Regulation No. 136 on machines and parts.

Alcoa agrees to cut prices of fabricated aluminum products beginning June 15

Aluminum Company of America at the request of Price Administrator Henderson has agreed, beginning June 15, 1942, to make substantial reduction in the prices of fabricated aluminum products.

Lower costs, greater profits

These reductions will effect substantial savings to the Government in its purchases of planes and other essential war materials.

"OPA has been studying the prices of fabricated aluminum products for some time," Mr. Henderson stated. "The production of these products, principally aircraft sheet, castings and forgings, has tremendously increased and will continue to increase to meet the expanding plane program. This has meant lower costs and substantially greater profits to ALCOA. A price reduction under these circumstances is clearly warranted. The reduction effected, while substantial, will not work undue hardship upon ALCOA or in any way impair its financial position."

To ask similar cuts of others

The reduction in prices will range from more than 20 cents per pound on some of the high cost fabrications down to 1 cent per pound in cases where margins are small. Particularly significant reductions were made in the prices of 24S sheet and plate and forgings going into airplane production. These reductions will apply to all deliveries made on and after June 15, 1942, even if made pursuant to contracts entered into at higher prices prior to June 15.

OPA plans to request the other aluminum fabricators to make similar reductions. The requested reductions when applied to the entire industry will amount to many millions of dollars a year.

All sales of Douglas fir peeler logs placed under ceiling

Because of increased demand for straight-grained Douglas fir lumber in war production, all sales of Douglas fir logs with peeler log qualifications have been brought under the provisions of Revised Price Schedule 54 (Douglas Fir Peeler Logs), Price Administrator Henderson announced May 14.

Copper scrap premium control shifted to new clause

Special purpose premiums granted to certain users of copper scrap by Order No. 1 under Revised Price Schedule No. 20 (Copper and Copper Alloy Scrap) were revoked May 11 by Price Administrator Henderson, since they have been replaced by the special use premium in Revised Price Schedule No. 20, as amended.

The revocation becomes effective May 21, 1942.

Conditions for premium

The special use premium of 1¼ cents per pound may be paid only if the following conditions exist, Mr. Henderson stated:

1. The scrap has been prepared to meet the consumer's specifications and is suitable for his direct use without further preparation, and

2. The scrap is not sold or delivered to a copper refiner, a brass and bronze ingot manufacturer, a ferrous or non-ferrous foundry, or a brass mill.

Companies named in Order No. 1 will be permitted, by the new provision, to pay the same 1¼ cents per pound premium above the price of No. 1 copper scrap as they were permitted to pay under the "special purpose" provisions of Order No. 1.

Adams named chief of furniture and bedding branch

Appointment of William A. Adams as chief of the furniture and bedding branch of the Bureau of Industry Branches was announced May 12 by Philip D. Reed, Bureau chief. Mr. Adams has been deputy chief of the branch since February 8.

John M. Brower, retiring chief of the furniture and bedding branch, will continue to serve the branch as chief technical consultant.

★ ★ ★

Book match definition for resale is changed

The definition of "resale book matches" is changed by Amendment No. 2 to Maximum Price Regulation No. 129 (Paper and Paper Products) issued May 9 by Price Administrator Henderson. As now defined in the amendment, "resale book matches includes paper matches in books sold by a manufacturer for distribution to retailers." Inadvertently, s e v e r a l words had been omitted from the definition in the regulation.

MIXED SCRAP SHIPMENT REGULATIONS LIBERALIZED

A new amendment liberalizing the provisions governing mixed shipments of iron and steel scrap was announced May 13 by Price Administrator Henderson.

The amendment states that when grades of scrap commanding different maximum prices are included in one vehicle, the maximum price of the scrap in the vehicle shall be that of the lowest-priced grade in the shipment. It provides, however, that this limitation shall not affect shipments involving vessel movement if each grade commanding a different maximum price is segregated in the vessel.

The amendment—titled Amendment No. 4 to Revised Price Schedule No. 4—was to become effective May 18, 1942.

. . . . . .

Cold and hot finished tubing

Price Administrator Henderson on May 9 warned jobbers and warehousemen of iron and steel products not to use list prices for cold finished mechanical tubing in computing their prices on hot finished mechanical tubing.

. . . . .

Firm changes subcontractors without boosting tool price

Defiance Machine Works, Inc., of Defiance, Ohio, is permitted to sell 150 specified machine tools manufactured by a subcontractor—the Haughton Elevator Co. of Toledo, Ohio—at maximum prices originally named by OPA to take care of their manufacture by another subcontractor, Administrator Henderson announced May 11. Permission is granted under Amendment No. 9 to Revised Price Schedule No. 67 (New Machine Tools) to sell the 150 tools as follows:

Type	Quantity	Maximum price each
Model No. 112-21" production drilling machine	100	$1,600
Model No. 200-26" heavy duty production drilling machine	50	2,062

While prices agreed upon with Haughton are in excess of those at which the other subcontractor had indicated its willingness to manufacture, Defiance has advised OPA that it will absorb the increased manufacturing cost by Haughton, as subcontractor.

Five steel companies permitted to pass on extra freight costs

Orders permitting several steel companies to pass on to some customers certain heavier freight costs stemming from war business were announced May 11 by Price Administrator Henderson.

The orders were issued under Revised Price Schedule No. 6, governing sales of iron and steel products.

The companies granted certain exceptions from terms of the price schedule are:

South Chester Tube Co., Chester, Pa.; Sheffield Steel Corporation, Kansas City, Mo.; Colorado Fuel & Iron Corporation, Denver, Colo.; Seneca Wire & Manufacturing Co., Fostoria, Ohio; and Follansbee Steel Corporation, Pittsburgh, Pa.

The exceptions, for the most part, were granted under the section of the price schedule which provides that OPA may give producers relief from "excessive or unusual" freight absorption resulting from war orders on allocations.

"In general, Revised Price Schedule No. 6 allows a producer of steel who must ship out of its usual market area, or by other than usual means of transportation, because of the war program, to use the basing point closest to the mill rather than the normal governing basing point," OPA said. "However, although this provision affords ample relief in the great majority of cases, it does not completely alleviate the situation on those mills which are not located at basing points, and which are compelled to ship toward their emergency basing point because of an allocated or other high-rated order. Although the Office of Price Administration will not relieve a mill of all freight absorptions of this type, in unusual situations where excessive freight absorption is compelled in this manner, an exception may be granted under section 1306.7 (c).

"In certain cases on which orders are now being issued by the Price Administrator, freight absorptions of this unusual type were involved."

★ ★ ★

Merchant bar rise denied

A request by Pollak Steel Co. for permission to raise prices on merchant bars has been denied, OPA announced May 12. OPA said that "an exception will not be granted merely to make a particular item more profitable when over-all profits are good."

Ceilings on "fluid milk," "fluid cream" include virtually every household form

"Fluid milk" and "fluid cream"—the retail prices of which are controlled by OPA's general maximum price regulation—are defined so broadly as to include virtually every form that finds its way into American households, according to a "statement of examples" issued May 13 by Price Administrator Henderson.

Controlled at retail level only

The statement also lists examples of what OPA considers as "ice cream" within the meaning of the regulation. Ice cream is controlled at all levels of selling—manufacturing, wholesale, or retail—while fluid milk and fluid cream are only controlled at the retail level. The retail price ceiling, establishing maximum prices at the highest levels reached in March by each individual seller (whether store or home-delivered), went into effect May 18.

Text of the "statement of examples" follows:

Examples of Fluid Milk, Fluid Cream, and Ice Cream as Covered by the General Maximum Price Regulation Bulletin No. 1 of April 28

A. EXAMPLES OF PRODUCTS COVERED BY THE REGULATION:

I. *All fluid milk—Examples:*
1. All standard grades of milk—Examples: (a) Certified milk, (b) Grade A, (c) Grade B, and (d) all other standard grades whether sold under special label or not.
2. *all special milk—Examples:* (a) Homogenized milk, (b) soft curd milk, (c) Vitamin D milk, (d) all other vitamin fortified milk, and (e) all other special milk.
3. *Flavored milks and skim milk drinks—Examples:* (a) chocolate milk, (b) chocolate drink made with skim or partially skimmed milk, (c) fruit flavored milk, (d) fruit flavored skim milk, and (e) all other flavored milk or milk drinks.
4. *Cultured milk—Examples:* (a) cultured buttermilk regardless of fat content, (b) Bulgarian type buttermilk, (c) Acidophilus cultured milk, and (d) all other cultured milk or cultured skim milk.
5. *Miscellaneous types of fluid milk—Example:* (a) skim milk.

II. *All fluid cream—Examples:* 1. table cream, coffee cream, or light cream; 2. whipping cream, or heavy cream; 3. cultured or sour cream; 4. combinations of milk and cream known as "cereal special," "half-and-half," etc.; and 5. all other cream (milk from which a portion of the serum solids have been removed and which is not classed as fluid milk, evaporated, or condensed milk).

III. *Ice Cream—Examples:* 1. ice cream of all flavors and grades, both bulk and packaged, regardless of fat content and overrun; 2. frozen desserts and frozen custards; 3. ices and sherbets*; 4. all ice cream and frozen dessert specialties, such as bars, pies, molds, and cups; 5. fancy or decorated ice cream in any form; 6. ice milk; 7. malted milk base (similar to ice milk); and 8. all other ice cream or frozen desserts.*

B. TYPE OF SALES COVERED BY THE REGULATION:

I. Sales at retail of fluid milk, fluid cream, and ice cream; II. Sales at wholesale and by manufacturers of ice cream.

*(All ices and frozen desserts are included in the General Maximum Price Regulation either as ice cream or nondairy products.)

Government contracts exempt from GMPR until May 18

Effective date of the general maximum price regulation with respect to Government contracts was postponed from May 11, 1942, until May 18, 1942, under Supplementary Regulation No. 2, Price Administrator Henderson announced May 11.

After May 18, 1942, contracts with the Government must be entered into at prices not topping applicable maximum prices. Deliveries remaining to be made under Government contracts made prior to May 18, 1942, may continue to be made at contract prices until June 15, 1942.

Machines, parts also exempt

Postponement of effective dates on Government contracts is made in order to avoid overburdening the contracting officers of the military forces and of the Government agencies in bringing their contracts into conformity with the regulation.

The supplementary regulation also exempts machines and parts and machine work from provisions of GMPR. These items are subject to provisions of Maximum Price Regulation No. 136, which does not become effective until May 18, 1942.

Fat, oil-bearing items not covered by raw fats schedule

Because they are fat or oil-bearing material rather than raw fats, the following commodities are not covered by Revised Price Schedule No. 53 (Fats and Oils) but are covered by the general maximum price regulation and supplemental regulation No. 1 thereto, Price Administrator Henderson ruled May 11:

Butcher shop fats and suet, slaughterhouse fats and suet, offal collected at butcher shops and slaughterhouses, poultry offal, bones, fallen animals, and greases collected from hotels and restaurants.

GMPR ceilings to control retail sales in case of conflict with State fair trade agreements

Ceilings established by the general maximum price regulation will control retail selling prices in cases of any conflict with State Fair Trade Laws, Price Administrator Henderson announced May 14.

"Fair trade agreements cannot require a retailer to sell above his ceiling price," Mr. Henderson said. "To the extent that any fair trade agreement or State Fair Trade Act is inconsistent with the regulation, the regulation will control."

Basic points in fair trade agreements

Three basic points on fair trade agreements were outlined for the retailer by Mr. Henderson:

1. Fair trade agreements may establish a minimum price which is binding upon a retailer only if that minimum is not higher than the ceiling prices of that retailer.
2. No new fair trade agreement effective after May 18 may establish minimum prices for a retailer higher than the March ceiling price of that retailer.
3. If the highest price charged by a retailer during March was below the minimum price established by a fair trade agreement, the retailer is nevertheless "frozen" to the prices he actually charged, regardless of the fact that in charging such price he may have violated a fair trade agreement or a State Fair Trade Act.

However, in the last instance, where a retailer is "frozen" at a *maximum* price which forces him to sell below the *minimum* price set in a fair-trade agreement that was in effect in March, he may apply under Section 18 (a) of the Regulation for an adjustment of his ceiling on the ground that it is "abnormally low in relation to the maximum prices of the same or similar commodities established . . . for other sellers at retail."

Basis for trade agreements

Trade agreements controlling minimum retail prices are generally based on one of two types of State Law.

State Fair Trade Acts permit manufacturers or distributors of branded articles to establish minimum retail prices through agreements with the trade.

State Unfair Practices Acts control minimum prices without supplementary agreements, usually by forbidding a retailer from selling below cost or at less than a specified percentage—often 6 percent—above cost. This type of law was directed particularly at "loss leaders."

Under either type of law, Mr. Henderson stated, minimum prices may be established only to the extent that they do not require a retailer to sell above his ceiling prices.

Three Navy requisitions get exception from price regulation

To enable the United States Navy to accept bids for approximately a year's supply of certain types and kinds of woolen fabrics, Price Administrator Henderson on May 12 excluded bids under three specific Navy requisitions from the provisions of the general maximum price regulation.

Under the terms of Supplementary Regulation No. 3, sales and deliveries of goods exempted are those specified in Navy Regulations 489, 496, and 497, under which the Navy is accepting bids for 4,959,500 yards of flannel, melton and kersey.

Specific prices established

Specific maximum prices are established under the supplementary regulation applying to the woolen fabrics under these three Navy requisitions as follows:

Type:	Price per yard
11-ounce flannel	$2.575
16-ounce melton	3.85
30-ounce kersey	5.475

OPA officials find that the prices allowed permit manufacturers to cover their requirements at the wool ceiling which was established in March 1942 and reflect a proper price relationship with costs as of that period. Furthermore, they say that these prices are sufficiently low so as to prevent dissipation of defense appropriation and to effectuate the purposes of the Emergency Price Control Act of 1942.

Mixed wool clothing house clips regulated, OPA points out

In order to correct a trade misinterpretation, Price Administrator Henderson May 11 stated that mixed wool clothing house clips fall within the definition of raw wool waste materials covered by Maximum Price Regulation No. 123 and are therefore subject to its provisions.

Trowbridge named consultant on apparel manufacture

Appointment of Sherman Trowbridge as special consultant in charge of apparel manufacturing problems was announced May 11 by OPA Administrator Henderson.

NO PRICE CHANGE INTENDED FOR OLD MANILA ROPE

The present price ceiling of $115 per ton for old manila rope established in Revised Price Schedule No. 47 (Old Rags) will remain in effect and no changes in the maximum price are contemplated by OPA, Price Administrator Henderson said May 13.

He urged dealers in old manila rope to release their supplies to manufacturers of rope—papers and other items essential in the war effort.

Imported wood pulp governed by prices established April 20

Delivered prices for the various grades of imported wood pulp which purchasers in the United States may pay may not exceed the maximum delivered prices at the consumer's mill as established by Maximum Price Regulation No. 114 (Woodpulp), Price Administrator Henderson stated May 13.

The regulation, which became effective April 20, established a single-pricing system and maximum prices for the various grades of domestic and foreign wood pulp. The order, however, also provides for freight allowances for producers of domestic wood pulp based on the geographic location of the producing mill.

Any consumer prepared to show that because of the transportation charges involved he cannot purchase wood pulp produced in a foreign area at the ceiling prices established by the regulation, may file a petition with OPA for exception from the maximum prices fixed by the order.

Text of newsprint regulation corrected by OPA

Amendment No. 1 to Maximum Price Regulation No. 130 (Standard Newsprint Paper) was issued May 11 by Price Administrator Henderson and effected the correction of an error printed in the text of the regulation.

The phrase ". . . no consumer shall buy or receive standard Newsprint Paper in the course of trade or business, . . ." in the first sentence of section 1347.271 (Maximum Prices for Standard Newsprint Paper) has now been changed, as was intended, to read "no person shall buy or receive Standard Newsprint Paper in the course of trade or business, . . .".

Price for seven rayon grey goods aligned with 229 others

Adjustments in maximum prices of 7 rayon grey goods constructions to bring them into proper relationship with the 229 types of these goods recently brought under the ceilings are provided by Amendment No. 2 to Revised Price Schedule No. 23 effective May 12.

Two acetate warp crepe constructions are increased ½ cent per yard to correct an inadvertence contained in the schedule. Fabric No. 4—20 is raised from 23½ to 24 cents and Fabric No. 4—30 from 28½ to 29 cents. This brings these two numbers into correct relationship with Fabric No. 4—25.

The maximum selling price of Fabric No. 2—195 has been lowered from 23½ to 22⅞ cents to bring the per loom return of this twill number into line with per loom return of the 41 other fabrics of this group.

In the taffeta group, three changes are effected. The ceiling of Fabric No. 1—170 has been increased from 19¾ to 21 cents, since OPA studies find that the per loom return allowed for this fabric is lower than for any of the similar fabrics in this group. The selling prices of Fabric No. 1—240 is raised from 19 to 19½ cents and of Fabric No. 1—245 from 19¾ to 20¼ cents to take into consideration the increased differential in the manufacture of an all-acetate fabric above that of an all-viscose fabric. This increase recognizes the differential between all-acetate and all-viscose constructions under the revised schedule.

One number in the marquisettes, ninons, and voiles group, Fabric No. 7—50, is advanced from 19½ to 20¼ cents in recognition of the increased costs in producing this type over the other constructions.

Provision is made for an extra premium for 16 shafts of 1½ cents per yard over the basic plain construction by changing paragraph (b) (2) of the appendix to the schedule which sets forth maximum prices. This was inadvertently omitted.

★ ★ ★

All-cotton goods pricing simplified

A simplified method for determining maximum prices of goods made entirely of cotton which come under the provisions of Maximum Price Regulation No. 118 (Cotton Products) was announced May 12 by Price Administrator Henderson through Amendment No. 2 to this regulation.

Since the "sliding scale" feature in establishing all cotton yarn and textile prices covered by various schedules has been eliminated, the base maximum price for cotton products covered by Regulation No. 118 is increased by 5 cents for each pound of cotton content, by Amendment No. 1.

Amendment No. 2, effective May 16, provides that sellers of goods consisting wholly of cotton, in invoicing such cotton products, need state only the unadjusted maximum price, the loom weight and the maximum price. Buyers may determine the correctness of the adjustment by simple arithmetic.

Henderson denies favoring wage "freeze," explains position on taxes and savings

Leon Henderson, Administrator of the Office of Price Administration, issued on May 12 the following statement:

The variety of reports that appeared after my testimony yesterday before the Ways and Means Committee of the House of Representatives impels me to release a general outline of my expressed position on several important questions.

WAGES

It is essential to the success of President Roosevelt's seven-point program for control of the wartime cost of living that wages be stabilized and that general wage increases be avoided. Without wage stabilization there can be no effective administration of the price level. However, as a part of real wage stabilization, the wage levels of substandard groups of workers in our population must be raised. Substandard groups cannot be condemned to a continuation of a substandard existence at a time when the country's welfare demands that every citizen's health and productive capacity be maintained and improved. Further, real wage stabilization requires adjustments to remove inequities as between higher-paid groups. This is necessary to continued effective production of war material at the highest possible rate.

Reports that I have intimated the need for wage "freezing" are untrue, but it is true that I oppose general increases in the level of wages.

Also untrue are intimations that the Office of Price Administration desires additional powers to deal with the wage question. I have repeated time and again, and take occasion to repeat once more, my firm conviction that the laws and problems related to the administration of prices are unsuitable for stabilization of wages.

THE SALES TAXES

I am unalterably opposed to a national sales tax. Such a measure would raise the prices of the necessities of life and would fall with heaviest burden on those persons whose standard of living is already below safe levels. By making higher the prices of goods, the sales tax also would greatly increase the difficulties of rationing essential products equitably, particularly for substandard income persons.

TAXES

The Treasury's program on higher taxes to meet the mounting cost of war and to absorb the dangerous excess of purchasing power over supplies of goods is a vital part of the President's over-all attack on the cost-of-living. I have urged the adoption of the entire program advanced by the Treasury, including reductions in individual exemptions. In fact, I would support an even sharper cut in personal exemptions.

COMPULSORY SAVINGS

I did not discuss compulsory savings before the House Committee. The Treasury is launching its drive to stimulate each individual to save 10 percent of his income voluntarily. I am supporting, and I feel everyone should support, this campaign to the utmost of his ability.

★ ★ ★

Two salvage firms excused from general price regulation

Exception from the terms of the general maximum price regulation of all sales and deliveries made by The Underwriters Salvage Co. of Chicago and the Underwriters Salvage Co. of New York was announced May 13 by Price Administrator Henderson.

Both of these firms, the Administrator said, had registered with OPA and had satisfactorily demonstrated that they were engaged solely in the business of reconditioning and selling damaged merchandise received from insurance companies, transportation companies, and agencies of the United States Government.

. .

Service charge report required for Pennsylvania hard coal

Producers and distributors of Pennsylvania anthracite who make any charges for special services must report the charges to OPA monthly, Administrator Henderson announced May 13.

In a second provision of the amendment, OPA refused to exempt the Franklin-Lykens Coal Co. of Ashland, Pa., from the price regulation but granted the company a premium of from 30 cents to $1.25 a ton on sizes larger than pea and 10 cents per net ton of rice (buckwheat #2) marketed under the trade name, "The Only Genuine Franklin Coal of Lykens Valley."

Several more items excepted from general price regulation

Amendment No. 1 to Supplementary Regulation No. 1, excepting selected additional commodities and services from the provisions of the general maximum price regulation, was announced May 12 by Price Administrator Henderson.

Amendment No. 1 to the Supplementary Regulation perpetuates, among others, the exceptions previously granted in specific price schedules or maximum price regulations for imported silk wastes, copper scrap or copper alloy scrap sold to a foundry by a person operating, owning or maintaining rolling stock, and green coffee sold in Puerto Rico.

Added to the list of commodities excepted were cotton mill waste, ground grain feed, hog cholera virus and antihog cholera serum, block mica of strategic grades and fabricated mica produced from such grades, and diamond dies smaller than 0.002 inch diameter. Appalachian hardwood lumber was exempted, but only until May 18, 1942 when a specific regulation was to be issued.

Salvage firms exempt

All sales or deliveries by companies engaged solely in reconditioning and selling damaged commodities received from insurance companies, transportation companies, and agencies of the United States were also excepted, provided such persons or companies registered with and were approved by OPA as engaging solely in such business.

The supplying of dry cleaning services by dry cleaning establishments to others than those owning the garments cleaned, was excepted until July 1, 1942, when the supplying of such services at retail are to be brought within the terms of the general maximum price regulation. The Administrator pointed out, however, that such wholesale dry cleaning establishments are specifically subject to the record-keeping requirements of that regulation.

Interior's Bituminous Division to handle inquiries on prices

Correspondence and personal inquiries relating to Maximum Price Regulation No. 120—Bituminous Coal Delivered from Mine or Preparation Plant—should be referred directly to the Bituminous Coal Division of the Department of the Interior, according to a procedure outlined May 12 by Price Administrator Henderson.

Wastepaper ceilings adjusted to route higher-grade fibers to mills needing them

Price ceilings over unsorted wastepaper, containing two or more grades, sold to a dealer for the purpose of grading and sorting for resale to consumer mills, are removed as the result of Amendment No. 3 to Revised Price Schedule No. 30 (Wastepaper) issued by Price Administrator Henderson. The action is designed to increase the supply of higher-grade fiber papers to mills which have specific need for them.

Allowances for processing made in combed cotton yarn revisions

Allowances for loss in weight of combed cotton yarn when it is processed by merchants through such finishing operations as bleaching or "gassing" are given consideration in an amendment issued May 14 by Price Administrator Henderson to Revised Price Schedule No. 7.

Fine-gage hosiery machines put first for fine rayon yarn

The WPB May 15 issued Amendment 1 to the supplementary rayon order (M-37-c), granting hosiery manufacturers operating fine-gage machines preferences in deliveries of the fine denier sizes from the amount of rayon viscose and cuprammonium yarn which has been set aside for hosiery.

WPB limits grinding, pressing of cocoa beans to 70 percent

WPB acted May 11 to curtail the supply of cocoa products used in making such confections as chocolate candy, chocolate coated foods, powdered cocoa, chocolate covered ice cream, cocoa butter, and chocolate syrup.

The chocolate in these products is obtained from cocoa beans. Order M-145 and Supplementary Order M-145-a, issued May 11, restrict the amount of cocoa beans that may be ground or pressed during the balance of May and the month of June to 38.8 percent of the grindings during the 3 months ended June 30, 1941. This percentage represents 70 percent of the total grindings during the 1941 period, prorated over the remaining portion of the current quarter.

Sperm oil placed under complete allocation

Sperm oil was placed under complete allocation control May 16 by the Director of Industry Operations.

Crude ceilings adjusted in two areas

Maximum prices for crude oil produced in the Loco Hills area of Eddy County, N. M., were set May 13 at $1.12 per barrel for 40-degree gravity, with customary differentials for lower gravities, Price Administrator Henderson announced.

The amendment also set a maximum price of $1.25 a barrel for crude petroleum of 40 degree gravity produced in Garvin County, Okla., from the Tussy field.

★ ★ ★

Solid fuel regulation made more inclusive

The first amendment to the sweeping regulation which on May 18 placed the wholesale and retail prices charged by 45,000 dealers in solid fuels under rigid control at levels prevailing in the period from December 15-31, 1941, was announced May 16 by Price Administrator Henderson.

Amendment No. 1 to Maximum Price Regulation No. 122 (Solid Fuel Delivered From Facilities Other Than Producing Facilities—Dealers) reinforces the regulation by providing a method of pricing solid fuels appearing in new markets and any sales of solid fuels which might not have been originally covered by the regulation (for example, seasonal movements for special uses, such as bunker fuel on the Great Lakes).

Nonmetallic materials for repairing, relining lamp shades

The restrictions of WPB order L-33 governing the manufacture of portable electric lamps and shades do not apply to the repairing, recovering, retrimming, or relining of lamp shades in which no new metal frame is used, the WPB held May 15 in an interpretation to the order.

Large producers' sales, deliveries of softwood "construction" lumber frozen

The WPB May 13 froze for a period of 60 days all sales and deliveries by large producers of softwood "construction" lumber, except to meet the needs of the Army, Navy, and Maritime Commission.

The order (L-121) affects approximately 70 percent of this country's softwood lumber production and applies particularly to timbers, framing items, and boards commonly used in building construction. It leaves factory, shop, and box lumber, and all hardwood lumbers, free to move in the customary trade channels.

Stocks in retail yards, estimated to be approximately 7,000,000,000 feet, are sufficient to supply the essential civilian demands during the period the order is in force, the WPB lumber and lumber products branch said.

The definition of producer does not include sawmills which produced less than 5,000 feet, board measure, per average day of eight hours of continuous operation during the 90 days preceding May 13.

★ ★ ★

Some high lauric acid oil allowed in food this summer

Because soya bean oil and other substitutes grow rancid in hot weather, the WPB announced May 11 that a limited use of high lauric acid oils in food products will be permitted during summer.

Restrictions removed on molasses deliveries

Restrictions on deliveries of molasses from producers and importers to primary distributors (bulk wholesalers) were removed May 11 by the Director of Industry Operations in Amendment No. 1 to General Preference Order M-54.

★ ★ ★

Pencil order modified

The WPB May 15 issued Amendment No. 1 to the pencil order (L-113), prohibiting the use of any finishing materials for pencils containing any pigments other than carbon black, lamp black, bone black, white, domestic earth colors, and ultramarine blue.

Plant committees use car-pooling maps and other ways to help transport workers

American ingenuity has been applied to transport so that reports to the War Production Drive headquarters provide a blueprint on successful car-pooling methods that are widely adaptable.

Labor-Management committees working for greater production of planes, tanks, guns, and ships have reported that the task of working out systems for car pooling plays a vital part in getting all employees † work on time every day. Many of the largest war plants are not on main street car and bus lines and private transportation is the only means many employees have of getting to work. As irreplaceable tires wear out, the sharing of rides is the only means of transportation.

Many ingenious methods are being devised to further car pooling.

Maps with thumbtacks help

The War Production Drive Committee in the Hunter Manufacturing Corporation plant at Croydon, Pa., reports that one-third of their workers who formerly drove to work now arrive after shared rides. The committee prepared a large map of the territory in which employees lived. For each person driving a car a red tack with his shop number located his home; a white tack with his shop number located the residence of each person without a car. This enables workers to form their car pools quickly and efficiently.

The War Production Drive Committee at the Grayson Heat Control, Ltd., plant at Lynwood, Calif., used a variant of this plan. Three maps were erected, one for each shift—the Sunshine Shift, the Matinee Shift, and the MacArthur Shift. Each employee was issued a tab on which to write his name, address, and pertinent facts about his means of transportation. Tabs were pinned to appropriate maps, locating each worker's residence. By this means, car pools are arranged.

One company adds housing service

The transportation subcommittee at the Cleveland (Ohio) Tractor Co. reported it was going ahead on doubling-up and car pooling plans, but was working on the possibility that there be no private transportation in the future. With this in mind, a housing rental service has been added to help the transportation committee enable workers to move nearer the plant or to where public transportation is assured.

The American Cable Division of the American Chain & Cable Co., Bridgeport, Conn., reported that voluntary car pooling was so successful that the number of cars used now have been reduced two-thirds. Some drivers are bringing from four to seven friends with them.

Buses and railroads adjust schedules

Many committees have reported that after they had obtained exact information as to how many employees came from each section, and at what hours, they were able to obtain full cooperation from bus companies and railroads. One special bus arranged for the plant of the De Laval Steam Turbine Co., at Trenton, N. J., was of help to this plant and two other plants in the vicinity. A railroad was persuaded to stop an express train to bring workmen to the Bridgeport, Pa., plant of the Summerill Tubing Co. The AGA Aviation Co. is cooperating with other plants in its vicinity. Other production drive committees are making a study of the Pontiac plan, which is being developed by the Michigan State Highway Commission. The plan, in addition to the encouragement of car pooling, provides for the coordination of shifts. Plants in one end of town start shifts half an hour later than those in the other end, leveling off the traffic peak and enabling some buses to carry full loads in both directions. School hours were also changed so they would not conflict with plant hours, and paydays were spread through the week. Parking lots were subdivided according to the residential districts of the workers so people without cars would know where to go to arrange transportation.

The Doehler Die Casting Co. plant is cooperating with the Montgomery County (Pa.) Committee to work out a county-wide solution of transportation problems.

2,764 trucks, trailers released in week ended May 9

WPB announced May 12 that during the week ended May 9, 2,764 trucks and trailers and 119 miscellaneous vehicles were released under the truck rationing program that began March 9. Since the start of the program, 94,709 trucks and trailers and 2,011 miscellaneous vehicles, such as station wagons, ambulances and hearses, have been released.

10,000 miles, 2 years' wartime service—goal for recapped tires

Recapped passenger car tires that will travel as much as 10,000 miles and give motorists 2 years' service under wartime driving restrictions are the aim of the Government's most recent tire conservation program.

The standards section of the Consumer Division, OPA, announced May 12 that it had released to camelback manufacturers suggestions outlining the average properties of the industry's product, so that each camelback maker can bring his own brand up to the industry level.

Motorist's only hope

Auto tires recapped with some of the better grades of reclaimed rubber now being produced may last through as much as 10,000 miles of city driving, the Consumer Division points out. If auto travel is cut 50 percent by wartime measures, this means tires will last 2 years or more.

Camelback is the motorist's only hope for prolonging the life of the tires he now has. Local tire rationing boards may permit drivers to have their tires recapped, if they can show definite need bearing on the war effort.

The WPB has specified two kinds of camelback. Grade C, for truck tires, can be made with restricted amounts of crude rubber. Grade F, for passenger car tires, must be made wholly of reclaimed rubber.

Regulations for replenishing camelback stocks modified

Retreaders may replenish camelback stocks on the basis of the amounts actually needed for retreading or recapping a tire larger than those now provided for by the replenishment table in the Revised Tire Rationing Regulations, OPA Administrator Henderson announced May 13.

Amendment No. 9 to the regulations, which became effective May 15, has been issued to accomplish this purpose.

Where possible, the amount of camelback for replenishment still must be calculated on the basis of the replenishment table. But when more than 55 pounds is necessary for tires 12.00–24 and larger, a retreader who wishes to replenish his stock for the amount used must attach to Part D of Form R 9 (the replenishment part of the certificate issued by the local board) a statement of the amount actually used in performing the service.

TO WIN THIS WAR ... MORE PEOPLE HAVE GOT TO ENJOY RIDING IN FEWER CARS

Anti-freeze production to go on quota basis

Production of anti-freeze will be placed upon a quota basis by Order L–51, issued May 14 by the Director of Industry Operations.

Quotas have not yet been set, but they are expected to approximate 50 percent of the amount of anti-freeze sold by each producer in 1941.

Anti-freeze manufactured for the Army, Navy, other governmental agencies, Lend-Lease, or for the governments of the British Empire, Belgium, China, Greece, the Netherlands, Norway, Po-

This cartoon was drawn especially for VICTORY *by Dr. Seuss. This notice constitutes full permission to reprint the drawing. Engravings may be made direct from this reproduction, or three-column mats will be furnished on application to Distribution Section, Division of Information, Office for Emergency Management, Washington, D. C. Refer to V–1.*

land, Russia and Yugoslavia may be made in addition to quotas.

The reason for the order is that anti-freeze compounds are made of ethyl, methyl and isopropyl alcohol and ethylene glycol, all critical war materials.

Dean denies gasoline rules leave loophole for Congressmen

Reports covering a supposed loophole in the gasoline rationing regulations favoring Congressmen are based on an inaccurate interpretation of the regulation, Joel Dean, chief of the fuel rationing branch of OPA, announced May 13.

"X" cards may be issued for a vehicle if the owner certifies that all or substantially all of the use of the vehicle is for the official business of the Federal, State, local, or foreign governments. No one is entitled to an "X" card because of his position as a Government employee.

OPA lists price schedules still effective; others are subject to general regulation

The following tabulation shows the status of all existing OPA price schedules and regulations as of May 9, 1942.

Particular attention should be paid to the class of seller affected, since sellers to whom these price schedules or regulations do not apply become subject to provisions of the general maximum price regulation.

Three classes of orders

In the past year the Office of Price Administration and its predecessor, the Office of Price Administration and Civilian Supply, have issued three types of price orders, each applying to specified commodities and to specified classes of sellers:

1. Price schedules (issued prior to February 10, 1942).

2. Maximum price regulations (issued under authority of the Emergency Price Control Act of 1942 after February 10, 1942).

3. Temporary maximum price regulations, effective for only 60 days and replaced in most instances by maximum price regulations.

In addition, OPA has made informal agreements with members of industry groups to stabilize prices at various levels.

Price schedules and maximum price regulations are permanent and remain in full force even after the general maximum price regulation becomes effective.

Sellers whose maximum prices have been controlled under price schedules or maximum price regulations must continue to observe the limitations imposed by those schedules or regulations.

Others subject to general regulation

Sellers who are not covered by these price schedules or maximum price regulations become subject to the general maximum price regulation.

The following table indicates in simplified reference form the status of price schedules and maximum price regulations which remain in effect, and shows the class of sellers generally covered and the approximate price level determined by the schedule:

No. 1—Second-hand machine tools; all sellers; percentage of March 1, 1941 list price of new tool.
No. 2—Aluminum scrap and secondary aluminum ingots; all sellers; prices listed in schedule.
No. 3—Zinc scrap and secondary slab zinc; all sellers; prices listed in schedule.
No. 4—Iron and steel scrap; dealers and brokers; prices listed in schedule.

No. 6—Iron and steel products; producers; April 16, 1941.
No. 7—Combed cotton yarns and the processing thereof; manufacturers and jobbers; March 1942.
No. 8—Pure nickel scrap, monel metal scrap, stainless steel scrap, nickel steel scrap and other scrap materials containing nickel, secondary monel ingot, secondary monel shot, and secondary copper-nickel shot; all sellers; prices listed in schedule.
No. 9—Hides, kips and calfskins; all sellers; prices listed in schedule.
No. 10—Pig iron; producers; prices listed in schedule.
No. 11—Fine cotton gray goods; see Note A; March 1942.
No. 12—Brass mill scrap; all sellers; prices listed in schedule.
No. 13—Douglas fir plywood; mill sales; prices listed in schedule.
No. 15—Copper; all sellers; prices listed in schedule.
No. 16—Raw cane sugars; all sellers; prices listed in schedule.
No. 17—Pig tin; all sellers; prices listed in schedule.
No. 18—Burlap; all sellers; prices listed in schedule.
No. 19—Southern pine lumber; mill sales; prices listed in schedule.
No. 20—Copper and copper alloy scrap; sellers to consumers; prices listed in schedule.
No. 21—Formaldehyde; all sellers; prices listed in schedule.
No. 23—Rayon grey goods; all sellers; prices listed in schedule.
No. 24—Washed cattle tail hair and winter hog hair; all sellers; prices listed in schedule.
No. 26—Douglas fir timber; mill sales; prices listed in schedule.
No. 28—Ethyl alcohol; manufacturer; prices listed in schedule.
No. 29—By-product foundry, by-product blast furnace coke; all sellers; prices listed in schedule.
No. 30—Wastepaper; all sellers; prices listed in schedule.
No. 31—Acetic acid; all sellers; prices listed in schedule.
No. 32—Paperboard sold east of the Rocky Mountains; producer; prices listed in schedule.
No. 33—Carded cotton yarns; manufacturers and jobbers; March 1942.
No. 34—Wood alcohol; all sellers; prices listed in schedule.
No. 35—Carded grey and colored-yarn cotton goods; see Note A; March 1942.
No. 36—Acetone; all sellers; prices listed in schedule.
No. 37—Normal butyl alcohol; all sellers; prices listed in schedule.
No. 38—Glycerine; all sellers' prices listed in schedule.
No. 39—Upholstery furniture fabrics; manufacturer; 5 percent above Sept. 10, 1941.
No. 40—Builders' hardware and insect screen cloth; all sellers except retail; October 1-15, 1941.
No. 41—Steel castings; producers; July 15, 1941.
No. 42—Paraffin wax; all sellers; prices listed in schedule.
No. 43—Used steel barrels or drums; all sellers; prices listed in schedule.
No. 44—Douglas fir doors; manufacturers; prices listed in schedule.
No. 45—Asphalt or tarred roofing products; manufacturers; prices listed in schedule.
No. 46—Relaying rail; all sellers; prices listed in schedule.
No. 47—Old rags; all sellers; prices listed in schedule.

No. 49—Resale of iron or steel products; jobbers or warehouse men; April 16, 1941.
No. 50—Green coffee; all sellers; prices listed in schedule.
No. 51—Cocoa beans and cocoa butter; all sellers; prices listed in schedule.
No. 52—Pepper (berries); all sellers except retail; prices listed in schedule.
No. 53—Fats and oils, all sellers; Oct. 1, 1941 or 111 percent of November 26, 1941; schedule lists specific prices for cottonseed oil.
No. 54—Douglas fir peeler logs; sales to lumber & plywood mills; prices listed in schedule.
No. 55—Second-hand bags; all sellers; Oct. 1-15, 1941.
No. 56—Reclaimed rubber; all sellers; Nov. 5, December 5, 1941.
No. 57—Wool floor coverings, manufacturers; 5 percent above Oct. 13, 1941.
No. 58—Wool and wool tops and yarns; all sellers; prices listed in schedule.
No. 59—Kapok; all sellers; prices listed in schedule.
No. 60—Direct-consumption sugars; all sellers except at retail; prices listed in schedule.
No. 61—Leather; all sellers except at retail; Nov. 6-Dec. 6, 1941.
No. 62—Cigarettes; manufacturers; Dec. 26, 1941.
No. 63—Retail prices for new rubber tires and tubes; retail sellers; prices listed in schedule.
No. 64—Domestic cooking and heating stoves; manufacturers; Nov. 1941.
No. 65—Resale of floor coverings; distributors; Oct. 1-13, 1941, Dec. 1-31, 1941.
No. 66—Retreaded and recapped rubber tires, the retreading and recapping of rubber tires, and basic tire carcasses; all sellers; prices listed in schedule.
No. 67—New machine tools; all sellers; October 1, 1941.
No. 68—Hide glue stock; all sellers; prices listed in schedule.
No. 69—Primary lead; all sellers; prices listed in schedule.
No. 70—Lead scrap materials, secondary lead (including calking lead), battery lead scrap, and primary and secondary antimonial lead; all sellers; prices listed in schedule.
No. 71—Primary and secondary cadmium; all sellers; prices listed in schedule.
No. 73—Fish meal; all sellers except at retail; prices listed in schedule.
No. 74—Animal product feedingstuffs; all sellers except at retail; January 17, 1942.
No. 75—Dead-burned grain magnesite; all sellers; prices listed in schedule.
No. 76—Hide glue; all sellers; prices listed in schedule.
No. 77—Beehive oven furnace coke produced in Pennsylvania; sellers to consumers; prices listed in schedule.
No. 78—Oxalic acid; all sellers; prices listed in schedule.
No. 79—Carbon tetrachloride; all sellers; prices listed in schedule.
No. 80—Lithopone; all sellers; prices listed in schedule.
No. 81—Primary slab zinc; all sellers; prices listed in schedule.
No. 82—Wire, cable and cable accessories; manufacturers; October 15, 1941.
No. 83—Radio receiver and phonograph; manufacturers; October 15, 1941.
No. 84—Radio receivers and phonograph parts; manufacturers; October 15, 1941.
No. 85—New passenger automobiles; all sellers; prices listed in schedule.
No. 86—Domestic washing machines and ironing machines; manufacturers; October 1-15, 1941.
No. 87—Scrap rubber; sellers to consumers; prices listed in schedule.
No. 88—Petroleum and petroleum products; all sellers except at retail; Oct. 1, 1941, in most cases.
No. 89—Bed linens; see Note A; March, 1942.
No. 90—Rayon waste; all sellers; prices listed in schedule.

No. 91—Tea; all sellers except at retail; prices listed in schedule.
No. 92—Soy bean and peanut oils; all sellers except retail and wholesale; October 1, 1941.
No. 93—Mercury; all sellers; prices listed in schedule.
No. 94—Western pine lumber; mill sales; prices listed in schedule.
No. 95—Nylon hose; all sellers except at retail; prices listed in schedule.
N°. 96—Domestic fuel oil storage tanks; all sellers; prices listed in schedule.
No. 97—Southern hardwood lumber; mill sales; prices listed in schedule.
No. 98—Titanium pigments; all sellers; [1] prices listed in schedule.
No. 99—Acetyl salicylic acid; all sellers; [1] prices listed in schedule.
No. 100—Cast iron soil pipe and fittings; manufacturer, jobber, wholesaler; prices listed in schedule.
No. 101—Citric acid; all sellers; prices listed in schedule.
No. 102—Household mechanical refrigerators; manufacturer; Dec. 2, 1941-Feb. 2, 1942.
No. 103—Salicylic acid; all sellers; [1] prices listed in schedule.
No. 104—Vitamin C; all sellers; [1] prices listed in schedule.
No. 105—Gears, pinions, sprockets and speed reducers; all sellers; [1] October 15, 1941.
No. 106—Domestic shorn wool; all sellers; prices listed in schedule.
No. 107—Used tires and tubes; all sellers; prices listed in schedule.
No. 108—Nitrate of soda, sulphate of ammonia and cyanamid; all sellers; [1] margins listed in schedule.
No. 109—Aircraft spruce; all sellers; prices listed in schedule.
No. 110—Resale of new household mechanical refrigerators; retailers and wholesalers; prices listed in schedule.
No. 111—New household vacuum cleaners; retailers and wholesalers; prices listed in schedule.
No. 112—Pennsylvania anthracite; producer and distributor; prices listed in schedule.
No. 113—Iron ore produced in Minnesota, Wisconsin, and Michigan; all sellers; 1941 shipping season.
No. 114—Woodpulp; all sellers; [1] prices listed in schedule.
No. 115—Silk waste; all sellers; prices listed in schedule.
No. 116—China and pottery; manufacturers; Oct. 1-5, 1941.
No. 117—Used egg cases and used component parts; all sellers except a poultrymen's cooperative association; prices listed in schedule.
No. 118—Cotton products; see Note A; July-August, 1941, plus 5¢ per pound of cotton content.
No. 119—Original equipment tires and tubes; all sellers; 1941 maximum.
No. 120—Bituminous coal; sales at the mines; October 1-15, 1941.
No. 121—Miscellaneous solid fuels delivered from producing facilities; producer; Dec. 15-31, 1941.
No. 122—Solid fuels delivered from facilities other than producing facilities; dealers; Dec. 15-31, 1941.
No. 123—Raw and processed wool waste materials; all sellers; prices listed in schedule.
No. 124—Rolled zinc products; producer and manufacturer; prices listed in schedule.
No. 125—Nonferrous foundry products; all sellers; October 1-15, 1941.
No. 126—Fluorspar; producers; January 2, 1942.
No. 127—Finished piece goods; converters and wholesalers; March 16-April 15, 1942.
No. 128—Processing piece goods; sales by processors; March 16-April 15, 1942.
No. 129—Waxed paper, envelopes, paper cups, paper containers and liquid tight containers, sanitary closures and milk bottle caps, drinking straws, certain sulphate and certain sulphite papers, certain tissue papers, rope and jute papers, technical papers, gummed papers, tags, pin tickets and mark-

Henderson lauds landlords supporting rent control

Landlords who have been quick to cooperate with the Federal Government's rent control program were commended May 14 by Price Administrator Henderson.

Mr. Henderson said many letters expressing 100 percent support of the program had come into OPA headquarters, along with similar expressions from real estate organizations throughout the country.

ing machine tickets, glazed and fancy papers, standard grocer's and variety bags, resale book matches, unprinted single weight crepe paper in folds, certain bag papers, certain wrapping papers; manufacturers; prices listed in schedule.
No. 130—Newsprint; all sellers; prices listed in schedule.
No. 131—Camelback for recapping and retreading tires; manufacturers; prices listed in schedule.
No. 132—Waterproof footwear; manufacturers; prices listed in schedule.
No. 133—Farm equipment (retail prices); retailers; manufacturers' price list effective during or prior to March 1942.
No. 134—Construction and road equipment (rental prices); all persons; rentals listed in schedule.
No. 135—Mixed fertilizer, super phosphate and potash; all sellers; [1] February 1942.
No. 136—Machines and parts; all sellers; October 1, 1941.
No. 137—Motor fuel sold at service stations; all sellers; March 1942, adjusted.
No. 138—Standard ferromanganese; all sellers; prices listed in schedule.
No. 139—Used household mechanical refrigerators; sellers to consumers; prices listed in schedule.
No. 140—Sanitary napkins; all sellers; prices listed in schedule.

The following temporary maximum price regulations have been replaced by maximum price regulations:

No. 1—Mixed fertilizers; Regulation No. 135.
No. 2—Used egg cases; Regulation No. 117.
No. 7—Silk waste; Regulation No. 115.
No. 10—Finished piece goods; Regulation No. 127.
No. 11—Motor fuel sold at service stations; Regulation No. 137.
No. 16—Newsprint; Regulation No. 130.

The following temporary regulations will be allowed to run their course and, after expiration, the commodities will automatically be brought under the General Maximum Price Regulations.

No. 3—Manufacturers and distributors; Novelty floor coverings; expires April 30; GMPR effective May 11.
No. 4—Manufacturers; Sisal pads; expires May 2; GMPR effective May 11.
No. 5—Manufacturers; Bedding, metal beds, mattresses, springs, studio couches; expires May 2; GMPR effective May 11.
No. 6—Wholesale; Canned fruits and vegetables; expires April 30; GMPR effective May 11.
No. 9—Retail; Used typewriters; expires May 11; GMPR effective May 18.

The following temporary price regulations have been specifically revoked, the revocation to be effective May 11. The commodities thereafter will be subject to the General Maximum Price Regulation.

. No. 12—Domestic washing machines and ironing machines—distributors and retailers.
No. 13—Resale of new domestic cooking and heating stoves and ranges.
No. 14—Resale of new radio receiving sets and phonographs—distributors and retailers.
No. 15—New typewriters.
No. 17—Plumbing fixtures.
No. 18—Domestic electrical appliances.
No. 19—Oil paints and varnish.

Temporary Maximum Price Regulation No. 8 on dressed hogs and wholesale pork cuts does not expire until May 21. It is anticipated that a maximum price regulation will supplant this temporary regulation.

Permanent maximum price regulations are established for the following commodities previously covered by informal price actions issued by OPA:

124—Rolled zinc products.
125—Nonferrous foundry products.
126—Fluorspar.
129—(Certain paper and paper products).
131—Standard newsprint.
132—Camelback.

The following commodities now covered by informal price actions will come under the General Maximum Price Regulation:

Building materials: High tension porcelain insulators, basic refactory brick.
Chemicals, drugs and paints: Dry colors (Western differential only). Copper sulphate, cotton linters, lead pigments, light oils, coal tar derivatives.
Copper and brass: Brass and bronze alloy ingots.
Fertilizers: Rotenone, calcium arsenate, sulphate of ammonia and nicotine sulphate.
Lumber: Wire-bound boxes, cork, doors, etc., of western pine, gypsum rock, redwood lumber, rotary cut veneer.
Rubber and rubber products: Friction scrap, rubber sundries.
Iron and steel products: Gray iron castings. Zinc, lead and tin: Antimony, zinc oxide, zinc dust, zinc alloys, bonded abrasive products, lead products and coated abrasives.
Consumers' durables: All products covered by informal actions.
Food and food products: Bread and salmon.
Fuels: Industrial lubricating oils and grease.
Paper and paper products: Writing papers, printing papers, boxes, converted paper products as follows: towels, napkins, patterns, facial tissue; tickets, coupons and checks; liquid tight containers and paper milk bottles; dishes, spoons and plates; lace papers; specialty paper bags and envelopes; paper shipping sacks. Agreements with wholesalers and retailers.

[1] Certain sales to the Government excepted.
[1] Quantity limitations.
[1] Sellers cannot charge higher prices than those listed in schedule. But Distributors may pay higher than these prices, the difference going to Defense Supplies Corp. in compensation for added transportation costs in shipments to abnormal sales areas.

NOTE A.—All sellers except legitimate non-manufacturing distributors.

INDUSTRIAL OPERATIONS...

New installations of air-conditioning, commercial refrigeration equipment banned except for war, vital civilian needs

The WPB May 15 banned new installations of air-conditioning and commercial refrigeration equipment except to meet war and essential civilian requirements.

Production curbed

New installations designed solely for personal comfort, such as in theaters, restaurants, hotels, etc., will not be permitted.

Limitation Order L-38 also places rigid restrictions on the production and sale of air-conditioning and commercial refrigeration equipment.

For the next 90 days, only the Army, Navy, and Maritime Commission will be entitled to contract for production of such items as beer dispensers, carbonated beverage dispensers, bottled beverage coolers, low temperature mechanical refrigerators designed to store frozen food or to "quick-freeze" food, individual room coolers, florist boxes and display cases, and fountainette-type soda fountains. After that time, production of those items must be stopped completely.

Order L-38 prohibits the installation, effective immediately, of any new equipment except on "preferred orders." These orders apply only to the Army, Navy and Maritime Commission, certain other Government agencies, Lend-Lease requirements, and persons possessing a preference rating of A-9 or higher issued directly to them and designating the type of equipment desired.

"Essential" uses

In considering applications for preference ratings under the order's terms, the branch will consider the following uses of equipment as "essential":

1. Processing, transportation, storage, preservation, and distribution of food and food products only in those expanding defense communities where adequate minimum facilities do not exist in the opinion of the War Production Board.
2. Production, processing, transportation, storage, preservation, and distribution of milk and dairy products. (This does not include equipment for the manufacture, sale, or distribution of ice cream, frozen confections, carbonated or malt beverages.)
3. Mining, manufacturing processes, communication equipment, and processing methods (including water and liquid cooling) where control of temperature or humidity can be proved necessary for production of the product or products.

4. Ice manufacture and storage only where, in the opinion of the War Production Board, adequate facilities do not now exist.
5. Miscellaneous applications in connection with testing and research laboratories; defense production drafting rooms which can demonstrate proof of actual need; operating rooms in regularly constituted hospital buildings; preservation of drugs, medicine and serums, mortuaries (body storage); production inspection test rooms.

Machine tool orders excluded from benefits unless adequate description is submitted

Purchasers of machine tools must include in their orders to manufacturers specifications or other description in sufficient detail to enable the producer to place the tools in his production schedule, WPB ruled May 15.

Some prospective purchasers of machine tools have advised tool builders of their intention to purchase machines of a given type, but the tool is frequently described in such vague terms that it cannot be placed in a production schedule according to the provision of E-1-b, until additional information is furnished. Advices of this kind, the interpretation ruled, should not be treated as purchase orders as defined by E-1-b.

... .

11 merchandise items exempt from L-63 inventory control

Eleven categories of merchandise have been specifically exempted from the restrictions imposed by Suppliers' Inventory Limitation Order L-63.

Interpretation No. 1 of this order, issued May 15, lists seeds, plants, livestock, fertilizer, clocks, watches, sporting goods, furniture, pottery, china, and glass ware as items which need not be included in calculation of the dollar volume of inventories permitted by L-63. Inventories of these items remain subject to the terms of Priorities Regulation No. 1, which provides that all inventories must be kept to a practicable working minimum.

Farm equipment makers can't dispose of surplus iron, steel, except for A-1-k, A-3 or higher

The WPB assumed control May 15 over the disposition of any surplus inventories of iron and steel held by manufacturers of farm machinery and equipment.

Under the terms of Supplementary Limitation Order L-26-b, manufacturers, except under certain conditions, cannot dispose of inventories of iron or steel in raw or partially fabricated condition which are in excess of requirements under Limitation Order L-26 establishing production quotas for most types of farm equipment.

Surplus inventories may be disposed of as follows: on orders for alloy steel bearing a preference rating of A-1-k or higher, on other orders assigned a rating of A-3 or higher, to the Defense Supplies Corporation or Metals Reserve Company or any other corporation organized under the Reconstruction Finance Corporation Act, to any iron or steel mill for reprocessing or resale within the limitation of various WPB orders, and upon specific authorization of the Director of Industry Operations after application has been filed on Form PD-479.

Farm equipment removed from M-148; L-26 to cover exports

Farm equipment has been removed from the list of "critical materials" subject to the terms of General Exports Order M-148, which gives preferential treatment to purchase orders for such materials when accompanied by a license for export to Latin America.

Amendment prepared

An amendment to the farm machinery limitation order, L-26, has been prepared by the farm machinery and equipment branch of WPB in cooperation with the Board of Economic Warfare and the Office of Lend-Lease Administration to cover exports of farm equipment. This amendment to L-26, which was to be issued shortly, makes it unnecessary to include farm equipment under the terms of M-148.

Changed designs, substitutes asked in fluorescent fixtures to cut steel consumption

Manufacturers of industrial fluorescent lighting fixtures have been requested by the building materials branch of the WPB to use open-end reflectors and in other ways to change their designs in order to reduce steel consumption.

Investigation has revealed at least five possibilities: pressed wood composition boards, cement-asbestos compositions, special bonded papers, plastics, and glass.

A number of sample fixtures using substitute materials have already been completed. It is expected that lighting results will be as efficient as those obtained when metal reflectors are used, but in general, the reflectors made from substitute materials will have a limited life, estimated at from 3 to 5 years.

Oil company punished; accused of violating conservation order

In the first action of its kind involving the petroleum industry, the War Production Board has issued a suspension order directed against a West Coast oil company.

Suspension Order S-45, announced May 11, charges that the Bel-Air Oil Co., Los Angeles, Calif., violated the terms of Conservation Order M-68 by using scarce material to drill a well which did not conform to the uniform well-spacing pattern, required by the conservation order, of not more than one well to each 40 acres.

The Bel-Air Oil Co. is enjoined from the production of any oil from the particular well in question for the next three months, unless the Director of Industry Operations determines that such production is "necessary and appropriate in the public interest and to promote the war effort."

In addition to this penalty, no preference ratings will be assigned to deliveries of materials to the Bel-Air Co., and no allocation of restricted materials will be made to it, during the life of the order.

★ ★ ★

SHOEMAKERS ASKED TO OMIT STEEL TRIM

The leather and shoe section, WPB, on April 23 asked shoe manufacturers not to use steel "nailheads," or brads, to decorate uppers and "platforms" of women's shoes. A "platform" is a middle sole between the outsole and the insole.

First "production concentration" confines stove manufacture to small factories

(Continued from page 1)

more than three times the average monthly amount used in the base period.

5. Effective May 15, Class C manufacturers of domestic cooking appliances are limited to a monthly iron and steel use of 70 percent of monthly average use during the base period.

6. Effective May 15, Class C manufacturers of domestic heating stoves are limited to a monthly iron and steel use of 50 percent of the monthly average use during the base period.

7. After July 31, the average weight of iron and steel used per unit by any manufacturer of domestic heating stoves must not exceed 70 percent of the average weight of iron and steel per unit produced during the base period.

Steel per unit limited for ranges

8. After July 31, the average weight of iron and steel used per unit by any manufacturer of permitted types of coal or wood ranges must not exceed 70 percent of the average weight of iron and steel per unit produced during the base period.

9. After July 31, no manufacturer of domestic cooking appliances is permitted to produce more than one model of permitted type gas range.

10. Permitted type gas ranges must be manufactured so as to comply with the performance and safety requirements set forth in the American Emergency Standard Approved Requirements for Domestic Gas Ranges Z21, ES 1942.

11. Use of any iron or steel in the production of cover tops or lids for the cooking surfaces of domestic cooking appliances or the production or assembly of any domestic cooking appliances equipped with such cover tops or lids is prohibited.

1,200,000 new stoves in existence

The WPB plumbing and heating branch, which is administering the L-23-c order, said that present civilian and war requirements for cooking and heating stoves are a small percentage of the normal productive capacity of the industry. In a normal year there are produced approximately 4,000,000 cooking stoves and 3,500,000 heating stoves, representing a total volume of $215,000,000.

It is estimated that there are at present approximately 1,200,000 new stoves in existence, and in the period to July

31, an additional 800,000 will be produced. The total of 2,000,000 stoves is expected to satisfy the essential requirements for at least a year. All manufacturers are permitted to continue without restriction the production of repair and replacement parts.

Of the production of permitted types by firms which will continue to manufacture cooking and heating stoves, approximately 75 percent will be available for civilian use. This is believed to allow a sufficient number of stoves for all essential civilian purposes.

Expected to release 25,000 workers

The requirement that all firms in tight labor markets discontinue production in order to relieve a severe labor supply situation, together with the cessation of stove production by the larger companies is expected to release about 25,000 workers for war industry. The industry as a whole normally employs 35,000 people.

The labor shortage areas are as follows:

Alabama—Huntsville.
California—Beverly Hills, Culver City, Huntington Park, Irvington, Los Angeles, Monrovia, North Hollywood, Oakland, Petaluma, San Francisco, San Rafael, Stockton.
Connecticut—Hartford, New Britain.
Indiana—Indianapolis, South Bend.
Kansas—Wichita.
Maine—Portland.
Maryland—Baltimore, Perryville.
Michigan—Milan.
New Hampshire—Salmon Falls.
New Jersey—Cranford, Newark, West Berlin.
New York—North Tonawanda.
Ohio—Akron, Cleveland, Massillon.
Oregon—Portland.
Pennsylvania—Erie, Lansdale, Middletown, Philadelphia, Pottstown, Royersford.
Washington—Everett, Seattle.

The plumbing and heating branch estimates that 92 companies out of a total of 245 affected by the order will be required to discontinue stove manufacture after July 31.

★ ★ ★

Baggs to head truck section, automotive branch

Thomas A. Baggs, of New York City, has been appointed chief of the truck section of the automotive branch, R. L. Vaniman, deputy chief of the branch, announced May 14.

For the past 16 months, Mr. Baggs has been an industrial specialist with the OPM and the WPB.

WPB diverting 300,000 tons of copper, brass from frozen stocks to arms

Three hundred thousand tons of copper and brass products, saved for military uses by limitation and conservation orders of the WPB, will soon be on their way to munitions factories for conversion into implements of war, the Division of Industry Operations announced May 14. Metal once intended for ash trays, door knobs, and roofing will go into rifle cartridges and artillery shells, and the engines and motors of fighting ships and airplanes.

It is estimated that the 300,000 tons of metal will yield 255,000 tons of copper and approximately 45,000 tons of zinc. This is enough copper for the production of three and one half billion rounds of armor-piercing .30 caliber rifle or machine gun ammunition, two million 75 mm. field howitzer shell casings, 33 destroyers, 28 cruisers, and 2,000 bombers.

Within the next few days some 20,000 copper fabricators were to receive notification from the inventory and requisitioning branch of WPB of the method by which the Government will buy their inactive stocks of primary and fabricated copper. Eighty thousand other owners of copper inventories will receive similar notices in the near future.

Scarcity of copper for military and essential civilian uses has been the source of serious difficulties for nearly a year. Since the attack on Pearl Harbor threw the Nation's armament program into high gear, the current available output of the metal is considerably less than the expanded munitions industry requires to operate at one hundred percent capacity. The Nation-wide salvage campaign announced May 14 is designed to round up all of the red metal frozen in the hands of owners by previous WPB orders.

Prices from 15 to 30 cents a pound

Prices at which the Government will buy copper inventories range from 15 cents a pound for certain types of drawn copper wire to 30 cents a pound for copper in certain other forms. Fabricated copper products will be purchased at prices up to two and one-half times their value as scrap.

Accompanying WPB's price schedule is a set of forms on which manufacturers will report the precise nature of the copper and copper-base alloys in their inventories and indicate their willingness to sell them to the Government.

When the completed reports and replies to the Government's offer to buy are received by WPB, they will be reviewed to determine the most efficient and economical disposition of the material for immediate war use. Arrangements for the physical transfer of stocks acquired and for payments to holders will be made by the Copper Recovery Corporation, a nonprofit organization formed to act as agent for the Metals Reserve Company, a subsidiary of RFC. The costs of the program will be paid by Metals Reserve out of a fund set up by RFC to cover a number of such commodity salvage programs.

WPB may use requisition

In cases of refusal to accept the established prices, the WPB probably will requisition such copper and copper-base alloys as it must obtain for the war effort.

It is believed that substantial quantities of partially and wholly assembled copper products may be used in their present form, and it is urged that manufacturers working on war orders notify the WPB, % Copper Recovery Corporation, 155 East 44th Street, New York, N. Y., of particular needs which they are experiencing difficulty in filling. In such cases, the WPB will endeavor to bring together potential buyers and sellers, without involving the Government in purchase of the material. Metal which must be reprocessed before it can be used for war purposes will be sold by the Government to brass millers, refiners, and ingot makers at the ceiling prices set by OPA.

Dental firm penalized on charge of priority violation

A suspension order denying priority assistance and allocations of restricted materials to the Ruby Dental Manufacturing Co., New York City, for a period of 2 months, was announced May 14 by WPB.

Suspension Order S-50 charges that when the offending company was authorized under the health supplies rating plan to assign a preference rating of A-10 to the delivery of 4,275 molded trays, it applied the rating issued for this limited quantity to orders for a total of 50,000 molded trays and a quantity of aluminum castings, although these latter items were specifically disapproved.

The rating was also illegally applied by this company to obtain deliveries of large quantities of other materials not specifically authorized by the WPB.

Suppliers of repair parts to copper, brass mills get A-1-c to replenish stocks

Suppliers of maintenance and repair parts to copper and brass mills were given an A-1-c rating May 14 by the Director of Industry Operations to enable them to replenish inventories when they have filled orders bearing an A-1-c or higher rating from the mills.

Their previous rating for this purpose, A-3, was found insufficient to keep them supplied.

The action was taken in an amendment to Order P-106, which grants a rating of A-1-a to mills for actual breakdowns and A-1-c to avert a threatened breakdown. No change is made in these ratings.

The expiration date of the order, which was indefinite, was set as June 30, 1942.

Acrylonitrile under allocation to guard Buna rubber output

To insure continued full production of Buna N Type oil-resistant synthetic rubber, Acrylonitrile (vinyl cyanide) May 14 was placed under complete allocation control by the Director of Industry Operations.

The order, M-153, prohibits the delivery or use of Acrylonitrile in any amount except upon specific authorization of the Director of Industry Operations.

The production of Buna N Type synthetic rubber is the sole use for Acrylonitrile, and it is manufactured by only three companies.

For the period between the present and June 1, 1942, applications for supplies of Acrylonitrile should be made with respect to requirements for that period. Thereafter, applications should be made for each monthly period, prior to the first of each month. Provision is made in the order for allotment of additional amounts during the month to cover emergency requirements.

Golf club makers may use up plastic caps and ferrules

WPB on May 12 issued Amendment No. 2 to the golf club order (L-93) permitting golf club manufacturers to use completely fabricated plastic ferrules and caps they now have on hand.

Alloy iron, steel production subject to monthly melting schedules after June 1

Production of alloy iron and steel will be subject after June 1 to monthly melting schedules to be issued by the Director of Industry Operations, the WPB announced May 11.

No orders below A-1-k

Amendment No. 3 to Supplementary Order M-21-a provides that no iron or steel may be melted or delivered to fill orders with ratings lower than A-1-k, except for certain National Emergency and other low alloy steels, which may be produced for orders down to A-3 ratings.

Purchasers, after June 1, must accompany each order with a statement giving the end use to which the materials ordered will be put, the Government contract number, the date on which delivery is needed and a statement that the delivery date is not earlier than necessary for the purchaser to meet his own delivery on production schedules.

Producers must file their schedules monthly with the WPB on Forms PD-391, 391-a and 440. Producers who melt less than 4,000 pounds of chromium and 500 pounds of nickel in a month need not file the schedules.

Meltings and deliveries must be made in accordance with schedules approved by the Director of Industry Operations. Meltings may not be made after June 1, except as approved, nor deliveries after July 15. These restrictions apply to iron or steel containing chromium, cobalt, molybdenum, nickel, tungsten or vanadium.

Ways to increase plywood production discussed

Methods of increasing production of plywood were discussed at a recent meeting of the softwood plywood industry advisory committee, it was announced May 11 by Arthur T. Upson, chief of the lumber and lumber products branch.

Manufacturers present were advised of the necessity for expanding production of essential types of plywood lumbers (Douglas-fir and Ponderosa Pine). Simplification as a means of increasing output of essential items was also considered.

. . . . . .

ISTLE USES CURBED

The use of istle, a fiber grown in Mexico, was restricted in an order (M-138) announced May 11 by the WPB. The order restricts the use of raw istle to brushes and twine and cordage. In addition, it may be used for padding on orders rated higher than A-2.

PHOSPHATE ROCK INVENTORY RESTRICTIONS LIFTED

Inventory restrictions on phosphate rock were removed May 11 by the Director of Industry Operations to permit consumers to take advantage of transportation facilities when and as they are available.

Order M-149, issued May 11, removes the minimum working inventory restrictions of Priorities Regulation No. 1 and any other inventory restrictions, insofar as they apply to phosphate rock.

Approximately 75 percent of phosphate rock is used in the production of fertilizers. The remainder is used in chemical warfare, in the manufacture of baking powder, and in soaps, water-softening compounds and boiler cleansers.

The order became effective immediately.

★ ★ ★

Batt names Garst to help get Alaskan mines into production

Appointment of Jonathan Garst to represent the WPB Materials Division in Alaska was announced May 11 by William L. Batt, Director of Materials.

Mr. Garst has been loaned to WPB by the Agricultural Marketing Administration for the tour of duty in Alaska. He is regional director at San Francisco for the AMA, covering 11 Western States.

Mr. Garst's duties, Mr. Batt explained, will be to work with the Bureau of Mines and the Geological Survey who are conducting an extensive survey of Alaska for deposits of critical minerals.

As new deposits are uncovered by the surveying agencies, Mr. Garst will assist in getting mines into production and their output on the way to shipping centers for transport to United States smelters.

★ ★ ★

Nelson urges coal stock piling now to avoid future haul clogs

Donald M. Nelson, WPB Chairman, May 11, called on all consumers of coal, especially industrial users and war plants, to stock pile coal at once to the limit of storage capacity.

Mr. Nelson made his appeal in an open letter in which he said that transportation difficulties will increase in future months, but that there is still more available carrying capacity on railroads and other transportation facilities which can be used now to transport coal.

The letter included a warning that serious transportation difficulties will ensue in the coming fall and winter months unless the stock piling of coal is started at once and carried on effectively.

30 percent more glass containers planned through simplified designs, weights

This country is going to have thinner and less fancy glass containers, but will probably have 30 percent more of them to help meet the shortage of tin cans and other metal containers.

A sweeping order of the WPB, effective May 11, moves toward these objectives, together with the saving of considerable amounts of soda-ash and other glass-making materials, by standardizing certain glass container sizes and weights.

At the same time, the WPB issued two accompanying schedules to the order (L-103), limiting the production of bottles for distilled spirits (whiskey, gin, brandy, and rum) and for malt beverages (beer, ale, porter, and stout) to specified sizes and weights.

Mass production sought

The Limitation Order has five general objectives:

1. To reduce unnecessary weights.
2. To require simpler designs using less glass per bottle.
3. To permit the industry adequate time for the manufacture of new molds in which glass bottles are made, so that mold-making shops will not be overburdened.
4. To establish a trend to "stock" containers which many consumers can use, and which can be made on a mass production basis.
5. To allow private designs to be used only on efficient long runs, and only designs which meet the same weight limits assigned stock items.

The order provides for the issuance of schedules of simplified practices by the Director of Industry Operations, prohibiting the manufacture of glass containers not conforming to the terms outlined. The schedules covering distilled spirits and malt beverages (Schedule A and Schedule B, respectively) are the first two such schedules to the order.

The order also freezes all glass container designs to existing molds except when certain conditions are met. One of these exceptions allows the manufacture of glass containers on machines normally used for other container materials. Other exceptions cover the use of a specifically authorized design never previously made in glass, the packing of a product not previously packed in glass, and allow minor changes to permit a lighter or more efficient glass container.

⌒ ⌒

Heat-treating furnace rating extended to June 30

Preference Rating Order P-74, which grants a rating of A-1-c to enable producers to obtain materials for the construction of heat-treating furnaces, was extended May 11 until midnight, June 30, by the Director of Industry Operations. The order was due to expire on May 15.

WPB centers activities in field, giving broad powers to 13 regional offices; Washington to plan program and policy

One of the most important steps yet taken in the decentralization of WPB activities throughout the Nation was announced May 12 by James S. Knowlson, Director of Industry Operations, with the issuance of orders and regulations officially setting up 13 regional offices and vesting broad authority in the regional directors.

Policy determination in Washington

The new step, which is in line with general policy to decentralize WPB operations as much as possible, involves 2 documents—(1) a general administrative order formalizing the 13 regional offices, and (2) a set of administrative instructions outlining the functions and duties of the regional directors.

The broad duties to be assumed by the regional directors are given in section 2 of the administrative instructions, which says:

In general, the regional offices shall provide the focal point in each region for all War Production Board business, and the regional director will be the representative of the Chairman of the War Production Board within the region.

It is intended that the decentralization of War Production Board activities shall be progressively developed to the end that, so far as practicable, the work of the War Production Board in Washington shall center in policy determination, program planning, the institution of major procedures and general coordination, while the day-to-day operations shall be conducted through the regional offices.

As this development progresses, and it becomes practicable to define the function of the regional directors in greater detail, supplementary instructions for this purpose will issue.

Preliminary organization of the 13 regions was announced previously, but the administrative instructions issued May 12 go much further in giving the regional directors specific and effective authority over WPB activities in the field.

The 13 regional offices established are:

Region No. 1 Boston; No. 2 New York; No. 3 Philadelphia; No. 4 Atlanta; No. 5 Cleveland; No. 6 Chicago; No. 7 Kansas City; No. 8 Dallas; No. 9 Denver; No. 10 San Francisco; No. 11 Detroit; No. 12 Minneapolis; and No. 13 Seattle.

So far, six regional directors have been appointed. They are: Orville H. Bullitt in Philadelphia, Ernest Kanzler in Detroit, Frank H. Neely in Atlanta, John C. Virden in Cleveland, Joseph L. Overlock in Chicago, and Walter H. Wheeler in Boston.

The effect of the May 12 action is to center policy and planning work in Washington, but to put operations, insofar as possible, in the field. It is expected that additional functions and duties will be vested in the field directors as soon as possible, in order that businessmen and industrialists in various parts of the country may deal as much as possible with the field offices.

The new step involves replacement of the former bureau of field operations established on February 12. Regional directors will report to the chairman of the War Production Board through the Director of Industry Operations. These reports will be made through a deputy.

WPB Bureau to consolidate priority, conservation actions in construction field

Organization of a Construction Bureau consolidating the construction functions of WPB was announced May 12.

William V. Kahler, on leave as chief engineer of the Chicago area, Illinois Bell Telephone Co., and since May 1941 head of the construction branch, Production Division, will be chief of the new Bureau. In this capacity he will be a member of the Plant Site Board.

A part of the Production Division, the Bureau will:

1. Service all construction essential to the war effort.
2. Recommend construction project priority ratings.
3. Apply the principles of conservation of essential materials to construction projects.
4. Administer Conservation Order L-41 which places all private construction under rigid control.

The consolidation makes it possible for all applications for construction, except those of the Army and Navy, to be handled by a single WPB agency. It will permit a central integration of requirements for construction material, information of which is basic to planning building programs. It also will make it possible to study from one point of view the essentiality of any building project.

In general, the Bureau will service essential construction projects so that scheduled completion dates are met. It will work closely with industry and with the Army, Navy, and other Government agencies to eliminate construction delays wherever possible.

The Bureau will recommend the issuance of limitation and conservation orders to conserve construction materials, equipment and labor required for the war program, and administer such orders. The policies of the Bureau of Industrial Conservation will be applied by the Construction Bureau to project applications to insure a minimum use of essential materials.

The Government Requirements Branch, now under the direction of Maury Maverick, will continue to have all contacts with Federal, State, and local government agencies in regard to applications concerning their construction projects.

The procedure for handling publicly and privately financed defense housing is not affected by this consolidation, but the Housing Branch in the Division of Industry Operations, under Sullivan Jones, which recommends the assignment of priority ratings to such projects, is transferred to the new Bureau.

A. I. Henderson named Materials Director; Batt busy with Requirements, other posts

Donald M. Nelson on May 12 appointed A. I. Henderson Director of Materials of the WPB. The announcement was made by William L. Batt, who has been in charge of materials since early in the defense program.

Mr. Henderson was deputy director of the Division, and has been closely associated with Mr. Batt in the materials field since the creation of the National Defense Advisory Commission in 1940.

In announcing Mr. Henderson's appointment, Mr. Batt explained that the pressure of his many other duties has been such that he has been forced to withdraw more and more from actual administration of the Materials Division and that Mr. Henderson has been performing most of the duties of the director for several months.

Mr. Batt is chairman of the WPB Requirements Committee; American member of the Combined Raw Materials Board established by joint action of the President and Prime Minister Churchill last January; Coordinator of the Russian Aid program, and chairman of the United States-Canada Coordinating Committee. He will continue in all of those capacities.

Schoenlaub named acting chief, production requirements branch

Appointment of Charles M. Schoenlaub as acting chief of the Production Requirements Branch was announced May 10 by C. H. Matthiessen, Jr., chief of the Bureau of Priorities.

Questions and Answers on Priorities

1. Q. What is an "escalator clause" in a contract?

A. An "escalator clause" in a contract is an advance guarantee from a buyer that he will meet, at a fixed ratio, any increase in price that occurs between the date of the contract and the date of the delivery.

2. Q. What is the "steel warehouse plan"?

A. The steel warehouse plan is a plan based on a percentage of previous consumption, whereby a steel warehouse is given a preference rating to obtain a quota of steel with which to supply small civilian users.

3. Q. Do orders for steel have to follow preference ratings?

A. Unless the steel is directly allocated, orders for steel must be produced in proper sequence of preference rating regardless of the product involved. No iron or steel may be shipped by a producer without a preference rating of A–10 or higher.

4. Q. What sequence of deliveries must be followed under the new export order M–148?

A. Exports of critical materials listed in Exhibit A of M–148 are given preference, within limitations, over other orders bearing high preference ratings, if the order for these materials is for export to Latin America and is accompanied by an export license bearing a specified delivery date. When such an order is served on a producer, he must meet the specified delivery date, regardless of his other delivery schedules.

5. Q. Will "L" and "M" orders apply to companies under the Production Requirements Plan?

A. All ratings assigned under the Production Requirements Plan will be subject to the controls imposed by "L", "M", and other priority orders and regulations.

PRIORITY ACTIONS

Preparation of the Priority Action list for VICTORY was delayed this week. The record for 14 days will be published next week.

PD-25X to be dropped

Because standard applications under the Production Requirements Plan have been simplified by new instructions issued earlier last week, use of the special PD–25X application blank for firms with an annual business of less than $100,000 a year will be discontinued after May 23, the Director of Industry Operations announced May 15.

The PD–25X application, known as the Modified Production Requirements Plan, was designed to reduce the paper work required from small manufacturers applying for priority assistance under PRP.

The new instructions for filling out the regular PD–25A application permit applicants to leave a considerable number of the columns blank, and thus reduce the amount of information required. A further simplification of Form PD–25A is being studied, and may be put into effect for subsequent quarters.

Applicants who have used Form PD–25X in the past should now apply on Form PD–25A, as simplified.

Metal household furniture order adjusted to use processed iron, steel parts of no other value

Amendment of the metal household furniture order (L–62) to permit the use of iron and steel contained in inventories of manufacturers prior to March 20, provided that such inventory consisted of parts so processed as to be worthless for any purpose other than metal household furniture, was announced May 15 by the Director of Industry Operations.

No additional materials may be acquired or processed, but the furniture quotas contained in the order may be exceeded to permit the full utilization of parts in inventories which are so fabricated or processed.

The following changes are also made by the amendment:

1. It permits production of Venetian blinds containing less than 15 ounces of metal per blind.

2. The definition of "manufacturer" is amended to include manufacturers of parts specifically intended for incorporation into metal household furniture.

3. Manufacturers are permitted to acquire from other manufacturers, and use, zinc or zinc die castings containing less than 2 percent of aluminum which had been made into Venetian blind parts prior to March 20.

4. The production cut-off date is changed from May 31 to June 30 in order to permit additional time for the assembly of inventory parts. No new quota is permitted for June, the inventory production being the only additional production which will be permitted.

Production requirements applications simplified for third quarter

A revised form of application for priority assistance under the Production Requirements Plan to be used for the third quarter of 1942 was announced May 13 by Director of Industry Operations Knowlson.

New instructions to applicants for preference ratings under the Production Requirements Plan will allow them to omit a considerable part of the information which has previously been required. Users of materials will also be able to supply the same reports on PRP applications which they are now preparing in answer to the general metals questionnaire, Form PD–275, and duplication of paper work will thus be avoided.

Ratings on books to weigh less

The new instructions will simplify the preparation of PRP applications by the many additional companies which must begin operating under the Production Requirements Plan in the quarter starting July 1.

Under the new program, assignment of ratings to PRP applicants will depend increasingly on the nature and use of the applicant's product, less on the pattern of preference ratings on the orders which he has on his books. For example, high ratings would be assigned to a manufacturer of parts which would ultimately be incorporated in military planes or tanks, without his having to prove that 75 percent of his orders were A–1–a, 15 percent A–1–b, etc.

For the present, the revised PD–25A application form for the Production Requirements Plan which was prepared for the April–June quarter will continue to be used, but the instructions specify that many of the columns may be left blank. These instructions are now available in War Production Board field offices, and applications on the simplified basis will be accepted, effective immediately.

PETROLEUM INDUSTRY AID

Preference Rating Order P–98, which provides priority assistance for the petroleum industry, has been extended to July 1, 1942. It was scheduled to expire at midnight May 15. A new procedure for granting preference ratings to the petroleum industry will be announced before July 1.

Ruffles and sweeping skirts removed from lingerie to save 15 percent of yardage

The use of unnecessary yardage in women's and children's lingerie is prohibited in a WPB order (L-116) which took effect at midnight May 10.

The order applies to nightgowns, slips, petticoats and pajamas. It does not apply to other types of underthings, in which as a rule little extra cloth is used.

The WPB apparel section estimates that the order will result in a saving of approximately 15 percent of the yardage used by the lingerie industry.

Tucks and full sleeves are out

Ruffles, all-over pleating or tucking, full sleeves, and excessive length or sweep of garments are prohibited.

The new order follows the basic principles of the order governing women's and children's outer garments (L-85).

All stocks, either on hand May 11 or in process of manufacture prior to May 11, are exempt from the lingerie order.

Under general restrictions, no nightgown, slip, petticoat or pajamas may have double material yokes; balloon, dolman or leg-of-mutton sleeves; all-over tucking, shirring or pleating; more than one pocket; a hem wider than an inch, or a ruffle bottom or a ruffle attached or applied below the waistline.

No more than one article of lingerie may be sold at a unit price. This provision is similar to the prohibition in L-85 against the sale of "ensembles" at a unit price.

In addition to the general restrictions, the order contains the following prohibitions:

NIGHTGOWNS

Nightgowns may not be made, sold or delivered with a separate or attached jacket, robe, sacque, negligee, fichu, shawl, cape, slip, chemise, teddy bear, mittens, cap, hood, hot-water bottle cover, or shoes at a unit price.

A nightgown may not be longer than 54 inches for a size 36, with corresponding lengths for different sizes. The sweep for a size 36 is limited to 72 inches.

A belt of self or contrasting material may not be more than half an inch wide.

SLIPS AND PETTICOATS

A slip or petticoat may not be made, sold or delivered with a separate or attached pantie, brassiere, teddy bear, chemise, gown, robe, negligee or housecoat at a unit price.

It may not have a sweep of more than 60 inches for a size 36, with corresponding measurements for other sizes. Length is not restricted because it is governed by the length of a skirt or dress, restricted in L-85.

A slip or petticoat may not have a shadow or double skirt panel of any kind.

PAJAMAS

Pajamas may not be made, sold or delivered with a separate or attached jacket, robe, sacque, negligee, hood, cap, mittens, belt or shoes at one unit price.

Maximum measurements for a size 36 permitted under the order are: length top, 25 inches; length trousers, including waistband, 41 inches; circumference of trouser leg, 24 inches.

★ ★ ★

COAT HANGERS FREED FROM DEATH SENTENCE

WPB on May 9 lifted a previously imposed death sentence on coat hangers. Amendment No. 2 to Order L-30 excludes from the list of restricted household articles coat hangers made of wood or paper board if their only scarce-material content is a steel wire hook.

The amendment also removes restrictions on the use of joining hardware, such as nuts, nails, bolts and screws, in the manufacture or assembly of kitchen and household articles, provided the weight of such joining hardware is not more than 5 percent of the weight of the completed article.

⌃ ⌃ ⌃

End to colored bed sheets asked, to save civilian dyes

To help stretch limited civilian supplies of dyestuffs as far as possible, manufacturers of bed sheets have been requested by the Bureau of Industrial Conservation to cease manufacturing and selling colored sheets, colored sheeting, and sheets with colored edges by July 1.

+ ★ +

War workers expected to gain by WPB cotton program

Millions of American war workers will benefit from the long-range plan which began with the recent War Production Board order converting a large part of the cotton textile industry to military production.

Sturdy work clothes for the great army of citizens on war production lines are the ultimate aim of WPB, the OPA Consumer Division said. Although the order actually switches another substantial number of cotton looms from civilian to war work, it was regarded as paving the way for other orders increasing the total production of cotton goods and converting more and more looms to essential civilian fabrics.

Ceiling set on shearlings; price high enough to encourage production, WPB believes

Specific maximum prices are established for "shearlings"—a type of sheepskin now used principally for the armed forces in the linings of flying suits and garments for cold climates—by Maximum Price Regulation No. 141, effective May 13.

The regulation applies both to domestic raw shearlings in their unprocessed stage and to tanned shearlings for the armed forces. Raw shearlings are defined in the order as the untanned skins of sheep or lambs slaughtered in the United States and sold with a wool growth of one inch or less.

This price action by the Office of Price Administration in the case of domestic raw shearlings conforms with the opinion of the War Production Board that the maximum prices established by the regulation are sufficiently high to encourage production of shearlings.

Ceilings established by the price regulation follow in dollars and cents per skin f. o. b. shipping point for domestic raw shearlings:

Grade No. 1 (½" to 1"), $2.15; Grade No. 2 (¼" to ½"), $1.90; Grade No. 3 (½" to ¼"), $1.00; Grade No. 4 (bare to ¼" and clipper cut skins less than ¼" and all shearlings with a wool count of less than 46's), $0.40.

A commission of 2½ cents per skin is permitted to be added to the maximum price when a broker is employed by the buyer. Such commission is payable only if (1) the domestic raw shearlings are purchased at a price not exceeding the applicable ceiling, (2) it is shown as a separate charge in an invoice or similar document delivered to the purchaser, and (3) the commission is not split or divided with the seller or with an agent or employee of the seller.

For tanned shearlings for the armed forces, a list of maximum prices is established by the regulation for various types and finishes for No. 1 skins graded according to established trade practice and to meet Quartermaster specifications. Ceilings for other types, finishes, and grades shall be in line with prices set forth.

★ ★ ⌃

Woolen firm given 30 days to complete civilian orders

The Susquehanna Woolen Co., New Cumberland, Pa., has been authorized by the WPB to use reprocessed or reclaimed wool for a period of 30 days to complete nonmilitary orders on its books at the time that Suspension Order S-39, issued against it for violation of priority regulations, prohibited this mill from putting into process any wool at all for civilian purposes.

New industry advisory committees

The Bureau of Industry Advisory Committees, WPB, has announced the formation of the following new industry advisory committees:

ANNULAR BALL BEARING

Government presiding officer—George C. Brainard, chief of the tools branch.

Members:

F. O. Burkholder, vice president, Ahlberg Bearing Co., Chicago, Ill.; G. W. Nordstrum, president, Aetna Ball Bearing Mfg. Co., Chicago, Ill.; C. D. Adams, vice president, Bearings Co. of America, Lancaster, Pa.; R. B. Nichols, general manager, Bantam Bearings Corporation, South Bend, Ind.; M. Stanley, president, Fafnir Bearing Co., New Britain, Conn.; F. G. Hughes, general manager, New Departure Division, General Motors Corporation, Bristol, Conn.; George Carleton, Jr., vice president, Nice Ball Bearing Co., Philadelphia, Pa.; R. J. Ritter, vice president, Norma-Hoffmann Bearings Corporation, Stamford, Conn.; George R. Bennett, Jr., president, Federal Bearings Co., Poughkeepsie, N. Y.; Frank Lennox, sales manager, Hoover Ball & Bearing Co., Ann Arbor, Mich.; J. P. Vogt, president, Western Corporation, Chicago, Ill.; A. C. Davis, president, Marlin-Rockwell Corporation, Jamestown, N. Y.; Chas. S. McGill, president, McGill Manufacturing Co., Valparaiso, Ind.; S. F. Wollmar, S. K. F. Industries, Inc., Philadelphia, Pa.; C. H. Talcott, sales manager, Torrington Co., Torrington, Conn.

CHURCH GOODS

Government presiding officer—Louis C. Upton, chief of the consumers durable goods branch.

Members:

Donald C. Fendler, president, C. M. Almy & Son, Inc., 562 Fifth Avenue, New York, N. Y.; James P. Hayes, president, H. M. H. Co., 48 Bagley Street, Pawtucket, R. I.; Bernard A. Benziger, president, Benziger Brothers, Inc., 12 West Third Street, New York, N. Y.; John R. Thomas, Thomas Communion Service Co., 322 N. W. Street, Lima, Ohio; Louis J. Meyer, president, Louis J. Meyer, Inc., 804 Walnut Street, Philadelphia, Pa.; Jack C. Deagan, secretary, J. C. Deagan, Inc., 1770 W. Berteau Avenue, Chicago, Ill.; Lawrence Daleiden, Lawrence Daleiden Col., 218 W. Madison St., Chicago, Ill.

CONTINUOUS FORM, AUTOGRAPHIC REGISTER & SALESBOOK

Government presiding officer—E. W. Palmer, assistant chief, printing & publishing branch.

Members:

W. R. Baker, United Autographic Register Co., Chicago, Ill.; R. J. Blauner, American Lithofold Corporation, St. Louis, Mo.; Carl W. Brenn, Autographic Register Co., Hoboken, N. J.; W. A. Daley, W. S. Gilkey Printing Co., Cleveland, Ohio; R. S. Daugherty, The Shelby Sales Book Co., Shelby, Ohio; Clark Dunlap, Stephen Greene Co., Philadelphia, Pa.; R. D. Hopkin, Gilman-Fanfold Corporation, Niagara Falls, N. Y.; Talbot T. Speer, Baltimore Sales Book Co., Baltimore, Md.; Clarence L. Johnston, Sunset McKee Sales Book Co., Oakland, Calif.; W. N. McLeod, American Sales Book Co., Niagara Falls, N. Y.; Fred Merrick, The Gilmanton Salesbook Co., Cleveland, Ohio; Lawrence Rauh, The Egry Register Co., Dayton, Ohio; R. L. Robinson, The Natl. Carbon Coated Paper Co., Sturgis, Mich.; William N. Ryan, American Register Co., So. Boston, Mass.; M. A. Spayd, The Standard Register Co., Dayton, Ohio.

ELECTRIC FUSE

Government presiding officer—John L. Haynes, chief, building materials branch.

H. T. Bussman, vice president, McGraw Electric Co., Bussman Manufacturing Co. Division, St. Louis, Mo.; C. Carroll, sales manager, The Chase-Shawmut Co., Newburyport, Mass.; O. H. Jung, treasurer and general manager, Trico Fuse Manufacturing Co., Milwaukee, Wis.; F. C. LaMar, president, Great Western Fuse Co., Pittsburgh, Pa.; L. R. Popp, vice president, Pierce Renewable Fuse Co., Inc., Buffalo, N. Y.; James Bennan, vice president, Jefferson Electric Co., Chicago, Ill.; T. D. Foster, manager, Wiring Device Sales, General Electric Co., Bridgeport, Conn.; T. W. Kirkman, president, Kirkman Engineering Corporation, New York, N. Y.; A. L. Eustice, president, Economy Fuse and Manufacturing Co., Chicago, Ill.; J. G. Riksman, president, Royal Electric Co., Pawtucket, R. I.; P. J. Shelley, president, Metropolitan Electric Manufacturing Co., Long Island City, N. Y.

FIBER CAN

Government presiding officer—Douglas Kirk, chief of the containers branch.

A. J. Baumgardt, Seften Fibre Can Co., St. Louis, Mo.; J. H. Crones, W. C. Ritchie & Co., Chicago, Ill.; W. H. Hopple, The Cin-Made Corporation, Cincinnati, Ohio; William C. Stelk, American Can, New York City; W. L. Stevens, Improved Mailing Case Co., New York City; L. C. Tienken, Cross Paper Products Corporation, New York City; W. F. Walker, The Cleveland Container Co., Cleveland, Ohio.

FISH NET

Government presiding officer—John E. Bromley, chief, nets and laces unit.

Walter Adams, Adams Net & Twine Co., St. Louis, Mo.; Walter Conklin, general manager, E. J. Ederer Co., Chicago, Ill.; Louis Lichtenstein, vice president, Fish Net & Twine Co., Jersey City, N. J.; Sam Barbour, vice president, Linen Thread Co., New York, N. Y.; P. T. Pauls, president, Pauls Fish Net Co., Chicago, Ill.; Robert Starr, A. M. Starr Net Co., East Hampton, Conn.

HOSPITAL STERILIZERS

Government presiding officer—Milton H. Luce, administrator of the health supplies branch.

L. L. Lunenschloss, vice president, Scanlon Morris Co., Madison, Wis.; Walter S. Yahn, secretary-treasurer, American Sterilizer Co., Erie, Pa.; W. C. Castle, president, Wilmot Castle Co., Rochester, N. Y.; Dr. L. L. Watters, president, Hospital Supply Co., New York, N. Y.; C. R. Pelton, president, Pelton & Crane Co., Detroit, Mich.; Harold B. Bunzi, general manager, Prometheus Electric Corporation, New York, N. Y.

MUSICAL INSTRUMENT

Government presiding officer—Jesse L. Maury.

William F. Ludwig, president, W F L Drum Co., 1728 North Damon Ave., Chicago, Ill.; Henry Wickham, vice president, Wickham Piano Plate Co., Box 348, Red Bank, N. J.; Charles Pfriemer, president and general manager, Charles Pfriemer, Inc., Wales Ave. and 142d Std., New York, N. Y.; Alfred L. Smith, executive vice president, C. G. Conn, Ltd., Elkhart, Ind.; Robert Pancotti, president, Excelsior Accordions, Inc., 333 Sixth Ave., New York, N. Y.; Jack Schwartz, president, Micro Musical Accessories Corporation, 10 West 19th St., New York, N. Y.; Maurice J. Strauss, president U. S. Harmonica Corporation, 321 West Putnam Ave., Greenwich, Conn.; L. P. Bull, vice president and general manager, Story and Clark, 64 East Jackson Blvd., Chicago, Ill.; Julius A. White, president and general manager, Kohler & Campbell, Inc., 614 West 51st St., New York, N. Y.; E. R. McDuff, president, Grinnell Bros., 1515 Woodward Ave., Detroit, Mich.; Paul H. Bilhuber, research engineer, Steinway and Sons, 109 West 57th St., New York, N. Y.; Victor J. Kraus, vice president, The Baldwin Co., 1801 Gilbert Ave., Cincinnati, Ohio; H. J. Cook, president and general manager, The Cornwall & Patterson Co., 938 Crescent Ave., Bridgeport, Conn.; Harry Buegeleisen, president, Buegeleisen & Jacobson, 5 Union Square, New York, N. Y.; George H. Stapely, president, Everett Piano Co., South Haven, Mich.; Neil Abrams, sales manager, Gibson, Inc., Kalamazoo, Mich.; A. G. Sabol, vice president, Reuter Organ Co., 613-18 New Hampshire St., Lawrence, Kans.; O. Albert Jacob, Jr., president and general manager, Mathushek Piano Manufacturing Co., 79 Alexander Ave., New York, N. Y.; Vincent Bach, president, Vincent Bach Corporation, 621 East 216th St., New York, N. Y.

REFRIGERATION CONDENSING

Government presiding officer—Sterling F. Smith, section chief, air conditioning and commercial refrigeration branch.

W. C. Allen, Lynch Manufacturing Corporation, Defiance, Ohio; W. W. Higham, Universal Cooler Co., Marion, Ohio; Frank H. Faust, General Electric Co., Bloomfield, N. J.; Byron E. James, York Ice Machinery Co., York, Pa.; Charles Knox, Baker Ice Machine Co., Omaha, Nebr.; B. J. Scholl, Brunner Manufacturing Co., Utica, N. Y.; H. C. Morrison, Curtis Refrigerating Machine Co., St. Louis, Mo.; Lars Hanson, Carrier Corporation, Syracuse, N. Y.

SNUFF

Government presiding officer.—John B. Smiley, chief, beverage and tobacco branch.

Charles W. Bumstead, George W. Helem, Co., 9 Rockefeller Plaza, New York, N. Y.; Thomas A. Clark, U. S. Tobacco Co., New York, N. Y.; M. E. Finch, American Snuff Co., Memphis, Tenn.; T. V. Hartnett, Brown & Williamson Tobacco Co., Louisville, Ky.; Benjamin Pierson, Byfield Snuff Co., Byfield, Mass.

WALL PAPER

Government presiding officer—E. W. Palmer, assistant chief, printing and publishing branch.

E. R. Barlett, Richard E. Thibaut, Inc., New York, N. Y.; George A. Birge, The Birge Co., Inc., Buffalo, N. Y.; W. R. Buttorff, Gilbert Wall Paper Co., York, Pa.; C. E. Charlstrom, The Joliet Wall Paper Mills, Joliet, Ill.; Harry Freund, Globe Mills, Inc., Chicago, Ill.; H. W. Hennings, The Chicago Wall Paper Mfg. Co., Steubenville, Ohio; W. S. Hevenor, Commercial Wall Paper Mills, Inc., Hammond, Ind.; E. M. Lennon, Lennon Wall Paper Co., Joliet, Ill.; Wm. C. Macey, Sears Roebuck Co., Division No. 653, Chicago, Ill.; Alexander Martinek, The Prager Co., Inc., Worcester, Mass.; George F. Mellen, Wall Paper Division, Imperial Paper & Color Corporation, Glens Falls, N. Y.; F. G. Snedden, Superior Wall Paper Co., Joliet, Ill.; Charles H. Stoner, Cook Paint & Varnish Co., Kansas City, Mo.; W. H. Yates, United Wall Paper Factories, Inc., Chicago, Ill.

WPB frees road building by U. S., States, counties from individual project approval

WPB moved May 12 to permit governmental road departments to begin construction of many public roads without individual authorization of each project under provisions of Conservation Order L-41, which places construction of all kinds under rigid control.

Authority No. L-41-600, issued by Industry Operations Director Knowlson, makes it possible for Federal, State, county and municipal agencies to continue their spring and summer programs for building essential public roads by simply filing monthly reports of material commitments.

Only local materials permitted

Neither Order L-41, nor the authority issued under it May 12, restricts road construction for which P-19-e preference rating orders are issued. Although projects that require preference rating orders for obtaining material come under the provisions of L-41, upon issuance of a P-19-e series order, they are automatically authorized to begin construction. For such projects the road departments should make application as in the past for a P-19-e Limited Highway Project Preference Rating Order.

Only materials which are ordinarily available locally such as sand, gravel, etc. may be used in building roads under the May 12 authority, since it is provided that no important types of steel, except from stocks already in the hands of road departments or contractors, may be incorporated in the projects.

The Director of Industry Operations may at any time order the road department to cease work upon any road project permitted under the May 12 authorization, if he determines that the labor, material and construction equipment needed to complete the project are more urgently needed in the war effort.

KELLER NAMED CONSULTANT ON STATE BARRIERS

ODT Director Eastman May 11 announced the appointment of Joseph E. Keller, Washington, D. C., attorney, as consultant on State barriers.

Mr. Keller will deal with problems affecting the interstate movement of petroleum and other liquids needed in the War Production Drive.

TANK CAR CONTROL ORDER POSTPONED TO JUNE 1

The effective date of an order establishing a Nation-wide system of tank car control has been postponed from May 15 to June 1, ODT Director Eastman announced May 9.

The postponement was authorized by Mr. Eastman to give shippers more time to file applications for permission to move cars affected by the order.

The order, which sets up a section of tank car service to administer the program, prohibits the movement of any loaded tank car without special or general permission of the ODT, except for cars covered by blanket exemptions.

Specifically exempted by the order (General Order ODT No. 7) are all cars consigned to or by any Government agency.

Exempted under a companion order (Exception Order ODT No. 7-1) are cars hauling petroleum or petroleum products into 17 Eastern States and the District of Columbia and into two ·Northwestern States, and cars used in hauling any commodity for a distance of more than 100 miles over the shortest available published rail tariff route.

★ ★ ★

31 percent saving achieved 2 days after l. c. l. regulation

ODT Director Eastman May 9 disclosed a savings of 31 percent in closed freight cars loaded with less-than-carload merchandise 2 days after ODT's General Order No. 1 became effective. The order, setting up a 6-ton weight minimum on merchandise loading and prohibiting use of closed cars in intraterminal movement, took effect May 1.

★ ★ ★

Limits on local deliveries put off until June

The effective date of a portion of a recent Office of Defense Transportation order placing certain restrictions on local delivery services has been postponed from May 15 to June 1, ODT Director Eastman announced May 12.

The effective date of section 501.32 was ordered postponed to give industries affected by the order more time in which to revise their delivery schedules and work out plans for conservation of tires and equipment under wartime standards deemed imperative by the ODT.

310,000 tons a week set as goal in solid-train coal movement to New England

Bituminous coal movement by railroad to New England at the rate of 310,000 tons a week for the remaining 34 weeks of 1942 will be necessary to maintain the off-peak tonnage spread and thus aid to forestall any possibility of a fuel shortage in the Northeastern States through overtaxed rail facilities.

ODT Director Eastman, May 9 pointed to this goal and to the rise in tonnage handled when he revealed that, for the week ending April 25, a total of 5,006 cars were hauled in the all-rail eastward movement, or more than 250,000 tons, as compared with 2,266 cars hauled for the week ending January 10, 1942.

Decline in water haul

Solid-train movement of this coal, wherever practicable, was brought about a short time ago through ODT efforts when it became apparent that an ever-decreasing coastwise water haul, through the Norfolk gateway, would make heavier demands on the all-rail facilities.

Mr. Eastman emphasized the necessity for continued cooperation on the part of coal consumers in constantly adding to their stock piles by protective storage through the off-peak months.

The coastwise collier water movement, which last year carried through the Norfolk gateway to New England points a total of 13,000,000 net tons has been curtailed this year due to submarine activity and other factors, Mr. Eastman pointed out. Rail rerouting via Baltimore, Philadelphia, New York, and other points to New England consumers has thus become necessary.

It is possible, Mr. Eastman said, that a substantial increase will have to be made in tonnage moved to tidewater by rail and then carried by barges.

★ ★ ★

WOOD NAMED FULL-TIME ASSISTANT ON LAKE CARRIERS

Joseph B. Eastman, Director of Defense Transportation, May 12 announced the appointment of A. T. Wood, of Cleveland, Ohio, former vice president of the Wilson Transit Co., as full time assistant on Great Lakes carriers. Mr. Wood who has been serving part time in this capacity since last January, will have offices in the Terminal Tower, Cleveland.

GIVING THEM A LIFT

Cartoon by Elderman for OEM. Publishers may obtain mats of these charts weekly in either two- or three-column size.   Requests to be put on the mailing list should be addressed to Distribution Section, Division of Information, Office for Emergency Management, 2743 Temporary R, Washington, D. C.

Tires, tubes, auto replacement parts exempted from L–63

Tires, tubes, and automotive replacement parts have been removed from the supplies covered by Limitation Order L–63, by Exemption No. 3 to the order, issued May 12 by the Director of Industry Operations. Because these particular supplies are adequately covered by other WPB and OPA orders, it is unnecessary to keep them under the general inventory control imposed by L–63.

Uses of cashew nut shell oil curbed

The use of cashew nut shell oil in the manufacture of brake linings, except for the Army and Navy, was prohibited May 14 by the Director of Industry Operations, in an amendment to Order M–66 which restricts the use of such oil.

The amendment does not restrict use of cashew nut shell oil for the manufacture of molding resins or resin solutions for electrical uses on ratings of A–2 or higher, or of brake linings on A–2 ratings, provided the oil comes from inventory.

Plans for Nation's first war transportation program explained to mayors by Eastman

Letters clarifying the procedure to be followed in setting up and operating the country's first war transportation program have been sent out by ODT Director Eastman, to the mayors of all cities, towns, and boroughs with a population of 10,000 or more.

Lack of understanding apparent

Mr. Eastman said he had received "many gratifying assurances of cooperation" from the chief executives of municipalities throughout the country but that the responses had indicated "quite clearly a lack of understanding insofar as the nature of the national organization is concerned."

The Highway Traffic Advisory Committee to the War Department, Mr. Eastman explained, has assumed responsibility for the national operation of the program. J. Trueman Thompson, Willard Building, Washington, D. C., has been named national director of the program, it was announced, and a staff and field force have been assembled to assist him.

Every governor, Mr. Eastman explained, is expected to appoint a committee to take charge of the program in each State, with the chairman acting as State administrator of the program. Mr. Thompson's staff will work through these State committees.

"It is highly desirable," Mr. Eastman said in his letter to the mayors, "that your local administrator keep in touch with the national program through the State administrator and his committee. These State organizations will be fully advised and equipped to render assistance to your local group, and from an organization standpoint it is advisable that your local administrators work through the State organization and not directly with the national office."

Purpose of program

The purpose of the Nation-wide war transportation program is:

(1) to prolong the life of all transportation facilities now in use and (2) to increase the efficiency of mass transportation facilities.

These objectives are to be accomplished through:

(1) systematic staggering of office, factory, and school hours; (2) group riding in private automobiles on a planned, neighborhood-by-neighborhood basis, and (3) improved regulation of local traffic.

LABOR . . .

Davis asks labor, industry to exercise "greatest of self-restraint on wage front"

William H. Davis, chairman of the National War Labor Board, last week asked labor and industry to exercise the "greatest of self-restraint on the wage front," to stabilize wages and thus help make the President's seven-point program to keep down the cost of living a success.

Addressing the Industrial Relations Council of Metropolitan Boston, Mr. Davis said: "The wage stabilization part of the cost-of-living program was left to collective bargaining. It was left not to regimentation but to democratic self discipline. That is as it should be.

"License is freedom without self discipline. Liberty is freedom with self discipline. We are not fighting this war for privileges and we cannot win this war without self restraint. Both labor and management will have to show the greatest of self restraint on the wage front. Each one of you will have to read the President's message and apply that message to your own people and to your own plants.

"I appeal to those of you in the audience who represent the workers of New England to forego wage demands which are not consonant with the President's program. I appeal to those of you who are employers to refrain from bidding up the price of labor in your own shops for the selfish purpose of luring manpower away from your competitors. With good will and a realization of our common purpose, we will succeed and we will win this war."

Scouts wage freezing

Mr. Davis scouted suggestions that wages be "frozen" for the duration. "If anybody talks about freezing wages—well there ain't no such animal," he said. "We talk glibly about the wage levels in America. Wages in America are about as level as the Himalaya Mountains. There is not any wage level to be frozen."

Man on subsistence has no standard

"The question really is," Mr. Davis said, "how far can we maintain the standards that have been attained. Simply translated, this means, how much of the increases which have occurred in the cost of living can we add to the wage rates and still get stability of prices.

"But you cannot maintain the level of real wages, and our problem is to find out how much of the purchasing power we can restore at the higher level and still look out for the fellow at the bottom. You have got to look out for the fellow at the bottom. A man who has a high wage, a machinist, for instance, has got a standard of living. He can talk about a standard of living. He can talk about his and I can talk about mine.

"But a man who is on a subsistence wage has no standard. All he has is a living. If prices go up, that man does not decrease his living standards, he increases his privations! And there is not any sense in trying to win the war with workers who are suffering privations. It is a matter of common efficiency, insofar as we can, to lift up the low levels."

Plaster base for war orders now included in quotas

Permission to produce metal plastering bases and accessories for direct war contracts in addition to established quotas has been removed from Limitation Order L–59, it was announced May 16 by the Director of Industry Operations.

Man-days lost from strikes in April were 8/100 of 1 percent of total man-days worked

Man-days lost from war production due to strikes in April of this year were 8/100 of one percent of total man-days worked during the month, William H. Davis, chairman of the National War Labor Board, announced last week.

A total of 173,500 man-days was lost in April compared with a total of 166,700 in March and 1,031,000 in April of last year. At the same time, employment on war materials increased from 59 million man-days during April last year, and 200 million man-days during March to a new high of 213 million man-days in April of this year.

The following table gives a detailed picture of the strike situation as it affected war production during April, compared with March of this year:

	April 1942	March 1942
Man-days lost	173,500	166,700
Man-days worked	213,000,000	200,000,000
Percentage—time lost to time worked—percent	8/100 of 1	8/000 of 1
Number of strikes	[1] 95	74
Number of men involved	43,000	39,250

[1] 1 of this number was a lock-out.

★ ★ ★

Job discrimination outlawed in ship firms carrying war cargo

Steamship lines engaged in the transportation of war materials are war industries and come under Executive Order 8802, which outlaws discrimination based on race, creed and national origin, according to an opinion rendered by John Lord O'Brian, general counsel of the WPB, to the President's Committee on Fair Employment Practice, and announced May 18 by Lawrence W. Cramer, executive secretary of the committee.

DRAWINGS FOR VICTORY

and

FOR YOUR PUBLICATION

VICTORY PRESENTS, on facing page, 4 drawings by well-known American artists who have volunteered their talents to help emphasize, in their own medium, the scarcity of rubber, the desirability of car pooling and other matters vital to winning the war. These drawings are the work of Otto Soglow, Alain, Chon Day, and Gregory d'Alessio. VICTORY will print four drawings by these and other artists each week. Permission to reprint is hereby granted. Mats in two-column size (larger than appears here) are available weekly. Requests to be put on the mailing list regularly, or for individual mats should be addressed to Distribution Section, Division of Information, Office for Emergency Management, 2743 Temporary R, Washington, D. C.

"Catch him! That's rubber!"

"Ed is pooling his car today, dear."

"We're getting places with this war production drive. There's a rudder I painted this morning."

". . . And you're the man, Jones, who said car pooling wouldn't work."

Over 75,000 Japanese evacuees from west to be offered voluntary Work Corps jobs

Beginning within a few days, more than 75,000 Japanese workers—both men and women—who have been evacuated by the Army from Pacific Coast military areas, will be given an opportunity to enlist in the War Relocation Work Corps for work useful to their new communities and to the national production effort.

All over 16 years may apply

This announcement was made May 15 by M. S. Eisenhower, Director of War Relocation Authority, the agency recently established by Executive order to supervise the employment of and to operate relocation centers for all Japanese evacuated to such centers from the West Coast.

Official enlistment forms for the work program are now being distributed by the Authority in assembly centers throughout the West Coast military area where evacuees are being housed pending transfer to other areas for the duration of the war. All employable evacuees over 16 years of age may apply for enlistment in the Corps for the duration of the war. This enlistment is voluntary.

Director Eisenhower pointed out that one of the first jobs for enlistees at relocation communities will be to start agricultural production.

"It is hoped that relocated communities will become self-sufficient in production of foodstuffs within the turn of a season, and will be producing additional crops for the Food for Freedom program shortly thereafter."

When an evacuee enlists in the Work Corps, he or she swears or affirms loyalty to the United States; agrees to serve for the duration of the war and 14 days thereafter; agrees to perform such tasks as may be assigned; and agrees to accept in payment such cash and other allowances as may be provided by the Authority.

As its part of the bargain, the Authority agrees to furnish the enlistee and his unemployable dependents with basic housing, food, health service, and educational facilities at a Relocation Center.

No wages as such

The income that enlistees may earn will depend, very largely, on the success the relocated communities have in organizing and managing their various agricultural and manufacturing enterprises. There will be no wages, as such, but enlistees will receive small cash advances, which will be charged against their enterprises.

WAR EFFORT INDICES

MANPOWER

National labor force, April	53,400,000
Unemployed, April	3,000,000
Nonagricultural workers, March	40,298,000
Percent increase since June 1940	**14
Farm employment, May 1, 1942	10,796,000
Percent increase since June 1940	**1

FINANCE *(In millions of dollars)*

Authorized program June 1940—	
April 30, 1942	‡156,362
Airplanes	36,557
Ordnance	32,122
Miscellaneous munitions	19,552
Industrial facilities	16,288
Naval ships	15,457
Posts, depots, etc.	13,176
Merchant ships	7,484
Stock pile, food exports	5,791
Pay, subsistence, travel for the armed forces	4,930
Housing	1,392
Miscellaneous	6,613
Total expenditures, June 1940— April 30, 1942	*26,534
Sales of War Bonds, cumulative May 1941–April 1942	5,389
April 1942	531

PRODUCTION *(In millions of dollars)*

June 1940 to latest reporting date

Gov. commitments for war plant expansion; 1,428 projects, Mar. 31	10,677
Private commitments for war plant expansion; 7,366 projects, Mar 31	2,333

EARNINGS, HOURS, AND COST OF LIVING

		Percent increase from June 1939
Manufacturing industries— February:		
Average weekly earnings	$35.76	38.7
Average hours worked per week	42.2	12.5
Average hourly earnings, 80.3¢		19.5
Cost of living, April (1935– Index 39=100)	115.1	14.5

* Prelim. Includes revisions in several months.
‡ Preliminary and excludes authorizations in Naval Supply Act for fiscal year 1943.
**Adjusted for seasonal variations.

OFFICE FOR EMERGENCY MANAGEMENT

WAYNE COY, *Liaison Officer*

CENTRAL ADMINISTRATIVE SERVICES: Dallas Dort, *Director.*

DEFENSE COMMUNICATIONS BOARD: James Lawrence Fly, *Chairman.*

INFORMATION DIVISION: Robert W. Horton, *Director.*

NATIONAL WAR LABOR BOARD: Wm. H. Davis, *Chairman.*

OFFICE OF SCIENTIFIC RESEARCH AND DEVELOPMENT: Dr. Vannevar Bush, *Director.*

OFFICE OF CIVILIAN DEFENSE: James M. Landis, *Director.*

OFFICE OF THE COORDINATOR OF INTER-AMERICAN AFFAIRS: Nelson Rockefeller, *Coordinator.*

OFFICE OF DEFENSE HEALTH AND WELFARE SERVICES: Paul V. McNutt, *Director.*

OFFICE OF DEFENSE TRANSPORTATION: Joseph B. Eastman, *Director.*

OFFICE OF FACTS AND FIGURES: Archibald MacLeish, *Director.*

OFFICE OF LEND-LEASE ADMINISTRATION: E. R. Stettinius, Jr., *Administrator.*

OFFICE OF PRICE ADMINISTRATION: Leon Henderson, *Administrator.*

CONSUMER DIVISION: Dexter M. Keezer, *Assistant Administrator,* in charge. Dan A. West, *Director.*

OFFICE OF ALIEN PROPERTY CUSTODIAN: Leo T. Crowley, *Custodian.*

WAR MANPOWER COMMISSION: Paul V. McNutt, *Chairman.*

WAR RELOCATION AUTHORITY: Milton Eisenhower, *Director.*

WAR SHIPPING ADMINISTRATION: Rear Admiral Emory S. Land, U. S. N. (Retired), *Administrator.*

WAR PRODUCTION BOARD:
Donald M. Nelson, *Chairman.*
Henry L. Stimson.
Frank W. Knox.
Jesse H. Jones.
William S. Knudsen.
Sidney Hillman.
Leon Henderson.
Henry A. Wallace.
Harry L. Hopkins.

WAR PRODUCTION BOARD DIVISIONS:
Donald M. Nelson, *Chairman.*
  Executive Secretary, G. Lyle Belsley.
PLANNING COMMITTEE: Robert R. Nathan, *Chairman.*
PURCHASES DIVISION: Houlder Hudgins, *Acting Director.*
PRODUCTION DIVISION: W. H. Harrison, *Director.*
MATERIALS DIVISION: A. I. Henderson, *Director.*
DIVISION OF INDUSTRY OPERATIONS: J. S. Knowlson, *Director.*
LABOR DIVISION: Sidney Hillman, *Director.*
LABOR PRODUCTION DIVISION: Wendell Lund, *Director.*
CIVILIAN SUPPLY DIVISION: Leon Henderson, *Director.*
OFFICE OF PROGRESS REPORTS: Stacy May, *Director.*
REQUIREMENTS COMMITTEE: Wm. L. Batt, *Chairman.*
STATISTICS DIVISION: Stacy May, *Director.*
INFORMATION DIVISION: Robert W. Horton, *Director.*
ADMINISTRATIVE DIVISION: James G. Robinson, *Administrative Officer.*
LEGAL DIVISION: John Lord O'Brian, *General Counsel.*

VICTORY

OFFICIAL WEEKLY BULLETIN OF THE AGENCIES IN THE OFFICE FOR EMERGENCY MANAGEMENT

WASHINGTON, D. C.　　　　　MAY 26, 1942　　　　　VOLUME 3, NUMBER 21

Axis has ⁹⁄₁₀ of rubber areas, situation is "grim," top officials reveal; war to take every pound for two years

Four leading war agency officials joined May 22 in a statement designed to clarify the facts about the severe rubber shortage.

Issued because many confusing and conflicting stories have been circulated about rubber, the statement points out that the shortage is extremely serious, reports to the contrary notwithstanding, and that no rubber of any kind can be spared for purposes not directly connected with the war effort.

Optimism about rubber "misleading"

Donald M. Nelson, Chairman of the War Production Board; Arthur B. Newhall, Rubber Coordinator; Joseph B. Eastman, Director of the Office of Defense Transportation; and Leon Henderson, Administrator of the Office of Price Administration and Director of the WPB Division of Civilian Supply, all joined in the statement, which follows in part:

There has been a great deal of confusion about the rubber situation, much of it caused by optimistic stories about the availability of synthetic rubber at an early date, or the large amount of scrap rubber which can be reprocessed.

But there is little real basis for such optimism. Our rubber shortage is one of the worst materials shortages we face. We can spare no rubber of any kind for nonessential uses. Statements to the contrary are misleading, and do the country a great disservice, for the facts

as we see them are grim, and we need 100 percent cooperation in conservation measures by the general public and by industry.

New arms program changed picture

Before Pearl Harbor, it appeared that this country had an adequate supply of rubber, in the light of the situation as it then existed. We had stock piled substantial tonnages in anticipation of interruption in shipments from the Far East, and steps had already been taken to regulate civilian consumption.

Events following Pearl Harbor, however, created a wholly new series of problems. The President announced a new military program on January 6. This very greatly increased our military requirements for rubber. Then, our major sources of rubber supply were lost. In addition, our Allies were forced to look to the United States as a source of military rubber.

Thus, despite precautionary steps taken in 1941, it has become necessary to develop a rationing program for rubber which eliminates all but the most necessary uses.

All of synthetic must go to war

War Production Board figures show three facts:

1. We cannot spare any rubber to make new tires for ordinary passenger cars; the tires we do have
(Continued on page 8)

Adjusting Shipping Costs *
of carrying Petroleum and Petroleum Products to East Coast in Gov't-requisitioned tankers

WAR SHIPPING ADMINISTRATION WILL ASSUME THE ADDITIONAL COSTS DUE TO SUBMARINE ACTIVITY

COST AS OF APRIL 1942

BASIC RATE PER BARREL ESTABLISHED JAN. 20, 1942

Each coin = 5 cents

* TANKERS IN EXCESS OF 3,000 GROSS TONS

DATA OPA

461959°—42

Review of the Week

America's position with regard to rubber, an indispensable material of war, is grim. That word was used by four leading war agency officials who last week painted this picture:

The Axis occupies 90 percent of the world's rubber-producing areas and straddles the sea lanes to 7 percent of the rest.

The new armament program after Pearl Harbor changed the comparatively secure position reached by stock piling.

The present plans for synthetic rubber encompass the production of only 300,000 tons in the year of 1943.

No rubber at all can be spared this year or next for any purpose not directly connected with the war effort.

The tires on automobiles are necessary to the war effort whether or not the tires will be yielded to the Government, and it is unpatriotic to use them up for pleasure.

Moreover, the public was informed in a press conference later in the week that Nation-wide gasoline rationing awaits only development of a system and the prime object will be conservation of rubber. The Office of Defense Transportation, for its part, forbade sightseeing bus service after June 1 and strictly limited charter bus service.

Priorities on skilled manpower

The War Manpower Commission last week announced it was preparing directives to the United States Employment Service and the Selective Service System designed to give war plants priority on skilled manpower, in order of urgency to be determined by the War Production Board. Manpower Chairman McNutt emphasized that insofar as the Nation voluntarily cooperates with this program, legal controls will be unnecessary. WPB announced meanwhile that the drive to establish management-labor committees to speed production of war materials is being extended to all shipyards and machine-tool factories.

No more building for amusements

Construction of stadia, moving picture palaces and all other buildings for the amusement of the public, except playgrounds, was ruled out for the duration. WPB began a survey of all types of building in progress to determine their essentiality.

The Division of Industry Operations restricted manufacture, delivery, and sale of heavy power and steam equipment to war purposes and repairs. Dairy, coffee grinding, and food slicing and grinding machinery was added to a list of restricted industrial machines.

Arsenic and the alloying element tantalum were placed under allocation. The use of tin and terneplate was restricted to a few specified items. Strict control was set over quartz crystals.

Steps to get more war chemicals

Coal coking and oil processing plants were given operating directions calculated to make available 200,000 more gallons a month of toluene, from which TNT is produced. Priority aid to the vital chemical plants was stepped up.

Shipments of iron ore on the Great Lakes continued to break records. WPB directed steel companies to curtail production of other items and increase output of structural shapes in June, to keep pace with the expanded flow of plates.

WPB named an agent to salvage the scarce and vital tin collected by the enforced return of tooth paste tubes and others to retailers. The Bureau of Industrial Conservation announced that a cooperative public had collected a surplus of waste paper but warned that prospective needs require a continuation of the campaign, and suggested that the same enthusiasm if applied to reclaiming rubber could go a long way to relieve the shortage of this direly needed material.

Reaching the cross-roads store

The Office of Price Administration intensified its effort to acquaint every crossroads storekeeper with the details of general price control. A permanent maximum price schedule was set up for pork, based on February 16-20 levels with certain additions to compensate for increased raw-material costs up to March 7. OPA continued to tighten and adjust its ceilings on textiles.

Large-scale Federal adjustments of the price structure were undertaken when OPA worked out a system with the Reconstruction Finance Corporation to absorb part of the increased cost of carrying coal to the Northeast, and with the War Shipping Administration to do the same for tanker transport of petroleum products to the East. OPA also put maximum prices on pickled sheepskins, to take the squeeze off tanners who were pinched between increased costs beneath and a ceiling above.

Tire quotas reduced

As a preliminary to rationing bicycles, OPA unfroze these increasingly important vehicles to the extent of permitting shipment to distributors. An inventory was started. The Division of Industry Operations, meanwhile, put the most rigid form of allocation over deliveries of completed trolley cars, commercial buses, and bodies for either. OPA, reflecting the more serious rubber situation, announced a counter-seasonal reduction in tire quotas for June.

★ ★ ★

TOLUENE FOR TNT

To provide manufacturers of TNT and other war materials with an additional 200,000 gallons of toluene per month, an amendment to General Preference Order M-34 was issued May 22 by the Director of Industry Operations.

Every person who cokes coal or processes oil to operate his plant is forbidden to sell, use, or deliver any oils containing toluene until the maximum amount of toluene has been extracted or unless the purchaser is equipped to extract the toluene himself. Oils from petroleum sources are not affected. "Oils," for the purposes of this order, means drip oil from the gas industry, and light oil produced in coal coking.

★ ★ ★

WAR EFFORT'S PROGRESS TOLD VISUALLY

The charts appearing every week on the front cover of VICTORY tell the story of America's battle as it is fought here at home. One-column mats are available for publication by newspapers and others who may desire them. Requests should be sent to Distribution Section, Division of Information, OEM, Washington, D. C.

VICTORY

OFFICIAL BULLETIN of the Office for Emergency Management. Published weekly by the Division of Information, Office for Emergency Management, and printed at the United States Government Printing Office, Washington, D. C.

Subscription rates by mail: 10¢ for 53 issues; 25¢ for 13 issues; single copies 5¢, payable in advance. Remit money order payable directly to the Superintendent of Documents, Government Printing Office, Washington, D. C.

On the Home Front

We have been a restless, nomad people since our pioneers braved the perils of ocean to carve out a new society in a new world. This quality civilized the frontiers, built a great nation. And it established a habit of movement. By train, by motorbus and most of all by private automobile we traveled 280 billion passenger-miles last year within our own borders. We have considered it one of our inalienable rights to move about from one place to another as our fancy or interests dictated.

Taking the rubber out of rubberneck

Today, too, we are on the move—but we move as one and in a single direction. We are a solid phalanx pressing toward destruction of the Axis. Our armed forces are being marshalled in the East and in the West and our warships mount guard from the Irish Channel to the Coral Sea. And it is because they must have the utmost freedom of movement that the Home Front is voluntarily giving up its freedom to move at will.

Already we have given up hope of new automobiles, new tires, and unlimited supplies of gasoline for the duration, and last week we moved closer to Nation-wide rationing of travel. Last week the Office of Defense Transportation prohibited operation of "rubberneck" bus tours and cut chartered bus service to essential tasks like transporting troops, war workers, and school children.

Transportation experts estimate this step will save 100,000 pounds of crude rubber, or enough to equip more than 60 medium tanks. The day may come when American expeditionary forces will roll toward the enemy on this very rubber.

Ball fans are in the war too

As the transportation crisis deepens, the great American game of baseball has been asked to do its bit to relieve traffic congestion. Joseph B. Eastman, director of the ODT, has suggested to Baseball Commissioner Judge Kenesaw Mountain Landis that ball clubs move game time either ahead or back so that departing crowds will not reach the streets at the height of the evening rush hour. Even the hour at which the umpire cries "Play Ball" is important when the game is total war.

ODT also has requested the United States Chamber of Commerce, American Bankers' Association, and Institute of Life Insurance to urge that member groups schedule vacations so that employees leave and return in midweek, taking some of the strain off week-end travel. It's not going too far, perhaps, to assume that if we start our vacations on Tuesday instead of Saturday, for example, we may speed ammunition to an embarkation point in time to catch an outgoing transport. Certainly we'll

REPRINTING PERMISSIBLE

Requests have been received for permission to reprint "On the Home Front" in whole or in part. This column, like all other material in VICTORY, may be reprinted without special permission. If excerpts are used, the editors ask only that they be taken in such a way that their original meaning is preserved.

be speeding soldiers and sailors toward well-earned furloughs.

It isn't a stationary war

Mr. Eastman summed up the transportation problem last week in a speech before the American Trucking Association in Chicago. ". . . transportation is today an indispensable factor all along the line," he said. "We can't fight or live without it, and if transportation ever bogs down the war effort will bog down with it." That's why you may be asked to stay put—except for the most necessary travel—for the remainder of the war. The prices of almost everything we wear, eat and use now have been put under a rigid roof at the retail level to beat the rising cost of living. And as you go about your shopping remember that price control requires your sympathetic cooperation as well as that of your storekeeper. Familiarize yourself with, 1, exceptions, 2, highest legal prices, 3, posting of prices, 4, service charges, and 5, enforcement. Don't deputize yourself as an amateur price policeman, be tolerant and patient.

Manpower: Swinging to war

The place of manpower in the mosaic of total war was sketched last week by Federal Security Administrator Paul V. McNutt, chairman of the War Manpower Commission. To the National Industrial Conference Board he said that "... American workers will switch to Uncle Sam freely and enthusiastically." WMC has outlined its eight-point program toward manpower mobilization, expects that the job of transferring 10,500,000 workers from civilian to war production by Jan. 1, 1943, will be done on a voluntary basis. But WMC is determined that the fate of the Nation and its defenders "shall not be jeopardized by anybody's private interest."

Womanpower: Keep your powder dry

Glamour as usual—but less variety . . . WPB says that lipstick, rouge and face powder will come in fewer shades, sizes and kinds to save glycerine, alcohol, waxes and colors.

What becomes of those tooth paste and shaving cream tubes you turn in to the druggist when you buy new supplies? WPB has named the Tin Salvage Institute, of Newark, N. J., as the sole organization authorized to collect and salvage them for their tin—tin to solder the bonds of democracy . . . If you order a beverage in a public place for drinking on the premises and it's unmixed it comes under the price ceiling. Mixed drinks do not . . . Brass screws or other copper products can no longer be used to attach handles to blades of saws . . . The installation of air conditioning or commercial refrigeration in public places solely to cool the fevered brow has been banned to save materials for war . . . All construction started since April 9 will be inspected in a Nation-wide survey to see that scarce materials have not been used in violation of the WPB conservation order.

Watch for wartime pajamas

Watch out for a WPB order saving cloth in men's pajamas as has already been done with women's nightgowns and lingerie . . . It probably will restrict pajamas to three styles, cut down the number of fabrics used, eliminate collars, lapels, cuffs and pockets, shorten trousers and coats . . . The first textile goods bearing OPA type label are beginning to appear on retail counters in the form of sheets and pillow-cases . . . It shows you what you're buying . . . Steamship lines which transport war materials are war industries and must hire employees without regard to race, creed or national origin, WPB asserts . . . Three midwestern companies have drawn WPB suspension orders as a result of transactions involving illegal dealings in aluminum . . . While Jones and Laughlin Steel Corporation, of Pittsburgh, a smaller steel concern and three iron and steel scrap brokers have been restrained by a Federal court order from buying and selling scrap at prices in excess of the legal ceilings . . . Iron ore shipments on the Great Lakes up to May 1 were almost 24 percent above the total for that date last year.

MANPOWER . . .

Plants get priority on registered workers in order of urgency set by WPB, under voluntary plan to be tried by McNutt

An eight-point program of immediate steps to promote "the fullest utilization of the manpower of this Nation," was announced May 21 by Paul V. McNutt, chairman of the War Manpower Commission.

After consultation with the Commission, Mr. McNutt said directives calling for immediate action will be issued to various agencies of the Federal Government having to do with manpower.

Urges use of Employment Service

Mr. McNutt added that the directives will be helpful in focusing and coordinating the various activities of Government agencies.

"However," Mr. McNutt emphasized, "these directives cannot be entirely successful unless the people of this Nation cooperate fully with their Government.

"I specifically urge that all employers recruit their new workers through the United States Employment Service, and that all persons desiring war work register with the United States Employment Service."

He said that he would also urge "that the publishers of this Nation refrain from accepting advertisements which are designed to steal workers from employers engaged in essential war production."

"In those cases," he added, "where labor unions have an agreement with an employer to furnish workers, I urge that they observe the same priorities in furnishing workers that the United States Employment Service is requested to observe.

"Unless there is orderly recruitment of workers, it will be impossible to bring about the fullest utilization of the manpower of this Nation.

Cooperation will make legislation unnecessary

"I should also like to emphasize that insofar as it is possible to insure the full and effective utilization of our manpower through voluntary cooperation with the Government, it will be unnecessary to put into effect legal controls which will inevitably limit the freedom of action of workers and employers alike." .

The following are the subjects of the directives that are now being drafted to become effective June 1:

1. To the United States Employment Service to prepare and maintain a list of those skilled occupations essential to war production in which a national shortage exists. Such occupations will be designated as critical war occupations.

2. To the War Production Board to classify war plants and war products in the order of their urgency in the war program.

3. To the United States Employment Service to make preferential referrals of workers to employers engaged in war production in the order of their priority before making referrals to other employers.

4. To the United States Employment Service to proceed immediately to analyze and classify the occupational questionnaires distributed by the Selective Service System, to interview those individuals with skills in critical war occupations, and to refer them to job openings in war production work.

5. To the Selective Service System to instruct all its local boards located in a community served by the United States Employment Service to secure the advice of the local public employment office before classifying or reclassifying an individual skilled in a critical war occupation.

6. To the United States Employment Service to increase its activities and facilities necessary to provide additional agricultural workers.

7. To the Farm Security Administration to increase the number of mobile labor camps in order to make available workers in agriculture to achieve the "Food For Victory" objective.

8. To the Office of Defense Transportation and the Farm Security Administration to assure adequate transportation facilities to move migrant agricultural workers.

★ ★ ★

From watches to planes

Possibility of converting part of the watch industry to the manufacture of aviation and navigation instruments was discussed last week.

Women could do 80 percent of jobs in 21 key war industries, survey shows

A survey of occupations in 21 key war industries indicates that 80 percent of the jobs could be done by women, Paul V. McNutt, chairman of the War Manpower Commission said May 22.

Employed in wide variety of jobs

The survey, he explained, covered 1,859 jobs in war industries, and also 937 nonwar jobs. It was made by the occupational analysis section of the U. S. Employment Service of the Social Security Board.

War industries covered by the survey were:

Manufacture of aircraft and parts, air transportation and service, aluminum products, munitions manufacture, automobile, motorcycle, truck and tank manufacture, and equipment, communications, electrical machinery, firearms, industrial chemicals, iron and steel and their products, machine tools, machine models and patterns, foundries, professional and scientific instruments, railroad equipment, shipbuilding and repairing, utilities and petroleum production and refining.

Among the occupations which women are performing satisfactorily are a wide variety called for in the manufacture and assembly of parts for motors, radios, recording instruments, and airplane gages, Mr. McNutt said. The development of new machinery, he added, now makes possible the employment of women even in the manufacture of heavy shells and other types of munitions.

Can do almost any kind of work

Even in the ship and boat building industry, it was found women could be satisfactorily used as boilermakers' helpers, draftsmen, machinists' helpers, blueprint machine operators, and flash welders. It was also found that women could be satisfactorily employed in foundry work as casting cleaners, finishers, and polishers, as machine core makers and facing mixers.

The results of the study have been published by the Employment Service in a form easily usable by employers and personnel managers. The booklet, "Occupations Suitable for Women," lists the jobs, and indicates for each one how long a period of training is required, whether or not women are already employed in such work, or can be, given training, and the industries in which the occupation occurs.

Pay stabilized for 1,700 Breeze workers; General Motors Sunday premium ended

The National War Labor Board last week issued its first wage decision since the President sent his message to Congress outlining a seven-point program to freeze the cost of living. During the week, a seven-agency interdepartmental committee headed by William H. Davis, chairman of the Board, studied the question of securing additional authority from President Roosevelt to stabilize the Nation's wage situation.

An agreement was also reached between the General Motors Corporation and the United Automobile Workers, CIO, and the United Electrical, Radio and Machine Workers, CIO, settling the entire question of overtime payments for 230,000 workers by putting an end to premium payments for Saturday, Sunday, and holiday work as such.

Four officials study plan

The committee, which met to consider ways of strengthening the wage stabilization plank of President Roosevelt's seven-point program to keep down the cost of living, appointed Paul V. McNutt, chairman of the War Manpower Commission, Frances Perkins, Secretary of Labor, Leon Henderson, OPA Administrator, and Mr. Davis to discuss the entire question with Philip Murray, president of the Congress of Industrial Organizations, and William Green, president of the American Federation of Labor, before taking the matter to the President.

The group faces the problem of dealing with the 95 percent of collective bargaining cases which never reach the War Labor Board but are settled by agreement of both parties.

In announcing the program, Mr. Davis told reporters: "The problem of freezing the cost of living is the problem of American labor. It will wreck all of us if we don't do it, but it will wreck labor first. If I were a labor leader, I would make sure that I had yielded enough to effect stabilization. I would rather overshoot the mark than undershoot it. If we can freeze the cost of living for 6 months, it will stay frozen and then labor can get back the amount by which it overshot the mark in giving up possible inflationary wage increase demands. Otherwise, if you undershoot the mark, rising prices may take all of labor's gains away."

Shipyard settlement a guide

No definite level was selected as a possible minimum standard under the plan. Mr. Davis pointed out, however, that well-paid workers could expect to get no more than shipyard workers received at the recent Chicago meeting of the Shipbuilding stabilization conference. There, shipyard workers agreed to take only half of the $235,000,000 in increases which rises in the cost of living entitled them to under the terms of a legally binding contract. That half was paid in defense bonds.

First wage decision

The Board's first wage decision since the President asked the Board to stabilize wages as part of his seven-point program concerned the dispute between the Breeze Corporation, Inc., Newark, N. J., and the International Union of United Automobile, Aircraft and Agricultural Implement Workers of America, Locals 823, 752, 8710, CIO.

By a unanimous vote, the Board issued a directive order which stabilized the rates of pay for the 1,700 employees of the company's four Newark plants in accordance with ten classifications of jobs which the company and the union had previously accepted.

The Board order raised the standard hiring rate for the company from 55 to 60 cents an hour but at the same time turned down a union request for a general wage increase. The order also set classification rates for the plants which in effect raised the pay of workers receiving substandard compensation.

The union originally sought a general increase of 15 cents per hour for employees receiving more than the standard rate of pay. The three-man mediation panel which heard the case recommended on April 24 that instead each employee receive a 4 cent an hour general increase in pay. On April 27, President Roosevelt sent his message to Congress outlining the Administration's seven-point program to keep down the cost of living. Shortly thereafter the Board asked the panel to revise its recommendations in the light of the wage stabilization plank of this seven-point program. The panel then withdrew the recommendation of a 4-cent-an-hour increase and also suggested that proposed standards in the two highest classifications be reduced from $1.10 an hour in Classification 9 to $1.07, and from $1.20 an hour in Classification 10 to $1.15. No one, however, had his wages cut as a result of the decision.

New standard rates

The following table contains for each of the 10 classifications: (1) The standard rate per hour ordered by the Board; (2) The lowest rate now paid by the company; and (3) The highest rate now paid by the company:

Classification:	(1)	(2)	(3)
I	$0.74	$0.60	$0.70
II	.76	.60	.85
III	.78	.60	.85
IV	.81	.60	.98
V	.83	.60	.90
VI	.86	.60	.98
VII	.94	.60	1.00
VIII	1.00	.71	1.00
IX	1.07	.75	1.13
X	1.15	1.00	1.35

Under the Board order the pay of employees receiving more than standard rates will not be reduced because of the establishment of the rates. They will continue to be paid their present rates with the understanding that they be reclassified or reassigned as soon as practicable so that their present rates may become appropriate for the job performed.

The original recommendations of the panel were signed by Robert K. Burns, panel chairman, representing the public, and Hugh Lyons, associate member, representing employees, with panel member W. H. Doran, representing employers, dissenting.

General Motors agreement

Mr. Davis, chairman of the National War Labor Board announced that interim agreements on the entire question of overtime had been reached between the General Motors Corporation and the United Automobile Workers and between the Corporation and the United Electrical, Radio and Machine Workers. Both unions are affiliated with the CIO.

The tentative agreements put an end to premium payments for Saturday, Sunday, and holiday work as such. They provide that straight time shall be paid for work up to 40 hours a week; time and a half for work over 8 hours in any one day or for work over 40 hours in any one week, and also for the sixth day of the work week. Double time will be paid for the seventh consecutive day worked. These overtime payments for the sixth and seventh days will be diminished by all time lost for personal reasons.

The new agreements provide for the establishment of overlapping shifts designed to guarantee maximum utilization of machinery and the achievement of continuous war production. Employees on such three-shift operations will receive a full 8 hours' pay, a 20-minute lunch period being absorbed in the overlap.

The agreements were reached with the assistance of a three-man mediation panel of the Board, which is now conducting negotiations between the two unions and the corporation for new collective bargaining agreements to replace existing agreements which expired April 28, 1942. The panel consists of Fowler Harper for the public, Wilbur Doran for employers, and Patrick Fagan for labor.

The overtime agreement between the U. A. W. and the corporation will go into effect Monday, May 25, at 12:01 a. m. The Board had extended, by directive order, the existing agreement with respect to overtime to that date. The effective date of the overtime agreement between the corporation and the U. E. R. M. W. A. has not been determined as yet. Meanwhile the overtime provisions of the 1941 U. E. R. M. W. A. agreement will continue in effect. The corporation and the unions have agreed that all other provisions of both the U. A. W. and the U. E. R. M. W. A. agreements with the corporation will remain in effect until such time as negotiations for new agreements are completed by the parties and ratified by the membership of each union. The overtime agreements will be incorporated in the completed contracts. It was further agreed by the parties that any wage adjustment or other economic concessions would be retroactive to April 28, 1942, the date on which the old collective bargaining agreements expired.

A total of 200,000 employees are affected by the U. A. W. agreement. A total of 30,000 are affected by the U. E. R. M. W. A. agreement.

Lawn mower makers can produce at full 1941 rate until June 30

Lawn mower manufacturers, restricted in Order L-67 to 50 percent of their rate of production in 1941, May 22 were permitted by the WPB to produce until June 30, 1942, at the full rate of their 1941 output, provided that in the extra production they may use only fabricated iron or steel in their possession prior to March 31.

TRANSPORTATION . . .

Bus sightseeing banned, charter limited to save 100,000 pounds of rubber a year

The Office of Defense Transportation on May 20 issued an order banning all sightseeing bus services and limiting chartered bus services to such essential operations as transportation of members of the armed forces, war workers, and school children.

It was estimated that the order, which becomes effective June 1, will result in a saving of more than 100,000 pounds of crude rubber a year.

Buses are defined by the order (General Order ODT No. 10) as all rubbertired vehicles having a seating capacity of 10 or more.

June 1 is deadline

On and after June 1, no such vehicle will be allowed to carry pasengers for the primary purpose of sightseeing, and no such vehicle may be chartered by any individual or group except those specifically exempted by the order.

Special exemptions apply to:

1. Members of the armed forces.
2. Persons participating in organized recreational activities at military establishments, provided their transportion is requested by the appropriate commanding officer.
3. Selectees traveling to or from examining or induction stations, provided their transportation is requested by Selective Service officials.
4. Students, teachers, and school employees traveling to and from school.
5. Employees traveling to and from work.
6. Boys and girls under 18 years of age traveling to and from summer camps, provided such transportation is requested by a regional office of the Office of Defense Health and Welfare Services, Division of Recreation.
7. Persons or groups traveling to and from places of religious worship.
8. Civilians traveling to and from their homes in the event of evacuation on orders of governmental or military authorities.

Local authorities' aid asked

Mr. Eastman called on local and State police authorities and the general public to aid in enforcing the order.

Purposes of the order, prepared by the local transport division of ODT, are "to assure maximum utilization of the facilities, services, and equipment of carriers by motor- vehicle for the preferential transportation of troops and material of war and to prevent shortages in motor vehicle equipment necessary for such transportation, . . . to conserve and providently utilize vital equipment, material and supplies, including rubber, and to provide for the prompt and continu-

ous movement of necessary traffic, the attainment of which purposes is essential to the successful prosecution of the war."

Advisory committees on port, shipping problems named

Appointment of two coastwise and intercoastal carriers' advisory committees was announced May 18 by ODT Director Eastman, one in Baltimore and the other in Philadelphia.

The committees will work with Ernst R. Holzborn, director of ODT's division of coastwise and intercoastal transport on port and shipping problems.

Members of the Baltimore committee are:

T. J. Hooper, of the Eastern Transportation Co., *chairman;* George E. Rogers, Harbor Towing Corporation; H. C. Jefferson, Curtis Bay Towing Co.; John F. Bittner, Chesapeake Lighterage Co.

Members of the Philadelphia committee are:

S. C. Loveland, of the S. C. Loveland Co., Philadelphia, *chairman;* Thomas J. Donnelly, Schuylkill Transportation Co., *vice-chairman;* Thornton D. Hooper, Interstate Oil Transport Co.; William Meyle, Independent Pier Co.; D. T. Sheridan, Sheridan Transportation Co., all of Philadelphia; and L. C. Campbell, Wilson Line, Inc., Wilmington, Del.

Ball games may start earlier to ease traffic rush

That famous American battle cry, "Play Ball," may be heard at a different time of day before the current season is ended.

ODT Director Eastman announced that he had written Judge Kenesaw M. Landis, Commissioner of Baseball, asking that the various clubs under his jurisdiction consider changing the starting time of their games as an aid to the war transport conservation program.

Most major league baseball games now start at 3:15 and let out between 5 and 6, at the height of the evening traffic rush.

Blanket curb modified on use of closed freight cars for intraterminal movement

Blanket restrictions on the use of closed freight cars in any kind of intraterminal freight movement, recently imposed by an amendment to General Order No. 1, have been modified by the ODT to apply only to less-than-carload merchandise where such cargo can be conveniently handled by motor vehicle, it was announced May 19 by ODT Director Joseph B. Eastman.

The general order, which became effective May 1, is designed to regulate merchandise traffic loadings through minimum weight limits, in order to release equipment for the movement of urgent war materials.

Exceptions

The new amendment (No. 2) specifies that, with certain exceptions, no carrier may load or forward between points in the same municipality, or between contiguous cities, or within adjacent zones, "any railway closed freight car containing merchandise."

The exceptions provide that closed freight cars may be used: (a) Where necessary to relieve freight house facilities because of inability to obtain transportation by motor vehicle; (b) where motor vehicles are not available; (c) where carrier, shipper or consignees' facilities make motor transport impracticable, and then only if such car contains the net tonnage demanded by the general order; (d) where authorized by special or general permit of ODT.

Organizations asked to urge midweek vacation travel

The ODT has requested the United States Chamber of Commerce, American Bankers' Association, and the Institute of Life Insurance to ask member organizations to aid in relieving week-end travel demands on the railroads and bus lines by scheduling midweek departure and return of employees who plan vacation trips.

In letters addressed to these organizations, ODT called attention to Director Joseph B. Eastman's recent appeal to all Government agencies.

Tank car commodity movements exempt from permits if over 100 miles by shortest route

The ODT made it clear that, until further notice, a special or general permit will not be needed to move any commodity by tank car to a destination more than 100 miles away as measured by the shortest available published rail tariff route.

The shortest available published rail tariff route is to be used, the ODT explained, merely as a yardstick for determining whether or not a special or general permit is required.

This point was clarified in an amendment (No. 1) to Exception Order ODT No. 7-1.

The general order, together with the exception order and the amendment, was to go into effect June 1.

Also exempt from the permit requirements established in General Order No. 7 are shipments of petroleum and petroleum products into 17 Eastern States and the District of Columbia from any other State and into the States of Washington and Oregon from any outside point. Shipments of less than 100 miles within these areas are not exempt.

★ ★ ★

Emergency tire, tube reserves for long-haul operators

An extension of time within which long-haul truck and bus operators may apply for emergency reserves of tires and tubes under a plan put into effect April 22 by the OPA was announced May 19 by Price Administrator Henderson.

Applications to local rationing boards for the special certificates needed to set up the reserves will be accepted through June 15.

⌐ ⌐ ⌐

Railway authorized to use bus, truck service in place of trains

ODT Director Eastman, May 16, authorized the Northern Pacific Railway to substitute bus and truck service for mail-express-passenger trains No. 235 and No. 236 between Logan and Butte, Mont.

The authorization was contained in ODT Supplementary Order No. 2-1, the first to be issued under the provisions of General Order No. 2 which became effective April 1, and which prevents railroads from substituting bus service for train service without ODT permission.

100-CITY TRAVEL SURVEY IS UNDER WAY

An exhaustive survey of intercity bus and railroad passenger travel originating in one hundred cities was inaugurated May 22 by the ODT.

The survey was to extend over a week, and a complete count of all intercity tickets sold was to be kept by all carriers at the hundred points named. The cities were selected on the basis of geographical importance and traffic density.

ODT Director Eastman also announced the launching of a passenger-interview program through the cooperation of field workers of the Work Projects Administration who hope to contact more than 20,000 intercity travelers during the week.

⌐ ⌐ ⌐

ODT to make Nation-wide check of carload freight on May 27

A Nation-wide check on all carload freight billed and forwarded from each station on the Nation's railroads on a given date was announced May 22 by the ODT.

ODT Director Eastman asked the railroads to furnish his office with complete copies of waybills on all carload freight originating on their lines on May 27. ·

★ ★ ★

3,304 trucks, truck trailers, 227 other vehicles released

During the week ended May 16, the WPB released 3,304 trucks and truck trailers and 227 miscellaneous vehicles under its truck-rationing program, the automotive branch announced May 18.

Since the program began March 9, a total of 28,100 trucks and truck trailers and 2,238 miscellaneous vehicles, including station wagons, hearses, ambulances, etc., have been released.

⌐ ⌐

Railway transport appointments

Two appointments to the division of railway transport were announced May 20 by ODT Director Eastman.

Charles B. Colpitts, of New York City, has been named associate director of the Division, in charge of rail-truck coordination for the eastern and southern regions. Holly Stover, of Washington, D. C., has been appointed special assistant to V. V. Boatner, director of the division.

Bus service between Washington, New York placed on war footing

Bus service between Washington, D. C., and New York City was placed od a war footing May 22 by the ODT.

Bus lines submit voluntary plan

Effective June 3, the four bus lines operating between the two cities are directed by a special order to pool services, stagger schedules, permit the interchange of tickets and eliminate duplicating operations on certain routes.

The order (Special Order ODT B-1) is based on a voluntary plan submitted by the bus lines in accordance with a request by ODT Director Eastman that they conserve rubber and equipment by elimination of unnecessary mileage.

Great Lakes iron ore shipments reach new all-time high

Iron ore shipments this year on the Great Lakes up to May 1 reached a new all-time high of 8,581,740 gross tons, the WPB announced May 18. This tonnage represents an increase of 1,626,947 tons, or 23.9 percent, over the same period in 1941.

Tire lease contract plan opened to new bus firms

As a step in rubber conservation, Price Administrator Henderson, May 22, announced an amendment to the tire rationing regulations which will permit bus transportation companies to enter into new tire and tube leasing contracts with tire manufacturers or wholesalers.

The necessary changes to open the way to new contracts are contained in Amendment No. 10 to the Revised Tire Rationing Regulations. Effective date of the amendment was May 23.

★ ★ ★

Trolley car, bus deliveries subject to rigid allocation

Deliveries of completed trolley cars and commercial motorbuses, and of bodies designed to be mounted upon chassis for either, are placed under the most rigid form of allocation control by the provisions of an order (L-101) issued May 21 by the Director of Industry Operations.

Axis has ⁹⁄₁₀ of rubber areas

(Continued from page 1)

must be strictly rationed to essential uses.

2. All the synthetic rubber we get must go to the war effort.

3. The most optimistic estimates for this year and next indicate no rubber for anything but the most essential uses.

Actually, the rubber shortage is far worse than most people seem to realize; the enemy controls 90 percent of the world's rubber-producing areas, and every ounce of our stock pile is needed desperately for the armed forces.

Biggest stock pile is on autos

Worst of all, the optimistic stories may keep us from recognizing what we are up against until too late. Our biggest stock pile of rubber is on our cars; these tires must be preserved. Autos shelved for the duration for lack of tires put more burden on already overcrowded buses and trolleys.

Every citizen can and must adopt a five-point conservation program:

1. Stop driving your car except when necessary; make it last.

2. Drive under 40 miles an hour.

3. Shift tires from wheel to wheel and inflate them properly.

4. If you drive to work, drive your friends and neighbors; car-pooling is essential.

5. Remember that rubber is precious; save it; every car is now a vital part of the Nation's transportation system.

Needless driving today is unpatriotic. Deliberate waste of rubber helps the enemy. We call on Americans to ration themselves strictly.

BACKGROUND

This is the situation which faces us: the amount of rubber which can be made available for civilian, industrial, and essential transportation purposes this year must be held down to not more than 150,000 tons, which is 79 percent less than the 700,000 tons consumed for all civilian purposes in 1941. The actual current rate of use—10,000 tons a month—is 83 percent less than the 1941 rate of civilian consumption.

The 1942 allotments do not include any rubber for new passenger car tires.

It has been reported that some drivers are not taking conservation measures seriously, in the belief that eventually their tires will be requisitioned.

But if we wear out the tires on the 30 million passenger cars, the truck, bus, and train transportation systems of the Nation will be swamped. On the other hand, if it is possible to preserve cars in the hands of their owners, it will be an advantage to all transportation and to the war effort. If the time should come when the Government had to call on civilians to sacrifice their tires, we know they would respond patriotically. In the meantime, no American should deliberately waste the mileage left in his tires.

The following figures show how the war effort demands rubber that must be made available: A medium tank requires 1,750 pounds; a gas mask, 1.8 pounds; a 10-ton pontoon bridge, 3,200 pounds; a half-ton truck, 125 pounds; a Flying Fortress, 1,250 pounds. A 35,000-ton battleship alone requires 150,000 pounds—or enough to equip 2,000 passenger automobiles complete with spare tires.

Other factors in the rubber supply and demand situation are as follows:

SYNTHETIC

The War Production Board is making every effort to expand the production of synthetic rubber, and is investigating every possible new process, but all the information we have shows that every pound of synthetic rubber which this country will be producing at forced draught between now and the end of 1943 must be reserved for direct and indirect military purposes. None can be made available for the manufacture of tires for nonessential civilian purposes.

The War Production Board has set a goal of 800,000 tons as the production rate to be reached by the end of 1943. But reaching a rate, of course, is a much simpler thing than actually producing that much rubber in a year. The present program calls for production of over 300,000 tons during the calendar year of 1943.

RUBBER SALVAGE

All old scrap rubber can be reclaimed and used over again. Reclaimed rubber can be mixed with crude rubber to form a compound usable in many products, military as well as civilian.

But we cannot process rubber that is in the basements or back yards or garages of the country. Old tires, tubes, rubber shoes, hose, bathing caps, and other articles must be turned in, in ever increasing quantities, if we are to maintain the capacity of reclaiming plants.

Since Pearl Harbor, the flow of scrap rubber to reclaiming plants has greatly diminished. It must be started again. Every American must see to it that every ounce of old rubber he owns gets into war channels. Scrap rubber can be sold to junk dealers or can be given to charitable organizations.

GUAYULE

All available Guayule seeds in the United States have been planted, but it will take 4 to 6 years to grow enough Guayule rubber to make an appreciable contribution to the supply. Not more than 10,000 tons annually can be expected soon from Mexican Guayule.

SOUTH AMERICA

Negotiations are in progress with all Latin American countries, and agreements have recently been made with Brazil, Peru, and Nicaragua in which the United States will take the entire exportable surpluses of their rubber for the next 5 years. This will meet only a small part of our needs. Brazil will be able to ship this country from 10,000 to 15,000 tons of crude rubber this year, and, we hope, perhaps 25,000 to 30,000 tons in 1943. The Peruvian agreement is expected to provide between 6,000 and 10,000 tons over the 5-year period.

WORLD PRODUCTION OF CRUDE RUBBER, 1940

Origin	Tonnage	Status
Malaya	540,000	Area controlled by Axis.
Netherlands Indies	536,000	Do.
Ceylon	89,000	Shipments uncertain.
French Indo China	64,000	Area controlled by Axis.
Thailand	44,000	Do.
Sarawak	35,000	Do.
North Borneo	17,500	Do.
South America	17,600	
India	11,500	Shipments uncertain.
Burma	9,600	Area controlled by Axis.
Liberia	7,350	
Other African	1,300	
Mexican Guayule	4,108	
Nigeria	2,903	
Philippines	2,267	Do.
Total	1,390,000	1,260,000 tons, or 90 percent, is in Axis controlled areas; and 1,380,-000 tons or 97 percent either Axis controlled or originating in areas from which shipment is now uncertain.

GANGWAY! *This poster, showing in graphic fashion the need for saving rubber here at home, has been distributed by the OEM Information Division for display by filling stations, chain stores, tire companies, mail order houses, automobile accessory stores, automobile dealers, and shipyards. Other persons desiring the poster should write to the Division of Information, OEM, 430 Delaware Avenue, Washington, D. C. Two-column mats of the illustration above are available for publication on request to Production Section, Information Division, OEM, 2743 Tempo R, Washington, D. C.*
Refer to Mat V–6

Operator enjoined from selling gasoline unless card is presented

A temporary restraining order enjoining C. P. Stevenson, operator of the Whitehall Service Co. of Anderson, S. C., from selling gasoline without calling for presentation of a gasoline rationing card was secured May 21 by the OPA.

It was the first action against violators of the gasoline rationing regulation.

Tire quotas lowered

A quota of tires for rationing in June lower than the quota for May was announced May 22 by OPA Administrator Henderson in a further step to conserve rubber. This decrease is contrary to the seasonal pattern of replacement sales in previous years.

The June quota makes available 49.584 new tires for List A passenger vehicles, 479,-051 recapped tires or recapping services for List A and List B together, and 265,007 inner tubes. These figures compare with May quotas of 55,573 new tires, 578,092 recaps and 315,058 tubes.

The truck tire quota, which provides for buses, trucks, industrial tractors and farm equipment, includes 247,715 new tires, 365,-014 recaps and 309,116 tubes, compared with 238,259 new tires, 379,060 recapped tires and 326,836 inner tubes made available in May.

30.8 percent of car owners got "A" cards, partial returns show

Partial returns on the gasoline rationing registration indicate that percentage estimates made by OPA on the number of the various types of rationing cards to be issued were substantially correct.

The OPA reported May 21 that 30.8 percent of 1,486,806 car owners for whom returns are now in, received "A" cards, giving them the minimum allotment of gasoline under the emergency rationing plan. OPA had estimated that "A" cards would constitute about one-third of the number of cards to be issued.

Of the nearly 1½ million registrations reported, 10.8 percent of car owners received "B–1" cards; 11.3 percent received "B–2" cards; 37.5 percent received "B–3" cards and 9.6 percent were issued "X" cards for unrestricted amounts of gasoline.

Volunteers get extra gasoline to carry on war work

Volunteers engaged in war activities, including American Red Cross services, and work of the OCD, may get supplemental rations of gasoline needed to carry on such work. This was provided by the OPA May 21 in an amendment to the gasoline rationing regulations.

The new order also allows supplemental rations when they are needed, to members of volunteer firemen's organizations, as well as to any organization "solely engaged" in any civilian defense activity that is under the supervision or direction of the Army, Navy, Marine Corps, or Coast Guard.

War construction workers assured of gasoline to work, and from job to job

Thousands of workers on war construction jobs in the East Coast gas ration area who need their cars not only to drive back and forth to work, but also to travel from job to job, are assured adequate supplies of gasoline for these purposes, the OPA declared May 16.

The gasoline rationing regulations permit supplemental rations of gasoline whenever they are needed for cars that must be driven in pursuit of a gainful occupation. Supplemental rations may also be issued to migrant workers who need their cars to travel from job to job.

Hints to motorists on how to stretch gasoline rations

Hints to motorists on how to stretch gasoline rations were issued May 18 by the Consumer Division of the OPA.

Drive less and walk more. Cut out pleasure driving and concentrate on essential driving.

Fill up the empty seats in your car. Form a car club; pool essential driving with your neighbors; take turns at driving the crowd to the office or factory; make shopping day a neighborhood enterprise, with five or six people to each car.

Drive slowly. Your gasoline will take you farther if you drive under 40. Every mile you knock off your speed means a saving in gas.

Cut out jackrabbit starts and stops—they waste gasoline. Make sure your tires are properly inflated; it takes more gasoline to drive a car with underinflated tires.

Use lighter oils. Heavy oil drags on your engine, and more gasoline is needed to overcome this drag.

Use first and second gear as little as possible. Accelerate slowly, but shift to high at 15 miles an hour.

Have a slipping clutch adjusted at once. Go easy on your hand choke. Improper choking floods the engine with too much gasoline. Driving with the choke out also wastes gasoline.

Make these checks every 5,000 miles or oftener: Have the spark plugs cleaned and adjusted. Have the distributor points checked and adjusted. Clean the air cleaner. Have the carburetor cleaned and adjusted.

Park in the shade whenever you can. Gasoline evaporates more quickly from your tank in the hot sun.

Cosmetics being studied for relative essentiality

The toiletries and cosmetics branch of WPB said May 20 that it is making a study of the relative essentiality of toiletries and cosmetics and the materials used in their manufacture.

PHILLIPS NAMED CHIEF OF TIRE RATIONING BRANCH

Appointment of Dr. Charles F. Phillips as chief of the tire rationing branch of the OPA was announced May 19 by Price Administrator Henderson.

Dr. Phillips, who has been acting chief of the branch for several weeks, takes the place formerly occupied by Granville R. Holden, who had been called in to act as special assistant to Mr. Henderson during the formation of the tire rationing division.

Have facts ready when asking supplementary gas, OPA urges

Applicants for additional rations of gasoline were urged by the Office of Price Administration May 20 to arm themselves with the necessary facts about their driving requirements before asking their local rationing boards for supplemental cards.

Not only must the applicant sign his statement of fact, but, if he is an employee and the supplemental ration is needed to carry on his work he must also present the affidavit or affirmation of his employer, or an authorized representative of his employer.

Under the gasoline rationing regulations, the board is authorized to grant supplemental rations only if it finds that they are "essential to life or to the pursuit of a gainful occupation and that no reasonably adequate alternative means of transportation are available." The board in granting a supplemental ration will issue an A card or whatever B card or combination of cards, are necessary to provide for the amount of the ration.

The applicant must state why his present ration is insufficient. He must support this reason with facts. Next, the applicant must state what means of public transportation are available to him.

Other questions ask the applicant to state what vehicles owned by members of his family, or by friends or business associates are available to his use, and to specify what effort has been made to "double-up" with other car owners.

If, by his answers to all these questions, the applicant has indicated his present supply of gasoline is inadequate, he is asked to state "the minimum mileage which you declare is absolutely essential to you up to midnight, June 30, 1942?" The calculations made in arriving at this estimate must be set down on the application.

"B" card holders who save on ration, free to use balance as they please, Henderson says

Legitimate holders of "B" gasoline ration cards who can cut down on their requirements by doubling up with other motorists in driving to and from work or economize otherwise in use of gasoline are free to use the balance of the gasoline to which they are entitled under the "B" card for any purpose they desire, Price Administrator Henderson announced May 18.

To check "X," "B-3" cards

At the same time the Administrator announced that local rationing boards throughout the eastern area affected by the rationing plan will be relied upon to check applications for "X" and "B-3" cards to determine whether anyone has received such cards without justification. If it should become necessary to check the use which "X" card holders make of their cars, by spot inspections along the highways, such checking will be done by inspectors from OPA regional and State offices, the Administrator stated.

Some Government employees can get gasoline without card

Government employees with official travel orders directing use of their cars may get gasoline without a ration card.

The OPA May 18 directed service station attendants throughout the rationed area to honor such orders on two conditions: that they be on an official form, and that these orders specifically direct the employee to use his car for the trip.

Gasoline rationing regulations provide, however, for sale without a ration card to any vehicle that is designated by license plate, registration card or other document indicating that it is in use by a Federal, State, local, or foreign government or government agency.

Charles Kenney appointed to feed and grain unit

Appointment of Charles Kenney as senior business specialist in the feed and grain unit, food section, of the OPA was announced May 18 by H. R. Tolley, director of the food and apparel division.

MERRILY WE ROLL ALONG

U.S.
MISUSE
OF
AUTOMOBILE
TIRES

Cartoon by Elderman for VICTORY: Publishers may obtain mats of these cartoons weekly in either two- or three-column size. Requests to be put on the mailing list should be addressed to Production Section, Division of Information, Office for Emergency Management, 2743 Temporary R, Washington, D. C. Refer to V–8.

Home fruit canners to get sugar in proportion to amount canned

The OPA May 20 took steps to conserve the Nation's fruit crop through the issuance of a new sugar rationing regulation which will permit persons who do home canning to obtain sugar in proportion to the amount of fruit canned.

Under the new regulation, home canners may obtain 1 pound of sugar for every 4 quarts of finished canned fruit, and an additional pound of sugar for each member of the family unit for the packing of preserves, jams, jellies, and fruit butters.

OPA permits bicycle shipping preliminary to rationing

As a preliminary to bicycle rationing, which will begin early in June, Administrator Henderson announced on May 16 issuance of Ration Order No. 7, permitting manufacturers to ship adults' bicycles to distributors for the first time since April 2, when sales and transfers were frozen by the War Production Board to forestall a possible run of buying. Effective date of the order was May 15, and it remains in effect until rationing goes into operation.

At the same time, the Administrator said that he had requested all dealers, distributors and manufacturers to report their May 8 inventories of all bicycles except children's sizes.

Manufacturers may ship now

Manufacturers may begin shipments to distributors immediately, even before they have reported their inventories.

Shipments in limited quantity to dealers for resale only also are permitted, but such transfers must await word from the OPA to the manufacturer or distributor that the dealer receiving the bicycles has first filed his inventory report. After this requirement is complied with, a dealer may buy as many as 10 adults' bicycles for each of his sales outlets, in addition to those he has on hand.

The dealer who intends to make such purchases must state on his inventory report the names of the suppliers with whom he wishes to place his orders and the number he wishes to buy. On receipt of the inventory, the OPA will give the suppliers named permission to release to the dealer the number of bicycles designated. However, no sales to the ultimate consumer may be made before the rationing program, yet to be announced, has begun.

50-percent war plants can get bikes

An exception is made to this rule in cases where a war production plant needs bicycles for employee transportation. In such cases, OPA headquarters in Washington may grant permission for the purchase. This exception applies only to plants that can show more than 50 percent of their orders or deliveries in April bore a priority rating of A-10 or better.

Children's bicycles—the difference between adults' and children's is determined by the size of the frame—will not be subject to rationing and are not to be included in the inventory reports to OPA. Manufacture of children's sizes was halted by WPB order on April 1.

PRICE ADMINISTRATION . . .

Booklets unacceptable for posting prices, should be changed by June 1, says OPA

Acceptable and unacceptable methods for retailers to mark maximum allowed prices on cost-of-living articles, under the general maximum price regulation,

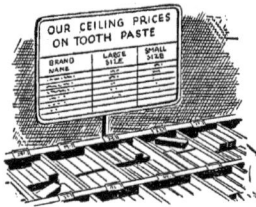

Where ceiling prices are displayed for group of related items, listed by brand name and size, ceiling price need not be marked on each separate item in bin or on counter.

were outlined May 18 by Price Administrator Henderson.

OPA has ruled that posting ceiling prices in booklet form, or in layers of lists, is not acceptable. Mr. Henderson announced, however, that due to the fact some merchants apparently have misunderstood the posting requirements, and hence have gone ahead with preparation of price booklets as means of satisfying section 13 (a) of the regulation, OPA will accept this method as of May 18. But he urged such merchants to change as soon as possible to some acceptable method. In no event, he said, should such change be delayed beyond June 1.

Three acceptable markings

Mr. Henderson stressed particularly the fact that cost-of-living commodities are not the only ones subject to the price regulation. The regulation, he pointed out, applies to all items not specifically excluded. The cost-of-living commodities are those for which visible marking or posting of maximums is required.

The marking provision for cost-of-living commodities, Mr. Henderson said, "may be complied with in three different ways: (1) By marking the ceiling price on the item itself, (2) by marking the

shelf, bin, rack, or other holder of container, upon which the item is kept by the seller, or (3) by posting ceiling prices at the place in the business establishment where the item is offered for sale."

To ease the retailer's work in cases where related merchandise in different price lines is frequently mixed together

DISPLAYING PRICES

Reproduced on this page are two of eight approved methods of displaying prices on cost-of-living commodities illustrated in the OPA booklet, *What Every Retailer Should Know About the General Maximum Price Regulation*. The booklet also shows ceiling price display cards for table, counter or bin, using one price card for group of articles all having same ceiling price; shelf marker displaying same ceiling price for group of articles on shelf; method of identifying selling price as ceiling price where ceiling price sign for a group is not used; and display by price lines, permitted in some specified cases where lines are physically mixed. Another illustration stresses graphically that ceiling price must be shown even if sale price is below ceiling.

in the store, the regulation permits him to display the ceiling prices of certain goods by price-lines, Mr. Henderson pointed out. This may be done only for articles marked by asterisks in appendix B of the regulation. In such cases, the ceiling prices may be indicated on a card posted near the merchandise to which the prices refer. In addition, each separate item in the indicated price-line must be marked with its actual selling price.

The guiding rule in marking cost-of-living commodities, Mr. Henderson said, is:

Consumers should be able to see the "ceiling price" marker clearly when standing at the point of purchase without having to ask or look for it, and without having to thumb through pages. This is the "eye" test.

In other words, the customer should be made aware of the "ceiling price," whether

or not he has a special interest in seeing it. For the same reason, care should be taken when lists are used to make the printing large and clear enough, and to post the list conspicuously enough, so that the customer cannot miss it. . . .

Among the specific methods of posting which the OPA regards as unsatisfactory is posting in a store a sign such as: "All prices in this store are no higher than our ceiling," or a counter mark such as "All prices on merchandise on this counter are ceiling prices."

"COST-OF-LIVING" COMMODITIES

TOBACCO, DRUGS, TOILETRIES, AND SUNDRIES

(All brands, grades, and sizes, except where otherwise indicated)

Tobacco: Cigarettes; smoking tobacco in cans and packages.

Packaged household drugs: Aspirin tablets; milk of magnesia (liquid); cod liver oil (liquid); epsom salts; boric acid; castor oil and mineral oil; witch-hazel and rubbing alcohol.

Toiletries and sundries: Hand and toilet soaps; dentifrices (paste, powder, and liquid); shaving cream; toothbrushes; sanitary napkins; razor blades; facial tissues.

Infants' food: All types.

Ice cream: Bulk and packaged.

APPAREL AND YARD GOODS

Men's and boys' clothing: Suits, business and sport*; overcoats, topcoats, and raincoats, business and sport*; trousers and slacks, dress, sport, and wash*; men's shirts, other than formal*; pajamas and nightshirts, cotton, wool, and part wool*; shorts, cotton; undershirts, cotton knit; union suits; hosiery, other than pure silk and pure wool*; felt hats*; work shirts; work pants; overalls and coveralls; sweaters; mackinaws*; jackets, boys' only*; men's work gloves; boys' gloves and mittens; boys' blouses and shirts; boys' snow suits*.

Women's and girls' clothing: Coats, untrimmed and fur-trimmed, sport and dress*;

Approved arrangement of individual ticket so that ceiling price and sale price may be shown separately.

suits*; dresses, street and house*; hosiery, including anklets*; panties and slips*; foundation garments and brassieres*; women's gloves, children's gloves and mittens*; skirts; blouses and shirts, tailored, rayon or cotton*; sweaters; children's jackets*; nightgowns and pajamas, other than silk*; robes and house coats, flannel and cotton*; children's overalls, slacks, sun suits and shorts (cotton Infants' clothing: Diapers; dresses other only)*; children's snow suits*.

than silk; shirts; binders; sleeping garments; coats, cotton, wool, part wool; snow suits; sweaters; sunsuits (cotton only).

Yard Goods: Cotton yard goods; rayon yard goods; wool and mixtures of wool.

Footwear: Street, work, dress, and sport shoes for men, women, and children*; infants' shoes; rubber footwear.

FOOD AND HOUSEHOLD SUNDRIES

Meat—Fresh beef: Rib roast; chuck steak; top round steak; rump roast; chuck roast; beef liver; ground round steak.

Pork: Loin whole roast; rib end roast; best center cut chops; loin end roast; bacon; ham whole, half, or sliced; salt pork.

Other meat products: Cooked or smoked ham; frankfurters.

Canned Fruits, Vegetables and Juices.— Canned peaches; canned pears; canned pineapples; canned corn; canned peas; canned tomatoes; canned pork and beans; canned green beans, cut; canned tomato juice; canned grapefruit juice; canned pineapple juice.

OTHER GROCERIES AND HOUSEHOLD SUNDRIES

Canned salmon; canned vegetable soup; canned tomato soup; packaged flour mixes (cake, pancake, biscuit mixes only); macaroni and spaghetti, dried, bulk and packaged; rolled oats, bulk and packaged; corn flakes; bread, all types; soda crackers; fresh milk and cream; lard, bulk and print; vegetable shortening; sugar, all types packaged and bulk; coffee; cocoa; table salt; corn meal, bulk or packaged; rice, bulk or packaged; toilet paper; soaps (bar, flakes, powder, chips, granular, and cleansing powders); paper napkins.

HOUSEHOLD FURNITURE, APPLIANCES, AND FURNISHINGS

Appliances and equipment: Radios and phonographs; vacuum cleaners and carpet sweepers; refrigerators and iceboxes; washing machines; sewing machines; stoves and ranges; small appliances (irons, toasters, glass coffee makers, and mixers); floor lamps and bridge lamps; light bulbs; ironing boards; step-on cans; floor brooms; china and pottery tableware, in sets; cooking utensils (10-quart pail, 2-quart saucepan, 5-quart teakettle).

Furniture: All living room, dining room and bed room suites (sets or individual pieces); kitchen tables and chairs; studio couches and sofa beds; mattresses; bedsprings.

Furnishings: Rugs and carpets, size 6 by 9 feet and larger; linoleum; felt base floor coverings; bed sheets and sheeting, cotton;* towels, cotton bathroom and kitchen;* blankets and comforts;* house curtains;* bed spreads, cotton;* tablecloths and napkins, plain and print (cotton only);* window shades.

HARDWARE, AGRICULTURAL SUPPLIES MISCELLANEOUS

Hayforks; garden and lawn rakes; dirt shovels; axes, single bit; claw hammers; handsaws; inside and outside house paints (ready mixed); fertilizer, bulk and packaged; vegetable seeds, bulk and packaged*; insecticides; bicycles, adult sizes; bicycle tires; flashlights.

ICE, FUEL AND AUTOMOTIVE

Ice; coke; coal (hard and soft); charcoal; firewood; kerosene; fuel oil; gasoline; oil tires and inner tubes.

* Maximum prices may be posted by pricelines at the place in the business establishment where the commodities are offered for sale, provided that, in addition, the selling price of each commodity in such classification shall be marked on the commodity itself.

Buying public urged to learn salient points of general price control bill

Price Administrator Henderson last week urged the buying public to acquaint itself thoroughly with the following points regarding the general maximum price regulation which went into effect May 18:

1. All commodities sold at retail, excepting only those specifically excluded in the regulation, are price-controlled.

2. The maximum prices are the highest prices charged by each individual seller during March 1942. (Each store—even though part of a chain—is considered an individual seller.)

3. This means that different stores will have different maximum prices for the same article—just as they did last March. And you still can shop around for lower prices.

4. There is nothing in the regulation to prevent a retailer from reducing his prices. But, no price can be raised above the maximum.

5. Important groups of commodities have been selected as "cost-of-living" items. The ceiling prices for these must be displayed by every retailer in his store beginning May 18. However, the fact that an item does not have a "ceiling price" publicly shown does not mean it is exempt from price control. Everything, whether it has a posted "ceiling price" or not, is covered unless it is specifically excluded in the regulation.

Not an easy task

"It is no easy task for the retailers in this country to adjust their operations to the price control program and I urge the public to be tolerant of misunderstandings and honest mistakes over the next few weeks," Mr. Henderson said. "Willful violators will be punished, of course, and penalties are severe."

Since the regulation's exceptions most important in the average family's shopping will be found in food markets, Mr. Henderson issued the following list and recommended that both shoppers and storekeepers keep it for reference purposes.

THESE FOOD PRODUCTS ARE CONTROLLED

*All fluid milk (at retail)—All standard and special grades: homogenized milk, chocolate milk, all other flavored milk, cultured buttermilk and other cultured milk, skim milk, etc.

*All fluid cream (at retail)—table cream, whipping cream, sour or cultured cream, and all combinations.

All canned goods (except for canned milk products)—canned fruits, vegetables, juices, soups, fish, meats, stews, etc.

All bottled goods—soft drinks, ketchup, sauces, etc.

Fresh bananas.

All frozen fruits, vegetables, meat, and fish.

Cake mixes and all flour mixes in packages.

All cuts of beef and pork.

All smoked, spiced, and pickled fish and meats (bacon, hams, sausage, frankfurters, etc.).

Bread—all kinds—white, rye, whole wheat, raisin, bran, etc.

All cakes, pies, cookies, and crackers.

Jams, jellies, and all other preserves.

All sugar, molasses, prepared honey, and all other syrups, flavors, and sweetenings.

All dried fruits with one exception (dried prunes).

Most packaged dry foods—such as rice, barley, cornmeal, cracker meal, cereals, noodles, spaghetti, macaroni, gelatin and gelatin desserts, puddings, etc.

Soaps in all forms—bar, cake, flakes, chips, powder, or liquid.

Shortening—lard, cooking oils, etc.

Salad oils—salad dressing, etc.

Candies, confections, and chewing gum.

Coffee, tea, cocoa, and other beverages.

Salt, pepper, and other spices and condiments.

Also cleaners and housekeeping items—scouring powders, ammonia, bleaching and cleaning fluids, waxes, polishes, brooms, mops, dusters, pails, etc.

Peanuts, peanut butter, and other peanut products.

Tobacco products—cigars, cigarettes, smoking and chewing, etc.

*Retail sales include home deliveries as well as store sales.

THESE FOOD PRODUCTS ARE NOT CONTROLLED

Butter and cheese.

Evaporated, condensed, and other canned milk products.

Poultry and eggs.

Fresh fruits and vegetables (except bananas).

Flour.

Fresh fish, sea food, and game.

Mutton and lamb.

Nuts.

Dried prunes.

Dry beans.

Obviously, Mr. Henderson pointed out, the foregoing list is not complete as to items covered—there are many more sold in food markets. However, the list is complete as to the "excepted" foods. In other words, everything sold in a food market is covered by the price ceiling unless it is one of the things in the second list above.

Very few things of common use sold in other retails stores are excluded from the General Regulation, the sole exceptions being: living animals, birds and fowl; books, magazines, newspapers, and periodicals; used automobiles; stamps, coins, precious stones (but not jewelry, which is covered); antiques; knotted oriental rugs; paintings, etchings, sculptures, and other objects of art.

★ ★ ★

Carpet firm allowed to change fabrics, lower ceilings

Permission to manufacture certain carpet fabrics containing substitute materials at prices reflecting the decrease in cost of the new materials was granted May 20 by Price Administrator Henderson to Mohawk Carpet Mills, Inc., of Amsterdam, N. Y.

Sales of armaments to U. S. Government excluded from general price order

Sales of armaments to the United States Government were excluded from the general maximum price regulation May 19 in a new order issued by the OPA.

Assembled combatant items excluded

Price Administrator Henderson announced that effective May 18, the general price order will not apply to purchases by the United States Army, Navy, Maritime Commission or any other Government agency of completely assembled combatant items including:

Aircraft, ammunition, armored vehicles and armored trains, artillery, balloon barrage equipment, bombs, bomb sight., caissons, fire control equipment, gas masks, gun sights, military bridges, military searchlight units, mines, mortars, projectiles, small arms, ships and boats and torpedoes, military propellants and explosives, grenades, primers, fuses, boosters and other pyrotechnics.

The exceptions from the general price order of such purchases by Government agencies are provided in Supplementary Regulation No. 4 to the General Maximum Price Regulation, made public May 19.

Also excluded

The new supplementary regulation also excludes from the general maximum price regulation sales to Government agencies of the following:

(1) Noncombatant ships and boats; (2) goods produced under Government-authorized developmental war contracts; (3) goods produced under secret war contracts; (4) goods needed for emergency repair or servicing of combatant items, noncombatant ships, boats and aircraft owned by the Government and parts and assemblies for such units; (5) any commodity for which there is an emergency need, provided the purchase does not amount to more than $1,000; and (6) Brazilian rock quartz crystals.

Parts, subassemblies excepted too

Parts and subassemblies of combatant items are also excluded from the general maximum price regulation, but some of these parts and subassemblies are subject to the provisions of other orders—particularly Maximum Price Regulation No. 136 on machines and parts.

All completely assembled aircraft are excepted from the general maximum price regulation, regardless of by whom purchased.

Commenting on the exclusion from the general order of sales or deliveries to the Government of all completely assembled combatant items, guns and explosives, Mr. Henderson said:

"These items are excluded from price control at this time in order to prevent any possibility that their sudden wholesale subjection to price control under the general maximum price regulation might interfere with essential war production."

Trucks still subject to order

The supplementary regulation provides, however, that trucks which are not armored vehicles still remain subject to the general maximum price regulation. Passenger automobiles continue subject to Revised Price Schedule No. 85 covering such vehicles—even if bought by the Army or Navy. Unarmored trucks do not present large conversion problems.

The Supplementary Regulation excludes from the general order sales or deliveries to the United States or its agencies of noncombatant as well as combatant ships and boats.

Supplementary Regulation No. 4 also permits adjustments from established maximum prices to be made in order to prevent any threat of impeding production.

Ceilings on sales, deliveries to War, Navy effective July 1

The effective date of price ceilings established by the general maximum price regulation has been extended until July 1, 1942, for sales or deliveries to and contracts with the War and Navy Departments, Price Administrator Henderson announced May 19.

★ ★ ★

GMPR doesn't authorize sales below "fair trade" prices

Nothing in the general maximum price regulation authorizes sales below the minimum prices established under State Fair Trade laws if these minimums are equal to or less than the ceiling prices set by the Regulation Price, Administrator Leon Henderson stated May 22.

OPA to tell thousands of small stores about price control

At least half the country's 1,900,000 retailers have been reached in the first phase of an intensive program to acquaint them with the purpose, meaning and mechanics of the general maximum price regulation, Price Administrator Henderson said May 22.

The regulation, setting maximum retail prices on nearly all goods sold at retail at the highest price charged by each storekeeper in March went into effect May 18.

To date, the educational campaign has included about 1,000 trade meetings, releases to newspapers and trade press, radio speeches, distribution of literature through the mail, the widespread campaign of OPA's Consumer Division, and educational programs arranged by trade organizations, chambers of commerce, and other business associations.

The campaign's second phase is now getting under way, and will concentrate on the "grass roots," hundreds of thousands of small owner-operated country and city stores, whom the OPA now seeks to inform more thoroughly on the how-to-do-it of price control.

Special handling of some fats, oils sales to determine ceilings

Where sellers of fats and oils are unable to determine their maximum prices under any of the five methods indicated in Revised Price Schedule No. 53 (Fats and Oils), specific provision now is made by the OPA for handling such cases, Price Administrator Henderson announced May 21.

Universal price ceilings effective June 18 in Hawaii

Because of delays in transportation and communications between continental United States and Hawaii, Price Administrator Henderson announced May 18 the postponement until June 18 of the date on which universal price ceilings, now in effect in the United States, would apply in Hawaii.

The provision that persons subject to the regulation must at once preserve all existing records showing their prices during the March base period remains unchanged.

Pickled sheepskin prices "rolled back" to take squeeze off tanners

Tanners of sheepskin leather, squeezed between a ceiling on their own product and advancing prices for pickled sheepskins, were afforded relief May 19 by Price Administrator Henderson who "rolled back" the price for pickled sheepskins to the basis of levels prevailing last October in the first action of this character since the issuance of the general maximum price regulation.

The effect will be to remove any reason for price advances in consumer articles derived from this commodity such as shoes, clothing, gloves, belts and handbags, according to the Administrator. Pickled sheepskins rank next to cattle hides, kips and calfskins in the United States as a source of leather.

Maximum Price Regulation No. 145, issued May 19 and effective May 23, 1942, establishes ceilings at an average of about $1 per dozen pickled sheepskins below levels that prevailed during the first three months of 1942. This, in effect, "rolls back" a price advance that had occurred between October 1941 and March 31, 1942, and adjusts the October prices for seasonal factors.

⋏ ⋏ ⋏

Adjustment protest procedure modified for bituminous coal

A slight change in the procedure for filing protests, petitions for amendment, or petitions for adjustment or exception involving Maximum Price Regulation No. 120 (Bituminous Coal Delivered from Mine or Preparation Plant) was effected by Amendment No. 1 to Procedural Regulation No. 1, announced May 18 by Price Administrator Henderson.

Under the provisions of the amendment, one original and six copies of any protest, petition for amendment, or petition for exception or adjustment, and of all accompanying documents and briefs shall be filed. Formerly five copies were all that were required.

The amendment, effective May 18, further provided that the Administrator may appoint or designate an officer or employee of the Bituminous Coal Division of the United States Department of the Interior to conduct the oral hearing when held in connection with such a protest.

OPA seeks to protect maximum price level from disturbance by imports, yet assure satisfactory volume of goods from abroad

Plans are being developed by the Federal Government to prevent prices paid abroad for imported merchandise from disturbing the level of domestic prices established by OPA's general maximum price regulation, Price Administrator Henderson announced May 21.

At the same time, the Administrator emphasized that the general maximum price regulation applies to imported as well as domestic commodities. This means that imported commodities cannot be sold in this country for more than the highest prices charged by the importer on resale last March, notwithstanding the fact that the selling price in the country of origin may have risen since, or may rise in the future.

Will hold March figures

"The highest March price level is going to be held, whether the commodity is of domestic or foreign origin," Mr. Henderson stated. "We recognize, of course, that the importer cannot in every case dictate the price he will pay for goods bought in a foreign country for resale in the United States. Neither can the United States Government. It is equally true, however, that to allow prices abroad to disturb prices in this country, either for the actual commodity or for products made in whole or in part of foreign material, would make difficult, if not impossible, the success of the whole price-control program.

"The two objectives to be obtained are protection of the domestic price level and the assurance of a satisfactory volume of imports needed in this country. Solution of these problems is being worked out by the Office of Price Administration in collaboration with other Government agencies . . ."

Issues clarifying rules

For purposes of clarification, Mr. Henderson issued the following rulings on the applicability of the general regulation to imports:

1. The price at which goods may be imported from a foreign country is not subject to the general maximum price regulation if the domestic importer or his agent deals directly with the seller in the foreign country. However, a domestic resale of the imported goods is subject to the regulation unless specifically exempted.

2. If the importer places his order with a representative in this country of the foreign seller, the sale is subject to the regulation.

3. Where the order is placed with the representative in this country, the representa-

tive is considered a different seller from his principal for the purpose of determining the maximum price.

4. Where the representative in this country acts for several foreign principals, he is considered a different seller with respect to the goods he sells for each different principal, for the purpose of determining the maximum price.

5. Where the fact that the representative in this country is acting as a representative, and not as a principal, is not disclosed to or otherwise known by the importer, the maximum price must be determined exactly as if the representative of the seller were himself a principal.

6. If the imported goods are already in this county at the time they are sold or contracted to be sold, the sale is subject to the regulation, whether or not the buyer deals directly with the foreign seller.

OPA has previously ruled that those of its regulations which fix maximum prices in dollars and cents apply to purchases abroad for import into this country, unless such purchases are expressly excepted by the regulation involved. These rulings, Mr. Henderson stated, stand unchanged. They are not, however, applicable to regulations which, like the general maximum price regulation, set maximum prices for each individual seller by reference to the prices he charged during a base period.

★ ★ ★

Agents, subsidiaries of U. S. exporters bound by ceilings in foreign sales

Agents or subsidiaries of American exporters selling to foreign consumers in Latin America or other foreign countries must abide by the ceiling prices established by OPA's maximum export price regulation under an amendment issued May 22 by Price Administrator Henderson.

Newsprint export prices adjusted to war costs

Exporters of standard newsprint paper may add certain actual freight charges incurred as the result of wartime conditions to maximum prices established by the Maximum Export Regulation on April 30, Price Administrator Henderson announced May 22.

U. S. to absorb higher costs in moving bituminous coal to New York, New England

Arrangements whereby the Federal Government will absorb the increased transportation costs involved in keeping New York and New England industry supplied with bituminous coal in the face of dislocation of the normal tidewater by vessel from Hampton Roads, Va., were announced May 17 by Price Administrator Henderson.

The plan, worked out jointly by OPA, the Reconstruction Finance Corporation, and the War Shipping Administration, is in line with wartime policy to use whatever means the Federal Government has available to hold the general level of prices and prevent an inflationary increase in the cost of living. Primary result of the program will be to enable the maintenance in New York and New England of OPA's maximum prices for bituminous coal and for coke, extremely important industrial commodities, without imposing unreasonable hardship on coal receivers who have been compelled by the war to obtain supplies from other-than-normal sources and to make use of higher cost transportation.

Ceiling prices at the highest levels prevailing in the period December 15-31, 1941, were announced for wholesale and retail sales of bituminous coal, coke, and other solid fuels in Maximum Price Regulation No. 122 issued April 30 and effective May 18.

Four main features of program

Following are the four main features of the program:

1. War Shipping Administration will reduce rates for transporting bituminous coal by tidewater from Hampton Roads, Va., to New York and ports north in vessels of 1,000 gross tons or more. These rates will be brought back to approximately the levels that prevailed during the last 2 weeks in December 1941.
2. Reconstruction Finance Corporation will make funds available to compensate New York and New England receivers of southern bituminous coal for the increased transportation costs involved in moving coal by all-rail, instead of by tidewater.
3. Reconstruction Finance Corporation also will make funds available to compensate New York and New England receivers who formerly used coal from the southern fields, but are now dependent for supplies on northern fields.
4. Adjustments also will be made by Reconstruction Finance Corporation for New York and New England dealers who have stocked bituminous coal within recent months at higher transportation costs reflecting increases since December 15-31 and who are now being compelled by Maximum Price Regulation No. 122 to lower their prices.

'Receivers" who will be entitled to apply for adjustments under (2) and (3) include industrial consumers, distributors and dealers.

In every case the amount of the compensatory adjustment will be certified by the OPA to the Reconstruction Finance Corporation.

Mr. Henderson called special attention to the fact that the new program will not conflict with the minimum prices administered by the Bituminous Coal Division of the Department of the Interior.

Eligible for adjustment

Eligible to apply to OPA for compensatory adjustments, according to the new Compensatory Adjustment Regulation No. 1, issued May 19, are the following classes of New York and New England receivers of bituminous coal:

1. Those who prior to January 1, 1942, normally brought in southern bituminous coal from Hampton Roads via tidewater but who now have to resort to higher-cost transportation, such as all-rail or rail and barge or small vessel.
2. Dealers who normally handled southern bituminous coal shipped from Hampton Roads by tidewater prior to January 1, 1942, provided (a) that during the period January 1, 1942, to May 17, 1942, they have taken delivery of bituminous coal at a higher cost than southern bituminous coal was brought in prior to January 1, 1942; and (b) that prior to May 18, 1942, they have not disposed of the higher-cost coal or of an equivalent amount of inventory of prices adjusted upward over their selling prices during the period December 15-31, 1941.
3. Persons who since January 1, 1942, have converted over from burning oil to burning bituminous coal, providing that (a) they are not obtaining southern coal by collier from Hampton Roads, and (b) demonstrate, to OPA satisfaction, that their receiving point is such that a southern bituminous coal shipped from Hampton Roads to the nearest unloading port would have involved lower transportation costs, but was unavailable.

Applications by receivers described in paragraphs (1) and (2) above may be filed with OPA on or before June 20, 1942, and on or before the 20th day of each month thereafter these applications, which must contain all of the information required by the new regulation, may request compensation in connection with costs actually incurred during the preceding calendar month for the transportation of bituminous coal. Applications by those in the group described in paragraph (3) above may be filed on or before July 20, 1942.

Provision is made for the receipt of special application from those who for some reason or other are compelled to pay higher tidewater rates than those to which they were subject during the last 2 weeks of December 1941.

Petroleum tanker charges over basic rate to be absorbed by Shipping Administration

War-inflated costs of shipping petroleum and petroleum products by tanker will be brought down sharply under a Government-aid plan announced jointly May 19 by the War Shipping Administration and OPA.

The plan, advanced by OPA as a means of preserving the existing price levels by relieving oil consumers of the heavy burden of increased marine transportation expenses, provides that the War Shipping Administration will assume all costs of the movement by vessel of crude petroleum and petroleum products into the United States and between coastal and tidewater points in the United States over and above the basic maximum charter rates established by the United States Maritime Commission on January 20, 1942, or in effect on that date. This underwriting will be retroactive to the effective date, April 20, or subsequent thereto, when the War Shipping Administration requisitioned or chartered the individual vessels.

It was emphasized that the program only applies to shipments in tankers in excess of 3,000 gross tons requisitioned by or under charter to the War Shipping Administration.

Sub warfare boosted costs

Basic charter rates were set by the Maritime Commission on January 20, 1942, for petroleum transportation from the Gulf and Caribbean to the East Coast as follows: 40 cents per barrel for gasoline and kerosene; 42 cents per barrel for light fuel oil; 43 cents per barrel for 30° gravity crude or under; and 48 cents per barrel for heavy crude and residual fuel oils. Subsequently, because of submarine warfare, the commission established surcharges ranging from 100 to 200 percent of these basic rates. As a result, by April of this year, the costs of tanker movement from the Gulf to the East Coast north of Cape Hatteras had risen to about 85 cents a barrel more than the basic charter rates.

The new plan, as previously stated, provides that the charterers will only have to pay the January 20 basic charter rates and the War Shipping Administration will absorb anything in excess of those rates. It further provides that where no charter rates have been established, the War Shipping Administration will set charter rates predicated upon basic rates in effect on January 20, 1942.

"YEAH, BUT THINK OF THOSE UNFORTUNATE PEOPLE AT HOME WHO'LL HAVE TO WALK TO THE MOVIES!"

Dr. Seuss

Waste paper response results in surplus for time being

According to reports received by the Bureau of Industrial Conservation, the response of the American people to the salvage for victory waste-paper program has been so whole-hearted that there is an unusual surplus of this important war material.

Asked to check local markets

Commenting upon the success of the waste paper collection campaign, Lessing J. Rosenwald, chief of the Bureau said, "If similar intensive efforts in the collection of scrap rubber and scrap metals

This cartoon was drawn especially for VICTORY by Dr. Seuss. This notice constitutes full permission to reprint the drawing. Engraving may be made direct from this reproduction, or three-column mats will be furnished on application to Production Section, Division of Information, Office for Emergency Management, Washington, D. C. Refer to V–7.

can now be carried out, the public can go a long way toward filling the Nation's need for these vital materials."

Meanwhile, the Bureau advised each community to check its local markets to learn how much waste paper local dealers can handle. In many instances, paper-board mills have been offered more waste paper than their present inventory and production capacity can handle. The surplus backs up on the dealers whose storage facilities become overtaxed with the result that they either reject waste paper or accept it only on reduced terms. Then in turn junk dealers refuse to accept or purchase waste paper.

May be shortage next winter

Mr. Rosenwald pointed out that there is the possibility of a new shortage developing next winter, in view of the fact that the potential supply of waste paper will tend to decrease as the war progresses, whereas the demand for paper-board containers will increase as the volume of war production develops.

Wholesale pork under permanent ceiling; raw material cost rises added to base

Ham, bacon, and other pork products which are American dinner table favorites and constitute nearly half our national meat supply, representing about 10 percent of the consumer's total food dollar spent, were placed under permanent price ceilings at the wholesale level May 21 by Price Administrator Henderson.

The 250-pound "porker," mostly cornfed and the farmer's most important animal for sale, is indirectly affected by the price order (Maximum Price Regulation No. 148, effective May 21). The order fixes prices of dressed hogs and wholesale pork cuts at levels no higher than those actually prevailing for each individual packer seller during the March 3–7, 1942, period. Individual ceilings for each seller's prices are established, based on his price lists and highest sales of the period February 16–20, 1942, plus certain stated additions representing the rise in raw material costs from February 16 to March 7.

Retailers under GMPR

The new regulation at the wholesale level replaces a temporary 60-day order, which expired May 21. Neither hog producers nor retail outlets are covered directly by the new permanent order. However, retail prices are fixed by the general maximum price regulation, OPA pointed out.

Coincident with issuance of the new regulation, OPA announced a new joint meat study to be made in cooperation with the Agricultural Marketing Administration. This will include a further survey of costs involved in meeting Government specifications on meat products designed for use of the armed forces and for the Lend-Lease requirements of our allies.

Under the temporary regulation, sales to the Federal Surplus Commodities Corporation and to the military forces of the United States were allowed at maximum prices 2 cents per pound higher than the top figures established for comparable sales in the domestic trade. This 2-cent differential was intended to compensate sellers for extraordinary costs incurred by them in complying with the stringent Government sales specifications. However, further OPA investigations revealed that this differential was too great and gave such sellers an inequitable advantage in bidding for hogs—the raw material. Hence, the new regulation lowers the differential on such Government sales to 1½ cents per pound.

Prices well above requirements

Another feature of the permanent regulation is the provision that all sales of dressed hogs may be made on the basis of a percentage figure over the live hog price, regardless of the seller's previous practice.

The OPA chief stated that the maximum prices established in the new regulation are well above those which reflect to hog raisers a price equal to the highest of the four alternatives provided for in farm product section 3 (a) of the Emergency Price Control Act of 1942.

OPA quarters are confident that the new price ceilings will not hamper the Department of Agriculture's "all-out" production program of hogs.

Maximum Price Regulation No. 148 covers all wholesale pork cuts derived from the carcass of the hog, dressed with head off and kidney and leaf lard out, and all canned meats consisting entirely of pork. It also defines each different grade and brand, as well as each weight classification, as a separate wholesale pork cut. This coverage is somewhat broader than that of the temporary regulation.

Over-all dollar limit may be set on stocks of goods for sale

As a result of recent surveys, which show that stocks of civilian goods in the hands of retailers and wholesalers have taken a sharp upward turn in the past few months, the WPB inventory and requisitioning branch is preparing to take immediate steps to limit all inventories to practicable working minimums.

Present proposal is to set an over-all dollar limitation on inventories of goods for sale. This will mean that the presence of excesses in one or more lines of merchandise will operate to prevent purchases in other lines which the retailer or wholesaler may wish to replenish.

Swollen inventories in the hands of some retailers are preventing others from obtaining merchandise in sufficient quantities to supply the needs of the communities they serve.

Imports of all known commercial oils placed under control

Control of imports of all known commercial oils not previously under such restriction was taken May 22 by the Director of Industry Operations.

In addition to the oils, the action places fats, seeds and nuts, cinchona or other bark from which quinine is derived, and corundum under import control.

ADDITIONS TO BASE TO DETERMINE PORK PRICES

[Cents per pound]

	Fresh or frozen	Cured	Smoked	Boiled	Baked or dried	Canned
1. Regular hams:						
Bone in	½	½	¾	1	1¼	----------
Boneless	¾	¾	1	1	1¼	1¼
2. Skinned hams:						
Bone in	1	1	1¼	1¾	2	----------
Boneless	1½	1½	1½	1¾	2	2
3. Virginia style hams	----------	----------	----------	----------	2½	----------
4. Shoulders:						
Bone in	1	1	1½	----------	----------	----------
Boneless	1½	1½	1¾	2	2	2
5. Picnics:						
Bone in	1	1	1¼	----------	----------	----------
Boneless	1½	1½	1¾	2	2	2
6. Butts:						
Bone in	1¼	1½	1½	----------	----------	----------
Boneless	2	2	2½	2¾	3	3
7. Bellies:					Sliced	
For bacon	¾	¾	1	----------	1¼	1¼
For dry salt	1½	1½	1¾	----------	2	2
8. Loins:						
Bone in	2	2	2½	----------	----------	----------
Boneless	3	3	4	----------	4	4
9. Spare ribs	½	½	¾	----------	----------	----------
10. Fat backs	[illegible]	[illegible]	[illegible]	----------	----------	----------
11. Plates	1¼	1¼	1½	----------	----------	----------
12. Jowl butts	1	1	1½	----------	----------	----------
13. Feet, tails, bones	½	----------	----------	----------	----------	1
14. Pork trimmings	1½	----------	----------	----------	----------	----------
15. Canned meats made entirely from pork	----------	----------	----------	----------	----------	½

War chemical producers get more priority aid

The vital chemical war industries were granted further priority assistance in obtaining maintenance and repair materials by the terms of Amendment No. 1 to General Preference Order P-89 as Amended, issued May 22 by the Director of Industry Operations.

The amendment allows the chemical producer to use an A-1-c rating to obtain 30 percent of his regular supplies, and A-3 for the remaining 70 percent. The amendment also allows an A-1-c rating to be extended by suppliers to replenish their stocks.

★ ★ ★

Army Engineer lumber auctions not included in ceiling delay

The postponement of the effective date of the general maximum price regulation in the case of contracts with the United States Government or its agencies does not apply to sales of lumber in bid-lettings conducted by the U. S. Army engineers, OPA announced May 21.

∧ ∧ ∧

Interior to handle complaints on bituminous coal prices

Investigation of complaints and checks of compliance with OPA's Maximum Price Regulation No. 120—Bituminous Coal Delivered From Mine or Preparation Plant—will be undertaken by the Bituminous Coal Division of the Department of the Interior, Price Administrator Henderson announced May 22.

∧ ∧ ∧

Second-hand bag prices

Several changes in the provisions of the maximum price regulation applying to second-hand bags were announced by Price Administrator Henderson May 22, chiefly for the purpose of making the regulation conform to other OPA orders or to general trade practice.

★ ★ ★

Arsenic placed under allocation

Arsenic was put under allocation control May 22 by General Preference Order M-152, issued by Director of Industry Operations Knowlson.

BEVERAGE PRICING

Prices of beverages sold by hotels, restaurants, soda fountains, bars, and cafes for consumption on the premises are controlled by the general maximum price regulation, provided such beverages are not mixed on the premises, under an interpretation issued May 19 by Price Administrator Henderson.

..

Dollars-and-cents ceilings set for 8 leading groups of cotton fabrics

Dollars-and-cents ceiling prices, chiefly at the manufacturer's level, for eight leading cotton fabric groups falling under the provisions of Maximum Price Regulation No. 118 (Cotton Products) were announced May 21 by Price Administrator Henderson to replace individual ceilings which are determined from the weighted average price of each seller during a base period.

The plan of supplying definite average prices was announced last month when Regulation No. 118 was issued. The May 21 specific prices, supplied through Amendment No. 3, represent only a portion of those which the Office of Price Administration ultimately will incorporate in the cotton product schedule.

The eight groups for which prices are supplied consist of ducks, flannels, grey self-filled sheeting, warp sateens, woven table and laundry felts, grey carded gabardines, grey coutils (corset fabrics), and grey moleskins.

Prices for leading numbers are:

Numbered duck, 35 percent off list; Army duck, 33 percent off list; single-filling ounce duck, 19¾ cents per pound; double-filling ounce duck, 20¾ cents per pound; 36-inch 4.75 bleached flannel, 13¾ cents per yard; 8-ounce glove-and-mitten flannel, 20¾ cents per yard; 34-inch 118 by 64 2-yard warp sateen, 22¾ cents per yard; 54-inch 19–20-ounce table and laundry felt, 54 cents per yard; 34½-inch 1.60–1.70 yard grey moleskin, 26 cents per yard.

The prices took effect May 25, 1942.

∧ ∧ ∧

TANTALUM TO BE ALLOCATED

Tantalum, the entire output of which is going into vital war uses, was placed May 22 under complete allocation control by the Director of Industry Operations (Order M-156) so flow of the metal may be channeled among the various users.

Civilian needs for colorfast, preshrunk clothes can be met

Colorfast and preshrunk clothing for civilians can be manufactured without interfering with military production, the Consumer Division of the OPA reported May 20, in a statement designed to clear up misunderstandings regarding supplies of fast dyes and preshrinking machinery.

⁎ ★ ⁎

Rayon and wool waste rules adapted to licensing

Amendments to the rayon waste price schedule and the raw and processed wool waste materials maximum price regulation have been issued by Price Administrator Henderson to bring the enforcement sections into conformity with the licensing provisions of Supplementary Order No. 5 (Licensing).

Amendment No. 1 to Revised Price Schedule No. 90 (Rayon Waste) and Amendment No. 1 to Maximum Price Regulation No. 123 (Raw and Processed Wool Waste Materials) are necessary to conform these two with Supplementary Order No. 5.

.. ∧ ⁎

Ceilings on 4 weights of canton flannels to be adjusted

Maximum prices for four weights of canton flannels (jobber type) will be revised downward by 1 cent per yard in a forthcoming amendment to Maximum Price Regulation No. 118 (Cotton Products) the OPA announced May 22.

This revision will be for the purpose of correcting an error in ceiling prices for these flannels issued May 21, 1942, as a part of Amendment No. 3 to Regulation 118.

⁎ ★

Ceilings imposed on milled rice

Rice—a $64,000,000 farm crop constituting a major source of agricultural income in Louisiana, Texas, Arkansas, and California, and an essential item in the food diet of our territorial possessions—May 22 was put under specific price regulation, at the processed stage, by Price Administrator Henderson.

Ceilings were established on milled rice in Maximum Price Regulation No. 150 at prices approximating the peak levels of end–December 1941, or the first fortnight in March 1942.

Bolts, nuts, screws, rivets under ceiling; sizes cut from 450,000 to 250,000

Maximum manufacturers' prices for bolts, nuts, screws, and rivets were announced May 20 by Price Administrator Henderson.

Prices of bolts, nuts, screws, and rivets, with the exception of cap and set screws, are stabilized at the levels prevailing October 1, 1941. Prices of cap and set screws are stabilized at the levels of June 1, 1941.

The maximum prices are set forth in Maximum Price Regulation No. 147, on ferrous and nonferrous bolts, nuts, screws, and rivets, and become effective May 28, 1942.

Simplification to save steel

In conjunction with the regulation, OPA issued a simplified stock list of standard sizes of bolts, nuts, and other fastenings reducing the number of stock sizes from approximately 450,000 to 250,000.

"The exclusion of hundreds of odd diameters and lengths will conserve many tons of steel and increase total production of standard stock sizes in line with the War Production Board's program of conservation and greater production," the Price Administrator said.

The simplified list was prepared by OPA with the assistance of the industry and with the approval of the Army, Navy, Maritime Commission, WPB, Bureau of Standards, and the Panama Canal Commission.

Delivery charges and allowances provided for in the new price regulation are, with one exception, those historically developed and adopted by the industry in its basing point system which came into being about 1910.

The one exception is the provision allowing a manufacturer to make a charge for all-rail freight to the Pacific Coast insofar as the cost exceeds the amount of freight which, in general, would normally have been absorbed by the producer if the shipment had been made by rail and water.

OPA gets temporary injunction on Jones & Laughlin, another steel firm, three scrap brokers

A temporary restraining order enjoining Jones & Laughlin Steel Corporation of Pittsburgh, Pa., fourth largest independent producer, Allegheny-Ludlum Steel Co. of Brackenridge, Pa., and three iron and steel scrap brokers from buying and selling in excess of the legal ceilings was secured May 19 in Federal district court in Pittsburgh by OPA.

It was the second complaint to be lodged against Jones & Laughlin Steel Corporation within a period of 4 weeks. The company has already been accused of violation of priority ratings in an action brought by the War Production Board on April 20.

Named with the two steel companies were Glosser & Sons, Johnstown, Pa., Staiman Brothers, Williamsport, Pa., and the Hodes Coal & Junk Co., Lock Haven, Pa.

In the OPA presentation, the defendants were charged with "upgrading" and "top dressing" scrap. Glosser & Sons were also accused of accepting commissions on "upgraded" and "top dressed" materials, a practice expressly forbidden under Iron and Steel Scrap Schedule No. 4.

Price relief taken from one steel firm, another cut

Two steel companies which some time ago were granted permission by the OPA to charge higher than maximum prices for certain products because of high-cost production were ordered by OPA May 21, in the light of a study of their earnings positions, to reduce prices on the products.

Central Iron & Steel Co. of Harrisburg, Pa., which on May 22, 1941, was granted permission to charge a maximum price for steel plates of $2.35 per hundred pounds, base, at established basing points, was ordered to restore the $2.10 per hundred pounds maximum base price provided in Revised Price Schedule No. 6 on such iron and steel products.

Eckels-Nye Steel Corporation, of Syracuse, N. Y., which since September 17, 1941, has been permitted to charge $2.50 per hundred pounds at established basing points for rail merchant bars, have grade, was ordered to charge not over $2.40 per hundred pounds for the bars. While a reduction from the previous allowable price, the new price the company may charge is still higher than the $2.15 per hundred pounds maximum provided in Revised Price Schedule No. 6.

36 steel men asked to serve on advisory liaison groups between OPA and industry

Price Administrator Henderson May 18 invited 36 steel men to become members of four advisory committees to serve as liaison groups between the OPA and the industry on any problems which may arise with respect to prices.

The four advisory units, created under the terms of the Emergency Price Control Act of 1942, are to be known as: General steel products advisory committee, armament steels and alloys advisory committee, wire products advisory committee, and cold finished bars advisory committee.

GENERAL STEEL PRODUCTS ADVISORY COMMITTEE

Avery C. Adams, United States Steel Corporation, Pittsburgh, Pa.; J. W. Anderson, Sheffield Steel Corporation, Kansas City, Mo.; Homer Butts, Niles Rolling Mill Co., Niles, Ohio; Norris J. Clarke, Republic Steel Corporation, Cleveland, Ohio; J. A. Henry, Weirton Steel Co., Weirton, W. Va.; Paul Mackall, Bethlehem Steel Co., Bethlehem, Pa.; J. L. Neudoerfer, Wheeling Steel Corporation, Wheeling, W. Va.; N. H. Orr, Colorado Fuel & Iron Corporation, Denver, Colo.; L. V. Parsons, Jones & Laughlin Steel Corporation, Pittsburgh, Pa.; A. C. Roeth, Inland Steel Co., Chicago, Ill.; and W. E. Watson, Youngstown Sheet & Tube Co., Youngstown, Ohio.

ARMAMENT STEELS AND ALLOYS ADVISORY COMMITTEE

R. M. Allen, Allegheny Ludlum Steel Corporation, Pittsburgh, Pa.; W. H. Colvin, Jr., Rotary Electric Steel Co., Detroit, Mich.; Norman L. Deuble, Copperweld Steel Corporation, Warren, Ohio; Horace D. Disston, Henry Disston & Sons, Inc., Philadelphia, Pa.; A. T. Galbraith, Crucible Steel Co., of America, New York, N. Y.; F. L. Gibbons, Carnegie-Illinois Steel Corporation, Chicago, Ill.; J. H. Parker, Carpenter Steel Co., Reading Pa.; Martin H. Schmid, Republic Steel Corporation, Massillon, Ohio; Rufus Tucker, Bethlehem Steel Corporation, Bethlehem, Pa.; and H. H. Ziesing, Midvale Co., Nicetown, Pa.

WIRE PRODUCTS ADVISORY COMMITTEE

H. J. Blaser, Seneca Wire & Manufacturing Co., Fostoria, Ohio; John Graham, American Steel & Wire Co., Cleveland Ohio; N. L. Hite, Continental Steel Corporation, Kokomo, Ind.; Ernest C. Low, John A. Roebling's Sons Co., Trenton, N. J.; Henry Roemer, Jr., Pittsburgh Steel Co., Pittsburgh, Pa.; Ford Schusler, Keystone Steel & Wire Co., Peoria, Ill.; C. F. Stone, Atlantic Steel Co., Atlanta, Ga.; E. C. Stout, Wickwire Spencer Steel Co., New York, N. Y.; and G. F. Wright, G. F. Wright Steel & Wire Co., Worcester, Mass.

COLD FINISHED BARS ADVISORY COMMITTEE

W. R. Howell, Bliss & Laughlin, Inc., Harvey, Ill.; V. A. Jevon, Jones & Laughlin Steel Corporation, Pittsburgh, Pa.; W. N. Lynch, Seystone Drawn Steel Co., Spring City, Pa.; E. L. Parker, Columbia Steel & Shafting Co., Pittsburgh, Pa.; J. T. Somers, Wyckoff Drawn Steel Co., Pittsburgh, Pa.; F. C. Young, Union Drawn Steel Division of Republic Steel Corporation, Massillon, Ohio.

Agricultural insecticides, fungicides placed under seasonal regulation

The OPA, May 18 declared retail sales of agricultural insecticides and fungicides to be seasonal and issued Maximum Price Regulation No. 144 to determine the manner in which maximum retail prices are to be established.

The regulation became effective May 18, 1942.

Under its terms, any seller at retail is to determine his selling price of each brand and package size during the calendar month between April 1, 1941, and March 31, 1942, in which he made the largest deliveries of the item to users. He is to determine the cost to him of the goods he delivered to users in that month, then compute the dollar and cents margin between the ceiling price and the cost price.

The margin is to be added to the maximum price that can be charged to the retailer by his supplier under the terms of the general maximum price regulation. The resulting figure is the maximum retail price for the item, and is to remain the maximum price unless changed by special order.

✦ ✦ ✦

Household insecticides added to summer seasonal regulation

Household insecticides May 18 were added by the OPA to the restricted list of summer seasonal goods on which retailers may establish their ceiling prices through methods provided by Maximum Price Regulation No. 142 (Retail Prices for Summer Seasonal Commodities).

These insecticides were inadvertently omitted from the specified list which includes summer apparel, furniture and certain other warm-weather merchandise.

A retailer of these summer seasonal commodities, in order to arrive at his ceiling prices is required to apply last season's percentage mark-up to a cost figure that cannot be more than the highest manufacturer's price in March and may be less.

Sliding scale revoked for ethyl alcohol from molasses

Price Administrator Henderson has revoked the sliding-scale method of pricing ethyl alcohol produced from the fermentation of molasses because, through United States Government purchases of the Cuban crop and resale of such purchases, molasses market price fluctuations have been eliminated.

RAG, WASTE PAPER DEALERS MADE SUBJECT TO LICENSING

Provisions of Supplementary Order No. 5 to the general maximum price regulation, which licenses dealers to sell scrap, waste, and salvage materials to consumers are specifically made applicable to dealers in old rags and waste paper in actions announced May 20 by Price Administrator Henderson.

Amendment No. 4 to Revised Price Schedule No. 30 (Wastepaper) and Amendment No. 2 to Revised Price Schedule No. 47 (Old Rags) were issued to make these schedules conform with the provisions of the general licensing order. All dealers who sell, deliver, or transfer to consumers the commodities covered by these schedules are now automatically licensed.

🌂 🌂 🌂

Forms ready for registry by scrap dealers

Forms for registration of all dealers selling waste, scrap, and salvage material to consumers (and in the case of iron and steel scrap, to consumers or their brokers) were to be mailed to dealers by the end of last week. They also were to be available at all OPA offices by the middle of this week.

The licensing regulation (Supplementary Order No. 5), which automatically licenses such dealers and requires them to register with OPA on or before June 20, 1942, became effective May 20.

All registration statements are to be mailed by dealers to the Bureau of Census, which is acting as collecting and compiling agent for OPA.

PRICING OF SAMPLES, MEMORANDUM GOODS

Emphasis was placed May 18 by Price Administrator Henderson on the recent ruling by OPA that wholesalers and manufacturers who delivered articles as samples, or on memorandum, during March 1942, may not use the prices at which these articles were offered, to price them under the general maximum price regulation.

The samples or memorandum goods, Mr. Henderson pointed out, probably would have been priced higher than goods actually delivered in March.

Cut-rate gas stations given 3-cent margin in curtailed area, but must file prices

Operators of cut-rate filling stations in the gasoline curtailment area who have increased their maximum prices so as to provide a gross selling margin of 3 cents a gallon must file a new statement of their ceiling prices with OPA, Administrator Henderson announced May 19.

Maximum Price Regulation No. 137—Motor Fuel Sold at Service Stations—on May 18 replaced Temporary Price Regulation 11, and holds maximum prices at each service station to the highest prices charged at the station during March. This permanent regulation, as announced April 28, also allowed service stations in 17 East Coast States and the District of Columbia, beginning May 18, to add 0.4 cents per gallon for gasoline and 0.2 cents per gallon for Diesel fuel to the highest March price to offset higher transportation costs.

Amendment 1 to Maximum Price Regulation No 137, effective May 19, continues a provision in the temporary regulation which permitted stations in the gasoline curtailment area, as defined by the War Production Board, to raise maximum prices to the extent necessary to obtain a gross selling margin of three cents a gallon above the price the retailer pays to his supplier for gasoline.

Each station must set prices

The amendment, however, requires a filling station operator taking advantage of this provision to file with OPA within five days a new certified statement of the price he charges for each grade of motor fuel and the maximum price otherwise applicable.

The amendment also defines a term "seller" to make clear that each service station, regardless of ownership, is a unit for pricing purposes and must set its own maximum prices on the basis of its highest March prices.

★ ★ ★

Top prices approved for two new stove models

Prices proposed by the Samuel Stamping and Enameling Co., of Chattanooga, Tenn., for two new gas heating stoves have been approved by Price Administrator Henderson in Order No. 2 under Revised Price Schedule No. 64 (Domestic Cooking and Heating Stoves).

INDUSTRIAL OPERATIONS . . .

Industrial machine production permitted for stock; three new classes regulated

WPB, in a general revision of Limitation Order L-83 regulating distribution of many types of industrial machinery, May 18 added three groups of machinery—dairy, coffee grinding, and food slicing and grinding—to the 14 classes in the original order.

Rigid control of orders, deliveries

While retaining rigid control over acceptance of orders and deliveries by manufacturers, distributors, and all other persons of new, used, and reconditioned machinery, the amended order permits production of new machinery for stock without authorization.

Manufacturers, however, were cautioned by L. S. Greenleaf, Jr., chief of the special industrial machinery branch, that if they produced machinery in anticipation of receiving an approved order, they would run the risk of having the machinery tied up for considerable periods of time.

11 exempted transactions

The amended order lists 11 specific types of exempted transactions, most of them dealing with transfers of used or reconditioned machinery, where inequity or hardship would otherwise result. They deal principally with seizures upon default under conditional sales, transfers in bankruptcy, mergers, leases of plant, shipments for repair, trade-ins, etc. Sales at auction, sheriff's sales and tax sales in liquidation proceedings are restricted unless they are made to a dealer, who is covered by the order.

Only on approved orders

In general, no person may accept an order for machinery covered by the limitation or deliver any machinery except upon an approved order. Approved orders include those for the Army and Navy, certain Government agencies, the governments of the United Nations, Lend-Lease requirements, and any orders bearing an A-9 or higher preference rating issued at any time on an original PD-1, PD-1A, or P-19h certificate or on a PD-3, PD-3A or any rating in the P-19 series issued prior to the effective date of the order.

Manufacturers or distributors who, on the date at which the order affects any specific kind of machinery, had orders on their books which are not in the approved category may apply to WPB for permission to fill them. The Director of Industry Operations will authorize fulfillment of such orders if he deems them necessary to promote the war program. The effective date of the order for the first 14 classes of machinery was April 9 and for the rest, May 18.

Machinery affected by the order follows:

Leather working; tanning; textile machinery and equipment; packaging and labeling; pulp and paper making; paper converting; printing and publishing; bakery; confectionery; beverage bottling; industrial sewing; cotton ginning and delinting; shoe manufacturing; shoe repairing; coffee grinding; food slicing and grinding, and dairy machinery and equipment.

Certain of these classes of machinery are exempted where the value of the individual machine is below a specified minimum.

WPB PROVIDES RENEGOTIATION OF "OPEN-END" CONTRACTS

To promote spread of orders, speed in delivery, and wider use of existing facilities, the War Production Board has issued Directive No. 3, providing for the renegotiation of Government contracts of the "open-end" type used in peacetime.

These contracts require a Government purchase all of its requirements of a specified article from one company over a definite period of time.

In some cases, wartime needs for articles which the Government has agreed to purchase from one company under an "open-end" contract far exceed the amounts contemplated when the contracts were originally signed, and participation of other companies is desirable both to obtain faster delivery and to use facilities of smaller companies which might otherwise go unused.

Most of these contracts have been entered into by Treasury Procurement. Contracts of the War Department, Navy Department, Maritime Commission, or any Government corporation are excluded from the terms of the directive.

Heavy power, steam equipment limited to war, other vital use

The WPB May 18 restricted the manufacture, delivery, and sale of heavy power and steam equipment to orders for defense agencies, United Nations, Lend-Lease, and orders, other than repair and maintenance, rated A-9 or higher.

Only on approved orders

The purpose of the order is to make certain that no power equipment is put into production for any but highly essential purposes. It prevents consumers from using their repair and maintenance ratings to obtain new equipment.

Under the May 18 order (L-117) new heavy power and steam equipment may be manufactured, sold, and delivered only on an approved order.

An approved order is limited to the following:

1. An order accompanied by PD-3A certificate for delivery to the Army, Navy, Maritime Commission, or certain other Government agencies.
2. An order accompanied by a PD-3A certificate from the Government of any of the United Nations.
3. An order placed by any agent of the United States for any of the Lend-Lease countries.
4. Any order bearing a preference rating of A-9 or higher assigned by a PD-3 or PD-3A certificate countersigned prior to May 18, or by a PD-1 or PD-1A certificate or a P-19h order issued at any time.

Other provisions

The restrictions do not apply to the sale or shipment of equipment to regular distributors or dealers to fill approved orders previously received. Nor does the order prohibit the delivery of equipment which was actually in transit at the time of issuance of the order.

Manufacturers of the equipment may extend any preference rating certificate to obtain materials to be incorporated in equipment to be used to fill an approved order.

The order requires equipment manufacturers to file with the WPB on or before June 1, 1942, their production schedules for heavy power and steam equipment and a list of all unfilled orders received before the issuance of the order, whether or not such orders are approved orders.

A list of all equipment regarded as heavy power and steam equipment is set out in schedule A attached to the order.

Production of structural steel shapes to be pushed by curtailing other items

Plans to increase materially the output of structural steel shapes used in shipbuilding were announced May 19 by C. E. Adams, chief, iron and steel branch.

Curtailment of other items made on the same mill equipment will make the increase possible.

Production of structural shapes has not kept pace in recent months with the expanded output of steel plates made possible by the conversion of strip mills to plate production. Therefore, it is necessary to expand shape production in June.

A directive to steel companies to carry out the program has been issued by Director of Industry Operations Knowlson.

*   ★ *

All construction started since April 9 being surveyed

A Nation-wide survey of all construction started since April 9, effective date of Conservation Order L-41, has been inaugurated by the compliance branch, WPB announced May 20.

Home Owners' Loan Corporation is lending the services of approximately 3,000 of its examiners for a detailed check on the degree of observance of the terms of the conservation order, issued last month to assure use of scarce materials only in essential building operations.

Reports of the HOLC examiners will be reviewed by the compliance branch, and appropriate action will be taken in cases of violation of priorities procedures or the provisions of L-41.

This operation is in addition to the compliance survey of the transactions of builders engaged in construction of privately financed war housing projects, currently being made for WPB by some 200 inspectors loaned by the Wage and Hour Division of the Department of Labor.

Two other surveys

Other compliance surveys announced May 20 by WPB include operations of silverware manufacturers, who normally use considerable quantities of copper, and inventories and uses of jewel bearings. The field investigations for both will be carried out by attorney-examiners of the Federal Trade Commission, on behalf of WPB.

WPB HALTS ALL BUILDING FOR PUBLIC'S AMUSEMENT

In a move to free more material and equipment for the war program, WPB on May 23 ordered all construction costing $5,000 or more which is primarily for the amusement of the public to be stopped before June 6. Construction already underway is included.

The May 23 order (L-41-a) exempts only playgrounds for children, strictly temporary construction, and construction costing less than $5,000. To continue construction of any other projects of this type, specific authorization must be obtained from the War Production Board.

Included in the stop order are amusement parks, stadia, race tracks, movie theaters, arenas, baseball parks, and the like.

Other kinds of nonessential construction may be halted by subsequent orders, the WPB warned.

In many instances where construction is stopped, immediate steps will be taken by the WPB to requisition the materials and equipment.

Two firms make restitution, are returned to good standing

Restitutions by two violators of priority regulations have brought about termination of suspension orders issued against them, it was announced May 19 by the Director of Industry Operations.

The companies are Stearns-Mishkin Construction Co., of Washington, D. C., and Enterprise Oil Co., Enterprise, Ala.

*   *

Penn named head of used construction machinery section

Establishment of a used construction machinery section in the construction machinery branch of the Division of Industry Operations was announced May 18 by Joseph F. Ryan, branch chief.

Hamilton O. Penn, former president of the H. O. Penn Machine Co., New York City, has been named head of the new section, which will survey the used construction equipment situation throughout the country and work out plans under which all available machinery can be put to use.

Utilities' excess stocks to be used for electric extensions to housing projects

The WPB has notified electric utilities that it has worked out plans for using materials in excess stocks of utilities in making electric extensions to housing projects.

To conserve critical materials

Henceforth the WPB will not grant authority for the purchase of such material in the open market for use in extensions to housing projects. All such material must come from excess stocks now on hand. These measures were taken because of the shortage of critical materials, especially copper.

As a part of this plan, the WPB power branch has received from electric utilities reports on their excess stocks of wire and other materials. It is preparing a catalogue of such stocks—copper wire, distribution transformers, and meters—which will be furnished to all electric utilities.

When a utility wishes to make an extension of more than 250 feet it must make application to the WPB, as Order P-46 requires WPB approval for extensions in excess of 250 feet. If the WPB approves the application, the utility will be authorized to use materials from its own stock or to acquire them from another utility company.

The Administrative Letter also notified utilities of a new WPB requirement that no new housing project be started prior to obtaining approval for extensions of utility services. These services include not only electric service but also other utilities, including gas and water.

In order to reduce the quantity of critical materials used in making electric, gas, and water extensions to housing projects, the WPB power branch has reduced the allowable weights of materials and distances for such extensions.

The new standards apply to houses on which construction began after April 22, 1942.

. . . . . .

Brass screws illegal for saw handles

Use of brass screws or other copper products to attach handles to blades of saws was declared illegal May 19 in an interpretation of Order M-9-c issued by the Director of Industry Operations. Steel screws are a satisfactory substitute.

Questions and Answers on Priorities

1. Q. Is the Production Requirements Plan something new?

A. The PRP grew out of the old Defense Supplies Rating Plan of more than a year ago. Many companies have been operating under the present plan since its announcement in January, and the number is increasing steadily.

2. Q. How will producers know when they are expected to switch over to the PRP?

A. They are notified, industry by industry, when to make this change. In the meantime, the present tools of the priority system will remain in full use.

3. Q. Will "l" and "m" orders still be issued to companies under the PRP?

A. All ratings assigned under the Production Requirements Plan will be subject to the same controls.

4. Q. Are priority ratings used under the Production Requirements Plan?

A. Under the plan, priority ratings are assigned only to specified materials for specified purposes.

5. Q. What is the steel warehouse plan?

A. The steel warehouse plan is a plan based on a percentage of previous consumption, whereby a quota of steel is allocated to steel warehouses who supply small civilian users.

6. Q. Does the industrial machinery order L-83 affect every kind of industrial machinery?

A. Limitation Order L-83 applies only to industrial machinery included in List A of the order. Machinery affected includes the following: leather working, tanning, textile machinery and equipment; packaging and labeling, pulp and paper making, paper converting, printing and publishing, bakery, confectionery, beverage bottling, industrial sewing, cotton ginning and delinting, shoe manufacturing, shoe repairing, and in the revision of May 18th (L-83 as amended) 3 new groups of machinery: dairy, coffee grinding, and food slicing and grinding were added to the list. Certain of these classes of machinery are exempted from the restrictions where the value of the individual machine is below a specified minimum, such as industrial sewing machinery, for example, on orders for a single machine of a value below $200.

PRIORITY ACTIONS			*From May 7 *Through May 20		
Subject	Order No.	Related form	Issued	Expiration date	Rating
Air conditioning machinery and equipment:					
a. Industrial and commercial:					
1. Forbids new installations except for war and essential civilian needs, and restricts production and sale.	L-38		5-15-42		A-9 or higher.
Aircraft:					
a. Material for production:					
1. Allows A-1-a rating to be extended for necessary operating supplies.	Amend. No. 1 to P-109 as amended.		5-8-42		A-1-a.
Antifreeze:					
a. To restrict production:					
Automobiles—Passenger and light Trucks:	L-51		5-14-42		
a. Material for production of replacement parts:					
1. Further production restrictions.	Supplementary order		5-5-42		
2. Change of expiration date of production.	L-4-c, Amend. No. 1.		5-8-42		
Bicycles:					
a. To permit the sale of new adult bicycles to specified Government agencies or authorized persons acquiring them for export or use in a foreign country.	Suppl. order L-52-a, Amend. No. 2.		5-13-42		
Cashew nuts:					
a. Restriction on importation to insure maximum extraction of oil from cashew nut shells.	M-147		5-9-42		
b. Prohibits the use of cashew nut shell oil in the manufacture of brake linings except for Army and Navy.	M-6, Amend. No. 1		5-14-42		
Chemicals—To conserve supply and direct distribution:					
a. Acrylonitrile:					
1. Complete allocation prohibits delivery or use except with specific authorization of the Director of Industry Operations.	M-153 Amend. No. 2		5-14-42		
b. Chlorine:					
1. Removes the reports requirement.	M-19 as amend.	PD-190	5-1-42		
Cocoa:					
a. To restrict amount of cocoa beans that may be ground, processed, or sold.	M-145	PD-473	5-11-42		
b. Restricts amount that may be ground or processed in May and June.	Suppl. Order M-145-a.	PD-473	5-11-42		
Coffee:					
a. Restrictions on roasters inventory to a 2 months' supply.	M-135 Amend. 1		5-8-42		
Construction:					
a. Permits building by Government roads departments of essential public roads by monthly reports of material requirements under L-41, without individual authorization of each project.	Authority No. L-41-600.	Pr-46 (Public Road).	5-8-42		
b. Makes 3 minor changes in text of L-41; "defense housing" changed in 2 instances to "war housing," designation place where PD-200 & PD-200A forms may be filed including phrases as may be prescribed, omission of preference to P-115.	L-41, Amend. to Schedule A.		5-16-42		
Construction equipment:					
a. Restrictions on the sale and production of power cranes and shovels.	L-82	PD-445, 446	5-2-42		
b. Restrictions on sale and production of rubber-tired construction equipment.	L-82-a	PD-445, 446	5-2-42		
Cooking appliances—domestic:					
a. Domestic electric ranges, forbids the sale or distribution except on a preference rating of A-9 or higher or by specific authorization.	Suppl. order L-23-b	PD-192	5-2-42		
b. To "concentrate" production for war, orders all end to manufacture of domestic cooking appliances by latter films after July 31, and permits limited number of light weight models to be produced by smaller films, also designated 29 "labor shortage areas" in 5 States.	Suppl. order L-23-c		5-14-42		
Copper:					
a. Copper and copper base alloys:					
1. Limits shipments to ratings of A-1-c or higher unless specific authorization is given for a lower rated shipment.	Amend. to M-9-a as amend. 1-7-42 and 2-6-42.		5-7-42		A-1-k or higher.

Subject	Order No.	Related form	Issued	Expiration date	Rating
Copper—Continued.					
a. Copper and copper base alloys—Con.					
2. Prohibits use in all but essential operating parts of motor vehicles.	L–108		5–6–42		
b. Copper scrap, copper base alloy scrap:					
1. Amended to include "ingots" and provide for monthly reports from foundries on PD–459.	Suppl. order M–9–b as amend. 5–9–42.	PD–121, 130, 228, 459.	5–9–42		
c. To facilitate sales of frozen brass mill or wire mill products to brass or wire mills without WPB approval.	Amend. to M–9–c as amend.		5–15–42		
d. Forbids use of brass screws or other copper products to attach handles to blades of saws.	M–9–c as amend. Int. No. 1.		5–19–42		
e. Forbids manufacture of any article omitted from List A and A–1 if it contains copper or copper products where substitution is practicable.	M–9–c, Int. No. 3		5–19–42		
f. Material for repair, maintenance, or operating of mills which roll, draw or extrude copper or copper base alloys:					
1. A–1–c rating to suppliers to replenish inventories when they have filled orders bearing an A–1–c or higher rating.	Amend. to P–106		5–14–42	6–30–42	A–1–c.
Electric lamps and shades (portable):					
a. Holds that restrictions of L–33 do not apply to repairing, recovering, retrimming or rallning of lamp shades in which no new metal frame is used.	L–33, Int. No. 1		5–15–42		
Electroplating and anodising equipment:					
a. Controls production, sale, and delivery to orders rated A–1–j or higher.	L–110	PD–1A	5–11–42	Until revoked.	
Exports of critical materials:					
a. Giving preference in exports for Latin America and assuring delivery of listed export materials in required delivery dates.	M–148		5–12–42		
b. Removes farm equipment from materials listed in Schedule A of the order.	M–148, Amend. 1		5–15–42		
Farm machinery:					
a. Provides shipments to specified countries up to 112 percent of net shipping weight of total quantity of those countries in 1940, listing countries used in determining the percentage quota.	L–26, Amend. 3	PD–388, 387	5–18–42		
b. Controls disposition of surplus inventories of iron and steel held by manufacturers in excess of production quotas.	Suppl. order L–26–b	PD–478, 479	5–15–42		A–1–k or higher.
Feminine apparel order:					
a. Includes fur coats in restrictions of original order with other minor changes.	L–85, Amend. 2		5–20–42		
Feminine lingerie and certain other garments:					
a. To prohibit the use of unnecessary yardage in women's and children's lingerie.	L–116		5–9–42		
Ferrous material:					
a. Assigns A–1–c rating for deliveries for ferrous material to be used in manufacture of nonmetal containers for food products.	P–79, Amend. 1		5–18–42		
Fire protective equipment:					
a. Permits the manufacture of carbon dioxide extinguishers according to specifications of the Armed Services and Maritime Commission, restricting delivery to orders rated A–1–j or higher; also permits manufacturing of brass fire hose couplings for Maritime Commission.	L–89, Amend. 3		5–21–42		
Fuel—motor:					
a. Reduction in deliveries of gasoline 17 Eastern States and the District of Columbia, similar 50 percent cut in deliveries effective June 1 in Washington and Oregon States, and complete cut in deliveries for race cars and facing motorboats in restricted areas.	L–70, Amend. 2	PD–367	5–13–42		
b. Restrictions on deliveries for use in space and central heating, coal spraying, and the operation of domestic and commercial water heating equipment.	L–56, as amended		5–13–42	Until revoked.	
Freight cars:					
a. Provides that producers may accept deliveries of parts and materials from suppliers if they are not subject to other rated orders.	Suppl. order L–97–a–1, Amend. 1.		5–14–42		

(Continued on page 26)

WPB formalizes procedure for ordering machine tools allocated to foreign countries

A directive formalizing the procedure to be followed in the placing of orders for machine tools allocated to foreign countries was issued May 20 by Donald M. Nelson, WPB Chairman.

Monthly deliveries apportioned

Under the provisions of General Preference Order E–1–b, previously announced, each producer's monthly deliveries of each size of each type of machine tool is apportioned, 75 percent to Service purchasers (Army, Navy, Maritime Commission) and 25 percent to other purchasers.

The latter 25 percent is divided among foreign purchasers and essential industries in this country and Canada, and scheduled for delivery in accordance with preference ratings. Tool orders for foreign purchasers are given a blanket A–1–a preference rating and no preference rating certificates are required. The percentage allocated to foreign purchasers as a group is determined by the machine tools subcommittee of WPB. Within these allocated quantities the Office of Lend-Lease Administration will make recommendations to the machine tools subcommittee with respect to the apportionment of machine tools among various foreign countries.

Use of tin, terne plate limited to few specific items

Use of tin and terne plate, except by special authorization, was limited to a few specific items by the Director of Industry Operations May 18 in a revision of Supplementary Order M–21–c.

Permitted uses

The permitted uses are:

For cans, as authorized by Conservation Order M–81; for closures, as authorized by Conservation Order M–104; for baking pans for institutions and commercial bakers, hot-dipped tin plate up to 1.25 pounds per base box and electrolytic plate up to 0.50 pound; for dairy equipment, hot-dipped tin plate up to 3.30 pounds per base box; for cheese vats, dipped plate up to 11 pounds per base box; for gas meters, dipped plate up to 3.30 pounds, electrolytic up to 0.50, short ternes up to 1.30 and long ternes to 4 pounds; for oil lanterns, short ternes and long ternes with the same coating limits, and for textile spinning cylinders and card screens, dipped plate of the basic 1.25 limitation.

Farm equipment makers given greater leeway in determining types for export

The WPB May 18 modified its restrictions on exports of farm machinery and equipment to allow manufacturers greater discretion in determining the types of equipment to be exported.

Under Limitation Order L–26, manufacturers were permitted to export up to 80 percent of each class or type of equipment exported by them in 1940 and use in the production of attachments and repair parts for export up to 150 percent of the amount of materials used to produce these items for export in 1940.

These provisions are replaced by amendment No. 3 to this order, issued May 18, which authorizes manufacturers to ship to foreign countries, except Canada, and to United States territories and possessions up to 112 percent of the net shipping weight of the total quantity of those countries in 1940. The amendment lists the countries used in determining this percentage quota. Shipments to these and other countries will be regulated through the operations of the Board of Economic Warfare and the Office of Lend-Lease Administration.

The amendment sets up quotas on various types of equipment for shipment to Canada.

. . . ..

Construction lumber for completion of vital war housing

Director of Industry Operations Knowlson announced May 22 that clause (b) (1) (iv) of the Construction Lumber Freeze Order (L–121) would be invoked to take care of the needs of war housing projects, where vital need for completion of such projects is determined by the WPB and the various housing agencies concerned.

The clause permits any producer to sell, ship, or deliver construction lumber upon the specific authorization of the Director of Industry Operations on Form PD–423.

Four new housing critical areas

Four new areas were added May 20 to the Defense Housing Critical Area list. They are: Camp Atterbury, Ind., and Marion, Ohio; Illiopolis, Ill.; and Hondo, Tex.

PRIORITY ACTIONS	*From May 7 *Through May 20

(Continued from page 25)

Subject	Order No.	Related form	Issued	Expiration date	Rating
Glass:					
a. Container and closure simplification order:					
1. Standardizing certain glass container sizes and weights specified in accompanying schedules A and B for liquor and malt beverage bottles.	L–103		5–11–42		
Golf clubs:					
a. Permits use of completely fabricated plastic ferrules and caps on hand.	L–93, Amend. No. 2		5–12–42	5–31–42	
Heat-treating furnaces:					
a. Extension until June 30 of P–74	P–74, Ext. No. 1		5–11–42	6–30–42	A–1–e.
Incendiary units:					
a. Prohibit production and distribution of incendiary bombs, for use as "demonstrators," by civilian group.	L–115	PD–449	5–7–42		
Industrial machinery:					
a. Addition of 3 groups of machinery—dairy, coffee grinding and food slicing and grinding to 14 classes of original order.	L–83 as amend		5–18–42	Until revoked.	
Istle:					
a. Restricts the use of raw istle in brushes, twine, and cordage, permits use for padding on orders rated higher than A–2.	M–138		5–9–42		
Jute and jute products:					
a. Formalizing telegraphic restrictions on processing of jute for manufacture of carpet yarns in April.	M–70, Amend. No. 2		5–1–42		
b. Restrictions on use of jute in manufacture of rugs, carpets, and linoleum for civilian use.	M–70, Amend. No. 3	PD–222–B	4–30–42		A–2; A–3.
c. Restrictions imposed by amend. 3 to M–70 relaxed by telegram, permit wool carpet and rug manufacturers to use jute and jute carpet yarns in process in their mills.	M–70, amend. No. 3, relaxed by telegram.		5–8–42		
Kitchen and household articles:					
a. Removes restrictions on coat hangers made of wood or paperboard if sole source material content is a steel wire hook, further restrictions on use of joining hardware.	L–30, Amend. No. 2		5–9–42		
Lauric acid oils:					
a. Cocoanut oil, babassu oil, palm kernel oil and other high lauric acid oils:					
1. Permits food manufacturer to use in June and July, 50 percent of amount be used in corresponding month of 1941, and in August and September 25 percent.	M–60, Amend. No. 1		5–11–42		
Lumber—construction, softwood:					
a. 60-day freeze on sales and deliveries by large producers, except to meet the needs of the Army, Navy, and Maritime Commission.	L–121	PD–3, 3A, or 4, 423.	5–13–42		
Machine tools:					
a. Provides that purchase orders should include all information needed by the producer to enable him to schedule the tools for production.	E–1–b, Int. No. 1		5–15–42		
Metal household furniture:					
a. Permits use of iron and steel in manufr. inventories which consist of parts so processed as to be worthless for any purpose other than metal household furniture.	L–62, Amend. 2		5–14–42		
Metal plastering bases and accessories:					
a. Removes permission to produce items for war contracts in addition to established quotas.	L–59, Amend. 1		5–16–42		
Mines:					
a. Eliminates special reference to gold and silver mines from original order.	Amend. 2 to P–56 as amend. 3–2–42.		5–15–42		
Mining machinery and equipment:					
a. Addition explosives and explosive equipment to list of mining machinery and equipment in Schedule A of the order.	P–56, Amend. No. 1		4–28–42	Varies	
Molasses:					
a. Removes restrictions on deliveries from producers and importers to primary distributors (bulk wholesalers).	Amend. No. 1 to M–54 as amend. 3–27–42	FB 155, 157, 158	5–11–42		
Naphthenics and naphthenic acid:					
a. Placed under strict use and allocation control.	M–142	PD–438, 439	5–5–42		A–18 or higher.

Subject	Order No.	Related form	Issued	Expiration date	Rating
Office machinery: a. Modifies restrictions on distribution of various types of new office machinery to enable dealers to return new equipment to manufacturers willing to accept it.	L–54–b, Amend. 2		5–8–42		
Pencils: a. Prohibits use of finishing materials containing any pigments other than carbon black, lamp black, bone black, white, domestic earth colors and ultramarine blue.	L–113, Amend. 1		5–15–42		
Petroleum: a. Extension of preference rating P–98: 1. Extends effective date of order from issued March 14, 1942, to July 1, 1942.	P–98		5–16–42	7–1–42	
Phosphate rock: a. Removes inventory restrictions to permit consumers to take advantage of any available transportation facilities.	M–149		5–11–42	Until revoked.	
Plumbing and heating: a. Removal of restrictions on iron body, brass, or bronze valves for use in Navy or Maritime Commission Vessels.	L–42, Schedule 1, Amend. 1.		5–16–42		
b. Removal of restrictions on gray cast, malleable iron, and brass and bronze pipe fittings for use in Navy and Maritime Commission Vessels.	L–42, Schedule 2, Amend. 1.		5–16–42		
Power: a. Heavy power and steam equipment: 1. Heavy power and steam equipment may be manufactured, sold and delivered only on approved order.	L–117	PD–3A	5–15–42		A–9.
Power—electric: a. To provide for the curtailment in the United States.	L–94	PD–424	5– 1–42	Until revoked.	
Project: a. Material for use in construction road projects may be assigned ratings under Preference Rating Order P–19–e.	P–19–e, Amend. 2, (relaxes restrictions of amendment No. 1).	PD–100	5– 9–42		
Quartz crystals: a. To control use for specified purposes.	M–146	PD–484, 485.	5–18–42		
Railroad equipment: a. Makes clear that freight car producers may accept deliveries of parts and materials from suppliers if they are not subject to other rated orders.	L–97, A–1, Amend. 1.		5–13–42		
Rail and rail joints—used: a. Permits shipments up to 10 tons during any calendar month.	L–88, Amend. 1		5–18–42		
Rayon yarn: a. Grants hosiery manufacturers operating 5-gage machines preferences in deliveries of the fine denier sizes from the amount of rayon viscose and cuprammonium yarn set aside for hosiery.	Suppl. order M–37–c, Amend No. 1.		5–15–42		
Safety equipment: a. Prohibits use of specified scarce materials and limits the use of others.	L–114		5–5–42		A–2 or higher.
Sperm oil: a. Complete allocation control.	M–40, Amend. 1	PD–481	5–16–42		
Spices: a. Restrictions on distribution of black and white pepper, pimento (allspice), cassia (cinnamon), cloves, ginger, nutmeg, and mace.	M–127		5–6–42		
b. Fixes percentage quotas for deliveries.	M–127–a		5–8–42		
Steel: a. Alloy iron and alloy steel: 1. Sets monthly melting schedule to be issued by the Director of Industry Operations, further restrictions on metal or delivery.	Suppl. Order M–21–a, Amend. No. 3.	PD–391, 391–a, 440.	5–11–42		
b. Warehouses and dealers: 1. Forbids deliveries by warehouses on ratings lower than A–10 except in certain specified cases, inventory restrictions also imposed.	Suppl. Order M–21–b, Amend. No. 4.	PD–83–a, 83–f rev., 83–g.	5–4–42	Until revoked.	A–1–k; A–3.
Steel and iron: a. Limits the use of tin and terne plate to a few specific items, except by subordination.	Suppl. Order M–21–e as amend. 5–16–42.		5–16–42		
Supplier's inventory order: a. Removal of tires, tubes, and automotive parts from supplies covered by L–63.	L–63, Exemption No. 3.		5–12–42		
b. Exempts seeds, plants, livestocks, fertilizer, clocks, watches, sporting goods, furniture, pottery, china or glassware from restrictions of the order.	L–63, Int. 1	PD–1A	5–15–42		

(Continued on page 29)

Alien Property Custodian takes over two firms, five copyrights to further war effort

Leo T. Crowley, Alien Property Custodian announced May 20 that he had taken over the following assets of foreign nationals:

The 25 shares, representing 100 percent control of the capital stock of Steel Union, Inc., a California corporation organized in 1934 to act as selling agent for Stahlunion-Export, the export subsidiary of Vereinigte Stahlwerke, A. G. Both of the latter companies have their principal offices in Dusseldorf, Germany. (Vesting Order No. 7)

Five copyrights, copyright applications and copyright claims owned by German nationals. (Vesting Order No. 8)

Five hundred thirty-five thousand shares of the capital stock of American Bosch Corporation, representing 77.24 percent stock interest in that corporation, presently deposited with City Bank Farmers Trust Co. of New York as agent for a voting trustee. (Vesting Order No. 9)

The Bosch action, Mr. Crowley added, implies no criticism of the present management or directorate of the American Bosch Corporation, which have made an excellent record in the war effort.

★ ★

Petroleum orders adjusted to clarify export provisions

Because the export of supplies for the petroleum industry is now controlled by the Foreign Petroleum Material Rating Plan, the petroleum industry conservation orders, M–68 and M–68–c, have been amended to make it clear that their provisions apply only in the United States, United States territories and possessions, and the Dominion of Canada.

Use of equipment as security exempt from plumbing order

Limitation Order L–79, which freezes the sale and shipment of most types of plumbing and heating equipment, is not intended to limit the use of the equipment covered as security for a loan, it was announced May 22.

WPB to give high priority to fabrics for work clothes, restrict cloth per garment

Representatives of the work clothing industry were informed May 20 by WPB, at a meeting of the industry's advisory committee with WPB clothing officials, that two orders to be issued soon will grant a high priority rating to certain fabrics used in the manufacture of work clothes and will restrict the use of cloth and buttons in such garments.

The fabric order will specify certain garments as work clothes and the priority rating for fabrics to be used in making such garments will not be available for the same fabrics for use in other garments.

Work clothes will consist of the following: Waistband overalls, or dungarees, bib overalls, overall jumpers or coats, blanket-lined overall jumpers or coats, one-piece work suits, work pants, work breeches, cossack jackets, work shirts, work aprons, oil slickers, men's lined work coats, and white surgical garments for health and safety.

The fabrics to be made available for these garments in specified constructions (that is, weight or thread count) are denims, chambrays, coverts, whipcords, cottonades, shirting flannel, blanket linings, moleskins, corduroy, suedes, poplins, drills, twills, jeans, print cloth yarn fabrics, and sheetings.

★

Uses of quartz crystals curbed

Strict control over the products for which quartz crystals may be used was ordered May 18 by the Director of Industry Operations.

Order M–146 provides that, except for specific authorization, they may be used only for these purposes:

Products for use in implements of war, as defined in the order, produced for the Army, Navy, or other Government agencies or Lend-Lease; oscillators and filters for use in radio systems operated by Federal agencies or commercial airlines; and telephone resonators.

Purchasers must certify to the fabricator of products containing quartz crystals that the products will be used only for these purposes.

Holders of 25 pounds or more of quartz crystals, or 10 pieces in a manufactured form not incorporated in a mounting, as of May 18, must report to the WPB by June 20, on Form PD–484. Consumers also must report monthly on this form by the 20th of the month.

PAJAMA STYLES

Suggestions for conserving cloth in the manufacture of men's pajamas were discussed at a meeting May 18 of WPB clothing officials and the men's clothing industry advisory committee.

★ ★ ★

Feminine apparel order modified to include fur coats

The feminine apparel order (L–85) has been amended to bring fur coats within the restrictions of the original order and to make a number of other relatively minor changes.

A special maximum measurement schedule has been set up for "girl stouts" and "teen-age stouts."

Imported wearing apparel for women and children arriving in United States customs after June 1 must comply with all restrictions of the order.

The original order exempted a person of "unusual height" from the size restrictions. The new amendment (No. 2) defines such a person as one who is 5 feet 8½ inches or more in height without shoes.

A garment manufactured as a certain size must be sold as that size.

Other changes

Other changes follow:

1. Double back yokes may be used on knitted fabrics to eliminate the possibility of a knitted shoulder pulling out of shape. Only single yokes were permitted before.
2. Bias sleeves of plaid material may be used if they are set-in sleeves.
3. Measurements for slacks have been increased ½ inch in width and 1 inch in length on fabrics other than wool to allow for shrinkage.
4. Toddlers' wool coats in sizes 3 and 4 are brought under the order. They were formerly exempt.
5. Robes for the judiciary are exempt from the measurement restrictions.

Tin, lead scrap order modified

Minor revisions in Order M–72, governing tin and lead scrap, were announced May 18 by the Director of Industry Operations.

The first change specifies that on or before the 10th of each month dealers must file with the Bureau of Mines reports on Form PD–249. Consumers must file similarly, using Form PD–254.

The second authorizes the Director of Industry Operations to issue specific directions as to shipments of scrap or materials produced from scrap.

Makers of nonmetal food containers get A–1–c for ferrous materials

In order to speed the manufacture of nonmetal containers to be used for food products, the WPB has assigned a rating of A–1–c for deliveries of ferrous material to be used in such containers.

The order (Amendment No. 1 to Preference Rating Order P–79) was effective on May 16. Manufacturers of nonmetal food containers formerly had an A–7 rating, which proved too low to secure necessary nails and wire.

Without the high rating granted by the amendment boxes, hampers, and crates, necessary for harvesting of many crops, could not be built.

The amendment sets up a procedure for application of the higher preference rating to deliveries of ferrous material to which preference ratings have already been assigned under P–79, by notification to suppliers.

Metal container users warned to use substitutes for steel

Users of metal containers were warned May 19 by the WPB containers branch that an urgently critical situation exists in steel, and that immediate and extensive use of substitutes for steel containers, particularly drums, must be undertaken.

Even though substitute materials may be more expensive and less satisfactory, their use may be the means of keeping such companies in business. Substitution of materials not needed in war production should be used wherever possible, but even more critical materials which are less critical than steel can be used where necessary.

The containers branch pointed out that it is quite possible that steel container users may soon be forced to suspend operations until they are able to develop suitable containers which do not use steel.

★ ★ ★

Marcus to leave WPB

H. Stanley Marcus, chief of the WPB clothing section, is resigning to return to his business, the Neiman-Marcus Co. of Dallas, Tex. He plans to leave about June 1 but in any event will serve until his successor has been appointed and is on the job.

New industry advisory committees

The Bureau of Industry Advisory Committees, WPB, has announced the formation of the following new industry advisory committees:

ANTIFRICTION BEARING INDUSTRY

Government presiding officer—George C. Brainard, chief, tools branch.

Members:

S. F. Wollmar, executive vice president, SKF Industries, Inc., Philadelphia, Pa.; H. O. K. Meister, general manager, Hyatt Bearing Division, General Motors Corporation, Harrison, N. J.; A. C. Davis, president, Marlin-Rockwell Corporation, Jamestown, N. Y.; Fred Hughes, general manager, New Departure Division, General Motors Corporation, Bristol, Conn.; William E. Unnstattd, president, Timken Roller Bearing Co., Canton, Ohio; F. O. Burkholder, vice president, Ahlberg Bearing Co., Chicago, Ill.; S. A. Strickland, president, Bower Roller Bearing Co., Detroit, Mich.; R. B. Nichols, general manager, Bantam Bearings Corporation, South Bend, Ind.; G. A. Strom, president, Strom Steel Ball Co., Chicago, Ill.; C. H. Talcott, vice president and general manager, The Torrington Co., Torrington, Conn.; R. F. Moyer, vice president, Standard Machinery Co., Providence, R. I.; George Carleton, vice president, Nice Ball Bearing Co., 30th and Nicetown Lane, Philadelphia, Pa.

BRASS & BRONZE FOUNDRIES INDUSTRY

Government presiding officer—H. O. King, chief of the copper branch.

Members:

B. J. Flaherty, president, Johnson Bronze Co., Newcastle, Pa.; Damon Wack, assistant to president, National Bearing Metals, 230 Park Avenue, New York, N. Y.; L. M. Nestlebush, vice president, Falcon Bronze Co., 218 South Phelps Street, Youngstown, Ohio; N. H. Schwenk, vice president, Cramp Brass & Iron Foundries Division, Baldwin Locomotive Works, Paschall Station, Philadelphia, Pa.; J. P. Jefferis, Janney Cylinder Co., Philadelphia, Pa.; William C. Hardy, secretary, Wm. A. Hardy & Sons Co., 133 Water Street, Fitchburg, Mass.; W. V. Storm, Western Brass Works, 1441 Naud Street, Los Angeles, Calif.; W. C. Peare, treasurer, E. A. Williams & Son, 111 Plymouth Street, Jersey City, N. J.

BRASS AND BRONZE INGOT MAKERS INDUSTRY

Government presiding officer—H. O. King, chief of the copper branch.

Members:

L. Chapman, president, H. Kramer & Co., 1347 South Kedzie Avenue, Chicago, Ill.; Leo Halpern, manager, Federated Metals Division, American Smelting & Refining Co., 120 Broadway, New York, N. Y.; George Avril, proprietor, G. A. Avril Smelting Works, Este Avenue and B. & O. Railroad, Cincinnati, Ohio; Melvin Butter, president, Harry Butter & Co., Inc., 151 Mount Vernon Street, Dorchester, Mass.; W. J. Bullock, president, W. J. Bullock, Inc., Box 662, Birmingham, Ala.; David B. Rosenthal, general manager, Eastern Iron and Metal Co., 2300 East 11th Street, Los Angeles, Calif.

COFFEE INDUSTRY

Government presiding officer—John N. Curlett, chief, imported foods and desserts section, food supply branch.

Members:

Russell E. Atha, Folger Coffee Co., Kansas City, Mo.; Frank W. Buxton, American Coffee Corporation, New York, N. Y.; R. H. Cardwell, Jr., O. W. Antrim & Sons, Richmond, Va.; J. K. Evans, General Foods Corporation, New York, N. Y.; Albert Hanemann, Brazilian Warrant Co., New Orleans, La.; William Whitney Pinney, New York Coffee & Sugar Exchange, New York, N. Y.; Traver Smith, Standard Brands, Inc., New York, N. Y.; George R. Mueller, The C. D. Kenny Co., Baltimore, Md.; P. R. Nelson, Ruffner McDowell & Burch, Inc., New York, N. Y.; James M. O'Connor, Green Coffee Assn., of New York City, N. Y.; P. R. Phillips, W. R. Grace & Co., San Francisco, Calif.; George C. Thierbach, Jones-Thierbach Co., San Francisco, Calif.; John H. Wilkins, Sr., John H. Wilkins Co., Washington, D. C.

FOUNTAIN PEN AND MECHANICAL PENCIL INDUSTRY

Government presiding officer—M. D. Moore, section chief of the consumers' durable goods branch.

Members:

Ellery A. Boss, president, A. T. Cross Pencil Co., Providence, R. I.; A. G. Frost, president, Esterbrook Steel Pen Mfg. Co., Camden, N. J.; Julius M. Kahn, president, David Kahn, Inc., North Bergen, N. J.; W. K. Kerr, president, W. K. Kerr Pen Co., Tulsa, Okla.; Clinton E. Marshall, Marshall and Meier, New York, N. Y.; Craig R. Sheafer, president, W. A. Sheaffer Co., Fort Madison, Iowa; E. J. Stern,

president, Scripto Manufacturing Co., Atlanta, Ga.; Lawrence P. Keller, president, Weidlich Pen Co., Cincinnati, Ohio; W. F. Wallace, sales manager, Inkograph Co., New York, N. Y.; Frank Waterman, president, L. E. Waterman Co., New York, N. Y.; Thomas H. Wright, president, Rite-Rite Manufacturing Co., Downers Grove, Ill.

OVER-ALL CONSTRUCTION MACHINERY INDUSTRY

Government presiding officer—Joseph F. Ryan, chief, construction machinery branch.

Members:

P. H. Birckhead, general sales manager, Bucyrus, Erie Co., South Milwaukee, Wis.; Ralph E. Boyd, vice president, Galion Iron Works & Mfg. Co., Road Machinery, Galion, Ohio; Neal Higgins, government sales manager, International Harvester Co., 180 North Michigan Avenue, Chicago, Ill.; John H. Jay, president, Quickway Truck Shovel Co., 4150 Josephine Street, Denver, Colo.; J. F. Richardson, secretary, The Buffalo Springfield Roller Co., Springfield, Ohio; Carl H. Frink, owner, Frink Snow-Plows, 205-227 Webb Street, Clayton, N. Y.; Lion Gardiner, vice president, Jaeger Machine Co., 560 West Spring Street, Columbus, Ohio; Thomas W. Rosholt, president, Rosco Mfg. Co., 3128 Snelburg Avenue, Minneapolis, Minn.; Harold G. Smith, executive engineer, The Buda Co., Harvey, Ill.; C. B. Smythe, vice president, Thew Shovel Co., Lorain, Ohio; Larry B. West, owner, The Simplicity System Co., Chattanooga, Tenn.

PRIORITY ACTIONS

*From May 7
*Through May 20

(Continued from page 27)

Subject	Order No.	Related form	Issued	Expiration date	Rating
Tin: a. Tin-coated and alloy tubes—collapsible: 1. No retailer shall sell Class III tube to purchaser without one used tube of any kind for each Class III tube sold.	M-115, Amend. 1		5-11-42		
Tin plate and terne plate: a. Increases use of cans which may be produced from tinplate.	M-81, Amend. 2 (supersedes telegraphic permissions).		4-30-42		
Tin scrap: a. Lead and tin; and alloys thereof: 1. Announces forms to be used by dealers and consumers. Authorizes Director of Industry Operations to issue specific directions as to shipments of scrap or material produced from scrap.	M-72 (as amend. 5-18-42).	PD-249, 254	5-18-42		
Toys and games: A. Clarified meaning of term "raw material form" in the order.	L-81, Int. 1		5-8-42		
Zinc: a. Conserve supply and direct distribution of zinc: 1. Limits consumer's and distributor's supply of zinc. Lists forms to be used by both.	M-11 (as amend. 5-1-42).	PD-450, 94A	5-1-42	Until revoked.	
b. General preference order: 1. To conserve supply and direct distribution of zinc oxide and zinc dust.	M-11-s	PD-62	5-1-42	Until revoked.	
c. Supplemental order: 1. Determines amount of metallic zinc, zinc oxide, and zinc dust to be set aside by producer for month of May.	M-11-k		5-1-42		

(Lack of space forbids printing Suspension Orders this week. They will appear next week.)

TOP CARTOONISTS DRAW

FOR YOUR PUBLICATION

VICTORY PRESENTS, on facing page, a second group of 4 drawings by well-known American artists who have volunteered their talents to help emphasize, in their own medium, matters vital to winning the war. VICTORY will print four drawings by these and other artists each week. Permission to reprint is hereby granted. Mats in two-column size (larger than appears here) are available weekly. Requests to be put on the mailing list regularly, or for individual mats should be addressed to Distribution Section, Division of Information, Office for Emergency Management, 2743 Temporary R, Washington, D. C.

Production drive spread to shipyards, machine-tool plants of Nation

With more than 750 American war plants now engaged in the War Production Drive, the War Production Board is now conducting its own drive to get labor-management committees established in all shipyards and in all machine-tool factories.

Urgent need for ships, machine tools

A number of shipyards and machine-tool works have successful labor-management committees and their War Production Drives have increased the output of these war essentials.

Since the need for ships and machine tools is one of the most pressing problems of the war economy, War Production Drive Headquarters decided that extension of the labor-management plan to these plants was urgent.

Official plan books and a report book in which successes of the labor-management committees have been recorded are being sent to all shipyards and machine-tool works, together with a statement of posters, streamers, literature, etc. available for War Production Drives.

Wisconsin plant doubles production

A number of recent successes in other than shipyards and tool shops were made public by War Production Drive Headquarters this week.

The committee at the Sheboygan, Wis., plant of Vollrath Co. reported that although its daily production of 3,000 items of war material had been considered the maximum, after the committee was formed production was increased to 6,000 units a day.

The committee of the Westinghouse Manufacturing Co. at East Pittsburgh, Pa., reported that shipments for the first quarter of 1942 were 60 percent ahead of the corresponding period in 1941. The number of employees had increased 24.4 percent and the pay roll had been increased 48.3 percent.

The Philco Corporation, Philadelphia, reported that production in the metal division had increased more than 4,000 units since April 1.

The committee of the Great Lakes Steel Corporation reported that Blast Furnace B at Ecorse, Mich., broke a world's record by producing 43,478 tons during March.

Other achievements

The committee of the Thompson Machine Products, Inc., Cleveland, Ohio, telegraphed:

March production of war materials broke company records. Aircraft output alone exceeded that of the entire year 1939. Actual production first half of April exceeded same period March by 26 percent. New monthly records are definitely ahead with continued team work.

Officials at War Production Drive Headquarters expressed the opinion that, in view of these and similar records of achievement, there would be no difficulty in extending the drive widely among shipyards and machine-tool plants.

GIVE IT YOUR BEST!

POSTERS in the style pictured above, colored red, white, and blue, are obtainable on request to Distribution Section, Division of Information, Office for Emergency Management, 430 Delaware Avenue, Washington, D. C., in the following sizes: 56'' x 40'', 28¼'' x 40'', 28½'' x 20'', 14'' x 20'', and 10'' x 14''. Two-inch stickers, 6 to a sheet, in the same style are available also at that address. Two-column mats of the poster are available on request to Production Section, Division of Information, OEM, 2743 Tempo R, Washington, D. C.

Drive booklet reports progress toward production goal

War Production Drives are increasing production in American plants, War Production Drive Headquarters reported in a booklet mailed May 19 to Government contractors and labor-management committees.

The report booklet reviews a few drives "chosen either because their reports were in soon enough to include before the book went to press, or because they had some idea or suggestion that has worked, is working, and might work for you."

Charts take on deeper meaning

The booklet tells how production was increased at an upstate New York plant of the Symington-Gould Corporation. The plant was new and the labor-management committee set to work to get the men working together. The booklet tells how they did it:

A completed tank made with Symington-Gould castings was driven through the plant. The results were electrifying. When the workers got a glimpse of the finished fighting machine they realized the vital importance of those peculiar-shaped castings they had been making!

They talked and studied the tank excitedly—pointed with justified pride to the parts they had made—realized that they were really helping to win the war.

From then on, posters, suggestion boxes, production charts had a deeper meaning. Competition between departments became keener, any lagging department got a proper needling from the other departments it held up, production was on the upswing.

The Q4V campaign

The booklet also described the Q4V campaign in the Cleveland (Ohio) Westinghouse plant. Q4V is an abbreviation of the slogan "Quicker for Victory." One of the most successful stunts was the use of two big cardboard figures. One was a heroic figure of General MacArthur saluting and bearing the legend "A Salute from Gen. MacArthur" which is awarded weekly to the department or group showing the greatest increase in production efficiency. The other was a figure of a slinking Jap with such reminders as "Hirohito say, 'Thanks for forgetting to wind the alarm clock—make worker come late.'"

"I haven't had to fix a single flat since I started pooling my car."

"He's been hearing about this here war production drive."

"You mean I can't have some extra gas to go visit my mother-in-law?"

"Of course, I'll only use the lighter when I'm out of matches."

OCD charged with new action program to guard U. S. facilities against sabotage

The President, by Executive order, has directed the Office of Civilian Defense to assure the development and execution of protective measures against sabotage for many types of the Nation's essential facilities.

Subject to approval of Secretary of War

The program, announced by the White House May 20, is known as the Facility Security Program. It will supplement the protective programs of the Army, Navy, and Federal Power Commission, previously authorized by the President, and will correlate with them the anti-sabotage activities of other Government agencies. The new plan of action will be developed in conjunction with and subject to the approval of the Secretary of War.

The order makes it clear that protective measures are the primary responsibility of the owners and operators of essential facilities, public as well as private. The purpose of the program is to assure that this responsibility is carried out, and it will be operated through nine already established agencies of the Federal Government listed in the President's directive, as follows: Federal Communications Commission, Department of Commerce, Public Roads Administration, Office of Defense Transportation, Public

Buildings Administration, Department of Agriculture, Department of the Interior, Federal Power Commission, and the Public Health Service.

The OCD program will not affect the investigative duties of the Federal Bureau of Investigation with respect to acts of sabotage and espionage.

The Executive order defines "facilities" to include, among other things, communication systems, air commerce, highways, railways, forests, mines, gas and water utilities, public buildings and storage facilities.

Landis denies Government delayed delivery of helmets

Any stoppage in delivery of some 22,000 steel helmets for New York is not due to action of OCD or any other Federal Department, Director Landis asserted May 21. He said that "On two occasions . . . the Mayor of New York has stated that the delivery of some 22,000 steel helmets destined for New York had been stopped by action of the Federal Government—'presumably the OCD.'"

WAR EFFORT INDICES

MANPOWER

National labor force, April	53,400,000
Unemployed, April	3,000,000
Nonagricultural workers, March	40,298,000
Percent increase since June 1940	**14
Farm employment, May 1, 1942	10,796,000
Percent increase since June 1940	**1

FINANCE *(In millions of dollars)*

Authorized program June 1940– May 15, 1942	$158,362
Airplanes	35,557
Ordnance	32,122
Miscellaneous munitions	19,552
Industrial facilities	16,813
Naval ships	15,457
Posts, depots, etc.	13,176
Merchant ships	7,459
Stock pile, food exports	5,791
Pay, subsistence, travel for the armed forces	4,930
Housing	1,392
Miscellaneous	6,613
Total expenditures, June 1940– May 15, 1942	*28,740
Sales of War Bonds cumulative May 1941–May 15, 1942	5,707
May 1–15 1942	318

PLANT EXPANSION *(In millions of dollars)*

June 1940 to latest reporting date Gov. commitments for war plant expansion; 1,428 projects, Mar. 31	10,677
Private commitments for war plant expansion; 7,366 projects, Mar. 31	2,333

EARNINGS, HOURS, AND COST OF LIVING *Percent increase from June 1940*

Manufacturing industries— March:		
Average weekly earnings	$36.15	40.2
Average hours worked per week	42.5	13.3
Average hourly earnings	80.9¢	20.4
Cost of living, April (1935–89 = 100)	115.1	14.5

*Prelim. Includes revisions in several months.
‡ Preliminary and excludes authorizations in Naval Supply Act for fiscal year 1943.
**Adjusted for seasonal variations.

OFFICE FOR EMERGENCY MANAGEMENT

WAYNE COY, *Liaison Officer*

CENTRAL ADMINISTRATIVE SERVICES: Dallas Dort, *Director.*

DEFENSE COMMUNICATIONS BOARD: James Lawrence Fly, *Chairman.*

INFORMATION DIVISION: Robert W. Horton, *Director.*

NATIONAL WAR LABOR BOARD: Wm. H. Davis, *Chairman.*

OFFICE OF SCIENTIFIC RESEARCH AND DEVELOPMENT: Dr. Vannevar Bush, *Director.*

OFFICE OF CIVILIAN DEFENSE: James M. Landis, *Director.*

OFFICE OF THE COORDINATOR OF INTER-AMERICAN AFFAIRS: Nelson Rockefeller, *Coordinator.*

OFFICE OF DEFENSE HEALTH AND WELFARE SERVICES: Paul V. McNutt, *Director.*

OFFICE OF DEFENSE TRANSPORTATION: Joseph B. Eastman, *Director.*

OFFICE OF FACTS AND FIGURES: Archibald MacLeish, *Director.*

OFFICE OF LEND-LEASE ADMINISTRATION: E. R. Stettinius, Jr., *Administrator.*

OFFICE OF PRICE ADMINISTRATION: Leon Henderson, *Administrator.*

CONSUMER DIVISION: Dexter M. Keezer, *Assistant Administrator,* in charge. Dan A. West, *Director.*

OFFICE OF ALIEN PROPERTY CUSTODIAN: Leo T. Crowley, *Custodian.*

WAR MANPOWER COMMISSION: Paul V. McNutt, *Chairman.*

WAR RELOCATION AUTHORITY: Milton Eisenhower, *Director.*

WAR SHIPPING ADMINISTRATION: Rear Admiral Emory S. Land, U. S. N. (Retired), *Administrator.*

WAR PRODUCTION BOARD:
Donald M. Nelson, *Chairman.*
Henry L. Stimson.
Frank W. Knox.
Jesse H. Jones.
William S. Knudsen.
Sidney Hillman.
Leon Henderson.
Henry A. Wallace.
Harry L. Hopkins.

WAR PRODUCTION BOARD DIVISIONS:
Donald M. Nelson, *Chairman.*
   Executive Secretary, G. Lyle Belsley.
PLANNING COMMITTEE: Robert R. Nathan, *Chairman.*
PURCHASES DIVISION: Houlder Hudgins, *Acting Director.*
PRODUCTION DIVISION: W. H. Harrison, *Director.*
MATERIALS DIVISION: A. I. Henderson, *Director.*
DIVISION OF INDUSTRY OPERATIONS: J. S. Knowlson, *Director.*
LABOR DIVISION: Sidney Hillman, *Director.*
LABOR PRODUCTION DIVISION: Wendell Lund, *Director.*
CIVILIAN SUPPLY DIVISION: Leon Henderson, *Director.*
OFFICE OF PROGRESS REPORTS: Stacy May, *Director.*
REQUIREMENTS COMMITTEE: Wm. L. Batt, *Chairman.*
STATISTICS DIVISION: Stacy May, *Director.*
INFORMATION DIVISION: Robert W. Horton, *Director.*
ADMINISTRATIVE DIVISION: James Q. Robinson, *Administrative Officer.*
LEGAL DIVISION: John Lord O'Brian, *General Counsel.*

VICTORY

OFFICIAL WEEKLY BULLETIN OF THE AGENCIES IN THE OFFICE FOR EMERGENCY MANAGEMENT

WASHINGTON, D. C.   **JUNE 2, 1942**   **VOLUME 3, NUMBER 22**

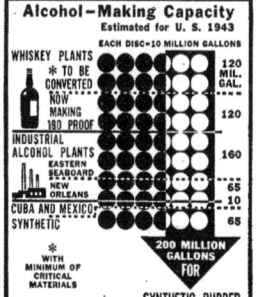

Alcohol—Making Capacity
Estimated for U. S. 1943
EACH DISC=10 MILLION GALLONS

WHISKEY PLANTS
  * TO BE   120 MIL. GAL.
  CONVERTED
  NOW
  MAKING   120
  190 PROOF
INDUSTRIAL
ALCOHOL PLANTS   160
  EASTERN SEABOARD
  NEW ORLEANS   65
CUBA AND MEXICO   10
SYNTHETIC   65

  * WITH MINIMUM OF CRITICAL MATERIALS

200 MILLION GALLONS FOR SYNTHETIC RUBBER

DATA . WPB

Army, Navy, WPB will curb war plant and other construction to save materials for weapons now instead of "much later"

In a move to make all possible material and effort available for immediate war production, top officials of the War Production Board and the War and Navy Departments have established broad principles governing all wartime construction which will bring such building under more rigid conservation control.

The program means that no new plants will be built unless they are absolutely essential and can meet seven newly established criteria. This applies not only to direct war plants but to all other construction.

One of the main reasons for the new policy is that all critical materials are needed for war production now, and no materials can be spared for building new facilities except when they are absolutely necessary. The policy means simply that, in the light of existing shortages, it is necessary to put materials and effort into planes, ships, tanks and guns now, rather than putting them into plants which would not produce fighting weapons until a much later date.

The principles were outlined in a directive, effective immediately, signed by Donald M. Nelson, Chairman of the War Production Board, William H. Harrison, Director of Production, Henry L. Stimson, Secretary of War, and Frank Knox, Secretary of the Navy.

The seven criteria which must be met before any project will be approved for construction follow:

1. It is essential for the war effort.
2. Postponement of construction would be detrimental to the war effort.

3. It is not practical to rent or convert existing facilities for the purpose.
4. The construction will not result in duplication or unnecessary expansion of

ALCOHOL FOR RUBBER DOESN'T MEAN TIRES FOR YOUR CAR

The chart on this page indicates WPB's intention to turn 200,000,000 gallons of the alcohol produced in 1943 to the production of butadiene. It is estimated that butadiene from this amount of alcohol will, when processed with other ingredients, furnish 200,000 tons of Buna synthetic rubber. WPB officials envision the use of 140 to 150 million bushels of grain for industrial alcohol in 1943. Leaders of war agencies have stressed that "the most optimistic estimates for this year and next indicate no rubber for anything but the most essential uses."

existing plants or facilities now under construction or about to be constructed.
5. All possible economies have been made in the project, resulting in deletion of all nonessential items and parts.
6. The projects have been designed of the simplest type, just sufficient to meet the minimum requirements.
7. Sufficient labor, public utilities, transportation, raw materials, equipment and the like are available to build and operate the plant. The manufactured product can be used at once or stored until needed.

Review of the Week

The War Production Board, Army and Navy last week decreed rigid controls over all construction, with the expressed intent of turning all possible materials to the production of weapons immediately instead of building new factories which would not produce until "much later."

The battle of materials

Other developments in the battle of materials:

Three new Government-owned aluminum plants started operations in May, the Materials Division reported. Four more are expected to come in by August 1, the seven together to have a capacity of 640 million pounds a year. First plants in a duplicate program are expected to begin production about December.

An alcohol-producing capacity of 540 million gallons for 1943 was forecast by the Materials Division, which explained that the total would be reached by conversion of whiskey plants, that practically the whole would be from grain, and that 200 million gallons was scheduled for butadiene, synthetic rubber ingredient.

Junked automobiles yielded 350,-000 tons of metal for war production in April, the Bureau of Industrial Conservation announced. Included was 6,000 tons of the urgently needed copper. The bureau revealed plans for a tin-can salvage campaign in 36 cities accessible to detinning and copper-precipitating plants.

WPB took control over many types of general industrial machinery, from elevators to pumps; put drastic restrictions on delivery and use of mahogany, which is a war material; set aside a quantity of fine cotton yarn production for the armed forces; took over horsehide fronts suitable for military garments; issued a cloth-conserving order for women's and children's robes, negligees, beachcoats and lounging pajamas; froze all safety razors in the hands of

manufacturers and jobbers; announced rules for distribution of 600,000 refrigerators for essential uses; and ordered canners to set aside their entire 1942 pack of salmon, sardines, Atlantic herring and mackerel for military use—the public to get a share if there proves to be enough.

Some supplies released

The Division of Industry Operations also found occasion to release some supplies not needed for war. Chief among these was a quantity of softwood construction lumber of several types. Small-gage shotguns and certain other firearms were "unfrozen"; manufacturers were permitted to use up stocks of zippers on various garments; restrictions on plumbing were relaxed somewhat; and additional quotas of coffee and tea were provided for 60 areas where war activity has caused an influx of workers.

With the shipping situation crucial, the Office of Defense Transportation acted to prevent piling up at the docks, by conditioning all shipments into port areas on prior arrangements for space in outgoing vessels. ODT also moved to find millions of square feet of storage space in idle business buildings.

Steps to end "pirating" of workers

The War Manpower Commission considered plans to make the United States Employment Service the sole hiring agency for certain critical skills in some areas, to prevent "pirating" of workers between factories. It was announced at the same time that "if a worker refused to accept suitable employment in a war industry without reasonable cause, it would of course be the duty of the United States Employment Service to report the circumstances to the Selective Service System for consideration in connection with any request for deferment on occupational grounds."

The Office of Price Administration applied Federal control of rents in 20 of the "defense rental" areas previously designated, and also added 19 more which are given 60 days to reduce their rents to stated levels. Several "defense rental" areas were enlarged.

OPA also issued price regulations on canned vegetables; ice; wide osnaburgs; fall styles of women's, girls' and children's cloth outerwear garments; new bags made of cotton and burlap; Appalachian hardwood lumber shipped from mills; and manufacturers' prices for mechanical rubber goods.

Producers of gray iron castings were given a formula for prices not determinable under the general price regulation.

Meanwhile, OPA took a number of actions adjusting prices in special cases, particularly with regard to coal.

Special bus services out for ball parks, racetracks

Joseph B. Eastman, Director of Defense Transportation, May 30 issued a statement clarifying application of General Order ODT No. 10, which bans operation of sightseeing buses and limits charter buses to essential services, effective June 1.

Mr. Eastman's statement follows (in part):

The intent of General Order O.D.T. No. 10 is to restrict the use of bus tires to services which are necessary, and certainly to prohibit bus operation for purposes that relate primarily to entertainment. For this reason sightseeing has been specifically prohibited.

It is the intent of the order, therefore, to eliminate entirely special services which are operated primarily to serve places of entertainment, such as baseball parks, race-tracks, bingo games, circuses, musical and dramatic entertainments and similar occasional events. This is not to be construed by any means as an indication on the part of this office that such events should be eliminated from our social life. Events of this nature, if prudently managed, are staged at centers of population or on established transit lines.

WAR EFFORT'S PROGRESS TOLD VISUALLY

The charts appearing every week on the front cover of VICTORY tell the story of America's battle as it is fought here at home. One-column mats are available for publication by newspapers and others who may desire them. Requests should be sent to Distribution Section, Division of Information, OEM, Washington, D. C.

VICTORY OFFICIAL BULLETIN of the Office for Emergency Management. Published weekly by the Division of Information, Office for Emergency Management, and printed at the United States Government Printing Office, Washington, D. C.

Subscription rates by mail: 75¢ for 52 issues; 25¢ for 13 issues; single copies 5¢, payable in advance. Remit money order payable directly to the Superintendent of Documents, Government Printing Office, Washington, D. C.

On the Home Front

We have reached a point in this war, in our progress toward victory, where plans crystallize quickly into accomplishment and programs are transmuted from the bronze of words to the gold of action without long delay. In many fields, that about which we used to talk has become that which we are doing. We talked of total war, for example, and were aware that total war meant giving everything we had to wage a war. Now, however, we actually are *waging* such a war. Now we aren't merely talking about the need for completely mobilizing American manpower, we're doing it.

"Able to dish it out"

This is the way we had to go, this is the road we had to travel. And it is well that we travel swiftly, for we have need of every minute. But we're getting along. We're getting tough. We've learned to take it, and because we have learned to take it we are able to dish it out, to dish out the tanks and planes and ships and weapons which will lick our enemies.

Right now Home Fronters are taking in their stride things which might have thrown many of us temporarily off balance a few months ago. In our progress toward the efficient practice of total war we have been like the Army recruit whose training takes off fat, puts on muscle and sinew.

Fighting a three-sided war

The past few days brought new proof that we are growing lean and hard, that we are putting everything we have into our punches. For instance, the great program for complete mobilization of our manpower.

We are fighting a three-sided war—war on the field of arms, war under the factory roofs, war on the rolling farms. To win this war we are raising a fighting force of at least 8,000,000 soldiers and sailors together with a labor force of 20,000,000 and an agricultural force of 12,000,00—men and women. If any one of these armies fails, all will fail.

It is the job of the War Manpower Commission to find these armies; to see, too, that American manpower and womanpower is used efficiently. WMC estimates that 7,000,000 to 8,000,000 will come from suspended civilian industries, 400,000 to 600,000 from the farms, 400,000 from the professions, 1,500,000 from the temporarily unemployed, and 2,000,000 from the home. The peacetime me-

chanic, the mechanically inclined farm hand, retired workers, women without children, boys under the draft age and girls in their late teens—all are eligible for enlistment in the army of the Home Front.

Can't afford square pegs in round holes

A primary rule of total war is that manpower must not be wasted, the Nation at war cannot afford the luxury of square pegs in round holes. Proper employment of manpower on farm and in

REPRINTING PERMISSIBLE

Requests have been received for permission to reprint "On the Home Front" in whole or in part. This column, like all other material in VICTORY, may be reprinted without special permission. If excerpts are used, the editors ask only that they be taken in such a way that their original meaning is preserved.

factory requires care that the man with mechanical training and aptitudes doesn't wind up behind the plow, or the good agriculturist turn up as a second-rate worker in a munitions plant.

The U. S. Employment Service is all-out in the work of mobilization. Placements in factories, shipyards, offices, and farms for April totalled 605,200, 19 percent more than were placed in March. Meanwhile the Nation-wide training drive continues, with 2,400 vocational schools and 10,000 public school shops offering technical courses; as well as 3,195 factories which provide "in plant" training for their employees, employees who learn as they work.

Rice is a $64,000,000 crop, staff of life to millions in our southeastern States and Territories, one of our principal exports to Cuba. Rice was brought under the price ceiling last week and its price frozen at levels existing from late December 1941 to mid-March 1942. This represents one more step to make certain the family budget is not upset by skyrocketing prices.

Rents rolled back in 20 key areas

Federal control of residential rents went into effect last week for the first time in our history—more proof that we are willing to get tough with ourselves.

The Office of Price Administration rolled back rents of all habitations from hotel rooms to trailers in 20 key areas to dates as far back as January 1941. OPA acted because local authorities had failed to halt the upsurge in rents within a 60-day period. The order affects the rents of 9,000,000 persons in 13 States.

Still time to "get in the scrap"

Tolling of school bells for the last time this spring should be the signal for a Nation-wide campaign of salvage. Boys and girls, scouts and guides and other juvenile organizations have shown themselves invaluable in collecting rubber, iron, tin, and copper—all waste materials needed by our military machine. And WPB's Bureau of Industrial Conservation is launching a program to salvage tin cans in 36 selected cities.

Steps toward travel rationing

More evidence of our ability to take it and dish it out: Price Administrator Leon Henderson has warned members of the meat industry not to try to get out from under the price ceiling. "Ignorance—professed or actual—," Henderson said, "Will not be accepted . . . as an excuse . . .". . . . WPB has cut down drastically on civilian use of mahogany, domestic and Philippine, in such kinds as are used in building combat ships and airplanes . . . On the other hand, it modified the "freeze" on softwood construction lumber so that it now affects only about 55 percent of production . . . ODT has started a survey of inter-city bus and rail travel out of 100 cities as a step toward travel rationing and has placed bus service between Washington and New York on a war footing.

Auction sales bound by ceilings

OPA decrees that the 1942 fall lines of women's, girls' and children's outer clothing shall be priced at the same level as in 1941 . . . and that goods sold at auction shall not go above the price ceiling . . . The price ceiling over ice has been lifted a trifle to permit dealers to sell ice in the summer months at the same prices they got in the summer of 1941 instead of at the March 1942 levels . . . WPB has liberalized the rules under which distributors may sell molasses to farmers for use in preparations to kill insects . . .

Federal Security Administrator Paul V. McNutt reports that 2,500 of the 3,070 counties in the country have organized nutrition committees in the past year . . . The number of new passenger automobiles to be rationed in June throughout the country has been set at 40,000, not including reserves, or the same as in the past 3 months.

MATERIALS . . .

540-million-gallon alcohol production to be attained in 1943 by conversion of whiskey plants; 200 million for rubber

A report on the alcohol-making facilities of the United States and the outlook for this year and next was made May 25 by A. I. Henderson, Director of Materials.

Military and essential civilian demand for 1943 is now estimated at 476 million gallons, including 200 million for butadiene, an ingredient of synthetic rubber. Production capacity is estimated at 540 million gallons, to which will be added a stock pile of 50 million gallons plus surplus from 1942.

This production capacity will be achieved by conversion of the whiskey distilling industry to industrial alcohol and full-time operation of all industrial alcohol plants in the country.

This is the way the total will be reached:

	Gallons
Synthetic (from ethylene gas)	65,000,000
Whiskey plants now making 190 proof	120,000,000
Whiskey plants to be converted	120,000,000
New Orleans industrial alcohol plants	65,000,000
Seaboard industrial alcohol plants	160,000,000
Cuba and Mexico	10,000,000
	540,000,000
Surplus from 1942	50,000,000

Practically all this production will be made from grain. Beverage alcohol plants use grain exclusively, of course, and grain-handling equipment now is being installed in all eastern seaboard plants so they can use either grain or blackstrap molasses, if the latter is available. Because sufficient blackstrap, residue from sugar production, is available at New Orleans from domestic sources, plants in that area will continue to use it. Blackstrap from seaboard plants came, in the past, from Cuba and other sugar-producing islands off the East Coast.

The beverage alcohol industry falls into two distinct classifications, those with facilities to make 190 proof alcohol and those with facilities to make only 120-140 proof. The first class already is engaged full time in the production of alcohol for war uses. Many of the second type now are shipping their low proof alcohol to industrial plants for rectifying into 190 proof. This will con-

tinue on a rising scale throughout the year.

Negligible amounts of critical materials

For complete conversion of the latter type, 20 rectifying stills from Pacific Coast plants and six from idle distilleries in other parts of the country will be installed in whiskey distilleries, chiefly in Kentucky, center of the straight run whiskey industry. These stills will make it possible to produce 190 proof from straight run plants.

Object of this conversion program is production of the necessary amounts of alcohol without using critical materials to build new equipment. Necessity for this is demonstrated by the fact that 550 tons of steel plates, 790 tons of structural steel, 70 tons of copper and four tons of bronze as well as other materials are necessary for the construction of a plant that will turn out 2,500,000 gallons of alcohol a year.

Almost a hundred plants this size would be necessary to equal the output of the beverage alcohol industry. Under the program adopted, necessary amounts of alcohol can be produced with the use of a negligible amount of new equipment.

To use 136 million bushels

The 1943 program will consume approximately 136 million bushels of grain. Corn, rye and wheat now are being used, in approximately that order, but a large increase in the use of wheat for alcohol production is being arranged. The larger part of the new installations will be for wheat as the source material.

Because existing plants are located in regard to markets, no alcohol shipping problems of importance will be encountered. This is best shown by the production and consumption records of the various sections of the United States. These are:

	Production	Consumption
	Percent	Percent
North Atlantic States	57.45	57.75
Southern and Gulf States	20.08	19.42
North Central States	15.53	17.32
Midwest and Southwest	4.87	3.06
Pacific Coast States	2.17	2.42

Three new aluminum plants producing, four more to begin by August 1

Three new Government-owned aluminum plants have started operations so far this month, a fourth is expected to begin production early in June, and the entire first expansion program of seven plants will be in production by August 1, A. H. Bunker, chief, aluminum and magnesium branch, announced May 30.

All ahead of schedule

All seven plants will be completed ahead of schedule, he said. The first two were finished in 6 months, as compared to a normal building time of 11 months. The plants will get into full production from 60 to 120 days after completion, depending upon size.

The completed plants are located in Oregon, Washington, and New York. The Alabama plant will be completed next, followed by ones in Arkansas, California, and a second plant in Washington, in that order. All were built for the Government by the Aluminum Co. of America, which also will operate the plants.

Plants in the second expansion program, also of 640 million pounds annual capacity, will start coming in about December of this year. The flow of aluminum metal is expected to increase every month from now on until the early part of 1943, when the entire aluminum capacity as planned by WPB will be operating at its peak.

Iron, steel scrap users urged to stock up; limit removed

WPB on May 23 called upon consumers of iron and steel scrap to build up inventories to the largest extent possible during the summer.

To make this possible, the Director of Industry Operations issued an amendment to Order M-24 removing inventory restrictions of Priorities Regulation No. 1 on iron and steel scrap.

C. E. Adams, chief, iron and steel branch, voiced the warning to steel producers that only by building up inventory will it be possible to continue extensive steel operations next winter.

Nelson lauds ship workers for giving up part of raise to achieve stabilization

Donald M. Nelson, Chairman of the War Production Board, commended the Nation's shipyard workers May 24 "for their splendid action in sacrificing some of their rightful claims to pay increases in order to achieve a new wage stabilization agreement in the crucial shipbuilding industry."

The WPB Chairman released a report made to him and to Wendell Lund, Director of the Labor Production Division, by Paul R. Porter, Chairman of the Shipbuilding Stabilization Committee, who conducted the shipbuilding wage stabilization conference at Chicago.

Supporting President's program

Representatives of the shipbuilding unions "have demonstrated their willingness to support President Roosevelt's seven-point program against inflation, by not seeking the full percentage of pay raise provided for in their contracts," Mr. Nelson said.

According to Mr. Porter's report:

The conference agreement also extends to the entire shipbuilding industry the abolition of Saturdays and Sundays as premium days per se.

The agreed-upon wage adjustment provides for an increase of eight cents an hour for all workers in shipyards covered by the stabilization program, with two exceptions:

(1) In order to abolish a wage differential of five cents per hour less for standard skilled mechanics in the Gulf Zone, an increase of 13 cents an hour was agreed upon for this classification of workers. Workers in other classifications in the Gulf Zone will, under the terms of the agreement, receive increases ranging from 9 to 12 cents an hour.

(2) In the Pacific Northwest, approximately 6,000 standard skilled mechanics who have been receiving three cents an hour over the established scale of $1.12 will receive an increase of only five cents per hour.

Agreement called for more

The scheduled increases, including the elimination of both the Gulf and Northwest differentials, will result in a national uniform wage rate of $1.20 per hour for standard skilled mechanics.

Under the terms of the zone agreements entered into while we were still a Nation at peace, the shipyard workers on the West Coast were entitled to a wage increase of approximately 14½ cents an hour for first-class mechanics in accord with cost of living adjustments in their contracts. These contracts expired on April 1 of this year but wage adjustments were held in abeyance pending the outcome of the conference. Shipyard workers in the Gulf Zone, by the terms of their agreement, would probably have been entitled to an increase of 18 cents an hour on August 1. On the East Coast, as in the Great Lakes region, the workers have likewise yielded their contractual rights to wage increases under cost of living schedules.

MANPOWER . . .

McNutt considers making U. S. sole hiring agency for critical skills in some areas

After receiving reports from various sections of the country on the practice that has developed of "pirating" from essential war activities workers possessing critical skills, the War Manpower Commission at its session May. 27 announced that it would issue a policy statement designed to remedy this condition. WMC Chairman McNutt stated that it was probable that the policy would apply initially only to a few critical occupations in a small number of war production areas where the situation has become particularly serious.

Mr. McNutt stated that consideration was being given to requiring that all hiring in the specified areas for jobs requiring these critical skills should be carried on only through the United States Employment Service or in accordance with methods approved by the United States Employment Service. He stated that utilization of the United States Employment Service as the sole hiring agency has been operating successfully on a voluntary basis for the southern California airplane plants for some time.

Policy might be restricted to workers already in war plants

Mr. McNutt further stated that at the outset it might very well be that the use or approval of the United States Employment Service would be required only when an employer desired to hire a worker already employed in an essential war industry, no restrictions being placed upon the hiring of workers not employed in an essential war industry.

Under any of the plans now contemplated the restrictions will apply only to employers. There will be no restrictions placed upon the freedom of a worker to work where he chooses except that he will be expected to secure any new job requiring a critical skill through the United States Employment Service or in accordance with methods approved by the United States Employment Service. However, every effort would be made to induce workers possessing critical skills to accept employment in war industries in accordance with the relative urgency of need for the product of these industries.

In the event that an employer engaged in methods of recruitment contrary to the policy promulgated and failed to correct such method upon due notice from the United States Employment Service, the United States Employment Service would be required to make a report to the War Manpower Commission, the War Production Board, the War and Navy Departments, and other authoritative agencies so that appropriate action could be taken. If a worker refused to accept suitable employment in a war industry without reasonable cause, it would be the duty of the United States Employment Service to report the circumstances to the Selective Service System for consideration in connection with any request for deferment on occupational grounds.

Some job shifts justified

Mr. McNutt pointed out that in each area that might be designated as a critical area a local committee of labor and management representatives would be established to advise, hear, and make recommendations on appeals by either workers or employers in order that the interests of individual worker and employer might be fully considered and protected.

Mr. McNutt also pointed out that there would always be some cases where a worker was justified in changing his job and an employer was justified in hiring him, even though he was already working in a war industry but that he believed that workers and employers of this country were fully prepared to sacrifice private convenience to public necessity and would cooperate fully with the Government in any reasonable policy promulgated.

8 war industries ordered to stop discrimination

Orders to "cease and desist" from discriminating against workers because of their race and religion were directed May 26 to eight war industries in New York and New Jersey by the President's Committee on Fair Employment Practice. The committee's action was based on the record of its public hearings held in New York City in February.

Pay stabilized for 1,600 brass workers; Sunday premium eliminated for Mack Co.

Acting in accordance with President Roosevelt's seven-point program to freeze the cost of living, the National War Labor Board last week issued an order stabilizing wages in the Cleveland plant of the Chase Brass & Copper Co.

Other Board decisions issued during the week included one putting an end to premium pay for work on Saturdays, Sundays, and holidays as such in the Mack Manufacturing Corporation plant at New Brunswick, N. J.; an order providing for preferential hiring procedure for licensed deck officers employed by the United States Lines Co., New York; and an order disposing of the 10 issues in the dispute between the Scott Lumber Co., Inc., Burney, Calif., and the International Woodworkers of America, Local 6-269, C. I. O.

The Board also referred two jurisdictional disputes involving A. F. L. and C. I. O. unions to labor members of the Board for settlement.

Chase Brass wage decision

The Board by a vote of 8 to 4 with labor members dissenting ordered an upward adjustment of 4 cents an hour in the Cleveland mill of the Chase Brass & Copper Co.

At the same time, the Board directed the company to begin negotiations with the International Association of Machinists, Local 54, A. F. L. union involved in the dispute, to iron out inequalities in rates paid occupational groups within the plant to an extent that will result in an average total increase of not less than 2 cents an hour or more than 3 cents an hour for the entire pay roll.

The wage adjustments ordered were designed to stabilize rates within the plant, between the plant and other plants in the Cleveland area and between the plant and other brass industry plants. All adjustments were made retroactive to January 1, 1942, in accordance with a unanimous interim order of the Board issued April 8. The increases will provide the workers 20 percent more pay than the bonus ordered because of the bonus system now in effect at the plant. A total of 1,600 workers are employed at the plant. The majority opinion was written by Dr. George W. Taylor, Board vice chairman, and concurred in by William H. Davis, Board chairman, Frank P. Graham and Wayne L. Morse, representing the public, and George H. Mead, Cyrus Ching, H. L. Derby and E. J. McMillan, representing employers. Matthew Woll, R. J. Thomas, Robert Watt, and Emil Rieve, representing labor, dissented.

Part of the upward wage adjustments should be made in the form of allowing reclassifications within occupational groups, Dr. Taylor stated.

The majority opinion said:

The inequalities in the wage scales and the rectification of resulting inequalities at the Cleveland mill are to receive immediate attention as an important part of the wage stabilization program, particularly since it was the judgment of the majority of the panel that further delay in the accomplishment of such standardization will foster unrest and dissatisfaction within the plant and will thereby interfere with the attainment of maximum production.

In line with program

The War Labor Board has the definite responsibility for settling wage cases which come before it in line with the wage stabilization program as outlined by the President when he wrote that wages in general can and should be kept at existing scales. Such stabilization is to be carried out, of course, with due regard to adjustments necessary to eliminate inequalities and substandard conditions. The adjustment which is made in this case recognizes existing scales and adjusts the Chase rates to them with the objective of attaining the contemplated stabilization....

All of the facts available in this case indicate that a greater increase than that provided by the Board order would not only fail to carry out the objective of the National wage stabilization Program but would actually create instability by increasing the wages of the Cleveland plant of the Chase Brass Co. somewhat above other comparable plants in Cleveland and substantially above other plants in the brass industry.

It has been suggested by the minority of the Board in this case that a greater increase, even to the extent of 10 cents per hour in the base rates, should be granted for various reasons, but particularly in view of the company's admitted ability to pay.

It is evident that, if the wage stabilization program is to have any meaning, wage instability should not be created solely because individual concerns may at a certain time be able to pay an increase above prevailing wage standards. The stabilization of wages is a part of a seven-point program. The effectuation of that program requires certain steps along seven lines of which wage stabilization is one. Nor is the wage stabilization phase of that program to be nullified merely because some employers have at the moment ability to pay an unstabilizing wage. If it should be the fact that the employers' returns would be excessive under resulting costs and prices, that matter must be considered by those agencies whose activities are affected by other phases of the seven-point program.

Premium pay eliminated

An overtime pay formula which puts an end to premium pay for work on Saturdays, Sundays, and holidays as such was made the unanimous directive order of the National War Labor Board in settling the dispute between the Mack Manufacturing Corporation, New Brunswick, N. J., and the International Union of United Automobile, Aircraft and Agricultural Implement Workers of America, Local 824, C. I. O.

The new overtime formula follows the principle originally laid down by the

A. F. L. and C. I. O. in an agreement with the President. It was incorporated by the Board in the International Harvester case and is virtually the same formula as the one agreed to by the same union and the General Motors Corporation on May 23.

The formula provides:

(A) There shall be no overtime pay for Saturdays, Sundays, or holidays, as such.

(B) Time and one-half shall be paid to employees for any sixth consecutive day of work.

(C) Work shifts shall be so arranged that every worker will have at least one day's rest in seven, except in cases of emergency. If an employee is required to work a seventh consecutive day, he shall be paid for that day at the penalty rate of double time.

Commenting on Clause 6, the Board order stated:

It is our view that maximum productive efficiency can best be achieved under a work schedule whereby the workers have some time off for rest and relaxation. The company may proceed, however, to set up swing shift operations so that the full productive capacity of the plant can best be utilized and at the same time provide that employees will have one day of rest in seven. Now that the union has agreed to the elimination of overtime payments for Saturdays, Sundays, and holidays as such, there has been removed what may well have been a financial deterrent to the institution of swing shifts.

Preferential plan ordered

The National War Labor Board last week settled the dispute between the United States Lines Co., New York City, and the Masters, Mates and Pilots, Local No. 88, A. F. L., by spelling out a union security clause which gives the company two choices of preferential plans for hiring licensed deck officers.

The case was certified to the Board on March 19, 1942, after the United States Maritime Commission and the United States Conciliation Service were unable to secure an agreement on union security. Hearings were held before the Board panel on April 7 and 8, after which the panel prepared a unanimous decision which was made the directive order of the Board by a unanimous vote.

The union security issue revolved about the nature of a preferential clause for licensed deck officers. The panel prepared its own draft of this clause after both the company and the union submitted proposed clauses. The Board, in its directive order, pointed out that the company has two choices of hiring procedure under the union security clause finally approved, as follows:

(a) The company may make its own selection of men to fill vacancies for licensed deck officers, even though those selected are not union members, as long as they become members of the Union upon their employment. This particular procedure may apply either as respects the hiring of deck officers "from the outside" or as respects the promotion of seamen in the employ of the company.

(b) The company may employ licensed deck officers under the preference requirements of the clause. This requires the giving of preference to qualified union members. If such qualified officers cannot be provided by the Union from its members, however, the company may then employ deck officers who are not members of the Union and who are not obligated to become members of the Union.

Scott lumber case

The National War Labor Board by a unanimous vote issued a directive order disposing of the ten issues in the dispute between the Scott Lumber Co., Inc., Burney, Calif., and the International Woodworkers of America, C.I.O., Local 6–269.

In issuing the directive order the Board adopted as its own with one amendment the unanimous recommendations of a three-man panel of the Board which tried to mediate the dispute. Mediation was unsuccessful because of the failure of the company to send to the hearings representatives with authority to make final decisions.

At the first hearing before the panel—on May 8—the company was represented by Isreal Greene, a Newark, N. J., attorney who was only authorized to move for a postponement. In reply to a request from the Board that the company be represented at a hearing on May 13 by persons "whose approval is necessary for final decisions," the company designated Raymond H. Berry, a member of the company's Board of Directors, to be present.

At the May 13 hearing, Mr. Berry told the panel that the company did not consider it proper to submit the issues to the Board because the company had placed the matter before the Superior Court of California in a suit for an injunction against the union. Judge Walter P. Stacy of the Supreme Court of North Carolina, chairman of the panel, asked Mr. Berry whether he was authorized to represent the company in any regard. Mr. Berry replied, "No. I am sort of a glorified messenger boy to present the determination of the company and have presented it." In further discussion, Mr. Berry stated that he could not and would not mediate, arbitrate, or discuss.

After the panel devoted the entire day to an effort to find some procedure to settle the issues amicably, Mr. Berry announced that he would not return on the following day, May 14, at which time the union submitted its case. The panel then drew up its own recommendations on the basis of the material before it.

Two disputes to labor members

Two jurisdictional disputes between the A. F. L. and C. I. O. unions have been referred to labor members of the National War Labor Board for settlement in accordance with the procedure agreed to by William Green and Philip Murray, the presidents of the A. F. L. and the C. I. O.

One of the disputes—at the General Motors Corporation Frigidaire Division in Dayton, Ohio—is between the A. F. L. Building and Construction Trades of Dayton and Local 801 of the United Electrical, Radio and Machine Workers, C. I. O., over which union should do a painting job. The United Electrical, Radio and Machine Workers of America has a collective bargaining agreement with the company covering the plant, but the A. F. L. Building Trades group contends that the painting is more properly a job to be done by its members.

The other dispute is in the Kingston Products Corporation plant at Kokomo, Ind., and involves the United Steelworkers of America, C. I. O., and the A. F. L. Metal Polishers, Buffers, Platers, and Helpers International Union. At issue is which union 12 metal polishers should belong to. Both unions have collective bargaining agreements covering parts of the plant.

Both disputes were certified to the Board by Secretary of Labor Frances Perkins on the recommendation of the United States Conciliation Service of the Department of Labor.

PRODUCTION DRIVE drawing, made by Garrett Price to symbolize the might of the American worker, will be made into a poster. Posters will not be available until further notice, but 2- and 3-column mats for publication may be had on request to Distribution Section, Division of Information, OEM, Washington, D. C. Refer to Mat V–14.

605,200 jobs filled by U. S. Employment Service in April

More than half a million jobs in factories, shipyards, and offices, and 50,600 jobs on farms were filled by the United States Employment Service during April, it was announced May 27 by Paul V. McNutt, Chairman of the War Manpower Commission.

Both agricultural and nonagricultural placements by United States employment offices rose sharply in response to rapidly expanding war and food production efforts, Mr. McNutt said. In all, 605,200 placements were made—19 percent more than in March. Farm placements were 42 percent greater than in March.

With the increase in placements, there has been a continuing decrease in the number of individuals available for jobs. By the end of April, the number of job seekers registered in the active files of United States employment offices had dropped to 4.4 million—4 percent below the previous month, and 14 percent below the number in April 1940.

TRANSPORTATION . . .

Movement of goods to ports conditioned on prior arrangements for ship space

The Office of Defense Transportation on May 23 issued instructions to carriers designed to prohibit the shipment of export goods into United States ports until shipping space is available. The new system went into effect June 1 and will involve shipments originating in both Canada and the United States.

The new plan is designed to prevent congestion and delays which handicapped overseas shipping in the first World War.

Government and commercial shipments under control

After the new regulations go into effect, no export shipments by any governmental agency will be permitted to move into a port area until block permits authorizing such movement have been issued by the Chief of Transportation in the War Department.

Working along the same lines as presently in effect through the Board of Economic Warfare, unit permits will be required before any overseas shipment of commercial goods may be moved into a port area. In order to obtain a unit permit, the shipper must first obtain a license and priority number from the Office of Export Control, Board of Economic Warfare, Washington, D. C. Present holders of licenses from the Board of Economic Warfare do not require new licenses. For the present, at least, materials moving under so-called "general licenses by BEW designation," may continue to move without application to the Board of Economic Warfare.

Must book ship space

The shipper then must obtain a definite space booking from the ocean carrier, and this booking must be approved by the War Shipping Administration and, if the shipment is to be handled by a British or British-controlled ship, by the British Ministry of War Transport.

Commercial shipments originating in Canada will be handled by ODT block permits the same as shipments involving governmental agencies.

Applicants for block permits will submit their applications through the procuring agencies with which their governmental contracts were negotiated, while all Canadian requests will be forwarded directly to the Office of Defense Transportation.

Unit permits for shipment by rail will be issued by G. C. Randall, Manager of Port Traffic, Association of American Railroads, 30 Vesey Street, New York City, and by his field officers.

Special rules for l. c. l.

Unit permits for shipment by truck will be issued by the field offices of the Division of Motor Transport of the ODT, and unit permits for barge line shipments will be issued by the ODT's Division of Inland Waterways, Washington, D. C.

Separate regulations have been established for shipment of less-than-carload, bargeload or truckload lots. There are no restrictions on such shipments by or for Government agencies, and shipment of other goods for Cuba, the Dominican Republic, and Puerto Rico may move without restriction through Tampa, Fla. All other such shipments must bear the Board of Economic Warfare License and the number of the steamship contract.

★ ★ ★

Great Lakes coal movements curbed to augment iron ore shipping facilities

In a further move to assure maximum capacity for the transportation of iron ore, the ODT has issued an order prohibiting certain Great Lakes coal movements, it was announced May 25.

ODT in another order, recently banned, with few exceptions, all Great Lakes grain shipping to bring more than 300 vessels into the ore traffic.

The coal order (General Order No. 9), which became effective June 1, forbids Lake carriers, unless authorized by special or general permits, to move coal from any Lake Erie port to: (a) Any port on the Detroit and St. Clair Rivers south of and including Port Huron; (b) The Chicago area; (c) Any port on Lake Erie and Lake Ontario, and connecting or tributary waters.

Simultaneously, ODT Director Eastman issued a general permit, worked out in cooperation with the Office of Solid Fuels Coordination, to allow vessels of the self-unloading type to move coal to: (1) Any Canadian port on Lake Erie, Lake Ontario, or on the Welland Canal; (2) Any port on the Detroit and St. Clair Rivers; (3) Any port in the Chicago area. These self-unloaders, of which there are 97 under United States registry, are equipped with a belt-conveyor device for unloading, and are not considered suited to ore transportation.

General Order No. 9 and its accompanying general permit, will make available Great Lakes shipping facilities for an additional 2,000,000 tons of iron ore.

★ ★ ★

Great Lakes dock operators given relief on train fuel

Dock operators on the upper Great Lakes are permitted to add specific handling and storage charges to mine prices plus transportation charges in determining maximum prices for the sale of railroad fuel, as the result of Amendment No. 2 to Maximum Price Regulation No. 122 (Solid Fuels Delivered from Facilities Other Than Producing Facilities—Dealers), Price Administrator Henderson announced May 22.

ODT moves to acquire millions of square feet of storage space in unused business buildings

Acquisition of millions of additional square feet of storage space, when and where required by any Government agency, without the erection of new buildings, is embraced in the Office of Defense Transportation's group warehousing plan for 40 of the Nation's largest cities.

The expanded scope of the program, under which idle buildings of small manufacturers and other business enterprises will be utilized for storage purposes, was revealed May 23 by ODT Director Eastman, in announcing the signing of ODT's first group warehousing contract with the Federal Emergency Warehouse Association, of Philadelphia. This association, Mr. Eastman said, was recently formed by Philadelphia merchandise warehouse operators who, under the terms of their contract with the Government, have pooled their facilities to make available 400,000 square feet of storage space.

Col. Leo M. Nicolson, director of ODT's division of storage, who is in direct charge of the group warehousing program, emphasized the benefits that will accrue to the small business man whose production has been curtailed or whose plant has been closed down through inability to get raw materials for production of non-essential items.

★ ★ ★

One line allowed to substitute electric buses for street cars

The Office of Defense Transportation has authorized the Des Moines Railway Company, Des Moines, Iowa, to substitute electric buses for street cars on its Ingersoll-West, Des Moines line, it was announced May 23.

ODT explained that overhead wires had been installed on the Des Moines line, that the company already had received delivery of 17 trolley coaches ordered for the purpose a year ago, that the street car line was in a dilapidated condition and would require costly repairs and replacements, and that the 10 street cars to be released by the substitution are needed on other lines.

Transportation committee named to study needs, recommend preferential movements

Formation of a transportation committee to obtain information from the various divisions of the WPB as to anticipated transportation requirements and to make recommendations with respect to preferential movement of traffic, within the United States was announced May 26, by Director of Industry Operations Knowlson.

Chairman of the committee is Edgar B. Stern, of New Orleans, La., who since last October has been OPM and WPB representative to the Board of Economic Warfare. Mr. Stern will devote full time to the committee. Other members represent interested divisions and branches of WPB.

Committee members

They are:

Dr. Reavis Cox, Division of Civilian Supply; H. W. Dodge, Materials Division; Dr. William Y. Elliott, Stockpile and Shipping Branch; and John J. Fennelly, Division of Industry Operations.

Additional members may be appointed from time to time.

To determine order of preference

Recommendations of the committee will be submitted to the Director of Industry Operations, who may transmit them in the form of certifications, instructions and directives concerning preferential movement of materials to the Office of Defense Transportation.

When transportation facilities are inadequate to move all freight ready to be shipped between certain points within a definite period of time, the transportation committee will determine on the basis of information obtained from various divisions of WPB which types of freight should be given preference, and will so inform the Director of Industry Operations. The Director will then transmit the recommendations to the Office of Defense Transportation for appropriate action.

Drive to conserve farm trucks by pooling, economical use, launched by ODT, Agriculture

The Office of Defense Transportation and the United States Department of Agriculture on May 28 asked farmers throughout the country to cooperate in a comprehensive program for conservation and more efficient use of farm trucks and automobiles.

Because of the rubber shortage, the limited supply of new vehicles and the increasing scarcity of repair parts, farmers are urged to use their trucks and cars as little as possible and to take better care of such equipment.

Farm truck pools planned

The two Government agencies recommended that farmers not only eliminate unnecessary driving but also form transportation pools both for hauling their produce to market and for transporting needed supplies to the farms.

The program has the double aim of conserving vital equipment and assuring a continuous flow of farm commodities to market. It will be carried out by State and County War Boards already functioning under the Department of Agriculture.

NEW APPOINTMENTS

Three appointments to the staff of the Office of Defense Transportation were announced May 26 by Director Eastman.

C. M. Sears, Jr., of Providence, R. I., former president of the Short Line, Inc., interstate bus system, has been named associate director of the division of transport conservation.

Charles F. Kellers, of New York City, former president of the New Haven Towing Co., has assumed duties as associate director of the division of coastwise and intercoastal transport.

F. L. Thompson, of Chicago, until recently vice president in charge of engineering on the Illinois Central Railroad, was named consultant on rail maintenance in the division of railway transport.

Bayliss appointed in ODT

ODT Director Eastman announced May 23 the appointment of Arthur E. Bayliss, of New York City, to be executive assistant to Henry F. McCarthy, director of ODT's division of traffic movement.

MAKE WAY! . . . This OEM poster was distributed by the Bituminous Coal Consumers' Counsel. Persons wishing to reproduce the poster should write to Bituminous Coal Consumers' Counsel, Box 483, Washington, D. C. Two-column mats for publication are available on request to Distribution Section, Division of Information, OEM, Washington, D. C.; refer to V–16.

PRICE ADMINISTRATION . . .

OPA takes over rent control in 20 areas as 60-day test period expires

Price Administrator Henderson May 27 ordered housing rents reduced in twenty of the Nation's most important war production and military training areas. The orders restore rents to levels prevailing as far back as January, April and July of 1941.

Federal control for first time

With this action, Federal control of rents for every type of housing accommodation in the 20 areas—houses, apartments, hotels, rooming houses, trailers— became effective with rents payable for June.

The twenty areas, located in 13 States, embrace a population of 9 million persons, and with the opening of area offices, Federal control of residential rent begins for the first time in this country's history. The areas were originally designated on March 2.

Since the areas have not met Mr. Henderson's recommendations in the 60 days provided by statute the Price Administrator was required to make Federal control effective.

19 directors named

At the same time Mr. Henderson released the maximum rent regulations for housing accommodations other than hotels and rooming houses for the control of rents in these areas, and announced the appointment of 19 area rent directors who will administer the regulations. Regulations for hotels, rooming and boarding houses were to be issued before June 1, on which date both sets of regulations became effective.

The maximum rent regulations place a ceiling on rents as of a specified date, varying as to locality, and call for the registration by landlords of all rental dwelling units whether occupied at present or not. This registration is to start some time during June.

While immediately affecting only 20 areas, regulations similar except for the maximum rent date will be applied to other of the 342 defense-rental areas so far designated when any such areas are brought under Federal control.

Also issued was a procedural regulation which sets up machinery for protest and amendment of the maximum rent regulations and for adjustments under them.

The reduction of rents to these levels will be automatic. Beginning June 1, as a general principle with a few exceptions, tenants are to cut their rents back to what was being charged on the maximum rent date set for their respective areas.

Exceptions to this principle are made in the maximum rent regulations for housing accommodations, other than hotels and rooming houses, in which provision is made for adjustment in the maximum rent as set by date in special cases.

Provision is also made to care for rents affected by seasonal demand.

20 areas listed

The twenty areas and the maximum rent date beyond which rents cannot go save in certain special cases are:

Bridgeport, Conn., Hartford-New Britain, Conn., Waterbury, Conn., Schenectady, N. Y., Birmingham, Ala., Mobile, Ala., (all April 1, 1941).

Columbus, Ga., Jan. 1, 1941; Wilmington, N. C., Hampton Roads, Va., area, Detroit, Mich., Akron, Ohio, Canton, Ohio (all April 1, 1941).

Cleveland, Ohio, July 1, 1941; Ravenna, Ohio, April 1, 1941; Youngstown-Warren, Ohio, April 1, 1941; South Bend, Ind., Jan. 1, 1941;

Burlington, Iowa, Jan. 1, 1941; Wichita, Kans., July 1, 1941; San Diego, Calif., Jan. 1, 1941; and Puget Sound, Wash., area, April 1, 1941.

Directors and location of office

Area rent directors appointed by Mr. Henderson, and the location of the rent offices are:

CONNECTICUT: *Bridgeport,* Walter Stapleton, 27 Harrison Street; *Hartford-New Britain,* G. Ray Smith, 110 Ann Street; *Waterbury,* George J. McDuff, Buckingham Building.

NEW YORK: *Schenectady,* Robert W. Christie, New York Central Arcade.

OHIO: *Akron,* Halley T. Waller, 5th Floor, First Central Tower; *Canton,* John A. Pearl, Commercial Bldg., 205 S. Market Street; *Cleveland,* Alfred A. Benesch, Room 855, Union Commerce Bldg.; *Ravenna,* Francis E. Richardson, 257 W. Main Street; *Youngstown-Warren,* Judge George J. Carew, 9th Floor Union National Bank Bldg.

MICHIGAN: *Detroit,* Patrick V. McNamara, 7th Floor, Penobscot Bldg.

INDIANA: *South Bend,* Carl L. Hibberd, 106-108 West Monroe Street.

ALABAMA: *Birmingham,* John G. Million, Phoenix Bldg., 17th Street and 2d Avenue, N.; *Mobile,* Henry J. Kittrell (no office selected).

GEORGIA: *Columbus,* Shelby Compton (no office selected).

VIRGINIA: Hampton Roads, (director to be announced shortly; no office selected).

NORTH CAROLINA: *Wilmington,* George W. Jeffery, 120 Princess Street.

KANSAS: *Wichita,* Mrs. Margie Charles, 5th Floor, Yorkrite Bldg.

IOWA: *Burlington,* Oscar Brandt (no office selected).

CALIFORNIA: *San Diego,* John A. Arvin, Room 682, Spreckels Bldg.

WASHINGTON: *Seattle,* Alfred Harsch, Room 1106 White-Henry-Stuart Bldg.

19 more war production, training areas told to reduce rents in 60 days

Nineteen more communities from Georgia to Alaska were named "defense-rental" areas May 26 by Price Administrator Henderson as OPA continued its move against inflated rents in the Nation's war production and military training areas.

Mr. Henderson recommended that rents in these areas be reduced to the levels prevailing on March 1 of this year, and gave them the customary 60 days as prescribed by the Emergency Price Control Act to meet the recommendations.

The May 26 designations extend the number of "defense-rental" areas from 323 to 342, and add one million persons to the 86 million living in areas already named by the Price Administrator.

Defense-rental areas named May 26 (identified by principal center of population) are listed below:

Hot Springs-Malvern, Ark.—Garland,

Hot Springs and Clark Counties; *Modesto, Calif.*—Stanislaus County; *Ventura, Calif.*—Ventura County; *Bainbridge-Cairo, Ga.*—Decatur and Grady Counties; *Brunswick, Ga.*—Glynn, Brantley, Camden, McIntosh and Wayne Counties; *Decatur, Ind.*—Adams County; *Wabash, Ind.*—Wabash, Huntington and Miami Counties; *Ludington, Mich.*—Manistee, Mason and Oceana Counties; *Sault St. Marie, Mich.*—Chippewa County; *Anaconda, Mont.*—Deer Lodge County; *Monroe, N. C.*—Union County; *Chillicothe, Ohio.*—Ross County; *Sidney, Ohio.*—Shelby County; *Borger, Tex.*—Hutchinson, Carson and Gray Counties; *Dumas-Sunray, Tex.*—Dallam, Hansford, Hartley, Moore and Sherman Counties; *Yakima, Wash.*—Yakima County; *Brigham, Utah*—Box Elder and Cache Counties; *Casper, Wyo.*—Natrona County; *Alaska—*Territory of Alaska.

Entire 1942 pack of salmon, 3 other fishes, set aside; some for civilians possible

The WPB May 26 ordered canners to set aside for the Government their entire 1942 pack of salmon, sardines, Atlantic herring, and mackerel.

The order, M–86–b, is a companion to the previously issued M–86 and M–86–a which required canners to set aside for the Government certain percentages of their 1942 pack of fruits and vegetables.

Lawrence Hopkinson, in charge of fishery products for the WPB, said that the May 26 order does not mean that none of the 1942 pack of fish covered by the order will be available for civilians.

"Because of uncertainty as to the supply and the demand it was thought best to require that the entire pack of these fish be set aside, then if the full supply is not needed for military and Lend-Lease requirements it can be released for civilian purposes," Mr. Hopkinson said.

Six "defense-rental" areas enlarged

Expanding war production activities and construction of additional Army camps has prompted Price Administrator Henderson to increase the size of six "defense-rental" areas, effective May 22.

In an amendment to the designation on March 2, 1942, of the Hampton Roads, Va., defense-rental area, the Price Administrator extended the area to include the Independent City of Suffolk, the previously undesignated portions of Norfolk and Princess Anne Counties, and all of Nansemond County.

An amendment was also issued to extend five of the areas designated April 28, 1942, for which the recommended maximum rent date was March 1, 1942. These areas are:

Ind., Columbus, originally designated as Bartholomew and Brown Counties, extended to include Johnson, Morgan and Shelby Counties;

Kans., Baxter Springs, originally designated as Cherokee County in Kansas and Ottawa County in Oklahoma, extended to include Crawford County, Kans.;

Northeastern New Jersey, originally designated as Counties of Bergen, Essex, Hudson, Middlesex, Monmouth, Morris, Passaic, Somerset and Union, extended to include Sussex County;

Tenn., Clarksville, originally designated as Montgomery County, extended to include Steward County in Tennessee and Christian, Todd and Trigg Counties in Kentucky;

Tex., Amarillo, originally designated as Potter County, extended to include Randall County.

Major canned vegetables under formula for pricing outside general regulation

Because the Nation's canned vegetable processors did not have sufficient stocks on hand in March 1942 to enable them to make sufficient sales to permit a ready determination of price ceilings, Price Administrator Henderson has issued Maximum Price Regulation No. 152 to supplant the general maximum price regulation insofar as it affects hermetically sealed, canned or glass-packed vegetables at the canner level only.

Sales of hermetically sealed, canned or glass-packed vegetables at wholesale and retail will continue to be governed by provisions of the general maximum price regulation, so that prices may not exceed the highest charged during March 1942. Preliminary studies indicate that the formula used in arriving at canner ceiling prices will generally ease the burden on wholesalers and retailers. Should it become necessary in order to prevent undue pressure on the retail price structure, wholesalers' maximum prices will be established for a base period earlier than March 1942.

Support program arranged

To avoid any substantial dislocation of distributor channels, the Department of Agriculture, after consultation with OPA, has announced that if necessary it will purchase the most important canned vegetables at prices equal to 92 percent of the canner's ceiling prices established by the new regulation.

The new maximum prices for canned vegetables are individual ones for each canner. They are arrived at by use of a formula, previously outlined to the industry by OPA after a series of conferences in which the Department of Agriculture participated and announced a price-support program based on 92 percent of the OPA ceiling prices.

Pricing formula outlined

The new OPA pricing formula on canned vegetables arrives at the canner's maximum price per dozen f. o. b. factory for each kind, grade and container size of canned vegetables packed after the 1941 pack by taking:

(1) The weighted average price per dozen charged by the canner f. o. b. factory for such kind, grade and container size during the first 60 days after beginning of the 1941 pack; plus

(2) Eight percent of the weighted average price per dozen f. o. b. factory, plus

(3) The actual increase per dozen cans in the cost of the raw agricultural commodity as of May 4, 1942, over cost of the 1941 pack.

The Department of Agriculture's price-support program applies to ten of the canned vegetables covered by the new OPA regulation. The ten commodities covered by both price-support and specific price ceilings under the new regulation are asparagus, lima beans, snap beans, beets, sweet corn, carrots, peas, spinach, tomatoes, and tomato juice.

The OPA's price ceilings in the new regulation also apply to 25 other canned vegetables and products. These include artichokes, baby foods (chopped vegetables and vegetable purees), bamboo sprouts, bean sprouts, carrots and peas, celery, chili sauce, hominy, okra, okra with tomatoes, onions, parsnips, peppers, pickles, rhubarb, succotash, tomato catsup, tomato paste, tomato puree, tomato sauce, turnips, vegetable greens, vegetables (mixed), vegetable juice (except sauerkraut juice), and vegetable juice (mixed).

The Department of Agriculture's price-support program also covers two canned vegetables—pumpkin and squash—that are not included in the specific list of commodities upon which price ceilings are set by OPA in the new regulation.

Others still under GMPR

On these two canned vegetables—and all others which are not specifically covered by the regulation—the Administrator explained that the canner's maximum selling prices remain the highest March 1942 prices, as provided by the general maximum price regulation.

The new regulation was effective as of May 25.

★ ★ ★

Follow grade preference before size, canners told

WPB on May 25 amended Canned Foods Supplementary Order M–86–a, to make it clear that the grade preference of fruits or vegetables packed in 1942 for military and Lend-Lease consumption takes precedence over the can-size preference. (The grade preference varies among commodities, but in most cases fancy, choice, or extra standard grades are first preference.)

For example, if a packer is able to furnish choice grade (first grade preference) apricots in a No. 2½ can (second can-size preference) or top standard apricots (second grade preference) in a No. 10 can (first can-size preference), but is unable to pack choice grade in a No. 10 can, he is required to pack choice grade in a No. 2½ can.

★ ★ ★

Only 3 types of packing boxes

The WPB containers branch emphasized May 23 that types of boxes other than those specified by Amendment No. 1 to Order M–86–a will not be allowed for this year's pack of canned fruits and vegetables.

The order specifies that either wire-bound, nailed wooden, or weatherproof solid fiber boxes, made in accordance with the terms of the order, must be used for the packing of such canned fruits and vegetables.

Mechanical rubber goods under ceilings; formula provided for "tailor-made" items

OPA has established ceilings on manufacturers' prices for standard mechanical rubber goods items and has outlined a formula for computing maximum prices on specially designed items, Price Administrator Henderson announced May 23.

The ceilings and the formula are contained in Maximum Price Regulation No. 149, which went into effect May 27, 1942, except that effective dates applicable to purchases by governmental agencies are postponed to conform to Supplementary Regulation No. 2 of the general maximum price regulation.

One purpose of the order is to establish the maximum prices of most standard mechanical rubber goods, which are used largely in connection with machinery, at a level of prices paralleling that previously set by OPA for other machine parts not made of rubber. These standard items, which are included in Appendix A of Maximum Price Regulation No. 149, may not be sold at a price higher than the manufacturer's list price, less all discounts, as of October 1, 1941.

Belting, hose and tubing, jar rings and container sealing compounds, lined tanks, pipes and fittings, packing, plumbers' supplies and specialties, tape and thread, made in whole or in part of rubber. These items constitute the bulk of mechanical rubber goods sold on a list price basis.

"Tailor-made" goods—items which ordinarily are sold on a bid basis—are not to be sold at prices in excess of those computed by application of a pricing formula that is set forth in the regulation. To determine the maximum price that may be charged a "bid price" purchaser under this formula, the manufacturer takes the sum of the direct labor and direct materials costs as of a "base date," and to that total adds the gross margin, expressed in dollars and cents, which he would have added to the total direct costs in arriving at his selling price to a purchaser of the same class as of the base date.

The base date to be used in computing the maximum price of most such items is January 5, 1942. However, if an article included in Appendix A had no list price on October 1, 1941, the same formula must be used, except that the base data is October 1, 1941.

Two "listed cities" added for iron, steel products

Two more cities—Tacoma, Wash., and Sioux Falls, S. D.—have been added to "listed cities" recognized by OPA as distribution centers for iron and steel products sold from warehouses.

A listed city is defined as one recognized to have a seller or sellers stocked with a full and representative line of iron and steel products whose price lists may serve as basing lists for the city.

★ ★ ★

Longer lengths of iron, steel scrap included in No. 2

Pieces of iron and steel scrap 15 inches wide and as much as 5 feet long, with some exceptions, may be sold in the future as No. 2 heavy melting steel, Price Administrator Henderson has announced.

Previously the maximum lengths and widths permitted in the No. 2 heavy melting category under Revised Price Schedule No. 4 on iron and steel scrap were pieces 3 feet long and 15 inches wide, excepting car sides.

Ceiling adjustment granted firm producing iron ore

Moore and Crago, of Duluth, Minn., a partnership firm engaged in the production of iron ore, May 23 was granted relief by the OPA from its ceiling prices under Maximum Price Regulation No. 113, covering iron ore.

Price Administrator Henderson said that from a study of the concern's books for 1939, 1940, and 1941, it appears impossible for it to operate at 1941 selling prices, which are the ceiling prices.

The requested relief was granted in Order No. 1 under Maximum Price Regulation No. 113. The order became effective May 23.

Coal firm granted price relief

The Parker Seam Coal Corporation of Cumberland, Md., is permitted to charge $3.90 per net ton f. o. b. the mine for mine run coal shipped by truck or wagon, by Order No. 5 under Maximum Price Regulation No. 120 (Bituminous Coal Delivered From Mine or Preparation Plant).

Producers of gray iron castings given formula for determining ceilings on many products

Producers of gray iron castings were given a formula by the OPA May 23 for determining the maximum price for any gray iron casting produced for which the maximum price cannot be determined under Section 1499.2 of the general maximum price regulation.

Products not uniform

Price Administrator Henderson pointed out that there are more than 3,000 producers of gray iron castings, and that their products are not at all uniform. Castings, for the most part, are custom made to fit particular designs and specifications.

In Order No. 1 under Section 1499.3 (b) of the GMPR—made public May 23 and effective May 25—the Price Administrator gave this formula for pricing gray iron castings whose prices cannot be determined under Section 1499.2:

The producer's maximum price for each such casting shall be a net price (after adjustment for all applicable customary extra charges, discounts or other allowances) not in excess of that at which he would have sold such a casting during March 1942 under the pricing formula or method of calculating price used by him in March 1942, employing the same cost factors (wage rates, prices of materials, and overhead) and profit margins which were in effect for him in March 1942 even though his costs or profit margins may have increased since that date.

The Price Administrator added that on or before the last day of each month, beginning with June 30, 1942, a seller must report the prices of all gray iron castings priced under Section 1499.3 (b) during the preceding month to OPA in Washington on forms which are to be supplied. Each price so reported shall be subject to adjustment at any time by the OPA.

Longer base period optional in computing dealers' inventories

The method of computing inventories permissible under Suppliers' Inventory Limitation Order L-63 has been altered to allow dealers affected by the order to base their calculations on their sales during the preceding quarter, rather than on the second preceding month.

Amendment No. 3 to the suppliers' order, announced May 25 by the Director of Industry Operations, effects this change, which is optional.

Bed-linen pricing provisions adjusted

Under Amendment No. 6 to Revised Price Schedule No. 89 (Bed Linens), effective May 28, 1942, the following changes were made:

1. Sales of "domestic-type grey wide sheetings" become subject to the schedule and are removed from the provisions of Maximum Price Regulation No. 118 (Cotton Products).

2. Specific maximum prices are established for "domestic-type grey wide sheeting" at a level ¾¢ per yard less than 97 percent of the ceiling for brown sheeting of the same type and dimensions.

3. Trade discounts on sales of "domestic-type grey sheetings" are fixed at net 10 days to conform to established trade practice in this class of sales.

4. Specific maximum prices are determined for substandard back-filled type grey sheetings at 49.5¢ per pound net of such sheeting.

5. Sales of bed linens to a manufacturer, converter, or finisher become subject to the schedule.

6. Sales of brown sheeting are made subject to the schedule no matter to whom sold.

7. Specific maximum prices for bleached pillow tubing are established, for various types and dimensions at 1¢ per yard below current levels.

★ ★ ★

Wholesale, retail ceilings on single-weight crepe paper

Maximum prices for the wholesale and retail sale of single-weight, unprinted crepe paper in folds of 9 feet by 20 inches are the same under the general maximum price regulation as the wholesale and retail prices for it in folds of 10 feet by 20 inches during March 1942, Price Administrator Henderson announced May 25.

The maximum price determination applies to the above single-weight crepe paper in 9 foot by 20 inch folds having ratios of 2¼ to 1, 2½ to 1, and 2 to 1.

★ ★ ★

Some contracts for Army field jackets exempt from GMPR

The OPA May 28 excluded from the scope of the general maximum price regulation certain specified contracts for the manufacture of field jackets (wind breakers) for the United States Army.

This action, taken under Supplementary Regulation No. 7, is for military expediency in order to facilitate the procurement of such jackets by the Army. The exception applies only to the Army request for informal bids No. 669-42-NEG 320 for the fabrication of field jackets to meet Quartermaster Corps Tentative Specification PQD No. 20 (b) March 17, 1942.

RUG DISTRIBUTORS WARNED

Distributors of wool floor coverings were warned May 27 by Price Administrator Henderson that the practice of refusing to accept orders for 9' x 12' rugs and offering instead a slightly different size is an evasion of Maximum Price Regulation No. 65 (Resale of Floor Coverings).

Some distributors, OPA has been informed, have refused orders for the 9' x 12' size and offer their customers a slightly different size such as 9' x 12'1'' in order to obtain the cut order price which is approximately 17 percent higher.

Fall prices of women's, girls', children's outerwear garments must not exceed last season's

All 1942 fall styles of women's, girls' and children's cloth outerwear garments—coats, suits, dresses, and many other items—cannot be sold for prices above those charged last season under a new regulation issued May 26 by Price Administrator Henderson. Retailers, wholesalers and manufacturers of such garments are required to establish their price lines for the 1942 fall season at no higher than their 1941 fall season price lines.

Yardage savings taken into account

The regulation—No. 153, Women's, Girls' and Children's Outerwear Garments—the first applying solely to finished wearing apparel, sets as the maximum price for each seller the highest price charged by him for a garment of substantially equal workmanship and quality during a base period of July 1 through September 30, 1941. It became effective May 29.

While specifying that prices for the types of apparel covered by the new regulation shall be no higher than those charged last year's selling season, Mr. Henderson pointed out that the order takes into account simplification of styles and reductions in the yard goods going into a garment, as provided by War Production Board orders.

As used in the regulation, the term "women's, girls' and children's outerwear garments" includes garments of the following types: coats, suits, separate jackets, separate skirts, dresses, blouses, snowsuits, legging sets, and separate leggings.

All bag osnaburg, sheeting needed for war, agriculture

The entire production of bag osnaburg and bag sheeting provided for in the recent WPB textile conversion order (L-99) will be needed to meet minimum military and agricultural demands, T. M. Bancroft, chief of the carded cotton fabrics unit of the WPB, said May 25.

Mr. Bancroft made his statement because of recent reports in some quarters that an overproduction of osnaburg would result from the conversion order.

Mr. Bancroft said that some months ago the Defense Supplies Corporation was authorized to purchase large yardages of bag osnaburg and bag sheetings for stock pile, but because of the great need of bags for agricultural products and the limited supply, only a very small yardage was purchased.

The situation has not changed. The Defense Supplies Corporation still stands ready to make such purchases, but no offers have been received.

Ceilings lowered on wide osnaburgs

Ceiling prices for wide osnaburgs, a type of cotton cloth used chiefly for bagging, were lowered by Price Administrator Henderson May 25 by placing them under the provisions of Revised Price Schedule No. 35 (Carded Grey and Colored Yarn Goods) and removing them from Maximum Price Regulation No. 118 (Cotton Products).

The effect of the May 25 Amendment No. 4 to Price Schedule No. 35 is to bring osnaburgs in widths of 42 inches and over into line with maximum prices for osnaburg less than 42 inches wide. A differential of 10 percent over the narrow goods, which represents the customary trade practice, is established by the change. The amendment became effective May 30, 1942.

Ceilings on cotton, burlap bags

Ceilings for all types of new bags made from cotton and burlap fabrics were established May 25 by the OPA in order that containers may be available for the packaging of the Nation's grain harvest. Maximum Price Regulation No. 151 (New Bags) will affect chiefly sales and deliveries by manufacturers to consumers.

Coal price relief granted ˙ in 5 special situations

Special situations—i n c l u d i n g one where an explosive plant must be assured fuel to operate on Government orders—are provided for in two amendments to and three orders under Maximum Price Regulation No. 120 (Bituminous Coal Delivered From Mines or Preparation Plants).

Amendment No. 2, effective May 25, 1942, establishes a maximum price of $2.20 per net ton for 1¼″ by 0 coal resulting from the crushing of run-of-mine coal produced at a Southwestern mine of the Leavell Coal Company, when sold for use at an ordnance works.

Because of the relatively small production of coal in the area, it has become necessary to develop new mining properties to provide a dependable source of supply for the power plant.

Amendment No. 1 to Maximum Price Regulation No. 120 also effective May 25, establishes a special maximum price for smithing coal produced at the Salem No. 1 Mine of the Keystone Coal and Coke Company in Production District No. 2 (Western Pennsylvania) of $4 per ton.

Order No. 2 under Maximum Price Regulation No. 120 grants some relief asked in a petition of Durham Coals, Inc., Chattanooga, Tenn.

Order No. 3 grants some exceptions to the Elmira Coal Company, Excelsior Springs, Mo.

Order No. 4 grants relief to certain coal producers in Production District No. 10 (Illinois) who made representations to justify exceptions from established maximum prices on the ground that the maximums were below the going prices prevailing in October 1941.

★ ★ ★

Coal mine granted exception

Price Administrator Henderson announced May 23 that an exception, effective immediately, to Maximum Price Regulation No. 120 (Bituminous Coal Delivered From Mine or Preparation Plant) has been granted, permitting the sale of certain sizes of high quality coal produced from the Glen Rogers Mine (Mine Index No. 73), at Glen Rogers, Wyoming County, W. Va., District No. 7, at prices above the maximum.

In its review of the case, OPA found that the mine would be burdened with genuine hardship unless an adjustment of prices was made.

ICE CEILINGS ADJUSTED FOR HEAVY SUMMER SEASON

Because in certain sections of the United States the ice industry's established practice has been to have higher seasonal prices during the heavier consuming summer season, Price Administrator Henderson May 25 ruled that the "winter period" prices of March 1942—set as peaks under the general maximum price regulation—would cause unnecessary hardship to sellers during the summer months.

Therefore, the Administrator May 25 issued Maximum Price Regulation No. 154, which under certain terms and conditions, permits such ice merchandisers during April to October inclusive only to sell at the same prices charged by them in the corresponding month of 1941. During the winter period, the ceiling shall be the March 1942 peaks. The new regulation on ice became effective May 25.

★ ★ ★

Relief given coal distributor; procedure set up for others

Less than three days after a petition to Price Administrator Leon Henderson indicated that a coal distributor—bound by long-term contractual obligations—faced unjustified hardship in complying with a price regulation, an amendment to the regulation, issued May 26, granted relief. The amendment, however, permits no increase in the retail levels.

This action by the Administrator, which also sets up a special procedure under which other similarly situated persons may apply for relief, came in Amendment No. 3 to Maximum Price Regulation No. 122 (for solid fuel dealers, other than producers) and Order No. 1 under the same regulations. (Both are effective as of May 25, 1942.)

The petition was filed May 25, 1942, by George B. Newton Coal Co., Philadelphia.

Houston's crude oil price

A maximum price of $1.30 per barrel for East Texas crude petroleum sold by the Houston Oil Company of Texas at its Tank No. 11, Peterson Tank Farm, Isaac Ruddle Survey, Rusk County, Texas was permitted by OPA in an amendment May 26 to its petroleum and petroleum products price schedule. All of this product is bought under contract by Shell Oil Company, Inc.

Pricing change aids States; cities in storing solid fuel

In a move to encourage storing of solid fuels by States, cities and other political subdivisions to meet any unexpected contingencies, Price Administrator Henderson on May 26 issued Amendment No. 4 to Maximum Price Regulation No. 122 (Solid fuel dealers other than producers). The amendment was effective as of May 25, 1942.

In a new section added to Appendix A of the price regulation, the amendment declares that, in sales of solid fuels by a person subject to the price regulation to a state or other political subdivision, contracts may be entered into at prices not exceeding applicable maximum prices which are in effect at the time of delivery; and, in addition, for special services rendered by the seller, at specified charges, in connection with storage, maintenance or delivery of solid fuels.

These special charges, however, are permitted only for novel services not provided for in the original regulation.

Requirements for imposition of these special charges include the stipulation that any such contract shall state the charges for special services separately from the price paid for the fuel as a commodity; that such contracts shall be awarded by open bids, and that two copies of any such contract shall be filed with OPA.

★ ★

Petroleum sellers required to maintain discounts

Sellers of petroleum or petroleum products must maintain discounts which they allowed buyers on comparative sales during the October 1–15, 1941, period, Price Administrator Leon Henderson ruled May 27 in issuing Amendment No. 17 to Revised Price Schedule No. 88 (Petroleum and Petroleum Products). The amendment was effective as of May 27, 1942.

★ ★

Soft coal producers shipping to own docks given aid

Bituminous coal producers who ship fuel to their own dock facilities in the Northeast and distribute it from those points are given the same benefits accorded other distributors under Compensatory Adjustment Regulation No. 1 by an amendment to the regulation effective May 23, 1942, and issued by Price Administrator Henderson.

The compensatory regulation provided for compensation of dealers and distributors who incur increased transportation costs in keeping New York and New England supplied with coal in the face of dislocated normal tidewater transportation from Hampton Roads, Va

Rules governing auctions prevent sales above ceiling

Rules governing auction sales, which will prevent goods being sold at auction at prices above legal maximums, were announced May 27 by the OPA.

The maximum price for each item, under the general maximum price regulation in general is the maximum price for which that item was sold by each seller, in March 1942.

An important exception to the rules controlling maximum prices at auctions is a bona fide auction of used household or personal effects. Such a sale is not covered by the price regulations at all.

At many auctions, the goods sold will be partly those covered by the price regulation, partly those not covered.

Sales in bulk will be permitted at public auction sales, provided:

(a) Items not under price control are not included in the same bulk with controlled items.

(b) The maximum price for each separate item in the "controlled" bulk has been itemized.

(c) The price for the sale of the "controlled" bulk does not exceed the aggregate of the maximum prices.

In case of a "tie"

Foreseeing a situation in which two or more persons might all bid the maximum allowed or ceiling price, leading to a "tie," OPA stated that "The determination of which bid is to be accepted is not OPA's concern. However, a practical solution is drawing lots."

Items may be included in the "controlled" bulk, even though they are uncontrolled in sales to certain classes of purchasers, or have different controlled prices depending upon the class of purchasers. The itemization of the maximum prices should include a separate itemization of the maximum price for each level, and should state a reasonable price on the uncontrolled level. The maximum price for the bulk will, in such cases, vary with the successful bidder.

★ ★ ★

Ceilings adjusted on unrepaired used tires, tubes

Used tires or tubes that are not serviceable without repairs, may not be sold at the ceiling price which would apply to them if they were undamaged or already repaired, Price Administrator Henderson stated May 25.

To clear up any misunderstanding that may have existed on this score, the Administrator has issued Amendment No. 2, effective May 26, to Maximum Price Regulation No. 107.

The amendment provides that the maximum price for any unrepaired used passenger car or truck tire or tube is the level established in Regulation No. 107, less an amount equal to the charges prevailing in the locality of the seller on March 7, 1942, for the repairs necessary.

FUNERAL SERVICES UNDER RETAIL PRICE RULE

Charges for funeral services must conform to ceilings established by the general maximum price regulation, Price Administrator Henderson stated May 27.

"The funeral service industry in all its operations is subject to the requirements laid down in the General Maximum Price Regulation," Mr. Henderson said.

"It does not matter whether a funeral director bills a lump sum for all his various professional and personal services, facilities and merchandise, or sends an itemized bill. In any event, the charges must conform to the price ceilings and none can exceed the highest charges in effect last March."

The OPA interpretation holds that since the services of a funeral director and his staff are performed in connection with the sale of a commodity—the casket—the general maximum price regulation applies. Hence funeral directors must determine their maximum prices in the same way as others selling at retail.

– – –

Sales by War, Navy Department stores exempt till July 1

Sales by commissaries, ships' stores ashore and other sales stores of the War and Navy Departments will be exempt from price ceilings until July 1, Price Administrator Henderson announced May 27.

The postponement, contained in Amendment 3 to Supplementary Regulation No. 2 of the general maximum price regulation, was made effective as of May 18, the date retail sales came under the regulation.

OPA previously exempted from the General Maximum Price Regulation sales to the War and Navy Departments until July 1. The May 27 action removes the two departments from the possibility of having to buy goods at higher than March prices up to July 1, and yet having to sell the goods at the March prices.

The amendment does not, however, apply to sales, deliveries, or contracts with stores operated as army canteens or post exchanges or as ships' service activities. Sales or deliveries to these stores became subject to the general maximum price regulation May 11 and sales by these stores became subject to that regulation on May 18.

Some processed grain products excepted from universal ceiling

Some processed grain products—which are prepared mainly for food—have been excepted from the March ceiling provisions of the general maximum price regulation, Price Administrator Henderson announced May 25. However, the exception does not prevail when these products are sold in packages of 3 pounds or less.

Commodities excepted

These new exceptions to the universal ceiling are listed in Amendment No. 2 of Supplementary Regulation No. 1, which became effective May 26.

The commodities upon which GMPR shall not apply to sales or deliveries, except when packaged in containers holding 3 pounds or less, include the following:

1. Such specified wheat products as farina, semolina, ground wheat, and malted wheat.

2. Such specified corn products as malted corn and such dry corn milled products as meal, hominy, and grits. (Dry corn milled products such as bran, hominy feed, oil cake and meal, germ cake and meal and oil are not excepted.)

3. Such specified barley products as pearled barley, ground pearled barley, hulled barley, malted barley, barley needles, and ground barley.

4. Such specified oat products as groats, hulled oats, ground groats, rolled hulled oats (table or feeding), cereal oats, and ground oats.

5. Such specified rye products as malted rye and ground rye.

6. Ground soy beans.

7. Ground buckwheat.

Some of these commodities excepted consist of whole grains after processing. OPA quarters explained that they are priced by adding to the price of the grain a constant moderate milling charge. Others are principal products after the byproducts have been removed. They are priced by crediting the value of the byproducts to the cost of the grain and adding a constant moderate milling charge.

Pottery sales on U. S. contracts

Simplification of the procedure for pottery manufacturers who enter bids for Government contracts and an alternative method of determining maximum prices for semivitreous ware customarily priced on a pound sterling basis are effected in Amendment No. 1 to Maximum Price Regulation No. 116 issued May 22 by Price Administrator Henderson.

Prices of Appalachian hardwood lumber shipped from mills cut 7 to 8 percent

Prices of Appalachian hardwood lumber shipped from mills were cut about 7 to 8 percent from present levels as Price Administrator Henderson established a list of separate price ceilings for this type of lumber through the issuance of Maximum Price Regulation No. 146—Appalachian Hardwood Lumber.

Prices "rolled back"

The regulation bases maximum prices approximately on quotations prevailing during the October 1 to 15, 1941 period and, in effect, "rolls back" these lumber prices from the highest levels of March 1942. All sales of Appalachian hardwood lumber had been excluded from the provisions of the general maximum price regulation up to the time this special regulation was issued. Although Regulation No. 146 became effective June 1, 1942, it immediately excluded from the application of the general regulation sales which fall within the scope of the Appalachian regulation. All sales of Appalachian lumber which will not be controlled by Regulation No. 146 are immediately subject to the general regulation.

Hardwood lumber produced from the Appalachian area has long enjoyed a favorable price differential over lumber produced in the Southern hardwoods area which since February 20 has been controlled by Revised Schedule No. 97. The May 22 order restores the normal competitive relationship between Appalachian and Southern hardwood lumber.

Area designated

The Administrator has designated the Appalachian hardwood area to include all of West Virginia, the eastern parts of Kentucky and Tennessee, the northeastern part of Georgia, the western parts of Maryland, Virginia, and North Carolina, and the northwestern part of South Carolina. The species of lumber included are yellow poplar, tough white ash, beech, soft maple, ash (other than tough white ash), butternut, chestnut, hard maple, red oak and white oak, hickory, basswood, birch, buckeye and cherry.

The regulation covers all sales and deliveries of Appalachian hardwood lumber where the shipment originates at the mill rather than at a distribution yard.

The Appalachian regulation by express terms does not apply to direct mill shipments which are retail sales. However,

such retail sales are covered by the general maximum price regulation.

The May 22 order provides a fixed scale of dollars and cents prices for Appalachian hardwood lumber sold in standard or near standard grades, and also establishes maximum prices for special grades and items.

Advertising allowance to seller not covered by price rule

Advertising allowances granted by a manufacturer for promotional services to a distributor or a retail outlet are not covered by the general maximum price regulation, Price Administrator Henderson said May 28.

In an interpretation of the regulation, the Office of Price Administration stated:

Advertising allowances granted by a seller for promotional services rendered by a buyer are not "frozen" by the general maximum price regulation and are not to be considered as an element in the price at which goods were delivered during March [the base period under the universal price ceiling].

The seller is, therefore, not required to continue to grant the advertising allowances customarily granted by him to different purchasers or classes of purchasers.

If, however, allowances, even though designated as "advertising allowances," actually constituted a reduction in the price of merchandise and were granted by the seller without regard to promotional services to be rendered by the buyer (the distributor or retail outlet), the seller is required to treat such allowances in the same way as his customary allowances, discounts and price differentials prevailing in March.

Ceilings set on most feed items

Ceiling prices are established under the general maximum price regulation on the majority of feed items, the OPA indicated May 23 in an interpretation.

The following feed items are included under the general maximum price regulation, OPA stated:

wheat bran, wheat standard middlings, malt sprouts, wheat flour middlings, wheat red dog, wheat mixed feed, brown, gray and white wheat shorts, alfalfa meals, dried beet pulp, oat mill feed, distillers' dried grains, cottonseed meal, citrus pulp, corn gluten feed, corn gluten meal, soybean oil meal, coconut meal, brewers' dried grains, molasses, and all other commodities used for feeding purposes except hay, whole grains and seeds, or grains and seeds processed expressly for use as feeds.

Citric acid ceilings revised to check evasions

A revision of the maximum price schedule for citric acid, striking at evasive practices which have grown up since the schedule became effective in February, was announced May 25 by Price Administrator Henderson.

Wholesalers classed as "resellers"

Citric acid is widely used in pharmaceutical manufacture and for flavoring soft drinks, confectioneries, and foods. The changes are set forth in the new citric acid schedule entitled, "Revised Price Schedule No. 101, as amended," which became effective May 26.

One of the important provisions makes it clear that wholesalers are classified as "resellers" and hence are subject to the maximum prices established for resellers.

Another provision specifies that persons selling at maximum prices must continue the practices on cash discounts prevailing at the time the original schedule took effect.

One of the principal changes reduces the amount that may be charged for sales of large quantities of citric acid when delivered in small-sized containers. In an attempt to obtain higher prices, some sellers have been repackaging large quantities of citric acid in small packages in order to obtain the differential that had been allowed for five-pound packages without regard to the quantity sold.

One important effect will be to prevent the wasting of scarce container materials.

Export provisions deleted

Because of the recent issuance of the Maximum Export Price Regulation, which superseded the export provisions of the original citric acid schedule, the amendment deletes the provisions on exports and provides that they shall be governed by the over-all export regulation.

Flour, cake mixes, other terms clarified by OPA

In order to clarify certain ambiguities regarding some terms used in the general maximum price regulation, the OPA has issued specific definitions of "flour," "cake mixes," and "flour mixes," and made clear what the term "packaged" means, Administrator Henderson announced May 28.

Fuel briquette terms changed

A paragraph defining "miscellaneous solid fuels" in Maximum Price Regulation No. 121 (Miscellaneous Solid Fuels Delivered From Producing Facilities) is revised to substitute the words "briquettes made from coal or coke" for "briquettes made from coal and coke," by Amendment No. 1, effective immediately, OPA announced May 28.

New industry advisory committees

The Bureau of Industry Advisory Committees, WPB, has announced the formation of the following new industry advisory committees:

HAND SHOVEL INDUSTRY

Government presiding officer—John L. Haynes, chief, building materials branch.

Members:

W. W. Rector, American Fork & Hoe Co., Cleveland, Ohio; L. P. Finley, Union Fork & Hoe Co., Columbus, Ohio; Richard Harte, Ames Baldwin Wyoming Co., Parkersburg, W. Va.; Edwin T. Nipher, The Wood shovel & Tool Co., Piqua, Ohio; Arvid P. Zetterberg, Ingersoll Steel & Disc Division, Borg Warner Corporation, New Castle, Ind.; James W. Leis, Magor Car Corporation, Clifton, N. J.; John Pfeifer, John Pfeifer Co., Philadelphia, Pa.; E. W. Hamlin, The Hamlin Metal Products Co., Akron, Ohio.

HARDWOOD LUMBER MANUFACTURERS INDUSTRY

Government presiding officer—Arthur Upson, chief, lumber and lumber products branch.

Members:

A. O. Anderson, Michigamme, Mich.; J. W. Damron, president, W. M. Ritter Lumber Co., Columbus, Ohio; Owen Johnson, president, Johnson Lumber Co., Manchester, N. H.; Walter W. Kellogg, president, Kellogg Lumber Co., Monroe, La.; Campbell Pancake, president, Pancake Lumber Co., Inc., Staunton, Va.; C. W. Parham, president, C. W. Parham Lumber Co., Memphis, Tenn.; Lee Robinson, president, Mobile River Sawmill Co., Mount Vernon, Ala.; O. T. Swan, secretary-manager, Northern Hemlock & Hardwood Manufacturers Assn., Oshkosh, Wis.; E. M. Vestal, vice president, Vestal Lumber & Mfg. Co., Knoxville, Tenn.; Carl L. White, president, Breece White Mfg. Co., Eudora, Ark.

HOUSE TRAILER INDUSTRY

Government presiding officer—Francis Palms, chief, house trailer section of the lumber and lumber products branch.

Members:

D. D. Arehart, president, Palace Travel Coach Corporation, Hemphill Road, Flint, Mich.; Wilbur J. Schult, president, Schult Trailers, 1708–1900 South Main Street, Elkhart, Ind.; E. H. Becker, president, Glider Trailer Co., 1824 West Kinzie Street, Chicago, Ill.; George F. Miles, vice president, Vagabond Coach Mfg. Co., Brighton, Mich.; H. L. Bartholomew, president, Indian Trailer Corporation, 122 East 63d Street, Chicago, Ill.; E. E. Raymond, president, Raymond Products Co., 411 Rust Avenue, Saginaw, Mich.; W. E. Case, president, Main Line Trailer Co., 8825 Avalon Boulevard, Los Angeles, Calif.; H. D. Platt, president, Platt Trailer Co., Inc., 530 McDonald Street, Elkhart, Ind.; Charles R. Smith, president, Travelodge Corporation, 65 North Madison Street, Tulsa, Okla.; R. J. Miller, president, Miller Auto Cruiser Co., 812-12th Street, Bradenton, Fla.

MEN'S PAJAMA INDUSTRY

Government presiding officer—H. Stanley Marcus, chief of the clothing section.

Members:

Leon L. Chock, Reliance Mfg. Co., 200 Fifth Avenue, New York, N. Y.; Sylvan Geismar, Manhattan Shirt Co., 444 Madison Avenue, New York, N. Y.; Felix Gundersheimer, Stadium Mfg. Co., 1501 Guilford Avenue, Baltimore, Md.; Harry S. Jacobson, F. Jacobson & Sons, 1115 Broadway, New York, N. Y.; Peter K. Karberg, H. B. Glover Co., Fifth and Iowa Streets, Dubuque, Iowa; Andrew Krein, Krestie Mfg. Co., 208 South Pulaski Street, Baltimore, Md.; Louis Lublin, Lublin Weeker Co., 1270 Broadway, New York, N. Y.; Harold W. Mittelstadt, Wilson Brothers, Box 772, Chicago, Ill.; A. R. Richtmyer, Knothe Brothers, 24 West 40th Street, New York, N. Y.; Harold A. Steiner, Harold Steiner, Inc., 350 Fifth Avenue, New York, N. Y.

PORTLAND CEMENT INDUSTRY

Government presiding officer—John L. Haynes, chief, building materials branch.

Members:

M. M. Alexander, Missouri Portland Cement Co., St. Louis, Mo.; Garner A. Beckett, Riverside Cement Co., Los Angeles, Calif.; L. N. Bryant, Green Bag Cement Co., Pittsburgh, Pa.; R. W. Crum, Highway Research Board, Washington, D. C.; A. E. Douglass, Allentown Portland Cement Co., Catasauqua, Pa.; Edwin P. Lucas, Superior Portland Cement Inc., Seattle, Wash.; L. Morris Mitchell, Merritt, Chapman & Scott, New York City, N. Y.; John F. Neylan, Lone Star Cement Co., New York City, N. Y.; W. C. Russell, Peerless Cement Co., Detroit, Mich.; Blaine S. Smith, Universal Atlas Cement Co., New York City, N. Y.; S. W. Storey, Trinity Portland Cement Co., Chicago, Ill.; W. A. Wecker, Marquette Cement Mfg. Co., Chicago, Ill.; Joseph S. Young, Lehigh Portland Cement Co., Allentown, Pa.; Herbert A. Snow, Portland Cement Co. of Utah, Salt Lake City, Utah.

PULP AND PAPER INDUSTRY TRANSPORTATION

Government presiding officer—F. E. Hufford, transportation consultant.

Members:

W. J. Bailey, West Virginia Pulp & Paper Co., New York, N. Y.; J. E. Bryan, Wisconsin Paper & Pulp, Mfrs. Traffic Assn., Chicago, Ill.; G. L. Fenstenmaker, Sutherland Paper Co., Kalamazoo, Mich.; James P. Friel, Central Fibre Products Co., Chicago, Ill.; R. J. Henderson, Minnesota & Ontario Paper Co., Minneapolis, Minn.; Hugo Ignatius, International Paper Co., New York, N. Y.; Frederick F. Kator, The Mead Corporation, Dayton, Ohio; J. D. Patterson, Union Bag and Paper Corporation, New York, N. Y.; J. A. Quinlan, St. Regis Paper Co., New York, N. Y.; A. A. Raphael, New England Pulp & Paper Traffic Assn., Boston, Mass.; H. T. Ratliff, The Champion Paper & Fibre Co., Hamilton, Ohio; J. J. Seid, Crown-Zellerbach Corporation, San Francisco, Calif.

SOFTWOOD LOGGERS AND LUMBER MFRS. INDUSTRY

Government presiding officer—Arthur Upson, chief, lumber and lumber products branch.

Members:

Carl W. Bahr, California Redwood Distributors, Ltd., 35 East Wacker Drive, Chicago, Ill.; J. M. Brown, president, Long Lake Lumber Co., Spokane, Wash.; M. L. Fleishel, president, Putnam Lumber Co., Shamrock, Fla.; Everett Hancock, M. S. Hancock & Son, Casco, Maine; C. R. McPherson, president, Wilson Cypress Co., Palatka, Fla.; Orville R. Miller, vice president, Mt. Jefferson Lumber Co., Portland, Oreg.; F. C. Mills, Mills Lumber Co., Acworth,

Ga.; L. K. Pomeroy, president, Ozark-Badger Lumber Co., Wilmar, Ark.; Forest H. Himes, F. H. Himes Lumber Co., Crandon, Wis.; Lacy H. Hunt, Tilford Hunt Co., Nacogdoches, Tex.; W. B. Greeley, secretary-manager, West Coast Lumbermen's Assn., Seattle, Wash.; Dana E. McDuffee, Blagen Lumber Co., Stockton, Calif.; W. G. Savage, president, Lake Washington Mill Co., Renton, Wash.; C. C. Sheppard, president, Louisiana Central Lumber Co., Clarks, La.; Charles Snellstrom, manager, Snellstrom Bros., Inc., Eugene, Oreg.; F. K. Weyerhaeuser, president, Weyerhaeuser Sales Co., St. Paul, Minn.

TOILETRIES AND COSMETICS INDUSTRY

Government presiding officer—C. A. Willard, acting chief, toiletries and cosmetics branch.

Members:

Joseph A. Danilek, comptroller, Elizabeth Arden Sales Corporation, New York, N. Y.; R. L. Evans, Ralph L. Evans Associates, Hoboken, N. J.; Davis Factor, general manager, Max Factor Co., Los Angeles, Calif.; Manning O'Connor, Colgate-Palmolive-Peet, Jersey City, N. J.; John W. Smith, president, Aladdin Laboratories, Minneapolis, Minn.; Paul H. Douglas, vice president, Bourjois, Inc., New York, N. Y.; E. W. Golden, Jr., general manager, Keystone Laboratories, Inc., Memphis, Tenn.; Jule Gordon, sales representative, F. W. Fitch Co., New York, N. Y.; Joseph D. Nelson, vice president, Andrew Jergens Co., Cincinnati, Ohio; John H. Wallace, Jr., president, Wallace Laboratories, New Brunswick, N. J.; Northam Warren, president, Northam Warren Corporation, New York, N. Y.; J. E. Wiedkorf, general manager, Parfums Ciro, New York, N. Y.

UNIVERSAL ELECTRIC TOOL INDUSTRY

Government presiding officer—E. P. Waller, chief, industrial specialties group.

Members:

E. E. Morrison, Albertson & Co., Sioux City, Iowa; L. J. Walker, Chicago Pneumatic Tool Co., 6 East 44th Street, New York, N. Y.; R. L. Hamilton, Dunmore Co., Racine, Wis.; A. W. Mall, Mall Tool Co., 7740 South Chicago Street, Chicago, Ill.; D. J. Ridings, Porter-Cable Machine Co., Syracuse, N. Y.; H. F. Tideman, Signal Electric Mfg. Co., 600 West Jackson Boulevard, Chicago, Ill.; L. M. Knouse, Stanley Electric Tool Division, Division Stanley Works, New Britain, Conn.; C. E. Hahn, Cincinnati Electrical Tool Co., Madison & Edwards Road, Cincinnati, Ohio; Philip Rogers, Millers Falls Co., 57 Wells Street, Greenfield, Mass.; S. P. Black, Black & Decker Mfg. Co., Towson, Md.; B. W. Ristau, Skilsaw, Inc., Chicago, Ill.; Steven Scace, Speedway Mfg. Co., 1834 South 52d Avenue, Cicero, Ill.; D. G. Black, Syntron Co., Homer City, Pa.; George E. Smith, U. S. Electrical Tool Co., Cincinnati, Ohio; Kennedy M. Clark, James Clark Jr. Electric Co., 600 East Bergman Street, Louisville, Ky.; O. P. Wodack, Wodack Electric Tool Corporation, Chicago, Ill.; Neil C. Hurley, Jr., Independent Pneumatic Tool Co., 600 West Jackson Boulevard, Chicago, Ill.; J. F. Willey, Louisville Electric Mfg. Co., Louisville, Ky.; John E. Penniman, Power King Tool Corporation, 1941 Heinz Street, Warsaw, Ind.; Andrew Wyzenbeek, Wyzenbeek & Staff, Inc., 838 West Hubbard Avenue, Chicago, Ill.; A. G. Decker, Jr., Van Dorn Electric Tool Co., 600 East Pennsylvania Avenue, Towson, Md.

Two members have been added to the refrigeration condensing unit industry advisory committee:

Clyde Ploger, Servel, Inc., Evansville, Ind.; Forest Jernberg, Mills Novelty Co., Chicago, Ill.

CONSERVATION . . .

Cans will be collected in 36 cities to salvage tin, steel, copper for war

A tin-can salvage program to reclaim large quantities of tin, steel scrap, and copper urgently needed for war materials will be sponsored and directed by the WBP Bureau of Industrial Conservation.

Plans for tin can collection in 36 metropolitan areas, advantageously located for rail shipping to detinning and copper precipitation plants now in operation, were announced June 1 by the Bureau.

Collections will be restricted to these areas at present because authorities estimate it will take only 250,000 tons of tin cans a year to keep existing detinning facilities running at maximum capacity.

In 32 areas, householders will be asked to prepare the cans by cleaning, removing the label and both ends, and compressing slightly for shipment to detinning plants.

In four designated centers, Los Angeles, Dallas, Houston, and Kansas City, Kans., and Kansas City, Mo., unprepared cans will be collected for shredding and delivery to copper mines where they are used in the process of reclaiming copper through precipitation.

The metropolitan centers selected to collect tin cans for detinning plants and to be asked to inaugurate collection programs are:

Boston, Mass.; Hartford-New Britain, Conn.; Providence, R. I.; Springfield-Holyoke, Mass.; Lowell-Lawrence, Mass.; New York, N. Y.; northern New Jersey, Albany-Schenectady-Troy, N. Y.; Philadelphia, Pa.; Scranton-Wilkes Barre, Pa.; Baltimore, Md.; Washington, D. C.; Rochester, N. Y.; Buffalo, N. Y.; Pittsburgh, Pa.; Youngstown, Ohio; Cleveland, Ohio; Detroit, Mich.; Columbus, Ohio; Cincinnati, Ohio; Louisville, Ky.; Indianapolis, Ind.; Chicago, Ill.; Milwaukee, Wis.; Minneapolis-St. Paul, Minn.; St. Louis, Mo.; Denver, Colo.; Atlanta, Ga.; Birmingham, Ala.; New Orleans, La.; San Francisco, Calif.; Seattle, Wash.; Portland, Oreg.

Increased use of casein to release vital materials

The dairy cows of America may be called on to play an unusual part in helping the United Nations to victory, the Bureau of Industrial Conservation pointed out May 31.

Cow's milk, in the form of skimmed milk not otherwise used, is the source of casein, a basic chemical product. Substitution of casein for more essential chemicals will release quantities of vital materials for essential war production, the conservation and substitution branch of the Bureau of Industrial Conservation says.

The Bureau of Industrial Conservation's chemical experts have at their fingertips formulas for the use of casein in numerous industrial processes.

Among the industrial concerns which can be served by the Bureau with the latest technical advice on casein substitution are the makers of paint, adhesives, plastics, furniture, plywood, insecticides, polishes and metal cleansers, and all manufacturers who employ solvents that might be replaced with casein emulsions.

Nation's housewives called upon to ease load on junkman

The WPB June 1 called on the Nation's housewives to cooperate in easing the load on junkmen caused by success of Salvage for Victory campaigns.

The junkmen, with decrepit wagon or battered pickup truck, is a front-line fighter in the battle of waste, a key man in the Salvage for Victory campaign.

To help the junkman, WPB makes the following suggestions:

Long before the junkman arrives on the scene there are many ways you can make his task lighter. As you drag the scrap from attic, basement, and backyard, sort the various metals—steel, copper, aluminum, zinc, tin—into separate piles and try to strip them of any worthless encumbrances.

If you come across any old tires, hot water bottles, shower curtains or galoshes place them in a separate pile marked "rubber." Sort out your old rags according to their type of material and separate oily ones from clean ones. Flatten out your cartons, boxes and paper bags. Stack your newspapers in a pile until they reach a height of 6 feet and tie them up securely. Put as much of your junk as possible in boxes and bags.

If you're not interested in selling your scrap, call your favorite charity to dispose of it. Or phone your local Salvage for Victory committee.

Production committee praised for saving 100 tons of iron, much scarce metal

Lessing J. Rosenwald, Chief of the Bureau of Industrial Conservation, May 25, congratulated the War Production Drive Committee of the Grasselli, N. J., plant of E. I. duPont de Nemours Co., on its report of an outstanding salvage campaign.

Copper sent back to war

The labor-management committee reported that the salvage campaign in one month netted the following materials: 100.5 tons of scrap iron, 9.5 tons of hard lead, 5.25 tons of copper, 3 tons of brass, 1.75 tons of aluminum, 1.75 tons of stainless steel, 0.25 ton of monel.

In addition, receptacles for rubber placed throughout the plant gathered 1,073 pounds of scrap rubber.

How they do it

Details of the report follow:

The company formerly burned off the rubber insulation from copper wires and cables so as to salvage the copper. It now salvages the rubber by squeezing the wire or cable through a set of rollers, thus permitting the rubber to be easily removed from the wire.

All the short stubs of welding rods are saved for return to the welding supplier for credit.

All worn-out or broken steel punches, dies, drills and high-speed tools are salvaged.

On its lead-burning operations, it is supplying the lead burners with wooden buckets so that the lead scrapings can be salvaged.

All burned-out electrical fuse cases are collected and returned to the manufacturer for refilling.

Dry cell batteries of all types, including flashlights, are collected when worn out for the zinc salvage.

All waste burlap is being collected.

Wiping rags are being collected when dirty and are being washed for reuse.

Metal motor covers, coupling guards, machine guards and brackets are being standardized to conserve steel.

★ ★ ★

Data on national emergency steels available to industry

Technical information on the national emergency steels is accumulating and is available to industry, it was announced May 27 by the metallurgical section, iron and steel branch, and the Bureau of Industrial Conservation, who are cooperating on the proposed new specifications. The Iron and Steel Institute has collected all existing data and published it in loose-leaf form.

HELPING TO BRING IT UP.

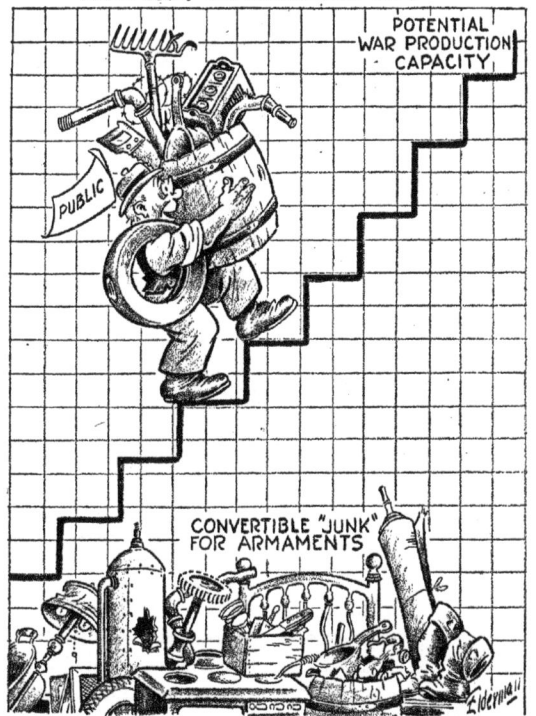

Cartoon by Elderman for VICTORY. Publishers may obtain mats of these cartoons weekly in either two- or three-column size. Requests to be put on the mailing list should be addressed to Distribution Section, Division of Information, Office for Emergency Management, Washington, D. C. Refer to V–15.

Machine regulation put off

Effective date of Maximum Price Regulation No. 136 on machines and parts has been advanced to July 1, 1942, from June 1, 1942, Price Administrator Henderson announced May 30. "An extensively and extremely important amendment to Maximum Price Regulation No. 136 is in process," he said.

San Francisco regional director

Harry H. Fair, of San Francisco, has been named San Francisco regional director of WPB, it was announced May 30. The San Francisco region includes California, Arizona, and Nevada. All WPB field offices in these three States will be directly responsible to the San Francisco regional office.

350,000 tons of metal collected from old autos in April

Evidence that automobile graveyards are aiding substantially in relieving the Nation's scrap metal shortage was offered May 28 by the WPB Bureau of Industrial Conservation.

According to reports made public by the automobile graveyard section of the Bureau, the yards have yielded approximately 350,000 tons of scrap metal from more than 400,000 junked cars during April. This is about 200,000 tons more than the monthly average of scrap metal recovered from them during 1941. The figure includes about 6,000 tons of copper urgently needed for war material.

Officials of the Bureau are confident that the Government's campaign begun last March to induce auto graveyard owners to turn over the contents of their yards on a 60-day schedule will help considerably in meeting the Nation's 1942 scrap shortage. They point to reports from a number of mills recording a pick-up in scrap inventory concurrent with the development of the auto graveyard campaign.

Tire shortage expected to help

Merrill Stubbs, chief of the automobile graveyard section, said:

Reports from the field indicate that the months following April should show an even greater increase in the amount of scrap metal recovered from automobile graveyards. There are at present in this country 6,837,781 cars more than 10 years old. Limitations on tires and gasoline, and the difficulty of securing replacement parts, is convincing owners of these old cars that their continued existence represents a loss to them as well as to their country's war economy. We are making a special appeal to the owners of cars no longer economically usable or repairable to haul them to the nearest graveyard. Only those cars offering safe, practical transportation should be withheld.

Chemical cotton pulp under full allocation

Chemical cotton pulp is placed under full allocation control by Conservation Order M–157, issued May 28 by the Director of Industry Operations.

Effective July 1, 1942, no producer may deliver, and no buyer may accept, any chemical cotton pulp except as specifically authorized by the Director of Industry Operations. Exceptions to this are deliveries to the Army, Navy, Coast Guard, and Maritime Commission; and small orders of 500 pounds or less to any one consumer per month, provided that the total of such small deliveries is less than 2,000 pounds a month by any one producer. June deliveries are not affected. The filing of inventory and purchase intention forms is required.

INDUSTRIAL OPERATIONS . . .

WPB releases some lumber suitable for war housing and farm purposes

The War Production Board on May 28 amended the Construction Lumber Order (L–121) to release from the restrictions several grades and items no longer being bought by Federal agencies, which are usable for war housing and farm purposes.

Among types of construction lumber released from the freeze provisions are 2-inch dimension shorter than ten feet; scant size 1-inch boards and 2-inch dimension; No. 1 heart common in three species not usually used for construction purposes; all No. 3 common dimension; all No. 2, 3, and 4 common boards in some species, No. 3 and No. 4 in other species, and No. 4 in still others; one grade of drop siding and flooring; and railway ties.

War housing to be reexamined

No specific exemption has been provided for the sale to war housing contractors of construction lumber of types still covered by the order.

Representatives of the WPB, the National Housing Authority, the Federal Housing Agency, and other housing officials have agreed that all war housing projects must be reexamined so as to reduce the requirements of construction lumber to the minimum essentials.

It was pointed out by Arthur T. Upson chief of the WPB lumber and lumber products branch, that "the majority of construction lumber now being produced is required by the armed services and other Government agencies directly prosecuting the war, so that for the next several months, construction lumber will not be generally available for many civilian purposes."

In addition, the amendment (No. 1) to the order includes the following within the permitted classes of purchasers: Panama Canal, Defense Plant Corporation, Lend-Lease governments, shipbuilding plants, and operators of mining enterprises qualified under Preference Rating Orders P–56, P–58, and P–73.

Local distributing yards not covered

The amendment also permits sales to any person for use in construction or repair of buildings for storage of agricultural products, for packing and boxing of agricultural products, and also for manufactured articles for the Army, Navy, or other governmental agencies.

In addition to reducing the proportion of soft-wood construction lumber frozen by the order from about 70 percent to 55 percent of production, the amendment makes it clear that local retail yards, whose principal operation involves the local distribution of lumber, are not covered by the order.

... .

Some guns released for sale to public

Small-gage shotguns, odd-caliber and certain .22-caliber rifles, and other types of firearms not needed by the armed forces or for other essential purposes were released by WPB May 26 for general sale to the public.

Several types reserved

An amendment to the limitation order on new firearms (L–60) unfreezes such guns, which dealers and wholesalers have been forbidden to sell since February 27, except for the following types:

Pistols.—Any .22-caliber Harrington and Richardson "Sportsman" Model Target revolver, or any manufactured by Colt's, Smith and Wesson, or the High Standard Manufacturing Company.

Rifles.—Any rifle chambered for Government .30/06-caliber cartridge or any of the following rifles of .22-caliber: Mossberg Model 42-B and Repeating Model 42 MB; Remington Models 513 Target and 511; Winchester Models 75 Target and G–6941–R; Stevens Model 416–2; Savage Model 33, and Ranger Sears-Roebuck Target.

Shotguns.—Any 12-gage; any 16-gage automatic; and any 16-gage pump action repeater.

The above types of firearms may be sold by jobbers, dealers, and wholesalers:

1. On a specific order of the Director of Industry Operations,

2. For Federal, State, or local government use,

3. For Lend-Lease purposes,

4. On an order on hand as of May 26, to which a preference rating of A–1–j or higher has been applied, or

5. To the Defense Supplies Corporation.

Sales of "war use" mahogany restricted to military purposes

The WPB May 26 imposed drastic restrictions on the delivery and use of the kinds of mahogany and Philippine mahogany which are suitable for combat watercraft, in aircraft, and for other military purposes.

Conservation of supplies is necessitated by a shortage of shipping space for the transportation of mahogany from its foreign source to the United States.

Of existing stocks in this country, it is estimated that about 25 percent is of a quality usable in combat ships and aircraft. It is planned to restrict future imports from Central America to those grades of mahogany which are suitable for military and naval use.

Can fill certain orders only

The restrictions, embodied in Conservation Order M–122, prohibit the sale or delivery of "war-use" mahogany or "war-use" Philippine mahogany except for the following categories of orders:

1. United States Government or Lend-Lease.

2. For use in plywood and parts, for aircraft, boats and ships to the extent that it is permitted by controlling specifications.

3. For use in patterns and models used in the manufacture of products bearing a preference rating of A–10 or higher.

4. Orders specifically authorized by the Director of Industry Operations.

The restrictions on sale and delivery do not apply to those persons who have an inventory of 100 board feet or less on the date of issuance of the order.

* ★ * *

American mahogany freed from shipping certification

Mahogany logs imported from Mexico and Central America no longer require shipping space certificates for shipment to this country, it was announced May 29 by Dr. W. Y. Elliott, chief of the stock pile and shipping branch. Mahogany logs from Africa, however, remain on the "Emergency Shipping Priority List" still subject to certificate.

★ ★ ★

Curb on grain bin production doesn't apply to wooden ones

Manufacturers of farm equipment were advised by the WPB May 30 that they may produce an unlimited quantity of grain bins which are made of wood and contain no metal except for nails, strappings, and small hardware.

Use of metal barred in plumbing fixtures after June 20 except reinforcing, coating

Use of metals other than joining hardware, coating, or reinforcing mesh will be prohibited after June 20 in a list of plumbing fixtures common in the home and commercial establishments.

. This action, effected by Schedule 12 to Limitation Order L–42, is expected to save 46,000 tons of iron and 7,200 tons of steel annually.

The schedule bars the use of metal (except for the hardware, etc.), in the manufacture of plumbing fixtures, but permits iron and steel to be used in the following specified cases: In shower receptors, 15 pounds; in shower stall and receptor combinations, 25 pounds; in plaster interceptors, 5 pounds; in grease interceptors, 5 pounds; and in septic tanks, the minimum required for reenforcement and connections.

Restriction of the use of iron and steel to the above items in effect halts the production after June 20 of the following plumbing fixtures:

Sinks (except scullery), sink and laundry tray combinations, foot baths, drinking fountains, wash fountains; water closet bowls, frost closets or hoppers, and tanks for water closets or urinals (other than pressure tanks for frost proof closets).

★ ★ ★

A–3 on materials for buses, trucks extended to June 30

The A–3 preference rating made available under Preference Rating Order P–54 for deliveries of materials going into the manufacture of buses and truck trailers, and bodies and cabs for medium and heavy trucks has been extended until June 30, the WPB announced May 26.

Under Amendment No. 4 and Extension No. 6 to the order, however, no deliveries of materials can be made on the A–3 rating after June 30 unless producers have filed, prior to June 1, an application for assistance under the Production Requirements Plan.

The A–3 rating, under the terms of the amendment, may be used only for delivery of material to be physically incorporated into passenger carriers, truck trailers, and bodies and cabs for medium and heavy trucks, provided existing limitation orders or other directions by WPB permit such production. The rating cannot be used to obtain material going into the manufacture of medium and heavy trucks, but merely for bodies and cabs for these types of vehicles.

CHLORINE ORDER ADJUSTED

Users of chlorine are permitted to accept delivery in the smallest practical delivery unit, and the date for filing of orders for chlorine with producers is advanced to the tenth of the preceding month in which delivery is sought by an amendment to General Prefernce Order M–19, released May 22 by the Director of Industry Operations.

★ ★ ★

14 types of industrial machines directed into war channels

The WPB assumed control May 26 over the distribution of many types of general industrial equipment so that they will be directed into war channels.

Deliveries on A–9 or higher

The order, L–123, affects such machinery as passenger and freight elevators, electric motors of more than one horsepower, industrial fans, industrial compressors and pumps, and a number of other classes of machinery used generally in various industrial operations. Some types of machinery within these classes are covered by other WPB orders and are therefore not restricted under L–123.

The order provides that no one may accept any order for or deliver any equipment listed in the 14 classes set forth except upon a preference rating of A–9 or higher or upon specific authorization of the Director of Industry Operations.

A list of the machinery covered is contained in List A attached to the order.

BUTYL ALCOHOL UNDER COMPLETE ALLOCATION

All grades of butyl alcohol were placed under complete allocation May 28 by the Director of Industry Operations through issuance of General Preference No. M–159. Allocation will start on July 1.

Purchasers will apply for allocations on Form PD–505 and producers and distributors will report on Form PD–506. Deliveries to persons using less than 54 gallons a month may be made without allocation, providing the total of these deliveries does not exceed 2 percent of a producer's monthly output.

Producers also are required to use grain to the fullest possible extent in making butyl alcohol and may not use molasses unless their grain facilities are in use to the utmost.

Technical instruments controlled by WPB to conserve metals

In a move to conserve nickel, chromium and their alloys, the WPB has assumed control over the production and distribution of many types of instruments, regulators, and control valves used in general industrial processing and in the manufacture of war material.

With the assistance of technical personnel of all interested Government agencies, and of the industry, WPB's general industrial equipment branch has drafted specifications for the production of various types of instruments and restrictions on their use, which are incorporated in Conservation Order L–134.

The order covers 28 specific items forming component parts of industrial processing instruments and valves and regulators.

Under the general restrictions, manufacturers are prohibited from processing any chromium, nickel or alloys of these metals in producing any instrument parts except for use under the operating conditions specified. Thirty days after the date of order's issuance (May 26), manufacturers may not deliver any parts except for the specified uses. Effective immediately, they cannot deliver these instrument parts, no matter what the intended use is, except upon a preference rating of A–10 or higher.

Manufacturing specifications set forth in the order take effect 60 days after the date of issuance. Deliveries intended for the Army, Navy, and Maritime Commission will not be affected by the restrictions until 90 days after the issuance date.

Fence wire, posts, roofing released for unrated sales

Amendments to Orders M–21 and M–21–b to permit the sale on unrated orders of fence wire, barbed wire, poultry netting, fence posts, gates, staples and corrugated roofing and siding have been issued by Director of Industry Operations Knowlson.

The action was taken because these items are constantly used by farmers and householders for maintenance and repair.

An optional change in the quota basis for wire and wire products delivered to warehouses also is contained in the amendment to M–21–b.

WPB permits zipper stocks to be used for many items; "reconditioning" provided

The slide fastener (zipper) order was amended May 28 to permit the use of slide fasteners fabricated prior to April 1, 1942, in a long list of garments and articles.

The original order (L–68) prohibited the use of slide fasteners in garments and articles listed in an appendix to the order after June 1, 1942.

The WPB clothing section said that the amendment will result in a conservation of materials, since the materials for some garments and articles have been cut out for zipper closures and would be useless without such closures. The section also pointed out that the amendment will not result in the use of additional quantities of copper or copper base alloy, inasmuch as the processing of such metals in the manufacture of slide fasteners has already been stopped.

As a result of the amendment, several thousand manufacturers may continue to use their stocks of slide fasteners in the production of a wide variety of articles including bags, bathrobes, billfolds, cases, coats, corsets, cosmetic sets, coveralls, covers, footwear, gloves, hoods, kits, knit goods, linings, luggage, muffs, negligees, and lingerie, notebooks, overalls, pads, pouches, purses, raincoats, robes, shirts, slips and petticoats, sporting goods, sport jackets, sweaters, swim suits, toys, and upholstery.

The amendment also permits the reconditioning and sale of used slide fasteners. Only existing parts of slide fasteners may be used in the reconditioning process.

The amendment also provides for the use of snap fasteners for men's wear on the same basis as that provided in the original order for work clothing and women's and children's wear.

The clothing section pointed out that there is nothing in the order to prohibit the manufacture and use of slide fasteners from sterling silver or plastics, except the restrictions as to length.

"Strategic mica" for Army, Navy items under WPB control

Use of "strategic mica" in products for the Army and Navy is made subject to complete control of WPB by an amendment of Conservation Order M–101, issued May 23 by the Director of Industry Operations.

Cellar drainers simplified to save vital copper

Simplification of electric cellar drainers (sump pumps) in order to save considerable amounts of copper and copper base alloy has been ordered by the War Production Board, effective on June 16.

* * *

Clothes pressing machinery sales, deliveries curtailed

Pressing machinery used by custom tailors or by pressing establishments has been made subject to General Limitation Order L–81, as amended, imposing drastic restrictions on the production and sale of commercial laundry and dry cleaning equipment.

WPB corrects information on steel product reporting

Producers of iron and steel products on Schedule B of Order M–21–b must file Form PD–83–f quarterly with WPB, and warehouses must report to the Bureau of Census on Form PD–83 before the fifteenth of each month, with respect to products on Schedule A.

WPB press release T–269, issued May 4, stated the requirements of Amendment No. 4 to the order incorrectly.

* * *

Percentage of fine cotton yarns reserved for military use

WPB acted May 28 to make available sufficient quantities of fine cotton yarns to meet requirements of the armed forces for fabrics made from such yarns.

Order M–155, issued May 28, requires combed yarn mills to earmark at least 40 percent of their production of medium combed yarns and not less than 65 percent of their coarse combed yarn for the armed services. They must begin this earmarking as soon as necessary to fill orders made mandatory by the WPB order, but not later than the week beginning June 29.

Ban lifted on plumbing, heating equipment for civilian needs

The WPB May 23 moved to relax the restrictions which were imposed upon the sale of plumbing and heating equipment in Limitation Order L–79 by removing the ban on equipment necessary for civilian needs.

Aids conversion to coal use

One important effect of the order as amended is to release the sale to householders of cooking and heating stoves and water heaters where no other equipment for these purposes is available.

At the same time, the amended order facilitates the conversion of oil and gas burning equipment to the use of coal by permitting the sale and delivery of any equipment—as for instance, grates—needed to convert such burners to the use of coal.

The revised order permits the shipment until June 30 of equipment for bona fide contractual orders which had been received no later than April 16, the date of issuance of the original L–79 regulations.

Another exemption from the previous provisions permits delivery of plumbing and heating equipment until July 31, 1942, for completion of projects started after July 31, 1941, and through April 9, 1942, if the purchaser certifies the necessity of such equipment. (April 9 was the date of issuance of L–41, the Construction Limitation Order.)

Hot water heaters, radiators, and other types of equipment which use electricity are excluded from the terms of the amended order. Thus, the ban contained in the original order on sale of many types of equipment connected to both water and electric systems is removed.

· · · · · ·

Order distinguishes between large and small machinery

WPB on May 29 clarified General Limitation Order L–83, as amended, so that certain types of machinery covered by the order will not be confused with small household types regulated by other WPB orders. Amendment No. 1 to the order stipulates that coffee grinding machinery and food slicing and grinding machinery, the production and sale of which have been restricted, means machinery of one horsepower or over.

New method set up for handling rated orders for cotton duck

The WPB May 28 amended the cotton duck order (M–91) to provide a new procedure for handling preference-rated orders for cotton duck.

Up to the present such orders have been served on cotton mills or cotton mill agents regardless of their effect on orders previously placed with the mills by the armed services. At times this has resulted in the displacement of a previous order even though the old order was just as important for the armed services as the new one.

Under Amendment No. 2, issued May 28, a mill is required to refer to procurement officials of the Army, Navy, and the Marines any preference-rated orders received by such mill whenever such orders, if filled, would result in the deferment of previously placed preferential orders rated better than A–2. These officials will then determine whether the orders referred to them duplicate other purchasing arrangements made directly by the Army or the Navy for cotton duck.

★ ★ ★

Use of rubber thread curbed in some health products

The WPB May 26 prohibited the use of bare rubber thread, and of covered rubber thread of size 60 and coarser, in the manufacture of a list of health and medical products.

Covered rubber thread, size 61 and finer, however, may continue to be used in such products.

The May 26 action was taken in Amendment 3 to Order M–124.

Products affected by the May 26 amendment are:

Edging, industrial shoes, belting and flexible metallic hose, repair cords and webs, sanitary belts, surgical elastic bandage, surgical stockings, trusses, webbing for respirators, hose masks, gas masks and inhalators, and surgical supports for abdomen, back, and breast.

★ ★ ★

Shoe makers allowed to use brass findings in stock

Shoe manufacturers are permitted to use findings containing copper if such findings were in stock on March 31, 1942, and if no steel or other nonmetallic findings are available, according to an amendment to Supplementary Conservation Order M–9–c–1, released May 23 by the Director of Industry Operations.

CHEMICAL COTTON PULP UNDER ALLOCATION

Chemical cotton pulp was placed under full allocation control by Conservation Order M–157, issued May 28 by the Director of Industry Operations.

Effective July 1, 1942, no producer may deliver, and no buyer may accept, any chemical cotton pulp except as specifically authorized by the Director of Industry Operations. Exceptions to this are deliveries to the Army, Navy, Coast Guard and Maritime Commission; and small orders of 500 pounds or less to any one consumer per month, provided that the total of such small deliveries is less than 2,000 pounds a month by any one producer. June deliveries are not affected.

. . . . .

Styles in women's, children's robes, other garments restricted to save cloth

A cloth-conserving order covering women's and children's robes, housecoats, negligees, beachcoats and lounging pajamas was issued May 25 by the WPB.

Wool banned

The order places the following restrictions on the manufacture of these garments, beginning May 27:

1. They may not be made of cloth containing any wool, except from cloth owned by a manufacturer on the effective date of the order (May 27).
2. None of the garments may be sold at a unit price with a sleeping pajama, nightgown, slip, or any kind of accessory.
3. They may not be made (a) French facings, (b) balloon, kimona, dolman, or leg-of-mutton sleeves, (c) shirring, tucking, or pleating, except on skirts which do not exceed the sweep restrictions before the shirring, tucking or pleating operation, (d) with more than one pocket, (e) with more than ¼ inch hem at the bottom, (f) with a hood, (g) with a belt longer than 50 inches for women's ranges and 40 inches for children's ranges.

Exceptions

In addition, the order provides maximum measurements for all of the garments covered by the order. Long robes and housecoats are not eliminated, but they may not be as full and sweeping as formerly.

Unrestricted by the order are garments for infants and toddlers (sizes 1–3), historical costumes for theatrical production, and lounging wear for women of unusual height or abnormal size.

A similar order, governing men's and boys' robes, is expected soon.

Mills must earmark enough cotton yarn for armed services

The WPB acted May 28 to make available sufficient quantities of fine cotton yarns to meet requirements of the armed forces for fabrics made from such yarns.

Order M–155, issued May 28, requires combed yarn mills to earmark at least 40 percent of their production of medium combed yarns and not less than 65 percent of their coarse combed yarn for the armed services. They must begin this earmarking as soon as necessary to fill orders made mandatory by the order, but not later than the week beginning June 29, 1942.

The yarns so earmarked are to be used, sold or delivered only upon orders for physical incorporation into materials or equipment for the Army, Navy, U. S. Maritime Commission, and other war agencies, Lend-Lease, United Nations, Defense Supplies Corporation, manufacturers of officers' uniforms, manufacturers of tracing cloth, typewriter ribbons, and electrical insulation material, and persons specifically authorized by WPB to purchase reserved combed yarns.

. . . .

Horsehide fronts to be set aside for military use

The WPB May 25 took control of horsehide fronts which can be made into leather suitable for gloves, leather jackets, windbreakers, and other military garments.

The order (M–141) directs that any raw or in-process horsehide which in the judgment of a tanner's most qualified expert can be made into leather meeting military specifications must be set aside for such purposes. Military specifications include all Federal and United States Army, Navy, and Marine Corps specifications.

★ ★ ★

Conversion of goose, duck feathers sped for war use

The WPB acted May 27 to speed up the conversion of goose and duck feathers covered by Order M–102 into grades of down and feather mixtures suitable for military sleeping bags, pillows, and other military articles.

The May 27 action was taken in Amendment 1 to Order M–102, under which the sale, delivery, and use of goose and duck feathers was restricted to orders having a preference rating of A–1–j or higher.

All stocks of safety razors in hands of manufacturers, jobbers frozen for Military

The WPB May 23 froze the sale and delivery of all safety razors in the hands of manufacturers and jobbers except safety razors in transit and safety razors for the Army and the Navy. Retailers' stocks are not affected.

The order (L-72-a) was effective May 23, at 2:01 a. m., Eastern War Time.

Pending production of substitute

The purpose of the order was to make present stocks of safety razors available for the armed forces.

A previous order, L-72, restricted the use of copper in the manufacture of safety razors for 60 days and prohibited its use thereafter except for plating.

Pending the production of a substitute type safety razors, the army will require 700,000 razors a month during the next 2 months.

The only way to meet the demand is to make all present stocks in the hands of manufacturers and jobbers available to the Army and Navy, which is achieved through the freeze order.

Exceptions to the freeze order are:

1. Safety razors in transit at the time the order takes effect may be delivered to their immediate destination. Thus, safety razors in transit from a jobber to a retailer may be delivered to the dealer and sold without restriction, since the retailer is not affected by the order. On the other hand, safety razors in transit from a manufacturer to a jobber may be delivered to the jobber and then frozen.

2. Safety razors may be sold and delivered to the Army and the Navy for free distribution to men in the services. They may not be sold or delivered to the Army and Navy for resale, whether at post exchanges or other retail outlets.

3. Jobbers may sell or deliver safety razors to other jobbers or to manufacturers. This is to permit a jobber to dispose of his stock if he wishes to. Safety razors thus transferred are, of course, frozen at the point of transfer.

Brass used in one razor would make 3 .30 caliber cartridges

The WPB order freezing sale of safety razors by manufacturers and jobbers, except to the armed forces, makes interesting these facts about safety razors.

The safety razor industry turned out about 10,000,000 units last year, using 1,662,000 pounds of brass in the process. That's enough to make 81,570,000 .30 caliber cartridges or 3,947,000 cartridge clips for the Garand rifle. The brass used in one razor, one-sixth of a pound, would produce three .30 caliber cartridges.

Subject	Order No.	Related form	Issued	Expiration date	Rating
Arsenic:					
a. Regulates sales, deliveries of arsenic. Persons requiring arsenic for any use must submit form to producer on or before 5th day of last month of the preceding quarter. Records must be kept by producers for inspection by WPB officials, and must notify customers of order.	M-152	PD-490; 491; PD-492.	5-22-42		
Construction:					
a. All construction costing $5,000, or more which is primarily for the amusement of the public to be stopped before June 6.	L-41-a		5-23-42		
Copper:					
a. Shoe manufacturers permitted to use findings containing copper if such findings were in stock on March 31, 1942.	M-9-c-1		5-23-42		
Chemical:					
a. Production of chemical maintenance, repair, and operating supplies:	P-89, amended (Amend. No. 1.)		5-22-42	6-30-42	A-1-c; A-3.
1. Chemical war industries granted further priority assistance by amendment to P-89.					
Dyestuffs:					
a. Conservation order M-103 amended to increase the quantity of dyes available for civilian use.	M-103 (as amend.)		5-26-42		
Electric lamps and shades:					
a. Portable:					
1. Redefines "portable lamps" under Order L-33, and adds to the list of essential parts in which iron and steel may be used in the manufacture of lamps.	L-33 (Amend. No. 2.)		5-25-42		
Equipment:					
a. Plumbing and heating:					
1. Permits use of new plumbing and heating equipment as collateral in security transactions with no physical movements of equipment other than for storage or warehousing.	Int. No. 1 L-79	PD-422	5-22-42		
b. Laundry equipment, dry cleaning equipment and tailor's pressing machinery:	L-91 (as amed.)	PD-418; 419; PD-25a; 25.	5-22-42	Until revoked.	P-90.
1. Places control over selling, manufacturing, and use of new equipment. Nonapplicability to repair or maintenance of existing equipment. Manufacturing of equipment prohibited after May 15, 1942 unless granted Preference Rating by WPB.					
c. Metal plumbing and heating equipment:					
1. Removes ban on equipment necessary for civilian needs. Sale and delivery of any equipment on an A-10, or better, preference rating is permitted.	L-79 (as amend. 5-23-42).	PD-423	5-23-42		A-10.
d. Heavy power and steam equipment:	L-117 (Amend. No. 1).		5-26-42		
1. Only heavy power and steam equipment designed for other than marine use is subject to Order L-117.					
e. General industrial equipment:					
1. Restrictions on acceptance of orders for, and production and distribution of general industrial equipment.	L-123		5-26-42		
Feminine apparel:					
a. For outer wear and certain other garments:					
1. Amends limitation order L-85 in regard to clothing.	L-85 (Amend. No. 2)		5-19-42		
b. Feminine lounging wear and certain other garments:					
1. Places control over cloth used in women's and children's robes, house-coats, negligees, beach-coats and lounging pajamas.	L-118		5-25-42		
Fire protective equipment:					
a. Permits manufacturing of carbon dioxide extinguishers according to U. S. Army or Navy or U. S. Maritime Commission specifications, provided they are used to fill orders with preference rating of A-1-j or higher.	L-66 (Amend. No. 3).		5-21-42		A-1-j or higher.

Subject	Order No.	Related form	Issued	Expiration date	Rating
Foods, canned: a. States that the grade preference of fruits and vegetables packed in 1942 for military and Lend-Lease consumption takes precedence over the can-size preference.	M-86-a (as amended—5-25-42).	PD-342.	5-25-42		
b. Canned foods: 1. Supplementary order. WPB orders canners to set aside for the Government their entire 1942 pack of salmon, sardines, Atlantic herring, and mackerel.	M-86-b.		5-26-42		
Glass container and closure simplifications: a. Malt beverages: 1. Prohibits manufacturing of glass containers which can not be returned to brewery for refilling, beginning July 1, 1942.	L-103 (Amend. No. 1 of Sch. B).		5-21-42		
Goose and duck feathers: a. Places allocation on sales, deliveries, and use of goose and duck feathers.	M-102 (Amend. No. 1).		5-26-42		
Horsehide: a. Places complete control over horsehide fronts which can be made into leather suitable for gloves, jackets, windbreakers and other military garments.	M-141.	PD-475.	5-25-42		
Imports: a. Strategic materials: 1. Addition of commodities to list A in General Limitation Order M-63. Places all oil imports under control.	M-63 (Amend. No. 6).		5-22-42		
Instruments: a. Valves and regulators used in industrial processes. 1. Restrictions placed on mfr., sales, and deliveries of instrument end or instrument connection, control valve, regulator, or safety valve except on rating of A-10 or better, to conserve nickel, chromium and their alloys.	L-134.		5-26-42		A-10.
Leather, sole: a. Places restriction on sole cutters, in regard to sales, deliveries, and use of reserved cut leather stock. Those affected by order must file imports with WPB.	M-80 (as amended 5-22-42).		5-22-42		
Lawn mowers: a. Use of iron and steel: 1. Permits mfr. to use iron or steel which had been fabricated or processed prior to March 31, 1942 which could be used for any other purpose than production of lawn mowers.	L-67 (Amend. No. 1).		[5-22-42		
Mahogany: a. Drastic restrictions placed on delivery and use of the kinds of mahogany and Philippine mahogany which are suitable for combat watercraft, in aircraft, and for other military purposes.	M-122.		5-26-42		A-10.
Material: a. Material entering into the construction of defense projects: 1. Only material which will be incorporated into defense construction projects may be delivered under preference ratings assigned by Preference Rating Order P-19-a.	P-19-a (Amend. No. 1).		5-23-42		
Mica: a. Use of "strategic mica" in products for Army and Navy: 1. No such mica may be used in any product for Army and Navy which is not an implement of war, after June 1, 1942, and none may be used in any product whatever after July 1, 1942, except by autorization by WPB.	M-101 (as amended—5-23-42).	PD-480; 326.	5-23-42	Until revoked.	
Molasses: a. For insecticides purposes: 1. Farmers given permission to acquire molasses equal to their purchases in corresponding quarter for year ending June 30, 1941.	M-54 (As amended—3-27-42) (Amend. No. 2).		5-25-42		
Motor trucks, truck trailers, and passenger carriers: a. Amended and extended. Assignment of preference rating.	P-54 (Amend. No. 4; Ext. No. 6).	PD-25a.	5-25-42		A-3.
Passenger carriers: a. Places restriction on delivery of passenger carriers. Production and delivery of passenger carriers maintained by WPB.	L-101.		5-21-42	Until revoked.	

(Continued on page 26)

Aromatic petroleum solvents diverted to aviation gasoline, nitration toluol

With the objective of increasing the production of aviation gasoline and nitration-grade toluol, the WPB has issued an order limiting the delivery of aromatic petroleum solvents, normally used in paint and other protective coatings, to orders bearing high preference ratings.

The order (M-150, effective May 25) is designed to divert more than half of the two principal aromatic constituents of petroleum solvents—toluol and xylols—from use in the protective coating field to the more important production of aviation gasoline and nitration toluol.

Principal provisions

The principal provisions of the order follow:

1. Deliveries may be made only to fill orders to which certain preference ratings have been assigned. During the period June 4 to June 14, the required rating is A-10; beginning June 15, the required rating is A-2. A person purchasing solvents for resale without physical or chemical change is not required to show a rated use.

2. A purchaser, other than a person buying for resale, is required to attach to the order a certification showing the purposes for which the solvents are to be used.

3. Each producer of solvents must accumulate before July 1, or as soon thereafter as possible, a minimum inventory amounting to not less than 25 percent of his average monthly production of each solvent produced during the first four months of 1942. This reserve stock will be held for distribution by the Director of Industry Operations in emergency situations.

To the extent that withdrawals from the pool are ordered by the WPB, a producer must replenish the reserve at a rate of not more than 5 percent of average daily production.

4. After making deliveries on rated orders and setting aside the inventory stock, each producer must divert his remaining supply of solvents, whether in the form of finished product, intermediate fraction, or crude petroleum, to the production of nitration toluol or aviation gasoline as ordered by the Director of Industry Operations. The aviation gasoline so produced must be delivered solely in fulfillment of contracts or subcontracts of the Army or Navy.

5. No person is to use the solvents for any purpose if suitable substitutes are available.

6. Solvents may not be received by any producer or distributor if the delivery would result in a supply in excess of 30 days' needs.

Dallas regional director

Appointment of Ross Eugene Risser as regional director of the WPB for the Dallas region was announced May 27. The region includes the States of Texas, Oklahoma, and Louisiana.

Questions and Answers on Priorities

Q. When will people begin to feel the shortage of consumers' durable goods?

A. By the middle of the summer stocks in retail stores will begin to disappear due to sweeping curtailment in the production of durable household goods.

Q. What protection does an industry have against unreasonably deferred deliveries?

A. A complaint setting forth the circumstances can be sent to the Director of Industry Operations in Washington, who will take appropriate action.

Q. How are preference ratings for military items assigned?

A. The contracting officer will give you a PD–3A certificate when he places the order. Like PD–1A's, these forms can also be extended to suppliers and subsuppliers.

Q. What is a defense order?

A. Any order bearing an A–10 or higher rating is a defense order, and any order placed by the Army, Navy, or specified divisions of the Government, certain foreign countries or any Lend-Lease contract is a defense order, whether it bears a rating or not. In addition to this any subcontract of a defense order is in itself a defense order if the material will be a physical part of the basic order.

Q. Must all defense orders be accepted?

A. All defense orders whether they have an A or B rating must be accepted unless: (1) your entire production is devoted to orders bearing higher or equal ratings which would make delivery on schedule impossible, (2) the material is not the kind usually produced or able to be produced by you, (3) the order doesn't meet established prices and terms, (4) the order specifies delivery within 15 days and meeting it would hold up completion of previously accepted orders, even though they bear lower ratings. Adjustments must be made on your delivery schedule, however, if it is an AA-rated order or a specific direction of the Director of Priorities.

Q. Is it necessary to accept a B-rated order if your schedule is filled with orders bearing higher ratings?

A. No, if meeting the delivery date of the B-rated order would hold up delivery on your previously accepted orders.

PRIORITY ACTIONS
*From May 21
*Through May 27

(Continued from page 25)

Subject	Order No.	Related form	Issued	Expiration date	Rating
Petroleum, aromatic solvents:					
a. Restrictions placed on deliveries. Placing of orders, and restrictions on use of aromatic solvents petroleum.	M–150		5–25–42		
b. Material for oil industry:					
1. Provided for deliveries of material between persons in U. S. and Possessions and Dominion of Canada, but not elsewhere.	M–68 (Amend. No. 4)		5–21–42		
c. Conservation of material for oil industry:					
1. Supersedes Int. No. 1 of Order issued Feb. 7, 1942, and provided for deliveries of material between persons in U. S., its territories and possessions, or Dominion of Canada, but not elsewhere.	M–68–C (As amended 3–23–42).		5–21–42		
Pistols, rifles, and shotguns:					
a. Releases certain types of firearms not needed by the armed forces or for other essential purposes, for general sale to the public. Pistols, rifles, and shotguns still under control.	L–60, (Amend. No. 1).		5–26–42		
Refrigerators, domestic mechanical:					
a. Establishes rules for disposition of domestic mechanical refrigerators now frozen in the hands of distributors and manufacturers:	L–5–d	PD–426; 427; 430; 431; 432.	5–25–42		
1. Procedure for distribution of refrigerators under L–5–d.		PD–429			
2. Supplementary Directive 1–I, amendment of delegation with respect to rationing of refrigerators.					
Rhodium order interpreted:					
a. Term "Jewelry" as used in Conservation Order M–96 includes silver deposit glassware.	M–96 (Int. No. 1 as amend. 4–17–42).		5–21–42		
Rubber yarn and elastic thread:					
a. Prohibits use of bare rubber thread and of covered rubber thread of size 60 and coarser, in manufacture of a list of health and medical products.	M–124 (Amend. No. 4).		5–26–42		
Safety razors:					
a. Freezes sale and delivery of all safety razors in hands of manufacturers and jobbers except those in transit and those for the Army and Navy.	L–72–a		5–22–42		
Sextants:					
a. Int. No. 1 to limitation order L–58 defines sextants in regard to mariner's, and as used in order L–58.	L–58 (Int. No. 1)		5–22–42		
Steel:					
a. Iron and steel:					
1. Places restriction on iron and steel products after May 15, 1942, except on preference rating of A–10 or better.	M–21 (Amend. No. 5).		5–26–42		A–10.
b. Supplementary order, iron and steel, warehouses and dealers:					
1. Quota restrictions on iron and steel products for dealers.	M–21–b (Amend. No. 5).		5–25–42		
c. Iron and steel scrap:					
1. Consumers of scrap are authorized to accept deliveries of scrap without regard to restrictions set forth in Priorities Reg. No. 1, as amended, until further notice.	M–24 (Amend. No. 1).		5–23–42	Until revoked.	
d. Shot and bullet core steel:					
1. Steel for 90 mm. armor-piercing and semi-armor-piercing shot is placed under complete allocation by WPB.	M–21–f (Amend. No. 1).		5–26–42		
e. Iron and steel conservation:					
1. Interpretation of iron and steel conservation order M–126, as it affects beds and bed springs, and general limitation order L–49, relating to springs and mattresses.	M–126 (Int. No. 1)		5–23–42		
f. Steel, sheet:					
1. Reserve allotments of steel sheets expanded to include both hot and cold rolled sheets, to relieve shortage of steel drums.	M–45 (Amend. No. 2)		5–25–42		
Supplies:					
1. Inventory order amended:					
1. Allows dealers to base their calculations on their sales during the preceding quarter rather than on the second preceding month.	L–63 (Amend. No. 3).		5–23–42		

Subject	Order No.	Related form	Issued	Expiration date	Rating
Tantalum: a. Places restriction over sales and deliveries of tantalum. Order M-63 (applicable to tantalum) is unaffected by this order. Entire output of tantalum placed under complete allocation by WPB.	M-156...............	PD-488; 487; PD-489.	5-22-42	....	
Toluene (toluol): a. Places strict control over material containing toluene, to provide manufacturers with ample supply. Excludes oils derived from petroleum.	M-84 (Amend. No. 2).	....	5-22-42		

SUSPENSION ORDERS, MAY 7 THROUGH 20

Company	No.	Violation	Penalty	Issued	Expiration date
Susquehanna Woolen Co., New Cumberland, Pa.	S-39..	Amendment No. 1 to S-39.....	Permitted to use reprocessed or reclaimed wool for period of 30 days to complete non-military orders on books at time of Suspension Od. S-39.	4-23-42	5-24-42
Twin City Brass & Aluminum Foundry Co., Minneapolis, Minn.	S-43..	Charged with illegal acceptance and delivery of aluminum and aluminum scrap between September 1941 and February 1942.	Prohibited from accepting or delivering any form of aluminum for 3 months; 10 days after order, must cease all processing of the metal.	5-14-42	8-17-42
Everett Sales & Equipment Corporation, New York, N. Y.	S-44..	Charged with manufacturing cellophane packages for textile products; a use prohibited by limitation order CL-20.	For period of 1 month is prohibited from accepting or delivering any cellophane or similar material; after 10 days grace, company will also be enjoined from processing any cellophane.	4-28-42	5-31-42
Bel-Air Oil Co., Los Angeles, Calif.	S-45..	Used scarce material to drill oil well which did not conform to the uniform well-spacing pattern, required by Order M-68.	Enjoined from production of any oil from well in question for next 3 months.	5-7-42	8-11-42
Ruby Dental Mfg. Co., Inc., New York, N. Y.	S-50..	Charged with extending Preference Rating P-29, which it had been issued, to receive larger quantities of material than specified.	For period of 2 months no deliveries of material shall be made to company and no priority over deliveries shall be given to the company.	5-13-42	7-13-42
Superior Metal Co., Chicago, Ill., and Bethlehem, Pa.	S-52..	Company certified that it needed 150 nickel anodes to complete certain contracts which was later learned that this quantity of material was not needed for completion of listed contracts.	For period of 2 months is prohibited from accepting or delivering, processing or dealing in any manner with nickel products.	5-8-42	7-8-42
Paine Heating & Tile Co., Jackson, Miss.	S-54..	Charged with misrepresentation to WPB under Preference Rating P-100 to obtain material with rating of A-10.	For period of 1 month deliveries of material shall not be accorded priority and no restricted material will be allocated to it.	5-15-42	6-15-42
O. D. Jennings & Co., Chicago, Ill.	S-55..	Charged with purchasing aluminum scrap for castings into parts for gaming machines, with knowledge that it was prohibited by Sup. Order M-1-c.	For period of 2 months deliveries of material or equipment shall not be accorded priority, and no allocation to materials shall be made.	5-12-42	7-14-42
Columbia Metal Co., Chicago, Ill.	S-56..	Charged with selling aluminum scrap in violation of Sup. Order M-1-c.	For period of 3 months is prohibited from purchasing or selling any aluminum. No preference rating to be given company.	5-12-42	8-14-42
Ewing Foundry Co., Indianapolis, Ind.	S-57..	Charged with making deliveries of aluminum scrap with knowledge that it was in violation of M-1-c.	No restricted material shall be allocated to it, and all priority assistance withdrawn for period of 2 months.	5-12-42	7-14-42

Steel for 90 mm. armor-piercing shot placed under allocation

Steel for 90 mm. armor-piercing and semi-armor-piercing shot was placed under complete allocation May 26 by the Director of Industry Operations.

This size was added to others under allocation in Order M-21-f, which was issued February 17.

Exchange of rail parts freed from M-21 restriction

WPB ruled May 28 that equipment used in the construction or repair of railroad cars may be sold between producers or suppliers of materials regardless of the restrictions on deliveries of iron and steel products contained in General Preference Rating Order M-21.

Heavy power, steam equipment solely for marine use not subject to L-117

The WPB acted May 25 to clarify Limitation Order L-117, which restricts the manufacture, delivery, and sale of heavy power and steam equipment.

The original order did not specify that equipment of this type manufactured solely for marine use was not intended to be covered by the restrictions. In Amendment No. 1 to the definition of heavy power and steam equipment is amended so that only equipment designed for other than marine use is subject to the restrictions.

The order, in its amended form, limits the manufacture, delivery and sale of new heavy power and steam equipment to orders for war agencies, United Nations, Lend-Lease, and orders other than repair and maintenance rated A-9 or higher.

★ ★ ★

Fluorescent lighting fixtures, parts to be inventoried

In order to determine the extent of existing stocks of fluorescent lighting fixtures and parts which might be used directly in the war effort, the WFB has requested all producers and distributors to provide complete information on their inventories as of June 2, on form PD-499.

★ ★ ★

Industrial, other lamps excluded from "portable lamps" order

The WPB May 25 redefined "portable lamps" under Order L-33, and added to the list of essential parts in which iron and steel and any other metal may be used in the manufacture of lamps.

The May 25 changes were made in Amendment 2 to the Portable Electric Lamp and Shade Order, L-33, which applies to portable lamps illuminated either by incandescent or by fluorescent bulbs or tubes. These include such lamps as floor lamps, desk lamps, table lamps, and bed lamps.

The amendment clarifies the definition of "portable lamps" by stating that the following lamps are excluded from the order: Industrial lamps, which are used in conjunction with industrial machines, tools, assembly benches, and similar factory equipment; and any overhead suspended fixtures, either portable or nonportable.

RATIONING . . .

600,000 "frozen" refrigerators to be released under rules for essential uses

The WPB May 26 established rules for the disposition of the approximately 600,000 domestic mechanical refrigerators now frozen in the hands of distributors and manufacturers.

Must meet needs for duration

Production of refrigerators was discontinued on April 30, 1942, and the supplies now on hand must meet essential needs for the duration of the war.

The order issued May 26, L–5–d, becomes effective June 15, 1942. It supersedes the original freeze order, L–5–b, which was issued on February 14, 1942. The new order sets up what is expected to be a permanent arrangement for the withdrawal from frozen stocks of refrigerators required for military and essential civilian needs.

The order does not affect the right of retailers to sell all of the electric refrigerators they had in stock at the time of the issuance of the freeze order, including refrigerators which they had ordered and paid for prior to the issuance of the original order but which were not in their possession at the time the order was issued. However, only those gas or kerosene refrigerators which were fully paid for by an ultimate consumer and were in the hands of the seller at the time of the original freeze order may be delivered after the effective date of the new order. Restrictions on gas and kerosene refrigerators in the hands of dealers are more severe than on electric refrigerators because the available supply is considerably less.

Under the May 26 order, new domestic mechanical refrigerators may be sold, shipped, or delivered, beginning June 15, 1942, only as follows:

1. To fill contracts or purchase orders for the Army, Navy, Maritime Commission or the Panama Canal.
2. Upon a Certificate of Transfer issued by the Director of Industry Operations of the WPB. Such certificates are expected to be issued only on approval of the National Housing Agency (for war housing), the United States Public Health Service, the Board of Economic Warfare (for export to Latin-American countries), Lend-Lease, and the Procurement Division of the Treasury.

In addition, manufacturers may sell refrigerators to the Defense Supplies Corporation or to any other RFC agency.

The order permits repossession of new refrigerators for default in payments,

but refrigerators so obtained may not be resold except upon a certificate from the WPB or to fill an Army or Navy order.

Refrigerators whose sale and delivery was permitted under the original freeze order as amended and which were in transit prior to the effective date of this order, June 15, may be delivered.

* * *

NO DECISION ON LIMITING WHOLESALE, RETAIL STOCKS

James S. Knowlson, Director of Industry Operations, May 23 made the following announcement in connection with published reports about considerations which are now being given by the WPB to possible ways and means of limiting wholesale and retail inventories to practicable working minimums:

1. Considerable confusion has been caused in business circles by speculations about the announcement that the WPB is considering action to require stores to reduce their stocks to "practicable working minimums."
2. This problem is being considered by the War Production Board, as reported, but no definite decisions have been made. Further deliberations are necessary, because of the many practical problems involved, and a final decision will probably not be made for some time.
3. It appears that preliminary drafts of such an order have been circulated, and it should be understood that these are ideas and suggestions only and do not in any sense represent a decision on the part of the War Production Board.

. . .

Gasoline card rationing called off in Washington, Oregon

Plans for card rationing of gasoline in the States of Washington and Oregon beginning June 1 were cancelled May 25 by the OPA, which has been authorized by the WPB to ration gasoline in those areas.

Cancellation was announced by OPA Administrator Henderson, following a conference with Harold L. Ickes, Coordinator of Petroleum. They will recommend to the WPB that the curtailment of gasoline deliveries to dealers in those States be continued at 33⅓ percent.

40,000 new passenger cars available for rationing in June, plus unused May quota

The number of new passenger automobiles made available for rationing in June will be the same as was allocated monthly in March, April, and May—40,000—plus any unused quota carried over at the end of May, the OPA announced May 28.

In making allotments of quotas to the various States in June, the OPA has taken into consideration the increased industrial activity in some areas, new construction work on war production plants and military establishments in others, and similar factors that might swell the need for new passenger automobiles.

. . .

Dyes order amended to increase quantity for civilian use

The dyestuffs conservation order (M–103) was amended May 26 to increase the quantity of dyes available for civilian uses.

The original order, issued March 28, 1942, prohibited the sale and use of ten dyes for civilian purposes and restricted the civilian use of all other anthraquinone vat dyes for the second quarter of 1942 to 12½ percent of the quantity of these dyes used during 1941.

The May 26 amendment removes one of the dyes—Golden Orange G—from the prohibited list of military dyes and changes the quota basis from a percentage of only the civilian vat dyes used in 1941 to a percentage of all the vat dyes used in 1941.

Other changes

Other changes effected are:

1. One producer may sell or deliver dyestuffs to another producer without having the amount charged against his quota.
2. A person may obtain up to 25 pounds of each color for experimental purpose without having it charged against his quota.
3. Canada is exempted from the export restrictions.
4. Dye consumers are permitted to purchase military dyes from the Defense Supplies Corporation in excess of minimum working inventories.
5. A mixture does not become a military dye until it has more than 10 percent of a military color in it. In the original order not more than 2 percent of a military color was permitted in a mixture for civilian use.

Military on special duty at war plants can get new autos, or tires for own cars

Army and Navy personnel assigned to special duty at industrial establishments, on construction jobs or in similar activities may establish eligibility as war workers to buy new automobiles, or tires for use on their own cars, by meeting requirements announced May 25 by the OPA.

Commanding officer must certify need

After conferences with the OPA, the War and Navy departments have agreed that applications by Army and Navy personnel under the pertinent sections of the automobile or tire rationing regulations must be reviewed by the senior commanding officer at the post or in the area in which the duties of the applicant are performed. When the application is presented to the local rationing board, it should be accompanied by a letter from the commanding officer certifying that:

1. The automobile or the tires are to be used for necessary travel in the performance of the duty assigned.
2. No quarters can be provided the applicant at his post of duty.
3. There is no other means of transportation available.
4. Every effort has been made to arrange for "doubling up," so that the personally owned cars of the men involved are used to the maximum.
5. The applicant has agreed to use his car only for the purposes for which the application is made, except for minimum incidental use for other than pleasure driving.

Even after these requirements are complied with, military personnel, in going before a local board, still must make the same showing of need for the tires or car that is required of civilians.

★

3,032 commercial vehicles released week ended May 23

The WPB May 25 announced that during the week ended May 23 it released 3,032 commercial vehicles under the rationing program that went into effect March 9.

Anderson joins machines staff

Ivan Anderson, of Mamaroneck, N. Y., has been appointed assistant chief of the special industrial machinery branch, Lewis S. Greenleaf, Jr., branch chief, announced May 27.

Additional tea and coffee granted to over 60 areas of war activity

WPB on May 28 granted additional coffee and tea quotas to more than 60 areas of war activity in 32 States whose population has increased by 10 percent or more during the past year.

Douglas C. Townson, chief of the WPB food branch, announced that coffee roasters and tea packers may deliver a "relief quota" of coffee and tea to receivers in specified areas, in addition to the regular quota already assigned under Supplementary Order M-135-a (Coffee) and Supplementary Order M-111-b (Tea).

The additional coffee or tea obtained on this basis must be sold for consumption within the specified defense area.

Mr. Townson said that action has been taken to relieve the most critical areas first. Results of further studies are being awaited before extending such relief to other areas which may be entitled to it.

The areas involved in the May 28 action, and the increase expressed in percentage of original quota, are as follows:

Alabama: Calhoun County, 15; Decatur, 20; Florence (restricted to a 15-mile radius), 35; Huntsville (restricted to 5-mile radius), 35; Mobile Metropolitan District,[1] 15; Talladega County (and territory within a 25-mile radius of Childersburg), 20.

Arkansas: Fort Smith, 10; Hope, 20; Pine Bluff, 22.

Arizona: Phoenix Metropolitan District,[1] 12.

California: Los Angeles Metropolitan District,[1] 10; Oakland Area (Alameda, Contra Costa, Solano, and Napa Counties), 10; Sacramento Metropolitan District,[1] 10; San Diego Metropolitan District,[1] 35; Santa Barbara County 15.

Colorado: Colorado Springs 15.

Connecticut: Bridgeport Metropolitan District,[1] 15.

District of Columbia: Washington, D. C., Metropolitan District,[1] 15.

Georgia: Augusta Area, 22.

Illinois: Marion, 12.

Iowa: Burlington, 27.

Kansas: Parsons Area, 45; Wichita Metropolitan District,[1] 25.

Kentucky: Elizabethtown, Hardin County, 20; Louisville Defense Area (Jefferson County, Ky., and Clark and Floyd Counties, Ind.), 10.

Louisiana: Alexandria, Rapides Parish, 30.

Maine: Bath-Brunswick, 12; Portland, South Portland Metropolitan District,[1] 11.

Maryland: Baltimore Metropolitan District,[1] 10.

Michigan: Detroit Metropolitan District,[1] 15.

Missouri: Joplin, 12.

Nevada: Las Vegas, 100.

New Jersey: Middlesex County,[2] 10.

New Mexico: Roswell, 10.

New York: Elmira Area (and those cities and towns within a 20 mile radius of Elmira and Elmira Heights, Horseheads, Corning, Painted Post, and Montour Falls), 11; Massena, 20.

North Carolina: Elizabeth City Area, 12; Fayetteville, 80; Jacksonville, Morehead City, Kinston, 40; Wilmington, 50.

Oklahoma: Choteau-Pryor Area (includes

Choteau, Pryor, Claremore, Wagoner, Vinita), 80; Lawton, 20.

Oregon: Pendleton Area (includes Hermiston), 10; Portland Metropolitan District,[1] 15.

Pennsylvania: Philadelphia Metropolitan District,[1,2] 10.

South Carolina: Columbia, 20.

Texas: Abilene, 22; Austin Metropolitan District,[1] 10; Beaumont, Port Arthur, Orange (Jefferson and Orange Counties), 25; Corpus Christi Metropolitan District,[1] 22; Dallas County, 10; Tarrant County, 10; Galveston Metropolitan District,[1] 10; San Antonio Metropolitan District,[1] 15; Texarkana, 20; Wichita Falls Area, 18.

Utah: Salt Lake City Area (comprises all territory with rectangle bounded by Santaquin on south, Grantsville on west, Logan on north, and Heber on east, and also includes cities of Wendover, Dugway, Delta, Halper, Price, Maryville, Crescent Junction, Moab, Cedar City, and Monticello), 15.

Virginia: Blackstone (towns and localities within 15 mile radius, 100; Norfolk, Portsmouth, Newport News, Hampton, Phoebus, South Norfolk, 35; Petersburg, 15.

Washington: Seattle Metropolitan District,[1] 20; Takoma Metropolitan District,[1] 15.

West Virginia: Charleston Metropolitan District,[1] 10.

[1] Represents metropolitan area as defined by the Bureau of the Census in the 1940 Census.
[2] May only.

Some war agencies can get trucks without special permit

WPB on May 28 modified its new commercial motor vehicle rationing program so that the Army and Navy and certain other war agencies can obtain trucks without applying for special permits, when trucks are built to order for such agencies.

The agencies are:

The Army or Navy of the United States, the United States Maritime Commission, the Panama Canal, the Coast and Geodetic Survey, the Coast Guard, the Civil Aeronautics Administration, the National Advisory Committee for Aeronautics, the Office of Scientific Research and Development.

The government of any of the following countries: Belgium, China, Czechoslavakia, Free France, Greece, Iceland, Netherlands, Norway, Poland, Russia, Turkey, United Kingdom including its Dominions, Crown Colonies and Protectorates, and Yugoslavia.

Any agency of the United States Government, for delivery to, or for the account of, the government or any country listed above, or any other country, including those in the Western Hemisphere, pursuant to the Act of March 11, 1941, entitled "An Act to Promote the Defense of the United States." (Lend-Lease Act)

Under Amendment No. 1 to Order M-100, WPB provides that these agencies need not go through the procedure of obtaining an exemption permit in any case where commercial vehicles are produced for them under contract and title is transferred at the time of delivery.

Over 9 million volunteers enrolled for civilian defense, Daniels reports

More than 9,000,000 volunteers are now enrolled for civilian defense work, Jonathan Daniels, assistant director of OCD in charge of civilian mobilization, reported May 29. This includes both the protective services and community activities. Mr. Daniels had just concluded the first conference since the organization of the Citizens' Service Corps with assistant regional directors in charge of this program.

3 million gain since March 1

This represents a gain of approximately 3,000,000 in volunteer enrollment since March 1, when 6,066,748 were on OCD rosters, Mr. Daniels said. The civilian Mobilization reorganization, begun when Mr. Daniels took charge of this program in February, is now virtually complete, he added, and each of the units is functioning effectively.

Approximately 9,500 local defense councils are now organized, including a number of county councils representing several community organizations. This represents an increase of more than 500 since March 1. The number of volunteer offices, some of which serve as many as four or five local defense councils, has risen during the same period from 1,950 to 2,403.

Mr. Daniels declared:

Reports from all sections of the country may be summed up in a few words. America is awake. We no longer need to say "this is war." People know it, and they know the urgency of mustering all our forces for a maximum civilian effort in war. They are asking, "How can I help?" and we are doing our best to provide the answer.

Nutrition groups in ⅚ of counties reported on anniversary of conference

Paul V. McNutt, Federal Security Administrator and Director of the Office of Defense Health and Welfare Services, reported May 26 on the anniversary of the National Nutrition Conference that gratifying progress has been made within the past year in carrying out the objectives of the National Nutrition Program to promote health through proper food habits. The National Nutrition Conference, called by President Roosevelt, was held on May 26· 27, and 28 of last year.

6 million children get lunches

"More than 2,500 of the 3,070 counties in the country have organized nutrition committees within the last year," he said. "These committees, and the State and city committees, have enlisted to help coordinate and carry out the objectives of the national nutrition program, which includes the activities of twenty Federal Government Agencies. In addition to spreading needed information on how to eat for better health, they are cooperating in projects designed to get more healthful food to those who need it most and often can least afford it.

"Among these plans are penny-milk and free school-lunch programs. By March of this year more than 6,000,000 children in 93,000 schools were receiving free lunches made possible by the distribution of surplus commodities. This meant an increase of 1,300,000 children in 26,200 schools within a year. Another activity of the nutrition committees is the organization of classes and discussion groups in which guidance is given in selecting low-cost foods high in nutritive value.

"One direct contribution to the war effort resulting from the national nutrition program has been the interest aroused among employers in the food eaten by their employees. Many employers are conducting education programs among their employees stressing that their health and strength are greatly dependent on the food they eat. In some industrial plants, meals are served at less than cost in the cafeterias as one way to help employees maintain their health and efficiency under the added strain of the war effort."

Eight new housing critical areas

WPB has added eight new areas to the Defense Housing Critical Area List. They are Bagdad, Ariz.; Blythe, Calif.; Seneca, Ill.; Rising Sun, Ind.; Greenville, Tex.; Bellingham, Wash.; Hanna, Wyo., and Reliance-Superior, Wyo.

TOP CARTOONISTS' WORK IS AT YOUR DISPOSAL

VICTORY PRESENTS, on facing page, a third group of 4 drawings by well-known American artists who have volunteered their talents to help emphasize, in their own medium, matters vital to winning the war. VICTORY will print four drawings by these and other artists each week. Permission to reprint is hereby granted. Mats in two-column size (larger than appears here) are available weekly. Requests to be put on the mailing list regularly, or for individual mats should be addressed to Distribution Section, Division of Information, Office for Emergency Management, Washington, D. C.

. . .

Eastman gives more time on truck conservation, but says goals must be reached

Several changes in the four general orders for conservation of trucks and tires were announced May 29 by the Office of Defense Transportation.

Such changes as were made, Director Eastman said, have been approved only to give industries affected additional time to work out their own plans for attaining the objectives of the orders. It is imperative, he declared, that such programs for the conservation and more efficient use of motor transport be instituted immediately for the successful prosecution of the war.

Major changes outlined

In the major changes announced May 29, the ODT:

1. Postponed from June 1 to July 1 the effective date of a provision of Orders 3, 4, and 5 prohibiting the operation of trucks in over-the-road deliveries unless loaded to 75 percent of capacity on the return trip.

2. Relaxed a provision of Order No. 6 with respect to newspapers and set up two alternate plans for conservation of trucks engaged in newspaper delivery services.

3. Extended jurisdiction of the local delivery order to 25 miles beyond the corporate limits of the municipalities.

4. Exempted trucks engaged exclusively in the pick-up or delivery of telegraphic, radio and cable communications and the U. S. mails from the provisions of Order No. 6.

5. Relaxed Order No. 6 with respect to coal trucks and set July 1 as the effective date of the mileage reduction program for such vehicles.

6. Extended to July 1 the effective date of Order No. 6 with respect to trucks primarily equipped for the transportation of bulk liquids.

MAÑANA AMERICANS

"You'll love it—It smells like gasoline."

"We think you've misunderstood the word, Mr. Murgatroyd. Its a SLOGAN contest we're running."

Lend-lease aid to U. S. by other nations important and growing, Stettinius reports

Edward R. Stettinius Jr., Lend-Lease Administrator, on May 31 made the following statement:

More and more supplies are being furnished to American troops abroad through lend-lease in reverse without money payment by us. As the number of American troops abroad increases, these reciprocal lend-lease benefits to the United States are growing in importance.

From the time American troops first arrived in Northern Ireland the British government has provided them with food, other essential supplies and labor to help in the construction of facilities, without dollar payment on our part. The goods and services received are offset against the materials which the United States has supplied to the British under the lend-lease program. The Australian government is performing similar services for the United States forces in Australia.

This is one phase of a larger program of reciprocal aid which is expanding rapidly and has been a major development of the last three months on both the supply fronts and the fighting fronts. Through lend-lease, the United States is providing the British Commonwealth of Nations, Russia, China and others of the United Nations with supplies to help them help us beat the Nazis and Japan. Through lend-lease in reverse they are now doing the same for us. Measured in dollars, the value of this reciprocal aid is not yet large. Measured in terms of need at the place where the aid is furnished, it is already significant.

Under the joint control of combined boards sitting in Washington and London, the resources of the United Nations are now in effect in one big pool. Each nation contributes to the pool to the extent permitted by its economic resources and its military position.

The United States has received from Britain many types of military equipment, including a complete gun factory. We have received equipment for experimental purposes and invaluable information on new improvements in various weapons of war, all without dollar payment. On the same basis Russia has supplied us with vital information on tank construction and has sent us technical experts to assist us in manufacturing explosives.

American ships in British ports are repaired and refitted on the lend-lease account. United States air forces and the United States air ferry services, operating to the far corners of the earth, are supplied by local British and Australian authorities without expense.

WAR EFFORT INDICES

MANPOWER

National labor force, April	53,400,000
Unemployed, April	3,000,000
Nonagricultural workers, April	40,773,000
Percent increase since June, 1940	**14
Farm employment, May 1, 1942	10,796,000
Percent increase since June 1940	**1

FINANCE *(In millions of dollars)*

Authorized program June 1940–May 15, 1942	‡166,435
Airplanes	36,223
Ordnance	35,403
Miscellaneous munitions	21,330
Naval ships	16,445
Industrial facilities	16,338
Posts, depots, etc.	14,037
Merchant ships	7,465
Pay, subsistence, travel for the armed forces	6,155
Stockpile, food exports	4,851
Housing	1,392
Miscellaneous	6,796
Total expenditures, June 1940–May 15, 1942	*28,740
June 1940–April 1942	
Authorized program	166,435
Contracts and other commitments	108,176
Expenditures	26,762

PLANT EXPANSION *(In millions June 1940 to latest reporting date of dollars)*

Gov. commitments for war plant expansion; 1,644 projects, April 30	12,131
Private commitments for war plant expansion; 7,836 projects, April 30	2,574

EARNINGS, HOURS, AND COST OF LIVING

		Percent increase from June 1940
Manufacturing industries—March:		
Average weekly earnings	$36.15	40.2
Average hours worked per week	42.5	13.3
Average hourly earnings	80.9¢	20.4
Cost of living, April (1935–39=100)	*Index* 115.1	14.5

*Prelim. Includes revisions in several months.
‡Preliminary.
**Adjusted for seasonal variations.

OFFICE FOR EMERGENCY MANAGEMENT

WAYNE COY, *Liaison Officer*

CENTRAL ADMINISTRATIVE SERVICES: Dallas Dort, *Director.*

DEFENSE COMMUNICATIONS BOARD: James Lawrence Fly, *Chairman.*

INFORMATION DIVISION: Robert W. Horton, *Director.*

NATIONAL WAR LABOR BOARD: Wm. H. Davis, *Chairman.*

OFFICE OF SCIENTIFIC RESEARCH AND DEVELOPMENT: Dr. Vannevar Bush, *Director.*

OFFICE OF CIVILIAN DEFENSE: James M. Landis, *Director.*

OFFICE OF THE COORDINATOR OF INTER-AMERICAN AFFAIRS: Nelson Rockefeller, *Coordinator.*

OFFICE OF DEFENSE HEALTH AND WELFARE SERVICES: Paul V. McNutt, *Director.*

OFFICE OF DEFENSE TRANSPORTATION: Joseph B. Eastman, *Director.*

OFFICE OF FACTS AND FIGURES: Archibald MacLeish, *Director.*

OFFICE OF LEND-LEASE ADMINISTRATION: E. R. Stettinius, Jr., *Administrator.*

OFFICE OF PRICE ADMINISTRATION: Leon Henderson, *Administrator.*

CONSUMER DIVISION: Dexter M. Keezer, *Assistant Administrator, in charge.* Dan A. West, *Director.*

OFFICE OF ALIEN PROPERTY CUSTODIAN: Leo T. Crowley, *Custodian.*

WAR MANPOWER COMMISSION: Paul V. McNutt, *Chairman.*

WAR RELOCATION AUTHORITY: Milton Eisenhower, *Director.*

WAR SHIPPING ADMINISTRATION: Rear Admiral Emory S. Land, U. S. N. (Retired), *Administrator.*

WAR PRODUCTION BOARD:

Donald M. Nelson, *Chairman.*
Henry L. Stimson.
Frank W. Knox.
Jesse H. Jones.
William S. Knudsen.
Sidney Hillman.
Leon Henderson.
Henry A. Wallace.
Harry L. Hopkins.

WAR PRODUCTION BOARD DIVISIONS:

Donald M. Nelson, *Chairman.*
Executive Secretary, G. Lyle Belsley.
PLANNING COMMITTEE: Robert R. Nathan, *Chairman.*
PURCHASES DIVISION: Houlder Hudgins, *Acting Director.*
PRODUCTION DIVISION: W. H. Harrison, *Director.*
MATERIALS DIVISION: A. I. Henderson, *Director.*
DIVISION OF INDUSTRY OPERATIONS: J. S. Knowlson, *Director.*
LABOR DIVISION: Sidney Hillman, *Director.*
LABOR PRODUCTION DIVISION: Wendell Lund, *Director.*
CIVILIAN SUPPLY DIVISION: Leon Henderson, *Director.*
OFFICE OF PROGRESS REPORTS: Stacy May, *Director.*
REQUIREMENTS COMMITTEE: Wm. L. Batt, *Chairman.*
STATISTICS DIVISION: Stacy May, *Director.*
INFORMATION DIVISION: Robert W. Horton, *Director.*
ADMINISTRATIVE DIVISION: James G. Robinson, *Administrative Officer.*
LEGAL DIVISION: John Lord O'Brian, *General Counsel.*

VICTORY

OFFICIAL WEEKLY BULLETIN OF THE AGENCIES IN THE OFFICE FOR EMERGENCY MANAGEMENT

| WASHINGTON, D. C. | JUNE 9, 1942 | VOLUME 3, NUMBER 23 |

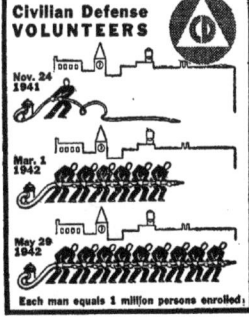

Civilian Defense VOLUNTEERS

Nov. 24 1941

Mar. 1 1942

May 29 1942

Each man equals 1 million persons enrolled

Lack of material may halt some production in future, says Batt; we must resort to new specifications, scheduling, scrap

War production demands have created a shortage of materials in the United States that will grow more serious as the war progresses, William L. Batt, chairman of the Requirements Committee, WPB, and A. I. Henderson, newly appointed Director of Materials, warned both industry and civilian consumers June 3.

Mr. Batt said he could not overemphasize the difficulties of the job he has turned over to Mr. Henderson as his successor as Director of Materials.

"As the vast production machine which has been created over the last 2 years swings into action, the difficulty of providing materials to feed it will become more and more apparent," Mr. Batt said.

"This comes as no surprise to us who have been living with the problem. I can see times ahead when a shipway may stand idle for lack of steel and an ammunition line may slow down for lack of copper and brass.

"Our civilian economy is fast going on a minimum subsistence standard. Vital materials no longer can be used except for war and for the maintenance of those things necessary to carry on the war.

"The past months have been relatively easy. The military has taken from the civilian to meet its needs. This pool is nearly dry. From here on out it will be a continuous problem to provide materials to meet the needs of our fighting forces. Industry must get ready to 'patch and pray' to keep existing equipment at work."

These steps will be necessary, the officials said, to keep the military machine running full blast and to produce enough goods for essential civilian requirements:

1. Long-range planning of requirements for materials and careful scheduling to meet them.

2. Revision of specifications to reduce the amounts of scarce materials used.

3. Widespread use of substitutes.

4. A vast increase in civilian cooperation with the national salvage program to speed up the flow of scrap, particularly metals and rubber.

5. Careful handling of scrap and secondary metal by industry to get the greatest possible use from it.

They pointed out that the War Production Board now is engaged in stimulating production in every possible way: By building new plants, exploiting low-grade ores, paying premium prices for copper, lead and zinc, and recommending Federal financing for new projects in materials production.

Some revision of the war plant expansion program has been made necessary because of the shortage of materials, particularly metals, although in most instances this is caused by a lack of fabricating facilities as much as by a shortage of the materials themselves.

464518°—42

Review of the Week

With war production going into the mass stage, Requirements Committee Chairman Batt warned last week that:

"I can see times ahead when a shipway may stand idle for lack of steel and an ammunition line may slow down for lack of copper and brass."

The pool of civilian demands from which the military program has taken its needs is nearly dry, Mr. Batt said, and we shall now have to resort to careful scheduling, revision of specifications, widespread substitutions and a vast increase in the reclaiming of scrap materials if we are to keep our armed forces supplied.

Total mobilization of food

One basic material of war was given recognition last week when a nine-agency committee was established to control production and allocation of all civilian and military food supplies. The Foods Requirements Committee, under the chairmanship of Secretary of Agriculture Wickard, will assemble complete information on needs and will decide, on the basis of equipment necessary to produce and transport them, how foods shall be grown and distributed.

This action implied attention to the best use of outgoing shipping. Incoming shipping, too, will be subject to further supervision; the War Production Board last week added civilian items to the list of commodities under import control.

Moving toward allocation

Allocation of materials for manufacture on the basis of our total needs took another step forward when the Division of Industry Operations announced that all but a few types of large metal-using companies would be placed under the production requirements plan for the third quarter of 1942. This system involves application for preference ratings on calculated quantities of materials in advance, and enables WPB to divide up available supply in a way that was impossible under blanket priorities.

Meanwhile, limitations and allocations

were broadened. Manufacture of musical instruments and of tableware and cutlery was sharply restricted. Drastic curbs were placed on the use of copper in farm tractors and engine power units. Office machinery makers, undergoing conversion to war work, were given new limits and their products were subjected to distribution control. Meanwhile, WPB established a policy for all appeals to manufacture beyond deadlines or in excess of quotas.

Placed under allocation control were 3 chemical sources of nitrogen, important in making fertilizer and explosives; chlorate chemicals, also important to explosives; beryllium, a vital hardening element for copper; and styrene, a basic ingredient of synthetic rubber. Scrap metals and alloys of various types were put under import control. The privilege of importing reclaimed rubber was reserved for the military forces and the Reconstruction Finance Corporation.

WPB Chairman Nelson appointed a committee to investigate all possibilities of cargo planes, and Junkers airplane patents were among 608 newly seized by the Alien Property Custodian.

Employing and housing manpower

The War Manpower Commission issued a booklet telling employers and workers specific steps they can take to see that our human resources are mobilized for our urgent needs. WMC revealed that a growing army of "physically handicapped" persons is being used for war production tasks it can perform.

The Office of Price Administration ordered rents cut back in 24 more areas of war activity. The Division of Industry Operations moved to speed new accommodations by giving more than 100,000 housing units relief from lumber restrictions.

OPA also announced a new gasoline rationing system for the East Coast which will eliminate "X" or unrestricted cards.

Price work included a ceiling on bicycles, and action on a wide variety of items, including lumber, textiles, foods, and fuels.

SPECIAL COMMITTEE TO STUDY EAST COAST PETROLEUM

Appointment of a special committee to consider the status of petroleum supplies in the East Coast region was announced June 4 by WPB Chairman Nelson.

Wayne Johnson, special adviser to Mr. Nelson on petroleum matters, is chairman of the new committee, which has been instructed to report its findings to the WPB as soon as possible.

The committee will also consult with the Maritime Commission and with the Office of the Petroleum Coordinator in regard to recent pipe-line recommendations made by the Petroleum Coordinator's office.

Members of the committee are Jesse Jones, Federal Loan Administrator; Gen. W. B. Pyron, representing the Secretary of War; Commander W. M. Callaghan, representing the Secretary of the Navy; Isidor Lubin, representing Harry L. Hopkins; Charles Rayner, representing Vice President Henry A. Wallace; A. R. Glancey, representing Lt. Gen. William S. Knudsen, and Glennon Gilbey, representing Price Administrator Henderson.

MACHINE TOOL DELIVERIES CONTINUE TO RISE

The value of new machine tools, presses, and other metal working machinery shipped during April was $114,-100,000, it was announced May 30 by Production Director Harrison.

Shipments of machine tools alone amounted to 25,415 units, with a total value of $103,364,496. During March, 24,300 units, valued at $98,358,299 were shipped.

WAR EFFORT'S PROGRESS TOLD VISUALLY

The charts appearing every week on the front cover of VICTORY tell the story of America's battle as it is fought here at home. One-column mats are available for publication by newspapers and others who may desire them. Requests should be sent to Distribution Section, Division of Information, OEM, Washington, D. C.

VICTORY

OFFICIAL BULLETIN of the Office for Emergency Management. Published weekly by the Division of Information, Office for Emergency Management, and printed at the United States Government Printing Office, Washington, D. C.

Subscription rates by mail: 75¢ for 52 issues; 25¢ for 13 issues; single copies 5¢, payable in advance. Remit money order payable directly to the Superintendent of Documents, Government Printing Office, Washington, D. C.

On the Home Front

Total war involves creation of a tremendous human pyramid. At the apex stands the soldier with gun in hand, facing the enemy. Below him are skilled workmen turning out tools of war, and farmers producing the staff of life, and transportation workers and the workers in mines and forests who produce the raw materials. At the bottom are millions of civilians doing a hundred-and-one everyday tasks that keep the home fires burning. It's just like a circus act, too—if one performer falls out of place the whole pyramid is in danger of collapse.

The right person in every job

That's why the War Manpower Commission is going so carefully about the task of mobilizing all our brawn and brains for the crucial struggle with the Axis. They must see that the pyramid is staffed from apex to base with exactly the right man—and the right woman—in the right job. The soldier must be the finest physical specimen available, the workman must possess the most precise skills, the farmer must be a master craftsman of the soil, all the rest of us must be doing the jobs for which we are best fitted.

In the final analysis there is scarcely anyone who doesn't have a part to play in this gigantic effort—whatever his age, sex, race, color, birthplace or physical condition. This was reemphasized last week when Chairman Paul V. McNutt of the WMC gave out some figures from the United States Employment Service showing that "a steadily growing army" of physically handicapped men and women is going on the production line. More than 7,500 such workers—many with a missing limb, poor eyesight or other disability—were placed in jobs in April.

Keep fit for victory

Those of us who are blessed with normal faculties owe it to ourselves and our country to keep fit and healthy in the long, grueling days ahead. This applies especially to men and women directly engaged in war work. Six high officials charged with boosting production called this to the attention of the War Production Drive Committees in more than 800 plants last week. They pointed out that sick and injured war workers lose 6,000,000 work-days every month and emphasized that "only healthy workers

can put into the drive what it takes—vigor, staying power and the will to win." Posted on plant bulletins and published in plant papers was the slogan: "Save a day for Victory."

Any idea that the gasoline shortage in the Eastern States was a temporary one or that the rationing system would be

REPRINTING PERMISSIBLE

Requests have been received for permission to reprint "On the Home Front" in whole or in part. This column, like all other material in VICTORY, may be reprinted without special permission. If excerpts are used, the editors ask only that they be taken in such a way that their original meaning is preserved.

short lived has been dispelled by the Office of Price Administration. Administrator Leon Henderson last week disclosed the outlines of a permanent rationing plan which will give motorists a basic quota of fuel for household driving and limited extra allotments for carrying on their business—if they can prove their need.

You can fight shortages

Because we are pouring everything we have into the war effort we are faced with shortages in vital materials, shortages which, according to WPB's Division of Materials, will grow more serious as the war progresses. This has meant and will continue to mean less and less for the civilian, widespread substitution, and an increasing necessity for getting scrap metals and other materials back to the processing plants.

That last necessity, more than ever before, indicates a spare-time job for each of us. WPB stresses the urgent need for civilian collection of scrap, especially metals and old rubber. Only by scraping the bottom of the barrel shall we have enough for victory. This was true some months ago, today it is a matter of pressing, immediate, continual need. Unless we get in the scrap, furnaces will grow cold and cold furnaces can lose wars.

The U. S. A. is going to have less melody so that our aviators may sing a song of destruction over Germany and Japan. A recent WPB order stops manufacture of almost all musical instruments in order that more guns may

be fired, more bombs dropped. The 15,000 tons of war materials which went into pianos, saxophones and other musical instruments in 1940 would have supplied the iron for 11,500 6-ton army trucks, steel for 83 medium tanks, brass for 49,000,000 rounds of .30 calibre ammunition, copper for 500 155-mm. field pieces, aluminum for 40,000 aircraft flares.

We're going to get along without any new carving sets, pen and pocket knives, and manicuring scissors. WPB decided they weren't necessary in wartime.

Here's what the saving means in terms of metals and materials badly needed in the fight for freedom: 6,000 tons of iron and steel, 2,000 tons of stainless steel, 600 tons of copper alloy, and smaller amounts of nickel, chrome, rubber, and plastics.

Another record falls

With more than 800 plants now operating under the War Production Drive program, one of them, the Colorado Fuel & Iron Corporation, of Pueblo, reports that it broke previous ingot production records in May by 8,000 tons. . . . All typewriter production will end early next autumn when enough typewriters will have been made to take care of Army and Navy needs for two full years. . . . OPA has designated 24 more communities as defense rental areas and ordered the rents rolled back to earlier levels, making 366 such areas in all. . . . WPB has exempted more than 100,000 war housing units from the restrictions on lumber deliveries.

Nearly 10,000 bicycles have been released to war production plants for transportation of workers and for messenger service . . . OPA reminds you that if you're still looking for a war ration book or a sugar purchase certificate the place to apply for it is at your local War Price and Rationing Board—not the schoolhouse where the original registration took place. . . . OPA once more advises home owners on the Atlantic Seaboard and in the Pacific Northwest whose furnaces burn oil to convert to coal, if they can . . . WPB has ruled you can't get new telephone service unless you're in war or essential civilian work and can prove that without the telephone installation you can't do your job properly . . . Rubber is in the news again in these ways: Styrene, one of the chemical compounds used in making rubber, has been brought under rigid WPB control; a plastic substitute for rubber hose has been developed for use with air raid stirrup pumps; sale of rubber lifesaving suits has been restricted to cargo ships and tankers.

9-agency Foods Requirements Committee in WPB to control production, allocation

A Foods Requirements Committee with control over production and allocation of all civilian and military food supplies was established within the War Production Board June 5 under chairmanship of Secretary of Agriculture Claude R. Wickard.

The new committee, named by Donald M. Nelson, Chairman of WPB, will determine civilian, military, and foreign food requirements and has authority to step up or limit the domestic production of foods as well as the importation of foods and agricultural materials from which foods are derived.

Administration of rationing remains in OPA

Administration of food rationing remains in the hands of the Office of Price Administration.

In addition to Secretary Wickard, the committee will consist of representatives of the State, War, and Navy Departments, Office of Lend-Lease Administration, Board of Economic Warfare, and the WPB Divisions of Industry Operations, Materials and Civilian Supply.

Decisions of the Foods Requirements Committee will be final, subject to the over-all direction and approval of WPB.

The order creating the committee served to clarify and define the respective functions of the Department of Agriculture, State Department, Office of Lend-Lease Administration, OPA, Board of Economic Warfare, and WPB as far as they relate to the total wartime picture of food production, supply, allocation, rationing, and importing.

Powers delegated to agencies

Although the order retains final authority in the hands of the chairman of the WPB, the top agency concerned with the Nation's vast problems of production and supply, the Foods Requirements Committee has received broad powers in the food field. Those powers and functions, in turn, are given to the Department of Agriculture and other agencies, many of them already familiar with the job.

In charting its far-reaching decisions affecting the eating habits of every man and woman in the country, the Foods Requirements Committee will receive estimates and programs from agencies representing users of food, such as the Army and Navy and the Division of Civilian Supply of the WPB. The Committee will

then balance this information against data supplied by agencies representing food producers, such as the Department of Agriculture.

Definite information channels

When all of the facts, programs, and estimates have been assembled and studied, the Foods Requirements Committee will, broadly speaking, make a final decision on how all foods shall be produced and allocated in the light of their availability and of the material and equipment necessary to produce, process, transport, and store them.

To guide the Committee in reaching its decisions, each Government agency concerned with the production or use of food will act as a channel of information. The Department of Agriculture will report regularly on the progress of domestic food production and, after consulting with the State Department and the Board of Economic Warfare, on programs formulated for the importation of foods and agricultural materials from which foods are derived. The War and Navy Departments will report on their special wartime requirements for food. The Division of Civilian Supply of the WPB will draw up lists of food supplies considered essential for home civilian consumption. The Division of Industry Operations of WPB will report on available stocks of nonfood materials, such as cotton and rubber, which are processed from agricultural materials. And the Board of Economic Warfare and the Office of Lend-Lease Administration, together with the State Department, will estimate the food requirements of our allies.

To carry out the final decisions of the Foods Requirements Committee, the order assigns definite functions to various agencies concerned with the food problem.

Agriculture Department's functions

The Department of Agriculture will be responsible for:

1. Increasing or limiting domestic agricultural production in accordance with decisions of the Committee.

2. The earlier stages of food production in general.

3. The importation of foods and agricultural materials from which foods are derived. These powers have been delegated to the Com-

modity Credit Corporation within the Department of Agriculture by the Board of Economic Warfare.

4. The formulation of programs for conservation of critical foods or agricultural materials from which foods are derived.

The Division of Industry Operations of the WPB will be responsible for the later stages of food production in general, such as baking and the manufacture of candy and soft drinks.

The Materials Division of the WPB will be responsible in general for the processing of nonfoods derived from agricultural materials which are a source of food. Soap would be an example of this.

Members of the Foods Requirements Committee and the agencies they represent are as follows: Chairman, Claude R. Wickard, Secretary of Agriculture; L. S. Stinebower, State Department; Brig. Gen. Carl A. Hardigg, War Department; Rear Adm. W. B. Young, Navy Department; W. B. Parker, Board of Economic Warfare; Dr. John Orchard, Office of Lend-Lease Administration; Roland S. Vaile, Division of Civilian Supply of the WPB; Douglas C. Townson, Division of Industry Operations of the WPB; and T. L. Daniels, WPB Materials Division.

★ ★ ★

3d Lend-Lease forwarding contract is signed

Continuing its efforts to carry out the directives of the Bland freight forwarding bill, the War Shipping Administration announced May 30 that it had executed a contract with the West Gulf Forwarders Incorporated for the handling of all Lend-Lease cargo at Houston and Galveston, Texas, on and after June 1st.

The War Shipping Administration previously had signed contracts with forwarding groups at the ports of Boston and New Orleans.

★ ★

Petroleum shipment aid includes war risk insurance

The Government-aid plan announced jointly on May 19 by the War Shipping Administration and Price Administrator Henderson, for maintenance of January 20, 1942, levels of charter rates on vessel movements of petroleum and petroleum products, was interpreted June 4 to include war risk insurance on petroleum cargoes.

RATIONING . . .

"X" cards for gasoline to be dropped under new plan effective in July; coupons to provide only for proven need

"X" cards, providing for unrestricted purchases of gasoline, are eliminated in the new coupon plan for rationing gasoline which the Office of Price Administration will put into effect in the East Coast area next month, Price Administrator Henderson announced June 4. This plan will supplant the emergency plan now in operation. No motorist under the new plan will receive gasoline in excess of what he needs to carry on his work, except that all motorists will have a basic ration to provide for household and other necessary family driving.

Slips to be torn out and returned

Coupon books will take the place of the "meal ticket" type cards, Mr. Henderson said. In fact, the new plan will require coupons for all gasoline purchases. Coupons, issued to car owners in several types of books, will be torn out by the dealer when gasoline purchases are made. The dealer in turn must turn in these coupons when getting new stocks from his supplier. This "flow back" of coupons, it was explained, will provide an audit control of every gallon of gasoline distributed under rationing.

Under the new plan there will be 6 types of books for highway uses. The A book, containing 48 coupons, will provide the basic ration to which every passenger car owner is entitled. These 48 coupons will be good for 1 year. B and C books will provide supplementary rations for passenger cars for vocational, governmental, and war purposes in addition to that provided by the A book.

The D book will provide a basic ration for motorcycles, and "S–1" and "S–2" books will be issued to trucks, buses, and similar vehicles.

Extra forms for extra gas

OPA announced that only A and D books will be issued at the time of registration. The dates and places for registration will be announced later. Upon filling out a simple form and presenting his registration card, any automobile owner may receive the basic ration book.

To obtain additional rations, through either a B or a C book, the car owner must fill out a much more detailed application and present it to a local rationing board for action. The application forms for these higher rating books will be available at the registration place.

In order to satisfy a local board that he should have a supplementary book of coupons, a car owner will have to prove that an A book will not provide him with enough gasoline to carry on his occupation or other work. On his application he will have to prove (1) that he has formed a club of four members who plan to "double up" or rotate use of their cars, or (2) that alternative means of transportation are inadequate. He will also have to establish the minimum amount of driving that he must do.

Books to be "tailored" to need

All B books will contain 16 coupons, which must last persons to whom they are issued a minimum of 3 months, according to the mileage need he has proved. If the B book will meet the needs of the user for a period longer than 3 months, the board will "tailor" the book by fixing an expiration date which will allow the exact mileage required. The expiration date will be determined by the local board, and the date will be stamped on the book cover at time it is issued. It will be impossible, save in exceptional cases, for the holder to receive another B card before that expiration date.

C books, containing a maximum of 96 coupons, will be issued to drivers who prove that neither an A book, nor an A book plus a B book, will supply them with sufficient gasoline to carry on work related to the war effort or to the maintenance of essential public or civilian services. Such drivers will receive gasoline only for driving in connection with specified work or services of this type. Among the services for which such rations will be issued are medical care, maintenance of public utilities, carrying farm labor, giving religious comfort or assistance, and making official trips on Government business.

Only journeys authorized by any Federal, State, local, or foreign government for their employees or officials will be considered official trips.

Each C book, it was explained, will be tailored to fit the needs of the person receiving it. While all C books will contain 96 coupons, coupons will be removed to provide the exact mileage required.

S books will be issued for trucks, buses, and taxis, and will provide sufficient gasoline for the needs of such vehicles for a 4-month period.

OPA emphasized that while all applicants for rations for trucks, buses, and similar vehicles must show how much gasoline they will need, there is no intention at the present time to curtail the operations of such vehicles except as the Office of Defense Transportation may provide in its rules and regulations.

In addition to the various coupon books for highway users, there will be E and R books for nonhighway users, including boats.

★ ★ ★

Local boards authorized to examine card holders

Specific authority for local rationing boards to call in holders of gasoline ration cards for personal questioning to determine whether the card was obtained by mistake or fraud is provided in a new amendment to the gasoline rationing regulations, the OPA announced June 4. This authority applies to the emergency plan now in operation throughout the Atlantic Seaboard area.

The board may also require "X" card holders to be examined as to whether they are using their cards for the purpose for which the cards were issued. If the examination convinces the board that the card was wrongfully obtained or that an "X" card is being used illegally, it may order that the card be surrendered.

Betten associate chief

Appointment of Robert S. Betten as associate chief of OPA's tire rationing branch was announced June 2 by Administrator Henderson.

MORE RATIONING NEWS

appears on pages 22 and 23.

INDUSTRIAL OPERATIONS . . .

WPB adds civilian items to import control to insure best use of shipping space

The War Production Board will take control of imports of commodities for civilian use as well as strategic war materials beginning July 2, under a revision of General Imports Order M-63 issued June 2 by Industry Operations Director Knowlson.

Purpose of the order is to take advantage of available shipping space by requiring that commodities be imported in the order of their importance. This is accomplished by attaching to the order lists I, II, and III and setting up rules for the importation of the commodities on each list.

List I restrictions

List I.—No person, except Government agencies, may import, purchase for import or contract for importation of any material on this list except by special authorization of the Director of Industry Operations. Applications for this permission must be made on Form PD-222-C. Imports may continue to be made under existing contracts, but all such contracts must be reported immediately to the War Production Board.

After commodities on this list are imported the owner cannot sell, process, or move them beyond the place of initial storage. He can sell them to Government agencies, or apply for authorization to process or move them on Form PD-222-A.

Reports of imports must be made on Form PD-222-B by all persons, including Government agencies, to collectors of customs before the materials are entered for consumption, for warehouse, or withdrawn from warehouse. With the exception of this provision regarding Government agencies, this method of handling imports is substantially the same as that now in force.

List II restrictions

List II.—Commodities on list II are subject to the same import regulations as those on list I. Permission to import must be sought on Form PD-222-C, existing contracts must be reported, and reports on PD-222-B must be made to the collector of customs.

After legal importation has been made, however, commodities on list II may be sold, processed, or consumed without restriction, insofar as M-63 is concerned. These commodities either are covered by other orders which provide sufficient control over their use, or no control is deemed necessary.

List III restrictions

List III.—Existing contracts for importation of commodities on list III will not be allowed to stand, as are those on the other two lists. Specific authorization for import must be obtained on Form PD-222-C, regardless of existing contracts.

After materials on this list are imported they may be disposed of without restriction, insofar as this order is concerned, except that reports must be made to the collector of customs.

It was emphasized that the granting by the Director of Industry Operations of authorization to import is not a guarantee of shipping space. This must be obtained in the usual way at the point of origin of the shipment.

Issued simultaneously with M-63 is Supplementary Order M-62-a, which releases from the provisions of M-63 commodities imported overland or by air from Canada and Mexico.

LIST I

The numbers listed after the following materials are commodity numbers taken from Schedule A, Statistical Classification of Imports of the Department of Commerce (issue of January 1, 1941, as supplemented January 1, 1942). Materials are included in the List to the extent that they are covered by the commodity numbers listed below.

Beef and mutton tallow—includes oleo stock—0036.6; beef and mutton tallow (inedible)—includes oleo stock—0815.6; berl ore and beryllium ore—6270.0; metallic beryllium—898.870; *beryllium oxide, carbonate and other beryllium salts; castor beans—2231.0; castor oil—226.02; cattle, ox, and calf tail hair—3696.1; cinchona bark or other bark from which quinine may be extracted—2201.0; cod-liver oil—0805.0; cod oil—0804.0; columbite—6270.3; corn or maize oil (edible)—1422.0; corundum and emery in grains, or ground, pulverized, or refined—547.01; corundum ore—5460.0; cottonseed oil—226.22; cottonseed oil—crude—1423.1; cottonseed oil—refined—1423.2.

Flax—3261.0, 3262.5, 3262.6, 3262.7, 3262.8, 3262.9; flaxseed (linseed)—2233.0; glycerine-crude—6290.0; g l y c e r i n e—refined—6291.1; goat and kidskins, including cabrettas—0241.0; goose down—0932.3, 0933.0; graphite or plumbago—amorphous—5730.1, crystalline, flake—5730.5, crystalline, lump, chip, or dust—5730.6; hempseed—2238.0; horse mane and tail hair—3694.0, 3694.1.

Lead—6505.0, 6506.1, 6506.5, 6507.0, 6509.0; linseed oil, and combinations and mixtures,

in chief value of such oil—2254.0; muru muru nuts—2239.63; muru muru kernels—2239.64; neatsfoot oil—0808.95; oiticica oil—2255.6; ouricury (uricury) kernels—2239.62; *ouricury (uricury) oil; ouicury (uricury) nuts—2239.61.

Peanut (ground nut) oil—1427.0; quebracho extract—2344.0; quicksilver or mercury—6662.0; rotenone bearing roots—221.26, 222.36, 221.30, 222.37; rubber seed—2239.5; *rubber seed oil; rutile—6270.2.

Sesame seed—2234.0; shark oil and shark-liver oil—0808.7; sperm oil—crude—0803.0; sperm oil—refined—0803.1; sunflower seed—2240.0; sunflower oil (edible)—1421.0; sunflower oil (denatured)—2247.0; tantalite or tantalum ore—6270.4; tucum nuts—2239.65; tucum kernels—2239.66; Whale oil—0803.5.

Wool (apparel, finer than 44's)—3520.0, 3521.0, 3521.1, 3521.2, 3521.3, 3522.0, 3523.0, 3523.1, 3523.2, 3523.3, 3526.0, 3527.0, 3527.1, 3527.2, 3527.3, 3528.0, 3529.0, 3529.1, 3529.2, 3529.3; wool grease—including degras or brown wool grease, containing of free fatty acids more than 2 percent—0813.2; wool grease, including degras or brown wool grease, containing of free fatty acids 2 percent or less and not suitable for medicinal use—0813.3; wool grease—including degras or brown wool grease suitable for medicinal use, including adeps lanae, hydrous or anhydrous—0813.5; zirconium ore—6270.5.

LIST II

The numbers listed after the following materials are commodity numbers taken from Schedule A, Statistical Classification of Imports of the Department of Commerce (issue of January 1, 1941, as supplemented January 1, 1942). Materials are included in the List to the extent that they are covered by the commodity numbers listed below.

Aluminum scrap—6302.3; a n t i m o n y—6650.0, 6651.0, 6651.1, 838.180, 838.210; babassu nuts—2239.13; babassu kernels—2239.15; babassu nut oil—2257.1; cashew nuts and cashew nut kernels—1377.0; cashew nut oil and cashew nut shell oil—2257.2; chromium—6213.0; coconut oil—2242.5; *cohune nuts and kernels.

Copper—6400.8, 6417.1, 643.00; copper scraps—6400.9, 6418.3, 6453.0, 674.19, 676.02; copra—2232.0; cotton linters, munitions, or chemical grades only (Grades 3-6 according to Department of Agriculture Classification)—3005.0; ferrous scrap—6004.0, 6004.1.

Hides and skins—0201.0, 0202.0, 0203.0, 0203.1, 0205.0, 0206.0, 0207.0, 0208.0; istle or tampico fiber—3405.0.

Asbestos (originating in Rhodesia or Union of South Africa)—5500.0, 5500.1, 5501.0, 5501.1, 5501.9, 5502.1; kapok—3403.0; kyanite and sillimanite—939.95; lead—6504.0; lead scraps—6505.1, 6506.5, 6506.9.

Mica—5560.7, 5560.8, 5560.9, 5561.0, 5561.8, 5561.9, 5564.0, 5564.2; *mercury-bearing ores and concentrates; palm kernels—2239.6; palm kernel oil—2248.0; palm oil—2243.0; pig and hog bristles—0917.0, 0979.1.

Rapeseed oil—2253.0, 2246.0; rapeseed—2237.0; seed lac—2105.5; *shearlings, sheepskin; shellac—2107.2, 2108.0; tin scraps—6651.0; tung oil—2241.0; tungsten—6232.0; vanadium ore—6260.0.

LIST III

The numbers listed after the following materials are commodity numbers taken from Schedule A, Statistical Classification of Imports of the Department of Commerce (issue of January 1, 1942). Materials are included in the List to the extent that they are covered by the commodity numbers listed below.

Animal and vegetable fats, oils, and greases: bois de rose or lignaloe oil—228.27; cacao butter—1420.0; oleo stearin—0036.3; tallow, vegetable—2250.0; *animal products, edible:* beef and veal, pickled or cured—0099.0; canned beef, including corned beef—0028.0; meat extracts, including fluid—0096.0; sausage casings, sheep and lamb only—0034.0; sausage casings—0035.5; offal, edible—0028.6; *animal products, inedible:* blood, dried—8505.0; bone black, bone char, and blood char—099.0; bones, crude—0911.2; bones, ground, ash, dust, meal, and flour—0911.3; tankage—0975.0.

Argols—8339.0, 8330.0, 837.11; asphalt—5394.0, 5078.1, 5079.1; balsams, crude, not containing alcohol—2141.0, 2141.3, 2141.4, 2141.5, 2141.9; baskets, wood and straw—4221.0-4221.9, incl., 676.03, 838.981; boxwood (logs)—4033.0.

Bromine compounds—838.223, 838.224; casein or lactarine—0943.0; charcoal—5011.0; chicle—2131.0, 2189.3; cocoa or cacao beans—1501.3.

Coffee—1511.0, 1511.1; cotton linters, Grades 1 and 2 (other than munitions and chemical grades—3005.0; cotton, raw—3001.0, 3003.6, 3003.7, 3003.8; cotton waste—3006.1, 3006.2, 3006.31, 3006.35, 3006.6, 323.38, 323.39, 985.902, 985.903, 985.905; *dairy products:* butter—0044.0; cheese—0045.1-0046.99 incl.; eggs, chicken—0088.1; milk, condensed and evaporated—0040.0, 0040.1, 0040.7.

Dog food—1190.7, 1190.8; *drugs, herbs, leaves, roots, etc.:* caffein—811.10, 811.11, 811.12; coca leaves—222.03; fish livers—221.97; kola nuts—221.49; soap bark seed or quillaya—221.62. Fabrics, woven of vegetable fiber other than cotton and jute—3287.3; fabric footwear—0369.1-0369.9, incl.; *fibers:* caroa fiber (included in "Paper Base Stock"); *Hibiscus ferox;* *piassava fiber.*

Fluorspar—5801.0, 5801.1; fish and shellfish and their products—0047.0-0087.9, incl.; fish scrap and fish meal—0976.0, 8509.7.

Fruits: Bananas—1301.0, 133.17; grapes—1318.3, 1318.5, 1319.1, 1319.2, 1319.5; melons—133.42, 133.43; peaches—133.61, 133.62, 133.65; pears—133.66, 133.67, 133.68.

Furs, undressed—0700.0-0729.5 incl.; glass—5204.0-5298.5, incl.; glue and glue stock (animal and vegetable)—0940.5, 0934.0, 0940.1, 0940.3, 0930.8, 0930.9, 2946.0, 2946.1.

Grain and Grain preparations: Barley malt—1080.0; bran shorts—1181.0, 1182.0; cracked corn—109.18; corn—1081.0; corn meal, flour, grits, and similar products—109.19; rice meal, flour, polish, and bran—1059.1; broken rice—1059.2; red clover seed—2402.0, 2404.0; rye—1044.0; tapioca, tapioca flour, and cassava—1226.0.

Guano—8504.0; gums and resins natural—2161.0-2171.9, incl.; hair—goat and kid hair except Angora (mohair) and cashmere—3696.2.

Hides and Skins: Coney, rabbit fur and hare skins (included in "Furs, undressed"); deer and elk—0293.1, 0293.2; horse, colt, and ass—0211.1, 0211.3, 0212.1, 0212.2, 0212.3, 0212.5; reptile—0295.0; sharkskins—0298.3; sheep and lamb (no wool)—0232.0, 0234.0, 0234.1, 0234.3.

Ilmenite and ilmenite sand—6270.1; iodine—8300.0, 838.630; leather—0300.1-0345.9, incl.; leather purses—6092.6-0692.9, incl.; *leche caspi;* mahogany logs—4031.0; monazite sand and other thorium ore—593.30; nitrates, sodium and potassium—8506.0, 8527.5, 8527.9.

* *Note:* Commodity numbers for these materials have not been assigned by the Department of Commerce, Statistical Classification of Imports.

JUNE LEAD POOL

The lead pool for June was set at 15 percent of April production June 1 by the Director of Industry Operations. The amount is unchanged from recent months.

All but a few types of large industries to file under requirements plan by July 1 as WPB fits demand to available supply

Another step toward strict allocation of scarce materials and improved control of inventories was taken May 30 in an announcement by Industry Operations Director Knowlson that all but a few classes of companies requiring more than five thousand dollars' worth of metal for the third calendar quarter of 1942 must apply for priority assistance under the production requirements plan before July 1.

Over 10,000 companies covered

More than 10,000 companies, including most of those handling large war contracts, will be required to operate under production requirements plan by the terms of a revision of Priorities Regulation No. 3 which was to be issued within a few days. About 7,000 companies are now using the plan.

Preference ratings are assigned under the production requirements plan only for specified quantities of materials to be obtained during a calendar quarter. Major metal using plants affected by the revised regulation will not be permitted to use any preference rating except ratings assigned to them by production requirements plan during the third quarter of 1942. During that quarter they will not be allowed to accept delivery of any scarce metal in excess of a quota established for them under the plan.

It is anticipated that only the following classes of companies which will use more than five thousand dollars' worth of metal in the third quarter will continue under existing procedures instead of under the production requirements plan: Producers engaged in primary production of basic metals; distributors; wholesalers; builders; companies engaged in transportation; utilities, including light, heat, water, and gas companies; mining companies and petroleum enterprises; communications, including telephone and telegraph; companies engaged in sewage and drainage operations.

System reveals total needs

All large metal users have recently been required to report their use of metal to WPB on Form PD-275. Those affected by the revision of Priorities Regulation No. 3 may use exactly the same information in filling out production requirements plan application Form

PD-25A, adding the other information called for.

As a result of this step, the WPB will be able to determine in advance of each quarter the total quantities of material required by industry. It will also obtain information as to available inventories in the hands of each manufacturer. With this information at hand, demand can be brought into approximate equality with supply, and the available supply will then be distributed in accordance with the established quotas.

^ ^ ^

Production of office machines curtailed to speed conversion; distribution control provided

In a move to hasten conversion of the industry to 100 percent war work, the WPB has sharply curtailed the manufacture of various types of office machinery and set up a system of distribution control so that only essential users may obtain the machines produced.

Previous orders revoked

Such items as adding machines, dictating machines, accounting and bookkeeping machines, addressing machines, time recording machines and other types of office equipment are covered by the order, L-54-c. Previous orders, L-54-b and amendments thereto, had governed the distribution of office machinery but placed no restriction on production. These orders are now revoked.

Production of many types of familiar office equipment, including cash registers, change making, coin handling, check handling and envelope handling machinery and autographic registers, was halted under the terms of the steel conservation order, M-126.

To build up stock pile

Order L-54-c is designed to regulate production until the end of the year so that a sufficient stock pile of essential types of machinery will be built up to take care of all requirements until June 30, 1944. Production quotas fixed for various types of machinery are based on a survey of estimated minimum requirements of Government and essential civilian users.

Nelson sets up committee on cargo planes to study use, production, and materials

WPB Chairman Nelson announced June 2 the creation of a special committee on cargo planes.

Purpose of the committee is to obtain all the available facts relating to cargo planes, including the past use of airplanes for carrying cargoes and the future possibilities of such transportation techniques as they relate to production problems arising from the war effort.

For all kinds of cargo

Considerable interest has been shown recently in the possibilities of increasing the use of large-size, long-range airplanes capable of carrying substantial cargoes of all kinds.

Mr. Nelson has charged his new committee with the job of making an objective study of the situation to see what the facts are as they relate to production problems, including the problem of raw materials for possible cargo plane construction.

Membership of the Committee is as follows:

Harold E. Talbott, deputy director of the WPB Production Division; T. P. Wright, assistant chief, aircraft branch, WPB Production Division; William Barclay Harding, vice president of the Defense Supplies Corporation (American Republic Division) of the Reconstruction Finance Corporation; Lewis Douglas, deputy to Admiral Land in the War Shipping Administration.

Dr. Jerome C. Hunsaker, chairman of the National Advisory Committee for Aeronautics; Robert Hinckley, Assistant Secretary of Commerce, in charge of aviation; Col. Royal B. Lord, assistant director, Board of Economic Warfare.

Grover Loening, one of the country's pioneer aeronautical designers and manufacturers, is the technical consultant to the committee. Gerard B. Lambert, member of the executive staff of WPB and chief of liaison for WPB, will be executive secretary to the committee.

WPB to allocate principal chemicals for industrial and agricultural nitrogen

Six chemicals were placed under complete allocation control May 30 by the Director of Industry Operations. The order numbers, chemicals, and date allocation is effective follow:

General Preference Order M-163, byproduct ammonia and sulphate of ammonia, June 1; General Preference Order M-164, synthetic ammonia, June 1; General Preference Order M-165, cyanamid, June 1; General Preference Order M-167, capryl alcohol, July 1; General Preference Order M-168, isopropyl alcohol, July 1; and General Preference Order M-169, methyl ethyl ketone, July 1.

Orders M-163, M-164, and M-165 cover chemicals representing the principal sources of industrial and agricultural nitrogen, and are likewise needed in large volume for manufacture of explosives. To insure adequate supplies for war purposes, and to distribute as equitably as possible all amounts available for agricultural purposes, the WPB now prohibits delivery of these chemicals by a producer or seller except by specific authorization by the Director of Industry Operations. Manufacturers and retailers of fertilizer and their agents are *not* included in this restriction.

Producers and distributors of these chemicals are required to file Form PD-237 prior to the tenth day of each month, beginning with June. In addition, fertilizer manufacturers must file Form PD-503 prior to July 1, and consumers of synthetic ammonia must file, when requested by WPB, reports on Form PD-504.

Orders M-167, M-168, and M-169 provide that no producer may use and no producer or distributor may deliver the chemicals covered, except by express permission of the Director of Industry Operations. Certain forms are provided which must be filed with the WPB, where they will be the basis for allocation. Under M-167, Forms PD-525 and PD-526 must be used; under M-168, PD-521 and PD-522, and under M-169, PD-523 and PD-524.

Under the latter three orders, quantities of 54 gallons or less (ten gallons in the case of capryl alcohol) are exempt from the restrictions, provided that the purchaser certifies that he is complying with the order, and provided that the amount so delivered by any producer is less than 2 percent of his production for that month.

Junkers plane patents among 600 newly seized by Alien Property Custodian

Six hundred patents, most of recent date and many of immediate importance to the American war effort, were taken over June 3 from their German and Italian owners by the Alien Property Custodian. Processes and equipment covered by the patents will be made available to American industry.

Instruments also included

Covering recent developments in their respective fields, the patents include many owned heretofore by Junkers and Arado, two of the large German manufacturers of airplanes.

Patents owned by Robert Bosch and covering electrical equipment, particularly in the ignition field, were seized, as were many patents in the fields of radio, television, and aircraft instruments.

Several of the seized patents related to the electron microscope, currently of great importance in scientific fields.

Several thousand seized

Several thousand patents have been seized thus far by the Alien Property Custodian in accordance with the April 21 directive of the President to "seize all patents controlled by enemy aliens, either directly or indirectly."

Surveys currently in progress at the Patent Office will disclose all patents and pending patent applications held in the name of foreign nationals and will permit the Custodian to complete his vesting of the holdings of enemy aliens.

Chlorate chemicals under allocation

Chlorate chemicals were put under complete allocation control by General Preference Order M-171, issued June 1 by the Director of Industry Operations.

The chlorate chemicals are used normally for making matches, fireworks and explosives, for killing weeds, oxidizing, and preventing rust, and in chemical processes. The equipment on which one chlorate is made is usually suitable for making other chlorates, so that, the supply situation of all chlorates may be considered as a unit. The WPB may specify which chlorates a producer may manufacture.

Copper use cut sharply for farm tractors, engine power units

Drastic limitations on the use of copper in the manufacture of farm tractors and engine power units are imposed by an order issued June 3 by the Director of Industry Operations.

Beginning June 15, producers are prohibited from manufacturing for sale or receiving from suppliers for resale any copper products or copper base alloy products for tractors or engine power units except for certain specified uses.

Substitutes being developed

The order, Supplementary Limitation Order L–26–c, will reduce the amount of copper used in radiators by 40 or 50 percent, and, at the current production rate for tractors, will reduce copper requirements by approximately 60 tons a month.

No provision is made for the use of copper in starting motors, generators or electrical lighting equipment for farm tractors. The farm equipment industry has had its engineers working for several months to develop substitutes for copper, and considerable progress in this direction has been reported.

The order specifies that no copper products or copper base alloy products may be used, even from inventory, in the production of farm tractors, or engine power units, other than for the following:

Radiators (only for water courses and tanks of copper alloy containing not more than 71 percent copper); cooling control devices, such as thermostats and radiator sealing caps of pressure type only; electrical equipment, confined to magnetos, switches, and wiring; bearings, bushings, thrust washers and similar parts; carburetor parts; plating for functional parts in connection with carburizing where substituted for solid copper or copper base alloy; gaskets.

In addition, copper products may be used as minor alloying elements for functional parts where substitutes are prohibitive from a standpoint of tool cost, or as brazing material for jointing functional parts. Powdered copper may be used for certain operations.

Restrictions contained in the order are in addition to those provided in the General Copper Conservation Order, M–9–c.

San Francisco deputy

Harry H. Fair, newly appointed San Francisco regional director of WPB, announced June 1 the selection of Henry S. Wright as Deputy Director in charge of operations.

WPB controls platinum sales to keep supplies from Germany, believed in need

The War Production Board on June 2 took steps to prevent Germany's getting any of the platinum she needs so badly for her munitions production.

All traffic in platinum except that conducted through normal, approved trade channels was halted by General Conservation Order M–162, announced June 2 by the Director of Industry Operations. Where transfer of platinum is permitted, the transaction, as well as inventories, must be filed with WPB on forms designated by WPB.

A strategic war material

Platinum is a strategic material of war. That this country has adequate supplies is suggested by the 100 percent operation of the platinum jewelry industry, and the even course of platinum prices. The Axis powers are not so fortunate. It is believed by United States authorities that Germany lacks this vital metal, so important to the production of nitric acid for explosives, for alloys, instruments, fire-control apparatus, fuses, chemical processes and other war products. Germany imported most of its platinum before the war, and it is now known that these sources are cut off, strengthening the belief that the German shortage is critical.

To prevent any American platinum being smuggled out of the country, or otherwise finding its way into the hands of our enemies, the present order forbids anyone to buy, sell, transfer, or otherwise dispose of any platinum (by which is meant any compound or alloy containing one percent or more of platinum) except to a person known to the seller to be a dealer, distributor, processor, or consumer of platinum.

Inventory reports required

It is made a particular responsibility of every person selling, delivering, or disposing of platinum to assure himself that the purchaser is entitled to receive it under this order.

Every person who has 1 troy ounce or more of platinum in his possession on the last day of the month must file, beginning May 31, 1942, Form PD–512 with WPB describing the circumstances under which he holds such platinum. A list of fabricated products containing platinum (Schedule A attached to the order) are exempted from this reporting provision.

Every person who sells, transfers, or otherwise disposes of platinum (except items on schedule A) during any calendar month must file Form PD–513 with WPB before the 15th of the following month describing the persons and circumstances involved in the disposal.

Illicit traffic known to exist

Purchasers of platinum must also file pertinent information on Form PD–514 by the 15th of the following month, relative to their purchases during the preceding calendar month.

Compliance with the provisions of this order by American citizens is expected to stop the illicit international traffic in platinum which is known to exist, and without which Germany cannot hope to get the metal it needs.

Violators of this order are subject to severe fine and imprisonment under the Second War Powers Act.

Items on Schedule A are:

Dental alloys and appliances, including, but not limited to, castings, pins and foil; electrical equipment and parts; fuse wire for use in detonators or in temperature limiting fuses; glass furnace parts; industrial equipment and parts; jewelry, except scrap or uncompleted forms thereof; laboratory equipment; platinum metal catalysts; rayon spinnerets; thermocouples or resistance thermometers.

Scrap metals, alloys placed under import control

Scrap metals and alloys of various types were placed under import control June 1 by the Director of Industry Operations with the addition of these items to Order M–63.

The new list includes iron and steel, aluminum, copper, lead, tin and magnesium in various categories of scrap and alloys.

The June 1 amendment became effective immediately.

Camouflage paint may be made through June

Infra-red reflecting camouflage paint may be manufactured by any company, on a strictly competitive basis, it was announced June 2 by the protective coatings section, chemicals branch, WPB, in an attempt to correct a general misunderstanding.

Manufacture of most musical instruments to cease; stocks frozen for armed forces

The manufacture of practically all musical instruments will be stopped soon as a result of an order announced May 31 by the WPB.

Using over 10 percent critical items

One provision of the order freezes present stocks of 27 different kinds of band instruments in the hands of manufacturers, jobbers, and wholesalers. These frozen stocks will be made available to the armed forces for use by Army, Navy, and Marine bands.

The stop provision applies to instruments containing more than 10 percent, by weight, of critical materials. Critical materials include not only metals but also cork, plastics, and rubber. The order therefore affects almost all musical instruments except violins, cellos, and some guitars.

The order is an amendment to General Limitation Order L–37, issued February 17, 1942, which curtailed the use of critical materials in musical instruments.

Under this amendment (Supplementary Limitation Order L–37–a), instruments containing more than 10 percent, by weight, of critical materials are treated as follows:

1. Beginning Monday, June 1, 1942, no critical materials may be processed for the manufacture of such instruments.
2. For a period of one month all of the affected instruments except pianos and organs may be assembled, on a restricted basis, from fabricated and semifabricated parts in the hands of manufacturers prior to May 29. Manufacturers may use such fabricated materials at the same rate as was permitted during the preceding 3 months under L–37.
3. After June 30, no more of these instruments may be completed. Production must stop entirely.
4. For a period of 2 months beginning June 1, pianos and organs may be completed or assembled out of fabricated or semifabricated materials. Such fabricated and semifabricated materials may be used at the same rate as was permitted during the preceding three months under order L–37.
5. After July 31, no more pianos or organs may be completed or assembled. Production must stop.

Piano and organ manufacturers are given a month longer for the assembly of such instruments than the manufacturers of other musical instruments because the production cycle of pianos and organs is longer and because their plants will not be able to start production of war materials until September.

Instruments containing not more than 10 percent, by weight, of critical materials may be manufactured at a rate of 75 percent of the use of critical materials in those instruments in 1940.

Replacement parts for all types of instruments may be produced at a rate of 75 percent of their production in 1940.

Being converted to war

Essential accessories containing not more than 10 percent of critical materials may be produced at a rate of 35 percent of 1940 production.

Critical materials are listed in the order as follows: iron, steel, lead, zinc, magnesium, aluminum, rubber, copper and copper base alloy, tin, phenol formaldehyde plastics, methyl methacrylate plastics, neoprene, cork, nickel, and chromium.

The musical instrument industry is being converted to the manufacture of direct war equipment. Piano manufacturers will manufacture gliders. Organ manufacturers will produce blowers for link trainers, used in ground training of pilots. Manufacturers of other instruments, such as brasses, will manufacture precision instruments, mostly for airplanes.

* * *

Some wood cabinets exempt from metal furniture ban

Wood filing cabinets containing not more than 2 pounds of essential steel hardware for each drawer have been removed from the limitations of the Metal Furniture Order, L–13–a.

This change is made by Amendment No. 2 to the order, effective June 1. The wooden cabinets are expected to be widely substituted for metal ones.

Order L–13–a required that production of most types of metal office equipment and furniture cease on May 31.

. . .

Fishing tackle can be made through June

Fishing tackle manufacturers may continue to produce their wares until the end of June 1942 under an amendment to Limitation Order L–92 issued June 1 by the Director of Industry Operations.

The June 1 amendment permits another month of production provided the critical materials needed for such articles were in the manufacturer's possession in fabricated form on or before April 23.

Cutlery manufacture sharply restricted; pocket knives limited to gold or silver

The manufacture of tableware, pocket knives, scissors and other cutlery is sharply restricted in General Limitation Order L–140, announced June 1 by WPB.

The order divides these articles into four classes. It permits limited production of three classes and prohibits production of the fourth, the latter representing a long list of everyday articles that are regarded as unnecessary.

The use of alloy iron or alloy steel in any of the articles covered by the order is prohibited. The only metals that may be used are unalloyed iron or steel, gold, and silver.

The restrictions do not apply to sterling silver flatware, which is not covered by the order.

Restrictions by classes effective June 1, 1942, are as follows:

Class I.—This class consists of industrial food processing machinery—that is, knives, forks, spoons, saws, cleavers, and other hand-operated cutlery used in packing, canning, dehydrating, and other food plants. In the manufacture of these items as much iron and steel may be used quarterly, beginning June 1, 1942, as the aggregate weight of metals used quarterly during the year ending June 20, 1941, in the manufacture of these same articles.

Class II.—This class includes cutlery used in homes, butcher shops, hotels, and other commercial establishments in the preparation of foods. It also includes commercial pocket knives, trimmers, and shears. The quarterly use of iron and steel in the manufacture of articles in class II must not exceed 60 percent of the weight of metals used quarterly in the manufacture of these same items during the year ending June 30, 1941.

Class III.—This class includes cutlery used in serving and eating food, and ordinary cutting scissors. Carving sets are not included in this group. The quarterly use of iron and steel in the manufacture of articles in class III is restricted to 35 percent of the weight of metals used quarterly in the production of these same articles during the year ending June 30, 1941.

Class IV.—This is the class of unessential cutlery. It includes domestic carving sets, pen knives, boys' pocket knives, and manicure implements. These articles may be produced through June 30, 1942, at the same rate of production as during the year ending June 30, 1941. After June 30, 1942, no metal other than gold or silver may be used in these articles.

It is estimated that the order will save annually on cutlery items about 6,000 tons of iron and steel, including 2,000 tons of stainless steel; 600 tons of copper alloy and small amounts of nickel, chrome, aluminum, antimonial lead, rubber, and plastics.

The cutlery and silver-plated flatware industries affected by this order consist of approximately 80 companies, which normally have an annual business of about $60,000,000.

Assembly of small stokers allowed, to speed conversion

The WPB, June 4, acted to speed the conversion of oil-burning equipment to coal by permitting the assembly of small stokers from materials which were in manufacturers' hands on May 31.

Norris to head operations section

At the same time, W. W. Timmis, chief of the plumbing and heating branch, announced the creation of an operations section which will continue an over-all study, under way in the branch for some time, of the various problems involved in the conversion of oil burners to use of other fuels.

Permission to assemble small coal stokers is contained in Amendment 1 to Limitation Order L–75. The original terms of the order ended the production of such stokers on May 31. The amendment, which was approved by the Office of Petroleum Coordinator and the Office of Solid Fuels Coordinator, permits the assembly until September 30 of small stokers composed wholly of fabricated parts in a manufacturer's physical possession on the former cut-off date.

The new operations section will be headed by Henry S. Norris, of Adamstown, Md., and will have the major responsibility of handling the demand for stokers, grates, and other equipment needed for conversion to coal.

Coatings for steel drums restricted after June 20

Coatings containing certain organic binders or pigments may not be used for coating steel containers of 2 gallons or greater capacity after June 20, by the terms of General Conservation Order M–158, announced June 1 by the Director of Industry Operations.

This order is expected to save nearly a million pounds a year of critical oils and resins, which are needed for military purposes. Normally, about 1,600,000 pounds each of critical oils and resins are used for drum coating each year.

The order divides coatings into two classes: "Class A," and others. Class A coatings, containing tung, oiticica, perilla or dehydrated castor oils; alkyd, phenolic, vinyl, urea or melamine resin; or cellulose esters or ethers, may not be used for drum coating after June 20 except for export (the export exception does not apply to Class A coatings containing tung or oiticica), or orders for the Army, Navy, Coast Guard or Maritime Commission.

WPB establishes policy on appeals to produce over quotas after deadlines

A uniform policy to be followed in the consideration of all appeals for permission to continue production which has been halted by WPB conservation and limitation orders was announced June 2 by the War Production Board.

The policy adopted by WPB will govern decisions on appeals to assemble processed or semiprocessed inventories beyond cut-off dates or in excess of limitation quotas. In general, such appeals will not be granted except when the materials involved have already been fabricated to such an extent that their use as scrap would be grossly wasteful.

WPB has issued more than two hundred conservation and limitation orders restricting or stopping production of hundreds of different articles.

Other relief considered first

The granting of appeals will be considered only after it has been determined that no other adequate relief is available to the applicant. Relief available in many cases without granting an appeal from the terms of a WPB order includes:

1. Assistance in disposing of frozen inventory materials to other companies permitted to use them, or to Government agencies.

2. Resale to the source of supply.

3. Assistance in securing war orders or in conversion of facilities to direct war production.

4. Advice on obtaining financial assistance from the Bureau of Finance in the Division of Industry Operations.

5. Assistance in the disposal of idle production equipment.

Before filing an appeal under an order, any company which considers itself subjected to undue hardship should consult with the nearest WPB field office to find out whether any of the forms of assistance outlined above will solve its difficulties.

Conditions for approval

When an appeal is filed in proper form for permission to assemble processed inventories in excess of limitation or conservation orders, no such appeal will be granted unless:

(a) The amount of unprocessed critical material is exceptionally small.

(b) The following tests are met:

1. The processed inventory must be

without salvage or reclaim value to war production, and, if not assembled, must have small scrap value, compared to the worth of the completed item.

2. The appellant must not be in violation of existing conservation, limitation, or priority orders.

3. The appellant must not have purposely processed a large inventory with the view of requesting preferential treatment or have otherwise violated the spirit of the order from whose terms he is appealing.

4. The labor to be employed for the assembling of the inventory will thus be trained for war work, or if this is not the case, the labor so used for assembly should not be required immediately for war production.

5. Consideration will be given if granting the appeal will help finance conversion to war work, or if this is not the case, will relieve the appellant's financial stress, and in no way interfere with the war effort.

6. Granting the appeal must not give the appellant any substantial advantage over competitors in a like situation.

7. No permission will be granted to use or procure materials which are very scarce, such as nickel and tungsten, except when the amount is extraordinarily small and the article manufactured will have an unusually large value to the national economy.

Primarily, appeals will be granted only if the successful prosecution of the war is furthered thereby. However, there may be certain appeals for relief where to deny the appeal would injure civilian economy without corresponding benefit to the war effort. In those instances the tests above will be treated as the basic points to be taken into consideration in determining whether or not to grant the appeal.

BENZENE UNDER ALLOCATION

Benzene was placed under complete allocation control by the issuance June 1 of an amendment of General Conservation Order M–137 by the Director of Industry Operations.

Because of the rapidly growing demand for benzene in making aviation gasoline, synthetic rubber, phenol for plastics, and aniline for the high explosive tetryl, it is deemed necessary to prohibit delivery or acceptance of any benzene after July 1, 1942, except by specific authority of the Director of Industry Operations. Quantities of 50 gallons or less to one person in one month are excepted.

Further provisions of the order prohibit the use of benzene as a motor fuel, either pure or in mixture, or its sale when the seller has reason to suspect that it may be so used.

More than 100,000 war housing units picked for relief from lumber curb

More than 100,000 of the most essential war housing units now under construction have been given relief from the restrictions on lumber deliveries contained in Limitation Order L-121, it was announced by the WPB June 3.

Both publicly and privately financed

After thorough investigation by the National Housing Administration and the WPB lumber and lumber products branch, these war housing projects were selected as the ones whose completion were most urgently needed in the war effort.

John B. Blandford, Jr., National Housing Administrator, reported that construction activity on these projects would have ceased almost immediately unless relief had been granted.

The 100,000 war housing units involved are divided almost equally between those publicly financed and privately financed. In the former category are 76 projects in 25 States, covering 54,039 units. The privately financed projects include 51,350 units in 32 localities in 20 States.

"Specific authorization" clause invoked

All of these projects are being constructed to house war workers and employees of war production plants and military and naval establishments. Local retail lumber stocks in the affected areas are not sufficient to permit the completion of the projects.

The method adopted for administering relief for these emergency demands was use of the "specific authorization" clause of Order No. L-121 which J. S. Knowlson, Director of Industry Operations, announced on May 22 would be invoked to take care of the needs of essential housing projects already under construction.

The authorization covering the publicly financed housing permits the purchase and delivery of construction lumber needed for the completion of a list of specified projects. The Federal Public Housing Authority superintendent for each project must certify the necessity for the lumber being bought under this authorization.

Demand far exceeds supply

The authorization covering the privately financed housing is similar. However, since the individual projects could not conveniently be specified, both the contractor and an authorized agent of

the FHA are required to certify the necessity for the lumber being bought under this authorization.

WPB officials emphasized that present demand for lumber of certain kinds greatly exceeds the supply, and that housing contractors who receive authorization to purchase lumber in accordance with the present plan cannot expect prompt deliveries in every case.

Limitation Order L-121, which was issued on May 13, prohibited sales of construction lumber by large producers for a period of 60 days with the exception of sales and deliveries to the Army, Navy, and Maritime Commission.

The lists of the public and private war housing projects covered and the number of dwelling units involved follow:

PUBLIC PROJECTS

ALABAMA—Mobile, 1,060.
ARIZONA—Higley, 110.
CALIFORNIA—Long Beach (Compton), 500; Pittsburg-Antioch, 86; San Francisco, 40; and Vallejo, 2,700.
CONNECTICUT—Bristol, 200; Hartford, 146; (West Hartford), 345; (Manchester), 300; (Glastonbury), 200; (Weathersfield), 200, 130, 100; (East Hartford), 150; and New London, 1,600.
DISTRICT OF COLUMBIA—Washington, 278, 1,150 dorm, 720, 750, 350 dorm, 3,000, 3,550.
FLORIDA—Banana River (Cocoa), 80, (Eau Gallie), 80, Key West, 210, Sebring,[1] 118.
ILLINOIS—Crab Orchard (Herrin), 200; (Marion), 200; Granite City, 264, 143; Joliet, 500, and Rockford, 150, 200.
INDIANA—Charlestown, 750, and La Porte, 3,130.
IOWA—Burlington, 400.
KANSAS—Parsons, 400, and Wichita, 2,300.
MARYLAND—Elkton, 350.
MASSACHUSETTS—Holyoke, 220, and North Weymouth, 142.
MICHIGAN—Detroit, 210.
NEW YORK—Niagara Falls, 450.
NORTH CAROLINA — New Bern-Moorehead City, 270.
OHIO—Dayton, 750, and Sandusky, 200.
OKLAHOMA—Pryor, 250, 100, 150.
OREGON—Portland, 400.
PENNSYLVANIA—Beaver County, 104, 50, 50; Chester, 350, and Erie, 224.
SOUTH CAROLINA—Charleston, 2,000.
TEXAS—Brownwood, 84 and Texarkana, 400.
UTAH—Ogden, 200.
VIRGINIA—Newport News, 5,200, 350; Norfolk-Portsmouth, 750, 900, 3,300; and Quantico, 250.
WASHINGTON—Bremerton, 1,750, 1,000; Keyport, 300; Seattle, 900, 350, 500, (Kirkland), 100; and Vancouver, 4,000.
WISCONSIN—Sturgeon Bay, 400.
Total, 54,039.

PRIVATE PROJECTS

ALABAMA—Huntsville, 675; Mobile, 450.
ARIZONA—Litchfield Park - Phoenix - Salt River Valley, 200.
CALIFORNIA—Oakland-A l a m e d a, 2,000; Richmond, 1,500; San Diego, 550; and Vallejo, 500.

[1] Exception made for this number out of total of 193 units.

DISTRICT OF COLUMBIA—Washington, 11,000.
KANSAS—Parsons, 125, and Wichita, 2,000.
LOUISIANA—New Orleans, 550.
MAINE—Portland, 250.
MARYLAND—Baltimore, 1,500.
MICHIGAN—Detroit, 11,000.
NEVADA—Las Vegas-Boulder City, 450.
NEW JERSEY—Paterson, 1,500.
NEW YORK—Buffalo, 1,500, and Utica-Rome-Ilion, 200.
OHIO—Akron, 400, and Dayton, 750.
OREGON—Portland, 900.
PENNSYLVANIA—Philadelphia, 5,000.
SOUTH CAROLINA—Charleston, 600.
TEXAS—Fort Worth, 400, and Orange-Beaumont-Port Arthur, 300.
UTAH—Ogden, 500, and Salt Lake City, 1,000.
VIRGINIA—Newport News, 500, and Norfolk-Portsmouth, 3,000.
WASHINGTON—Seattle, 1,500, Tacoma, 300, and Vancouver, 250.
Total, 51,350.

Phone companies given time to balance stocks

In order to permit telephone companies to balance inventories, swollen as a result of increasing demands by war agencies for service, WPB on June 3 postponed until September 1 the inventory restrictions contained in orders assigning preference ratings for materials necessary to the operation of the companies.

Averts indiscriminate junking

The telephone industry has been placed in the position of having inventories long on some items and short on others. Amendment gives telephone companies an opportunity to balance inventories without indiscriminate junking of excess stocks.

PLUMBING, HEATING REPAIRS ARE MADE EASIER

Installation of equipment calling for more material than that being replaced is permissible under the plumbing and heating repair and maintenance order (P-84), if the substitution is one of less critical material.

This is made clear by Interpretation No. 1, issued June 1, which also declares that the prohibition against a substitution "more extensive than that which is necessary to replace" worn-out or damaged parts does not mean that the identical part or parts must be replaced.

Furthermore, installations calling for a different kind of equipment are not necessarily more extensive within the terms of the order, if the new parts do not contain a greater weight of metal.

Scrap, reclaimed rubber impost confined to Military, RFC

WPB, on the recommendation of the Board of Economic Warfare, prohibited June 6 the importation of rubber and rubber products, including Balata, except by the military forces or by subsidiaries of the Reconstruction Finance Corporation.

The Rubber Reserve Company of the RFC which has heretofore been the sole importer of crude rubber and latex, will now also undertake the purchasing of reclaimed and scrap rubber in any form, as well as finished rubber products.

This action was effected by Amendment No. 10 to Supplementary Order M-15-b. "Imports" as used in the amendment cover a release from the bonded custody of the United States Bureau of Customs, as well as any shipment from a foreign country or from any territory or possession of the United States into continental United States.

* * *

Grade crossing, highway signals exempt from metal sign curb

The WPB June 2 exempted all mechanical and electrical railroad, grade crossing, and highway signals from the restrictions of Limitation Order L-29. In the original order, traffic lights alone were exempt.

In addition, the amendment restates the lamp or bulb exemptions for electrical signs to make it clear that not only incandescent and fluorescent lamps and tubes, but also neon and all other kinds of tubing used as a source of light, are exempt. Previously, the order exempted only lamps or bulbs.

* * *

Plant efficiency booklet released

A booklet on plant efficiency has been published by the Division of Information, WPB, and is now available for distribution, on request.

The booklet is called "Plant Efficiency—Ideas and Suggestions on Increasing Efficiency in Smaller Plants."

Copies may be obtained from regional and local offices of the War Production Board, located in 120 cities; from local offices of the Division of Information, OEM; or by writing to the Division of Information, OEM, in Washington.

Bureau of Construction opens headquarters in New York City; five branches move

The Bureau of Construction, recently established to coordinate all construction functions of the WPB, has moved to New York and opened headquarters in the Empire State Building.

Liaison staff to remain

Except for a small office staff which will remain in Washington for liaison work, the entire organization under William V. Kahler, chief of the Bureau, is affected by the change. Thomas L. Peyton, assistant to the chief, will be in charge of the Washington office.

Five operating branches

The Bureau is divided into five operating branches: Project analysis branch, materials control branch, project service branch, housing branch, and consultation branch.

The Project Analysis Branch handles all applications for private construction and recommends priority ratings for them. It administers limitation and conservation orders covering construction. Various agencies interested in construction have designated representatives to be stationed in New York to work with the Bureau in determining the essentiality and urgency of projects.

These include the Materials Division, Bureau of Industry Branches, Bureau of Priorities, Bureau of Governmental Requirements, the Army-Navy Munitions Board, the Plant Site Board, the Federal Works Administration, the Federal Housing Administration and the Federal Public Housing Authority.

The Materials Control Branch reviews the use of materials in projects which have been designated as essential by the project analysis branch. The former branch is guided by criteria established in the Bureau of Industrial Conservation, WPB, and applies these principles to insure a minimum use of critical materials.

The Project Service Branch works closely with industry and with the Army, Navy, Defense Plant Corporation, and other Government agencies, rendering whatever service is needed to eliminate construction delays so that scheduled completion dates are met. It advises and assists these groups on design and construction matters including the procurement and expediting of needed materials.

The Housing Branch recommends priority ratings for publicly and privately financed war housing. It works closely with other housing and related agencies in the Government, reviewing with them such matters as the type of housing as it relates to the use of materials, availability of utilities, services, etc.

The Consultation Branch acts as liaison between the public and the Bureau. It interprets the needs and problems of the construction industry and recommends procedures consistent with the over-all war program. Through its knowledge of trends and the requirements for essential military construction, the branch recommends the issuance of limitation and conservation orders and amendments, as may from time to time become necessary.

Direction and decisions of the Bureau will be handled in the New York Office.

All contacts with Federal, State, and local government agencies in regard to applications concerning their construction projects are the function of the bureau of governmental requirements, under the direction of Maury Maverick. This branch, part of the Division of Industry Operations, will remain in Washington.

The facilities of several other agencies of the Government have been made available to the War Production Board for receiving and processing applications for authorization to begin construction.

Applications for farm building, either agricultural or residential, should be filed with the local county and State War Boards of the United States Department of Agriculture which recommends essential building to the Bureau of Construction for approval.

Applications for residential building, other than on farms, should be filed at local office of the FHA. Publicly and privately financed defense housing programs also are processed by the FHA. Recommendations are made by FHA to WPB, but in each instance final approval for a project must be given by the Bureau of Construction which then assigns it a priority rating.

Applications for commercial and other construction should be filed directly with the Bureau of Construction. Each project of this type is reviewed by an end-product branch in the WPB which makes recommendations as to essentiality and urgency to the Bureau.

Correspondence concerning projects handled by the Bureau of Construction should be addressed to: War Production Board, Bureau of Construction, Empire State Building, New York, N. Y.

* * *

Switching temporary phones to permanent permitted

Restrictions on telephone installations have been modified so that temporary equipment may be replaced by permanent equipment and other special operations may be carried out without undue hardship to subscribers.

In Amendment No. 1 to General Conservation Order L-50, as amended, WPB makes it possible for a subscriber to substitute less telephone facilities in cases where his existing facilities exceed his requirements.

* * *

Status of preferred applicants

Preferred applicants for new telephone service must demonstrate that the service is necessary to discharge the war or essential public activity in which they are engaged, the WPB ruled June 2 in Interpretation No. 1 of General Conservation Order L-50.

Questions and Answers on Priorities

Q. Once you have obtained a preference rating for materials, how do you go about getting your requested supplies?

A. By endorsing a purchase order for these supplies, and stating on the face of it a prescribed certification of the preference rating that entitles you to them. You extend this purchase order to your suppliers, who, in turn, can extend it to subsuppliers.

Q. In applying for priority assistance is it necessary to specify a definite delivery date on the application form?

A. Priorities Regulation No. 1 as amended requires every applicant for priority assistance to specify in his application the latest date on which such items requested can be delivered to him to meet his contract obligations or production schedules. All applications specifying "immediately" or "at once" will be returned to the applicant. Place and exact delivery date must be filled in.

Q. Does the fact that WPB is going into an allocation system mean that there will be no more priority ratings?

A. Priority ratings will remain to supplement and implement the allocation system.

Q. What is a blanket rating?

A. A limited blanket rating or "P" order covers certain vital industries important to defense, assigning a rating or ratings for all the materials required to produce a specified product, within the limits of the order.

Q. What are project ratings?

A. They're preference ratings for material going into essential construction; plant expansion to fill war orders, for example, or defense housing for war workers. No building project will qualify for this, however, unless it is important to the war effort or vital to the public health and safety.

Juke and slot-machine parts brought under limitation order

General Limitation Order L–21–a was amended June 4 to bring manufacturers of parts for automatic phonographs and weighing, amusement and gaming machines under the terms of the order. By an oversight, they were omitted in the original order.

PRIORITY ACTIONS			*From May 28 *Through June 3			
Subject	Order No.	Related form	Issued	Expiration date	Rating	
Agave fiber: a. Further restrictions placed on production of agave wrapping twine.	M–84 (Amend No. 6)		6–1–42			
Alcohol: a. Butyl alcohol: 1. Effective July 1 all grades of butyl alcohol placed under complete allocation by WPB. Persons using less than 54 gallons a month not subject to allocation, provided deliveries do not exceed 2 percent of a producer's monthly output.	M–159	PD–505; 506	5–28–42			
Benzene: a. Prohibits delivery or acceptance of benzene after July 1, 1942.	M–137	PD–223–A; PD–224–A	6–1–42			
Beryllium: a. To conserve supply and direct distribution. Complete allocation placed by WPB.	M–160	PD–496; 497	6–1–42			
Calcium-silicon: a. Order M–20–a extended indefinitely.	M–20–a (Amend. No. 1)		5–30–42			
Chemical: a. Chemical cotton pulp: 1. Effective July 1, chemical cotton pulp placed under full allocation.	M–157	PD–507; 508; 509	5–28–42			
b. Byproduct ammonia and sulfate of ammonia placed under allocation.	M–163	PD–237; 503	5–30–42			
c. Synthetic ammonia placed under allocation.	M–164	PD–237; 503; 504	5–30–42			
d. Cyanamid placed under allocation.	M–165	PD–237; 503	5–30–42			
e. Capryl alcohol placed under allocation.	M–167	PD–525; 526	5–30–42			
f. Isopropyl alcohol placed under allocation.	M–168	PD–521; 522	5–30–42			
g. Methyl ethyl ketone placed under allocation.	M–169	PD–523; 524	5–30–42			
Closures and associated items: a. Slide fasteners: 1. Order amended to permit use of slide fasteners fabricated prior to Apr. 1, in a list of garments and articles.	L–68 (Amend. No. 1)		5–28–42			
Chlorate chemicals: a. Chlorate chemicals placed under complete allocation.	M–171	PD–515; 516	6–1–42			
Closures for glass containers: a. Limits supply of tonnages of blackplate to be used for nonalcoholic beverages' bottle caps. Prohibits use of blackplate after Aug. 1, and of tin, in the manufacture of closures for wine and distilled spirits.	M–104	PD–519	5–30–42			
Coal stokers: a. Permits assembly of small stokers from materials in manufacturer's hands on May 31.	L–75 (Amend. No. 1)		6–4–42			
Communications: a. Applicants for telephone service must show need for such.	L–50 (As Amend. 4–29–42) (Int. No. 1).		6–2–42			
b. Maintenance, repair, and operating supplies. 1. Postpones effective date of 27½ percent restriction to Sept. 1.	P–129 (Amend. No. 1)		6–3–42			
2. Postpones effective date of 27½ percent restriction to Sept. 1.	P–130 (Amend. No. 1)		6–3–42			
Copper: a. Permits use of bronze powder in manufacture of paste, ink, leaf, and paint until Dec. 15, 1942. Prohibits all use of products made with bronze powder for these purposes after Dec. 31, 1942.	M–9–c–3 (As Amend. 5–30–42).		5–30–42			
Cotton duck: a. Provides new procedure for handling preference-rated orders for cotton duck.	M–91 (Amend. No. 2)	PDL–1	5–28–42		A–2.	
b. Allocation placed on use, sales, and deliveries of combed cotton yarn.	M–155		5–28–42			
Cutlery: a. Manufacture of tableware, pocket knives, scissors, and other cutlery restricted by WPB.	L–140		5–30–42			
Drum exterior coating: a. Restrictions placed on coatings containing certain organic binders or pigments after June 20.	M–156		5–30–42			
Farm machinery and equipment and attachments and repair parts therefor: a. Restrictions placed on use of copper in manufacture of farm tractors and engine power units, effective June 15.	L–26–c		6–3–42			

Subject	Order No.	Related form	Issued	Expiration date	Rating
Furniture (metal office and equipment):					
a. Restrictions on amount of steel for use in wood filing cabinets listed.	L-15-a (Amend. No. 2).		6-1-42		
Fishing tackle:					
a. Fishing tackle manufacturers permitted to continue to produce their wares until June.	L-92 (Amend. No. 1).		6-1-42		
General inventory order:					
a. Inventory restriction exceptions on manufacturing of refractory brick, including 16 materials.	M-161.		6-1-42		
Goatskins, kidskins, and cabrettas:					
a. Sets quota for processors and tanners for months of June and July to 140 percent of monthly average of skins put into process during 1941.	M-114 (Amend. No. 2).		5-30-42		
Goose and duck feathers:					
a. Feathers less than 4 inches in length to be reserved for military orders.	M-102 (Amend. No. 2)		6-1-42		
Imports of strategic materials:					
a. Scrap metals and alloys placed under import control.	M-63 (Amend. No. 7).		6-1-42		
b. WPB places control over imports of commodities imported for civilian use, beginning July 2.	M-63 (As Amend. 6-2-42).	PD-222-C; PD-222-B.	6-2-42		
c. Releases from the provisions of M-63 commodities imported overland or by air from Canada and Mexico. Order effective 30th day after date of issuance.	M-63-a.		6-2-42		
Kapok:					
a. Extends order to June 30, 1942.	M-85 (Amend. No. 3).		6-1-42		
Laundry equipment, dry-cleaning equipment, and tailors' pressing machinery:					
a. Adjusted to conform to customary manufacturing practices of the industry.	L-91 (Amend. No. 1).	PD-418.	6-3-42		
Lead:					
a. Lead pool for June set at 15 percent of April production.	M-38-I.		6-1-42		
Lumber, construction:					
a. Releases restrictions on several grades and items of lumber no longer being bought by Federal Agencies, which are usable for War Housing and farm purposes.	L-121 (Amend. No. 1).		5-28-42		
Machinery (industrial):					
a. Food slicing and grinding machinery as restricted in L-83, defined as machinery of one horsepower or over.	L-83 (A m e n d e d) (Amend. No. 1).		5-29-42		
Metal signs:					
a. Mechanical and electrical railroad, grade-crossing, and highway signals exempted from Lim. Od. L-29.	L-29 (Amend. No. 1).		6-2-42		
Motor fuel:					
a. 30 percent cut in gas deliveries in Oregon and Washington rescinded by WPB.	L-70 (Amend. No. 3).		6-1-42		
Musical instruments:					
a. Certain musical instruments placed under allocation by WPB.	L-37-a.	PD-498.	5-29-42		A-1-k.
Naphthenic acid and naphthenates:					
a. Specifies products excepted by an amendment to Gen. Preference Od. M-142.	M-142 (Amend. No. 1).		6-1-42		
Office machinery:					
a. Regulates production and sets up distribution control for office machinery.	L-54-c.		6-1-42		
b. Revocation of Order L-54-b.	L-54-b (Revoked).		6-1-42		
c. Manufacturer authorized to maintain present rate of production of typewriters, etc., during June and July.	L-54-a (Amend. No. 2).		5-30-42		
d. Supplementary order.	L-54-a-1.		5-30-42		
Pencils, wood cased:					
a. Lifts restrictions of order L-113 to allow manufacturer to use stock on hand, and prohibits manufacturer from acquiring any pigments to be used in production of pencils, other than specified colors.	L-113 (Amend. No. 2).		5-30-42		
Platinum:					
a. Restrictions placed on sale, purchase, and delivery of platinum. To conserve supply and direct distribution.	M-162.	PD-512; 513; 514.	5-30-42		
Plumbing and heating simplification:					
a. Prohibits use of metals other than joining hardware, coating, or reinforcing mesh, after June 20, in plumbing fixtures.	L-42.		5-28-42		
Plumbing and heating equipment P-84:					
a. Interpretation of P-84 in regard to installation of equipment.	P-64 (Int. No. 1).		6-1-42		

(Continued on page 18)

Bureau helps 429 war firms obtain $54,476,358 in May

The Bureau of Finance of the WPB reported June 5 that during May it assisted manufacturers engaged in war production to obtain $54,476,358 of financing from local banks, Federal Reserve banks, the Reconstruction Finance Corporation, the Army, Navy, Maritime Commission and other public and private agencies.

This compared with $55,109,966 in the preceding month. This financing was utilized by 429 companies throughout the country, compared with 289 companies in April.

The Bureau has representatives in 35 WPB field offices who give advice and assistance to firms engaged in war production or seeking war-orders. It makes no loans itself but directs qualified firms to public and private agencies that do.

Flashlight makers allowed to use up plated iron, steel stocks

General Limitation Order L-71 was amended June 5 to permit flashlight manufacturers to use up inventories of plated iron and steel at a rate not exceeding their 1940 production.

The original order, issued March 27, prohibited the use of aluminum, crude rubber, chromium, nickel, tin, brass, or copper in flashlights after March 31, 1942.

The June 5 amendment permits use of these materials if they were plated on steel prior to March 31, 1942, and provided such plated steel was in the possession of the manufacturer or his supplier prior to March 31.

The original order also prohibited the use of iron and steel in flashlights and batteries after May 31, 1942, except in reflectors, contact fittings, battery top seals, battery under jackets, eyelets, rivets, and caps and end ferrules.

The June 5 amendment permits the use in flashlight cases and batteries of iron and steel which was in fabricated form and in the possession of manufacturers or their suppliers prior to April 1, 1942. Such use may not exceed the rate of production in 1940.

Relaxations permitted in the amendment are subject to previously issued metal conservation orders. Under General Conservation Order M-126 no iron or steel may be used in flashlight tubes after August 3, 1942.

Survey of war production committees reveals quick results in majority of cases

Coincident with the announcement that the number of plants with labor-management committes for war production drives had risen to 800, WPB made public June 1 the results of an unsolicited, voluntary survey of a cross-section of plants in the drive.

Results of this analysis were submitted to WPB Chairman Nelson by the editors of "Mill & Factory," a trade magazine published by the Conover-Nast Corporation of New York City.

Private advantage not sought

Summarizing their survey, the examiners said that it indicated conclusively that the labor-management plan "has not, up to this point, been used by labor for its own benefit, as many spokesmen prophesied. On the other side of the question, it is equally apparent that management has not attempted to use the new committees to its own advantage at the expense of labor."

The surveyors picked 88 plants with labor-management committees, reporting "they were chosen at random and represent a cross-section of industry, being large, medium, and small plants manufacturing many different products." To insure frankness, the names of the plants were kept confidential.

A sincere effort to increase production

The questions asked, the replies, and some of the investigators' comments follow:

HAS ANY ATTEMPT BEEN MADE BY LABOR TO USE THE COMMITTEE AS A MEANS OF ENCROACHING ON MANAGEMENT FUNCTIONS?

	Percent
Yes	8
No	87
Don't know yet	5

HAS THERE BEEN ANY ATTEMPT TO CHANGE THE FUNCTION OF THE COMMITTEE FROM ITS PRIMARY PURPOSE INTO A BARGAINING UNIT?

	Percent
Yes	4
No	95
Don't know yet	1

HAS LABOR TO DATE USED THESE MEETINGS IN A SINCERE EFFORT TO INCREASE PRODUCTION?

	Percent
Yes	74
No	21
Too early to tell	5

HAS IT INCREASED THE NUMBER OF WORTHWHILE SUGGESTIONS BY EMPLOYEES AND THUS BENEFITED PRODUCTION?

	Percent
Yes	51
No	31
Don't know yet	18

"Among those reporting no increase, four have long had well-run suggestion systems and can see no particular increase in the number or quality of the material received. Four companies have not as yet put their systems into operation."

HAS ANY ATTEMPT BEEN MADE BY LABOR TO SUGGEST TO EMPLOYEES THAT THIS PLAN IS ACTUALLY AN ADAPTATION OF THE MURRAY MANAGEMENT-LABOR PLAN?

	Percent
Yes	6
No	89
Don't know yet	5

DOES THE EXPERIENCE OF THE PLAN TO DATE LEAD YOU TO BELIEVE THAT IT IS OF GREAT ENOUGH BENEFIT TO THE WAR PRODUCTION PROGRAM IN YOUR PLANT TO JUSTIFY THE TIME IT CONSUMES?

	Percent
Yes	54
No	27
Don't know yet	19

HAS THE PLAN RESULTED IN THE IMPROVEMENT OF YOUR LABOR-MANAGEMENT RELATIONS?

	Percent
Yes	47
No	47
Don't know yet	6

"The answers to this question may be misinterpreted until it is pointed out that all but fourteen companies replying in the negative stated specifically that their labor-management relations were already very good before establishing the Committee."

IS THE CHAIRMAN OF THE COMMITTEE A MEMBER OF THE LABOR OR MANAGEMENT GROUP?

	Percent
Management group	72
Labor group	14
Co-chairman or alternate chairmen for each meeting	14

The analysis concluded:

"Although the plan is still largely in the process of being set up, it is significant that 73 percent of those answering the queries report a sincere effort on the part of labor to help increase production."

United States officials appeal to production drive committees to keep workers fit and on job

Six high officials charged with increasing American war production June 4 appealed to War Production Drive committees to keep the American workman healthy to save man-hours for victory.

Need vigor, staying power

The appeal was signed by Donald M. Nelson, Chairman of the War Production Board; Paul V. McNutt, Chairman of the War Manpower Commission; Robert P. Patterson, Under Secretary of War; James V. Forrestal, Under Secretary of the Navy; E. R. Stettinius, Jr., Lend-Lease Administrator, and E. S. Land, Chairman of the Maritime Commission.

Their joint statement was sent to each labor-management committee in the more than 800 plants which are participating in the War Production Drive. The text follows:

Sick and injured war production workers lose 6,000,000 workdays every month.

We must save as many of those lost days as we possibly can for the Production Drive.

Only healthy workers can put into the drive what it takes—vigor, staying power, and the will to win.

It is your job to fight sickness and accidents. See to it that every medical and engineering means of prevention is provided in your plant. Make it a healthful working place.

Help the men and women in your plant to keep themselves healthy and on the job. You can do this by training them in health conservation and safety as carefully as you train them in efficiency.

Use your influence to see that your community has an active public health department; enough doctors, nurses, and hospital beds to care for your workers and their families. Your Federal and State governments are doing their part. Make sure your community does its part.

If your plant is not already conducting a sound industrial hygiene program, write to the United States Public Health Service, Washington, D. C., for advice. Do it today. You can boost production, save time and lives if you start now. Save a day for Victory.

The committees were urged to post the text, in large letters, on bulletin boards and to reprint it in plant newspapers.

Production Drive extended into mines to speed metals "more precious than gold"

WPB Chairman Donald M. Nelson announced June 5 extension of the War Production Drive into the nonferrous metal mining industry in an all-out effort to step up production of the basic war metals which have become more precious than gold to the Nation's armed forces.

Mr. Nelson announced that the Drive will be launched at a joint labor-management rally June 13 (Miners Day) at Butte, Mont., an important copper and zinc producing center. Mr. Nelson will speak to the rally in Butte by long-distance phone.

Materials Director A. I. Henderson announced the establishment of a nonferrous metals committee to integrate the work of the copper, lead, and zinc branches of WPB in connection with the War Production Drive in nonferrous metal mines.

This committee will work jointly with the Labor Production Division in the establishment of local labor-management committees throughout the mining areas involved.

Personnel of 2 committees named

In commending the management of the Anaconda Copper Company for its cooperative spirit and its leadership in establishing j o i n t labor-management committees at its Butte properties, Mr. Henderson stated: "With this good start, we expect that 'Victory Committees' will soon be functioning in all the nonferrous metal mining areas."

Members of the new committee in the Materials Division will be: H. O. King, chief of the copper branch; George Heikes, chief of the zinc branch; and Erwin Vogelsang, chief of the lead branch. Mr. King will head the committee.

Wendell Lund, Director of the Labor Production Division, announced the formation of a special section in his division to work with the Materials Division in promoting the campaign.

The new section will be headed by Dr. Allen Buchanan, formerly of the United States Tariff Commission and at present labor consultant to the copper and zinc branches of the Materials Division. Bela Low, E. M., principal consultant in metal mining to the Labor Production Division, will be assigned to the new unit.

ANOTHER WAR PRODUCTION RECORD IS SMASHED

Smashing of one more war production record was reported June 4 by the labor-management committee of the Colorado Fuel and Iron Corporation, Pueblo, Colo.

Robert Leech, secretary of the War Production Drive Committee, telegraphed War Production Board headquarters:

"Colorado Fuel & Iron Corporation employees smashed all previous ingot production records during May with total of 106,000 tons. Best previous record 98,000 tons. Also set more than 20 major production marks in other departments."

Donald M. Nelson, chairman of the War Production Board, telegraphed congratulations.

Multiple plant corporations active in production drive

Corporations with multiple plants have been especially enthusiastic about labor-management production committees, it was pointed out June 4, at War Production Drive headquarters.

War Production Drives to bring the output of war material up to the victory level are now under way in more than 3 plants each of 16 companies.

A list of the companies and the number of plants in which labor-management committees are functioning follows:

DU PONT GROUP

E. I. du Pont de Nemours & Co...	51
General Motors Corporation...	9
Remington Arms Co...	6

U. S. STEEL GROUP

American Steel & Wire Co...	18
Carnegie Illinois Steel Corporation...	18
Tennessee Coal, Iron & R. R. Corporation...	10
Columbia Steel Co...	4

ANACONDA COPPER GROUP

Anaconda Wire & Cable Co...	7
American Brass Co...	4

OTHER CORPORATIONS

Westinghouse Electric & Manufacturing Co...	25
Johns-Manville Products Corporation...	10
Owens-Illinois Glass Co...	6
Borg-Warner Corporation...	6
Curtiss Wright Corporation...	6
Revere Copper & Brass, Inc...	6
R. C. A. Manufacturing Co...	4

War plants click to rhythm of slogans; half a million take part in contests

Wheels in the war plants of America are clicking to the rhythm of slogans. More than half a million men and women on the war production line have participated in slogan contests in 300 plants, a recapitulation at War Production Drive Headquarters shows. Contests are under way or are being planned in most of the remainder of the 855 plants in which voluntary labor-management committees have been organized for War Production Drives.

Slogan contests have been one of the most successful features of War Production Drives, labor-management committees report. They dramatize the part a plant and each man in it plays in the war; they provide a means for wide participation in the Production Drive and in the war itself, and they provide an ever-present stimulant to increased production. Also, men and women like to write them.

War Bonds frequently given

Under the plan of the War Production Drive, a committee within the plant conducts the slogan contest, making its own rules and providing its own prizes. More often than not, prizes are War Bonds contributed for the most part by the management or persons associated with the management. Some committees have had weekly or monthly contests.

Some typical slogans and the plants in which they originated follow:

T. N. T.—TODAY NOT TOMORROW, Western Electric & Manufacturing Co., Canton, Ohio.

SPEED THE WHEELS TO BEAT THE HEELS, American Steel and Wire Co., Waukegan, Ill.

SPEED 'EM FOR FREEDOM, Curtiss Wright Corporation, Beaver, Pa.

FIGHT 'EM IN THE FACTORY, Eastman Kodak Company, Rochester, N. Y.

IF IT'S NIP AND TUCK, MAKE IT THE NIP THAT GETS TUCK, E. I. du Pont de Nemours & Company, Joliet, Ill.

PRODUCTION QUOTAS MUST BE BEAT TO KNOCK THE AXIS OFF ITS FEET, Globe-Union, Inc., Milwaukee, Wis.

HYPRODUCTION MEANS AXIS DESTRUCTION, Cincinnati (Ohio) Planer CO.

JAPPY, WE'LL KNOCK YOU SLAP HAPPY, Boye and Emmes Tool Co., Cincinnati, Ohio.

THE NAZIS CHEER EACH IDLE GEAR, American Steel & Wire Co., Worcester, Mass.

WPB to survey operations of 800 steel warehouses

Operations of 800 large steel warehouses are to be surveyed shortly by the compliance branch of WPB.

Questionnaires designed to establish the practices of these warehouses and the degree of their conformity with priorities orders are to be mailed, while 200 investigators of the Wage and Hour Division of the Department of Labor will make the necessary field examinations.

Approximately 15 percent of all iron and steel production is distributed through warehouses and it is essential that these products be stocked and distributed in accordance with the needs of the war program.

The compliance branch will analyze the completed questionnaires and will initiate punitive action in cases of demonstrated violation of WPB orders.

Blackplate curbed for beverage caps, tin barred

Because of the serious shortage of steel, WPB on May 30 sharply limited the tonnages of blackplate which may be used for beer and nonalcoholic beverage bottle caps, and at the same time completely prohibited use of blackplate after August 1, and of tin, effective at once, in the manufacture of closures for wine and distilled spirits.

In addition, WPB enlarged the list of other products for which the use of tinplate or terneplate covers is prohibited.

Rubber life suits restricted

WPB on June 1 restricted sales and purchases of rubber life-saving suits in order to make the necessary equipment available for oceangoing and coastwise cargo and tank vessels of over 1,000 gross tons.

The United States Coast Guard recently issued regulations requiring that each such cargo boat and tanker be equipped with one lifesaving suit for each person on board.

Supplementary Rubber Order M-15-e provides that the suits can be sold only for uses prescribed by the Coast Guard, or if the sale has been expressly authorized by the Director of Industry Operations. Purchases made by or for the account of the Army, Navy, Coast Guard, or for Lend-Lease purposes are exempted from the restrictions.

PRIORITY ACTIONS

*From May 28
*Through June 3

(Continued from page 15)

Subject	Order No.	Related form	Issued	Expiration date	Rating
Radio receivers and phonographs: a. Clarifies certain subjects contained in Lim. Od. L-44.	L-44 (Int. No. 1)		6-1-42		
Railroad equipment: a. Provides for sale and delivery of railroad car parts designed for construction or repair, if material obtained under preference rating.	L-97-a-1 (Amend. No. 2).		5-28-42		
Rationing of new commercial motor Vehicles. a. Modifies Od. M-100 to allow the Army and Navy and certain other war agencies to obtain trucks without applying for special permits, when trucks are built to order for such agencies.	M-100 (Amend. No. 1).		5-28-42		
Rubber and products and materials of which rubber is a component. a. To restrict transactions in rubber lifesaving suits.	M-15-e		6-1-42		
Styrene: a. Styrene placed under complete allocation by WPB.	M-170		6-1-42		
Wool: a. Consolidates the second quarter order and all amendments thereto. Lifts some restrictions.	M-73 (As Amended—6-1-42) (Extended—7-4-42).		6-1-42		

SUSPENSION ORDERS

Company	Number	Violation	Penalty	Issued	Expiration date
Brandtjen and Kluge, Inc., St. Paul, Minn.	S-49	Unauthorized melting of aluminum scrap, contrary to Sup. Od. M-1-d. Acquiring material under false representation of Preference Rating P-100, for printing presses.	Prohibited from delivering any printing or publishing machinery for 4 months. 10 days after effective date of order, company may not manufacture machinery of this type on orders in excess of $200, except on ratings of A-1-k, or higher.	5-27-42 (effective 5-30-42).	9-30-42

PRIORITIES REGULATIONS

Number	Subject	Issued
Prior. Reg. No. #10	Allocation Classification System established requiring use of symbols by every person placing purchase orders or contract after June 30, 1942. Purchases by retailers and purchases by distributors for resale exempt from requirements of regulation.	6-2-42

Styrene placed under complete allocation

Styrene, one of the basic raw materials from which synthetic rubber is made, was placed under complete allocation control June 1 by the Director of Industry Operations.

Golf club production permitted to June 30

Manufacturers have been given an additional month in which to manufacture golf clubs out of their inventories of iron and steel which had been fabricated into golf club parts prior to April 9, 1942, the date of issuance of Limitation Order L-93.

Brett named deputy rubber coordinator

Alden C. Brett, treasurer and comptroller of the Hood Rubber Co., Watertown, Mass., has been appointed deputy coordinator for rubber, Coordinator Arthur B. Newhall announced June 2.

Mr. Brett will be Mr. Newhall's representative in negotiations with South American Countries and other Government Agencies for expanding supply.

★ ★ ★

Safety equipment sales

Permission to sell safety equipment assembled from parts which were in inventory on May 5 on A-10 or higher orders was granted June 4.

Auto plants will scrap obsolete machinery to provide war materials

An effective move in the field of industrial salvage, and one that should help satisfy the war demand for scrap metal was outlined in the announcement made in Detroit by WPB and the Automotive Council for War Production that the automotive industries will put on an intensive campaign to scrap obsolete machinery, equpiment, and buildings.

The proposal, according to officials of the Bureau of Industrial Conservation, comes as the result of months of intensive study of the problems involved. The most serious of these concerned the formulation of a method by which the degree of obsolescence could be measured to determine whether particular items should be scrapped. The announced procedure under which the salvage authority in each plant will make the decision, meets with the approval of the bureau.

★

Ban on use of bronze powder relaxed for some purposes

Because there is no apparent military demand for the remaining small stocks of bronze powder in the country, its use by the printing and publishing industry and for other decorative purposes was permitted June 1 by the Director of Industry Operations.

An amendment of Supplementary Order M-9-c-3 permits the use of bronze powder in the manufacture of paste, ink, leaf, and paint until December 15' 1942, and prohibits all use of these products made with bronze powder, and bronze powder itself, for these purposes after December 31, 1942.

The order does not permit further manufacture of bronze powder and permits the use of stocks in the hands of other than manufacturers only.

Tucker WPB representative to Economic Warfare Board

Appointment of Joe M. Tucker as WPB representative to the Board of Economic Warfare was announced June 4 by WPB Chairman Donald M. Nelson. Mr. Tucker replaces Edgar B. Stern, who was recently named chairman of the WPB transportation committee.

BERYLLIUM UNDER ALLOCATION

Complete allocation control over beryllium, alloying material used to harden copper, was ordered June 1 by the Director of Industry Operations with the issuance of Order M-160.

Consumers must file requests for allocation on Form PD-496 by the twentieth of the month preceding the month in which they wish delivery and must file a monthly report to the WPB on Form PD-497. The latter form also must be used by any person who has as much as 10 pounds of beryllium in his possession in any month for a report to WPB.

Until July 1, beryllium may be delivered without allocation to produce an article with a rating of A-1-c or higher.

. . .

Salvage firm's sales of repaired goods exempt from GMPR

Sales of the J. B. Shelnutt Salvage Co., of Louisville, Ky., a firm engaged solely in reconditioning and selling damaged merchandise received from insurance companies, transportation companies, and agencies of the United States Government, have been excepted from the general maximum price regulation.

The firm was the third to register with the OPA for the exemption allowable to salvage companies dealing only in this type of merchandise.

The exemption, contained in Order No. 2 under Supplementary Regulation No. 1 to the general maximum price regulation, was effective June 4.

. . . .

Stored shells will be shipped to England, not scrapped here

The British Purchasing Commission has informed the WPB that in accordance with instructions from London, a large number of 9.2'' shells which have been in storage in the United States will be shipped to England.

These shells were originally made for a type of gun no longer manufactured. Nevertheless, a considerable number of these guns are still in use, requiring ammunition.

Previously, the WPB had been notified by the British Purchasing Commission that the shells would be scrapped in the United States.

Delay in scrap dealers' yards may force direct buying by mills making steel

A threatened bottleneck in scrap metal dealers' yards in some localities may force the Government to request steel mills to buy scrap metal direct, and prepare it for the furnaces in their own yards, Lessing J. Rosenwald, Chief of the Bureau of Industrial Conservation, said on June 4.

Mr. Rosenwald pointed out that while the bottleneck was due in some cases to the increased volume of scrap metal piling into the yards, there is a real need for increasing and facilitating the rate of scrap turn-over in yards where additional quantities are being received.

Prices to collectors suffering

"The increased volume of scrap metal now being offered to them," said Mr. Rosenwald, moreover "in some instances has prompted dealers to lower scrap prices to the prejudice of the owners and collectors, who should not be asked to take a loss in return for their cooperation with the salvage program. The steel mills that buy direct will be prepared to purchase scrap in any amount at ceiling prices, less the cost of freight and handling."

Direct buying by steel mills, Mr. Rosenwald noted, would also make it possible for them to build greater reserves, thus eliminating shut-downs that may be caused by bottlenecks or price cutting in particular areas.

"The movement of scrap," concluded Mr. Rosenwald, "must not be permitted to falter. Steel production is now reaching record heights. Ninety days ago the lack of scrap metal caused 20 furnaces to draw their fires. A month back, 6 furnaces were down, while on June 1 no furnace was down for this cause. The flow of iron and steel scrap from all sections of the country has been accelerating at a rapid rate; it must not bog down in dealers' yards."

Westberg to head textile joint procurement committee

George E. Westberg, New York City, has resigned as chief of the combed fabrics unit of the WPB textile branch to accept the chairmanship of the textile joint procurement committee set up by the purchase policy committee of WPB's Division of Purchases. Mr. Westberg succeeds the late A. J. Rice, who died.

PRICE ADMINISTRATION . . .

24 new areas get 60 days to cut rents; total now 366, with 89 million population

Price Administrator Henderson announced June 4 the addition of 24 more communities to this Nation's rapidly growing list of "defense-rental areas," and increased the size of one area already designated.

This action by the OPA in its continuing move against inflated rents in the country's war production and military training centers, makes a total of 366 communities thus far designated. In the first 20 of these areas, Federal control of residential rents other than hotels and rooming houses became effective June 1. Areas now designated contain more than 89 million persons.

March 1 date set

In the designations made June 4, the Price Administrator recommended that rents in the 24 new areas be reduced to levels prevailing on March 1 of this year. Among other points covered in the recommendations were that provisions be made to protect tenants from unwarranted evictions, to prevent evasion of maximum rents by any means whatsoever, and that provisions be made for establishing maximum rents for housing accommodations not rented on March 1, newly constructed or substantially altered since then. As prescribed by the Emergency Price Control Act the areas were given 60 days in which to meet the recommendations.

Parsons, Kans., originally designated on April 28, is the area which was increased in size. Originally the area was defined as all of Labette County. An amendment to the original designation adds the counties of Montgomery, Neosho, and Wilson to the area. Maximum rent date is July 1, 1941.

24 areas listed

The 24 newly designated areas (identified by principal center of population) are listed below. All have March 1, 1942, as the recommended maximum rent date.

Tuscaloosa, Ala.—Tuscaloosa County; Dover-Seaford, Del.—Sussex and Kent Counties; Pocatello-Idaho Falls, Idaho—Bannock, Bingha, Bonneville, and Power Counties; Tippecanoe, Ind.—Davis and Knox Counties in Indiana, and Lawrence County in Illinois; Rockland, Maine—Knox County; Aberdeen, Miss.—Chickasaw, Clay, Itawamba, Lee, and Monroe Counties in Mississippi, and Lamar County in Alabama; Centerville, Miss.—Adams, Amite, Pike, and Wilkinson Counties in Mississippi, and the Parishes of East Feliciana and West Feliciana in Louisiana; Grenada, Miss.—Calhoun, Carroll, Grenada, Leflore, Montgomery, Tallahatchie, Webster, and Yalobusha Counties.

Cape May, N. J.—Cape May County; Carlsbad, N. Mex.—Eddy County; Deming N. Mex.—Luna County; Hobbs, N. Mex.—Lea County; Goldsboro, N. C.—Lenoir, Wayne, and Wilson Counties; Mansfield, Ohio—Ashland, Crawford, and Richland Counties; Chickasha, Okla.—Caddo and Grady Counties; North Bend-Marshfield, Oreg.—Coos County.

Warren, Pa.—Warren County; Sioux Falls, S. Dak.—Lincoln, Minnehaha, and Turner Counties in South Dakota; Lyon County in Iowa; and Rock County in Minnesota; Dyersburg, Tenn.—Crockett, Dyer, and Lauderdale Counties; Murfreesboro, Tenn.—Rutherford County; Eagle Pass, Tex.—Maverick County; Greenville, Tex.—Hunt County; Pecos, Tex.—Reeves and Ward Counties; Parkersburg, W. Va.—Wood County in West Virginia, and Washington County in Ohio.

★ ★ ★

Two rental control areas extended, one transferred

In two amendments to previous designations of "defense-rental" areas, Price Administrator Leon Henderson June 1 extended two areas and transferred a district in one area to an adjacent one, effective May 30.

The Clinton-Newport (Indiana) defense-rental area, originally designated as Parke and Vermillion Counties in Indiana, was extended to include Edgar and Vermillion Counties in Illinois. The recommended maximum rent date is March 1, 1942.

The Point Pleasant-Gallipolis area, originally designated as Gallia County in Ohio and Mason County in West Virginia, was extended to include Meigs County in Ohio and Jackson County in West Virginia. The recommended maximum rent date is March 1, 1942.

The defense-rental area of Richmond, Va., was decreased in size by the transfer of the Magisterial District of Matoaca in Chesterfield County to the Petersburg, Va., defense-rental area. The Richmond area is now defined as Independent city of Richmond, and the County of Henrico; and in Chesterfield County, the Magisterial District of Bermuda, Clover Hill, Dale, Manchester, and Midlothian. The recommended maximum rent date is March 1, 1942.

The Petersburg, Va., defense-rental area was increased by the transfer of the Magisterial District of Matoaca, from Chesterfield County, and the addition of independent city of Hopewell. As now defined, the Petersburg defense-rental area includes Independent cities of Hopewell and Petersburg; Counties of Dinwiddie and Prince George, and in Chesterfield County, the Magisterial District of Matoaca. The recommended maximum rent date is April 1, 1941.

Central hardwood lumber area created; ceilings set on lumber shipped from mills

Creation of a Central hardwood lumber area with maximum prices for lumber shipped from mills in the area was announced May 30 by Price Administrator Henderson.

A regulation for "twilight zones"

The new region, with its maximum prices, is set up through Maximum Price Regulation No. 155, which became effective June 1.

It includes Illinois, Indiana, and Ohio, and all of Kentucky and Tennessee not included in the Appalachian hardwoods area excepting a portion of western Tennessee which remains in the Southern hardwoods area.

The portions of Kentucky and Tennessee included in the Central area were formerly a part of the Southern area.

It was a matter of bringing "twilight zones" which are neither Appalachian nor Southern so far as texture of lumber is concerned into a regulation particularly suited for them, the Price Administrator explained.

Texture differences recognized

The new Central hardwoods area—the new intermediate zone—recognizes the difference between the Appalachian and Southern textures through an internal division into a North Central and South Central area, for which separate prices are provided.

The maximum prices provided for the North Central area are lower than those in the Appalachian zone, but are higher than those in the South Central area and Southern hardwoods zone.

The South Central maximum prices, though lower than the North Central quotations, are higher than those in the Southern price schedule.

By the issuance of Maximum Price Regulation No. 155, Mr. Henderson pointed out, the competitive relationships of lumber produced in the Central area to lumber produced in the Appalachian and Southern areas will be preserved.

The regulation covers all sales and deliveries of Central hardwood lumber where the shipment originates at the mill rather than at a distribution yard.

A number of lumber items are specifically exempted from Regulation No. 155.

New conscientious objector camps soon to be ready

(Information furnished by Office of Defense Agricultural Relations, U. S. Department of Agriculture)

Three new conscientious objector camps are being established in California under supervision of the Forest Service, United States Department of Agriculture. These camps, technically known as Civilian Public Service Camps, have been approved for establishment at former CCC camps in the Sierra, Los Padres, and Mono National Forests. Work at the Camps will be concerned primarily with fire control. The Sierra National Forest camp will be occupied by Mennonites, Los Padres camp by Brethren, and the Mono Forest camp by Friends. A number of men are under order to report to these camps and occupation was to begin within the next 2 or 3 weeks.

Other camps established

Other conscientious objector camps under supervision of the Forest Service are at San Dimas, Calif.; Marietta, Ohio; Petersham, Royalston, and Ashburnham, Mass.; Cooperstown, N. Y.; Stoddard, N. H.; Kane, Pa.; Stronach, Mich.; Cascade Locks, Oreg.; Jasper-Pulaski, Ind.; and Placerville, Calif.

· ··

Evacuees to Wyoming area may work on reclamation projects

Evacuees from the Pacific Coast military area who will be moved shortly into the Heart Mountain Relocation Area near Cody, Wyo., as announced recently by Lt. Gen. J. L. DeWitt of the Western Defense Command and Fourth Army, will be given an opportunity to develop the land for irrigation and produce vitally needed crops, M. S. Eisenhower, Director of the War Relocation Authority, said June 5.

Under engineers' guidance

The main job to be undertaken by the Japanese-American evacuees will be to carry forward irrigation and land development work already begun by the Reclamation Bureau. Engineers and other technicians of the Bureau will provide the War Relocation Authority with expert guidance both in planning and carrying out the program. Evacuees will work the soil directly under War Relocation Authority supervision and will not obtain any rights or interest in the land.

Dried farm products, ruled "unprocessed," are excepted from universal ceiling

Agricultural commodities, such as peas, lentils, seeds, and hops, that merely are dried, remain "unprocessed" and, as such, are excepted from the general maximum price regulation, Price Administrator Henderson ruled June 6 in Amendment No. 4 to the "universal ceiling."

Under the original definition of "processing," drying constituted processing and subjected any agricultural commodity dried to the provisions of the regulation unless it was otherwise excluded.

The new amendment became effective June 5, 1942.

Other highlights

Other highlights of the new amendment include clarification of the following points:

1. All dried imported agricultural commodities definitely *are* covered by the general maximum price regulation.
2. Sales or deliveries of dried fruits and dried berries—other than dried prunes and other than sales or deliveries "in natural condition" by growers to packers—definitely *are* covered by the general maximum price amendment.
3. The amendment, with relation to drying, causes most seeds to be excluded from provisions of the general maximum price regulation. Under the regulation as originally enacted, some seeds that were processed further by fumigation or otherwise were covered by the regulation. As such further processes are not expensive, a likely result of price control on processed seeds would be to discourage such processing. This would be undesirable. Hence, *all* seeds, flowers, and bulbs have been excluded from the regulation by the new amendment as raw and unprocessed agricultural commodities, as long as they maintain their original identity without being processed further into products commonly designated by other names.
4. Shelling of peanuts is defined as processing in the general maximum price regulation to distinguish it from shelling of corn, which is a separate process accidentally bearing the same name. However, nuts—other than peanuts—are not presently under the general maximum price regulation. The possibility of subjecting other nuts to the regulation from time to time is covered by the present amendment.
5. In the new management, it is recognized that cooking and distilling clearly are processes which remove a commodity from the raw state—where it is *not* covered by the general maximum price regulation—to the processed state—where it *is* so covered.

List of items covered

The following items remain under the general maximum price regulation, except so far as they are excluded by qualifications below:

> In the hands of packers (including grower-packer and cooperative) and commercial channels: all dried fruits and berries (except prunes), including apples, apricots, peaches, pears, nectarines, raisins, currants, figs, and dates.
>
> At all levels of distribution: alfalfa meal (chopped, leaf), clover meal, lespedeza meal; all peanuts with the exception of farmer

stock peanuts; spices and condiments such as cassia, cloves, cinnamon, ginger, vanilla beans, nutmeg, and others; tapioca, mandioca; chicle, mate, desiccated and shredded coconuts.

The following items are excluded from the "universal ceiling":

> In the hands of the grower: all dried fruits and berries, including apples, apricots, peaches, pears, nectarines, raisins, currants, figs, and dates.
>
> At all levels of distribution: prunes; dry edible beans, peas, lentils; all hay and such farm grains as corn, oats, wheat, barley, buckwheat, soybeans, rye; vegetable and field seeds; hops; all shelled and unshelled nuts (except peanuts after they leave the hands of the farmer); sunflower seed, mustard seed, caraway seed, unbleached cardamon seed.

Rotenone may be used to combat cattle grubs, banned for fruits

Rotenone may be used as an insecticide in the treatment of cattle for grubs, but may not be used as a germicide for citrus fruits, by the terms of an amendment to Conservation Order M-133, issued June 5 by the Director of Industry Operations.

Citrus fruits are one of the products that can be protected adequately with an insecticide other than one containing rotenone; cattle grubs are combatted best with the rotenone compound, acceptable substitutes not being available.

Poles, posts, mine timbers, piling are subject to GMPR

Poles, posts, piling, split stock, mine timbers, and similar semifinished timber products are subject to the general maximum price regulation, Price Administrator Henderson announced June 3.

Cordwood, the Price Administrator said, is covered by the general maximum price regulation if sold as firewood, but not if sold for processing into lumber or wood pulp. However, the provision of the general maximum price regulation which exempts sales by a farmer of commodities grown and processed on his farm if the total of such sales or deliveries does not exceed $75 in any one calendar month, would apply to such sales of semifinished timber products and cordwood.

Ceilings set on distributors', dealers' sales of "War Model" bicycle in 3 zones

The "War Model" bicycle that is expected to solve part of the Nation's problem of getting workers to their jobs as gasoline, tire, and automobile rationing restricts the use of private passenger cars, June 5 was put under a price ceiling by Price Administrator Henderson.

Maximum prices for this standardized type of bicycle, the only kind that the WPB will permit to be manufactured, and which almost overnight has grown to such importance that purchases may be made hereafter only by those who qualify under rationing regulations soon to be announced by OPA, are established in Maximum Price Regulation No. 158, effective June 5.

In the East, the highest retail price that a dealer may charge for the War Model is $32.50, in the middle zone it is $33.50, and in the Far West zone $34.50.

May add sales or use taxes

There is special provision for sales by mail-order. The maximum price applicable in such cases is $29.50 f. o. b. the seller's usual point of shipment in the East, $30.50 in the middle zone, and $31.50 in the Far West.

In certain cases where a dealer's net costs are usually low because of proximity to a bicycle factory or as a result of volume purchases, retail ceilings will be relatively lower under a section of the regulation which limits the permissible mark-up.

The difference in maximum permissible prices as between the three zones is to compensate for freight cost variation. Sales or use taxes may be added to the ceiling prices.

Retailers are required to post the maximum price in their stores by June 10.

Sales curbed until rationing begins

Until the OPA begins rationing bicycles, no retail sales of adults' sizes of any model may be made at any price, except to war production plants for transportation of workers, and then only on written authorization from OPA headquarters in Washington.

Manufacturers' prices for the War Model are not covered by the regulation. Maximums for sales at the manufacturers' level already have been established by voluntary agreement between the individual manufacturers and OPA.

The maximum levels in the order announced June 5 apply only to the War Model. Selling prices of all other new bicycles are covered by the general maxi-

mum price regulation, which sets each seller's ceiling price at the highest price charged by him in March of this year.

May affect other models

In issuing the ceiling order on the War Model, however, Mr. Henderson called attention to the fact that prices on other new bicycles had been rising substantially before the WPB froze sales of all adults' sizes on April 2.

"It is the expectation of the Price Administration," he said, "that the setting of a maximum price for the War Model will result in sympathetic adjustments downward in the prices of bicycles that were manufactured before the changeover to the War Model and have not yet been sold."

Distributors' sales covered

Maximum Price Regulation No. 158 sets ceiling prices on distributors' as well as dealers' sales of War Model bicycles. For distributors, the top price at which these bicycles may be sold to a dealer in the Eastern zone is $23.75 f. o. b. point of shipment, subject to a discount of 2 percent for cash within 10 days; a distributor who delivers to a dealer in the middle zone from his own stock may add 75 cents to the Eastern basic maximum, and for such deliveries in the Far West he may add $1.50 to the Eastern maximum.

The middle zone includes the States of Alabama, Arkansas, Florida, Georgia, Kansas, Louisiana, Mississippi, Nebraska, North Dakota, Oklahoma, South Dakota, and Texas (except the counties of El Paso, Hudspeth, Culberson, Jefferson Davis, Presidio, Brewster, Terrell, Pecos, and Reeves).

The Far West zone is Arizona, California, Colorado, Idaho, Montana, Nevada, New Mexico, Oregon, Utah, Washington, Wyoming, and the counties in Texas that are not included in the middle zone.

The Eastern zone is all parts of the United States not embraced in the middle and Far Western zones.

✦ ✦ ✦

Regional tire reserves

Regional reserve quotas of tires and tubes upon which regional administrators of OPA may draw for adjustment of emergency needs are provided for in Amendment No. 11 to the Revised Tire Rationing Regulations, announced May 30 by Price Administrator Henderson.

10,000 bicycles released for workers in war plants

Almost 10,000 bicycles have been released already by the OPA to war production plants which are qualified to buy them for transportation of workers and for messenger service, Administrator Henderson announced June 4.

Heaviest demand has come from California aircraft plants.

⌃ ⌃ ⌃

Careless, unskilled recapping of tires investigated by OPA

The serious rubber situation necessitates immediate steps to eliminate careless workmanship in the recapping of tires and to arrange for technical advice for retreaders who are not skilled in applying the new camelback made almost entirely of reclaimed rubber, the OPA said June 2.

In a letter to all OPA State directors, Deputy Administrator John E. Hamm requests the directors to ask local rationing boards for names and addresses of retreaders against whom there have been an apparently excessive number of consumer complaints.

⌃ ⌃

Newspapers asked to reprint lists of local rationing boards

Price Administrator Henderson June 1 asked newspapers throughout the country to republish complete lists and addresses of local war price and rationing boards in the cities or areas which they serve.

⌃ ⌃

Price-posting for motor fuels

To bring price-posting requirements for retail motor fuel sales in line with provisions of the general maximum price regulation covering many other commodities, Price Administrator Henderson June 4 issued Amendment No. 2 to Maximum Price Regulation No. 137 (Motor Fuel Sold At Service Stations).

The amendment was effective immediately.

The amendment also extends to July 1, 1942, the time limit for the filing by retail dealers of maximum prices charged their customers in reports to the War Price and Rationing Board of the OPA.

WHAT A FEW NUTS CAN DO

Cartoon by Elderman for VICTORY. *Publishers may obtain mats of these cartoons weekly in either two- or three-column size. Requests to be put on the mailing list should be addressed to Distribution Section, Division of Information, Office for Emergency Management, Washington, D. C. Refer to V–17.*

Pawned typewriters can be returned

Persons who have pawned typewriters as pledges on loans will be permitted to secure their return, according to an interpretation of rationing regulations issued June 5 by OPA.

A concession to persons unfamiliar with the provisions of Revised Rationing Order No. 4, which prohibited the pledging of typewriters for loans after March 13, the interpretation was designed to clear up a misunderstanding which had existed relative to the status of pawned machines.

OPA officials emphasized at the same time that deliberate violators will be held liable under the provisions of the regulations.

Person buying a business to operate is now allowed to acquire its typewriters

An amendment broadening the classification of those eligible to acquire both new and used typewriters and alleviating certain hardships that have arisen under the typewriter rationing program was announced June 2 by OPA.

Under the amendment—No. 2 to Revised Rationing Order No. 4—the most widely affected groups are purchasers of used office machines.

Some eligible without certificates

Declared eligible to obtain certain used office machines without rationing certificates after June 4 are (1) persons who buy or otherwise acquire a business or manufacturing concern for the purpose of continuing the enterprise at the same location; (2) persons who had traded in typewriters to manufacturers, wholesalers, or dealers and had failed to obtain new machines because of the general freeze order of March 6.

Two groups added for rationing

Under the original order, purchasers of the assets of a business were not permitted to buy the typewriters used in that business.

Two groups were added to those eligible to purchase used office machines upon presentation of a rationing certificate: accredited representatives and official missions of the governments of the United Nations for official use in the United States, its Territories, and possessions; Army Exchanges and Ship's Service Stores for their official use.

Portables obtainable for the blind

Portables may also now be obtained by persons who are blind, near blind, or otherwise physically handicapped, if these typewriters are adapted for the use of persons so handicapped.

In addition, a procedure was established for obtaining specially built used machines, reconditioned or rebuilt, where the special features were installed or ordered prior to March 6. Applications may be made to the Office of Price Administration in Washington for these machines, now in manufacturers' or dealers' stocks, providing that the design is such that the machine is unusable except by the applicant or a small class of persons similarly situated and that it cannot be made generally usable by moderate alterations.

Ceilings set on textiles, apparel, other items sold to military after July 1

Taking into consideration special circumstances surrounding the production of many military articles, Price Administrator Henderson June 4 announced a method for pricing such items that may be sold or delivered to war procurement agencies after July 1, 1942.

Commodities affected

Maximum Price Regulation No. 157 (Sales and Fabrication of Textiles, Apparel and Related Items for Military Purposes) establishes maximum prices for the following commodities when made in accordance with military specifications:

1. Yarns, textiles, and textile products;
2. Leather, fur, and products thereof;
3. Rubber fabrics, apparel, and footwear; and
4. Wearing apparel, including findings, and other individual, organizational, or ship's personnel equipment made in whole or in part of any of the materials listed in (1) and (2) or from rubber, except rubber drug sundries.

Maximum prices are established at the highest price at which sale or delivery of a particular article was made prior to April 1, 1942, plus an amount proportionate to the seller's increases in material and labor costs between the time the contract was placed and March 31, 1942, plus increases in wage rates pursuant to certain collective bargaining contracts or other wage agreements entered into before April 27, 1942.

For any U. S. war procurement agency

No further increase in costs beyond the dates specified will be allowed, Mr. Henderson stated.

"Today's action was taken," he said, "in order to avoid disruption of orderly procurement for the armed forces. The nature of military requirements does not permit the adjustments to provide for absorption of increased material and labor costs which are being called for in civilian production."

The provisions of the regulation apply to sales or fabrication of the articles specified, or to contractors selling or subcontractors handling such articles destined for any war procurement agency of the United States Government, including the War and Navy Departments, the Maritime Commission, the Lend-Lease Section in the Procurement Division of the Treasury Department, and any agency of any of the foregoing.

Other provisions

The maximum prices determined by this regulation do not apply to any sale or fabrication service for which a maximum price is in effect at the time of such sale or delivery, under the terms of any other maximum price regulation except the general maximum price regulation.

However, if the buyer and seller are unable in good faith to determine whether a particular commodity or fabrication service falls within the term "textiles, apparel, and related articles" as defined, then it is deemed subject to all provisions of the regulations.

Specific provision is made for a seller's increase in costs, as determined in accordance with customary accounting policy of the seller.

Maximum Price Regulation No. 157 goes into effect with respect to Government contracts on July 1, 1942. Prior to that date, sales or deliveries by prime contractors to the United States Government war procurement agencies are exempt from the general maximum price regulation. This exemption does not apply to subcontractors.

★ ★ ★

OPA working on pricing formula for cold-weather apparel

A new maximum price regulation providing a method for establishing ceiling prices on fall and winter knitted garments and certain other cold-weather wearing apparel is under preparation, Price Administrator Henderson announced June 5.

To relieve uncertainty of manufacturers

His statement was made in advance of the issuance of the pricing formula in order that manufacturers of such fall and winter articles will not delay the start of their production season because of uncertainty as to whether their products will be priced equitably. OPA is now making a thorough study of seasonal pricing problems as they apply to these goods.

Types of apparel being considered for inclusion under the new regulation are woolen knit goods, such as hosiery, underwear and sweaters; heavyweight cotton underwear, woolen and leather jackets, and heavy gloves. This is a preliminary listing and the actual regulation may cover a broader or narrower scope according to OPA officials. They cautioned, however, that so-called hardship cases are not to be construed as seasonal pricing problems.

Production of wrapping twine from agave further restricted

Still further restrictions in the production of agave wrapping twine, used widely in lumber mills, paper mills, and newspaper plants, are provided for in an amendment to General Preference Order M–84 issued June 1.

Processing of agave fiber into wrapping twine had been restricted previously to 65 percent of the rate of production in 1941. The June 1 amendment (No. 6) reduces the amount for this purpose to 57.5 percent in June, 50 percent in July and 40 percent in August and each month thereafter.

★ ★ ★

Invoice details explained to piece goods converters

Details which must be shown by converters of finished piece goods on their sales contracts or invoices under the terms of Maximum Price Regulation No. 127 were explained June 3 by the OPA.

Reports have been received by OPA that converters of finished piece goods interpret paragraphs (a) and (b) under section 1400.77 to require that the actual division factor—used in determining the actual *selling* price be specified on the invoice or contract of sale.

This trade interpretation is incorrect, according to OPA officials. The regulation requires only "a statement of the division factor—used in determining the *maximum price*."

★ ★

Seconds in bag osnaburg, sheeting, freed at mills

Limitation Order L–99 was amended June 5 to permit mills to sell or deliver without restriction bag osnaburg and bag sheeting irregulars, seconds, or cuts under 40 yards in length up to 6 percent of a mill's production of bag osnaburg and bag sheetings.

★

Forms sent to weavers for rayon grey goods report for May

The four report forms to be used by weavers of rayon grey goods under the provisions of Revised Price Schedule No. 85, as amended (Rayon Grey Goods), are now being mailed in time for manufacturers to file their reports on May production, the OPA announced June 1.

CHANGES IN WOOL PRICING

Numerous changes in the wool and wool tops and yarns price schedule to establish additional dollars and cents ceilings or pricing formulas, to permit jobbers' premiums, and to make other technical or corrective changes were provided in an amendment June 5 by OPA.

Among the most important provisions in the June 5 Amendment No. 5 to Revised Price Schedule No. 58 are those setting forth a price-determining formula for manufacturers of woolen sales yarns and the granting of a premium of 7½ cents per pound for jobbers of specified worsted yarns.

Types of wools for which specific maximum prices are established in the amendment include scoured shorn domestic wools, South American shorn wools scoured in the United States, and certain grades of processed noils.

..

Curb on civilian use of duck, goose feathers made uniform

Restrictions on the use of duck and goose body feathers for civilian purposes are made uniform by Amendment No. 2 to Conservation Order M-102, issued June 1 by the Director of Industry Operations.

Under the terms of Amendment No. 1, use of duck body feathers over 3 inches in length for nonmilitary products was permitted. The June 1 amendment requires all such feathers less than 4 inches in length to be reserved for military orders, as are goose feathers up to 4 inches long. This corrects an error in Amendment No. 1.

Plan offered to "roll back" work clothing prices

A plan to "roll back" the price of men's and boys' work clothing at the wholesale, manufacturing, and cloth stages in order to relieve a price squeeze on retailers was presented by an industry committee to OPA June 3, Administrator Henderson announced.

The proposal submitted by the committee representing retailers, wholesalers, work-clothing manufacturers and cloth mills was looked upon by OPA officials as a "very constructive" effort and assurance was given the group that it will be given careful consideration.

Wool restrictions relaxed to permit some for floor coverings, draperies, other use

Some restrictions in the wool, Conservation Order M-73 as amended and extended through the second quarter of 1942 were relaxed in an order issued June 2 which consolidates the second quarter order and all amendments thereto, the Director of Industry Operations has announced.

The June 2 order reenacts the orginal second quarter allocation of new wool to the woolen and worsted systems and makes the following changes in amendments to the second quarter order:

1. It removes the complete prohibition against the use of wool in floor coverings, draperies, and upholstery for nonmilitary use.

The June 2 order permits the use of the following wools in the manufacture of drapery and upholstery fabrics: Coarse carpet wool, mohair, skin alpaca, coarse alpaca fleece, alpaca seconds; Huarizo, Llama, or coarse pieces or locks of alpaca or llama.

It permits the use of coarse carpet wool in the manufacture of floor coverings.

Coarse carpet wool takes in the following: Persian Gulf (excluding fleeces); Aleppo stuffings and pieces (excluding fleeces); Egyptian fleeces and colors (excluding pulled, white); Indias (other than Joria, Kandahar, Vicanere Super, Vicanere No. 1); Awassi, Karadi, Cyprus, Oporto, Thibet (other than No. 1 and No. 2 white), Iceland (skin). Scotch, Irish, & English Blackfaced, Irish Kerry, Haslock,

Herdwick, Swalesdale, Devon; Cordoba 40's, 36's combing 12 months growth only; B. A. 5's, 6's combing 12 months growth only; Balkan pulled wools.

A manufacturer is permitted to use such wools in the production of floor coverings, drapery and upholstery fabrics up to 25 percent of his rate of use for such purposes during the first half of 1941.

2. Lower grade alpaca and llama and kid mohair are added to those lower grades of wool which may be used on a more liberal basis than fine wools on the woolen and worsted systems.

3. The order requires that acetate staple fiber also be made available to manufacturers for blending with wool. Formerly only viscose staple fiber had to be set aside for such purposes.

4. The prohibition against the use of more than 80 percent wool in nonmilitary blankets is removed in the case of blankets made solely from used papermakers' wool felts and used processing wool felts.

5. The provision in the previous order assigning a preference rating to orders for fabrics used in officers' uniforms has been removed. It is expected that a separate order assigning a rating for materials to be used in uniforms for officers other than United States Army officers will be issued soon. Uniforms for Army officers will hereafter be acquired by the Quartermaster Corps and thus no rating will be necessary. However, rated orders already placed for fabrics for officers' uniforms are not to be disturbed by the June 2 amendment but retain their status as rated orders.

Ceilings set on 10½-ounce shirting flannel for Army

Ceiling prices of 10½-ounce shirting flannel containing various proportions of foreign and domestic wool applying to sales and deliveries to the United States Army were provided by the OPA June 5 through Amendment No. 4 to Revised Price S c h e d u l e No. 58, as amended (Wool and Wool Tops and Yarns).

The maximum prices now provided, which become effective July 1, 1942, for sales and deliveries to the United States Army of 10½-ounce shirting flannel of the specifications set forth in United States Army Requisition No. 8-54C are as follows, in dollars and cents per yard:

	Sales and deliveries by integrated mills	Sales and deliveries by nonintegrated mills
100 percent domestic wool	$2.13	$2.17
50 percent domestic, 50 percent foreign wool	2.10	2.14
100 percent foreign wool	2.07	2.11

For other proportions of foreign and domestic wool the amendment provides that maximum prices shall be determined in proportionate relation to the prices given above.

Maximum export premiums set for finished piece goods

Maximum export premiums that may be charged in the sale of finished textile piece goods for shipment abroad have been established at 6 to 8½ percent of the domestic maximum price, the percentage varying according to the function performed by the exporter, Price Administrator Henderson announced June 6.

At the same time Mr. Henderson gave notice that the OPA might prescribe a specific maximum export premium for other trades or industries when necessary to eliminate hardship or when the trade or industry found "great difficulty" in determining the premium from the base period set in the maximum export price regulation.

.. ж ..

Special cartons for shoes not necessary, says Henderson

In order to correct a misunderstanding in the shoe trade, Price Administrator Henderson June 5 stated that shoe manufacturers and other sellers who furnished retailers with special carton wraps in March 1942 need not continue such a practice.

Dollars-and-cents ceilings put on 10 meat items sold to Government

Specific ceiling prices for certain canned meat and frozen boneless beef items sold to the Federal Surplus Commodities Corporation and other Government purchasing agencies are established in Maximum Price Regulation No. 156, announced June 3.

The new ceilings will effect substantial savings to the Army, as compared with recent prices paid for such commodities.

Articles covered by the regulation include, in addition to boneless beef, the following canned commodities: Vienna sausage, corned beef, corned beef hash, meat and vegetable stew, meat and vegetable hash, chili con carne, and rations 1, 2, and 3.

The regulation, effective June 2, applies to deliveries of these items to specified Government buying agencies on and after July 1, 1942. The general maximum price regulation will apply after June 15, 1942, to deliveries to the FSCC, and after July 1, 1942, to deliveries to the armed forces of this country, of all other commodities not specifically excepted and not otherwise subject to particular OPA price regulations.

Other purchasers under GMPR

Sales of the items covered by Regulation No. 156 to any purchasers other than the Government remain subject to the maximum prices established by the general maximum price regulation, it was emphasized.

Meat scraps, digester tankage priced by zone system

A zone pricing system has been established for meat scraps and digester tankage in Maximum Price Regulation No. 74 (Animal Feedingstuffs) as amended, Price Administrator Henderson announced June 1. This amended regulation became effective June 5, and places all manufacturers on an equal competitive position, relative to raw material purchases.

Certain sales by retailers (who are not processors) of meat scraps and digester tankage are exempt under the present order. These are continued at the March ceilings under the general maximum price regulation. However, it was indicated that these retail sale maximums will be adjusted after further OPA study.

Curb on natural resins lifted

Restrictions on the use of natural resins in the manufacture of playing cards, pencils, house paint, label varnishes, toys, and farm equipment finishes were removed by an amendment to General Conservation Order M–56, issued June 5 by the Director of Industry Operations.

★ ★ ★

Processors' ceilings on refined lard cut to February 1942 level

Price Administrator Henderson June 3 cut back processors' maximum selling prices on refined lard to the wholesaler and retailer to the February 1942 level. Maximum prices of refined lard to consumers remain unchanged at the March 1942 peak levels under the general maximum price regulation.

Simultaneously, in a move designed to readjust more equitably the internal margin of profits in lard at all stages of distribution—without increasing the ultimate price to the consumer—the OPA increased permissible ceilings on various grades of lard and steam-rendered pork fat in the pre-retail state.

★ ★ ★

Laundry machine assembly rules fitted to trade practice

The production curtailment program for commercial laundry and dry-cleaning machinery has been adjusted to conform to customary manufacturing practices of the industry.

In Amendment No. 1 to Limitation Order L–91, issued June 3, manufacturers are authorized to assemble machinery after the dates for shutdown of the industry in cases where delivery has been approved by the Director of Industry Operations and the only operation necessary to prepare the machinery for delivery is to assemble the completely fabricated parts.

The industry has long engaged in the practice of not completing final assembly until an order for machinery is actually received.

Canned citrus fruits, juices removed from scope of GMPR

Canned citrus fruits and citrus juices were removed from the scope of the general maximum price regulation June 1.

Resources Protection Board gathering information on relative importance of plants

The Resources Protection Board, named by WPB Chairman Nelson May 16, is gathering information on which to base evaluations of the relative wartime importance of all industrial plants, war installations, facilities, and vital economic resources, and recommendations for their protection.

The board, under the chairmanship of William K. Frank, of the WPB Production Division, will cooperate closely with the Army and Navy, the Maritime Commission, and Office of Civilian Defense in furnishing ratings and recommendations by which they may be guided in planning the protection of resources.

It will make an over-all study of the relative importance to the war effort of all plants, installations, including factories, shipyards, railroads, and communication networks, and mines and other natural resources. The hazards that will be considered will include bombing, sabotage, espionage, or actual invasion, as well as natural hazards such as fire and flood.

Other members of the Resources Protection Board include Col. Carl G. Richmond of the War Department, Joseph Fennelly of the Navy Department, Philip Bastedo, Office of Civilian Defense, and William J. Kearny, Materials Division of WPB. Emerson Ross of the Statistics Division of WPB was named Director of Resources Analysis. James W. Fesler of the Office of the Executive Secretary of WPB was appointed Secretary.

Dollars-and-cents ceilings put on oleo, oleo stearine

Specific dollars-and-cents maximum prices for oleo stock, oleo oil, and oleo stearine to all classes of buyers for any purpose are established by Amendment No. 4 to Revised Price Schedule No. 53 (Fats and Oils), Price Administrator Henderson announced June 5.

The amendment is effective June 9, 1942.

The specific ceiling prices set for oleo—packed in used drums or barrels, f. o. b. Chicago—are as follows in cents per pound:

Extra oleo stock, 12.75; prime oleo stock, 12.50; extra oleo oil, 13.04; prime oleo oil, 12.75; prime oleo stearine, 10.61.

New industry advisory committees

The Bureau of Industry Advisory Committees, WPB, has announced the formation of the following new industry advisory committees:

BOYS' SHIRTS, PAJAMAS, WASH SUITS AND SPORTSWEAR INDUSTRY

Government p r e s i d i n g officer—H. Stanley Marcus, chief of the WPB clothing section.

Members:

Louis B. Baer, Strouse-Baer Co., Baltimore, Md.; Robert L. Hays, The Kaynee Co., Cleveland, Ohio; Joe Isaacson, L. Isaacson & Sons, New York, N. Y.; Leon Kahn, De Luxe Wash Suits Co., New York, N. Y.; Louis Rosensweig, S. Liebovitz & Sons, New York, N. Y.; Edward Rowan, Elder Mfg. Co., St. Louis, Mo.; Irving Rubenstein, Don Juan Mfg. Co., New York, N. Y.; Elias Savada, Savada Brothers, New York, N. Y.

DISTILLED SPIRITS & WINE INDUSTRY TRAFFIC

Government presiding officer—John B. Smiley, chief, beverage and tobacco branch.

Members:

Charles W. Braden, National Distillers Products Corporation, New York, N. Y.; E. M. Fleischmann, Harford County Distillery, Inc., Baltimore, Md.; James H. Gentlemen, Park & Tilford, Inc., New York, N. Y.; Edward Gusky, Schenley Distillers Corporation, New York, N. Y.; Frank H. Luther, Joseph E. Seagram & Sons, Inc., Louisville, Ky.; John A. Margolis, Bisceglia Bros. Corporation, Philadelphia, Pa.; J. Campbell Moore, Garrett & Co., Inc., Brooklyn, N. Y.; E. J. Plover, The American Distilling Co., Pekin, Ill.; E. Stewart Underhill, Jr., Urbana Wine Co., Inc., Hammondsport, N. Y.; James L. Val, Padre Vineyard Co., Los Angeles, Calif.; William Widmer, Widmer's Wine Cellars, Inc., Naples, N. Y.

FARM MACHINERY AND EQUIPMENT EXPORT INDUSTRY

Government presiding officer—William R. Tracy, chief, farm machinery and equipment branch.

Membership:

H. S. Eastwood, export manager, The De Laval Separator Co., New York, N. Y.; W. F. Haberer, export manager, Deere & Co., Moline, Ill.; A. R. Hauschel, export manager, J. I. Case Co., Racine, Wis.; D. A. Himes, export manager, Oliver Farm Equipment Co., Chicago, Ill.; G. C. Hoyt, vice president, International Harvester Co., Chicago, Ill.; A. G. Jacoby, export sales manager, S. L. Allen & Co., Philadelphia, Pa.; W. B. Kellogg, export manager, F. E. Myers & Brothers Co., Ashland, Ohio; Roger M. Kyes, vice president, Ferguson-Sherman Mfr. Co., Dearborn, Mich.; C. M. Lancaster, export manager, B. F. Avery & Sons Co., Louisville, Ky.; W. B. Taylor, export manager, Minneapolis-Moline Power Equipment Co., Minneapolis, Minn.; W. O. Taylor, export manager, Allis-Chalmers Mfr. Co., Milwaukee, Wis.; Lewis C. Walker, president, Aermotor Co., Chicago, Ill.

FISH INDUSTRY COMMITTEE

CANNED SALMON SUBCOMMITTEE

Government presiding officer—Lawrence T. Hopkinson, in charge of fishery products for the WPB.

Members:

Aubin Barthold, Alaska Packers Assn., 111 California Street, San Francisco, Calif.; E. M. Brennan, manager, P. E. Harris & Co., Dexter Horton Building, Seattle, Wash.; William Calvert, Jr., San Juan Fishing & Packing Co., Foot of Stacy Street, Seattle, Wash.; Victor H. Elfendahl, vice president, Alaska Pacific Salmon Co., Skinner Building, Seattle, Wash.; Laurence Freeburn, Pyramid Packing Co., Colman Building, Seattle, Wash.; John A. Green, vice president, Pacific American Fisheries, South Bellingham, Wash.; Frank Lloyd, president, Ketchikan Packing Co., White-Henry-Stuart Bldg., Seattle, Wash.; Thomas Sandos, Columbia River Packers Assn., Astoria, Oreg.; E. E. Willkie, vice president, Libby McNeill & Libby, Union Stockyards, Chicago, Ill.; A. W. Wittig, Shepard Point Packing Co., Colman Building, Seattle, Wash.

GYPSUM INDUSTRY

Government presiding officer—J. L. Haynes, chief of the building materials branch.

Members:

John C. Best, National Gypsum Co., Buffalo, N. Y.; H. E. Chism, Texas Cement Plaster Co., Oklahoma City, Okla.; F. G. Ebeary, The Ebeary Gypsum Co., New York, N. Y.; Gordon C. Estes, Certain-Teed Products Corporation, Chicago, Ill.; W. L. Keady, U. S. Gypsum Co., Chicago, Ill.; W. H. Kellogg, Jr., The Connecticut Adamant Plaster Co., New Haven, Conn.; James Letohouts, Grand Rapids Plaster Co., Grand Rapids, Mich.; Ezra Sensibar, Cardiff Gypsum Co., Chicago, Ill.; Vincent S. Villard, Newark Plaster Co., New York, N. Y.; Martin Uidall, Pacific Portland Cement Co., San Francisco, Calif.

JEWELED WATCH MANUFACTURERS INDUSTRY

Government presiding officer—Robert Beatty, section chief in the consumers' durable goods branch.

Members:

I. E. Boucher, general manager, Waltham Watch Co., Waltham, Mass.; Roland Gsell, president, Mt. Vernon Watch Co., Inc., New York, N. Y.; Benjamin Learus, president, Benrus Watch Co., Waterbury, Conn.; John H. Ballard, president, Bulova Watch Co., New York, N. Y.; C. M. Kendig, president, Hamilton Watch Co., Lancaster, Pa.; T. Albert Potter, president, Elgin National Watch Co., Elgin, Ill.

MEN'S SHIRTS, SPORT SHIRTS, AND ENSEMBLES

Government presiding officer—H. Stanley Marcus, chief of the clothing section.

Members:

J. H. Bonck, J. H. Bonck Co., New Orleans, La.; Harry Doniger, David D. Doniger & Co., New York, N. Y.; James G. Dulin, James G. Dulin, Inc., Washington, D. C.; John R. Frizzell, Henderson & Erwin, Inc., Charlottesville, Va.; E. M. Jette, C. F. Hathaway Co., New York, N. Y.; Morriss Kessler, Raritan Shirt Co., New York, N. Y.; Henry Louis, Brownstein-Louis Co., Los Angeles, Calif.; E. C. Pfeffer, Cluett, Peabody & Co., Inc., New York, N. Y.; Louis Rosensweig, S. Liebovitz & Sons, New York, N. Y.; Edward Rowan, Elder Mfg. Co., St. Louis, Mo.

OFFICERS' MILITARY INSIGNIA MANUFACTURERS

Government presiding officer—M. D. Moore, section chief of the consumers durable goods branch.

Members:

F. A. Ballou, Jr., B. A. Ballou & Co., Providence, R. I.; Earl Congelton, American Emblem Co., Utica, N. Y.; Irvin H. Hahn, The Irvin H. Hahn Co., Baltimore, Md.; Thomas Kelliher, American Metal Crafts Co., Attleboro, Mass.; Abner A. Raeburn, N. S. Meyer, Inc., New York, N. Y.; Paul Simmerson, American Insignia Co., New York, N. Y.; John F. Williams, Lilley Ames Co., Columbus, Ohio; E. R. Wilmarth, V. H. Blackinton & Co., Attleboro Falls, Mass.

PHARMACEUTICAL MANUFACTURERS

Government presiding officer—Francis M. Shields, chief of the health supplies branch.

Members:

Robert Lincoln McNeil, president, McNeil Laboratories Inc., Philadelphia, Pa.; Elmer Bobst, president, Hoffman LaRoche Inc., Nutley, N. J.; Carleton H. Palmer, E. R. Squibb & Sons, Inc., New York, N. Y.; Dr. Theodore G. Klumpp, president, Winthrop Chemical Co., New York, N. Y.; D. E. Baughman, president, Fort Dodge Serum Co., Fort Dodge, Iowa; C. H. Nelson, Jr., president, Hart Drug Corporation, Miami, Fla.; Paul R. Frohring, president, General Biochemicals, Inc., Chagrin Falls, Ohio; George R. Flint, president, Flint, Eaton & Co., Decatur, Ill.; S. DeWitt Clough, president, Abbott Laboratories, North Chicago, Ill.; Dr. A. W. Lescochier, president, Parke, Davis & Co., Detroit, Mich.; Eli Lilly, president, Eli Lilly & Co., Indianapolis, Ind.

PROPRIETARY DRUG MANUFACTURERS

Government presiding officer—Frances M. Shields, chief of the health supplies branch.

Members:

C. S. Beardsley, vice president, Miles Laboratories, Elkart, Ind.; J. M. Buck, director, Public Relations, Plough, Inc., Memphis, Tenn.; H. M. Clark, vice president, Dr. Hess & Clark, Inc., Ashland, Ohio; W. Y. Preyer, Vick Chemical Co., Greensboro, N. C.; Raymond E. Taylor, president; Takara Laboratories, Los Angeles, Calif.; James Hill, Jr., president, Sterling Products, Inc., New York, N. Y.; W. J. Kirn, vice president, American Home Products, New York, N. Y.; George H. Miller, president, The Musterole Co., Cleveland, Ohio; J. G. Ayars, president, Allen & Company, Inc., St. Louis, Mo.; Dr. Frank L. Dewees, president, S. F. Baker & Co., Keokuk, Iowa.

REFRIGERATOR VALVE AND FITTINGS MANUFACTURERS

Government presiding officer—A. H. Baer, of the air conditioning and commercial refrigeration branch.

Members:

W. H. Pape, sales manager, Crane Co., Chicago, Ill.; Charles Benson, The Imperial Brass Mfg. Co., Chicago, Ill.; F. L. Riggin, president, Mueller Brass Co., Port Huron, Mich.; E. J. Ferguson, treasurer, Weatherhead Co., Cleveland, Ohio; G. J. Henry, president, Henry Valve Co., Chicago, Ill.; Edward G. Mueller, president, Kerotest Manufacturing Co., Pittsburgh, Pa.; K. M. Newcum, Superior Valve & Fitting Co., Pittsburgh, Pa.; V. L. Graf, president, V. L. Graf, Co., Detroit, Mich.

TRANSPORTATION . . .

Driver-salesmen operating beyond local area must cut mileage ¼, but are exempt from over-the-road restrictions

The ODT announced June 1 a further revision of General Order ODT No. 6 to include driver-salesmen whose operations extend beyond the local delivery areas defined by the order.

To conserve tires and vehicles

Order No. 6 now applies in all cases where "property is transported solely for the purpose of sale to retail dealers in a vehicle operated by the seller or an employee thereof," provided the vehicle returns to the point of origin on the same calendar day.

General Order ODT No. 5 has been changed to conform with Order No. 6 as revised. The change takes such operations as delivery of bread, groceries, ice cream, soft drinks and tobacco by driversalesmen out of the jurisdiction of Order No. 5 and places them under the jurisdiction of Order No. 6.

In effect, this means driver-salesmen engaged in such enterprises must conserve tires and vehicles by reducing their delivery mileage by 25 percent, as compared with the corresponding month of 1941, but will be exempt from requirements imposed on over-the-road operators.

In an amendment announced May 28, the local delivery area was defined as extending 25 miles beyond the corporate limits of the municipality in which a delivery originates. All other deliveries involving a distance of not more than 25 miles are defined in the order as local deliveries.

Newspaper deliveries affected

Another major change in the local delivery order permits newspapers to adopt either of two plans for the conservation of delivery trucks and tires.

Under one plan, papers must limit the number of their daily deliveries according to a population scale set up by the ODT and then reduce their total delivery mileage by an additional 25 percent, as compared with their total delivery mileage in the corresponding month of 1941.

Papers located in metropolitan districts of less than 200,000 must limit to one the number of their daily deliveries to the same person, under this plan. Papers in metropolitan districts with a population of 200,000 to 700,000 are allowed two deliveries; papers in metropolitan districts with a population of 700,000 to 2,000,000 are allowed three deliveries, and papers in metropolitan districts with a population of more than 2,000,000 are allowed four deliveries.

The population is to be determined by means of Series PH-1 of the United States Census, made up by the United States Department of Commerce for 140 cities.

Under the alternate plan, papers may make an unlimited number of deliveries but must cut their total delivery mileage by 40 percent, as compared with the corresponding month of 1941.

Each plan prohibits special deliveries and call-backs, and the reductions in delivery mileage resulting from the elimination of such services is to be considered as additional to other reduction provided by the two plans.

The alternate plans for newspapers are set up in General Permit ODT No. 6-1. General Permit ODT No. 6-2, announced at the same time, provides that operators of trucks hauling coal and other solid fuels may base their 25-percent mileage reduction on miles per ton delivered, rather than on total mileage alone.

This provision was included to allow for the off-season increase in local coal deliveries resulting from the war. The 25-percent mileage reduction does not become effective for such trucks until July 1.

Amendment No. 2 to General Order No. 6, also announced on May 28, exempts trucks used exclusively for the pick-up and delivery of telegraphic, radio, and cable communications and United States mails.

This amendment also permits a company to make one additional delivery a day to transport a commodity requiring the use of special equipment. This would permit an ice and coal concern, for example, to deliver a load of ice and a load of coal to the same person on the same day.

The ODT also issued Amendment No. 3 to General Order ODT 5 to correct an error in Amendment No. 2, redefining over-the-road service.

* * *

Two western bus lines ordered to coordinate operations

A special order coordinating the operations of two long-distance western bus lines was issued June 2 by ODT.

The Burlington Transportation Co. and the Interstate Transit Lines are directed by the order to reduce schedules, permit limited interchange of tickets, share certain terminal facilities and otherwise revise their operations to save tires and equipment.

Service between Omaha, Nebraska, and Los Angeles, California, and between Omaha and Sioux City, Iowa, is affected by the order, which became effective June 10.

Tank trucks exempt from mileage cut until July 1

The ODT June 1 released the text of General Permit ODT No. 6-3 postponing until July 1 application of General Order ODT No. 6 with respect to tank trucks.

Order No. 6, which became effective June 1 for all vehicles engaged in local delivery service except those specifically exempted, requires a 25 percent monthly mileage reduction as compared with the corresponding month of 1941, and prohibits certain types of deliveries.

★ ★ ★

4,214 vehicles released in week

The WPB, during the week ended May 30, released 4,214 trucks, truck trailers, and miscellaneous vehicles to civilian users and holders of Government Exemption Permits, the automotive branch announced June 1.

Last week 510 light, 1,201 medium, and 402 heavy trucks; 253 trailers; and 14 miscellaneous vehicles were released to civilian users. Holders of Government Exemption Permits, which include permits for export by private individuals, received 662 light, 729 medium, and 220 heavy trucks; 101 trailers; and 122 miscellaneous vehicles.

★ ★ ★

Lake iron ore shipments break all records in May

All-time records for iron ore shipments were broken in May by Lake Superior ports, it was announced June 2. From the 10 ore docks at Duluth; Superior, Wis.; Two Harbors, Minn.; Ashland, Wis.; and Escanaba and Marquette, Mich., there were shipped to lower Lake ports in May 12,622,872 tons.

★ ★ ★

Eastern motorists urged to make further gasoline, tire savings

Don't try to "live up" to your gasoline ration. Stay under it—try to cut your present mileage at least 50 percent.

This was the urgent request of Joel Dean, chief of the fuel ration branch.

Under no circumstances, the statement emphasized, will such savings result in penalties for the card holder.

LABOR . . .

Board sets pattern on union security issue by ordering union maintenance in four disputes over open versus closed shop

The National War Labor Board by its action in four cases last week revealed that it had developed a pattern for the handling of the union security issue—a matter which proved a storm center during the first days of the Board's existence.

In four important cases last week the Board ordered similar maintenance of union membership clauses inserted in collective bargaining contracts settling in each case bitter disputes over the open versus the closed shop. Typical was the one provided to settle the union security issue in a dispute between the Brown & Sharpe Co., Providence, R. I. and the International Association of Machinists, A. F. L. The full text of the union maintenance clause ordered in this case follows:

All members who at the date of the signing of this contract are members of the Union in good standing in accordance with the constitution and bylaws of the Union, and those employees who may hereafter become members shall, as a condition of employment, remain members of the Union in good standing during the life of the agreement.

Immediately after the signing of the agreement, the Union shall furnish to the National War Labor Board a notarized list of members in good standing as of that date. If any employee named on that list asserts that he has withdrawn from membership in the Union, the assertion or dispute shall be adjudicated by an arbiter appointed by the National War Labor Board whose decision shall be final and binding upon the Union and the employee.

Other cases in which maintenance of membership was ordered included the dispute between the Hotel Employers Association of San Francisco, Calif., and the San Francisco Local Joint Executive Board of Hotel and Restaurant Employees, A. F. L.; the Nevada Consolidated Copper Corporation, Chino Mines Division, Santa Rita and Hurley, N. Mex., and the Metal Trades Department of the A. F. L.; and the Robins Dry Dock & Repair Co., Brooklyn, N. Y., and the Industrial Union of Marine & Shipbuilding Workers of America, C. I. O.

Although employer members dissented in each case, observers viewed the almost identical decisions as an indication that this maintenance of membership plan was the answer which the Board would probably provide whenever a certain measure of union security was required to settle a dispute between labor and management.

The struggle over union security originally centered around three major cases of the Board; namely, Walker-Turner, International Harvester, and Federal Shipbuilding & Drydock Co. In these three cases various forms of maintenance of membership were ordered,

as the Board on a case-by-case basis hammered out its program. On these three cases the Board was sharply divided with employer members dissenting. Many observers feared that the corporations involved would use this sharp division as an excuse for refusing to comply with the Board's orders.

Discussion in the public press centered around this threat and for a time, it appeared that the Board was faced with a major crisis on the union security issue. After some delay, the three concerns accepted the decision of the War Labor Board—the umpire which was set up by the President of the United States to finally determine all labor disputes for the duration of the war. Since that time, the going on this issue has been relatively smooth.

Clarification of the union security issue now leaves the field open to develop a working program to handle another big issue—the settlement of disputes over wages in line with the President's 7-point program to freeze the cost of living.

Spotlight now on wages

Already the Board has made two important "pilot" decisions on the question of wage stabilization—one settling the dispute between the Breeze Corporations, Inc., Newark, N. J., and the United Automobile Workers, C. I. O., and the other in the dispute between the Chase Brass & Copper Co., Cleveland, Ohio, and the International Association of Machinists, A. F. L.

In both cases the Board decided that stabilization of wage rates within an individual plant was clearly permissible under the President's program. Orders providing for standardization of wage rates in each of these two plants were designated to make sure that workers sitting side by side, doing the same work with the same skill, received the same rate. In both cases the Board either turned down or sharply reduced union demands for blanket increases in wages on the ground that the granting of such demands would upset the wage stabilization program.

In the Breeze case, the Board raised the standard hiring rate for the company from 55 to 60 cents an hour, but at the same time flatly turned down a union request for a general wage increase. An increase of 4 cents an hour had been recommended by a three-man panel of the Board before the President sent his stabilization message to Congress. The union had originally asked for a 15 cents an hour increase.

In the Chase Brass & Copper Co. case the Board allowed an upward adjustment of 4 cents an hour to provide for a measure of stability between the plant and other brass mills throughout the country and similar plants in the Cleveland area. In this case the union had requested a flat 10 cents an hour increase which was cut to "6 to 8 cents" by a Board panel, and then further reduced by the full Board.

In two other cases—both decided last week—the Board approved limited wage

increases for the expressed purpose of equalizing rates of pay among each concern's employees.

In the Nevada Consolidated Copper Corporation case (where the Board order also provided for union maintenance), the Board ordered wages paid to 600 craft employees of the company's Chino Mines Division, Santa Rita and Hurley, New Mexico, increased 50 cents a "day or shift," retroactive to January 16, 1942.

"This adjustment," the directive order of the Board states, "is necessary to eliminate an inequality in wages paid employees in these crafts as compared with employees represented by the Railroad Brotherhoods working at the New Mexico properties of the company. The latter employees received a wage increase, comparable to that provided by this order, as of January 16, 1942. For about 35 years, practically identical wages have been paid to employees in the two categories in question. This relationship is reestablished by the present Board order."

A 2 cents an hour wage increase retroactive to December 15, 1941, for nonbonus employees of the Pacific States Cast Iron Pipe Co., Provo, Utah, was ordered by unanimous vote of the Board last week, "as the first step in eliminating marked inequalities within the wage-rate structure within this plant." The order of the Board finally determining the dispute between the company and the United Steelworkers of America, C. I. O. was originally referred to the National Defense Mediation Board on August 19, 1941. In the formal opinion accompanying the directive order, Dr. George W. Taylor, public member of the Board, stated: "There was undoubtedly an improper balance between earnings of hourly rated employees and employees working under the bonus plan. The management recognized this in the exception which it filed to the investigator's report."

In the Hotel Employers Association of San Francisco case, in addition to granting a maintenance of membership, the Board ordered the hotels to continue their existing practice of giving preference to members of unions affiliated with the San Francisco Local Joint Executive Board of Hotel and Restaurant Employees when hiring new employees.

Crack down on wildcat strike

An unauthorized week-long strike of 56 weavers at the Hathaway Manufacturing Co.'s plant at New Bedford, Mass., ended last week as a result of the intervention, at the request of the Board, of the international officers of the American Federation of Labor and the officers of the United Textile Workers of America, A. F. L.

After conferences between Chairman Davis of the Board, George Meany, and Robert Watt, A. F. L. members of the Board, Francis Gorman, president of the U. T. W. A., and other representatives of the U. T. W. A., it was decided to discipline any weavers who failed to return to work the following day by summoning them before the International Executive Council of the U. T. W. A. on charges of wilfully violating the contract and the International's constitution. The union officials agreed to provide substitutes for the weavers who persisted in striking. Within a few hours after this decision was made, the weavers in a secret mass meeting voted overwhelmingly to return to work. The company was able to resume full operations the next morning.

MANPOWER . . .

Booklet tells what workers and employers can do for all-out manpower mobilization

What workers, employers,. and labor unions can do to aid in all-out manpower mobilization is outlined in a pamphlet, "Work Will Win," issued June 3 by the War Manpower Commission.

After explaining the scope of the manpower problem and the needs of industry, agriculture and the armed forces, the pamphlet outlines the Commission's voluntary program of training and recruiting the right workers for the right jobs at the right time.

For employers

Under the heading "Here Is Our Job," the booklet asks cooperation of employers, labor unions and all governmental officials to:

1. Utilize all local sources of labor, relaxing frivolous hiring requirements based on prejudice which now bar from jobs qualified Negroes, women, older workers and persons of foreign birth or foreign-sounding names.

2. Train and employ women immediately in the service trades and in labor-shortage areas, to take the places of men called to war.

3. Upgrade workers into supervisors and foremen to organize the greater production effort of the next few months.

4. Employ young persons, women and white-collar workers in the farm labor scarcity areas to help in this summer's harvest.

5. Discourage pirating of labor among war contractors who thereby hinder each other's production, and thereby the whole of war production.

For workers

Each worker, the booklet says, can help in the following ways:

1. By staying on his war job until the Government advises him he is more needed in another war job (through the United States Employment Service), or that his services are needed by the armed forces (through the draft board).

2. By looking for a war industry job for which he is fitted, if he is now in a peacetime job. But he should not migrate around the country looking for war work on the basis of

incomplete information. He should check with the United States Employment Service to find out where the present and future jobs are opening, and what kind of workers are needed, before going into a war area which probably will have inadequate housing and transportation and difficult working conditions.

3. Whether employed now or not, by exploring the possibility of obtaining training for an essential war job, preferably in or near his own community.

4. College and. advanced high-school students should stay in school and seek to prepare themselves for technical work, either through the regular courses or in the short courses set up in the technical colleges and universities for war workers.

McSHERRY NAMED OPERATIONS DIRECTOR

Appointment of Brig. Gen. Frank J. McSherry as director of operations of the War Manpower Commission was announced June 2 by Commission Chairman Paul V. McNutt.

★ ★ ★

Hiring of handicapped increases rapidly

A steadily growing army of physically handicapped men and women is taking its place in war production, according to United States Employment Service figures released June 3 by Paul V. McNutt, Chairman of the War Manpower Commission.

In April, the United States employment offices made more than 7,500 placements of handicapped workers—about 2,000 more than in March and 3,000 more than in February. New York accounted for 1,700 of the April placements, Illinois for 1,100, Texas for 860, and Michigan for 670.

Complete utilization of the skills and talents of the physically handicapped, however, has not yet been reached, Mr. McNutt said.

West Coast ship repair representatives adopt new agreement to keep costs down

Representatives of West Coast ship repair workers have followed the lead of shipbuilding labor in approving a wage stabilization agreement conforming to President Roosevelt's program to keep down the cost of living, Paul R. Porter, chairman of the Shipbuilding Stabilization Committee, reported June 3, to Wendell Lund, director of the WPB Labor Production Division.

All crafts to work shifts

Under the new agreement just reached by the Pacific Coast ship repair conference conducted by Mr. Porter, double-time pay for overtime will be dropped to time-and-a-half. In addition, all crafts agree to work shifts, and uniform shift premiums are established for all Pacific ports.

All repair jobs are to pay the repair rate, with the repair rate to maintain the previous differential over the construction rate, the stabilization pact provides. Ship conversion work done before service runs will carry the construction wage rate.

The new agreement suspends the former provision for cost-of-living adjustments during the duration of the war.

WELL-KNOWN ARTISTS WILL DRAW FOR YOUR PAPER OR MAGAZINE

VICTORY PRESENTS, on facing page, a fourth group of 4 drawings by well-known American artists who have volunteered their talents to help emphasize, in their own medium, matters vital to winning the war. VICTORY will print four drawings by these and other artists each week. Permission to reprint is hereby granted. Mats in two-column size (larger than appears here) are available weekly. Requests to be put on the mailing list regularly, or for individual mats should be addressed to Distribution Section, Division of Information, Office for Emergency Management, Washington, D. C.

(In individual orders for the four drawings displayed this week, please refer to the serial number printed on the drawings and add the letter A, thus: V 12 A, V–13–A, V–14–A, V–15–A.)

"But Dad, remember you said we were to share the car."

Drawn for O. E. M.

"Oh, how nice! A rubber check!"

Drawn for O. E. M.

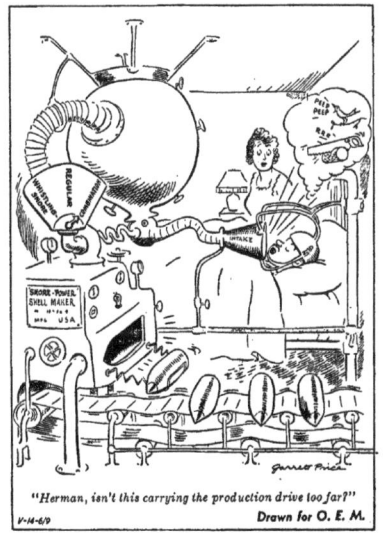

"Herman, isn't this carrying the production drive too far?"

Drawn for O. E. M.

"No, No, McShane! Not his tires! Don't aim at his tires!"

Drawn for O. E. M.

Questions and answers on price regulation

(The following are selected from a list of questions and answers released by OPA June 6.)

Q. A retail store sold coffee during March at 2 pounds for 64 cents, 1 pound for 34 cents. It now continues its 34-cent price for 1 pound, and will permit customers to buy 2 pounds at the same time for double the price of 1. Does this violate the general maximum price regulation?

A. Yes. If 2 pounds are sold to a customer at one time, the March highest price for that quantity must not be exceeded.

Q. A store has made a practice of giving customers cash checks constituting a 3¾-percent discount with purchases. Can the store discontinue giving these cash checks?

A. No; unless an equivalent reduction in price is made.

Q. Is taxi service subject to the general maximum price regulation, or any other OPA control? ·

A. No.

Q. Are embroidered textile products, produced in commercial quantities, included within the scope of the term "objects of art," which are specifically exempt from the general maximum price regulation?

A. No. The term "objects of art" refers to items which are unique, and in no case to items produced in commercial quantities.

Q. Where a seller, in March, had the practice of giving free repair service and replacement of defective parts for a certain period after the sale, may the length of the period for free service or free replacements or both, be reduced without diminishing the prices?

A. The period for either the free service, or the free replacements, or both, may not be reduced without proportionately reducing the price.

Price formula is provided for malleable iron castings

Producers of malleable iron castings and high alloy steel castings were given price formulas June 2 by the OPA for establishing maximum prices for such castings as cannot be priced under Section 1499.2 of the general maximum price regulation.

⋇ ⋇ ⋇

KAPOK ORDER EXTENDED

Amendment No. 2 to the kapok order, M–85, extending from May 31, to June 30, 1942, the time in which dealers may sell, transfer title to, or deliver kapok to manufacturers within the restrictions of the order was issued June 1 by the Director of Industry Operations.

WAR EFFORT INDICES

MANPOWER

National labor force, April	53, 400, 000
Unemployed, April	3, 000, 000
Nonagricultural workers, April	40, 773, 000
Percent increase since June 1940	**14
Farm employment, May 1, 1942	10, 796, 000
Percent increase since June 1940	**1

FINANCE *(In millions of dollars)*

Authorized program June 1940–May 1942	‡166, 435
Airplanes	36, 223
Ordnance	35, 403
Miscellaneous munitions	21, 330
Naval ships	16, 445
Industrial facilities	16, 338
Posts, depots, etc	14, 037
Merchant ships	7, 465
Pay, subsistence, travel for the armed forces	6, 155
Stockpile, food exports	4, 851
Housing	1, 392
Miscellaneous	6, 796
Total expenditures, June 1940–May 1942	*30, 615
Sales of War Bonds—	
Cumulative May 1941–May 1942	6, 023
May 1942	634
May quota exceeded	5.7%

PLANT EXPANSION *(In millions of dollars)*

June 1940 to latest reporting date	
Gov. commitments for war plant expansion; 1,644 projects, April 30	12, 181
Private commitments for war plant expansion; 7,836 projects, April 30	2, 574

EARNINGS, HOURS, AND COST OF LIVING

	Percent increase from June 1940
Manufacturing industries—March:	
Average weekly earnings	$36. 15	40. 2
Average hours worked per week	42. 5	13. 3
Average hourly earnings	80. 9¢	20. 4
Cost of living, April 1935– 89=100)	*Index 115. 1	14. 5

*Prelim. Includes revisions in several months.
‡Preliminary.
**Adjusted for seasonal variations.

OFFICE FOR EMERGENCY MANAGEMENT

WAYNE COY, *Liaison Officer*

CENTRAL ADMINISTRATIVE SERVICES: Dallas Dort, *Director.*

DEFENSE COMMUNICATIONS BOARD: James Lawrence Fly, *Chairman.*

INFORMATION DIVISION: Robert W. Horton, *Director.*

NATIONAL WAR LABOR BOARD: Wm. H. Davis, *Chairman.*

OFFICE OF SCIENTIFIC RESEARCH AND DEVELOPMENT: Dr. Vannevar Bush, *Director.*

OFFICE OF CIVILIAN DEFENSE: James M. Landis, *Director.*

OFFICE OF THE COORDINATOR OF INTER-AMERICAN AFFAIRS: Nelson Rockefeller, *Coordinator.*

OFFICE OF DEFENSE HEALTH AND WELFARE SERVICES: Paul V. McNutt, *Director.*

OFFICE OF DEFENSE TRANSPORTATION: Joseph B. Eastman, *Director.*

OFFICE OF FACTS AND FIGURES: Archibald MacLeish, *Director.*

OFFICE OF LEND-LEASE ADMINISTRATION: E. R. Stettinius, Jr., *Administrator.*

OFFICE OF PRICE ADMINISTRATION: Leon Henderson, *Administrator.*

CONSUMER DIVISION: Dexter M. Keezer, *Assistant Administrator,* in charge. Dan A. West, *Director.*

OFFICE OF ALIEN PROPERTY CUSTODIAN: Leo T. Crowley, *Custodian.*

WAR MANPOWER COMMISSION: Paul V. McNutt, *Chairman.*

WAR RELOCATION AUTHORITY: Milton Eisenhower, *Director.*

WAR SHIPPING ADMINISTRATION: Rear Admiral Emory S. Land, U. S. N. (Retired), *Administrator.*

WAR PRODUCTION BOARD:
Donald M. Nelson, *Chairman.*
Henry L. Stimson.
Frank W. Knox.
Jesse H. Jones.
William S. Knudsen.
Sidney Hillman.
Leon Henderson.
Henry A. Wallace.
Harry L. Hopkins.

WAR PRODUCTION BOARD DIVISIONS:
Donald M. Nelson, *Chairman.*
Executive Secretary, G. Lyle Belsley.

PLANNING COMMITTEE: Robert R. Nathan, *Chairman.*

PURCHASES DIVISION: Houlder Hudgins, *Acting Director.*

PRODUCTION DIVISION: W. H. Harrison, *Director.*

MATERIALS DIVISION: A. I. Henderson, *Director.*

DIVISION OF INDUSTRY OPERATIONS: J. S. Knowlson, *Director.*

LABOR DIVISION: Sidney Hillman, *Director.*

LABOR PRODUCTION DIVISION: Wendell Lund, *Director.*

CIVILIAN SUPPLY DIVISION: Leon Henderson, *Director.*

OFFICE OF PROGRESS REPORTS: Stacy May, *Director.*

REQUIREMENTS COMMITTEE: Wm. L. Batt, *Chairman.*

STATISTICS DIVISION: Stacy May, *Director.*

INFORMATION DIVISION: Robert W. Horton, *Director.*

ADMINISTRATIVE DIVISION: James G. Robinson, *Administrative Officer.*

LEGAL DIVISION: John Lord O'Brian, *General Counsel.*

VICTORY

OFFICIAL WEEKLY BULLETIN OF THE AGENCIES IN THE OFFICE FOR EMERGENCY MANAGEMENT

WASHINGTON, D. C.	JUNE 16, 1942	VOLUME 3, NUMBER 24

IN THIS ISSUE

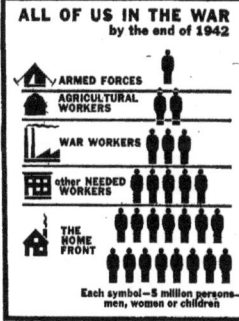

ALL OF US IN THE WAR
by the end of 1942

ARMED FORCES

AGRICULTURAL WORKERS

WAR WORKERS

other NEEDED WORKERS

THE HOME FRONT

Each symbol—5 million persons—
men, women or children

Nation-wide collection of scrap rubber under way at President's direction to determine extent of United States supply

Detailed plans for the all-out, Nation-wide scrap rubber collection campaign to be conducted in accordance with the President's direction were announced June 14 by Lessing J. Rosenwald, chief of the WPB Bureau of Industrial Conservation.

To reach every home and plant

The campaign is designed to reach into every home and industrial plant, to stimulate the flow of as much scrap as possible into the Nation's war supply. Main points of the plan are as follows:

1. The campaign began at 12:01 a. m. June 15, and will end at midnight June 30.

2. The Bureau of Industrial Conservation will supervise the campaign, working in close cooperation with the Office of the Petroleum Coordinator for War and the Petroleum Industry War Council.

3. Local salvage committees set up by the BIC in every State—there are now over 12,000 such committees—will play a major role in the effort locally and will work with regional and local representatives of the petroleum industry.

To be turned in at filling stations

4. All scrap rubber coming from citizens during the campaign will be turned in by them at filling stations.

5. Filling stations will pay for reclaimable rubber at the uniform rate of a penny a pound.

6. Oil companies which serve the filling

stations will collect the rubber and take it to central concentration points.

Companies will not profit

7. The oil companies, taking title to the rubber, will sell mixed scrap to the Rubber Reserve Company (RFC) at the rate of $25 per short ton (2,000 pounds) in carload lots.

8. The excess resulting from the difference between $20 a short ton, paid to the citizen, and the price paid by the Government to oil companies will be turned over to designated charities.

9. The Government will store the scrap rubber in warehouses and it will then be allocated to reclaimers' plants at the direction of the War Production Board.

10. Industrial scrap, as differentiated from scrap uncovered by private citizens may either be sold to oil companies at bulk distributing stations or sold through the usual channels of trade.

Check to be kept on amounts

11. The oil companies, playing a major role in the effort, will, in addition to making filling stations available as collection points, use much of their personnel to stimulate the flow.

13. A report on the total amount of rubber collected at filling stations in this special campaign will be made available to the Government within a short time after the close of the effort.

Instructions to executive secretaries
(Continued on page 4)

Review of the Week

The whole Nation prepared last week for a campaign to find out how much we have of one of the scarcest and most strategic materials—rubber, which comes from areas 90 percent controlled by the Axis. The scrap collection drive, requested by President Roosevelt and carried out by the War Production Board's Bureau of Industrial Conservation with the help of gasoline filling stations, was to begin on June 15 and end on June 30.

Joint board to weld war production of two nations

Distribution of scarce materials will be one of the prime purposes of the Combined Production and Resources Board, set up by the United States and Great Britain with Donald Nelson as American representative. In its larger aspect the joint board will weld the war production of the two nations into one gigantic program, centrally planned for speed and volume and economy of transportation.

Keyed to the mutual production program will be the WPB's new system for allocation of materials here in America. As forecast a week previously, the production requirements plan will be used to determine over-all needs of the large industries and spread the supply where it will do the most good. In announcing the order which applies this principle, Requirements Chairman Batt and Industry Operations Director Knowlson revealed the plan's place in a system of control extending all the way from the general staffs of the United Nations to the individual factory.

Far-reaching changes in civilian life

Looking at the whole picture from the civilian point of view, Joseph L. Weiner, deputy director of the WPB Division of Civilian Supply, predicted far-reaching changes in the life and habits of everyone within the next few months as a result of necessary restrictions on food, clothing, transportation, and housing.

With respect to several of these matters the hand was writing on the wall last week. The Office of Defense Transportation placed intercity bus operations under wartime regulation throughout the country, ordering discontinuance of some services and pooling of others. The United States and Britain announced simultaneously with the Combined Production and Resources Board, a Combined Food Board which is to regard the entire food resources of Great Britain and the United States as "in a common pool, about which the fullest information will be interchanged." The WPB Division of Industry Operations continued restrictions on wool, and gave high priorities to materials which will go into uniforms.

United States output for war exceeds expectations

As compensation for all these deprivations, present and to come, Donald Nelson last week told us their direct result: American war production is proving greater than the leaders of the effort ever thought it could be.

Materials alone do not operate the mass production factories that are rolling out the undreamed-of quantities of planes and tanks and guns and ships. As a guide in the problem of supplying all-important skilled labor, the War Manpower Commission last week named a management-labor policy committee composed of seven leaders from each of the two fields. The Labor Production Division of WPB also set up a policy committee, composed of labor men. And war production drive headquarters announced awards to be given individual working men for ideas that will speed and improve production of weapons.

The Office of P_{rice} Administration postponed the new "tailor-made" system of gasoline rationing for the East Coast until July 15, to give time for training registrars and ration boards.

Clothing and textiles continued to occupy a great deal of OPA's attention. Pricing of fall and winter garments for women and children was changed to a present-cost-plus-normal-profit basis. Eleven additional groups of cotton fabrics were brought under ceilings stated in dollars and cents. OPA also set maximum prices for the sale and rental of used typewriters, the only kind now generally available to the public.

Nelson sees 60,000 planes in 1942; total war production greater than expected

We shall make 60,000 planes this year, WPB Chairman Nelson assured the graduating class of his alma mater, the University of Missouri, in a speech June 9. Our total production of war goods has proved greater than we had any reason to suppose from the blueprints it could be, he revealed. Excerpts:

As you of course know, a very large number of new factories for the manufacture of arms and munitions were built in this country during the past year. During the past winter, a great many of these began to swing into production; and since then we have been discovering a rather unexpected thing—that in many, many instances the rate of output of a new factory has proved to be a great deal higher than the output which was anticipated when the factory was designed and built. In other words, we have found that our total production of war goods is higher than we had any reason to suppose it could be when we looked at the blueprints.

Natural result of mass technique

Why is that happening? In part, of course, I think it is due to the fact that the men who are making the goods—the managers, the engineers, the foremen and the workers alike—are working as they never worked before to make the things we need so desperately on the battle line. But beyond that, I think that what we are seeing is the natural result of the application to munitions production of the best mass production techniques.

A new aircraft factory was put into production some time ago. It had been designed to produce fifty airplanes a month, working at full capacity. Now we have discovered that its real capacity is much closer to one hundred and fifty planes a month. And I would like to remind you that it is just two years since the President announced that we ought to try to reach a point at which we could make fifty thousand airplanes a year. Well, this year we shall make sixty thousand airplanes, and by the end of the year was shall still be picking up speed for an even vaster production in 1943.

VICTORY

OFFICIAL BULLETIN of the Office for Emergency Management. Published weekly by the Division of Information, Office for Emergency Management, and printed at the United States Government Printing Office, Washington, D. C.

Subscription rates by mail: 75¢ for 52 issues; 25¢ for 13 issues; single copies 5¢, payable in advance. Remit money order payable directly to the Superintendent of Documents, Government Printing Office, Washington, D. C.

On the Home Front

The soldiers on the production front are gaining ground every day. We are producing tanks and guns and ships and planes on a constantly increasing scale, but these soldiers now have sent back a hurry call for support. They have sent this call to the home front and it is a call as urgent as that call for artillery or aviation which sometimes comes from hard-pressed ground forces caught in some desperate sector of a fierce action.

Call has new ring of urgency

But as of this moment the call has a new ring of urgency. The need for raw materials in certain war operations is so great that it is almost a case of "now or never." Shortage of metals threatens to close down some of the blast furnaces which work for war, and every blast furnace closed down means fewer steel plates for cargo vessels, fewer tanks for the front, fewer weapons for our fighting men.

"Patch and pray" not enough

The War Production Board has warned war industry that it must prepare to meet these shortages as best it can and that it must be prepared, in the words of William L. Batt, chairman of the WPB Requirements Committee, to "patch and pray" in an effort to keep its equipment busy.

Industry, however, can only do a certain amount of praying and patching just as the military commander awaiting needed aerial or artillery support can hang on just so long without that support. By this time there must be a need indeed on the home front who fail to realize that part of the answer to the shortage of metals and the shortage of rubber and the shortage of all types of materials is scrap—and that scrap is everywhere.

Must match industry's efforts

The one great remaining source of scrap is in the homes and on the farmsteads of America. In the next few weeks we must make a supreme effort to do our part as families and as individuals as efficiently as industry has been doing its part. Ours has been the leak, ours the unforgivable waste. If you doubt the importance of scrap rubber to our military effort consider that the rubber reclaimed from a thousand pairs of rubber galoshes from a thousand closets will provide all the rubber needed in a single medium bomber; that the rubber left in

that old casing at the back of the garage would make 18 pairs of rubber boots for paratroopers; that the rubber in one old bicycle tire and tube provide all the rubber needed in building six military field radio sets or a gas mask.

The next few weeks and the months that follow until victory must see a continuing effort to gather from city apartment, suburban home and country farm

REPRINTING PERMISSIBLE

Requests have been received for permission to reprint "On the Home Front" in whole or in part. This column, like all other material in VICTORY, may be reprinted without special permission. If excerpts are used, the editors ask only that they be taken in such a way that their original meaning is preserved.

every possible piece of scrap iron and steel, copper and brass, of zinc, of lead, of aluminum.

"Blackplate" for tin plate

If anything is needed to underline the importance of tin in the war effort, an importance which led to recently announced plans for tin can collections in 36 major United States cities and to a further 10 percent cut in use of tin for unnecessary civilian purposes effective July 1, it is present in the proposal discussed at a recent meeting of WPB's fruit, fish, and vegetable canning industry advisory committee. At this meeting it was proposed that chemically treated steel—"blackplate"—to the trade—should be substituted for tin plate in making ends of cans for packing some commodities and that another process be substituted for the present method of making the ends of cans used to pack another group of commodities, principally vegetables. If this were done, proponents of the change insist, about 6,000 tons of tin a year might be saved.

The achievements of the War Production Drive are something to dismay the dictators quite as much as the fierce and dedicated resistance of the Russians. Last week produced two typical examples of what American workers can do of their own free will. Officials of the War Production Drive and the War Production Board journeyed to Rochester, N. Y., for a

ceremony resembling that which accompanies an award of decorations on the fighting front. They went to the war plant of the Symington-Gould Corporation which had increased its war production 14 percent in a single month. And in Hamilton, Ohio, men of the American Rolling Mill Co. fulfilled a pledge to WPB chairman Donald M. Nelson by breaking production records for the third successive month. Every such achievement lessens the distance between the United Nations and triumph.

Awards of merit to the production line

That WPB is well aware of this is shown by its announcement of a plan of individual awards to workmen who devise ways of increasing or improving the output of their factories. "The Army and Navy," said Mr. Nelson, "have systems of commending merit of high order in the line of duty. There is also merit of a high order on the production line in this war. I propose that the production soldier shall also be recognized for production in this war."

Bound by a tighter tether

As a Nation we send our soldiers and our warships out toward flaming horizons thousands of miles away; as individuals, millions of us will be tied to our home by a tighter tether in the months to come because we must have transportation for the men and the materials and the weapons needed for war. Passenger trains will be fewer and slower and crowded to the point of discomfort. And so with buses. As for the automobile, anyone who grinds rubber from the tires of his car in unnecessary driving these days wilfully is aiding our enemies. There are still those who do not realize this or do not care and they are the people who in the Eastern States, where gasoline is rationed, have been getting extra gasoline from bootleg gasoline stations in order that they might pursue their empty "pleasure as usual" existence in the face of national danger. But these people, measured against the rest of us, are few enough and they will profit little. After July 15 the new gasoline rationing system will make it difficult to bootleg gasoline without going to jail.

We're quite likely to find ourselves living in a darker world and that not because of military black-outs against enemy antiaircraft but because we must save electric power to keep our war industries running. . . . Fewer houses for war workers will be built because war industry needs the steel which would have gone into them.

WE NEED THIS MUCH RUBBER
TO FIGHT THE WAR THIS YEAR . . . .

RECLAIMED　　SYNTHETIC　　　CRUDE

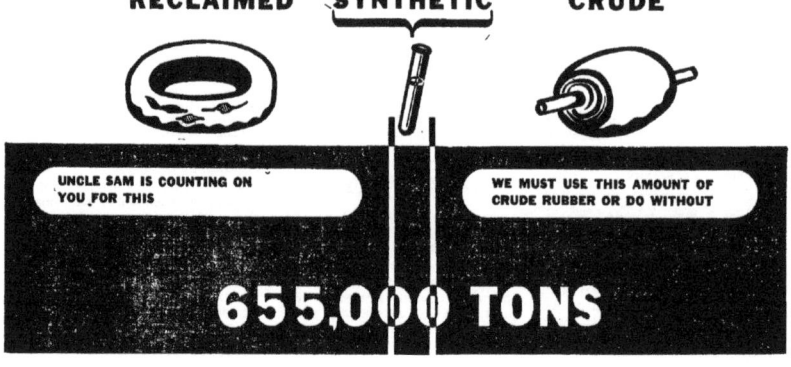

UNCLE SAM IS COUNTING ON YOU FOR THIS

WE MUST USE THIS AMOUNT OF CRUDE RUBBER OR DO WITHOUT

655,000 TONS

National scrap rubber collection begins

(Continued from page 1)

and State chairmen of all State salvage committees from Herbert L. Gutterson, chief of general salvage, Bureau of Industrial Conservation, included the following:

The oil industry will turn over to the national headquarters of USO, Army Relief, Navy Relief, and the American Red Cross, on an equal basis, any receipts in excess of purchase price. There will be no profit to the oil industry.

Reclaimable rubber which is acceptable will include all kinds of rubber except used battery boxes, and parts thereof and tire beads. Metal, wood and leather should be removed from such articles as leather shoes, baby buggy tires, etc.

Aside from the obvious purpose of bringing in vitally needed scrap rubber, one of the important purposes of this drive is to provide immediate factual data on the amount of reclaimable rubber in the country. For this reason the following important policies have been set down:

1. Accurate and complete reports will be requested of every unit in the oil industry of the amount of

scrap rubber collected, immediately after the end of the drive.

2. All scrap rubber salvaged by the public should flow through the oil industry's filling stations and bulk plants. In addition, large quantities of scrap rubber such as may be in the hands of industrial plants, auto graveyards, etc., may be sold directly to the nearest oil company bulk station.

. . .

Buses carrying children to summer camps get tires

A vehicle used to transport children under 18, and their attendants, to and from a summer camp will be eligible for tires and tubes, provided requirements announced June 7 by the OPA are met.

The OPA announced that under certain conditions a bus may be used to carry Army selectees to and from examination or induction centers.

Amendment No. 12 to the Revised Tire Rationing Regulations, which became effective June 8, sets forth the requirements to be met in both instances.

SCRAP RUBBER'S IMPORTANCE

THE CHART on this page reveals in graphic fashion the large place occupied by scrap in our 1942 rubber program. The proportion shown represents the amount WPB believes factories can reclaim if it is collected, and Uncle Sam is counting on us to bring it in.

(Two- and three-column mats of this chart will be available within a week for publication. Address requests to Distribution Section, Division of Information, OEM, Washington, D. C.; refer to Mat V-23 and specify size.)

More reclaimed, less crude rubber allowed industrial tires

Almost 300 tons of crude rubber will be conserved for war production by an amendment to the rubber specifications order, M-15-b-1, effective June 12.

The Amendment (No. 6) requires the use of more reclaimed rubber and less crude in the manufacture of industrial pneumatic and solid tires. This is expected to save from 75 to 100 tons of crude rubber each year without materially diminishing quality.

The tires affected are used on industrial trucks and similar equipment generally found in factories and shipyards.

Present emergency plan for gasoline rationing in East extended to July 15

Extension of the present emergency plan for gasoline rationing on the East Coast to July 15 was announced June 12 by the OPA. This change was made to permit training of registrars and ration boards on the new coupon system to go into effect on that date. Originally, the emergency plan was to end June 30.

Unit value of cards raised

At the same time OPA raised the unit value of the "A" and "B" cards now in use from 3 gallons to 6 gallons, effective at 12:01 A. M. June 15. The purpose of doubling the unit value was to provide card holders with enough gasoline to tide them over the 2-week extension period.

Card holders who have exhausted all units on their cards by June 15 may apply to a local rationing board for an extra ration. OPA pointed out, however, that such a ration should be for gasoline needed between July 1 and July 15 only, since the rations allowed by the present cards were expected to cover all driving needs through June 30. Applicants for additional supplies of gasoline in all cases will be required to pass the usual tests for supplemental rations.

* * *

Service station operators warned not to play favorites

Any service station operator who engages in "black market" activities or favors his best customers with extra gasoline will force himself out of business and make himself liable to criminal prosecution under the permanent gasoline rationing program scheduled to take effect next month.

Subject to strict audit

The OPA June 8 warned station operators that they will be subject to strict audit control and will be required to turn over to suppliers the exact number of stamps for the amount of gasoline delivered to their stations on essentially the same basis his customers must turn coupons over to him.

If a station operator persists in selling gasoline in amounts greater than the total number of coupons his customers turn in, he will not have sufficient coupons himself to turn over to his supplier and will eventually find himself with no gasoline in his storage tanks and no means of obtaining any.

WPB approves pipe line from Texas to Illinois to supply crude oil to East

The War Production Board June 11 approved immediate construction of a 24-inch pipe line from Longview, Tex., to the Salem, Ill., area. It took this action after considering the changed situation with respect to oil tankers and military requirements, and after receiving assurances that prompt construction of the line will not interfere with delivery of steel or motor equipment orders for the War and Navy Departments or for the Maritime Commission's shipbuilding program.

The 550-mile pipe line, which will carry crude oil to relieve shortages in the East Coast area, will require 125,000 tons of finished steel. Consumption of critical materials, however, will be minimized by the substitution of cast iron for steel in some places, and by the use of seamless steel tubing in place of valuable steel plate. The line is expected to be completed by December 1, 1942.

The WPB's approving action was taken after Wayne Johnson, chairman of a special committee investigating the pipe line proposal, reported to WPB Chairman Nelson that the line could be built with a minimum of disturbance to the war production program and would provide an increased supply of oil to the East Coast area within 6 months.

OPA tells how gasoline books will be "tailored" to needs

Further details of tailoring of supplemental rations to fit the needs of individual car owners under the new coupon rationing plan that will go into effect in the East Coast area next month, were announced June 11 by OPA.

Supplementary "B" or "C" books will be issued to car owners who can prove that the "A" book, to which every registered car owner is entitled, will not provide enough gasoline to meet his needs.

Methods differ between "B" and "C"

"B coupon books will have a variable expiration date, while "C" books will have coupons torn out and, if necessary, so that the applicant will receive no more coupons than he has established a need for.

This is how the tailoring will be done:

A car owner who drives to work, or who needs his car in his work, may find that an "A" book, which he obtains when he registers for rationing, does not meet his requirements.

He may ask the registrar for an application form for a supplemental ration. This he will present to a local rationing board after he has filled it out.

The Board will determine if the applicant is entitled to any supplemental ration, and if so, whether it should be in the form of a "B" or a "C" book. No applicant may receive both.

The "B" book, to be issued for necessary vocational use, will contain 16 coupons. This is a fixed number, and will not be varied by tearing out any of the coupons. These 16 coupons will have to last the applicant for at least 3 months. If he does not need 16 coupons' worth of gasoline to meet his requirements during the next three months, the rationing board will extend the period so that the 16 coupons will last him a longer time.

A "C" coupon book can be issued only for vehicles proving occupational needs greater than can be met by the maximum "B" allowance, in addition to the "A" ration. Also, the applicant must belong to a certain category of essential drivers in order to be eligible for "C" books. Among the services for which such rations will be issued are medical care, maintenance of public utilities, carrying farm labor, giving religious comfort or assistance, and making official trips on Government business.

Motorcycles will be issued "D" books as a basic ration, and one, or more, "D" books as a supplemental ration. Each book will be good for one year, and coupons will be torn out to tailor any supplemental ration to the applicant's need. Each "D" coupon will be worth 40 percent of the gallonage value of the "A" coupon.

* * *

First copies of "A" gasoline coupon book reach OPA

First copies of the new "A" gasoline coupon book, which motorists in the East Coast rationed area will need to obtain their basic rations of gasoline when the coupon plan goes into effect in July, were delivered June 10 to the Office of Price Administration.

The book contains six sheets of eight coupons each, representing a year's supply of gasoline for the holder.

Each sheet of coupons will be good for a 2-month period. Unused coupons are void after the period for which they were issued is over.

On the outside of the front cover, the book will carry a description of the car for which the book is issued, as well as the name and address of the owner.

INDUSTRIAL OPERATIONS ...

Over-all control of scarce materials established under requirements plan; priorities inadequate, WPB chiefs explain

A pattern for flow of materials to the Nation's wartime industry was announced June 10 in a joint statement by William L. Batt, chairman of WPB's Requirements Committee, and J. S. Knowlson, Director of Industry Operations.

It is the first over-all effort to coordinate control of the distribution and use of scarce materials, and is embodied in a new Priorities Regulation No. 11.

Batt and Knowlson explain system

The regulation provides for establishing definite quantitative limits to the acquisition of metals and other scarce materials by any person or company using more than $5,000 worth of metal in a calendar quarter. Government arsenals, shipyards, etc., are subject to the requirements, as well as manufacturers of munitions, ships, airplanes, and all other large users of metal.

The joint statement by Mr. Batt and Mr. Knowlson follows in part:·

The huge materials requirements of the growing war production · program make it necessary to institute much stricter controls over the use of metals and other scarce materials. The priorities system as it was developed last year as a means of giving preference to defense orders no longer provides adequate control.

General staffs to advise joint board

Creation by the President [June 9] of a Combined Production and Resources Board to coordinate the distribution of· materials and the production programs of the United States and its Allies gives the War Production Board increased responsibility for directing every available pound of material into the war program and adequately essential civilian uses.

The general staffs of the United Nations will advise the Combined Production and Resources Board as to strategic requirements of weapons and ships. In the same way, the Armed Services of the United States and the Maritime Commission will inform the War Production Board of the types of materials and equipment most vitally needed, and their order of urgency.

The Requirements Committee of WPB, on the basis of these statements of direct war requirements, and other information on essential civilian needs, will establish broad policies for the distribution of scarce materials. The policy decisions of the Requirements Committee, on which the Army and Navy are represented, will determine the part of the total available supplies of basic materials which can be made available in each calendar quarter to war industries and other consuming groups.

Within these broad policy limits established by the Requirements Committee, the Bureau of Priorities will determine the maximum quantities of scarce materials which may be acquired by each individual company required to qualify under the plan in each three-month period beginning July 1. In making these determinations, the Bureau of Priorities will be guided by the recommendations of the Armed Services, and of the other divisions of the War Production Board.

The basic instrument which will be used in this quarterly apportionment of materials to individual companies is the production requirements plan. It should be emphasized, however, that the produc-

Details of Priorities Regulation No. 11

Priorities Regulation No. 11, issued June 10, affects any company, business, person, plant or division of a company maintaining a separate inventory whose past or anticipated quarterly receipt or withdrawals from inventory of metals in the forms covered by an accompanying Metals List aggregate $5,000 or more, with the following exceptions:

United States or other Government agencies (not including those engaged in manufacture, such as shipyards, arsenals, prison factories, etc., which are subject to the requirements); companies or persons engaged in: transportation; furnishing heat, light, power, electricity, gas or water; mining or quarrying; production, refining, transportation, distribution or marketing of petroleum. or associated hydrocarbons; communications; sewerage or drainage; wholesaling, retailing, warehousing, or other similar operations which do not involve the manufacture or processing of materials; extracting, smelting, refining, alloying, or processing metal ores or scrap into raw metal; construction.

Must file by June 30

With these exceptions, all companies using over $5,000 worth of metal quarterly are defined as Class I Producers, and are required to file a PRP application not later than June 30, 1942.

An interim procedure is provided, allowing companies which have properly filed an application but have not yet received a rating certificate under PRP to continue applying preference ratings under any appropriate "P" order (even if the "P" order was scheduled to expire on June 30) or individual preference rating certificate, or to extend preference ratings on orders which the company is engaged in filling. However, the company may not use any such preference rating or ratings to obtain more than 40 percent of the amount of any given material which has been indicated in its PRP application as the estimated requirement for the quarter, and any material so obtained must be deducted from the amount authorized on the PRP certificate when it is received. No Class I Producer who fails to file a PRP application by June 30 may use any preference rating after that date except ratings specifically assigned for construction or capital equipment.

Other ratings mostly forbidden

No company which has received a PRP certificate may apply or extend any other preference rating except for capital equipment or construction, and no such company may accept delivery of materials listed in Materials List No. 1 of the PRP application form, PD-25A, or other materials for which he has sought priority assistance, in greater quantities than those authorized on the certificate, even if the materials can be obtained without use of a preference rating. Companies operating under PRP which need capital equipment or priority assistance for construction or expansion may apply in the usual way on PD-1A or PD-200 and PD-200A application forms.

tion requirements plan under this program will no longer be primarily a mechanism for the assignment of preference ratings to each applicant on the basis of the rated orders the applicant has on his books. PRP now becomes the chief means by which the War Production Board will execute general policies. The emphasis from now on will be on the end use of materials rather than on preference ratings. A classification system, already announced, will be used to obtain information on end use to assist in controlling the distribution of metals during the fourth quarter.

Can relate rated quantities to supply

For the first time, by this means, the War Production Board will have centralized control of the distribution of materials, and will be able to relate the total quantities of materials for which preference ratings are assigned to the available supply.

This ambitious program cannot be put into full operation in one step. For the third quarter of this year, therefore, the primary emphasis will be on the distribution and use of metals. Only companies which use more than $5,000 worth of basic metal in a calendar quarter will be required to apply under the production requirements plan for the quarter beginning July 1. A few special classes of companies, such as those engaged in transportation, construction, mining, and public utility services, will be controlled by existing procedures for the present. The branches of the War Production Board which handle allocations and assignment of priority ratings will be guided by the broad policy determinations made by the Requirements Committee for each group of metals users.

WPB to govern monthly shipments

Every large user of metal will be required to obtain a quarterly authorization for all his scarce material requirements under the production requirements plan. It should be understood, however, that a rating under PRP does not constitute a guarantee of delivery of materials covered by the rating. Actual shipments of critical materials now under allocation control will be governed by month-to-month directions from the War Production Board, as heretofore, on the basis of the appropriate forms required for each material.

For the benefit of companies which use less than $5,000 worth of basic metal in a quarter, and are therefore not now required to apply under the production requirements plan, a percentage of the total supply materials will be set aside, and

Simple standard certification set up for applying and extending all ratings; requirement for copy of order abolished

The use of preference ratings will be simplified and standardized by the terms of an amendment to Priorities Regulation No. 3, announced June 12 by the Director of Industry Operations.

Effective July 1, any preference rating, no matter how it has been assigned, may be applied or extended by a single form of certification, which states merely that the purchaser certified to the seller and to the War Production Board that he is entitled to use the preference ratings indicated on his purchase order, in accordance with the terms of Priorities Regulation No. 3.

Needn't furnish copies of orders

Provisions of existing orders which require a purchaser to furnish his supplier with copies of preference rating orders or other special certifications are all rescinded, except for the special provisions of Priorities Regulation No. 9 with respect to the application of preference ratings for certain types of exports. This change does not, however, affect any provision of existing preference rating orders which limits the kinds of material which may be obtained by use of the assigned rating, or which requires specific information on purchase orders.

In addition to the standard certification, orders on which a preference rating is applied or extended after July 1 must also include the identification symbols required by Priorities Regulation No. 10, which established the Allocation Classification system.

Extension is restricted

The amended Regulation No. 3 restricts extension of preference ratings, in most cases, to material which will be delivered to, or physically incorporated in a product delivered to the person to whom the rating was originally assigned, or which will be used to replace in inventory materials so delivered, subject to definite limitations. A rating may not be extended to replace materials in inventory except to the extent necessary to restore the inventory to a practicable

they may obtain their minimum requirements from this reserve by use of the regular priorities procedures which have been in effect up to now.

working minimum. No rating higher than A-1-b may be assigned to orders for replacement of materials in inventory, even though the order for which the materials were used may have carried a higher rating.

A "basketing" provision permits the simultaneous extension of ratings which have been assigned by different preference rating certificates or orders on a single purchase order. When ratings are basketed in this way, the lowest rating may be extended for the whole order, or the various items in connection with which the ratings are extended may be listed separately, with the corresponding rating applied to each.

Provisions for small manufacturers

Special provision is made for small manufacturers not operating under the production requirements plan. Such producers may extend ratings to deliveries of operating supplies including lubricants, small perishable tools, etc., which are required and will be consumed in filling the rated order which they are extending, but the cost of such operating supplies must not exceed 10 percent of the cost of the materials to which the rating is extended and which such supplies are used to process. Not more than 25 percent of the operating supplies obtained in this way during any month may be metals in the forms described in the metals list of Priorities Regulation No. 11.

Class I producers as defined in Priorities Regulation No. 11—large users of metals required to apply under the production requirements plan—are prohibited from extending ratings for any purpose after July 1. They must file PD-25A applications to obtain their materials requirements, and they may apply only ratings assigned on their PRP certificates or ratings specifically assigned to them for construction or acquisition of capital items. Ratings assigned on PRP certificates, like all other ratings, will be applied by the standard form of certification prescribed by the amended Regulation No. 3.

This is the metal control program for the third quarter of 1942. It will require the wholehearted cooperation of everyone concerned.

U. S. and Britain pool production, food programs through new joint boards

The President announced June 9, on behalf of himself and the Prime Minister of Great Britain, the creation of a Combined Production and Resources Board and a Combined Food Board.

The general purpose of the two boards was announced with release of memoranda addressed by the President to WPB Chairman Donald Nelson, who will act as the American representative on the Combined Production and Resources Board and to Secretary of Agriculture Claude Wickard, who will act as the American representative on the Combined Food Board.

PRODUCTION AND RESOURCES BOARD

The text of the memorandum to Mr. Nelson follows:

In order to complete the organization needed for the most effective use of the combined resources of the United States and the United Kingdom for the prosecution of the war, there is hereby established a Combined Production and Resources Board.

1. The Board shall consist of the Chairman of the War Production Board, representing the United States, and the Minister of Production, representing the United Kingdom.

2. The Board shall:

(a) Combine the production programs of the United States and the United Kingdom into a single integrated program, adjusted to the strategic requirements of the war, as indicated to the Board by the Combined Chiefs of Staff, and to all relevant production factors. In this connection, the Board shall take account of the need for maximum utilization of the productive resources available to the United States, the British Commonwealth of Nations, and the United Nations, the need to reduce demands on shipping to a minimum, and the essential needs of the civilian populations.

To adjust plans to military position

(b) In close collaboration with the Combined Chiefs of Staff, assure the continuous adjustment of the combined production program to meet changing military requirements.

3. To this end, the Combined Chiefs of Staff and the Combined Munitions Assignments Board shall keep the Combined Production and Resources Board currently informed concerning military re-

quirements, and the Combined Production and Resources Board shall keep the Combined Chiefs of Staff and the Combined Munitions Assignments Board currently informed concerning the facts and possibilities of production.

4. To facilitate continuous operation, the members of the board shall each appoint a deputy; and the board shall form a combined staff. The board shall arrange for such conferences among United States and United Kingdom personnel as it may from time to time deem necessary or appropriate to study particular production needs; and utilize the Joint War Production Staff in London, the Combined Raw Materials Board, the Joint Aircraft Committee, and other existing combined or national agencies for war production in such manner and to such extent as it shall deem necessary.

FOOD BOARD

The text of the memorandum to Secretary Wickard is as follows:

By virtue of the authority vested in me by the Constitution and as President of the United States, and acting jointly and in full accord with the Prime Minister of Great Britain, I hereby authorize, on the part of the Government of the United States, the creation of a joint Great Britain-United States board to be known as the Combined Food Board.

In order to coordinate further the prosecution of the war effort by obtaining a planned and expeditious utilization of the food resources of the United Nations, there is hereby established a Combined Food Board.

The board will be composed of the Secretary of Agriculture and of the Head of the British Food Mission who will represent and act under the instruction of the Minister of Food.

The duties of the Board shall be:

To consider, investigate, enquire into, and formulate plans with regard to any question in respect of which the Governments of the United States of America and the United Kingdom have, or may have, a common concern, relating to the supply, production, transportation, disposal, allocation or distribution, in or to any part of the world, of foods, agricultural materials from which foods are derived, and equipment and nonfood materials ancillary to the production of such foods and agricultural materials, and to make recommendations to the

Governments of the United States of America and the United Kingdom in respect of any such question.

"A common pool"

To work in collaboration with others of the United Nations toward the best utilization of their food resources, and, in collaboration with the interested nation or nations, to formulate plans and recommendations for the development, expansion, purchase, or other effective use of their food resources.

The board shall be entitled to receive from any Agency of the Government of the United States and any Department of the Government of the United Kingdom, any information available to such Agency or Department relating to any matter with regard to which the Board is competent to make recommendations to those Governments, and in principle, the entire food resources of Great Britain and the United States will be deemed to be in a common pool, about which the fullest information will be interchanged.

LEND-LEASE FARM PRODUCTS NEAR 5 BILLION POUNDS

Approximately 5 billion pounds of farm products had been delivered to representatives of the United Nations for lend-lease shipment up to May 1, the United States Department of Agriculture has reported. Total cost of the 4,977,475,000 pounds bought by the Agricultural Marketing Administration and delivered at shipping points since the program began in April 1941, was $651,529,000.

Improved food dehydration detailed in new plans

Detailed plans and specifications for improved driers used in dehydrating vegetables have now been made available to the food industry and processors by the United States Department of Agriculture.

Information sheets on commercial dehydration and blueprints of equipment have been prepared by the Bureau of Agricultural Chemistry and Engineering, for beets, cabbage, carrots, several kinds of greens, onions, sweet potatoes, Irish potatoes and rutabagas. Other vegetables and foods are to be covered later.

$30,615,000,000 spent for war; May figure over 3.8 billion

A total of $30,615,000,000 has been laid on the line by the Federal Government for the prosecution of the war since intensive military effort began in the middle of 1940, WPB announced June 10.

This sum was paid out by the Treasury and Reconstruction Finance Corporation over a 23-month period beginning in July 1940 and ended May 31, 1942.

Expenditures in May came to $3,853,-000,000—2½ times the figure for November, the month before Pearl Harbor, and more than 4 times expenditures in May 1941. A 10 percent gain over the $3,505,-000,000 expended in April was recorded.

★ ★ ★

Steel stamps for marking metal available to war plants

Steel stamps used for marking metal were excepted from the restrictions of General Conservation Order M-126, covering iron and steel, by an amendment issued June 9 by the Director of Industry Operations.

Stamps for marking metal are extensively used in many war plants, though such stamps are rarely bought by the armed forces themselves. To permit plants to buy needed stamps, "Stamps and tablets" is deleted from List A of M-126 by Amendment No. 1, and "Stamps (except for marking metal)" and "tablets" are added.

Further tin curb for containers discussed by committee

A proposed amendment to Conservation Order M-81 to curtail further the use of tin in the manufacture of containers for vegetables and certain other specified products was discussed at a recent meeting of the fruit, fish, and vegetable canning industry advisory committee.

Under the proposed order, chemically treated blackplate would be substituted for tinplate and terneplate in the making of the ends of cans for the packing of specified commodities. Experiments have proven that blackplate can be used for such purposes.

In addition, it is proposed to substitute electrolytic tinplate for hot dipped tinplate in making the ends of cans for the packing of another group of specified commodities, principally vegetables.

Tin for noncritical products to be cut further to meet war, civilian food needs

To provide additional tin for the urgent needs of military operations and civilian food supply, tin used in noncritical products will be cut another 10 percent, effective July 1, 1942, the Director of Industry Operations announced June 6. This reduction, plus certain others are contained in an amended version of Tin Conservation Order M-43-a. While the June 6 order was issued as an amendment, it is actually a rewriting and consolidation of the several previous amendments, and supersedes the previous restrictions.

Banned for 28 types of products

Use of tin in some 28 types of products (those on List A) is forbidden, as in the original order. All other products, except those covered by other specific WPB orders, may, after July 1, 1942, use only 30 percent of the amount of tin used in the corresponding quarter of 1940. Until June 30, 1942, 40 percent of the 1940 amount may be used. This will effect a 10 percent reduction of tin consumption in all products not specifically excepted to the order.

Exceptions

Restriction to the 40-percent and 30-percent use does not apply (where substitutes are impracticable) to manufacture of products carrying a preference rating of A-1-k or higher, to bearing metals produced with the rating of A-3 or higher, to the manufacture of terneplate and tin plate under the terms of Order M-21-e, or to certain kinds of solder for cans and containers under Orders M-81 and M-86.

The order as amended prohibits the manufacture and use of tin oxide except on orders carrying a rating of A-1-k or higher, restricts the amount of tin that may be used in solder, and in printing plates.

Other changes

Certain imperative military and civilian operations were being jeopardized by restrictions in the original order.

To avert an unnecessary hardship the order is changed to permit tinning of dairy implements (as defined in the order), to permit tin to be used in (1) blasting caps for mineral extraction, (2) babbitt for repair of certain diesel engines, and (3) repair and maintenance of ships for which a preference rating has been assigned by the Maritime Commission under PD-800.

No restrictions in the order apply to the use of tin for implements of war

(combat weapons and field service equipment) for the armed services, where such use of tin is required by service specifications.

All tin under allocation

Parts of the original order which are not changed continue to permit tin to be used, under certain circumstances, in:

(1) packaging food for human use, (2) health supplies, under Order P-29, (3) collapsible tubes under Order M-115, (4) certain amounts of secondary tin in type metal and printing plates, (5) scientific control instruments, and (6) bearing metals.

M-43 places all tin under allocation. In addition to this order, the country's total tin supply is controlled by these other orders: M-81, M-86, M-86-a, cover cans; M-21-e, M-104 deal with tin and terne plate; M-72 controls disposition of scrap; and M-115 limits collapsible tubes.

Texas smelter expanded

The amended order is issued concurrently with the announcement that the new tin smelter being erected in Texas has been expanded from an original capacity of 18,000 tons to 52,000 tons per year capacity. An A-1-a priority rating has been assigned to this smelter, built primarily to refine Bolivian ore, so that production may be increased at the earliest possible date.

Cobalt-nickel oxide may be used in ground coat frit

Cobalt-nickel oxide may be used in the manufacture of ground coat frit by the terms of Amendment No. 1 to Conservation Order M-39-b, issued June 9 by the Director of Industry Operations.

Consumption of cobalt in the manufacture of ground coat frit, an important ingredient in the enamelling of steel, was limited, in any one quarter, to 35 percent of the amount of cobalt used in the first 6 months of 1941. The amendment permits use of cobalt-nickel oxide which cannot be practicably separated into cobalt and nickel, and at the same time prohibits use of cobalt or compounds which can be so separated.

The amendment also provides that no restriction is placed on sale or use of ground coat frit containing cobalt in commercially nonrecoverable form.

WPB takes over car rationing for 11 Government agencies including Army, Navy, Marines

WPB set up machinery June 8 for rationing passenger cars to the Army, Navy and Marine Corps, and Government agencies engaged directly in the prosecution of the war.

A Government Exemption Permit, issued on Form PD-501 by the Director of Industry Operations, will be necessary in order for specified Government agencies to obtain new passenger cars after June 12.

Agencies operating under the plan are Army, Navy and Marine Corps, Maritime Commission, War Shipping Administration, Panama Canal, Coast and Geodetic Survey, Civil Aeronautics Administration, National Advisory Committee for Aeronautics, Office of Scientific Research and Development, and the Office of Lend-Lease Administration.

In addition a Government Exemption Permit must be obtained from WPB by persons desiring to export passenger cars under an export license issued by the Board of Economic Warfare.

Manufacturers, distributors, dealers, or sales agencies must honor a Government Exemption Permit regardless of the terms of any contract or any other commitment entered into with any other person, provided, of course, they have the specified type of passenger car in stock.

Transfers may not be made of "pool" cars—cars which were frozen under OPA regulations for rationing in 1943—except by special authority, which must be stated on the face of the Government Exemption Permit.

New passenger cars have been distributed to the Army and Navy and other Government agencies under OPA regulations. The new WPB order, M-130, places the distribution of cars to these agencies in the hands of WPB. OPA still controls rationing to private individuals and to Government agencies not included in the Government Exemption Permit plan.

Delivery restrictions on industrial equipment explained

An interpretation of General Limitation Order L-123, restricting deliveries of many types of general industrial equipment on and after May 26, was issued by the Director of Industry Operations June 13 stating that equipment covered by the order is considered to have been delivered prior to May 26 if it had been placed in the hands of a common or contract carrier for shipment to the purchaser before that time.

The interpretation, No. 1, makes it clear that equipment in transit at the time the order became effective is not subject to the restrictions.

PRIORITY ACTIONS					*From June 4 *Through June 10	

Subject	Order No.	Related form	Issued	Expiration date	Rating
Aircraft control and pulley bearings: a. Concentration of production of certain sizes of antifriction aircraft control and pulley bearings ordered by WPB.	L-145		6-6-42		
Amusement and gaming machines: a. Automatic phonographs and weighing machines: 1. Order amended to include manufactures of parts for machines.	L-21-a (Amend. No. 2).		6-4-42		
Cellophane and similar transparent material derived from cellulose: a. Further restrictions placed on use of cellophane.	L-20 (As Amend. 6-8-42).		6-8-42	Until revoked.	A-10.
Cobalt: a. Permits use of cobalt-nickel in manufacture of ground coat frit.	M-39-b (Amend. No. 1).		6-6-42		
Cocoa: a. To prevent excessive quota-exempt processing of cocoa beans.	M-145 (Int. No. 1)		6-9-42		
Communications: a. To permit temporary equipment to be replaced by permanent equipment on telephone installations.	L-50 (As Amend. 4-23-42) (Amend. No. 1).		6-4-42		
b. Restrictions on inventories in the radio and wire communications industries modified.	P-130 (Int. No. 1)		6-5-42		A-3.
c. Restrictions modified	P-129 (Int. No. 1)		6-5-42		A-3.
Construction: a. Series of interpretations of Conservation Order L-41, placing all construction under field control.	L-41 (Int. No. 1)		6-6-42		
Farm machinery and equipment and attachments and repair parts therefor: a. Further restrictions on sale of above equipment.	L-26-d		6-8-42		A-2.
b. Permits deliveries of iron and steel after June 30.	P-95 (Amend. No. 3).		6-8-42	6-30-42	
Flashlight cases and flashlight batteries: a. Permits flashlight manufacturer to use up inventories of plated iron and steel at rate not exceeding 1940 production.	L-71 (Amend. No. 1).		6-5-42		
Foundry equipment and repair parts: a. Material for production: 1. Suppliers and Subsuppliers, permitted to use Preference Rating assigned under P-31 to complete deliveries after expiration date of original order, which expired May 30.	P-31-a		6-5-42		
Golf clubs: a. Manufacturers given extension to June 30, in which to manufacture golf clubs.	L-93 (Amend. No. 3).		6-4-42		
Imports of strategic materials: a. Balsa wood placed under import control.	M-63 (Amend. No. 8).		6-10-42		
Incandescent and fluorescent lamps: a. Use of critical materials in manufacturing of light bulbs to be curtailed without curtailing the production of light bulbs themselves. Effective July 1.	L-28 (Amend. No. 1).	PD-532; 423; 417	6-8-42		A-2.
Istle and istle products: a. Tightens restrictions on istle waste and waste istle.	M-138 (Amend. No. 1).		6-8-42		
Jute and jute products: a. Restrictions on acceptance of delivery and use of imported jute and jute products.	M-70 (Amend. No. 4).		6-8-42		
Material entering into the production of officers uniforms: a. Grants high priority rating for cloth and other materials needed for manufacturing of uniforms, for armed forces.	P-131	PD-25A	6-8-42		A-1-i.
Natural resins: a. Restrictions removed on use of natural resins in manufacture of playing cards, pencils, house paint, label varnishes, toys and farm equipment finishes.	M-56 (As Amend. 6-5-42).	PD-339	6-5-42		
Osnaburg (bag and bag sheetings): a. Permits mills to sell or deliver without restrictions, seconds or cuts under 40 yards in length up to 6 percent of mill's production of bag osnaburg and bag sheetings.	L-99 (Amend. No. 1).		6-6-42		
Oil burners: a. "Class A" burners, may be produced to fill orders bearing A-10 preference rating.	L-74 (Amend. No. 1).		6-4-42		
Passenger automobiles: a. Sets up machinery for rationing passenger cars to Army, Navy, Marine Corps and Government agencies engaged in prosecution of war.	M-130	PD-501; 502	6-8-42 (Effective 6-12-42)		

PRIORITY ACTIONS

*From June 4
*Through June 10

Subject	Order No.	Related form	Issued	Expiration date	Rating
Pigs' and hogs' bristles: a. Permits users to buy and accept delivery of bristles to replace their inventory of finished products shipped on war orders.	M-51 (Amend. No. 1).		6-6-42		
Power (electric): a. Heavy power, and steam equipment, order amended to permit production, sale, and delivery of heavy equipment not provided for in original order.	L-117 (Amend. No. 2).		6-8-42		
Protective helmets: a. Permission given to assemble and sell protective helmets parts which were in process on April 29, and to sell those which have already been manufactured.	L-106 (Amend. No. 1).		6-5-42		
Rotenone: a. Permits use of rotenone as an insecticide in treatment of cattle for grubs, but restricts use as a germicide for citrus fruits.	M-133 (Amend. No. 1).		6-6-42		
Rubber: a. Rubber and products and materials of which rubber is a component: 1. Prohibits importation of rubber and rubber products, except by military forces or subsidiaries of Reconstruction Finance Corporation.	M-15-b (Amend. No. 10).		6-6-42		
Safety equipment: a. Change of required rating for sale of equipment using already fabricated materials.	L-114 (Amend. No. 1).		6-4-42		
Springs and mattresses (beds): a. Restrictions placed on use of wire in springs and mattresses. Production of mattresses containing iron and steel prohibited after Sept. 1.	L-49 (Amend. No. 1).		6-8-42		A-3.
Steel and iron (conservation): a. Steel stamps used for marking metal are exempt from original order.	M-126 (Amend. No. 1).		6-9-42		
Tin: a. Effective July 1, tin used in noncritical products to be cut another 10 percent.	M-43-a (As Amend. 6-5-42).	PD-229.	6-5-42		
Welding rods and electrodes: a. To conserve supply and direct distribution. Allocation control placed by WPB. Order effective seven days after date of issuance.	L-146.	PD-528.	6-6-42		A-9; A-1-J.

PRIORITIES REGULATIONS

No.	Subject	Issued
Prior. Reg. No. 11.	Provides for establishing definite quantitative limits to the acquisition of metals and other materials by any person or company using more than $5,000 worth of metal a year. Government arsenals, shipyards, etc., are subject to requirements as well as manufacturers of munitions, ships, airplanes, and all other large users of metal.	6-10-42

Welding rods, electrodes placed under strict control

Distribution of welding rods and electrodes has been placed under strict control by an order announced June 9 by the Director of Industry Operations.

Welding rods and electrodes, under the terms of Limitation Order L-146, may be delivered without restrictions only to the Army and Navy, specified Government agencies, governments of the United Nations, for operations under the Lend-Lease program, and to accredited schools which are training welding operators under a course conforming to the American Welding Society's code for minimum instruction requirements, or schools established within industrial plants which meet certain instruction qualifications. Other deliveries of ordinary rods and electrodes are confined to orders bearing a preference rating of A-9 or higher. In the case of alloy electrodes or rods, which mean ferrous-base electrodes or rods whose core wire contains more than 2 percent by weight of materials other than iron or carbon, deliveries may not be made except on orders of A-1-J or higher.

The order also provides for the setting aside each month, for repair and maintenance purposes only, 6 percent of each type of rod or electrode delivered by a manufacturer during that month.

No one is permitted to acquire rods or electrodes if the result will be to increase his inventory beyond a 60-day supply. Manufacturers must file a record of all shipments with WPB on Form PD-528 on or before the 18th day of each month. The order became effective June 13.

Production of specific sizes of aircraft control bearings concentrated among companies

Concentration of production of certain sizes of antifriction aircraft control and pulley bearings among the various companies making them was ordered June 6 by the WPB.

Limitation Order L-145, issued June 6, provides that after June 9 a producer of bearings may not accept any purchase order for any of the sizes specified on an exhibit attached to the order, unless he is designated as an "authorized producer" of the size sought to be purchased.

It is suggested by WPB that customers requesting a producer to furnish a size of bearing formerly made by him, but which is not now permitted under the order, should be referred to another company designated as an "authorized producer" of such a size.

Other provisions

In case a producer has completed parts or completed bearings on hand, however, he may deliver these to purchasers. The order does not restrict producers from filling purchase orders received prior to June 10.

Another section of L-145 prohibits a company which manufactured a size of bearing for which it is not now designated as an "authorized producer" from disposing of the tools and equipment used by it in making such bearings. A company must keep these tools and equipment and preserve them in such condition that it can recommence production on one month's notice.

★ ★ ★

WPB prohibits diversion of farm equipment from farms

To assure delivery of essential equipment to the American farmer, WPB has ordered that products manufactured under its farm machinery and equipment program must actually reach the farm, and must not be diverted to industrial or other nonagricultural uses.

In Supplementary Limitation Order L-26-d, WPB makes it plain that its program is designed solely for production of essential machinery and equipment for farms, including such items as domestic water systems and garden tractors, which have been found to have been diverted in many instances to nonagricultural activities.

Critical materials cut for light bulbs; substitutes permit increase in output

The use of critical materials in the manufacture of electric light bulbs will be curtailed without curtailing the production of the light bulbs themselves, by an amendment to Limitation Order L-28 ·issued June 8.

To use substitutes

This will be made possible through the use of substitutes that will not affect the efficiency of the light bulbs.

The base, formerly made of solid brass, will be made of steel, plated with brass. Lamp leads, formerly made of a 50-50 combination of nickel and copper, will be made of iron wire plated with nickel and copper. Filament supports, formerly made of nickel and molybdenum, will be made of iron wire plated with nickel. · The filament itself will continue to be made of tungsten, since no satisfactory substitute has been found. The plating process will require only about a tenth as much of the critical metals as was used before.

The substitution provisions of the order will go into effect July 1, 1942.

Not only will there not be a curtailment in the production of lamp bulbs, but the amendment permits greater production than in 1940. During the 3-month period beginning July 1, 1942, and for each 3-month period thereafter, a manufacturer is permitted to produce bases for incandescent and fluorescent lamps at a rate of 125 percent of his production in 1940. In addition, he may exceed even that rate of production in one 3-month period if he will reduce his production during the succeeding 3 months accordingly.

Decorative lights banned

Between now and July 1 brass may be used in the manufacture of bases but it is restricted to 6⅔ percent of the amount of brass used for such purposes in 1940. This amounts to a rate of 80 percent of 1940 usage.

The amendment also prohibits the manufacture of Christmas tree, advertising and decorative or display lights. The original order reduced such production by 50 percent. The amendment eliminates such production entirely, effective June 1, 1942.

On and after June 15, no black-out lamps· may be produced except to fill orders rated higher than A-2.

The substitute provisions will not apply until September 6, 1942, to orders placed by or for the Army, Navy, or United States Maritime Commission.

To clear the deck for the use of the substitute material, no manufacturer is permitted to accept delivery of or produce lamp parts after June 15, 1942, that do not comply with the substitute provisions if such delivery or production will leave any of the presubstitute parts in his inventory after July 1.

★ ★ ★

Communications inventories

Restrictions on inventories in the radio and wire communications industries have been modified so that material for specific Army, Navy and other war projects may be stocked without interference with normal operating inventories, the Division of Industry Operations announced June 10.

This action was taken in interpretations of Preference Rating Orders P-129 and P-130.

Cosmetics makers urged to find substitutes

The toiletries and cosmetics branch urged manufacturers June 11 to seek substitutes for mannitol, sorbitol, and their derivatives, which are available only for orders bearing high priority ratings. In addition, it was emphasized that a tight supply situation also exists for wetting agents and emulsifiers, such as sulphonated coconut oil or lauryl alcohol.

★ ★ ★

Balsa under import control

Balsa wood was placed under import control June 10 by an Amendment to General Imports Order M-63, issued by the Director of Industry Operations. Effective immediately, no balsa wood may be imported except by certain governmental agencies, or with the express permission of WPB.

General Imports Order M-63 controls the import of a list of strategic materials. The June 10 amendment adds balsa wood to this list.

On July· 2, 1942, the import control will be broadened to include import of materials for civilian use as well as strategic materials. The amendment will be superseded by the amended order, which was issued on June 2, and takes effect July 2, 1942.

Cellophane use cut still further in rewritten order

Use of cellophane was further restricted June 8 by an amendment to Limitation Order L-20, issued by the Director of Industry Operations.

The order as amended covers cellophane · or other transparent cellulose sheets of 0.003 inch or less. The original order covered sheets of 0.005 inch or less. A new plastics conservation order is being drawn which will cover use of sheets over 0.003 inch in thickness. Further restrictions imposed by this amendment prohibit use of cellophane in window cartons, for carton overwraps, for packaging animal food, rubber nipples, and candy.

New restrictions added

The amendment rewrites the entire order, consolidates previous amendments, clarifies certain ambiguous provisions of the original order, and adds new restrictions to the use of cellophane.

While this amendment does rewrite the entire order, the following points are new:

1. Products covered by the order are those of 0.003 inch thickness or less;
2. "Cellulose caps or bands of any gage" are added to the definition of products covered by the order;
3. The prohibition against using cellophane is changed to read "no person shall use cellophane . . . for the packaging, sealing, or manufacture of the materials included in the following categories . . ." The word "sealing" is added to the previous wording;
4. Rubber nipples may not be packaged in cellophane;
5. Added to the list of prohibitions is "Candy products and chewing gum, except where used as a protection for the product itself";
6. Added to the list of prohibitions is "All animal foods . . ."; "All window cartons and overwraps where used as a protection for the carton rather than the product itself."

Also added in the amended order is provision for reporting by middlemen to producers, by the tenth of each month, the amount of cellophane sold by them to various industries during the preceding month. Also to be reported are Government orders, and those bearing a rating of A-10 or better, ·by industries.

★ ★ ★

Fluorescent lighting inventory

Manufacturers, assemblers, wholesalers, distributors, and retailers· of fluorescent lighting fixtures have been notified· that the date for filing their inventories with WPB has been advanced from June 5 to June 15. The action was made necessary by delays in the distribution of the report form, PD-499.

Uniforms sped by high rating on fabrics and other materials needed in manufacture

In order to make certain that officers of the Army, Navy, Marine Corps, and other War agencies will be able to obtain uniforms when they need them, the Director of Industry Operations has issued an order (P–131) granting a high priority rating for cloth and other materials needed for the manufacture of such garments.

Buttons and thread covered

The rating—A–1–i—is assigned to materials, such as cloth, buttons and thread to be used by a manufacturer in the production of uniforms, including shirts, overcoats, caps, ties, etc. The rating may be extended to the cloth manufacturer or other supplier to cover the materials furnished by a supplier to the manufacturer of officers' uniforms. The supplier, in turn, may extend the rating on all materials except metals.

Covers all types of fabrics used

The order applies to all types of fabrics used in the official uniforms of all the agencies covered by the order. Uniforms included are for the Army, Navy, Marine Corps, Coast Guard, United States Military and Naval Academy and Training School students, Maritime Commission, Coast and Geodetic Survey, Public Health Service, Women's Army Auxiliary Corps and any similar Navy organization, and the Army Specialist Corps.

On and after July 1, 1942, suppliers of buttons, zippers, grippers, fasteners, closures or findings made of metal may not apply the A–1–i rating provided under the order to obtain material used in the manufacture of metal closures and finders. Instead, they may apply for priority assistance to obtain such material on form PD–25A under the Production Requirements Plan.

JUTE ORDER AMENDED

General Conservation Order M–70 has been amended to exempt processors of jute covering, twine, and rope from the provisions in the original order requiring certification of bales on deliveries of such products. It was explained that the amendment corrects an error in the original order.

PROTECTIVE HELMETS

Permission to asemble and sell protective helmet parts which were in process on April 29, and to sell those helmets which have already been manufactured, has been granted by the Director of Industry Operations in an amendment to Limitation Order L–105.

The amendment (No. 1, effective June 5) will make available a substantial number of helmets which are either completed or semifabricated. Officials of the safety and technical equipment branch said that the sale of these helmets will help meet the demand which is not supplied by the OCD.

The finished helmets and parts already semifabricated cannot be readily used for purposes other than those for which they were designed.

The original order prohibited the production and sale of protective helmets, except on order by an Agency of the United States or by one of the other United Nations. Production from parts not fabricated at the time the order was originally issued remains subject to this restriction.

⊥ ⊥ ⊥

Willard named chief of toiletries, cosmetics branch

C. A. Willard, who has been acting chief of the toiletries and cosmetics branch for the past several weeks, has been named chief of the branch by Philip D. Reed, chief of the Bureau of Industry Branches.

Bristle order amended

Circumstances under which users of pigs' and hogs' bristles may buy and accept delivery of bristles to replace their inventory of finished products shipped on war orders are clarified in an amendment, No. 2, to General Preference Order M–51. The amendment was issued June 6 by the Director of Industry Operations.

This action is taken in response to requests from the industry for clarification of the regulations covering purchase of bristles. The amendment does not change the effect of the order, nor does it change the course of action required of bristle users.

Production of mattresses, pads containing iron or steel banned after September 1

The production of mattresses or pads containing iron or steel is prohibited after September 1 in Amendment 1 to Limitation Order L–49, issued June 8 by the Director of Industry Operations.

During July and August, a manufacturer of innerspring mattresses or pads may produce twice his average monthly production of such products in the 12 months ended June 30, 1941.

The order does not affect the manufacture of mattresses or pads filled with cotton, felt, or hair.

Other provisions

Effective June 8, no manufacturer of innerspring mattresses or pads may acquire any wire for the production of such products, except from the inventories of other manufacturers of innerspring units.

In addition, a manufacturer may not sell or deliver any of his inventory of iron or steel, except as follows:

For use by other manufacturers of bedsprings and mattresses; for use to fill orders bearing a preference rating of A–3 or higher; or for sale to the Defense Supplies Corporation, Metals Reserve Company, or any other Government purchasing agency. No restrictions are placed on the sale or delivery of any finished products a manufacturer has on hand or is permitted to manufacture under L–49.

★ ★ ★

ISTLE CURB TIGHTENED

Conservation Order M–138 has been amended to tighten restrictions on istle, a fiber grown in Mexico which is coming into increasing demand as a substitute for such fibers as jute and other cordage fibers formerly imported from the Far East.

Amendment No. 1 controls both istle waste and waste istle. The distinction is this: Waste istle results from preparing the fiber for use in istle products; istle waste results from the processing of the prepared fiber.

The amendment redefines "istle product" to include any product made from istle, alone or in combination with other materials.

The inventory provision has been modified to include a person who processes istle products, to give him the benefit of a 2 months' supply instead of the 1 month's supply allowed him under the original order.

Scientific laboratories not engaged in war work can obtain equipment for vital uses only

Because of the critical shortage of scientific equipment, university and other private laboratories engaged in research work unrelated to the production of materials, or in other research not directly connected with the war effort, will be unable to secure new laboratory equipment unless the particular use is approved by the Director of Industry Operations.

To save critical materials

This is the result of Limitation Order L-144, issued June 12. The order prohibits the sale and delivery of laboratory equipment except for certified essential uses in order to save highly critical materials and to make certain that such equipment will be available for vital war purposes.

Manufacturers will obtain the necessary amounts of critical materials for purposes permitted by the order by filing PD-25A applications under the Production Requirements Plan. Distributors, wholesalers, and jobbers needing priority assistance should file PD-1X forms with the Distributors Branch of the War Production Board.

★ ★ ★

U. S. may buy burlap stocks

Conservation Order M-47 (burlap) was amended June 12 to enable the Commodity Credit Corporation to purchase frozen stocks of burlap and make them available to growers to relieve a shortage of crop-covering material on the West coast.

★ ★ ★

Telephone equipment committee

Government presiding officer—Bruce H. McCurdy, chief, telephone section, communications branch.

Members:

Fred Clarke merchandise manager, Western Electric Co, 195 Broadway, New York, N. Y.; R. A. Gantt, vice president, International Telephone & Telegraph Co., New York, N. Y.; F. R. McBerty, president, North Electric Co., Galion, Ohio; M. K. McGrath, president, Kellogg switchboard & Supply Co., 6650 Cicero Avenue, Chicago, Ill.; W. L. Runzel, president, Runzel Cord & Wire Co., 4727 Montrose Avenue, Chicago, Ill.; A. F. Gibson, assistant treasurer, Stromberg-Carlson Telephone Manufacturing Co., 100 Carlson Road, Rochester, N. Y.; W. C. Hasselborn, president, Cook Electric Co., 2700 Southport Avenue, Chicago, Ill.; J. W. Shipman, vice president, Automatic Electric Co., 1000 West Van Buren St., Chicago, Ill.; R. W. Siemund, vice president, Leich Electric Co., 427 West Randolph St., Chicago, Ill.

CONSTRUCTION CLARIFIED

WPB on June 6 announced a series of interpretations of Conservation Order L-41, which was issued April 9 to place all construction under rigid control.

The order (WPB-831) made it necessary for builders to obtain authorization from WPB to begin residential construction costing $500 or more; agricultural construction costing $1,000 or more; or commercial and other construction costing $5,000 or more during any continuous 12-month period.

Authorized building outside quota

It was ruled that construction authorized by WPB does not have to be included in the cost quota allowed in the order. For instance, an owner specifically authorized by WPB to remodel an industrial plant, may still spend, in addition, up to $5,000—the limit allowed without authorization—during any 12-month period.

It also was ruled that where a building is used for two or more purposes, as defined in the order, it should be classified according to its predominant use.

Another interpretation provides that the estimated cost need not include the cost of used material, including equipment, which has been taken from a building and is to be used in other construction work, provided there is no change of ownership. It is not necessary, likewise, to include in the total cost estimate the cost of labor in incorporating such used material.

Cost of certain equipment included

The estimated cost of a project, under the interpretation, shall include the cost of certain equipment. These include articles, chattels or fixtures physically incorporated in the building and used as a part of the building. Also included are items that cannot be detached without materially injuring them or the construction.

The term "without change of design," as it applies to repair work permitted by the order, is interpreted to allow change in material or type of equipment if the architectural or structural plan is not substantially altered in effecting the change.

It was ruled that movement of earth—ditch digging, grading, etc.—where no material except earth or other unprocessed material is involved should not be included in the cost of the project.

Wood casket committee

Government presiding officer—Anthony F. Bisgood, section chief, consumers' durable goods branch.

Members:

L. S. Ashley, Northwestern Casket Co., Minneapolis, Minn.; Everett Halliday, New Castle Casket Co., New Castle, Ind.; John A. Dolan, Wellsville Casket Co., Wellsville, N. Y.; E. H. McCowen, Hardwood Casket Co., Cleveland, Tenn.; E. Lawrence Mory, Boyertown Burial Casket Co., Boyertown, Pa.; George D. Richards, Chicago Casket Co., Chicago, Ill.; H. L. Stein, National Casket Co., Boston, Mass.; J. T. Tidwell, Texas Coffin Co.; Waco, Tex.; John Bertelsen, Hollywood Casket Co., Hollywood, Calif.

Deliveries of mine machines made from rated materials limited to rated orders

Mining machinery produced from materials obtained under a preference rating cannot be delivered except on rated orders, the Division of Industry Operations ruled June 12.

Amendment No. 3 to Preference Rating Order P-56-a provides that in the future mining machinery made from material obtained on a preference rating shall be delivered by the producer only to an operator as defined in Preference Rating Order P-56 or P-58, or to a producer as defined in Preference Rating Order P-68 or P-73 and only to fill an order bearing a preference rating assigned under these orders.

The division also announced that material necessary for repair and maintenance of houses owned by a mining operator and used for the housing of miners cannot receive as high a preference rating as material necessary for the actual operation of the mine.

Interpretation No. 1 to Preference Rating Order P-56, as amended, provides that an A-10 rating is available for such repair and maintenance material. Material necessary for operation has an A-8 rating.

★ ★ ★

Restriction removed from metal used in wooden pails, tubs

Limitation Order L-30 was amended June 12 to encourage a return to the wooden pail and tub.

The original order required a 30 percent reduction in the use of iron and steel in the manufacture of pails and tubs. This restriction was aimed chiefly at metal pails and tubs but its effect was to cut retail production by WPB.

Amendment No. 3, issued June 12, removes from the restrictions of the order any pail or tub which contains metal only in hoops, bails, ears, and handles, provided the total weight of this metal does not exceed 15 percent of the weight of the article.

Metal pails and tubs may be produced, under the limits of the original order, until the end of June. But the unrestricted production of wooden pails and tubs is expected to result in a return to the wooden article.

The June 12 amendment also affects carpet sweepers, curtain rods and fixtures, and drapery attachments.

Type of steel limited for use in hand service tools; orders restricted to A–10, higher

General Preference Order E–6, issued June 12, limits the type of steel which may be used in producing hand service tools and also limits the orders which producers of such tools may fill.

Included among the hand service tools covered by the order are chisels, hammers, snips, pliers, punches, screwdrivers, and wrenches. The order provides that such tools may not be manufactured out of any alloy steel except those series specifically designated in an exhibit attached to the order.

It was provided, however, that producers who, prior to June 12, had already received alloy steel of a series not listed are permitted to use it up.

Quota-exempt processing of cocoa butter, powder clarified

Interpretation 1 to Conservation Order M–145 was issued June 9 by the Director of Industry Operations to prevent excessive quota-exempt processings of cocoa beans to fill Army, Navy, and other quota-exempt orders requiring cocoa butter and cocoa powder.

The June 9 interpretation makes it clear that when a processor produces cocoa butter, for example, to fill an order for the Army, Navy, or other quota-exempt persons or agencies, he must give consideration to the cocoa powder produced in the same processing operations.

While he may use that powder to fill any type of order, if subsequent quota-exempt orders requiring the same amount of powder, or less, are received, he may not again process quota-exempt beans to supply that powder.

The same is true in the reverse type of situation when a quota-exempt order requires cocoa powder.

★ ★ ★

Deliveries of power and steam equipment broadened

Limitation Order L–117 has been amended to permit the production, sale, and delivery of heavy power and steam equipment not provided for in the original order. Amendment No. 2, just issued, permits deliveries on ratings of A–9 or higher assigned by PD–2, PD–4, PD–5, P5–B, and PD–25A certificates.

New industry advisory committees

The Bureau of Industry Advisory Committees, WPB, has announced the formation of the following new industry advisory committees:

ASPHALT ROOFING

Government presiding officer—John L. Haynes, chief, building materials branch.

Members:

C. O. Brown, Dixie Asphalt Products Corporation, Savannah, Ga.; Otto Cervenka, Globe Roofing Products Co., Whiting, Ind.; John J. Flood, American & Asphalt Roof Corporation, Kansas City, Mo.; Lloyd A. Fry, Lloyd A. Fry Roofing Co., Chicago, Ill.; T. H. Kashuba, T. K. Roofing Manufacturer Co., Chester, W. Va.; W. H. Lowe, Paraffine Companies, Inc., San Francisco, Calif.; Benjamin H. Roberts, Bird & Son, Inc., E. Walpole, Mass.; P. C. Rowe, The Flintkote Co., New York, N. Y.; R. J. Tobin, Tilo Roofing Co., Inc., Stratford, Conn.; A. L. Wall, Weaver-Wall Co., Cleveland, Ohio.; D. D. Hamilton, Koppers Co., Pittsburgh, Pa.; S. P. Moffit, The Ruberoid Co., New York, N. Y.

BISCUIT, CRACKER, AND PRETZEL SUB-COMMITTEE OF BAKING INDUSTRY

Government presiding officer—John T. McCarthy, chief, bread and bakery products section, food branch.

Members:

George Burry, president, Burry Biscuit Co., Elizabeth, N. J.; Stuart Johnston, vice president, Robert A. Johnston Co., Milwaukee, Wis.; K. F. MacLellan, president, United Biscuit Co., Chicago, Ill.; Hanford Main, president, Loose-Wiles Biscuit Co., Long Island City, N. Y.; Victor F. Miller, president, Miller-Parrot Co., Terre Haute, Ind.; Charles F. Montgomery, vice president, National Biscuit Co., New York, N. Y.; A. R. Petrie, vice president, H. W. Clark Biscuit Co., N. Adams, Mass.; H. G. Schneider, president, Laurel Biscuit Co., Dayton, Ohio; Gross Williams, president, Consolidated Biscuit Co., Chicago, Ill.

COPPER PRODUCERS

Presiding Officer—Harry O. King, chief of the copper branch.

Members:

K. C. Brownell, vice president, American Smelting & Refining Co., 120 Broadway, New York City; A. E. Petermann, Calumet & Hecla Consolidated Copper Co., Calumet, Mich.; Robert E. Dwyer, vice president, Anaconda Copper Mining Co., 25 Broadway, New York City; J. F. McCelland, vice president, Phelps Dodge Corporation, 40 Wall Street, New York, N. Y.; A. J. McNab, vice president, Magma Copper Co., 14 Wall Street, New York, N. Y.; Carl T. Ulrich, vice president, Kennecott Copper Corporation, 120 Broadway, New York City; B. N. Zimmer, vice president, American Metal Co., 61 Broadway, New York, N. Y.

DAIRY EQUIPMENT AND MACHINERY MANUFACTURERS

Government presiding officer—L. S. Greenleaf, Jr., chief of the special industrial machinery branch.

Members:

E. Roy Alling, Rice & Adams, Buffalo, N. Y.; John Colony, Manton-Gaulin Mfg. Co., Everett, Mass.; E. C. Damrow, Damrow Brothers,

Fond du Lac, Wis.; John W. Ladd, Cherry-Burrell Corporation, Chicago, Ill.; Harry L. Miller, Chester Dairy Supply Mfg. Co., Chester, Pa.; Timothy Mojonnier, Mojonnier Brothers, Chicago, Ill.; Gilbert R. Olsen, General Dairy Equipment Co., Minneapolis, Minn.; George W. Putnam, Creamery Package Co., Chicago, Ill.; Roland F. Smith, Waukesha Foundry, Waukesha, Wis.; H. J. Walker, Thomas D. McHale, Manufacturing Co., Los Angeles, Calif.

HAND SAWS

Government presiding officer—John L. Haynes, chief, building materials branch.

Members:

G. W. Dunnington, E. C. Atkins & Co., Indianapolis, Ind.; S. Horace Disston, Henry Disston & Sons, Inc., Tacony, Philadelphia, Pa.; F. G. Acomb, Pennsylvania Saw Corporation, York, Pa.; E. A. Todd, Simonds Saw & Steel Co., Fitchburg, Mass.; H. J. Bradbury, Ohlen Bishop Mfr. Co., Columbus, Ohio; Walter C. Hecker, Curtis Saw Division of Curtis Manufacturing Co., St. Louis, Mo.; James J. Dougherty, Central Hardware Co., Philadelphia, Pa.

HIGH PRESSURE STEEL GAS CYLINDER MANUFACTURERS

Government presiding officer—Charles Dailey, chief, steel drums and tight cooperage section, containers branch.

Members:

Wilbert Wear, Harrisburg Steel Corporation, Harrisburg, Pa.; G. R. Hanks, Taylor-Wharton Iron & Steel Co., Easton, Pa.; H. E. Passmore, National Tube Co., Pittsburgh, Pa.; H. O. Brumder, Pressed Steel Tank Co., Milwaukee, Wis.; Walter H. Freygang, Walter Kidde & Co., New York, N. Y.; Edward E. O'Neill, American LaFrance-Foamite Corporation, Elmira, N. Y.

PORCELAIN ENAMELED UTENSILS

Government presiding officer—Anthony F. Bisgood, section chief, consumers' durable goods branch.

Members:

F. S. Barnshaw, U. S. Stamping Co.; Moundsville, W. Va.; Ralph M. Fawcett, Republic Stamping & Enameling Co., Canton, Ohio; D. S. Hunter, Enameled Utensil Mfrs. Council, Cleveland, Ohio; Frank E. Jones, The Jones Metal Products Co., West Lafayette, Ohio; W. F. Lewis, Lisk Manufacturing Co., Canandaigua, N. Y.; W. J. Vollrath, Polar Ware Co., Sheboygan, Wis.

TIGHT COOPERAGE

Government presiding officer—Charles Dailey, chief, steel drums and tight cooperage section, containers branch.

Committee members are:

Harold R. Clark, Allied Barrel Corporation, Oil City, Pa.; W. R. Foley, Chickasaw Wood Products Co., Memphis, Tenn.; Walter O. Johnson, T. Johnson Co., Inc., Chicago, Ill.; Isadore Levine, H. Levine Cooperage Co., Los Angeles, Calif.; Pat Lynn, Ozark Gateway Cooperage Co., Joplin, Mo.; A. L. Nelson, Jr., St. Louis Cooperage Co., St. Louis, Mo.; Paul M. Ripley, Brooklyn Cooperage Co., New York, N. Y.; L. R. Steidel, J. H. Hamlen & Son, Little Rock, Ark.; William G. Tyler, The Kimball Tyler Co., Baltimore, Md.; M. Edward Verdi, Verdi Brothers Cooperage Co., North Bergen, N. J.; W. I. Wymond, Chess & Wymond, Inc., Louisville, Ky.

CIVILIAN SUPPLY . .

Changes to be felt soon in food, clothing, transportation and housing, Weiner warns

Far-reaching changes in the lives and habits of every citizen during the next few months were forecast June 8 by Joseph L. Weiner, deputy director of the Division of Civilian Supply, in a statement describing how the war economy must reach into every home in the Nation.

Food, clothing, transportation, and housing are the four principal fields in which changes have developed and in which even greater changes may be expected, Mr. Weiner said.

Specialists in the division have been working for many months to determine the needs of the civilian population and to correlate these needs with the exigencies of a war economy. Mr. Weiner's statement, based on these studies, follows in part:

FOOD

It may be said categorically that there is no danger that this country will lack a sufficient supply of staples, or that the American diet will lack its vital elements.

But on the other hand, while we can be sure of a balanced, nourishing diet, it is also clear that some of our eating habits may have to be revised.

For example, sugar is being rationed. That cuts down our supply of sweets. Coffee and tea are not as freely available as they used to be, because of the shipping situation. The same problem comes up in the case of bananas. Other things which must be imported may be lacking from our customary menus.

Some of our fishing areas are being closed by the war, or are concentrating on Army, Navy, and Lend-Lease requirements, and this may at times affect the supply of fish. And naturally the job of sending our allies food, such as pork, imposes an increased demand on the supply, although, as is generally known, efforts are being made to increase essential crops and farm products.

Americans can help greatly in this situation in a number of ways.

First, don't hoard. Don't overbuy. This is what the enemy wants people to do.

Second, don't waste food.

Third, eat fresh fruits and vegetables as much as possible, so as to diminish the tin requirements for tin cans.

Fourth, try to get locally grown vegetables, so as to diminish the requirements for food transportation.

Fifth, eat substitutes for fish and pork. There are plenty available.

CLOTHING

It appears now that the rationing of clothing can be avoided this year.

But there are some other changes that can be expected.

It appears that the public will have to wear more cotton, because of the wool situation. It appears also that the military demand for wool will bring about additional minor style changes. Cloth manufacturers will have to blend wool with other materials in order to conserve, but we still can be sure that we will be well clothed.

The division is now making a survey of the wool, cotton, and rayon situations to see exactly what the situation is from the civilian point of view, and so that we will be able to anticipate any difficulties in good time.

Leather is another problem, for the demands of our armed forces for shoes increase rapidly. There are plenty of shoes in the stores, so there is nothing in the leather picture to get excited about now. But it is a problem, and future developments may very well affect our civilian supply.

TRANSPORTATION

Everyone is familiar with the gasoline shortage. Many people, however, do not recognize that there is also a shortage of fuel oil, largely caused by transportation difficulties. This shortage will be felt most keenly in Eastern States. We are facing a serious problem in our efforts to find means of making available fuel oil to keep our factories running and our houses warm next winter. We have just so much transportation equipment and no more. Everyone who can possibly do so ought to convert now from oil-burning heating apparatus to coal-burning appliances. Also we should lay in our supplies of coal now in order to take some of the strain off our transportation facilities this fall.

Transportation difficulties undoubtedly will have a broad effect upon our daily lives. There will be less social life in the evening unless it is confined to the neighborhood. Mr. and Mrs. America will have to get acquainted with their neighbors, trade at their neighborhood stores, attend their neighborhood movies, accept a greatly curtailed variety of goods and dispense with the customary desire for a change of scenery.

The division has been authorized by the War Production Board to make a study of all the energy resources of the country—electric power, natural gas, manufactured gas, etc. It is becoming more necessary daily to divert our fuel and power from nonessential to essential uses. This may mean that we will have to live in a somewhat darker world. Main Street may lose its glow of electricity.

HOUSING

We will have to reexamine the housing situation in order to make certain that all available space in so-called critical defense areas is being utilized. The demands of the war program upon our output of steel are going to make it impossible for us to build homes in areas where adequate housing facilities already exist, but have not been put to work because of reluctance on someone's part to make them available. Compulsory billeting of war workers has been resorted to in England. In that country, unoccupied houses have been commandeered. These 2 methods furnish means of solving housing problems, but I hope they will not have to be adopted here.

Most war workers are not in a position to buy a home, either because their incomes are not sufficient or because they may have to be moved at any time. Therefore, I believe we should discourage privately financed home construction for sale, and concentrate our priority assistance on those projects that will be made available for rental to war workers.

This represents only a general picture of what the future holds in store for us. The Division of Civilian Supply is charged with the responsibility of seeing to it that materials left over after the demands of the war program have been met are allocated for various civilian operations in the order of their importance to our daily lives. The division will continue to act as the guardian of our civilian economy.

"YOU KNOW, DEAR....SOMETIMES I WISH WE'D GONE EASY ON OUR TIRES BACK IN 1942!"

Dr. Seuss

Drawn for Division of Information, O. E. M.

Intercity bus curb not meant for Jones Beach vacationists

An order of the ODT calling for elimination of unnecessary intercity bus services has no direct application to transportation of recreation seekers to Jones Beach, near New York, ODT Director Eastman made plain June 11.

This policy was set forth in a telegram from Mr. Eastman to Robert Moses, president of the Long Island State Park Commission and the Jones Beach State Parkway Authority, who had asked for an interpretation of the intercity bus order, General Order ODT No. 11.

The order does not apply to service

This cartoon was drawn especially for OEM by Dr. Seuss. This notice constitutes full permission to reprint the drawing. Engravings may be direct from this reproduction, or three-column mats will be furnished on application to Distribution Section, Division of Information, Office for Emergency Management, Washington, D. C. Refer to V–24.

extending less than 15 air miles beyond the corporate limits of a city or on which the average fare is 35 cents or less. Jones Beach is less than 15 air miles from the outer boundaries of New York. The order is effective July 1.

ODT will take monthly sampling to forecast transport needs

As an aid to bringing about greater utilization of existing freight transportation facilities, the Office of Defense Transportation has initiated a plan designed to provide monthly an accurate forecast of the Nation's freight equipment requirements.

ODT Director Eastman has asked a large representative group of manufacturers, producers and distributors to submit, beginning June 15, an advance monthly estimate of traffic movement from their establishments. The information, to be provided on a special form, will include the commodity to be shipped.

TRANSPORTATION . . .

Intercity bus lines throughout Nation made subject to pooling and limitations

A general order placing intercity bus operations under wartime regulations throughout the country was issued June 9 by the Office of Defense Transportation.

The order becomes effective July 1.

Intercity service, as defined by the order, does not include bus runs within 15 miles of the limits of a city, nor schedules on which the average fare is 35 cents or less.

Five requirements

Operators of buses used in intercity service are required to:

1. Discontinue all limited or express service.

2. Discontinue schedules which do not come up to certain efficiency standards as determined by the average load.

3. Discontinue service to places of amusement.

4. Pool competitive services which cover the same or closely parallel routes.

5. Freeze present routes.

Round-trip schedules operated primarily for the purpose of transporting workers to and from their jobs are not subject to the regulations, and an exception also is made for buses serving military and naval establishments.

Less-used routes discontinued

The order (General Order ODT No. 11) prohibits the operation of more than one round-trip schedule a day over any route where experience shows that the average load in both directions will be less than 40 percent of the seating capacity in any month.

Operators are required to keep records of passenger-miles and seat-miles and report to the ODT any round-trip schedule which fails to meet these requirements.

Since local bus service involves constantly changing loads, the order requires that the average load for the entire journey be used as a basis for determining the degree of efficiency of the operation.

Service for amusements banned

A bus might start out fully loaded, the ODT explained, and still fail to meet the 40-percent-average-load requirement when it had completed its round trip.

Intercity bus service, as defined by the order, may not be operated after July 1 "for the primary purpose of supplying transportation to or from a golf course, athletic field, race track, theater, dancing pavilion, or other place conducted primarily for the purpose of amusement or entertainment."

Express service was ordered discontinued, the ODT said, to release buses for needed local service.

Extensions must be approved

The order further provides that no bus route may be extended after July 1 without special permission of the ODT.

Operators of competing bus lines are required to make joint plans for maximum utilization of equipment through pooling of services, staggering of schedules, exchange of operating rights, or other methods. These plans, or statements giving the reasons why such plans have not been agreed upon, must be submitted to the ODT by July 30.

Other special orders coming

Two special orders based on operators' plans already have been issued by the ODT, affecting four bus lines operating between New York and Washington and two bus lines operating in the West.

Other special orders of this type are forthcoming.

★ ★

Paper work lightened in moving goods to ports

Revised instructions to shippers governing movement of goods into United States ports for offshore shipment have been issued by the Office of Defense Transportation, it was announced June 9.

Shippers now are not required to apply directly to the War Shipping Administration or the British Ministry of War Transport for permission to move export goods through the ports.

No other major change has been made in the regulations, which became effective June 1.

Many miles' savings expected from 2 intercity bus orders

The ODT June 9 issued two more special orders in its Nation-wide program for more efficient operation of intercity bus lines.

Special Order ODT No. B–3 governs operations of the Pacific Greyhound Lines, the Santa Fe Trail Transportation Co., and the Santa Fe Transportation Co. between Los Angeles, Calif., and Albuquerque, N. Mex. This order becomes effective July 1.

Based on companies' plans

Special Order ODT No. B–4, effective June 16, governs operations of the Pacific Greyhound Lines and the Burlington Transportation Co. between San Francisco, Calif., and Salt Lake City, Utah.

Both orders are based on plans submitted by the companies affected. It is expected that the orders will result in a total saving of 186,840 scheduled bus miles a month.

The companies are required to honor each other's tickets between all points where equal fares apply, eliminate duplicating departure times, and share depot and ticket agency facilities wherever practicable.

Each company, moreover, is required to eliminate one daily round-trip run on each route.

Five motor transport field managers named

Appointment of five more field office managers in the division of motor transport, ODT, was announced June 8 by ODT Director Eastman.

The division will have a total of 51 field offices. Managers of 43 now have been appointed.

The five new managers and the cities where they will make their headquarters are:

Billings, Mont.—Emmett Fogarty, of Butte, former engineer for the Montana Railroad Commission.

Milwaukee, Wis.—Russell R. Lynch, of Milwaukee, formerly on the staff of the Wisconsin Public Service Commission.

Oklahoma City, Okla.—William W. Warren, of Oklahoma City, former manager of the Warren Transportation & Storage Co.

Salt Lake City, Utah.—Richard W. Candland, of Salt Lake City, former secretary and general manager of the Utah Motor Carriers Association.

Wichita, Kans.—W. R. Bartling, of Wichita, former traffic manager of the Universal Motor Oils & Fuels Co.

ODT acts to ease burden on workers in plans for truck, tire conservation

The Office of Defense Transportation on June 6 issued a five-point statement of policy to be used by industry and labor as a guide in developing programs for conservation of trucks and tires in accordance with ODT orders.

Text of the statement

Several disputes between employers and employees have arisen over methods for applying Office of Defense Transportation orders for conservation of trucks and tires. These disputes are hampering the prompt and effective application of these orders.

In view of this, the Office of Defense Transportation deems it necessary to emphasize that its regulations are intended solely to save vitally needed rubber and rolling stock.

In drawing up specific plans for compliance with ODT orders carriers are expected to cooperate with their employees where dislocation of employment is likely to be involved or where existing labor agreements are affected.

The Office of Defense Transportation is not endorsing any particular plan or plans. Its primary concern is that conservation goals are achieved and that legal requirements are not violated.

In order to hold labor controversies to a minimum, to insure fair treatment of employees and to achieve necessary conservation goals without delay, the ODT urges that in the event of labor controversies the following principles be applied in arriving at a settlement:

1. All conservation plans must comply fully with the terms of the applicable order.
2. As between feasible alternative plans, either of which will result in compliance, that plan should be adopted which will result in the least burden on employees.
3. Savings directly resulting from the application of an order should be used to afford employees reasonable protection against losses of earnings and jobs.
4. Savings remaining after such provision has been made for employees should be passed on to consumers in the form of lower prices.
5. Conservation plans instituted to comply with ODT orders should be limited to the duration of the emergency.

GASOLINE RATIONING FOR TRUCKS, BUSES

Regulations of the Office of Defense Transportation will control the amount of rations to be issued trucks, buses, and Government-operated cars under the new coupon plan for gasoline rationing which the OPA will put into effect on the East Coast next month.

The rationing plan, itself, will not restrict operations of these vehicles, OPA announced June 7. But they will not receive gasoline than will be required for carrying out the operations permitted by ODT.

Trucks, buses, and certain passenger car types operated for commercial or governmental purposes, will apply for S coupon books. These applications will be filed with a local rationing board, or, if the vehicle is operated under an Interstate Commerce Commission license, at a local office of the Office of Defense Transportation.

Must report 3-month needs

The applications will require specific information on mileage requirements for a period of three months. All claims for mileage set out in this application must be strictly in accordance with the ODT regulations.

The S category, OPA explained, will include the following types of passenger cars: (1) taxis, jitneys, and cars for hire; (2) cars owned by Federal, State, local, or foreign governments; (3) cars held by dealers for resale.

··· ·· ···

Vacation-at-home a patriotic gesture, says McCarthy

While no restrictions on individual railroad or bus travel now exist, the ODT feels that planning a vacation close to home this year will not only relieve public transportation facilities, but will be a patriotic gesture.

The possibilities of such a holiday are discussed in an article by Henry F. McCarthy, director of ODT's division of traffic movement, appearing in the current issue of *Public Safety* magazine.

The vacation-at-home idea is stressed by Mr. McCarthy who says: "Joseph B. Eastman, Director of the Office of Defense Transportation, concurs with a number of high Government executives in the belief that a vacation planned at home this year is really a highly patriotic vacation. . . ."

Most milk trucks to be out of use in less than 2 years unless conserved, says ODT

Most of the country's milk trucks will be off the streets in less than 2 years as a result of the rubber shortage unless effective programs for conservation of equipment are instituted without delay, ODT asserted June 10.

Survey reveals need

That long-range conservation of tires and trucks in the milk distribution industry is needed, the ODT said, is indicated in a report prepared by the Milk Industry Foundation on the basis of data collected by the International Association of Milk Dealers.

The survey, requested by the ODT, covered 389 milk distributing industries in all parts of the country.

206 say 1 year at normal rate

Two hundred and six dealers and dairymen advised the association that they could continue to make retail deliveries for a year, at the most, if no conservation programs were put into effect.

Many of them said they could continue to operate no longer than 6 months without cutting down on the use of equipment.

Virtually every dealer questioned said his retail delivery service would have to end within 2 years if continued on the normal basis.

A majority of the dealers questioned either had instituted conservation programs or were drawing them up at the time the survey was made.

154 on every-other-day basis

One hundred and fifty-four of the 389 dairymen had put their deliveries on an every-other-day basis.

The plans in process of adoption when the survey was made also included elimination of Sunday deliveries, discontinuance of call-backs, making of collections in conjunction with deliveries, and conversion to horse-drawn vehicles.

A few dealers combined deliveries with other dealers, and a small percentage of them consolidated routes and put two men on the trucks.

The ODT emphasized, in disclosing results of the survey, that the situation confronting the milk distribution industry is symptomatic of the entire local delivery problem.

PRODUCTION DRIVE . . .

Individual awards established for workers devising ways to produce more and better

A plan of individual awards to workmen who devise means for more or better war production was announced June 15 at War Production Drive Headquarters.

Three awards are planned. They are restricted to plants with voluntary labor-management committees organized in accordance with the plan put forth by the WPB.

First award

The first award is the "Award of Individual Production Merit," which plant committees are authorized to grant.

This may be given to any workman after the plant committee decides that his suggestion improves quality or production or conserves a critical material or in other tangible ways increases the effectiveness of the war production of the plant.

The award will be attested in a document signed by labor and management chairmen of the War Production Drive committee within the plant. Should the same worker submit additional suggestions worthy of the same award, additional seals will be attached to the award.

For outstanding suggestions

The second award is the "Certificate of Individual Production Merit." This will be awarded by War Production Drive Headquarters and it will be granted to those making outstanding suggestions.

War Production Drive Headquarters will require that the suggestion first be adopted in the plant and that the labor-management committee submit a complete report of its adoption, including full facts bearing on the actual results coming from the suggestion. The suggestion will then be carefully studied and a certificate be awarded. The certificate will be signed by a representative of the War Production Board.

Third and highest award

The third and highest award will be the "Citation of Individual Production Merit," which will be awarded to the maker of a suggestion that will have an outstanding effect on the entire war effort.

The citation will be granted only after a suggestion has been found worthy of the distinction by a technical committee of the War Production Board. Donald M. Nelson, WPB Chairman, will sign the citation. A distinctive emblem in addition to a certificate will go to the originator of the idea.

The awards were set up at the direction of Mr. Nelson, who wrote:

"Our Army and Navy have systems of commending merit of high order in the line of duty. . There is also merit of a high order on the production line in this war. I propose that the Production Soldier shall also be recognized for meritorious service to his country. . . ."

Importance of men on production line

The awards constitute a recognition of the importance of suggestions from men on the production line. From the first, these have played a large part in the great increase in American war production. In announcing the award plan June 15, the War Production Drive Headquarters statement said:

Grand plans alone are not going to win this war for our side. It will require also the sum of millions; of one-man assignments successfully carried out by the men and women at the bench, at the machine, and on the assembly lines—by individual Americans, each knowing the proper technique of his or her job. It is a trait of American character that, no matter what the job, the American war production worker is not merely putting in time in order to make a full pay week but also studying the job with an eye to turning out just a little better piece than the one before—and a little faster, too, if possible.

Suggestions plans differ

Suggestion plans differ from plant to plant. One of the most successful systems has included the distribution of suggestion forms, which are numbered and which have a corresponding number on a stub. Men with suggestions, are asked to submit them anonymously and to retain the stub.

How to handle bargaining issues

In other plants, committees have found that the psychological value of permitting a worker to sign his suggestion is more effective than the anonymity. War Production Drive Headquarters does not recommend one plan over the other but does recommend that all suggestions be promptly acknowledged by the local committees. It adds one other strong recommendation:

In such cases where the nature of the suggestion deals with matters which come within the jurisdiction of the collective bargaining machinery of the plant and of other agencies established by law, the plant labor-management War Production Drive committee, or its designated subcommittee, will refer such suggestions to the proper agency.

Ohio plant breaks production records three months running

Fulfilling a pledge to Donald M. Nelson, WPB Chairman, men in the Hamilton, Ohio, plant of the American Rolling Mill Co. have broken production records for the third successive month.

C. R. Hook, president of the company, forwarded to Mr. Nelson a report from L. F. Reinartz, division manager, showing that a final compilation of production figures from the Hamilton plant disclosed an output of 41,099 tons for the month of May.

Beats all-time high first month

A labor-management committee was formed at Hamilton in March immediately after Mr. Nelson issued the first call for such a committee. The committee launched a campaign with such success that in the first month the plant broke the all-time American Rolling Mill record with a tonnage of 38,141. At the end of the month, Ora Clark, chairman of the labor-management committee, telegraphed Mr. Nelson that the committee was not satisfied with this record and would try to beat it in April.

In April the plant produced 38,785 tons. Again the committee sent its promise of a new record.

★ ★ ★

New York plant reports 14 percent jump in 1 month

War Production jumped 14 percent in 1 month under the stimulus of a War Production Drive, the labor-management committee of the Symington-Gould Corporation of Rochester, N. Y., reported to War Production Drive Headquarters.

Far from being satisfied with this achievement, the committee has launched a campaign to increase production 30 percent over the present output. A large production chart will be unveiled to start the campaign.

The unveiling of the production chart will be attended by considerable ceremony. A large number of officials and civic leaders have been invited to participate. A recorded speech by Donald M. Nelson, chairman of the War Production Board, will be heard and Ray Millholland, representative of the WPB, will make an address.

Committee named to supervise war work in railroad shops

Formation of a committee composed of representatives of railroad employers, railroad employees, and the Government to supervise the performance of war production work in railroad shops was announced June 12 by ODT Director, Eastman.

Under railroad labor standards

The committee was named as the result of a recent agreement between railroad management and representatives of shop craft and clerical employees to produce war materials in railroad shops under the labor standards provided for in existing labor contracts.

To make it possible for the railroads to produce war work under railroad labor standards, exemption has been obtained for the railroad companies from the application of the Walsh-Healy Act and the hours provisions of the Fair Labor Standards Act.

Otto S. Beyer, director of the ODT's division of transport personnel, heads the newly-formed committee. Other members are:

George A. Landry, chief of the staff service branch, Production Division, WPB; Andrew Stevenson, chief of the transportation branch, Division of Industry Operations, WPB; M. W. Clement, president, Pennsylvania Railroad; W. M. Jeffers, president, Union Pacific Railroad; Ernest E. Norris, president, Southern Railway; B. M. Jewell, president, Railway Employes' Department, AFL; F. H. Knight, general president, Brotherhood of Railway Carmen of America; H. J. Carr, vice president, International Association of Machinists.

George M. Harrison, grand president of the Brotherhood of Railway and Steamship Clerks, Freight Handlers, Express and Station Employes, will serve as an alternate for one or the other labor members when there is a matter up which affects his organization.　●

Mr. Beyer said that railroad officials are now working with representatives of the War Production Board, and with agencies engaged in contracting for war materials, on the types of war goods that railroad shops can produce.

※　※　※

Defense housing critical areas

The WPB has added 10 new areas to the Defense Housing Critical Area list.

They are:

Rosiclaire, Ill., Decatur, Ind., Richmond, Ind., Louisiana Ordnance Works. Doyline, La., Saulte Ste. Marie, Mich., Tonopah, Nev., New Castle, Pa., McGregor, Tex., Elkton, Va., and New Martinsville, W. Va.

FARM WOMEN PERFORM VITAL WAR SERVICE, SAYS WICKARD

"If we are going to meet our farm production goals, we will have to depend more and more on the women," Secretary of Agriculture Claude R. Wickard declared in a radio broadcast June 5 on the subject 'Farm Women Are War Workers.

"Already there are plans," he said, "for getting groups of city women and high-school boys and girls to help out on the farms. This is a fine thing. But for getting most of the steady, day-to-day work done, farm families will have to depend on themselves. That means more work than ever for farm women."

⋅　⋅　⋅

Gavit named general counsel of War Manpower Commission

War Manpower Commission Chairman Paul V. McNutt announced June 11 the appointment of Bernard Campbell Gavit, dean of the School of Law, Indiana University, as General Counsel of the War Manpower Commission.

⋅　⋅　⋅

Railroad executives' committee to work with ODT on manpower

A committee of railroad executives has been named by the Association of American Railroads to work with the ODT division of transport personnel on railroad manpower problems, ODT Director Eastman said June 11.

The committee, headed by J. H. Parmalee, director of the A. A. R.'s Bureau of Railway Economics, was appointed following a series of conferences between ODT and the association.

The unused reserve of skilled railroad employees is now so small that railroads must look to new sources of manpower, Mr. Eastman said. Expansion of recruiting and training programs, and more effective utilization of the existing labor force is necessary in order to meet this situation.

Besides Mr. Parmalee the other members of the A. A. R. committee are:

H. A. Debutts, vice president (operating), Southern Railway; H. A. Enochs, chief of personnel, Pennsylvania Railroad; W. H. Flynn, general superintendent of motive power and rolling stock, New York Central; John P. Morris, general mechanical assistant, Atchison, Topeka & Santa Fe; J. B. Parrish, assistant vice president, Chesapeake & Ohio; C. R. Young, personnel manager, Illinois Central System.

6-man group to pass on labor production problems

Appointment of a six-man policy committee made up of three high officials from each of the major labor organizations was announced June 9 by Wendell Lund, Director of the WPB's Labor Production Division.

To determine major policies

The Labor Production Division's policy committee, Lund said, will determine major questions of production policy with him. The committee will pass on questions of organization as well as policies and will have contact through its chairman, Mr. Lund, with Chairman Nelson and with the other branches of the War Production Board.

The policy committee held its organization meeting last week with Mr. Lund and will meet frequently to discuss current and future problems relating to labor's participation in the war effort.

"No major policies will be made or changed by my division except with prior consultation and agreement of this committee," Lund said. "This is a representative group of the highest officials of the American Federation of Labor and the Congress of Industrial Organizations. President Green and President Murray have approved this plan and they also will be consulted by me and by the committee on major problems."

The members of the committee follow.

Representing the American Federation of Labor:

Frank P. Fenton, director of organization, A. F. L., Washington, D. C.; John P. Frey, president, Metal Trades Department, A. F. L., Washington, D. C.; and George Masterton, president, United Association of Journeymen Plumbers and Steamfitters, A. F. L., Washington, D. C.

Representing Congress of Industrial Organizations:

Clinton S. Golden, assistant to the president, United Steel Workers of America, C. I. O., Pittsburgh, Pa.; John Green, president, Industrial Union of Marine and Shipbuilding Workers of America, C. I. O., Camden, N. J.; and Walter P. Reuther, member of International Executive Board, United Automobile, Aircraft, and Agricultural Implement Workers of America, C. I. O., Detroit, Mich.

⋅　⋅　⋅

Coal prices for railroad

Permission to continue certain sales of bituminous coal to the New York, New Haven & Hartford Railroad at maximum prices established for commercial uses, when the fuel is used by the railroad for generating electricity, was granted by Price Administrator Henderson June 7.

MANPOWER . . .

Manpower policy committee appointed to guide commission in major issues

The management-labor policy committee of the War Manpower Commission, to be composed of seven national labor leaders and seven leaders of war production and transportation management was set up June 9 by Commission Chairman Paul V. McNutt.

The manpower policy committee held its first meeting June 9, to discuss basic policies and immediate problems. Meetings are planned to be held weekly, on Tuesdays. The commission meets on Wednesdays.

Chairman McNutt announced that the policy committee, as well as the commission itself, would be consulted on all major questions.

The committee was created by Order No. 1 issued by Mr. McNutt as chairman of the commission.

To recommend and initiate policies

The order authorizes the committee "to consider and recommend to the chairman matters of major policy concerning the activities and responsibilities of the commission.

The order also directs the committee to make studies on its own motion, and to initiate the formulation of manpower policies, in addition to considering policies referred to it by the chairman.

One representative of railroad labor and one of railroad management, as well as three C. I. O. and three A. F. L. officials, plus six war production management executives, will make up the committee.

"The War Manpower Commission has been directed by the President to assure the most effective mobilization and maximum utilization of the Nation's manpower to fight this war," Mr. McNutt said.

"We are starting out by enlisting the leaders of labor and of business management. They will not only aid and assist us, they will also guide us.

"The manpower policy committee is charged with considering and recommending policies, and also to initiate policies. Its recommendations will have great weight in determining the fateful steps we shall take."

Those who thus far have accepted membership on the policy committee, and their organizations, are:

Representing Management:

R. Conrad Cooper, assistant vice president, Wheeling Steel Corporation, Wheeling, W. Va.; H. A. Enochs, chief of personnel, The Pennsylvania Railroad Co., Broad Street Station Building, Philadelphia, Pa.; R. E. Gillmor, president, Sperry Gyroscope Co., Inc., Brooklyn, N. Y.; R. Randall Irwin, director, industrial relations, Lockheed Aircraft Corporation, Burbank, Calif.; and C. J. Whipple, president, Hibbard, Spencer, Bartlett & Co., Chicago, Ill.

Representing Labor:

Frank P. Fenton, director of organization, A. F. L., Washington, D. C.; John P. Frey, president, Metal Trades Department, A. F. L., Washington, D. C.; George Masterton, president, United Association of Journeymen Plumbers and Steamfitters, A. F. L., Washington, D. C.; Clinton S. Golden, assistant to the president, United Steel Workers of America, C. I. O.; John Green, president, Industrial Union of Marine and Shipbuilding Workers of America, C. I. O., Camden, N. J.; and Walter P. Reuther, member of international executive board, United Automobile, Aircraft and Agricultural Implement Workers of America, C. I. O., Detroit, Mich.

★ ★ ★

Committee urges appropriations to find labor for farms

War Manpower Commission Chairman Paul V. McNutt was requested June 9 in a resolution adopted by the Commission's labor-management policy committee to "impress upon the Bureau of the Budget and the Congress their responsibility to provide means for the harvesting of food and other agricultural production for our armed forces, our allies, and our civilian population."

The committee's resolution stated that if such appropriations are not promptly provided, President Roosevelt should be requested to allocate the necessary money out of his emergency funds.

The resolution was adopted at the first formal meeting of the committee.

The farm labor resolution asserted that "the inability of existing Government agencies to recruit and place agricultural labor in an orderly manner is resulting in the proposal of plans for the importation of alien labor by private contractors."

The two operating agencies functioning in recruitment and placement of agricultural workers are the United States Employment Service and the Farm Security Administration.

Voluntary medical recruiting must work fast or yield to new methods, says McNutt

Unless the voluntary plan promptly recruits enough physicians for our armed forces and war industry areas, "some other and more vigorous plan will have to be produced," Manpower Chairman McNutt told a meeting of the American Medical Association June 8. Although he praised the canvassing and classifying job done by the association, he said that "the careful safeguards that were set up by the Procurement and Assignment Service have apparently slowed down the rate of recruitment."

Excerpts from Mr. McNutt's speech:

We are not getting as many volunteers as the Procurement and Assignment Service expected we would have by this time. It is absolutely necessary that there be an immediate and significant increase in the number of volunteers, or else some other method of procurement will be required soon.

Slightly over 3,000 physicians, who were not obligated by reserve commissions, volunteered in the first 6 months of this war. By contrast, 12,000 volunteered in the first 6 months of the last war.

Forces need two-thirds of younger doctors

An army of 9 million will take 12 percent of our male population. Present Medical Corps ratios indicate the armed forces will require 33 percent of all our physicians, (including retired men)—two-thirds of all those under the age of 45.

For the military services younger men must go. They must realize their duty now. The armed forces need thousands of young doctors immediately—to be exact, 5,000 by July 1; 20,000 during the next 7 months.

The older men . . . must not only stay, but must extend the scope of their activities to meet the medical needs of the civilian communities.

★ ★ ★

Electricity on essential list

Production, transmission, and distribution of electric power were listed, June 5, as essential to the war effort by National Headquarters, Selective Service System.

Detroit may need 746,000 employees at war peak

A careful and comprehensive check of Detroit's peak labor requirements conducted by the WPB in cooperation with the United States Employment Service reveals that 524,000 were employed in war manufacturing in May and that 660,-000 would be employed by November. New estimates of employers indicate that when the war peak is reached, more than a year from now, 746,000 employees may be required.

Women, minority groups, included

A careful recheck of earlier employer forecasts has confirmed predictions that the Detroit area faces a labor-supply problem which will require complete use of all possible local labor resources, including especially the employment of women and all minority groups.

"By using these local resources effectively, intensifying training programs and planning the transfer of workers from nonmanufacturing pursuits and nonessential manufacturing occupations to war work, the labor needs of Detroit plants can be met during the next 6 months without large-scale migration of workers from other areas," said Ernest Kanzler, regional WPB director in Detroit.

Long range employment forecasts, based on present plans which may be subject to change, indicate that the manufacturing employment may reach a level of 728,000 in May 1943 and 746,000 at the war peak in a few months later.

Scrapping of oil well derricks suggested in search for scrap

Widespread scrapping of oil well derricks to secure needed iron and steel scrap, has been suggested to the Petroleum Industry War Council by M. R. Singleton, salvage director of the petroleum industry for the industrial salvage section of the Bureau of Industrial Conservation.

Most of the oil wells in this country, according to Mr. Singleton, can dispense with fixed derricks by using itinerant truck-drawn hoisting equipment.

By scrapping useless oil derricks in Oklahoma, Kansas, Texas, and California, over 300,000 tons of steel could be directed into essential war production.

Drawn for Division of Information, O. E. M.
KID SALVAGE

KID SALVAGE, a character drawn by Steig especially for OEM, will appear in VICTORY every week. Mats for publication are available in either 2- or 3-column size. Requests to be put on the mailing list should be addressed to Distribution Section, Division of Information, OEM, Washington, D. C. When ordering individual mats, refer to code number and specify size.

New recruitment organization set up to provide seamen

The War Shipping Administration June 6 announced establishment of a Recruitment and Manning Organization, designed to provide an uninterrupted flow of seamen for America's steadily increasing Merchant Marine, and to cooperate with representatives of the United Nations in securing personnel.

Rear Admiral Emory S. Land, War Shipping Administrator, named Marshall E. Dimock as director of the Recruitment and Manning Organization. Mr. Dimock was formerly Associate Commissioner of Immigration and Naturalization, and Second Assistant Secretary of Labor. The new organization will operate under the general supervision of Captain Edward Macauley, assistant to the administrator and member of the United States Maritime Commission.

"The principal responsibility of the new organization is to see that seamen and officers are available for American and foreign ships when and where needed," Mr. Dimock said.

Japanese evacuees to cultivate 10,000 Arkansas acres

Ten thousand acres of raw but rich Mississippi Delta land in southeastern Arkansas will be cleared, drained, and put into cultivation by Japanese evacuees from Pacific Coast States, the War Relocation Authority announced June 8.

Under military protection

The area selected by the Army and War Relocation Authority as the seventh site for relocation of Japanese evacuees is in Desha County near Rohwer, about 15 miles north of Arkansas City. Approximately 10,000 evacuees will be moved in as soon as basic housing can be provided.

Announcement of the selection was made several days ago by the Wartime Civil Control Administration, which is moving all Japanese, both aliens and citizens, from restricted areas along the Pacific Coast. The relocation project will be administered by the War Relocation Authority and will be designated by the War Department as a military area under military protection.

First emphasis on own food

Emphasis will be primarily on production of foods for the evacuee population and secondarily on crops to meet national needs. The area is well adapted to produce long-staple cotton, alfalfa, soybeans, oats, corn, and truck crops.

Elementary schools and high schools will be maintained by the War Relocation Authority in cooperation with the Arkansas State Department of Education and the United States Office of Education. Doctors and nurses will be recruited insofar as possible from the evacuee population.

Evacuees to produce food at eighth relocation center

Development of irrigation facilities and production of food crops will constitute the principal work program for Japanese-American evacuees in the recently announced relocation center near Granada, Colo., M. S. Eisenhower, director of the War Relocation Authority, stated June 11.

The new relocation site, announced on June 3 by Lt. Gen. J. L. DeWitt of the Western Defense Command and Fourth Army, is the eighth to be selected.

Labor Board orders upward pay adjustment for 1,150 Long Island aircraft workers

The National War Labor Board last week issued a major wage decision, provided union security for two unions, and issued an ultimatum to striking textile workers in Fall River, Mass., to return to work or lose their jobs. The Board also referred a jurisdictional dispute to the National Labor Relations Board to avoid usurping "the function of another Government agency." The monthly report on strikes in war industries issued during the week showed time lost from war production due to strikes has been reduced to 6/100 of one percent during May.

Major wage order

To remove "glaring" inequalities between the wages paid to employees of the Ranger Aircraft Engines Division of the Fairchild Engines and Airplane Corporation at Farmingdale, Long Island, and the level of wages paid in comparable Long Island plants and by competing firms in the industry, the National War Labor Board unanimously ordered an upward adjustment of 10¢ an hour to the 1,150 men employed at the plant.

The Board also unanimously ordered the wage increase to be retroactive to April 10 and raised the hiring rate from 50¢ to 60¢ an hour. The hiring rate will then be increased to 65¢ an hour after 30 days from hiring, to 70¢ after 60 days, and to 75¢ after 90 days. The hiring rates ordered by the Board are in line with those in the industry and in the immediate area of the Ranger plant.

In this case the Board granted union security to the United Automobile Workers' CIO union, which has bargaining rights in the plant, by ordering the inclusion of a maintenance of membership clause in the contract between the company and union. This clause will not go into effect for 15 days, after which time all members of the union in good standing and those who may later become members will be required to remain members for the duration of the agreement as a condition of employment. An arbiter appointed by the Board will make final decisions on any disputed cases arising under this clause.

The Board's decision on the wage issue was made after a careful study by the Bureau of Labor statistics of wages in comparable plants in Long Island and in the aircraft industry. This study was brought up to date by the Bureau during the first week in June. A public hearing was held on the dispute May 27.

The opinion written by Wayne L. Morse and concurred in by the three other public members of the Board and the four labor members who participated in the decision, stated flatly that wage stabilization "cannot be accomplished by freezing existing wage rates."

The opinion states in part:

The War Labor Board has accepted as a solemn obligation, the President's instructions that it should stabilize wages. It appreciates the fact that the obligation calls for the highest degree of judicial impartiality and fairness in reaching its wage determinations.

There is, moreover, not such a singular thing as an American wage level, but rather, there are many wage levels in this country and they are in constant flux. The interplay of economic forces which produce these varying wage levels cannot be changed from a dynamic to a static phenomenon. However, the coordinated program suggested by the President permits sufficient flexibility in adjusting certain wage rates with the facts and needs of a given situation. Such a program can succeed in stabilizing our war economy. Thus if all groups involved in the President's seven-point program meet the tests of their duties and obligations in the premises, our national economy will be saved from the ravages of inflation. . . .

It needs to be emphasized that there is no rule of thumb or static wage formula that can be applied mechanically to wage cases to the end of producing wage stabilization. Hence, it is not surprising that the President's message on wage stabilization permits of that degree of flexibility necessary to a fair and just balancing of the various interests which are involved in wage dispute cases. It gives to the War Labor Board that reasonable degree of discretion which is necessary if it is to decide individual cases on their merits and at the same time stabilize wages by checking unwarranted wage demands. Through a wise exercise of the discretionary power granted to it in the President's stabilization program, the Board can do much toward preventing the cost of living from spiraling upward.

In the instant case, the Board is confronted with an exceptional wage situation insofar as wage inequalities are concerned. The wage comparison data made available to the Board by the Bureau of Labor statistics leads to the inescapable conclusion that there are glaring inequalities in the wage scales of the Ranger Company when compared with the wage rates paid for like work in other plants, both in the Long Island area and outside of that district. It simply would not be fair to the workers involved to deny them a wage increase in view of the unfavorable wage position in which they find themselves when compared with other workers who perform like work.

This is particularly true in view of the fact that the record makes clear that it has become the common practice for employers in the Long Island area to refrain from employing persons who seek to improve their economic position by moving from one war industry plant to another. It cannot be questioned that it is very desirable to eliminate to the maximum extent possible, the migration of workers from one plant to another. There certainly is a need for stabilization of manpower, as well as of wages. However, it is not fair or reasonable to require a worker, either by employer practice or by Government policy, to remain on his job for the duration of the war unless reasonable adjustments are made in his wages so that he is not discriminated against economically as a result of such a manpower stabilization program.

Thus, in this case, precisely because it is desirable to have the employees remain in steady employment at the Ranger plant for the duration of the war, they are entitled to have their wage inequalities ironed out by a reasonable wage adjustment. . . .

The decision was unanimous, except that two of the employer members, dissented on the union security issue.

Textile strikers rebuked

Asserting that the Nation-wide industry-labor no-strike agreement "cannot be flouted by a small group of selfish and willful workers," William H. Davis, Chairman of the National War Labor Board, called upon 125 fixers and changers employed at the Arkwright Corporation, Fall River, Mass., textile concern, to end an unauthorized week-long strike or lose their jobs.

A demand for an immediate wage increase precipitated the strike. The War Labor Board now has before it a request for a general wage increase from the CIO United Textile Workers of America, which, if granted, would be extended to the jobs held by the strikers. The strike has been repudiated both by the CIO union, which has bargaining rights for the plant, and by the American Federation of Textile Operatives, an independent union to which a majority of the strikers belong. The strikers are among the highest paid workers in the plant.

Garment workers made secure

By a vote of 8 to 1 the Board ordered the Ranger type of maintenance of membership clause included in the contract between the E-Z Mills, Bennington, Vermont, and International Ladies Garment Union, AFL.

Under the directive order of the Board, parties to the dispute are to conclude the contract in 15 days. This contract is to remain in full force and effect until August 31, 1943.

A total of 450 employees are involved.

NLRB functions protected

The Board adopted as its own the recommendations of a five-man mediation panel to refer a case to the National Labor Relations Board to avoid usurping "the function of another Government agency." The case involves a dispute over representation at the Holt, Ala., plant of the Central Foundry Co. Unions involved are the United Steelworkers of America (CIO) and the International Molders and Foundry Workers Union of North America (AFL).

Under the Board order, all dues collected by the AFL union under a union shop contract from persons claiming membership in the CIO are to be "held in escrow" by the AFL while the National Labor Relations Board acts on a CIO petition to be recognized as exclusive bargaining agent for the plant's production and maintenance employees. If the NLRB should find the existing contract between the company and the AFL invalid, the dues held in escrow will be refunded. However, if the NLRB should find otherwise, the dues will be retained by the AFL. The plant employs about 1300 men. The case was certified to the WLB on June 3, while a strike which started on May 27 was in progress.

PRICE · ADMINISTRATION . . .

Women's and children's fall and winter garments put on cost-plus basis if price cannot be set under GMPR

Methods of pricing fall and winter outerwear garments for women, girls and children originally established in Maximum Price Regulation No. 153 were revised June 10 by Price Administrator Henderson, in order to make the regulation more workable.

Virtually every section of the regulation is changed and a different method of pricing is provided for the coats, suits, and dresses and many other items specified.

Based on cost plus last year's mark-up

Under the pricing method provided by the amended regulation, sellers are required, in general, to establish their ceiling prices in accordance with a formula based upon this season's cost to which is added the mark-up or margin they obtained on their sales during last selling season of garments of the same classification.

The original regulation established as the maximum price for each seller the highest price charged by him for a garment of "substantially equal workmanship and quality" during a base period of July 1 through September 30, 1941.

Types of garments covered

The amended regulation applies to cloth garments of the following types:

Coats, suits, separate jackets and separate skirts and dresses for feminine wear in sizes 3 and up; blouses in sizes 30 and up, snowsuits for children in sizes from 3 to 14 for two-piece suits and sizes from 1 to 6 for one-piece suits, legging sets and separate leggings for children in sizes from 1 to 10 years. Dresses in girls' teen age and children's sizes which were not covered by the regulation as originally issued are included under the amendment. Otherwise the garments covered are the same.

In keying selling prices to cost plus last year's mark-up, the amendment takes into consideration the cost to the seller of the garment being priced. In the case of a manufacturer, this includes the cost of the material and trimmings plus the labor costs of producing the garment computed on the basis of wage rates paid by the manufacturer on March 31, 1942.

A manufacturer may include increased labor costs subsequent to March 31, 1942, for the purpose of computing his maximum price, only where the increase was

made pursuant to a collective bargaining contract or other wage agreement, which contract or agreement was entered into on or before April 27, 1942, and unconditionally provided for the wage increase in question.

Contracts may be carried out

Garments falling within the provisions of the amended regulation are designated as "new lines." A "new line" is defined to mean any woman's, girl's or child's outerwear garment whose maximum price cannot be established under Section 2 (a) of the general maximum price regulation.

The regulation became effective on June 15, 1942, and is applicable to deliveries of "new lines" on and after the effective date. However, contracts entered into prior to June 15 in compliance with the general maximum price regulation or with Regulation No. 153 as originally issued may be carried out at contract price.

Rubber footwear sales to war agencies exempt from MPR 132

Sales of waterproof rubber footwear under contract with any war procurement agency of the United States, or with anyone who buys for resale to such an agency, are specifically exempted from Maximum Prize Regulation No. 132 by amendment No. 1 to that order, announced June 6 by Price Administrator Henderson.

The Administrator pointed out, however, that the sales exempt from the rubber footwear order are subject to Maximum Price Regulation No. 157, which sets ceiling prices on sales of apparel for military purposes.

The agencies exempt from the provisions of Regulation No. 132 by Amendment No. 1, effective June 4, are the War and Navy departments, the Maritime Commission, and the Lend-Lease section of the Treasury Department's procurement division.

11 more cotton fabric groups come under dollars-and-cents ceilings; products redefined

Eleven additional cotton fabric groups will come under dollars-and-cents ceilings, Price Administrator Henderson announced June 10 as the OPA continued its plan of supplying definite maximum prices in place of individual sellers' weighted averages for the "cotton products" covered by Maximum Price Regulation No. 118.

Other changes

Other changes in the regulation are provided through Amendment No. 4. The more important of these are redefinition of "cotton products," extension of the permission to continue selling or delivering "on memorandum" under specified conditions, and revision of the "war procurement" clause to conform with other regulations.

Also provided are an extension of the "cotton content adjustment" feature to take into consideration the flax noil content of articles covered, and the correction of inadvertent errors in maximum prices for Canton flannels, hose and belting duck, enameling duck, and filter twills.

All but one of these errors were previously reported in press releases and three of the corrections are effective as of May 25, 1942, the effective date of Amendment No. 3. The "memorandum" provision also takes effect May 25. Otherwise, Amendment No. 4 became effective June 15, 1942.

Fabrics included

The 11 groups for which specific maximum prices are supplied are:

Industrial fabrics; frock cloth; gingham, seersuckers and related fabrics; carded filling sateens and sateen-yarn twills; blanket linings; nursery products, including gauze diapers, pads and bibs, bird's-eye cloth and diapers, and flannelette diapers; wide laundry cover cloth; paper maker dryer felts; cheesecloth and bunting; yarn dyed slack suitings, and miscellaneous special products, such as individual construction of waffle cloth and bagging.

This brings the total of groups specifically priced under the regulation to 19, representing many of the fabrics covered and many of the principal groups. Dollars-and-cents ceilings for other products regulated are under preparation.

Some pork product sellers may seek adjustment or exception from price regulation

Certain classes of dressed hog and wholesale pork cut sellers who suffered peculiar hardships because of special circumstances existing during the February 16–20, 1942, base period now may file petition for adjustment or exception under Amendment No. 1 to Maximum Price Regulation No. 148, Price Administrator Henderson announced June 8.

Three classes specified

Previously, the regulation provided only for petitions for amendment.

In the new amendment, effective June 9, 1942, adjustment of or exception from the maximum prices set by the regulation may be granted to any person who shows to the Administrator's satisfaction that he falls within any of the following three specific classes of pork product packers and slaughterers:

1. Persons whose operations were curtailed or adversely affected during the February 16–20, 1942, period by reason of plant alterations, repairs, remodelling, or construction which hampered them in processing or marketing their pork products in the usual manner.

2. Persons whose dealings consisted primarily of disposing of inventory acquired at a time substantially earlier than that at which other comparable sellers acquired dressed hogs or wholesale pork cuts of the type on which adjustment is being requested.

3. Persons whose dealings during the February 16–20, 1942, period were confined to dressed hogs or wholesale pork cuts derived from a type of hogs only regionally and seasonally available and not regularly quoted on major livestock markets.

Packer's price protest dismissed, another denied

The OPA has issued an order dismissing protest of the Lima Packing Co. of Lima, Ohio, against Temporary Maximum Price Regulation No. 8 (Dressed Hogs and Wholesale Pork Cuts), Administrator Henderson announced June 11.

Dismissal was based on grounds that this protest does not comply with provisions of Procedural Regulation No. 1 necessitating filing of such protest within 60 days after issuance date of the temporary regulation.

Simultaneously, OPA in another order denied the protest of the Humphrey Supply Co. of Reno, Nev., asking for specific higher ceiling prices than were allowed under Temporary Maximum Price Regulation No. 8 and its successor Maximum Price Regulation No. 148.

FROZEN FOOD PACKERS' PROTEST DISMISSED

A protest of the National Association of Frozen Food Packers against the general maximum price regulation has been dismissed in an order issued by the OPA. Dismissal was based on the fact that the protest was not in substantial compliance with requirements of the Emergency Price Control Act of 1942 and of Procedural Regulation No. 1.

The protestant is a trade association whose members are persons engaged in the cold-packing and quick-freezing of strawberries. The dismissal order was entered without prejudice to the right of any individual member of this trade association to file a proper protest.

★ ★ ★

Prices for Vitamin A oils to be discussed at industry meeting

A meeting of producers and concentrators of fish liver oils will be held in San Francisco on June 22, to discuss prices of Vitamin A oils, Price Administrator Henderson announced June 11.

The meeting has been called by the chemical branch of the industrial material price division of the OPA.

Heretofore, Vitamin A oils have been subject to the provisions of Revised Price Schedule No. 53, covering a wide variety of fats and oils. Studies made by the OPA indicate that the special problems of the Vitamin A oil industry may be more adequately met by a regulation establishing maximum prices for Vitamin A oils specifically.

Vitamin producers recently asked the chemical branch of the OPA to call an industry meeting to discuss a special price regulation to provide a level of prices which would encourage wider sales.

Burry wools' price control shifted to Regulation 58

Amendment No. 3 to Maximum Price Regulation No. 106—Domestic Shorn Wool—was issued May 6 by OPA to eliminate from the regulation provisions applying to seedy or burry wools sold in the carbonized state. Amendment No. 5 to Revised Price Schedule No. 58—Wool and Wool Tops and Yarns—now makes provision for these wools.

Seasonal wooden containers for farm products given special pricing formula

A maximum price regulation providing special pricing formulas for boxes, baskets and other seasonal wooden containers used for fruits and vegetables was announced June 8 by OPA.

The regulation was made necessary by the fact that the containers, because of the seasonal nature of their sales, could not be priced equitably in many areas on the basis of deliveries made in March 1942, the base pricing period provided by the general maximum price regulation.

Titled Maximum Price Regulation No. 160 (Seasonal Wooden Agricultural Containers), the measure became effective June 6, 1942.

The regulation covers all wooden containers used for fruits and vegetables except cooperage products and used containers, and covers the whole country with the exception of what is known to the trade as the Western area—California, Washington, Oregon, Idaho, Montana, Wyoming, Utah, Nevada, Arizona, New Mexico, and Colorado.

The Western States not included were to receive a separate specific regulation shortly.

The Price Administrator said Price Regulation No. 160 is only a temporary measure. It will be replaced as soon as possible by a permanent regulation setting forth dollars-and-cents price schedules.

Margin added to off-season price

Maximum prices for manufacturers are computed on the basis of a formula which is designed to convert off-season prices of the first three months of 1942 into on-season prices by the device of adding to the 1942 off-season prices the margin of last year's on-season over off-season prices.

Maximum prices for wholesalers and retailers simply will be the seller's average cost for this season's containers plus the margin of his last season's average price above his last season's average cost.

The regulation is limited to "seasonal containers." These are defined as containers, deliveries of which by the seller in the first three months of 1941 constituted less than 15 percent of the total deliveries of the same container for the full year 1941, and not more than 8 percent in any one of the 1941 months of January, February or March.

Alcohol antifreeze ceilings to be much lower than some prices now charged

Maximum prices for alcohol antifreezes were to be established by the OPA by mid-June at levels substantially below those now charged by some manufacturers, Price Administrator Henderson announced June 8.

"During the spring there was an abnormal off-season demand for alcohol antifreeze," Mr. Henderson explained. "Some manufacturers increased prices."

As now contemplated by the OPA, the regulation will hold manufacturers' prices to levels perhaps as low as 69 cents per gallon for high-cost-production alcohol antifreeze delivered by the carload in drums, container included. This ceiling would be approximately 10 cents a gallon under prices now charged by some manufacturers.

The regulation also will probably set maximum retail prices at approximately 35 cents per quart for high-cost-production alcohol antifreeze and about 25 cents per quart for low-cost-production alcohol antifreeze.

The schedule will also cover ethyleneglycol antifreeze solutions, prices of which have remained relatively stable at established levels.

★ ★ ★

Ceilings set on 1942 line of refrigerators

Maximum prices at which the Edison General Electric Co., Chicago, may sell to distributors its 1942 line of Hotpoint refrigerators are established in Order No. 1 to Revised Price Schedule No. 102, announced June 6 by Price Administrator Henderson.

On sales to distributors

The Edison General Electric Co. is a wholly owned subsidiary of the General Electric Co., Bridgeport, Conn., which manufactures the Hotpoint refrigerators and sells them to the Chicago subsidiary.

There is great similarity of prices and models existing between the models sold by the Hotpoint Co. and the General Electric Co. The prices approved in the order bear the usual relationship to the prices for General Electric Co. refrigerators. The price relationship between the two 1942 lines of $model^s$ is the one which existed between them in 1941.

The approved maximum Hotpoint prices to distributors, which became effective June 5, are as follows:

Model EA–63–42, $68.74; Model EA–7–42, $82.50; Model EAS–7–42, $89.00; Model EB–7–42, $93.63; Model EBP–7–42, $99.79; Model EC–7–42, $110.49; Model EC–8–42, $120.22; Model ED–8–42, $130.17; Model ED–12–42, $219.46; and Model ED–16–42, $249.08.

OPA explains landlord registration for 20 rental areas under Federal control

Registration by landlords of houses, apartments, flats, tenements, and all other similar housing accommodations was to begin the week of June 15 in the first 20 Defense-Rental Areas brought under Federal regulation June 1 by the OPA. This registration is to be completed by midnight July 1.

Details of registration are explained in part in excerpts from a question-and-answer digest prepared by the OPA. The Q. and A. applies to housing accommodations other than hotels and rooming houses.

Q. Where are forms for this registration statement usually made available?

A. At banks, city and county offices, real estate offices, fire houses, police stations, light and gas company offices, and at the area rent office.

Q. What if a place isn't rented at the time of the registration?

A. Whether rented or vacant, the accommodations must be registered.

Q. What if a landlord fails to register by July 1?

A. Willful violation of the registration requirements subjects the landlord to the penalties provided by the Emergency Price Control Act, which are a fine of $5,000 or 1 year's imprisonment.

Q. What housing accommodations must be registered in this registration?

A. Houses, apartments, flats, tenements, and all similar dwelling units.

Q. Must a landlord make out a separate registration statement for each dwelling unit he rents or is offering for rent?

A. Yes. A statement must be made for each unit, rented or not rented.

Q. Are there any circumstances by which a tenant would have to submit a registration statement?

A. Yes. The tenant is told on the reverse side of his copy of the statement that if he sublets all or any part of the dwelling unit he must also submit a registration statement.

Q. Exactly what does this mean?

A. It means, for the registration of housing accommodations other than hotels and rooming houses, that if a tenant rents to one or two paying tenants not members of his family, he must register. If he rents to three or more, then he is to wait for the registration of hotels, rooming and boarding houses.

Q. Would the same hold true of a person who owned the home he lived in and rented to one or two paying tenants?

A. Yes. He would have to register. And if he rented to more than two, he would have to register later.

Q. What comprises a dwelling unit?

A. A dwelling unit is a room, or group of rooms, for which a single rent is paid.

Q. What about hotels, rooming and boarding houses?

A. These are not to be registered at this time. Registration of this type living quarters is to be made at a later date.

Bed linen makers, agent allowed premium change

Two manufacturers and one selling agent were granted permission June 9 by the OPA to charge premiums for two specific types of bed linens which fulfill special pricing requirements laid down by the bed linens price schedule (No. 89).

Joseph Bancroft & Sons Co., Wilmington, Del., and Rhoads & Co., Philadelphia, Pa., may sell "Basco" Hospital sheets at a premium not to exceed an amount equal to 3½ percent of the applicable base price for type 128 sheets set forth in the schedule under Order No. 5 to Schedule 89.

Pacific Mills, New York City, is granted permission to sell pillow cases having colored selvage at a premium of 5 cents per dozen over the ceiling price and a premium of 20 cents per dozen for sheets with a similar selvage, less trade and all other discounts applicable under the schedule. This action is permitted under Order No. 6.

★

Ceilings set on new gas-range models of Ohio firm

Maximum prices at which the Newark Stove Co., Newark, Ohio, may sell two new models of private-brand gas ranges to the Phillips Petroleum Co., Detroit, are established in Order No. 3 under Revised Price Schedule No. 54 (Domestic Cooking and Heating Stoves) issued June 6 by Price Administrator Henderson.

The new models, designated in the order as Model Nos. 342 Philgas and 442 Philgas, are to be sold at prices no higher than those established by the schedule for two formerly manufactured models—Nos. 341 and 441, respectively.

The new models are the same as Models 341 and 441 except for two minor construction changes. The order became effective June 6.

10 classes of military items exempt from price control on sales to U. S. war agencies

Ten classifications of military equipment and supplies, ranging from ski stoves to paratroop knives, are now excluded from provisions of price control regulations when sales of these essential items are made to Federal war procurement agencies, Price Administrator Henderson announced June 10.

The June 10 action was effected through the issuance of Amendment No. 2 to Supplementary Regulation No. 4 to the general maximum price regulation and Amendment No. 1 to Revised Price Schedule No. 64 (Domestic Cooking and Heating Stoves.)

The following are now excepted until January 1, 1943:

(1) The following ski troop equipment: carabiners, ice axes, pitons, ski bindings, ski poles, ski wax, mountain and ski goggles;
(2) Mountain and ski stoves (gasoline, one burner);
(3) Field ranges, model-1937 (Quartermaster Corps); spare parts therefor, Class A: accessories therefor, parts 222, 223, 224, 225, 226, 227, 228, 229 230, as listed in Instructions for Operation and care of Gasoline Field Range, model-1937 (Quartermaster Corps);
(4) Canteens, canteen cups, and meat cans, model M-1942 (Quartermaster Corps);
(5) Helmet liners, model M-1 (Quartermaster Corps);
(6) Wire Cutter, model M-1938 (Quartermaster Corps);
(7) Identification tags, model M-1940 (Quartermaster Corps);
(8) Metal insignia, cap and collar (for enlisted men);
(9) Paratroop knives;
(10) United States Army field rations C, D, and K.

★ ★ ★

Paperboard prices must be approved by OPA

Prices for new specialty paperboard items must be submitted to the OPA for approval, Price Administrator Henderson stated June 6 in response to inquiries from paperboard manufacturers.

Also, proposed prices must be approved by OPA for paperboard items which do not fall into at least one of the following categories: items sold, contracted for sale or price-listed by manufacturer during the base period of October 1, 1940 to October 15, 1941.

Revised Price Schedule No. 32 (Paperboard Sold East of the Rocky Mountains) established prices for paperboard which the manufacturers contracted for sale, sold or for which he listed prices during the base period referred to above. Top prices also were established in specific dollars and cents figures for specified paperboard items.

ALASKA LUMBER EXEMPT FOR 60 DAYS

An amendment excepting deliveries of lumber produced in Alaska from the provisions of the general maximum price regulation for a period of 60 days was announced June 12 by Price Administrator Henderson.

The measure—titled Amendment No. 4 to Supplementary Regulation No. 1 to the general maximum price regulation—became effective June 10. It applies to all deliveries between that date and August 10, 1942.

··· ··

Ceilings set on fabricated concrete reinforcing bars

A maximum price regulation for fabricated concrete reinforcing bars—the steel rods worked into concrete to give it strength in building, bridge, and road construction—was announced June 10 by Price Administrator Henderson.

The measure—Maximum Price Regulation No. 159, fabricated concrete reinforcing bars—became effective June 15.

50-cent margin allowed

The regulation establishes, as a ceiling, prices based on an allowance to the fabricator of a margin of 50 cents per hundred pounds of bars over and above the cost of the bars to the fabricator at the steel mill, excluding freight and extras.

These are the prices at or under which approximately 75 percent of the Nation's fabricators were operating in April 1941.

The pricing provisions of the regulation pass on to the consumer all charges for freight from mill to fabricator and from fabricator to consumer. There are, however, these two modifications of this rule:

1. Where a fabricator obtains an advantage as the result of an "in transit" freight rate, the regulation requires him to pass this advantage on to the consumer.
2. Where delivery is made by truck instead of by railroad an arbitrary charge of 10 cents per hundred pounds may be made.

★ ★ ★

Cohen named OPA attorney for Region IX

Appointment of Wallace Cohen as regional attorney for Region IX embracing all the territories and possessions of the United States, was announced June 12 by OPA General Counsel David Ginsburg.

Sales of imported commodities in original form not under GMPR

Sales of an imported commodity, if kept in its original form when sold to the Federal Government or a governmental agency, are exempt from the general maximum price regulation, Price Administrator Henderson emphasized June 11. This applies to sales of imported commodities by subcontractors as well as by contractors.

The Price Administrator explained that this point was covered in Amendment No. 1 to Supplementary Regulation No. 4, Exceptions. The exemption does not include sales of a commodity made from an imported commodity, nor does it include sales of an imported commodity if it is processed.

Mr. Henderson's clarification was necessitated by trade inquiries regarding the status of cocoa powder sales to the Army.

Ceilings set on 2-, 3- 5-gallon used steel paint pails

Maximum prices for used steel paint pails of 2-, 3-, and 5-gallon capacity were announced June 6 by Price Administrator Henderson.

The prices were issued in Revised Price Schedule No. 43, as amended, which formerly covered only used steel drums.

Also, in Revised Price Schedule No. 43, as amended, certain deductions have been made from the maximum prices established for reconditioned drums.

The new maximum prices established by Revised Price Schedule No. 43, as amended became effective June 10.

Wool skins exempt from GMPR

Wool skins (the pelts of sheep and lambs with the wool left on) are exempted from the general maximum price regulation because of special pricing problems, the OPA announced June 11.

In exempting wool skins from the general regulation by Amendment No. 5 to Supplementary Regulation No. 1, OPA pointed out that such action cannot result in any marked rise in prices, because the products of wool skins are covered by specific maximum price regulations. The amendment took effect June 12.

Provisions of cotton products and finished piece goods regulations correlated

Any fabric covered by Maximum Price Regulation No. 118 (Cotton Products) is exempt from the provisions of Maximum Price Regulation No. 127 (Finished Piece Goods) under an amendment to the latter regulation issued June 12 by the OPA.

The practical effect of Amendment No. 3 to Regulation 127 is to correlate this regulation with Regulation 118 as recently amended and to place under 118 sales of all finished carded cotton piece goods of a character predominantly finished and marketed by integrated or vertical mills (those which weave as well as finish or fabricate the cloth) whether or not a lot of such goods is actually finished and marketed in a particular instance by an independent converter.

A second effect of this amendment is to bring under Maximum Price Regulation 127 all sales of finished piece goods of a type predominantly finished and marketed by independents, regardless of who actually finishes and markets a particular lot. Such sales are exempted from Regulation 118. Moreover, since finished goods made from combed cotton yarns are specifically exempted from 118, they will now become subject to Regulation 127, even though they may be of a type predominantly marketed by vertical organizations.

Maximum price set on new type of sponge sweatband

The OPA June 12 announced a maximum price for a new type of sponge sweatband that American Allsafe Co., Buffalo, N. Y., has begun to manufacture to take the place of one it previously made of materials that no longer are available for the purpose.

The OPA issued Order No. 9 under the general maximum price regulation, establishing the following formula for determining the ceiling level for the new band:

To the maximum selling price at which the old type of sponge sweatbands were delivered in March 1942 to each class of purchaser, American Allsafe Co. may add 53 percent of the increase in the direct cost of the manufacture of the new sponge sweatband over the old, based upon the March 1942 direct costs of manufacturing both the new and old types.

OPA retains authority to review the company's selling prices determined by the formula, and to revoke Order No. 9 at any time. Effective date of the order was June 10.

CEILINGS ON USED MACHINES

Maximum prices for second-hand machinery and electrical products will be established July 1, 1942, under the terms of Maximum Price Regulation No. 136, on machines and parts, Price Administrator Henderson reminded June 8.

Used processing, mining, construction, electrical, and railroad machinery and equipment, together with parts of such machines, are included in the machines or parts covered by the regulation.

★ ★ ★

Somers heads cold finished bars advisory committee

Joseph T. Somers, president of the Wyckoff Drawn Steel Co., of Pittsburgh, Pa., has been elected chairman of the cold finished bars advisory committee of the OPA, Price Administrator Henderson announced June 8.

The committee is one of four iron and steel industry advisory units created by the Price Administrator last month to serve as liaison groups between OPA and the industry on any problems which may arise with respect to prices.

Other members

Other members of the cold finished bars advisory group are:

W. R. Howell, of Bliss & Laughlin, Inc., Harvey, Ill.; T. L. Kelby, of LaSalle Steel Co., Chicago; V. A. Jevon, of Jones & Laughlin Steel Corporation, Pittsburgh, Pa.; W. N. Lynch, of Keystone Drawn Steel Co., Spring City, Pa.; E. L. Parker, of Columbia Steel & Shafting Co., Pittsburgh, Pa.; and F. C. Young, of Union Drawn Steel Division of Republic Steel Corporation, Massillon, Ohio.

Special prices set on two types of latex footwear

Maximum prices at which Transcontinental Rubber Corporation of New York City may sell two items of waterproof footwear which it is manufacturing under special War Production Board permit, have been established by Order No. 1, under Maximum Price Regulation No. 132, announced June 9 by Price Administrator Henderson. The items on which ceilings were set are two kinds of latex women's footholds—rubbers that cover the forepart of a shoe only.

Ceilings lifted on sales of canned tomatoes and peas to war agencies

In order to effectuate purchases of canned tomatoes and peas for use by the military forces, Price Administrator Henderson June 12 excluded such sales and deliveries to the Army, Navy, Marine Corps, Lend-Lease Administration, Veterans' Administration, and Treasury Procurement from provisions of Maximum Price Regulation No. 152 (Canned Vegetables) and the general maximum price regulation.

This exemption is made in Amendment No. 1 to the regulation, effective June 15.

Prefer better grades, larger cans

The purchasing agencies of the armed forces prefer the better grades and larger can sizes of tomatoes and peas. This preference was shown officially in the issuance of WPB Order M-86A, which in the Administrator's judgment, will aid in conservation of containers and in procurement by the Army of the preferred grades.

The Department of Agriculture's support prices, announced December 19, 1941, of 95 cents per dozen and $1.10 per dozen for Grade C or Standard tomatoes and peas respectively, packed in 16-ounce, number two size cans, have provided the incentive for heavy production and packing of such grades.

★ ★ ★

Outgoing shipments cancelled from eastern beet sugar area

Orders for emergency movements of refined beet sugar by processors in Ohio, Indiana, and the lower peninsula of Michigan were cancelled, effective June 12, 1942, Price Administrator Henderson announced June 11.

This action does not affect the orders under which sugar is moved from other areas of supply.

Mr. Henderson pointed out that if outgoing shipments from this area—commonly referred to as the eastern beet sugar territory—were made, such shipments will have to be made up by arrivals from western beet processors and cane refiners. Such a double movement would entail higher cost to DSC and would require unjustified use of rail facilities. Therefore, such shipments are being discontinued.

New ceilings on sale and rental of used typewriters are below March levels

Maximum prices for the sale and rental of used typewriters, at levels considerably lower than those which prevailed during March 1942, are established in specific dollars and cents figures for all makes and models in Maximum Price Regulation No. 162, announced June 12 by Price Administrator Henderson.

The ceiling prices set forth in the order for second-hand typewriters, demand for which has increased rapidly since the production of new machines has been restricted and earmarked for military needs by the WPB, reflect price levels which existed October 1–15, 1941, adjusted for reconditioning and rebuilding costs charged in March 1942. Resulting retail top prices are about 4.3 percent less than March 1942 prices and about 3.5 percent above October 1941 prices. Rental rates fixed by the regulation are generally those which existed during October 1–15, 1941, but do not include pick-up and delivery charges.

The sale of used typewriters, as well as new typewriters in the hands of dealers, is now limited to persons who have obtained the prerequisite purchase certificates from War Price and Rationing Boards. Rentals, however, are not subject at present to rationing regulations.

Consumers affected by the regulation, which becomes effective July 1, 1942, range from the most vital war agencies, industrial plants, professional and small business men to the average household, school, and student.

The June 12 action fixes specific top prices for "rough" or "as is," "reconditioned" and "rebuilt" typewriters according to the age, make, and model of the machine.

Until June 12 the sale of used typewriters was covered by the general maximum price regulation which, on May 18, superseded Temporary Maximum Price Regulation No. 9.

Illinois steel and wire firm denied price relief

Northwestern Steel & Wire Co., of Sterling, Ill., June 9 was denied permission by the OPA to charge higher than the maximum prices in Revised Price Schedule No. 6 for certain steel products, even though its manufacturing costs of some items exceed mill realization at ceiling prices.

OPA ruled that in view of the "extremely satisfactory" over-all profits position of the company, higher prices were not warranted.

★

Examples of milk products not under general regulation

The OPA gave further examples June 12 of milk products not covered by the

Additional examples of milk products not covered are:

Sweetened condensed milk; sweetened condensed skim milk; condensed and evaporated buttermilk; dry or powdered milk; dry or powdered skim milk; dry or powdered buttermilk; dry or powdered whey; casein; malted milk powder; and plastic cream for manufacturing.

Two firms allowed to base fats ceilings on nearest sales date

Price Administrator Henderson June 12 granted applications of Distillation Products, Inc., of Rochester, N. Y. and Grayslake Gelatin Co. of Grayslake, Ill., setting maximum prices for these companies on products that hitherto could not be priced by these concerns with the base periods used in the freeze technique of Revised Price Schedule No. 53 (Fats and Oils), as no sales were made on those dates.

In both instances, the Administrator permitted the firms to set their prices based on the nearest possible sales date to November 26, 1941, and multiplying by 111 percent of that sales figure. The schedule provides that in instances where a specific ceiling price has not been set, the ceiling price is the individual seller's October 1, 1941, price or 111 percent of the November 26, 1941, figure, whichever is higher.

★ ★ ★

Goodman named OPA director for Kentucky

Appointment of George H. Goodman, of Louisville, as Kentucky State Director of the OPA was announced June 9 by Administrator Henderson.

Mr. Goodman has been State WPA director since July 1935.

Three biggest soap makers voluntarily roll back prices

Three large manufacturers producing the bulk of the Nation's soap, acting voluntarily in a joint move to relieve a "price squeeze" on retailers, wholesalers and jobbers, June 12 announced rescinding of price rises averaging 3¼ percent posted in February and March of this year.

The three — biggest soap makers in the country — are Colgate-Palmolive-Peet Co., Procter & Gamble Co. and Lever Brothers.

Another roll-back of major importance, the action carries the prices of soap at their factory doors back to the levels prevailing before February 28, 1942.

The reductions were made at the request of the OPA.

Hide glue 'jobbers' redefined to allow sales between producers

The definition of jobbers in the hide glue industry has been changed so as to permit the continuance of the traditional practice of producers purchasing hide glue produced by others, Price Administrator Henderson announced June 11. The change was effected through Amendment No. 3 to Revised Price Schedule No. 76, on hide glue, and became effective June 10.

WELL-KNOWN ARTISTS WILL DRAW FOR YOUR PAPER OR MAGAZINE

VICTORY PRESENTS, on facing page, a fifth group of 4 drawings by well-known American artists who have volunteered their talents to help emphasize, in their own medium, matters vital to winning the war. VICTORY will print four drawings by these and other artists each week. Permission to reprint is hereby granted. Mats in two-column size (larger than appears here) are available weekly. Requests to be put on the mailing list regularly, or for individual mats should be addressed to Distribution Section, Division of Information, Office for Emergency Management, Washington, D. C.

(In individual orders for the four drawings displayed this week, please refer to the serial numbers printed on the drawings.)

Gregory d'Alessio — Drawn for Division of Information, O. E. M.

"He carries me a block and I carry him a block. We save our rubber heels that way."

O. SOGLOW — Drawn for Division of Information, O. E. M.

"Hey! Don't you know how bad the rubber shortage is?"

O. SOGLOW — Drawn for Division of Information, O. E. M.

"Mrs. Van Pyster is wearing the family heirloom tonight."

O. SOGLOW — Drawn for Division of Information, O. E. M.

"I feel like a hoarder."

Civilian amateurs to provide two-way radio communication in raid emergencies

Two-way radio communication in air raid emergencies, employing the skill of civilian technicians, including radio amateurs, was envisaged June 13 in a joint statement by the Office of Civilian Defense and the Federal Communications Commission which announced a new War Emergency Radio Service, providing for the use of "Civilian Defense" stations. Under authority granted in Order No. 9 of the Defense Communications Board, the two agencies are collaborating their activities relative to proposed emergency civilian defense radio systems to be available in the event air raids damage or destroy other means of communication.

To augment OCD services

Thousands of compact radio stations to be constructed and operated under prescribed restrictions largely by persons who have had amateur radio experience are expected to augment the services of the OCD organizations throughout the Nation. According to radio engineers the two-way radio stations can be constructed of the unused "junk" material which amateurs and radio repairmen usually accumulate in their "storerooms." The transmitters will use not more than 25 watts input power, which will tend to limit their effective communicating range to approximately 10 miles—the longest distance ordinarily necessary for this type of service.

Persons holding commercial radio operator licenses, including radio engineers employed in broadcast stations, qualified repairmen, and others interested, are expected to join the civilian defense communication system. One amateur organization as well as broadcast stations are encouraging their members to participate in building up the new radio system. Printed manuals designed to facilitate administrative operation will be distributed by the OCD, through its regional offices.

U. S. INFORMATION SERVICE AIDS VISITING BUSINESSMEN

Businessmen and industrialists coming to Washington who require information, or are in doubt as to the proper Government official or officials to see for a discussion of their problems, will avoid confusion and save time by making use of the expanded services of the United States Information Service, conveniently located at 1400 Pennsylvania Avenue, NW., the United States Information Service has announced.

Trained information clerks are available to answer questions, and staff specialists are available for personal interviews. Telephone inquiries may be made by calling Executive 3300.

The United States Information Service is a division of the Office of Government Reports, Executive Office of the President.

WAR EFFORT INDICES

MANPOWER

National labor force, April	53,400,000
Unemployed, April	3,000,000
Nonagricultural workers, April	40,773,000
Percent increase since June 1940	**14
Farm employment, May 1, 1942	10,796,000
Percent increase since June 1940	**1

FINANCE
(In millions of dollars)

Authorized program June 1940–May 1942	‡166,345
Airplanes	36,223
Ordnance	35,403
Miscellaneous munitions	21,330
Naval ships	16,445
Industrial facilities	16,165
Posts, depots, etc.	14,037
Merchant ships	7,465
Pay, subsistence, travel for the armed forces	6,155
Stockpile, food exports	4,851
Housing	1,892
Miscellaneous	6,879
Total expenditures, June 1940–May 1942	*30,595
Sales of War Bonds—	
Cumulative May 1941–May 1942	6,023
May 1942	634
May quota exceeded	5.7%

PLANT EXPANSION
(In millions of dollars)
June 1940 to latest reporting date

Gov. commitments for war plant expansion; 1,644 projects, April 30	12,131
Private commitments for war plant expansion; 7,636 projects, April 30	2,574

EARNINGS, HOURS, AND COST OF LIVING

		Percent increase from June 1940
Manufacturing industries— March:		
Average weekly earnings	$36.15	40.2
Average hours worked per week	42.5	13.3
Average hourly earnings	80.9¢	20.4
	Index	
Cost of living, April (1935–39=100)	115.1	14.5

*Prelim. Includes revisions in several months.
‡Preliminary.
**Adjusted for seasonal variations.

OFFICE FOR EMERGENCY MANAGEMENT

WAYNE COY, *Liaison Officer*

CENTRAL ADMINISTRATIVE SERVICES: Dallas Dort, *Director.*

DEFENSE COMMUNICATIONS BOARD: James Lawrence Fly, *Chairman.*

INFORMATION DIVISION: Robert W. Horton, *Director.*

NATIONAL WAR LABOR BOARD: Wm. H. Davis, *Chairman.*

OFFICE OF SCIENTIFIC RESEARCH AND DEVELOPMENT: Dr. Vannevar Bush, *Director.*

OFFICE OF CIVILIAN DEFENSE: James M. Landis, *Director.*

OFFICE OF THE COORDINATOR OF INTER-AMERICAN AFFAIRS: Nelson Rockefeller, *Coordinator.*

OFFICE OF DEFENSE HEALTH AND WELFARE SERVICES: Paul V. McNutt, *Director.*

OFFICE OF DEFENSE TRANSPORTATION: Joseph B. Eastman, *Director.*

OFFICE OF FACTS AND FIGURES: Archibald MacLeish, *Director.*

OFFICE OF LEND-LEASE ADMINISTRATION: E. R. Stettinius, Jr., *Administrator.*

OFFICE OF PRICE ADMINISTRATION: Leon Henderson, *Administrator.*

CONSUMER DIVISION: Dexter M. Keezer, *Assistant Administrator,* in charge. Dan A. West, *Director.*

OFFICE OF ALIEN PROPERTY CUSTODIAN: Leo T. Crowley, *Custodian.*

WAR MANPOWER COMMISSION: Paul V. McNutt, *Chairman.*

WAR RELOCATION AUTHORITY: Milton Eisenhower, *Director.*

WAR SHIPPING ADMINISTRATION: Rear Admiral Emory S. Land, U. S. N. (Retired), *Administrator.*

WAR PRODUCTION BOARD:
Donald M. Nelson, *Chairman.*
Henry E. Stimson.
Frank Knox.
Jesse H. Jones.
William S. Knudsen.
Leon Henderson.
Henry A. Wallace.
Harry L. Hopkins.

WAR PRODUCTION BOARD DIVISIONS:

Donald M. Nelson, *Chairman.*
Executive Secretary, G. Lyle Belsley.

PURCHASES DIVISION: Houlder Hudgins, *Acting Director.*

PRODUCTION DIVISION: W. H. Harrison, *Director.*

MATERIALS DIVISION: A. I. Henderson, *Director.*

DIVISION OF INDUSTRY OPERATIONS: J. S. Knowlson, *Director.*

LABOR PRODUCTION DIVISION: Wendell Lund, *Director.*

CIVILIAN SUPPLY DIVISION: Leon Henderson, *Director.*

REQUIREMENTS COMMITTEE: Wm. L. Batt, *Chairman.*

VICTORY

OFFICIAL WEEKLY BULLETIN OF THE AGENCIES IN THE OFFICE FOR EMERGENCY MANAGEMENT

WASHINGTON, D. C.　　　　**JUNE 23, 1942**　　　　**VOLUME 3, NUMBER 25**

First halt in living cost's rise since 1940 follows general ceiling

For the first time since November 1940 the steady rise in living costs has been checked as a direct result of the general ceiling on retail prices established on May 18 -and the accompanying measure to reduce rents, Price Administrator Henderson asserted June 18.

Commenting upon a special study by the Bureau of Labor Statistics of living costs in 21 cities for the period from May 15 to June 2, Mr. Henderson stated:

"The first returns are in. They are good. They show that at last the upward movement in living costs has been checked and that they actually declined slightly in the period under study. The survey demonstrates that if we are really serious about it, the battle against inflation can be won. . . .

"The program for the months ahead is one of joint effort by consumers, retailers, wholesalers, manufacturers, and the Government to see that the provisions of the general maximum price regulation are followed scrupulously. We have seen what this regulation can do to hold down prices. We must all join to see that it works as well in the future. . . .

"We must also backstop the ceiling by seeing that the buying power of the country is brought down to levels approximating the supply of goods and services that are available. This means that we will have to have increased savings, greater purchases of war bonds, larger diversion of incomes into taxes, repayment of debts and stabilization of wages and of farm

prices not covered by the price law. With these additional steps, we are bound to succeed."

The Bureau of Labor Statistics study shows that the increase in living costs, which has mounted 17½ percent since the outbreak of the war in Europe, stopped in its tracks during the May 15 to June 2 period, and actually declined 0.1 percent on the average for the 21 cities surveyed.

The greatest decline came in rents, which dropped 1.2 percent as the result of, or in anticipation of, rent regulations setting inflated rents back to earlier dates. Clothing prices also declined one-half of 1 percent as the result of restoration of March levels, and house furnishings declined 0.3 percent. Food prices, some of which, because of special provisions of the price control law, cannot be brought under control, rose 0.3 percent. Fuel, electricity, and ice rose one-tenth of 1 percent. Utility rates are not covered by the general maximum price regulation, while special provisions of the regulation permitted winter discounts on ice to be removed and ordinary summer levels to be restored.

Among the cities covered, Birmingham showed the greatest decline in living costs, amounting to 1.4 percent, and was followed by Cleveland and Detroit with declines of 1.3 percent each. In Savannah and Seattle living costs dropped 0.7 percent. Some cities showed slight increases in living costs, largely because of increases in prices of those foods which are not under control.

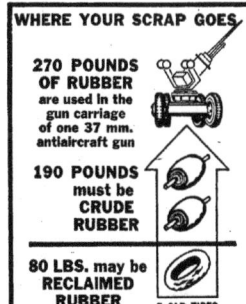

WHERE YOUR SCRAP GOES

270 POUNDS OF RUBBER are used in the gun carriage of one 37 mm. antiaircraft gun

190 POUNDS must be **CRUDE RUBBER**

80 LBS. may be **RECLAIMED RUBBER**

5 OLD TIRES

Review of the Week

While the concrete job of providing America's needs for war went forward in thousands and thousands of plants, the civilian war agencies last week made a series of adjustments to prepare for the sustained and ever-growing effort of the months to come.

Code to indicate "end use" of product

The War Production Board announced that a code number signifying the final use of the product will be attached to every order for production, and the same number will filter down through suborders and sub-suborders to every component of the product. This system, to be applied in the third quarter of 1942, will enable WPB by the beginning of the fourth quarter to judge the "end use" of every article being produced—whether it is for a tank, an airplane, or a machine tool. Then under the production requirements plan each manufacturer will be permitted to buy scarce materials in proportion to the important products he is making.

Rubber scrap drive ends June 30

While Government and public alike awaited the results of the rubber scrap collection designed to reach into every home, dealers throughout the country were agreeing to sell their complete inventories of rubber scrap to Uncle Sam before the campaign ends June 30. The WPB Bureau of Industrial Conservation meanwhile disclosed preliminaries for a drive in which every housewife will be asked to save fats for the glycerine which is vital to war. The Division of Industry Operations ordered users of alloy steels to separate by types all scrap so that the indispensable elements they produce will not be lost.

Nelson acts to speed lumber output

The increased importance of lumber to war production moved WPB Chairman Nelson to appoint a western lumber administrator with full powers to carry out action programs. Mr. Nelson also asked Pacific Coast operators to log immediately the best and most accessible lumber in the region. The Office of Price Administration put a ceiling on many types of logs and lumber, with the explanation that peak war demands coming in a period of decreased production had started prices on the way up.

At the same time, OPA found it necessary to remove ceilings from synthetic rubber, aviation gasoline, toluene, and materials essential to their manufacture, in order to encourage greater output.

The Division of Industry Operations continued its restrictions on manufacture, with cuts in the use of scarce materials for products ranging from church goods to baby carriages.

Workers keep seniority under new policy

For materials are a limiting factor in production and each last pound must be put into the goods that will deliver the biggest wallop on the battle line. But the same is true of labor. War Manpower Commission Chairman McNutt and WPB Chairman Nelson last week corrected a situation that was keeping several thousand of the best workmen out of new war plants. These plants were afraid to hire the workers because Government policy gave former employers the right to recall the employees on a week's notice, with loss of seniority rights the penalty for refusal. Now workers who have been trained for new war jobs may stay on them with full rights, unless the old employer offers them places which will use their new skills.

Rise in living costs checked

Moreover, to develop a stable labor force for maximum airplane production, the WPB Labor Production Division prepared to hold the first of a series of wage stabilization conferences in that industry on July 6.

A second purpose of the conferences is to put wages on a sound level that will tend to check inflationary influences on the general economy. And there was news of primary importance on this front last week; the Office of Price Administration announced that the rise in living costs has been checked.

The war information services operated last week without drastic outward change under the new Office of War Information.

Elmer Davis named director of new Office of War Information

By Executive Order 9182 dated June 13, 1942, a new information agency was established within the Office for Emergency Management.

The President has named Elmer Davis, news analyst and radio commentator, director of the new Office of War Information to coordinate the war informational activities of all Federal departments and agencies.

According to the terms of the order, the functions of the Division of Information of OEM with respect to the provision of press and publication services relating to the specific activities of OEM agencies were to be transferred to those agencies themselves.

In other respects, the powers and duties of the OEM Division of Information relating to the dissemination of general public information on the war effort were to be consolidated in the new Office of War Information along with various other information agencies.

· · ·

OEM HANDBOOK ISSUED

An "OEM Handbook," describing the functions and organization of the war agencies within the Office for Emergency Management, was issued June 17.

The 72-page booklet describes in detail the organization of the War Production Board, the Office of Price Administration and the other constituent agencies of the OEM.

Copies of the booklet are available in room 1501, New Social Security Building, and from the Superintendent of Documents, Washington, D. C., and at OEM field offices.

★ ★ ★

WAR EFFORT'S PROGRESS TOLD VISUALLY

The charts appearing every week on the front cover of VICTORY tell the story of America's battle as it is fought here at home. One-column mats are available for publication by newspapers and others who may desire them. Requests should be sent to Distribution Section, Division of Information, OEM, Washington, D. C.

VICTORY

OFFICIAL BULLETIN of the Office for Emergency Management. Published weekly by the Division of Information, Office for Emergency Management, and printed at the United States Government Printing Office, Washington, D. C.

Subscription rates by mail: 75¢ for 52 issues; 25¢ for 18 issues; single copies 5¢; payable in advance. Remit money order payable directly to the Superintendent of Documents, Government Printing Office, Washington, D. C.

On the Home Front

We have confounded the predictions of our enemies, we have notched up our belts, we have tightened our economy so that almost nothing needed for war is wasted on the nonessentials of ordinary living. And now, as we gather our forces for the supreme effort which shall overthrow Axis tyranny, we are fighting another sort of waste.

The waste we are fighting now is waste of what we call "manpower" but which actually embraces almost everybody—man or woman or adolescent child—in the U. S. A.

The manpower mobilization program, its goal a job for everyone and everyone in the right job, is one attack on the problem of manpower waste. And another line of attack is that which hits at the waste of war manpower caused by accidents and ill health.

Under compulsion to remain fit

Ill health and accidents fight for our enemies on the production front and the home front just as on the field of battle. The malarial fevers which seeped from the steaming, miasmic jungles of Bataan were allies of the Japanese, and disease and illness are their allies—and allies of the Nazis, too—in the war production centers of America.

But the compulsion to remain fit extends beyond the camps of our Army and the warships of our Navy and the walls of our factories. It is a compulsion laid upon all of us. Indifferent health means indifferent morale and indifferent morale is an invitation to defeat.

Fighting ill health on two fronts

The weapons with which ill health is fought on the home front are weapons familiar to every housewife—proper food, proper rest, proper exercise, proper medical care. On the industrial front the problem is complicated by other factors.

Among these factors are preventable accidents and preventable illnesses, especially venereal infections. The President last week called upon industrial communities to eliminate that "major source of infection," the red-light district, in the same way that such districts have been eliminated from the vicinity of army camps and naval stations. And War Manpower Commission Chairman

Paul V. McNutt, addressing 8,500 key executives in war production plants, called venereal disease "one of the most menacing" hazards to the health of war workers. Illness and injury cost us 6,000,-000 work days every month—work days

REPRINTING PERMISSIBLE

Requests have been received for permission to reprint "On the Home Front" in whole or in part. This column, like all other material in VICTORY, may be reprinted without special permission. If excerpts are used, the editors ask only that they be taken in such a way that their original meaning is preserved.

which would have brought victory over the Axis that much nearer.

Rise in living costs checked

The fight against the high cost of living hasn't been won yet, but the enemy no longer is advancing, he is on the defensive. The Office of Price Administration announces that for the first time since November 1940 the steady rise in living costs has been checked as a direct result of the general price ceiling established at the retail level a little more than a month ago. "The first returns are in," Price Administrator Henderson said. "They show that at least the upward movement in living costs has been checked, and that they actually declined slightly . . . if we are really serious about it, the battle against inflation can be won."

A new spirit abroad

That is encouraging news. Encouraging, too, is the news from the War Production Drive. More than 900 industrial plants doing war work now have established joint management-labor committees to devise ways of increasing and speeding the flow of weapons and ships toward the fighting fronts. Summing up the really astonishing achievements of these committees, reviewing the long list of production records shattered, WPB Chairman Donald M. Nelson said last week that "there is a new spirit abroad in this land—or perhaps it is just a spirit that was always there." And he added:

"America today is really beginning to

work at full speed for the first time. We are just beginning to realize what our strength really is. We are just starting to use it."

Berlin, Rome, and Tokyo newspapers please copy.

New ways of doing things

The face of change—even wartime change—is not always unpleasant. Out of the needs and scarcities of war come, sometimes, new ways of doing things which are better than the old ways; new shapes and textures and materials for common things which are better than the old shapes and forms and textures. WPB's Division of Civilian Supply recently called attention to the fact that house furnishings formerly made of strategically important aluminum and copper and stainless steel now are appearing in pottery and glass and wood and plastics. The stream of American design has not dried up because of the war, nor has American technology lost its drive.

Fats and oils campaign in the offing

To the campaigns for saving all our scrap metals and rubber and rags and paper, our campaign to get these metals and materials back to the plants which will refabricate them into the things we need for war, add another campaign which will begin shortly.

This new campaign will be a drive to replace fats and oils we are unable to get, these days, from the Far East. We need these fats and oils for many reasons, but principally because they make glycerine and glycerine helps make the explosives used by our British allies and also is used in the recoil mechanisms of our own guns and for other military purposes.

There is a ready way of replacing our lost fats and oils and that is to recover and save part of the estimated 2,000,-000,000 pounds of cooking fats wasted every year. The household fats salvage program won't begin until sometime in July, according to WPB's Bureau of Industrial Conservation. But when it does, BIC hopes to collect more than half a billion pounds of cooking fats a year from the kitchens of American homes. Neighborhood chain stores, meat markets and frozen food locker plants will serve as collection centers.

As the concentrated 2-week drive to get scrap rubber out of the attic and garage and into the reclaiming plants draws to its close, BIC says scrap rubber dealers throughout the country have agreed to sell accumulated piles of such rubber immediately. This will swell the total we can remake into rubber products our armed forces must have.

LABOR

Two Labor Board employer members cast first union membership maintenance votes

The ranks of the employer members of the National War Labor Board split on the union security question last week, as two of the employer members for the first time joined public and labor members in ordering a form of maintenance of membership. The Board also set the "Little Steel" public hearing for June 29 and approved the award of an arbitrator stabilizing wage rates in the West coast Douglas Fir area.

New form of membership maintenance clause

The employer members of the Board last week broke a consistent record of solid dissents on maintenance of membership clauses when two of them split away and voted with the public and labor members for such a clause in the Ryan Aeronautical Company case.

By a vote of 10 to 2 the Board ordered the San Diego, Calif., company to include in a contract with the United Automobile Workers, C. I. O., a clause providing that all employees who, 15 days from the date of the order, are members of the union in good standing or who thereafter become members shall, as a condition of employment, remain members in good standing and any dispute over the status of any employee will be finally decided by an arbiter appointed by the Board.

Dr. Frank P. Graham, public member of the Board, in writing an opinion on the membership maintenance provision, stated that the Ryan case is significant because it is "the first time two employer members of the War Labor Board voted for maintenance of union membership as a condition of employment." In his opinion, which was signed by the three other public members of the Board, Chairman William H. Davis, Vice-Chairman George W. Taylor, and Wayne L. Morse, Dr. Graham traces the history of union security in both the National Defense Mediation Board and the present Board to show that "a pattern of decisions on union security" was evolved, in "a relentless search for a reconciliation of stability and freedom."

"To many thoughtful minds," Dr. Graham wrote, "the test of the liberty of the worker is not, as some spokesmen for business think, in the consent of the corporation to the abridgment of this liberty, or even in the sanction by the government of the compulsion upon the individual by the corporation, or by the union, or by both. This individual liberty inheres in the prior knowledge and the consequent consent of the worker himself, whether expressed in a certification, which he himself expresses freely and individually in writing before being bound, or in a majority vote in which he freely participates with knowledge of what his vote binds him to, or in the freedom of a member of the union, for a brief period of two weeks or so to withdraw from the union or to stay in the union with express knowledge as to the nature of the particular provision for union security by which he is to be bound for the remainder of the contract."

Roger D. Lapham and R. R. Deupree were the employer members who went along with the Board majority. E. J. McMillan and H. B. Horton dissented. In a concurring opinion, Mr. Lapham said in part: "The Directive Order of the Board in this case is noteworthy because for the first time it recognizes one of the main principles the employer members have contended for:

"In simple language, it states that for the next 15 days (or until July 3, 1942) employees of the Company who are now members of the Union may withdraw from the Union before the maintenance of membership clause in the agreement between the Company and the Union becomes effective. * * *

"In previous union maintenance decisions, the employer members of this Board in their dissenting decisions emphasized that the Directive Orders of the Board did not allow the individual affected to exercise in some form the right of withdrawal or resignation within a reasonable time. (See dissenting opinions in International Harvester Company case, NDMB 4, and Federal Shipbuilding and Drydock Company case.) In the latter case, the majority opinions, but not the Directive Order, did explicitly state the individual's right to withdraw from the Union before the agreement between the Company and the Union was executed." Mr. Lapham added a statement that his concurring opinion in the Ryan case covered his affirmative vote for the membership maintenance clauses in the Ranger Aircraft Engines and 2-Z Mills cases as well as Ryan. The clause in these three cases is identical.

The Board by unanimous vote ordered the company to bring its wage rate up to the level of all other Southern California aircraft plants set last summer as the result of the OPM stabilization agreement by:

1. Making retroactive to the first pay period of July 1941 a basic hiring rate of 60 cents an hour, to be increased 5 cents an hour each four weeks until it reaches 75 cents an hour.

2. Making retroactive to October 15, 1941, a blanket increase of 10 cents an hour over the rates set in the contract signed January 22, 1941. These two provisions were ordered to bring the company's wage rates into line with the rest of the Southern California aircraft industry.

The Board refused to grant a current wage increase, since the WPB has called a wage stabilization conference for this section of the industry.

"Little Steel" hearing set

Monday, June 29, has been set by the Board as the date for the public hearing on the dispute between the "Little Steel" companies — B e t h l e h e m, Republic, Youngstown and Inland — and the United Steel Workers of America, CIO.

The Board also set June 25 as the final date for the fact-finding panel to submit its report to the Board. The union is demanding a wage increase of $1 a day and the union shop and checkoff for 182,000 workers.

Arbitrator's award approved

By unanimous vote, the Board has approved the arbitration award of Prof.

Vernon H. Jensen of the University of Colorado, in the dispute between the Employers' Negotiating Committee and the International Woodworkers of America, C.I.O.

The award provides that employees of the operators represented by the Employers' Negotiating Committee shall receive an increase of 7½¢ an hour as of April 1, 1942. A total of 10,000 employees are affected by the award. The Employers' Negotiation Committee represents 187 Douglas fir region operators in the Puget Sound Area, Wash.

The record of the case showed a need for stabilizing manpower in the West Coast lumber industry to prevent a migration of lumber workers to better paying jobs in shipyards, aircraft and other West Coast war industries. At the same time Professor Jensen's award had the effect of stabilizing wage rates within the Douglas fir area.

Professor Jensen's award in this case provided employees who have worked at least 1,400 hours during a year with a week's paid vacation. Employees who worked less than 1,400 hours are to receive proportionately less vacation. The award also recommended that employees who are drafted or enlist in the armed services be granted a proportionate vacation for the weeks worked during the year.

The parties to the dispute had entered into an arbitration agreement on April 17, 1942, which provided that the award of the arbitrator was to be submitted to the War Labor Board for approval before it was submitted to the parties, and that if the Board approved the award, a directive order should be entered, making the award the order of the Board.

Textile strikers resume work

After a meeting with War Labor Board officials in Washington, representatives of the American Federation of Textile Operatives returned to Fall River, Mass., to urge back to work 125 fixers and changers who had been on an unauthorized strike for 9 days.

As a result the men agreed to return to work June 22. The United States Employment Service had previously hired workers to replace those on strike, and production was at 90 percent of normal. A demand for an immediate wage increase had precipitated the strike. The War Labor Board has before it a request for a general wage increase from the C. I. O. United Textile Workers, bargaining agent for the plant, which, if granted, would cover the strikers.

Wage stabilization award

A 5-cent per hour wage increase over basic wage rates for boatmen and warehousemen employed by the W. J. Connors Contracting Co., Terminals and Transportation Corp., and the Great Lakes Transit Corporation, was ordered by a unanimous vote of the Board.

In an opinion accompanying the Board order, Wayne L. Morse, public member of the Board, pointed out that the wage increase "appeared amply justified * * * when viewed from the standpoint of wages paid for comparable work in the Buffalo area. • • •

McNutt meets with Federal and State officials to consider unemployment in New York City

At the direction of the President, Paul V. McNutt, Chairman of the War Manpower Commission, met June 19 with Governor Lehman of New York State, Mayor LaGuardia of New York City, and representatives of the Federal agencies concerned with war production, to review the situation in New York City arising out of the unemployment caused by the curtailment of civilian production and of distribution of consumer goods, as well as the idle metal working and other production facilities in the Metropolitan area.

It was the consensus of the conferees that:

New York City presents currently one of the most serious manpower problems of this country.

In New York there is a great reservoir of manpower which is not now being adequately utilized in the war production program.

New York City has already been hard hit by the curtailment of civilian production and it seems probable that further curtailment may cause additional unemployment. The present unemployment estimate is almost 400,000 workers, many of whom are skilled.

Metropolitan New York has idle plant facilities, some of which can readily be adapted to war production. Housing transportation and community facilities are also available.

It was agreed that each of the Federal agencies would reexamine the New York City situation in the light of problems in its own field.

★ ★ ★

First in aircraft series of wage stabilization conferences scheduled for West Coast

Wendell Lund, Director of the Labor Production Division of the WPB June 18 announced the first of a series of wage stabilization conferences in the aircraft industry. The meeting will be held at Los Angeles on July 6.

Representatives of the nine air frame manufacturers on the Pacific Coast and the two principal labor organizations in the industry, the United Automobile, Aircraft, and Agricultural Implement Workers of America (CIO and the International Association of Machinists (AFL) will attend. The War Department and the Navy Department are also being asked to participate in the conference.

Paul R. Porter, chief of the newly-established wage stabilization branch of the Labor Production Division, was named by Mr. Lund to preside at the conference.

900 plants now in War Production Drive; many records broken

The establishment of labor management committees in 10 General Electric plants brings to 900 the number of plants participating in the War Production Drive, it was announced June 19 at War Production Drive Headquarters.

Electric companies participate

With this participation in force at General Electric plants, all of the three largest electric manufacturers are engaged in the drive to increase war production. There are labor management committees in 25 Westinghouse plants and in 3 Western Electric plants. One General Electric plant established a committee earlier, bringing to 11 the number of its plants in the drive.

These electric manufacturing companies make hundreds of different things for the armed services. They not only produce almost all of their peacetime articles for the Army and Navy, but they also have converted a large part of the plants for the manufacture of new devices for fighting men.

Production progress reported

Coincident with the rise in number of plants with War Production Drives, a large number of increases in production have been reported by labor-management committees in the last few days.

The committee in the plant of Associated Shipbuilders, Seattle, Wash., reported that a ship keel previously requiring 98 days, had been laid in 21 days.

The committee in the New Haven, Conn., plant of the American Steel & Wire Co. of New Jersey, reported that six production records were broken during the first 5 months of 1942 against five records for the entire year of 1941.

The committee in the Torrance (Calif.) Works of the Columbia Steel Co. reported:

The joint labor-management production drive committee for this plant wishes you to know that the steel foundry at this plant broke all existing records for production during the month of April. This has come about in some degree through the cooperation of all concerned with the War Production Drive and it is with pride in the work that these men have done that we pass this information on to you.

The committee in the Philadelphia plant of the J. G. Brill Co. reported that "in the last couple of months production of practically all items has been doubled."

The bulletin of the Continental Foundry Co., of East Chicago, Ind., stated:

"Exceeding previously set quotas for vital parts in Army tanks, the East Chicago plant is well on its way to break its present production schedule. . . ."

The committee in the East Pittsburgh plant of the Westinghouse company reported that shipments in the terms of carloads reached a new high for the month of May, exceeding the April high by 55 carloads.

Segregation of alloy steel scrap ordered

Mandatory segregation of alloy steel scrap to conserve scarce alloying materials and permit their reuse was ordered June 18 by J. S. Knowlson, Director of Industry Operations.

The order, M–24–c, sets up classifications of alloy steels, provides for their segregation by classifications and prohibits mingling of segregated alloy scrap except in the melting process.

Important savings in the principal alloying elements, nickel, chromium, tungsten and molybdenum, are expected as a result of the order.

Eighteen classifications are set up. The first nine are alloy constructional steels containing combinations of nickel, chromium and molybdenum. Classes 10, 11, and 12 are high-speed tool steels

containing tungsten and molybdenum, chromium and vanadium. The remaining classes except the 18th, are corrosion and heat-resistant alloys containing chromium and nickel. Class 18 is all other heat- and corrosion-resistant steels containing chromium, nickel, molybdenum, cobalt or copper.

Doesn't apply to scrap dealers

Persons who produce 10 tons or more of alloy scrap per month in the first nine classes must segregate them and those who produce one ton or more of the last nine classes must do likewise.

The order does not apply to scrap dealers as they have no means to analyze the alloy content of scrap. It is directed primarily to steel fabricators.

MANPOWER . . .

20 million to be needed in war factories and transportation, 12 million on farms; eventually perhaps 10 million in Army

Following is a series of questions and answers released last week by the War Manpower Commission to explain some of the more important aspects of the manpower program:

Q. How many men will be required for the armed forces?

A. We have 2,000,000 under arms now; we shall have 4,200,000—maybe 4,500,000—by the end of the year; in 1943, 6,000,000 to 7,000,000 (according to General Hershey) and eventually we may have as many as 10,000,000.

Q. How many men will be required for the industrial army—for the army on the farms?

A. We must have a force of 20,000,000 in direct war production and transportation in 1944 and 12,000,000 in the fields for 1943's harvest.

Women must fill the gaps

Q. Will women be needed in these jobs?

A. Women must fill the gap created by the departure of men for the fighting fronts; a million and a half already are doing war work and four million more will be needed in the next 2 years.

Q. Where are we going to get these millions of men and women?

A. Seven to eight million are expected to come from suspended or converted peacetime industries, 400,000 to 600,000 from the farm, 400,000 from professional ranks, 1,500,000 from the unemployed, and 2,000,000 from the home—housewives, youths, and retired workers.

Q. What Federal agencies are in charge of this task?

A. The War Manpower Commission, headed by Federal Security Administrator Paul V. McNutt, will direct the job. Its principal field agency will be the United States Employment Service. Many training agencies and industry will also help.

Q. Does that mean a "labor draft"?

A. No; this is a voluntary movement to place every man and woman in the job for which he or she is best fitted, and most needed.

Q. How large is our total labor force?

A. 55,000,000 persons.

Q. Do we have any potential reserves?

A. There are an additional 13,000,000 housewives without small children, youths, and retired workers.

Q. How many more workers will be needed in war industry and agriculture?

A. 11,000,000 in industry and 2,500,000 on the farms at the heaviest peak.

Q. What war industries must be expanded most?

A. Shipbuilding personnel will be about tripled, aircraft increased four times, ordnance nearly tripled, and Government employment in navy yards, Army arsenals, and air depots raised five-fold.

Q. How many skilled occupations are involved?

A. Nearly 100.

Q. What are some of these occupations?

A. For every tool designer available, 51 are needed; for every toolmaker, 25; for every ship carpenter, 7; for every marine machinist, 22, and for every aircraft riveter, 4.

Q. Are war workers needed *now*?

A. Yes; they are desperately needed in some war industry communities, and in some farm regions.

Q. Where do I apply for such work?

A. At your nearest United States Employment Service office.

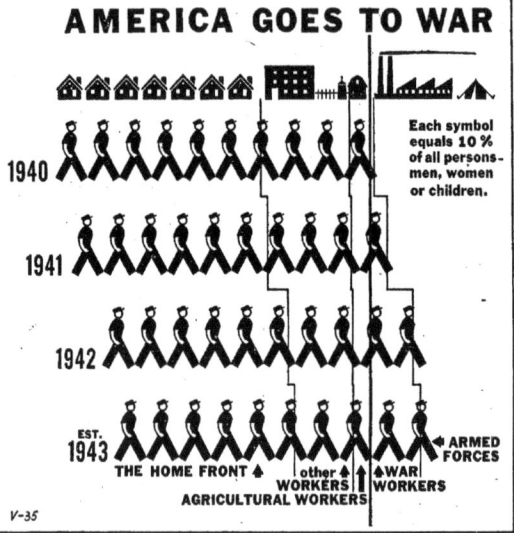

AMERICA GOES TO WAR

1940

1941

1942

EST. 1943

Each symbol equals 10 % of all persons-men, women or children.

THE HOME FRONT ♠ other ♠ ♠ WAR
WORKERS ♠ WORKERS
AGRICULTURAL WORKERS

♠ ARMED FORCES

V-35

Grant for OEM

Two-column mats for publication will be available within a week. Address Distribution Section, Division of Information, Office for Emergency Management, Washington, D. C., and refer to V-35.

McNutt names division heads of War Manpower Commission

Chairman Paul V. McNutt June 17 announced the following appointments to the War Manpower Commission, completing most of the national organization:

Edward C. Elliott, president of Purdue University, to be chief of the Professional and Technical Employment and Training Division.

Lt. Col. Sam Seeley, United States Army, to be chief, Office of Procurement and Assignment Service.

Dr. Leonard Carmichael, National Roster, Scientific and Specialized Personnel. Dr. Carmichael, president of Tufts College, Medford, Mass., organized the Roster in 1940 and has directed it since.

John J. Corson, chief, Industrial and Agricultural Employment Division.

Lt. Col. Clinton Roy Dickerson, United States Army, chief, Military Division. Lt. Col. Dickerson is assistant to Maj. Gen. Lewis B. Hershey, director of the Selective Service System.

Dr. Elliott, Mr. Corson, and Lt. Col. Dickerson are responsible to Brig. Gen. Frank J. McSherry, Director of Operations, War Manpower Commission.

Serving under Altmeyer

Serving under Arthur J. Altmeyer, Executive Director of the Commission, will be the following:

Dr. William Haber, chief, Planning and Progressive Reports Division. Dr. Haber, on leave from the University of Michigan, has been on the staff of the Director of the Budget and is on detail from the Bureau of the Budget to direct the planning activities of the War Manpower Commission.

Frederick F. Stephan, chief, Statistical Analysis and Coordination Service. Mr. Stephan is president of the American Statistical Association.

Robert C. Weaver, chief, Negro Manpower Service. Dr. Weaver was formerly Negro affairs adviser to the Interior Department and the USHA and has headed the Negro Employment and Training Branch of the Labor Division of the OPM and WPB for the last 2 years.

Will W. Alexander, chief, Minority Groups Service. Dr. Alexander, former Farm Security Administrator, directed a minority groups program in the WPB's Labor Division, and is on detail from the Julius Rosenwald Fund.

Harold Dotterer, chief, Administrative Services. Mr. Dotterer, chief clerk of the Federal Security Agency, has been detailed to the Manpower Commission.

Chairman McNutt also announced appointment of Raymond Rubicam, president of the advertising firm of Young and Rubicam, New York City, as a special assistant. Mr. Rubicam is serving without compensation.

Auto workers may stay with new war jobs under amended labor transfer policy

War Manpower Commission Chairman Paul V. McNutt and War Production Board Chairman Donald M. Nelson by joint action June 18 amended the Government's automobile industry labor transfer policy to facilitate employment of trained workers at their top skills.

Retain seniority rights

A joint McNutt-Nelson statement amends the Government's official transfer policy for this industry, announced September 17, 1941, by Associate Director General Sidney Hillman of the OPM.

The statement points out that under the former policy, a former employer could recall a worker to his original job on one week's notice. If the worker did not answer such a call, he would lose his accumulated seniority rights with the original employer. This had the effect of disrupting essential war occupations in the new plants, especially where the worker had been retrained for a new job in the new plant.

Consequently the statement directs that workers originally from nonwar plants who have been fully trained by the new employers for new jobs may, if they choose, stay with their new employers, retaining their accumulated seniority rights, unless they are offered jobs by their former employers, which will utilize their newly acquired skills.

The original recall provision has operated to prevent the employment of several thousand skilled employees of the closed or converted civilian plants. This is because the new war plants feared the original employer would recall the workers as soon as the civilian plant was converted. Meantime the converted automobile industry has reached a new peak in employment, surpassing previous peacetime peaks, and many of the new employees have been drawn in from outside of the Detroit area.

In addition there are thousands of employees in the new war plants who are not being trained for jobs for which they could be qualified because the new employers fear they may be recalled.

Reports from some employers indicate they have discouraged the employment of people with long seniority records, because of the necessity of protecting future production in the new plant.

"This nation cannot afford such disruptions of essential war production and the loss of precious man-hours of work from the war effort," the McNutt-Nelson joint statement said.

Two unions ordered to stop racial discrimination

In two stiffly worded decisions, the President's Committee on Fair Employment Practice has sustained charges of race discrimination against two Chicago labor unions which have prevented Negro steamfitters and plumbers from working on certain defense projects.

Texts made public

The texts of these decisions were made public June 14 by Lawrence W. Cramer, executive secretary of the committee, who pointed out that Local 597, Steamfitters Protective Association, and Local 130, Chicago Journeymen Plumbers Union, had been given until June 18, to "alter or construe" their present policies in such a manner that qualified steamfitters and plumbers may be employed "in the ordinary course of business" on the basis of merit. The unions have another five days in which to notify the contractors to whom they supply workers.

Lund names Keenan, Clowes associate directors

Reinforcing his recently announced policy of labor representation in the WPB Labor Production Division, Director Wendell Lund June 14 appointed Joseph O. Keenan of the Chicago Federation of Labor, AFL, and Philip J. Clowes of the United Steel Workers of America, CIO, as his associate directors.

THANKS FOR THE NIPPONESE

War Production Drive Headquarters reports that a table has been installed to hold rejected parts in the plant of the Grayson Heat Control, Ltd., at Lynwood, Cal. Over it is a large caricature of Hirohito with a happy grin and a line saying, "Thank you so much please for helping Japanese soldier."

CONSERVATION . . .

Waste of rubber in past years created scrap which may save U. S. now

Scrap rubber has long been a factor in the American rubber industry although in the past we made no determined effort to save rubber, WPB observed this week.

Proper mixture doesn't lower quality

Nevertheless reclaimed rubber has always been important to the manufacture of all sorts of rubber products, not excepting tires. A proper mixture of reclaimed with crude rubber doesn't decrease the quality of the product; as a matter of fact, in the case of tires, some manufacturers claim a proper mixture increases this durability.

Reclaimed about ¼ of total in 1938

Figures on the percentage of reclaimed rubber used in the rubber industry over the period 1938–41, inclusive, are interesting when compared with figures on the importation of crude rubber during that period. In 1938 our reclaiming plants produced 121,000 tons of reclaim, while we imported 457,000 tons of crude rubber. In 1939 we produced 170,000 tons of reclaim, imported 592,000 tons of crude; in 1940, 190,000 tons of reclaim, 648,000 tons of crude; and in 1941, 270,000 tons of reclaim, 775,000 tons crude.

Taken cold, these figures do not do full justice to the importance of reclaimed scrap rubber in our rubber economy. After 1938 there was a growing spread in the margin between crude rubber imports and the amount of reclaim, but this does not represent a decline in the use of reclaim rubber by manufacturers; it merely reflects growing fear of war in the Far East, fear which brought mild efforts to create a reserve of crude rubber against an uncertain future. The figure for 1938, in which reclaimed rubber amounts to just a little less than 25 percent of the total quota, affords a truer picture of the relative importance of scrap to crude in the rubber industry.

One of the reasons why the U. S. A. did not develop a more considerable reclaiming industry than now exists was the fact that crude rubber often was available at extremely low prices during the years since the last war.

But just because we weren't making full use of our rubber scrap, because scrap was only a lesser factor in the rubber industry and vast quantities of scrap rubber were cast aside, we piled up—during the years when we were the world's greatest consumer of rubber—a tremendous reserve of scrap rubber.

This reserve, unlike the great stock pile of rubber on the wheels of America's 28,000,000 privately owned passenger vehicles is not visible. It is hidden away in attic and cellar. It is forgotten beneath the bath tub and lies in dark recesses of the barn. It is piled in odd corners of garages, it is oxidizing on battered jalopies in auto graveyards.

How large is this reserve? We'll find out, but at the moment this isn't important. Large or small we must have all of it; all the worn out tires, all the hot water bottles and overshoes and girdles and mats and nipples and balls and fly swatters and garden hose and galoshes and all the other now useless items among 50,000 different articles of common use which contain rubber. Our immediate need is to collect scrap rubber enough to keep the rubber reclaimers' plants operating at capacity—and that we can do.

★ ★

Typewriter users told how to save rubber

By taking advantage of a new rubber-saving process for renovating typewriter rollers, large business firms and other typewriter users can make an important contribution to the Nation-wide rubber conservation campaign now under way, technical experts of the OPA said June 20.

A recently developed process makes old typewriter rollers as good as new, increases their service by several years, and requires the use of no rubber whatever.

An ordinary sand or grit blasting machine, of the type used by metal polishers, can be shifted to the job of renovating typewriter rollers. Hard films of dirt and dried ink are blasted from the surface of the rollers, leaving the live rubber beneath clean and smooth.

Duties of war price, rationing board members outlined by OPA

The first two in a series of administrative letters detailing the duties of local war price and rationing board members under the expanded program of Nation-wide price control have been mailed out to OPA State officers for distribution, the OPA announced June 19.

Five major duties listed

The instructions, in the form of a letter from Price Administrator Henderson to the local boards, list five major duties which the board members will be asked to handle. They are:

1. To distribute explanatory materials relating to the general maximum price regulation and to give out such information as is included in the materials.

2. To receive and file price lists of cost-of-living commodities filed by retailers.

3. To supply forms upon which retailers may apply for adjustments under the price ceiling and to maintain records of adjustments made by the OPA regional offices.

4. To receive complaints of violations of price regulations, and other types of complaints, and to forward them to the proper OPA office.

5. To forward to the appropriate OPA office communications, applications and inquiries which are submitted to local boards but fall outside the jurisdiction of the board itself.

★ ★ ★

Rubber imports banned except by RFC subsidiaries

The WPB on the recommendation of the Board of Economic Warfare, June 19 prohibited the importation of rubber and rubber products, including balata, except by subsidiaries of the Reconstruction Finance Corporation.

The Rubber Reserve Company of RFC, which has heretofore been the sole importer of crude rubber and latex, will now also undertake the purchasing of reclaimed and scrap rubber in any form, as balata.

This action was effected by Amendment No. 10 to Supplementary Order M–15–b. "Imports" as used in the amendment cover a release from the bonded custody of the United States Bureau of Customs, as well as any shipment from a foreign country or from any territory or possession of the United States into continental United States.

INVISIBLE BARRIER

CIVILIAN MISUSE OF AUTOMOBILE TIRES

Cartoon by Elderman for Victory. *Publishers may obtain mats of these cartoons weekly in either two- or three-column size. Requests to be put on the mailing list should be addressed to Distribution Section, Division of Information, Office for Emergency Management, Washington, D. C. Refer to V–34.*

Dealers agree to sell rubber scrap stocks to Government

Reports received June 17 by the Bureau of Industrial Conservation indicate that scrap rubber dealers throughout the country are agreeing to sell their complete inventories of scrap rubber to the Government within the 2-week period of the Nation-wide scrap rubber collection campaign.

Auto mats reclaimable but won't make retreads

Rubber experts of the Bureau of Industrial Conservation and the WPB's rubber branch made it clear that while the rubber in automobile floor mats could be reclaimed, it was not of a quality that would make adequate camelback stock for retreading purposes.

11,173,979 pounds of aluminum, other scrap collected in 1941

A report on the amount of aluminum collected in the National Aluminum Collection Campaign last year was made public June 19 by the Bureau of Industrial Conservation.

Excerpts from the report follow:

Collections during the national aluminum campaign were scheduled for the period of July 21–29, 1941. Actually, the collection of this aluminum, which was under the supervision of the Office of Civilian Defense, extended over a considerable period of time subsequent to July 29.

Falls short of expectations

According to complete returns now available, 11,173,979 pounds of aluminum and other scrap were collected during the campaign. The amount is somewhat less than was indicated earlier on the basis of reports received from local chairmen at the various concentration points.

The best relative showing was made in the New England States, while the poorest showing was made in the Southern States particularly in Mississippi, Georgia, and South Carolina.

It was hoped that around 15,000,000 pounds of aluminum would be collected as a result of the drive. Actually, only 6,398,051 pounds, or 57.4 percent of the total scrap collected was in the form of aluminum. The remainder was largely scrap iron with smaller quantities of copper, brass, pewter, and other materials present.

The reasons for this disappointing showing are not difficult to discern. The collection was undertaken by the Office of Civilian Defense without adequate preparation and without cooperation of the dealers who were left entirely out of the program. Also, the expected results were based upon two sample drives in Madison, Wis., and Richmond, Va. These two particular drives were of an intensive nature and should not have been regarded typical of what we could expect from the country as a whole.

The delay in the shipment of aluminum scrap from the various concentration points to the plants of the smelters can be traced in large measure to the by-passing of dealers, since adequate facilities for cleaning, sorting, and treating aluminum scrap were not available and smelters had to undertake this work themselves.

INDUSTRIAL OPERATIONS . . .

Code numbers on all orders will show end use of product at any stage, provide basis for authorizing material

The effect on the priorities system of the new regulations concerning the production requirements plan was explained June 18 in a statement issued by the Bureau of Priorities of the Division of Industry Operations.

Preference ratings will still be used

"The production requirements plan is the basic material authorization to buy, and supersedes all other priority instruments in the field it covers," according to J. S. Knowlson, Director of Industry Operations. "The other priority instruments will continue in effect, however, for the groups not covered by PRP, and preference ratings will still be used as directives of d e l i v e r y on finished products."

Excerpts from the statement follow:

The production . requirements plan is the chief method of authorizing the purchase of basic materials. With a few exceptions, it is mandatory for all concerns using $5,000 worth of metal a quarter and it may be used by other concerns. Approximately 90 percent of the metal used will be covered by the plan.

Special conditions to be weighed

For the third quarter of this year, PRP is based primarily upon one form, PD–25A. This form is filled out by manufacturers as a specific application for authority to buy materials during the quarter. The PD–25A's will be reviewed and processed by the end products branches, including branches of the Armed Services, within the limitations of the general policy determinations as set forth by the Requirements Committee. Specific conditions within the individual company will be taken into account, however. The PD–25A will then be returned to the applicant as an authority to buy the amounts of material approved on the form.

Advance over-all information already has been gathered from all large metal users on their metal requirements for the third quarter. The facts learned from them, together with information on supply furnished by the materials

branches of the WPB, will be used by the Requirements Committee to determine how metal use can best be distributed.

A third part of the picture is the allocation classification system, which will be started during the third quarter so that it may become an effective part of PRP during the following quarter. The allocation system fits in as follows:

Code to reveal end use

The present PD–25A requires information on the end uses of the applicant's . products. However, the applicant often has no way of determining these end uses, especially if he is a sub-subcontractor. And even when he knows the end use, he has had no standard method of stating it on the PD–25A. The allocation system, designed to rectify this, is an end use code in numerical symbols. Numbers from 1.00 to 23.00 have been assigned to all major classes of military, industrial and civilian uses. These classifications are subdivided as necessary. For instance, class 9.00—power, light and heat—has under it subclass 9.10, electricity; 9.20, petroleum; 9.30, coal and coke; 9.40, gas. In addition, there are purchaser symbols such as USN for the Navy.

Priorities Regulation No. 10 requires that the code be used on orders placed after July 1 and on all previously placed orders calling for delivery after July 31. In this way the end use will filter down through all layers of contractors and subcontractors to the concerns buying the basic materials.

As a result, when the applications are made under PRP for the fourth quarter, it will be possible for each manufacturer to state exactly, in terms of the code, what proportion of his products will go to what particular end uses, such as tanks, machine tools, or airplanes.

WPB to govern monthly shipments

As previously stated, PRP grants authority to buy a definite amount of specific materials and also authorizes a lump allowance for operating supplies. Actual shipments of critical material now under allocation control still will be governed by month to month directions from

the War Production Board through the "M" orders covering the various materials. In brief, the "M" orders continue in effect just as before, except for the substitution of the new allocation classification for the various classifications now used. PRP, however, is intended to reduce the problem of allocation under the "M" orders by bringing total demand into approximate balance with total supply. This will make the specific scheduling of shipments the most important function of the "M" order.

Priorities Regulation No. 11, the legal basis of PRP, provides that in addition to companies using less than $5,000 worth of metals a quarter, the users engaged in nine classes of business (see Victory, June 16) may continue to work through the existing priority procedures.

Several priority tools continue

Several important priority instruments will continue to be used:

The "P" Orders, which eventually will be greatly reduced in number. In the immediate future, however, certain orders will continue in effect for the users of less than $5,000 worth of metal a quarter and for the special groups. For instance, P–46 for the public utilities, and broad orders such as P–148, the export order, and P–100 as it applies to concerns not covered by PRP will continue.

PD–1A's may still be issued for capital equipment for all classes of producers, and for all requirements of the industries not operating under PRP. A PD–1A certificate may be used to obtain a finished item from a company covered by PRP, but the rating cannot be extended by such a producer to get necessary materials for manufacture since he will be required by the terms of PRP to obtain his basic materials through that plan. Where a rating assigned on a PD–1A is served on a manufacturer outside the terms of PRP (for example, the manufacturer who uses less than $5,000 worth of metal for the quarter), the rating can be extended for the necessary materials. .

PD–3A's will be used for military requirements in almost exactly the same way as PD–1A is used. Officers of the Army and Navy will continue to assign the PD–3A certificate for the delivery of finished items. The rating then serves as a directive of delivery—the manufacturer will be required to deliver the finished item in accordance with the degree of preference rating assigned. But if the manufacturer is operating under PRP he cannot get materials for production by extending the rating. Instead, he will rely on PRP. (The degree of preference rating and the end use code assigned to the finished items will show up in the manufacturer's application under PRP for the next quarter.)

Project Ratings (P–19 Series) will continue to be used for practically all building or construction activities with the usual exceptions of a limited amount of military construction and certain classes of housing.

Limitation (L) and Conservation (M) Orders will continue to govern the things a manufacturer cannot make even though he may be able to get the material.

Critical metal for baby buggies forbidden after August 1; use of iron and steel curbed

The WPB issued an order June 14 that permits continued production of baby carriages but requires that they contain none of the more critical metals and only a minimum of iron or steel.

Allowed time for conversion

The order, L–152, is expected to convert the baby carriage industry from a steel to a wood-working industry.

Baby carriages are divided into three groups. Between now and July 31, 1942, carriages in all three groups may be manufactured at the same rate as, they were manufactured during the base year ending June 30, 1941. The amount of metal to be used in these carriages is not restricted, companies affected may have time in which to get lined up for the production of wooden models.

Restrictions vary for each group

On and after August 1 no metal other than iron, steel, gold, or silver may be used in the production or assembly of any carriage in any of the three groups.

To conserve manufacturers' inventories of steel, the order prohibits the sale or delivery of steel intended for use in baby carriages except for use in carriages permitted by the order.

At least six of the companies expect to have sample all-wood models (except for steel axles and fittings) ready for display later this month.

. .   . .   . .

Copper banned for pipes in water systems

In an interpretation of Copper Conservation Order M–9–c, the Director of Industry Operations on June 15 prohibited the use of copper and copper alloys in the manufacture of pipes and fittings for use in water supply and distribution systems, except corporation cocks and curb stops.

M–9–c provides that copper cannot be used where any less scarce material is an acceptable substitute. Iron and steel may be used satisfactorily for pipes and fittings, hence copper and copper alloys cannot be used for these purposes.

The interpretation does not apply to plumbing fixtures in buildings, in which the use of copper is already specifically prohibited by Order M–9–c, nor does it apply to water meters.

Critical material banned in church goods; religious leaders approve substitutions

The use of critical material in the manufacture of church goods was ordered curtailed in General Limitation Order L–136 issued June 14 by the War Production Board.

Critical materials such as brass and copper are to be replaced by other less critical materials such as iron, steel, silver, gold, and selected wood stock.

Products affected by the order include articles of religious devotion and articles used in the conduct of religious services.

No conflict with church laws

Louis Upton, chief of the WPB consumers' durable goods branch, said that leaders of large religious groups consulted by WPB during preparation of the order said that other substances can be substituted for the scarce metals prohibited by the order. All of these leaders, Mr. Upton added, expressed a willingness to cooperate in the conservation program.

"None of the restrictions in the order conflict with any provision of Canon and other church laws," Mr. Upton said.

The order provides that on and after June 23, 1942, no manufacturer may produce or assemble any church goods containing any of the following materials: Aluminum, cadmium, chromium, copper and copper base alloys, cork, phenolic plastics, methacrylate plastics, lead (except for solder), magnesium, mercury, nickel, rhodium, rubber, silk, tin and tinplate, zinc, and alloy steel.

Iron and steel limited

During the 3-month period beginning June 1 and for each 3 months thereafter until otherwise ordered, a manufacturer may use an amount of iron and steel which may not exceed 50 percent, by weight, of the total amount of iron, steel, and critical material he used during a corresponding 3 months in 1940 in the manufacture of church goods. The use of gold and silver is unrestricted.

The order prohibits the sale of a manufacturer's stock of iron, steel, and restricted material, except (a) in articles he is permitted to produce under the order; (b) to other church goods manufacturers for articles they are permitted to produce; (c) to fill orders with a preference rating of A–1–j or higher; (d) to the Defense Supplies Corporation, the Metals Reserve Corporation, or other Government agency set up by the RFC.

30-watt fluorescent fixtures freed from sales restrictions

Fluorescent lighting fixtures using tubes rated at 30 watts or less—types which are used in kitchens, retail stores, and for similar purposes—have been released from the sales restrictions of Order L–78, it was announced June 13 by the Director of Industry Operations.

This action, effected by Amendment No. 2 to the order, was taken because the types released have little direct use in war plants.

The amendment also makes the following changes:

1. Permits high voltage (cold cathode) fixtures to be made of materials already fabricated.
2. Eliminates replaceable starters from the restrictions of the order.
3. Permits the interchange of fixtures and parts among manufacturers for uses as defined in the order.
4. Extends the life of the order until September 1. It would have expired on June 30.
5. Permits delivery, but not sale, of fixtures or parts for purposes of demonstration, test, and storage, and also delivery within branches of a single enterprise.

The amendment also makes clear that portable lamps regulated by Order L–33 are not covered by Order L–78.

Water meters sharply cut in use of critical materials

The use of critical metals in the manufacture of water meters is sharply restricted in a WPB order issued June 18.

No stainless steel or nickel alloys may henceforth be used in water meters. Tin is prohibited except as an alloy in copper, and copper and copper base alloys are eliminated from all parts of the meter except internal gears and workings.

The order, Schedule I to Limitation Order L–154, was issued concurrently with issuance of L–154, which empowers the Director of Industry Operations of WPB to issue, from time to time, schedules restricting the use of critical material in the production of any power, steam and water auxiliary equipment.

★ ★ ★

New housing critical areas

The War Production Board has added seven new areas to the Defense Housing Critical Area List—Santa Ana, Calif.; Sansalito, Calif., Milledgeville, Ga.; Sycamore, Ill.; New Castle, Ind.; Sidney, Nebr.; and Chillicothe, Ohio.

Shipments of some types of space-heating equipment limited to military, naval orders

Shipments of certain types of space-heating equipment were limited by the WPB June 13 to orders of the Army, Navy, Maritime Commission, and Coast Guard.

Replaces "freeze" order

This action, embodied in Limitation Order L-107, replaces a telegraphic "freeze" order, issued on March 24, which prohibited shipment except on specific approval by the Director of Industry Operations.

The L-107 order covers extended surface heating equipment, including unit heaters, unit ventilators, blast heating coils, convectors, and winter air conditioners. These products are m a d e largely from steel, copper, and copper alloys, and are used for heating large spaces or for industrial drying purposes.

The order prohibits delivery, regardless of the terms of any prior commitment or preference rating, except for the military or naval services noted above, unless delivery is expressly authorized on Form PD-412a by the Director of Industry Operations.

Cadmium restricted to vital military, civilian uses

Use of cadmium will be restricted to essential military and civilian uses by an amendment to General Preference Order M-65 issued June 18 by the Director of Industry Operations. On and after June 24, 1942, the order as amended will permit the delivery of cadmium to distributors and to users only upon specific authorization by WPB.

Users of cadmium must obtain authorization from WPB by filing Form PD-441 before delivery can be made or accepted.

★ ★ ★

Safety equipment rules alined with over-all rubber order

Issuance of an amendment to Limitation Order L-114 on safety equipment to permit the use of rubber for purposes detailed by Rubber Order M-15-b was announced June 17 by the Director of Industry Operations.

| PRIORITY ACTIONS | | | | *From June 11 *Through June 17 | |

Subject	Order No.	Related form	Issued	Expiration date	Rating
Agar: a. Order M-96 broadened to include wet as well as dry forms of agar.	M-96 (Amend. 1)		6-13-42		
Baby carriages: a. Permits manufacture of baby carriages but requires that they contain a minimum of iron and steel.	L-162	PD-423, 417	6-13-42		
Burlap and burlap products: a. Enables Commodity Credit Corporation, to purchase frozen stocks of burlap to release shortage of material on West Coast.	M-47 (as amended May 2, Amend. 1).		6-12-42		
Chromium and nickel in automotive valves: a. Rigid specifications for the manufacture of exhaust valves used in automotive equipment established by WPB to consume quantities of chromium and nickel.	L-128		6-17-42, effective 7-1-42		
Church goods: a. Use of critical material in manufacture of church goods ordered curtailed by WPB.	L-136	PD-417	6-13-42		A-1-1
Coffee: a. Coffee roasters given aid in handling excess green coffee.	M-135 (Amend. 2)	PD-533	6-12-42		
Corsets, combinations and brassieres: a. Amended to allow use in specified cases.	L-60 (Amend. 1)		6-13-42		
Copper: a. Curtailing use of copper in certain items, with respect to pipes and fittings for water supply and distribution systems.	M-9-c (as amend. Int. No. 4).		6-15-42		
Domestic mechanical refrigerators: a. Extension of time in which to submit reports from June 26 to July 3, because of delay in delivery of printed forms.	L-5-d (Amend. 1)		6-15-42		
Douglas fir plywood (moisture-resistant type): a. Restrictions placed on deliveries after July 1 by WPB to conserve supply and direct distribution.	L-150		6-15-42		
Extended, surface heating equipment: a. Shipments of space-heating equipment limited by WPB to orders of Army, Navy, Maritime Commission, and Coast Guard.	L-107	PD-412a, 467	6-13-42		
Fluorescent lighting fixtures: a. Releases certain fixtures for sale and extends life of order to Sept. 1.	L-78 (Amend. 2)		6-13-42	9-1-42	A-2
Gages, precision measuring tools, testing instruments, and chucks: a. Strict distribution of instruments brought under control by WPB.	E-5		6-15-42		A-10
General industrial equipment: a. Definition of equipment covered by L-123.	L-123 (Amend. 1)		6-13-42		
Kitchen, household, and other miscellaneous articles: a. Removes certain restrictions on tubes. Amendment effects carpet sweepers, curtain rods, fixtures and drapery attachments also.	L-30 (Amend. 3)		6-12-42		
Laboratory equipment: a. Prohibits sale and delivery of laboratory equipment except for certified essential uses.	L-114		6-12-42		
Mahogany and Philippine mahogany: a. States that mahogany veneers not subject to Conservation Order M-122.	M-122 (Int. No. 1)		6-15-42		
Mining machinery and equipment (material entering into the production of): a. Mining machinery cannot be delivered except on rated orders. b. Provides A-10 rating for repair and maintenance material.	P-56-a (Amend. No. 3). P-56 as amended (Int. No. 1).		6-19-42 6-12-42		
Pyrethrum: a. Complete allocation control placed by WPB. To conserve supply and direct distribution.	M-179	PD-591	6-13-42		
Rubber and products and material of which rubber is a component: a. Requires use of more reclaimed rubber and less crude in manufacture of industrial pneumatic and solid tires. b. Supplementary order. c. Restricts transactions in new aircraft tires and tubes.	M-15-b-1 (Amend. No. 6). M-15-b-1 (as amended). M-15-d		6-12-42 6-12-42 6-12-42		
Safety equipment: a. Permits use of rubber for purposes detailed by Rubber Order M-15-b.	L-114 (Amend. No. 2).		6-17-42		

Subject	Order No.	Related form	Issued	Expiration date	Rating
Spices: a. Food processors, manufacturers of medicines, and other types of industrial receivers of restricted spices are directed to compute monthly spice quotas on amount used in corresponding quarter in 1941.	M-127 (Amend. No. 1).		6-12-42		
b. Supplementary order	M-127-a (as amended).		6-12-42		
Suppliers in inventory: a. Railroad supplies removed from controls imposed by L-63.	L-63 (Amend. No. 4).		6-15-42		
Tin (collapsible tin, tin coated, and alloy tubes): a. Sale of tooth paste and shaving cream permitted without turn-in of tube to armed forces.	M-118 (Amend. 2)		6-15-42		
b. Amended to include various amendments issued since original issuance date, and to remove obsolete provisions.	M-43 (as amended June 17)	PD-213	6-17-42		
c. Tin plate and terneplate: Manufacturers of cans ordered to use electrolytic tin plate and chemically treated black plate for tin plate where possible.	M-81-a		6-13-42		
Tools (hand service): a. Limits type of steel which may be used in producing hand service tools. Track-laying tractors and auxiliary equipment: a. Tightening of control by WPB of above equipment.	E-6		6-12-42		A-10.
	L-53 (Amend. 1)		6-15-42		
Wool: a. Order extended a month, to August 2, 1942, to allocate new wool for July.	M-73 (as amended for period July 5 to Aug. 2, 1942.)		6-11-42, effective 7-5-42.		

PRIORITIES REGULATIONS

Number	Subject	Issued
Prior. Reg. No. 3, as amended June 10, 1942.	Establishes a uniform method of application and extension of preference ratings, effective July 1, and preference rating may be applied or extended by a single form of certification.	6-10-42

Rigid specifications set on automotive valves to save nickel, chromium

Rigid specifications for the manufacture of exhaust valves used in all types of automotive equipment were established by WPB June 17 in order to conserve large quantities of chromium and nickel.

Limitation Order L-128, effective July 1, specifies the maximum amount of chromium and nickel that may be used in the manufacturing formula for automotive exhaust valves.

All manufacturers, the order provides, must use a two-piece, welded head type of construction, permitting chromium and nickel to be used in the valve head only. It is estimated that this restriction alone will result in saving more than 40 percent of chromium and nickel used in former standard manufacturing practices.

Although it is unlikely that any additional chromium or nickel will be made available to manufacturers of exhaust valves for civilian use, issuance of order L-128 is regarded as a necessary step in attempting to achieve conservation in

the manufacture of valves that may be possible without additional allocations of the two critical metals.

Old valve must be turned in

In addition to setting up manufacturing specifications, the order prohibits distributors, retailers or jobbers from selling an exhaust valve to a consumer unless the consumer turns in a used exhaust valve, which cannot be reconditioned.

Distributors, retailers or jobbers must dispose of returned valves through customary channels within thirty days after receiving them. They must recondition valves whenever possible.

Consumers are prohibited from using in passenger cars or light trucks valves manufactured under the specifications for medium and heavy trucks.

Restrictions contained in the order do not apply to the production of valves on contracts placed within ninety days after July 1 by the Army, Navy or Maritime Commission.

Makers of cans for vegetables, fats, other products ordered to use new types of plate

Manufacturers of cans for several vegetables, fats, and a score of other products have been ordered by the WPB to substitute wherever possible electrolytic tin plate and chemically treated black plate for tin plate so as to further conserve the country's supply of tin. This regulation became effective June 13 with the issuance of Conservation Order M-81-a.

Since electrolytic plate mills are experiencing difficulty in obtaining materials necessary to build their lines, the order issued June 13 was somewhat less rigid than it would be if production during the next few months could have been accurately forecast.

Products affected

The regulations require the use of the electrolytic tin plate and chemically treated black plate "to the greatest extent available" for the following products:

Electrolytic tin plate—asparagus; green and wax beans; certain fish and shell fish; frozen foods; honey; beets; carrots; carrots and peas; pumpkin and squash; green leafy vegetables; okra; mixed vegetables; soups, except tomato; sweet syrups; chili con carne; and liquid soap.

Chemically treated black plate—hardened edible oils and lard and other fats; dry baby formulas; milks; dehydrated vegetables; liquid oils; coconuts; fly spray; lighter fluids; acetone; oleic acid; dry cleaners; naphtha and other benzols; turpentine; paste polish and waxes; dry disinfectants; and health supplies, except liquid drugs such as chloroform and ether.

Other provisions

Manufacturers of cans for beans, lima and green soybeans, peas, corn, succotash, and meats, except for chili con. carne, are also required to use to the greatest extent available either chemically treated black plate or electrolytic tin plate according to a formula outlined in the order.

Tin allocation order revamped; rules unchanged

The tin allocation order, M-43, was amended June 17 by the Director of Industry Operations to include in the order itself the various amendments issued since the original issuance date, December 17, 1941, and to remove obsolete provisions.

No change is made in either the method of allocation or in the effect of the order upon tin users.

Civilian wool allocation plan submitted by industry committee, to run 6 months

Officials of the WPB textile, clothing and leather branch are considering recommendations of the woolen and worsted industry advisory committee, for a new civilian wool allocation program beginning in August and running for 6 months.

Objectives

The objectives of such a program—to conserve wool to insure an adequate supply for the armed forces, and to make certain that the remaining civilian allotment is used in the production of maximum yardage for woolen civilian fabrics—keynoted a statement to the committee in Washington June 18 by K. W. Marriner, chief of the WPB wool section.

Explaining the need for an order to bring about that objective, Mr. Marriner said that a definite rule, which applies to all alike, provides protection for those who are doing a good job of blending.

The advisory committee submitted recommendations for a three-point allocation program, as follows:

1. That a 6-month allocation be provided for in a WPB order, with new wool allocated for civilian supply on the following basis:

(a) *For the Worsted System*—20 percent of a manufacturer's basic quarterly poundage to be used during the 6-month period for any type of wool product, and a bonus of an additional 25 percent to be used during the same period to produce fabrics and yarns containing less than 65 percent new wool and more than 20 percent of any wool fiber. This 45 percent of a mill's basic quarterly poundage for a 6-month period represents an increase over the 20 percent allocation for the present 3 months under the present order.

(b) *For the Woolen and any other system*—5 percent of a manufacturer's basic quarterly poundage to be used during the 6-month period for any type of wool product, and a bonus of an additional 25 percent to be used during the same period to produce fabrics and yarns containing less than 65 percent new wool and more than 20 percent of any wool fiber. This likewise represents an increase over the 10 percent allocation for the second quarter.

2. That independent yarn spinners should be allowed to make 100-percent wool yarn from their blended quota providing they receive certification from the weaver or knitter that such yarn will be used in a blended fabric.

3. That the 20-percent minimum new wool clause be interpreted to apply only to cloth containing new wool and not to cloth containing reused or reprocessed wool, or to a line of goods heretofore manufactured which contains less than 20 percent new wool.

The governmental officials took the recommendation under advisement and were to meet later to consider the recommendation and prepare the WPB order.

WOOL'S IMPORTANCE to our armed forces is displayed in this first of a series of "FOTOFACTS." Two-column mats are available for publication. Requests should be addressed to Distribution Section, Division of Information, OEM, Washington, D. C. In ordering, refer to V–33.

BAG OSNABURG RESALES

In response to trade inquiries, T. M. Bancroft, chief of the carded fabrics unit of the WPB, June 18 clarified a point on which there has been some confusion in connection with the resale of bag osnaburg and bag sheeting by a person who has acquired them under General Preference Order M–107.

Paragraph (f) of M–107 provides that a bag manufacturer may apply a preference rating to the purchase of bag osnaburg and bag sheeting provided he certifies that the fabric will be placed in process solely for the manufacture of agricultural bags.

The impression has become prevalent, Mr. Bancroft said, that if conditions of the bag manufacturer's business change after he has purchased bag fabrics under the order to an extent which will not require the prompt use of any particular yardage of bag osnaburg or bag sheeting, he is at liberty to resell these goods for some other purpose than the manufacture of agricultural bags.

This is definitely not the case, Mr. Bancroft said. The bag manufacturer is given the right, under the order, to assign a preference rating to certain cotton piece goods for a specific purpose—the manufacture of agricultural bags—and these goods cannot be used for other purposes without authorization of the WPB.

More elastic permitted in some surgical garments

The use of additional elastic fabric in surgical type corsets is permitted for the benefit of expectant mothers, physically disabled persons, and persons having sagging muscles, by Amendment No. 1 to Limitation Order L-90. The amendment was issued June 15 by the Director of Industry Operations.

In addition, manufacturers are allowed to use various other kinds of elastic fabric in other types of corsets, girdles, panty-girdles, and combinations to enable them to use up inventories of elastic fabric.

The amendment also permits the production of inner belts for corsets, girdles, panty-girdles, and combinations, under specified restrictions. In the original order, the use of elastic fabric in such belts was prohibited.

On the other hand, the amendment further curtails the use of elastic fabric in hose supporters.

Corsets, girdles, and combinations are reclassified into four different types.

Track-laying tractors under tighter WPB control

Tightening of WPB control of the distribution of track-laying tractors and auxiliary equipment was ordered June 15 by the Director of Industry Operations.

Amendment No. 1 to Limitation Order L-53 prohibits any person from selling, leasing, delivering, or transferring any new track-laying tractor or new auxiliary equipment, regardless of any preference rating, except upon a specific release issued prior to June 15, or upon specific authorization.

Railroad supplies removed from L-63 restrictions

Because railroad supplies are such slow-moving items that no vendor can turn over his stock within the period required by Suppliers' Inventory Limitation Order L-63 for inventory calculations, they have been removed from the controls imposed by that order. The change was effected in Amendment No. 4 to L-63, issued June 15 by the Director of Industry Operations.

ETHYL CELLULOSE UNDER ALLOCATION

Ethyl cellulose was placed under complete allocation control by General Preference Order M-175, issued June 18 by the Director of Industry Operations. This action was taken to provide adequate supplies for military and essential civilian use and to prevent its use for purposes where substitutes are available.

By the terms of the order, no person may deliver, and no person may accept delivery, of ethyl cellulose except by specific authorization of the Director of Industry Operations. Deliveries of 50 pounds by any one person to any one other person in one month are excepted.

Ethyl cellulose is used in lacquers, coated textiles, and plastics. While production is now larger than ever before, orders carrying preference ratings of A-10 or higher are drawing off stocks for which comparatively plentiful nitrocotton, pitch, tar, or other substitutes are available.

★ ★ ★

Gum naval stores, wood and gum for stores excepted from GMPR

Wood and gum for naval stores and gum naval stores are excepted from the general maximum price regulation, Price Administrator Henderson ruled June 13 in Amendment No. 5 to the regulation. The exemption became effective June 19, 1942.

Wood naval stores, including pine oil, however, remain under provisions of the general maximum price regulation at all levels of distribution.

Gages under stricter control

Distribution of gages, precision measuring tools, testing instruments and chucks was brought under stricter control June 15 with the issuance of General Preference Order E-5.

Under the order no gage, precision measuring tool, chuck or testing instrument, may be sold except pursuant to a rating of A-10 or higher.

Producers' present delivery schedules for gages, precision measuring tools, testing instruments and chucks should be maintained for 30 days from June 15 without change.

General Preference Rating Order E-1-a, revised, which formerly controlled the distribution of gages and chucks, was revoked and replaced by E-5.

Gifts to fighting men excluded from tube turn-in

The War Production Board announced June 15 an amendment to the collapsible tube order (M-115) which permits retailers to dispose of existing stocks of gift toilet kits containing tooth paste or shaving cream to members of the armed forces without requiring a turn-in of an old tube, provided that the box is sent directly by the seller to a soldier, sailor, marine, or member of the United States Coast Guard.

Also exempt

The amendment also exempts from the turn-in requirement sales or distribution of tooth paste and shaving cream made through Army exchanges, ship service stores, ship stores, and Marine exchanges at certain locations to newly inducted selectees and enlistees, or to casualties of war in Army or Navy hospitals.

Distribution or sales through the designated Government agencies aboard ship, in the territory of Alaska, or outside the continental limits of the United States are also excluded from the turn-in requirement.

★ ★

Plane suppliers not in PRP can continue extending ratings

Preference Rating Orders P-109 and P-109-a, which expire June 30, were amended June 18 to permit suppliers who are not required by the terms of Regulation 11 to come under PRP to extend ratings for the purpose of filling purchase orders of producers rated under P-109 and P-109-a, even after the orders have expired.

P-109 has assigned A-1-a ratings to production of military and naval tactical types of aircraft and P-109-a has assigned A-1-b ratings to producers of trainer types.

★ ★ ★

Pyrethrum under allocation

Pyrethrum, a floral derivative used in insecticides, was on June 13 placed under complete allocation and end use control by General Preference Order M-179, issued by the Director of Industry Operations and effective immediately. Each producer must file reports.

RATIONING . . .

Rationing violators' gasoline deliveries suspended by OPA; 175 cases submitted

Price Administrator Henderson on June 16 suspended for periods of from 15 to 30 days deliveries of gasoline to 8 service station operators in metropolitan New York and 6 in the Philadelphia area who admitted flagrant violation of OPA's gasoline rationing regulations.

The June 16 suspension orders, eight in the New York area and six in the Philadelphia area, will be followed shortly by others from a total of 175 reports of violations that were uncovered 10 days ago in "spot checks" carried out in Eastern cities by OPA investigators and citizen volunteers operating under special instructions from OPA enforcement officials.

The orders, copies of which are served on the dealer and sent to his gasoline supplier and the Office of the Petroleum Coordinator, are issued by the Price Administrator under the authority conferred upon him by the President and the War Production Board. They prohibit delivery of gasoline to the affected dealer for a specified period, but do not apply to sales of such supplies as may be in his storage tanks. Neither do the orders prevent him from performing any other auto service operations, such as car washing, greasing, etc.

"It's not smart to chisel"

"Gasoline means life to our transportation in the East and death to many American seamen in our tanker fleets," Mr. Henderson stated.

"Every gallon is precious. Filling station operators know this: the public knows it, too.· It's not smart to chisel."

The 14 dealers were the first of 175 whom OPA had summoned to answer charges of violating the gasoline rationing regulations. Investigation of the remainder of the 175 cases, drawn from the Philadelphia, New York, and Newark, N. J., areas was under way on June 17.

2,000 checked stations

The suspension orders came as the result of a program of enforcement launched early in June. At that time more than 2,000 men and women—some drawn from the staff of OPA at New York, Philadelphia and Washington, and other volunteer citizens trained for the task set out to determine what dealers did when motorists asked for gasoline without a rationing card.

Investigators were instructed to drive into a filling station or garage and say: "I haven't my rationing card with me and I want 3 gallons of gasoline."

The 2,000 checkers visited several thousand retailers and turned up 175 cases for further investigation. In each, OPA sent to the station proprietor a summons to a hearing, a statement of the charge specifying the date and the amount of the sale or sales alleged to be contrary to the regulations, and a copy setting forth OPA procedure and informing the accused as to his rights.

Hearings were public

Preliminary hearings were held in public in the metropolitan area in which the violation was alleged to have occurred. If the dealer did not deny the fact of violation, he was given an opportunity to make an explanation, and a full report was then sent to Washington for final action. If the dealer denied the charge, the case was set down for hearing before an authorized OPA presiding official.

At this second public hearing, the investigator who originally reported the violation testified, the dealer was permitted to present witnesses and to cross-examine Government witnesses, and he was permitted to be represented by counsel. The official who conducted the hearing then reported the case directly to Price Administrator Henderson for final action.

A person against whom an order has been issued has the right to appeal to the Price Administrator for reconsideration of the order and to submit affidavits and briefs. Pending action on the review, the Price Administrator may lift the suspension.

★ ★ ★

Rationing certificate needed to withdraw own tire for own use

Consumers who have new tires or tubes or retreaded or recapped tires in public warehouses, may withdraw them for their own use only if the vehicle is eligible and only on presentation of a rationing certificate obtained in the usual way. This point was made by Price Administrator Henderson on June 17, in issuing a clarifying amendment (No. 14) to the revised tire rationing regulations. The amendment was effective June 22.

Only drivers showing need may have extra gasoline through July 15

Motorists who have used all units on their A or B ration cards will not be able to get any more gasoline until July 15 without showing need before a local rationing board.

The OPA issued this warning as its order raising the value of the unit from 3 gallons to 6 gallons went into effect June 15. The unit value was doubled to enable the present emergency plan to operate until July 15 when the new coupon plan will be instituted on the East Coast. The temporary plan was originally scheduled to end June 30, and units on the various types of cards were intended to meet the driving needs of card holders until that date.

"Some motorists have the impression that if their units are all used they should automatically receive more units for the 2-week period between June 30 and July 15," said Joel Dean, chief of the fuel ration branch of OPA. "This is not the case. The cards now in use were issued to car owners with enough units to provide for their gasoline needs through June 30."

· ★ ★

Register for gasoline at public schools July 1, 2, 3

Motorists in the East Coast States will register July 1, 2, and 3 at public schools for basic gasoline ration books, it was announced June 14 by OPA. ·

This announcement was made following conferences with the office of John W. Studebaker, United States Commissioner of Education. Commissioner Studebaker is requesting superintendents of schools in the States covered by the rationing plan to take responsibility in organizing staffs of volunteers—teachers and others—to register the motorists.

Registrars at the schools will issue only the A books. Car owners who feel that this basic ration is not sufficient to meet their driving needs will be required to submit applications for supplemental rations to a local rationing board for action. Local rationing boards, OPA said, will be ready to receive these applications for supplemental B or C books any time between July 1 and July 15, when the new coupon plan will go into effect.

Diplomats' official cars made eligible for tires

Vehicles operated principally for official use by heads of foreign diplomatic missions formally accredited to this country have been made eligible for tires under the revised tire rationing regulations, Price Administrator Henderson announced June 18.

Foreigners in war work aided

Eligibility is also extended to foreign government employes engaged in functions essential to the war effort under a section of the regulations which heretofore has applied only to our own Federal, State and local government employes.

The diplomats, under amendment No. 15 to the revised tire rationing regulations are made eligible under List A. Only one vehicle for each is eligible.

In bringing the automobiles of foreign government employes within List B—this list includes vehicles whose use is second in importance only to the uses that qualify for List A—the Office of Price Administration pointed out that many of them are engaged in work essential to the war effort. Under the amendment, cars used by foreign military, technical, purchasing, air and shipping missions are eligible, provided the other conditions for eligibility are satisfied. Eligibility under the same conditions also extends to foreign diplomatic officials, other than the head of the mission, and consular officials using automobiles principally to perform official business in furtherance of their mission in this country.

Effective date of Amendment No. 15 was June 22.

Sell unusable tires for scrap when changing, OPA urges

In line with President Roosevelt's scrap rubber collection drive to determine the supply available for reclaiming, Price Administrator Henderson on June 15 called attention to a section of the tire rationing regulations which requires anyone who gets tires or tubes under rationing to dispose of any in excess of the number he is permitted to have under the regulations.

Tires disposed of at the time of replacement purchases should be sold for scrap if they are so old or have been so badly damaged that they are no longer usable as tires, Mr. Henderson said.

50,668 ADULT BICYCLES SOON TO BE RATIONED

United States stocks of adults' new bicycles, soon to be rationed, totaled 150,668 as of May 8, according to inventory reports filed with OPA.

This figure, while not final, is substantially larger than preliminary reports had indicated. It includes 122,243 in dealers' and distributors' stocks and 28,425 held by manufacturers. Of the 150,668 total, 114,008 were men's bicycles and 36,660 women's.

Over 11,000 bicycles have been released under a section of Ration Order No. 7, which permits production establishments that can show their April orders or deliveries bore a priority rating of A–10 or better to get bicycles for transportation of their workers.

★ ★ ★

Migratory farm workers assured of gasoline to reach jobs

Migratory farm workers, now engaged in harvest activities in many sections of the East Coast gasoline rationed area, may obtain whatever supply of gasoline they need to travel from job to job, the OPA declared June 17.

Rationing regulations, OPA pointed out, provide for any supplementary rations needed for cars that must be driven in pursuit of a gainful occupation. Many migrant workers, like thousands of workers on war construction jobs throughout the East, need their cars to travel from one place of employment to another.

Application for additional supplies of gasoline for such travel should be made at a local rationing board.

*

U. S. cheese supply ample for all needs, says Wickard

Secretary of Agriculture Wickard, who a year ago asked American consumers to cut down their use of cheese so that urgent British requests could be met, advises that the current rate of production has been sufficiently boosted to meet Lend-Lease requirements, supply the armed forces, have an adequate reserve, and allow for increased civilian consumption. The current rate of cheese production is almost one-half more than in 1941.

Nonhighway gasoline users to get "E" and "R" books

All gasoline for occupational nonhighway purposes, including commercial boats, will be rationed through "E" and "R" coupon books tailored to needs under the permanent rationing plan which the OPA will put into effect on the East Coast on July 15.

These coupon books, containing enough coupons for a six-month supply, may be obtained at local rationing boards. OPA announced that applicants may be issued one or more "E" or "R" books depending upon the amount of gasoline for which need can be established during this period.

An "E" book will contain 48 coupons with an exchange value of one gallon each, and an "R" book will have 96 coupons with an exchange value of five gallons each. In addition, bulk purchase coupons in 100-gallon and 1-gallon denominations may be issued when the ration totals 250 gallons or more a month. Bulk purchase coupons are to be issued for the convenience of large users, who store gasoline in tanks. However, "E" and "R" books may also be used for deliveries of gasoline into storage tanks as well as into vehicles.

"E" books will be issued for small engines, including power lawn mowers and outboard motors. "R" books and bulk purchase coupons will be issued for larger motor equipment, including tractors and heavy farm equipment, and other machinery, such as ditch diggers, using large engines.

★ ★ ★

Five-ply tires freed from rules causing virtual freeze

Sale of five-ply tires, heretofore restricted to special uses under OPA rationing regulations, now may be made to any holder of a certificate for a four-ply casing, Administrator Henderson announced June 15.

Before the revision, the regulations required that an applicant who wished to buy tires of more than four-ply had to show that the vehicle on which the casing was to be mounted could not be operated satisfactorily in its intended use with a tire of lighter construction. The effect of this provision was virtually to freeze the sale of five-ply casings, as an applicant who qualified for tires for special uses usually preferred to buy six-plies.

The amendment, No. 13, became effective June 15.

Sugar books available for consumers who have used excess stocks in canning

Consumers who registered for sugar rationing but were not issued War Ration Books because they had excess amounts of sugar will be permitted to obtain books upon application to the local War Price and Rationing Boards if their excess sugar supplies have been depleted by allowances made for home canning.

This revision of the sugar rationing regulations was announced June 17 by OPA along with six other new provisions, all of which are incorporated into Amendment No. 2 to OPA Rationing Order No. 3, effective June 19.

The amendment flatly prohibits any sugar trading outside of the rationing program in a provision which states that "except as otherwise expressly permitted in Rationing Order No. 3, deliveries of sugar shall be made only by and to, and accepted only by and from registered consumers, registering units and primary distributors."

OPA takes over zoning

At the same time, the amendment incorporates into the sugar regulations two provisions of WPB Order M–55 dealing with primary distributors which were not invalidated when rationing took effect.

One section, which now becomes a section of the rationing regulations, defines the zones into which primary distributors may and may not ship refined sugar.

The other section carried over from M–55 requires beet sugar refiners to hold for delivery as OPA may direct the sugar the WPB order required them to hold, and to set aside 15 percent of each month's production for delivery as OPA may direct.

The purpose of the zoning section is to retain in the Northeast all of the sugar refined in that area and to attract into that area as much sugar as possible from zones where it is more plentiful.

July 15 deadline

Sugar delivered by primary distributors before the effective date of the new amendment (June 19) but still owned by the distributor on this date, which was not delivered in compliance with the zoning restrictions, must be sold and delivered prior to July 15, 1942, at or near the points to which such deliveries were made.

This section does not apply to raw sugar, invert sugar, soft sugar in bulk or to confectioner's, brown, loaf, tablet, and other specialty sugars in 1- and 2-pound packages, except fine granulated sugar, or to sugar refined or processed outside the continental United States.

Also included in Amendment No. 2 is a provision which adds three new fruits, blackberries, boysenberries, and pineapples to the list of those for which sugar may be obtained for the purpose of freezing under table IV of section 1407.241 of Rationing Order No. 3.

★ ★ ★

Institutions allowed more sugar in proportion to meals served

Restaurants, hotels, boarding houses and other institutional users of sugar may obtain increases in their sugar allotments in proportion to an increase in the number of meals they are serving, the OPA announced June 19 in an operating instruction to State OPA Directors and to Local War Price and Rationing Boards.

Applications for increases in institutional allotments in addition to those provided in the regulations may be filed on OPA Form No. R–315 which is the Special Purpose Application for a Sugar Purchase Certificate. Institutional users should continue to apply for regular allotments on OPA Form R–314.

★ ★ ★

Honey will pinch hit for sugar in many foods

Several million additional pounds of honey are made available in 1942 as a sugar substitute in such foods as bakery goods, ice cream, candy, and soft drinks through an amendment to General Preference Order M–118, issued June 18 by the Director of Industry Operations.

The quantities of honey that manufacturers are permitted to use, however, are still subject to quota regulation.

Under the amendment, manufacturers may use, during any quarter beginning July 1, up to either 120 percent of their consumption of honey during the corresponding 1941 quarter, or 600 pounds, whichever amount is larger. During June, such consumers may use either 100 percent of the amount consumed in June 1941, or 200 pounds.

Wickard shifts staff to handle food requirements tasks

To assist in handling new responsibilities imposed on the Department and Secretary of Agriculture by the creation of the Food Requirements Committee of the WPB, Secretary Wickard has named four Department officials to new posts.

M. Clifford Townsend, director of the Office of Agricultural War Relations, becomes Administrator of the Agricultural Conservation and Adjustment Administration, succeeding R. M. Evans, who recently was appointed a Governor of the Federal Reserve System.

Replacing Mr. Townsend as OAWR head will be S. B. Bledsoe, as assistant to Secretary Wickard. H. W. Parisius, another assistant to the Secretary, will serve as associate director of OAWR.

A new division is set up in OAWR to be known as the Division of Food Requirements headed by D. A. FitzGerald, formerly of the Bureau of Agricultural Economics.

★ ★ ★

Sugar firm denied price relief

Price Administrator Henderson June 19 dismissed protest of Revere Sugar Refinery of Charlestown, Mass., against provisions of Revised Price Schedule No. 60 (Direct Consumption Sugars) on grounds that it does not comply with provisions of the Emergency Price Control Act of 1942. Protest was not filed within 60 days after effective date of the revised schedule, as required by the act.

Revere asserts generally that the protest is based upon grounds arising after expiration of such 60 days. However, the protest reveals that such grounds arose—at least in substantial part—prior to expiration of such 60 days, and in no way indicates the extent to which such grounds arose after such expiration date.

Prices on new stove models

Maximum price at which the Samuel Stamping & Enameling Co., Chattanooga, Tenn., may sell two new stoves it manufactures exclusively for Sears, Roebuck & Co., Chicago, are established in Order No. 7 under Revised Price Schedule No. 64 (Domestic Cooking and Heating Stoves), announced June 18 by Price Administrator Henderson.

OPA defines eggs, poultry exempt from general ceiling

An interpretation of the meaning of "eggs and poultry" under the general maximum price regulation was issued June 17 by OPA.

The designation "eggs and poultry" covers a number of those foods that are not subject to the regulation, which places a general ceiling at the highest levels reached in March over practically all of the commodities and services important to the cost-of-living.

Exempt from control

According to the interpretation, the following items are considered to be "eggs and poultry" and, hence, exempt from control under the regulation:

Eggs—shell eggs; dried whole eggs; dried egg yolk; dried egg albumen; frozen whole eggs, frozen albumen and frozen yolk, with or without sugar, salt, or an emulsifying agent; and tanner yolk; tanner whole egg.
Poultry—live poultry; full drawn chicken, turkey, etc.; other dressed poultry; disjointed chicken, turkey, etc.; split chicken; cooked whole chicken; frozen chicken, turkey, etc.; smoked chicken, turkey, etc.; and New York dressed chicken.

The following canned products are not deemed to be "eggs and poultry" within the meaning of the general maximum price regulation, and, accordingly, are subject to the maximum prices established by the regulation:

Canned dried egg products; canned boned chicken, turkey, etc.; canned whole chicken, turkey, etc.; potted chicken, turkey, etc.; chicken a la king; chicken bouillon cubes; chicken and egg noodle; chicken paste or spread; chicken and noodle soup; chicken soup; chicken broth soup; dried chicken broth; chicken gumbo soup; and country style chicken soup.

FATS AND OILS PRICES

An amendment clarifying the meaning of Revised Price Schedule No. 53 provides that certain fats and oils, otherwise exempt from the ceiling prices of that schedule, are covered by the schedule if a method for computing the top price for such commodities is set forth in section 1351.151 (b) (6), (8), (9) or any subsequent subparagraph hereafter added to paragraph (b) of that section, Price Administrator Henderson announced June 13.

The section of the schedule referred to in the new Amendment No. 5, which became effective June 18, provides for alternate pricing methods.

OPA acts to increase sugar inventories where needed to assure rations

To assure consumers that they will not suffer inconvenience in obtaining sugar to which they are entitled under the sugar rationing regulations, the Office of Price Administration on June 18 made provision for increasing the inventories of retailers, and, in some cases, of wholesalers.

Instructions have been sent to local war price and rationing boards to guide them in handling requests for such increases when State directors delegate powers to make such adjustments.

Transport an important factor

In making these adjustments, local boards and State directors will take into consideration circumstances affecting the operations of the business, including the frequency of delivery service, time required to transport sugar supplies from wholesaler to the retailer and also the time necessary for the transfer of stamps and certificates from the retailer to the wholesaler.

While retailers are not to be allowed inventories beyond actual needs, adjustments may be made in all cases where they are needed to provide an inventory adequate to maintain uninterrupted distribution of sugar.

Two types of adjustment are provided: Permanent adjustments to cover the continuing needs of the business and temporary adjustments to cover abnormal "peaks."

A retailer may apply to a local rationing board for a permanent increase in his allowable inventory, and the board may increase his allowable inventory to an amount equal to one pound for each dollar of gross weekly sales reported in his application at the time of registration.

Application for an amount which will result in a permanent increase in excess of one pound of sugar for $1 of weekly sales reported, will be considered if transportation difficulties or other reasons, require the retailer to maintain a larger inventory. Local boards, in such cases, may make recommendations to State directors who shall make the final decision.

Temporary rise for seasonal need

In addition to these permanent adjustments, rationing boards may grant temporary increases (up to 100 percent of the permanent allowable inventory) in the case of retailers and wholesalers who need amounts of sugar to meet peak demands caused by home canning or other seasonal business. The local board and the applicant must agree on the period during which the temporary increase is to be allowed. In any event, such an adjustment must not continue beyond November 1, 1942. Before the end of the adjustment period, the retailer must surrender to the board stamps or certificates equal to the amount of the temporary increase.

★ ★

Sugar stamps 5 and 6 to buy 28 days' ration each;

The OPA announced June 18 that stamps Nos. 5 and 6 in the War Ration Books will be valid for sugar purchases for 4 weeks instead of 2 as were the first four stamps, but the individual consumer ration of half a pound of sugar a week remains unchanged.

For greater convenience

The new stamp schedule is included in Amendment No. 3 to Rationing Order No. 3 which also contains a provision liberalizing the sugar rationing regulations under which institutional and industrial users obtain their sugar allowances. The amendment was effective June 20.

The size of consumer rations and institutional and industrial allotments remain precisely what they are at present, the revision having been made for the greater convenience of consumers and trade users of sugar.

Stamp No. 4, now good for the purchase of a single pound of sugar, expires at midnight, June 27, after which Stamp No. 5 becomes valid for the purchase of 2 pounds of sugar for a period extending until midnight of July 25. Stamp No. 6 also good for a 2-pound purchase, may be used from July 26 to August 22.

Sometime before August 22, the OPA will announce the periods of validity of subsequent stamps.

More liberal terms

In issuing the new amendment, the OPA asked all housewives to tear out of their War Ration Books and destroy all stamps which are no longer valid. As of the present moment, these are stamps Nos. 1, 2, and 3.

Amendment No. 3 provides that applications for allotments of institutional and industrial users subsequent to June 30 shall be for consecutive 2-month periods, the first of which commences on July 1.

PRICE ADMINISTRATION . . .

Ceilings lifted on synthetic rubber, aviation gasoline, toluene, components to spur industrial expansion for war use

Price ceilings on synthetic rubber, aviation gasoline, toluene, and materials essential to their manufacture were removed June 13 by Price Administrator Henderson to spur industrial expansion deemed necessary to produce an increasing volume of these vital war necessities.

Exemptions sought by Government agencies

Mr. Henderson's action came in an amendment (No. 7) to Supplementary Regulation No. 1 to the general maximum price regulation, and an amendment (No. 18) to Revised Price Schedule 88, covering petroleum and petroleum products. Both were effective June 13.

Aviation gasoline of 91 octane rating or higher already had been excepted from provisions of Revised Price Schedule No. 88 but it still came under ceiling provisions of the general maximum price regulation on May 11. This ceiling is removed now.

Commodities excepted from regulation

The amendment to Supplementary Regulation No. 1 declares that the general maximum price regulation shall not apply to any sale or delivery of the following commodities:

1. Aviation gasoline of 91 octane rating or higher, as mentioned above.
2. The following, to the extent sold or delivered for use in the manufacture of such aviation gasoline: Components of such gasoline, including but not limited to alkylate, neohexane, iso-octane, hydrocodimers, isomate, and hot acid octanes; isopentane, isobutane, normal butane and butylenes; and aromatic hydrocarbons and base stocks or fractions thereof.
3. Synthetic rubber, including rubber of the butadiene-styrene Copolymer, parbunan, neoprene, theokol, butyl, koroseal, flammenol and acrysol types.
4. The following, to the extent sold or delivered for use in the manufacture of synthetic rubbers: Components of synthetic rubbers, including but not limited to butadiene and styrene; all hydrocarbons and petroleum fractions used in the manufacture of butadiene and styrene, including but not limited to ethylene, propylene, butylene, isobutylene, propane, butane and iso-butane; hydrogen, acetaldehyde, acetylene, vinylacetylene, vinyl chloride, vinyl acetate, sebacate esters, phthalate esters tricresyl phosphate, hydrochloric acid, calcium carbide, ethylene dichloride, dichlorethyl ether, sodium polysulphide, butylene glycol, and acrylonitrile
5. Toluene manufactured from petroleum.
6. The following to the extent sold or delivered for use in the manufacture of such

toluene: Base stocks from which toluene is to be extracted, and selected charging stocks to be processed for the synthesis of such toluene.

The amendment requires that duly authenticated copies of all contracts involving sale, purchase or exchange of the exempted commodities be filed with OPA within 15 days after the signing of such contracts.

The amendment to Revised Price Schedule No. 88 excepts from the revised schedule the components of aviation gasoline and synthetic rubber to conform with the exceptions in Supplementary Regulation No. 1. It also excepts from ceiling provisions toluene manufactured from petroleum.

★ ★ ★

"Package deals" violate GMPR, Henderson warns

Certain "package deals," in which customers are required to purchase unwanted merchandise in order to obtain radios, phonographs, or household appliances, are violations of the general maximum price regulation, Price Administrator Henderson warned June 19.

A recent investigation conducted by OPA regional offices showed that in some localities, particularly in the New York area, many retailers are compelled to buy household items or other commodities when they place an order for a radio or phonograph.

In other instances, it was reported retailers are practically compelled to purchase from wholesale distributors some slow-selling model such as an expensive radio-phonograph combination, in order to obtain popular models ordered from distributors.

The Price Administrator pointed out that under certain conditions the package deal is legal. Dealers may offer a merchandise plus deal if the price is as low as or lower than the aggregate price of the items in the assortment.

Makers of wood furniture, bedding may set tentative prices on new articles

Manufacturers of wood household furniture and bedding may set tentative prices on all new articles which were not offered for sale during March 1942. Price Administrator Henderson announced June 19 in a telegram sent to bedding and furniture manufacturers and trade associations.

To facilitate trading at market

The ruling to allow open-pricing was made to facilitate trading at a furniture market held June 22 in New York. Under the provisions of the general maximum price regulation the manufacturers would have had to submit their prices for OPA's approval and this procedure might not have been possible to complete in some instances before the opening of the market.

The telegram also informed the manufacturers that the OPA soon would issue a regulation providing a method for determining maximum prices for certain new goods, including bedding, wood household furniture, lamps, housewares, and many other consumer durables.

Determination of "in line" wastepaper ceilings

The method for determining maximum prices of various grades of wastepaper, including specialty grades, which are not specifically listed in Revised Price Schedule No. 30 (Wastepaper) was announced June 18 by Price Administrator Henderson.

The action, effected through the issuance of Amendment No. 5 to Revised Price Schedule No. 30, provides that the maximum price for any grade of wastepaper not listed in the schedule must be a price "in line" with the maximum price designated in the schedule for the nearest related grade of wastepaper.

In order to determine the "in line" price, all persons, prior to buying or selling such wastepaper, must submit certain cost and materials data, set forth in the amendment, to the OPA. Prices will then be adjusted if found to be not in line.

Maximum export premium on piece goods sales clarified by OPA

The maximum export premium on the sale of finished textile piece goods that may be charged by an exporter other than the converter or the manufacturer was clarified through an amendment to the maximum export price regulation announced June 18 by Price Administrator Henderson, effective June 30.

Inasmuch as some question has been raised as to the precise method of determining the premium for this type of transaction, Amendment No. 3 is designed to make clear that the maximum export premium on a sale of piece goods for shipment abroad by a person other than the manufacturer or converter shall be:

1. 13½ percent of the cost of acquisition when the exporter acquired the goods from a converter or manufacturer.
2. 8½ percent of the cost of acquisition when he acquired them from a person other than a converter or manufacturer.

★ ★ ★

Ceiling set on small-lot sales of metallic cadmium

Small-lot sales of metallic cadmium—going mostly to distributors or laboratories for experimental purposes—will be permitted at levels no higher than those at which the individual seller did business during October 1941 or the last date previous thereto on which such a small-lot sale was made, Price Administrator Henderson announced June 18.

In Amendment No. 1 to Price Schedule No. 71 (Primary and Secondary Cadmium), issued June 18, OPA will allow sellers of cadmium in containers of 5 pounds or less to sell metallic cadmium at prices not higher than their individual October 1941 peak or the last date previous thereto on which a sale in such container was made.

★ ★ ★

Ceilings set on Pennsylvania firm's 3 new floor fabrics

Maximum prices at which the Hardwick & Magee Co., Philadelphia, may sell three new floor coverings it proposes to manufacture are established in Order No. 5 under Revised Price Schedule No. 57 (Wool Floor Coverings), announced June 19 by Price Administrator Henderson, effective the same day.

TRANSPORTATION CEILING PUT OFF TO JULY 1

The effective date of the general maximum price regulation as it applies to transportation, storage, and related services has been postponed to July 1, Price Administrator Henderson announced June 17.

The extension was made, OPA said, because of "the vital need of avoiding any possible interruption in the flow of commodities. Accordingly, persons furnishing such transportation and allied services are given further time in which to conform their establishments to the requirements of the general maximum price regulation."

★ ★ ★

Carpet firm allowed to make two new fabrics to replace others

Order No. 3 under Revised Price Schedule No. 57 (Wool Floor Coverings), announced June 8 by Price Administrator Henderson, authorized the Bigelow-Sanford Carpet Company, Inc., New York, to manufacture two new floor coverings and established the maximum prices at which they may be sold by the company.

The new fabrics—designated in the order as "Gedney" and "Rodney"—are similar in construction specifications to "Consort" and "Waldon" and will replace the latter fabrics in the company's line.

Scrap burlap, scrap bagging, cotton mill waste restored to general price regulation

Scrap burlap, scrap bagging and cotton mill waste—materials used variously for bagging, lining, and padding—are again placed under the provisions of the general maximum price regulation in order to preserve ordinary channels of distribution, Administrator Henderson announced June 15.

Supplementary Regulation No. 1, which originally exempted these commodities up to the level of the industrial consumer from the general regulation, is now changed through Amendment No. 6 to provide that sales of these materials at all levels are covered by the general price order.

War agencies may contract for certain textiles, other items pending ceiling adjustment

In order that there may be no delay in the production of certain textiles, apparel and related articles essential for the war program, Price Administrator Henderson June 19 announced a method by which war procurement agencies of the Government may enter into contracts and receive deliveries of these commodities pending OPA action on applications for adjustment of ceiling prices.

This action was taken through Amendment No. 2 to Maximum Price Regulation No. 157 (Sales and Fabrication of Textiles, Apparel and Related Items for Military Purposes), effective July 1.

The June 19 amendment provides that an application for adjustment of ceiling prices established by the regulation may be made by a present or prospective contractor or subcontractor who believes that the applicable maximum price impedes or threatens to impede the production of a commodity which is essential to the war program. The procedure for filing such an application will be issued by OPA.

Having filed an application for adjustment, contracts or subcontracts may be entered into and deliveries may be made at the price requested in the application. Final settlement, however, must be made in accordance with the OPA order issued in connection with such application. If then required, the amendment provides that refunds shall be made.

The regulation applies to the following commodities when sold or fabricated for a war procurement agency in accordance with military specifications:

1. yarns, textiles and textile products;
2. leather, fur and products thereof;
3. rubber fabrics, apparel and footwear; and
4. wearing apparel, including findings, and other individual, organizational or ship's personnel equipment made in whole or in part of any of the materials listed in (1) and (2) or from rubber, except rubber drug sundries.

★ ★ ★

Pricing outlined for fuels not sold in base period

Price Administrator Henderson has amended Maximum Price Regulation No. 121 (Miscellaneous Solid Fuels Delivered From Producing Facilities) to establish maximum prices for new sizes and qualities of fuels not covered in the regulation and for fuels, although not new, which may not have been sold in the price-basing period December 15–31, 1941.

The change in the regulation is made in Amendment No. 2, effective June 16, 1942.

Four grades of iron and steel scrap added; specifications changed for some types

An amendment providing for changes in specifications for certain grades of iron and steel scrap, along with the addition of several new grades to those already in Revised Price Schedule No. 4, was announced June 16 by Price Administrator Henderson. The amendment, No. 6, became effective June 17, 1942.

Principal changes

Principal changes made by the amendment include the following:

1. Four new listed grades of steel scrap are added to the schedule. They are No. 3 bundles, cast steel, tube scrap, and automotive springs and crankshafts.
2. A number of changes are made in the specifications of grades already listed in the schedule.
3. Premiums are established for certain contained alloys.
4. The method of setting forth basing point prices has been simplified by stating the prices of particular grades in terms of differentials over and under the price of the base grade—No. 1 heavy melting steel.
5. Specific switching charge deductions to be subtracted from basing point prices in computing shipping point prices within basing points have been established in the schedule.
6. A specific shipping-point price of $15.33 per gross ton has been defined for the base grade—No. 1 heavy melting steel—at all shipping points in New York City and Brooklyn. A 50-cent per gross ton loading charge is authorized where shipment is by deck scow or railroad lighter.
7. Louisiana has been made a "remote State," thereby enabling more distant consumers to obtain scrap from Louisiana by absorbing a higher freight charge.
8. Limitations on freight absorptions have been relaxed to facilitate the movement of scrap from northern New England to New England consumers.
9. A "preparation in transit" privilege has been established for unprepared railroad scrap.

The four new grades

For the four new grades of steel scrap, the amendment establishes the following differentials:

No. 3 bundles, $2 under the base grade.
Cast steel, $2.50 over the base grade.
Tube scrap, $3 over the base grade.
Automotive springs and crankshafts, $1 over the base grade.

In the case of cast steel, tube scrap, and automotive springs and crankshafts, these differentials apply only to sales for electric furnace, acid open hearth, and foundry use.

Definitions of types

No. 3 bundles are defined as galvanized sheet scrap or galvanized wire hydraulically compressed into charging box size and weighing not less than 75 pounds per cubic foot. They may not include terneplate or vitreous enameled stock.

Cast-steel scrap is defined as all cast steel not over 48 inches long or 18 inches wide, and not over 0.05 percent phosphorus or sulphur, free of alloys and attachments. It may include heads, gates, and risers.

Tube scrap is defined as seamless or welded, not over 0.05 percent phosphorus and sulphur, free of alloys. It shall not be more than 18 inches in length and not over 6 inches inside diameter. It may be mashed or unmashed. Pieces over 6 inches inside diameter may be included when thoroughly flattened. The scrap must be new material.

Automotive springs and crankshafts are defined as clean automotive springs and crankshafts.

Open-hearth premium abolished

The most important changes in specifications of grades already listed in the schedule include the following:

No. 2 busheling may now be 16-gage in thickness, instead of 12-gage.

The maximum phosphorus and sulphur analysis of "low phos" grades has been raised to 0.05 percent.

Basic open hearths may no longer purchase alloy-free "low phos" and sulphur turnings at a price in excess of the maximum established for open-hearth turnings.

Alloy-free "low phos" and sulphur turnings must now come to the consumer direct from the industrial producer.

Chemical borings are now divided into two types—No. 1 and No. 2. No. 1 chemical borings are priced at $1 below the base grade, and may not contain more than 1 percent oil—No. 2 chemical borings, priced at $2 below the base grade, may not contain more than 1.5 percent oil. Where either of these grades is loaded in boxcars instead of gondolas, an additional charge of 75 cents per gross ton for loading is permitted.

Premiums for nickel steel scrap containing 5.25 percent nickel and under, heretofore established in Price Schedule No. 8, have been transferred to Revised Price Schedule No. 4.

New premiums have been inserted for certain "low phos" grades containing 0.15 percent or more molybdenum, and for certain "low phos" grades conforming to specifications S. A. E. 52,100 and sold for electric furnace use.

Top price set for new floor covering

The maximum price at which the Karastan Rug Mills, a division of Marshall Field & Co., Chicago, may sell a new floor covering, is established in Order No. 4 under Revised Price Schedule No. 57 (Wool Floor Coverings), announced June 18 by Price Administrator Henderson. The top price for Kara-Lana, as set forth in the order, is $6.89 per square yard f. o. b. mill, subject to discounts, allowances, rebates and terms no less favorable than those in effect for the manufacturer's sales of Karashah.

Sellers of scrap "as is" risk penalties, says OPA

Persons who buy and sell aluminum scrap on an "as is" basis are running the risk of making themselves liable to the heavy penalties provided for violation of Revised Price Schedule No. 2 on aluminum scrap, Price Administrator Henderson warned June 16.

The schedule, which establishes maximum prices for aluminum scrap, specifically provides that maximum prices may be charged and paid only for scrap which meets generally accepted standards of the .rade, the Price Administrator pointed out.

"Low-grade scrap, scrap which is not clean and dry, and scrap which for any other reason fails to meet trade standards must be sold at prices proportionately below the established maximum prices," he pointed out. "Proper deductions must be made for oil, water and other contamination contained in borings, turnings and similar machinings."

"The safe and proper way to buy and sell aluminum scrap," the Price Administrator added, "is to agree upon a price for a given lot only on a 'clean and dry' basis, so that the payment will be confined to the actual clean scrap content, to be determined by analysis or other method established in the trade."

★ ★ ★

Domestic rules cover most sales to British purchase commissions

Sales of goods and commodities to such agencies as the Lend Lease Administration, British Purchasing Commission, and British Air Commission are, in general, domestic sales subject either to specific domestic price schedules or regulations or to the general maximum price regulation, Price Administrator Henderson pointed out June 16.

In general, he added, they are subject to such schedules and regulations rather than the maximum export price regulation.

"In all cases in which an agency such as the Lend Lease Administration, the procurement agencies of the Treasury, or the British Purchasing Commission buys material f. o. b. or f. a. s., and takes title and all responsibility for the material at the factory door or on the shipping dock, the seller performs no exporting function and the sale is a domestic and not an export sale," the Price Administrator explained.

Fabricators get special ceiling on frozen copper products to speed flow into war

The March price lists of five leading brass and wire mills have been established as the ceilings at which fabricators may sell their excessive or frozen inventories of brass and wire mill products if they are otherwise unable, under the general maximum price regulation, to determine their ceilings, Price Administrator Henderson announced June 13.

The action, set forth in Order No. 10 to the general maximum price regulation, was taken to facilitate the salvage program of the War Production Board in bringing idle and excessive inventories of copper and copper base alloy products into immediate war use.

"These inventories are held by thousands of fabricators throughout the country," Mr. Henderson stated. "As a result of WPB curtailment in production of civilian goods, the inventories are largely frozen."

The mills whose March prices determine the ceilings are American Brass Co., General Cable Corporation, Revere Copper & Brass, Inc., Bridgeport Brass Co., and Anaconda Wire & Cable Co.

The brass or wire mill products covered by the order include new plate, sheet, strip, roll, coil, wire, rod, bar, tube, tubing, pipe, extrusion, forging, anode or other shape made from copper or copper base alloy by a brass or wire mill.

The order does not apply to any rod, coil, wire or other shape for which Revised Price Schedule No. 82—Wire, Cable, and Cable Accessories—establishes a maximum price.

"Precious stones" defined

Price Administrator Henderson June 13 defined "precious stones" which are exempt from provisions of the general maximum price regulation.

In order to clear up trade uncertainties that may have existed, the Administrator defined "precious stones" as follows:

"Precious stones" are any mounting into which a precious stone is set. A precious stone is any ruby, sapphire, emerald, natural pearl, or any diamond weighing more than 1.00 carat, or any semiprecious stone after sale by the cutter, when the cutter has received more than $100 for sale of the stone. Any other stone shall not be deemed precious, except that when two or more diamonds with an aggregate weight of 1.50 carats are set in one mounting, the diamond shall be deemed "precious." Synthetic stones and cultured pearls are not precious.

SPECIAL STEEL SCRAP GIVEN OWN CEILING

A maximum price for a type of chrome-vanadium-steel scrap sold by the Tennessee Coal, Iron & Railroad Co. of Birmingham, Alabama—a high-speed tool steel scrap similar to the "molybdenum type," but differing in alloy content—has been established, Price Administrator Henderson announced June 16.

As this particular type of scrap was not sold by any company during March 1942, a maximum price could not be set under section 2 of the general maximum price regulation, Mr. Henderson stated. Maximum prices of $51.82 per long ton, f. o. b. mill for the solid grade and $44.04 for the turnings and borings grade were established, the Price Administrator announced.

★ ★ ★

Watson heads advisory group on general steel products

Walter E. Watson, vice president of Youngstown Sheet & Tube Co., Youngstown, Ohio, has been elected chairman of the general steel products advisory committee of OPA, Administrator Henderson announced June 15.

Other members of the committee are:

Avery C. Adams of United States Steel Corporation, Pittsburgh; J. W. Anderson, Sheffield Steel Corporation, Kansas City, Mo.; Homer Butts, Niles Rolling Mill Co., Niles, Ohio; Norris J. Clarke, Republic Steel Corporation, Cleveland, Ohio; J. A. Henry, Weirton Steel Co., Weirton, W. Va.; Paul Mackall, Bethlehem Steel Co., Bethlehem, Pa.; J. L. Neudoerfer, Wheeling Steel Corporation, Wheeling, W. Va.; N. H. Orr, Colorado Fuel & Iron Corporation, Denver; L. M. Parsons, Jones & Laughlin Steel Corporation, Pittsburgh; and A. C. Roeth, Inland Steel Company, Chicago.

The committee, purely advisory, meets at the call of the chairman to discuss any price questions or problems arising in connection with Revised Price Schedule No. 6 on iron and steel products.

★ ★ ★

35 percent lead zinc oxides returned to April 1 price

The maximum price for leaded zinc oxides containing 35 percent or more lead, which was reduced one-fourth cent per pound by the general maximum price regulation, has been allowed to return to the April 1, 1942 level of 7 cents per pound, Price Administrator Henderson stated June 18. This price, which corrects an inadvertent omission, became effective June 22.

Ceilings on sales of pig tin made by electrolytic process same as for top grade

OPA's maximum price schedule for pig tin—No. 17—has been amended to permit sale of certain metal produced by the electrolytic process at a price equal to that of the top grade of tin, Price Administrator Henderson announced June 17.

The Administrator pointed out that a plant has been established recently to undertake the electrolytic production of pig tin. Output is still in the experimental stage. The tin is produced from the Bolivian ores not utilized by the Metals Reserve Co. With the exception of its lead content, the impurities in this tin are well below the maximum tolerances permitted by the United States Treasury Department for Grade A tin. Aside from this the tin is of a very high grade, and for certain uses is equal or superior to tin meeting the specifications of the Treasury Department's Procurement Division.

The maximum price is established in Amendment No. 2 to Revised Price Schedule No. 17, effective June 22, 1942.

The amendment in addition permits the payment of differentials for tin in special shapes. An amount not exceeding 1¼ cents per pound may be added, on and after the effective date of the amendment, to current maximum prices, for tin made and sold at the request of the buyer in special shapes weighing not more than seven pounds.

Firm converted to steel plates granted rise to avert loss

The Granite City Steel Co. has been granted authority to increase the base price of all carbon steel plates, base grade, to $47 per net ton, f. o. b. Granite City, Ill., Price Administrator Henderson announced June 15.

The change was effected by Order No. 12 under Revised Price Schedule No. 6 on iron and steel products, and became effective as of June 6, 1942.

The company, which has increased its plate production from approximately 25 percent of total output to well in excess of 50 percent, based its request for an increase on the assertion that current high output of plates, with subsequent decline in production of more profitable products, would result in a loss if plates were sold at ceiling prices.

Prices of many suit, coat fabrics cut by seasonal formula for makers, jobbers

Prices of woolen and worsted fabrics that go into men's and women's suits and overcoats are lowered in many instances at the manufacturing and jobbing levels through a special seasonal pricing formula for these goods, announced June 17 by Price Administrator Henderson.

To facilitate flow of goods

Maximum Price Regulation No. 165 (Woolen and Worsted Civilian Apparel Fabrics), in providing a method for pricing these fabrics, will facilitate the flow of goods to garment makers, Mr. Henderson said. Deliveries by mills and jobbers for the fall season have been postponed pending the establishment of a method of pricing, according to information reaching the OPA. The regulation took effect June 22.

The June 17 regulation establishes individual ceilings for each manufacturer by going back to his last season's selling period some 8 to 16 months earlier for the same class of fabrics. The manufacturer then adds a specified percentage markup to allow for advance in basic costs from that time to March 1942.

A jobber's maximum selling price is set by the actual price he paid for the fabric plus a percentage markup varying with the size of the lot of goods sold and the class of the purchaser.

Savings passed on to buyer

The effect of the pricing formula will result in reductions from March 1942 deliveries on individual types of fabrics ranging up to 25 cents per yard, OPA said. In some special cases the reduction is even greater.

An important phase of the June 17 regulation will be to pass along to the buyer, savings in less costly new fabrics made of blends of wool and substitute fibers under the WPB program. The pricing formula for such blended fabrics is designed to encourage the manufacture and substantially to increase the supply of these new and blended fabrics. Ceilings in these cases are based on the actual cost of the materials plus a markup.

Three price-determining formulas

Three different price determining formulas are provided for various types of fabrics. These apply (a) to fabrics previously sold by the manufacturer, (b) to fabrics comparable to those previously sold and (c) to new fabrics.

Under the first grouping of fabrics previously sold by manufacturers, two applicable base periods are provided.

The first applies to woolen or worsted apparel fabrics sold for the spring season only or for both the spring and fall seasons. The last selling period by mills for these goods was mostly from June through August 1941, and the formula allows percentage mark-ups of from 10 to 12½ percent from the "opening price" for various constructions of fabrics.

The second covers fabrics sold only for the fall season. Sales for the fall season of 1941 were made chiefly between December 1, 1940, and February 28, 1941. Percentage mark-ups allowed of from 20 to 30 percent from the "opening price," take into consideration the additional cost increases over the longer period.

For comparable fabrics

For "comparable fabrics" a special pricing formula is provided. These are types which, although not previously sold by the manufacturer, are substantially similar to the ones that he did sell during the applicable selling period. The ceiling is determined by taking the maximum price which may be charged for the fabric previously made and increasing or reducing the price by the difference in the cost of raw materials used.

For new fabrics

For "new fabrics" not comparable to any fabrics previously produced by a manufacturer, a simple formula to establish his selling price is provided. The manufacturer determines the raw material and manufacturing cost on the basis of March 1942 levels. He then multiplies this by the ratio of his 1941 weighted average selling price of all civilian woolen or worsted apparel fabrics he produced to his weighted average manufacturing cost of these same fabrics.

Used materials at public sale exempted for Army and Navy

The prices which the War and Navy Departments receive for used, damaged, and waste materials disposed of at public sale do not fall under the provisions of the general maximum price regulation, Administrator Henderson ruled June 15.

The one exception to the general exemption is sales of waste fat and oil bearing materials for which a special provision was being considered.

Some textiles, apparel bought or sold by war procurement stores exempt from regulations

Purchases and sales of certain textiles, apparel and related articles by stores of "war procurement agencies" are exempted from the provisions of OPA regulations under the terms of two amendments announced June 17 by Administrator Henderson.

Amendment No. 3 to Supplementary Regulation No. 4 exempts from the general maximum price regulation sales to or by army canteens, post exchanges and ships' service activities of the types of articles specified. This is for the purpose of placing these stores on the same basis as stores actually owned and operated by the War and Navy Departments. These were previously excluded from the provisions of the general regulation until July 1.

Amendment No. 1 to Maximum Price Regulation No. 157 (Sales and Fabrication of Textiles, Apparel and Related Items for Military Purposes) in general, makes a similar provision in connection with sales of the specified articles by any war procurement agency including stores operated as army canteens, post exchanges and ships' service activities.

"Textiles, apparel and related articles" which are excepted by the two June 17 amendments are those covered by Maximum Price Regulation No. 157.

The amendment to Regulation 157 also makes clear that it is the intention of OPA that the general maximum price regulation shall be applicable to transactions by subcontractors on the types of textiles covered until July 1, 1942. On that date Regulation 157 takes effect.

★ ★ ★

FLUORSPAR CEILINGS

The OPA has granted permission to the Fluorspar Processing Co., Colorado Springs, Colo., to sell its glass grade fluorspar at a maximum price of $27.40 per ton, f. o. b. Salida, Colo. This is the same maximum price previously authorized for the company's sales of acid grade fluorspar.

Mr. Henderson also announced that The Western Feldspar Milling Co., of Denver, Colo., has been granted authority to sell its 40-mesh fluorspar, 76 percent calcium fluoride, at a maximum price of $14.50 per ton, f. o. b. Denver. Approval of this maximum price was contained in Order No. 2 under Maximum Price Regulation No. 126.

Truck operators apply science to prolong haulage facilities

Wartime requirements are making motortruck haulage much more efficient in terms of safe, speedy, continuous operation, Fred M. Lautzenhiser, technical consultant of WPB's automotive branch, said June 16 at a meeting of the National Safety Council's Institute for Traffic Training at Yale University.

"Operators and shippers are recognizing that certain scientific principles applied to such factors as load distribution give results of considerable importance when rubber is scarce and the number of trucks available under the Nation's rationing procedure is strictly limited," Mr. Lautzenhiser said.

★ ★ ★

Two Carolina-Virginia bus lines ordered to consolidate services

The fifth in a series of special orders pertaining to the operation of intercity bus lines was issued June 15 by the Office of Defense Transportation.

The new order (Special Order ODT B-5) affects the operations of the Atlantic Greyhound Corporation, Charleston, W. Va., and the Carolina Coach Co., Raleigh, N. C.

Points jointly served include Charlotte, Lexington, Greensboro, Durham, Raleigh, and Fayetteville in North Carolina, and Norfolk, Suffolk, Portsmouth, Emporia, Petersburg, Martinsville, Danville and Richmond in Virginia.

The companies are required, effective June 20, to honor each other's tickets between the points named and to divert traffic for the purpose of relieving overloads and reducing operation of extra sections.

⌃ ⌃ ⌃

Three field officers named

ODT on June 17 announced the appointment of three more field office managers in the division of motor transport, making 46 office managers named, with five more such to be chosen.

Those whose appointments were announced June 17 and the cities where they will make their headquarters are:

Boise, Idaho—Maurice H. Greene, of Boise.

Davenport, Iowa—Paul V. Kortkamp, of Rock Island, Ill.

Nashville, Tenn.—Victor E. Nichol, of Nashville.

New industry advisory committees

The Bureau of Industry Advisory Committees, WPB, has announced the formation of the following new industry advisory committees:

BLANK BOOK, LOOSE LEAF & BINDER INDUSTRY

Government presiding officer—E. W. Palmer, assistant chief of the printing and publishing branch.

Members:

Hubert O. Auburn, The Tenacity Mfg. Co., Cincinnati, Ohio; F. D. Barnhill, Charles R. Handley Co., Los Angeles, Calif.; G. W. Brownlee, Ekonomic Binder Co., Atlanta, Ga.; James Cooper, Hall & McChesney, Inc., Syracuse, N. Y.; C. T. Dean, American Beauty Cover Co., Dallas, Tex.; W. C. Horn, W. C. Horn Bros. & Co., Newark, N. J.; Benjamin Kulp, Wilson-Jones Co., Chicago, Ill.; James J. McNulty, Loose Leaf Metals Co., St. Louis, Mo.; John W. Tamany, Boorum & Pease Co., Brooklyn, N. Y.; Richard P. Towne, National Blank Book Co., Holyoke, Mass.; Murray Vernon, S. E. & M. Vernon, Inc., New York, N. Y.; W. T. Wood, The Heinn Co., Milwaukee, Wis.

BRASS MILL INDUSTRY

Government presiding officer—Francis R. Kenney, research advisor, copper branch.

John A. Coe, Jr., vice president, The American Brass Co., 414 Meadow St., Waterbury, Conn.; Robert L. Coe, vice president, Chase Brass & Copper Co., 236 Grand St., Waterbury, Conn.; J. A. Doucett, vice president, Revere Copper & Brass, Inc., 230 Park Ave., New York, N. Y.; W. M. Goss, vice president, Scoville, Mfg. Co., Waterbury, Conn.; J. P. Lally, president, C. G. Hussey & Co., 2850 Second ave., Pittsburgh, Pa.; H. L. Randall, president, Riverside Metal Co., Riverside, N. J.; F. L. Riggin, president, Mueller Brass Co., Port Huron, Mich.

CANE & BEET SUGAR PACKAGING INDUSTRY

Government presiding officer—A. E. Bowman, chief, sugar section, food supply branch.

R. S. Stubbs, American Sugar Refining Co., New York, N. Y.; W. O. L. Stanton, National Sugar Refining Co., New York, N. Y.; Louis V. Place, Jr., W. J. McCahan Sugar Refining & Molasses Co., Philadelphia, Pa.; Thomas Oxnard, Savannah Sugar Refining Co., Savannah, Ga.; Goyn M. Talmage, Henderson Sugar Refinery, Inc., New Orleans, La.; David M. Keiser, Colonial Sugar Co., New York, N. Y.; C. F. Dahlberg, South Coast Corporation, New Orleans, La.; Frank A. Kemp, Great Western Sugar Co., Denver, Colo.; Frank J. Belcher, Jr., Spreckels Sugar Co., San Francisco, Calif.; A. W. Beebe, Lake Shore Sugar Co., Detroit, Mich.; J. Stewart, The Garden City Co., Colorado Springs, Colo.; A. A. Smith, California & Hawaiian Sugar Corporation, San Francisco, Calif.

CAST IRON BOILER AND RADIATOR INDUSTRY

Government presiding officer—W. W. Timmis, chief, plumbing and heating branch.

R. E. Daly, American Radiator & Standard Sanitary Corporation, Pittsburgh, Pa.; V. A. Good, sales manager, Burnham Boiler Corporation, Irvington, N. Y.; L. N. Hunter, vice president, National Radiator Co., Johnstown, Pa.; John P. Magos, Crane Co., Chicago, Ill.; J. F. McIntire, vice president, United States Radiator Corporation, Detroit, Mich.; H. F. Randolph, vice president, International Heater Co., Utica, N. Y.; Stanley E. Smith, vice president, The H. B. Smith Co., Inc., Westfield, Mass.; Lester O. Stearns, vice president, Columbia Radiator Co., McKeesport, Pa.; W. R. Stockwell, Weil-McLain Co., Michigan City, Ind.

COPPER WIRE & CABLE INDUSTRY

Government presiding officer—Francis R. Kenney, research advisor, copper branch.

W. E. Sprackling, Anaconda Wire & Cable Co., New York, N. Y.; D. R. G. Palmer, General Cable Corporation, New York, N. Y.; H. L. Erlicher, General Electric Co., Schenectady, N. Y.; Wiley Brown, Phelps Dodge Copper Products Corporation, New York, N. Y.; C. A. Scott, Rome Cable Corporation, Rome, N. Y.; F. C. Jones, Okonite Co., Passaic, N. J.; Everett Morss, Simplex Wire & Cable Co., Cambridge, Mass.

FERROCHROMIUM PRODUCERS INDUSTRY

Government presiding officer—Andrew Leith, chief, manganese and chrome branch.

W. J. Priestly, Electrometallangical Co., New York, N. Y.; Ward A. Miller, Vanadium Corporation of America, New York, N. Y.; Charles F. Colbert, Jr., Pittsburgh Metallurgical Co., Niagara Falls, N. Y.; L. G. Pritz, Ohio Ferro-Alloys Corporation, Canton, Ohio.

FERTILIZER INDUSTRY

Government presiding officer—T. E. Milliman, chief, agricultural chemicals section.

Horace M. Albright, U. S. Potash Co., New York, N. Y.; John T. Burrows, International Agricultural Corporation, Chicago, Ill.; Louis H. Carter, American Agricultural Chemical Co., New York, N. Y.; M. K. Derrick, Farm Bureau Co-operative Association, Indianapolis, Ind.; N. E. Harman, Meridian Fertilizer Factory, Hattiesburg, Miss.; Sidney B. Haskell, The Barrett Division, Allied Chemical & Dye Corporation, New York, N. Y.; Chester F. Hockley, Davison Chemical Corporation, Baltimore, Md.; M. H. Lockwood, Eastern States Farmers' Exchange, Springfield, Mass.; John A. Miller, Price Chemical Co., Louisville, Ky.; Weller Noble, Pacific Guano Co., Berkeley, Calif.; John E. Sanford, Armour Fertilizer Works, Atlanta, Ga.; C. D. Shallenberger, Shreveport Fertilizer Works, Shreveport, La.; Oscar F. Smith, Smith-Douglass Co., Norfolk, Va.; W. B. Tilghman, Wm. B. Tilghman Co., Salisbury, Md.; J. A. Woods, Chilean Nitrate Sales Corporation, New York, N. Y.

⌃ ⌃ ⌃

Hurley appointed chief of consumers' durable goods

John A. Hurley, of St. Joseph, Mich., has been appointed chief of the consumers' durable goods branch by Philip D. Reed, chief of the Bureau of Industry Branches.

Western log and lumber administrator named to push all-out production

In order to facilitate a program of all-out lumber production, WPB Chairman Donald M. Nelson June 18 designated Frederick H. Brundage as western log and lumber administrator of the lumber and products branch. Mr. Brundage has been granted a leave of absence from his position as associate regional forester in the Sixth Region by the United States Forest Service. As western log and lumber administrator, he will have the full powers of the War Production Board to carry out such action programs as may be necessary in order to obtain the qualities and quantities of lumber required by the war program, Mr. Nelson said.

Advisory board to be named

To advise and assist Mr. Brundage, a board was to be appointed shortly for the western lumber industry. This advisory board, including management and labor members, will be representative of the various segments in the industry.

Through the International Woodworkers of America and the International Brotherhood of Carpenters and Joiners, Mr. Nelson has asked that those who work in the woods and in the sawmills forego their vacations this year, accepting instead the money payment for the vacation while working for wages during the vacation period.

Asked to log best timber now

Excerpts from Mr. Nelson's statement follow:

At the same time I am requesting the owners and operators in the Pacific Coast lumber industry to log at this time the best and most accessible timber in the region. Lumber this year is much more important to the war program than lumber next year or in 1944.

Similarly I am directly an appeal to the Governors of the Pacific Coast States requesting that they review State legislation and practices which may restrict lumber production. . . .

Lumber from every region in the United States is an important and critical material in our whole war program. It is needed for the construction of cantonments, ships, planes, gliders, pontoons, war housing, for Lend-Lease, for packaging war products, and as a substitute for critical materials in the war program.

The War Production Board is making arrangements for improved methods of granting priority assistance to the lumber industry, especially for the loggers who sell their product to the sawmills and do not sell directly to the Government. It is hoped that through this new priority system for the lumber industry throughout the United States the loss of time in logging and milling operations as a result of lack of material for repairs and maintenance will be considerably reduced.

★ ★ ★

Higher rating on materials helps railroads move war items

Seeking to expedite rail transportation of vital war supplies, the Director of Industry Operations June 18 assigned a higher preference rating to the country's railroads for deliveries of materials essential for repair and maintenance of track, structures, signal and communications systems, cars and locomotives, and other important operating equipment.

Previously, under Preference Rating Order P–88, an A–3 rating was made available for deliveries of these materials. The new order, Amendment No. 1 to P–88, raises the rating to A–1–j.

Nickel scrap order modified

Order M–6–c, covering nickel scrap, was amended June 19 by the Director of Industry Operations to make it conform to the new alloy steel scrap segregation order, M–24–c.

Changes in M–6–c provide:

1. Nickel scrap covered by the order is scrap containing 1 percent nickel or over, instead of 0.50 percent as originally specified.

2. Nickel scrap does not include metal the principal part of which is aluminum nor metal containing over 40 percent copper. Both such alloys are covered by orders M–1–d and M–6–b respectively.

3. Ferrous nickel scrap must be segregated in the same manner as provided in order M–24–c covering alloy steel scrap.

4. The provision of the original order limiting the amount of scrap which may be melted in any month to 300 pounds nickel-content is removed.

5. Any melter may receive nickel scrap which he requires to fill orders bearing preference ratings higher than A–2, without regard to primary nickel which may have been allocated to him in conformity with the original order.

6. Dealers must not melt nickel scrap without specific authorization of the Director of Industry Operations.

Restrictions relaxed on sales of some industrial refrigerator and air-conditioning equipment

Manufacturers and distributors of industrial and commercial refrigerator and air-conditioning equipment are afforded some degree of relief from the restrictions imposed by Limitation Order L–38, by Amendment No. 1 to the order, announced June 20 by the Director of Industry Operations.

Preferred group enlarged

Main provision of the amendment permits sale of certain items of equipment listed under paragraph (e) of the order, without the necessity of obtaining a preference rating to cover the installation of the finished product. Under the order as originally issued such items could be sold only on an A–9 or higher preference rating, or to agencies listed in a preferred order group.

Added to the preferred order group are Army exchanges, Naval ship-stores, officers' messes, and officers', noncommissioned officers' and enlisted men's clubs.

Repair parts are defined, and excluded from the provisions of the order and may now be sold without preferred status.

Added to the list of items which may no longer be manufactured, save on direct Army or Navy orders, are ice cream cabinets and evaporative coolers. All producers' inventories of the items listed under paragraph (e), including these cabinets and coolers, remain frozen.

Junked autos yield 383,253 tons of scrap in May

The pile of scrap iron and steel necessary to keep the Nation's steel mills charging at full capacity has been substantially augmented in the last 2 months by the activity of the auto graveyard section of WPB's Bureau of Industrial Conservation.

Figures just released by this section show that a total of 383,253 tons of scrap iron and steel were shipped out of the auto wreckers' yards in the month of May. This is an increase in tonnage of 10 percent over the yield in April and an increase of more than 100 percent over the monthly recovery rate of scrap iron from auto graveyards in 1941.

Dollars and cents ceilings set on red cedar shingles

Dollars and cents maximum prices for red cedar shingles, which constitute 95 percent of all wood shingles produced in the United States, have been established under Maximum Price Regulation No. 164, on red cedar shingles, Price Administrator Henderson announced June 18. The regulation, which becomes effective June 29, applies to shipments which originate at mills.

Except for the lower grades the ceiling prices are approximately the same as those which prevailed under the general maximum price regulation.

Canadian imports subject to ceilings

While the maximum prices for the No. 1 grade of shingle are the same as the average March ceiling prices, the ceiling for the other two grades is somewhat lower. Prices for the lower grades were computed on the basis of the average differential which prevailed from October 1941 to March 1942, he said.

Canadian imports are subject to ceiling prices, and it is estimated that more than 99 percent of total production of red cedar shingles falls within the scope of the regulation.

Prices f. o. b. mill

The regulation establishes prices f. o. b. the mill, but in order to permit the seller to quote and sell on a delivered basis, a provision allows the seller to add his actual transportation costs where he delivers the shingles to the purchaser.

Wet-resistant Douglas plywood sizes cut from 4,300 to 300

Reduction of the number of sizes of moisture-resistant Douglas Fir Plywoods has been ordered by the War Production Board in order to create an additional production of about 20 million feet per month.

Limitation Order L-150 prohibits the production of delivery after July 1 of types and sizes of Douglas Fir Plywoods other than those listed in the order, except upon the specific authorization of the Director of Industry Operations.

It is expected that the simplification practices ordered will result in a reduction of sizes about 4,300 to approximately 300.

Dollars-and-cents ceilings extended to additional West Coast lumber items

The extension of dollars-and-cents maximum price schedules to additional lumber items produced from Douglas fir, West Coast hemlock, and all species of true fir, which previously were subject to the general maximum price regulation, was announced June 18 by Price Administrator Henderson.

Ceilings below current levels

The changes were made by amending Revised Price Schedule No. 26 on Douglas Fir Lumber, and reissuing it as Maximum Price Regulation No. 26 on Douglas Fir Lumber and other West Coast Lumber, effective June 29, 1942.

The maximum prices established for the additional lumber items which are included in Regulation No. 26 are substantially below current levels. The prices of those items for which maximums had been established previously under Revised Price Schedule No. 26 have not been changed.

Among the lumber items for which dollars-and-cents maximum prices have been established under the regulation are many which are extensively used in the manufacture of military equipment.

Larger areas included

While Revised Price Schedule No. 26 applied only to lumber produced in those parts of Oregon and Washington lying west of the crest of the Cascade Mountains, Maximum Price Regulation No. 26 includes those mills located in the counties of Del Norte, Humboldt, Mendocino and Sonoma, in California, as well as Canadian imports of lumber processed from Douglas fir, West Coast hemlock, and all true species of fir.

The dollars-and-cents maximum prices for West Coast hemlock and all species of true fir have been established at a level $1.00 lower than the maximum for Douglas fir prices as contained in Revised Price Schedule No. 26 on all items except boards. The maximum for boards has been set at the same level as Douglas fir. The maximum prices for these additional items are approximately the same as those which prevailed from October 1, 1941, to October 15, 1941, he stated.

Prices higher on vital war items

In the case of ship decking, pontoon lumber, aircraft lumber, and other items vital to the war effort the maximum prices are somewhat higher than the

October 1941 prices, but somewhat lower than those of March 1942. The price history of many of these items, Mr. Henderson said, is so short as to be unreliable and, in some instances, the production of these items in abnormal quantity has led to increased manufacturing costs.

Formula for special items

Any special or nonstandard item of lumber must be priced under a formula by which each individual seller may compute his maximum. Prices determined in this manner must be filed with the Office of Price Administration, Washington, D. C.

Maximum prices for sales where shipment originates at a "distribution yard," whether wholesale or retail, remain subject to the general maximum price regulation.

Maximum prices set for major West Coast logs

Maximum prices for the major species of West Coast logs were announced June 15 by Price Administrator Henderson. The prices are established by Maximum Price Regulation No. 161 on West Coast logs, effective June 20.

Under the regulation prices of West Coast logs—which have shown increases ranging from 30 to 55 percent in the past 9 months—will be established at levels above those of October 1941, but under prices now prevailing.

Species of logs covered

The species of logs covered by the regulation include Douglas fir peeler logs and all other grades of Douglas fir logs, western red cedar logs, western hemlock logs, western white fir logs, Noble fir logs, and Sitka spruce logs, of all grades and types produced in those parts of Oregon, Washington, California, and Canada lying west of the crests of the Cascade and Sierra Nevada mountain ranges. Maximum prices previously established for Douglas fir peeler logs in Revised Price Schedule No. 54 have been incorporated in Regulation No. 161.

Wage differentials have been given consideration in the prices set.

HEALTH AND WELFARE . . .

President and McNutt call on executives to clean up "off-the-job" conditions

Some 8,500 key executives of war production plants have received a letter from the President, transmitted to them June 17 by Paul B. McNutt, Director of the Office of Defense Health and Welfare Services and Chairman of the War Manpower Commission, calling for the active encouragement of physical and moral fitness.

Work near camps praised

The President's letter to Mr. McNutt commended government and community efforts in improving health and morale and "in eliminating from the vicinity of camps and naval stations that major source of infection—the red-light district." Mr. McNutt, in turn, underscored the President's emphasis on the need for similar measures in war industry areas.

President Roosevelt's letter to Mr. McNutt follows:

From every quarter come evidences of our national concern for total physical and moral fitness in this war for survival, fitness for the freedom we cherish. So far as the Federal Government is concerned. I have reports of the recent meeting between the United States Public Health Service and the War Production Board looking to a vigorous emphasis on industrial hygiene and health education in the current war production drive. Cooperation of the Public Health Service and the Department of Labor in accident prevention has been continuous. The Interdepartmental Committee on Venereal Disease has made splendid progress in eliminating from the vicinity of camps and naval stations that major source of infection—the red-light district. The War Production Board is cooperating in the extension of that effort to industrial areas where, incidentally, a major part of military and naval infection is derived. The community facilities program is rapidly supplying the necessary sanitation, and hospital and clinic facilities in the communities surrounding camps and industrial areas. The Procurement and Assignment Service is spreading our medical manpower to serve these new population centers. Our program for the rehabilitation of rejected selectees is rapidly taking form, as well as health education in our schools and other agencies.

Job depends on people

But this job depends ultimately upon the people themselves and their moral fibre. Increasingly State and local officials are giving leadership in public health and law enforcement. From religious leaders and responsible citizens come to me, almost daily, expressions of their concern, which they are translating into active local cooperation for total effectiveness. In fact, only good local community organization can meet many of these needs.

I, therefore, call for the united efforts of government—Federal, state, and local—of business and industry, of the medical profession, of the schools, and of the churches; in short, of all citizens, for the establishment of total physical and moral fitness. No one can doubt the objective, or fail to cooperate in the various programs when he understands them. This is one effort in which every man, woman, and child can play his part and share in ultimate victory.

Mr. McNutt's letter to the executives follows in part:

I am deeply concerned, as I know you are, over preventable absences of workers in war jobs. There is no question that many millions of lost work days could be saved and that needless accidents and spoilage of materials could be prevented by simple safeguards to workers' health.

Effect of off-the-job conditions

Nine times out of ten when a man is physically unfit for work, the cause, so experts say, lies in off-the-job conditions.

One of the most menacing of these hazards is venereal disease. Intelligent attack upon this hidden enemy could reduce it to the same relative unimportance as smallpox or diphtheria.

More than 2 years ago the Army, Navy, and Public Health service approved an eight-point program. Near the camps the vigorous help of the commanding officers has brought great progress. The Army venereal disease rate is now the lowest in wartime and the lowest ever recorded except for one peacetime year.

Protection section ready to help

But Army and Navy jurisdiction and that of the Federal Government under the May act does not extend to prostitution or similar conditions in industrial areas. The Social Protection Section of the Office of Defense Health and Welfare Services, however, stands ready to cooperate fully in war industry communities, as in those near military posts. The assistance and guidance it has already given in many local communities speaks for its experience and effectiveness.

In line with the President's letter, I am, therefore, asking your help in securing the repression of prostitution and in supporting local law enforcement to eliminate red-light districts and other conditions adversely affecting your manpower.

★ ★ ★

Use of elastic fabrics cut for athletic supports, other items

The use of elastic fabrics in the manufacture of sanitary belts, sanitary crotch shields, and athletic supports and suspensories was restricted June 18 by WPB in Limitation Order L–137.

Smart to supervise Japanese relocation centers in two areas

Joseph H. Smart has been appointed regional director of the War Relocation Authority, to supervise relocation centers in the Rocky Mountain and Great Plains area which will be the wartime homes of Japanese Americans evacuated by the Army from the strategic military areas of the Pacific Coast.

Mr. Smart's appointment was announced June 20 at Washington headquarters of the War Relocation Authority.

Stocks of anti-malarial agents reserved for armed forces

Because large amounts of anti-malarial agents will be needed by our armed forces fighting in the tropics, the WPB June 19 took two important actions designed to prevent the use of stocks of any such drugs for nonessential purposes.

An amendment to Conservation Order M–131, issued June 19 by the Director of Industry Operations, revokes the provision which exempted quinine or totaquine stocks of less than 50 ounces from the sales restrictions of the order.

A new order, M–131–a, prohibits the sale of any amount of Cinchonine or Cinchonidine for other than anti-malarial purposes, or the sale of Quinidine except for anti-malarial purposes or the treatment of cardiac disorders.

The health supplies branch explained that the tightening of the restrictions on quinine and totaquine is necessitated by the expectation of a severe shortage of all anti-malarial agents.

KEEP ON THE JOB!

Time irrevocably lost to the war effort through absenteeism is under attack at the Kearney & Trecker Corporation plant at Milwaukee, Wis. According to a report to War Production Drive Headquarters, newspaper headlines recounting our defeats and our set-backs, such as "Mother Loses Three Sons at Pearl Harbor," carry the subscription: "Dedicated to each of you 115 men who were absent the day after pay day."

New division on maritime labor relations established

The War Shipping Administration June 17 announced the creation of a Division of Maritime Labor Relations. The division will be under the supervision of Captain Edward Macauley, who was named deputy administrator of the War Shipping Administration on the same day.

The Division of Maritime Labor Relations will formulate the general labor policy of the War Shipping Administration, cooperating closely with other activities of the Administration concerned with the recruitment of personnel and the manning of vessels of the United States and United Nations.

Hubert Wyckoff has been appointed director, and Erich Nielsen, assistant director, of the new division.

ODT STAFF APPOINTMENTS

Two appointments to the staff of the division of railway transport, ODT, were announced June 19 by Director Eastman.

Horace M. Wigney, of Chicago, was named chief of the refrigerator car section.

W. T. Long, of Dallas, Tex., was made deputy director of rail-truck coordination for the southwestern region.

Van Shaick named director of Second Civilian Defense Region

James M. Landis, Director of the United States Office of Civilian Defense announced on June 16 that President Roosevelt had approved the appointment of George S. Van Schaick as regional director of the Second Civilian Defense Region with headquarters in New York City.

Col. Walter W. Metcalf has been acting regional director for the Second Region since the resignation of Col. Franklin D'Olier in January. He will continue his present post as Army liaison officer of the Second Region in charge of civilian protection.

Mr. Van Schaick, an attorney, is vice president of the New York Life Insurance Co.

CIVILIAN DEFENSE . . .

Volunteers organized to help guard Nation's forests against fire hazards

To mobilize the manpower necessary to protect the Nation's forests against the hazards of forest fires during the war, the United States Office of Civilian Defense has established a Forest Fire Fighters Service of volunteers, it was announced June 19 by Director James M. Landis.

Organized and developed through State and Local Defense Councils, the Forest Fire Fighters Service will function through the cooperation of the Forest Service of the Department of Agriculture, the land management agencies of the Department of Interior and other established forest protection agencies. Members of the Forest Fire Fighters Service will be enrolled as units in the Civilian Defense Auxiliary groups and will be furnished with arm bands, identification cards and automobile plates for purposes of identification in an emergency.

Federal agencies to train volunteers

Director Landis has issued instructions to the nine regional directors of OCD to assist in the organization of local units and the enrollment of personnel of the Forest Fire Fighters Service and to cooperate in establishing and strengthening of forest protection programs advanced by Federal, State, and local agencies.

Participating in the program will be the United States Forest Service, the Indian Service, the National Park Service, the Grazing Service, the General Land Office, the Fish and Wild Life Service, State Forestry Departments and private protection associations. These agencies will direct the operations of the fire-fighting groups on forest lands under their respective jurisdictions and will develop training programs for the enrolled volunteers.

Normal seasonal hazards enhanced

The possibility of incendiary bombing by enemy planes and the danger of sabotage enhance the normal seasonal hazards and make the menace of forest fires this year the greatest the country has ever faced.

Diversion of men to the armed forces and to war industries necessitate the dependence of Federal and State Forest Services upon volunteers to help to control outbreaks of fire in the forests.

"Enrollment in local Forest Fire Fighters Service units provides the opportunity for civilians to participate actively in a vitally important war service on the home front," Director Landis said.

"Forest fires could cause as much damage and could hamper the war effort just as seriously as direct enemy bombs. They could disrupt transportation and communication facilities, impede war industry by destroying the resources so imperatively needed, and damage power lines and aqueducts."

Nelson commends program

Donald M. Nelson, Chairman of the War Production Board, heartily commended the program as a contribution to war production.

Public will be informed of any new, safe method of handling incendiary bombs, Landis says

Extensive experiments on methods of dealing with incendiary bombs and the resultant fires are being conducted by the Office of Civilian Defense, Director James M. Landis said June 20 in response to inquiries. The results, which may result in some drastic changes in technique, will be made available as soon as certain scientific questions have been resolved, he said.

"Publication of reports in this country on new British methods of fighting incendiaries has caused us to receive numerous inquiries in the matter," Mr. Landis said. "For some weeks we have been making careful experiments and checking against the British experience. Public announcement will be made as soon as we are certain of the existence of safer methods of dealing with magnesium bombs.

"Certainly," he said, "we shall not endorse any new methods of handling incendiary bombs until we are sure that they are in fact more effective than the methods which we currently advocate."

Deferment of all meetings, conventions not related to war sought by Eastman

Deferment for the duration of all meetings, conventions, and group tours which are not closely related to furtherance of the war effort was called for June 19 by ODT Director Eastman. Mr. Eastman asked also that all State and county fairs be postponed.

Appeals for voluntary restrictions

Attendance at meetings which are closely related to the war program should be skeletonized, Mr. Eastman said.

Pointing to the steady rise in the volume of passenger traffic on railroad and bus lines, Mr. Eastman appealed to the American people voluntarily to impose certain restrictions on their travel.

Vacations should be staggered throughout the year, he said, and vacation travel should be scheduled so that trips would neither start nor terminate on week ends. Private passenger cars should not now be used for extensive vacation travel, he added.

"Do not travel, aside from vacations, for mere pleasure or when travel can readily be avoided," Mr. Eastman said.

★ ★

WPB releases 2,397 trucks, other vehicles in week

The automotive branch of WPB announced June 15 that during the week ended June 13, it authorized the release of 2,397 trucks, truck trailers, and miscellaneous vehicles to civilian users and holders of Government exemption permits under the rationing plan that became effective March 9.

Some mahogany veneers released from restrictions

Among mahogany veneers not subject to the sales restrictions of Conservation Order M–122 are ½₈-inch veneers which do not meet the joint Army-Navy specifications for aircraft construction.

This is made clear by Interpretation No. 1 of the order. The ½₈-inch veneers, and all other non-war-use mahogany woods, may be sold freely in the usual channels of distribution.

NELSON ANSWERS TRUMAN COMMITTEE

Donald M. Nelson, WPB Chairman, June 19 issued the following statement:

I am sorry that the Truman committee, which has done and is doing such valuable work, should have been critical of the work of Philip Reed.

During the past 5 months American industry has been converted from peace to war. Mistakes have of course been made. But the record of the War Production Board speaks for itself. The production we are getting is due to the teamwork of many able men.

Mr. Reed is entitled to full credit for his participation in this work. I have full confidence in him and sincerely hope that he will continue his valuable assistance in the war effort as long as he can do so.

··

Proposed curb on motion picture theater equipment discussed

The manufacturers of motion picture theater equipment, sitting as an industry advisory committee, discussed with representatives of the WPB at a meeting in Washington last week, conservation of critical materials and conversion of certain plant facilities to war work, and a proposed limitation order curtailing the manufacture of motion picture theater equipment.

Harold Hopper, Government presiding officer, told the industry committee that the importance of the motion picture business as a medium of training, education, information, and morale building, is recognized and it is intended to keep the theaters operating. On the other hand, the manufacture of motion picture theater equipment uses many critical materials, such as copper, nickel, aluminum, and steel, and it is imperative that such materials be conserved for the war program.

· · ·

SAVE EVERYTHING!

The War Production Drive committee of the Du Pont Indiana Ordnance Works erected a V-shaped bulletin board on which a daily and cumulative record of rubber bands, paper clips, found on floors and in wastebaskets was posted. In addition, a daily conservation communiqué, written by a different office worker each day, was posted.

Colored stickers displayed on cars expected to forestall gasoline chiseling in East

Would-be gasoline chiselers are expected to have a difficult time getting gasoline they don't deserve when the OPA's permanent gasoline rationing plan goes into effect July 15 in the East Coast area.

In addition to the new style gasoline rationing coupon books, the OPA will issue with the books, colored "A," "B," "C," and "S" stickers which every driver of an automobile or commercial motor vehicle will be required to display on his vehicle thereby informing the public as to the type of book he has obtained.

South African amosite asbestos saved for war use

To conserve the supply of imported South African amosite asbestos for essential military purposes, the circumstances under which it may be used are changed in several respects by an amendment to Conservation Order M–79, issued June 19 by the Director of Industry Operations.

·· ·· ··

WELL-KNOWN ARTISTS WILL DRAW FOR YOUR PAPER OR MAGAZINE

VICTORY PRESENTS, on facing page, a sixth group of 4 drawings by well-known American artists who have volunteered their talents to help emphasize, in their own medium, matters vital to winning the war. VICTORY will print four drawings by these and other artists each week. Permission to reprint is hereby granted. Mats in two-column size (larger than appears here) are available weekly. Requests to be put on the mailing list regularly, or for individual mats should be addressed to Distribution Section, Division of Information, Office for Emergency Management, Washington, D. C.

(In individual orders for the four drawings displayed this week, please refer to the serial numbers printed on the drawings.)

"I guess they're looking for that rubber bone Swankie buried."

Drawn for Division of Information, OEM.

"No wonder we aren't winning the war! The Salvage Committee won't call for that clock, they expect me to bring it to them!"

Drawn for Division of Information, OEM.

"Pappy, what is car pooling?"

Drawn for Division of Information, OEM.

"I could tell those boys down in Washington a thing or two about rationing."

Drawn for Division of Information, OEM.

Meeting called to discuss saving household fats needed in war production

Lessing J. Rosenwald, chief of the Bureau of Industrial Conservation, invited editors of trade publications in the food distributing field to attend a conference to be held June 23, in Washington, to discuss ways of salvaging household fats to further our war effort.

The public will not be asked to save household fats until some time early in July.

"War in the Pacific has seriously reduced our imports of fats and oils from the Far East," said Mr. Rosenwald. "A ready means is at hand of getting a substitute to replace this loss; that is, recovery and use of part of the estimated 2 billions of pounds of household cooking fats that are now wasted each year. The war effort requires glycerine for explosives and other war needs, both for our own forces and those of our allies. Fats make glycerine. To insure our supply of glycerine, the Bureau of Industrial Conservation is setting up the Household Fats Salvage Program, and hopes to secure over half a billion pounds a year of wasted cooking fats from the kitchens of American homes.

"Neighborhood chain food stores, meat markets, and frozen food locker plants should serve as ideal centers for the collection of household fats. These centers will weigh and buy waste fats from the housewife and sell them to the renderer. The renderer in turn will buy and transport the fats to his plant for processing and then forward the refined product to industrial centers."

Housewives are asked not to dispose of less than a pound of fats.

Drawn for Division of Information, O. E. M.
V-32-4/23.
KID SALVAGE

KID SALVAGE, a character drawn by Steig especially for OEM, will appear in VICTORY *every week. Mats for publication are available in either 2- or 3-column size. Requests to be put on the mailing list should be addressed to Distribution Section, Division of Information, OEM, Washington, D. C. When ordering individual mats, refer to code number and specify size.*

WAR EFFORT INDICES

MANPOWER

National labor force, April	53,400,000
Unemployed, April	3,000,000
Nonagricultural workers, April	40,773,000
Percent increase since June 1940	**14
Farm employment, June 1, 1942	11,917,000
Percent increase since June 1940	**1

FINANCE *(In millions of dollars)*

Authorized program June 1940–May 1942	‡164,673
Airplanes	35,978
Ordnance	35,220
Miscellaneous munitions	21,281
Industrial facilities	16,697
Naval ships	15,538
Posts, depots, etc.	13,220
Merchant ships	7,465
Pay, subsistence, travel for the armed forces	6,150
Stockpile, food exports	4,851
Housing	1,392
Miscellaneous	6,881
Total expenditures, June 1940–May 1942	*30,595
Sales of War Bonds—	
Cumulative May 1941–June 15, 1942	6,357
June 1–15, 1942	334

PLANT EXPANSION *(In millions of dollars)*

June 1940 to latest reporting date	
Gov. commitments for war plant expansion; 1,644 projects, April 30	12,131
Private commitment for war plant expansion; 7,836 projects, April 30	2,574

EARNINGS, HOURS, AND COST OF LIVING — *Percent increase from June 1940*

Manufacturing industries— April:		
Average weekly earnings	$36.63	42.0
Average hours worked per week	42.4	13.1
Average hourly earnings	81.9¢	21.9
Cost of living, (1935–39 = 100):	*Index*	
May 1942	116.0	15.4
June 2, 1942	115.9	15.3

*Prelim. includes revisions in former months.
‡Preliminary.
**Adjusted for seasonal variations.

OFFICE FOR EMERGENCY MANAGEMENT

WAYNE COY, *Liaison Officer*

CENTRAL ADMINISTRATIVE SERVICES: Dallas Dort, *Director.*

BOARD OF WAR COMMUNICATIONS: James Lawrence Fly, *Chairman.*

INFORMATION DIVISION: Robert W. Horton, *Director.*

NATIONAL WAR LABOR BOARD: Wm. H. Davis, *Chairman.*

OFFICE OF SCIENTIFIC RESEARCH AND DEVELOPMENT: Dr. Vannevar Bush, *Director.*

OFFICE OF CIVILIAN DEFENSE: James M. Landis, *Director.*

OFFICE OF THE COORDINATOR OF INTER-AMERICAN AFFAIRS: Nelson Rockefeller, *Coordinator.*

OFFICE OF DEFENSE HEALTH AND WELFARE SERVICES: Paul V. McNutt, *Director.*

OFFICE OF DEFENSE TRANSPORTATION: Joseph B. Eastman, *Director.*

OFFICE OF FACTS AND FIGURES: Archibald MacLeish, *Director.*

OFFICE OF LEND-LEASE ADMINISTRATION: E. R. Stettinius, Jr., *Administrator.*

OFFICE OF PRICE ADMINISTRATION: Leon Henderson, *Administrator.*

OFFICE OF WAR INFORMATION: Elmer Davis, *Director.*

OFFICE OF ALIEN PROPERTY CUSTODIAN: Leo T. Crowley, *Custodian.*

WAR MANPOWER COMMISSION: Paul V. McNutt, *Chairman.*

WAR RELOCATION AUTHORITY: Milton Eisenhower, *Director.*

WAR SHIPPING ADMINISTRATION: Rear Admiral Emory S. Land, U. S. N. (Retired), *Administrator.*

WAR PRODUCTION BOARD:
Donald M. Nelson, *Chairman.*
Henry L. Stimson.
Frank W. Knox.
Jesse H. Jones.
William S. Knudsen.
Sidney Hillman.
Leon Henderson.
Henry A. Wallace.
Harry L. Hopkins.

WAR PRODUCTION BOARD DIVISIONS:

Donald M. Nelson, *Chairman.*
  Executive Secretary, G. Lyle Belsley.

PURCHASES DIVISION: Houlder Hudgins, *Acting Director.*

PRODUCTION DIVISION: W. H. Harrison, *Director.*

MATERIALS DIVISION: A. I. Henderson, *Director.*

DIVISION OF INDUSTRY OPERATIONS: J. S. Knowlson, *Director.*

LABOR PRODUCTION DIVISION: Wendell Lund, *Director.*

CIVILIAN SUPPLY DIVISION: Leon Henderson, *Director.*

REQUIREMENTS COMMITTEE: Wm. L. Batt, *Chairman.*

VICTORY

OFFICIAL WEEKLY BULLETIN OF THE AGENCIES IN THE OFFICE FOR EMERGENCY MANAGEMENT

WASHINGTON, D. C.   JUNE 30, 1942   VOLUME 3, NUMBER 26

BAD NEWS FOR THE AXIS

By the President

We ordinarily do not release production figures because they might give aid and comfort to the enemy. I am going to give today just a few which are definitely going to give the Axis just the opposite of "aid and comfort."

We are well on our way towards achieving the rate of production which will bring us to our goals.

In May, we produced nearly 4,000 planes and over 1,500 tanks. We also produced nearly 2,000 artillery and anti-tank guns. This is exclusive of anti-aircraft guns and guns to be mounted in tanks.

And here is a figure which the Axis will not be very happy to hear—in that one month alone we produced over 50,000 machine guns of all types—including infantry, aircraft and anti-aircraft. That does not include sub-machine guns. If we add those in, the total is well over 100,000. All these figures are only for one single month.

While these figures give you some idea of our production accomplishments this is no time for the American people to get overconfident. We can't rest on our oars. We need more and more, and we will make more and more. And we must also remember that there are plenty of serious production problems ahead—particularly some serious shortages in raw materials, which are receiving the closest consideration of the Government and industry.

June 25, 1942

CEILING ON RENTS
July 1, 1942

IN
Defense-Rental Areas

WHERE MAXIMUM RENT REGULATIONS ARE IN EFFECT

21%

46%   67%

WHERE OPA HAS RECOMMENDED STABILIZATION

OTHER AREAS (NO CEILING)   33%

Each symbol = 10% of U. S. population.

DATA OPA

Review of the Week

News from the war front last week was mixed and, with Tobruk and fresh assaults on Russian line, not very good. But in America, the news was definitely good.

The best news was President Roosevelt's release of war production figures, which, the President pointed out, were of no aid and comfort to the enemy. He revealed that in May we produced nearly 4,000 planes, more than 1,500 tanks, 2,000 artillery and anti-tank guns and more than 100,000 machine and submachine guns.

To his big news, the President attached an emphatic warning against over-confidence and a call for more and more production. He warned "we must also remember that there are plenty of serious shortages ahead."

A hint of one way in which production is being increased came in a release from the War Production Board citing an increase of 63½ percent since a labor-management committee started a War Production Drive in the plant of the Cleveland (Ohio) Tractor Company. In May alone the increase was 33 percent.

More good news

Other good news of the week:

Issuance of OPA orders extending the price ceiling to services in connection with commodities, effective July 1.

The extension of rent control to 60 new areas by Price Administrator Henderson.

The price ceiling on services is the third step in the price control program. The first step was the limiting of wholesale prices. The second step was the limiting of retail prices. Both of these steps were taken in May. In each step, the highest price at which sales were completed in the month of March became the highest price that may be charged now.

The third step places under price control only those services involving commodities. A doctor or a masseur is exempt; a radio repairman and a shoe shiner are affected because their services involve commodities: radio sets and shoes.

Controls strengthen each other

Supporting this program and gaining support from it, is the rent control program. As rapidly as it becomes necessary, areas in which war production flourishes are being put under rent control. In rents, the March maximum is not always the ceiling figure. Some rents have been rolled back to levels in 1941. In extending the control areas, Mr. Henderson has brought Federal protection against rising rents to regions in which 38,000,000 Americans live—one quarter of the Nation.

The OPA believes that the price ceiling and the rent ceilings are effective barriers against runaway inflation in America.

At this writing, the exact amount of rubber salvaged by the gas stations and other agencies has not been totalled. The amount obtained, however, was less than hoped for but it was sufficient to encourage the President to continue the drive for 10 more days.

One flash of fireworks in the battle for salvage: Paul C. Cabot, deputy chief of the Bureau of Industrial Conservation, WPB, wrote a long, long letter to Phillip Murray, President of the CIO, recounting the bureau's successes in salvaging scrap metal. His point: "The statement . . . in which you are quoted as having said the Government's failure to gather scrap was 'almost criminal' would appear to be unwarranted."

Of burs and beef and beehives

The WPB stopped the production of nonmilitary truck trailers; limited the use of elastic fabric to essential health and military uses; limited the types and sizes of dental burs; and froze all large stocks of canned corn beef to make them available for the Army. The board's other orders during the week were largely taking bugs out of earlier restrictions. Civilian quotas of certain dyes were increased, the use of already manufactured zippers was permitted, and orders were relaxed to permit more drilling for gas in certain areas and to permit the making of more beehives and farm packing machinery.

Gas ration plan changes

The WPB reduced by 14 percent the amount of cocoa beans that may be processed in the next 3 months and reduced by 10 percent the civilian apricot pack. On the other hand, it increased the quota of cloves by from one-third to one-half.

It was a busy week for the OPA. In addition to orders on rents, the OPA changed the date for the new gas rationing plan in the east from July 15 to July 22. Registration dates were changed from July 1, 2 and 3 to July 9, 10 and 11.

The OPA demonstrated that gas rationing rules have teeth when it suspended deliveries to 64 filling stations and garages in the metropolitan areas of New York, Newark and Philadelphia for selling gasoline to persons without a ration card.

More tires for war workers

The OPA issued several score orders ironing out inequalities in the price control picture, announced it would set ceiling prices on toys, arranged to get more tires to war workers and still found time to urge the use of a new sand-blast method of rehabilitating typewriter rollers instead of replacing the rollers.

War Manpower Commissioner McNutt issued eight directives to the U. S. Employment Service, the WPB, the Director of Selective Service and the Secretary of Agriculture, setting up the machinery by which men will be found for war jobs and cared for on the job. The Commissioner also established a Negro Manpower Service to broaden the opportunities for Negroes to help in war work.

★ ★ ★

WAR EFFORT'S PROGRESS TOLD VISUALLY

The charts appearing every week on the front cover of VICTORY tell the story of America's battle as it is fought here at home. One-column mats are available for publication by newspapers and others who may desire them. Requests should be sent to Distribution Section, Division of Information, OEM, Washington, D. C.

VICTORY

OFFICIAL BULLETIN of the Office for Emergency Management. Published weekly by the Division of Information, Office for Emergency Management, and printed at the United States Government Printing Office, Washington, D. C.

Subscription rates by mail: 75¢ for 52 issues; 25¢ for 18 issues, single copies 5¢, payable in advance. Remit money order payable directly to the Superintendent of Documents, Government Printing Office, Washington, D. C.

On the Home Front

We launched our attack on the high cost of living—inflation to the economists—in three waves. On May 11 we clamped a ceiling on the prices of almost everything we eat, wear, and use at the manufacturing and wholesale levels. On May 18 we extended this ceiling to cover commodity prices at the retail level. This week we stretched it over the prices of most consumer services. In less than two months, then, we have set our economic house in order—won the first battle in our fight to avert economic chaos.

$5,000,000,000 a year for consumer services

Price control of consumer services is important to everybody. The American people spend upwards of $5,000,000,000 a year in nearly 1,000,000 shops and stores on such services and the fact that they are being brought under control will go a long way toward stabilizing the budgets of 33,000,000 American families.

"Consumer service" is a fancy term for something which is a part of our daily living. Every time you have your shoes shined or your suit pressed or your watch fixed you are buying a consumer service. When you put your automobile in a parking lot or send your clothes to the laundry or have a roll of film developed you are getting a consumer service. There are a thousand-and-one consumer services which add to our enjoyment of life—and tap our pocket books.

Fewer new goods, more repairs

Under the terms of the Office of Price Administration's order, tradesmen cannot charge more for most consumer services than in the month of March. It's important to remember, however, that price control extends only to service rendered in connection with a commodity. That exempts work done by dentists, for example, or barbers or hairdressers—but it includes services rendered by the undertaker.

One of the most important types of service covered by the ceiling are repair services. As time goes on and new consumer goods vanish from the shelves we are going to call on the repair man at more frequent intervals. We will then be grateful that the cost of repairing automobiles, electrical appliances, furniture, luggage, and a host of other things has been stabilized.

The mobilization of manpower for maximum service at the front, in the factory, and on the farm is going to occupy our attention for many months to come. The War Manpower Commission already has taken some big strides toward the goal and took additional steps last week. Commission Chairman Paul V. McNutt issued eight directives to the

REPRINTING PERMISSIBLE

Requests have been received for permission to reprint "On the Home Front" in whole or in part. This column, like all other material in VICTORY, may be reprinted without special permission. If excerpts are used, the editors ask only that they be taken in such a way that their original meaning is preserved.

U. S. Employment Service, the War Production Board, the Selective Service System and the Department of Agriculture designed to "promote effective mobilization and utilization of the Nation's manpower." These agencies were allotted a specific task in the program to make certain that healthy young men without special skills go into the fighting forces, that the skilled mechanic of middle years stays at his lathe and that trained farm workers remain in the fields. A Democracy engaged in total war cannot tolerate misfits, malingerers or madcaps on any front.

Many skilled workers unemployed

Mr. McNutt attacked another manpower problem last week—that of the temporary unemployment of skilled and semiskilled workers caused by the shutting down of nonessential civilian industries. He conferred with Governor Lehman of New York, Mayor LaGuardia of New York City and Donald M. Nelson, chairman of WPB, over the situation in New York City, where nearly 400,000 men, many of them highly skilled, are idle at the very time when we need the highest production in our history. Much of this unemployment is due to the shutdown of nonessential civilian industry—but men—and plants, too—must be converted to the work of war.

Training program for Negroes

The vital stake of America's 13,000,000 Negroes in the fight for freedom has been emphasized by creation of a Negro Manpower Service within the War Manpower Commission. Under the direction of Dr.

Robert C. Weaver, an expert on Negro employment, the Service will carry out a program of training and placement of colored workers. The unhappy race discriminations of peacetime are fast disappearing.

Campaign launched to save trucks

Transportation must not be a bottleneck if men and materials are to move to far-flung fronts in sufficient quantities to defeat the Axis. Highly-trained soldiers waiting in cantonments, finished weapons piling up on steamship docks, are of no value on the battlefield. The Office of Defense Transportation has opened a new offensive on the transportation front with the formation of a "U. S. Truck Conservation Corps." This corps will enlist the owners and drivers of our 5,000,000 trucks and thousands of others who service and supply them in a Nation-wide campaign to save their machines and their tires. The President opened the offensive, saying that "it has become the patriotic duty of every truck operator in America to help in every possible way to make his truck and tires last longer." Our trucks, like our passenger cars, and our trains, must last for the duration.

Enemy-owned patents seized

Automobile graveyards yielded more than 383,253 tons of scrap metal in May, 10 percent more than in April and 100 percent more than the monthly rate in 1941 . . . Last summer's aluminum collection drive resulted in the recovery of 6,398,051 pounds, only 42½ percent of the amount expected . . . Several million additional pounds of honey have been made available as a substitute for sugar in bakery goods, ice cream, candy and soft drinks . . . And beekeepers have been encouraged to produce more honey by a WPB order increasing the output of wooden beehives.

Your landlord has *not* been prohibited from repainting or redecorating your apartment if it constitutes normal "maintenance or repair" . . . Enemy-owned patents seized by the U. S. Alien Property custodian cover a wide variety of machines and processes—among one group of more than 750 seized last week were patents for coal mine conveyors, automatic drills for use in airplane construction, oil refining processes, and chemical compounds . . . the patents were owned by German, Italian, Japanese, and Hungarian corporations and individuals . . . WPB has amended its regulations to expedite the piping of gas, water and electricity to thousands of war housing units . . .

MANPOWER . . .

U. S. agencies concerned with various aspects of manpower given specific tasks in 8 directives issued by McNutt

War Manpower Commissioner Paul V. McNutt June 25 issued eight directives to "promote effective mobilization and utilization of the Nation's manpower."

To channel manpower where needed

The directives are addressed to Federal agencies concerned with various aspects of manpower, including the War Production Board, the Selective Service System, and the U. S. Employment Service. Collectively, these directives constitute a program to coordinate information regarding manpower supply and to channel available manpower where it is needed—in war industry and in agriculture.

Employment Service has primary role

Four of the directives are addressed to the U. S. Employment Service, making clear the primary role which that agency is to play in all-out mobilization along the home front.

The employment service is directed to prepare and maintain lists of essential activities and occupations, as well as lists of occupations in which shortages exist. It is directed to analyze and classify occupational questionnaires distributed by the Selective Service system, to interview individuals with skills in critical war occupations, and to refer such individuals to job openings in war production. The U. S. Employment Service is further instructed to alleviate critical war production shortages by making preferential referrals of workers to war industry employers in order of priority, and to enlarge its activities so as to insure an adequate supply of agricultural workers.

Data on job priorities from WPB

The plan by which a system of job priorities is established will be buttressed by information supplied by the War Production Board. The board is charged, in Mr. McNutt's directive to it, with the task of furnishing the War Manpower Commission "current information with respect to the relative importance, in connection with the maintenance and effectuation of the national war supply program, of filling job openings in plants, factories or other facilities . . ."

Selective Service to collaborate

WPB, in securing this information, may seek the aid of the War and Navy departments, the Maritime Commission, the Department of Agriculture, the Army and Navy Munitions Board, "and such other departments and agencies as it may deem appropriate."

The directive to the Director of Selective Service calls for "close collaboration" between the Selective Service System and the U. S. Employment Service to the end that persons engaged in essential war activities are temporarily deferred from military training and service and that individuals not now engaged in essential activities, but who are qualified for such occupations, be afforded "reasonable opportunity" to become so engaged.

Housing of transient farm workers

Two of the directives, addressed to the Secretary of Agriculture and to "certain Government agencies" respectively, concern the housing and transportation of the additional transient agricultural workers essential to this summer's "Food for Victory" harvest.

The Secretary of Agriculture is instructed to gather information regarding housing facilities in areas which will require nonlocal agricultural workers and to make certain that additional labor camp facilities are established where necessary.

Transportation needs coordinated

The transportation directive calls on the U. S. Employment Service, the Department of Agriculture and "any other department or agency having information concerning workers transferring to, moving between or engaged in essential activities" to transmit information regarding transportation needs to the Office of Defense Transportation. Under the Executive order by which it was established, the ODT is responsible for assuring adequate transportation facilities for war workers. .

Other provisions

The directive to the U. S. Employment Service establishing priorities in recruitment of war industry workers and that dealing with recruitment of transient agricultural workers both safeguard the workers' interests from the point of view of wages and working conditions.

The "Placement Priorities Directive" provides that the employment service may except from the priority provision an employing establishment in which "wages and conditions of work are not at least as advantageous to a worker referred to a job opening therein as those prevailing for similar establishments in the industrial area." And the "Directive to Expedite the Recruitment and Placement of Essential Agricultural Workers" provides that the service shall not recruit agricultural workers for "any agricultural employment in which the wages or conditions of work are less advantageous to the worker than those prevailing for similar work in the locality."

Weaver named director of new Negro manpower division

Chairman Paul V. McNutt June 20 announced establishment within the War Manpower Commission of a Negro Manpower Service to work for the full utilization of Negroes in the training and employment phases of the war production program. Dr. Robert C. Weaver has been appointed director of the new division which will operate under Arthur J. Altmeyer, executive director of the War Manpower Commission.

Second Arkansas site selected for Japanese evacuees

Nearly 8,000 acres of potentially productive Mississippi Delta land in Chicot and Drew Counties, Arkansas, near Jerome will be cleared and brought under cultivation by Japanese evacuees from the Pacific Coast military zone, the War Relocation Authority announced June 26.

Ninth in national program

The new Delta relocation site is the second war-duration work center for West Coast evacuees to be selected in Arkansas and the ninth in the national relocation program. Others are situated in the eastern part of California and in Arizona, Idaho, Wyoming, and Colorado.

ARMS AND THE MAN

Cartoon by Elderman for VICTORY. *Publishers may obtain mats of these cartoons weekly in either two- or three-column size. Requests to be put on the mailing list should be addressed to Distribution Section, Office of War Information, Washington, D. C. Refer to V–44.*

Training of war workers pushed by joint committees, says McNutt

"Joint management-labor committees are operating effectively to push the training programs for essential war production workers, Paul V. McNutt, Chairman of the War Manpower Commission, said June 29 in reviewing apprenticeship training results during the past 6 months.

"Joint committees, particularly apprenticeship committees, which represent management and labor have been most effective in shaping policies for general training programs to be conducted in the plants," Mr. McNutt pointed out.

A 6 months' progress report of the apprenticeship section submitted to Mr. McNutt as a result of the recent transfer to the Federal Security Agency from the Department of Labor, reported the training of more than 500,000 war workers, which helped solve 97,000 in-plant training problems in war industries.

Mr. McNutt urged immediate expansion of in-plant training programs. "Increased production is paramount now," he said. "All-round workers are needed not only for supervisors and foremen for the tremendously expanded labor supply in war production plants, but they are needed, too, as lead, set-up and quartermen and for installation, maintenance and repair work. . . ."

★ ★ ⊥

Colorado steel firm granted relief on Lend-Lease shipments

Colorado Fuel and Iron Corporation, of Denver, Colo., has been granted permission to pass on to the buyer a larger share of heavy freight costs on shipments of iron and steel products to the Eastern seaboard for the account of the Lend-Lease Administration, Price Administrator Henderson announced June 26.

Such shipments, the Administrator explained, go far beyond this company's usual market area.

In Order No. 14 under Revised Price Schedule No. 6 on iron and steel products, effective June 30, 1942, Colorado Fuel and Iron is permitted on sales for Lend-Lease account to charge maximum Chicago basing point prices, freight on board, Minnequa, Colorado.

Order No. 14 extends to Lend-Lease shipments of all types of products by the company the same transportation cost relief granted it last month on a Lend-Lease shipment to the Eastern seaboard of 300 gross tons of galvanized steel fencing wire.

May machine tool production up 80 percent over 1941

The value of new machine tools, presses, and other metal-working machinery shipped during May was $118,500,000, 80 percent more than the same month last year, it was announced June 26 by the War Production Board.

Price cut on aluminum products postponed to August 1

Reductions in prices of fabricated aluminum products previously scheduled by the OPA to take effect July 1, have been postponed until August 1, Price Administrator Henderson announced June 26.

LABOR . . .

Steel Workers' demand for dollar-a-day increase, union security analyzed as Board gets "Little Steel" fact-finding report

William H. Davis, chairman of the National War Labor Board, June 30, made public the report of the Board's fact-finding panel in the wage and union security dispute between four "Little Steel" companies and the United Steelworkers of America, CIO. A public hearing before the full board is scheduled for this week.

The fact-finding panel, which is composed of Arthur S. Meyer, chairman of the New York State Board of Mediation, representing the public; Cyrus S. Ching, vice president of the U. S. Rubber Co., representing employers; and Richard T. Frankensteen, director of Aircraft Organization, United Automobile Workers of America, CIO, representing labor, and assisted by Sidney A. Wolff, New York attorney, submitted its report to the Board after four and one-half months of hearings and study. The panel has condensed over 2,500 pages of testimony and hundreds of exhibits, including scores of complicated economic and financial charts, down to a report of 67 pages.

The panel was not asked to make recommendations to the Board but "to define and investigate the issues in dispute between the parties" and to "submit to the Board its findings of fact."

The dispute concerns the union's demands for a wage increase of $1 a day, union security and check-off, and, in the case of the Republic Steel Corporation and the Bethlehem Steel Company, a demand for a minimum wage guarantee. The other two companies are the Youngstown Sheet and Tube Company and the Inland Steel Company. The union represents 157,000 employees of the four companies.

HIGHLIGHTS OF FINDINGS

If any wage increase is granted by the Board in this case, it will be made retroactive to the date of certification of the case, in accordance with an interim order of the Board issued April 24. The cases were certified at different dates, between February 6 and 10.

Briefly summarized, the highlights of the panel's findings are as follows:

1. The panel finds that all four companies are able to pay the requested wage increase of $1 a day."

2. "Profit taxes represent the Government's opinion of the extent to which the Government should share in the net profits of business after all other expenses including labor costs, have been deducted. To propose that wages should be affected by profit taxes, is to propose that labor's return should be conditioned by the Government's impost on industry."

The companies' earnings before Federal profit taxes are ample and represent the proper criterion of ability to pay, the panel pointed out. The panel also pointed out, however, that the companies would pay only a small part of any increased labor costs—11¼ percent under the Treasury profits tax proposal and 6 percent under the Ways and Means proposal. The balance would cost the companies nothing, since it would come out of a decrease in taxes.

3. "The panel finds that if a wage increase otherwise proper, is withheld because of its effect on governmental revenues per se, such withholding would involve an unauthorized tax on workers."

4. The panel found that in March 1941, the month before the steel wage increase last year, the hourly earnings in the durable goods industries were 12% less than they were in the steel industry. During the past year, this relationship has changed so that for the year 1942 the panel estimates the hourly earnings in durable goods will be only 7.9% less than steel, a shift of 4.1%.

In March 1941, the hourly earnings in all manufacturing industries were 20% less than steel, whereas, for the year 1942 they are estimated to be only 17.2% less, a shift of 2.8%.

The panel estimates an even greater shift in the relationships, when calculated on a weekly basis. Its figures show that in March 1941, the weekly earnings in durable goods were 4.2% less than the weekly earnings in steel, whereas for the year 1942 durable goods will be 7.8% above steel, a shift of 12%. In March 1941, the weekly earnings in all manufacturing were 16.6% below steel, whereas, for the year 1942 they will be only 7.5% below, a shift of 9.1%.

5. The panel's estimates have been made on the assumption that there will be no increase either in wage rates or in hours of work after the month of May 1942. The panel, however, has drawn attention to the fact that it is highly probable that hours of work will continue to increase throughout the year, except in steel. Steel is a three-shift industry working at capacity and there is no elasticity for increase or hours. The fairly stable weekly hours worked in steel and the continually increasing hours in durable goods and all manufacturing have accounted in great degree, according to the panel, for the shift in relationships which have occurred during the past year.

6. "The panel further finds that a greater weight is normally given to hourly earnings because hourly earnings fix costs and because it is proper that the worker should be paid according to the extent of his labor . . . weekly earnings should be given more than their usual weight in the present determination of a just wage for the steelworkers.

The panel also found that the comparisons between steel and durable goods and steel and all manufacturing are pertinent, though the former is more to the point. It also found that "contrasts between present comparative relations of industries and past comparative relations are pertinent though not controlling."

7. "The panel finds that from March, 1941, to March, 1942, the cost of living for steel towns advanced 14%; average weekly earnings in the steel industry advanced approximately 13.1%, and average hourly earnings advanced approximately 14.6%."

The panel then compared the changes in the cost of living which had taken place since the general steel wage increase in April, 1941, with the changes in weekly earnings since April, 1941, and concluded:

"The panel believes that weekly earnings are the proper criterion for measuring the impact of rising living costs and therefore finds that the buying power of the earnings of the steel worker has decreased approximately 13.3% since the last general change of wage rates in the steel industry."

8. "Inland has said that in the past, increases in steel wages spread like wildfire throughout the other industries in the country and that the same thing would happen again . . . . The panel believes that general economic conditions are the principal cause of changes in wage rates, rather than any specific change in a particular industry. . . .

"It is clear that the national money income shares importance with the consumer's pie, and that, though the latter will shrink, the former will grow. To ask labor to accept less than its proportionate share of the Nation's money income in order to prevent labor from acquiring too much pie leaves out of account that money has value even when it must be saved."

9. "Inland and Youngstown are either presently complying with or are willing to comply with" the union's request for a minimum daily wage guarantee. "Granting the request would involve no direct additional cost to the companies."

10. "The functions of this union, in particular, are today of vital significance and its maintenance is socially desirable . . . Union security, in the form of maintenance of membership, united with the checkoff would— (a) make shop conditions more peaceful by diminishing friction and eliminating the solicitation of dues, (b) reduce the cost of dues' collection and benefit the union accordingly, (c) release the time of union officials and thus permit frequent contact with both union membership and management addressed to the elimination of grievances and to a concerted effort to achieve maximum production."

Cyrus Ching dissents from this finding because "he does not believe union maintenance should be imposed in these cases". Richard T. Frankensteen dissents because "he finds the facts in these cases warrant . . . the union shop." The panel was unanimous on everything except this issue.

Other excerpts from the report

1. The United Steelworkers of America has contracts with firms producing 60% of the total tonnage of the entire steel industry covering more than 600,000 employees. This does not include the four companies involved in this case, which produce about 32% of the total tonnage.

2. The union's dues are $1 a month. The initiation fee is $3. The union has never levied special assessments.

3. The union was designated the sole collective bargaining agent in the plants of the four companies in the summer and fall of 1941 when it won National Labor Relations Board elections in Bethlehem by a majority of 70% and showed the NLRB by a check of

union membership records that between 70% and 75% of the eligible employees in the other three companies were members of the union.

The wage demand

4. The union bases its demand for a general wage increase of $1 a day on the following arguments:

"(1) The steel worker has not received his share of the savings through increased productive efficiency in the steel industry.

"(2) The wages of the steel worker are inadequate when judged by standards of health and decency.

"(3) The companies are able to pay the increase demanded.

"(4) Comparable wages justify the demand.

"(5) The change in the cost of living justifies the demand."

5. "The panel finds that the union cannot ground a demand for a wage increase on the reallocation of savings through increased productive efficiency in the steel industry."

6. "The average annual income of steel workers was $1,926.72 in the year 1941 . . . The panel finds that the union has not sustained its contention that wages in the steel industry are inadequate when judged by standards of health and decency."

Ability of the companies to pay

7. The $1 a day increase would cost Bethlehem, $23,000,000; Republic, $16,500,000; Youngstown, $4,700,000; Inland, $3,300,000.

The 1941 earnings of the four companies before Federal profit taxes were: Bethlehem, $119,758,000; Republic, $70,288,000; Youngstown, $37,624,000; Inland, $38,079,000.

8. If the union receives the $1 a day increase, the 1942 earnings of the companies prior to Federal income taxes would be in round figures as follows: Bethlehem, $90,000,-000; Republic, $50,000,000; Youngstown, $30,-000,000; Inland, $30,000,000.

"It will be noted that in each case the figure is substantially greater than any year in the 1931-1940 decade, and is in the case of Bethlehem over 6 times, Republic over 13 times, Youngstown over 20 times and Inland over 3 times the average annual earning for the period."

Comparative wages

10. "The panel finds that for the year 1942 hourly earnings in the steel industry will be greater than hourly earnings in durable goods and greater still than hourly earnings in all manufacturing but in both cases the percentage difference will be less than it was in the past."

11. "The panel finds that for the year 1942 weekly earnings in durable goods will probably be substantially greater than weekly earnings in the steel industry whereas in March 1941, they were slightly less. Weekly earnings in all manufacturing will probably be in the neighborhood of weekly earnings of steel workers, whereas, in March 1941, they were substantially less."

Earnings of all workers for the year 1942

	Hourly earn-ings	Rela-tion to steel	Weekly earn-ings	Rela-tion to steel
	Cents	Percent		Percent
Steel	99.1	....	$40.93	....
Durable goods	91.3	−7.9	44.12	±7.8
All manufacturing	82.0	−17.2	37.86	−7.5

"The month of March 1941 will be chosen for comparison because that was

the month preceding the steel wage increase of April 1941."

Earnings of all workers for the month of March 1941

	Hourly earn-ings	Rela-tion to steel	Weekly earn-ings	Rela-tion to steel
	Cents	Percent		Percent
Steel industry	87.3	....	$34.94	....
Durable goods industries	76.8	−12	33.48	−4.2
All manufacturing industries	69.7	−20	29.11	−16.6

(The two above tables are quoted verbatim from the report.)

Cost of living

12. "The wage rates in the steel industry advanced ten cents an hour on April 1, 1941. Giving effect to this advance, the Panel further finds that:

"(d) From April 1941 to March 1942, the cost of living in steel towns advanced 13.3%.

"(e) Over the same interval, average weekly earnings in the steel industry decreased a fraction of 1%.

"(f) Over the same interval, average hourly earnings in the steel industry advanced approximately 3.2%."

13. "On the presumption that the present policies of price freezing of most goods, rationing of scarce goods and control of rents in defense areas will continue and prove effective, and solely on the basis of the material in the record, the Panel has allowed nothing for increases of living costs after March 15, 1942."

Inflation

14. "The Panel further finds that the country is committed to fighting inflation on a seven point front, that one of the seven points is the stabilization of wages and that every wage increase has an inflationary effect proportionate to its size and base."

"The 'national income' represents the total sum distributed to individuals plus a sum which represents business savings. It is, therefore, the whole dividend of the Nation after the subtraction of depreciation and corporate taxes. For the years 1939 to 1941, the total compensation of employees has represented between 68% and 66½% of the national income. Labor's proportion has, in other words, remained practically constant. An important shift in the allocation of the national income would, at this time, justly cause concern. . .

"It is clear that the national money income shares importance with the consumer's pie and that, though the latter will shrink, the former will grow. To ask labor to accept less than its proportionate share of the Nation's money income in order to prevent labor from acquiring too much pie leaves out of account that money has value even when it must be saved.

"The Panel does not, however, intend to imply that a technique of forced savings can properly be worked out in the course of adjusting labor disputes."

Minimum wage guarantee

15. Many workers (50% of Bethlehem's; 20% of Republic's) are paid on a piece-rate or incentive basis, rather than solely on an hourly rate basis. Some days their piece-rate earnings do not equal the guaranteed minimum hourly wage multiplied by the number of hours worked. Other days they earn more than the guaranteed minimum. Bethlehem and Republic guarantee these workers that their daily wage will equal the minimum when averaged over the pay period, which varies from one to two weeks. The

union requests that they pay the guaranteed minimum as of each day. Youngstown and Inland are either complying with the union's request or are willing to comply.

16. The panel finds that: "The workers desire the change requested. The union represents the employees and its word should be accepted as to their wishes. Granting the request would involve no direct additional cost to the companies." Since no wage increase is intended, there is no reason for retroactive adjustment, the panel found.

If the Board grants the union's request the panel suggests that the Bethlehem and Republic companies negotiate with the union regarding any changes that need to be made in the incentive, tonnage, or piece-work rates, "on the assumption that the companies will have to bear no direct, additional cost, and that the steel workers' pay for performing a given quantity and type of work shall not be decreased."

~ ~ ~

Sellers of motor fuel at service stations given price adjustment privilege

Sellers of motor fuel, including Diesel fuel, at service stations are given the same privilege of asking for maximum price adjustments, as sellers of other commodities, in Amendment No. 31 to Maximum Price Regulation No. 137 (Motor Fuel Sold at Service Stations), issued June 26 by Price Administrator Henderson. The amendment was effective June 30.

The amendment was issued because, when Temporary Procedural Regulation No. 2 was issued to guide applications for adjustment under the general maximum price regulation, it was so phrased that it was inapplicable to the service station regulation.

Drive for scrap rubber continued 10 days by the President

President Roosevelt on June 29 called for a 10-day extension of the scrap rubber drive. He was advised that a great amount of scrap could still be gleaned.

As the whirlwind national rubber campaign went into its second week June 22, Lessing J. Rosenwald, chief of the WPB's Bureau of Industrial Conservation, issued a special appeal asking members of over 12,000 local salvage committees to redouble their efforts to bring in as much scrap rubber as possible.

PRICE ADMINISTRATION . . .

Ceiling put on charges for consumer services of million U. S. businessmen

Price Administrator Leon Henderson June 23 transferred all consumer services connected with commodities—from shoe shining to watch repairing—from the general maximum price regulation and placed them under a separate ceiling with provisions to meet the distinct price control problems involved.

In Maximum Price Regulation No. 165—Consumer Service, effective July 1—the Price Administrator set the highest prices charged last March by each individual seller as a wartime ceiling over consumer services for which the American public pays more than $5,000,-000,000 yearly.

The new regulation completes the over-all price ceiling program that began when President Roosevelt outlined his seven-point anti-inflation drive in a special message to Congress.

"Services to the ultimate consumer are a special problem in the field of price control," Mr. Henderson stated.

"The new regulation does not change in any way the main objectives of the Office of Price Administration, which are to stabilize the cost of living under wartime conditions at levels reflected in the highest prices charged for commodities and services during March 1942.

1,000,000 establishments affected

"Estimates place the number of establishments supplying the consumer services covered by today's order at nearly 1,000,000. While the prices of some so-called wholesale services are controlled by the new regulation, for the most part it applies directly to services sold at retail and hence affects the budget of every family."

The general maximum price regulation established each seller's highest March prices as a ceiling for practically every article and service sold in the United States at all levels of selling—producer, manufacturer, wholesaler, and retailer. The only exceptions important to the average family's cost of living were a limited number of food commodities and various personnel and professional services exempt from any control by OPA under the Emergency Price Control Act of 1942.

By its different effective dates, the general regulation, in effect, divided the over-all price control program into three main parts:

First came the ceiling of May 11, which applied to all sales of services and commodities at the manufacturing and wholesale level.

Second was the ceiling of May 18, applying to all sales of commodities at retail.

The third phase, effective as of July 1, applied to sales of services at retail.

"Wholesalers" included in order

While retail sales of services are the focal point of the third regulation, the new order goes beyond the retail level by defining a "consumer service" as "any service when sold to an ultimate consumer other than an industrial or commercial user, whether sold directly or through any other person to such ultimate consumer, or integrated with further servicing sold to the person with whom such ultimate consumer contracts." The phrase "integrated with further servicing" brings within the scope of the new regulation such operations as wholesale dry cleaning on behalf of a tailor shop—whether or not the wholesale dry cleaner or the tailor presses the garment being "serviced."

Outstanding features

Outstanding features of the new consumer service regulation include:

1. The automatic licensing on July 1 of all persons covered. No physical evidence of license is issued, but all sellers of the consumer services covered, are nonetheless licensed and subject to OPA action for revocation in the event of violations.

2. A provision permitting sellers of seasonal services—rental of beach equipment at a summer resort, for example—to determine their maximum prices by (a) taking the highest price charged in the corresponding season of 1941 and (b) adding an amount arrived at by multiplying that price by the percentage increase in the cost of living between last season and March 1942. A table showing these percentage increases is part of the regulation.

3. Provision for prompt adjustment upward of the March ceiling prices of any seller of consumer service who can prove he is suffering substantial hardship because his top prices do not reflect cost increases between February 1 and April 27, 1942, and that continuance of his service is threatened.

Copies of Maximum Price Regulation No. 165, Consumer Service, may be obtained by writing Distribution Section, Office of War Information, Social Security Building, Washington, D. C.

Henderson denounces splitting of iron, steel orders into near carloads to get higher prices

Selling of iron and steel products in quantities just under carload weight with the view of obtaining the higher prices permitted for less-than-carload shipments is an evasion of Revised Price Schedule No. 49 on such products, Price Administrator Henderson warned.

"Revised Price Schedule No. 49 provides that mill carload prices shall be charged for straight carloads sold out of warehouse stock," said Mr. Henderson. "The schedule establishes 40,000 pounds as a minimum carload shipment on iron and steel products with the exception of rails, where a minimum carload lot is 56,000 pounds.

"Splitting of orders into near carload shipments, or encouraging customers to place orders for not over 39,999 pounds with the intent of getting the higher less-than-carload price is an evasion . . .

"The War Production Board now prohibits carload shipments from warehouses, other than mixed cars, except on certification. This is not to be construed, however, to mean, that the War Production Board legislates generally against shipments in carload quantity from warehouses. They may exclude specific shipments for specific reasons, but it is their wish, along with the Office of Price Administration, that a certified carload shipment be made at proper carload price as established by the Office of Price Administration. . . ."

★ ★ ★

Consumer service ceiling explained to trade at meetings

A series of State and local meetings designed to carry to proprietors of retail service establishments information on the application of the consumer service maximum price regulation is planned by the OPA.

The first of the series was held in Washington June 25 when trade association representatives of close to 100,000 establishments supplying consumer services met with OPA officials.

The morning session was given over to an explanation of the new regulation. The afternoon session was devoted primarily to questions and answers on the application of the regulation to particular situations.

Scope of new order on consumer services

The scope of the new order placing ceilings on consumer services beginning July 1 is explained by the following questions and answers:

Q. What is the maximum price regulation for consumer services?

A. A separate price regulation placing a ceiling on consumer services.

Q. What is a consumer service?

A. A consumer service under the regulation is a service rendered in connection with a commodity for the ultimate consumer such as the housewife, the motorist or the farmer. But consumer service as used in this regulation does not include an industrial or commercial service, the ceiling prices for which were set by the General Maximum Price Regulation and became effective last May 11.

Examples of consumer services

Q. What are examples of consumer services?

A. Laundry, dry-cleaning and shoe repairs are some of the most common services performed for consumers. Others are the lubrication or repair of a private passenger car, the developing and printing of amateur films, the repair and servicing of home radio sets and electrical appliances, and the sharpening of household knives and scissors.

Q. What are examples of industrial or commercial services, which remain under the general maximum price regulation?

A. The sponging and shrinking of cloth after it has left the manufacturer and before it has been sold for cutting into garments; the services of a stevedoring company, and the warehousing of products on the way from a mill to a retail store.

Parking lot charges affected

Q. Is the charge made by a parking lot covered by the regulation?

A. Yes, an automobile is a commodity and the storage of a commodity is therefore under the price ceiling.

Q. What are the maximum prices on consumer services?

A. The highest prices which the supplier of the service charged in March 1942.

Q. Are prices on services standardized by this regulation?

A. No, the regulation simply places a ceiling for each establishment at the highest price it charged for a service in March 1942. But ceiling prices will vary from shop to shop just as uncontrolled prices varied in March.

Q. May prices be charged below the ceiling?

A. Yes, the regulation does no more than place a top limit beyond which prices cannot go.

Q. Some members of a chain of shoe-repair shops during March made a special rate of 75 cents for half-soling men's shoes. Other members of the chain held to the customary price of $1.00. What is the ceiling price in these establishments?

A. The ceiling price has nothing to do with the ownership of the store or service business. The ceiling price is determined for each separate establishment on the basis of the highest price which it charged for a service supplied during March. For any stores which cut the price to 75 cents during the entire month the ceiling is 75 cents. For those which sold as high as $1.00, the ceiling is $1.00.

Professional services excluded

Q. Does the consumer service price regulation put a ceiling on charges for such personal services as haircuts and manicures?

A. No, the definition of "service" in the consumer service price regulation is limited to those rendered in connection with a commodity.

Ceiling on auto repairs

Q. What about the charges of a garage for the repair of a private automobile? Is there a ceiling on the rate for a standard repair job, such as a motor tune-up?

A. Yes, if the garage in March made a standard charge of, for example, $3 for a motor tune-up, that is the highest price the garage may charge for a motor tune-up after July 1.

Q. Is any provision made for determining the ceiling prices on seasonal services (such as the sharpening of ice skates) which are not generally rendered during March?

A. Yes, for such services the maximum charge is the highest charge made during the last season, plus an adjustment for the percentage increase in the cost of living between the time of the last service and March 1942. A table of living cost rises is included in the consumer service regulation.

Automatically licensed

Q. What are the provisions about licenses?

A. Every person selling a consumer service is automatically licensed under this regulation, and every new seller automatically is licensed. There is no certificate or other actual license, but the seller is licensed nevertheless.

Q. What is the purpose of the license?

A. It is a method of enforcement. If a seller, after a warning from OPA, violates the regulation, a court of proper jurisdiction may suspend the license for as long as 12 months. Without a license it is illegal to sell services which are under this regulation.

Q. Must a service establishment post any ceiling prices in a manner similar to the "cost-of-living" posting rules of the general maximum price regulation?

A. No, the regulation does not require any service establishment to display a list of the ceiling prices.

Q. But does not the consumer service establishment have to make some list or report of its ceiling prices?

A. Yes, every person supplying a consumer service over which this regulation sets a price ceiling must prepare by September 1 a complete list of the highest prices he charged for all services he supplied during March for which prices were regularly quoted in that month. This report must also show any pricing method regularly used in March, and all customary allowances and discounts.

U. S. emergency purchases excluded from GMPR

Purchases by the United States Government for immediate delivery of any commodity for which there is an emergency need are excluded from the general maximum price regulation through an amendment announced June 24 by Price Administrator Henderson.

Originally Supplementary Regulation No. 4 in exempting sales of armaments to the Government from the general regulation, provided in addition for the exclusion of emergency purchases of goods not exceeding $1,000 in value. Amendment No. 5 to this supplementary regulation, effective June 30, 1942, removes this monetary limitation on such purchases.

The person making an emergency purchase on behalf of the United States or any of its agencies must file a report with the Washington office of OPA certifying that it was made in a situation in which it was imperative to secure the commodity immediately and in which it was impossible to secure or unfair to require, immediate delivery at the applicable maximum price.

Price regulations changed to make them easier understood and enforced

A series of amendments to simplify the application of the general maximum price regulation were announced by Price Administrator Leon Henderson.

The changes, none of which affects the level of price ceilings, are contained in Amendment No. 7 to the general maximum price regulation and in Supplementary Order No. 6, both effective June 25.

Chief points covered follow:

State and Federal taxes

The amendment rewrites the section on Federal and State taxes to make clear that a seller is required to absorb a tax only if, during March 1942 he paid the tax and did not pass it on when reselling the article on which he had paid the tax.

This section also permits a seller who absorbed a tax in March to pass on an *increase* in a tax effective after March provided the amount of the increase is separately stated from the selling price and provided the tax law or ordinance does not prohibit the tax from being passed on.

Now the section, for example, will permit a retailer to pass on to the consumer an increase paid by the retailer in the cigarette tax if the retailer separately states the actual amount of the increase.

Price ceilings for distributors and jobbers

The definition of a "sale at wholesale" has been changed to permit a person who buys a commodity and resells it to an industrial or commercial user without substantially changing its form to use the method of a wholesaler rather than that of a manufacturer in establishing his ceiling prices.

Purchases by war procurement agencies

A section has been added to the over-all price regulation eliminating war procurement agencies and contracting and paying officers from liability to penalties for paying more than ceiling prices. This enables contracting officers of the Army, Navy, Maritime Commission and the Lend-Lease Section to buy war materials without waiting to determine whether the seller's prices were in conformity with the general maximum price regulation.

This change, however, *in no way* lifts the price ceiling for the seller.

Institutional sales

A special category releases persons selling cost-of-living commodities exclusively to governmental agencies, or to religious, educational, or charitable institutions, institutions for the sick, deaf, blind, disabled, aged or insane, or any school, hospital or library from the rule requiring them to display or report their ceiling prices on cost-of-living commodities.

Mixed feed for animals

The definition of "mixed feed" for animals has been rewritten so as to bring under the general maximum price regulation mixed feed resulting from the mixing or blending of byproducts from a single vegetable, plant or other agricultural product, including molasses, beet pulp, and mixtures of cottonseed hulls and meals.

Screenings—the materials removed in cleaning grain or seeds—were also brought under the regulation.

Clarifying earlier regulation

Although price ceilings established under the general maximum price regulation do not apply to commodities covered by separate price regulations, the amendment makes clear that *certain basic provisions* of the general maximum price regulation apply to *all* OPA price regulations, unless the particular commodity price regulation specifies to the contrary.

These provisions cover (a) the licensing and registration of wholesalers and retailers, (b) the issuance of sales receipts or slips, and (c) the posting and reporting of ceiling prices on retail sales of cost-of-living commodities.

Posting ceiling prices

To eliminate any conflict or overlapping between the general maximum price regulation and separate price regulations on the posting of ceiling prices of cost-of-living commodities, Supplementary Order No. 6 adjusts the posting requirements of eight price regulations.

Ceiling adjusted on dead-burned grain magnesite for 2 consumers

To insure an adequate supply of maintenance grade dead-burned grain magnesite for the Vanadium Corporation of America and the Mathieson Alkali Works, Inc., Price Administrator Henderson has granted permission to the Westvaco Chlorine Products Corporation to increase its selling price for this commodity to $40.50 per ton in sales to these two consumers.

The change in the maximum price, which applies only to these two customers and to shipments from Westvaco's Patterson, California, plant, was effected by Amendment No. 2 to Revised Price Schedule No. 75. The amendment became effective June 20.

The higher maximum price which Westvaco is permitted to charge to these two consumers will not result in an increased selling price for any of their products, Mr. Henderson stated.

Adjustable pricing allowed on contracts for steel castings pending action on freight costs

To speed the Nation's war program, Revised Price Schedule No. 41 has been amended to allow foundries to apply for permission to charge buyers of steel castings the abnormal freight costs on shipments of castings directly related to the war effort if such costs are occasioned by unusual circumstances such as deliveries beyond the normal shipping area.

Category of exceptions created

In order that the production of defense material may not be impeded during the time that such permission is being obtained, the schedule has further been amended to permit the Price Administrator to allow foundries to adjust their prices on deliveries made during the period their application is being considered by OPA.

Formerly, adjustable pricing was permissible only on contracts for steel castings where delivery was not required until 6 months or more after date of contract.

The changes have been effected through Amendment No. 2 to Revised Price Schedule No. 41, Steel Castings, Price Administrator Henderson announced June 22. The amendment became effective June 25.

"The amendment creates a category of exceptions so that the Price Administrator may permit a seller to charge more than maximum prices in cases where he would otherwise be forced to absorb abnormally high transportation costs resulting from dislocated tonnage shipments needed for the emergency requirements of the war effort," Mr. Henderson said.

CARTOONS HELP PRODUCTION DRIVE

The War Production Drive committee of the E. I. du Pont de Nemours plant at Louisville, Ky., gathers cartoon ideas from workers in the plant and distributes them in mimeograph. A recent picture of a Jap with a hot-foot was captioned, "We are not making foot powder but its good for de-feet of our enemies." A drawing of an arrogant Nazi was captioned, "How would you like to have him for a shift supervisor?"

Rents paid by roomers, boarders in 20 defense-rental areas ordered under Federal control

Rents paid by roomers and boarders in 20 defense-rental areas were ordered under Federal control, effective July 1, by Price Administrator Henderson June 26. These areas have been under Federal regulation for housing accommodations other than hotels and rooming houses since June 1.

Cuts ordered in Baltimore area

At the same time, the Price Administrator issued regulations for the Baltimore, Md. defense-rental area, ordering rents reduced to levels prevailing in Baltimore on April 1, 1941. One regulation for Baltimore covers hotels and rooming houses, the other covers housing accommodations other than hotels and rooming houses. Both are effective July 1.

Under the regulations issued for hotels and rooming houses in the 20 defense-rental areas, landlords are to register the rooms they rent, or are offering for rent, within 45 days of the effective date of the regulation. That means this registration is to be concluded by midnight of August 15.

Rental properties which come under the regulation for hotels and rooming houses include: hotels, rooming houses, boarding houses, dormitories, auto camps, trailers, residence clubs, tourist homes or cabins, and all other establishments of a similar nature.

Excluded from this regulation are rooms in hospitals, or rooms of charitable or educational institutions used in carrying out their charitable or educational purposes.

Other provisions made in the regulation cover such points as: prohibitions; minimum services; adjustments; restrictions on removal of tenant; inspection; evasion; enforcement; procedure; petitions for amendment; and definitions.

Areas affected

The 20 areas, in addition to Baltimore, for which this regulation for hotels and rooming houses applies, with the maximum rent dates follow:

Bridgeport, Conn., April 1, 1941; Hartford-New Britain, Conn., April 1, 1941; Waterbury, Conn., April 1, 1941; Schenectady, N. Y., April 1, 1941; Birmingham, Ala., April 1, 1941; Mobile, Ala., April 1, 1941; Columbus, Ga., Jan. 1, 1941; Wilmington, N. C., April 1, 1941; Hampton Roads, Va., area, April 1, 1941; Detroit, Mich., April 1, 1941; Akron, Ohio, April 1, 1941; Canton, Ohio, April 1, 1941; Cleveland, Ohio, July 1, 1941; Ravenna, Ohio, April 1, 1941; Youngstown-Warren, Ohio, April 1, 1941; South Bend, Ind., April 1, 1941; Burlington, Iowa, Jan. 1, 1941; Wichita, Kans., July 1, 1941; San Diego, Calif., Jan. 1, 1941; Puget Sound, Wash., area, April 1, 1941.

OPA may act to cut rents July 1 in 60 more defense-rental areas in 30 States

Present indications are that the OPA will act to reduce rents in 60 more Defense-Rental Areas on July 1 by issuing maximum rent regulations, Price Administrator Henderson said June 22.

Voluntary efforts not enough—Henderson

The areas under consideration for this action embrace a population of 28 million persons and include such cities as Chicago, Philadelphia, San Francisco, Pittsburgh and Newark. The areas are scattered through 30 States.

"Demands for rental housing are increasing everywhere," Mr. Henderson said. "Voluntary efforts—good as they have been to control the rent problem—have not been effective enough. Our defense workers—and that means everyone these days—must be protected from soaring rents and threats of evictions. Our investigations in Defense-Rental Areas are continuous, and we will act wherever necessary and whenever necessary."

For the 60 areas under consideration, the Price Administrator made recommendations as to stabilizing rents on April 28, giving the 60-day period prescribed in the emergency price control act to meet his recommendations. Investigations in these areas as to what extent the recommendations have been met have been going on during this month.

Areas considered for action

The areas now being considered for action on July 1, with 1940 population and maximum-rent date are:

San Luis Obispo, Calif., 33,246; Gainesville-Starke, Fla., 59,792; Alexandria-Leesville, La., 107,359; Montgomery-Prince Georges, Md., 178,402; Jackson-Milan-Humboldt, Tenn., 124,928; Tullahoma, Tenn., 97,309; Brownwood, Tex., 65,740; Mineral Wells, Tex., 38,938; Alexandria-Arlington, Va., 131,492; *Jan. 1, 1941.*

Anniston, Ala., 76,946; Huntsville, Ala., 150,107; Muscle Shoals, Ala., 80,323; Talladega, Ala., 108,130; New Haven, Conn., 300,667; New London, Conn., 181,447; Jacksonville, Fla., 210,143; Macon, Ga., 105,464; Joliet, Ill., 114,210; LaPorte-Michigan City, Ind., 75,918; Junction City-Manhattan, Kans., 35,839; Bath, Maine, 35,417; Baltimore, Md., 1,195,966; Niles, Mich., 89,117; Biloxi-Pascagoula, Miss., 71,400; Hattiesburg, Miss., 34,901; Rolla-Waynesville, Mo., 46,930; Massena, N. Y., 91,098; Watertown, N. Y., 84,003; Fayetteville, N. C., 74,257; Dayton, Ohio, 567,040; Lawton, Okla., 38,988; Sharon-Farrell, Pa., 101,039; Abilene, Tex., 79,093; Beaumont-Port Arthur, Tex., 162,711; El Paso, Tex., 131,067; Radford-Pulaski, Va., 50,963; Morgantown, W. Va., 119,985; *April 1, 1941.*

Indianapolis, Ind., 460,926; Parsons, Kans.,

30,352; Louisville, Ky., 451,473; Minden, La., 33,676; Joplin-Neosho, Mo., 107,744; Lorain-Elyria, Ohio, 112,390; Texarkana, Tex., 82,082; *July 1, 1941.*

San Francisco Bay, 2,066,091; Savannah, Ga., 117,970; Chicago, 4,418,122; Rockford, Ill., 136,380; Springfield, Mass., 404,568; Flint, Mich., 227,944; Saginaw-Bay City, Mich., 232,543; St. Louis, Mo., 1,476,865; Northeastern, N. J., 3,115,160; Buffalo, N. Y., 958,487; Portland-Vancouver, Oreg., 501,275; Erie, Pa., 180,889; Philadelphia-Camden, 3,199,637; Pittsburgh, 2,593,780; Charleston, S. C., 141,033; San Antonio, Tex., 437,854; *March 1, 1941.*

Bangor firm's proposed increase in power rates opposed by OPA

Permission to intervene in opposition to a proposed increase in secondary power rates of the Bangor Hydro-Electric Company was sought June 27 by Price Administrator Henderson in a petition filed with the Maine Public Utilities Commission in Bangor.

Would be inflationary

The Administrator's petition said that, on the basis of information supplied by the power company, the effect of the proposed increase would be to raise the annual operating costs and expenses of certain manufacturers of pulp and paper, which products are under OPA price ceilings.

Further, according to the petition, "it appears that the proposed increased rates are predicated principally upon alleged estimated increases in Federal income taxes to be levied in 1942." Approval of the increase under these circumstances, the commission was told, would be contrary to the intent of the Congress, inflationary in character, and would adversely affect the programs and policies of OPA to stabilize prices.

★ ★ ★

CRITICAL HOUSING AREAS

The War Production Board has added eleven new areas to the Defense Housing Critical Area List. They are:

Corona, Calif.; Ontario-Pomona-Upland, Calif.; Twentynine Palms, Calif.; Peru, Ind. (for conversion and rehabilitation purposes only); Claremont, N. H.; Sioux Falls, S. D. (for conversion and rehabilitation purposes only); Big Springs, Tex.; Fort Stockton, Tex.; Brigham, Utah; Magna, Utah; Windsor, Vt.

Three steps to stabilize cost of iron and steel products announced by Henderson

Three steps designed to stabilize further and make "fair and reasonable" the cost of iron and steel products to buyers, particularly to the Nation's armament makers, were announced June 26 by Price Administrator Henderson.

In Amendment No. 6 to Revised Price Schedule No. 6, on iron and steel products, effective June 30, these actions were taken:

1. Producers of iron and steel products were directed to file with the OPA data covering conversion and processing charges. The data, the Price Administrator said, will be studied to determine whether such charges are fair and reasonable; and whether any future regulation of them is necessary.

2. Uniform rules for the application of extras and other charges on cold finished steel bars and shafting were issued. These rules are designed to clarify such charges, and eliminate the possibility of the charging of several overlapping extras on the same product. This step, the Price Administrator said, will result in "substantial savings" to buyers. In many instances members of the industry have already voluntarily adopted the revised practices, so that the amendment, to some extent, merely standardizes existing pricing practices.

3. Conditions under which producers of concrete reinforcing bars are required to give discounts were defined by OPA. The Tennessee Valley Authority and Bureau of Reclamation, as well as concrete reinforcing bar fabricators, were listed as customers entitled to the discount of 25 cents per hundred pounds on such bars.

Commenting on the request for data on conversion or processing charges, the Price Administrator said that in the past, steel mills have sometimes purchased billets or other steel from persons who were able to obtain such steel on the market and have processed or converted it under an agreement to resell. In these cases, the purchases by the steel producer and subsequent resale to the former owner have been at ceiling prices. With these sales, the Office of Price Administrator is not greatly concerned so long as the prices are within the permissible maximums, Mr. Henderson said.

In regard to the new uniform rules for the application of extras, the Price Administrator said that extras applicable to sales of cold finished steel bars and shafting, both in the carbon steel and alloy steel classifications, have for some time been confused. Both bars and shafting are highly important in the war program.

64 gasoline violators penalized by suspension of deliveries

Gasoline deliveries to 64 filling stations and garages in the metropolitan areas of New York, Newark and Philadelphia were suspended June 26 by Paul M. O'Leary, acting deputy administrator in charge of rationing, for periods of 15 to 30 days for violation of OPA rationing regulations.

The June 26 suspension orders are the largest group which the OPA has served against filling stations and garages for selling gasoline without requiring a rationing card of the motorist.

In the initial enforcement drive opened by the OPA earlier this month, inspectors for OPA made a "spot check" from which came 175 cases for further investigation. Thus far, 78 suspensions have been ordered. Final action has not been taken on a number of remaining cases.

The suspension orders, served on the retail dealer and on his gasoline supplier, prohibit delivery to the dealer for the specified period but do not prevent sales of such supplies as may be in his storage tanks. The orders also do not bar the dealer from performing any other service operations.

Housewife will be able to judge quality of meat under new order

Housewives are assured of a simple and accurate guide for buying beef and veal when the new OPA price regulation on these meats becomes effective July 13, the Consumer Division of the OPA said June 28.

Under the new order, all beef and veal sold at wholesale must be graded according to Government specifications of quality. Ceiling prices asked by beef and veal wholesalers must be related to the grades stamped on each meat carcass.

The new grading requirement is a guarantee to the homemaker that she will obtain the quality she pays for.

When the new regulation goes into effect, shoppers will find all beef, yearling, and veal stamped with a grade letter. Government grades now called "prime" and "choice" will be combined into the new grade "AA." The present Government grade known as "good" will be stamped "A," and will cover most of the better grades of beef and veal bought by housewives. The "commercial" grade will be stamped "B," and the "utility" grade will be stamped "C."

Provisions of general price regulation modified for Puerto Rico, Virgin Islands

Special conditions peculiar to two territories of the United States—Puerto Rico and the Virgin Islands—were recognized June 17 by Price Administrator Henderson in a supplementary regulation (No. 13) modifying several features of the general maximum price regulation as they affect the islands.

Base period changed

The modifications are:

1. The base period for determination of ceiling prices under the general maximum price regulation in Puerto Rico and the Virgin Islands has been changed from the month of March, to the period from April 10 to May 10, 1942.

2. The date by which sellers on these islands must have their statements of ceiling prices ready has been extended to August 1, 1942.

3. Sellers in these islands must show in these statements their maximum prices, both for the month of March 1942, and for the period from April 10 to May 10. It is the April 10–May 10 period, however, that establishes their ceilings.

4. The date by which sellers in these islands must post conspicuously in their stores their maximum prices for the list of nearly 200 cost-of-living commodities is extended to August 1.

5. Power to adjust cases in which sellers claim the regulation causes them substantial hardship has been delegated to the administrator of the Ninth Region, subject to review by the Price Administrator on appeal. Applications for adjustment are to be filed with the Territorial Directors of Puerto Rico and the Virgin Islands in accordance with Procedural Regulation No. 7.

New cosmetics order expected to limit shades, odors

One of the features of a forthcoming limitation order on production of cosmetics will be a reduction in the number of permitted shades and odors of a wide variety of items ranging from lipsticks to "cosmetic" stockings.

Simplification of shades and odors is expected to lead to a reduction of dealer and wholesaler inventories and a consequent saving in container and closure material.

Vanadium melting restricted

Melting of vanadium was placed under complete control of the Director of Industry Operations in an amendment to the vanadium conservation order, M-23-a, dated June 23.

Prices on all kinds of scrap rubber alined with maximums on tire, tube scrap

Acting to smooth out distortions in the scrap rubber market, Price Administrator Henderson June 27 announced issuance of Revised Price Schedule No. 87 as amended, effective June 26, which brings prices to consumers for all kinds of scrap rubber into line with the maximums already established on tires, tire parts, and tubes.

The Administrator emphasized that the ceiling order in no way affects either Rubber Reserve Company's offer to buy scrap tires and miscellaneous scrap rubber at $25 a ton in carload lots at any shipping point in the country, or the price paid to individuals by filling stations and other collection agents in the national campaign.

California-processed sugar raised 15¢ per 100 pounds on DSC sales in 10 States

Because of demand in the eastern deficit area under rationing regulations and surpluses in West Coast refiners' hands, Price Administrator Henderson June 26 ruled that California-refined cane sugar hereinafter may be sold by Defense Supplies Corporation or its designees at $5.60 per 100 pounds in ten Northeastern States.

This increase of 15 cents per 100 pounds, requested by DSC was to be effective June 27, by Amendment No. 2 to Order No. 1 under Revised Price Schedule No. 60 (Direct Consumption Sugars).

Dead animals ascend through price ceiling

Dead animals, usually termed fallen animals, were exempted from provisions of the general maximum price regulation by Amendment No. 9 to Supplementary Regulation No. 1, effective June 25, 1942.

The value of the carcasses depends largely upon the hides and the distance the animals must be transported for rendering and in certain areas no fallen animals were sold during March.

Drawn for Division of Information, O. E. M.
V-42-6/30
KID SALVAGE

KID SALVAGE, a character drawn by Steig especially for OEM, will appear in VICTORY *every week. Mats for publication are available in either 2- or 3-column size. Requests to be put on the mailing list should be addressed to Distribution Section, Office of War Information, Washington, D. C. When ordering individual mats, refer to code number and specify size.*

Single payment lease plan for typewriters illegal

Rental of typewriters under schemes which permit the seller to collect the full sales price of a machine at the outset of the transaction or to accept payment in installments are in violation of typewriter rationing regulations, OPA warned June 25.

The ruling was made as the result of so-called "Lend-Lease" or "Single Payment Lease" plans advertised by certain New York department stores through which the customer pays the full price of the machine with the promise that he will automatically acquire title when OPA regulations permit.

★ ★ ★

Lewis named special aide

Appointment of Ben W. Lewis, Oberlin, Ohio, price executive of the rubber price branch, as a special representative aiding in field price administration was announced June 23 by J. K. Galbraith, deputy administrator of the OPA in charge of prices.

Gasoline raised 2½ cents per gallon on Eastern Seaboard to pay higher cost of moving

A special increase in the price of gasoline, kerosene and light fuel oils along the Eastern Seaboard—to finance the increased cost of transporting petroleum products into the restricted area and assure unrestricted movement—was to be made June 29, Price Administrator Henderson announced June 27.

Users to bear costs

The increases are: gasoline, 2½ cents per gallon; kerosene, range oil, tractor fuel, distillate Diesel fuel oils, gas house oils and Nos. 1, 2, 3 and 4 fuel oils, 2 cents per gallon. There will be no increase on residual fuel oils. The advances are permitted also on retail sales.

★ ★ ★

FANCY BED LINEN PRICES

Specific prices that one manufacturer may charge for fancy bed linens were established June 27 by the OPA.

Sales and deliveries of certain sheetings, sheets and pillow cases by Defender Manufacturing Co. of New York City are exempted from the provisions of Revised Price Schedule No. 89 (Bed Linens) through Amendment No. 7. Simultaneously maximum prices for these bed linens are provided under Order No. 12 to the general maximum price regulation. Both actions took effect June 23.

Amendment No. 7 to Schedule 89 at the same time provides that deliveries of grey sheetings and bleached pillow tubing against contracts entered into between May 4 and May 27, 1942 will be governed by Maximum Price Regulation 118 (Cotton Products). Deliveries against contracts made after May 27, come under the scope of Schedule 89.

Burning of old tires to prevent frost damage prohibited

Rubber Coordinator Arthur B. Newhall June 25 called attention to the fact that WPB regulations prohibit the burning of old or cut-up tires for the purpose of preventing frost damage in fruit or citrus groves.

Supplementary Order M-15-b contains a general ban on the destruction of certain rubber products except where essential to manufacturing or reclaiming operations.

Retailers' price ceiling statements

An explanation in question and answer form, of the price ceiling statements which all retailers must prepare by July 1, was released June 25 by the OPA. Some of the questions and answers follow:

1. Q. What are the statements that a retailer is required by the general maximum price regulation to have finished by July 1?
A. He is required to prepare:
1. A statement of the maximum prices at which he is offering "cost-of-living commodities" for sale on June 30, or on the day he files the statement. The great majority of these maximum prices will be the highest prices at which he sold or offered for sale cost-of-living commodities during March. The maximum prices for articles which the seller began to deal in after March. 1942 will be determined on the basis of similarity, or shopping competitors, or applying the formula in Section 3A of the Regulation. The nearly 200 "cost-of-living commodities" are listed in Appendix B of the Regulation.
2. A statement of the highest price at which during March he sold, or offered for sale, each article in his store on which the regulation places a ceiling. (These prices are his own price ceilings.) This statement must also show customary allowances, discounts and other price differentials.

Must file first statement

2. Q. What must the retailer do with these statements when he has finished them?
A. (1) He must file the first statement, covering the articles on the cost-of-living commodity list which he handles, with the nearest War Price and Rationing Board by July 1. If he does not know where this nearest board is located, he may call his local newspaper, the police department, city hall or county courthouse.
(2) He must keep the second statement, covering all his items having price ceilings, at his place of business, starting July 1, for examination by any customer or interested person during business hours.

Why necessary

3. Q. Why does the Office of Price Administration require these statements of retailers?
A. To provide a quick means for each retailer to prove that he is obeying the general maximum price regulation, and is thus doing his full part in the battle against inflation.
4. Q. In what form should a retailer prepare his statement of maximum prices for such of the cost-of-living commodities as he handles?
A. OPA suggests that the retailer use standard letter-size paper; that if he does not have a typewriter he prepare his statement carefully in ink; that the exact name and address of the establishment be indicated on a separate title page, or at the top of the first page; that items be listed in the order shown in Appendix B of the general maximum price regulation, of course omitting groups, classes and items not handled.

5. Q. How does OPA suggest that the retailer arrange his items and prices if he uses this standard size paper?
A. The following would be a typical arrangement for a typical clothing store: The name and address of the store appears at the top of the first sheet. The rest of this sheet, and the other sheets are divided into four columns, headed respectively "Name of commodity"; "Manufacturer, name or code number and style number"; "Other identification"; and "Maximum Price." Under "Name of Commodity" the first heading is "Apparel and yard goods." Under that comes "Men's and boys' clothing". Under that "Men's pajamas". etc. Beside "Men's pajamas" in the second column, the pajamas are described as "John Smith Co. or (No. 22) style C 49." In the "Other identification" column, the pajamas are further identified as "Jacket style, plain colors, cotton." Maximum Price is listed as $1.98. And so on through the retailer's stock.

Chain may not file blanket statement

10. Q. May a chain of stores file a blanket statement of maximum prices with OPA covering all cost-of-living items being handled in all stores, although every store may not have all those items?
A. No. The regulation requires a separate list for each store. But if all the stores in the chain have the same price ceiling for each article, the central office may mimeograph or print a list containing all such items with the maximum prices for each item, and these lists can be submitted separately by each store. If the prices are different in some stores, a list of items could be prepared, and the prices filled in by each store.
11. Q. In what form should the retailer's statement of all March maximum prices, which he keeps in his store, be prepared?
A. It does not at present have to be prepared in any specified form, so long as it is perfectly clear from the statement what the maximum price is for each particular article. Each article described in the statement must be described in such manner as to be easily identified by any person. Identification should include manufacturer's name, style, brand, size, etc.
17. Q. How may the record-keeping provisions of the general maximum price regulation be summarized?
A. The record-keeping provisions require the retailer to do six things:
1. Preserve all existing records of March 1942 prices.
2. Keep the same kind of records or documents relating to prices charged after May 18.
3. Prepare a statement of highest prices charged in the base period (March).
4. Keep records showing the basis for determining the maximum price of any item sold after May 18.
5. Continue to provide customary sales slips and give receipts.
6. Properly identify all merchandise in displaying prices or preparing statements of maximum prices.

Retailers may use catalogues, other printed lists in preparing ceiling statements

Catalogues or similar printed merchandise lists supplied by wholesalers, manufacturers or trade organizations may be used by retailers in preparing statements of maximum prices which every seller under the general maximum price regulation must have by July 1, the OPA stated June 22.

Two statements required

Such lists may prove particularly helpful to drug stores, hardware retailers, jewelers and others carrying a large assortment of items.

In compiling the list of March prices, printed lists are acceptable as long as there is included, in one way or other, every item in stock that is covered by the general maximum price regulation. This statement, OPA said, is not to be filed with any OPA office but is to be retained in the place of business beginning July 1 for examination by any customer or interested person.

A second statement which retailers must prepare is the list of ceiling prices on the designated cost-of-living commodities shown in Appendix B of the general maximum price regulation. This is a restricted list of the store's maximum prices on a representative group of items that enter into the family cost-of-living and must be filed with the nearest War Price and Rationing Board by July 1.

★ ★ ★

Maximum prices set on antifreeze

American motorists will be able to obtain antifreeze at reasonable levels during the coming winter, Price Administrator Henderson stated June 25 in announcing maximum prices for this commodity.

The retail price has been established at levels well under the speculative quotations prevalent at the end of last winter, he said. In addition to prices at retail, ceilings for antifreeze have been determined for manufacturers and distributors.

Since May 18 retail maximum prices for antifreeze have been governed by the provisions of the general maximum price regulation—that is, the highest price which the individual seller charged during March. The dollars and cents maximums announced June 25 were established by Maximum Price Regulation No. 170, Antifreeze, effective June 30, 1942.

New ceilings set on beef, veal at packer and wholesale levels

The basis for maximum prices of beef and veal at the packer and wholesale levels is changed by a special regulation (Maximum Price Regulation No. 169), announced June 20 by Price Administrator Henderson. The regulation, effective July 13, provides that packers and wholesalers' ceilings for each grade of carcass and quarter of $_{beef}$ (or carcass and saddle of veal) shall be a price no higher than the lowest price at which each individual merchandiser sold at least 30 percent of his total quantity of that grade during March 16–28, 1942.

To relieve squeeze against retail ceilings

Maximum retail prices to consumers are not changed by the regulation, and continue to be governed by the general maximum price regulation.

As a necessary part of price control on beef and veal, provision also has been made for standard grading of these meats by all packers and wholesalers in accordance with the grading specifications of the Agricultural Marketing Administration of the United States Department of Agriculture.

"The new regulation will relieve an inordinate squeeze against the retail price ceilings on these commodities," Mr. Henderson pointed out.

★ ★ ★

Licenses necessary to sell used egg cases

All persons who sell used egg cases and used component parts and who are subject to the maximum price regulation established for these goods are being licensed as a condition of selling, Price Administrator Henderson announced June 20.

The licensing provision is contained in Amendment No. 1 to Maximum Price Regulation No. 117—Used Egg Cases and Used Component Parts—and became effective June 22.

★ ★ ★

WAR SHIPPING APPOINTMENTS

Admiral Emory S. Land, War Shipping Administrator, June 23 announced the appointment of Charles H. C. Pearsall as WSA manager in the Caribbean area with headquarters in Havana, Cuba. At the same time Admiral Land announced the appointment of Charles M. Colgan as WSA representative at the Canal Zone.

20 food industry leaders named to help solve price adjustment problems

Twenty leaders of the food industry, representing virtually every phase of processing and distribution, were appointed by Price Administrator Henderson June 24 as a national food industry advisory committee to work with OPA in the solution of problems and adjustments under the general maximum price regulation.

To advise on adjustment problems

The committee, representing canners, processors, wholesalers, and chain and independent retailers will advise with OPA on problems of adjustment under the general maximum price regulation.

"The job of the committee," Mr. Henderson stated, "will be to work out a full and complete solution of the problems of the food industry in a spirit of mutual understanding."

Trade associations to help

The first meeting was to be held on June 26 and was to concern itself largely with the problem of the "squeeze" created for retailers and wholesalers under the general maximum price regulation, and to over-all discussion of OPA policy and the maintenance of ceiling prices.

The new committee has been recruited largely from special committees and groups which already have been engaged in working with various war agencies. It will be assisted in the collection of information by representatives of the nine trade associations in the food field, and representatives of these associations were invited to attend the meeting.

Personnel of committee

Appointed to the national food industry advisory committee were:

P. M. Brinker, Dallas, Tex., and D. E. Robinson, Pittsburgh, *independent retailers;* John T. Menzies, Baltimore, Austin Iglehart, New York, and H. S. Meinhold, New York, *packers and manufacturers;* E. N. Richmond, San Jose, Calif, and H. L. Cannon, Bridgeville, Del., *canners;* Jack Wilson, Cambridge, Mass., *soap and shortening manufacturers;* French Fox, Charlerois, Pa, and Frank J. Grimes, Chicago, *voluntary group wholesalers;* W. H. Albers, Cincinnati, and Sidney Rabinowitz, Boston, *supermarkets;* Alfred Dorman, Statesborough, Ga., and A. C. McCune, McKeesport, Pa., *smaller independent wholesalers;* William B. Mackey, Philadelphia, and Francis Whitmarsh, New York, *larger independent wholesalers;* William D'Miller, Chicago, and Isaac Jacobson, Washington, D. C., *cooperative group distributors;* and Hunter Phelan, Norfolk, Va., and Ralph Burkhard, Somerville, Mass., *proprietary chains.*

Two mines allowed to make adjustable-pricing contracts

Issuing orders under Maximum Price Regulation No. 120 (Bituminous Coal Delivered from Mine or Preparation Plant), Price Administrator Henderson has permitted two mines—one in West Virginia and the other in the State of Washington—to enter into adjustable-pricing contracts pending disposition of petitions asking price adjustment.

The contracts would fix interim sales at existing maximum prices, with the provision that they be adjusted to price changes, if any are permitted, in OPA's final decision on the company's petitions.

Order No. 11 permits the West Virginia Coal and Coke Corporation, Cincinnati (on and after May 18, 1942, the effective date of Maximum Price Regulation No. 120), to enter into such agreements with buyers of bituminous coal produced at its Norton Mine, at Norton, W. Va., in Production District No. 3, to adjust prices upon deliveries made during the pendency of its petition for adjustment or exception, in accordance with the disposition of the petition.

Order No. 14 permits the Pacific Coast Coal Company, Seattle, on and after May 27, 1942 (date of filing of the petition), to enter into adjustable-pricing contracts pending disposition of its petition.

Phillips to direct automotive supply rationing

Appointment of Dr. Charles F. Phillips of Syracuse, N. Y., to the newly created position of director of the automotive supply rationing division was announced June 22 by Price Administrator Henderson.

In his new capacity, Dr. Phillips, a former professor of economics at Colgate University and marketing consultant to a food store chain, will supervise tire and passenger automobile rationing activities and rationing of bicycles, which is soon to begin.

Announcement of his new position follows by only a few weeks his appointment as chief of the tire rationing branch, a post to which Robert S. Betten succeeds.

Simultaneously with Dr. Phillips' appointment, Mr. Henderson named Hubert G. Larson as chief of the automobile rationing branch and Robert E. Stone as associate chief. Both had been assistants to Rolf Nugent, the former automobile rationing chief, who recently became head of the Price Administration's consumer requirements branch.

Importers may sell commodities to industrial, commercial users at prices above ceilings under certain conditions

Importers are given permission by the OPA to sell imported commodities, under certain conditions, to industrial and commercial users at prices above those paid in March 1942, the established ceiling prices provided by the general maximum price regulation.

To assure free flow of imports

This permission is granted in Supplementary Regulation No. 12 to the general maximum price regulation, effective June 20.

The purpose of the new supplementary regulation is to make possible a continued free flow of imported commodities into this country.

Buyer must process commodity

Under the supplementary regulation, persons who import any commodity after March 31, 1942, and sell it to an industrial or commercial user in substantially the same condition in which it was imported, are permitted to sell such a commodity above their ceiling price in March to the extent of the difference between their delivered costs of the commodity and their delivered costs for the same commodity delivered by them in March.

Mr. Henderson stated:

The supplementary regulation further provides that the importer may only sell above his maximum price in March to an industrial or commercial user, who is defined as a person who does not resell the commodity he purchases in substantially the same form as he received it. In other words, the buyer must process the commodity in some manner before he resells it.

User to absorb increased costs

The industrial or commercial user is placed on notice that he will have to absorb any increased costs which he paid for the imported commodity to the importer. In this manner, any possibility of a resulting inflationary tendency from such transactions will be stopped at the point of first resale of the imported commodity in this country.

As a safeguard, the importer is obliged under the regulation to notify the industrial or commercial user that he is selling the imported commodity to him above his March ceiling price, and in that manner the latter can determine for himself whether he is in a position to absorb the increased delivery costs before he enters into the transaction.

No effect on Government purchases

The supplementary regulation is limited in its coverage to imports into the continental United States from its territories and possessions and from foreign countries. It does not apply to imports into its territories and possessions from any origin. This limitation is necessary, it was explained, because there are other regulations covering the territories and possessions.

Lumber from Canada is excepted because specific coverage of imported Canadian lumber is to be provided under other regulations.

The Price Administrator pointed out that sales by domestic sellers of imported commodities, unprocessed by them, to the United States or any of its agencies or to any person who will use the imported commodity to fulfill a contract or a subcontract with the United States or any of its agencies were excepted from the provisions of the general maximum price regulation under Amendment No. 1 to Supplementary Regulation No. 4. Supplementary Regulation No. 12, therefore, has no effect on Government purchases of import commodities which have already been excepted.

Combed yarns, woven goods for war use not under MPR 157

All combed yarns of the types covered by Revised Price Schedule No. 7 and all finished woven goods of the descriptions governed by Maximum Price Regulation No. 127 remain under the provisions of these two price orders, even when sold or fabricated for military purposes, the OPA made clear June 23.

Questions had arisen in the trade, according to information received by OPA, as to whether goods or yarns of these types were exempted from these two price orders and came under the provisions of Maximum Price Regulation 157 (Sales and Fabrication of Textiles, Apparel and Related Items for Military Purposes) when made in accordance with military specifications for a war procurement agency.

The June 23 statement was made at the request of the Army Quartermaster Corps and the War Production Board, OPA said.

OPA further pointed out that Regulation 157 does not apply to any other commodity for which a maximum price is in effect, except those covered by the general maximum price regulation.

Paper products regulation revised by OPA to include other grades

Certain grades of paper omitted erroneously from the section of Maximum Price Regulation No. 129, which established conditions of sale for these grades, are now included by Amendment No. 4 to the regulation (paper and paper products) issued June 23 by the OPA.

The amendment corrected subparagraph (3) of section 1347.12 (d) by adding the words "and (d) (2)" so that the conditions of sale affecting maximum prices includes the grades set forth specifically in (d) (2)— "all other grades of Machine Finish Kraft Wrapping Paper, and all grades of Machine Glazed Kraft Wrapping Paper, Machine Finish Variety Bag Paper, Machine Glazed Kraft Bag Paper, including but without limitation Unbleached Kraft Butchers Paper."

The amendment also qualifies Unbleached Kraft Butchers Paper in the same subparagraph by adding to the clause "where the basis weight is 40 pounds and up." No basis weight for this type of paper was originally listed.

Other corrections

Other corrections made by the amendment are:

Variety bag papers, glassine, greaseproof, fruit wrapping and manifold are now listed among those excluded from the papers set forth in subparagraph (6) of section 1347.11 (a), and the word "converting" is inserted to conform with the statement of considerations issued with the regulation.

The addition of the words "Machine Finish and Machine Glazed" to the headnote in paragraph (d) of Section 1347.12 and the addition of the words "Machine Finish to Grades" clarify the types of wrapping and bag paper originally intended to be covered by the regulation.

Paper makers must bear increased freight costs

Manufacturers of industrial paper and converted paper products may not add increased freight costs to their maximum prices which were established in some cases by Maximum Price Regulation No. 129 and in others by the general maximum price regulation, the OPA announced June 24.

Under this interpretation, announced to clarify the problems of freight costs which have arisen since the issuance of the general maximum price regulation, manufacturers who allowed partial freight must absorb the 6 percent increase in freight rates, effected in March 1942, and any other increase in freight costs incurred as the result of wartime emergency conditions such as the rerouting of shipments by rail instead of water.

Markups adjusted on resales of new bags made from cotton and burlap fabrics

Markups which sellers, other than manufacturers, of new bags made from cotton and burlap fabrics may charge were adjusted by the OPA June 24 through an amendment to Maximum Price Regulation No. 151 (New Bags). At the same time the definition of "new bags" was also clarified.

May add highest "cents per bag" margin

Amendment No. 1 to the regulation takes into consideration the variation in markups customarily - charged by re-sellers according to the type of bag and the section of the country where sold. Persons purchasing bags for resale are permitted by the amendment to add to the "delivered cost" a margin which is, generally, equivalent to the highest markup, in cents per bag, charged during the month of March 1942.

While the highest "cents per bag' margin obtained by resellers during March 1942 is permitted, OPA officials pointed out that this represents a smaller percentage marking because of the increased cost of the bags they resell.

Other provisions

When a seller made no sales or deliveries of a new bag of the same type during March 1942, other methods are provided for determining his markup under various situations such as basing it upon his most nearly similar new bag or the markup of his most closely competitive seller.

Definition of new bag clarified

Markups to be charged by sellers other than manufacturers are based on the "delivered cost" of the bag to the seller. This delivered cost must not exceed the maximum price established for the regulation, plus actual transportation charges incurred by the seller in transporting the bags to the point of shipment.

The definition of new bag is amended to read:

"New bag" means a previously unused container which (i) is manufactured within the United States, (ii) is to be used for packaging a commodity therein for transportation or storage (iii) is manufactured from burlap or cotton textile material which has not previously been used for any commercial purpose. It shall not include seamless cotton bags.

Jobbers of woolen or worsted civilian apparel fabrics may use optional pricing

An optional method of establishing a maximum price for woolen or worsted civilian apparel fabrics sold by jobbers under Maximum Price Regulation No. 163 and two clarifications of provisions applying to jobbers' sales were announced June 24 by Price Administrator Henderson.

Amendment No. 1 to Regulation 163 makes the optional pricing method applicable only to those jobbers who dealt in the same fabric during the period October 1 to December 1, 1941. It provides that they may use as their ceiling for a fabric the highest price at which they sold or delivered the same fabric during that period so long as such optional maximum is not higher than the replacement cost of the fabric plus the permitted mark-up. Otherwise the percentage mark-ups over the manufacturer's invoice price set by the regulation originally are applicable.

Affects those who supply custom tailors

"The mark-up presently permitted by the regulation in many cases would establish a maximum lower than the prices at which the same fabrics were sold to customers of jobbers during the fall of 1941," Mr. Henderson explained.

The June 24 amendment will, for the most part, affect those jobbers who supply custom tailors and who, of necessity, maintain large inventories to be able to fill orders out of stock. A substantial proportion of current inventory was acquired by them some time ago, at prices considerably below replacement cost.

Another provision of the amendment makes it clear that the division factor applicable to sales of cut lengths of 9 yards or less to merchant tailors also applies to sales of such lengths to the custom tailoring departments of retail stores for which the jobbers perform the same service.

It is also provided that the jobber in establishing his mark-up by using the manufacturer's invoice price uses the gross price rather than the price after any discount.

Simultaneously with the June 24 amendment to Regulation 163, OPA issued corrections of typographical errors appearing in the text of the regulation. In Section 1410.11 (a), the word "or" is corrected to read "of" and in Section 1410.115 (a) (5), the word "not" is corrected to read "nor."

Converters' prices on rayon yarn "rolled back;" formal ceilings set

Prices which converters of rayon yarn may charge were "rolled back" June 22 by Price Administrator Henderson at the same time that he issued a companion regulation placing formal ceilings over rayon yarns and staple fibers.

6 regulations on rayon

The two regulations of June 22 bring to a total of six the number of OPA schedules specifically covering various phases of the rayon industry. All forms of rayon or its products not specifically covered by any of these six regulations are controlled by the general maximum price regulation on the basis of March 1942 levels.

Maximum Price Regulation No. 167 (Rayon Yarn and Staple Fiber) issued June 22 establishes maximum prices at the levels which rayon yarn producers have observed for their products since October 1941 at OPA request.

Maximum Price Regulation No. 168 (Converted Yarn and Converting Charges) applies to commission converters and sellers of converted yarns. By converting is meant the changing of the original form of the yarn by operations such as twisting, warping, dyeing, and spooling, in order to prepare it for the weaving and knitting industries.

Set at lower prices

The ceilings provided under this regulation are set at substantially lower prices than most converters charged in March 1942, which were the prices established as the ceilings under the general maximum price regulation. The June 22 regulation supersedes the general regulation for these converting operations and establishes uniform specific charges.

PRODUCTION DRIVE . . .

War plant reports 63½ percent production increase in three months' drive

An increase in war production of 63½ percent, one of the greatest since the start of the War Production Drive, was reported on June 25 to Donald M. Nelson, chairman of the War Production Board, by the War Production Drive Committee of the Cleveland (Ohio) Tractor Company.

Cites monthly increases

The committee cited its production increases as follows:

March—greatest production in the history of the company.

April—23 percent greater than March.

May—33 percent greater than April, or approximately 63½ percent greater than at the start of the War Production Drive.

The report was signed by Nick Nardolillo, John J. Bergman and W. G. Schultz, representing labor; and H. R. Buckner, L. F. Hawkins, and L. H. Grutsch, chairman, representing the management. The labor representatives are members of the International Association of Machinists, A. F. L.

In acknowledging the report, War Production Drive Headquarters sent this message:

"Your remarkable production record is outstanding even during these times when millions of men are striving toward the same goal."

Work behind the increase

The committee reported the activities of its subcommittees in detail. The report gives an interesting picture of the work behind the production increase.

The housekeeping committee has cleared a bottleneck in transportation, reducing the waiting time for stock.

The safety committee is stimulating departmental rivalry for the best safety record. It also distributes safety bulletins.

The material saving committee, through weekly educational meetings, reduced labor loss 3 percent and material loss by 24 percent. The report states, "This savings percentage is actually a greater ratio when the production increase for 33 percent for the month of May is taken into consideration." Losses, the committee said, will be even lower in June.

The fire prevention committee makes a weekly inspection of the plant and arranges for the installation of new fire-fighting equipment, signs, etc., when needed. It holds weekly training classes.

The transportation committee erected three large city maps, one for each shift, and located the homes of each employee with numbered pins. A master file gave information necessary for the formation of car pools. A test in one department showed employees had reduced their cars by fifty percent. The committee expects poolings will eventually eliminate 300 cars.

The publicity committee is developing a slogan contest and has erected a production bulletin board. The committee discovered four cartoonists among employees and their work is being utilized in publicity.

The absentee committee, not satisfied with reducing absenteeism 25 percent during the month of May, is making personal contact with habitual absentees this month.

The suggestion is about to put its program into effect, offering war bonds and stamps on 10 percent of a year's saving from the suggestion.

★ ★ ★

Nielsen to attend London maritime conference

The Maritime Commission and the War Shipping Administration June 20 announced that Erich Nielsen, assistant director of the Division of Maritime Labor Relations of the War Shipping Administration, will attend as an observer the conference of the Joint Maritime Commission of the International Labor Office to be held in London, commencing June 22.

Chief aim of the conference, the twelfth of its kind, will be to help coordinate efforts of all United Nations' seamen's organizations and shipowners to secure maximum coöperation between these groups and the United Nations in carrying out the wartime responsibility of shipping.

"DON'T LET THEM DOWN"

The Chrysler Corporation plant at Detroit labor-management committee reports to War Production Drive Headquarters that bulletin boards have been erected showing the number of brothers, sons, uncles, cousins, fathers, nephews, and husbands in the Army, Navy, Marine Corps, and Army Air Corps. The bulletin board carries the words: "Don't let them down! Their lives may be in your hands."

Foreign requirements branch to act as priorities liaison

Establishment of a foreign requirements branch in the Bureau of Priorities was announced June 22 by Henry Nelson, assistant bureau chief in charge of requirements.

Functions of new branch

The new branch will be headed by Fred Lavis, Jr. who has been a priorities specialist in the automotive branch of OPM and WPB since September 1941.

The foreign requirements branch will serve as liaison on priority matters between the War Production Board, the Lend-Lease Administration, and the Board of Economic Warfare, and will receive all applications for priority assistance from foreign governments or purchasers in foreign countries (except Canada) received through these agencies. In cooperation with existing agencies, the foreign requirements branch will develop improved procedures for handling priorities on materials and products for export.

CUTS REJECTS 25 PERCENT

Thomas Muckenfuss, an inspector of purchasing material in the Camden, N. J. plant of the R. C. A. Manufacturing Co., Inc., which has an active War Production Drive Committee, suggested a change in parts on a piece of essential war equipment which eliminated 25 percent of the number of rejects and saved the cost of grinding, finishing and the cost of parts bought from a subcontractor.

Germany scours occupied countries for labor

Nazi agents have been forced to scour the occupied countries for labor because Germany has been drained of all able-bodied men for war service and because the efficiency of labor has dropped because of war conditions, according to a statement issued June 17 by the Office of War Information.

Further excerpts follow:

A recent order by Himmler calls for replacing the men in provincial police stations with women, so that the men may go to the front. Radio Moscow has reported the presence of pale, hastily-trained German factory workers who have been thrown into the battle to replace shock weary troops.

Various recruitment methods

Hitler has used various methods in recruiting labor for Germany.

1. The Germans, as in Norway, order forced mobilizations of workers and load them into freight cars bound for Germany.
2. The occupation chiefs threaten to reduce food rations unless workers "voluntarily" go to Germany.
3. Occupations forces order a flat percent of workers laid off, so they can be shipped to Germany. The Swedish radio reported that the Nazis ordered 30 percent of the Norwegian workers 1 id off, and the Athens City Council was told to halt its public projects.
4. Nazi diplomats have concluded agreements with friendly nations to deliver work-

ers. Radio Ankara reported that Laval agreed to send 150,000 additional workers to Germany, in return, according to the Free French, for 10,000 sick war prisoners. Several hundred thousand Italians are in Germany, and 130,000 were reported to have arrived in May. The Falangist party of Spain has encouraged workers to go to Germany. Approximately 83,000 Bulgarians are in the Reich.

5. The Nazi labor agents promise the workers higher wages, better food and special privileges. Special broadcasts paint a picture of Germany as a "labor utopia." The Nazis, however, do not mention that all foreign workers in the Reich must pay a "worker's tax," which ranges from 25 to 30 percent of the wages, nor the barracks in which the workers live under the watchful eye of the Gestapo, nor the long hours of work, nor the order that factory workers must devote their free time to farm labor.

Stripped of their own labor, the occupied and dominated countries are forced into an agonized position. Radio Vichy said that without the 800,000 French peasants, prisoners of war in Germany, France was faced with famine. Hungary has been forced to mobilize girls from 14 to 60 to serve in war industries. All men between 18 and 60 in Croatia may be called up for farm work, public works, swamp draining and other manual tasks.

"HE'S WATCHING YOU"

Poster design prepared by Grohe for the Division of Information, Office for Emergency Management, scheduled to appear in war plants during the week. Requests for 14 x 10 inch posters and two-column mats may be addressed to the Distribution Section, Office of War Information, Washington, D. C. A limited supply of 28¼ x 40 inch posters are available and requests for single copies will be filled until supplies are exhausted.

Butadiene placed under allocation from producers

Butadiene, basic ingredient for the manufacture of Buna-type synthetic rubber, was placed under allocation from producers June 27 by the Director of Industry Operations with the issuance of Order M–178, effective July 1.

Producers seeking to deliver and persons asking delivery of butadiene are required to make application to the Director of Industry Operations, Reference M–178. They are requested to use Form PD–33, which covers the production and shipment of all chemicals used in the manufacture of synthetic rubber.

PRIORITIES . . .

AAA now highest rating as WPB devises new high preference series

Provision for rerating war orders and for applying a new series of high preference ratings is made in Priorities Regulation No. 12, and amendments to Priorities Regulations 1 and 3, issued June 27 by the Director of Industry Operations.

AA abolished

The new ratings are AAA, AA-1, AA-2, etc., all of which will take preference over A-1-a ratings. Heretofore the highest rating has been AA, whose use was permitted only by special authorization of the Director of Industry Operations. This rating is now abolished, and all outstanding AA ratings are automatically changed to AA-2.

For urgent war materials

The chief purpose of the rerating is to permit greater flexibility in the assignment of preference ratings to definite quantities of military and related non-military items, most of which have recently been either AA or in the A-1 series. It will permit use of top ratings for a balanced program of urgent war materials without seriously disturbing the pattern of ratings for other war and essential civilian orders.

Assignment of ratings

The new high ratings may be assigned either directly by the Director of Industry Operations or by appropriate officers of Government war agencies expressly authorized to issue reratings. A special form, PD-4X, called a "Rerating Direction," is prescribed for use where the Army, Navy or other Government war agency rerates deliveries of war materials to be made directly to it.

Whenever a rerating direction is issued, it must include the Allocation Classification and Purchasers' Symbols required by Priorities Regulation No. 10.

Reratings by manufacturers

A separate form called a "Rerating Certificate," PD-4Y, is provided for use by a manufacturer whose deliveries to a war agency have been rerated, so that he may in turn rerate related deliveries to be made to him. The test for determining what deliveries may thus be rerated by a manufacturer or his suppliers is substantially the same as the test for

determining to what deliveries an original rating may be applied or extended, as specified in Priorities Regulation No. 3, which was recently amended to provide a uniform standard in this respect.

A manufacturer may apply or extend the rerating to material which will be delivered by him on a rerated order, or physically incorporated in material so delivered, or to restore inventories to a practicable working minimum when material has been taken from inventory to fill a rerated order.

Other provisions

The new ratings may also be used by small companies for certain operating supplies which will be consumed in filling the rated order, up to 10 percent of the cost of materials to be processed, provided that not more than 25 percent of such operating supplies are metals in the forms listed in Priorities Regulation No. 11. Such reratings may not be used to obtain operating supplies by any company whose use of the metals listed in Regulation 11 amounts to more than $5,000 in a quarter. Most such companies obtain ratings for their operating supplies under the production requirements plan.

Companies operating under the production requirements plan are specifically authorized, like other companies, to apply or extend the higher ratings to rerate deliveries to themselves, but may not use the ratings to obtain greater quantities of material than they are authorized to receive on their PRP Certificate (Form PD-25A) or a supplementary certificate issued upon application on Form PD-25F or PD-25H.

Displacement of rated orders

Priorities Regulation No. 1 has been amended by altering the provision with respect to displacement of rated orders by new orders bearing a higher rating. Previously, no producer was required to divert material already processed to fill an order rated A-10 or higher which was within 15 days of completion, even when he received a new order with a higher rating, unless the new rating was AA. Hereafter, this provision applies only in case the rating on the original order was higher than A-2. Such an order

within 15 days of completion must be displaced only by a new order with an AAA rating, or by specific direction from the Director of Industry Operations.

In no case, however, is a company required to terminate existing production schedules in less than 15 days after receipt of a new rated order, and a company may continue on its existing production schedule up to a maximum of 40 days if change is necessary, unless specifically instructed to change the schedule by the Director of Industry Operations.

To rate items separately

Priorities Regulation No. 3 is amended to conform to the provisions of Regulation 12, and the amendments to Regulation 3 also modifies the previous provision with respect to simultaneous extension of several different ratings. Whereas previously a company having several different ratings to be extended to orders for the same material could put them all together and write one purchase order for the entire quantity, using the lowest rating for all of it, this will now be permitted only when it is not commercially practicable to rate and obtain the items separately.

Procedure for importing coffee contracted for prior to July 2

The WPB and the Board of Economic Warfare June 20 issued an explanation of the procedure to be followed under General Imports Order M-63 for importing coffee already contracted for or which may be contracted for prior to July 2, 1942.

Order M-63 in general prohibits the importation of coffee without prior authorization by the Director of Industry Operations of the WPB. The procedure to be followed by an applicant seeking such authorization is as follows:

He should file with the War Production Board, Washington, D. C. (Ref. M-63) in duplicate, an application for authorization on Form PD-222-c, attaching to such application a letter in duplicate certifying that the application covers a contract existing on the effective date of the inclusion of coffee under the order (July 2) and giving details concerning the contract (including date, original quantity, quantity still undelivered, price, and whether coffee is afloat or for prompt shipment or, if for future shipment, the month of scheduled shipment or availability at port.)

Adjusted steel order permits metal for keys, tags, other uses

Three changes in the steel conservation order, M–126, were made June 26 by the Director of Industry Operations.

The first permits the use of iron and steel for maintenance and repair of coffee roasting machinery. This requires only a small amount of metal and was not permitted by the original order.

"Manicure implements" are eliminated from List A of M–126 as their manufacture now is covered in detail by Order L–140.

The original order prohibited the use of iron and steel in the manufacture of identification, key, name and price tags. The June 26 amendment (No. 2) permits the manufacture of tags or badges for these uses: To identify workers in governmental agencies; to identify workers in industrial plants; metal tags required by Federal or State law for livestock or poultry; and pin or wire attached tickets for price marking of soft goods.

Higher priority to enable canners to increase 1942 pack

Fruit and vegetable packers are assigned higher preference ratings for material and machinery under Amendment No. 1 to Preference Rating Order P–115, issued June 23 by the Director of Industry Operations.

The amendment will aid approximately 3,000 canneries to pack the 1942 fruit and vegetable pack, which is expected to be approximately 15 percent larger than that in 1941.

The rating for materials for repairs, maintenance and operation is raised from A–3 in the original order to A–1–j.

Civilian apricot pack cut another 10 percent

In order to make apricots available for Lend-Lease purposes without allocating additional tinplate, an additional 10 percent reduction in the civilian apricot pack was ordered by the Director of Industry Operations June 22.

This is accomplished by Amendment No. 3 to Conservation Order M–81, reducing the permitted civilian pack for 1942 from 75 percent to 65 percent of the 1940 pack.

DYNAMIC NAMES

The Douglas Aircraft Corporation, of Santa Monica, Calif., reported to War Production Drive Headquarters that it had offered prizes for the best names for planes it is building for the Army. Among the names suggested for bombers were: Scorpion, Dingo, Diablo, Banshee, Guardsman, Bolo, Dragon, and Dominator. Prize winners will get additional prizes if the Army adopts their names.

★ ★ ★

Restrictions on copper and brass ironed out

Restrictions governing the use of copper and brass in certain civilian products were revised by an amendment to Conservation Order M–9–c announced June 20 by the Director of Industry Operations.

Permission is granted to attach and use zippers, snappers, fasteners and other copper and brass clothing findings, though none may be manufactured.

Other effects of the amendment are:

1. Watches and clocks may be assembled from parts completed prior to June 15, 1942 into cases not containing brass or copper.

2. The prohibition on use of copper and brass in manufacture of bells is lifted, under certain circumstances, to permit such use for conducting electricity.

3. The prohibition on use of copper or brass in radio manufacture is lifted to permit manufacture of replacement vacuum tubes and various special types of radio apparatus under certain circumstances.

★ ★ ★

800 new gas wells in three States authorized

Threatened curtailment of war production and essential civilian activities in Missouri, Kansas, and Oklahoma because of lack of sufficient natural gas has been averted through modification of existing conservation laws, announced June 20 by the Director of Industry Operation. Approximately 800 new wells will be allowed.

Supplementary Order M–68–2, issued by the Division, provides that in Missouri and in certain areas of Kansas and Oklahoma, the size of the unit required before drilling, completing, or providing additions to any well can be carried out will be sharply reduced from the original minimum of 640 acres. Necessary material for such work may now be obtained if the unit is 40 acres or more.

New version of laundry, cleaning equipment order issued

A reissue of General Limitation Order L–91, as amended to June 22, was announced June 23 by the Director of Industry Operations. This is the order which controls the production and distribution of laundry and dry cleaning equipment and tailors' pressing machinery.

Further changes made

The new version embodies the terms of previous amendments and itself makes certain further changes. Principal among these are the requirements that distributors, as well as manufacturers, must file monthly reports of orders, production, and shipments on Form PD–419, and the addition to the list of deliveries authorized by paragraph (b) (I) of shipments to fill orders for bagloading or other ordnance plants where the hazard is such that the machinery has been specified as necessary by the Army or Navy.

Another change adds vessels constructed for the U. S. Navy to the list of those entitled to receive the equipment controlled by L–91.

Attached to the amended order is List A, naming the types of machinery covered by the order.

War rejects of olive drab wool waste may be used for civilians

Olive drab wool waste remnants, ends, seconds or rejects more than 1⅛ yards long may be sold or used for civilian garments if the Army or Navy, having been offered them, rejects them. This is provided for in Amendment No. 2 to General Preference Order M–87 issued June 22. The same applies to blankets made from remnants, ends, seconds or rejects of any length.

The amendment also changes the word "wool" to "wool fiber" to make clear that the wool referred to in the order means any wool fiber rather than only new wool.

DYE QUOTA INCREASES

More of the better dyes will become available for civilian use during the third quarter of 1942 as a result of an amendment to Conservation Order M–103 issued June 26. The amendment provides civilian quotas for anthraquinone dyes from July 1 to September 30 at the rate of 70 percent of their use in 1941. The current quarter's quota is at the rate of 50 percent of last year's use.

Curb lifted on coal and coke inventories

Chemical producers are permitted to build up inventories of coal and coke by Amendment No. 2 to Preference Rating Order P–89, issued June 24 by the Director of Industry Operations. The action was taken as part of a Nation-wide drive to encourage the accumulation of fuel stocks in anticipation of shortages expected to be caused next winter by war demands on transportation facilities.

Amendment No. 2 also makes the order, and all amendments to the order, effective until revoked.

Order P–89 assigns preference ratings to chemical producers for repair, operating, and maintenance supplies. Amendment No. 2 removes the restrictions on inventories of coal and coke in conformity with General Inventory Order M–97, which permits any person to deliver or accept any amount of coal or coke, even though such delivery may be in conflict with other WPB orders, including General Priority Regulation No. 1.

All large stocks of canned beef set aside for armed forces

All large stocks of imported canned beef in the United States were frozen June 22 and made available to the armed forces.

Under order M–172 all stocks held by any person in excess of 5,000 pounds in any one place, in contiguous places, or in transit in the United States are required to be set aside for 90 days under allocation to the armed forces.

In addition, all stocks of canned beef in transit from abroad also must be set aside for the Government upon arrival at U. S. Ports, unless imported by a Government agency or under General Imports Order M–63. Beginning July 2, 1942, all imports of canned beef will be licensed under M–63. It is likely that such licenses will be limited to importations for the armed forces.

Any person having a stock to be set aside must file a report with WPB on Form PD–555 by July 22.

★ ★ ★

DENTAL BUR TYPES LIMITED

The War Production Board on June 25 ordered a reduction in types and sizes of dental drills to increase production of necessary types.

This action, which will reduce the present number of types and sizes by about 50 percent, is embodied in Schedule I to Limitation Order L–139.

PRIORITY ACTIONS
*From June 17
*Through June 24

Subject	Order No.	Related form	Issued	Expired date	Rating
Air conditioning machinery and equipment: (industrial and commercial refrigeration):					
a. Manufacturers and distributors afforded some relief from provisions of L–38.	L–38 (Amend. 1)....	PD–520.....	6–18–42		
Aircraft products (material entering into the production of):					
a. Amended to permit suppliers who are not required by terms of Reg. 11 to come under FRP to extend ratings for purpose of filling purchase orders of producers listed under P–109 and P–109-a, even after the orders have expired.	P–109-a (Amend. 1).	....	6–17–42		A–1–b
b. Amended with P–109-a.	P–109 as amend. 3–11–42 (Amend. 2).	....	6–17–42		A–1–a
Asbestos:					
a. Circumstances under which amosite asbestos may be used are changed in several respects.	M–79 as amend 6–18–42.	....	6–18–42		
Canning fruits and vegetables:					
a. Assigns higher preference rating to fruit and vegetable packers.	P–115, Amend. 1....	PD–285.....	6–23–42		A–1–f A–1–c
Cellulose, (ethyl):					
a. Ethyl cellulose placed under complete allocation. To conserve supply and direct distribution.	M–175..............	PD–550, 549.....	6–18–42		A–10
Cadmium:					
a. Effective June 24—permits delivery of cadmium to distributors and to users only upon specific authorization.	M–65 as amend. 6–7–42.	PD–441.....	6–17–42	Until revoked.	
Chemicals (production of maintenance, repair, and operating supplies):	P–89 Amended (Amend. 2).	....	6–24–42	Until revoked.	A–1–c; A–3
a. Chemical producers permitted to build up inventories of coal and coke.					
Copper (curtailing use of copper in certain items):					
a. Use of zippers, snappers, fasteners and other copper and brass clothing findings permitted but none may be manufactured.	M–9-c (Amend. 2) (As amend. 5–7–42).	....	6–17–42		
Elastic fabrics, knitted, woven or braided:					
a. Limits use to essential health articles and to military products.	M–174..............	....	6–20–42 (effective 6–24–42).		
Farm machinery and equipment and attachments and repair parts therefor:					
a. Permits manufacture of wooden beehives.	L–26 (amend. 4).....	....	6–20–42		
Honey:					
a. Several million pounds of honey made available to manufacturers, but still subject to quota restrictions.	M–118 as amend. 6–18–42).	PD–246.....	6–18–42		
Imported canned beef (canned goods):					
a. All large stocks of imported canned beef frozen and made available to armed forces.	M–172..............	PD–555.....	6–22–42	10–1–42	
Iron and steel scrap:					
a. Mandatory segregation of alloy steel scrap ordered by WPB. Sets up clarification of alloy steels.	M–24-c.............	....	6–17–42		
Laundry equipment, dry cleaning equipment and tailors' pressing machinery:					
a. Reissue of L–91 which embodies previous amendments and itself.	L–91 as amend. 6–22–42.	PD–419.....	6–22–42		
Leather, sole:					
a. Permits use of frozen stocks of heavy shoe sole leather and purchase of similar quality leather that dealer had on hand on May 22, 1942.	M–80 as amend. 6–22–42). (As amend.)	....	6–19–42		
Nickel:					
a. Amended to conform to new alloy steel scrap segregation order, M–24-c.	M–6-c as amend. 6–19–42.	....	6–19–42		A–2.
Petroleum (production, transportation, refining and marketing of):					
a. Extends provisions of P–98 to the Canadians.	P–98 (Amend. 1)....	....	6–19–42		A–1–a to A–10.
b. Material conservation: 1. Allows for drilling of approximately 800 new wells in Missouri, Kansas, and Oklahoma.	M–68–2.............	....	6–20–42		
Power, steam and water auxiliary equipment:					
a. Use of critical materials in mfr. of water meters sharply curtailed.	L–154.............	....	6–17–42		
Quinine, and other drugs extracted from cinchona bark:					
a. Revokes provisions which exempted quinine or totoquine stocks of less than 50 ounces from sales restrictions of the order.	M–131 as amend. 4–30–42 Amend. 1.	....	6–19–42		
b. Prohibits sale of any amount of cinchonine, quinidine or cinchonidine for other than medicinal purposes.	M–131-a.............	PD–401-a.....	6–19–42		
Railroad maintenance, repair and operating supplies (materials entering into):					
a. Assigns higher preference ratings for supplies.	P–58 Amend. 1.....	....	6–17–42		A–1–j.

Subject	Order No.	Related form	Issued	Expired date	Rating
Rubber and products and material of which rubber is a component:					
a. Prohibits importation of rubber and rubber products including balata, except by subsidiaries of the RFC.	M-15-b Amend. 10.	....	6-19-42	....	
Sanitary belts and supports:					
a. Use of elastic fabrics in the mfr. of sanitary belts and supports restricted.	L-137............	....	6-18-42	....	
Suppliers inventory:					
a. Exemption No. 5 releases from restrictions of L-63 large group of noncritical building material.	L-63 Exemption No. 5.	....	6-23-42	....	
Tin plate and terneplate:					
a. Additional 10 percent reduction in civilian apricot pact ordered.	M-81 Amend. 3.......	....	6-22-42	....	
Tools:					
a. Assigns higher preference rating to Canadian purchasers of machine tools.	E-1-c............	....	6-16-42	....	A-1-a.
b. Interpretation regarding productions and delivery of machine tools.	E-1-b Int. 1........	....	6-16-42	....	
Utilities (maintenance, repair and supplies):					
a. Assigns preference rating for utility extensions to housing projects.	P-46 Amend. to 3-26-42.	....	6-23-42	9-30-42	A-1-c.
Order extended..........	Ext. 1 and Amend. 1.				
Vanadium:					
a. Melting and delivery of any amount over 10 pounds per month placed under complete control.	M-23-a as amended June 1942.	P D-209-a, 209-b.	6-23-42	....	
Wool (O. D. clips, O. D. wool rags and O. D. wool wastes):					
a. Provides for sale of garments which Army and Navy reject.	M-87 Amend. 2.......	....	6-22-42	....	

PRIORITIES REGULATIONS

Number	Subject	Issued
Prior. Reg. No. 11 Amend. 1.	Operators of metal mills partially excluded from use of the PRP. Metal mills which do not buy more than $5,000 worth of metal in a quarter for processing into forms not included in the metal list of Priorities Reg. No. 11, and for maintenance and repair are not required to apply under the PRP, but may continue to receive and extend ratings as they have in the past.	6-19-42
Prior. Reg. No. 11 Amend. 2.	Amended to clarify the interim procedure to be followed by companies which have not yet received a PRP certificate; and also to redefine the permissible use of ratings by companies already operating under PRP.	6-22-42

Compliance branch begins audits under PRP

Continuous audit of a large segment of American industry will be inaugurated by the War Production Board on July 1, when the compliance branch will commence successive surveys of the records of manufacturers operating under the Production Requirements Plan.

Some 9,000 companies have elected to take advantage of PRP since the establishment last December of this over-all method of extending priority assistance. Beginning July 1, it is expected that this number will be doubled as a consequence of the mandatory provisions of Priorities Regulation No. 11, which requires that all manufacturing users of metals in excess of $5,000 worth per calendar quarter file PRP applications not later than June 30.

WPB's compliance branch has enlisted the aid of the field investigation staff of the Wage and Hour Division of the Department of Labor in its program. Field work will be directed by the eight regional compliance chiefs, and accountants' reports of audits will be reviewed by analysts on their staffs.

High rating assigned cloth for the American flag, and others

To encourage display of the American flag, the WPB June 27 issued an order (M-166) granting a preference rating of A-2 to purchase orders by flag manufacturers for certain cotton and rayon fabrics to be used in the manufacture of flags.

The preference rating assigned by the order applies not only to cloth for the manufacture of American flags but also to cloth for many others.

The following types of cotton fabrics are made available by the order for flags: 1. Cotton, mercerized bunting manufactured according to Federal specifications; 2. cotton scrim, 40 inches wide, 32 by 32 construction, 2.70 yds. per pound; 3. cotton sheeting, 40 inches wide, 48 by 44 construction, 3.25 yds. per pound; 4. cotton print cloth, 38½ inches wide, 64 by 60 construction, 5.35 yds. per pound.

Rayon fabric made available for flags are: 1 Rayon taffeta, 39 inches wide, 110 by 60 construction, made with 150 denier viscose or cupprammonium bright rayon yard; 2. rayon taffeta, 40 inches wide, 120 by 68 construction, made with 120 denier acetate rayon yarn.

More wooden beehives allowed under modified farm order

Beekeepers of the United States, called upon by the Government to increase honey production to assist in offsetting shortages of sugar and beeswax, will benefit by the terms of an amendment to the farm machinery and equipment order, announced June 22 by the Director of Industry Operations.

Amendment 4 to Limitation Order L-26 authorizes a substantial increase in the output of wooden beehives. Previously permitted production of all beekeepers' supplies was 100 percent of 1940 output. This is now altered to allow manufacture of 133 percent of the hives produced during the base period, provided those to be made are of wooden construction. Production of metal hives is still subject to the terms of the original order.

Another provision of the amendment permits the production of belt-driven, but not electric, irrigation turbine pumps of 1,200 gallons per minute capacity, and larger, in sufficient quantities to fill orders rated A-3 or better. Previously, production of any turbine pumps of these sizes was prohibited.

Noncritical building materials lifted from L-63 curb

A large group of slow-moving, noncritical building materials is specifically released from the restrictions imposed by Suppliers' Inventory Limitation Order L-63, under the terms of Exemption No. 5 to the order, issued June 23 by the Division of Industry Operations.

Dealers holding stocks of the following materials need no longer include them in the records and reports called for by L-63, although they remain subject to the inventory restrictions of Priorities Regulation No. 1:

Portland and natural cement, lime, gypsum and gypsum products, bituminous roofing materials, concrete pipe, cut stone, sand and gravel, crushed stone, clay products, insulation board, acoustical materials, mineral wool, paving materials, concrete products, glass, lumber, wooden mill work.

WPB asks fewer furniture fairs

The War Production Board on June 23 asked the furniture industry to hold only one instead of four markets each year to reduce unnecessary travel.

Utility extensions to war housing units get same preference ratings as projects

The WPB acted June 24 to expedite the extension of utility services, such as electricity, gas and water, to thousands of war housing units throughout the country.

Approval of applications decentralized

Under an amendment to P–46, utility extensions to housing projects are assigned the same preference ratings as are assigned to the housing projects themselves. Heretofore extensions to housing projects were specifically excluded from the automatic rating assigned by P–46. In order to facilitate the use of the preference rating, new procedures have been developed under which utility applications for housing extensions will be reviewed in the field and will be processed simultaneously with the housing project application.

Strict standards for use of materials

Materials needed for such extensions will be made available as far as possible from the inventories of the utility companies themselves. A catalog listing excess stocks has been compiled by the WPB power branch and has been sent to all utilities. To make certain that these materials will go as far as possible, the power branch has prepared strict standards for the use of scarce materials.

The new plan has been worked out by the power branch of the WPB in collaboration with the Board's housing priorities branch and Federal housing agencies. Utilities are being instructed in the new procedure by an administrative letter from the WPB power branch. Local offices of the FHA will be able to give full details to private builders in 2 or 3 days.

Other changes in the June 24 amendment and extension to P–46 include:

1. Utilities in Canada are brought under the terms of P–46, formalizing arrangements previously worked out by WPB with the Department of Munitions and Supply in Ottawa.

2. Material required for utility extensions to all projects rated A–5 or better is assigned the same rating as is assigned to the project itself.

3. An A–5 rating is assigned to material required by utilities for protection against air raids, provided such protection is directed by an authorized Federal or State agency.

Order extended to September 30

4. After July 1, 1942, a preference rating of A–1–c is assigned to deliveries of material required for repair of an actual breakdown of existing utility facilities or required to make reasonable advance provision for such repair. The amount of material that may be acquired under an A–1–c rating is restricted.

5. Automatic approval of 250-foot extensions, formerly permitted, is changed to apply only to projects if (1) the buildings affected are wired or piped and ready for service by July 1, 1942, or (2) in the case of new construction, foundations are completed prior to July 1. After July 1, no extension of any length can be made without special WPB approval.

6. The order, which was to have expired June 30, 1942, has been extended to September 30, 1942.

Pulp and paper policies to be explained at general meetings

The pulp and paper branch of the WPB June 24 announced that two general meetings were to be held this week to inform the industry of the policies and the work of the branch.

One meeting was scheduled July 1, in New York City, and the second on July 2, at Chicago.

1,957 vehicles released in week

The automotive branch announced June 22 that during the week ended June 20, it released 1,957 trucks, truck trailers and miscellaneous vehicles to civilian users and holders of Government exemption permits.

Motion picture producers tell of plans to save critical items

Motion picture producers advised the WPB at an industry advisory committee meeting in Washington June 23 of measures it is taking to save critical materials in the production of motion pictures.

Conservation efforts have been directed chiefly toward reducing the amount of film used by elimination of waste and revision of certain technical practices, and reducing the quantity of materials used in the construction of sets.

The same chemicals that go into the production of films also go into the manufacture of munitions. A WPB representative told the committee that the situation in regard to some of the chemicals used in films will become even tighter than at present, calling for utmost conservation on the part of producers.

Industry takes steps to push production of heat exchangers

Steps were taken June 25 by the newly organized heat exchanger industry advisory committee to seek facilities capable of producing $200,000,000 worth of heat exchangers needed in the war program before July 1, 1943.

Critically needed

During 1941 the industry, comprising 53 companies, produced heat exchangers valued at $60,000,000. It is estimated that present facilities can produce only about $80,000,000 worth in the required time, leaving a deficit of approximately $120,000,000.

Heat exchangers—condensers, coolers, feed water heaters and other such equipment—are critically needed for the manufacture of chemicals for explosives, synthetic rubber, aviation gasoline and other petroleum products and for land and ship power plants.

William K. Frank was Government presiding officer at the meeting. James B. Forbes, on leave as district sales manager for heat exchangers of the American Locomotive Co., of Chicago, has been appointed chief of the recently organized heat exchanger and equipment section of the WPB.

★ ★ ★

Production of heavy truck trailers halted except for war

The WPB has ordered a halt to production, effective July 1, of commercial-type truck trailers for nonmilitary use.

After the end of this month, no manufacturer will be permitted to produce any truck trailers having a load-carrying capacity of 10,000 pounds or more, except for the Army and Navy, certain designated Government agencies, governments of the United Nations and for deliveries under the Lend-Lease Act.

Buses removed from L–1 series

The stop-production order covering commercial-type truck trailers is contained in Supplementary Limitation Order L–1–g, which also removes buses from the terms of orders in the L–1 series. Buses are now covered by General Limitation Order L–101, which is administered by WPB's transportation equipment branch. Order L–101 was issued May 21, and the transfer of buses from orders in the L–1 series is simply a formality.

Restrictions on paper and ilmenite inventories lifted

Paper, paperboard, paper products, waste paper, and ilmenite, which is a source of titanium pigments, have been removed from the inventory restrictions of Priorities Regulation No. 1 and all other WPB orders by amendments to General Inventory Order M–161, issued June 26 by the Director of Industry Operations.

The action on paper and paper products was taken to permit building up inventories in anticipation of a transportation shortage next fall and winter.

Restrictions on ilmenite are unnecessary because the National Lead Company's new development at Tahawus, New York, is expected to produce all that is needed in the United States.

Curb in two petroleum orders doesn't apply to Canadian firms

Two orders providing for conservation of materials in the production and marketing of petroleum and petroleum products were amended June 25 by the Director of Industry Operations to restrict their application to the United States, its territories and possessions.

This action was taken to make it clear that the restrictions contained in orders M–68 and M–68–c do not apply to Canadian oil companies to which priority assistance has been extended by a recent amendment to Preference Rating Order P–98. Application of the ratings by Canadian companies will be subject to Canadian government restrictions.

. . .

Monthly clove quotas raised

Monthly clove quotas for food processors, manufacturers of medicines and clove packers June 25 were increased by one-third, and for other manufacturers and wholesale receivers they were doubled.

The increases, which are the result of larger supplies of cloves built up by greater imports during recent months, are granted by Amendment No. 1 to Supplementary Order M–127–a.

Under the amendment, the new quota for any industrial receiver is 100 percent of the average monthly amount of cloves he used in the corresponding quarter of 1941.

New industry advisory committees

The Bureau of Industry Advisory Committees, WPB, has announced the formation of the following new industry advisory committees:

FIBER DRUM INDUSTRY

Government presiding officer—Douglas Kirk, chief, containers branch.

Members:

R. C. Carlson, Emery-Carpenter Container Co., Cincinnati, Ohio.; Henry Craemer, Carpenter Container Corporation, Brooklyn, N. Y.; H. A. Eggers, The Container Co., Van Wert, Ohio; John W. Harris, Pacific Steel-fiber Drums, Inc., Alhambra, Calif.; W. J. Mahoney, The Master Package Corporation, Owen, Wis.; T. E. Shultz, Fibre Drum Co., Kankakee, Ill.

FIN COIL & COOLER INDUSTRY

Government presiding officer—A. H. Baer, air conditioning and commercial refrigeration branch.

Members:

R. C. Colman, vice president, McQuay, Inc., Minneapolis, Minn.; Morrill Dunn, vice president, McCord Radiator & Mfg. Co., Detroit, Mich.; J. W. Hatch, president, Bush Manufacturing Co., Hartford, Conn.; B. E. James, York Ice Machinery Corporation, York, Pa.; H. T. Jarvis, vice president and general manager, Refrigeration Engineering, Inc., Los Angeles, Calif.; O. Z. Klopsch, general manager, Wolverine Tube Division, Calumet & Hecla Consolidated Copper Co., Detroit, Mich.; William L. Lynch, president, Rome-Turney Radiator Co., Rome, N. Y.; Milnor Noble, general manager, Aerofin Corporation, Syracuse, N. Y.; Paul H. Schoepflin, president, Niagara Blower Co., New York, N. Y.; C. E. Sims, general manager, Larkin Coils, Inc., Atlanta, Ga.; Reuben Trane, president, The Trane Co., La Crosse, Wis.; E. R. Walker, general manager, Pedders Manufacturing Co., Buffalo, N. Y.

HEAT EXCHANGER INDUSTRY

Government presiding officer—William K. Frank, chief, resources protection board.

Members:

W. C. Beekley, vice president, Whitlock Manufacturing Co., Hartford, Conn.; H. M. Corrough, division manager, Alco Products Division, American Locomotive Co., New York, N. Y.; G. H. Cox, assistant works manager, Westinghouse Electric & Mfr. Co., South Philadelphia, Pa.; J. A. Coy, president, J. A. Coy Co., Tulsa, Okla.; Chas. Currier, vice president, Ross Heater and Manufacturing Division, American Radiator & Standard Sanitary Co., Buffalo, N. Y.; E. L. Durrell, manager refinery division, J. B. Beaird Co., Shreveport, La.; C. H. Latrial, vice president, Southwestern Engineering Co., Los Angeles, Calif.; Melvin Sack, chief engineer, Henry Vogt Machine Co., Louisville, Ky.

LIVESTOCK EQUIPMENT MANUFACTURERS INDUSTRY

Government presiding officer—William R. Tracy, chief, farm machinery and equipment branch.

Members:

Ben H. Anderson, Ben H. Anderson Mfr. Co., Madison, Wis.; L. J. Brower, Brower Mfr. Co., Quincy, Ill.; C. E. Butler, The Galloway Co., Inc., Waterloo, Iowa; J. B. Clay, Clay Equipment Corporation, Cedar Falls, Iowa;

Zur W. Craine, Craine, Inc., Norwich, N. Y.; A. R. Hill, The Buckeye Incubator Co., Springfield, Ohio; R. C. Hudson, H. D. Hudson Mfr. Co., Chicago, Ill.; H. B. Megran, Starline, Inc., Harvard, Ill.; T. W. Merritt, Babson Bros. Co., Chicago, Ill.; S. H. Smith, The Smith Incubator Corporation, Bucyrus, Ohio; George C. Stoddard, DeLaval Separator Co., New York, N. Y.; W. A. Zaloudek, Oakes Mfr. Co., Tipton, Ind.

MOTION PICTURE THEATRE EQUIPMENT MANUFACTURERS INDUSTRY

Government presiding officer—Harold C. Hopper, head of motion picture and photographic section.

Members:

C. S. Ashcraft, president, Ashcraft Manufacturing Co., Long Island City, N. Y.; Edward C. Cahill, general manager, R. C. A. Manufacturing Co., Camden, N. J.; G. L. Carrington, vice president, Altec Service Corporation, New York, N. Y.; William A. Gedris, president, Ideal Seating Co., Grand Rapids, Mich.; Louis B. Goldberg, president, Goldberg Brothers, Denver, Colo.; Walter E. Green, director, General Theatres Equipment Co., New York, N. Y.; E. W. Hulett, president, E. W. Hulett Mfg. Co., Chicago, Ill.; Albert B. Hurley, president, Hurley Screen Co., Long Island City, N. Y.; J. E. Robin, president, J. E. Robin, Inc., New York, N. Y.; E. J. Vallen, president, Vallen Inc., Akron, Ohio; E. Wagner, president, Wagner Sign Service, Chicago, Ill.; E. A. Williford, sales manager, National Carbon Co., New York, N. Y.

POWER CRANE AND SHOVEL INDUSTRY

Government presiding officer—Joseph F. Ryan, chief of the construction machinery branch.

C. B. Smythe, president, Thew Shovel Mfg. Co., Lorain, Ohio; Carlton R. Dodge, Northwest Engineering, 28 E. Jackson Blvd., Chicago, Ill.; Morgan Ramsay, president, Bay City Shovels, Bay City, Mich.; Doc Shelton, president, Marion steam Shovel, Marion, Ohio; Ray Dorward, manager, Insley Mfg. Co., 801 N. Olney Street, Indianapolis, Ind.; John Jay, Quickway Truck Shovel, Denver, Colo.; E. W. Botten, secretary and treasurer, Owen Bucket, Cleveland, Ohio.

ZINC PRODUCERS INDUSTRY

Government presiding officer—George C. Heikes, chief of the zinc branch.

Kenneth C. Brownell, vice president, American Smelting & Refining Co., 120 Broadway, New York, N. Y.; Frank E. Chesney, purchasing agent, American Steel & Wire Co., Rockefeller Building, Cleveland, Ohio.; Irwin H. Cornell, vice president, St. Joseph Lead Co., 250 Park Avenue, New York, N. Y.; Robert E. Dwyer, Executive vice president, Anaconda Copper Mining Co., 25 Broadway, New York, N. Y.; Benno Elkan, president, International Minerals & Metals Corporation, 19 Broadway, New York, N. Y.; Marshall L. Havey, vice president, The New Jersey Zinc Co., 160 Front street, New York, N. Y.; C. H. Klaustermeyer, manager, Metals & Ore Division, Grasselli Chemical Division, E. I. du Pont de Nemours & Co., Wilmington, Del.; J. M. Pomeroy, vice president, General Smelting Co., Westmoreland & Richmond Sts., Philadelphia, Pa.; George W. Potter, vice president, Eagle Picher Mining & Smelting Co., Fifth & Pearl Streets, Joplin, Mo.; Howard I. Young, president, American Zinc Lead & Smelting Co., 818 Olive Street, St. Louis, Mo.; Bernard N. Zimmer, vice president, American Metal Co., Ltd., 61 Broadway, New York, N. Y.

TRANSPORTATION . . .

Motor transport units would move troops, civilians in emergency, under joint plan

The Office of Civilian Defense and the Office of Defense Transportation are co-operating in a plan for the organization of motor transport units in various parts of the country to facilitate the movement of troops and civilians in event of emergency, it was announced June 24.

24 trucks in a unit

ODT has sent letters to the large transportation companies explaining the purposes of the plan. Each letter was accompanied by an application blank and tables of organization for use of companies desiring to participate.

Each unit would consist of 24 trucks or buses capable of transporting 40 passengers each. Depending on local conditions, each unit also may include a five-passenger automobile, a service truck, a tank truck, and a light pick-up truck.

The letter sent out to the transportation companies states:

The primary function of the motor transport units will be to serve the needs, if they should arise, of the War Department for the movement of troops and of the Office of Civilian Defense for evacuation or other civilian protection purposes. The Office of Defense Transportation, through its local offices, will exercise control over allotment or assignment of such motor transport units.

To be paid for actual use

The plan is based on an agreement among the War Department, the Navy Department, the ODT, and the OCD. Motor transport units already organized or in the process of being organized under the auspices of military or other authorities are expected to be incorporated into the new program.

Companies joining in the program will be compensated by the Federal Government to the extent their equipment actually is used in emergency transportation. The companies themselves will be expected to bear the cost of organizing the units and training personnel.

A representative of the OCD will assist the companies in perfecting organization of the units. It also is expected that a representative of each company will have the opportunity to attend a training course sponsored by the OCD.

Voluntary plans for saving milk trucks, tires cleared by ODT and Justice

Several voluntary plans for the conservation of milk trucks and tires have been cleared by the ODT, and the Department of Justice.

Estimated mileage reductions in several of the plans went beyond the 25 per cent. required by General ODT No. 6, which also prohibits special deliveries, call backs, and more than one delivery a day to the same person.

Cities or areas affected and the number of dealers involved in plans thus far approved include:

Washington, D. C., six dealers; Indianapolis, Ind., 19 dealers; Luzerno, Lackawanna and Susquehanna Counties, Pennsylvania, 38 dealers; Detroit, Mich., 15 dealers; Madison, Wis., six dealers; Flint, Mich., nine dealers; New York-New Jersey Metropolitan District, 97 dealers, and Niagara Frontier Milk Distributors, representing 51 dealers in and around Buffalo, New York.

"Frustrated" freight may be moved from U. S. ports at once under general order

Defense Transportation Director Eastman, June 27 issued a general order which makes it possible for ODT to remove from United States ports any freight cargo when necessary to assure expeditious movement of troops and war materials.

The order (General Order No. 12) makes it possible to relieve certain ports of cargoes on hand, or in storage, many of which were destined for foreign ports at about the time of enemy occupation of those ports.

Issuance of the order does not imply that there exists any serious port congestion, ODT officials said. The fact remains, they added, that certain of this so-called "frustrated" freight occupies needed cars, ground, and warehouse space while it awaits final disposition.

"KEEP 'EM ROLLING" DRIVE LAUNCHED BY ODT

With "Keep 'em Rolling" as the rallying call, the ODT has launched one of its major campaigns—organization of a U. S. Truck Conservation Corps designed to assure the continued and uninterrupted flow of the material of war and the necessities of civilian life.

A booklet entitled, "America's Trucks—Keep 'em Rolling," has been prepared by the vehicle maintenance section of the division of motor transport explaining in detail the basic rules which should be followed by every truck operator and maintenance man during the emergency.

★ ★ ★

APPEAL BOARD NAMED

The OTD June 22 announced the appointment of another local appeal board to pass on appeals taken by persons who have been refused permission by ODT local allocation officers to purchase new trucks.

The new board will serve District No. 7—Tennessee, Kentucky, and Mississippi—with headquarters at Nashville, Tenn.

Personnel of three more local appeal boards was announced June 24 by the ODT.

Areas they will serve follow:

District No. 10.—Nebraska, Kansas, Iowa, and Missouri; headquarters at Kansas City, Mo.

District No. 13.—Wyoming, Colorado, and New Mexico; headquarters at Denver, Colo.

District No. 16.—Southern California and Arizona; headquarters at Los Angeles, Calif.

★ ★ ★

STAFF APPOINTMENTS

Four appointments to the staff of the division of railway transport were announced June 23 by ODT Director Eastman.

C. T. Kenney, of Cedar Rapids, Iowa, was made supervisor of rail terminals, at Seattle, Wash.

William E. Curley, of Chicago, was named supervisor of rail terminals at Chicago.

Shannon Kuhn, of Cleveland, Ohio, was named locomotive assistant in the mechanical section to specialize in locomotive repair problems.

Frank J. Swanson, of Oak Park, Ill., was named service representative in the mechanical section, and will visit car builders and railway shops to aid in facilitating car building and repair.

Labor policy committee set up to help formulate price, rent, rationing policies

Creation of a labor policy committee in the OPA composed of representatives of the AFL, the CIO, and the Railway Labor Organizations was announced June 27 by Administrator Henderson.

Composed of three members from each of the labor groups, the committee will work with Mr. Henderson and other OPA officials in the formulation of price, rent, and rationing policies of interest to labor. The first meeting of the committee was held on June 25, and was devoted to an introductory discussion of OPA problems.

Committee members

Members of the committee include:

AFL—I. M. Ornburn, secretary-treasurer of the Union Label Trades Department; Frank P. Fenton, director of organization; and Boris Shiskin, economist.

CIO—Emil Rieve, president of the Textile Workers Union; Sherman Dalrymple, president of the United Rubber Workers; and Joseph Curran, president of the National Maritime Union. All three CIO members are vice presidents of the parent organization.

RAILWAY LABOR ORGANIZATIONS—T. C. Cashen, chairman, Railway Labor Executives' Association; J. G. Luhrsen, executive secretary, Railway Labor Executives' Association; and Martin H. Miller, national legislative representative of the Brotherhood of Railroad Trainmen.

"We look forward to a relationship of great importance to the OPA program," Mr. Henderson said. "Organized labor has a lot to contribute to the protection of the consumer interests and living standards during this period of decreasing consumer goods production. It won't be an easy job. I am glad to have this opportunity to deal directly with organized labor on all matters in which we have a joint interest. I hope that as a result of this relationship we shall not only be able to protect workers' interests as consumers but also to preserve and extend the legitimate aspirations of trade unionism."

The new committee will be assisted in carrying on its work by the staff of the recently established Labor Office in OPA and by staff members of the three organizations represented.

Separate order for toys coming

A maximum price regulation setting the top prices at which all toys and games may be sold will be issued soon, Price Administrator Henderson a n n o u n c e d June 26.

RATIONING . . .

New gas plan opening shifted to July 22; OCD enlists in drive to form car clubs

The Office of Price Administration last week postponed until July 22 the date for the inauguration of thé permanent gasoline rationing system on the Atlantic Seaboard to give motorists an additional week to form car-sharing clubs as the Office of Civilian Defense offered its facilities to bring automobile owners together.

At the same time OPA shifted the registration dates for obtaining basic "A" books for motor cars, "D" books for motorcycles and other special books to July 9, 10, and 11 in the public schools. Holders of the present "A," "B–1," "B–2," and "B–3" cards were allotted an additional ration of gasoline to get them through to July 22.

Coupon good for 4 gallons

Announcement of the regulations under which the permanent system will operate disclosed that each coupon in the new books will be valued at 4 gallons each but will be subject to change as the Eastern oil supply ebbs and flows. Every automobile owner is entitled to an "A" card regardless of his driving needs. It carries 48 coupons or enough to allow 2,880 miles of driving annually on the basis of 15 miles to the gallon. Eighteen hundred miles of this is ear-marked for occupational use and the remaining 1,080 miles for miscellaneous household use.

Extra rations for car-poolers

To obtain a supplementary "B" or "C" book, the motorist must prove that his driving needs are in excess of 1800 miles annually and that he is carrying three or more persons to work as a member of a car-sharing club; or that he has tried to form such a club and failed and that there are no adequate means of public transportation open to him. If he meets these requirements, he will be given additional rations tailored to fit his exact needs.

Local defense councils asked to help

James M. Landis, director of OCD, tendered the service of the 3,000 local defense councils in the rationed area in the campaign to form car-sharing clubs. Each council was asked to enlist service clubs, civic organizations and patriotic groups in matching up drivers with empty space in their cars and war workers in need of a ride. Business and factory executives will be urged to persuade employees living in the same neighborhood to ride together. District centers will be set up for the registration and organization of the clubs in every community.

War chiefs call for cooperation

To lend emphasis to his plan, Mr. Landis made public an open letter from Secretaries Stimson, Knox and Ickes, War Production Chief Nelson, Price Administrator Henderson and Transportation Director Eastman calling on all motorists to get behind the effort in order to save gasoline and rubber.

"We ask you to give your fullest cooperation to this car-sharing plan," the letter said. "It becomes one more direct way in which you, every one of you, can help to win this war."

Gasoline dealers may favor certain classes of consumers if supply unequal to demand

Dealers whose gasoline supply is not sufficient to meet all consumer demands may give preference to cars of defense workers, trucks and ambulances under provisions of an amendment No. 6 to the emergency gasoline rationing regulations, announced June 24 by the OPA.

As a condition for showing preference to one or more of the classes of consumers mentioned in the order, a dealer will be required to post a notice of his intention to do so. The notice shall specify which class or classes of consumers are to be preferred. A copy of the notice must be mailed to the State OPA office in the State where the dealer's establishment is located.

The amendment, which revises a section of the regulations requiring that a dealer shall not discriminate among consumers legally entitled to gasoline, specifies that by "defense worker" is meant a worker (including an executive, technician or office worker) employed at (1) naval, military or hospital establishments; (2) public utilities plants, including establishments operating public transportation and communication systems; (3) plants engaged in the production of machines, munitions and other materials used in the war.

AGRICULTURE . . .

*(Information furnished through Office of Agricultural War Relations,
U. S. Department of Agriculture)*

Dried fruit buying program for West Coast expected to encourage maximum output

The Department of Agriculture has announced the prices to be paid West Coast growers of dried peaches, apricots, pears, and apples in connection with the Department's program to encourage an adequate pack of dried fruits to meet the increasing demands of the armed forces, Lend-Lease shipments, and civilian consumers.

AMA purchases to support prices

The Department's dried fruit purchase program for the West Coast, announced June 9, provides that announced grower prices will be supported through purchases by the Agricultural Marketing Administration, and that processors would be requested to reserve a part of their 1942 pack for Government purchase.

Grower prices to be paid by the AMA for the four natural condition dried fruits will average, roughly, per ton: Peaches, $280, apricots, $340, pears, $220;

and apples, $260. Rough average prices for the two other major dried fruits produced on the West Coast, announced earlier, are raisins, $105 per ton, and prunes, $135.

Processors will probably be requested to reserve the following percentages of their 1942 pack of each dried fruit for Government purchase: Apples and pears, 70 to 75 percent; peaches, 45 to 50 percent; apricots, 50 to 55 percent; and raisins and prunes, 40 to 45 percent. Definite percentages will be announced later.

With a capacity production of dried fruits needed this coming year, these grower prices are expected to encourage maximum output of the dried-fruits, and also insure a proper relationship between the prices received by growers and processors. Purchases from processors will be made at prices in line with those received by growers plus a reasonable margin for handling, processing, packing and shipping.

Over $154,404,000 in farm products bought in May

Farm products costing more than $154,404,000 were bought in May by the U. S. Department of Agriculture under the general buying program for Lend-Lease and other needs, the Department reports.

For Lend-Lease, other needs

While this was less than April's high mark of $193,893,000, it was the second highest for any month since the program started March 15, 1941. The decline was attributed largely to seasonal factors.

Total value of all farm products bought for Lend-Lease shipment and other distribution needs for the 14½-month period ending May 30 approximated $1,225,660,315.

During May, meat again led the list of commodities bought, although the volume dropped from previous totals. Particularly heavy purchases were made of canned and cured pork, frozen pork loins, lard, dried eggs, dry skim milk cheese, dry beans, cornstarch, processed strawberries, and salad oil.

Sugar studies to determine possible ration increase

Further studies of the sugar situation to determine whether prospects for our future supplies will now make possible a moderate increase in the sugar ration, are being made by the OPA.

While final decision on any increase will depend principally upon prospects for shipments of sugar from Puerto Rico and Cuba during the coming 6 months, the decision will also be influenced by additional information which is now becoming available on actual distribution under rationing.

OPA officials stated flatly that the stocks of sugar now on hand in the United States, even though somewhat greater than they had been able to count on, do not themselves justify any increase in the ration. They declared that the invisible supply in the hands of consumers and others today is 50 percent less than a year ago; that stocks held by primary distributors are 20 percent below last year's, and that the total sugar stocks on hand in the country are one-third less than we had at this time in 1941.

Farm labor problem will be more difficult next year than this, Wickard warns

The problem of farm labor will be more difficult next year than this, although hardships have been faced in some areas this year, Secretary of Agriculture Claude R. Wickard warned in a radio broadcast June 19 on the National Farm and Home Hour.

"By then, farm machinery may be even more difficult to get than it is now and we will need more manpower to keep farm production high," he said. "At the same time the Army will need more men, and so will war factories. Then, we'll have to make good use of every lesson we learn this year."

Pointing out that labor problems are different in different areas, Mr. Wickard expressed the belief that, despite difficulties at some points, "most farmers can get by this year. In many sections plenty of help still is available. Average figures for the whole country show that there is enough farm labor to go around."

If insufficient first-class farm hands are to be found, the Secretary advised turning to other sources of help, such as farmers who have small farms and can spare some extra time, farm-bred boys who work in country towns and can give some time, older men who haven't been active lately but can still get a lot of jobs done, farm women and girls, high-school and college boys, white collar workers willing to assist in farm work on their vacations, and women in land army organizations.

The Secretary also suggested higher wages might be necessary in areas where they remain low both as a means of getting more farm workers and to make for a sounder agriculture in the long run.

Ice dealers get relief

Steps to permit price adjustments to retail sellers of ice in certain areas—where a dealer is the sole practical source of ice and where continued operations at unprofitable ceiling figures would result in a cutting off of supplies—were provided June 26 by Price Administrator Leon Henderson in Amendment No. 9 to Maximum Price Regulation No. 154 (Ice). The new amendment was effective June 30.

NEW EQUATION TABLES grow out of the war. This is the second in a series of "FOTOFACTS." Two-column mats are available for publication. Requests should be addressed to Distribution Section, Office of War Information, Washington, D. C. In ordering, refer to V-43

Solvents can be reclaimed 50 percent for further use, says salvage chief

Millions of gallons of valuable chemical solvents and oils which are now being discarded can be reclaimed for further production purposes, it was said June 23 by S. Donald Perlman, salvage director for the chemical and textile industries of the industrial salvage section of the Bureau of Industrial Conservation.

"Contacts and conferences with business firms engaged in the reclamation and recovery of commercial solvents," said Mr. Perlman, "indicate that they have facilities available for increasing by 50 to 75 percent the amount of solvent reclamation now going on in the country. Salvage of dirty, contaminated solvents so that they can be used again in industrial processes and channelled into war production is a problem to which every commercial user of solvents and oils should pay attention. We cannot afford to waste precious chemical resources."

War workers may become eligible for Grade II tires by new plan

An amendment to the tire rationing regulations that makes war workers eligible for third, fourth, and fifth line new tires under restrictive conditions and simultaneously provides a system designed to make each tire deliver the utmost in essential transportation was announced June 21 by Price Administrator Henderson.

Must present statement from plant committee

Amendment No. 16 to the Revised Tire Rationing Regulations sets up a procedure under which an employee of an establishment essential to the war effort and employing more than 100 workers must present to his local War Price and Rationing Board a statement from a committee set up in his own plant, showing that he needs tires and has agreed to make maximum use of them in carrying other employees to and from work.

The amendment also provides that a war worker whose eligibility is thus established may be granted a certificate to buy a new Grade II tire—third, fourth, and fifth lines fall within this classification—when the casings on his car are unfit for recapping. War workers heretofore have been eligible only for recapped casings or recapping services.

Effective July 15

To give all establishments affected by the plan time to set up the certifying committees and make arrangements for the requisite maximum use of cars, the amendment will not be put into effect until July 15.

The committee set up in a war production establishment will be required to certify to the local board that an applicant for a tire purchase certificate:

1. Is not a temporary or transient worker;
2. Has no other practicable means of transportation available to him; or that, using another means, he would have to spend more than one hour in getting to work or returning to his residence;
3. Resides at least two miles from his place of employment; and
4. Regularly carries with him at least three other workers of the establishment, none of whom lives less than two miles from his work. If the vehicle is of less than four-passenger capacity, the committee is required only to certify that it is used to capacity. Moreover, the committee may certify a vehicle whose driver is unable to get a full load because his residence is remote from that of others who might ride with him, or their working shifts do not coincide.

Selective Service boards to segregate registrants into broad induction groups

Emphasizing that "the national interest requires that all calls to meet the manpower requirements of the armed forces be filled on schedule," National Headquarters, Selective Service System, June 25 advised its agencies that insofar as is practical in meeting these calls local boards would segregate registrants into four broad categories from which men may be called for service.

New policy set-up

The announcement by National Headquarters, made coincident with the signing by the President of the bill recently adopted by Congress which provides family allowances for dependents of enlisted men in the armed forces, sets up a new policy under which registrants will be selected for induction from categories in the following order:

Category 1. Registrants otherwise qualified for military service who have no bona fide financial dependents.
Category 2. Registrants otherwise qualified for military service who have financial dependents other than wives or children mentioned in categories 3 or 4.
Category 3. Registrants otherwise qualified for military service who have wives with

whom they are maintaining a bona fide family relationship in their homes and who were married prior to December 8, 1941, and at a time when induction was not imminent.

Category 4. Registrants otherwise qualified for military service who have wives and children, or children alone, with whom they maintain a bona fide family relationship in their homes who were married prior to December 8, 1941, and at a time when induction was not imminent.

While setting up the four broad categories, National Headquarters made it emphatic that they do not provide for the permanent deferment of men with dependents but rather provide the order in which registrants with dependents will be inducted.

Local boards will continue to review the facts in the case of each individual, National Headquarters said, adding that in the selection of registrants for induction from any of the four categories the "full facts in each individual case shall be considered, and the local board, subject to the usual appeals, must judge whether or not there are sufficient unusual circumstances to justify a departure from the general rule of priority of induction."

That wrist motion won't be so important in cooking from now on, WPB remarks

The can opener will no longer be the most important utensil in American kitchens if the suggestions made by the Bureau of Industrial Conservation to save tin now used in cans are carried out on a Nation-wide scale. War production demands upon this critical metal already exceed prospective supply.

Tin cans will not be entirely eliminated from the household scene, but there will be fewer of them, and they will be of larger, metal-saving sizes. Tin plate must be conserved for packing large quantities of fresh fruits and vegetables to be consumed by the fighting men of America's Army and Navy.

Substitute containers urged

Food packers and processors and the manufacturers of containers in which food usually comes to the pantry shelf are being asked by the bureau to eliminate metal containers, especially tin cans. Paper, cardboard, corrugated paper containers, wooden boxes, pails, barrels and glass containers should be more generally used for holding and shipping

foods. Certain products requiring metal containers but not necessarily tin surfacing to keep them from deteriorating, will be packed in untinned black plate cans. No health hazards will result from these conservation practices and there will be plenty of food to go around.

The bureau points out that the housewife will help conserve the Nation's supply of tin by following these suggestions:

1. Order and eat perishable fruits and vegetables in season.
2. Make use of your cellar for storing foods that can be preserved in a dry, cool place for considerable periods of time. Take a leaf out of grandmother's book and lay in a supply of apples, potatoes, pumpkin, squash, carrots, beets, cabbage, cauliflower, onions, pears, ripe peas, and beans.
3. Do your own home packing, making use of glass jars. Almost any food that comes in a tin can may also be packed by the housewife in a glass jar. An adequate supply of rubber sealing rings is assured for this purpose.
4. Use sun-cured, dried and dehydrated foods. Excellent dishes can be prepared with dried apples, peaches, apricots, prunes, peppers, peas, and beans.
5. Plan to put up, store, and buy foods that can be successfully preserved in earthen crocks, wooden pails, and large glass jars. Such items are pickles, sauerkraut, olives, spiced and pickled fruits, and green tomatoes.

Alien Property Custodian seizes 750 more patents

The office of Leo T. Crowley, Alien Property Custodian, has seized an additional group of more than 750 enemy-owned patents and copyrights, among them about 200 patents of I. G. Farben-industrie not previously vested. Included were patents owned by Japanese, Italians, and Hungarians.

The patents cover an automatic drill and riveter for use in aircraft construction, a conveyor already widely used in American coal mines, certain processes in oil refining, and chemicals, including adrenalin compound and chlorinated rubber.

Vesting orders covered the seizure of control of the J. M. Lehmann Co., manufacturers of machinery used in the ink and paint industries. The seizure eliminated all barriers to immediate conversion of the company's plant to war production.

Also seized was the interest of German nationals in the estate of Anna M. von Zedlitz, who organized a personal holding company to control about $2,500,000 of improved New York City real estate.

A new order by the Alien Property Custodian requires all persons claiming any interest in patents or patent applications now or formerly owned by nationals of designated foreign countries to report their interest, including any license agreement or claims of ownership, on Form APC-2 by August 15, 1942.

★ ★

WELL-KNOWN ARTISTS WILL DRAW FOR YOUR PAPER OR MAGAZINE

VICTORY PRESENTS, on facing page, a seventh group of 4 drawings by well-known American artists who have volunteered their talents to help emphasize, in their own medium, matters vital to winning the war. VICTORY will print four drawings by these and other artists each week. Permission to reprint is hereby granted. Mats in two-column size (larger than appears here) are available weekly. Requests to be put on the mailing list regularly, or for individual mats should be addressed to Distribution Section, Office of War Information, Washington, D. C.

(In individual orders for the four drawings displayed this week, please refer to the serial numbers printed on the drawings.)

"Not only a firebug, Sergeant—he uses GASOLINE."
—Drawn for Division of Information, O. E. M.

"Before I sell you this, I want to know if you are in this for patriotism or because you're getting rich at it."
—Drawn for Division of Information, O. E. M.

". . . Let me think . . . Acme stole me from Excelsior . . . Thunder Bird stole me from Acme. . . . Ye gods! I don't work here any more!"
—Drawn for Division of Information, O. E. M.

"You'll have to come to it sooner or later, Melvin."
—Drawn for Division of Information, O. E. M.

U. S. speeds rubber-tapping equipment for other American republics

United States Government agencies in collaboration with the other Americas are planning for one of the biggest equipment tasks of the war—the outfitting of thousands of rubber tappers to collect wild rubber in the forests of South and Central America, according to information received from the office of the Co-ordinator of Inter-American Affairs.

Excerpts follow:

Officials studying rubber equipment needs, for instance, estimate 100,000,000 tapping cups may be required. In addition, thousands of machetes will be required, also knives, shotguns, stoves, spouts, wringers, files to sharpen tools and other paraphernalia.

Dr. Earl N. Bressman, director of the Agricultural Division of the Office of Inter-American Affairs, recently told a United States Senate Committee that a preliminary equipment order from Brazil included 5,000 tapping cups, 5,000 machetes, 10,000 files, 5,000 shotguns, 250,000 shotgun shells and 3,000,000 atebrine tablets for combating malaria. This order indicates the scope of the equipment task.

Some 40,000 rubber tappers are estimated to be at work now in the Amazon basin. Officials hope to get another 20,000 equipped this year.

United States authorities hope to arrange for production in Brazil and other rubber-producing countries of much of the needed equipment. This will help relieve already overwhelming demand upon United States manufacturing industry, and at the same time, would help build the rubber industry in those countries.

The United States is giving financial and technical aid to rubber production in the other Americas. Agreements for purchase of rubber export surpluses already have been made with Brazil, Peru, and Nicaragua. Negotiations have been under way with other rubber-producing countries of the hemisphere.

The United States has agreed to contribute $5,000,000 toward rubber development in Brazil and $1,125,000 to Peru. Similar financial aid, it is indicated, may be forthcoming for other American republics joining in this vast rubber program. Aside from direct aid, additional millions of dollars are to go into health and sanitation projects to protect workers engaged in production of rubber and other strategic materials.

★ ★ ★

INDEPENDENCE DAY

The following statement concerning the July 4 holiday was made June 27 by WPB Chairman Nelson (quoted in part):

. . . on Independence Day this year we can pay proper honor to our freedom only by working in the defense of that freedom. Our soldiers on the battlefields of the world celebrate no holidays. We at home dare not have a July 4 holiday in war production. . . .

WAR EFFORT INDICES

MANPOWER
National labor force, April --------- 53,400,000
Unemployed, April -------------- 3,000,000
Nonagricultural workers, April---- 40,773,000
Percent increase since June 1940_ **14
Farm employment, June 1, 1942-_ 11,917,000
Percent increase since June 1940_ **1

FINANCE	(In millions of dollars)
Authorized program June 1940– June 15, 1942 --------------	$164,673
Airplanes -----------------	35,978
Ordnance ------------------	35,220
Miscellaneous munitions-----	21,281
Industrial facilities---------	16,697
Naval ships ---------------	15,638
Posts, depots, etc ----------	13,220
Merchant ships ------------	7,465
Pay, subsistence, travel for the armed forces --------------	6,150
Stockpile, food exports-------	4,851
Housing ------------------	1,392
Miscellaneous -------------	6,881

Total expenditures, June 1940–June 15, 1942 -----------------	*32,762
Sales of War Bonds—	
Cumulative May 1941–June 15, 1942 -------------------	6,357
June 1–15, 1942 -------------	334

PLANT EXPANSION *(In millions of dollars)*
June 1940 to latest reporting date
Gov. commitments for war plant expansion; 1,644 projects, April 30___ 12,131
Private commitments for war plant expansion; 8,227 projects, May 31__ 2,738

EARNINGS, HOURS, AND COST OF LIVING		Percent increase from June 1940
Manufacturing industries— April:		
Average weekly earnings --------------	$36.63	42.0
Average hours worked per week ----------	42.4	13.1
Average hourly earnings_	81.9¢	21.9
Cost of living, (1935–39 = 100):	Index	
May 1942 --------------	116.0	15.4
June 2, 1942 -----------	115.9	15.3

-Prelim. includes revisions in former months.
‡Preliminary.
**Adjusted for seasonal variations.

OFFICE FOR EMERGENCY MANAGEMENT

WAYNE COY, *Liaison Officer*

CENTRAL ADMINISTRATIVE SERVICES: Dallas Dort, *Director.*
BOARD OF WAR COMMUNICATIONS: James Lawrence Fly, *Chairman.*
INFORMATION DIVISION: Robert W. Horton, *Director.*
NATIONAL WAR LABOR BOARD: Wm. H. Davis, *Chairman.*
OFFICE OF SCIENTIFIC RESEARCH AND DEVELOPMENT: Dr. Vannevar Bush, *Director.*
OFFICE OF CIVILIAN DEFENSE: James M. Landis, *Director.*
OFFICE OF THE COORDINATOR OF INTER-AMERICAN AFFAIRS: Nelson Rockefeller, *Coordinator.*
OFFICE OF DEFENSE HEALTH AND WELFARE SERVICES: Paul V. McNutt, *Director.*
OFFICE OF DEFENSE TRANSPORTATION: Joseph B. Eastman, *Director.*
OFFICE OF FACTS AND FIGURES: Archibald MacLeish, *Director.*
OFFICE OF LEND LEASE ADMINISTRATION: E. R. Stettinius, Jr., *Administrator.*

OFFICE OF PRICE ADMINISTRATION: Leon Henderson, *Administrator.*
OFFICE OF WAR INFORMATION: Elmer Davis, *Director.*
OFFICE OF ALIEN PROPERTY CUSTODIAN: Leo T. Crowley, *Custodian.*
WAR MANPOWER COMMISSION: Paul V. McNutt; *Chairman.*
WAR RELOCATION AUTHORITY: Milton Eisenhower, *Director.*
WAR SHIPPING ADMINISTRATION: Rear Admiral Emory S. Land, U. S. N. (Retired), *Administrator.*
WAR PRODUCTION BOARD:
Donald M. Nelson, *Chairman.*
Henry L. Stimson.
Frank W. Knox.
Jesse H. Jones.
William S. Knudsen.
Sidney Hillman.
Leon Henderson.
Henry A. Wallace.
Harry L. Hopkins.

WAR PRODUCTION BOARD DIVISIONS:
Donald M. Nelson, *Chairman.*
Executive Secretary, G. Lyle Belsley.
PURCHASES DIVISION: Houlder Hudgins, *Acting Director.*
PRODUCTION DIVISION: W. H. Harrison, *Director.*
MATERIALS DIVISION: A. I. Henderson, *Director.*
DIVISION OF INDUSTRY OPERATIONS: J. S. Knowlson, *Director.*
LABOR PRODUCTION DIVISION: Wendell Lund, *Director.*
CIVILIAN SUPPLY DIVISION: Leon Henderson, *Director.*
REQUIREMENTS COMMITTEE: Wm. L. Batt, *Chairman.*

U. S. GOVERNMENT PRINTING OFFICE: 1942

Lightning Source UK Ltd.
Milton Keynes UK
UKHW010635110119
335238UK00007B/512/P